Lecture Notes in Artificial Intelligence 13566

Subseries of Lecture Notes in Computer Science

Series Editors

Randy Goebel
University of Alberta, Edmonton, Canada

Wolfgang Wahlster
DFKI, Berlin, Germany

Zhi-Hua Zhou
Nanjing University, Nanjing, China

Founding Editor

Jörg Siekmann
DFKI and Saarland University, Saarbrücken, Germany

More information about this subseries at https://link.springer.com/bookseries/1244

Goreti Marreiros · Bruno Martins · Ana Paiva ·
Bernardete Ribeiro · Alberto Sardinha (Eds.)

Progress in Artificial Intelligence

21st EPIA Conference on Artificial Intelligence, EPIA 2022
Lisbon, Portugal, August 31 – September 2, 2022
Proceedings

Editors
Goreti Marreiros ⓘ
ISEP/GECAD
Polytechnic Institute of Porto
Porto, Portugal

Bruno Martins ⓘ
IST/INESC-ID
University of Lisbon
Lisbon, Portugal

Ana Paiva ⓘ
IST/INESC-ID
University of Lisbon
Porto Salvo, Portugal

Bernardete Ribeiro ⓘ
CISUC
University of Coimbra
Coimbra, Portugal

Alberto Sardinha ⓘ
IST/INESC-ID
University of Lisbon
Porto Salvo, Portugal

ISSN 0302-9743   ISSN 1611-3349 (electronic)
Lecture Notes in Artificial Intelligence
ISBN 978-3-031-16473-6   ISBN 978-3-031-16474-3 (eBook)
https://doi.org/10.1007/978-3-031-16474-3

LNCS Sublibrary: SL7 – Artificial Intelligence

This Springer imprint is published by the registered company Springer Nature Switzerland AG
The registered company address is: Gewerbestrasse 11, 6330 Cham, Switzerland

Preface

The EPIA Conference on Artificial Intelligence returned to Lisbon this year. EPIA's second edition, in 1986, followed by the 1989 and 2011 editions, already took place in this unique city. The 21st edition, EPIA 2022, took place at the University of Lisbon, during August 31 to September 2, 2022 (https://epia2022.inesc-id.pt/).

As in previous editions, this international conference was hosted with the patronage of the Portuguese Association for Artificial Intelligence (APPIA). The purpose of the conference is to promote research in all areas of AI, covering both theoretical/foundational issues and applications, and the scientific exchange among researchers, engineers, and practitioners in related disciplines. The program, as in previous editions, was based on a set of thematic tracks dedicated to specific themes of AI. EPIA 2022 was composed of 12 tracks:

AI4IS	Artificial Intelligence for Industry and Societies
AIL	Artificial Intelligence and Law
AIM	Artificial Intelligence in Medicine
AIPES	Artificial Intelligence in Power and Energy Systems
AITS	Artificial Intelligence in Transportation Systems
ALEA	Artificial Life and Evolutionary Algorithms
AmIA	Ambient Intelligence and Affective Environments
GAI	General Artificial Intelligence
IROBOT	Intelligent Robotics
KDBI	Knowledge Discovery and Business Intelligence
MASTA	Multi-Agent Systems: Theory and Applications
TeMA	Text Mining and Applications

The conference program included 3 invited talks:

João Gama (University of Porto, Portugal),
  with a talk on "Current Trends in Learning from Data Streams";
Luc De Raedt (KU Leuven, Belgium),
  with a talk on "From Probabilistic Logics to Neuro-Symbolic Artificial Intelligence";
Iryna GurevychIryna Gurevych (Technical University Darmstadt, Germany),
  with a talk on "Comment – Link – Revise: Towards a General Framework for Modelling Interconnected Texts".

EPIA 2022 had a special focus on young researchers. The conference included a doctoral symposium, where students in the early stages of their doctoral research presented their main research ideas and discussed them with other students and the senior

scientific community. The conference also included an AI Talent Fair, which connected companies with the best young talent in Portugal. The AI Talent Fair included a panel with the title "AI talent in the market: training, attracting, and engaging," in which C-level players in industry and key actors in training AI talented Human Resources discussed the AI Talent in a holistic perspective.

For this edition, 64 papers were accepted, with authors from 18 different countries (Austria, Brazil, Czechia, Ecuador, Egypt, Finland, France, Germany, Italy, Morocco, the Netherlands, Norway, Portugal, Slovakia, Spain, Ukraine, UK, USA). All accepted papers were carefully revised by at least three reviewers from the Program Committee of the corresponding track.

The conference organizers are thankful to the student volunteers, the AI talent fair organizers, the doctoral symposium chairs, and the thematic track organizing chairs, together with their respective Program Committee members. All these individuals did an amazing work, contributing to a very successful conference. The organizers would also like to express their gratitude to all the members of the EPIA International Steering Committee, for their guidance regarding the scientific organization of EPIA 2022.

July 2022

Goreti Marreiros
Bruno Martins
Ana Paiva
Bernardete Ribeiro
Alberto Sardinha

Organization

Event and Program Chairs

Goreti Marreiros   GECAD, Polytechnic of Porto, Portugal
Ana Paiva   INESC-ID, Instituto Superior Técnico, University of Lisbon, Portugal
Bernardete Ribeiro   CISUC, University of Coimbra, Portugal

Local Organizers

Bruno Martins   INESC-ID, Instituto Superior Técnico, University of Lisbon, Portugal
Alberto Sardinha   INESC-ID, Instituto Superior Técnico, University of Lisbon, Portugal

Steering Committee

Ana Bazzan   Universidade Federal do Rio Grande do Sul, Brazil
Ann Nowe   Vrije Universiteit Brussel, Belgium
Ernesto Costa   University of Coimbra, Portugal
Eugénio Oliveira   University of Porto, Portugal
Helder Coelho   University of Lisbon, Portugal
João Pavão Martins   University of Lisbon, Portugal
José Júlio Alferes   NOVA University Lisbon, Portugal
Juan Pavón   Universidad Complutense Madrid, Spain
Luís Paulo Reis   University of Porto, Portugal
Paulo Novais   University of Minho, Portugal
Pavel Brazdil   University of Porto, Portugal
Virginia Dignum   Umeå University, Sweden

Track Chairs

Artificial Intelligence for Industry and Societies

Filipe Portela   University of Minho, Portugal
Teresa Guarda   State University Santa Elena Peninsula, Ecuador
Valentina Lenarduzzi   University of Oulu, Finland
Beatriz De La Iglesia   University of East Anglia, England

Artificial Intelligence in Medicine

Manuel Filipe Santos	University of Minho, Portugal
Carlos Filipe Portela	University of Minho, Portugal
Allan Tucker Brunel	University London, UK
Manuel F. Delgado	University of Santiago de Compostela, Spain

Artificial Intelligence and Law

Pedro Freitas	Catholic University of Portugal, Portugal
Ugo Pagallo	University of Torino, Italy
Massimo Durante	University of Torino, Italy
Paulo Novais	University of Minho, Portugal

Artificial Intelligence in Power and Energy Systems

Zita Vale	Polytechnic of Porto, Portugal
Tiago Pinto	Polytechnic of Porto, Portugal
Pedro Faria	Polytechnic of Porto, Portugal
Elena Mocanu	University of Twente, The Netherlands
Decebal Constantinu Mocanu	Technical University of Eindhoven, The Netherlands

Artificial Intelligence in Transportation Systems

Alberto Fernandez	Universidad Rey Juan Carlos, Spain
Tania Fontes	INESC TEC, Portugal
Rosaldo Rossetti	University of Porto, Portugal

Ambient Intelligence and Affective Environments

Paulo Novais	University of Minho, Portugal
Goreti Marreiros	Polytechnic of Porto, Portugal
João Carneiro	Polytechnic of Porto, Portugal
Sara Rodríguez	University of Salamanca, Spain
Peter Mikulecky	University of Hradec Králové, Czech Republic

General Artificial Intelligence

Bruno Martins	University of Lisbon, Portugal
Alberto Sardinha	University of Lisbon, Portugal
Ana Paiva	University of Lisbon, Portugal
Bernardete Ribeiro	University of Coimbra, Portugal
Goreti Marreiros	Polytechnic of Porto, Portugal

Intelligent Robotics

Nuno Lau	University of Aveiro, Portugal
Luís Paulo Reis	University of Porto, Portugal
João Alberto Fabro	Federal University of Paraná, Brazil

Knowledge Representation and Reasoning

Eduardo Fermé	University of Madeira, Portugal
Matthias Knorr	NOVA University Lisbon, Portugal
Pedro Cabalar	University of Corunna, Spain
Rafael P. Nyssen	University of Milano-Bicocca, Italy
Ricardo Goncalves	NOVA University Lisbon, Portugal

Knowledge Discovery and Business Intelligence

Paulo Cortez	University of Minho, Portugal
Alfred Bifet	Université Paris-Saclay, France
Luís Cavique	Portuguese Open University, Portugal
João Gama	University of Porto, Portugal
Nuno Marques	NOVA University Lisbon, Portugal
Manuel Filipe Santos	University of Minho, Portugal

Multi-Agent Systems: Theory and Applications

Alberto Fernandez	Universidad Rey Juan Carlos, Spain
Daniel Castro Silva	University of Porto, Portugal
João Balsa	University of Lisbon, Portugal
Paulo Leitão	Polytechnic Institute of Bragança, Portugal
Jomi Hübner	University Rio Grande Sul, Brazil

TeMA - Text Mining and Applications

Joaquim Silva	NOVA University of Lisbon, Portugal
Pablo Gamallo	University of Santiago de Compostela, Spain
Paulo Quaresma	University of Évora, Portugal
Irene Rodrigues	University of Évora, Portugal

Program Committee

Artificial Intelligence for Industry and Societies

Alberto Simões	Polytechnic Institute of Cavado and Ave, Portugal
Alfonso González-Briones	University of Salamanca, Spain
Ana Azevedo	Polytechnic Institute of Porto, Portugal

Artificial Intelligence and Law

Ana Rodriguez	University of Santiago de Compostela, Spain
Arlindo Oliveira	University of Lisbon, Portugal
Carlisle George	Middlesex University London, UK
Clara Pereira	University of Oxford, UK
Cristina Alonso	University of Santiago de Compostela, Spain
Ehrwein Céline	University of Applied Sciences of Western Switzerland, Switzerland
Elsa Sequeira	Catholic University of Portugal, Portugal
Francisco Andrade	University of Minho, Portugal
Giovanni Sartor	European University Institute, Italy
Luis Xavier	Catholic University of Portugal, Portugal
Luisa Avitabile	University of Roma, Italy
Manuel Masseno	Polytechnic Institute of Beja, Portugal
Peggy Valcke	KU Leuven, Belgium
Pompeu Casanovas	Autonomous University of Barcelona, Spain
Radboud Winkels	University of Amsterdam, The Netherlands
Teresa Moreira	University of Minho, Portugal
Thomas Burri	University of St. Gallen, Switzerland
Vicente Julian	Polytechnic University of Valencia, Spain

Artificial Intelligence in Medicine

Álvaro Silva	Abel Salazar Biomedical Sciences Institute, Portugal
Andreas Holzinger	Medical University Graz, Austria
António Abelha	University of Minho, Portugal
António de Jesus Pereira	Polytechnic Institute of Leiria, Portugal
Barna Iantovics	Petru Maior University of Tîrgu-Mureş, Romania
Beatriz de la Iglesia	University of East Anglia, UK
Cinzia Pizzi	University of Padua, Italy
Daniel Castro Silva	University of Porto, Portugal
Danielle Mowery	University of Utah, USA
Do Kyoon Kim	Pennsylvania State University, USA
Francesca Vitali	Pavia, Italy
Giorgio Leonardi	University of Piemonte Orientale, Italy
Göran Falkman	University of Skövde, Sweden
Helder Coelho	University of Lisbon, Portugal
Helena Lindgren	Umeå University, Sweden
Inna Skarga-Bandurova	East Ukrainian National University, Ukraine
José Machado	University of Minho, Portugal
José Maia Neves	University of Minho, Portugal
Luca Anselma	University of Turin, Italy

Michael Ignaz Schumacher	University of Applied Sciences Western Switzerland, Switzerland
Miguel Angel Mayer	Pompeu Fabra University, Spain
Mohd Khanapi Abd Ghani	Technical University of Malaysia, Malaysia
Panagiotis Bamidis	Aristotelian University of Thessaloniki, Greece
Pedro Gago	Polytechnic Institute of Leiria, Portugal
Pedro Henriques Abreu	University of Coimbra, Portugal
Pedro Pereira Rodrigues	University of Porto, Portugal
Rainer Schmidt	Institute for Biometrics and Medical Informatics, Germany
Ricardo Martinho	Polytechnic Institute of Leiria, Portugal
Rui Camacho	University of Porto, Portugal
Salva Tortajada	Polytechnic University of Valencia, Spain
Shabbir Syed-Abdul	Taipei Medical University, Taiwan
Shelly Sachdeva	Jaypee Institute of Information Technology, India
Stelios Pavlidis	Imperial College, UK
Szymon Wilk	Poznan University of Technology, Poland
Ulf Blanke	Swiss Federal Institute of Technology in Zurich, Switzerland
Werner Ceusters	University at Buffalo, USA

Artificial Intelligence in Power and Energy Systems

Alfonso Briones	Complutense University Madrid, Spain
Bo Noerregaard Joergensen	University of Southern Denmark, Denmark
Dagmar Niebur	Drexel University, USA
Fernando Lopes	National Laboratory of Energy and Geology, Portugal
Germano Lambert-Torres	PS Solutions, Brazil
Gustavo Arroyo-Figueroa	National Institute of Electricity and Clean Energies, Mexico
Hugo Algarvio	National Laboratory of Energy and Geology, Portugal
Isabel Praça	Polytechnic Institute of Porto, Portugal
João P. S. Catalão	University of Porto, Portugal
Jose L. Rueda	Delft University of Technology, The Netherlands
Omid Abrishambaf	SOLUTE, Spain
Phuong Nguyen	Eindhoven University of Technology, The Netherlands
Pierluigi Siano	University of Salerno, Italy
Rui Castro	University of Lisbon, Portugal
Sérgio Ramos	Polytechnic Institute of Porto, Portugal

Artificial Intelligence in Transportation Systems

Achille Fonzone	Edinburgh Napier University, UK
Ana Paula Rocha	University of Porto, Portugal
António Pedro Aguiar	University of Porto, Portugal
Carlos A. Iglesias	Polytechnic University of Madrid, Spain
Carlos Bento	University of Coimbra, Portugal
Cristina Olaverri-Monreal	Johannes Kepler University Linz, Austria
Danyang Sun	LVMT-ENPC, France
Eduardo Camponogara	Federal University of Santa Catarina, Brazil
Eftihia Nathanail	University of Thessaly, Greece
Elisabete Arsenio	National Laboratory for Civil Engineering, Portugal
Eugénio Oliveira	University of Porto, Portugal
Fabien Leurent	ParisTech, France
Fenghua Zhu	Chinese Academy of Sciences, China
Francesco Viti	University of Luxembourg, Luxembourg
Gianluca Di Flumeri	Sapienza University of Rome, Italy
Gonçalo Correia	Delft University of Technology, The Netherlands
Hilmi Celikoglu	Technical University of Istanbul, Turkey
Holger Billhardt	Rey Juan Carlos University, Spain
Javier J. Sanchez Medina	University of Las Palmas de Gran Canaria, Spain
João Mendes Moreira	INESC TEC, Portugal
Joel Ribeiro	INESC TEC, Portugal
Josep-Maria Salanova	Centre for Research & Technology Hellas, Greece
Jürgen Dunkel	Hanover University for Applied Sciences and Arts, Germany
Lígia Conceição	Armis ITS, Portugal
Luís Nunes	University Institute of Lisbon, Portugal
Marin Lujak	University Rey Juan Carlos, Spain
Mobyen Uddin Ahmed	Mälardalen University, Sweden
Pedro D'Orey	Polytechnic Institute of Porto, Portugal
Rui Gomes	ARMIS Group, Portugal
Sara Ferreira	University of Porto, Portugal
Sara Paiva	Polytechnic Institute of Viana do Castelo, Portugal
Sascha Ossowski	Rey Juan Carlos University, Spain
Thiago Sobral	INESC TEC, Portugal

Ambient Intelligence and Affective Environments

Amílcar Cardoso	University of Coimbra, Portugal
Antonio Caballero	University of Castilla-La Mancha, Spain
Carlos Bento	University of Coimbra, Portugal

Dalila Duraes   Polytechnic Institute of Porto, Portugal
Davide Carneiro   Polytechnic Institute of Porto, Portugal
Esteban Jove   University of A Coruña, Spain
Fábio Silva   University of Minho, Portugal
Fernando de la Prieta   University of Salamanca, Spain
Florentino Fdez-Riverola   University of Vigo, Spain
Francisco Bellas   University of A Coruña, Spain
Grzegorz Napela   AGH University of Science and Technology,
                                      Poland
Hector Alaiz Moreton   University of León, Spain
Hoon Ko   Polytechnic Institute of Porto, Portugal
Ichiro Satoh   National Institute of Informatics Tokyo, Japan
Jason Jung   Chung-Ang University, South Korea
Javier Bajo   Polytechnic University of Madrid, Spain
Javier Jaen   Polytechnic University of Valencia, Spain
Jean Ilié   University Pierre et Marie Curie, France
Jose Luis Calvo-Rolle   University of A Coruña, Spain
José Machado   University of Minho, Portugal
José Molina   University Carlos III of Madrid, Spain
José Neves   University of Minho, Portugal
Lino Figueiredo   Polytechnic of Porto, Portugal
Luís Macedo   University of Coimbra, Portugal
Ricardo Costa   ·   Polytechnic of Porto, Portugal
Ricardo Santos   Polytechnic of Porto, Portugal
Rui José   University of Minho, Portugal
Tatsuo Nakajima   Waseda University, Japan
Tiago M. Fernandez-Carames   University of A Coruña, Spain
Vicente Julián   Polytechnic University of Valencia, Spain

General Artificial Intelligence

Amílcar Cardoso   University of Coimbra, Portugal
Amparo Alonso-Betanzos   University of A Coruña, Spain
Ana Paiva   University of Lisbon, Portugal
Ana Paula Rocha   University of Porto, Portugal
Andrea Omicini   University of Bologna, Italy
Arlindo Oliveira   University of Lisbon, Portugal
Bernardete Ribeiro   University of Coimbra, Portugal
Carlos Ramos   Polytechnic of Porto, Portugal
Davide Carneiro   Polytechnic Institute of Porto, Portugal
Ernesto Costa   University of Coimbra, Portugal
Goreti Marreiros   Polytechnic of Porto, Portugal
João Carneiro   Polytechnic of Porto, Portugal

João Leite	NOVA University of Lisbon, Portugal
John-Jules Meyer	Utrecht University, The Netherlands
José Cascalho	University of Azores, Portugal
José Júlio Alferes	NOVA University of Lisbon, Portugal
José Machado	University of Minho, Portugal
Jose Molina	University Carlos III of Madrid, Spain
José Neves	University of Minho, Portugal
Juan Pavón	Complutense University Madrid, Spain
Luís Camarinha-Matos	NOVA University of Lisbon, Portugal
Luis Paulo Reis	University of Porto, Portugal
Luís Seabra Lopes	University of Aveiro, Portugal
Paulo Cortez	University of Minho, Portugal
Paulo Novais	University of Minho, Portugal
Paulo Quaresma	University of Évora, Portugal
Pedro Barahona	NOVA University of Lisbon, Portugal
Pedro Rangel Henriques	University of Minho, Portugal
Ricardo Santos	Polytechnic of Porto, Portugal
Tatsu Naka	Waseda University, Japan
Vicente Julian	Polytechnic University of Valencia, Spain
Victor Alves	University of Minho, Portugal

Intelligent Robotics

André Marcato	Federal University of Juiz de Fora, Brazil
Andre Conceicao	Federal University of Bahia, Brazil
Andreas Birk	Jacobs University Bremen, Germany
Anibal Ollero	University of Seville, Spain
Anna Helena Costa	University of São Paulo, Brazil
Antonio Bicchi	University of Pisa, Italy
Antonio Paulo Moreira	University of Porto, Portugal
Armando Sousa	University of Porto, Portugal
Augusto Loureiro da Costa	Federal University of Bahia, Brazil
Axel Hessler	Technical University of Berlin, Germany
Brígida Mónica Faria	Polytechnic of Porto, Portugal
Bruno Siciliano	University of Naples Federico II, Italy
Carlos Cardeira	University of Lisbon, Portugal
Carlos Carreto	Polytechnic Institute of Guarda, Portugal
Chenguang Yang	Swansea University, UK
Christian Ott	DLR, Germany
Daniel Polani	University of Hertfordshire, UK
Fabrizio Caccavale	CREATE, Italy
Fernando Osorio	University of São Paulo, Brazil
Flavio Tonidandel	University Center FEI, Brazil

Federico Vicentini	Italian National Research Council, Italy
Fumiya Iida	Swiss Federal Institute of Technology in Zürich, Switzerland
Gabriella Sanniti Di Baja	National Research Council, Italy
Guy Theraulaz	University Toulouse III Paul Sabatier, France
Huosheng Hu	University of Essex, UK
Jacky Baltes	University of Manitoba, Canada
John Hallam	University of Southern Denmark, Denmark
José Luis Gordillo	Technological Institute of Monterrey, Mexico
Kai Arras	University of Freiburg, Germany
Kasper Hallenborg	University of Southern Denmark, Denmark
Lina Maria Paz	University of Zaragoza, Spain
Luca Iocchi	Sapienza University of Rome, Italy
Luís Correia	University of Lisbon, Portugal
Luis Moreno	University Carlos III of Madrid, Spain
Luís Seabra Lopes	University of Aveiro, Portugal
Marco Dorigo	Free University of Brussels, Belgium
Mikhail Prokopenko	The University of Sydney, Australia
Nicolas Jouandeau	University Paris 8, France
Nikolaos Tsagarakis	Italian Institute of Technology, Italy
Owen Holland	University of Essex, UK
Paulo Gonçalves	Polytechnic Institute of Castelo Branco, Portugal
Reinaldo Bianchi	IIIA-CSIC, Spain
Rodrigo Braga	Federal University of Santa Catarina, Brazil
Rolf Pfeifer	University of Zurich, Switzerland
Rudolph Triebel	University of Oxford, UK
Rui Rocha	University of Coimbra, Portugal
Saeed Shiry	Amirkabir University of Technology, Iran
Sanem Sariel Talay	Istanbul Technical University, Turkey
Stephen Balakirsky	NIST, USA
Sven Behnke	Bonn University, Germany
Sylvain Calinon	Idiap Research Institute, Switzerland
Urbano Nunes	University of Coimbra, Portugal
Wolfram Burgard	University Freiburg, Germany
Xiaoping Chen	University of Science and Technology, China
Yan Wu	Agency for Science, Technology and Research, Singapore
Zhijun Li	University of Science and Technology of China, China

Knowledge Discovery and Business Intelligence

Agnes Braud	University of Strasbourg, France
Amilcar Oliveira	Portuguese Open University, Portugal
Armando Mendes	University of Azores, Portugal
Carlos Ferreira	Polytechnic of Porto, Portugal
Elaine Faria	Federal University of Uberlândia, Brazil
Fátima Rodrigues	Polytechnic of Porto, Portugal
Fernando Bação	NOVA University of Lisbon, Portugal
Filipe Pinto	Polytechnic Institute of Leiria, Portugal
José Costa	Federal University of Rio Grande do Norte, Brazil
Leandro Krug Wives	University Rio Grande Sul, Brazil
Manuel Fernandez Delgado	University of Santiago de Compostela, Spain
Marcos Aurélio Domingues	State University of Maringá, Brazil
Margarida Cardoso	University Institute of Lisbon, Portugal
Murat Testik	Hacettepe University, Turkey
Philippe Lenca	IMT Atlantique, France
Rita Ribeiro	University of Porto, Portugal
Roberto Henriques	NOVA University of Lisbon, Portugal
Rui Camacho	University of Porto, Portugal
Sérgio Moro	University Institute of Lisbon, Portugal

Knowledge Representation and Reasoning

Alejandro Garcia	National University of the South, Argentina
Carlos Areces	National University of Córdoba, Argentina
Carmine Dodaro	University of Calabria, Italy
Cristina Feier	University of Bremen, Germany
David Pearce	Polytechnic University of Madrid, Spain
David Rajaratnam	University of New South Wales, Australia
Emmanuele Dietz Saldanha	Dresden University of Technology, Germany
Erman Acar	Free University of Amsterdam, Netherlands
Fabrizio Maggi	University of Tartu, Estonia
Francesca Alessandra Lisi	University of Bari Aldo Moro, Italy
Gerhard Brewka	Leipzig University, Germany
Guohui Xiao	Free University of Bozen-Bolzano, Italy
Inês Lynce	University of Lisbon, Portugal
Jesse Heyninck	University of Dortmund, Germany
João Leite	NOVA University of Lisbon, Portugal
José Júlio Alferes	NOVA University of Lisbon, Portugal
Jorge Fandinno	University of Nebraska at Omaha, USA
Mantas Simkus	Vienna University of Technology, Austria
Manuel Ojeda	University of Málaga, Spain

Maria Vanina Martinez	University of Buenos Aires, Argentina
Marco Ferreirinha Garapa	University of Madeira, Portugal
Mario Alviano	University of Calabria, Italy
Maurício Duarte Luís Reis	University of Madeira, Portugal
Nicolas Troquard	Free University of Bozen-Bolzano, Italy
Orkunt Sabuncu	TED University Ankara, Turkey
Rafael Testa	University of Campinas, Brazil
Ramon Pino Perez	Yachay Tech University, Ecuador
Salvador Abreu	University of Évora, Portugal

Multi-Agent Systems: Theory and Applications

Adriana Giret	Polytechnic University of Valencia, Spain
Agostino Poggi	University of Parma, Italy
Alberto Fernandez-Gil	University Rey Juan Carlos, Spain
Alberto Sardinha	University of Lisbon, Portugal
Ana Paula Rocha	University of Porto, Portugal
Andrea Omicini	University of Bologna, Italy
Andrei Ciortea	University of St. Gallen, Switzerland
Antonio J. M. Castro	University of Porto, Portugal
Carlos Martinho	University of Lisbon, Portugal
Cristiano Castelfranchi	Institute of Cognitive Sciences and Technologies, Italy
Daniel Castro Silva	University of Porto, Portugal
Dave De Jonge	IIIA-CSIC, Spain
Diana Adamatti	Federal University of Rio Grande, Brazil
Federico Bergenti	University of Parma, Italy
Gauthier Picard	Université de Toulouse, France
Graçaliz Dimuro	Federal University of Rio Grande, Brazil
Henrique Lopes Cardoso	University of Porto, Portugal
Jaime Sichman	University of São Paulo, Brazil
Javier Carbo	University Carlos III of Madrid, Spain
João Balsa	University of Lisbon, Portugal
João Leite	NOVA University of Lisbon, Portugal
John-Jules Meyer	Utrecht University, The Netherlands
Jordi Sabater Mir	IIIA-CSIC, Spain
Jorge Gomez-Sanz	Complutense University Madrid, Spain
Juan Carlos Burguillo	University of Vigo, Spain
Luis Macedo	University of Coimbra, Portugal
Luís Nunes	Lisbon University Institute, Portugal
Marin Lujak	University Rey Juan Carlos, Spain
Michael Ignaz Schumacher	University of Applied Sciences Western Switzerland, Switzerland

Onn Shehory	Bar Ilan University, Israel
Paulo Leitão	Polytechnic Institute of Bragança, Portugal
Paulo Novais	University of Minho, Portugal
Rafael Cardoso	University of Manchester, UK
Ramon Hermoso	University of Zaragoza, Spain
Rosa Vicari	Federal University of Rio Grande do Sul, Brazil
Viviane Silva	IBM Research Brazil, Brazil

Text Mining and Applications

Adam Jatowt	University of Kyoto, Japan
Alberto Simões	University of Minho, Portugal
Alexandre Rademaker	IBM, FGV, Brazil
Antoine Doucet	University of Caen, France
António Branco	University of Lisbon, Portugal
Béatrice Daille	University of Nantes, France
Bruno Martins	University of Lisbon, Portugal
Fernando Batista	Lisbon University Institute, Portugal
Francisco Couto	University of Lisbon, Portugal
Gaël Dias	Normandy University, France
Hugo Oliveira	University of Coimbra, Portugal
Iñaki Vicente	Elhuyar Foundation, Spain
Irene Rodrigues	University of Évora, Portugal
Jesús Vilares	University of A Coruña, Spain
Joaquim Silva	NOVA University of Lisbon, Portugal
Luisa Coheur	University of Lisbon, Portugal
Katerzyna Wegrzyn-Wolska	ESIGETEL, France
Manuel Vilares Ferro	University of Vigo, Spain
Marcos Garcia	University of Santiago de Compostela, Spain
Miguel A. Alonso	University of A Coruña, Spain
Nuno Mamede	University of Lisbon, Portugal
Pablo Gamallo	University of Santiago de Compostela, Spain
Paulo Quaresma	University of Évora, Portugal
Pavel Brazdil	University of Porto, Portugal
Sérgio Nunes	University of Porto, Portugal
Renata Vieira	University of Évora, Portugal

Contents

AIM - Artificial Intelligence in Medicine

AmIA - Ambient Intelligence and Affective Environments

GAI - General Artificial Intelligence

IROBOT - Intelligent Robotics

KDBI - Knowledge D.sicovery and Business Intelligence

MASTA - Multi-Agent Systems: Theory and Applications

TeMA - Text Mining and Applications

AI4IS - Artificial Intelligence for Industry and Societies

Estimating the Temperature on the Reinforcing Bars of Composite Slabs Under Fire Conditions

Carlos Balsa[1]([✉])[iD] and Paulo A. G. Piloto[2][iD]

[1] Research Centre in Digitalization and Intelligent Robotics (CeDRI),
Instituto Politécnico de Bragança, 5300-253 Bragança, Portugal
balsa@ipb.pt
[2] Institute of Science and Innovation in Mechanical and Industrial Engineering (INEGI),
Associate Laboratory of Energy, Transports and Aeronautics (LAETA), Instituto Politécnico de
Bragança, 5300-253 Bragança, Portugal
ppiloto@ipb.pt

Abstract. A three-dimensional computational model based on finite elements was developed to evaluate the thermal behaviour of composite slabs with steel deck exposed to a standard fire. The resulting numerical temperatures are then used to obtain a new analytical method, which is an alternative to the simplified method provided by the standard, to accurately determine the temperatures at the reinforcing bars (rebar). The fitting of the analytical model to the numerical data was done by solving a linear least squares problem using the singular value decomposition. The resulting formula fits very well the numerical data, allowing to make predictions of the temperature in the rebar with an approximation error equal to zero and an estimating error at least 77% lower than that obtained with the proposal included in the standard.

Keywords: Transient heat transfer problem · Computational simulation · Concrete-steel slab · Fire rating · Least squares method · Singular value decomposition

1 Introduction

Steel-concrete composite slabs consist of a profiled steel deck which can be used as permanent formwork, and a reinforced concrete. Usually the concrete is reinforced with an anti-crack mesh on top and individual reinforcing bars (rebars) within the ribs (see Fig. 1). The use of composite slabs in buildings is very popular as these building elements offer some advantages for the structures, such as reducing the dead weight of the structures while speeding up the construction process.

Composite slabs may suffer considerable damage in the event of a fire, as the steel elements responsible for the slabs bending resistance capacity are significantly impaired in the event of a fire. To ensure that this building element is fire-resistant, in accordance with the regulations and standards, it is, therefore, necessary to carry out a thermal analysis prior to the static analysis. The fire resistance of this type of element is then determined by standard fire tests, taking into account load-bearing capacity (R), thermal

G. Marreiros et al. (Eds.): EPIA 2022, LNAI 13566, pp. 3–14, 2022.
https://doi.org/10.1007/978-3-031-16474-3_1

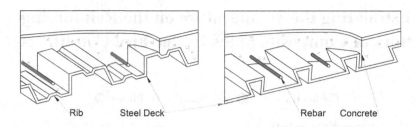

Fig. 1. Composite slab with trapezoidal (left) and re-entrant (right) steel deck.

insulation (I) and integrity (E). In order for a composite slab to demonstrate fire resistance according to the criteria of the European Standard EN13501-2 [7], it must be able to prevent large deformations or deformation velocities in case of fire, i.e. it must be load-bearing (R) and also provide thermal insulation that limits the temperature rise on the unexposed side (I). Finally, the composite slabs must prevent the passage of flames and hot gases through cracks or holes in order to contain the fire from below (E).

This paper deals with the determination of the thermal behaviour of composite slabs under a standard ISO -834 fire [11], focusing on the temperature evolution at the reinforcing bar (rebar). The rebar and the upper flange, web and lower flange of the steel deck are the structural components of the composite slab that are mainly affected by the temperature. An accurate and reliable estimation of the temperatures in these structural components is required, especially to determine the load-bearing criterion (R), as these temperatures have a direct influence on the reduction factors for the steel and concrete strength and thus on the bending resistance of the slabs.

Among the various ways to determine the fire rating of a composite slab, the development of standard experimental fire tests is the most expensive and time-consuming. Alternatively, Annex D of EN 1994-1-2 [6] provides the guidelines for estimating fire resistance based on the simplified calculation method, but this method is based on studies conducted long time ago and is currently outdated. The third method is to simulate computationally the experimental fire tests by means of numerical methods. Computer simulations are of great importance in this field because they allow a reliable and realistic description of the physical phenomena, including the effects of different fire scenarios, such as natural fires.

In [1,2], a series of computational simulations of the thermal effects on composite slabs where developed, with different steel deck geometries in a standard fire. The full-scale tests were simulated with 3D finite elements using Matlab Partial Differential Equations Toolbox (PDE Toolbox) [15]. The results were used to formulate a new proposal that enables to estimate of the temperatures in the slab components (lower and upper flange, web and rebar), which is an alternative to the EN1994-1-2 standard. Taking the numerical results as reference values, the proposed analytical method allows a more accurate estimation of the temperatures for different time values (45, 60, 90 and 120 min). However, since the coefficients of the new proposal are obtained by fitting the numerical data using the Generalised Reduced Gradient (GRG) optimisation method [13], there is no certainty that the solution is optimal or only quasi-optimal.

    In the present work, new coefficients for the analytical method are proposed. To
obtain the coefficients, the linear least squares method is used rather than an optimisation method. The resulting problem does not have full rank, so it must be solved using
the singular value decomposition method. This method guarantees that the calculated
solution is the one that minimises the sum of squared deviations.

    This paper is structured as follows. In Sect. 2 the thermal problem to be solved is
presented. Section 2.3 is devoted to the simplified method provided by the standard for
the calculation of temperatures in the rebar. The new analytical proposal for estimating the temperatures at the rebar is proposed in Sect. 3. This section also includes a
brief description of the calculation method used to perform the thermal analysis and
of the different approaches used to obtain the new proposal. The article ends with the
presentation of some final considerations in Sect. 4.

2   Transient Thermal Problem

This section is devoted to the description of the non-linear transient thermal problem
that must be modelled and solved in the multi-domain body corresponding to the composite slab under standard fire conditions. The heat flux acting on the unexposed side
depends on the ambient temperature and the heat flux acting on the fire exposed side
depends on the standard fire defined by the ISO -834 fire curve [11].

2.1   Physical Multidomains

The 3D heat transfer problems are solved for four different composite slabs with different geometries shown in Fig. 2. Two composite slabs with trapezoidal geometry, Confraplus 60 and Polydeck 59s, and two slabs with re-entrant geometry, Multideck 50 and
Bondek, were selected (see Fig. 2).

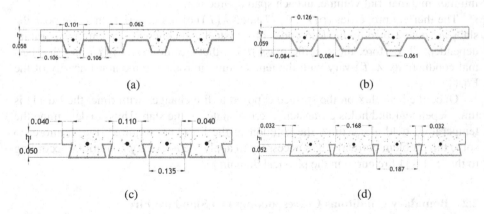

Fig. 2. Geometry and dimensions [mm] of the modelled slabs. (**a**) Confraplus 60. (**b**) Polydeck
59S. (**c**) Multideck 50. (**d**) Bondek.

The 3D computational models were developed in accordance with a realistic representation of the physical model of the composite slabs. The geometry of the models takes into account the exact shape of the surfaces from a representative volume of the slab. The selected cross-section has the side edges bounded by the centre of the upper flange and includes a rib and part of the anti-crack mesh. The length of the specimens is 200 mm in order to include the representative effect of all the components and the anti-crack mesh. The multidomain developed consists of four subdomains: the steel deck, the concrete, the reinforcing bars and the anti-crack. Thus, the materials that make up the physical sub-domains of the slabs are carbon steel (steel deck, rebar and anti-crack mesh) and concrete.

Confraplus 60 is a trapezoidal model profile manufactured by ArcelorMittal. The collaborating steel deck is made of S350 steel and the model uses a thickness of 1.25 mm. The geometric characteristics are shown in the Fig. 2a. The Polydeck 59S model is the second trapezoidal profile selected. The ArcelorMittal Polydeck 59S model, shown in Fig. 2b, consists of a steel deck with S450 steel and a thickness of 1 mm. The re-entrant model shown in Fig. 2c is the Multideck 50 manufactured by Kingspan Structural Products. This product has a steel deck with S450 steel grade and a thickness of 1 mm. The second type of re-entrant slab studied is Bondek, designed and manufactured by Lysaght. The slab consists of a steel profile with grade S350 and the model with a thickness of 1 mm was chosen (see Fig. 2d). These geometries were chosen based on geometric differences and current use.

The energy equation governs the heat conduction inside the physical domain

$$\rho(T)C_p(T)\frac{\partial T}{\partial t} = \nabla \cdot (\lambda(T)\nabla T), \tag{1}$$

where T represents the temperature [°C], $\rho(T)$ is the specific mass [kg/m^3], $Cp(T)$ is the specific heat [J/kgK], $\lambda(T)$ is the thermal conductivity [W/mK], t is the time [s] and $\nabla = (\partial_x, \partial_y, \partial_z)$ is the gradient. Equation (1), is based on the heat flow balance, for the infinitesimal material volume, in each spatial direction.

The thermal properties ($\rho(T)$, $Cp(T)$ and $\lambda(T)$) of the materials that compose the slabs are determined by the Eurocodes [4–6] (steel and concrete), and are temperature dependent. Therefore, the specific mass $\rho(T)$, the specific heat $Cp(T)$ and the thermal conductivity $\lambda(T)$ vary with the temperature, introducing the non-linearity of the Eq. (1).

Once the heat flux on the surface exposed to fire changes with time, the Eq. (1) is time-dependent and holds a transient thermal state for the slab. Thus, to determine the temperature field along time, the solution of the Eq. (1) is required. Furthermore, to solve the problem correctly, it is necessary to apply the boundary conditions according to the ISO-834 fire curve in the physical domain [3].

2.2 Boundary Conditions Corresponding to a Standard Fire

To set the boundary conditions, we need to master the different types of heat transfer acting on the slabs, i.e. conduction, convection and radiation. The composite slabs are subjected to three main boundary conditions, namely the exposed surface, the

non-exposed surface and the insulated surfaces. They all follow the guidelines of the Eurocode EN1991-1.2 [6].

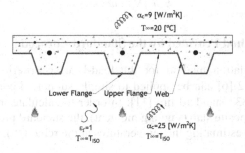

Fig. 3. Boundary conditions.

In the exposed side of the slab, the boundary conditions comprise the heat transfer by convection and radiation and are given by

$$\lambda\left(T\right)\nabla T.\overrightarrow{n} = \alpha_c\left(T_\infty - T\right) + \phi\varepsilon_m\varepsilon_f\sigma\left(T_\infty^4 - T^4\right) \tag{2}$$

where $\overrightarrow{n}$ is the unitary vector normal to the external face, ϕ is the view factor, α_c is the convection coefficient, ε_m is the emissivity of the material, ε_f is the emissivity of fire, σ is the Stefan-Boltzmann constant and T_∞ is the gas temperature of the fire compartment. Equation (2) represents the heat flux that arrives to the steel deck by radiation and convection based on the gas bulk temperature. The convection coefficient is $\alpha_c = 25$ W/m^{2}K, the emissivity of steel is $\varepsilon_m = 0.7$ and the fire emissivity is $\varepsilon_f = 1$. The boundary conditions parameters are represented in Fig. 3.

The view factor (ϕ) is a term that quantifies the geometric relation between the surface emitting radiation and the receiving surface. This parameter has no dimensions and depends on the rib surface's orientations and the distance between the radiative surfaces. The Crossed-Strings method, proposed by Hotell H. C. in 1950 [8], is used to determine the view factor.

Equation (2) includes the gas temperature, T_∞, of the fire compartment, which follows the standard fire curve ISO-834 ($T_\infty = T_{ISO}$) given by

$$T_{ISO} = 20 + 345\log_{10}\left(8t + 1\right), \tag{3}$$

where T_{ISO} is given in [°C] and t in [min] [11].

The top part of the composite slab (unexposed side) is also an important side to determine the temperature evolution. After all, it will determine the heat transfer from the slab to the above compartment. Following the standard EN1991-1-2 recommendations, the heat effect on the unexposed side may be defined by the heat flux by convection, using $\alpha_c = 9$ W/m^{2}K, to include the radiation effect [5]. The boundary condition in the upper surface of the slab is given by Eq. (4),

$$\lambda\left(T\right)\nabla T.\overrightarrow{n} = \alpha_c\left(T - T_\infty\right) \tag{4}$$

where T_∞ is the room temperature. The adiabatic boundary conditions, given by Eq. (5), are applied to the other four surfaces of the slab (front, back, left and right):

$$\lambda(T)\nabla T.\vec{n} = 0. \tag{5}$$

2.3   Analytical Method Provided by the Standard Eurocode

The simplified calculation method for the load-bearing criterion (R) presented in Eurocode EN1994 1.2 [6] can be applied to simply supported composite slabs when subjected to a ISO -834 standard fire [11]. In order to calculate the bending moment resistance of the composite slab (sagging moment), the standard provides the following analytical method for estimating the temperatures at the rebar (θ_r):

$$\theta_r = c_0 + c_1\frac{u_3}{h_2} + c_2 z + c_3\frac{A}{L_r} + c_4\alpha + c_5\frac{1}{l_3} \tag{6}$$

where the temperature θ_r are given in [°C]. The parameter l_3 is the distance within the ribs, u_3 represents the distance from the middle of the ribar to the lower flange in [mm], h_2 is the height of the rib in [mm], the z-factor represents the position of the rebar concerning the slab rib given by

$$\frac{1}{z} = \frac{1}{\sqrt{\frac{1}{u_1}}} + \frac{1}{\sqrt{\frac{1}{u_2}}} + \frac{1}{\sqrt{\frac{1}{u_3}}} \tag{7}$$

in [mm$^{-0.5}$], α corresponds to the angle formed between the web component of the steel deck and the horizontal direction in degrees [°], A/L_r is the ratio between the concrete volume and exposed area per meter of rib length of the steel deck, it is given in [mm], and its calculation is performed through

$$\frac{A}{L_r} = \frac{h_2\left(\frac{l_1+l_2}{2}\right)}{l_2 + 2\sqrt{h_2^2 + \left(\frac{l_1-l_2}{2}\right)^2}}. \tag{8}$$

The coefficients c_i in Eq. (6) are given by EN1994 1.2 [6], which depends on the time of fire resistance (fire rating) that must be achieved (60 min, 90 min or 120 min).

3   Improving the Analytical Method with Numerical Results

To improve the simplified method proposed by the standard, the thermal problem was solved computationally for different values of the concrete thickness (h_1). The values of the numerical temperatures obtained were used to define an alternative analytical method to the simplified method.

3.1 Computational Solution by Finite Elements Method

The Eq. (1) is discretised by finite elements within the physical subdomains corresponding to the different materials. Figure 4a shows the geometry of a representative volume of a composite slab Multideck, and Fig. 4b shows the corresponding mesh, both generated by Matlab PDE Toolbox.

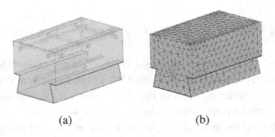

(a)   (b)

Fig. 4. Representative volumes of the Multideck 50 modelled in Matlab. **(a)** Geometry. **(b)** Finite-elements mesh.

The discretization of Eq. (1) by finite elements method (FEM) leads to the energy matrix formulae

$$C(T)\dot{T} + K(T)T = F \qquad (9)$$

where $\dot{T}$ is the vector of time derivatives of the nodal temperatures, C is the capacitance matrix, K is the conductivity matrix and F is the vector of the thermal loads that includes the boundary conditions (for details see, for example, [12]). The solution of the first order non-linear system of ordinary differential Eqs. (9), considering $T(t_0) = T^0$ and the respective boundary conditions, enables to determine the temperature at each node of the mesh, illustrated in Fig. 4b, over the time interval $[t_0, t_f]$.

Matlab (R2021a) PDE toolbox was used to develop and solve the nonlinear transient thermal analysis. The finite element model of the composite slab uses only the tetrahedron finite element type. This finite element is defined by four nodes and uses linear interpolation functions. The resulting mesh includes the four sub-domains concrete, steel deck, rebar and anti-crack mesh, each of which has its own thermal properties. The solution of Eq. (9) is computed by the built-in function ode15s [18].

The finite element computational model described here has been validated in previous work (see [1]) with the experimental results published by Lim and Wade [14] and Piloto et al. [17].

3.2 Improving the New Proposal with an Optimization Method

In [1] a parametric study was developed to determine the influence of concrete thickness h_1 on the temperatures used to determine the fire resistance of composite slabs according to the load-bearing criterion (R). A total of 20 numerical simulations were performed. The simulations considered h_1 values of 60, 70, 90, 110 and 125 mm for the

two trapezoidal geometries and of 50, 70, 90, 110 and 125 mm for the two re-entrant geometries. These values are the most frequently used dimensions in building practise.

Based on the results of the parametric study, new coefficients c_i where proposed for the simplified method given by the Eq. (6). In addition, the inclusion of a new term responsible for the inclusion of the effects of the variation of the thickness h_1 of the concrete slab was proposed. The thickness h_1 was explicitly included in the mathematical model multiplied by coefficient c_6:

$$\theta_{new} = c_0 + c_1 \frac{u_3}{h_2} + c_2 z + c_3 \frac{A}{L_r} + c_4 \alpha + c_5 \frac{1}{l_3} + c_6 h_1. \tag{10}$$

The coefficients for these new proposal methods were determined by fitting the mathematical model represented by the Eqs. (10) to the numerical results of the parametric study with h_1 considering the four different composite slab geometries. The coefficients were determined by minimising the sum of the squared deviations between the numerical and analytical temperatures. This sum was minimised using the Generalised Reduced Gradient (GRG) optimisation method [13].

Table 1. Coefficients of the new proposal obtained by optimization method (New OP).

Fire rating	c_0	c_1	c_2	c_3	c_4	c_5	c_6
45 min	99.82	100.20	106.00	−11.83	2.07	−3983.08	−0.06
60 min	−880.00	923.77	389.18	−30.70	2.96	−5263.73	−0.12
90 min	117.69	961.63	−526.70	28.09	0.74	−5803.21	−0.35
120 min	−151.22	834.65	31.95	−8.06	2.21	−7000.32	−0.60

The resulting coefficients for the estimation of temperatures on the rebar, through Eqs. (10), are included in Table 1. It is worth mentioning that, in addition to the standard fire resistance ratings of 60, 90, and 120 min, the new proposal also comprises the coefficients for the fire rating of 45 min. Analyzing the new coefficients presented in the Table 1, it turns out that c_6 is the smallest of the coefficients, showing that h_1 has a reduced effect on the rebar temperature, compared to the other parameters. However, it is a non-negligible effect that increases with time of fire resistance ratings. Although, as the coefficients in Table 1 were obtained by a numerical optimization method, there is no certainty that the solution is optimal. Consequently, a new approach is proposed to obtain these coefficients based on the linear least-squares method.

3.3   Improving the New Proposal by the Linear Least Squares Method

For each fire rating, new coefficients c_j, $j = 0, 1, 2, \ldots, 6$, must be provided so that the values calculated by Eq. (10) are approximately equal to the corresponding numerical temperatures θ_i, with $i = 1, 2, \ldots, 20$, for the four different types of steel deck geome-

tries and for the five different values of h_1. This results in the need for the approximate solution of the following overdetermined linear system of equations

$$\begin{cases} c_0 + c_1a_{1.2} + c_2a_{1.3} + c_3a_{1.4} + c_4a_{1.5} + c_5a_{1.6} + c_6a_{1.7} \approx \theta_0 \\ c_0 + c_1a_{2.2} + c_2a_{2.3} + c_3a_{2.4} + c_4a_{2.5} + c_5a_{2.6} + c_6a_{2.7} \approx \theta_1 \\ \vdots \qquad \vdots \qquad \vdots \qquad \vdots \qquad \vdots \qquad \vdots \qquad \vdots \\ c_0 + c_1a_{20.2} + c_2a_{20.3} + c_3a_{20.4} + c_4a_{20.5} + c_5a_{20.6} + c_6a_{20.7} \approx \theta_{19} \end{cases} \tag{11}$$

where $a_{i.2} = u_3/h_2$, $a_{i.3} = z$, $a_{i.4} = A/L_r$, $a_{i.5} = \alpha$, and $a_{i.6} = 1/l_3$ represents the geometrical parameters of one of the four composite slabs (Confraplus 60, Polydeck 59S, Multideck 50, or Bondek), and $a_{i.7} = h_1$ is the corresponding concrete thickness (50, 70, 90, 110 or 125 mm).

The solution of the system (11), in the least squares sense, corresponds to the solution $\mathbf{x} = [c_0 c_1, \ldots, c_6]^T \in \mathbb{R}^7$, which minimises the sum of the squared difference between the two sides of the 20 equations, viz,

$$\min_{\mathbf{x}} \sum_{i=1}^{20} \left(\theta_i - \sum_{j=0}^{6} c_i a_{ij} \right)^2. \tag{12}$$

The system (11) can be written in the matrix form as

$$\begin{bmatrix} 1 & a_{1.2} & a_{1.3} & a_{1.4} & a_{1.5} & a_{1.6} & a_{1.7} \\ 1 & a_{2.2} & a_{2.3} & a_{2.4} & a_{2.5} & a_{2.6} & a_{2.7} \\ \vdots & \vdots & \vdots & \vdots & \vdots & \vdots & \vdots \\ 1 & a_{20.2} & a_{20.3} & a_{20.4} & a_{20.5} & a_{20.6} & a_{20.7} \end{bmatrix} \cdot \begin{bmatrix} c_0 \\ c_1 \\ \vdots \\ c_6 \end{bmatrix} \approx \begin{bmatrix} \theta_0 \\ \theta_1 \\ \vdots \\ \theta_{20} \end{bmatrix} \Leftrightarrow \mathbf{Ax} \approx \mathbf{b} \tag{13}$$

where $\mathbf{A} \in \mathbb{R}^{20 \times 7}$ and $\mathbf{b} \in \mathbb{R}^{20 \times 1}$. The condition given by Eq. (12) is equivalent to the minimization of the squared norm of the residual, $\|\mathbf{r}\| = \|\mathbf{b} - \mathbf{Ax}\|$, of the system $\mathbf{Ax} \approx \mathbf{b}$, i.e.,

$$\min_{\mathbf{x}} \|\mathbf{b} - \mathbf{Ax}\|^2. \tag{14}$$

This least squares problem could be solved in different ways if $\mathbf{A}$ had full column rank, but $\mathbf{A}$ had only rank 5. In all four composite slab models, $u_3 = h_2$ is verified so that the second column of $\mathbf{A}$ is equal to the first ($a_{i.2} = 1$ for $i = 1, \ldots, 20$). As a result, the least squares problem has multiple solutions. However, of all the solutions to the Eq. (14), there is only one that also minimises the norm of $\mathbf{x}$ (see for example [10]). This solution can be obtained by decomposing it into singular values. The singular value decomposition of $\mathbf{A}$ is

$$\mathbf{A} = \mathbf{UDV}^T. \tag{15}$$

where $\mathbf{U} \in \mathbb{R}^{20 \times 20}$, $\mathbf{D} \in \mathbb{R}^{7 \times 7}$ and $\mathbf{V} \in \mathbb{R}^{7 \times 7}$. The matrix $\mathbf{D}$ is a diagonal matrix with the singular values of the matrix $\mathbf{A}$. Two of them are zeros because of the rank of the matrix $\mathbf{A}$. These matrices can be decomposed to separate the singular values that are not zero:

$$\mathbf{U} = [\mathbf{U}_1 \, \mathbf{U}_2], \quad \mathbf{D} = \begin{bmatrix} \mathbf{D}_1 & 0 \\ 0 & 0 \end{bmatrix}, \quad \text{and} \quad \mathbf{V} = \begin{bmatrix} \mathbf{V}_1^T \\ \mathbf{V}_2^T \end{bmatrix} \tag{16}$$

where $\mathbf{U}_1 \in \mathbb{R}^{20 \times 5}$, $\mathbf{D}_1 \in \mathbb{R}^{5 \times 5}$ and $\mathbf{V}_1 \in \mathbb{R}^{5 \times 5}$. The matrix $\mathbf{D}_1$ includes the non-singular values of $\mathbf{A}$. The solution of the least squares problem (14) is then given by

$$\mathbf{x} = \mathbf{V}_1 \mathbf{D}_1^{-1} \mathbf{U}_1^T \mathbf{b}. \tag{17}$$

The new coefficients obtained by this method are presented in Table 2.

Table 2. Coefficients for the new proposal obtained by least squares method (New LS).

Fire rating	c_0	c_1	c_2	c_3	c_4	c_5	c_6
45 min	1074.7	1074.7	−2005.1	123.02	−2.3751	−1833.9	−0.056628
60 min	1364.8	1364.8	−2510.3	154.60	−3.2784	−2307.9	−0.12413
90 min	1794.8	1794.8	−3272.5	203.24	−4.6096	−3018.4	−0.35139
120 min	2005.7	2005.7	−3580.4	222.61	−5.2642	−3328.4	−0.60330

3.4   Comparison of the Results

To compare the accuracy of the new coefficients, Table 3 shows the values of error measurements obtained with the new proposal, given by Eq. (10), and with the simplified method proposed by standard EN1994-1.2 [6] and given by Eq. (6). In the case of the new proposal, the results were obtained with the new coefficients derived in the previous section by the least squares method (New LS) and with the coefficients previously obtained by optimisation (New OP) and presented in the Table 1.

In Table 3, the values obtained by the analytical methods y_i for $i = 1, 2, \ldots, 20$ given by the simplified method or by the new proposal are compared with the numerical results θ_i for $i = 1, 2, \ldots, 20$ (right-hand side of the system (13)). According to the recommendations of Chai and Draxler [9], the Root Mean-Squared Error (RMSE) is used as an error measure to compare the results:

$$\text{RMSE} = \sqrt{\frac{1}{20} \sum_{i=1}^{20} (\theta_i - y_i)^2}, \tag{18}$$

and the Bias, given by

$$\text{Bias} = \frac{1}{20} \sum_{i=1}^{20} (\theta_i - y_i). \tag{19}$$

To complement the RMSE and Bias metrics, the Standard Deviation of the Error (SDE) is also considered. The SDE simply corresponds to:

$$\text{SDE} = \sqrt{\text{RMSE}^2 - \text{Bias}^2}. \tag{20}$$

From a statical point of view, the Bias is a basic indicator of the *systematic error* in a prediction and the SDE is the equivalent indicator of the *random error*. In the artificial

Table 3. Errors measures of the different proposals

Fire rating:	45 min			60 min			90 min			120 min		
Proposal	Bias	RMSE	SDE	Bias	RMSE	SDE	Bias	RMSE	SDE	Bias	RMSE	SDE
New LS	0	1.163	1.163	0	2.192	2.192	0	6.539	6.539	0	6.538	6.539
New OP	−10.62	21.38	18.56	−13.90	28.36	24.72	−15.64	31.69	27.56	−15.64	31.689	27.56
EN1994-1.2	−	−	−	46.21	54.18	28.28	202.2	204.1	28.29	202.16	204.13	28.29

intelligence (AI) context, the bias represents the *approximation error* and the SDE the *estimation error* [16].

The results obtained in Table 3 show that the temperatures obtained with the new proposal, with the coefficients obtained by the least squares method (New LS), fit the numerical results very well. It allows the smallest errors for all fire ratings, including a zero value for the bias (estimation error). In the context of machine learning (ML), the reduction to zero of the approximation error shows that the new proposal overfits the available numerical data [16]. The other errors are very small compared to the others proposals. Compared to the formulae provided in the standards, this new proposal makes it possible to reduce the SDE (approximation error) by 77%, in the case of fire ratings of 90 and 120 min, and by 92%, in the case of a fire rating of 45 min.

It can also be observed that the temperatures estimated by the simplified method of Eurocode EN1994-1.2 are usually lower than the numerical temperatures, as the Bias is always positive. Compared to the standard proposal, the new proposal, with New OP coefficients, helps to improve the temperature estimation for each fire rating time. However, they are not as efficient in reducing errors as the coefficients obtained by least squares (New LS).

4   Conclusion

In this work, a realistic computational model was used to simulate the thermal behaviour of composite slabs subjected to standard fire conditions. The results of the numerical simulations make it possible to determine the temperatures for different slab geometries and compare them with those resulting from the simplified calculation method of the standard EN1994-1.2.

The numerical values were compared with the simplified analytical method provided in the standard for estimating temperatures in the reinforcing bar (rebar). The results show that the simplified method gives temperatures that are very far from the numerical values, indicating that its formulation needs to be revised.

To improve the analytical calculation proposal, new coefficients are presented, obtained by fitting the numerical data using a linear least squares method. This method leads to the resolution of an overdetermined linear system where the coefficient matrix has an incomplete column rank, resulting in the problem having multiple solutions. Resolving this system by decomposition into singular values guarantees obtaining a solution that minimises the squared norm of the residue of the linear system. The results show that the new coefficients enable to improve the estimation of the temperatures in

the rebar, allowing to zero the estimation error and to get an approximation error at least 77% lower than that obtained with the formulae included in the standard.

Acknowledgements. This work has been supported by FCT - Fundação para a Ciência e Tecnologia within the Project Scope: UIDB/05757/2020.

References

1. Balsa, C., Silveira, M., Mange, V., Piloto, P.A.G.: Modelling the thermal effects on composite slabs under fire conditions. Computation **10**(6), 94 (2022). https://doi.org/10.3390/computation10060094
2. Balsa, C., Silveira, M.B., Mange, V., Piloto, P.A.G.: Computational modeling of the thermal effects on composite slabs under fire conditions. In: Guarda, T., Portela, F., Santos, M.F. (eds.) ARTIIS 2021. CCIS, vol. 1485, pp. 497–511. Springer, Cham (2021). https://doi.org/10.1007/978-3-030-90241-4_38
3. CEN: EN 1991-1-2: Actions on structures - part 1–2: General actions - action on structures exposed to fire (2002)
4. CEN: EN 1993-1-2: Design of steel structures. part 1–2: General rules - structural fire design eurocode (2002)
5. CEN: EN 1992-1-2: Design of concrete structures. part 1–2: General rules - structural fire design (2004)
6. CEN: EN 1994-1-2: Design of composite steel and concrete structures. part 1–2: General rules - structural fire design (2005)
7. CEN: EN 13501–2: Fire classification of construction products and building elements (2016)
8. Cengel, Y.A., Ghajar, A.J.: Heat and Mass Transfer: Fundamentals and Applications. McGraw-Hill Education - Europe (2014)
9. Chai, T., Draxler, R.R.: Root mean square error (RMSE) or mean absolute error (MAE)? – arguments against avoiding RMSE in the literature. Geosci. Model Dev. **7**(3), 1247–1250 (2014). https://doi.org/10.5194/gmd-7-1247-2014
10. Eldén, L.: Matrix Methods in Data Mining and Pattern Recognition. SIAM, Philadelphia (2007)
11. ISO: International standard ISO 834 - fire-resistance tests: Elements of building construction (1975)
12. Reddy, J.N., Gartling, D.G.: The Finite Element Method in Heat Transfer and Fluid Dynamics, 3rd edn. CRC Press, Boca Raton (2010)
13. Lasdon, L.S., Fox, R.L., Ratner, M.W.: Nonlinear optimization using the generalized reduced gradient method. Revue française d'automatique, informatique, recherche opérationnelle. Recherche opérationnelle **8**(V3), 73–103 (1974). https://doi.org/10.1051/ro/197408v300731
14. Lim, L., Wade, C.: Experimental fire tests of two-way concrete slabs - fire engineering research report 02/12. University of Canterbury, Technical report (2002)
15. MathWorks: Partial Differential Equation Toolbox™ User's Guide, Heat Transfer Problem with Temperature-Dependent Properties, The MathWorks Inc
16. Fernandes de Mello, R., Antonelli Ponti, M.: Machine Learning. Springer, Cham (2018). https://doi.org/10.1007/978-3-319-94989-5
17. Piloto, P.A.G., Prates, L., Balsa, C., Rigobello, R.: Numerical simulation of the fire resistance of composite slabs with steel deck. Int. J. Eng. Technol. **7**(2.23), 83 (2018). https://doi.org/10.14419/ijet.v7i2.23.11889
18. Shampine, L.F., Reichelt, M.W.: The MATLAB ODE suite. SIAM J. Sci. Comput. **18**(1), 1–22 (1997)

Hierarchically Structured Scheduling and Execution of Tasks in a Multi-agent Environment

Diogo Carvalho[1,2(✉)] and Biswa Sengupta[1]

[1] Zebra Technologies, London, UK
biswa.sengupta@zebra.com
[2] INESC-ID and Instituto Superior Técnico, University of Lisbon, Lisbon, Portugal
diogo.s.carvalho@tecnico.ulisboa.pt

Abstract. In a warehouse environment, tasks appear dynamically. Consequently, a task management system that matches them with the workforce too early (e.g., weeks in advance) is necessarily sub-optimal. Also, the rapidly increasing size of the action space of such a system consists of a significant problem for traditional schedulers. Reinforcement learning, however, is suited to deal with issues requiring making sequential decisions towards a long-term, often remote, goal. In this work, we set ourselves on a problem that presents itself with a hierarchical structure: the task-scheduling, by a centralised agent, in a dynamic warehouse multi-agent environment and the execution of one such schedule, by decentralised agents with only partial observability thereof. We propose to use deep reinforcement learning to solve both the high-level scheduling problem and the low-level multi-agent problem of schedule execution. The topic and contribution is relevant to both reinforcement learning and operations research scientific communities and is directed towards future real-world industrial applications.

Keywords: Hierarchical reinforcement learning · Multi-agent systems

1 Introduction

Tasks appear dynamically in a warehouse or retail store environment, and multiple agents must cooperate in executing them. The tasks themselves may consist, for example, of picking items, packing items, cleaning or replenishment, and usually have specific spatial requirements, whether those are the location of the item to be picked or packed, the place where cleaning is required or the shelf in need of replenishment. The dynamics of tasks coming into the environment are random and may be driven by various factors such as online promotions, weather changes, publicity, traffic, international events, and so on. Finally, tasks usually require one or more workers, be they humans or cobots, with a specific skill set to complete them. Within the described scenario, we set ourselves on a problem that presents itself with a two-level hierarchical structure. On the high level, a

G. Marreiros et al. (Eds.): EPIA 2022, LNAI 13566, pp. 15–26, 2022.
https://doi.org/10.1007/978-3-031-16474-3_2

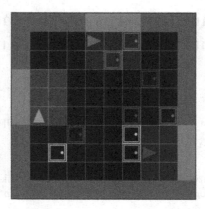

Fig. 1. 10×10 multi-agent grid world environment with 3 agents. Required tasks are represented as doors. Colors identify the agents and the available tasks. Agents have partial observability and can only see a 3-square around them.

centralised agent, which we refer to as scheduler, must come up with a schedule, matching decentralised agents, which we refer to as workers, with tasks. On the low level, workers must execute their schedule, respecting its order. The latter challenge composes a multi-agent partially observable Markov game.

Usually, in real-life environments, a human manager or management software that dwells on the high level does not try to capture the task-scheduling problem at the level of granularity we aim at with this work. Instead, workers are usually assigned categories of tasks they should be prepared to execute with days, weeks or months in advance. Consequently, such decisions are sub-optimal, and there often is excess or shortage of workforce to execute tasks, as schedulers fail to adapt to their dynamic environment rapidly. However, continuously changing workers' schedules, at the level of minutes or seconds, may become impractical: firstly, the action space of matching m tasks to n agents that can only take k tasks at a time amounts to $\binom{m}{n \cdot k} \cdot (n \cdot k)!$, which grows as fast as it precludes planning methods, designed to look for optimal solutions; then, more often than not, communication or observability issues are a reality in the environments we consider. Finally, on the low-level, we have a decentralised multi-agent problem, which becomes significantly challenging as the state and action spaces grow bigger downstream of increasing environment size, number of agents or tasks.

In this work, motivated by recent successes across the fields of multi-agent, deep and hierarchical reinforcement learning applied to resource management problems that we discuss in the next section; we make the point that hierarchical deep reinforcement learning algorithms are suited to solve the multi-agent warehouse environment problem, both at the upper level of task scheduling and the lower level of task execution. The contribution of this work is, therefore, two-fold: (i) a hierarchical multi-agent problem of scheduling and execution of tasks in a simulated warehouse environment; (ii) a deep hierarchical multi-agent reinforcement learning solution to the problem.

The document is outlined as follows. We start by reviewing the relevant literature on related problem settings and hierarchical reinforcement learning; we then provide the necessary background and notation to Markov decision problems, single and multi-agent reinforcement learning and hierarchical reinforcement learning; move to formalising the problem, its hierarchical structure and details of the implementation; describe the approach and present results; conclude and blaze a path for the future.

2   Related Work

2.1   Resource Management

One class of problems that have been addressed by reinforcement learning methods and may serve as an umbrella for our issue is the one of resource management. Particularly, some problems of resource management can be thought of as machine load balancing [2]. Planning has been used for commissioning tasks in multi-robot warehouse environments [6] and tabular reinforcement learning methods were early used for matching professors, classrooms, and classes [27]. More recently, through deep reinforcement learning, works have explored how to allocate resources such as bandwidth in vehicle-to-vehicle communications [36], power in cloud infrastructures [23] and computation jobs in clusters [25,26].

Another pair of problems that intersects with ours is the one of shared autonomous mobility [13] and particularly fleet management [22], as tasks and workers in a warehouse environment also have specific spatial attributes, and matching those, the upper level of our problem, has similarities with matching drivers and passengers. Nevertheless, contrarily to ours, work aiming at this problem assume the low-level policies are previously known across drivers, eliminating the added difficulty of a hierarchical reinforcement learning problem that we try to deal with. Different works have approached the high-level problem of dispatching through cascaded learning [10], both dispatching and relocation of drivers through centralised multi-agent management [15], or just the relocation [20]. Finally, graph neural networks have most recently been used to address the fleet management [12] and the multiple traveling salesman [16,17] problems.

2.2   Hierarchical Reinforcement Learning

Hierarchical reinforcement learning has long been promising to contribute to dealing with complex problems, particularly ones with large action spaces. Hierarchical reinforcement learning allows learning to happen on different levels of abstraction, structure and temporal extent. The first proposal of a hierarchical framework came through feudal reinforcement learning [7], where managers learn to produce goals to workers that learn how to satisfy them. Later, the Option framework [33] formalised and provided theoretical guarantees to hierarchies in reinforcement learning. More recently, these ideas have been successfully applied to new algorithms [3,29]. In the specific case of multi-agent systems, after a pioneering work [24], others have explored master-slave architectures [18], feudal multi-agent hierarchies [1] and temporal abstraction [34].

3   Background

3.1   Markov Decision Problems

Reinforcement Learning algorithms propose to solve sequential decision-making problems formally described as Markov decision problems. A Markov decision problem is a 5-tuple $(\mathcal{X}, \mathcal{A}, \mathcal{P}, r, \gamma)$, where $\mathcal{X}$ stands for the state space; $\mathcal{A}$ the discrete action space; $\mathcal{P}$ a set of $|\mathcal{A}|$ probability functions, each $P_a : \mathcal{X} \times \mathcal{X} \to [0, 1]$ assigning, through $P_a(x, x')$, the probability that state x' follows from the execution of action a in state x; $r : \mathcal{X} \times \mathcal{A} \to \mathbb{R}$ is a possibly stochastic reward function and γ is a discount factor in $[0, 1]$.

3.2   Reinforcement Learning

In the reinforcement learning setting, the agent does not know the dynamics description $\mathcal{P}$ nor the reward function r of the environment and its goal is to compute the best policy, $\pi^* : \mathcal{X} \times \mathcal{A} \to [0, 1]$, assigning the decision of which action to take in state x in a possibly stochastic manner. Such best policy is defined as the one yielding the biggest amount of summed discounted rewards, in the long run, no matter the state where the agent starts from. To make such notions precise, we define the action value-function of a given policy π as $Q^\pi : \mathcal{X} \times \mathcal{A} \to \mathbb{R}$ such that $Q^\pi(x, a) = \mathbb{E}[\sum_{t=0}^{\infty} \gamma^t r(x_t, a_t) \mid x_0 = x, a_0 = a]$, where $x_{t+1} \sim P_{a_t}(x_t, \cdot)$ and $a_t \sim \pi(x_t, \cdot)$. To solve a Markov decision problem, one possible partition of the set of reinforcement learning algorithms that do not explicitly try to learn a model of the world itself, called model-free, breaks them into two: value-based methods and policy-based methods.

On the one hand, value-based methods approximate π^* implicitly while approximating its action value-function Q^*, verifying the fixed point equation $Q^*(x, a) = \mathbb{E}[r(x, a) + \gamma \max_{a' \in \mathcal{A}} Q^*(x', a')]$. The most well-known method to perform such approximation is Q-learning, a tabular method that founds more sophisticated algorithms such as deep Q-networks [28]. On the other hand, policy-based methods are based on direct improvements over the policy. They do require an explicit representation of a policy π, known as the actor, commonly added of an estimate of its current value, known as the critic. For that reason, most policy-based algorithms are known as actor-critic algorithms. PPO [32] is one such actor-critic methods, where the baseline used is the state value function $b(x) = \mathbb{E}[Q(x, a)]$, added of the optimisation of a surrogate objective loss.

3.3   Multi-agent Markov Decision Problems

A decentralised partially observable Markov decision problem (Dec-POMDP) describes a fully cooperative multi-agent environment. More formally, it consists of a tuple $([n], \mathcal{X}, \mathcal{U}, \mathcal{P}, r, \gamma, \mathcal{Z}, O)$, $[n] = (1, 2, \ldots, n)$ representing the indexes of n agents. Identically to the way we formalised an MDP, in a dec-POMDP $\mathcal{X}$ consists of the set of states; $\mathcal{U} = \times_{i \in [n]} \mathcal{A}_i$, where $\mathcal{A}_i$ is the set of actions available for agent i; $\mathcal{P}$ is a set of transition probability functions, mapping a

triple $(x, u, x') \in \mathcal{X} \times \mathcal{U} \times \mathcal{X}$ to the probability that state x' follows from executing action u in state x; r is the immediate reward function, shared across agents, mapping pairs (x, u) to possibly stochastic rewards in $\mathbb{R}$. $\mathcal{Z} = \times_{i \in [n]} \mathcal{O}_i$ is the set of joint observations, where $\mathcal{O}_i$ is the set of observations for agent i, and O maps triples $(z, x, u) \in \mathcal{Z} \times \mathcal{X} \times \mathcal{U}$ to the probability that the joint observation z is emitted after the execution of action u in state x.

A partially observable Markov game is a more general setting than the one of dec-POMDPs, where rewards are not necessarily shared across agents. Consequently, a partially observable Markov game allows for modelling scenarios that are not fully cooperative, such as competitive or neutral ones. To formalize the relation between the two settings, a partially observable Markov game is a tuple $([n], \mathcal{X}, \mathcal{U}, \mathcal{P}, \mathcal{R}, \gamma, \mathcal{Z}, O)$, where $\mathcal{R}$ is a set of n reward functions $r_i : \mathcal{X} \times \mathcal{U} \to \mathbb{R}$.

3.4   Multi-agent Reinforcement Learning

Trying to address the multi-agent setting, methods have been developed that rely on either a fully-decentralised approach or through centralised training with decentralised execution, an approach firstly considered in planning [19] but that has become central in the reinforcement learning literature in the most recent years [11]. At the halfway point between the two (i.e., fully-decentralised and fully-centralised), we can also consider a multi-agent setting where multiple homogeneous agents can share and train a single policy, which can then be decentralised at test time. We refer to the last approach as parameter sharing [14].

The fully-decentralised approach has surprisingly had a few success stories. However, it is still tough for agents to learn independently due to the non-stationarity [30] of the environment caused by other agents' changing behaviour. Any single-agent reinforcement learning method can be implemented this way, including recent deep-RL methods, be them value-based or policy-based, by simply letting each agent learn as if it were in a single-agent setting.

The centralised training with a decentralised execution approach is, for scenarios where it is applicable, very promising. Most methods consist of a decentralised actor (policy) with a centralised critic (value-function) on learning time. On test time, only the actor is required, thus rendering the methods decentralised. Under the described umbrella, we can fit again extensions of the vanilla deep-RL methods, be them value-based or policy-based.

Finally, also parameter-sharing can be used to learn a single policy with any deep-RL algorithm for homogeneous multi-agent settings. The approach has been shown to mitigate the adverse effects of non-stationarity [5,35].

3.5   Hierarchical Reinforcement Learning

Among the frameworks that have formalised some interpretation of hierarchy within reinforcement learning, such as the one of feudal learning [7], hierarchical abstract machines [31] and MAXQ decomposition [8], the most popular one is the options formulation [33]. Options extend the traditional definition of actions and

Markov decision problems in the sense that, on top of the latter, an option also consists of a termination condition $\zeta : \mathcal{X} \to [0,1]$ and an initiation set $\mathcal{I} \subseteq \mathcal{X}$, determining respectively when the macro-action ends and when it starts.

4   Problem Setting

In our setting, the warehouse, location and specifications of tasks and agents are modelled as a multi-agent grid world. At each step, a cell of the grid world can be non-occupied, occupied with an agent or occupied with a task. Agents and tasks both have a set of attributes. In the case of agents, they have a colour identifier, a direction, and a schedule composed of their assigned tasks. In the case of tasks, they also have a colour identifier. Tasks appear randomly in the environment on each time step according to independent and identically distributed Bernoulli(p) random variables. The environment can only take up to m visible tasks, with m denoting the maximum size of the queue. If the queue is full and a new task arrives, it is added to a backlog with no limit number of tasks. When the queue is full, and a task is completed, another from the backlog is added to its place.

4.1   High-Level

On the high-level, an agent fully observes the state of the environment, including the location of tasks and their attributes, the location of agents, their attributes and their current schedules and the number of tasks in the backlog, and produces an action corresponding to the schedule each low-level agent must perform. Each high-level action is, therefore, a tuple in $m^{k \cdot n}$, where m is the size of the queue, k is the size of each low-level agent's schedule, and n is the number of agents.

The size of the action space, as described above, grows exponentially both on the size of the schedule k and the number of low-level agents n. To keep the action space linear in such quantities, the high-level agent recursively chooses one of m tasks to add to a low-level agent's schedule until either its buffer is full or the null action is chosen. Therefore, the high-level agent must output up to $m \cdot k$ tasks to output each schedule.

The high-level agent is rewarded the negative average job slowdown, which can be computed as $C = -\sum_{j \in (\mathcal{M} \cup \mathcal{L})} (D_j)^{-1}$, where $\mathcal{M}$ is the queue, $\mathcal{L}$ is the backlog, and D_j is the estimated time for actually executing job j. The high-level agent also receives a negative unit reward if it tries to schedule tasks that are already schedule or not present in the queue. Finally, the high-level agent is called to compute and communicate the new schedule to low-level agents when they have reached a maximum number of actions on the environment.

4.2   Low-Level

The low level is a decentralised, partially observable multi-agent problem. Since the reward is not shared across agents, the problem is, in particular, a Markov game. Consequently, the low-level does not present itself with a cooperative

nature, and there is no incentive for cooperation. However, competition, in a more intuitive sense, is also not particularly incentivised in our setting.

Each agent can see a v-square of cells around it, its location and direction and the location of tasks on its schedule and act without communicating with the other agents. At each time step, it is rewarded for the negative ratio of its progress, as the number of tasks of the schedule it still has to perform is divided by the total number of tasks it has been assigned, k.

4.3   Implementation Details

For all the algorithmic and learning implementation, we use the RLlib library [21]. To implement the warehouse environment, we build on an existing repository [4,9]. Figure 1 showcases a renderization of the environment.

Grid. The custom grid world is an $h \times w$ grid, with h denoting height and w denoting width. Each cell is then composed of a tuple encoding its content. The outer cells are walls. The inner cells have either a wall, an agent or a task.

Tasks. Tasks are represented as doors and have a certain colour, which identifies them. The task is complete, and the door disappears once an agent opens the corresponding door. To open a door, an agent must only navigate to the door and toggle it. The door then disappears from the environment. The environment may only contain, at a particular time step, m tasks at most. Any additional tasks are in a backlog. The number of tasks in the backlog is visible to the high-level agent, but its content is not.

Agents. The cells containing one of the n low-level agents, represented as isosceles triangles accounting for the direction they face, contain a tuple with its color, its direction and the tasks it is scheduled to perform.

Episodes. At the beginning of an episode, there are m_0 tasks in the environment. After each low-level step, a new task arrives with probability p.

Low-Level. Each low-level agent observes a v-sized grid around it, its current direction and the position of the the tasks it is scheduled to perform and must output an action in $\mathcal{A} = \{$do nothing, move front, turn right, turn left, toggle$\}$.

High-Level. The high-level agent must provide an action, a complete schedule, consisting of n sub-schedules of k tasks each, one for each low-level agent. Such a schedule is recursively computed to keep the action space linear in m.

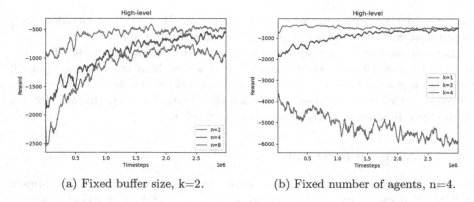

(a) Fixed buffer size, k=2.   (b) Fixed number of agents, n=4.

Fig. 2. High-level policy undiscounted episodic reward during training after $1 \cdot 10^6$ time-steps of low-level policy pre-training. Episodic rewards appear on the vertical axis, time-steps on the horizontal axis, regardless of happening on the higher or lower levels. In Fig. 2a, each agent's buffer size k is fixed and n varies. In Fig. 2b, the number of agents n is fixed and k varies.

5   Evaluation

5.1   Environment Settings

Along the section, we are set on a 10×10 grid where low-level agents observe a 3-square around them. We set the probability that a new task appears at a certain time-step as $p = (\frac{n \cdot k}{4} + 1)\%$. Finally, the maximum number of tasks visible on the environment is set as $m = m \cdot k + 1$. The initial number of tasks on the environment, at the beginning of an episode, is randomly and uniformly chosen as $m_0 \sim U(\{0, \ldots, m\})$. An episode ends once $4 \cdot h \cdot w$ low-level steps are made. A low-level episode ends once $h \cdot w$ episodes are made.

5.2   Experimental Results

We train the high-level agent with the PPO algorithm. The high-level policy network is composed of a convolutional neural network with a ReLU activation function. To leverage the power of the convolutional layers on RLlib, we zero-pad the grid world into a $h \times w \times f(k)$ tensor, $f : \mathbb{N} \to \mathbb{N}$ and each of the $h \cdot w$ $f(k)$-tuples are encoded with the attributes of agents or tasks.

Training both hierarchical levels at the same time may produce significant non-stationarities that may harm learning. Therefore before starting the high-level training, we train the low-level agents to perform randomly chosen schedules on a static environment ($p = 0$). After training the low-level agent for 10^6 time steps, we start training the high-level agent. Notice here that we allow the low-level policy to keep training. Training for the high level is performed using the PPO algorithm. In Sect. 5.3 we present results that validate our choice.

To examine how the high-level scheduler performs and scales with the number of agents, n, and the number of tasks each agent can be assigned, k, we show

learning plots for $n \in \{2, 4, 8\}$ when $k = 2$ and $k \in \{1, 2, 4\}$ when $n = 4$ on Fig. 2, the main set of results in the paper. Notice that, as n or k increases, the frequency p at which new tasks appear on the environment increases as per our construction, and as described above, rendering the environment more challenging when the workforce is also more capable. Figure 2a shows that, while the number of agents increases, the method can still learn a scheduler. Figure 2b shows that while each agent's maximum number of tasks assigned increases, the method may fail to learn a scheduler, particularly for $k = 4$. However, we hypothesise that the results are due to the difficulty of the environment itself— tasks appearing too frequently for $n = 4$ agents.

Low-level agents are trained with the PPO algorithm with shared parameters. The low-level policy networks are fully connected networks with a Tanh activation function. Learning hyperparameters are also default for PPO.

5.3 Additional Experiments

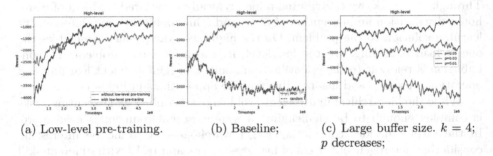

(a) Low-level pre-training.   (b) Baseline;   (c) Large buffer size. $k = 4$; p decreases;

Fig. 3. Additional experimental results. Vertical axis shows episode reward; horizontal axis time-steps taken.

We hereby include additional experimental results to the proposed hierarchical model for scheduling and executing tasks in a multi-agent warehouse environment described in the main document. The experiments add three insights: effects of low-level policy pre-training; performance of the high-level scheduler against a random baseline; performance of the high-level scheduler for a high buffer-size but as the difficulty of the environment itself decreases. Recall that the buffer size k is the number of tasks the high-level scheduler must assign to each agent and is consequently the number of tasks the low-level agents must perform until new tasks are assigned to it. Results are described in Fig. 3; the settings' details and analysis appear below.

Low-Level Pre-training. To confirm the benefits of the early training of the low-level policy, as described in Sect. 5.2, we compare the results of training both policy levels simultaneously against pre-training the low-level. We show the training plot after the first $1 \cdot 10^6$ time steps in Fig. 3a. As expected, due to the non-stationarity induced by training the two levels simultaneously, learning is worse without pre-training the low-level policy with a random scheduler.

Baseline. We are set on an environment of $n = 3$ agents, each with a buffer-size of $k = 3$ and a probability of new tasks coming in to the environment at a new time-step of $p = 0.05$. We compare the performance of the method we propose against a random scheduler, having pre-trained the low-level agents in both cases. Figure 3b shows the results. Clearly, the performance of our method surpasses the one of a random scheduler.

Large Buffer Size. Here, we examine if, when the buffer-size is large, $k = 4$, and the dynamics of the environment decrease (p decreases), the performance of the model increases. The environment is, as in the main document, of $n = 4$ agents and p varies in $\{0.01, 0.03, 0.05\}$. Figure 3c shows the results. We observe that, as expected, as the difficulty of the environment decreases (p decreases), the method is able to provide a better policy.

6   Conclusion

Through this work, we contributed a hierarchically structured problem of ware-house distribution and execution of tasks and a hierarchical deep reinforcement learning solution to the problem. On the high level, the problem resembles the one of load balancing. On the low level, it is a multi-agent problem. Thecontribution is relevant to the scientific communities of reinforcement learning and operations research and has possible real-life applications in industry.

While the hierarchical multi-agent problem of scheduling and executing tasks is complex enough to be challenging, a warehouse environment is even more. In the future, besides considering larger warehouses, it would be interesting considering heterogeneous fleets of low-level agents and tasks with different skill sets and requirements, respectively; multiple agents for executing a single task; different tasks with different levels of priority. To overcome the problems the added difficulties would imply, learning-wise, it may be valuable to add additional levels to the hierarchy, learn a latent embedded representation of actions in a continuous space or exploit the structuring capabilities of graph neural networks.

Acknowledgements. This work was supported by Fundação para a Ciência e a Tecnologia under project UIDB/50021/2020 and scholarship 2020.05360.BD.

References

1. Ahilan, S., Dayan, P.: Feudal multi-agent hierarchies for cooperative reinforcement learning. arXiv preprint arXiv:1901.08492 (2019)
2. Azar, Y.: On-line load balancing. In: Fiat, A., Woeginger, G.J. (eds.) Online Algorithms. LNCS, vol. 1442, pp. 178–195. Springer, Heidelberg (1998). https://doi.org/10.1007/BFb0029569
3. Bacon, P.L., Harb, J., Precup, D.: The option-critic architecture. In: Proceedings of the AAAI Conference on Artificial Intelligence, vol. 31 (2017)
4. Chevalier-Boisvert, M., Willems, L., Pal, S.: Minimalistic gridworld environment for openai gym (2018). https://github.com/maximecb/gym-minigrid

5. Christianos, F., Papoudakis, G., Rahman, M.A., Albrecht, S.V.: Scaling multi-agent reinforcement learning with selective parameter sharing. In: Meila, M., Zhang, T. (eds.) Proceedings of the 38th International Conference on Machine Learning. Proceedings of Machine Learning Research, 18–24 July 2021, vol. 139, pp. 1989–1998. PMLR (2021). https://proceedings.mlr.press/v139/christianos21a.html

6. Claes, D., Oliehoek, F., Baier, H., Tuyls, K., et al.: Decentralised online planning for multi-robot warehouse commissioning. In: International Conference on Autonomous Agents and Multiagent Systems, pp. 492–500 (2017)

7. Dayan, P., Hinton, G.E.: Feudal reinforcement learning. In: Hanson, S., Cowan, J., Giles, C. (eds.) Advances in Neural Information Processing Systems, vol. 5. Morgan-Kaufmann (1993)

8. Dietterich, T.G.: Hierarchical reinforcement learning with the maxq value function decomposition. J. Artif. Intell. Res. **13**, 227–303 (2000)

9. Fickinger, A.: Multi-agent gridworld environment for openai gym (2020). https://github.com/ArnaudFickinger/gym-multigrid

10. Fluri, C., Ruch, C., Zilly, J., Hakenberg, J., Frazzoli, E.: Learning to operate a fleet of cars. In: IEEE Intelligent Transportation Systems Conference (ITSC) (2019)

11. Foerster, J., Assael, I.A., de Freitas, N., Whiteson, S.: Learning to communicate with deep multi-agent reinforcement learning. In: Lee, D., Sugiyama, M., Luxburg, U., Guyon, I., Garnett, R. (eds.) Advances in Neural Information Processing Systems, vol. 29. Curran Associates, Inc. (2016)

12. Gammelli, D., Yang, K., Harrison, J., Rodrigues, F., Pereira, F.C., Pavone, M.: Graph neural network reinforcement learning for autonomous mobility-on-demand systems. arXiv preprint arXiv:2104.11434 (2021)

13. Guériau, M., Dusparic, I.: Samod: Shared autonomous mobility-on-demand using decentralized reinforcement learning. In: 2018 21st International Conference on Intelligent Transportation Systems (ITSC). IEEE (2018)

14. Gupta, J.K., Egorov, M., Kochenderfer, M.: Cooperative multi-agent control using deep reinforcement learning. In: Sukthankar, G., Rodriguez-Aguilar, J.A. (eds.) AAMAS 2017. LNCS (LNAI), vol. 10642, pp. 66–83. Springer, Cham (2017). https://doi.org/10.1007/978-3-319-71682-4_5

15. Holler, J., et al.: Deep reinforcement learning for multi-driver vehicle dispatching and repositioning problem. In: 2019 IEEE International Conference on Data Mining (ICDM), pp. 1090–1095. IEEE (2019)

16. Hu, Y., Yao, Y., Lee, W.S.: A reinforcement learning approach for optimizing multiple traveling salesman problems over graphs. Knowl.-Based Syst. **204**, 106244 (2020)

17. Kaempfer, Y., Wolf, L.: Learning the multiple traveling salesmen problem with permutation invariant pooling networks. arXiv preprint arXiv:1803.09621 (2018)

18. Kong, X., Xin, B., Liu, F., Wang, Y.: Revisiting the master-slave architecture in multi-agent deep reinforcement learning. arXiv preprint arXiv:1712.07305 (2017)

19. Kraemer, L., Banerjee, B.: Multi-agent reinforcement learning as a rehearsal for decentralized planning. Neurocomputing **190**, 82–94 (2016)

20. Lei, Z., Qian, X., Ukkusuri, S.V.: Efficient proactive vehicle relocation for on-demand mobility service with recurrent neural networks. Transp. Res. Part C: Emerg. Technol. **117**, 102678 (2020)

21. Liang, E., et al.: RLlib: abstractions for distributed reinforcement learning. In: International Conference on Machine Learning (ICML) (2018)

22. Lin, K., Zhao, R., Xu, Z., Zhou, J.: Efficient large-scale fleet management via multi-agent deep reinforcement learning. In: Proceedings of the 24th ACM SIGKDD International Conference on Knowledge Discovery & Data Mining (2018)

23. Liu, N., et al.: A hierarchical framework of cloud resource allocation and power management using deep reinforcement learning. In: 2017 IEEE 37th International Conference on Distributed Computing Systems (ICDCS), pp. 372–382. IEEE (2017)

24. Makar, R., Mahadevan, S., Ghavamzadeh, M.: Hierarchical multi-agent reinforcement learning. In: Proceedings of the Fifth International Conference on Autonomous Agents, pp. 246–253 (2001)

25. Mao, H., Alizadeh, M., Menache, I., Kandula, S.: Resource management with deep reinforcement learning. In: Proceedings of the 15th ACM Workshop on Hot Topics in Networks, pp. 50–56 (2016)

26. Mao, H., Schwarzkopf, M., Venkatakrishnan, S.B., Meng, Z., Alizadeh, M.: Learning scheduling algorithms for data processing clusters. In: Proceedings of the ACM Special Interest Group on Data Communication, pp. 270–288 (2019)

27. Ming, G.F., Hua, S.: Course-scheduling algorithm of option-based hierarchical reinforcement learning. In: 2010 Second International Workshop on Education Technology and Computer Science, vol. 1, pp. 288–291. IEEE (2010)

28. Mnih, V., et al.: Human-level control through deep reinforcement learning. Nature **518**(7540), 529–533 (2015)

29. Nachum, O., Gu, S.S., Lee, H., Levine, S.: Data-efficient hierarchical reinforcement learning. In: Bengio, S., Wallach, H., Larochelle, H., Grauman, K., Cesa-Bianchi, N., Garnett, R. (eds.) Advances in Neural Information Processing Systems, vol. 31. Curran Associates, Inc. (2018)

30. Papoudakis, G., Christianos, F., Rahman, A., Albrecht, S.V.: Dealing with non-stationarity in multi-agent deep reinforcement learning. arXiv preprint arXiv:1906.04737 (2019)

31. Parr, R., Russell, S.: Reinforcement learning with hierarchies of machines. Advances in Neural Information Processing Systems, pp. 1043–1049 (1998)

32. Schulman, J., Wolski, F., Dhariwal, P., Radford, A., Klimov, O.: Proximal policy optimization algorithms. arXiv preprint arXiv:1707.06347 (2017)

33. Sutton, R.S., Precup, D., Singh, S.: Between mdps and semi-mdps: a framework for temporal abstraction in reinforcement learning. Artif. Intell. **112**(1–2), 181–211 (1999)

34. Tang, H., et al.: Hierarchical deep multiagent reinforcement learning with temporal abstraction. arXiv preprint arXiv:1809.09332 (2018)

35. Terry, J.K., Grammel, N., Hari, A., Santos, L., Black, B.: Revisiting parameter sharing in multi-agent deep reinforcement learning. arXiv preprint arXiv:2005.13625 (2020)

36. Ye, H., Li, G.Y.: Deep reinforcement learning for resource allocation in v2v communications. In: 2018 IEEE International Conference on Communications (ICC), pp. 1–6. IEEE (2018)

AIL - Artificial Intelligence and Law

Content-Based Lawsuits Document Image Retrieval

Daniela L. Freire[1]([✉])[iD], André Carlos Ponce de Leon Ferreira de Carvalho[1][iD],
Leonardo Carneiro Feltran[1][iD], Lara Ayumi Nagamatsu[1],
Kelly Cristina Ramos da Silva[1][iD], Claudemir Firmino[1][iD],
João Eduardo Ferreira[1][iD], Pedro Losco Takecian[2][iD], Danilo Carlotti[1][iD],
Francisco Antonio Cavalcanti Lima[2][iD], and Roberto Mendes Portela[2]

[1] University of Sao Paulo, Sao Paulo, Brazil
{danielalfreire,andre}@icmc.usp.br,
{leonardo.feltran,lara.nagamatsu,kelly.ramos.silva,cfirmino}@usp.br,
{jef,danilopcarlotti}@ime.usp.br
[2] TJSP - Justice Court of São Paulo State, Sao Paulo, Brazil
plt@ime.usp.br, {franciscol,robertomp}@tjsp.jus.br

Abstract. The São Paulo Court of Justice has the highest number of lawsuits of all courts. The lawsuits are composed of raster-scanned documents enclosed in unstructured volumes, of which some are unreadable document images. Natural Language Processing techniques fail to extract from some of these documents due to the low quality of images. This article proposes a methodology to automatize the retrieval of document images from lawsuit databases based on the contents of the images. We developed a hybrid algorithm for feature extraction from document images and used a distance metric to retrieve similar images. The TJSP's database was used to validate our proposal, resulting in a system that allows finding similar images with an accuracy above eighty percent.

Keywords: Document image processing · Content-based image recognition · Deep learning techniques · Convolutional neural networks models · Feature extraction

1 Introduction

According to data from the report produced by the National Council of Justice [9], the São Paulo Court of Justice (in Portuguese, Tribunal de Justiça de São Paulo - TJSP) has the most significant number of lawsuits of all courts in the world, the congestion highest indicator (84%) and the longest average processing time (seven years and five months) among state courts in Brazil. Its lawsuits collection corresponds to 25% of the total lawsuits in Brazilian Justice, including lawsuits of the higher spheres, federal courts and superior courts. With that in mind, São Paulo Court has the largest workforce, comprising 2,500 magistrates and approximately 40,000 civil servants in 320 units. Despite the considerable

G. Marreiros et al. (Eds.): EPIA 2022, LNAI 13566, pp. 29–40, 2022.
https://doi.org/10.1007/978-3-031-16474-3_3

expense of the Judiciary and the public coffers, the grossing of the amount of money collected by the TJSP cases filed subject to the collection of costs in 2020 was R\$ 2,021.92. [12].

The lawsuits are composed of raster-scanned documents in PDF files-usually, several kinds of documents per file enclosed in unstructured volumes without any digital index. These documents have perspective distortions and uneven illumination because they were captured in an unrestrained environment and produced by a flatbed scanner, fax machine, or mobile devices, such as smartphones or tablets. Usually, Natural Language Processing (NLP) tools are used for extracting text from, classification and processing document images. However, many lawsuit document images are illegible or of low quality, so it negatively affects the performance carried out by NLP tools because extracted texts from them usually contain errors. Content-based image retrieval (CBIR) is equivalent to providing human vision to the computer for similarity-based image retrieval. CBIR can classify image database images according to the degree of similarity with the query image [4]. Image retrieval depends on its content, known as features, which can be low-level or high-level. Low-level features include colour, texture, and shape, and high-level features describe the features captured by a human-like brain. Several features are extracted in the image recovery process to identify the image with more fidelity. Examples of other features extracted from images are colour histogram, colour averaging, colour structure descriptor and texture for feature extraction [7]. Deep learning techniques, especially Convolutional Neural Networks (CNNs), have been successfully used to improve the performance of feature extraction and the classification efficiency of CBIR [10]. Compared to other feature extraction and classification algorithms, CNNs do not require pre-processing. They are responsible for developing their filters (unsupervised learning), which is not the case with other more traditional algorithms. The lack of initial parameterization and human intervention is a significant advantage of CNN.

This article proposes a CBIR to automatize the retrieval of document images from lawsuit databases. We use a TJSP database composed of 2,136 unrecognized document images by NLP tools. The first contribution is a hybrid algorithm for feature extraction of document images that combines two traditional computer vision techniques for feature detection (ORB and HOG) with one CNN (MobileNet). The second contribution is a content-based retrieval tool that uses the hybrid algorithm, specific for lawsuit document images. We validated our proposal by performing several experiments, reaching an accuracy above 80% in proposed models, and statistically confirmed the results with ANOVA and Tukey statistical tests. The rest of this article is organised as follows: Sect. 2 exposes the proposal of a content-based lawsuits document image retrieval; Sect. 3 describe the application of proposal; Sect. 4 reports experiments and statistics to validate the proposal; and, Sect. 5 presents our conclusions.

2   Proposal

This section describes our proposal of a methodology for automating the retrieving of similar images from lawsuits databases. Our goal is to offer an alternative for document processing when extracting information from document images is not feasible by NLP tools, i.e., when images are entirely blurred images or with stains or scribbles. The retrieving similar images occurs in three steps: Preprocessing, Features Extraction, Similarity Search, and Result Presentation. Figure 1 shows these stages. Preprocessing step of the document processing

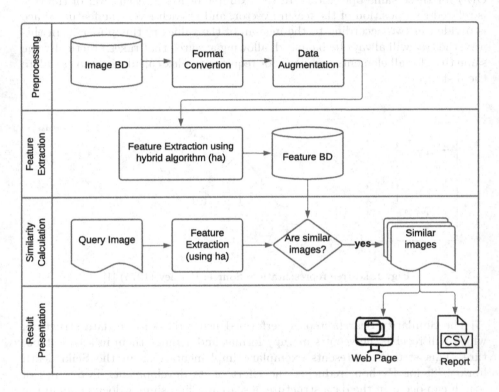

Fig. 1. Steps of retrieval.

pipeline has two activities: Format Conversion and Data Augmentation. In Format Conversion, the unrecognized documents images are read from a repository and converted from .pdf to .jpeg format. In Data Augmentation activity, since the unrecognized document images database is usually small (less than 1000 images), the data augmentation increases the database by applying several transformations such as rotation, width and height shift, shear, and zoom whitening, brightness, so on.

In the Features Extraction step, the features are extracted from all images and are stored as vectors in .npy format files. We developed a hybrid algorithm

based on ORB, HOG and MobileNet algorithms for feature extraction of images. The algorithm looks for points of great importance and edges in the images and compiles them into a descriptor vector used to compare the images. The descriptor vectors are written as files in the .npy format that is used by the data structure. Then the .npy files, which contain the vectors for each image, are read and stored in a kd-tree [1] for future searches. The kd-tree is a data structure in a binary tree that arranges the elements based on their values in each feature vector dimension. It has an average complexity of $O(logn)$ for inserting, removing and searching elements, while in the worst case, it has a complexity of $O(n)$ for these same operations. In the example of Fig. 2, each level of the tree is related to a position of the feature vector, and at each level, the feature space is divided in two according to the median of the values in this position. In this way, the tree will always be balanced, allowing a search that takes practically the same time for all elements and does not require complex calculations to calculate the distances.

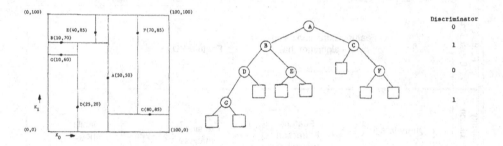

Fig. 2. kd-tree representation. Source: Bentley (1975) [1]

The Similarity Search step is performed using the kd-tree data structure, which will receive the vectors in .npy format and arrange them in a tree structure. This structure presents exemplary implementations in the Scikit-learn library [8] for Python, reducing the effort of its development. Two types of search can occur in the data structure, a search to find similar documents in the structure's database or a search based on a new image: *Query Image*. The first type results in a report on the relationship of which images present the most significant similarities to each other. In contrast, the second type presents a set of the N images most similar to the *Query Image*. The similarity between images is measured by the Euclidean distance similarity metric, comparing the feature vectors of the images to each other.

In the Result Presentation step, similar images and their similarity percentages are shown on a web page in the online process or on a report with this information saved into a file .csv format in the offline process.

3   Application

This section describes the application of the proposed CBIR in the São Paulo Court of Justice lawsuit document images. First, we contextualize how our research integrates with the document identification project in the TJSP environment and describe the database. Afterwards, we report the preprocessing and the feature extraction of the document images. Finally, we detail the image similarity search and the result presentation

3.1   Contextualization and Database

This experiment is part of the project to identify duplicates of the use of the same proof of payment of a lawsuit payment receipts issued by the TJSP, which gives evidence of fraud in the judicial system. The project's first stage seeks to identify document duplication through information obtained from texts extracted from images of scanned documents, using natural language processing techniques. The proposed pipeline deals with images of payment slip documents from which no information can be extracted and converted into texts. Usually, they are images whose text is unreadable or of low quality, containing much noise, low resolution, or even crumpled and poorly positioned document images.

The database used in the research project is composed of 139,603 processes that have 416,316 images of documents belonging to the 4th Civil Court of the Regional Forum XII - Nossa Senhora do Ó, in the city of São Paulo. Only 0.5% of the total number of documents were not recognized by the previous text extraction steps, leaving for our experiment 2,136 unrecognized document images, including lawsuit payment receipt images and other kinds of document images such as personal documents, reports, lawsuit decisions.

3.2   Preprocessing and Feature Extraction

We used Python Imaging Library (PIL) [3] to convert .pdf files to .jpeg format. PIL adds image processing capabilities to the Python interpreter and provides extensive file format support, an efficient internal representation, and fairly powerful image processing capabilities. After, we manually labelled the 2,136 unrecognized document images. As the number of the samples is small, We used the Keras ImageDataGenerator class that provides real-time data augmentation and ensures that the model receives new variations of the images at each epoch (or iteration) without adding them to the original image database. Furthermore, as the images are loaded in batches, much memory is saved.

We developed a hybrid algorithm for feature extraction based on HOG, ORB, and one CNN, MobileNet. We intended to combine the strengths of the three algorithms to obtain a more robust algorithm able to deal with the disturbances of document images. The internal structure of this algorithm is shown in Fig. 3.   The input image format changes according to each algorithm. HOG uses greyscale and 400 × 400 size images. ORG uses greyscale and 600 × 600 size images. Both algorithms require a larger size to capture more minor features,

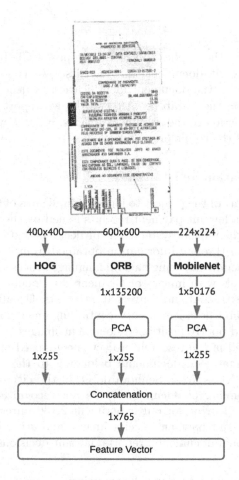

Fig. 3. Feature extractor diagram

such as small numbers and letters. MobileNet processing reduces the dimensionality of the images to a size of 224×224, which is the required size due to knowledge transfer, and colour images. In general, CNNs require inputs to have a specific value scale, as these scales lead to improved training. Keras library allows abstracting this part using a function that transforms the scale to the required format. The feature vectors produced for HOG, ORG, and MobileNet are 1×135200, $1X255$, and 1×50176 sizes. As feature vectors from HOG and MobileNet have many positions, we carried out a reduction dimensionality of the HOG and MobileNet output using Principal Component Analysis, or PCA, the most popular technique for dimensionality reduction. PCA is the orthogonal projection of the data onto a lower-dimensional linear space, such that the variance of the projected data is maximized [2]. All output feature vectors with the same size were concatenated, resulting in a vector with 765 positions which is normalized and then converted into a .npy format file.

3.3 Similarity Calculation and Result Presentation

The proposal CBIR can work out online or offline processes. In both processes, The `extractor.py` script extracts deep features from each database document image of the dataset using our hybrid algorithm. It stores `.npy` format files. In the online process, we developed a simple image-based image search engine using Keras and Flask, a micro web framework written in Python. The `server.py` script runs a web server, in which a query image is provided as input to the server via a Flask web interface. The server extracts the in-depth features from query images and compares them with dataset images using the Euclidean distance metric [11] to retry similar images. The `server.py` algorithm's output is a predefined number of best similar images. On the other hand, in an offline process, the `output.py` script reads a set of query document images from an input path, extracts deep features from these images, compares them with dataset images, finds a predefined number of best similar images, then returns a file `.csv` with query images and their respective similar images.

We tested the proposal CBIR using the dataset composed of 2,136 unrecognized document images to determine if there were images with 100% of similarity. The CBIR returned 32 images identified as equal to human experts.

4 Experiments

This section describes the experiments carried out to develop and evaluate the algorithm for feature extraction. First, we describe an experiment carried out to choose the CNN. After, we describe an experiment for hybrid algorithm evaluation.

4.1 CNN's Choice

We tested four CNNs: VGG16, ResNet50, MobileNet, and MobileNetV2. We performed an experiment with a set of 3448 document images from TJSP. Metrics measured were: execution time, CPU time, percentage of memory usage and accuracy. The execution time comprises the time elapsed to search for a more similar image. User CPU time is the CPU time spent executing the algorithm. The memory usage percentage is the percentage of the total memory size used in executing the algorithm. Accuracy indicates the number of correctly predicted cases concerning all existing cases. Table 1 summarizes the average of the values in the simulations, where the time unit of execution time and CPU time is second. We repeated the execution of each tested algorithm 30 times, collected the metrics and then performed tests to verify if there was a statistically significant difference between the CNNs. The tests applied were ANOVA and Tukey HSD test with a significance level of 0.05. The ANOVA test is a statistical technique that allows differentiating between the variations found in a set of measurements of an experiment derived from random factors due to real differences between the sources of variations (CNNs) under analysis. The parameter *F-value*, in the

ANOVA test, is a resource to find out if the variation between the population means is statistically significant. The *F-value* is a probability in which if its value is less than 0.05; it means that there is a statistical difference between the treatments (our CNNs). The *P-value* is a parameter that indicates the significance of the adding model terms. When there is such a difference in the experiment results, there are multiple comparison techniques to determine which treatments differ and which are similar. One technique is to use the Tukey HSD Test.

Table 1. Metric average of the convolutional neural networks

Metrics	CNNs			
	ResNet50	Vgg16	MobileNet	MobileNetV2
Execution time	**355.50**	365.83	362.40	363.20
CPU time	**4,893.33**	12,154.94	19,520.06	11,393.10
% Memory	23.03	23.03	**22.65**	23.35
Accuracy	0.86	0.85	**0.87**	0.87

Table 2 presents execution time analysis of variance (ANOVA). The resulting values for the *F-value* and the *P-value* were, respectively, 13.796 and 2.8523e–07. The ANOVA from execution time presents the sum of squares as 1,165.28 for the CNNs and 2,139.78 for error. The freedom degree was 3 for the CNNs and 76 for error. Table 3 presents CPU time analysis of variance. The resulting values for the *F-value* and the *P-value* were, respectively, 168.628 and 1.675e–33. The ANOVA from CPU time shows the sum of squares was 2.148961e+09 for the CNNs and 3.228426e+08 for error. The freedom degree was 3 for the CNNs and 76 for error.

Table 2. Execution time

Sources of variation	Degree of freedom	Sum of squares	*F-value*	*P-value* (>*F-value*)
CNNs	3.0	1,165.28	13.796	2.8523e–07
Error	76.0	2,139.78		

Table 3. CPU time

Sources of variation	Degree of freedom	Sum of squares	*F-value*	*P-value* (>*F-value*)
CNNs	3.0	2.148961e+09	168.628	1.675e–33
Error	76.0	3.228426e+08		

Table 4 presents memory percentage analysis of variance. The resulting values for the *F-value* and the *P-value* were, respectively, 21.128 and 4.706e–10. The ANOVA from memory percentage shows the sum of squares was 0.820917 for the CNNs and 0.984293 for error. The freedom degree was 3 for the CNNs and 76 for error. Table 5 presents accuracy analysis of variance. For the CPU time, the resulting values for the *F-value* and the *P-value* were, respectively, 1,497.11 and 1.76e–67. The ANOVA from accuracy shows the sum of squares was 0.002634 for the CNNs and 0.000045 for error. The freedom degree was 3 for the CNNs and 76 for error.

Table 4. Memory percentage

Sources of variation	Degree of freedom	Sum of squares	*F-value*	*P-value* (>*F-value*)
CNNs	3.0	0.820917	21.128	4.706e−10
Error	76.0	0.984293		

Table 5. Accuracy

Sources of variation	Degree of freedom	Sum of squares	*F-value*	*P-value* (>*F-value*)
CNNs	3.0	0.002634	1,497.11	1.76e−67
Error	76.0	0.000045		

Table 6, Table 7, Table 8, and Table 9 show the pairwise comparison of CNNs with Tukey HSD confidence intervals with a test significance level of 0.05. The group1 and group2 columns are the formed groups; the meandiff column is pairwise mean differences; p-adj is the adjusted *P-value* from the HSD test; the rejected column is "True" if we reject Null for group pair.

Table 6. Execution time

CNNs				
group1	group2	meandiff	p-adj	reject
MobileNet	MobileNetV2	0.7949	0.9000	False
MobileNet	ResNet50	−6.9039	0.0010	True
MobileNet	Vgg16	3.4298	0.1812	False
MobileNetV2	ResNet50	−7.6988	0.0010	True
MobileNetV2	Vgg16	2.6348	0.4029	False
ResNet50	Vgg16	10.3337	0.0010	True

Table 7. CPU time

CNNs				
group1	group2	meandiff	p-adj	reject
MobileNet	MobileNetV2	−8126.9605	0.0010	True
MobileNet	ResNet50	−14626.7325	0.0010	True
MobileNet	Vgg16	−7365.126	0.0010	True
MobileNetV2	ResNet50	−6499.772	0.0010	True
MobileNetV2	Vgg16	761.8345	0.6313	False
ResNet50	Vgg16	7261.6065	0.0010	True

Table 8. Memory percentage

CNNs				
group1	group2	meandiff	p-adj	reject
MobileNet	MobileNetV2	0.1399	0.0012	True
MobileNet	ResNet50	−0.0894	0.0706	False
MobileNet	Vgg16	−0.1214	0.0063	True
MobileNetV2	ResNet50	−0.2293	0.001	True
MobileNetV2	Vgg16	−0.2613	0.001	True
ResNet50	Vgg16	−0.0319	0.7876	False

Table 9. Accuracy

CNNs				
group1	group2	meandiff	p-adj	reject
MobileNet	MobileNetV2	−0.0002	0.7151	False
MobileNet	ResNet50	−0.0084	0.001	True
MobileNet	Vgg16	−0.0136	0.001	True
MobileNetV2	ResNet50	−0.0081	0.001	True
MobileNetV2	Vgg16	−0.0134	0.001	True
ResNet50	Vgg16	−0.0052	0.001	True

The experiment with the simulations for extraction features indicated that ResNet50 reached the best performance in terms of execution and CPU time. In contrast, MobileNet reached the best memory percentage and accuracy performance, c.f. Table 1. The lowest execution time average was 355.50 s with the ResNet50, but others reached similar values for this metric. The ANOVA showed a statistical difference, and the Tukey averages comparison test formed two groups: one with ResNet50 and another with the other CNNs, c.f. shown in Table 2 and Table 6. The lowest CPU time average was 4,803 s with the ResNet50. The ANOVA showed a statistical difference, and the Tukey averages comparison test formed two groups: one with ResNet50 and another with the other CNNs, c.f. shown in Table 3 and Table 7.

4.2   Hybrid Algorithm Evaluation

We carried out an experiment to evaluate the hybrid algorithm performance regarding the performance of each pure algorithm. We randomly selected 300 document images and applied five distortions in images: rotation, blurring, gamma level change, shift, and zoom level. The tests were performed by populating the data structure with unmodified images, while the query images were of modified images. The accuracy was collected for each level or type of distortion analyzed. Figure 4 presents the results for the four analyzed algorithms, the HOG, ORB, MobileNet and the hybrid algorithm. The best accuracy was reached by ORB, followed by the hybrid algorithm regarding rotation. HOG reached the best accuracy regarding blurring, followed by the hybrid algorithm. All algorithms reached similar accuracy regarding gama level change, shift, and zoom level.

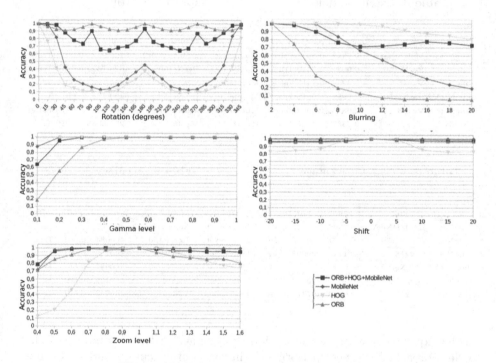

Fig. 4. Algorithm evaluation about distortions

We also applied five types of noises in images: Gaussian Noise, Localvar Noise, Poison Noise, Salt Noise, and Pepper Noise. The Gaussian Noise is a randomly generated noise value that affects the image pixels. In a Gaussian Noise added image, both the true pixel values and random Gaussian noise added values exist. It spreads the noise values by using the Gaussian probability density function [5,6]. Localvar noise is a zero-mean Gaussian white noise. The difference between Gaussian and Localvar noise is that the former is independent of the pixel intensity of an image, and the latter is dependent [13]. Poison Noise

depends on the measurement of light, photon direction and quantized nature of light [14]. Salt and Pepper are types of noise that combine black and white spots in an image. Salt noise is added to an image by adding random brightness all over the image. Pepper Noise modifies the image by adding random dark spots [5]. The accuracy collected for each noise analyzed is shown in Fig. 5 for the four analyzed algorithms, the HOG, ORB, MobileNet and the hybrid algorithm. There is also a significant performance increase in noisy images when using the proposed model, being very close to the performance of MobileNet, the best in this regard, reaching a better performance for Salt and Pepper types of noise. The hybrid algorithm generally showed greater robustness than the pure algorithms when considering both distortions and noise, although the accuracy was not the best in every case.

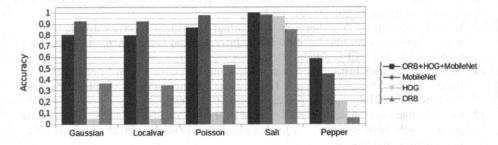

Fig. 5. Algorithm evaluation about noises

5   Conclusion

The lawsuit's document images often contain a lot of noise and distortions because they are captured in an unrestrained environment by different devices such as flatbed scanners, fax machines, smartphones, or tablets. The classification performance of these images with low quality is poor when NLP tools. We proposed a content-based lawsuits document image retrieval to search similar document images to solve this problem. The CBIR contains an algorithm for feature extraction based on three algorithms: HOG, ORB, and one CNN, MobileNet. We carried out exhaustive experiments to choose the best methodologies and techniques for developing the algorithm using the TJSP database. We concluded that the algorithm proposed has greater robustness in extracting features from images with distortions and noise than the pure algorithms.

References

1. Bentley, J.L.: Multidimensional binary search trees used for associative searching. Commun. ACM **18**(9), 509–517 (1975)
2. Bishop, C.M., Nasrabadi, N.M.: Pattern Recognition and Machine Learning. Springer, Heidelberg (2006)

3. Clark, A.: Pillow (pil fork) documentation. Readthedocs (2015). https:// Buildmedia.Readthedocs.Org/Media/Pdf/Pillow/Latest/Pillow.Pdf
4. Gudivada, V.N., Raghavan, V.V., Vanapipat, K.: A unified approach to data modeling and retrieval for a class of image database applications. In: Multimedia Database Systems: Issues and Research Directions, pp. 37–78. Springer, Heidelberg (1996). https://doi.org/10.1007/978-3-642-60950-3_2
5. Hoshyar, A.N., Al-Jumaily, A., Hoshyar, A.N.: Comparing the performance of various filters on skin cancer images. Procedia Comput. Sci. **42**, 32–37 (2014)
6. Luisier, F., Blu, T., Unser, M.: Image denoising in mixed poisson-gaussian noise. IEEE Trans. Image Process. **20**(3), 696–708 (2010)
7. Pattanaik, S., Bhalke, D.: Beginners to content-based image retrieval. Int. J. Sci. Eng. Technol. Res. **1**, 40–44 (2012)
8. Pedregosa, F., et al.: Scikit-learn: machine learning in python. J. Mach. Learn. Res. **12**, 2825–2830 (2011)
9. de Justiça Departamento de Pesquisas Judiciárias, C.N.: Justiça em números 2021. Justiça em números 2021 (2021 [Online])
10. Rian, Z., Christanti, V., Hendryli, J.: Content-based image retrieval using convolutional neural networks. In: 2019 IEEE International Conference on Signals and Systems, pp. 1–7. IEEE (2019)
11. Sergyan, S.: Color histogram features based image classification in content-based image retrieval systems. In: 6th International Symposium on Applied Machine Intelligence and Informatics, pp. 221–224. IEEE (2008)
12. de Tecnologia da Informação do Tribunal de Justiça de São Paulo, S.: Tribunal de justiça - estado de são paulo: a justiça próxima do cidadão (2022). https://www.tjsp.jus.br/QuemSomos
13. Tin, H.H.K.: Removal of noise by median filtering in image processing. In: Parallel and Soft Computing, pp. 1–3 (2011)
14. Unser, M.: Texture classification and segmentation using wavelet frames. IEEE Trans. Image Process. **4**(11), 1549–1560 (1995)

Lawsuits Document Images Processing Classification

Daniela L. Freire[1]([✉]) ⓘ, André Carlos Ponce de Leon Ferreira de Carvalho[1] ⓘ,
Leonardo Carneiro Feltran[1] ⓘ, Lara Ayumi Nagamatsu[1],
Kelly Cristina Ramos da Silva[1] ⓘ, Claudemir Firmino[1] ⓘ,
João Eduardo Ferreira[1] ⓘ, Pedro Losco Takecian[2] ⓘ, Danilo Carlotti[1] ⓘ,
Francisco Antonio Cavalcanti Lima[2] ⓘ, and Roberto Mendes Portela[2]

[1] University of Sao Paulo, Sao Paulo, Brazil
{danielalfreire,andre}@icmc.usp.br,
{leonardo.feltran,lara.nagamatsu,kelly.ramos.silva,cfirmino}@usp.br,
{jef,danilopcarlotti}@ime.usp.br
[2] TJSP - Justice Court of São Paulo State, Sao Paulo, Brazil
plt@ime.usp.br

Abstract. Natural Language Processing techniques usually fail to classify low quality lawsuit document images produced by a flatbed scanner or fax machine or even captured by mobile devices, such as smartphones or tablets. As the courts of justice have many lawsuits, the manual detection of classification errors is unfeasible, favouring fraud, such as using the same payment receipt for more than one fee. An alternative to classifying low-quality document images is visual-based methods, which extract features from the images. This article proposes classification models for lawsuit document image processing using transfer learning to train Convolutional Neural Networks most quickly and obtain good results even in smaller databases. We validated our proposal using a TJSP dataset composed of 2,136 unrecognized document images by Natural Language Processing techniques and reached an accuracy above 80% in the proposed models.

Keywords: Document image processing · Image classification · Deep learning techniques · Convolutional neural networks models · Feature extraction

1 Introduction

The São Paulo Court of Justice (in Portuguese, Tribunal de Justiça de São Paulo - TJSP) is the most significant in the volume of cases, with 25% of them in progress in Brazil. To ensure the excellent functioning and efficiency in the processing of these processes, the TJSP has 320 districts in the state and more than 40 thousand employees [26]. The parties must provide all documents necessary for the entry and processing of the lawsuit to the court, including proof of payment of court fees. The parties classify these and then pass through an

G. Marreiros et al. (Eds.): EPIA 2022, LNAI 13566, pp. 41–52, 2022.
https://doi.org/10.1007/978-3-031-16474-3_4

empirical conference by court officials. In many cases, classification errors favour fraud, such as using the same payment receipt for more than one fee. As the TJSP collection is physical and very voluminous, identifying these classification failures becomes unfeasible. Besides, the lawsuit documents are usually low-quality images captured in an unrestrained environment, so they typically have perspective distortions and uneven illumination.

The document image processing pipeline have used to automate the organization and indexing of document images. The first step of the pipeline is document image classification, which defines what class or classes a document belongs to. The survey [17] has been extended from the former search [4], presenting a current and broad literature analysis of document image classification, focusing on mostly-text document images, including non-mobile and mobile document images. The former regards document images produced by a flatbed scanner, fax machine, or converting an electronic document to the image format. In contrast, the latter refers to document images captured by mobile devices, such as smartphones or tablets.

Research works have dealt with problems with document image classification in Law, such as the identification of the parties in legal proceedings [19], classification of documents from lawsuits into administrative labels [3,21,23], and prediction of the lawsuit domain lawsuit [25]. Usually, Natural Language Processing (NLP) tools solve these problems. Meantime the particularity and lack of knowledge of the language used in Law turn this field into a challenge for NLP applications, especially in Brazil, where there is a more extensive jurisdiction with different expressions in the legal language to designate the same reality depending on regions of the country [22]. Furthermore, many legal documents are illegible, so it negatively affects the classification performance carried out by NLP tools since they can extract text containing errors of images with low quality. A solution to the classification of low-quality document images is visual-based methods. They describe the appearance of the document images roughly and catch information that enables one to recognize the documents "at a glance." [7]. One of the visual-based methods is the 'deep features' that use Convolutional Neural Networks (CNNs) to extract features from the images [17] automatically. CNN is a type of artificial neural network where individual neurons are arranged side by side so that they respond to overlapping regions in the visual field [14]. Two components make up a typical convolutional neural network architecture. The first component is faintly connected and is responsible for extracting images' features. The other component is fully connected and is responsible for classifying images using the features that, for this reason, are called deep features. This article proposes two classifications for lawsuit document image processing. The first is a classification model for eliminating images without useful information, and the second is a classification model for splitting lawsuits document images into different kinds of documents. We validated our proposal using a TJSP dataset composed of 2,136 unrecognized document images. The proposed models reached an accuracy above 80% in the proposed models. The rest of this article is organised as follows: Sect. 2 discusses works related to document

image classification and retrieving; Sect. 3 provides background information over image processing techniques; Sect. 4 exposes the proposal of a lawsuits document image processing pipeline; Sect. 5 reports experiments and statistics to validate the proposal; and, Sect. 6 presents our conclusions.

2   Related Work

This section gathers works that proposed using artificial intelligence techniques to support the work in the court system. Most works concern the automatic classification of court decisions by distinct techniques. Others predict the legal area from which a case belongs to and make the prediction of the court's decision based only on the textual content of the documents. Besides, we selected works that used Convolutional Neural Networks for classifying documents images or for content-based image recognition.

[25] developed a mean probability ensemble system combining the output of multiple Support Vector Machine (SVM) classifiers that reached 98% average F1 score in predicting a court decision, 96% F1 score for predicting the class of lawsuits, and 87.07% F1 score on estimating the date of a court decision. [3] proposed a classifier of 6,814 lawsuits [23] of the Supreme Court of Brazil into six classes. The authors used a Bidirectional Long Short-Term Memory model that reached an F1 score of 84%, dismissing the need to run an OCR on the remaining pages of the document. [27] mined the comprehensive information of enterprises and extracted features, combined with two models of machine learning. The first model is the combinatorial prediction model using the Light Gradient Boosting Machine (LightGBM) model, and its Top 1 accuracy was 40.868%, while its Top 2 accuracy was 21.826%. The second model is the Artificial Neural Network (ANN) model to classify and predict categories of lawsuits, its Top 1 accuracy is 40.803% and Top 2 accuracy is 21.243%. The dataset used is from the IEEE ISI World Cup 2019, which seventeen classes of lawsuits from 3,500 listed enterprises. [8] performed training of region-based classifiers and ensembling for document image classification. First, the authors used a primary level of 'inter-domain' transfer learning by exporting weights from a pre-trained VGG16 architecture on the ImageNet dataset to train a document classifier on whole document images. After, they studied the nature of region-based influence modelling and trained deep learning models for image segments in a secondary level of 'intra-domain' transfer learning. Finally, they integrated the predictions of the base deep neural network models with a stacked generalization based ensembling. The dataset was composed of a subset of the IIT-CDIP Test Collection known as the RVL-CDIP dataset [13], which consists of scanned grey-scale images of documents from lawsuits against American Tobacco companies, which is segregated into 16 categories or classes. The proposed method achieves state-of-the-art accuracy of 92.21%. [1] used an approach for learning visual features for document analysis in an unsupervised way, increasing the amount of data through a data augmentation technique. First, the authors used the feature extractor to represent document images s for an unsupervised classification task. Then, they used a

small amount of annotated data in the parameters initialization of the model used in a supervised classification task. In their experiments, the authors used the Tobacco-3482 [16], which contains 3,482 document images and 10 document classes and a small subset of the RVL-CDIP dataset [13], which contains 5,000 document images and 16 document classes. The median accuracy reached by the model in the classification task was 68.86%.

3   Background

Deep learning techniques are being used as feature extractors because these techniques are very robust when extracting complex features that express the image in much more detail, very efficient in learning the task-specific features and are very efficient [10,11,18,28]. The advantage of deep learning is that instead of providing the filters for performing convolution over an image to extract various features of an image (such as vertical edges, horizontal edges, noise distribution, son on), the model itself learn the filters and weights during each epoch. For this problem, we have used transfer learning for feature extraction. Transfer learning is a machine learning method that uses the weights of pre-trained models for a given task in models focusing on solving other problems. Due to this previous learning, training these networks takes less time and requires a smaller database to obtain good training.

There are several constructed convolutional neural networks models that use pre-trained models as starting points in computer vision problems, such as VGGNet [24]. VGGNet constructed CNNs with a depth of 16–19 layers. The VGG16 model comprises 13 convolutional layers, 3 fully connected layers, and five pooling layers. The 13 convolutional layers and the three fully connected layers have weight coefficients, composing a structure of 16 weighting layers, so it is called VGG16. The pooling layers do not count because they do not have weights. The model is constructed by piling several convolutional layers and pooling layers. The same convolution kernel parameters are used in every convolutional layer, and the same pooling kernel parameters are used in every pooling layer. The VGG16 structure is divided into blocks, and each block contains several convolutional layers and a pooling layer. In the same block, the number of channels of the convolutional layer is the same. Despite a simple structure, VGG is pretty adaptable because it contains many parameters, reaching 139,357,544 weights to convolution kernel and to fully connected layer. VGG19 is a CNN that comprises 19 layers of 16 convolution layers and 3 layers fully connected to classify the images, with 5 pooling layers. It uses multiple 3×3 filters in each convolutional layer because VGG19 is a popular method for image classification. These models are trained on the ImageNet dataset that contains a million images of 1000 categories.

In this article, we used Keras [15], an open-source software library that provides a Python interface for artificial neural networks and performs as an interface for the TensorFlow library. Keras Applications are deep learning models that are made available alongside pre-trained weights.

4   Proposal

This section describes our proposal of classification for unrecognized lawsuit document images. These documents make up a heterogeneous dataset containing document images with and without helpful information. We consider images without helpful information when they are entirely blurred, stains or small scribbles, while images with helpful information are those in which there is any content like text, figures, tables, and so on. The proposal has two main steps: preprocessing and classification.

4.1   Preprocessing

Preprocessing step has three activities: Format Conversion, Data Augmentation, and Histogram Equalization, as shown in Fig. 1. In Format Conversion, the unrecognized documents images are read from a repository and converted from .pdf to .tiff format. In contrast to other graphic formats such as JPEG, TIFF has an alpha channel that can store the transparency of individual pixels and colour information. The advantage of this method is the simple and, therefore, fast compression and decompression of such files with lossless quality. In Data Augmentation activity, since the unrecognized document images dataset is usually small (less than 1000 images), the data augmentation increases the dataset by applying several transformations such as rotation, width and height shift, shear, and zoom whitening, brightness, so on.

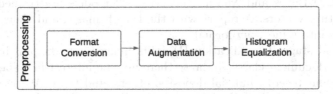

Fig. 1. Preprocessing step.

Then, in Histogram Equalization, we applied techniques to enhance the images' quality. First, we transformed the images into grey-scale and applied a Gaussian filter for smoothing out noises and for edge detection of the images. Simultaneously suppressing noise, the Gaussian filter can cause distortion, edge position shift, edge vanishing and ghost edges [9]. Furthermore, some images produced by data augmentation were distorted. Then, we use Contrast Limited Adaptive Histogram Equalization (CLAHE) technique for the histogram equalization. This technique carries out histogram equalization in small stains with high accuracy and contrast limiting. We used Otsu algorithm [20] to find the optimal value for a binary threshold. Otsu is the most popular global threshold iterative algorithm where the intensity levels are split into background and foreground for all possible intensity values in the image [2]. Then, we dismiss the

distorted images by calculating the percentage of black pixels of images binarized (*perc*), i.e., one minus the mean of pixel values divided by 255, because by convention, 0 is usually black, and 255 is white. Since we do not want to lose any image document with any helpful information, we assume a low value for the minimal percentage of black. Therefore, we considered an image with helpful information if it has at least 2% of black pixels, i.e., if an image has *perc* < 2, it is discarded. We use the resultant dataset to create a model for classifying new images into the classes: with and without helpful information.

4.2   Classification

The classification step is performed in two stages: Classification I and II. In the first stage (Classification I), we used the Haralick algorithm [12] to extract textural features from images. The Grey Level Co-occurrence Matrix (GLCM) is the main idea of Haralick Texture features. GLCM looks for pairs of adjacent pixel values that occur in an image and records them over the entire image. There are four types of adjacency: Left-to-Right, Top-to-Bottom, Top Left-to-Bottom Right, and Top Right-to-Bottom Left. First, the Haralick features are extracted for all four types of adjacency after obtaining the mean of all four types of GLCM. Then, the feature vector for the image which describes the texture is returned. The features are then stored as feature vectors in .npy format files to be used in the training of machine learning classification models. We created five machine learning classifiers to decide if an image has helpful information or not, namely Linear Support Vector Machine, Random Forest, Decision Tree, Gaussian Naive Bayes and Neural Networks. All models are trained with the Haralick texture vectors. A report with the list of images and their respective class is saved into a file .csv format.

The second stage (Classification II) splits images with helpful information into separate document classes because there may be interest in a specific class, such as payment receipt, judicial deposits, others, and trash. We used VGG19 because it is an advanced CNN with pre-trained layers and a great understanding of what defines an image in terms of shape, colour, and structure. We froze its layers and appended a shallow six-layer network on top of it to perform the classification task of identifying images with and without trees. A report with the list of images and their respective class is saved into a file .csv format. Figure 2 depicts the classification step.

5   Experiment

This section describes experiments to validation of the proposal of lawsuit document images classification in São Paulo Court of Justice. First, we contextualize how our research integrates the document image processing pipeline of the TJSP. Afterwards, we describe the database and the classification's models, and finally, we present the results obtained.

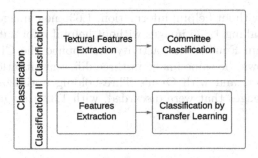

Fig. 2. Classification step.

This experiment is part of the project to identify failures of classification, mainly the reuse of the same payment receipt issued by the TJSP, which gives evidence of fraud in the judicial system. The project's first stage seeks to identify document duplication through information obtained from texts extracted from images of scanned documents, using natural language processing techniques. The proposed pipeline deals with images of payment slip documents from which no information can be extracted and converted into texts. Usually, they are images whose text is unreadable or of low quality, containing much noise, low resolution, or even crumpled and poorly positioned document images.

The dataset used in the research project is composed of 139,603 processes that have 416,316 images of documents belonging to the 4th Civil Court of the Regional Forum XII - Nossa Senhora do Ó, in the city of São Paulo. Only 0.5% of the total number of documents were not recognized by the previous text extraction steps, leaving for our experiment 2,136 unrecognized document images, including lawsuit payment receipt images and other kinds of document images such as personal documents, reports, lawsuit decisions.

5.1   Preprocessing

We used Python Imaging Library (PIL) [5] to convert `.pdf` files to `.tiff` format. PIL adds image processing capabilities to the Python interpreter and provides extensive file format support, an efficient internal representation, and fairly powerful image processing capabilities.

After, we manually labelled the 2,136 unrecognized document images into two classes: with and without helpful information. There were 230 images without helpful information and 1906 with helpful information. We separated 30 images of each class from testing, from which remained 200 images without helpful information and 1,876 with helpful information to train. Therefore, we needed to increase the number of images without helpful information to balance the training dataset.

In the Data Augmentation activity, we automatically used the Keras deep learning library for data augmentation by the ImageDataGenerator class. We used shift, brightness, zoom, and shear techniques to produce new images for each

of the 200 images without helpful information. 1,636 new images were produced in this activity, totalling 1,836 images without helpful information.

In the Histogram Equalization activity, we applied the CLAHE technique, c.f., Fig. 3 that shows the same image in three different situations: in greyscale, with Gaussian filter, and with Otsu's Thresholding optimization. It resulted in 511 distorted images that were discarded, with 1,325 images without useful information left.

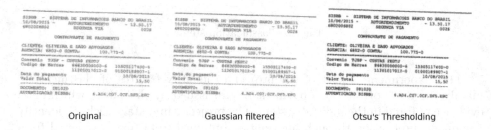

Original   Gaussian filtered   Otsu's Thresholding

Fig. 3. Example of CLAHE technique application.

5.2 Classification

In Classification I, we used Mahotas [6], a computer vision and image processing library for Python, to apply the Haralick Texture algorithm to extract features. We defined a function that computes features and takes the mean of for directions of the features, returned by `mahotas.features.haralick`. After feature extraction, we stored filed in `.npy` format because this way, we do not need to repeat the extraction for future training. Then, we created and trained five classifiers: Support Vector Machine (SVM), Random Forest (RF), Decision Tree (DT), Gaussian Naive Bayes (NB) and Neural Networks (NN). There were 1,325 images without useful information remaining, and we decided to use the same number of images with useful information to balance the training dataset. The five classifiers classified the 60 document images of the test dataset into with and without helpful information classes. Figure 4 shows the confusion matrix for this classification. All Classifiers correctly classified the thirty images with helpful information class, except the Linear SVM classifier, which misclassified the classes. Of the thirty images in the without helpful information class, SVM and NN correctly classified 21 images, RF correctly classified 16 images, DT correctly classified 14 images, and NN correctly classified 28 images. Table 1 lists the performance metrics of each classifier.

In the second stage (Classification II), we used a dataset with previously labelled document images into four classes: 175 payment receipts (class 1), 175 judicial deposits (class 2), 136 others (class 3), and 135 trash (class 4). As the number of the samples is small, We used the Keras ImageDataGenerator class that provides real-time data augmentation and ensures that the model receives new variations of the images at each epoch (or iteration) without adding them

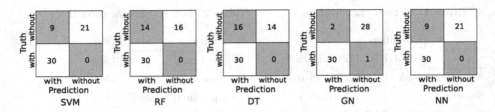

Fig. 4. Confusion matrix of classification I.

to the original image dataset. Furthermore, as the images are loaded in batches, much memory is saved. To monitor and control the training, we used some functions (callbacks) provided by Keras, namely, ModelCheckpoint and ReduceLROnPlateau. ModelCheckpoint function was used to save the model when a validation accuracy surpassed one previous reached. ReduceLROnPlateau was used to reduce the learning rate by 0.1 every five epochs when the validation accuracy has stopped improving. We used the weights of the VGG19 model. However, we did not train VGG19 any further. We only froze its layers and appended a shallow seven-layer network on top of it to perform the classification task of identifying document images in four classes, c.f. shown in Fig. 5.

```
conv_base = VGG19(weights='imagenet', include_top=False, input_shape=input_shape)
model = models.Sequential()
model.add(conv_base)
model.add(layers.GlobalAveragePooling2D())
model.add(layers.BatchNormalization())
model.add(layers.Flatten())
model.add(layers.Dense(128, activation='relu'))
model.add(layers.Dropout(0.6))
model.add(layers.Dense(4, activation='softmax'))
```

Fig. 5. Model used in classification II.

Global Average Pooling, a pooling operation that replaces fully connected layers, generates one feature map for each corresponding class of the classification task in the last layer, taking the average of each feature map. The resulting vector is fed directly into the softmax layer. The batch normalization layer normalizes its inputs, applying a transformation that maintains the mean output close to 0 and the output standard deviation close to 1. The Flatten layer is used to flatten the Dense layer's input with the RELU activation function that activates only certain neurons. A Dropout layer randomly selects neurons that will be ignored during training, thus creating less network computation and preventing overfitting. The Dense layer uses the SOFTMAX activation function, reducing the output to four neurons. Figure 6 shows the confusion matrix for this classification. Table 2 lists the performance metrics of each classifier.

Table 1. Metrics classification I.

	Classifiers				
	SVM	RF	DT	NB	NN
Accuracy	0.85	0.76	0.73	0.95	0.85
Sensitivity	1	1	1	0.96	1
Specificity	0.70	0.53	0.47	0.93	0.70

Table 2. Metrics classification II.

Metric	Value
Accuracy	0.968
Sensitivity	1.000
Specificity(class 0)	1.000
Specificity(class 1)	1.000
Specificity(class 2)	0.8857
Specificity(class 3)	1.000

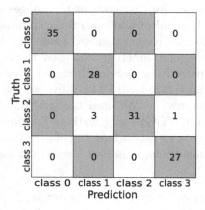

Fig. 6. Confusion matrix of classification II.

6 Conclusion

In this article, we present a proposal of classification for lawsuit document images. Our goal was to offer an alternative for document processing when extracting information from these document images is not feasible by NLP tools.

First, we carried out a preprocessing in images using Data Augmentation and Histogram Equalization techniques, then, we performed in two classification. In the first classification, we used the Haralick algorithm to extract textural features from images and created five machine learning classifiers to decide if an image has helpful information or not, namely Linear Support Vector Machine, Random Forest, Decision Tree, Gaussian Naive Bayes and Neural Networks. The Naive Bayes was the best model with 0.95 of accuracy, 0.96 of sensitivity, and 0.93 of specificity. In the second classification, we used VGG19, an advanced CNN with pre-trained layers, to extract features from . We froze its layers and appended a shallow seven-layer network on top of it to perform the classification task of identifying document images in four TJSP interest classes. This classifier obtained 0.96 of accuracy, 1 of sensitivity, and specificity above 0.88.

References

1. Abuelwafa, S., Pedersoli, M., Cheriet, M.: Unsupervised exemplar-based learning for improved document image classification. IEEE Access **7**, 133738–133748 (2019)
2. Ashir, A.M.: Multilevel thresholding for image segmentation using mean gradient. J. Electr. Comput. Eng. **2022** (2022)
3. Braz, F.A., et al.: Document classification using a bi-lstm to unclog brazil's supreme court. arXiv e-prints pp. arXiv-1811 (2018)
4. Chen, N., Blostein, D.: A survey of document image classification: problem statement, classifier architecture and performance evaluation. Int. J. Doc. Anal. Recogn. **10**(1), 1–16 (2007)
5. Clark, A.: Pillow (pil fork) documentation. Readthedocs (2015). https://Buildmedia.Readthedocs.Org/Media/Pdf/Pillow/Latest/Pillow.Pdf
6. Coelho, L.P.: Mahotas: Open source software for scriptable computer vision. arXiv preprint arXiv:1211.4907 (2012)
7. Csurka, G., Larlus, D., Gordo, A., Almazan, J.: What is the right way to represent document images? arXiv preprint arXiv:1603.01076 (2016)
8. Das, A., Roy, S., Bhattacharya, U., Parui, S.K.: Document image classification with intra-domain transfer learning and stacked generalization of deep convolutional neural networks. In: International Conference on Pattern Recognition, pp. 3180–3185 (2018)
9. Deng, G., Cahill, L.: An adaptive gaussian filter for noise reduction and edge detection. In: IEEE Conference Record Nuclear Science Symposium and Medical Imaging Conference, vol. 3, pp. 1615–1619 (1993)
10. DeTone, D., Malisiewicz, T., Rabinovich, A.: Superpoint: self-supervised interest point detection and description. In: IEEE Conference on Computer Vision and Pattern Recognition Workshops, pp. 224–236 (2018)
11. Dusmanu, M., et al.: D2-net: a trainable CNN for joint description and detection of local features. In: IEEE Conference on Computer Vision and Pattern Recognition, pp. 8092–8101 (2019)
12. Haralick, R.M., Shanmugam, K., Dinstein, I.H.: Textural features for image classification. IEEE Trans. Syst. Man Cybern. **1**(6), 610–621 (1973)
13. Harley, A.W., Ufkes, A., Derpanis, K.G.: Evaluation of deep convolutional nets for document image classification and retrieval. In: International Conference on Document Analysis and Recognition (2015)
14. Jain, S., Dhar, J.: Image based search engine using deep learning. In: 2017 Tenth International Conference on Contemporary Computing, pp. 1–7. IEEE (2017)
15. Ketkar, N.: Introduction to Keras. In: Deep Learning with Python, pp. 95–109. Apress, Berkeley, CA (2017). https://doi.org/10.1007/978-1-4842-2766-4_7
16. Kumar, J., Doermann, D.: Unsupervised classification of structurally similar document images. In: International Conference on Document Analysis and Recognition, pp. 1225–1229 (2013)
17. Liu, L., Wang, Z., Qiu, T., Chen, Q., Lu, Y., Suen, C.Y.: Document image classification: progress over two decades. Neurocomputing **453**, 223–240 (2021)
18. Liu, Y., Xu, X., Li, F.: Image feature matching based on deep learning. In: IEEE 4th International Conference on Computer and Communication, pp. 1752–1756 (2018)
19. Nguyen, T.-S., Nguyen, L.-M., Tojo, S., Satoh, K., Shimazu, A.: Recurrent neural network-based models for recognizing requisite and effectuation parts in legal texts. Artif. Intell. Law **26**(2), 169–199 (2018). https://doi.org/10.1007/s10506-018-9225-1

20. Otsu, N.: A threshold selection method from gray-level histograms. IEEE Trans. Syst. Man Cybern. **9**(1), 62–66 (1979)
21. Polo, F.M., Ciochetti, I., Bertolo, E.: Predicting legal proceedings status: approaches based on sequential text data. In: Proceedings of the Eighteenth International Conference on Artificial Intelligence and Law, pp. 264–265 (2021)
22. Polo, F.M., et al.: Legalnlp-natural language processing methods for the Brazilian legal language. arXiv preprint arXiv:2110.15709 (2021)
23. da Silva, N.C., et al.: Document type classification for Brazil's supreme court using a convolutional neural network. In: International Conference on Forensic Computer Science and Cyber Law (ICoFCS), Sao Paulo, Brazil, pp. 29–30 (2018)
24. Simonyan, K., Zisserman, A.: Very deep convolutional networks for large-scale image recognition. In: International Conference on Learning Representations, pp. 1–14 (2015)
25. Sulea, O.M., Zampieri, M., Malmasi, S., Vela, M., Dinu, L.P., Van Genabith, J.: Exploring the use of text classification in the legal domain, pp. 1–5 (2017). arXiv preprint arXiv:1710.09306
26. de Tecnologia da Informação do Tribunal de Justiça de São Paulo, S.: Tribunal de justiça - estado de são paulo: a justiça próxima do cidadão (2022). https://www.tjsp.jus.br/QuemSomos
27. Xu, Y., Zhang, M., Wu, S., Hu, J.: Lawsuit category prediction based on machine learning. In: IEEE International Conference on Intelligence and Security Informatics, pp. 176–178. IEEE (2019)
28. Zhang, Z., Lee, W.S.: Deep graphical feature learning for the feature matching problem. In: IEEE/CVF International Conference on Computer Vision, pp. 5087–5096 (2019)

A Rapid Semi-automated Literature Review on Legal Precedents Retrieval

Hugo Silva(✉) , Nuno António , and Fernando Bacao

NOVA Information Management School, Lisbon, Portugal
{hsilva,nantonio,bacao}@novaims.unl.pt

Abstract. Precedents constitute the starting point of judges' reasoning in national legal systems. Precedents are also an essential input for case-based reasoning (CBR) methodologies. Although considerable research has been done on CBR applied to legal practice, the precedent retrieval techniques are a relatively new and unexplored field of AI & Law. Only a few works have tested or developed methods for identifying such previous similar cases. This work uses text mining (TM), natural language processing (NLP), and data visualization methods to provide a semi-automated rapid literature review and identify how justice courts and legal practitioners may use AI to retrieve similar cases. Based on Preferred Reporting Items for Systematic Reviews and Meta-Analyses (PRISMA), automation techniques were used to expedite the literature review. In this study, we confirmed the feasibility of automation tools for expediting literature reviews and provided an overview of the current research state on legal precedents retrieval.

Keywords: Precedents retrieval · Rapid review · Automated

1 Introduction

There is a growing demand for the mediation of justice systems in society [1]. Whether in criminal justice, private civil justice, or administrative courts, the justice's action must also lead to timely and coherent decisions. Although many aspects of citizens' lives are affected by the decision-making process carried out by justice courts, these bodies have limited resources and struggle to keep up with the increasing cases demand [2].

In national legal systems, precedent constitutes the starting point of judges' reasoning. Most of the time, judges hew closely to precedent for legal certainty and fear that their decisions might be challenged before higher instances [3]. Common law jurisdictions, such as the United States and Great Britain, treat past cases as precedents, meaning that in some instances, a past case compels a particular result in a current case [4]. Even in jurisdictions where Civil law is adopted, courts are expected to consider past decisions when there is sufficient consistency in case law. Generally speaking, when uniform case law develops, courts treat precedents as a source of "soft" law, taking them into account when reaching a decision [5].

Precedents are also an essential input for case-based reasoning (CBR) methodologies. CBR means using old experiences to understand and solve new problems. It may involve

G. Marreiros et al. (Eds.): EPIA 2022, LNAI 13566, pp. 53–65, 2022.
https://doi.org/10.1007/978-3-031-16474-3_5

using old cases to explain new situations, critique new solutions, or reasoning from precedents to interpret a new situation (much like lawyers do) [6]. CBR is a broad field of research covering legal case-based reasoning, mainstream in Artificial Intelligence and Law (AI & Law), a subfield of AI [7].

Although considerable research has been done in CBR applied to legal practice, which dates to the 80s, the precedent retrieval techniques are a relatively new and unexplored field of AI & Law. Only a few works have tested or developed methods for identifying such previous similar cases. Nevertheless, they find good prospects given the advances observed in the areas of textual mining (TM), natural language processing (NLP), and machine learning (ML).

To the authors' knowledge, no work to date synthesized the techniques applied, and the research state on legal precedents retrieval. Nevertheless, this paper contributes to the development of this field by identifying the most promising results and research gaps. Specifically, the following research questions are addressed: How has the task of automating the identification of previous relevant cases been addressed by the researchers? What types of techniques are covered in the reviewed studies? What are the most promising strategies and research gaps in automating the retrieval of legal precedents?

This work uses TM, NLP, and data visualization methods on a semi-automated systematic literature review to identify how justice courts and legal practitioners can use AI to retrieve similar cases.

2 Materials and Methods

A systematic literature review (SLR) is a review of a clearly formulated question that uses systematic and explicit methods to identify, select, and critically appraise relevant research and collect and analyze data from the studies included in the review [8].

Systematic reviews are based on predefined criteria and protocol [9] and are highly valued evidence syntheses that inform decisions. However, the methodological rigor and process that makes SLR evidence trustworthy often take one to two years to complete and limit their utility in meeting the time-sensitive needs of stakeholders [10].

2.1 Rapid Reviews

Rapid reviews (RRs) emerged as an effective strategy for decision-makers with limited time and resources while still intended to respect the fundamental principles of knowledge synthesis [11]. Various mechanisms exist to enhance the timeliness of reviews, which can be used independently or concurrently. Among these mechanisms are review shortcuts, whereby one or more systematic review steps may be reduced or omitted, and the automation of review steps to fast-track the standard systematic review steps [11].

Despite the increased production and use of RRs, its methodology remains underdeveloped. There is no universally accepted definition of what constitutes a rapid review [12]. Although an extension to Preferred Reporting Items for Systematic Reviews and Meta-Analyses (PRISMA) for RRs is underway [13], until it is officially completed, authors are suggested to use the general PRISMA statement to the extent possible and adapt it accordingly [10]. This paper employs PRISMA's four phases as guidance for the essential items of an SLR: identification, screening, eligibility, and inclusion.

2.2   Literature Review Automation

Several researchers developed different techniques to automate the SLR process [14]. Conducting an SLR in line with good practices and the necessary rigor level is a complex, multi-stage, and time-consuming task [15]. Text analytics and ML techniques may help overcome this scaling problem while still maintaining the level of rigor expected of SRs [16], which is the reason why literature review has been employed in many different fields such as banking [17], tourism and hospitality [18], and marketing [19].

A recent analysis of forty-one studies on the automation of SLR revealed that they mainly automated the selection of primary studies. Although many studies have provided automation approaches for SLRs, no study has been found to apply automation techniques in the planning and reporting phases [14]. In thirty-two studies for SLR automation, solutions allowed identifying four types of applications: visual text mining (VTM), federated search strategy, automated document/text classification, and document summarization [15].

This study focuses on selecting primary studies for human screening by combining different TM techniques. We start by using VTM in the form of keyword extraction and word clouds to allow identifying the most relevant words and later as authors, keywords, and citation networks. Automated document classification was employed by deduplicating documents using their vectorial representation similarity and filtering documents by keywords. Finally, we used Latent Dirichlet Allocation (LDA) to perform eligibility screening by assigning a distribution of topics to each document. With each topic having a probability associated with it, it was possible to group documents and select the most relevant topic(s) in a *soft* clustering. Figure 1 shows the number of remaining documents after each dataset processing stage.

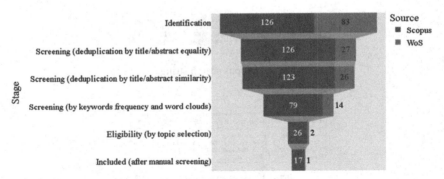

Fig. 1. The number of documents selected after each processing stage per electronic database.

The experimental procedure presented in this paper was conducted using Python. The source code and datasets used in this work can be downloaded from https://github.com/hugosaisse/semi-automated-rr-precedents.

2.3 Keyword Identification

A precedent is a court decision considered authoritative for deciding subsequent cases involving identical or similar facts or similar legal issues. If the facts or issues differ from those in a previous case, the previous case cannot be precedent [20].

From the cited references on the application of precedents in justice courts, and following the research questions, we identified the resulting set of key expressions used to refer to similar cases identification: 'precedents identification', 'precedent retrieval', and 'case similarity'. We also included 'case-based reasoning' as a possible term because identifying similar cases is essential for CBR models, despite being applied to many fields such as medicine or engineering. Attempting to narrow the search to the legal segment, we included the 'legal' keyword as a mandatory element.

2.4 Electronic Databases and Eligibility Criteria

Due to their extensive publications coverage, we used Thomson Reuters' Web of Science (WoS) and Elsevier's Scopus as the electronic databases for research. They are also the most used data sources for bibliometric analyses. The research language was limited to English to minimize the methodological difficulties with the mining techniques [18], and given that the most relevant research is published in English.

Finally, the 20-year timeframe ('Year' > 2001) was established to limit the search to only the most recent techniques, coinciding with advances in TM and NLP. Because the field of precedent extraction is relatively unexplored, we did not limit the types of publications returned. The search queries on Scopus and WoS are outlined in Fig. 2 and Fig. 3, respectively.

```
( TITLE-ABS-KEY ( {precedents identification}  OR  {precedent identification}
OR {precedent retrieval} OR {precedents retrieval} OR {case similarity} OR
{cases similarity} OR {case-based reasoning} ) AND TITLE-ABS-KEY (legal
)) AND ( LIMIT-TO ( LANGUAGE , "English")) AND (PUBYEAR > 2001
)
```

Fig. 2. Scopus search string.

```
((((TI=("precedent retrieval" OR "precedents retrieval" OR "case similarity" OR
"cases similarity" OR "case-based reasoning")) OR AB=("precedent retrieval" OR
"precedents retrieval" OR "case similarity" OR "cases similarity" OR "case-
based reasoning")) OR AK=("precedent retrieval" OR "precedents retrieval" OR
"case similarity" OR "cases similarity" OR "case-based reasoning")) AND
(TI=(legal) OR AB=(legal) OR AK=(legal))) AND LA=(English)
Timespan: 2002-01-01 to 2022-12-31
```

Fig. 3. WoS search string

2.5 Data Extraction and Pre-processing

The Scopus search result was exported to a comma-separated values (CSV) file using Scopus export functionality. The WoS search result was exported to a Microsoft Excel file. The inclusion of known studies in the field of interest was manually verified to ensure the relevance of the search terms. The datasets were merged into a single set. Considering

that both sources have different variables, the shared variables were identified, and the remaining were discarded. A variable called "Source" was created to identify the source database.

We extracted the document's country from the authors' affiliations and correspondence addresses for 167 entries (80% of the dataset). The correspondence address was used instead when extracting the country from the first authors' affiliation was impossible. Nonetheless, 20% of the samples did not have the country of origin identified.

The following step was removing duplicate samples. First, the titles of the documents were considered. The titles were preprocessed to remove extra spaces and punctuation and then converted to lowercase to prevent the text formatting (existence of white spaces, capitalization, and punctuation) from harming the identification of identical documents. This procedure resulted in the removal of 55 duplicates. All the preprocessing steps used the NLTK library, and, as a rule, the samples from Scopus were kept.

Next, the abstracts and the Digital Object Identifiers (DOIs) went through the same process, but no duplicates were identified. The processing of titles and abstracts was later deepened with tokenization and stemming. After that, one more duplicate title was identified, and the document was removed. In some cases, two documents in the database may represent two versions of the same study, for example, a conference paper that was revised and later published as a journal article. A strategy was then adopted to eliminate documents with abstracts or titles that are very similar but not identical: first, these variables were vectorized using unigrams and bigrams.

A bag-of-words model was used to represent the text in the vectorization step. For vectorial document representation, words' occurrence frequency was normalized by the number of documents each word occurs, i.e., through term frequency-inverse document frequency (TF-IDF). Also, in this case, words appearing in only one document or more than 80% of the corpus were ignored. Afterward, the cosine similarity between pairs of documents was calculated, and when abstracts had similarity above 0.8 or titles had similarity above 0.9, one of the documents was eliminated. The procedure above resulted in the identification of four duplicate documents. Three were reviews of the same study published in the following year, and one of them was a document published in more than one journal.

2.6 Screening Based on Keyword Frequency

Any studies related to legal precedents could be retrieved from the queries used in the research with the electronic databases, even if they did not involve any computational methods. Thus, a semi-automated screening process was applied to the remaining 149 documents to extract works that dealt with applying AI methods to identify legal precedents or similar past cases.

The screening process was carried out using the abstracts and started with the tokenization and stemming of the text when 3109 unique unigrams and 13559 bigrams were identified. The authors used word clouds to identify tokens that could indicate computer-aided precedent retrieval applications. In this visual representation of text, the bigger the words appear, the higher their frequency is in the corpus. First, the words with low discriminative power between documents ('legal', 'law', 'pap', 'new', 'research', 'result', 'using', 'used', 'use', 'analysil', 'two', 'work', 'one', 'elsevi', 'right', 'reserved',

'study', 'proposed', 'berlin', 'heidelberg', 'spring', 'natur', 'ieee') have been removed. When creating the cloud from unigrams, the 'cas', 'casebased', and 'reasoning' tokens, present in more than 50% of the documents, were also removed. The same was done with the 'casebased reasoning' bigram, present in more than 30% of the documents. The resulting word clouds were generated with the WordCloud Python library.

Observing the word clouds made it possible to identify 'artific intelligenc', 'machin learning', 'decision support', 'computat model' and 'syst' (including 'support syst') as the n-grams that directed to the most promising literature snippet. From this point on, only documents that contained these terms in the abstract, title, or keywords were kept, resulting in 93 samples.

2.7 Topic Modelling for Eligibility

The eligibility screening step of an SLR determines the scope of the evidence that may answer the research questions. It involves developing, testing, and applying inclusion and exclusion criteria by a review team based on pre-specified methods [21].

To select the studies that were more likely to answer the research questions in an expedite way, we adopted topic modeling to divide the documents among subjects. The use of topic modeling is not new. However, remarkably few papers utilize the method for categorizing research papers [22]. We decided to employ LDA [23], a state-of-the-art and preferred method for topic modeling [22], using the Gensim library.

The optimal number of three topics was obtained by comparing coherence and overlap measures bearing in mind that the higher the number of topics, the more challenging the model interpretation is. Coherence combines several measures to evaluate the degree of semantic similarity between high-scoring words in the topic [24]. On the other hand, the appearance of terms in multiple topics for a particular model and an overlap in topics due to lower numbers of unique terms across its topic descriptors may indicate less valuable (less coherent) models [25].

An analysis of the top 10 terms identified in each of the three topics and their respective weights showed that topic 0 was related to precedents' text processing and retrieval. Topic 1 seemed to be on argumentation and case-based reasoning. Additionally, Topic 2 seems to be related to decision support systems in the legal environment, having some degree of overlapping with Topic 1. These initial thoughts were then confirmed by screening the documents' abstracts. Therefore, the eligibility criterion adopted for each document was the dominance of topic 0, which showed the most significant correlation with the research questions.

2.8 Full-Text Screening for Inclusion

After selecting the topic, the remaining twenty-eight studies were screened by their full texts to remove studies unrelated to precedent retrieval or similar case identification. Although the results were limited to journal articles, a research note was found at the full-text screening stage and removed.

Consequently, ten documents were removed for the following reasons: one article focused on resolving counterintuitive consequences using logic program representation of statutes and Legal Debugging, one article proposed an approach using CNNs

to classify legal documents, two conference reviews summarized the conferences' contents, with no further details on the studies, one focused on legal statutes retrieval on existing cases, rather than precedents retrieval, one retrieved similar cases for dispute resolution in construction accidents, one proposed architecture for querying information systems using domain terminology for new product development (NPD), one proposed a rule-based classification system applied to construction litigation, one study proposed a method for text annotation, and one study could not have its full text retrieved from the databases. As a result, the eighteen articles detailed in Table 1 were included in the final analysis.

3 Results

3.1 Descriptive Analytics

The analysis of the sources revealed that the studies are sparsely distributed in several journals. Peer-reviewed articles were published in "Artificial Intelligence and Law", "International Journal of Engineering Research and Technology", "IEEE Access" and "Journal of Information Science and Engineering". Other studies have been published on a diversity of conference proceedings.

When we analyze publications by year and country of origin, a concentration of studies can be observed at the beginning of this century, followed by a long period with practically no publications in the field. From 2017 onwards, Indian researchers were the main contributors to the growing interest in the subject, probably following the developments observed in this field in the second half of the last decade, more precisely from 2013: word embeddings and neural networks (NN) applied to NLP, recurrent neural networks (RNN) and Long Short-Term Memory networks (LSTM), attention mechanisms, and pre-trained language models.

3.2 Content Analysis

It is possible to identify seven studies published in 2008 and before, in which the task of identifying similar cases was part but not the main object of the study. This step was performed using techniques requiring domain knowledge and manual screening. A standard limitation of these studies is scalability, i.e., as the number of cases increases, the application of the method of identifying similar cases becomes unfeasible.

After a significant gap of nine years, a second set composed of eleven papers exposes an essential move toward using TM and NLP, confirming the influence of the developments observed in this field after 2013. In this sense, we observed multiple text embedding techniques being employed in conjunction with variations of the BM25[26] ranking function and Bidirectional Encoder Representations from Transformers (BERT) model [27].

Table 1. Documents included in the final selection (Peer-reviewed articles are in italic).

Title	Year	Cited	Country
Unsupervised approaches for measuring textual similarity between legal court case reports	*2021*	*3*	*India*
Artificial intelligence as legal research assistant	2020	0	India
A study on lemma vs stem for legal information retrieval using R tidyverse. IMS UniPD @ AILA 2020 Task 1	2020	0	Italy
Cases without borders: Automating knowledge acquisition approach using deep autoencoders and siamese networks in case-based reasoning	2019	1	Germany
Removing named entities to find precedent legal cases	2019	3	India
FIRE 2019 AILA track: Artificial intelligence for legal assistance	2019	6	India
A Study of Precedent Retrieval System for Civil Trial	2018	0	Japan
Similarity analysis of court judgments using association rule mining on case citation data-a case study	*2018*	*1*	*India*
On the importance of legal catchphrases in precedence retrieval	2017	2	Botswana
Detection of catchphrases and precedence in legal documents	2017	1	India
An Ontological Chinese Legal Consultation System	*2017*	*18*	*China*
Concept and context in legal information retrieval	2008	24	UK
COMPUTER-AIDED LEGAL SUPPORT SYSTEM: An Initial Framework for Retrieving Legal Cases by Case Base Reasoning Approach	2008	0	Malaysia
Nonlinear nearest-neighbour matching and its application in legal precedent retrieval	2005	2	New Zealand
Case instance generation and refinement for case-based criminal summary judgments in Chinese	*2004*	*34*	*China*
Extensionally defining principles and cases in ethics: An AI model	2003	66	USA
A reduction-graph model of precedent in legal analysis	2003	19	USA
Classification and clustering for case-based criminal summary judgments	2003	7	China

4 Discussion

4.1 RQ1 (How has the Task of Automating the Identification of Previous Relevant Cases been Addressed by the Researchers?) and RQ2 (What Types of Techniques are Covered in the Reviewed Studies?)

The least recent study included in the final analysis proposed a theoretical reduction-graph model to assess precedents' relevance, accounting for such cases' key characteristics [28]. Another study proposed a model for retrieving principles and past cases based on content vectors and comparing cases according to actions and events levels [29]. Content vectors are flat summaries of the knowledge contained in complex relational structures. The content vector for a given description specifies which functors[1] (i.e., relations, connectives, object attributes, functions, among others) were used in that description and the number of times they occurred [30].

In 2004, a study proposed an algorithm for extracting important legal information from past lawsuits to build case instances, identify similar cases, and refine them by merging and removing irrelevant information. It involved representing the documents as lists of ordered keywords and assessing similarities in case instances using measures based on word counts. The nearest neighbors generated clusters using predefined crime classes [31]. The following study proposed a Nonlinear Nearest-Neighbor (NNN) matching function for legal precedents retrieval in accident compensation. The computational model compared cases in terms of "dimensions", which are factors that represent, analogize, and distinguish legal cases. Four groups of factors were used [32]. In 2008, a framework for retrieving legal cases based on CBR represented cases by attribute-value pairs based on expert knowledge and essential legal aspects. The method determined similar cases by executing a case-similarity calculation step and utilizing a distribution of values of fields to identify cases with high similarities [33].

To that point, the way of representing the cases was a predefined set of dimensions related to the characteristics of each case. In this sense, the dimensions or factors describing each case depend on the subject. Indeed, a study from 2008 highlighted two broad approaches to IR in the legal domain: those based on manual knowledge engineering (KE) and those based on NLP [34]. The authors mentioned the focus given so far to the KE-based retrieval and why this was not sustainable in the long term.

Considering the set of papers under analysis, we can identify a move toward TM and NLP with a study from 2017 [35] that proposed detecting precedents using rule-based Regular Expressions, cosine similarity between Doc2Vec embeddings [36], and topic modeling. Another study in the same year employed a genetic algorithm (GA) integrated with a k-nearest neighbor (KNN) algorithm for the same purpose [37]. The effectiveness of using legal catchphrases in precedence retrieval was also investigated. In this case, legal catchphrases extracted from current cases were compared to previous cases with gold standard catchphrases represented by TF-IDF vectors [38].

In a later study, the citations made in each document were used to identify similarities based on association rule mining. In this case, cases with citations that often occurred together were considered similar cases [39]. One study also proposed an ontology-based

---

[1] Functor is a function that maps elements of one set to those of another.

search for precedents, with rules that needed to be defined and manually followed by experts [40].

An unsupervised Autoencoder [41] was used in exchange for a neural word embedding such as Word2Vec [42], and has been combined with LSTM on unstructured text to retrieve similar texts. Reportedly resulting in less training time, faster retrieval, and more accurate results [43]. Another study [44] extracted information from legal documents using Named Entity Recognition (NER) [45], vectorized the resulting text using TF-IDF, and compared the documents using BM25 [44]. BM25 ranking function was also the method for identifying relevant precedents that achieved the best results on the Artificial Intelligence for Legal Assistance (AILA) track at FIRE 2019 [46]. In the following edition (FIRE AILA 2020), lemmatization and stemming were compared in the precedents retrieval task with no outstanding results for any techniques [47].

Top2Vec [48], a novel text embedding technique, was recently employed in a task to retrieve precedents. This study measured similarity among the Top2Vec embeddings using BM25 and achieved better results than those obtained with BM25 only [49]. The latest study of this SLR is an extensive investigation of 56 different assemblies, crossing eight document text representation techniques and seven similarity measurement techniques [50]. The applied methods included authors' designed methodologies, the BERT model, and legal domain Word2Vec (Law2Vec) [51].

While comparing the methodologies for measuring similarity, it was found that the embeddings learned by NN techniques (Word2vec, Doc2vec, Law2Vec) performed comparably with the other techniques for the stated task. When trained on the study's dataset, BERT yielded substandard results for the similarity estimation task. The authors also observed that the more traditional vectorization methods (such as the TF-IDF and LDA) that rely on a bag-of-words representation performed better than the more advanced context-aware methods (like BERT and Law2Vec).

4.2 RQ3: What are the Most Promising Strategies and Research Gaps in Automating the Retrieval of Legal Precedents?

The answers to RQ1 and RQ2 also support the existence of a diversity of approaches to identify legal precedents, all provided by the advances of the last decade in NLP and TM, i.e., network-based embeddings, LSTM, and transformers. There is still no clear path to follow, as most work has been carried out on very limited corpora. The only work that extensively compared methods for measuring similarity evaluated the results in only 50 pairs of documents. It concluded that vectorization methods such as the TF-IDF and LDA that rely on a bag-of-words representation performed better than the more advanced context-aware methods like BERT and Law2Vec [50]. In this sense, the techniques still need to be tested in more works, in different contexts, preferably with more extensive corpora and a ground truth provided by experts.

5 Conclusions, Limitations, and Future Research

By answering the research questions above, this paper confirmed the feasibility of automation tools for expediting literature reviews and provided an overview of the current research state on legal precedents retrieval. In what corresponds to the application

of machine learning methods to the retrieval of legal precedents, we conclude that the domain is still largely unexplored, and significant work needs to be developed to identify the most promising tools for this purpose. In this literature review, we identify some relevant limitations. first, the *status quo* is based on a small sample of eighteen publications. Second, the retrieval process itself is subject to decisions made by human reasoning that may limit or bias the results, e.g., the query used on the databases, the choice of keywords, or the topic selection for eligibility. Third, the different structures observed in the electronic databases limited working with the papers' references for finding related works by snowballing. Future work may explore the citation network derived from the selected papers and address the problem of defining keywords in an automated way, according to objective criteria.

Acknowledgments. Funding: This research was supported by a grant from the Portuguese Foundation for Science and Technology ("Fundação para a Ciência e a Tecnologia") [grant number DSAIPA/DS/0116/2019].

References

1. Gomez, A.R.: Demand side justice. Georg. J. Poverty Law Policy **XXVIII**(3), 411–436 (2021)
2. Susskind, R.: The future of courts. Practice **6**(5) (2020). https://thepractice.law.harvard.edu/article/the-future-of-courts/
3. Guillaume, G.: The use of precedent by international judges and arbitrators. J. Int. Disput. Settl. **2**(1), 5–23 (2011). https://doi.org/10.1093/JNLIDS/IDQ025
4. Rigoni, A.: Common-law judicial reasoning and analogy. Leg. Theory **20**(2), 133–156 (2014)
5. Fon, V., Parisi, F.: Judicial precedents in civil law systems: a dynamic analysis. Int. Rev. Law Econ. **26**(4), 519–535 (2006). https://doi.org/10.1016/j.irle.2007.01.005
6. Kolodner, J.L.: An introduction to case-based reasoning. Artif. Intell. Rev. **6**, 3–34 (1992)
7. Roth, A.: Case-based reasoning in the law: a formal theory of reasoning by case comparison. Universiteit Maastricht (2003)
8. Moher, D., Liberati, A., Tetzlaff, J., Altman, D.G.: Preferred reporting items for systematic reviews and meta-analyses: the PRISMA statement. J. Clin. Epidemiol. **62**(10), 1006–1012 (2009). https://doi.org/10.1016/j.jclinepi.2009.06.005
9. Jahan, N., Naveed, S., Zeshan, M., Tahir, M.A.: How to conduct a systematic review: a narrative literature review (2016). https://doi.org/10.7759/cureus.864
10. Garritty, C., et al.: Cochrane rapid reviews methods group offers evidence-informed guidance to conduct rapid reviews. J. Clin. Epidemiol. **130**, 13–22 (2021). https://doi.org/10.1016/J.JCLINEPI.2020.10.007
11. Tricco, A.C., Langlois, E.V., Straus, S.E.: Rapid reviews to strengthen health policy and systems: a practical guide. World Health Organization, p. 119 (2017)
12. Khangura, S., Konnyu, K., Cushman, R., Grimshaw, J., Moher, D.: Evidence summaries: the evolution of a rapid review approach. Syst. Rev. **1**(1), 1–9 (2012). Accessed 12 Apr 2022. https://doi.org/10.1186/2046-4053-1-10
13. Stevens, A., Garritty, C., Hersi, M., Moher, D.: Developing PRISMA-RR, a reporting guideline for rapid reviews of primary studies (Protocol) (2018)
14. van Dinter, R., Tekinerdogan, B., Catal, C.: Automation of systematic literature reviews: a systematic literature review. Inf. Softw. Technol. **136**, 106589 (2021). https://doi.org/10.1016/j.infsof.2021.106589

15. Feng, L., Chiam, Y.K., Lo, S.K.: Text-mining techniques and tools for systematic literature reviews: a systematic literature review. In: Proceedings - Asia-Pacific Software Engineering Conference APSEC, vol. 2017-Decem, pp. 41–50 (2018). https://doi.org/10.1109/APSEC. 2017.10

16. Zimmerman, J., et al.: Iterative guided machine learning-assisted systematic literature reviews: a diabetes case study. Syst. Rev. **10**(1) (2021). https://doi.org/10.1186/S13643-021-01640-6

17. Moro, S., Cortez, P., Rita, P.: Business intelligence in banking: a literature analysis from 2002 to 2013 using text mining and latent Dirichlet allocation. Expert Syst. Appl. **42**(3), 1314–1324 (2015). https://doi.org/10.1016/j.eswa.2014.09.024

18. António, N., de Almeida, A., Nunes, L.: Predictive models for hotel booking cancellation: a semi-automated analysis of the literature. Tour. Manag. Stud. **15**(1), 7–21 (2019). https://doi. org/10.18089/tms.2019.15011

19. Guerreiro, J., Rita, P., Trigueiros, D.: A text mining-based review of cause-related marketing literature. J. Bus. Ethics **139**(1), 111–128 (2015). https://doi.org/10.1007/s10551-015-2622-4

20. Self-defense|Wex|US Law|LII/Legal Information Institute. https://www.law.cornell.edu/wex/precedent. Accessed 12 Apr 2022

21. Frampton, G.K., Livoreil, B., Petrokofsky, G.: Eligibility screening in evidence synthesis of environmental management topics. Environ. Evid. **6**(1), 1–13 (2017). https://doi.org/10.1186/S13750-017-0102-2

22. Asmussen, C.B., Møller, C.: Smart literature review: a practical topic modelling approach to exploratory literature review. J Big Data **6**(1), 1–18 (2019). https://doi.org/10.1186/s40537-019-0255-7

23. Blei, D.M., Ng, A.Y., Jordan, M.I.: Latent Dirichlet allocation. J. Mach. Learn. Res. **3**(4–5), 993–1022 (2003). https://doi.org/10.1016/b978-0-12-411519-4.00006-9

24. O'callaghan, D., Greene, D., Carthy, J., Cunningham, P.: An analysis of the coherence of descriptors in topic modeling. Expert Syst. Appl. **42**(13), 5645–5657 (2015)

25. Arora, S., Ge, R., Moitra, A.: Learning topic models - going beyond SVD. In: Proceedings - Annual IEEE Symposium Foundation Computer Science, FOCS, pp. 1–10 (2012). https://doi.org/10.48550/arxiv.1204.1956

26. Robertson, S., Zaragoza, H.: The probabilistic relevance framework: BM25 and beyond. Found. Trends Inf. Retr. **3**(4), 333–389 (2009). https://doi.org/10.1561/1500000019

27. Devlin, J., Chang, M.W., Lee, K., Toutanova, K.: BERT: pre-training of deep bidirectional transformers for language understanding. In: NAACL HLT 2019 - 2019 Conference of the North American Chapter of the Association for Computational Linguistics: Human Language Technologies - Proceedings of the Conference, 2019, vol. 1, pp. 4171–4186 (2019). https://github.com/tensorflow/tensor2tensor

28. Branting, L.K.: A reduction-graph model of precedent in legal analysis. Artif. Intell. **150**(1–2), 59–95 (2003). https://doi.org/10.1016/S0004-3702(03)00102-4

29. McLaren, B.M.: Extensionally defining principles and cases in ethics: an AI model. Artif. Intell. **150**(1–2), 145–181 (2003). https://doi.org/10.1016/S0004-3702(03)00135-8

30. Forbus, K.D., Gentner, D., Law, K.: MAC/FAC: a model of similarity-based retrieval. Cogn. Sci. **19**, 141–205 (1994)

31. Liu, C.L., Chang, C.T., Ho, J.H.: Case instance generation and refinement for case-based criminal summary judgments in Chinese. J. Inf. Sci. Eng. **20**(4), 783–800 (2004)

32. Wang, R., Zeng, Y.: Nonlinear nearest-neighbour matching and its application in legal precedent retrieval. In: Proceedings - 3rd International Conference Information Technology Applications ICITA 2005, vol. I, pp. 341–346 (2005)

33. Raman, V., Palanissamy, A.: Computer aided legal support system: an initial framework retrieving legal cases by case base reasoning approach. In: 2008 International Conference Innovation Information Technology IIT 2008, pp. 317–321 (2008). https://doi.org/10.1109/INNOVATIONS.2008.4781663

34. Maxwell, K.T., Schafer, B.: Concept and context in legal information retrieval. Front. Artif. Intell. Appl. **189**(1), 63–72 (2008). https://doi.org/10.3233/978-1-58603-952-3-63
35. Kulkarni, Y.H., Patil, R., Shridharan, S.: Detection of catchphrases and precedence in legal documents. In: CEUR Workshop Proceedings, vol. 2036, pp. 86–89 (2017)
36. Le, Q., Mikolov, T.: Distributed representations of sentences and documents. In: 31st International Conference on Machine Learning, ICML 2014, vol. 4, pp. 2931–2939 (2014)
37. Zhang, N., Pu, Y.F., Yang, S.Q., Zhou, J.L., Gao, J.K.: An ontological Chinese legal consultation system. IEEE Access **5**, 18250–18261 (2017). https://doi.org/10.1109/ACCESS.2017.2745208
38. Thuma, E., Motlogelwa, N.P.: On the importance of legal catchphrases in precedence retrieval. In: CEUR Workshop Proceedings, vol. 2036, pp. 92–94 (2017)
39. Nair, A.M., Wagh, R.S.: Similarity analysis of court judgements using association rule mining on case citation data-a case study. Int. J. Eng. Res. Technol. **11**(3), 373–381 (2018)
40. Kiryu, Y., Ito, A., Kasahara, T., Hatano, H., Fujii, M.: A study of precedent retrieval system for civil trial. In: Moreno-Díaz, R., Pichler, F., Quesada-Arencibia, A. (eds.) EUROCAST 2017. LNCS, vol. 10672, pp. 151–158. Springer, Cham (2018). https://doi.org/10.1007/978-3-319-74727-9_18
41. Baldi, P.: Autoencoders, unsupervised learning, and deep architectures. In: ICML Unsupervised Transfer Learning, pp. 37–50 (2012). https://doi.org/10.1561/2200000006
42. Mikolov, T., Chen, K., Corrado, G., Dean, J.: Distributed representations of words and phrases and their compositionality. In: NIPS 2013 Proceedings of 26th International Conference on Neural Information Processing System, vol. 2, pp. 3111–3119 (2013)
43. Amin, K., Kapetanakis, S., Althoff, K.D., Dengel, A., Petridis, M.: Cases without borders: automating knowledge acquisition approach using deep autoencoders and siamese networks in case-based reasoning. In: Proceedings - International Conference Tools with Artificial Intelligence ICTAI, vol. 2019-Novem, pp. 133–140 (2019). https://doi.org/10.1109/ICTAI.2019.00027
44. More, R., Patil, J., Palaskar, A., Pawde, A.: Removing named entities to find precedent legal cases. In: CEUR Workshop Proceedings, vol. 2517, no. December 2019, pp. 13–18 (2019)
45. Mansouri, A., Affendey, L.S., Mamat, A.: Named entity recognition approaches. J. Comput. Sci. **8**(2), 339–344 (2008)
46. Bhattacharya, P., et al.: FIRE 2019 AILA track: artificial intelligence for legal assistance. In: ACM International Conference Proceeding Series, no. February 2018, pp. 4–6 (2019). https://doi.org/10.1145/3368567.3368587
47. Di Nunzio, G.M.: A study on lemma vs stem for legal information retrieval using R tidyverse. IMS UniPD @ AILA 2020 Task 1. In: CEUR Workshop Proceedings, vol. 2826, pp. 54–59 (2020)
48. Angelov, D.: Top2Vec: distributed representations of topics, pp. 1–25 (2020). http://arxiv.org/abs/2008.09470
49. Arora, J., Patankar, T., Shah, A., Joshi, S.: Artificial intelligence as legal research assistant. In: CEUR Workshop Proceedings, vol. 2826, no. December, pp. 60–65 (2020)
50. Mandal, A., Ghosh, K., Ghosh, S., Mandal, S.: Unsupervised approaches for measuring textual similarity between legal court case reports. Artif. Intell. Law **29**(3), 417–451 (2021). https://doi.org/10.1007/s10506-020-09280-2
51. Chalkidis, I.: Law2Vec: legal word embeddings (2018). https://archive.org/details/Law2Vec

The European Draft Regulation on Artificial Intelligence: Houston, We Have a Problem

Vera Lúcia Raposo[✉] [iD]

Coimbra University, Coimbra, Portugal
vera@fd.uc.pt

Abstract. The European Draft Regulation on Artificial Intelligence was presented in April 2021 with ambitious aims: to be a far-reaching regulation aimed to guarantee the highest level of protection for 'Union values, fundamental rights and principles', and at the same time promote innovation. However, several possible drawbacks are likely to jeopardize these ambitious purposes: the risk-based approach, grounded on different levels of risks, is imprecise; the conformity assessment has loopholes and might not be as protective as originally envisaged; some requirements are difficult to meet; the contextualization of this regulation within the European legal framework gives raise to overlaps and potential conflicts; the rights of the ones affected by this technology are not properly safeguarded; the European innovation boost might suffer a major setback. Instead of a solution for artificial intelligence, the European Union might have created a new problem.

Keywords: Artificial intelligence · Risk-based approach · Fundamental rights · Compliance · Innovation

1 Presentation of the European Draft Regulation

In April 2021 the European Commission released the proposal for a future European regulation on Artificial Intelligence (AI), the so-called AI Draft Regulation [1–3]. Even though the 2020 White Paper [4], that preceded the Draft Regulation, had already some clues on what was coming, there was a great deal of expectation, because the content of this Act can dictate the success (or failure) of many projects (business, research) in Europe and beyond, due to the extraterritorial effects envisaged in the Draft Regulation [5].

The main purpose of the Draft Regulation is to facilitate and develop AI within the European Union (EU) to create a true Digital Market [6], a long-lasting aspiration of the EU. This aim is not to be achieved through an uncontrolled rush towards a high-tech world, but through sustained technological development [7], respecting people's rights and basic European values and principles [8].

It is certainly an ambitious goal. As to this moment, and considering some of the amendments already suggested, several drawbacks can already be pointed out to the Draft Regulation (despite its laudable purposes).

G. Marreiros et al. (Eds.): EPIA 2022, LNAI 13566, pp. 66–73, 2022.
https://doi.org/10.1007/978-3-031-16474-3_6

2   Risk-Based Approach

The Draft Regulation bases its solutions on the categorization of the possible risks of AI systems. Therefore, the number and severity of the requirements to which each AI system will be subject depend on the respective level of risk [9]. The Draft Regulation refers to the following levels of risks [3]:

(a)   Unacceptably risk AI systems, which are prohibited (dark patterns, micro-targeting, social scoring and real-time biometric identification carried by public authorities in public spaces for law enforcement purposes);
(b)   High-risk AI systems, which are allowed, albeit within strict requirements;
(c)   Low-risk AI systems, for which the demands are mostly limited to transparency obligations.

The fact that some AI systems are considered unacceptable does not necessarily mean that they are forbidden in every single situation. This alleged ban actually contain several loopholes [9], in particular, the ban referring to facial recognition technology, which ends up being allowed in several situations [10].

Within the framework of the Draft Regulation, the quantity and quality (severity) of the requirements to which each AI system will be subject depends on the respective level of risk [11]. Therefore, the accuracy of the classification given to each AI system is crucial. As such, it is especially problematic the lack of clarification regarding several matters involving the levels of risk.

For a start, the definition of risk levels seems too focused on the respective software, neglecting its hardware, which, in turn, can crucially determine the level of risk posed by an AI system. Consider the following example: AI-based facial recognition software works connected to a camera, which, being a simple low-resolution camera, involves less risk than high-performance cameras or night vision cameras [12].

Secondly, the fact that the risk classification depends on the so-called 'intended purpose', that is, the purpose for which the AI systems was developed. It is a well-known fact that the declared purpose of a product does not determine the way it will effectively be used, and it is not uncommon to have on the market products being employed for completely different purposes from those for which they were designed. Moreover, in case of unlawful purposes (as the ones described in Article 5 of the Draft Regulation, which refers to 'unacceptable AI systems'), chances are that the real purpose is not declared by developers and/or manufacturers of the AI system. Therefore, the Draft Regulation should be based, not on the 'intended purpose', but on the 'foreseeable purpose' (or purposes), which, in turn, must be evaluated in light of the technical and functional characteristics of the AI system, the factual and human behaviours associated to it, and its joint use with other products [12, 13].

The very procedure to classify the AI system also raises doubts. For instance, it is not clear who decides what level of risk each system belongs to. The most plausible hypothesis is the national supervisory authority, but this is a mere assumption, as Article 59 of the Draft Regulation does not specifically provide for such competence. The timing of that decision – the decision on what level of risk each AI system belongs to - is also an issue. It cannot be too early, given that often, in the preliminary stage of developing

an AI system, it is still not possible to know the exact contours of the 'final product'. However, it cannot be too late either, since the requirements to be fulfilled by the AI systems depends on the respective level of risk, and many of them must be complied with from the initial stages of the procedure [3].

Linked to these questions, another arises: what happens if an AI system is wrongly labelled? Will the European authority – the European Artificial Intelligence Board - have the last word? Can the issue be decided by a court? Can damages be awarded for any losses suffered by the system's developers and/or manufacturers?

3   The Conformity Assessment

A troubling concern is that some features of the Draft Regulation are too flexible. For instance, it is stated that high-risk AI systems must be subject to demanding conformity assessments to get the CE marking [14, 15], without which they cannot be launched into the market (Recital 67 and Articles 16/i, 1/19, 1/26/c and 1/27 of the Draft Regulation). This compliance model is not exclusive to AI. It is very similar to the model in place for medical devices and not that different from the one applicable to medicines (even though in the latter the parallel with the CE conformity marking is the 'marketing authorisation' for drugs).

However, and unlike what happens in the context of those other compliance models, in the framework of the AI Draft Regulation, the assessment of compliance (the so-called 'conformity assessment') will be carried out, in most cases, by the manufacturer of the AI system himself (except for remote biometric identification systems, which must undergo the more rigorous procedure of third-party assessment). This solution has positive aspects since the manufacturer is the one who knows the product best and, therefore, who can best certify its compliance. However, it has an undeniable problem: how to trust a system in which the entity under control…controls itself [9, 13]?

The intervention of notified bodies, as referred to in Articles 30 et seq. of the Draft Regulation, (also not a novelty, as they are part of the conformity assessment of medical devices) might be aimed to provide some objectivity to the procedure. Notified bodies are supposed to be independent entities, operating autonomously and transparently. However, in practice, little is known about how they perform their functions [16, 17], and it might be the case that they are mere private entities, more concerned with ensuring that AI systems are approved in compliance with the formal requirements of the Draft Regulation, than with assuring effective levels of safety for the AI systems [18]. The risk of a 'privatized complaint industry' [18] cannot be underrated.

4   Difficulty in Complying with Some Requirements

In contrast to the flexibility that characterizes some aspects of the Draft Regulation, there are also extremely stringent impositions, that one can consider even utopian.

Take, for instance, Article 10(3) and its requirement that datasets for training and validation of AI systems must be 'error-free and complete'. I don't see how this requirement can be met, as it fails to recognize that perfect datasets simply do not exist [19].

Besides the excessive demand of this requirement, there is also the issue of its ambiguity [20], which adds another layer of difficulty with regard to compliance. It is not clarified to which specific type of error is the norm referring to: error in the data, error in the data classification, both types of errors, some other error not envisaged? Moreover, who assesses data quality and under what criteria?

Compliance difficulties will most likely also involve the transparency obligations, repeatedly invoked throughout the Draft Regulation (Recitals 14, 38, 39, 43, 47, 69 e 70; Articles 1/d e 13, e Titulo IV). Given that we are talking about an opaque technology (the famous 'black box') [21], it can be questioned how far such obligations are supposed to go.

5 Contextualization Within the EU Legal Framework

I envisage conflicts and overlaps, not only between norms from different legal texts but also between bodies and authorities.

The AI Draft Regulation appears in the aftermath of the European digital strategy [22], which, in turn, requires a bunch of new norms (some still in the pipeline) and new institutions. The legal framework covers e-commerce [23], data processing [24, 25], electronic communications [26], data governance [27], medical devices [28, 29] and pretty much everything directly or indirectly connected to the digital world. The million-dollar question is: how will all these norms and institutions relate to each other?

It will be almost impossible not to have overlaps between all these legal documents. Even if there are not actual conflicts, the challenge remains to take them all into account when acting or deciding. Let's take a concrete example: since AI systems work with data, frequently with personal data, it will be necessary to articulate the GDPR with the AI Regulation, which will not be an easy task, given that both include very detailed rules. Companies working in the field of AI (developers, manufacturers) can already anticipate challenging difficulties in what regards compliance, given the vast range of requirements to take into account for any simple act. Note, moreover, that the fact that some AI systems are accepted under the AI Draft Act does imply, without further ado, that they can be used. For example, facial recognition technology employed by private stakeholders is not prohibited by the Draft Act (most likely it will be a hight risk system and in some cases a low-risk system), but in practice, it turns out to be severely restricted in many scenarios by the GDPR [30].

Besides conflicts and overlaps between the norms, the same kind of issues might take place between bodies and authorities. The Draft Regulation calls for the creation of specific bodies at the national level (notifying authorities and notified bodies) as well as at the European level, namely the European Artificial Intelligence Board. The latter is a supranational supervisory authority, similar to the European Data Protection Board, created under the aegis of the GDPR. However, some national data protection bodies have already made it known that they consider them to be the most suitable to act as supervisory bodies for AI systems [31]. The 'suggestion' has, indeed, some advantages. Making use of authorities already established and with experience in this type of control (given the aforementioned use of personal data by AI systems, it is common for such entities to be called upon to comment on them) would make the model more effective.

In addition, it would reduce legal uncertainty and administrative complexity, as it would be possible to obtain greater consistency between the solutions given in the light of the AI Regulation and those given in the light of the GDPR [24] (and, by the way, of Directive 2016/680 [25], the control of which is also within the competence of the national data protection authorities). Another advantage is that the multiplication of supervisory authorities – with all connected difficulties and overlaps - would be avoided. In sum, there are indisputable advantages in the centralization of powers and functions in the national data protection authorities. However, a major concern must be considered: the reasoning underlying data protection does not entirely coincide with the reasoning necessary to monitor AI systems. AI raises many other issues beyond those typical of data protection and data protection authorities will probably lack proper expertise to deal with such issues [13].

6 Lack of Protection of CITizen's Rights

Some have criticized the Draft Regulation for having given in to business and technology instead of protecting fundamental rights and principles and the values of the European Union [32], as announced in the Explanatory Memorandum. One may agree that there are some loopholes in the protection of those affected by AI.

Note, for instance, that the Drat Regulation does not provide for a right to take legal action against developers, suppliers or users of AI systems who fail to comply with its standards (although non-compliance with those standards may be invoked in a civil liability case). Likewise, injured citizens do not have any legal base, under the Draft Regulation, to claim compensation for damages caused by AI (unlike what happens in Article 82 of the GDPR), which is a glaring omission. This has been a criticism repeatedly pointed out, both by European authorities (such as the European Data Protection Board and the European Data Protection Supervisor) [33] and by civil rights groups [18].

7 Discouragement to Technological Development

The fact that citizens' rights are not granted proper protection cannot be taken as a 'pro-technology' stance. If there is one thing missing from the Draft Regulation is precisely the boost to innovation. Apart from the 'regulatory sandboxes', referred to in Articles 53 and 54, and some measures to support small and medium-sized AI providers, in Article 55, there is not much encouragement to technological innovation. To this gap it must be added the massive list of compliance requirements (as referred to in Sect. 4) that hampers innovation, eventually with little added value in terms of rights protection. Research, manufacture, and commercialization of AI in the European space will suffer a heavy blow and AI investment in the EU may be hampered by such an 'innovation hole', which could advantage other leading players.

I dare to draw a parallel with what happens in relation to the GDPR. Nobody disputes that the level of demand in terms of requirements and limitations on what can be done in the field of data processing is practically at the maximum limit. The detail in regulation (hyper-regulation) has no equivalent in the rest of the world. That said, in terms of practical results, are the personal data of Europeans more protected than in other jurisdictions?

8 Houston, We Have a Problem

The Draft Regulation has an explicit aim: to be a far-reaching regulation aimed to guarantee the highest level of protection for 'Union values, fundamental rights and principles'. There is also a non-declared aim: to become the model in what regards the AI regulation for non-European jurisdictions, pursuing the so-called 'Brussels effect' (that is, the possibility to shape legal regimes worldwide by resorting to extraterritorial effects, forcing the consequent adoption of its solutions) that the GDPR so well embodies [34]. All these ambitious aims might fail due to the several issues referred to in this paper.

I fear that the AI Regulation will also become a hyper-regulation, with massive rules on practically everything, limitations that prevent the development of new technologies, excessive bureaucracy, absurd prohibitions, extremely heavy sanctions, but that do not necessarily result in higher protection for people's rights [3]. The EU may not be able to catch the train of technological transformation [35] and the alleged 'digital sovereignty' [36] might just be a flop.

References

1. Proposta de Regulamento do Parlamento Europeu e do Conselho que Estabelece Regras Harmonizadas em Matéria de Inteligência Artificial (Regulamento Inteligência Artificial) e Altera Determinados Atos Legislativos Da União, COM/2021/206 final. https://eur-lex.eur opa.eu/legal-content/PT/TXT/?uri=CELEX:52021PC0206. Accessed 11 Mar 2022
2. Meneceur, Y.: European Commission's AI Regulation Proposal: Between too Much and too Little? (2021). https://www.linkedin.com/pulse/european-commissions-ai-regulation-pro posal-between-too-meneceur/. Accessed 05 Mar 2022
3. Raposo, V.L.: Ex Machina: Preliminary critical assessment of the European draft act on artificial intelligence. Int. J. Law Inf. Technol. **30**(1), 88–109 (2022). https://doi.org/10.1093/ ijlit/eaac007
4. European Commission, White Paper on Artificial Intelligence - A European Approach to Excellence and Trust', Brussels, 19.2.2020 COM (2020). https://ec.europa.eu/info/sites/def ault/files/commission-white-paper-artificial-intelligence-feb2020_en.pdf. Accessed 15 Mar 2022
5. Gump, A.: New Proposed EU AI Regulation Extends Beyond Europe, JD Supra (2021). https://www.jdsupra.com/legalnews/new-proposed-eu-ai-regulation-extends-7373055/. Accessed 03 Mar 2022
6. Dąbrowski, L.D., Suska, M. (eds.): The European Union Digital Single Market Europe's Digital Transformation. Routledge, Abingdon (2022)
7. Raposo, V.L.: Digital Governance na Proposta de Regulamento da Comissão Europeia relativa à Inteligência Artificial: Breve Périplo sobre Good Governance e Direitos Fundamentais. In: Estudos em Homenagem Presidente Costa Andrade (forthcoming)
8. Fernández-Aller, C., Fernández de Velasco, A., Manjarrés, A., et al.: An inclusive and sustainable artificial intelligence strategy for europe based on human rights. IEEE Technol. Soc. Mag. **40**(1) (2021). https://doi.org/10.1109/MTS.2021.3056283
9. Raposo, V.L.: May I Have Some Artificial Intelligence with My Human Rights? About the Recent European Commission's Proposal on a Regulation for Artificial Intelligence, KSLR EU Law Blog (2021). https://blogs.kcl.ac.uk/kslreuropeanlawblog/?p=1569. Accessed 12 Mar 2022

10. Raposo, V.L.: The use of facial recognition technology by law enforcement in Europe: a non-orwellian draft proposal. Eur. J. Crim. Policy Res. (2022). https://doi.org/10.1007/s10610-022-09512-y
11. Currie, N.: Risk Based Approaches to Artificial Intelligence. https://www.crowe.com/-/media/Crowe/LLP/folio-pdf/Risk-Approaches-to-AI.pdf. Accessed 13 Mar 2022
12. European Consumer Voice in Standardisation (ANEC). ANEC commentson the European Commission Proposal for an Artificial Intelligence Act. Position Paper (2021). https://www.anec.eu/images/Publications/position-papers/Digital/ANEC-DIGITAL-2021-G-071.pdf. Accessed 22 Feb 2022
13. Raposo, V.L.: Proposta de Regulamento sobre Inteligência Artificial: the devil is in the details. Priv. Data Prot. Mag. **3**, 9–24 (2021), https://bo.europeia.pt/content/files/pdpm_003.pdf. Accessed 11 Mar 2022
14. European Commission, CE Marking. https://ec.europa.eu/growth/single-market/ce-marking_en. Accessed 04 Mar 2022
15. Decision No 768/2008/EC of the European Parliament and of the Council of 9 July 2008 on a common framework for the marketing of products, and repealing Council Decision 93/465/EEC. https://eur-lex.europa.eu/legal-content/EN/ALL/?uri=CELEX%3A32008D0768. Accessed 20 Jan 2022
16. Galland, J.-P.: The difficulties of regulating markets and risks in europe through notified bodies. Eur. J. Risk Regul. **4**(3), 365–373 (2013). https://doi.org/10.1017/S1867299X00002634
17. Veale, M., Borgesius, F.Z.: Demystifying the draft EU artificial intelligence act—analysing the good, the bad, and the unclear elements of the proposed approach. Comput. Law Rev. Int. **22**(4), 97–112 (2021)
18. Skelton, S.K.: Europe's Proposed Artificial Intelligence Regulation Falls Short on Protecting Rights, Computerweekly.com (2021). https://www.computerweekly.com/feature/Europes-proposed-AI-regulation-falls-short-on-protecting-rights. Accessed 02 Oct 2022
19. Floridi, L., Taddeo, M.: Romans would have denied robots legal personhood. Nature **557**(7705):309 (2018). https://doi.org/10.1038/d41586-018-05154-5. PMID: 29769676
20. Siemens, EU's AI Regulation Proposal (21/04/2021) Position & Recommendations (2021). https://ec.europa.eu/info/law/better-regulation/have-your-say/initiatives/12527-Artificial-intelligence-ethical-and-legal-requirements/F2662941_en?fbclid=IwAR1W6QQXqsZgrCkZM5Z9W22JVFg0RDrh-gc4dFlXvg8z-z-fAhAQi66y39Y. Accessed 25 Aug 2021
21. Cassauwers, T.: Opening the 'Black Box' of Artificial Intelligence, Horizon - The EU Research and Innovation Magazine (2020). https://ec.europa.eu/research-and-innovation/en/horizon-magazine/opening-black-box-artificial-intelligence. Accessed 20 Mar 2022
22. European Commission, Data Act: Commission proposes measures for a fair and innovative data economy. https://digital-strategy.ec.europa.eu/en. Accessed 14 Mar 2022
23. Directive 2000/31/EC of the European Parliament and of the Council of 8 June 2000 on certain legal aspects of information society services, in particular electronic commerce, in the Internal Market ('Directive on electronic commerce'). https://eur-lex.europa.eu/legal-content/EN/ALL/?uri=CELEX%3A32000L0031. Accessed 02 Mar 2022
24. Regulation (EU) 2016/679 of the European Parliament and of the Council of 27 April 2016 on the protection of natural persons with regard to the processing of personal data and on the free movement of such data, and repealing Directive 95/46/EC (General Data Protection Regulation). https://eur-lex.europa.eu/eli/reg/2016/679/oj. Accessed 02 Mar 2022
25. Directive (EU) 2016/680 of the European Parliament and of the Council of 27 April 2016 on the protection of natural persons with regard to the processing of personal data by competent authorities for the purposes of the prevention, investigation, detection or prosecution of criminal offences or the execution of criminal penalties, and on the free movement of such data, and repealing Council Framework Decision 2008/977/JHA. Accessed 02 Mar 2022

26. Proposal for a Regulation of the European Parliament and of the Council concerning the respect for private life and the protection of personal data in electronic communications and repealing Directive 2002/58/EC (Regulation on Privacy and Electronic Communications). COM/2017/010 final - 2017/03 (COD). https://eur-lex.europa.eu/legal-content/EN/TXT/?uri=CELEX%3A52017PC0010. Accessed 11 Mar 2022
27. Proposal for a Regulation of the European Parliament and of the Council on European data governance (Data Governance Act), COM/2020/767 final. https://eur-lex.europa.eu/legal-content/EN/TXT/?uri=CELEX%3A52020PC0767. Accessed 02 Mar 2022
28. Regulation (EU) 2017/745 of the European Parliament and of the Council of 5 April 2017 on medical devices, amending Directive 2001/83/EC, Regulation (EC) No 178/2002 and Regulation (EC) No 1223/2009 and repealing Council Directives 90/385/EEC and 93/42/EEC, https://eur-lex.europa.eu/legal-content/EN/TXT/?uri=CELEX%3A32017R0745. Accessed 02 Mar 2022
29. Regulation (EU) 2017/746 of the European Parliament and of the Council of 5 April 2017 on in vitro diagnostic medical devices and repealing Directive 98/79/EC and Commission Decision 2010/227/EU. https://eur-lex.europa.eu/eli/reg/2017/746/oj. Accessed 02 Mar 2022
30. Raposo, V.L.: (Do not) remember my face: uses of facial recognition technology in light of the general data protection regulation. Inf. Commun. Technol. Law (2022). https://doi.org/10.1080/13600834.2022.2054076
31. Commission Nationale de L'informatique et des Libertés (CNIL), Artificial intelligence: the opinion of the CNIL and its counterparts on the future European regulation (2021). https://www.cnil.fr/en/artificial-intelligence-opinion-cnil-and-its-counterparts-future-european-regulation. Accessed 15 Feb 2022
32. EDRI, Civil Society Calls on the EU To Put Fundamental Rights First in the AI Act (2021). https://edri.org/our-work/civil-society-calls-on-the-eu-to-put-fundamental-rights-first-in-the-ai-act/. Accessed 14 Mar 2022
33. European Data Protection Board and European Data Protection Supervisor, Joint Opinion 5/2021 on the Proposal for a Regulation of the European Parliament and of the Council Laying down Harmonised Rules on Artificial Intelligence (Artificial Intelligence Act) (2021). https://edpb.europa.eu/our-work-tools/ourdocuments/edpbedps-joint-opinion/edpb-edps-joint-opinion-52021-proposal_en. Accessed 03 Sept 2021
34. Bradford, A.: The Brussels Effect: How the European Union Rules the World. Oxford University Press, New York (2020)
35. Lewis, J.A., Has Europe Lost Both the Battle and War over Its Digital Future? (2020). https://www.csis.org/analysis/has-europe-lost-both-battle-and-war-over-its-digital-future. Accessed 19 Feb 2022
36. Michel, C., Digital Sovereignty is Central to European Strategic Autonomy (Speech) (2021). https://www.consilium.europa.eu/en/press/press-releases/2021/02/03/speech-by-president-charles-michel-at-the-digitaleurope-masters-of-digital-online-event/#:~:text=10%3A25-,Digital%20sovereignty%20is%20central%20to%20European%20strategic%20autonomy%20%2D%20Speech%20by,of%20digital%202021%22%20online%20event&text=Digital%20is%20one%20of%20the,had%20heard%20of%20COVID%2D19. Accessed 23 Jan 2022

Traffic Stops in the Age of Autonomous Vehicles

Tracy Hresko Pearl[✉]

University of Oklahoma, Norman, USA
tracy.pearl@ou.edu

Abstract. Autonomous vehicles have profound implications for laws governing police, searches and seizures, and privacy. Complicating matters, manufacturers are developing these vehicles at varying rates. Each level of vehicle automation, in turn, poses unique issues for law enforcement. Semi-autonomous (Levels 2 and 3) vehicles make it extremely difficult for police to distinguish between dangerous distracted driving and safe use of a vehicle's autonomous capabilities. Fully autonomous (Level 4 and 5) vehicles solve this problem but create a new one: the ability of criminals to use these vehicles to break the law with a low risk of detection. How and whether we solve these legal and law enforcement issues depends on the willingness of nations to adapt legal doctrines. This article explores the implications of autonomous vehicle stops and six possible solutions including: (1) restrictions on visibility obstructions, (2) restrictions on the use and purchase of fully autonomous vehicles, (3) laws requiring that users provide implied consent for suspicion-less traffic stops and searches, (4) creation of government checkpoints or pull-offs requiring autonomous vehicles to submit to brief stops and dog sniffs, (5) surveillance of data generated by these vehicles, and (6) opting to do nothing and allowing the coming changes to recalibrate the existing balance between law enforcement and citizens.

Keywords: Autonomous vehicles · Law & technology · Traffic stops

1 Background

Autonomous vehicles, also known as driverless cars, "are those in which at least some aspects of safety-critical control function (*e.g.*, steering, throttle, or braking) occur without direct driver input" [1]. Put more simply, autonomous vehicles take control out of the hands of human drivers and place it instead in complex onboard computer software, external sensors, and GPS. Working together, these systems allow the vehicle to change speed, direction, and route, and navigate the road environment with minimal input from their human occupants.

1.1 Autonomous Vehicle Development

The list of companies actively developing autonomous vehicles is growing, and includes both technology companies like Waymo and Lyft, and automobile manufacturers like Tesla, Ford, and Volvo. Progress, however, is coming in fits and starts, making it difficult

© The Author(s), under exclusive license to Springer Nature Switzerland AG 2022
G. Marreiros et al. (Eds.): EPIA 2022, LNAI 13566, pp. 74–84, 2022.
https://doi.org/10.1007/978-3-031-16474-3_7

to predict rollout with any accuracy. Additionally, companies are approaching the development and market release of autonomous vehicles differently, meaning that industry players are at differing stages of development.

The major implication of these varying approaches to autonomous vehicle development is that, for some period of years (if not decades), vehicles with differing levels of automation will populate public roads throughout developed countries. The U.S. National Highway Traffic Safety Administration (NHTSA), in an attempt to describe the significant benchmarks in vehicle autonomy, adopted a six-level taxonomy of these levels of automation [2]. Those levels are:

- Level 0: Vehicles with no automation whatsoever. A Level 0 vehicle is a conventional automobile without cruise control.
- Level 1: Vehicles with "function-specific automation" like basic cruise control. The driver can hand over one and only one driving function (like acceleration) to the vehicle, but must maintain control over all other driving tasks. Most vehicles currently on public roads are Level 1 vehicles.
- Level 2: Vehicles with "combined functioned automation" like cruise control with lane-centering. The driver can hand over more than one driving function (like acceleration and basic steering) to the vehicle, but must continuously monitor the vehicle and be ready to retake control quickly. A Tesla with Autopilot functionality is an example of a Level 2 Car.
- Level 3: Vehicles with "limited self-driving automation." The driver can hand over all driving functions to the vehicle and need not supervise, but must be ready to resume driving on fairly short notice. As of early 2022, Level 3 vehicles are in development, but are not yet available to consumers.
- Level 4: Vehicles that can drive completely autonomously, but "only in certain environments and under certain conditions." Human drivers need not be ready to retake control, but the vehicle may not be able to be used safely under certain conditions like extreme weather. Level 4 vehicles are in development.
- Level 5: Fully autonomous vehicles that "can perform all driving tasks, under all conditions that a human driver could perform them." Human drivers need not ever supervise or retake control of these vehicles and may lack the ability to do so even if they wished. Level 5 vehicles are in development.

One of the challenges that law enforcement may face as vehicles of these varying levels appear on public roads is knowing what level of autonomous vehicle (if any) a vehicle of interest is, and whether the human occupant is currently exerting any control. If a police officer spots a human in a driver's seat, for instance, it may be unclear whether the human is actively driving (as is possible in a Level 0, 1, 2, or 3 vehicle), whether the human is merely supervising the vehicle (as may be the case in a Level 2 or Level 3 vehicle driving semi-autonomously), or whether the human is a completely passive occupant (as will likely be the case in a Level 4 or 5 vehicle). Knowing the make, model, and year of the vehicle, moreover, may not be enough to resolve any uncertainty, as manufacturers like Tesla push greater levels of autonomy to existing vehicles via over-the-air updates over time, meaning that a vehicle that was Level 2 at purchase may evolve into a Level 3 or perhaps even Level 4 vehicle at some point in the future.

Despite these complexities, autonomous vehicles are expected to have a number of major societal benefits. These benefits include "improved safety and a reduction in roadway fatalities; improved quality of life; access, and mobility for all citizens; lower energy usage; and improved supply chain management" [3]. Additionally, wide adoption of these vehicles may yield other important gains such as "increased economic productivity and efficiency, reduced commuting time, and even the potential reduction of the environmental impact of conventional surface vehicles while increasing overall system energy efficiency" [4]. However, nations may never realize these benefits if existing laws do not adapt thoughtfully and carefully to this new technology, or if courts and legislatures adopt either too lax or too draconian of a stance on its regulation. This is particularly true with respect to traffic stops of autonomous vehicles, and what rights drivers and occupants may or may not have in that context.

1.2 Likely Impacts of Autonomous Vehicles on Traffic Stops

The growing number of semi-autonomous vehicles, and the eventual arrival of fully autonomous vehicles, on public roads will have far-reaching implications for traffic stops, some positive and some negative. A brief overview of the most significant of these can provide helpful context for the legal discussion that follows.

First, fully autonomous vehicles will likely drastically decrease the number of traffic violations and thus traffic stops each year. Because manufacturers will program these vehicles to obey all traffic laws and obey them perfectly, police will be less able to establish justifications for traffic stops, whether prextextual or not. In the U.S., for instance, even just a 30% reduction in traffic stops could mean a reduction of more than 5 million traffic cases each year, significantly reducing the caseloads of misdemeanor courts (and their equivalents elsewhere) and the costs associated with them.

Second, fully autonomous vehicles will likely reduce opportunities for police to racially profile. Studies have repeatedly shown that police stop Black and Latinx drivers at significantly higher rates than White drivers [6]. Without traffic violations to rely on as pretexts for traffic stops, police officers will have less opportunity to introduce subjectivity (or outright racial animus) into their decisions about which cars to stop, reducing the burden of over-policing on minority communities and perhaps even beginning to rebuild public trust in law enforcement.

Third, traffic stops of autonomous vehicles may be safer for both police and vehicle occupants alike. In fully autonomous vehicles, occupants may lack the ability to use the car to flee, a situation dangerous to both law enforcement and nearby civilians. Similarly, if autonomous vehicles are able to connect virtually to smart infrastructure (as many industry observers predict they eventually will), police may be able to gather a significant amount of information from a distance, reducing the likelihood of unjustified police shootings of drivers and passengers and reducing the risk to police inherent in close encounters with vehicle occupants who may turn out to be dangerous.

Fourth and finally, knowing that autonomous vehicles are significantly less likely to be stopped at all, criminals may use them to transport illegal contraband, victims of human trafficking, or worse. They may be able to do so, moreover, in vehicles with no human occupants at all, nearly eliminating the risk that a member of the criminal enterprise will be detained or apprehended. Such vehicles, when filled with explosives,

could also be turned into mobile bombs that could be driven into any publicly accessible location of choice. Law enforcement is already immensely concerned about these possibilities and their ability to respond effectively.

2 The Legal Complexities of AV Traffic Stops

The major question confronting nations now is how to apply existing traffic stop, search and seizure, and privacy laws in the brave new world of autonomous vehicles, a world in which the concepts of "driver" and "passenger" may no longer mean what they used to. This challenge, moreover, is immensely complicated by the uneven pace of development and adoption of these vehicles, meaning that automobiles on public roads may vary quite significantly in their levels of automation for quite some time before fully autonomous, Level 5 vehicles attain supremacy. What this array of automation means, most importantly, is that it would be a mistake for both courts and law enforcement to adopt a single approach to traffic stops of autonomous vehicles. As one group of scholars astutely observes: "Each [configuration of autonomous vehicles] includes different conceptions of and roles for "drivers," "passengers," "users," and "occupants"; different systems for communications and control; different systems of spatial organization; different commercial and political arrangements; and different consequences for societal and human values. Each imagination of autonomous automotive transport involves an entire world of reorganization for politics and values–each presenting different challenges for regulators and the public. Reckoning with the implications of these reconfigurations means... focusing on how each autonomous transport vision, promoted by various parties, moves toward a different future with particular political and ethical implications" [7].

Courts would be wise, therefore, to approach each level of autonomous vehicles as a distinct legal category unto itself, deserving of its own tailored application of law and precedent responsive to the unique aspects and challenges of that particular level. As discussed at greater length below, moreover, industry, law enforcement, and private citizens are all important stakeholders in the development of this new line of jurisprudence, and any new legal approach that overlooks the concerns of one of them is at risk to fail.

The following subsections are an attempt to identify the most significant legal issues presented by each unique level of automation. Each discussion seeks as its ultimate goals: (1) safety of public roads (and society more generally), and (2) protection of the rights of vehicle occupants.

2.1 Level 2 (Semi-autonomous) Vehicles

Level 2 vehicles, those in which the driver can both remove their hands from the wheel and their feet from the pedals but must continuously monitor the vehicle while in semi-autonomous mode, arguably place the least amount of stress on existing traffic stop jurisprudence. If anything, in fact, these vehicles may provide police with *more* reasons to initiate traffic stops than Level 1 vehicles. Indeed, Level 2 vehicles present unique risks on public roads because their drivers often (a) don't fully understand the limitations of the semi-autonomous systems within them, and/or (b) do not take their obligation to

constantly monitor the vehicle seriously, leading them to make reckless choices dangerous to everyone on the road [8]. This, in turn, means that police may have at least one
additional reason to initiate traffic stop of these vehicles, one that did not exist before
these vehicles arrived on the consumer market: failure to adequately monitor a vehicle
operating at a Level 2 measure of autonomy. Alternatively, this may merely be a new
version of a very old problem on public roads: distracted driving. Either way, a police
officer who witnesses the driver of a Level 2 vehicle doing something other than watch-
ing the road would certainly have probable cause to execute a standard traffic stop given
that there are no scenarios in which distracted driving in a Level 2 vehicle would be
justifiable.

Where Level 2 vehicles could theoretically complicate matters are situations in which
a Level 2 system either malfunctions or otherwise responds poorly to a sudden driving
condition, leaving even a very attentive driver with no time to respond. In those scenarios,
a nearby police officer might witness a car swerve, depart from a lane without signaling,
run off the road, or even hit another car, but lack the ability to determine whether this
traffic violation was the fault of the car's semi-autonomous system or the human driver.
= I would argue that, based upon what he or she has witnessed, a police officer would
absolutely have probable cause to execute a traffic stop under such circumstances despite
this uncertainty. Drivers in *many* scenarios may not be at fault for traffic violations (*e.g.*,
when those violations are caused by sudden brake failures, tire malfunctions, etc.) or
may have good reasons for violating traffic laws (*e.g.*, speeding to get a person in heavy
labor to the hospital), but courts have never found that such factors, discovered after the
fact, mean that police lacked justification to make a traffic stop.

2.2 Level 3 (Semi-autonomous) Vehicles

While Level 2 vehicles may not challenge policing or existing jurisprudence much, the
coming arrival of Level 3 vehicles on public roads will likely mark the start of much
greater uncertainty, both legally and functionally for traffic patrol officers. As discussed
above, Level 3 vehicles can drive themselves in some conditions, but may require a
human to retake control when signaled to do so by the vehicle itself. While drivers of
Level 2 vehicles must monitor their car constantly while using its autonomous features,
drivers of Level 3 vehicles have greater leeway to engage in other tasks, assuming they
can do so while remaining ready to retake control of the vehicle when alerted. Thus,
while distraction is never justified in a Level 2 vehicle, distraction may not only be safe
in a Level 3 vehicle, it is likely to be one of the major appeals of using this kind of
vehicle.

But, Level 3 vehicles will present law enforcement with the same kind of challenge posed by Level 2 vehicles: not knowing whether a given car is being piloted
autonomously or driven by a human driver at any given moment. The difference is that,
in a Level 2 vehicle, distracted driving arguably *always* provide justification for a traffic stop (since it is never justified in a Level 2 vehicle), whereas in a Level 3 vehicle,
distracted driving should not. The problem, of course, is that a police officer may not
know what level of autonomous vehicle it is, whether the autonomous system has been
activated, and whether, if activated, the driver has been signaled to retake control at that
moment. In short, when Level 3 vehicles become available to consumers, coexist with

Levels 0, 1, and 2 vehicles on public roads, and an officer witnesses a distracted driver, one of four scenarios is possible:

1. The distracted driver is driving a Level 0, 1, or 2 vehicle and is thus violating existing traffic laws;
2. The distracted driver is driving a Level 3 vehicle, has not activated the autonomous system, and is violating existing traffic laws;
3. The distracted driver is using a Level 3 vehicle, *has* activated the autonomous system, and is *not* violating existing traffic laws;
4. The distracted driver is using a Level 3 vehicle, has activated the autonomous system, but has been signaled to retake control of the vehicle, not done so, and is violating existing traffic laws.

This identification problem will be compounded by the fact that, as discussed above, manufacturers are releasing different levels of autonomy in their vehicles at different rates and even pushing new levels of automation to vehicles post-purchase via over-air-updates.

One potential solution would be to rule that the burden of identifying whether a distracted driver falls into Scenario 1, 2, 3, or 4 should not fall on law enforcement, and that witnessing a distracted person in a driver's seat always provides justification to initiate a traffic stop, regardless of the level of autonomy of the driver's vehicle and whether the autonomous system has been engaged. In fact, without meaningful changes in how these cars are manufactured, police may entirely lack the ability to determine what kind of vehicle someone is driving, particularly in the quickly moving world of traffic enforcement. The problem, of course, is that this kind of blanket approach could greatly undermine what will arguably be major appeal and utility of Level 3 vehicles: being able to engage in other tasks while the car is driving itself. If using the autonomous system of a Level 3 vehicle exposes drivers to a greater threat of traffic stops, some (if not many) consumers may opt not to purchase them at all, impeding the adoption and development of this technology and the many benefits it offers to society.

Another possible solution would be to use market share of Level 3 vehicles (as measured by percentage of vehicles on public roads with this level of automation) to determine whether police have justification to make stops for distracted driving more generally. Indeed, once the market share of Level 3 vehicles is high enough, police will arguably no longer have justification cause to suspect that a distracted driver is violating the law. If 80% of the cars are the road are Level 3, chances are better than not than a distracted "driver" is not doing anything dangerous or illegal.

A third possible solution to the quandary posed by Level 3 vehicles could come from industry rather than from courts or legislatures. One legal scholar has suggested that manufacturers outfit all autonomous vehicles with exterior indicator lights which, when illuminated, would indicate to any observer that the vehicle is being driven by its autonomous system rather than by a human driver. While at least one state in the U.S. has passed a law requiring autonomous vehicles to have "a visual indicator *inside* the cabin to indicate when the autonomous technology is engaged," no jurisdiction has yet demanded that these vehicles have exterior lights indicating the same, even though such lights would be tremendously helpful to law enforcement.

2.3 Level 4 & 5 (Fully Autonomous) Vehicles

Fully autonomous vehicles will likely eliminate the problem of distracted driving—and the appearance of districted driving—entirely. Early mockups of the interiors of these vehicles often show them without a driver's seat or even a steering wheel, so police should be able to determine fairly easily via simple observation that a vehicle is fully autonomous. However, fully autonomous vehicles may pose a different—and potentially very serious—problem for law enforcement. Since manufacturers plan to program fully autonomous vehicles to drive in near perfect compliance with traffic laws, the ability of police officers to establish legal justification to initiate a traffic stop could be significantly curtailed. This limitation, in turn, could create huge incentives for criminals to use these vehicles for nefarious purposes such as transporting drugs, other forms of contraband, and even victims of human trafficking or kidnapping. In more extreme scenarios, moreover, fully autonomous vehicles could be filled with explosives or biological weapons and used as lethal weapons. These possibilities should obviously be of concern to citizens and law enforcement alike.

Additionally, while there may be many benefits to an overall reduction in traffic stops resulting from the use of fully autonomous vehicles, these benefits are likely to come at the expense of detecting and stopping crime more generally. Indeed, "[c]onducting traffic stops has been a cornerstone of policing for decades, often leading to the identification of crimes unrelated to the act of driving" [9]. Police often use their ability to initiate traffic stops to conduct broader investigations of suspicious activity as traffic stops can—for better or worse—evolve into more significant stops involving searches of the interior of the vehicle, dog sniffs of the exterior of the vehicle, and/or extensive questioning of the occupants, all of which can result in evidence of non-traffic-related crimes. Stymieing law enforcement's ability to conduct these traffic stops could thus change the nature of policing and make it more difficult for police to detect crime of all types.

The relevant question, therefore, is the extent to which existing traffic jurisprudence truly impedes the ability of police to stop a fully autonomous vehicle. Are scholars and commentators right that police will have little to no ability to stop these vehicles, eventually rendering traffic stops mostly obsolete? Or, is the vast jurisprudence around traffic stops permissive enough to provide law enforcement with more opportunities than one might initially think to develop legal justification to stop a fully autonomous vehicle? The answer is almost certainly dependent on a number of factors. The most significant factor, however, is likely to be whether the vehicle is occupied or unoccupied by passengers.

Occupied Level 4 & 5 Vehicles. With respect to fully autonomous vehicles that are occupied, police could form justification to stop the vehicle in several ways. First and foremost, police could develop reasonable suspicion based on mere observation of the occupants. The U.S. Supreme Court, for instance, has said on repeated occasions that suspicious behavior on the part of car passengers can form the basis of both reasonable suspicion and even probable cause to stop a vehicle. In *United States v. Brignoni-Ponce*, for instance, the Court said that, in establishing reasonable suspicion for a traffic stop, officers may consider the number of passengers, the behavior of those passengers (*e.g.*, are they "trying to hide"), and even their "mode of dress and haircut" [10]. There is

seemingly no reason why police could not make similar observations about the occupants of fully autonomous vehicles and then execute traffic stops accordingly. Even something as simple as occupant failure to use seatbelts would, if observed by officers, be enough to execute a traffic stop.

Second, police could develop reasonable suspicion to stop a fully autonomous vehicle based on the type of vehicle (*e.g.*, truck vs. car), its location, and whether it appears to be carrying a significant amount of weight ("riding low"). In *United States v. Cortez*, the U.S. Supreme Court held that officers had reasonable suspicion to initiate a traffic stop to investigate suspected smuggling of undocumented immigrants based upon, among other factors, the number of passengers the vehicle could hold, its location near a known area of border crossing, and the time of night it was observed [11]. Even factors like out-of-state license plates and "travel patterns" might suffice. Again, there are no reasons to think this would no longer be true in the context of fully autonomous vehicles. Third, police could form justification to stop a fully autonomous vehicle based on a credible tip from an informant.

As this discussion makes clear, while autonomous vehicles may use utilize new and novel technologies, community members will still be able to use their eyes, ears, and life experience to identify suspicious or even outright criminal behavior and notify law enforcement. A strange vehicle with strange occupants slowly casing houses in the middle of the night will seem suspicious regardless of whether the vehicle is autonomous or not. Thus, while fully autonomous vehicles are likely to drive while causing few, if any, traffic violations, they will not be unstoppable if they are occupied. Police will be able to use observations about the passengers and the vehicle itself in addition to credible tips to establish reasonable suspicion to execute a traffic stop.

Unoccupied Level 4 & 5 Vehicles. Establishing justification to stop *unoccupied* fully autonomous vehicles will undoubtedly be more difficult. Without occupants, police officers will have less to observe and fewer indicia of potential criminal activity. While police will certainly retain the ability to use tips and observable characteristics of the vehicle itself to establish reasonable suspicion, even these factors are likely to be less meaningful in the context of unoccupied autonomous vehicles. For example, as discussed above, somecourts have held that police can use the location and/or route of a vehicle to establish reasonable suspicion. A car that seems out of place in a given neighborhood or to be taking an unusual route may be grounds for suspicion. However, in the context of unoccupied, fully autonomous vehicles: "Immediate observations like the route taken or even the neighborhood where the vehicle is being operated may be less indicative of criminal activity. When the AV takes control of the navigation of the vehicle and the route taken, these factors may simply be indicative of the programming of the vehicle, rather than an indication that criminal activity may be afoot. That is not to say that the location of the vehicle and route taken will become completely irrelevant, but the weight given to those factors should be reduced in many instances."

With so little to go on, moreover, even observable characteristics of the vehicle may not be enough to justify a traffic stop. For instance, if police witness an unoccupied, fully autonomous vehicle "riding low" in the back suggesting the vehicle is carrying a significant amount of weight, it is highly doubtful that factor alone, without something more, would be enough to establish justification for a traffic stop. Without any other

factors to consider, the situation could be described as something like "Schrodinger's Trunk;" police have no more reason to believe that the trunk is filled with contraband than they do to believe it is filled with lawful goods, and continued observation of the exterior of the car is unlikely to yield more clues. In a situation like that, a traffic stop would surely run afoul of established jurisprudence in many countries.

Troublingly, this analysis suggests that the concerns of industry observers are correct: criminals will be able to use unoccupied Level 4 and 5 vehicles to commit crimes successfully and with little risk of detection. If criminals take basic precautions to ensure that illegal goods (or victims) are not observable from the exterior of the car, program the vehicle to use well-traveled roads during normal hours, and otherwise make the vehicle inconspicuous, police will likely struggle mightily to establish reasonable suspicion to stop that vehicle in the absence of a credible tip. This situation begs the questions: (1) How big of a problem is this likely to become; (2) Is a solution needed?; and (3) If so, what are the potential options?

With respect to the first question—how big of a problem use of unoccupied autonomous vehicle for criminal purposes is likely to become—no data currently exists because fully autonomous vehicles are not yet available to consumers. However, we can use what we know about the risks associated with crime more generally to speculate. Currently, there are several significant risk factors associated with using occupied vehicles in the course of committing a crime:

- Human drivers frequently make mistakes and break traffic laws, making human-driven vehicles exponentially more likely than autonomous vehicles to be stopped by the police, pretextually or otherwise.
- Once a vehicle is stopped, police have a much better opportunity to see, smell, and hear the vehicle up close, increasing the risk police will develop justification to search the vehicle and find illegal contraband.
- If police find contraband or even merely have evidence that a traffic violation has occurred, they may be entitled to arrest the driver and/or the passengers of the vehicle, creating the risk that the relevant gang or criminal organization could lose a valuable member or, worse, find themselves confronted with a member who "flips" and cooperates with law enforcement.

Unoccupied fully autonomous vehicles not only have none of these risks associated with them, they are likely to be faster and more efficient than human-driven vehicles. The relevant question, therefore, is not "Will criminals use unoccupied, fully autonomous vehicles to commit crime," it is "Why would they not?"

How—or whether—we solve the problem of traffic stops and unoccupied fully autonomous vehicles is ultimately likely to turn on how politically, legally, and perhaps even culturally palatable the solutions are. Identifying those potential solutions is thus a critical component of this analysis, and the component to which we now turn.

3 Potential Solutions

Finding solutions to the challenges identified above requires a careful and nuanced balancing of the need to ensure that public roads are safe with the rights and privacy interests of vehicle occupants. The following, in order of least extreme to most extreme, are six possibilities.

First, state governments could pass restrictions on visibility obstructions in fully autonomous vehicles to give police a greater opportunity to detect contraband and perhaps even crime victims in the interiors of these vehicles. Such restrictions would almost certainly be reasonable extensions of existing window tinting laws and other such regulations although rest on a different justification: crime detection rather than driver visibility.

Second, governments could place restrictions on purchase and use of fully autonomous vehicles and prohibit their use by, for example, individuals with significant criminal histories. Such laws would be a new application of previous jurisprudence holding that operation of a motor vehicle is not a fundamental right in most countries, and, by extension, laws that permit governments to suspend or revoke driver's licenses for various driving offenses. Where such laws would be novel is in banning mere ownership of a particular category of vehicle, a restriction that arguably makes sense in the context of fully autonomous vehicles that can be dispatched by owners for nefarious purposes without any occupants.

Third, governments could require owners or users of fully autonomous vehicle to consent in advance to traffic stops and other forms of police scrutiny. While many nations already require drivers to provide implied consent to blood and breath alcohol testing as a condition of licensure, this solution would be a fairly dramatic extension of such laws since drivers would be asked to consent in advance to a wide range of potential police investigations. A better option might be to outfit fully autonomous vehicles with communication devices that would permit police officers to communicate remotely with owners.

Fourth, governments could establish checkpoints or pull-offs and require all fully autonomous vehicles to submit to brief stops and dog sniffs to determine if the vehicle is being used to carry contraband, much like cargo trucks are currently subjected to roadside weight checks in many nations. In the United States, however, The Supreme Court has indicated in multiple cases that it is likely to view such checkpoints as unconstitutional outside of very limited contexts given the extent to which such stops interfere with unfettered travel.

Fifth, governments could exploit existing AI jurisprudence to surveil data generated by autonomous vehicles. Some countries, for instance, currently hold that data shared with a third party is not entitled to privacy protection and can been used by law enforcement. Gathering this data from autonomous vehicles would greatly assist law enforcement in determining how, when, and where these vehicles are being used. However, given that such data could reveal a deep and wide variety of personal information, the privacy implications of such an approach would significant.

Finally, courts or the government could opt to do nothing about the problems created by autonomous vehicles, or even use these emerging issues as an opportunity to recalibrate both traffic stop and privacy laws. While autonomous vehicles may eliminate

(or at least drastically curtail) the use of pretextual traffic stops as a key method of law enforcement, police will still be able to use more conventional investigatory techniques to detect and stop the use of autonomous vehicles in crime. Such investigatory techniques, moreover, are less likely to result in the racial profiling and violence that have historically plagued pretextual traffic stops. Autonomous vehicles, therefore, as much as they may challenge an already fraught area of law, may create a valuable opportunity to rebalance both policing and privacy jurisprudence in greater favor of motorists who, for far too long, have seen a gradual but persistent erosion of many of their most significant rights.

References

1. U.S. National Highway Traffic Safety Administration, Preliminary Statement of Policy Concerning Automated Vehicles (2013)
2. U.S. National Highway Traffic Safety Admin., Federal Automated Vehicles Policy 9 (2016)
3. National Science & Technology Council & U.S. Department of Transportation, Ensuring American Leadership in Automated Vehicle Technologies, p. 1, January 2020
4. Ibid
5. Clark, J.D.: Driverless cars and criminal justice resource allocation. SMU Sci. Tech. Law Rev. **22**, 195–205 (2019)
6. Richardson, L.: Implicit racial bias and the perpetrator perspective: a response to reasonable but unconstitutional. Geo. Wash. Law Rev. **83**, 1008–1015 (2015)
7. Goldenfein, J.: Through the handoff lens: competing visions of autonomous futures. Berkeley Tech. Law J. **35**, 835–838 (2020)
8. Pearl, T.: Hands on the wheel: a call for greater regulation of semi-autonomous cars. Ind. Law J. **93**, 713, 731–738 (2018)
9. Cal. Veh. Code § 38750(c)(1)(B) (West)
10. Davis, K.: Preparing for a Future with Autonomous Vehicles. The Police Chief 83, July 2016
11. United States v. Brignoni-Ponce, 422 U.S. 873–885 (1975)
12. United States v. Cortez, 449 U.S. 411, 415–420 (1981)
13. Roseman, R.: When autonomous vehicles take over the road: rethinking the expansion of the fourth amendment in a technology-driven world. Rich. J. Law Tech. **20**, 3–28 (2014)

UlyssesSD-Br: Stance Detection in Brazilian Political Polls

Dyonnatan F. Maia[1](✉)(iD), Nádia F. F. Silva[1](iD), Ellen P. R. Souza[2](iD),
Augusto S. Nunes[3](iD), Lucas C. Procópio[3], Guthemberg da S. Sampaio[2],
Márcio de S. Dias[3,4](iD), Adrio O. Alves[3], Dyéssica F. Maia[6],
Ingrid A. Ribeiro[7](iD), Fabíola S. F. Pereira[5](iD),
and André P. de L. F. de Carvalho[3]

[1] Institute of Informatics, Federal University of Goiás, Goiânia, GO, Brazil
`dyonnatan@discente.ufg.br`, `nadia.felix@ufg.br`
[2] Centro de Informática, Federal University of Pernambuco, Recife, PE, Brazil
`ellen.ramos@ufrpe.br`, `gss6@cin.ufpe.br`
[3] Institute of Mathematics and Computer Science, University of São Paulo,
São Carlos, SP, Brazil
`{augustonunes,lucascbsi020,adrio20,andre}@usp.br`
[4] Federal University of Catalão, Catalão, GO, Brazil
`marciodias@ufcat.edu.br`
[5] Federal University of Uberlândia, Uberlândia, MG, Brazil
`fabiola.pereira@ufu.br`
[6] Pontifical Catholic University of Goiás, Goiânia, Brazil
`20202013000134@pucgo.edu.br`
[7] Faculdade de Ceilândia, University of Brasília, Brasília, DF, Brazil
`ribeiro.ingrid@aluno.unb.br`

Abstract. Political bill comments published in digital media may reveal
the issuer's stances. Through this, we can identify and group the polarity
of these public opinions. The automatic stance detection task involves
viewing the text and the target topic. Due to the diversity and emergence
of new bills, the challenge approached is to estimate the polarity of a
new topic. Thus, this paper evaluates cross-target stance detection with
many-to-one approaches in a collected Portuguese dataset of the political
pool from the Brazilian Chamber of Deputies website. We proposed a new
corpus for the bills' opinion domain and tested it in several models, where
we achieved the best result with the mBERT model in classification with
the joint input topic and comment method. We verify that the mBERT
model successfully handled cross-target tasks with this corpus among the
tested algorithms.

Keywords: Stance detection · Political comments · Cross-target

1 Introduction

Stance detection treats to identify and classify the polarity in a text towards a
topic [6,7]. Moreover, the polarity classification subtask evaluates whether the

G. Marreiros et al. (Eds.): EPIA 2022, LNAI 13566, pp. 85–95, 2022.
https://doi.org/10.1007/978-3-031-16474-3_8

text supports or is contrary to the topic. So, the input can be composed of the tuple (topic, text), and the output may be a ternary class (against, favour, none) or divided into identification (stance, none) and classification (against, favour). [6]. For political bill comments, the topic's representation can be the bill target itself or the subtopics that affect it. Thus, the topic could be any political, social or economic subject. When new bills get the public attention in Brazil, people can discuss the content and express opinions in public comments, social media debates, and specialised sites. This text data can reveal the yearnings of that population sample, so if we automatically determine their stance, then one advantage is that the author's bill may better comprehend its polarity of acceptance.

To automatically detect the texts' stance on each bill, it is interesting that the method detects points of view from new topics because the interest in these stances is more related to the popularity and deadline for the bill vote. This kind of problem may be treated as cross-target with many-to-one approach, which means it is tested the generalisation model capability with other targets/topics in the same context [7], many-to-one means that we will consider many topics to model training and evaluates each new topic.

Therefore, this paper presents a labelled corpus of surveys about Brazilian political bills extracted from the Chamber of Deputies website and evaluates some models by focusing on checking the cross-target capability with many-to-one approach. As a result, we verify that the BERT-based model overcomes the other tested models. We also make our corpus and models available for use[1] In the end, it discoursed the identified approaches' limitations and research opportunities.

The research reported in this paper has the following contributions: (i) A collected corpus from an online platform that enables all Brazilian citizens to interact and express their opinions concerning bills being discussed by the parliament; (ii) We discuss our annotation protocol and provide statistics about the stance detection corpus; (iii) We evaluate and compare Logistic Regression (LR), Naive Bayes (NB), Support Vector Machine (SVM), Feed-Forward Network (FNN) classical machine learning approaches and a pretrained multilingual BERT-based (mBERT) [4] deep learning model; and (iv) we make our considerations about the results.

This paper is organised into the following sections: Sect. 2 contains related works for stance detection applied to the Portuguese language and the cross-target approaches attached to stance detection. Section 3 relates the process of data collection and annotation and describes the resulting corpus. Section 4 describe the applied methods to generate the models. Section 5 contains the experiments and their results. Finally, Sect. 6 is a conclusion of this work with its contribution and future works.

---

[1] Dataset and code available at https://github.com/Dyonnatan/UlyssesSD-Br.

2   Related Works

Since the release of SemEval Task 6b [6], we had works exploring traditional methods to achieve the cross-target task, besides approaches that used neural networks with word embeddings and pre-trained models [7].

For architectures applied in Portuguese corpora, we have some baseline studies [8, 9, 12] that tested the Logistic Regression (LR), Naive Bayes (NB), Support Vector Machine (SVM), Feed-Forward Network (FNN), BiLSTM with FFN, BiLSTM with Attention Mechanism and FFN. Those are known techniques in the English domain, and newer methods have succeeded, whereas the Portuguese language has a drawback of low resources compared to English.

Nevertheless, earlier works in the English language indicate that contextual language representation achieves better results than static representation [11]. The BERT-like model [5] is the prior baseline with some variants; some works [2, 13] have an implemented model that consists of a BERT base model where topic and text are joint as input and fine-tuned for the task. The Allaway et al. (2021) [2] tested BERT-joint compared to BERT-sep. Both had a FFN with two layers to the classification output, and BERT-joint showed a better result.

In Reuver et al. [11] study, they proposed to verify whether stance detection is topic-independent and cross-topic generalisable. They conclude that the topic matters despite BERT showing better results than other tested models. The domain, linguistic characteristics and socio-cultural context are some of the main challenges.

We shall remark that our research differs from the existing works due to the aspects: We proposed an annotated corpus with several topics in the Portuguese language to achieve the stance detection cross-target with many-to-one approach in Brazilian Political Polls. We verify how our proposed model performs on elicited and Twitter corpora [12] adjusting for the cross-target with many-to-one task. We verify the capability of our trained model to evaluate on Santos and Paraboni's work [12] with that platform source variation.

3   UlyssesSD-Br Corpus

3.1   Data Collection

The Chamber of Deputies of Brazil website has a section about public opinion polls on political bills. There is a comment field in the poll where participants can write their opinions about the bill content with positive and negative points. Also, there is an option to download the comments on the page poll, whose data are collected anonymised.

Usually, famous political bills receive a nickname for referring to them, so these nicknames can be used to identify the main bill discussion. They are used to express or to represent an idea at the human comprehension level in replacement of the bills' formal names like "PL 10934/2004" to "Budget Guidelines Law", a translation of *"Lei de Diretrizes Orçamentárias"*. So, because this resource can be founded in the comment and brings words with semantic meaning, we picked

them as the target topic. We collected some known nicknames and linked each one to the comments that contain a citation to the nickname, generating a link between the comment and the related topic.

3.2 Annotation

We divided three teams with three volunteers each one for the annotation process. The volunteers were composed of undergraduates and graduates students randomly grouped. The possible classes were defined based on Mohammad (2017) [7]: Favor, to represent the comment towards the topic favourable. Against is a comment stance against the topic. None, when the topic is cited but there is no stance related to the topic. Furthermore, based on the Confortili et al. (2020) [3] was also added the not related class when the comment has no reference to the topic.

The annotation was divided into different documents per group, providing one document per day, varying in 50 to 100 comments per document. If at least one annotator gets confused or does not understand the comment, it is discarded.

In the first phase of conduction, we dedicated the first day to instructions and preparation testing with 50 comments, and a follow-up was carried out on the progress to the next two days. In the last phase, on the fourth day, we execute a new instruction to help with the emerged questions about the text interpretation. The annotation continues until the 13th day of work. Finally, we got the result data and kept the comments agreeing with at least two of the three annotators.

3.3 Data Analysis

We collected 215,712 comments in Portuguese language from 5,266 bills. Where 5093 bills have less than 100 comments, and 2,374 bills have just one comment. Only the four most popular have more than 10000 comments, whereas the most popular PL 3019/2020 have 26065 comments. There were 856 bills collected with their nicknames. They could have more than one nickname, like "*Lei de Diretrizes Orçamentárias*" is also "LDO".

After the annotation 1935 comments were accepted where it was discarded topics with fewer than 5 comments, resulting in 20 topics. Table 2 shows the stances and comments amount from this generated corpus.

4   Experimental Setup

We split the data by topics where the test has "subsistence allowance", "CLT", "LOAS", "Public Servants", and the training has all the other 16 topics that correspond to 22.4% and 77.6%, respectively. Table 3 shows the distribution of the label (Table 1).

Table 1. Examples of topics and comments collected.

Topic	Comment	Stance
CLT	*Falta de respeito com o trabalhador. Retrocessos na CLT.* [Lack of respect for the worker. Setbacks in the CLT.]	Favour
Estatuto do Desarmamento [Disarmament Statute]	*Nós já escolhemos sobre ter o direito e isso foi usurpado pelo "Estatuto do Desarmamento".* [We have already chosen about having the right and this has been usurped by the "Disarmament Statute"]	Against
Servidores Públicos [Public Servants]	*Retira a estabilidade dos futuros servidores públicos e não é justo.* [It takes away the stability of future public servants and it's not fair.]	Favour
Reforma Trabalhista [Labor Reform]	*Reduz direito dos trabalhadores e vai pior a crise brasileira. Chega de reforma trabalhista.* [It reduces workers' rights and will worsen the Brazilian crisis. Enough of labor reform.]	Against
Contratação [Hiring]	*Processo de contratação de servidores comissionados.* [Process of hiring commissioned servants.]	None

Table 2. Comments stance per topic

Topic	Favor	Against	None	NR	Total
Desarmamento [Disarmament]	83	273	24	2	382
Servidores Públicos [Public Servants]	185	46	35	0	266
Contratação [Hiring]	77	164	19	2	262
Código Penal [Penal Code]	194	19	38	0	251
Estatuto do Desarmamento [Disarmament Statute]	8	130	23	0	161
Reforma Administrativa [Administrative Reform]	9	101	4	1	115
Reforma Tributária [Tax Reform]	90	1	7	1	99
CLT	17	55	11	1	84
Reforma Trabalhista [Labor Reform]	1	78	3	0	82
Ajuda de custo [Subsistence allowance]	15	29	4	3	51
Reforma Previdenciária [Pension Reform]	6	29	0	0	35
LOAS	11	7	14	0	32
Partidos Políticos [Political Parties]	0	17	8	1	26
Seguro-Desemprego [Unemployment Insurance]	18	3	2	0	23
Porte de Armas [Possession of Arms]	14	0	2	0	16
Estatuto da OAB [OAB Statute]	5	4	5	0	14
Salário Mínimo [Minimum Wage]	11	0	3	0	14
LDB	7	1	1	0	9
Lei Maria da Penha [Maria da Penha Law]	0	5	1	0	6
Código de Defesa do Consumidor [Consumer Protection Code]	7	0	0	0	7
Overall	787	973	214	16	1935

The input test was followed by joint the topic with the comment (topic + comment). For both identification and classification subtasks, we apply the same methods. For NB, LR, SVM, RF and MLP, we tested some combinations from 1 to 5 n-grams, word and char representation, we found out the (1, 2) n-grams with char tokenisation and removing the diacritic by converting the text to Unicode format was the best configuration. The Majority score (Maj) is based on considering the majority class of each topic as the predicted label.

Table 3. Stance distribution by split corpus

	Favor	Against	None/NR	Total
Train	530	825	147	1502
Test	228	137	69	433

We generate the bag of words and TF-IDF features, compute chi-squared and select the features with a 0.95 p-value, resulting in 175 features. The models were trained with the default Scikit-learn framework [10] setup and received the joint input in a binary classification (stance, none) for the recognition task, where the not related class was also included for the none class. For the classification task, the same corpus was applied, but only comments with stance were included. Furthermore, the classes for this task were in favour and against.

For the BERT model, we used the PyTorch Transformers library version [14] getting pre-trained multilingual BERT base [4] and apply to pair sentence classification, in which the input is composed by joint the tokenised topic with the tokenised comment ($< CLS > topic < SEP > comment < SEP >$) and the output strategy remains the same from other models. We ran the train for 10 epochs and applied AdamW optimiser with a weight decay rate of 0.01 and a learning rate of 2e-5.

For the elicited and Twitter corpora, we also split the train and test set by topic to check the cross-target stance detection validation. We use the "Same sex marriage" and "Church tax exemptions" for testing and the other six topics for training for elicited corpus. We chose another two topics for the Twitter corpus because it does not have these topics, so we selected "Racial quotas and Drugs" legalisation and the other three topics for training. We also verify the mBERT model trained on UlyssesSD-Br to evaluate both corpora to check its performance on these topics from different corpora.

We use the metric weight-averaged F1 for the test validation to compare the models, aiming to minimise the impact of unbalanced data on the scores. To verify the score by polarity we use the macro F1.

5   Results and Discussion

5.1   Experiments in UlyssesSD-Br Corpus

Table 4 shows the weighted average F1 score evaluated in the identification sub-task by each model on political bills comments, the models represented were applied the BoW features because they perform better than TF-IDF for the sub-task. BERT model outperforms the other models. We can notice that all models, except BERT, have at least one topic with a score fewer than the majority class, which means they do not fully outpass the majority baseline (Maj), just the contextual word representation model did.

Table 4. Weighted-average F1 on the test identification set

Topic	Maj	NB	LR	MLP	SVM	RF	mBERT	Suport
S. allowance	0.799	0.779	0.806	0.777	0.762	0.742	**0.904**	51
CLT	0.791	0.817	0.656	0.522	0.560	0.573	**0.901**	84
LOAS	0.405	0.359	0.521	0.557	0.557	0.585	**0.875**	32
Public Servants	0.620	0.615	0.503	0.349	0.430	0.281	**0.973**	266

Table 5 shows the weighted average F1 score evaluated in the classifica-tion subtask by each model on political bills comments. Here we can see the BERT model with score superiority in all topics. The "subsistence allowance" and "CLT" topics have the same majority label (against); otherwise, the other two topics have the favour as the majority class. We can notice that the static models performed similar to the majority for two topics, but the topics with opposite class labels were poorly performed, indicating bias in some common set of tokens as identified polarity. Only the NB TF-IDF version outperforms "Public Servants" between the static token representation models.

Table 5. Weighted-averaged F1 on the test classification set

Topic	Maj	NB	NB*	LR	MLP	SVM	RF	mBERT	Suport
S.allowance	0.524	0.524	0.609	0.524	0.588	0.524	0.571	**0.887**	44
CLT	0.662	0.662	0.650	0.618	0.648	0.648	0.708	**1.000**	72
LOAS	0.464	0.218	0.218	0.218	0.492	0.425	0.615	**0.943**	18
Public Servants	0.712	0.092	0.760	0.092	0.413	0.134	0.364	**0.991**	231

* NB TF-IDF with word tokenization model

Table 6 shows the detailed macro-averaged F1 evaluated in the classification subtask by BERT model. We can verify that despite the unbalanced data, the model evaluates the polarity labels with a non-discrepant score, showing that

the model handled well with unbalanced topic polarity and amount, but overall it has more proportional polarity. The "CLT" topic was fully predicted correctly, and "Subsistence allowance" had the lowest, the only one with results below 0.9 in macro-weighted F1.

Table 6. Macro-averaged F1 on the test classification set for mBERT model

Topic	Against	Favor	All	Suport
Subsistence allowance	0.912	0.839	0.875	44
CLT	1.000	1.000	1.000	72
LOAS	0.923	0.956	0.940	18
Public Servants	0.978	0.994	0.986	231

5.2   Experiments in Elicited and Twitter Corpora

The elicited corpus has a little different context where people argue their opinion about some moral topics, but that relationship between moral topics and stance polarity may also be found in UlyssesSD-Br, once some dealt topics have moral points. Both elicited, and Twitter corpora have more texts by topic than UlyssesSD-Br and also implicit topics. However, it has significative fewer topics than UlyssesSD-Br; this is important to evaluate cross-target with many-to-one approach because we expect that, with more topics, the model has more capability to generalise and thus perform better in unknown topics.

Table 7 summarise the F1 evaluation on elicited corpus by mBERT model trained on Elicited train set for stance identification and also another model trained on the Twitter corpus.The Table 8 summarise mBERT model trained for stance polarity for both corpora.

Table 7. The mBERT weighted-average and macro (against, favor, all) F1 score on the elicited and Twitter corpus identification subtask.

Corpus	Topic	Weighted	Stance	None	All	Suport
Elicited	Same sex marriage	0.870	0.911	0.196	0.553	510
	Church tax exemptions	0.681	0.745	0.418	0.581	510
Twitter	Racial quotas	0.765	0.886	0.245	0.565	3,200
	Drugs legalisation	0.673	0.848	0.169	0.508	1,998

We notice the drop in results, two significant differences in these corpora from UlyssesSD-Br are the number of topics and the implicit topics are more present here too, which suggests that the amount of topic matter for this task, but we need to consider that we do not verify the linguistics phenomena issues for the model, that also impact on the results.

Table 8. The mBERT weighted-average and macro (against, favor, all) F1 score on the elicited and Twitter corpus classification subtask.

Corpus	Topic	Weighted	Against	Favor	All	Suport
Elicited	Same sex marriage	0.877	0.000	0.957	0.478	481
	Church tax exemptions	0.042	0.000	0.269	0.135	411
Twitter	Racial quotas	0.551	0.692	0.338	0.515	604
	Drugs legalisation	0.457	0.493	0.438	0.466	516

5.3 Experiments in Elicited and Twitter Corpora Using the UlyssesSD-Br Model Knowledge

The Table 9 and Table 10 shows the same trained mBERT applied to UlyssesSD-Br tested in the entire elicited and Twitter corpus, respectively. We can verify the model cannot perform so well compared to Table 4, but considering it has been evaluated on unknown corpora seems the model generalisation could perform the cross-target with many-to-one approach in this situation.

Table 9. mBERT weighted-average and macro F1 on the elicited corpus identification subtask

Topic	Weighted	Stance	None	All	Suport
Abortion legalisation	0.650	0.771	0.195	0.483	510
Same sex marriage	0.769	0.807	0.139	0.473	510
Gun ownership	0.690	0.856	0.125	0.491	510
Racial quotas	0.617	0.759	0.196	0.477	510
Church tax exemptions	0.709	0.831	0.202	0.517	510
Drugs legalisation	0.667	0.818	0.251	0.535	510
Criminal age	0.456	0.513	0.257	0.385	510
Death penalty	0.641	0.820	0.126	0.473	510

Table 10. mBERT weighted-average and macro (stance, none, all) F1 on the Twitter corpus identification subtask

Topic	Weighted	Stance	None	All	Suport
Abortion legalisation	0.682	0.835	0.051	0.443	3194
Racial quotas	0.592	0.687	0.186	0.436	3200
Drugs legalisation	0.393	0.425	0.303	0.364	1998
Death penalty	0.439	0.733	0.013	0.373	2563

6   Conclusion

From all tested algorithms, we find that the multilingual BERT-base model in a sentence pair classification, which tokenises the topic and text and joins them for the input model, achieves the best results in overcoming the baseline strategy in the identification and classification phases. We verify that only the contextual word representation model outperforms the majority baseline strategy for all topics. Our model is evaluated in a proposed annotated corpus based on Portuguese comments on Brazilian political polls from the Chamber of Deputies' Bills' opinion website section.

In future work, we plan to investigate other methods to achieve the cross-topic stance detection task and surpass the previous results, such as zero-shot and few-shot stance detection [1,2]. In addition, we will analyse in more detail the what are the semantic and linguistic phenomena barriers for the models.

Acknowledgements. We would like to thank the Ditec (Diretoria de Inovação e Tecnologia da Informação) from the Chamber of Deputies of Brazil for the support.

References

1. Allaway, E., McKeown, K.: Zero-shot stance detection: a dataset and model using generalized topic representations. In: Proceedings of the 2020 Conference on Empirical Methods in Natural Language Processing (EMNLP), pp. 8913–8931. Association for Computational Linguistics (2020). https://doi.org/10.18653/v1/2020.emnlp-main.717, https://aclanthology.org/2020.emnlp-main.717
2. Allaway, E., Srikanth, M., McKeown, K.: Adversarial learning for zero-shot stance detection on social media. In: Proceedings of the 2021 Conference of the North American Chapter of the Association for Computational Linguistics: Human Language Technologies, pp. 4756–4767. Association for Computational Linguistics (2021). https://doi.org/10.18653/v1/2021.naacl-main.379, https://aclanthology.org/2021.naacl-main.379
3. Conforti, C., Berndt, J., Pilehvar, M.T., Giannitsarou, C., Toxvaerd, F., Collier, N.: Will-they-won't-they: a very large dataset for stance detection on Twitter. In: Proceedings of the 58th Annual Meeting of the Association for Computational Linguistics, pp. 1715–1724. Association for Computational Linguistics (2020). https://doi.org/10.18653/v1/2020.acl-main.157, https://aclanthology.org/2020.acl-main.157
4. Devlin, J., Chang, M., Lee, K., Toutanova, K.: BERT: pre-training of deep bidirectional transformers for language understanding. CoRR abs/1810.04805 (2018). http://arxiv.org/abs/1810.04805
5. Devlin, J., Chang, M.W., Lee, K., Toutanova, K.: Bert: pre-training of deep bidirectional transformers for language understanding. arXiv:1810.04805 [cs] (2019). http://arxiv.org/abs/1810.04805, arXiv: 1810.04805
6. Mohammad, S., Kiritchenko, S., Sobhani, P., Zhu, X., Cherry, C.: SemEval-2016 Task 6: detecting stance in tweets. In: Proceedings of the 10th International Workshop on Semantic Evaluation (SemEval-2016), pp. 31–41. Association for Computational Linguistics, San Diego (2016). https://doi.org/10.18653/v1/S16-1003, http://aclweb.org/anthology/S16-1003

7. Mohammad, S.M., Sobhani, P., Kiritchenko, S.: Stance and sentiment in tweets. ACM Trans. Internet Technol. **17**(3), 26:1–26:23 (2017). https://doi.org/10.1145/3003433

8. Pavan, M.C., et al.: Morality classification in natural language text. IEEE Trans. Affect. Comput., 1 (2020). https://doi.org/10.1109/TAFFC.2020.3034050

9. Pavan, M., dos Santos, W., Paraboni, I.: Twitter moral stance classification using long short-term memory networks. In: Lecture Notes in Computer Science (including subseries Lecture Notes in Artificial Intelligence and Lecture Notes in Bioinformatics), vol. 12319 LNAI, pp. 636–647 (2020). https://doi.org/10.1007/978-3-030-61377-8-45

10. Pedregosa, F., et al.: Scikit-learn: machine learning in python. J. Mach. Learn. Res. **12**, 2825–2830 (2011)

11. Reuver, M., Verberne, S., Morante, R., Fokkens, A.: Is stance detection topic-independent and cross-topic generalizable? - a reproduction study. arXiv:2110.07693 [cs] (2021). arXiv: 2110.07693

12. Santos, W., Paraboni, I.: Moral stance recognition and polarity classification from Twitter and elicited text. In: Proceedings of the International Conference on Recent Advances in Natural Language Processing (RANLP 2019), pp. 1069–1075. INCOMA Ltd., Varna (2019). https://doi.org/10.26615/978-954-452-056-4-123

13. Vamvas, J., Sennrich, R.: X-stance: a multilingual multi-target dataset for stance detection. CoRR abs/2003.08385 (2020). https://arxiv.org/abs/2003.08385

14. Wolf, T., et al.: Transformers: state-of-the-art natural language processing. In: Proceedings of the 2020 Conference on Empirical Methods in Natural Language Processing: System Demonstrations, pp. 38–45. Association for Computational Linguistics (2020). https://www.aclweb.org/anthology/2020.emnlp-demos.6

Unraveling the Algorithms for Humanized Digital Work Oriented Artificial Intelligence

Monique de Souza Arruda[✉] [iD]

Porto Faculty of Law, Catholic University of Portugal, Rua Diogo Botelho, 1327,
4169-005 Porto, Portugal
marruda.advogada@gmail.com

Abstract. The present study analyzes the role of algorithms as an integral part of artificial intelligence (AI) and checks whether it is possible to interfere in the construction of the algorithmic system to generate benefits for platforms and gig workers or if the so-called complexity of the algorithms is an absolute impediment factor. to fulfill that ideal. The research methodology will be based on a qualitative approach, through bibliographic research in law, sociology, and programming. The research delves into the field of research on the relationship between algorithms and work aimed at creating algorithms oriented to providing decent worker-centered digital work and, for that reason, contributes to the emerging literature on algorithmic work.

Keywords: Algorithmic work · Gig work · Labor law

1 Introduction

In the era of digital revolution, the idea of having work and technology intricately linked is no longer terrifying: telework is no longer a discussion point with exclusively legal relevance, but, especially after the COVID-19 pandemic, it has become part of the everyday life of virtually all workers in times of mandatory isolation.

Digitalization, besides facilitating tasks and processes, has opened new paths for developing innovative solutions and inciting global markets to stimulate faster automatization and more efficient productive processes; resulting in decreased levels of waste, as well as, an increasingly better cost-benefit ratio, cost reduction, which in turn, enables access to goods and services in a more comprehensive way.

In this vein, this research aims to analyze the role of algorithms as an integral part of artificial intelligence (AI) and verify the possibility of interference in the construction of the algorithmic system, in order to generate benefits, not only to the platforms, but also to the workers who participate in it. This paper examines whether the algorithms' complexities function as an absolute impediment to achieving this ideal. The research methodology will be based on a qualitative approach, through bibliographical research in law, sociology, and programming.

G. Marreiros et al. (Eds.): EPIA 2022, LNAI 13566, pp. 96–107, 2022.
https://doi.org/10.1007/978-3-031-16474-3_9

2 Living the Age of Artificial Intelligence

Despite having just started, the "miracle" of the digital transformation, associated with the 4th Industrial Revolution, is breaking paradigms, generating impact that may have groundbreaking, ubiquitous applications. On the one hand, digitalization may contribute to the grater promotion of equalitarian values, what could lead to democratization and advances necessary for substantial social change. On the other hand, this process could be used as a tool for incentivizing mechanisms of greater segregation, marginalization, and precariousness.

To exemplify this issue, we can refer to the banking industry, which under the influence of digital transformation (more specifically, blockchain technologies such as: digital platforms, cybersecurity, and cloud computing) has fostered the growth of new companies in the fintech industry. Many customers have decided to move from the traditional sector to fintech industry on the grounds that similar or better services are offered in comparison to the financial markets monopolized by large companies. Nevertheless, these technologies, if misused, can be used to "hack" banking information, promote cyber-attacks, intercept transactions, and fraudulently use the information to purchase a product or service in e-commerce.

But what are the implications of the introduction of these innovative technologies on the marketplace and in everyone's lives? Even though, at first, they may seem highly beneficial and optimizing in the sectors where they are applied, in the era of interweaving technology in the fabric of society, it is critical to understand the consequences of this interaction. The question arises whether such interaction brings us closer to the evolution or regression, considering social welfare focused on the construction of a balanced society with minimum principles of equality aimed at the common good.

In the context of this new formatting of human lifestyle and production by the technological innovations of the 4th Industrial Revolution, it is essential to understand what IA consists of and the multidimensionality of its practical application. Gupta [8] explains that it consists of a science and engineering of making intelligent machines (endowed with human "intelligence" in a non-biological way), mainly intelligent computer programs. The application of this technology enables machines, equipped with their physical and computing components, to have the ability to interpret external data correctly, to learn from that data, and to use the learning (by computer processing of many paths of information and the results of applying the content - much faster and with much greater storage capacity than humans) to solve problems: achieving goals, performing specific tasks, or making decisions.

AI is applied to various fields of endeavor, such as natural language processing, robotics, machine vision, automatic proof of theorems, intelligent data retrieval systems, among others. Arshad[1] [3] adds that intelligent manufacturing is composed of

---

[1] For a better understanding, the author brings some examples of improvements made possible by the introduction of AI technologies on the factory floor, let us see:[…] improved quality control (e.g. turbofan blades can be 3D inspected by the manufacturer with micrometer accuracy), made predictive maintenance possible (e.g. failure can be stopped in equipment by detecting even subtle changes with the help of networked sensors), reduced energy and material costs, inventory optimization, product design (e.g. aircraft parts were created by airbus that are much lighter than those designed by humans), improved safety and environmental performance.

technologies that include industrial connectivity devices and services, big data processing capabilities, and robotic systems. He emphasizes that the application of AI in industries makes it possible to analyze, monitor, and make better decisions in the production process (based on logic and probabilities - the result of information processing by the machines).

Among the advantages of using AI we can highlight: the increase in the level of network operation management and the efficiency of information processing; the great capacity for reasoning and learning in network intelligence; the processing of information in the network management; the greater management of uncertainty information[3]; the ability to learn patterns from training data; the detection of faults in systems; reliability, greater cost-effectiveness and response speed. As well as the fact that it excels at human "limitations" since it has no stress, fatigue, need for rest or food.

From another perspective, the equipment and resources involved to create, repair, and rebuild the machines cost time and money; AI increases the competitive pressure in the market. Its decisions and solutions are not perfect, because they are not based on logical, clear, objective and detailed information inserted into the system, therefore it is not endowed with creativity, unable to explain the reasoning and logic it uses to reach a certain conclusion.

While it has the speed and logical capacity to interconnect and process information in a universe of options, through the probabilistic analysis that best results, according to the pre-selected objective for the decision, it can be the target of a malfunction arising from poor programming or information placed in the system that may cause a perception based on the literalness of the information, which leads it to produce wrong solutions to problems. As a result, it cannot be understood as a perfect solution, but relativized and studied case by case, because incorrect results can exist.

Moreover, AI can place its user in a content "bubble" that generates a distorted view of reality, which happens, e. g., when you have a taste for certain types of content on You Tube, Instagram, Tik Tok, Facebook, and the technology understands that you like certain subjects and dislike others, making you have a conditioned access to information, a very relevant fact when it comes to political opinions and elections. Borges & Filó [4] clarify that AI creates a personalized virtual environment for each user, shaped by algorithms that customize the space according to personal patterns, based on the choices that the network user makes, causing the technology, through pre-established information, to filter and anticipate options of choices.

Arshad [3] further warns that "if it falls into the wrong hands, hackers and terrorists gain the ability to manipulate and access it through security flaws in network protocols, potentially causing large-scale destruction if delivered into the hands of the wrong person." However, the most important disadvantage of applying AI, especially in the legal sphere, is related to the high potential of replacing human labor, causing unemployment.

From sociological point of view AI, contextualized with all the surroundings in which it is inserted, is not only a technological advance, as clarified by the advantages and disadvantages of its use, but also a production tool that, like financial capital in its time in history, unveils a series of "instruments of power" politically, economically, culturally and socially.

Such incidence is clarified by De Christo Hundertmarck & Weber [6] when they state that AI holds social political/violent power, besides being an extremely effective and influential market tool, for this reason they defend that its implementation should not be free, given maximum autonomy to programmers, but veiled by control mechanisms.

In this way, in order to know the implications of the use of AI in the great scope in which it incurs and to have a globalized perception of the social power of the technologies through which it is presented, namely algorithm, hardware and big data, there must be a strict control, both social and political-legal, of the actions and their results in society, because their free development, like absolute economic liberalism, can imply serious setbacks to society[2].

We highlight here some realities not always clarified to society, when implementing technologies endowed with AI to work tools, network search engines or social networks and its economic and social potential involved, besides the large amount of political, social and commercial information imposed on us, without consent and using technical ignorance, let us see:

Everything that is done on the Internet has a result of Artificial Intelligence: searches, the company that will appear to the consumer, the cost, the consumer profile, all these factors are evaluated by an AI, defined and presented to the consumer, dictating , therefore, which professional will you hire, in which bank will you open your account, which health plan will you have, what is the cost of your studies and the like. All these processes involve robots that take individuals to places (where there is advertising or not) and that return their tastes, goals and

---

[2] On this matter, the Proposal for regulation of the European Parliament and of the Council laying down harmonized rules on artificial intelligence (Artificial Intelligence Act) and amending certain union legislative acts, by the European Comission, of april 2021, is surgical. This is because it provides for a set of horizontal mandatory requirements that must be observed in the various systems equipped with AI, with the scope of limiting its use for purposes beneficial to society, based on ethical principles, enunciating mechanisms that endow automated decisions with transparency and of traceability to ensure security and protection of fundamental rights throughout the entire life cycle of AI systems. The "AI Act", in addition to being multidirectional and reaching several sensitive points of confluence of the use of these technologies in the different fields of application, guides them to the collective interest, addressing specific issues such as the necessary solutions for the effectiveness of regulation in the domain of employment, worker management and access to self-employment, lists high risk points for the misuse of algorithms in recruitment and selection processes, decision-making on promotions and dismissals, division of tasks and control or evaluation of people within the scope of contractual employment relationships, especially in terms of inspection and penalties arising from practices prohibited by law (e.g. in AI mechanisms that influence people or benefit from the vulnerabilities of specific groups of people due to age, disability, technical ignorance, causing physical or psychological damage to them) or the execution of high-risk AI systems that are not structured in accordance with the training, validation and testing data provided with the quality criteria established by law, which enable the governance and management of data externally. By conferring a high degree of risk to issues related to the algorithms applied to work, the proposal collaborates with the protection of the rights of workers of digital platforms, as it is concerned with the impacts that the misuse of AI generates on the career and in the livelihoods of these people.

influence their future decisions. At this point, the question is: to what extent does the Social Power of influence of AI prevail in the ethics and morals of the open market? [6].

3 Algorithms in the Constitution of AI

De Christo Hundertmarck & Weber [6] make an interesting allegory about the constitution of AI, dividing it into machinery, cognition, hardware and big data, which makes it possible to perceive it in a more playful way. In this case, the machinery (the whole system) would be what enables its practical realizations; the cognitive element – "the thought of the machine" would be the algorithms, which enable the "practical results of cognition in society, reality and practical vision, and determines the response time of information"; the hardware (physical part of the machine), the part that "underlies its realizations, determines the speed, deadline, estimates and quality of its processing"; and, the big data would be the data and information proper of artificial intelligence, since they consist of large volumes of data that need a tool capable of processing it, that is, of transforming the unstructured data captured from the environment by sensors and actuators, and parameterize them, to then apply them depending on their usefulness for decision making.

The algorithm is an integral part of the AI and, without it, this technology could not be built, because it is the element that creates the "routines" that make up the universe through which the machine processes a path, upon inputting an event and, after going through this tangle of logical sequences with extreme speed, analyzes all possible paths and gives a result, based on the internal analysis of the parameters that were programmed in the machine.

It is important to point out that "intelligent" machines are literal, they don't think, they just process the information they have and give a result by means of the parameters they contain, if we create an algorithm called "throw garbage from the kitchen", composed of the following sequence of actions: 1- open the garbage lid, 2- if garbage full, take out the garbage; 3- if it's not full, terminate action; 4- if it took out the garbage, open the door and take it out; 5- take the garbage out and throw it in the container. If the programmer makes a mistake and forgets, for example, to add the line to open the door, the "intelligent robot" goes to the door, knocks on it and comes back, because the programming line did not make it possible for it to execute all the steps, due to a flaw in its content. Thus, it is the algorithms that denote which paths the machine will be able to use as a solution, and which are the fundamentals for the choice of parameters. In short, behind the machines there is always a programmer, who has described the routines and parameters.

In words connected to programming, algorithms are finite and organized sets of steps, described by means of a computational flow, which, when executed, solve a certain problem, or in Manzano & Oliveira [11] concept:

Algorithm is a process of mathematical calculation or the systematic description of solving a group of similar problems. It can also be said that they are formal rules for obtaining a result or solving a problem, encompassing formulas of arithmetic expressions. In the area of software development, it is very common to relate the word algorithm to the block diagram (in this case, it would be a graphical algorithm), since many formulas are within the process symbology for solving a given problem, whether in the area accounting, whether in the financial area or on a payroll, as well as in any situation that requires a correct and/or coherent final result[3].

Thus, despite common sense designate algorithms as a "secret" formula that contains unintelligible and complex parameters, on the contrary, they consist of a rational, detailed, and coherent line, whose logical reasoning is developed by the programmer. Perhaps this is the reason why it is a "discipline" that, to the layman's eyes, can be considered extremely difficult, as it contains theorems that cannot be understood by an ordinary person, without the necessary technical knowledge, one more reason for the operators of law to keep in mind that the study and deepening in IT and programming areas will be essential to understand the world that unfolds ahead.

It turns out that, in their practical application, algorithms do not exist as a simple and unique cake recipe. For example, to build software for a video game, several algorithms are written that together derive into a system that operates according to its purpose. But one must always keep in mind that the machine "works" with the elements it has inserted into its database and does not think by itself, but only performs calculations based on its internal programming.

On the other hand, intelligent machines, through their internal calculations, the feedback of their parameters, by means of comparisons, the input of new data into the system, can create results beyond what was previously programmed, but always guided in terms of the pre-configured objectives for decision making. Despite this, it can be said that machines endowed with AI "solve problems autonomously" if machine learning is considered.

In this learning modality, AI machines create as if they were "new neural paths", and, considering the large universe of information contained in their programming system, for man it would be much more complex to unravel the paths chosen by the machine to solve a problem, which could lead one to believe that machines have a certain autonomous intelligence, but this autonomy is relative, as seen earlier, because the machine "thinks" according to programmed parameters.

---

[3] Free translation by the author.

Having made these considerations, some characteristics of the algorithms raised by De Christo Hundertmarck & Weber [6] can be verified. The first is that the algorithm can be perceived as a "biologymathematics[4]," the principal component of AI. This is programmed by humans and is endowed with capabilities such as: learning through a machine network; recognizing human voice and attitude patterns, and thus being able to reproduce them; performing predictive analytics (analyzing data to make predictions of future events), qualitative and quantitative, and spatial; storage; natural language processing; and coercion capabilities.

For the study of law, AI and its algorithms have major impacts on society, and, for this reason, cannot escape a careful legal understanding, to follow its evolution and lead it to produce beneficial effects to society. In this regard, Christin [5] highlights that there are connections between algorithms and the broader structures of social life, and understanding this system is essential to curb social processes such as discrimination, surveillance, and standardization, which may be implicit in the command lines of the algorithmic system.

Moreover, questions such as the replacement of human labor by intelligent machines, generating unemployment, as expressed by Zhang [21] must turn to "when this phenomenon will occur" and no longer around its possibility. In that vein, policy measures to retrain workers with the new skills that the digital marketplace demands should be prioritized, as well as providing to minimize the barriers that prevent researchers from predicting the impacts of this interaction [7], to mitigate the effects of this revolution.

However, one should also envision the positive market effects around IA, such as: the protection of workers' health in activities that require physical exertion, dangerous and extremely monotonous tasks in manufacturing, service, national defense, space exploration; the possibility of freeing workers from less complex activities to those that incite creativity, cognitive complexity, essentially emotional or artistically creative, as is the case of supervisory and management roles; the creation of new jobs linked to AI applications; the provision of various new flexible forms of employment, such as self-employment, independent contracting [21].

Another major issue surrounding automation by algorithms, without proper human "attention", is comprised in the issue of discrimination [16], to the extent that the algorithm is written by a programmer, who may insert into its programming lines data based

---

[4] Because AI targets the realization of human activities by machines. Therefore, it is analyzed in parallel with biological and cognitive activities. As clarify De Christo Hundertmarck & Weber [7], the machine equipped with AI is capable of learning, and this machine learning is derived from two strands, machine learning, "which are Artificial Intelligence systems, subjective, able to learn from their own experience, endowed with 'behavioral self-sufficiency'"; and machine deep learning, which uses "cytoartificial" neural networks (simplified simulations of how biological neurons behave) and extracts patterns and rules of human behavior via datasets, transcribing organic biological functions to machines in hardware format.

on their stereotypes of inequality and discrimination[5], which generates implicit biases[6] in "corporate walls and layers of code" [5], thus the algorithm will replicate human bias and learn to discriminate [14]. To alleviate incidences in this direction, it is essential that mechanisms for human intervention in the creation, maintenance, refinement, and evaluation of algorithmic processes, including at the audit level, be created.

The introduction of algorithms in the area of resources to provide models to support business decision and control, create projections and detect human patterns, oriented to optimize processes and reduce production costs in recruitment and selection processes [4], in performance evaluation and career progression analyses of workers [14], in monitoring productivity and work performance have evidenced the occurrence of gender, racial and other social prejudices, reinforcing inequalities and stereotypes, moving

---

[5] The Judgment of the Supreme Court of Spain ruled in a pioneering way in relation to the issue of algorithmic discrimination, in Judgment n. 805/2020, of September 25, 2020, in Appeal no. 4746/2019, of the Sala de lo Social Pleno for the unification of doctrine, in a lawsuit against the Glovo platform, in which it was declared that the relationship between the riders and the former is of a work-related nature. The decision highlights the functioning of the platform's algorithmic service management as a "subtle" way of exercising corporate power in relation to the way in which the service is provided by controlling its execution in real time (constant geolocation). This is how the domain of prices, of workers' evaluations, of the distribution of tasks is exercised. In the judgment of the "Tribunale Civile di Milano" (Sezione specializzata in materia di impresa Ricorso ex art. 840 sexiesdecies c.p.c.) against Deliveroo Italy srl, it is mentioned that the algorithm manages the complex planning system, the acquisition of the order by the user, identification of passengers receiving the delivery proposal, the distribution and organization of workflows, in addition to monitoring the different stages of delivery, receipts and payments. During this management, the judgment showed that the algorithm proceeded in a discriminatory way, as it started distributing a smaller amount of tasks as a form of sanction to pilots who "did not respect the work model imposed on them or engaged in non-conforming conduct through two appropriate parameters of 'reliability' and 'participation'" (n. 79). Thus, they were lowered in their scores by the algorithms and, as a result, began to receive fewer demands for work.

[6] The Deliveroo n.r.g. 2949/2019, judged by the Labor Section of the Ordinary Court of Bologna (Italy), of December 31, 2020, clearly expresses the issue of implicit prejudices that, if not visualized and against defendants, can harm equality at work. In this specific case, it was found that the conditions of access to reservations (bookings) of work sessions by pilots on the Deliveroo platform consist of indirect discrimination between these workers, creating disadvantages among them. First, because the algorithm penalizes the "pilot performance rating" in a generalized way (without observing the particular motivations) the non-compliance with work at the pre-scheduled time by the worker, using this statistic as a way of giving more opportunities to the pilots with the highest scores. to prioritize your work sessions. Second, because this first premise expresses another discriminatory attitude, since, as there is a priority for scheduling work for those with higher scores, work "slots" are increasingly scarce for other workers, harming, for example, those who had justifications. Legitimate reasons for not performing the service, as the judge explains: *"In sostanza, when you fly the piattaforma può togliersi la benda che la surrender "cieca" or "incosciente" rispetto ai motivi della mancata prestazione lavorativa on the part of the rider and, if not lo fa, è perché there is deliberately scelto di porre sullo stesso piano tutte le motivazioni – a prescindere dal fatto che siano o less tutelate dall'ordinamento – diverse dall'infortunio sul lavoro e dalla causa imputabile ad esse datrice di lavoro (which is evidently il app malfunction, che impedisce il log-in)".*

away the application of the ideals of justice and equity in smart work environments. Constituting such uses of the algorithm as new challenges to legal research.

4 Platforms and Algorithms: Working Against Workers

Regarding the use of algorithms, there is a debate between the question of the possibility or not of tracking the decisions taken in the scope of their data processing, since these can directly imply the rights of workers when AI is applied to the work environment.

The difficulty in this tracking lies in the fact that the algorithms are endowed, as stated [5] opacity and limitations in the concept of transparency of algorithmic systems. The opacity, first, may be a consequence of the algorithm's intentional secrecy due to the secrecy of companies, which classify it as intellectual property. Secondly, as already mentioned, it can be noticed by the fact that the algorithms are written in programming languages, which makes them incomprehensible to those who do not have knowledge in the area, the so-called "opacity due to technical illiteracy" factor. The third layer of opacity is founded on machine learning, as this capability makes it difficult to understand what factors the algorithm considered when making a decision. The fourth factor is linked to the size of the algorithms, as you can have algorithms chained together with billions of lines of code. For these reasons, algorithms are often referred to as "black boxes" devices that can only be understood in terms of their inputs and outputs, without any knowledge of how they work.

However, algorithms should not be considered static technological tools [5], because they were created to function as mediators in the technology/social networks interaction, or rather, they were created to merge and understand social behaviors, therefore, they never exist in the social vacuum, and their incidence is linked to social networks and institutional structures. Furthermore, in this process, they can be reconfigured (due to machine learning) and present results depending on how social actors position themselves in relation to them.

In the context of the gig economy or on-demand economy, the algorithmic management process has been used to control the provision of services in real time and in the definition of prices of goods and services, to increase efficiency and productivity in favor of interests. Companies in a unilateral way, which implies negative and precarious effects for the productive and psychological well-being. Workers are subject to heavy data collection, opaque automated processes, and asymmetrical power dynamics [21] due to the algorithmizing of platforms, despite companies hiding in arguments of algorithmic neutrality and objectivity and intellectual property secrecy, to selfishly benefit from the production factor.

Such precariousness even involves the insertion of gamification algorithms [1] at work, using avatars and a virtual competition system, based on the production of dopamine in the body of employees, to push workers beyond their limits on the production line, increasing productivity. In other words, it disguises a physical and mental effort by workers that can affect their physical and mental health.

Admittedly, in cases like Google's internet services that have more than two billion lines of code [5], given the size of the algorithm, it becomes difficult to identify which part of the system is responsible for a specific decision. However, this dimension applied

to work platforms is ridiculously small, which makes it possible to verify the parameters inserted in the algorithms in the protection of integrity and the implementation of a minimally dignified work environment for those who provide services in this new modality.

Or not? Will it be impossible to change unjust and degrading parameters of this relationship - to a certain extent atypical of work - in favor of the dignity of its workers? If, in the context of business interests, these algorithmic "routines" are changed according to the needs of the platform to make it increasingly better, more attractive, more efficient, more competitive through its internal algorithmic pricing scheme [17], with an eye on profit, why couldn't the algorithmic parameters be adapted to a reality of non-discrimination and non-productive exploitation? Or is the intention really to take advantage of the technological ignorance of others for business benefit, regardless of human exploitation linked to the activity? How they searched [2, 5, 9, 10, 12, 15, 17–21] it is possible to explore the relationships between algorithms, the performance of workers at work on digital platforms, in order to reorient the creation and promote the reconstruction of algorithms aimed at policies focused on granting decent work.

Even, A. Zhang et al. [20] propose changes in algorithm parameters judged deficient by the platform workers (through participatory design sessions), who, in view of the analysis of the deficiencies they perceive in the experience of working on the platform, design solutions that include translucency to the asymmetries of information and power existing, with the aim of promoting the fairness of the platform and the well-being of the workers, consequently, enabling a digital work centered on the worker.

Furthermore, it is essential that digital platforms are subject to external algorithmic audits [5, 13, 14], so that, when examining the algorithmic systems, it is possible to generate evidentiary content of labor proceedings for future protective measures in this bias, against discrimination and other abuses.

An interesting incentive to platforms, around the creation of a positive environment, according to the "win-win" model applied to business activity, where development is evidenced for both platforms and workers, in a directly proportional way, is placed by Moreira [14], when she suggests that employers undergo external audits to receive a kind of certification mark which would distinguish them favorably in the labor market.

5   Conclusion

The present study aimed to highlight important aspects about what algorithms really are to demystify them, such as absolute black boxes, which do not allow any degree of human intervention in their creation, reformulation and feedback process.

On the contrary, it became evident that, despite the relative technical difficulty, given the size of the algorithm or the absence of scientific programming knowledge, in penetrating and evaluating the parameters used for decision making, these are based on information and data entered by human hand, in computational language, considering that machines do what they were previously programmed for and, at least in the current phase, do not have the courage to "create" solutions at their own discretion, despite learning the machine exists, these possibilities are conditioned to what forms its database, which its programmers are aware of.

Finally, it should be noted that the field of research on the relationship between algorithms and work aimed at creating algorithms that go beyond a restricted view related to corporate secrecy and technological knowledge is under recent construction, in studies of a sociological nature and legal application, while, in a way, the barrier of limiting the study of algorithms to technological unemployment was broken. However, due to the speed with which it has been applied to the gig economy context, in the most varied ways, it has stimulated deeper research, which highlights the need for legal operators to immerse themselves in the search for technical improvement, so as not to be held hostage by "complexity" technology and the tools that will be placed, especially in the context of work.

Acknowledgments. This research was financially supported by Foundation for Science and Technology (FCT), within the scope of the doctoral research grant program.

References

1. Aloisi, A., de Stefano, V.: Il tuo capo è um algoritmo: contro il lavoro disumano. GLF Laterza (2020)
2. Ammannati, L., Canepa, A., Greco, G.L., Minneci, U.: Algoritmi, big data, piattaforme digitali: la regolazione dei mercati in trasformazione. Giappichelli (2021)
3. Arshad, Z.M.: An insight into artificial intelligence. Keep your dreams alive. Understand to achieve anything requires faith and belief in yourself, vision, hard work, determination, and dedication. Remember all things are possible for those who believe, p. 309
4. Borges, G.S., da Filó, M.C.S.: Artificial intelligence, gender, and human rights: the case of Amazon. Justiça Do Direito **35**(3), 218–245 (2021)
5. Christin, A.: The ethnographer and the algorithm: beyond the black box. Theory Soc. **49**(5–6), 897–918 (2020). https://doi.org/10.1007/s11186-020-09411-3
6. De Christo Hundertmarck, C.L., Weber, J.M.: Artificial intelligence and social environment: social power of algorithms facing society. Braz. J. Dev. 81529–81541 (2021)
7. Frank, M.R., et al.: Toward understanding the impact of artificial intelligence on labor. Proc. Nat. Acad. Sci. U.S.A **116**(14) 6531–6539 (2019). https://doi.org/10.1073/pnas.1900949116
8. Gupta, S.: Artificial intelligence in real life. In: Outcomes of Best Practices in Classroom Research, pp. 305–308. L Ordine Nuovo Publication (2021)
9. Chen, M.K.: Dynamic pricing in a labor market: surge pricing and flexible work on the uber platform (2016). https://doi.org/10.1145/2940716.2940798
10. Kusk, K., Bossen, C.: Working with Wolt: an ethnographic study of lenient algorithmic management on a food delivery platform. **6**(GROUP), 22 (2022). https://doi.org/10.1145/3492823
11. Manzano, J.A.N.G., de Oliveira, J.F.: Algoritmos: lógica para desenvolvimento de programação de computadores, vol. 29th edn. Editora Érica (2019)
12. Meisner, C., Duffy, B.E., Ziewitz, M.: The labor of search engine evaluation: making algorithms more human or humans more algorithmic? New Media Soc. (2022). https://doi.org/10.1177/14614448211063860
13. le Merrer, E., Pons, R., Trédan, G.: Algorithmic audits of algorithms, and the law. 1–15 (2022). https://doi.org/10.48550/arXiv.2203.03711
14. Moreira, T.C.: A discriminação algorítmica. Questões Laborais A **28**(58), 85–103 (2021)
15. Rosenblat, A., Stark, L.: Uber's drivers: information asymmetries and control in dynamic work. SSRN Electron. J. (2015). https://doi.org/10.2139/ssrn.2686227

16. da Rouxinol, M.S.: O agente algorítmico: licença para discriminar?: licença para discriminar?: (um [segundo] olhar sobre a seleção de candidatos a trabalhadores através de técnicas de inteligência artificial). Revista Do CEJ, 235–268 (2021)
17. Sanchez-Cartas, J.M., Katsamakas, E.: Artificial intelligence, algorithmic competition and market structures. IEEE Access 10, 10575–10584 (2022). https://doi.org/10.1109/ACCESS. 2022.3144390
18. Sun, P.: Your order, their labor: an exploration of algorithms and laboring on food delivery platforms in China. Chin. J. Commun. 12(3), 308–323 (2019). https://doi.org/10.1080/175 44750.2019.1583676
19. Waldkirch, M., Bucher, E., Kalum Schou, P., Grünwald, E.: Controlled by the algorithm, coached by the crowd-how HRM activities take shape on digital work platforms in the gig economy. Int. J. Hum. Resour. Manag. 32, 2643–2682 (2021). https://doi.org/10.1080/095 85192.2021.1914129
20. Zhang, A., Boltz, A., Wang, C., Lee, M.K.: Algorithmic management reimagined for workers and by workers: centering worker well-being in gig work. In: CHI Conference on Human Factors in Computing Systems (2022)
21. Zhang, Y.: The impact of artificial intelligence on China's labor legislation. Int. J. Front. Sociol. 22(4), 542–554 (2011). https://doi.org/10.1016/j.chieco.2011.07.002

The Compatibility of AI in Criminal System with the ECHR and ECtHR Jurisprudence

Nídia Andrade Moreira[✉]

Católica Research Centre for the Future of the Law, Porto, Portugal
nidiandrademoreira@gmail.com

Abstract. The admissibility of AI systems that focus on determining the measure of punishment must be analyzed in light of ECHR and ECtHR jurisprudence. We cannot live the AI evolution in a passive way and is a matter of time before it is adopted in the criminal justice system. The following paper focuses on the respect for fundamental rights as a filter of such instruments. We highlight the right to a fair trial (article 6), the principle of legality (article 7) and the prohibition of discrimination (article 14). Predictability can justify the adoption of predictive tools, ensuring fairer decision. On the other hand, explainability is an essential requirement that has been developed by explainable artificial intelligence. There are several AI models that must be adopted depending on domain and intended purpose. Only a multidisciplinary approach can ensure the compatibility of such instruments with ECHR. Thus, a confrontation between legal and engineering concepts is essential so that we can design tools that are more efficient, fairer and trustable.

Keywords: Artificial intelligence · Criminal system · European Convention on Human Rights

1 The Use of AI Systems as an Aid in Determining Sentence Length

We can divide two main branches of AI (i) symbolic AI and (ii) sub-symbolic AI. The first expresses knowledge by representing it according to rules. In these, the inference mechanisms are solidified and there are several representation languages (as logic or imperative languages). Nevertheless, sometimes there are areas in which we do not have the full extent of knowledge, being necessary to learn based on cases.

Symbolic AI is based on classic logic. In sub-symbolic AI we are faced with the ability to learn based on data. The legal universe is more associated with the symbolic world. Thus, we can think of the adoption of Expert Systems that are based on rules previously defined by experts. However, there are cases in which it is necessary to attend to data. In these scenarios, there is an extraction of knowledge through generalization and there is always an error associated with the model itself. The latter models can help detect inconsistencies between cases, for example.

We cannot choose which branch of AI we will use in the justice domain. In fact, we believe that both will be used, depending on the specific function assigned to such a tool.

G. Marreiros et al. (Eds.): EPIA 2022, LNAI 13566, pp. 108–118, 2022.
https://doi.org/10.1007/978-3-031-16474-3_10

Nevertheless, for aid in determining the measure of the punishment we believe that the analysis of previous decision will be a fundamental step.

As set out above, AI can be applied in the justice systems in various ways. At the investigation level, it can assist in analyzing evidence. It can also help by benchmark legislation. So, there are several possible applications. To understand them, it is necessary to analyze the function for which it can help the judge and how it will change the judge's work.

To fully understand the limitations of AI and the domains in which it can act we appeal to the distinction of (Searle 2002). We can distinguish AI and human performance by resorting to the concepts of syntax and semantics. Computer have syntax, i.e., a formal structure of operation. However, they do not possess semantic, i.e., they do not understand the meaning of these operations. There are no algorithms capable of replacing the judge, actin in a human way. So we do not admit the existence of an AI Judge. However, we consider that there are court function that can be performed by AI, namely analytical functions (such as the distribution of cases, for examples); meanwhile others imply a human dimension that will be very difficult to be compatible with AI (for example, the analysis of guilt).

1.1 Supporting Decision in the Criminal Sentencing

Technology is changing the way of thinking about the criminal law, but also the criminal process. In fact, technology has already changed some aspects of the justice system.

At a first level, technology can be a support tool for the judicial systems. This technology already exists in European systems, namely for enable management of court proceeding allowing, for example, the monitoring of cases online, the delivery of documents or case distribution.

At a last level, we have disjunctive technologies that change the judicial process and the judge's role. In this domain we can think of Artificial Legal Intelligence (ALI), i.e., AI systems capable of providing expert legal assistance or taking decisions (Sourdin 2018, p. 1122). Although predictive tools are not yet used in criminal systems of European countries, it seems that it is a matter of time to their adoption. Currently, the University of Cambridge is testing the Harm Assessment Risk Tool to be used in this domain.[1] Moreover, (Aletras et al. 2016) designed an AI model that can predict ECtHR decision with 79 per cent accuracy.

In fact, some studies reveal that AI systems will become more relevant (Sourdin 2018), although it is not clear the concrete domain where they will be used. We exclude the admissibility of such tools as substitutes for the judge, admitting them as auxiliaries to the jurisdiction task, particularly in the area of determining the length of the sentence in order to combat inconsistency between penalties. Thus, we restrict the scope of our study to the use of AI as a tool at the service of human being, as an aid to the judge. This is a consensual point in the doctrine and guidelines of Council of Europe (CoE).

The use of AI systems as tools to assist the judges in measuring sentencing has been seen as a potential way to ensure efficiency and equality in decisions. The use of such

---

[1] University of Cambridge Homepage, https://www.cam.ac.uk/research/features/helping-police-make-custody-decisions-using-artificial-intelligence.

tools constitutes a new form of knowledge available to the judge and will change the judicial systems (see. Re, Solow-Niederman 2019).

Most decision forecasting systems involve statistical techniques (Hall et al. 2005, p. 16). It would be interesting to develop systems that also allow translating legal reasoning. This will involve continuous and careful work between legal experts and engineers.[2]

2   The Use of AI in Light of ECHR

Recognizing the emergence of technological mechanisms in the justice system, the CoE and the European Union have developed studies in order to understand this topic.

In its study "Algorithms and Human Rights", the CoE expressed concerns in the field of criminal justice – namely, regarding the fair trial and the due process -, which were answered by the "European Ethical Charter on the use of Intelligence in Judicial Systems and their Environment" (2018).

The European Ethical Charter recognizes the need to encourage the use of instruments that promote the efficiency and quality of justice. Furthermore, the need for such instruments to respect fundamental rights, namely the ECHR, is reinforced.[3] However, the compatibility with human rights will depend on the domain in which it is used and the purpose of it. The choice of system used will be influenced by its functionality, complexity and accuracy (Recommendation CM/Rec(2020)1 of the Committee of Ministers to member States on the human rights impacts of algorithmic systems).

Note that the use of algorithms in the judicial system is recognized as a high risk to human rights (paragraph 11 Recommendation CM/Rec(2020)1 of the Committee of Ministers to member States on the human rights impacts of algorithmic systems). Thus, the adoption of such instruments should be preceded by a careful study of their risks and benefits. With this in mind the CoE intends the formulation of common framework of standards for the use of AI by courts (cf. Recommendation 2102 (2017). Technological convergence, artificial intelligence and human rights, paragraph 9.2.) and CEPEJ Working Group proposed the creation of a publicity accessible Resource Centre where all AI applications in the field of justice would be registered (cf. CEPEJ (2021)16- Revised roadmap for ensuring an appropriate follow-up of the CEPEJ Ethical Charter on the use of artificial intelligence in judicial systems and their environment).

Following the European studies, we propose to analyze the compatibility of the adoption of AI instruments to help do determine the punishment of the penalty with the ECHR and the ECtHR jurisprudence.

---

[2] See, *v.g.*, the project of (Hall et al. 2005) about a model of supporting discretionary sentencing decision-making that used Knowledge Discovery from Databases (KDD) to model the discretionary task of the judge.

[3] It should be noted that the present reflection aims at a general analysis. For a particular analysis, we must take into account the specificities of each country and its legislation. As an example, in the Portuguese case, we would have to consider the Portuguese judicial organization and its specific legislation, namely the Portuguese Charter on Human Rights in the Digital Era.

2.1 Right to a Fair Trial

Fairness is the fundamental principle of article 6. This principle requires particular attention in the context of criminal law, which contemplates stricter requirements (Moreira Ferreira v. Portugal (no. 2) [GC], §67; Carmel Saliba v. Malta, §67).

The principle is applicable since the pre-trial stage of the proceedings (inquiry, investigations), because the criminal process is seen as a whole (Dvorski v. Croatia, §76) and the fairness can be harmed since the beginning of the proceedings (Imbrioscia v. Switzerland, §36). It covers the whole proceeding, including the determination of the sentence (Aleksandr Dementyev v. Russia, §23).

The article establishes the right to be heard by an independent and impartial tribunal. Thus, impartiality and independence are the key words. Although predictive tools are not considered "judges" under article 6, it is important to analyze to what extent they may compromise the judicial system.

Independence is evaluated according to different criteria, namely, how judges are appointed, the duration of their term in office, the guarantees against external pressures and the appearance of independence (Fidlay v. United Kingdom, §73). Special emphasis should be given to the requirement that the judge must not be influenced by external pressures (Guðmundur Andri Ástráðsson v. Iceland [GC], § 234), regardless those influences are within the judicial system or outside of it. Specifically, the judge may not receive directives from other judges (Parlov-Tkalčić v. Croatia, § 8). But what if those directives come from AI systems?

Impartiality claims the absence of prejudice or subjectiveness (Kyprianou v. Cyprus [GC], § 118; Micallef v. Malta [GC], § 93). The judge must not attend to his or her personal interests or convictions. Subjectiveness is difficult to prove[4], but it has been pointed out as one of the reasons for the adoption of AI instruments. The use of AI has the potential to be seen as more neutral and reliable than human decisions, as long as they are not opaque (Simmons 2018, p. 1090). But caution is advised, because AI tools can also contain biases.

Given the link between independence and impartiality, we will analyze the two requirements together, similarly to ECtHR (Findlay v. the United Kingdom, §73).

AI can influence the decision of the judge to a point that he or she is strongly inclined to follow its suggestion (Quattrocolo 2020, p. 211). However, if such instruments are based only on previous decisions, in practice the judge is following the decisions of other judges, thus becoming subject to their peers' influence and biases.

If such tool is to be used, we believe that it should not be based solely on previous cases. The factors that contribute to the decision and the relationship between such factors should be identified, because they help to better understand how the sentence measure is determined, guide the criteria that judges should attend to and ensure sentence consistency across similar cases. Such tools should even detect flaws in previous decisions and correct them. Thus, the judge would not be influenced by peers, but rather rationalize his or her decision, making it more just.

---

[4] In fact, the ECtHR considers that the training and experience of the judges means that they are not influenced by external pressures (Craxi v. Italy (no.1), §104). For this reason, in most cases the objective aspect is evaluated. Thus, it is evaluated whether the judge has offered guarantees that exclude legitimate doubt as to his or her impartiality (Kyprianou v. Cyprus [GC], § 119).

The court must not only be independent, bust must also appear to be independent. Appearance of independence is important, in that it enables trust in the courts (Şahiner v. Turkey, § 44). For this reason, it must be guaranteed that the final decision maker is the judge, as an authority that can follow, ignore or change the recommendation made by a predictive algorithm (Simmons 2018, p. 1096). However, the judge must justify his or her choice.

The judge must know the system and its limitations. Several studies have pointed out explainability as the most critical. The level of explainability will depend on the application domain[5] and can be required from the moment of creation (by designing systems that are easy to understand, such as decision trees) or with the use of post-hoc techniques (Hamon et al. 2021, p.4). However, it should be noted that explainability is limited by the current state of the art and it should not be demanded of it what is not demanded to human deciders.

Thus, explainability must be taken into account when choosing the AI model used in the judicial systems, because different models have different approaches to this requirement. We can choose models that are considered inherently to be transparent (*v.g.*, linear regression or Bayesian models) or opaque models (*v.g.*, random forests or multi-laser Neutral Networks). Moreover, there are already authors who defend mixing the two models (hybrid models) in order to build explainable and accurate models.[6]

Transparency is different from explainability. A model is transparent if it is understandable by itself (Arrieta et al. 2020, p. 85). Transparency can be analyzed in three dimensions: simulability ("model's ability to be simulated by human"), decomposability ("ability to break down a model into parts and then explain these parts") and algorithmic transparency ("ability to understand the procedure") – cfr. (Belle et al. 2021, p. 3).

The first models are considered to be transparent and can have one or all of the levels of model transparency described. Although considered to be transparent, can become complex and require explainable artificial intelligence (XAI)[7] approaches to explain model decisions (Belle et al. 2021, p. 8).

Opaque models may achieve more accurate results, but their explainability requires the use of XAI, designing explainable models (Heaven 2020)[8], resorting to post-hoc

---

[5] For example, the use of AI by Spotify does not need an explanation. But if AI is used in areas that can influence human rights we should demand explainability.

[6] For example, (Wan et al. 2021) studied Neural-Backed decision tress (NBDTs) that combines neural networks and decision trees.

[7] There is no consensual definition of XAI. It aims to enable explainability of AI systems, ensuring greater confidence in their use. To understand the concept and the different purposes' of XAI see. (Arrieta et al. 2020).

[8] See the "Explainable AI- Rationale Generation" project which aims to develop machine learning models that automatically generate the machine's inherent reasoning in natural language. In this project, computer scientists have made efforts to justify automated systems, namely, through explanations made in the way that would be done by a human – see. https://gvu.gatech.edu/res earch/projects/explainable-ai-rationale-generation.

techniques (Belle et al. 2021).[9] By explainability we mean the ability for humans to understand the decision of AI systems.

Thus, it's crucial to choose the right model to develop a decision-support tool. This choice constitutes a relevant moment that will stipulate the level of explainability.

Furthermore, explainability is as important as the way is communicated to the target audience. So, explainability would only be satisfactory if its target audience understands it, which will increase confidence in the use of AI instruments.

The use of AI is not exclusive to its creators or to a fringe of society. AI has expanded to various domains and it is important that its users understand it. It would be interesting to develop studies that specifically target the legal application of such tools, in order to understand the explanations required and how should be legally regulated. AI should not be seen as a bubble, but as a tool to be integrated into various domains that deserves specific thought from each area in which it is used.

Although solutions can be found from XAI, other possible solutions include explaining AI-supported decision making as an alternative or addition to XAI (Bruijn et al. 2022, p. 5). In addition to the explanation of AI tools, we should also require an explanation of the decision that is based, even partially, on AI. In fact, the transparency of the model its different from the transparency of the decision. This implies that judges have the obligation to explain their decision, which forces them to critically analyze the result of AI tools. This requirement guarantees the judge's autonomy and addresses the CoE concern about the effects on the cognitive autonomy of individual (Decl(13/02/2019) - Declaration by the Committee of Ministers on the manipulative capabilities of algorithmic processes, paragraph 9).

Moreover, the accused has the right to an adversarial trial, which means that he has the right to participate effectively in the process by challenging the evidence presented. (Murtazaliyeva v. Russia [GC], § 91). It seems to us that this right allows the parties to challenge all the evidence presented, but also to syndicate the judge's decision and all the factors that contributed to it. Courts decisions must be justified, so that the defendant understands the decision (Moreira Ferreira v. Portugal (no. 2) [GC]. §84) and can exercise the right of appeal.

Additionally, the design of the AI is also important. A mere statistical model does not substantiate a sentence; legal meaning needs to be introduced alongside the empirical data (Reiling 2020, p.8).

2.2 No Punishment Without Law

Article 7 establishes the principle of legality - *Nullum crimen, nulla poena sine lege.* (There is no crime without law. there is no penalty without law). The law must provide in advance the conduct that constitutes a crime and the penalty cannot exceed the limits set (Del Río Prada v. Spain [GC], §80). This principle is important in the stages of prosecution, conviction and punishment (Del Río Prada v. Spain [GC], §77).

---

[9] There are several types of post-hoc explanations that will be appropriate depending on the model used that should be combined to obtain a more comprehensive explanation (Belle et al. 2021). See also (Arrieta et al. 2020).

The crime and the penalty must be clearly defined in law. According to the interpretation of the ECtHR the term "law" covers not only legislation, but also case law, comprising qualitative requirements, namely accessibility and foreseeability (Cantoni v. France, §29; Del Río Prada v. Spain, §91). Thus, the principle of legality covers both the law and the way the law is applied in a given case, which shows that foreseeability may be a factor to be taken into account.

These requirements apply to both the definition of the offense (Jorgic v. Germany, §§ 103–114) and the penalty. It is important to understand what the courts consider "foreseeability" to understand whether the concept coincides (at least in part) with the predictive justice we are writing about.

The term "predictability" is generally used as a way to ensure legal certainty. This requirement is seen as a counter power to *ius puniendi*. Knowing the possibility of a criminal consequence is different from predicting the concrete case (Quatrocollo 2020, p.219). When analyzing the jurisprudence of ECtHR we do not find express reference to the need to foresee the concrete case. Therefore, the concept does not seem to coincide with that of predictive justice.

When someone has committed a criminal act, it is important that it and its consequences are foreseen in previous law. When committing the criminal act, the agent acts even though he/she knows that the conduct is outside his/her field of freedom, to which a penalty corresponds (Amado 2018). But the agent is not expected to reflect on the penalty concretely applied. Even so, the agent knows that more serious conducts will have more severe penalties, there being a minimum of foresight regarding the scale of his/her penalty within the legal framework provided.

Predictability is different from prediction. Furthermore, it seems to us that the principle of legality requires something more than the mere provision of a criminal consequence in a previous law.

When we understand "law" in such a broad sense, it is not only the legislation that indicates criminal conduct. The ECtHR notes that we should be guided by the courts' interpretation. In the Camilleri v. Malta decision (see. §§39–45) the court refers the predictability of sentencing standards. It seems to us that, with the necessary adaptions, we can consider that, if there are serious and unjustified situations of inconsistency in sentencing, we are faced with a violation of this principle, because it does not correspond to the standard applicable by case law.[10]

This may have a contradictory effect. Judges may begin to adopt more severe penalties in cases that deserve more favorable sentences (Amado 2018, p. 185). We do not agree with this argument insofar as the judge will always have the possibility to decide differently from the applicable standard, if that is objectively justified.

Predictive justice can help predict the appropriate penalty for the case. The design of these tools will help to understand the factors that influence sentencing.[11] For this reason, it seems to us that such a tool could ensure a better application of this precept, by allowing the identification of cases that fall outside the predictable patterns of application in order to subsequently analyze whether this is justified in light of objective consideration.

---

[10] However, if the consequence is more favorable than the one corresponding to the foreseeable standard, there is no violation of the principle (Amado 2018, p. 180).

[11] In the opposite direction (Quattrocolo 2020, p. 219).

When it comes to penalties, the courts, faced with the penal framework, define the actual penalty for a case according to legal criteria. So, similar cases should have similar penalties. But if the penal frames are too broad, we could have a greater openness and discretion on the part of the judge, which could lead to unpredictability of penalties.

The ECtHR has a subsidiary nature in this matter and because of that cannot analyze the error of fact or law, unless the national court has violated rights and freedoms of ECHR (Vasiliauskas v. Lithuania [GC], §189).

The court cannot interfere in matters of determining the measure of the sentence. According to article 7, the court must confine to see whether the penalty imposed is not more severe than the penalty provided at the time of the practice of the fact and if the principle of retrospective application of more favorable criminal law was respected. However, the ECtHR cannot assess the length or type of applicable penalty (Vinter and Others v. the United Kingdom [GC], §105). However, we must not forget that the ECtHR can assess compliance with the ECHR. Thus, if there is a manifestly disproportionate penalty, this can be considered by the court under article 3 (Vinter and Others v. the United Kingdom [GC], §102) and, in our opinion, penalties that deviate from the standard application of the courts may also violate article 7.

2.3 Prohibition of Discrimination

The right not to be discriminated against complements the other articles of the ECHR and the Protocols. The article 14 is complemented by article 1 of Protocol No. 12 which establishes a general prohibition of discrimination. Both articles prohibit direct and indirect discrimination.

The application of this principle refers to the rights and freedoms of the ECHR, so its violation must be analyzed with another provision (Inze v. Austria, §36), which is why we refer to the rights analyzed above.

If AI tools are used in the criminal system, the right to a fair trial (article 6) must be guaranteed. This right will be violated if the decision takes discriminatory factors into account. The algorithm will be based on a theory (in the form of determining the penalty) translated into a code and also in data (depending on whether one opts for data-driven regulation or code-driven regulation, although it seems to us that both is ideal).

Although it is argued that the use of AI systems will allow the fight against human subjectivity, in fact, that may reveal the subjectivity of their creator or even discriminatory aspects reflected in their data. Therefore, we must be careful when building the algorithm and defining the data to be used. Some forms of AI that are currently used have proved this risk (Sourdin 2018, p. 1129). Recently, several studies have indicated the discriminatory aspects and biases that the COMPAS (an AI system used in US courts) suffers, which calls into question the very usefulness of the tool (Freeman 2016). When analyzing the data, if a rigorous choice is made, flaws may be detected in the justice system that would not be detected otherwise, but if data is not carefully chosen, it can result in discriminatory decisions that are intended to be countered.

Note that direct and indirect discrimination are prohibited. If the seemingly neutral AI discriminates based on the relationship with a group of people, there is indirect discrimination. So, it is important to ensure the quality and integrity of the used data.

However, the discrimination may not exist from the start, but results from machine learning. So, it is important to analyze the risk of bias throughout its use.

Therefore, its fundamental to understand the algorithm to detect these issues. In this respect, XAI could help to highlight bias in data (Arrieta et al. 2020)[12] and reverse engineering or reverse control is referred to as a solution that allows to review, discuss and contest the results (Quattrocolo 2019, p. 1527).

Furthermore, once ensuring respect for fundamental rights is an ongoing task, impact assessments must be carried out before and during the use of such tools.

3 Conclusions

The design and the implementation of AI systems must be compatible with fundamental rights and any discrimination must be prevented. Certified sources must be used; transparency, impartiality and fairness must be guaranteed. This will depend, to a large extent, on the algorithmic regulation and data processing model, which is why the tools must be designed in a multidisciplinary way.

Although XAI is quite recent, we believe that can make relevant contributions regarding explainability, which is the key concept here. It is important to understand the advances of AI in order to analyze its future integration into criminal justice. AI should be evaluated not only for its usefulness but also for the process it uses to achieve them.

The XAI research points out that AI systems should be used in more domains and their users should be part of the design from the very beginning because different people need different kind of explanations. In fact, we should think in explainability since the design: the required explanations must be defined and the model should be designed to provide the desired results and comply with the requirements demanded by law.

Throughout this paper we have noted that are several questions which have to be answered in collaboration with AI specialists and legal experts. An approach that takes into account the criminal law specificities and attempt fundamental rights is required. This knowledge exchange will create a link between XAI and legal world.

Engineering and social sciences should join efforts to establish metrics regarding the level of explainability required since this will be the guarantor of fundamental rights. This multidisciplinary approach requires continuous monitoring, since today's issues may be outdated tomorrow. Indeed, application of AI may be denied today, but as the capabilities of AI improves and confidence in it increases, it may be accepted.

It seems to us that only after testing several models can we state which one should be adopted and, consequently, which XAI solutions may be necessary. Thus, many questions will remain unanswered and should be taken up again when analysing and testing the concrete models. However, the adoption of these instruments must comply with the ECHR. We should anticipate interpretation/requirements made by ECtHR, given the particular aspects arising from the use of AI instruments in criminal proceedings.

Finally, engineering concepts do not coincide with legal concepts. For example, the efficiency sought by justice, in this particular case, the consistency of penalties, does

---

[12] For example, XAI techniques can be used to identify hidden correlations between data – see. (Arrieta et al. 2020, p. 104 ff.).

not have the same meaning as the efficiency sought by AI (Quattrocolo 2019, p. 1531). Thus, in the design of these models, a multidisciplinary conception that translates legal reasoning and guarantees fundamental rights is necessary. In fact, we must design reliable AI instruments that focus on human rights.

Several studies focus on the technical evolution of AI tools, making the use of such tools dependent on the evolution of computer science. For example, the demand for explainability is the fundamental issue in any discourse on the application of AI systems in the criminal justice system. This requirement depends on the evolution of AI systems and their transparency. However, this is an issue that does not exclusively concern engineering. It is a multidisciplinary field that should have at its core the respect for fundamental rights as a filter of these tools.

Acknowledgement. This research was funded by the Portuguese Foundation for Science and Technology (FCT) through the PhD grant 2021.07986.BD.

References

Aletras, N., Tsarapatsanis, D., Preotiuc-Pietro, D., Lampos, V.: Predicting judicial decisions of the European Court of Human Rights: a Natural Language Processing perspective. Peer J. Comput. Sci. **2**, e93 (2016). https://doi.org/10.7717/peerj-cs.93

Amado, J.A.G.: On the principle of criminal legality and its scope: foreseeability as a component of legality. In: Pérez Manzano, M., Lascuraín Sánchez, J.A., Mínguez Rosique, M. (eds.) Multilevel Protection of the Principle of Legality in Criminal Law, pp. 177–193. Springer, Cham (2018). https://doi.org/10.1007/978-3-319-63865-2_10

Arrieta, A., et al.: Explainable Artificial Intelligence (XAI): concepts, taxonomies, opportunities and challenges toward responsabile AI. Inf. Fusion **58**, 82–115 (2020). https://doi.org/10.1016/j.inffus.2019.12.012

Belle, V., Papantonis, I.: Principles and practice of explainable machine learning. Front. Big Data **4**, 688969 (2021). https://doi.org/10.3389/fdata.2021.688969

Bruijnm, H., Warnier, M., Janssen, M.: The perils and pitfalls of explainable AI: strategies for explaining algorithmic decision-making. Gov. Inf. q. **39**(2), 101666 (2022). https://doi.org/10.1016/j.giq.2021.101666

Freeman, K.: Algorithmic injustice: how the Wisconsin Supreme Court failed to protect due process rights in State v. Loomis. North Carol. J. Law Technol. **18**(3), 75 (2016)

Georgia Tech Homepage. https://gvu.gatech.edu/research/projects/explainable-ai-rationale-generation. Accessed 28 Apr 2022

Hall, M., Calabrò, D., Sourdin, T., Stranieri, A., Zeleznikow, J.: Supporting discretionary decision-making with information technology: a case study in the criminal sentencing jurisdiction. Univ. Ottawa Law Technol. J. **2**(1), 1–36 (2005)

Heaven, W.: Why asking an AI to explain itself can make things worse. MIT Technology Review (2020). https://www.technologyreview.com/2020/01/29/304857/why-asking-an-ai-to-explain-itself-can-make-things-worse/. Accessed 28 Apr 2022

Hamon, R., Junklewitz, H., Malgieri, G., Hert, P., Beslay, L., Sanchez, I.: Impossible explanations? Beyond explainable AI in the GDPR from a COVID-19 use case scenario. In: Proceeding of ACM FaaCT. ACM, New York (2021). https://doi.org/10.1145/1234567890

Quattrocolo, S.: Artificial Intelligence, Computational Modelling and Criminal Proceedings. A Framework for a European Legal Discussion. Springer, Heidelberg (2020)

Quattrocolo, S.: An introduction to AI and criminal justice in Europe. Revista Brasileira de Direito Processual Penal **5**(3), 1519–1554 (2019). https://doi.org/10.22197/rbdpp.v5i3.290

Reiling, A.: Courts and artificial intelligence. Int. J. Court Adm. **11**(2), 1 (2020). https://doi.org/10.36745/ijca.343

Re, R., Solow-Niederman, A.: Developing artificially intelligent justice. Stanford Technol. Law Rev. **22**(2), 242–289 (2019)

Searle, J.: Can computers think?. In: Chalmers, D.J. (ed.) Philosophy of Mind: Classical and Contemporary Readings. Oxford University Press (2002)

Simmons, R.: Big data, machine judges, and the legitimacy of criminal justice system. UC Davis L. Rev. **52**, 1067–1118 (2018)

Sourdin, T.: Judge v Robot? Artificial intelligence and judicial decision-making. UNSW Law J. **41**(4), 1114–1133 (2018)

Wan, A., et al.: NBDT: neutral-backed decision tree. In: ICLR Conference Paper (2021). https://doi.org/10.48550/arXiv.2004.00221

Enriching Legal Knowledge Through Intelligent Information Retrieval Techniques: A Review

Marco Gomes[1,2](✉) ⓘ, Bruno Oliveira[2] ⓘ, and Cristóvão Sousa[3] ⓘ

[1] CIICESI/ESTG, Polytechnic Institute of Porto, Felgueiras, Portugal
mfg@estg.ipp.pt
[2] ALGORITMI Centre, University of Minho, Guimaraes, Portugal
bmo@estg.ipp.pt
[3] INESC TEC, Porto, Portugal
cds@estg.ipp.pt

Abstract. This work aims to systematize the knowledge on emerging Intelligent Information Retrieval (IIR) practices in scenarios whose context is similar to the field of tax law. It is a part of a project that covers the emerging techniques of IIR and its applicability to the tax law domain. Furthermore, it presents an overview of different approaches for representing legal data and exposes the challenging task of providing quality insights to support decision-making in a dedicated legal environment. It also offers an overview of the related background and prior research referring to the techniques for information retrieval in legal documents, establishing the current state-of-the-art, and identifying its main drawbacks. A summary of the most appropriate technologies and research approaches of the technologies that apply artificial intelligence technology to help legal tasks is also depicted.

Keywords: Legal knowledge · Information Retrieval · Artificial intelligence · Legal domain

1 Introduction

Any technical domain, be it legal, tax, computational, or otherwise, is characterized by a highly specialized discourse using its terminology and style in the textual codification of the underlying themes. Thus, it is accepted that understanding a technical discourse requires a certain level of literacy suitable for the identification and analysis of the discourse. However, interpretation, as an act of inference about what is written from the perspective of its application to a given context, may require more than understanding the terminological and conceptual framework of the domain, implying a set of epistemic practices [7] from which new structures of knowledge emerge that tend to facilitate the process of interpretation. These practices contribute to meaning construction through collaborative activities, where experience and knowledge representation models

G. Marreiros et al. (Eds.): EPIA 2022, LNAI 13566, pp. 119–130, 2022.
https://doi.org/10.1007/978-3-031-16474-3_11

are crucial factors. Notwithstanding the importance of tacit knowledge and the models that facilitate its explanation, the interpretation process also depends on the quality of information and mechanisms of analysis and research of interrelated content, that is, identification of relationships between different types or categories of information.

The field of taxation and tax law is complex by nature, typically consisting of large volumes of highly technical textual information and categorized by codes (VAT, IRS, ...) and laws. Moreover, the different sources of information that make up this technical domain are characterized by a high degree of interdependence and dynamics, where inter and intratextual references and updates are frequent. Therefore, the correct and precise treatment of this information, its temporal location, and its availability in an organized and adequate way to the needs of different users can create added value for professionals and organizations, but, above all, it can serve to avoid legal disputes or promote necessary tools for support in resolving these, whether with the Tax Authority or with the Courts. In this work, the knowledge management process is assumed as a critical process, representing a key factor of organizational performance and an essential tool for competitiveness [26]. The availability and access to updated legislative information, complemented with objective and timely explanations, allows the users to comply with their tax obligations, promote tax efficiency, and reduce tax burdens. However, this process often results in querying data from multiple sources of information, where each document can handle updates and cross-references, which increases process complexity. In many cases, excessive, mismatched, and disorganized information can affect the entire data exploration process, which can lead to wrong decisions if improperly interpreted. For this, it is necessary to identify relevant information (Information Retrieval - IR), considering the existence of typically unstructured data and in large quantities [32]. However, considering the technological evolution in knowledge base management and new intelligent models of collection, processing, analysis, and representation of information, several of the existing gaps can be adequately explored. In this sense, the consortium presents this project, presenting complementary capabilities in the areas involved and proposing an intelligent solution to the problems encountered. This document contains four sections and is organized as follows. In the first section, the main problem is contextualized and described as the principal motivation for this work. Next, the following section (Sect. 2) presents an overview of different approaches for representing legal data and exposes the challenging task of providing quality insights to support decision-making in a dedicated legal domain. Section 3 proposes an overview of the related background and prior research referring to the techniques for information retrieval in legal documents, establishing the current state-of-the-art, and identifying its main drawbacks. A summary of the most appropriate technologies and research approaches for developing the research work is also depicted. Moreover, this section also gives an overview of the technologies that apply artificial intelligence technology to help legal tasks. Finally, the conclusion provides a summary of contributions to the main points of this work.

2 Legal Knowledge Representation

Legal data is typically represented using natural language framed within a specific domain and context. For that reason, expressing and sharing legal knowledge so that computers can explore is a challenging task. Therefore, the emergence of disruptive techniques for handling, modeling, and using data became very popular in the last decade, particularly with the advent of Artificial intelligence techniques used to implement Machine Learning algorithms that have enhanced the development of expert systems. However, systems cannot analyze and provide quality insights to support decision-making in a dedicated legal domain without a proper representation of knowledge. As stated by Ramakrishna and Paschke [24], knowledge represents a relation between a knower and a proposition, expressed by a declarative sentence. In [3], three types of knowledge are discussed: experiential knowledge is acquired based not only on experiences but also connects to the environment through the sensory before being processed by the individual, which means that the same experience may result in different knowledge (since it is associated with previous experiences and knowledge); the skills that represent the know-how resulting from doing specific actions; and claims that define what is known based on explicit knowledge (provided by, for example, by books or legislations). Each type is interconnected and is particularly relevant in the legislation domain since the same explicit knowledge (law) and its application by judiciary entities is influenced by experimental and know-how knowledge. In the last years, several research works have proposed technologies, methods, and languages to identify requirements and represent the specificities of the legal domain. The primary purpose is to capture information that can be processed and shared by computers. In [33] a categorization based on generations for describing the efforts to provide access to legal electronic data is presented. The first generation refers to a representation closer to word processing and database models; the second generation refers to the adoption of metadata for structuring and modeling, the third generation focuses on grammar for preserving consistency over time and the ability to share and integrate new knowledge to existing one (e.g., using ontologies). Finally, the four-generation provides prescriptiveness using constraint-based grammar. Some approaches have been used for legal knowledge representation during the last decades. For example, the LEXML [33] is a European model to promote interoperability for legal and legislative data. The LEXML was born from several countries' initiatives to find similarities between the national and international legal systems. However, LEXML is currently only implemented in Brazil and can be framed within the second generation of legal data representation. The EUR-Lex [33] provides European legal documents with Formex, an XML standard used for managing legal (not for representation) data in the EUR-Lex service that provides access to EU legislation such as the case law of the Court of Justice of the European Union, and other EU public documents. EUR-Lex supports multi-language to cover several European languages, supporting law or international agreements. Formex is widely adopted in the European community and defines the logical markup for legal documents. It can be framed in the first

generation of initiatives to standardize legal documents. The CEN MetaLex [2] is an XML standard used to represent sources of law and references to sources of law as CEN MetaLex documents. It provides the interchange of data in a standardized way. In addition, it provides mechanisms to link legal information from various levels of authority, supporting different countries and languages and information exchange and interoperability. These characteristics allow for the classification of this standard as the third generation. Akoma Ntoso [27] is an international technical standard for representing executive, legislative, and judicial documents in a structured way using a domain-specific XML vocabulary. It provides a framework for exchanging parliamentary, legislative, and judiciary documents. In addition, Akoma Ntoso maintains connected standards and languages that provide: document format (for open documents that cover areas such as Parliamentary Debates, Primary Legislation, or Judgements); a model for document interchange (supporting the generation, presentation, accessibility, and description of documents), data schema (all document types share the same basic structures), metadata schema and ontology (the ontology is designed to be extensible to accommodate extra elements and qualifiers to meet specific requirements), and a schema for citation and cross-referencing (relying on a name convention and a reference mechanism to connect a distributed document corpus). Due to these characteristics, Akoma Ntoso was originally a third-generation Initiative for legal knowledge representation. LegalXML[1] approach produces technical standards for structuring legal documents and information using XML, enabling the adoption and convergence of e-business standards for the legal domain. LegalXML has standards to support court documents, legal citations, or transcripts. In addition, it includes the LegalDocML, a legal rule representation language based on Akoma Ntoso for structuring legal content, the Electronic Court Filing for supporting interoperability among electronic courts, the LegalRuleML for representing legal norms and rules, among other technical specifications such as the LegalRuleML for supporting legal arguments representation and evaluation.

Among the presented approaches for representing legal data, the LegalXML initiative covers several aspects of legal knowledge representation [33]:

- Supporting the ability to represent different knowledge aspects with clear and expressive semantics.
- Provide mechanisms for knowledge sharing, reusability, and extensibility.
- Provide support for reasoning and inference over the legal content.
- The capacity to reference other legal documents, which is very useful in the jurisdiction context;
- Defining rules for legally checking
- Capacity to support authoring and to link the law context according to a specific temporal occurrence
- Support to track changes and amendments
- Support directions or injunctions indicate how a language should be used in specific contexts.

---

[1] http://www.legalxml.org/.

The main difference between LegalXML, CEN-Metalex, and Akoma Ntoso is related to the lack of prescriptiveness in CEN-Metalex and the original Akoma Ntoso version. With LegalRuleML, prescriptive statements are modeled by "If" conditions, describing rules application. Not only baseline rules but also the exceptions to the baseline.

3 Approaches for Information Retrieval in Legal Documents

Legal documents represent a complex knowledge composed of lengthy texts that need to be analyzed and interpreted by domain personnel (e.g., lawyers or judges) to extract meaningful information. In several cases, data is extracted with other related documents to select the right documents and for understanding the document content.

A legal document can involve several uses cases (such as contracts, regulations, or privacy documents). They typically involve several entities, relationships between, and the relationships between external documents, such as laws, amendments, or revocations. Thus, the complexity and time spent extracting relevant data in legal documents are challenging and error-prone. Since legal documents are subject to different interpretations, misinterpretations or precision loss are common problems related to text interpretation.

To analyze and reason over the documents, users need expert systems to support decision-making requirements. Due to their nature, extracting, organizing, and interpreting legal documents requires the application of several advanced techniques and algorithms. Techniques such as semantic web, text mining, and NLP (Natural Language Processing) techniques can be used to reveal understandings and patterns that can be used to support decision-making. Moreover, the knowledge extracted from legal documents will be used to support critical decisions related to its applications in judgments or legal decisions. This means the inappropriate legal data handling can lead to disastrous results and can be seen with mistrust from the decision-making personnel [5].

Legal search queries can be framed according to several dimensions (e.g., legal issues, jurisdictions), which imposes the evaluation of the proper algorithm, retrieval and ranking models to effectively extract meaningful data. Legal Information Retrieval (IR) and legal argument data mining represent two typical strategies to extract knowledge from legal documents. Despite focusing on different perspectives, several approaches can be used together [1]. The legal argument retrieval (AR) [1,36,37] use these two techniques for returning arguments and not just documents. In this context, Xu [39] addressed the possibility to automatically generate succinct summaries of legal documents through the identification of legal arguments.

3.1 Information Science

In the field of legal knowledge, there are several contributions not only for knowledge representation, as stated in the previous section, but also for rule

interchange [13]. Furthermore, for judicial interpretation based on domain, conceptualization [8].

The approach presented in [8] connects the knowledge coming from different decisions and highlights similarities and differences between them. The authors introduce JudO, an OWL2 ontology library of legal knowledge that relies on the metadata contained in judicial documents. JudO represents the interpretations performed by a judge while conducting legal reasoning toward adjudicating a case. JudO provides meaningful legal semantics while retaining a strong connection to source documents (fragments of legal texts). This approach detects and models jurisprudence-related information directly from the text and performs shallow reasoning on the resulting knowledge base.

In [14], the authors present a formal model of legal norms modeled in OWL. It is intended for semiautomatic drafting, semantic retrieval, and browsing legislation. Most existing solutions model legal norms by formal logic, rules, or ontologies. The proposed model formally defines legal norms using the elements of legal relations they regulate. The paper presents a formal model of legal norms used to develop expert systems for semiautomatic drafting and semantic retrieval and browsing of legislation.

Semantic web techniques are also used for modeling legal information and reason about related data. These networks represent the relevant entities, their properties, and their relationship considering the legal domain [38]. The research work presented in [9] describes the implementation of a semantic network. The authors implemented an entity recognition task using a NER Tagging tool to identify victims, places, or organizations as entities involved in the related legal case to produce nodes for the knowledge graph. To identify words and their context and their relationship with associated words, Part-of-speech [18] tagging was used for identifying edges (mainly verbs) between the entities previously identified. Additionally, they used an information Extraction tool to identify the relationships between entities from plain text. In [16], the authors present ALDA, a legal cognitive assistant to analyze digital legal documents. They addressed several components, including the development of ontological representation: the extraction of data to create knowledge bases (using text-mining and natural language processing), the cross-referencing between related documents (which results in the development of subgraphs), and the use of deep learning to extract semantically similar legal entities and terms.

3.2 Artificial Intelligence

Almost since 1970, it has been noticed the "information crisis in law" (an ever-increasing amount of legal data that is being generated and not plenty or properly used) encouraging the development of legal Information Retrieval systems [28]. Also, almost since 2007, the "natural language barrier" [23] has been discussed as a barrier that hinders artificial intelligence in the legal domain. However, even using artificial intelligence and other computing approaches almost since the 1970 s,s, there has been no breakthrough in such matter [25]. Most of the research performed on the use of Artificial Intelligence in the legal

domain appears to relapse into three main categories: Computer-Aided Reasoning (CAR), Knowledge-Based Systems (KBS), and Legal Language Processing (LLP). Those categories are highly coupled since CAR needs KBS, which relies on LLP, so those groups are a matter of research focus. This is suggested to be called a LIIS. Considering a legal system stack, CAR appears to be performed most by Case-based Reasoning. KBS seems to be built in most cases using one or another ontology strategy; on the other hand, on LLP, a commonly used approach appears not yet to exist. Regarding application, most of the research seems to aim one way or another at Legal Information Retrieval. Datastore and querying are ancient human needs performed by cataloging and retrieving systems [25,31]. Cataloging systems are used to handle structured data and retrieve the system's unstructured data. The first is related to SQL (or relational) within a computer science scope, yet the second is NoSQL (or non-relational) technology. Shall highlight that it is not a matter of choice but the impossibility to structure some types of information [22]. Moreover, Computer-aided Reasoning cannot only rely on formal logic [6]. It must also rely on a knowledge-based system that needs a legal language processor to be composed [31]. The stack sits on legal language processing. While it is not properly settled, it will not be possible to reach the expected breakthrough, called the "natural language barrier" [31]. The stack sits on legal language processing. While it is not properly settled, it will not be possible to reach the expected breakthrough, called the "natural language barrier" [23]. In this sense, it was realized that most natural language processing approaches do not adequately suit legal texts due to their idiosyncrasies, and legal language processing comes into use [6].

Specific issues of legal texts include sentences twice longer, and prepositional chaining is a third deeper than those used in newspapers [6]. Also, legal terms may present proper semantics being different from the regular use. Moreover, the law of each country is written in its official language and considers a particular legal structure [19]. Because of that, those concerns must be dealt with locally and hinders international cooperation. In other words, the "natural language barrier" in the legal field includes lexical, syntactic, semantic, pragmatic, and idiom obstacles. But once surpassed, it is believed that conventional approaches of Computer-aided Reasoning and knowledge-based systems are feasible to be used [23]. Meanwhile, researchers' efforts over the years led to tremendous advances in applying artificial intelligence (especially NPL) technology to help legal tasks. Nowadays, the Legal Information Retrieval datasets, including COLIEE, CaseLaw, and CM. Both COLIEE and CaseLaw are involved in retrieving the most relevant articles from a large corpus, while data examples in CM give three legal documents for calculating similarity. Moreover, these datasets provide benchmarks for the studies of LegalIR.

The difficulties are not restricted to legal language processing, although it typifies a barrier. Information retrieval itself presents several issues to be handled. The index formation (that can be static or dynamic), according to the complexity of data and the index itself, may lead to computational complexity (time and space) issues requiring some cluster processing and other big-data

approaches [11,22]. A significant data source may return more information than the user can handle, requiring a scoring system to rank the fetched documents. Due to the diversity of possible approaches, shall build an information retriever as specific as possible given a domain and user [25] within a user-centered design. Also another peculiarity of legal retrieving is the need to encompass juridical dynamics and context. CBR is a problem-solving method that addresses new problems by remembering and adapting solutions previously used to solve similar issues [17]. CBR is based on two tenets to understand intelligence: problems tend to occur repeatedly, and similar problems have similar solutions [20]. Also, the answer to each new problem in CBR becomes the basis for a new case, being learned and stored for potential reuse in the future [35].

The typical CBR cycle is composed of [17,34]: Retrieve, Reuse, Revise and Retain. The retrieving step is responsible for determining which case is most similar to the new problem. Two different approaches can calculate cases' similarities: the K-Nearest neighbours approach - which uses a weighted sum of features to identify the similarities - and the template retrieval approach - which returns all cases that fit within specific parameters. During the CBR cycle, some stages usually have human interaction. For example, while it may automate case retrieval and reuse, case revision and retention are performed by human experts. Reuse is the process that receives the retrieved cases and makes the necessary adapts to solve the new problem. There are two methods used to perform this action: transformational and derivational. While derivational methods modify the previous solution using domain-specific transformation operators, the transformational methods reuse the algorithms, techniques, or rules that generated the original solution to produce a new solution to the current problem.

Traditionally, intelligent systems procedures were described through rules called RBR. For Hayes [15], expressing knowledge using this model is difficult and time-consuming in real situations. In contrast, in CBR systems, the cases are knowledge, leading to automatic maintenance and updating of knowledge, while in RBR systems, new rules are created. This type of system proposes a solution to a given problem, from knowledge not wholly defined, low structured, or unknown, as well as allows it to pay attention during the process of constructing a solution to the aspects/characteristics of the problem considered a determinant for the construction the same solution.

In the legal context, CBR-based systems have found vast opportunities to develop their application methodologies and with satisfactory results [29]. The SCALIR is an example of a hybrid symbolic/sub-symbolic system that uses legal network knowledge to perform retrieval through spreading activation to perform the task [30], considering legal decisions as complex networks [21]. Indeed, the law may thus be thought of as a giant network containing information embedded in cases (nodes) and relationship information called citations (arcs) going from node to node. Measures such as betweenness, closeness, and Markov Centrality can help find the causes at the core of a judicial system. Likewise, measures such as clustering enable understanding the degree of interdependence of cases that comprise a jurisprudence database.

Meanwhile, as pointed out by Carneiro and Gomes [4,10,12], both RBR and CBR approaches to negotiation face criticism. Thus the main drawbacks can be briefly enumerated as follows [ibid]:

- Laws constantly change, thus implying updates to the rules that establish how solutions are generated in RBR. This may result in inconsistencies and/or redundancy. Moreover, this might be quite a complex task (depending on the complexity of the legal domain) that must be performed manually, despite the use of some supporting tool;
- The quality of an RBR tool is directly dependent on the quality of the work of the humans, translating the legal norms into rules. The quality of information of the rules may be hard to determine;
- RBR are static and will not shape changes in the legal domain unless these are coded manually by a human expert;
- The quality of a CBR tool is directly dependent on the quality and amount of past cases known;
- The fact that legal norms change frequently also has a negative impact on CBR approaches, rendering past cases potentially useless under the light of the new norms;
- Both CBR and RBR approaches are domain-dependent. This implies that rules are defined independently for each legal domain and that cases from a specific field can hardly be reused.

3.3 An Overview of the Related Background and Prior Research

According to the most recent literature, AI solutions in legal services can be grouped into document analysis, legal research, and practice automation. While the first two categories correspond to tools that support lawyers in their work, practice automation refers to the automation of a lawyer's work. Practice automation via AI tools might bring considerable gains in productivity and a significant change in the legal profession, with the automation of discovery (e-discovery) and the redaction of court briefs. However, datasets are essential for AI systems, both as training material for developing AI algorithms and as input material for its actual use. The data (or its lack) might constitute a barrier to entry for small law firms or solo practitioners who want to create their own AI systems. Data has been considered a bottleneck: In its decision v. Google (Shopping), the European Commission stated that the search data held by Google constituted a barrier to entry for other prospective market players. In the legal context, it has been described that most law firms are "document rich and data-poor", and public data such as judicial decisions and opinions are either not available or so varied in the format as to be challenging to use effectively.

4 Conclusion

The field of taxation and tax law is complex by nature, typically consisting of large volumes of highly technical textual information and categorized by codes

(VAT, IRS, ...) and laws. The development and deployment of techniques and approaches using AI and Law can help this field of knowledge to assist the legal professionals in interpreting this type of information, providing added value in a collaborative context that enriches the information and the professionals who use it. Bearing this in mind, this work intended to characterize the existing technological infrastructure and present the most relevant literature and understanding gathered related to these topics.

Acknowledgement. This work was supported by the Northern Regional Operational Program, Portugal 2020 and European Union, through European Regional Development Fund (ERDF) in the scope of project number 047223 - 17/SI/2019.

References

1. Ashley, K.D., Walker, V.R.: From information retrieval (IR) to argument retrieval (AR) for legal cases: report on a baseline study. Front. Artif. intell. Appl. **259**, 29–38 (2013). https://doi.org/10.3233/978-1-61499-359-9-29
2. Boer, A., Hoekstra, R., Winkels, R.: MetaLex: legislation in XML (2002)
3. Bolisani, E., Bratianu, C.: The elusive definition of knowledge. In: Emergent Knowledge Strategies. KMOL, vol. 4, pp. 1–22. Springer, Cham (2018). https://doi.org/10.1007/978-3-319-60657-6_1
4. Carneiro, D.: An agent-based architecture for online dispute resolution services. Ph.D. thesis, University of Minho (2013). https://hdl.handle.net/1822/28773
5. Devins, C., Felin, T., Kauffman, S., Koppl, R.: The law and big data. Cornell J. Law Public Policy **27**(2), 357–413 (2017)
6. Francesconi, E., Montemagni, S., Peters, W., Tiscornia, D. (eds.): Semantic Processing of Legal Texts. LNCS (LNAI), vol. 6036. Springer, Heidelberg (2010). https://doi.org/10.1007/978-3-642-12837-0
7. Frické, M.: Big data and its epistemology. J. Am. Soc. Inf. Sci. **66**(4), 651–661 (2015). https://doi.org/10.1002/asi.23212
8. Gangemi, A., Sagri, M.-T., Tiscornia, D.: A constructive framework for legal ontologies. In: Benjamins, V.R., Casanovas, P., Breuker, J., Gangemi, A. (eds.) Law and the Semantic Web. LNCS (LNAI), vol. 3369, pp. 97–124. Springer, Heidelberg (2005). https://doi.org/10.1007/978-3-540-32253-5_7
9. Giri, R., Porwal, Y., Shukla, V., Chadha, P., Kaushal, R.: Approaches for information retrieval in legal documents. In: 2017 10th International Conference on Contemporary Computing, IC3 2017 2018-January(November 2019), pp. 1–6 (2018). https://doi.org/10.1109/IC3.2017.8284324
10. Gomes, M., Carneiro, D., Novais, P., Neves, J.: Modelling stress recognition in conflict resolution scenarios. In: Corchado, E., Snášel, V., Abraham, A., Woźniak, M., Graña, M., Cho, S.-B. (eds.) HAIS 2012. LNCS (LNAI), vol. 7208, pp. 533–544. Springer, Heidelberg (2012). https://doi.org/10.1007/978-3-642-28942-2_48
11. Gomes, M., Silva, F., Ferraz, F., Silva, A., Analide, C., Novais, P.: Developing an ambient intelligent-based decision support system for production and control planning. In: Madureira, A.M., Abraham, A., Gamboa, D., Novais, P. (eds.) ISDA 2016. AISC, vol. 557, pp. 984–994. Springer, Cham (2017). https://doi.org/10.1007/978-3-319-53480-0_97
12. Gomes, M.F.V.: A conflict management environment to support decision-making process (2021)

13. Gordon, T.F., Governatori, G., Rotolo, A.: Rules and norms: requirements for rule interchange languages in the legal domain. In: Governatori, G., Hall, J., Paschke, A. (eds.) RuleML 2009. LNCS, vol. 5858, pp. 282–296. Springer, Heidelberg (2009). https://doi.org/10.1007/978-3-642-04985-9_26
14. Gostojić, S., Milosavljević, B., Konjović, Z.: Ontological model of legal norms for creating and using legislation. Comput. Sci. Inf. Syst. **10**(1), 151–171 (2013). https://doi.org/10.2298/CSIS110804035G
15. Hayes-Roth, F.: Rule-based systems. Commun. ACM **28**(9), 921–932 (1985). https://doi.org/10.1145/4284.4286
16. Joshi, K.P., Gupta, A., Mittal, S., Pearce, C., Joshi, A., Finin, T.: ALDA: cognitive assistant for legal document analytics. In: AAAI Fall Symposium - Technical Report FS-16-01-September, pp. 149–152 (2016)
17. Kolodner, J.: Case-Based Reasoning. Morgan Kaufmann, Burlington (2014)
18. Koniaris, M., Anagnostopoulos, I., Vassiliou, Y.: Evaluation of diversification techniques for legal information retrieval. Algorithms **10**(1), 1–24 (2017). https://doi.org/10.3390/a10010022
19. Lame, G.: Using NLP techniques to identify legal ontology components: concepts and relations. Artif. Intell. Law **12**(4), 379–396 (2004). https://doi.org/10.1007/s10506-005-4160-3
20. Leake, D.B.: Case-based reasoning: experiences, lessons, and future directions (1996)
21. Lupu, Y., Voeten, E.: Precedent in international courts: a network analysis of case citations by the European court of human rights. Br. J. Polit. Sci. **42**(2), 413–439 (2012). https://doi.org/10.1017/S0007123411000433
22. Manning, C.D., Raghavan, P., Schütze, H.: Introduction to Information Retrieval. Cambridge University Press, Cambridge (2008). https://doi.org/10.1017/CBO9780511809071
23. McCarty, L.T.: Deep semantic interpretations of legal texts. In: Proceedings of the 11th International Conference on Artificial Intelligence and Law, pp. 217–224 (2007)
24. Merkl, D., Schweighoffer, E., Winiwarter, W.: Exploratory analysis of concept and document spaces with connectionist networks. Artif. Intell. Law **7**(2), 185–209 (1999). https://doi.org/10.1023/A:1008365524782
25. Nissan, E.: Digital technologies and artificial intelligence's present and foreseeable impact on lawyering, judging, policing and law enforcement. Ai Soc. **32**(3), 441–464 (2015). https://doi.org/10.1007/s00146-015-0596-5
26. Omotayo, F.O.: Knowledge management as an important tool in organisational management: a review of literature. Libr. Philos. Pract. **1**(2015), 1–23 (2015)
27. Palmirani, M., Vitali, F.: Akoma-Ntoso for legal documents. In: Sartor, G., Palmirani, M., Francesconi, E., Biasiotti, M. (eds.) Legislative XML for the Semantic Web. Law, Governance and Technology Series, vol. 4. Springer, Dordrecht (2011). https://doi.org/10.1007/978-94-007-1887-6_6
28. Ramakrishna, S., Paschke, A.: Bridging the gap between Legal Practitioners and Knowledge Engineers using semi-formal KR. CoRR abs/1406.0 (2014). https://arxiv.org/abs/1406.0079
29. Rissland, E.L., Daniels, J.J.: A hybrid cbr-ir approach to legal information retrieval. In: Proceedings of the 5th International Conference on Artificial Intelligence and Law, pp. 52–61 (1995). https://doi.org/10.1145/222092.2221250
30. Rose, D.E.: A Symbolic and Connectionist Approach to Legal Information Retrieval. Psychology Press, London (2013)

31. Sanderson, M., Croft, W.B.: The history of information retrieval research. In: Proceedings of the IEEE 100(Special Centennial Issue), pp. 1444–1451 (2012). https://doi.org/10.1109/JPROC.2012.2189916
32. Schütze, H., Manning, C.D., Raghavan, P.: Introduction to Information Retrieval, vol. 39, p. 2. Cambridge University Press. Cambridge (2008)
33. Shelar, A., Moharir, M.: A comparative study to determine a suitable legal knowledge representation format. In: 2018 International Conference on Electrical, Electronics, Communication, Computer, and Optimization Techniques (ICEECCOT), pp. 514–519 (2018). https://doi.org/10.1109/ICEECCOT43722.2018.9001363
34. Slade, S.: Case-based reasoning: a research paradigm. AI Mag. **12**(1), 42–42 (1991). https://doi.org/10.1609/aimag.v12i1.883
35. Smyth, B., Keane, M.T.: Remembering to forget. In: Proceedings of the 14th International Joint Conference on Artificial Intelligence, pp. 377–382. Citeseer (1995)
36. Walker, V.R., Han, J.H., Ni, X., Yoseda, K.: Semantic types for computational legal reasoning: propositional connectives and sentence roles in the veterans' claims dataset. In: Proceedings of the International Conference on Artificial Intelligence and Law, pp. 217–226 (2017). https://doi.org/10.1145/3086512.3086535
37. Walker, V.R., Pillaipakkamnatt, K., Davidson, A.M., Linares, M., Pesce, D.J.: Automatic classification of rhetorical roles for sentences: comparing rule-based scripts with machine learning. In: CEUR Workshop Proceedings, vol. 2385 (2019)
38. Winkels, R., Boer, A., De Maat, E., Van Engers, T., Breebaart, M., Melger, H.: Constructing a semantic network for legal content. In: Artificial Intelligence Conference, Belgian/Netherlands, pp. 405–406(2005)
39. Xu, H., Savelka, J., Ashley, K.D.: Toward summarizing case decisions via extracting argument issues, reasons, and conclusions. In: Proceedings of the 18th International Conference on Artificial Intelligence and Law, pp. 250–254 (2021). https://doi.org/10.1145/3462757.3466098

AIM - Artificial Intelligence in Medicine

Region of Interest Identification in the Cervical Digital Histology Images

Tetiana Biloborodova[1,2]($\boxtimes$) (iD), Semen Lomakin[3], Inna Skarga-Bandurova[4] (iD), and Yana Krytska[3] (iD)

[1] University of Applied Science HTW Saar, Saarbrücken, Germany
beloborodova.t@gmail.com
[2] G.E. Pukhov Institute for Modelling in Energy Engineering, Kyiv, Ukraine
[3] Volodymyr Dahl East Ukrainian National University, Severodonetsk, Ukraine
[4] Oxford Brookes University, Oxford, UK

Abstract. The region of interest (RoI) identification has a significant potential for yielding information about relevant histological features and is imperative to improve the effectiveness of digital pathology in clinical practice. The typical RoI is the stratified squamous epithelium (SSE) that appears on relatively small image areas. Hence, taking the entire image for classification adds noise caused by irrelevant background, making classification networks biased towards the background fragments. This paper proposes a novel approach for epithelium RoI identification based on automatic bounding boxes (bb) construction and SSE extraction and compares it with state-of-the-art histology RoI localization and detection techniques. Further classification of the extracted epithelial fragments based on DenseNet made it possible to effectively identify the SSE RoI in cervical histology images (CHI). The design brings significant improvement to the identification of diagnostically significant regions. For this research, we created two CHI datasets, the CHI-I containing 171 color images of the cervical histology microscopy and CHI-II containing 1049 extracted fragments of microscopy, which are the most considerable publicly available SSE datasets.

Keywords: Region of Interest (RoI) · Cervical histology image · Bounding box

1 Introduction

Adoption of digital technology into histological practice increases the productivity and accuracy of the interpretation of the pathology slides [1], provides an objective quantitative assessment of the microscopy images, reduces the variability of the diagnosis, and improves differential diagnosis [2, 3]. Meanwhile, accurate automatic interpretation of histopathological images comes up against the difficulty that we still do not have a principled approach for identifying areas of interest. The lack of a gold standard for automatic RoI identification is explained by the morphological diversity of histological images, a wide variety of shapes of epithelial regions, density and shape of cells in these regions, the presence of artefacts, e.g., blood, mucus, staining in the tissue samples,

© The Author(s), under exclusive license to Springer Nature Switzerland AG 2022
G. Marreiros et al. (Eds.): EPIA 2022, LNAI 13566, pp. 133–145, 2022.
https://doi.org/10.1007/978-3-031-16474-3_12

the presence of columnar cellular regions and varying sizes of the RoI in images. For instance, cervical digital histology images are widely used for early diagnosis to prevent malignancy but only a relatively small part of the image containing SSE can be seen as a diagnostic area (see Fig. 1). Hence, considering the entire image for segmentation would add noise caused by irrelevant portions in the background and lead to the segmentation network being biased towards the background regions [4].

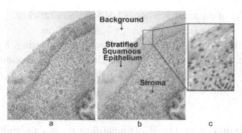

Fig. 1. An example of the CHI: (a) an initial image of 3288 × 4096 resolution at 40X magnification, (b) background, SSE and stroma (the yellow SSE region corresponds to the RoI in cervical histology microscopy and green line is picked to basement membrane, which separates the epithelium from the underlying stroma), (c) a zoomed-in view of the SSE

One of the possible solutions to increase detection performances is using bounding boxes (bb) around SSE as a region of interests (RoI) and then relying on region-based features for class identification [5]. This idea is both self-contained and attractive, but due to the highly diverse directions of SSE in histology images, it is often hard to come up with accurate RoI to pair with all the objects in a cervical image by using RoI with limited directions. The fine-grained, accurate RoI that follow directions and scales of actual boundaries of SSE suffer from high computational complexity during region identification and localization phases. For these reasons, most research has been focused on the analysis of manually selected RoI, making it difficult to replicate results on new data and ignoring the localization problem, which involves identifying RoI in new images. Early CHI image classification studies mainly focused on the discriminating models from the raw color input images to identify diagnostic elements for cell segmentation and differentiate them as RoI [6] or histological primitives [7, 8]. Most of them aim to image processing and identify areas of interest at the tissue level using histological primitives at the cellular level [9, 10] for cancer diagnosis. A set of studies on histology image analysis [11–13] utilize feature extraction and different attention strategies without relying on the RoI. However, as mentioned in [12], hand-crafted color and texture features are rarely sufficiently robust, and any unlabeled object without a corresponding bounding box can be the source of an incorrect learning signal [14]. Superior technical solutions for SSE identification can be found in [15, 16; however, to some extent, they also rely on the annotated SSE Finally, for many reasons, including concerns over privacy and confidentiality, a sufficient number of medical datasets of cervical histology microscopy could not be found in the public domain. We solve the problem of automatic localization and identification of the SSE on a new histological image dataset and propose a new multi-stage approach involving automatic bb extraction and subsequent

classification with a deep neural network to form the RoI representing the SSE in CHI. We demonstrate that this approach provides precise SSE identification even for the small size of the SSE in CHI with an overlapping clump of cells or masking by artifacts. Our specific contributions include:

- The CHDM-I dataset containing 171 full-size color images of the cervical histology microscopy, and CHI-II dataset containing 1049 fragments of microscopy. Compared with [13, 15, 16, 25], the CHDM-I proposes the largest number of samples among known public datasets.
- A method of automatic forming bb for RoI-based epithelium image segmentation.
- RoI construction pipeline based on bb, which guarantees efficiency and low complexity during region identification and localization phases.
- Assessment of the effectiveness of our approach through quantitative experiments with a validation of the findings by expert pathologists. Experiments also show that the proposed RoI identification approach can be used with other detector architectures providing significant improvements in the classification performance.

This paper is organised as follows. Section 2 discusses the related works. In Sect. 3, we present the pipeline for CHI processing and RoI identification. Section 4 describes experiments with presented datasets. Section 5 provides the conclusions.

2 Related Work

Although RoI localization and identification is a well-known problem in analyzing histological images, there is still no general approach to all kinds of histology images. Much recent progress on an interpretation of the histology slide images has benefited a lot from the deep learning modes [10, 15, 17–21], including adversarial neural networks [17], trained on labeled data for basal membrane segmentation to detect cancer micro invasions; DenseNet [18] for tumor metastasis detection as the RoI. The framework [18] comprises a patch-based classifier, an improved adaptive sampling method and a postprocessing filter on annotated data. A graph convolution network that admits a graph-based RoI representation [10] to incorporate local inter-patch context and, as in previous cases, RoI annotated data were used for RoI image classification. A comprehensive solution for identifying SSE as an area of interest is presented in [15]. RoI were used for differential diagnosis of cervical intraepithelial neoplasia (CIN). The procedure for epithelium localization was discussed in more detail in [19]. The classification of areas of interest in accordance with the CIN degree class using the DeepCIN network was proposed in [20, 21]. RoI identification was focused on differentially informative vertical segment regions [20]. Another group includes semi-supervised and weakly supervised techniques. A Multilayer Hidden Conditional Random Field framework for the CHI classification is an example weakly-supervised approach proposed in [13], where the CHI are mixed with the complex nucleus, interstitial and tissue fluid. Here, an immunohistochemical stained CHI dataset was used to test the effectiveness of the proposed model for the CHI classification. The classification was carried out without pre-processing in order to detect the area of interest. Early research on the analysis of digital slides of

cervical SSE [22] considers the threshold-based semi-automatic segmentation approach for obtaining the contours of cervical cancer RoI. Finally, a large group of unsupervised techniques [9, 23–25] demonstrate promising results in RoI identification and feature extraction. The detection framework using a bounding box to surround RoI for lung cancer images [9] offers fine-detailed, boundary-adherent super-pixel segmentation. This approach comprised super-pixel segmentation and super-pixel classification for RoI identification. Another approach [23] utilizes image-to-image translation for cancerous regions detection in histology images. It is based on training a model on tissues without pathological changes and then using it to detect visual abnormalities, which are cancerous tissue lesions. The paper [24] discusses RoI localization in whole slide images of breast biopsy slides based on understanding the visible patterns and predicting the diagnostically relevant areas. In [25], a region-based segmentation and grey-level co-occurrence matrix (GLCM) were applied for feature extraction and classification. It was noted that color and morphology of SSE show wide variability across different samples and even within the same image. Therefore, the simple segmentation approach demonstrates poor effectiveness for the SSE segmentation from cervical histological digital slides.

3   Method

In this section, we present the general pipeline of cervical digital histology image processing and RoI identification enriched with a new procedure of automatic bb construction embedded in this process. We start with data processing of cervical slide images to achieve out edge of SSE. Then we introduce the procedure of automatic bb construction. Third stage includes bb decomposition on patches and classification. Finally, we perform epithelium RoI identification and assessment. An overview of the methodology is shown in Fig. 2. Each stage consists of several procedures discussed below.

3.1   Cervical Slide Image Processing

The process begins with traditional image processing to form a curve that defines the lateral border (outer edge) of the tissue. Tissue can be epithelium or not. To accomplish this, the following procedures are used: (a) converting the RGB color model to the grayscale model, (b) blurring the image according to Gaussian, (c) image binarization using thresholding function, (d) cervical contour detection. All procedures are applied to low-resolution 15% reduced images (initial image size is 4096×3288, reduced size is 614×493). Threshold, the length of the tangent, and the width and height of the bounding boxes are chosen empirically based on the low-resolution images. The greyscale value is computed as the weighted average of the RGB values as Greyscale $= 0.299R + 0.587G + 0.114B$ [26]. Then Gaussian blur is applied to reduce the high-frequency components of the image [27]. Image thresholding converts a grayscale images to a black and white ones, where white pixels correspond to the background (no tissue), and the black pixels correspond to the tissue. The search for the contour of black pixels leads to the selection of the contours of the tissue surface and image boundaries. Further, the contours coinciding with the borders of the image are removed, and thus only the curve remains, indicating the outer surface of the tissue.

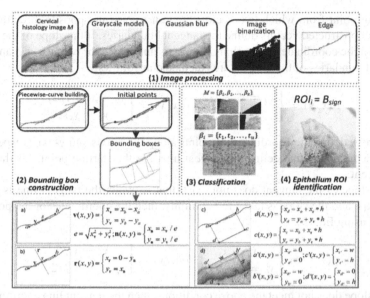

Fig. 2. An overview of proposed approach: (1) cervical slide image processing procedure, (2) bb construction presents piecewise curve and bb constraction (a, b, c, d shows bb constraction steps), (3) classification and (4) epithelium RoI identification.

3.2 Bounding Box (bb) Construction Procedure

When plotting the contour of the tissue, the coordinates are stored in two arrays, the coordinates along the x-axis and the coordinates along the y-axis. Images have an origin in the upper left corner; thus, the y-axis is inverted. Since the number of points per tangent and the length/width of the bb values are indicated relative to the initial dimensions of the image, we reduce these values proportionally to the image reduction.

$$q' = q \cdot \left(\tfrac{z}{100}\right),\tag{1}$$

where q denotes the initial value, z denotes the reduction percentage of the original image, and q' is the new value. Shaping bb involves shaping piecewise curves and shaping rectangles, which are the basis of bb.

The Contour Processing. The entire length of the contour is computed iteratively until all points of the contour have been achieved. During each iteration, a separate fragment of the contour is processed, and its length depends on the number of points included in the fragment. In addition, each iteration is accompanied by a search for a tangent of indefinite length by fitting a polynomial using the least squares method [28]. For each fragment of the contour, the average value of the coordinates along the x-axis is calculated. Resulting value is compared with the coordinates of each point along the x-axis. The point with the least difference is used to draw a tangent of fixed length.

Constructing a fixed-length tangent involves finding two points that define the tangent's boundaries. The input data are the length of the tangent, the slope of the tangent,

and starting point from which two vectors are constructed in opposite directions. The ends of the constructed vectors define the tangent boundaries. If the slope of the tangent is zero, then the coordinates (x, y) along the x-axis and y-axis for two points a and b that define the boundaries of the tangent are calculated as follows

$$a(x, y) = \begin{cases} x_a = x_s - l/2, \\ y_a = y_s, \end{cases} \quad b(x, y) = \begin{cases} x_b = x_s + l/2, \\ y_b = y_s, \end{cases} \tag{2}$$

where x and y define the coordinates of points along the x-axis and y-axis, respectively, a and b are the points that define the tangent line, s is the starting point, l is the length of the tangent.

If the slope of the tangent does not exist, that is, when the tangent line is parallel to the y-axis, and the slope is taken to be infinity, then the coordinates of the points are calculated using Eq. (3)

$$a(x, y) = \begin{cases} x_a = x_s, \\ y_a = y_s - l/2, \end{cases} \quad b(x, y) = \begin{cases} x_b = x_s, \\ y_b = y_s + l/2. \end{cases} \tag{3}$$

If the slope does not meet the above conditions, then the tangent line coordinates are calculated as follows. First, the change in coordinates Δx along the x-axis and Δx along the y-axis is calculated:

$$\Delta x = \frac{\frac{l}{2}}{\sqrt{1+m^2}}, \, \Delta y = \Delta x \cdot m, \tag{4}$$

where m is the slope. Then, the coordinates of the points of the tangent line are calculated using Eq. (5)

$$a(x, y) = \begin{cases} x_a = x_s - \Delta x, \\ y_a = y_s - \Delta y, \end{cases} \quad b(x, y) = \begin{cases} x_b = x_s + \Delta x, \\ y_b = y_s + \Delta y. \end{cases} \tag{5}$$

Owing this, the contiguous straight applied lengths are realized, making up a piecewise-specified curve, most closely corresponding to one obtained at the previous stage. As a result, it generates n-dimensional continuous piecewise linear function $f : \mathbb{R}^n \to \mathbb{R}$, where $\mathbb{R}$ is the set of points after processing stage, pointing to the tissue, and $\mathbb{R}^n$ is the set of points of the piecewise linear straight lines that best fits the original curve.

The bb Building and Extraction. The bbs are constructed through the forward and backward vectors. The coordinates of tangent line of a certain length are used to achieve the coordinates of the direction vector $v(x, y)$. Then, $\mathbf{v}$ is turned to the normalized direction vector $\mathbf{n}(x, y)$. First, the scalar e of the space of $\mathbf{v}$ is calculated as it is presented in Algorithm 1, and used to achieve coordinates of $\mathbf{n}$. Then $\mathbf{n}$ is rotated 90° to obtain a new normalized vector $\mathbf{r}(x, y)$ which is used to form the sides of the rectangle that is the basis of the bb. Next, $c(x, y)$ and $d(x, y)$ the coordinates of the two unknown vertices of the bb are calculated. Thus, having a and b, the known vertices of the bb rectangle, h is the height of the rectangle, and $\mathbf{r}$ is the normalized vector rotated by 90°, c and d, the unknown vertices of the rectangle are computed using Algorithm 1.

Algorithm 1: Bounding box construction

Input: $f: \mathbb{R}^n \to \mathbb{R}$
Parameter: a, b, h
Result: $\beta_i(a, b, c, d) \epsilon M$
Get the direction vector for given points a, b
$$\mathbf{v}(x, y) = \begin{cases} x_v = x_b - x_a \\ y_v = y_b - y_a \end{cases}$$
Normalize the vector $\mathbf{v}$
$$e = \sqrt{x_v^2 + y_v^2}$$
$$\mathbf{n}(x, y) = \begin{cases} x_n = \dfrac{x_v}{e} \\ y_n = \dfrac{y_v}{e} \end{cases}$$
Rotate the vector 90 degrees by swapping x and y, and inverting one of them
$$\mathbf{r}(x, y) = \begin{cases} x_r = 0 - y_n \\ y_r = x_n \end{cases}$$
Create a new line at b pointing in the direction of $\mathbf{v}$
$$\mathbf{c}(x, y) = \begin{cases} x_c = x_b + x_r * h \\ y_c = y_b + y_r * h \end{cases}$$
Create a new line at a pointing in the direction of v
$$\mathbf{d}(x, y) = \begin{cases} x_d = x_a + x_r * h \\ y_d = y_a + y_r * h \end{cases}$$

The obtained coordinates of all four vertices are used for bb β_i construction and visualization. The generated bbs provide necessary fragments from the original full-size image, and coordinates of the bb vertices correspond to the reduced version of the image. For this reason, additional calculations of the bb vertex coordinates are required for the full-size image:

$$a(x, y) = \begin{cases} x_a = 100 \cdot x_a / z \\ y_a = 100 \cdot y_a / z \end{cases}, \quad b(x, y) = \begin{cases} x_b = 100 \cdot x_b / z \\ y_b = 100 \cdot y_b / z \end{cases},$$
$$c(x, y) = \begin{cases} x_c = 100 \cdot x_c / z \\ y_c = 100 \cdot y_c / z \end{cases}, \quad d(x, y) = \begin{cases} x_d = 100 \cdot x_d / z \\ y_d = 100 \cdot y_d / z \end{cases}, \tag{6}$$

where a, b, c, and d are the vertices of the rectangle and z is the reduction percentage of the original image.

Next, the coordinates of the supplementary rectangle are determined, which has identical dimensions, but does not have a slope and is located at one of the vertices at the point of origin. The coordinates of the outlined rectangle are defined as

$$a'(x, y) = \begin{cases} x_{a'} = 0 \\ y_{a'} = 0 \end{cases}, \quad b'(x, y) = \begin{cases} x_{b'} = w \\ y_{b'} = 0 \end{cases},$$
$$c'(x, y) = \begin{cases} x_{c'} = w \\ y_{c'} = h \end{cases}, \quad d'(x, y) = \begin{cases} x_{d'} = 0 \\ y_{d'} = h \end{cases}, \tag{7}$$

where a', b', c' and d' are the vertices of the construction rectangle, and w and h are the width and height of bb.

The coordinates of the vertices of the construction rectangle and the bb, give the perspective transformation matrix, which is used to extract a fragment of an image from a full-size image by deforming the rotated bb to obtain a straightened rectangle.

3.3 Extracted bb Classification

After bb extraction, a new dataset of histological image fragments is generated. Depending upon the presence or absence of SSE, all extracted fragments are marked with a positive class label in there any SSE, and a negative class label in the absence of SSE in the bb. The resulting dataset is used to train the neural network model.

3.4 Epithelium RoI Identification

The microscopic image M includes a certain amount of bbs β which depends on settings of contour processing stage and number of obtained tangents. We model the microscopy image M as a set of k extracted bb β: $M = \{\beta_1, \beta_2, ..., \beta_k\}$, where each bb $\beta_i = \{t_1, t_2, ..., t_u\}$ is represented by a set of u patches t_i. Each patch is represented by the following expression $t_i = \left(P_i^O\right)$, $1 \leq i \leq u$. For the i-th patch t_i, P_i^O is a set of values of the probabilities of belonging of the patch to the labels of the classes of the set of labels O. The set of labels of the classes O in the proposed approach is represented as $O_k = \{o_k^{neg}, o_k^{pos}\}$, $1 \leq k \leq u$, where o_k^{neg} is the class label of the k-th patch t_i indicating the absence of SSE in the patch, and o_k^{pos} is the class label of the k-th patch t_i indicating the presence of SSE in the patch. Based on this, we describe P_i^O as follows: $P_i = \{p_i^{neg}, p_i^{pos}\}$, $0 \leq p \leq 1$. Since each selected bb may contain or may not contain SSE of cervical microscopy, they are defined as significant or insignificant, depending on the patch class labels obtained as a result of the classification and the probabilities of this class $\beta_i = \underset{i \in [o^{pos}, o^{neg}]}{argmax} \{t_i\}$. If a majority of the o^{pos} patch class positive labels are associated with presence of SSE, the β_i bb is defined as significant; otherwise, β_i bb is qualified as insignificant, i.e. $\beta_i' = \emptyset$. Hence, each image M can contain combined sets of two types of bb, B_{in} and B_{sign}, where B_{in} is a set of insignificant bb and B_{sign} denotes the dataset of significant bb containing SSE In these ways, the image defined as $M = B_{in} \cup B_{sign}$, $B_{in} \cap B_{sign} = \emptyset$, where insignificant set of bb B_{in} represents an empty set of objects $B_{in} = \emptyset$ subject to $\beta_i' = \emptyset$ and $1 \leq i \leq j$ and significant set of bb B_{sign} represents a set of patches labeled with class o^{pos} with a probability value $p = argmax_i\{P_i\}$. Thus, we get B_{sign} for β_i' subject to $\beta_i' \neq \emptyset$ and $1 \leq i \leq f$. As a result, RoI$_i$ of the i-th microscopic image M_i with SSE is defined as RoI$_i = B_{sign}$.

4 Experiments

The experiments were conducted on cervical histology images datasets CHI-I and CH-II developed with the assistance of medical professionals and expert pathologists and use of the proposed method for constructing bb and SSE RoI identification. The software implementation was carried out using the Python programming language [29] and the OpenCV library [30]. The consultations of medical experts was provided at the processing stage to determine the parameters of the SSE: (1) the threshold value that cuts off image fragments without a tissue site; (2) the size of the bounding box based on the height of the epithelium. Consultations with medical experts were carried out at the stage of training the model to annotate the obtained fragments and when testing the proposed approach for validating the obtained fragments for the presence of SSE.

4.1 Dataset

For this research, we created two CHI datasets captured during the years 2018, 2019 and 2020 and provided by the Department of Pathology at the Municipal Institution "Severodonetsk City Multidisciplinary Hospital", Severodonetsk, Ukraine. Histological slides were made by freezing and paraffin wire methods, stained by hematoxylin and eosin staining. The thickness of the sections and the degree of coloration vary. Data are fully anonymized. Written informed consent was obtained from all subjects (patients) in this study. Digital slides were acquired at 10 × objective magnification using Carl Zeiss Primo Star, SIGETA UCMOS camera and archived in 24-bit color JPEG format. Acquisition software is NIS-Elements F 3.2. The images have a resolution of 4096 × 3288 pixels.

The CHI-I dataset contains 171 color images of the cervical histology microscopy, 135 samples of cervix connective tissue with SSE and 36 samples without SSE CHI-I has two identifiers: (1) Image ID, the number of the histological specimen. One patient and, therefore, one diagnosis may correspond to several specimens belonging to one diagnostic case (visit); (2) Visit ID, the unique identifier for one diagnostic case (visit).

The CHI-II dataset contains 1049 fragments of microscopy, 644 bbs of positive class (contain SSE) and 405 bbs of negative class (background and/or artifacts without SSE). All extracted bbs inherit the visit ID from CHI-I. The set descriptions also specify the hyperparameters of the bb that make up the CHDM-II dataset: threshold lower limit, bb width and bb height. RoI from CHI-II were annotated by expert pathologists.

4.2 Procedure

The cervical image processing stage forms an outer edge curve of tissue. To process the image, the following parameters were used: Gaussian Kernel Size for Gaussian Blur function (25,25), threshold value = 230, number of points in one curve section = 1500. To avoid issues relating to edge detection, initial images must be set up horizontally so that the outer surface of SSE is directed to the right or upward, possibly at an angle.

Piecewise curves are formed iteratively until all points of the contour obtained at the previous stage have been processed. During each iteration, a separate contour fragment is processed, and its length depends on the set number of points included in the fragment. Each iteration is accompanied by the search and construction of a tangent of indefinite length. Further, for each fragment of the contour, the average value of the coordinates of the points along the x-axis is calculated. The obtained value is compared with the coordinates of each point of the fragment along the x-axis. The point with the least difference is determined by the original one and will be used to construct a tangent of fixed length. Finally, the coordinates of the starting points are used to calculate the angle of inclination of the straight line and form a rectangle. To obtain the rectangles (bb), the following parameters were used: bounding box width = 2250, bounding box height = 1500.

Bringing the reverse scaling of the resulting rectangles to the original image, we get bb - highlighted in green in the original image in Fig. 3a and in the form of separate highlighted fragments in Fig. 3b. The following image scaling options are used holds

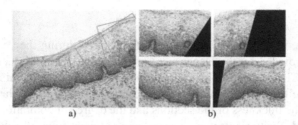

Fig. 3. Result of shaping and extracting bb.

the percentage by which image has to be scaled = 0.15. Depending on the specimen under study, the extracted fragments may not contain stratified squamous epithelium.

The extracted fragments were annotated by experts and formed the CHDM-II dataset. The fragment class was annotated as positive only if the extracted patch contains an SSE fragment image in height, i.e., from the basement membrane to the outer layer. The negative class includes microscopic fragments that do not contain an SSE, a background without tissue. Patches containing SSE, but not meeting the requirements of the positive class, were not included in the set - Single segments which are given "0". The number of fragments labeled with the positive class was 644 samples, the negative class 405 samples.

The fragments presented in the CHDM-II dataset are used to train the model. As was mentioned in [15, 24], the main challenges in this domain are the limited availability of annotated data, and images of varying sizes. To overcome these issues at the fragment classification stage, each of the extracted fragments was divided into 1000 overlapping patches with a patch stride s and fed to the network input. The total of 1,049,000 labelled image patches were generated, with 90% of the data used for training and 10% of data used for testing. The fragment class label is assigned according to the class of most patches.

The DenseNet [31] is trained for 100 epochs with an Adam optimizer with a learning rate of 0.0001 under early stopping conditions. Training parameters: batch size = 128, patch size = 224. Weights are used to balance the simulation results to obtain a correct model. The model is run on PyTorch platform [32] using nVidia GeForce RTX 2060 Super with 8GB of memory. Model training completed under 5 h.

4.3 Assessment

To evaluate the model, we used a test set consisting of 54 images, 28 images of the negative class and 28 images of the positive class. We evaluate the DenseNet network for classification as s.s.e/non-SSE RoI. The scoring metrics include accuracy (ACC), precision (PRC), recall (RR), F1-score (F1) [33]. The overall classification accuracy for both classes is 98%. We have used additional classification metrics, such as Fowlkes-Mallows index (FM), Matthews correlation coefficient (MCC). These metrics are more correctly reflected the quality of the prediction. With the test data we obtain FM = 1 and MCC = 0.959. Maximum possible value of these metrics is 1, which corresponds to the best classification possible, where all the elements have been perfectly classified. The proposed approach was validated using images that were not involved in training and

testing. The following parameters were used for validation: kSize = (25,25), threshold value = 240, one curve points = 1500, bb width = 1600, bb height = 1000, scale percent = 0.15. For model validation, we took several tough cases, e.g., SSE is highly compressed and skewed with respect to connective tissue, SSE boundaries and edges do not have a clear color delimitation with the fabric image. The selected fragments are classified using the trained model and analyzed by medical experts.

4.4   Comparison with State-Of-The-Arts

We compare our method to epithelium RoI identification with state-of-the-art histology slides RoI localization and detection. In the proposed approach the classifier is jointly trained on positive and negative image fragments. Table 1 summarizes the accuracy results of the current research. It shows the highest results achieved in the studies reviewed. The results show that the use of the proposed approach made it possible to achieve a higher classification accuracy compared to the breast cancer RoI allocation study by 18.4% and 19.44% than in studies [20] and [10], respectively.

Table 1. Quantitative comparisons with the state-of-the-art methods for RoI identification based on classification accuracy rates (%)

Histology RoI	ACC	PRC	RR	F1
Breast cancer [24]	79.60	–	–	–
Breast cancer[10]	78.56	–	–	–
Lung cancer [9]	–	71.27	73.33	–
Anomaly (cancerous) [23]	–	–	–	92
Basal membrane [17]	–	61.2	63.6	62.4
Cervical intraepitelial neoplasia [20]	88.5	–	–	88.0
Cervical cancer [13]	–	93.75	**100**	91.43
Cervical SSE [15]	97.8	–	–	95.6
Cervical SSE, Ours	**98**	**96**	**100**	**98**

The results show that the proposed approach to identifying epithelium RoI allows achieving more accurate classification results than the classification results in current research aimed at histology slides RoI detection.

5   Conclusion

In this paper, we presented an approach to identifying epithelium RoI in cervical digital slides. To implement the proposed approach, we have created a cervical digital slides dataset. We used a processing step that included color model transformation, image blurring, image binarization and edge detection to highlight the curve indicating the outer

edge of the cervical tissue. We proposed a new method for bb building and extraction, which allows isolating fragments of SSE from cervical digital slides, thus, creating a dataset of patches containing epithelium and not containing epithelium for further training of the classification model. The results demonstrate that the proposed approach made it possible to achieve classification accuracy up to 98% which is higher compared to the related works. Also, we have proposed a new method for identifying epithelium RoI in cervical digital slides. The proposed technique is also applicable in other histology images where the lateral border of epithelium should be seen as RoI. The CHI-I and CHI-II datasets, models, and code can be accessed on the CHI GitHub page [34]. We hope that the proposed approach for epithelium RoI identification in cervical digital slides will allow conducting more comprehensive studies to analyze the diagnostic patterns of cervical diseases in histopathology.

References

1. Ho, J., et al.: Can digital pathology result in cost savings? a financial projection for digital pathology implementation at a large integrated health care organization. J. Pathol. Inf. **5**(1), 33 (2004)
2. Gurcan, M.N., Boucheron, L.E., Can, A., Madabhushi, A., Rajpoot, N.M., Yener, B.: Histopathological image analysis: a review. IEEE Rev. Biomed. Eng. **2**, 147–171 (2009)
3. Jaume, G., et al.: Quantifying explainers of graph neural networks in computational pathology. In: CVPR, pp. 8106–8116 (2021)
4. Zamzmi, G., Sachdev, V., Antani S.: Trilateral attention network for real-time medical image segmentation. arXiv preprint arXiv:2106.09201 (2021)
5. Ding, J., Xue, N., Long, Y., Xia, G.-S., Lu, Q.: Learning RoI transformer for oriented object detection in aerial images. In CVPR, pp. 2849–2858 (2019)
6. Chen, K., Zhang, N., Powers, L., Roveda, J.: Cell nuclei detection and segmentation for computational pathology using deep learning. In: Spring Simulation Conference (SpringSim), pp. 1–5 (2019)
7. Ginley, B., Jen, K.-Y., Rosenberg, A., Yen, F., Jain, S., Fogo, A., Sarder, P.: Neural network segmentation of interstitial fibrosis, tubular atrophy, and glomerulosclerosis in renal biopsies. arXiv preprint arXiv:2002.12868 (2020)
8. Hermsen, M., et al.: Deep learning-based histopathologic assessment of kidney tissue. J. Am. Soc. Nephrol. **30**, 1968–1979 (2019)
9. Junzhou, H., Li., R.: Fast regions-of-interest detection in whole slide histopathology images. In: Histopathology and Liquid Biopsy. IntechOpen, vol. 67 (2021)
10. Aygüneş, B., Aksoy, S., Cinbiş, R.G., Kösemehmetoğlu, K., Önder, S., Üner, A.: Graph convolutional networks for region of interest classification in breast histopathology. In: Medical Imaging 2020: Digital Pathology, pp. 113200K (2020)
11. Gu, J., Fu, C.Y., Ng, B.K., Liu, L.B., Lim-Tan, S.K., Lee, C.G.L.: Enhancement of early cervical cancer diagnosis with epithelial layer analysis of fluorescence lifetime images. PLoS One **10**(5), e0125706 (2015)
12. Li, X., Xu, Z., Shen, X., Zhou, Y., Xiao, B., Li, T.Q.: Detection of cervical cancer cells in whole slide images using deformable and global context aware faster RCNN-FPN. Curr. Oncol. **28**(5), 3585–3601 (2021)
13. Li, C., et al.: Cervical histopathology image classification using multilayer hidden conditional random fields and weakly supervised learning. IEEE Access **7**, 90378–90397 (2019)
14. Yang, Y., Liang, K.J., Carin, L.: Object detection as a positive-unlabeled problem. arXiv preprint arXiv. 20202002.04672 (2020)

15. Sornapudi, S., et al.: Cervical whole slide histology image analysis toolbox. medRxiv 2020.07.22.20160366 (2020)
16. Gallwas, J., et al.: Detection of cervical intraepithelial neoplasia by using optical coherence tomography in combination with microscopy. J. Biomed. Opt. **22**(1), 16013 (2017)
17. Wang, D., Gu, C., Wu, K., Guan, X.: Adversarial neural networks for basal membrane segmentation of microinvasive cervix carcinoma in histopathology images. In: 2017 International Conference on Machine Learning and Cybernetics, pp. 385–389 (2017)
18. Ruan, J., Zhu, Z., Wu, C., Ye, G., Zhou, J., Yue, J.: A fast and effective detection framework for whole-slide histopathology image analysis. PlosOne **16**(5), e0251521 (2021)
19. Sornapudi, S., et al.: EpithNet: deep regression for epithelium segmentation in cervical histology images. J. Pathol. Inf. **11**, 10 (2020)
20. Sornapudi, S., et al.: DeepCIN: attention-based cervical histology image classification with sequential feature modeling for pathologist-level accuracy. J. Pathol. Inf. **11**, 40 (2020)
21. Sornapudi, S., et al.: Feature based sequential classifier with attention mechanism. arXiv preprint arXiv:2007.11392 (2020)
22. Weyn, B., Tjalma, W.A.A., Vermeylen, P., van Daele, A., van Marck, E., Jacob, W.: Determination of tumour prognosis based on angiogenesis-related vascular patterns measured by fractal and syntactic structure analysis. Clin. Oncol. **16**(4), 307–316 (2004)
23. Stepec, D., Skocaj, D.: Unsupervised detection of cancerous regions in histology imagery using image-to-image translation. In: Proceedings of the IEEE/CVF Conference on Computer Vision and Pattern Recognition, pp. 3785–3792 (2021)
24. Mercan, E., Aksoy, S., Shapiro, L.G., Weaver, D.L., Brunyé, T.T., Elmore, J.G.: Localization of diagnostically relevant regions of interest in whole slide images: a comparative study. J. Digit. Imaging **29**(4), 496–506 (2016). https://doi.org/10.1007/s10278-016-9873-1
25. Wang, Y., Crookes, D., Eldin, O.S., Wang, J., Hamilton, P., Diamond, J.: Assisted diagnosis of cervical intraepithelial neoplasia (CIN). IEEE J. Sel. Topics Signal Process. **3**(1), 112–121 (2009)
26. Bovik, A.C. (ed.): The Essential Guide to Image Processing. Academic Press, New York (2009)
27. Nixon, M., Aguado, A.: Feature Extraction and Image Processing for Computer Vision. Academic press, New York (2019)
28. Simanca, S.R., Sutherland, S.: Mathematical problem solving with computers. The University at Stony Brook (2002)
29. Van Rossum, G.: Python programming language. In: USENIX Annual Technical Conference, vol. 41, p. 36 (2007)
30. Bradski, G., Kaehler, A.: OpenCV. Dr. Dobb's J. Softw. Tools **3** (2000)
31. Huang, G., Liu, Z., van der Maaten, L., Weinberger, K.Q.: Densely connected convolutional networks. In: Proceedings of the IEEE Conference on Computer Vision and Pattern Recognition, pp. 4700–4708 (2017)
32. Paszke, A., et al.: Automatic differentiation in pytorch (2017)
33. Pal, A., et al.: Deep metric learning for cervical image classification. IEEE Access **9**, 53266–53275 (2021)
34. CHI. https://github.com/beloborodova-t/CHI/tree/main/Data

Audio Feature Ranking for Sound-Based COVID-19 Patient Detection

Julia A. Meister[1]([✉])(iD), Khuong An Nguyen[1], and Zhiyuan Luo[2]

[1] University of Brighton, Brighton, East Sussex BN2 4GJ, UK
{J.Meister,K.A.Nguyen}@brighton.ac.uk
[2] Royal Holloway University of London, Egham, Surrey TW20 0EX, UK
Zhiyuan.Luo@rhul.ac.uk

Abstract. Audio classification using breath and cough samples has recently emerged as a low-cost, non-invasive, and accessible COVID-19 screening method. However, a comprehensive survey shows that no application has been approved for official use at the time of writing, due to the stringent reliability and accuracy requirements of the critical healthcare setting. To support the development of Machine Learning classification models, we performed an extensive comparative investigation and ranking of 15 audio features, including less well-known ones. The results were verified on two independent COVID-19 sound datasets. By using the identified top-performing features, we have increased COVID-19 classification accuracy by up to 17% on the Cambridge dataset and up to 10% on the Coswara dataset compared to the original baseline accuracies without our feature ranking.

Keywords: COVID-19 classification · Audio event engineering · Sound feature ranking

1 Introduction

A widely accessible, non-invasive, low-cost testing mechanism is the number one priority to support test-and-trace in most pandemics. The advent of COVID-19 has abruptly brought respiratory audio classification into the spotlight as a viable alternative for mass pre-screening, needing only a smartphone to record a breath or cough sample [3].

It has long been common knowledge that respiratory diseases physically alter the respiratory environment in a way that often induces audible changes [17]. Consequently, manually listening to lung sounds (auscultation) is a common method to identify and diagnose respiratory disorders. However, many abnormalities only subtly affect auditory cues, making the inherently subjective auscultation process error-prone even when performed by a trained medical professional [2]. To counteract subjectivity, automated audio classification approaches with promising results have become more and more common in recent years [1,2,9].

One of the main limiting factors is the lack of ground truth data which may be difficult to obtain, prone to limited population diversity, and requires medical training to label correctly. Because COVID-19 detection is a widespread and

G. Marreiros et al. (Eds.): EPIA 2022, LNAI 13566, pp. 146–158, 2022.
https://doi.org/10.1007/978-3-031-16474-3_13

critical problem, multiple universities and research institutions have published COVID-19 audio datasets [3,19]. This offers a unique opportunity to verify classification solutions on independently collected samples from a diverse population. The datasets have supported the development of a variety of applications with Machine Learning (ML) audio classification. However, at the time of writing, none have yet been officially endorsed for medical usage, largely because of the high accuracy and reliability expectations for such a critical healthcare task.

The paper gives a comprehensive overview of relevant audio features (Sect. 2) and identifies the most indicative ones for COVID-19 (Sect. 3). Finally, the findings are put into the context of existing literature (Sect. 4).

1.1 The Paper's Contributions

The rigorous feature analysis presented in this paper improves COVID-19 respiratory classification by optimising and holistically evaluating audio signal representations for Machine Learning (ML). The following contributions are made:

- *Audio feature analysis and ranking.* We performed an extensive comparative analysis and ranking of 15 sound features prevalent and less-common in audio classification. The evaluation was carried out on two independent datasets, allowing the findings to be generalised.
- *Highlighted effective features.* We identified sound-based ML features with strong discriminative performance that go against common rules of thumb.
- *Increased COVID-19 detection accuracy.* We improved accuracy up to 17% by incorporating new training features based on our feature ranking.

2 Audio Features Overview

As in any Machine Learning (ML) application, feature engineering is a vital step for COVID-19 cough classification. We provide a detailed overview of 15 audio features from a variety of signal domains (Table 1) before rigorously evaluating their performance.

2.1 Time Domain

Low-level features extracted directly from the signal are in the time domain. They may identify crackling sounds caused by secretions in the throat and lungs [17], and have been previously used for COVID-19 classification [3,19].

Root Mean Square Energy (RMSE). A measure of the signal's amplitude over N frames, see Eq. (1). x_n is the average energy per frame [15].

$$\text{RMSE} = \sqrt{\frac{1}{N} \sum_{n=1}^{N} x_n^2} \tag{1}$$

Zero-Crossing Rate (ZCR). The signal's sign change rate (Eq. (2)). x_n is amplitude at frame n of N. $sign(a)$ returns 1 if $a > 0$, 0 if $a = 0$, and -1 else [15].

$$\text{ZCR} = \frac{1}{2} \times \sum_{n=2}^{N} |sign(x_n) - sign(x_{n-1})| \tag{2}$$

Table 1. *Audio feature selection.* The 15 audio features evaluated in the paper.

Domain	Feature category	Name	Intuition
Time	Signal energy	RMSE	Loudness of the signal
	Waveform	ZCR	Percussive vs tonal
Frequency	Spectral	S-BW	Perceived timbre
	Spectral	S-CENT	'Brightness' of a sound
	Spectral	S-CONT	Prevalence of formants
	Spectral	S-FLAT	Similarity to white noise
	Spectral	S-FLUX	Rate of frequency changes
	Spectral	S-ROLL	'Skewness' of the energy
Time-frequency	Cepstral	MFCC	Timbre, tone colour/quality
	Cepstral	MFCC-Δ	Velocity of temporal change
	Cepstral	MFCC-Δ^2	Acceleration of temporal change
	Tonal	C-ENS	Pitch
	Tonal	C-CQT	Pitch
	Tonal	C-STFT	Pitch
	Tonal	TN	Pitch & pitch height

2.2   Frequency Domain

To reveal frequency information of digital audio, it is decomposed into its constituent frequencies. This domain may identify abnormal lung sounds caused by an infection by examining the signal's intensity [17]. A subset has previously been used for COVID-19 detection [3,19].

Spectral Bandwidth. Equation (3) shows energy concentration, i.e. variance of expected frequency E given energy P_k and frequency f_k in $1 \leq k \leq K$ bands [16].

$$\text{S-BW} = \sqrt{\sum_{k=1}^{K}(f_k - E^2 \times P_k)} \tag{3}$$

Spectral Centroid. Equation (4) shows the weighted and unweighted sums of spectral magnitudes P_k in the k-th of K subbands. f_k is the corresponding frequency [20].

$$\text{S-CENT} = \frac{\sum_{k=1}^{K} P_k \times f_k}{\sum_{k=1}^{K} P_k} \tag{4}$$

Spectral Contrast. Compare spectral peaks P_k and valleys V_k in frequency band k, see Eq. (5). N is the number of frames and $x'_{k,n}$ the FFT vector [7].

$$\text{S-CONT}_k = P_k - V_k = (\log \tfrac{1}{N} \sum_{n=1}^{N} x'_{k,n}) - (\log \tfrac{1}{N} \sum_{n=1}^{N} x'_{k,N-n+1}) \tag{5}$$

Spectral Flatness. Eq. (6) measures similarity to white noise. P_k is the signal's energy at the k-th frequency band s.t. $1 \leq k \leq K$ [10].

$$\text{S-FLAT} = \frac{(\prod_{k=1}^{K} P_k)^{\frac{1}{K}}}{\frac{1}{K} \sum_{k=1}^{K} P_k} \tag{6}$$

Spectral Flux. Equation (7) measures a signal's energy change between frames. $E_{n,k}$ is the k-th of K Discrete Fourier Transform coefficients in frame n [20].

$$\text{S-FLUX}_n = \sum_{k=1}^{K} E_{n,k} - E_{n-1,k}^2 \tag{7}$$

Spectral Rolloff. Equation (8) finds frequency f_R s.t. the energy accumulated below is no less than proportion S of total energy. P_k is energy in one of K bands [20].

$$\text{S-ROLL} = \arg \min f_R \in \{1, \ldots, K\} \sum_{k=1}^{f_R} P_k \geq S \sum_{k=1}^{K} P_k \tag{8}$$

2.3 Time-Frequency Domain

This domain shows a signal's frequency as it varies over time. We consider two types of features: cepstral (timbre or tone colour) and tonal (pitch).

Cepstral Features. Non-linear Mel-frequency Cepstrum (MFC) is ubiquitous in respiratory classification because it explores a signal's temporal frequency content. It has been previously used for COVID-19 [3,12].

Mel-Frequency Cepstral Coefficients. Equation (9) shows the signal's transformation. $s(k)$ is the log energy of the k-th of K coefficients at frame n [3].

$$\text{MFCC}_n = \sum_{k=1}^{K} s(k) \cos \frac{\pi n (k - 0.5)}{K} \tag{9}$$

MFCC-Δ. The first-order derivative of MFCC, velocity, represents temporal change and is often included due to its low extraction cost [4].

MFCC-Δ^2. The second-order derivative, acceleration, is commonly included because it may improve audio classification [4].

Tonal Features. Based on the human perception of periodic pitch [13]. Two types are considered: chromagram and lattice graph. Secretions are a common consequence of COVID-19 which may alter the pitch of in- and expiration [17].

Chroma Energy Normalised. Chroma abstraction considering short-time statistics within chroma bands. Normalisation makes C-ENS resistant to timbre [13].

Constant-Q Chromagram. Extracted from a time-frequency representation. The constant-Q transform (C-CQT) has a good resolution of low frequencies [8].

Short-Time Fourier Transform Chromagram. The difference to C-CQT is the initial transformation, in this case the Short-time Fourier Transform (STFT) [8].

Tonnetz. A lattice graph of harmonic information. Distances between points become meaningful by encoding pitch as geometric areas [5].

Table 2. *Sample counts of the datasets.* Each coswara participant has 'shallow' and 'deep' breath (B), cough (C), and breathcough (BC) recordings.

Label	Cambridge			Coswara-deep			Cos.-shallow		
	B	C	BC	B	C	BC	B	C	BC
COVID-19	111	111	111	81	81	81	81	81	81
Healthy	194	194	194	1074	1074	1074	1074	1074	1074
$\sum$	305	305	305	1155	1155	1155	1155	1155	1155

3   Experimental Method and Results

The 15 investigated features range from prevalent to traditionally excluded from audio classification. They were ranked based on the empirical results analysis of two independent datasets. We assume that patterns repeated across both datasets are likely inherent to the COVID-19 respiratory recordings.

3.1   Research Questions

Three research questions were formulated to inform the experimental design and results analysis. Each is focused on improving COVID-19 audio classification.

- What are the most predictive audio features for Machine Learning?
- Are the feature rankings comparable across independent datasets?
- How much does the performance accuracy of Machine Learning models improve by using the most dominant features?

3.2   The Datasets

Two parallel independent datasets were considered throughout the paper to indicate whether feature rankings were likely generally applicable: the *Cambridge* and *Coswara* COVID-19 audio datasets. The sample counts are shown in Table 2.

Introduced in [3], the *Cambridge dataset* is a collection of healthy and COVID-positive cough and breath recordings. The data we used is a curated set of 48kHz WAV file samples, collected April-May 2020. Additionally, the Indian Institute of Science has collected shallow and deep breath and cough recordings in the *Coswara dataset* [19]. Compatible samples from April-December 2020 were considered. For consistency, we filtered for COVID-positive and healthy participants.

3.3   Feature Engineering

Cleaning the audio data was especially important because the recording devices and environments were not controlled. The pre-processing steps were carried out with the Python-toolkit `librosa`, and included trimming the leading/trailing silences and normalising the amplitude to $(-1, 1)$.

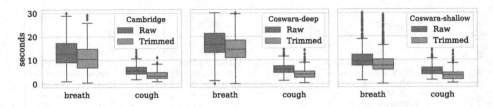

Fig. 1. *Sample lengths pre- and post-processing.* We trim leading and trailing silences (60 dB, empirically identified). Lengths were reduced by 1–3 s.

We evaluated 15 audio features from three signal domains (Sect. 2). To standardise feature dimensions for Machine Learning (ML) models regardless of sample length (1–30 s, Fig. 1), seven summary statistics were calculated to describe the feature distribution across frames: (i) minimum, (ii) maximum, (iii) mean, (iv) median, (v) variance, (vi) 1st quartile, and (vii) 3rd quartile. Only a small subset of features was considered for evaluation and ranking at a time to avoid overfitting (812 features total, Table 3).

Table 3. *Feature dimensions.* 812 features were considered. 7 Summary statistics were taken across frames to ensure consistent dimensions (sample length 1–30 s). To reduce overfitting risk, feature subsets were considered at a time for ranking.

Dimension	Features (min, max, mean, median, var, Q_1, and Q_3)
(1×7)	RMSE, ZCR, S-BW, S-CENT, S-FLAT, S-FLUX, S-ROLL
(6×7)	TN
(7×7)	S-CONT
(12×7)	C-ENS, C-CQT, C-STFT
(20×7)	MFCC, MFCC-Δ, MFCC-Δ^2

3.4 Results Description and Analysis

We identified the most informative features by evaluating two datasets in parallel. We propose that recurring predictive patterns are likely independent of the dataset, and should be strongly considered for future ML COVID-19 classification applications. Features were analysed in the following configurations:

- The Cambridge, Coswara-deep, and Coswara-shallow datasets.
- Breath (B), Cough (C), and BreathCough (BC) feature vectors. The latter is a concatenation of the previous two feature vectors, i.e. double the size.
- 5 models, selected for the variety in which they partition the label space: AdaBoost-Random Forest (ADA), K-Nearest Neighbours (KNN), Logistic Regression (LR), Random Forest (RF), and Support Vector Machine (SVM).

5-fold Cross-Validation ensured reliable results. We selected 3 metrics to compare the features' efficiency: *Receiver Operating Characteristic* (ROC), *Precision*

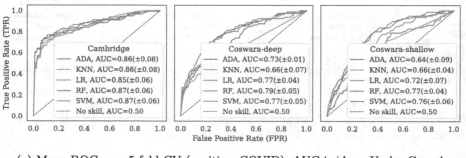

(a) Mean ROC over 5-fold CV (positive: COVID). AUC is 'Area Under Curve'.

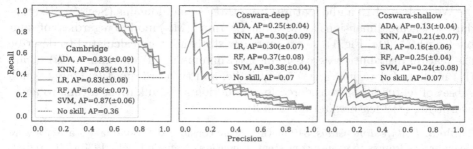

(b) Mean PR over 5-fold CV (positive: COVID). AP is 'Average Precision'.

Fig. 2. *BreathCough results.* Even though the ROC-curves look similar across datasets, the PR-curves reveal that Cambridge performed better overall. We also identified SVM and RF as the top-performing models. In PR-curves, the unskilled classifier corresponds to the dataset's positive label ratio.

(P), and *Recall* (R). PR curves are well suited to imbalanced data by omitting true negatives, counteracting ROC's optimism [18]. The mean over folds was a suitable indicator because the performance values passed the normality test [6].

Feature Categories. An overview of full feature vectors showed promising results, as most models outperformed their no-skill equivalent in ROC and PR-curves (Fig. 2). SVM and RF outperformed their counterparts across BC, B and C. Even though the two datasets had similarly shaped ROC curves, Cambridge had the best Average Precision (AP), and illustrates ROC's optimism on imbalanced datasets. An influential factor in Coswara's lower overall accuracies was the greater imbalance of COVID samples (Coswara 13:1 vs Cambridge 2:1, Table 2). Nonetheless, Coswara-trained models performed significantly better than their unskilled classifier counterparts (13–38% vs 7% AP, Fig. 2b).

BC signal domain results confirmed SVM and RF as the best performing models (Table 4). Considering SVM's BC ROC-AUC across all datasets, we note that the 4 feature categories were broadly ranked in increasing predictive efficiency (Cambridge, Coswara-deep, Coswara-shallow): *time domain* (79%, 64%, 56%), *tonal* (83%, 73%, 69%), *spectral* (85%, 74%, 72%), and *cepstral* (87%,

Table 4. *BreathCough 5-fold CV ROC-AUC results as mean(std).* SVM and RF achieved the highest accuracies across most domains. The feature categories were be ranked in the following increasing order: time, tonal, spectral, cepstral.

Dataset	Category	ADA	KNN	LR	RF	SVM
Cambridge	Time	67.17(.04)	77.96(.07)	76.01(.07)	78.21(.05)	**78.78**(.07)
	Spectral	87.09(.04)	85.34(.05)	84.17(.06)	**87.15**(.05)	84.84(.07)
	Cepstral	83.84(.05)	85.56(.07)	83.27(.06)	87.82(.07)	**87.15**(.06)
	Tonal	**84.74**(.09)	81.04(.05)	81.44(.04)	81.11(.07)	82.59(.07)
Coswara-deep	Time	55.65(.07)	62.34(.02)	54.21(.09)	**64.65**(.05)	63.94(.07)
	Spectral	65.77(.07)	68.18(.04)	72.03(.05)	71.76(.06)	**74.46**(.06)
	Cepstral	70.83(.06)	71.03(.03)	75.01(.05)	**77.55**(.06)	75.62(.08)
	Tonal	69.29(.06)	66.27(.02)	68.02(.03)	72.32(.06)	**72.98**(.03)
Coswara-shallow	Time	**61.63**(.04)	55.05(.06)	56.16(.09)	54.27(.07)	55.90(.09)
	Spectral	66.69(.04)	61.02(.05)	69.85(.05)	69.15(.05)	**72.32**(.04)
	Cepstral	63.13(.09)	68.35(.04)	65.83(.03)	**71.79**(.06)	70.62(.04)
	Tonal	58.37(.08)	63.98(.05)	65.21(.08)	67.17(.08)	**68.81**(.08)

76%, 71%). Spectral and cepstral categories achieved similarly high accuracies. Interestingly, the same ranking was prevalent for all 5 ML models, leading to the conclusion that the cepstral and spectral feature categories encode particularly informative COVID-19 data from breath and cough signals. A Repeated Measures ANOVA test [6] confirms that the feature domains lead to statistically significant differences in ROC score for all three datasets ($p < 0.02$).

Individual Features. We start with the best-performing SVM classifier before broadening to include all models to identify general predictive efficiency patterns. The results forming the basis of our analysis are available in Table 5. A Repeated Measures ANOVA test [6] verifies that the sample type leads to statistically significant differences in ROC score across all datasets ($p < 0.05$).

The majority of the 15 features significantly outperformed random guesses for COVID-19 classification across all datasets and sample types. The lowest accuracies were achieved by Coswara-shallow, matching previous findings. Similarities between Cambridge and Coswara-deep were underlined by sample types: BC achieved the highest mean ROC-AUC scores on average, whereas Coswara-shallow was split evenly between B and C. However, given all considered features, the Coswara-shallow dataset still showed its highest accuracy on BC samples since cepstral and tonal features were the most influential overall. MFCC (cepstral), S-CONT (spectral), and C-ENS/C-STFT (tonal) were the highest-scoring features in their categories, whereas the time domain was more variable.

Lastly, we note a surprising trend for MFCC. A prevalent rule of thumb suggests 12–13 coefficients for audio classification [3,7,19]. However, Fig. 3 shows that higher-order features provided discriminative information for COVID-19

Table 5. *5-fold CV ROC-AUC as mean(std).* The majority of features showed the most accurate results on the BreathCough (BC) vector. Feature categories were ranked in increasing accuracy: time domain, tonal, spectral, and cepstral.

(a) SVM, Cambridge data.

		B	C	BC
All	All	85.86(.07)	85.80(.05)	87.68(.06)
	All	72.77(.04)	74.90(.08)	78.78(.07)
Time	RMSE	72.28(.05)	76.45(.08)	77.88(.08)
	ZCR	64.59(.08)	69.73(.06)	71.40(.06)
	All	85.28(.06)	84.03(.07)	84.84(.07)
	S-BW	69.24(.08)	71.57(.04)	75.4(.08)
	S-CENT	73.45(.08)	70.06(.08)	78.07(.07)
Spectral	S-CONT	86.14(.06)	84.03(.08)	85.98(.08)
	S-FLAT	74.22(.07)	75.44(.05)	75.87(.06)
	S-FLUX	79.70(.08)	77.14(.06)	82.08(.06)
	S-ROLL	70.70(.07)	67.22(.04)	71.22(.06)
	All	86.25(.06)	83.98(.06)	87.15(.06)
Cepstral	MFCC	86.56(.04)	83.25(.05)	87.68(.04)
	MFCC-Δ	84.21(.04)	79.67(.08)	85.54(.08)
	MFCC-Δ^2	84.25(.09)	78.29(.07)	85.24(.09)
	All	79.69(.07)	78.06(.07)	82.59(.07)
	C-CQT	76.29(.06)	71.12(.09)	77.30(.06)
Tonal	C-ENS	77.56(.07)	72.11(.07)	83.50(.03)
	C-STFT	77.57(.05)	72.65(.03)	77.78(.07)
	TN	74.28(.04)	70.85(.04)	77.57(.05)

(b) SVM, Coswara-deep data.

		B	C	BC
All	All	76.79(.04)	70.85(.06)	77.15(.05)
	All	61.80(.04)	58.58(.06)	63.94(.07)
Time	RMSE	55.89(.10)	61.14(.07)	61.81(.07)
	ZCR	64.68(.03)	59.45(.13)	64.60(.04)
	All	76.34(.05)	66.74(.05)	74.46(.06)
	S-BW	61.63(.07)	63.51(.05)	65.46(.04)
	S-CENT	68.53(.06)	59.91(.06)	71.95(.05)
Spectral	S-CONT	74.89(.05)	63.42(.08)	73.57(.09)
	S-FLAT	61.77(.08)	59.86(.06)	61.14(.03)
	S-FLUX	63.79(.06)	62.76(.07)	67.20(.04)
	S-ROLL	65.35(.05)	63.16(.05)	67.58(.08)
	All	74.57(.03)	70.15(.09)	75.62(.08)
Cepstral	MFCC	74.24(.03)	70.74(.01)	75.38(.05)
	MFCC-Δ	64.85(.07)	68.90(.05)	68.99(.04)
	MFCC-Δ^2	66.65(.08)	67.72(.06)	70.72(.07)
	All	71.74(.05)	64.06(.06)	72.98(.03)
	C-CQT	67.87(.04)	62.78(.07)	61.50(.05)
Tonal	C-ENS	70.03(.07)	65.14(.03)	65.96(.05)
	C-STFT	67.01(.05)	61.80(.08)	68.19(.10)
	TN	60.90(.04)	62.84(.02)	61.33(.03)

on par with (Coswara-deep) or significantly outperforming (Cambridge) lower orders. This phenomenon was most noticeable in BC/B vectors and MFCC features. Since higher-order features contain information about details such as pitch and tone quality [11], we extrapolate that timber is highly relevant to COVID-19.

Discussion. Our extensive analysis, comparison, and ranking of 15 features has found recurring patterns of predictive efficiency for COVID-19 audio classification across independent datasets. There was a distinct category ranking consistent across models, sample types, and datasets (increasing): time domain, tonal, spectral, and cepstral. Contrary to the intuitive expectation, some 'complex' categories provided less discriminative information than 'simpler' ones (e.g. tonal/spectral features). However, this is justified when considering that tonal features describe pitch and so are more suited to tasks with melodic content.

The ranking underlines the significance of frequency-based features by elevating the spectral and cepstral categories describing timbral aspects and tone quality/colour. We have also shown that the common guideline to use only the first 13 MFCC features [3,7,19] was not applicable to COVID-19. Indeed, the

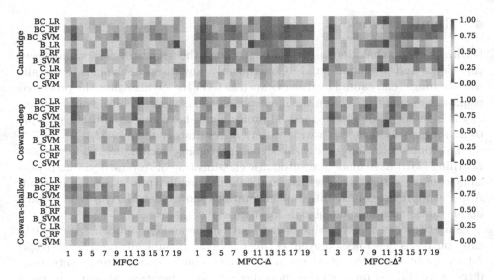

Fig. 3. *Normalised ROC-AUC of MFCC and derivatives for BreathCough (BC), Breath (B), and Cough (C) vectors.* Contrary to a common rule of thumb [3,7,19], 13+ features provided significant discriminatory data, and showed that timbral information is especially relevant to COVID-19 classification.

higher-order (timbre) features' predictive efficiency provided significantly more discriminatory information, especially for the BC and B feature vectors.

Taking a step back from the individual features, we note that the most prevailing pattern across all previous descriptions was that the concatenated BC feature vector outperformed the individual B and C vectors in most cases.

Given our insights, we compare our results to the published baselines, summarised in Table 6. The evaluated models were of similar type and complexity; The major difference was our introduction of new training features. We observe that our improved feature vectors significantly outperformed both the Cambridge and Coswara baseline accuracies by 10–17%, validating our feature selection.

Table 6. *Comparison to dataset papers' 5-fold CV baseline results.* The most comparable configurations are shown (feature processing and classification model).

Origin	Dataset	Sample	Model	ROC-AUC	Precision	Recall
This paper	Cambridge	BC	SVM	**87.68**(.06)	87.61(.07)	81.39(.07)
[3]	Cambridge	BC	LR	71.00(.08)	69.00(.09)	66.00(.14)
This paper	Cos-deep	BC	SVM	**77.15**(.05)	76.7(.05)	53.09(.03)
[12]	Cos-unknown	C	RF	67.45(—)	—	—

4   Related Work

During in- and exhalation, air travelling through the respiratory tract undergoes turbulence and produces sounds. Consequently, any physical changes to the airways or lungs (e.g. caused by diseases such as COVID-19) also alter the produced respiratory sounds [17]. Even though listening and evaluating lung sounds manually is inherently subjective, medical professionals have long used this technique to non-invasively diagnose a wide variety of respiratory diseases [2].

The popularisation of digital signal processing techniques and Machine Learning (ML) have made the automatic classification of respiratory sounds possible as a less subjective, low-cost, and patient-friendly (pre-)screening method. A literature review of existing implementations shows that ML can reliably pick up on subtle cues in audio signals for a variety of diseases.

Smartwatches and wearable devices have made audio monitoring for healthcare purposes feasible. Nguyen et al. apply a dynamically activated respiratory event detection mechanism to detect cough and sneeze events nonintrusively [14]. [1] presents classifiers distinguishing between asthma and pneumonia in pediatric patients. Lastly, an image classification solution with comparable results is developed in [2], using spectrograms as the input.

One of the first COVID-19 audio datasets containing breath and cough samples was presented in [3]. Using standard ML and audio processing techniques, the authors report 71% ROC accuracy for COVID classification. [12] and [19] consider further recording types such as vowel intonation and sequence counting, achieving 67% and 66% accuracy with ML models respectively.

5   Conclusion and Future Work

Our extensive comparative analysis of 15 audio features has provided significant insight into Machine Learning (ML) feature selection for COVID-19 respiratory audio classification and addressed the research questions laid out in Sect. 3.1. Primarily, we identified the most informative feature characteristics and verified their ranking across two independent datasets. Since the two feature rankings showed considerable overlap, we conclude that the features' relative salience was likely inherent to the respiratory signals rather than the evaluated datasets.

Throughout our analysis, a number of informative audio features were newly incorporated in the context of COVID-19 classification. In combination with our feature ranking, we achieved 88% and 77% accuracy on the Cambridge and Coswara datasets. Since the complexity of the signal processing and ML models is comparable to the baselines, the increase of up to 17% and 10% respectively was a consequence of our feature selection. Our established feature ranking could benefit future sound-based COVID-19 classification applications.

This paper provides a starting point for the holistic evaluation of respiratory audio features for COVID-19 classification. Considerations that could be addressed in future work are a comprehensive strategy to regularise different sample lengths, and to identify the most informative audio features for complex architectures such as Deep Learning neural networks.

Although sound-based COVID-19 detection was the primary purpose of this research, many other respiratory diseases and disorders could benefit from the development and improvement of automatic audio detection systems for diagnosis, treatment, and management. Therefore, the approach described in this paper could be generalised for the detection of other respiratory diseases.

Acknowledgements. We would like to thank Chris Watkins for the stimulating discussions, and University of Cambridge for access to the COVID-19 sound dataset. This research is funded by University of Brighton's Connected Futures, Radical Futures' initiatives, and Santander's Global Challenges Research grant.

References

1. Amrulloh, Y., Abeyratne, U., Swarnkar, V., Triasih, R.: Cough sound analysis for pneumonia and asthma classification in pediatric population. In: 2015 6th International Conference on Intelligent Systems, Modelling and Simulation, pp. 127–131. IEEE (2015)
2. Aykanat, M., Kılıç, Ö., Kurt, B., Saryal, S.: Classification of lung sounds using convolutional neural networks. EURASIP J. Image Video Process. **2017**(1), 1–9 (2017). https://doi.org/10.1186/s13640-017-0213-2
3. Brown, C., et al.: Exploring automatic diagnosis of COVID-19 from crowdsourced respiratory sound data. In: Proceedings of the 26th ACM SIGKDD International Conference on Knowledge Discovery & Data Mining, pp. 3474–3484 (2020)
4. Hossan, M.A., Memon, S., Gregory, M.A.: A novel approach for MFCC feature extraction. In: 2010 4th International Conference on Signal Processing and Communication Systems, pp. 1–5. IEEE (2010)
5. Humphrey, E.J., Cho, T., Bello, J.P.: Learning a robust Tonnetz-space transform for automatic chord recognition. In: 2012 IEEE International Conference on Acoustics, Speech and Signal Processing (ICASSP), pp. 453–456. IEEE (2012)
6. Iantovics, L.B.: Black-box-based mathematical modelling of machine intelligence measuring. Mathematics **9**(6), 681 (2021)
7. Jiang, D.N., Lu, L., Zhang, H.J., Tao, J.H., Cai, L.H.: Music type classification by spectral contrast feature. In: Proceedings, IEEE International Conference on Multimedia and Expo, vol. 1, pp. 113–116. IEEE (2002)
8. Korzeniowski, F., Widmer, G.: Feature learning for chord recognition: the deep chroma extractor. In: Proceedings of the 17th ISMIR Conference, pp. 37–43. International Society for Music Information Retrieval (ISMIR), New York (2016)
9. Laguarta, J., Hueto, F., Subirana, B.: COVID-19 artificial intelligence diagnosis using only cough recordings. IEEE Open J. Eng. Med. Biol. **1**, 275–281 (2020)
10. Madhu, N.: Note on measures for spectral flatness. Electron. Lett. **45**(23), 1195–1196 (2009)
11. Mitrović, D., Zeppelzauer, M., Breiteneder, C.: Chapter 3 - features for content-based audio retrieval. In: Advances in Computers, vol. 78, pp. 71–150. Elsevier (2010)
12. Muguli, A., et al.: DiCOVA challenge: dataset, task, and baseline system for COVID-19 diagnosis using acoustics. arXiv preprint arXiv:2103.09148 (2021)
13. Müller, M., Kurth, F., Clausen, M.: Audio matching via chroma-based statistical features. In: ISMIR, vol. 2005, p. 6 (2005)

14. Nguyen, K.A., Luo, Z.: Cover your cough: detection of respiratory events with confidence using a smartwatch. In: Conformal and Probabilistic Prediction and Applications, pp. 114–131. PMLR (2018)
15. Panagiotakis, C., Tziritas, G.: A speech/music discriminator based on RMS and zero-crossings. IEEE Trans. Multimedia **7**(1), 155–166 (2005)
16. Peeters, G., Giordano, B.L., Susini, P., Misdariis, N., McAdams, S.: The timbre toolbox: extracting audio descriptors from musical signals. J. Acoust. Soc. Am. **130**(5), 2902–2916 (2011)
17. Rizal, A., Hidayat, R., Nugroho, H.A.: Signal domain in respiratory sound analysis: methods, application and future development. J. Comput. Sci. **11**(10), 1005 (2015)
18. Saito, T., Rehmsmeier, M.: The precision-recall plot is more informative than the ROC plot when evaluating binary classifiers on imbalanced datasets. PLoS ONE **10**(3), e0118432 (2015)
19. Sharma, N., et al.: Coswara-a database of breathing, cough, and voice sounds for COVID-19 diagnosis. arXiv preprint arXiv:2005.10548 (2020)
20. Stolar, M.N., Lech, M., Stolar, S.J., Allen, N.B.: Detection of adolescent depression from speech using optimised spectral roll-off parameters. Biomed. J. **2**, 10 (2018)

Using a Siamese Network to Accurately Detect Ischemic Stroke in Computed Tomography Scans

Ana Beatriz Vieira[1]($\boxtimes$), Ana Catarina Fonseca[2], José Ferro[2],
and Arlindo L. Oliveira[1]

[1] INESC-ID/Instituto Superior Técnico, University of Lisbon, Lisbon, Portugal
{anabeatrizvieira,arlindo.oliveira}@tecnico.ulisboa.pt
[2] Department of Neurosciences and Mental Health, Neurology,
Hospital de Santa Maria, CHULN, Lisbon, Portugal
{acfonseca,jmferro}@medicina.ulisboa.pt

Abstract. The diagnosis of stroke, a leading cause of death in the world, using computed tomography (CT) scans, makes it possible to assess the severity of the incident and to determine the type and location of the lesion. The fact that the brain has two hemispheres with a high level of anatomical similarity, exhibiting significant symmetry, has led to extensive research based on the assumption that a decrease in symmetry is directly related to the presence of pathologies. This work is focused on the analysis of the symmetry (or lack of it) of the two brain hemispheres, and on the use of this information for the classification of computed tomography brain scans of stroke patients. The objective is to contribute to a more precise diagnosis of brain lesions caused by ischemic stroke events. To perform this task, we used a siamese network architecture that receives a double two-dimensional image of a CT slice (the original and a mirrored version) and a label that reflects the existence or not of a visible stroke event. The network then extracts the relevant features and can be used to classify brain-CT slices taking into account their perceived symmetry. The best performing network exhibits an average accuracy and F1-score of 72%, when applied to CT slices of previously unseen patients, significantly outperforming two state-of-the-art convolutional network architectures, which were used as baselines. When applied to slices chosen randomly, that may or may not be from the same patient, the network exhibits an accuracy of 97%, but this performance is due in part to overfitting, as the system is able to learn specific features of each patient brain.

Keywords: Ischemic stroke · Computed tomography · Symmetry detection · Image classification · Siamese network

1 Introduction

According to the *World Stroke Organization*, stroke is the second leading cause of death and disability in the world, with about 13 million cases annually [9].

© The Author(s), under exclusive license to Springer Nature Switzerland AG 2022
G. Marreiros et al. (Eds.): EPIA 2022, LNAI 13566, pp. 159–170, 2022.
https://doi.org/10.1007/978-3-031-16474-3_14

In this work only ischemic strokes were considered, since they represent a large fraction of all stroke events. Ischemic stroke occurs when a vessel supplying blood to the brain is obstructed, leading to damage or death of brain cells. It is usually caused by blood clots in a brain vessel or by narrowing of the blood vessels that irrigate the brain due to a process of atherosclerosis [15].

The diagnosis is made based on the evaluation of the symptoms and images resulting from Magnetic Resonance Imaging (MRI) or Computed Tomography (CT - used in this paper) exams. CT is most often chosen due to its widespread availability and short imaging time, but the resulting images are harder to interpret by automated means. The exams should be performed immediately upon admission, in order to identify and evaluate as rapidly as possible the existing lesions. The time elapsed since the onset of the stroke is crucial for the treatment and recovery of the patient. Recovery depends on the severity of the stroke, and the faster the diagnosis and treatment, the greater the chance of recovering the penumbra, which is the area around the ischemic region that can be recovered [15]. CT scans, obtained shortly after the incident, can detect the presence of ischemic or hemorrhagic lesions as well as the location and extent of the lesion, and exclude situations that can be confused with strokes [16].

There are several types of CT scans that can detect different changes in brain structures. The first exam most commonly performed is the Non-Contrast Computed Tomography (NCCT), since it enables the quick identification of the stroke type (ischemic or hemorrhagic) [14]. Depending on the type, other exams may follow. In our case, since only patients with ischemic stroke are considered, the exams that are usually performed later include Computed Tomography Perfusion (CTP) and Computed Tomography Angiography (CTA).

A human brain has two roughly symmetrical hemispheres, separated by the longitudinal fissure, which is a membrane filled with Cerebro-Spinal Fluid (CSF) [19]. This is usually known as the Mid-Sagittal Plane (MSP), because it is a virtual plane perpendicular to the brain, which divides it into left and right halves [19,21]. It is well known that the two hemispheres display both anatomical and functional asymmetries and this has been a significant topic of research [13]. Several results have shown that the asymmetry of the hemispheres is correlated with the presence of brain injuries [10,20], tumors [2,23], or mental illness [18].

The results presented in this paper are based on an approach that uses the level of symmetry between the two brain hemispheres to detect the presence or absence of stroke. The approach is based on the use of a siamese network, a particular neural network architecture developed to identify similarities between images, in this case symmetric ones[1].

After introducing the problem, we present some related work and describe the methodology used in the construction of the dataset, including image preprocessing and data augmentation. We then present and discuss the results obtained with the different architectures and the conclusions obtained from this work.

---

[1] Code available at: https://github.com/anagilvieira/siamese_network.git.

2   Related Work

One of the most effective methods for stroke segmentation was developed by Chen et al. [3], who proposed a framework consisting of two convolutional neural networks (CNNs) to segment stroke lesions using diffusion-weighted imaging (DWI), a specific MRI technique. One of the networks was a combination of two DeconvNets and the other one was a multiscale convolutional label evaluation network whose purpose is to evaluate the lesions detected by the first network, removing potential false positives.

Chin et al. [4] proposed a method that was used to assist neurologists in the diagnosis to improve the chances of recovery. This work developed a CNN for the early detection of ischemic stroke, which accepted as input CT images of the brain enriched with MRI data. Skull bone and other structures that might mislead the model were removed, since these structures exhibited similar pixel intensities as the ischemic area. The authors reported an accuracy of 93% in the classification task.

Recently, Herzog and Magoulas [8] proposed a method based on brain asymmetry to identify early dementia and its diverse stages, such as amnestic early mild cognitive impairment and Alzheimer's disease. They analyzed the structural and functional cerebral changes in both hemispheres using supervised machine learning algorithms and convolutional neural networks. The dataset was composed of brain asymmetries features, extracted from MRI scans from the Alzheimer's disease neuroimaging initiative database. The proposed pipeline achieved an accuracy that ranged from 75% to 93% for the mentioned diseases. Furthermore, this method offers a promising low-cost alternative for the classification of dementia and could potentially be useful in other brain degenerative disorders that are accompanied by visible changes in brain symmetry.

Inspired by the characteristics of the siamese network, Barman et al. [1] proposed a siamese neural network (DeepSymNet) for the detection of ischemic stroke from CTA images. This method enabled them to detect the changes in symmetry of vascular and brain tissue texture of the two brain hemispheres in parallel. The model was tested on a clinical dataset of 217 patients, and an AUC (Area Under the Curve) greater than 0.89 was obtained.

To perform brain symmetry studies on large neuroimaging archives, reliable and automatic detection of the mid-sagittal plane (MSP) is required to extract the brain hemispheres. However, traditional planar estimation techniques fail when the MSP presents a curvature caused by existing pathology or a natural phenomenon known as brain torque. As a result, midline estimates can be inaccurate. To address this matter, Gibicar et al. [6] suggested an unsupervised midline estimation method that consisted of three main stages: head angle correction, control point estimation, and midline generation. The technique was applied on a slice-by-slice basis for more accurate results and is able to provide accurate delineation of the midline even in the septum pellucidum (exactly in the middle of the brain), which is a source of failure for traditional approaches.

Our approach differs from these and other related works in that we use only CT data obtained at the time of hospital admission. This makes the problem

harder, since the changes in the brain images are more subtle, but also potentially more relevant in a clinical setting.

3   Dataset and Methods

The data used in this work was collected from ischemic stroke patients at *Hospital de Santa Maria*, in Lisbon. The dataset is composed of non-contrast computed tomography images, in DICOM format. The data was properly anonymized to preserve participant privacy and to meet all ethical requirements. In order to use only the most relevant slices of each NCCT, those in which the ischemic stroke can be detected, the 3D data was converted to 2D slices, each normalized to a size of 512×512 pixels. The final dataset used in the tests consists of slices chosen from different brain regions of different patients. The dataset is balanced and includes 340 images of each class, where one class corresponds to the absence of visible effects of stroke (and therefore expected symmetry of the hemispheres) and the other class corresponds to visible stroke effects (leading to a lack of symmetry). The images were annotated by one of the authors, Ana Catarina Fonseca, an expert neurologist.

Given the limited size of the dataset, we applied data augmentation techniques, namely Gaussian blur, to the data. In the experimental procedure, we used stratified 5-fold cross-validation where, besides making sure that all the folds contained approximately the same number of images for each class, we also ensured that all the slices corresponding to one patient were included in a single fold, in order to avoid overfitting and label information leakage.

3.1   Image Preprocessing

We used image preprocessing techniques to transform raw image data into a clean image data. This process was one of the most time-consuming since CT scan images are very complex and present several undesired characteristics.

Windowing. A CT scan consists of a set of points called voxels. The voxels represent elementary three-dimensional tissue volumes. The 'color' of each voxel is conventionally displayed as a shade of grey, corresponding to the density of brain tissue at that location and is called the attenuation value, which is given in Hounsfield Units (HU) [7]. It is a relative quantitative measurement of radio density used by radiologists in the interpretation of CT images, and is calculated as

$$HU = \frac{(\mu_v - \mu_w)}{\mu_w} \times K, \tag{1}$$

where μ_v is the calculated voxel attenuation coefficient, μ_w is the water attenuation coefficient, and K is an integer constant, standardized as taking the value 1000 [7]. To set the appropriate window for the color range, we define two parameters: windows level (WL), also known as windows center, and windows width

(WW). The windows level is the midpoint of the range of the CT numbers and is responsible for the image brightness, while the windows width is the range of the CT numbers that an image contains and is responsible for the image contrast.

All values above the upper level appear as white and all values below the lower level appear as black [22]. In our case we want to see the details of the brain, so we need to choose a window that maximizes contrast while not losing information. If the range is chosen poorly some gradations may poorly visible [22]. We found that picking a range between 0 and 80 for CTs, i.e., WL = 40 and WW = 80 provided best results, which coincides with the window most commonly selected for stroke analysis.

Figure 1 shows two sample images from an NCCT (WL:40, WW:80) and CTA (WL:60, WW:360), respectively, where a lesion caused by ischemic stroke can be seen near the left ventricle. The lesion is marked by a red circle. As is clear from the figure, the choice of the correct window enables us to see more details and, consequently, makes it easier to detect the asymmetry between the two hemispheres.

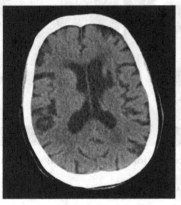 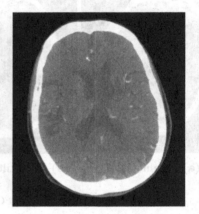

(a) Noncontrast Computed Tomography

(b) Computed Tomography Angiography

Fig. 1. Ischemic stroke lesions after two different windowing techniques were applied.

Head Tilt Correction. A common phenomenon in medical imaging devices is that they produce distorted brain images under certain circumstances, which can mislead visual inspection and lead to false clinical interpretation. The main reasons for this include the lack of a correct immobilization of the patients, inexperience of the technicians, and deficient calibration [10]. In order to correct the head tilt it is necessary to find the correct rotation angle, in order to align the MSP with the y-axis [8,19]. For that, the external contours of the brain were determined and an ellipse that best matches these contours was computed. Finally, the angle between the ellipse and the vertical axis was used to align the image. Figure 2 illustrates the same brain slice with and without head tilt correction.

Since the design of the external contours does not always fit the head optimally, there are images where the orientation of the head is not correctly aligned with the y-axis. This happens because of the slight (white) lines around the brain that causes interference in determining external contours.

Skull Stripping. Skull stripping is a fairly common process used with CT imaging because it is possible to focus only on the brain tissue, which is where the lesions are, and obtain a better segmentation of the different brain areas [4]. In fact, without the skull stripping step, the network attention was commonly focused on the eye region or on the bones around the brain.

Skull stripping was performed by subtracting from the original image an image where only the bone was visible, creating a resulting image with only the brain tissue. Figure 2 illustrates a slice before and after skull stripping.

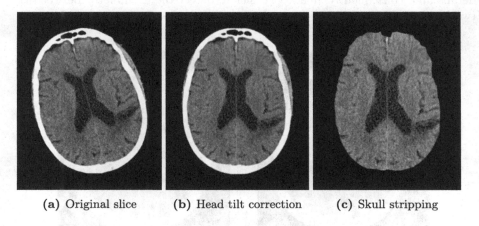

(a) Original slice   (b) Head tilt correction   (c) Skull stripping

Fig. 2. Main steps in CT images processing.

3.2   Symmetry Detection

Originally proposed for signature verification, similarity detection has been used extensively in various computer vision applications [1,5,11,12,17]. Similarity detection can be used to perform symmetry detection by using as inputs the original image and a mirrored image. We decided to use the siamese network (SiameseNet) to process two images, the original and a mirrored one. Unlike many other CNNs used in image recognition, this network does not assign a class to images, it only assesses the similarity between them.

The name is due to the fact that it is composed of two exactly equal convolutional neural networks that share the same parameters and weights. This network takes two images as input and calculates the similarity between them. Figure 3 represents the main stages of our siamese network. The first step is

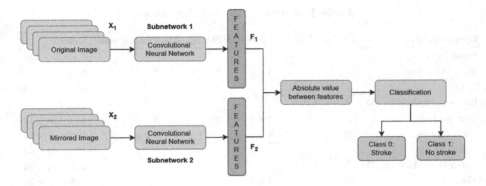

Fig. 3. Important stages of siamese network.

the feature extraction, where we used two CNNs (subnetwork 1 and subnetwork 2) to extract the features of each image. The network is trained with a label that reflects whether the two input images correspond to a visible stroke event (and are therefore less symmetric) or not. The output of each subnetwork was subsequently flattened (F_1 and F_2). The second step is the comparison between the two feature vectors. The difference of each subnetwork output is computed and the absolute value is used to generate a new feature vector D. Finally, the network output is the probability of the two input images being symmetric or not, reflecting the probability of stroke. The smaller the value of D, the more likely the images are to be symmetric and, therefore, to not exhibit evidence of stroke.

3.3 Proposed Architecture

Since the siamese network is made up of two equal networks, the network is trained, in each iteration, with a set of double images as input, the set size given by the batch size. One of the networks, subnetwork 1, takes as input the 'original' slices, with a resolution of 512×512, while subnetwork 2 takes as input the 'mirrored' slices, as shown in Fig. 3.

Table 1 shows in detail the characteristics of the different layers in our architecture. The feature extraction process is composed by 2D convolutional layers, 2D batch normalization layers, max pooling layers and a flatten layer, generating a feature vector with size 8192. The entire network uses ReLU activations, except for the prediction layer that uses softmax activation. After feature extraction and subtraction, two fully connected layers were used, the first generating a vector of size 1024 and the second generating a vector of size 2, one output unit for each class.

The model was trained and evaluated using stratified 5-fold cross-validation, for 200 epochs with a batch size of 32, using the ADAM optimizer with an initial learning rate of $\eta = 0.00001$. Since high weight values increase the chances of overfitting, L2 regularization with a weight factor $\lambda = 0.0005$ was used, applying a penalty for higher weight values. The model used 11M trainable parameters.

Table 1. Siamese network architecture.

Operation layer	Number of filters	Filter size	Stride value	Padding value	Output
Input layer					$1 \times 512 \times 512$
2D convolution	64	5×5	2	2×2	$64 \times 256 \times 256$
ReLU					$64 \times 256 \times 256$
Batch normalization 2D					$64 \times 256 \times 256$
Max pooling	64	2×2	2	0	$64 \times 128 \times 128$
2D convolution	128	5×5	2	2×2	$128 \times 64 \times 64$
ReLU					$128 \times 64 \times 64$
Batch normalization 2D					$128 \times 64 \times 64$
Max pooling	128	2×2	2	0	$128 \times 32 \times 32$
2D convolution	256	3×3	2	1×1	$256 \times 16 \times 16$
ReLU					$256 \times 16 \times 16$
Batch normalization 2D					$256 \times 16 \times 16$
Max pooling	256	2×2	2	0	$256 \times 8 \times 8$
2D convolution	512	3×3	2	1×1	$512 \times 4 \times 4$
ReLU					$512 \times 4 \times 4$
Batch normalization 2D					$512 \times 4 \times 4$
Flatten					8192
Fully connected					1024
Fully connected					2

3.4 Loss Function

When working with siamese networks, the most commonly used loss function is the contrastive loss, which is commonly used to compute a similarity score by calculating the Euclidean distance between the feature vectors [5]. However, since this is a classification task, we choose to use the cross entropy loss, given by $L(y_i, \hat{y_i}) = -(y_i \log \hat{y_i} + (1 - y_i) \log(1 - \hat{y_i}))$ where y_i and $\hat{y_i}$ are the actual class and the predicted class, respectively.

4 Results

To assess the performance of the siamese network architecture on this dataset, we performed an empirical comparison with two alternative baseline architectures, the SimResNet-18 and the ResNet-50. All models were trained using a PowerEdge C41402 server with an NVIDIA 32GB Tesla V100S.

ResNet-50. ResNet is a commonly used deep convolutional neural network architecture that normally exhibits good performance in image classification tasks. Other types of CNNs have difficulty optimizing the parameters during training because of vanishing gradients. ResNet minimizes these problem by using residual connections in parallel with the convolutional layers. We tested ResNets with 18 layers, 34 layers and 50 layers (three common variations of

ResNet) and found that the best performance was obtained using ResNet-50. With this model, we achieved 62% accuracy, using 23M parameters and 174 min of training time.

SimResNet-18. Initially motivated by the idea of combining ResNet and the siamese network architecture [17], we also tested an alternative approach where the ResNet is used only for the feature extraction step. The siamese network consists of two ResNets for feature extraction, where one of them accepts the original CT slice and the other accepts the mirrored slice. Since the ResNet uses a Global Average Pooling (GAP) layer after the last convolution layer, the resulting output is a feature vector with a size of 512, which is used to calculate the absolute value of the difference. The remaining components of the architecture are similar to those described for the SiameseNet. The feature vectors are subtracted, the absolute value of the difference is computed, and the images are classified into one of the two existing classes using a fully connected layer.

In this architecture, we tested different ResNet models, and after analyzing the number of parameters, the training time, and the results, opted for the 18-layer model. The hyperparameters used were the same as for the siamese network and the architecture used 11 M parameters. This approach reached 64% accuracy and required 154 min to train.

Experimental Results. Table 2 summarizes the classification performance of the proposed architecture, SiameseNet, compared with the SimResNet-18 and ResNet-50 baselines. The results presented in the table show that the siamese network clearly outperforms the other two models, with an accuracy and F1-values of 72%. The runtime for training the SiameseNet in the proposed dataset was 144 min. Although the overall accuracy was not very high in absolute terms, it is the best result known to us for this specific problem, ischemic stroke classification from CT scans.

Table 2. Model classification performance.

Model	Accuracy	Precision	Recall	F1-score
ResNet-50	0.62 ± 0.09	0.71 ± 0.14	0.47 ± 0.27	0.57 ± 0.17
SimResNet-18	0.64 ± 0.04	0.73 ± 0.12	0.48 ± 0.12	0.58 ± 0.07
SiameseNet	0.72 ± 0.13	0.75 ± 0.17	0.69 ± 0.25	0.72 ± 0.14

The low accuracy results obtained with ResNet-50 are most likely due to the fact that CT images have several features that make model learning difficult. When ResNet models are added to the Siamese network (SimResNet-18), we see an improvement in performance, although not very significant. Finally,

the siamese network architecture exhibits a considerable improvement in performance over the two baselines. However, the overall accuracy is still relatively low, mainly due to the fact that the dataset is small and the task very challenging.

The relatively high variance of the performance measures is essentially due to two factors. First, since the dataset is small and it cannot be guaranteed that all patients have the same number of samples, there is relevant variation on the fold size. In fact there are patients with 45 labeled slices and others with only 3 labeled slices. Imposing the restriction that all slices from the same patient were in only one of the folds is probably a significant source of performance variation between different folds.

In other experiments, when stratification was not used to guarantee that all the slices of one patient were in a single fold, we observed significant information leakage between the training and test sets, leading to the model not learning the features relevant to the problem but focusing on features that relate different slices of the same patient. In this case, when the dataset is split randomly, we obtained the results shown in Table 3. The results correspond to a very high accuracy for the SiameseNet (97%) but also for the two baseline networks. However, these results are not reliable nor reproducible in a clinical environment, since the network is using features that are not relevant to the problem, such as the dimension of the slices, or some other features that are only correlated with specific characteristics of the patient and not of the stroke effects.

Table 3. Model classification performance with random dataset splitting.

Model	Accuracy	Precision	Recall	F1-score
ResNet-50	0.89 ± 0.04	0.87 ± 0.08	0.92 ± 0.07	0.89 ± 0.05
SimResNet-18	0.91 ± 0.03	0.89 ± 0.04	0.93 ± 0.040	0.91 ± 0.03
SiameseNet	0.97 ± 0.02	0.96 ± 0.02	0.97 ± 0.03	0.97 ± 0.02

5   Conclusions and Future Work

We proposed to use a siamese network architecture for the detection of ischemic stroke, based on the fact that detected asymmetry of brain hemispheres is strongly correlated with evidence of stroke. The architecture obtained 72% accuracy and F1-score, on average, on an independent test set. Although the absolute value of the accuracy remains low and insufficient for clinical use, this architecture may become the starting point for other studies that use the lack of symmetry between the brain hemispheres to diagnose pathologies from CT scans.

During the development of the work, we took special care to avoid information leakage between the training and test sets, a phenomenon that leads to overfitting and limits reproducibility in a clinical setting. In some experiments,

we achieved unexpectedly high performance values, until we realized that the model was learning from features uncorrelated with the target task.

There are some aspects of the presented work that can be improved. One of these aspects is image preprocessing. Although the skull stripping process is mostly successful there are slices where small portions of non-brain tissue are mistakenly removed. This happens because all the white pixels in the image are removed when only the white pixels around the brain (bone) should be removed.

Another possible improvement is the removal of the CSF area since the intensity of the pixels is the same as the ischemic zone and can mislead the model.

Finally, the limited size of the dataset is one of the causes for the limited performance of the model. In total, slices from only 60 patients were used, with 35 patients associated with class 1 and 25 patients assigned to class 0. One avenue to increase the performance of the model would be to label more data and select the same number of slices from each patient, avoiding overfitting, data leakage, and selection bias.

Acknowledgments. This research was supported by the Portuguese Science Foundation, through the Projects PRELUNA - PTDC/CCI-INF/4703/2021 and UIDB/50021/2020.

References

1. Barman, A., Inam, M.E., Lee, S., Savitz, S., Sheth, S., Giancardo, L.: Determining ischemic stroke from ct-angiography imaging using symmetry-sensitive convolutional networks. In: 2019 IEEE 16th International Symposium on Biomedical Imaging (ISBI 2019), pp. 1873–1877. IEEE (2019)
2. Barzegar, Z., Jamzad, M.: Fully automated glioma tumour segmentation using anatomical symmetry plane detection in multimodal brain MRI. IET Comput. Vis. **15**(7), 463–473 (2021)
3. Chen, L., Bentley, P., Rueckert, D.: Fully automatic acute ischemic lesion segmentation in DWI using convolutional neural networks. NeuroImage Clin. **15**, 633–643 (2017)
4. Chin, C.L., et al.: An automated early ischemic stroke detection system using CNN deep learning algorithm. In: 2017 IEEE 8th International Conference on Awareness Science and Technology (iCAST), pp. 368–372. IEEE (2017)
5. Dey, S., Dutta, A., Toledo, J.I., Ghosh, S.K., Lladós, J., Pal, U.: SigNet: convolutional siamese network for writer independent offline signature verification. CoRR abs/1707.0 (2017)
6. Gibicar, A., Moody, A.R., Khademi, A.: Automated midline estimation for symmetry analysis of cerebral hemispheres in FLAIR MRI. Front. Aging Neurosci. **13**, 644137 (2021)
7. Goldman, L.W.: Principles of CT and CT technology. J. Nucl. Med. Technol. **35**(3), 115–128 (2007)
8. Herzog, N.J., Magoulas, G.D.: Brain asymmetry detection and machine learning classification for diagnosis of early dementia. Sensors **21**(3), 778 (2021)
9. Lindsay, M.P., et al.: World Stroke Organization (WSO): global stroke fact sheet 2019. Int. J. Stroke **14**(8), 806–817 (2019)

10. Liu, S.X.: Symmetry and asymmetry analysis and its implications to computer-aided diagnosis: a review of the literature. J. Biomed. Inf. **42**(6), 1056–1064 (2009)
11. Liu, X., Zhou, Y., Zhao, J., Yao, R., Liu, B., Zheng, Y.: Siamese convolutional neural networks for remote sensing scene classification. IEEE Geosci. Remote Sens. Lett. **16**(8), 1200–1204 (2019)
12. Melekhov, I., Kannala, J., Rahtu, E.: Siamese network features for image matching. In: 2016 23rd International Conference on Pattern Recognition (ICPR), pp. 378–383. IEEE (2016)
13. Miletto Petrazzini, M.E., Sovrano, V.A., Vallortigara, G., Messina, A.: Brain and behavioral asymmetry: a lesson from fish. Front. Neuroanatomy **14**, 11 (2020)
14. Öman, O., Mäkelä, T., Salli, E., Savolainen, S., Kangasniemi, M.: 3D convolutional neural networks applied to CT angiography in the detection of acute ischemic stroke. Eur. Radiol. Exp. **3**(1), 8 (2019)
15. Phipps, M.S., Cronin, C.A.: Management of acute ischemic stroke. BMJ **368**, l6983 (2020)
16. Pohl, M., et al.: Ischemic stroke mimics: a comprehensive review. J. Clin. Neurosci. **93**, 174–182 (2021)
17. Qiu, K., Ai, Y., Tian, B., Wang, B., Cao, D.: Siamese-ResNet: implementing loop closure detection based on siamese network. In: 2018 IEEE Intelligent Vehicles Symposium (IV), pp. 716–721. IEEE (2018)
18. Ribolsi, M., Daskalakis, Z.J., Siracusano, A., Koch, G.: Abnormal asymmetry of brain connectivity in schizophrenia. Front. Human Neurosci. **8**, 1010 (2014)
19. Ruppert, G.C.S., Teverovskiy, L., Yu, C.P., Falcao, A.X., Liu, Y.: A new symmetry-based method for mid-sagittal plane extraction in neuroimages. In: 2011 IEEE International Symposium on Biomedical Imaging: From Nano to Macro, pp. 285–288. IEEE (2011)
20. Vupputuri, A., Dighade, S., Prasanth, P.S., Ghosh, N.: Symmetry determined superpixels for efficient lesion segmentation of ischemic stroke from MRI. In: 2018 40th Annual International Conference of the IEEE Engineering in Medicine and Biology Society (EMBC), pp. 742–745. IEEE (2018)
21. Wu, H., Chen, X., Li, P., Wen, Z.: Automatic symmetry detection from brain MRI based on a 2-channel convolutional neural network. IEEE Trans. Cybern. **51**(9), 4464–4475 (2021)
22. Xue, Z., Antani, S., Long, L.R., Demner-Fushman, D., Thoma, G.R.: Window classification of brain CT images in biomedical articles. In: AMIA Annual Symposium proceedings 2012, pp. 1023–1029 (2012)
23. Yu, C.P., Ruppert, G., Nguyen, D., Falcão, A., Liu, Y.: Statistical asymmetry-based brain tumor segmentation from 3D MR images. In: Biosignals (2012)

Determining Internal Medicine Length of Stay by Means of Predictive Analytics

Diogo Peixoto[1], Mariana Faria[1], Rui Macedo[1], Hugo Peixoto[1], João Lopes[1], Agostinho Barbosa[2], Tiago Guimarães[1], and Manuel Filipe Santos[1]($\boxtimes$)

[1] Centro ALGORITMI, University of Minho, 4800-058 Guimarães, Portugal
hpeixoto@di.uminho.pt, {a80553,a81781,a70445}@alunos.uminho.pt,
mfs@dsi.uminho.pt
[2] Centro Hospitalar do Tâmega e Sousa, 4564-007 Penafiel, Portugal
a.barbosa@chts.min-saude.pt

Abstract. In recent years, hospital overcrowding has become a crucial aspect to take into consideration in inpatient management, which may negatively affect the quality of service provided to the patient. Inpatient management aims, through efficient planning, to maximise the availability of beds and conditions for the patient, considering cost rationalisation. In this way, this research has allowed the prediction of the length of stay (LOS) of each patient in the Internal Medicine specialty, with acuity, considering their demographic data, the information collected at the time of admission and clinical conditions, which may help health professionals in carrying out more assertive planning. For this study, were used data sets from the Centro Hospitalar do Tâmega e Sousa (CHTS), referring to a 5-year period, 2017 to 2021. The GB model achieved an accuracy of $\approx$96% compared to the DT, RF and KNN, proving that Machine Learning (ML) models, using demographic information simultaneously with the route taken by the patient and clinical data, such as drugs administrated, exams, surgeries and analyses, introduce a greater predictive capacity of the LOS.

Keywords: Length of stay · Machine Learning · Predictive analytics

1 Introduction

Currently, the constant increase in health expenses is notorious, and the financial pressures suffered by these are more and more striking. This highlights the high importance of resource management in this context and the relevance of finding ways to reduce these costs and optimise their use [1].

Furthermore, the increase in the volume of information stored by hospitals is significant, making it increasingly difficult to obtain useful information for decision-making. However, since this information is computerised, the application of Data Mining (DM) techniques has in recent years proved to be a valuable option for optimising hospital services. There are several applications of DM in health, both to assess the effectiveness of a treatment [2], the management of hospital resources [3], reduce health insurance frauds [4], among others.

G. Marreiros et al. (Eds.): EPIA 2022, LNAI 13566, pp. 171–182, 2022.
https://doi.org/10.1007/978-3-031-16474-3_15

In this study, is intended to predict the Length of Stay (LOS), corresponding to the number of days that a patient remains hospitalised in any health establishment. In this way, health professionals will be able to estimate how many patients will be admitted to the inpatient services, as well as the flow of future discharges, thus optimising hospital resources and reducing costs.

Within the scope of this project, the Design Science Research (DSR) methodology and the Cross Industry Standard Process for Data Mining (CRISP-DM) operational methodology were followed.

2 Background

2.1 Resources Planning in Hospital Settings

Overcrowding continues to be a problem faced by several hospitals worldwide. This problem is often caused by the lack of beds for inpatients, where hospitalisation management allows, based on an efficient planning, maximise the availability of beds considering the associated costs. However, this planning is complex due to limited resources and the need for prior knowledge of certain variables. It should be noted that ineffective planning leads to mismatches between resources and needs [5]. If resources exceed needs, there is a waste of resources that will lead to unnecessary costs, but if the opposite happens, there is overcrowding, which leads to a deterioration in the quality of service, an increased risk of spreading contagious diseases and a scrambling of human resources on an emergency basis [6].

It should also be noted that, due to the increase in the volume of information stored by hospitals, it is becoming increasingly difficult to understand that information and to obtain useful information for decision-making. Thus, the use of DM has become an increasingly viable and valuable option in recent years [7].

The LOS corresponds to the number of days that a patient remains hospitalized in any health care facility [8], undergoing a given type of treatment, from the date of admission to the date of discharge [9]. It should be noted that the use of this indicator (LOS), in addition to allowing the value of the costs that the patient represents for the hospital to be known, allows and evaluates the quality of the services provided to the patient, since a prolonged stay in hospital does not bring any benefits to the patient, exposed to a higher risk of adverse events [10].

2.2 Related Works

The use of Machine Learning (ML) techniques is increasingly applied to the prediction of LOS [8], allowing an optimization of hospital resources planning and management.

Hachesu et al. [8] estimated the length of stay of patients with coronary artery disease. In this study, 36 attributes referring to the patients' characteristics and clinical process (e.g., age, marital status, smoker, diabetes) were used. Decision Tree classification technique was applied to it, with an Accuracy of 83,5%, Specificity of 65,2% and Sensitivity of 97,1% (RW1).

Aghajani and Kargari [11] predicted the LOS in the general surgery department of Shariati Hospital. This study covered 30 variables regarding patient information available

at the time of admission and details of the discharge summary (e.g., number of surgeries and consultations). According to a classification approach, Decision Tree model was the one that performed best, with an accuracy of 88.9%, compared to the K-Nearest Neighbors model of 79.9%. It should be noted that three classes were considered, from 1 to 3 days, 4 to 5 days and 6 or more days. This study revealed that the type of surgery, the average number of consultations per day, the number of surgeries, and the number of days of hospitalisation before surgery were the attributes with the greatest influence on LOS (RW2).

More recently, Stone et al. [12] estimated the length of stay using data based on generic patient diagnoses from a hospital in Wales. This study treated LOS prediction as both a regression and a classification problem. However, the classification approach with the application of the Decision Tree algorithm stood out, with an accuracy of 75%, where two classes (short and long) were used. The attributes with the highest predictive value were age, postcode, gender, primary diagnosis and the first four secondary diagnoses (RW3).

Tien [13] also focused its study on predicting LOS, however, at the time of patient admission, based on a data source composed of patient demographic information, diagnoses, services, costs and treatments. To carry out this study, both in terms of data analysis and model building, approaching the problem from a multi-class perspective. This way, 6 classes were taken into consideration, namely, from 1 to 5, 6 to 10, 11 to 20, 21 to 30, 31 to 50 and 50 to 120 days. Among the developed models, Random Forest presented an accuracy of 65%, against 61% reached with Decision Tree model (RW4).

With the emphasis on the Covid-19 pandemic, the management of hospital resources proved to be an even greater challenge. Dina A. Alabbad et al. [14] predicted the LOS in the intensive care unit at King Fahad University Hospital, Saudi Arabia. The data source used included a total of 47 attributes related to information related to the patient's clinical history (e.g., age, gender, fever, comorbidities and laboratory results). Random Forest (RF) and Gradient Boosting (GB) were applied as ML algorithms, highlighting RF with an accuracy of 94.1%, compared to 88.1% for GB. Regarding the definition of classes, 9 possibilities were considered: class 1 is for patients who did not require intensive care, class 2 for patients who remained in the service in question for less than 1 day, and the remaining classes 3 to 9 were used to represent the various periods of days, 1–5, 6–10, 11–15, 16–20, 21–25, 26–30, and more than 30, respectively (RW5).

With the state-of-the-art analysis, it became clear that patient's LOS is a critical metric for hospital management. Thanks to the use of these models, a better planning of hospital resources is provided, allowing an increase in the number of beds available for new admissions and the reduction of waiting lists.

In general, it is possible to verify that the use of demographic information is related to good results in predicting the patient's LOS. However, little attention is paid to the entire path taken by the patient from the moment of admission, as well as to information related to the drugs administered and medical analysis. Therefore, the present problem will cross-reference all this information to analyse the implications on LOS. To this end, a multi-class approach was followed. In comparison with the various studies presented, LOS ranges were not previously defined for class identification, but all LOS possibilities were considered, adopting a more informative approach.

3 Materials and Methods

3.1 Methodologies

This document was developed according to the DSR (Design Science Research) research methodology which allows creating new knowledge from the design of innovative artefacts and analyse their performance [15]. This methodology is composed by six activities [16]: Problem Understanding (1), Suggestion (2), Development (3), Evaluation (4), Conclusion (5) and Communication (6).

The methodology adopted to support DM project was Cross Industry Standard Process for Data Mining (CRISP-DM), consisting of a reference model that describes the life cycle of a DM project. This consists on 6 phases [17]: Business Understanding (1), Data Understanding (2), Data Preparation (3), Modelling (4), Evaluation (5) and Deployment (6). The present work only addresses the first 5 phases since the last one will be developed in future works.

3.2 Tools and Algorithms

The Python programming language was used during work: Analysis of different sources, data preparation, cleaning, formatting, and modelling. To this end, a set of libraries were applied, highlighting:

- Numpy and Pandas for the analysis and preparation of data;
- Py2neo, to make the connection with Neo4j, a graphical data platform used to create flows, providing deeper data analysis;
- Matplotlib for graphic creation;
- Scikit-learn for the development of ML models.

3.3 Data Sets

All the data used for the development of this research were made available by the Centro Hospitalar do Tâmega e Sousa (CHTS), relative to a period of 5 years, containing data allusive to admissions, discharges, transfers between specialties, diagnoses, examinations, analyses, drugs administrated and surgeries carried out in the inpatient service and, still, demographic data of the patients.

4 Case Study

This section describes all processes and decisions taken in the first 5 phases of the CRISP-DM methodology. As previously mentioned, this study aims to predict the patient's LOS in a specific inpatient unit of the CHTS.

4.1 Business Understanding

This study aims to improving the efficiency in the planning and management of hospital beds, through the prediction of the LOS in the specialty of Internal Medicine, in the inpatient service.

The selection of this specialty is based on its inherent complexity, due to the difficulty in managing resources, and because of it, is the specialty with the greatest affluence, with approximately 20% of hospitalisation episodes having patients passing through the Internal Medicine service. In this way, having known how long a particular patient will remain hospitalised in a particular specialty, a more adjusted planning of the number of available beds is provided.

4.2 Data Understanding

The dataset provided refers to a 5-year period, from 2017 to 2021. Table 1 shows the various sources provided, as well as a brief description of them.

Table 1. Data sources

Data sources	Description
Patient information [F1]	Records alluding to information on patients hospitalised
Admissions inpatients [F2]	Composed of all the records relating to all inpatient admissions, containing data on the moment when it occurred, the type of admission and its origin
Transfers [F3]	Set of data containing all inpatient transfers, from the date and reason for admission to the service to which it is admitted, as well as the date of discharge from it
Diagnoses [F4]	Composed of all diagnoses carried out, recording the type of diagnosis and the date on which they were carried out
Specialties [F5]	Data source containing the record of all the specialties existing in the inpatient service
Clinical analyses [F6]	Referring to all the records of analyses carried out on the patients, as well as the respective prescribed quantity and date on which it is carried out
Exams [F7]	It contains all the records of the exams performed on the patients, as well as the respective prescribed quantity and date of performance
Drugs [F8]	Records, by inpatient service, of the drugs administered to patients, together with the date of the start of administration
Surgeries [F9]	Data source for all surgeries performed, containing the pathology code and respective date of performance

To understand the movement of patients in the specialty under study, a set of graphs representing the flow of patients was constructed. Figure 1 shows the most frequent origins and destinations of the patients admitted in this specialty.

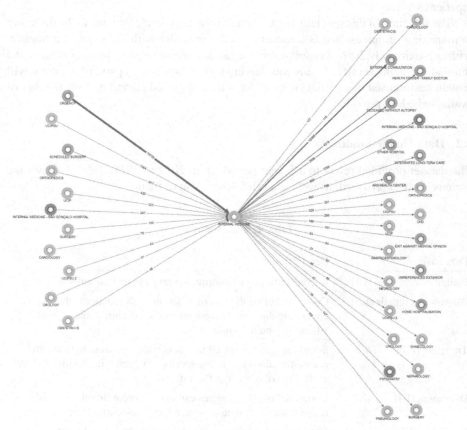

Fig. 1. Patient flow in internal medicine

A balance of classes in patient gender stands out, however in reference to the age range, approximately three quarters of the records correspond to patients aged 65 years or more, with a notable almost non-existence of underage patients (1%). It can be seen a large affluence in this service coming from the emergency service, 85% of the cases, compared to 3.5% of the cases of programmed surgery and 11.5% referring to transfers from other inpatient specialties (services).

Additionally, approximately 95% of the cases transferred to this specialty were admitted urgently, with the remainder being admitted on a scheduled basis. In this way, the high complexity and unpredictability in carrying out an efficient planning of the 355 beds assigned to Internal Medicine becomes evident, given all the uncertainty and instability inherent to these admissions, thus justifying the extreme importance of applying ML models.

4.3 Data Preparation

In this phase, the attributes that could demonstrate the highest predictive value for the models were initially selected, followed by the derivation of new attributes necessary for modelling in the later stages. Regarding the patient's characteristics, the variable age was constructed, using the patient's date of birth. We also highlight the transformations performed with the number of hospitalisations, the sequence of tests, analyses, medications and surgeries already performed, as well as the number of days of the patient's hospital stay until the moment when it was derived from the clinical record. At a global level, the attribute affluence was created to characterize the number of patients admitted in a certain specialty at the moment of admission of the patient in that specialty, and the type of register to show if it is the moment of admission or not.

As a target variable, the number of days was created referring to the remaining hospitalisation time. Regarding the definition of classes, these correspond to the possible values for the defined target, except for the first class that contemplates all records when the remaining LOS is between 1 and 3 days.

During this phase, atypical values were detected in terms of LOS (e.g., 193 days), the created target variable. These was clinically confirmed by the group of physicians as outliers, removing them.

4.4 Modeling

Supported by Sect. 2.2 and based on the objective of the study in question, several classification techniques were applied, namely Decision Tree (DT), Random Forest (RF), K-Nearest Neighbors (KNN) and Gradient Boosting (GB).

DT is a learning technique where a set of rules are inferred from the data in the form of if-then-else [18], whereas RF consists of a combination of DT [19]. As for GB, it is very similar to the RF technique, however, although it also combines several decision trees it does so in a sequential and iterative manner [20]. Finally, the KNN technique is based on the principle that similar things are closer to each other, thus classifying new data taking into account the majority class of the nearest k-neighbors [21].

For sampling and validation of results, the Cross Validation K-fold (CV) technique was used, since it provides greater reliability in the developed models, since it is possible to use all the data for train and test [22]. The value of k chosen was 5.

It is worth mentioning the presence of an imbalance of classes in the defined target, being necessary to apply an oversampling method to balance the respective classes.

This study was based on two distinct scenarios: A first one (C1) corresponding to the prediction of LOS at the time of admission and a second one (C2) mention the prediction of LOS both at the time of admission and at the time of analysis, examination, surgery or drug administration, resulting in 8 models (2 scenarios x 4 techniques).

4.5 Evaluation

To verify whether the developed models meet the defined objectives, it is crucial to evaluate them. To compare the various algorithms used, it was necessary to select the evaluation metrics, listed in Table 2. Such selection is based on the type of approach

adopted, since they are the most common and those equally applied in other referenced works.

Table 2. Evaluation metrics

Metric	Description
Accuracy (AC)	Indicates how often the classification model is correct [24]
Precision (PC)	Evaluates the model's ability to correctly classify against all records predicted to be positive [23]
Recall (RC)	Measures the proportion of actual positive predictions correctly made by the model [23]
F1-score (F1)	Returns the weighted average of PC and RC [23]
Kappa (KP)	Provides insight into the level of randomness of the model [24]
Area under the ROC curve (AUC)	Allows to evaluate the performance of the model regarding the distinction of classes [25]

To evaluate the model, success criteria were defined for each evaluation metric defined:

- AC, PC, RC, F1, AUC $\geq$ 85%;
- KP $\geq$ 80%.

5   Results and Discussion

In Table 3 it is possible to visualise for each scenario the best results achieved in the various models for the defined target.

Table 3. ML models results

Model	Metric	C1	C2
DT	AC	0,4472	0,7686
	PC	0,4045	0,7401
	RC	0,4472	0,7686
	F1	0,4136	0,7497
	KP	0,4047	0,7589
	AUC	0,9462	0,9919
RF	AC	0,5410	0,8573

(*continued*)

Table 3. (*continued*)

Model	Metric	C1	C2
	PC	0,5107	0,8552
	RC	0,5410	0,8573
	F1	0,5072	0,8486
	KP	0,5057	0,8581
	AUC	0,9594	0,9948
KNN	AC	0,5759	0,8597
	PC	0,6175	0,8439
	RC	0,5759	0,8597
	F1	0,5897	0,8492
	KP	0,5433	0,8538
	AUC	0,9763	0,9964
GB	AC	0,7534	**0,9598**
	PC	0,7409	**0,9593**
	RC	0,7534	**0,9598**
	F1	0,7416	**0,9595**
	KP	0,7344	**0,9581**
	AUC	0,9944	**0,9999**

C2 presents better results in terms of the metrics defined. Therefore, it is possible to conclude that the introduction of variables relating to the patient's clinical process during hospitalisation introduces greater predictive capacity into the model. Additionally, GB model stands out, since this model combines a set of "weak" models iteratively [26], with the purpose of increasingly shortening the error obtained in the previous model [20, 27].

In comparison with the related works analysed, Table 4 shows that, regarding the number of classes used, this approach presents a substantially higher value, which makes the model more specific and precise, enabling more assertive planning. In addition, it showed better performance than the other models, which leads to the conclusion that it stands out for updating the LOS at various times during hospitalisation.

Table 4. Comparison with related works

Study	Model	Number of classes	Accuracy
RW1	DT	3	83,50%
RW2	DT	3	88,90%
RW3	DT	2	75,00%
RW4	RF	6	65,00%
RW5	RF	9	94,10%
Case study	GB	25	95,98%

6 Conclusions

This study aimed to portray the ability to predict the LOS of a patient in the Internal Medicine specialty of the CHTS, both at the time of a patient's admission and during the clinical process, from the realization of tests, analyses and administered medications, in the period from 2017 to 2021, based on the application of ML techniques and using demographic data and medical records of the patients. For this purpose, two different scenarios were considered, with the application of four types of ML techniques. Based on the defined evaluation metrics, the GB model in C2 stood out with an accuracy of ≈96% compared to the DT, RF and KNN models. The importance of entering data regarding the patient's clinical record should be emphasised, namely the number of tests, analyses, medications and surgeries performed on a daily basis, as well as their accumulation during hospitalisation.

Thus, it is expected that, with the application of the developed prediction model, there is an increased probability that the quality of care provided to patients will be improved, as well as a more accurate discharge planning, providing greater efficiency in terms of operational workload and even better results in several quality measures, such as hospital readmissions.

To prepare the next steps of this research, it is expected to perform the deployment of this model. This will be achieved with the implementation of an Adaptive Business Intelligence (ABI) system [28] at CHTS. This is the ability to include DM and ML techniques in a data visualization system. Some prototypes are already being developed in this direction [29] and, in the future, this same ABI system will evolve. It is also expected that this presented GB model should not be independent, i.e., seeking to integrate new ML techniques that guarantee new alternatives to the one presented in this article. Therefore, it will be possible to optimise the results over time, as well as guarantee the correct maintenance and viability of the ABI system.

References

1. Veloso, R., et al.: Real-time data mining models for predicting length of stay in Intensive Care Units. In: KMIS 2014 - Proceedings of the International Conference on Knowledge Management and Information Sharing, n. Dm, pp. 245–254 (2014). https://doi.org/10.5220/0005083302450254

2. Koh, H.C., Tan, G.: Data mining applications in healthcare. J. Healthc. Inf. Manag.: JHIM **19**(2), 64–72 (2005). https://doi.org/10.4314/ijonas.v5i1.49926
3. Obenshain, M.K.: Application of data mining techniques to healthcare data. Infect. Control Hosp. Epidemiol. **25**(8), 690–695 (2004). https://doi.org/10.1086/502460
4. Priya, N., Anuradha, C., Kavitha, R., Vimala, D.: Analysing data mining applications in healthcare sector. Int. J. Innov. Technol. Explor. Eng. **8**(9), Special Issue 3, 1119–1122 (2019). https://doi.org/10.35940/ijitee.I3242.0789S319
5. Erenler, A.K., et al.: Reasons for overcrowding in the emergency department: experiences and suggestions of an education and research hospital. Turk. J. Emerg. Med. **14**, 59–63 (2014). 2.ª ed
6. Randhawa, S.A., Humayun, S.: Reasons of overcrowding in emergency department. J. Soc. Obstet. Gynaecol. Pak. **8**, 20–23 (2018). 1.ª ed
7. Boyle, J., et al.: Predicting emergency department admissions. Emerg. Med. J. **29**(5), 358–365 (2012). https://doi.org/10.1136/emj.2010.103531
8. Hachesu, P.R., Ahmadi, M., Alizadeh, S., Sadoughi, F.: Use of data mining techniques to determine and predict length of stay of cardiac patients. Healthc. Inform. Res. **19**(2), 121–129 (2013). https://doi.org/10.4258/hir.2013.19.2.121
9. Portela, F., et al.: Predict hourly patient discharge probability in intensive care units using Data Mining. Indian J. Sci. Technol. **8**(32), 2–11 (2015). https://doi.org/10.17485/ijst/2015/v8i32/92043
10. Barnes, S., Hamrock, E., Toerper, M., Siddiqui, S., Levin, S.: Real-time prediction of inpatient length of stay for discharge prioritization. J. Am. Med. Inform. Assoc. **23**(e1), e2–e10 (2016). https://doi.org/10.1093/jamia/ocv106
11. Aghajani, S., Kargari, M.: Determining factors influencing length of stay and predicting length of stay using data mining in the general surgery department. Hosp. Pract. Res. **1**(2), 51–56 (2016). https://doi.org/10.20286/hpr-010251
12. Stone, K., Zwiggelaar, R., Jones, P., Parthaláin, N.M.: Predicting hospital length of stay for accident and emergency admissions. In: Ju, Z., Yang, L., Yang, C., Gegov, A., Zhou, D. (eds.) UKCI 2019. AISC, vol. 1043, pp. 283–295. Springer, Cham (2020). https://doi.org/10.1007/978-3-030-29933-0_24
13. Tien, V.: Predicting Inpatient Length of Stay at Hospitals Using Python + Big Data. Towards Data Science (2020)
14. Alabbad, D.A., et al.: Machine learning model for predicting the length of stay in the intensive care unit for Covid-19 patients in the eastern province of Saudi Arabia. 14 de abril de 2022
15. Lacerda, D.P., Dresch, A., Proença, A., Antunes Júnior, J.A.V.: Design science research: método de pesquisa para a engenharia de produção. Gest. Prod. **20**(4), 741–761 (2013). https://doi.org/10.1590/S0104-530X2013005000014
16. Vijay, V., Kuechler, B., Petter, S.: Design Science Research in Information Systems, n. 1, pp. 1–66 (2012)
17. Pete, C., et al.: Crisp-Dm 1.0. CRISP-DM Consortium, p. 76 (2000)
18. Taylor, K.: Oracle Data Mining Concepts 11g Release 2 (11.2). Document E16808–07, Oracle, vol. 2, n. June (2013). [Em linha]. Disponível em: http://scholar.google.com/scholar?hl=en&btnG=Search&q=intitle:Oracle+Data+Mining+Concepts,+11g+Release+2+(11.2)#0
19. Suthaharan, S.: Machine Learning Models and Algorithms for Big Data Classification (2016)
20. Kuhn, M., Johnson, K.: Applied Predictive Modeling with Applications in R (2013)
21. Cios, K.J., Pedrycz, W., Swiniarski, R.W., Kurgan, L.A.: Data mining: a knowledge discovery approach (2007). https://doi.org/10.1007/978-0-387-36795-8
22. James, G., Witten, D., Hastie, T., Tibshirani, R.: Springer Texts in Statistics An Introduction to Statistical Learning - with Applications in R (2013)
23. Han, J., Kamber, M., Pei, J.: Data mining concepts and techniques (2014). https://doi.org/10.1109/ICMIRA.2013.45

24. McHugh, M.L.: Interrater reliability: the kappa statistic. Biochemia Medica **22**(3), 276–282 (2012). https://doi.org/10.11613/bm.2012.031
25. Pedregosa, F., et al.: Scikit-learn: Machine Learning in Python. JMLR **12**, 2825–2830 (2011)
26. Friedman, J.H.: Stochastic gradient boosting. Comput. Stat. Data Anal. **38**(4), 367–378 (2002). https://doi.org/10.1016/S0167-9473(01)00065-2
27. Masui, T.: All You Need to Know about Gradient Boosting Algorithm – Part 1. Regression (January 2020)
28. Michalewicz, Z., Schmidt, M., Michalewicz, M., Chiriac, C.: Adaptive Business Intelligence (2007). https://doi.org/10.1007/978-3-540-32929-9
29. Lopes, J., Guimarães, T., Santos, M.F.: Adaptive business intelligence: a new architectural approach. Procedia Comput. Sci. **177**, 540–545 (2020)

Improving the Prediction of Age of Onset of TTR-FAP Patients Using Graph-Embedding Features

Maria Pedroto[1,2]([✉])([iD]), Alípio Jorge[1,3]([iD]), João Mendes-Moreira[1,2]([iD]), and Teresa Coelho[4]

[1] Artificial Intelligence and Decision Support, INESC TEC, INESC, Campus da FEUP, Rua Dr. Roberto Frias, Porto, 4200-465 Porto, Portugal
maria.j.pedroto@inesctec.pt
[2] Department of Informatics Engineering, Faculty of Engineering, University of Porto, Rua Dr. Roberto Frias, s/n, Porto, Portugal
jmoreira@fe.up.pt
[3] Department of Computer Science, Faculty of Sciences, University of Porto, Rua do Campo Alegre, Porto, 4169-007 Porto, Portugal
amjorge@fc.up.pt
[4] Unidade Corino de Andrade, Hospital de Santo Antonio, R. D. Manuel II, Pavilhão 2 (ex-Cicap), 4050-345 Porto, Portugal
tcoelho@netcabo.pt

Abstract. Transthyretin Familial Amyloid Polyneuropathy (TTR-FAP) is a neurological genetic illness that inflicts severe symptoms after the onset occurs. Age of onset represents the moment a patient starts to experience the symptoms of a disease. An accurate prediction of this event can improve clinical and operational guidelines that define the work of doctors, nurses, and operational staff. In this work, we transform family trees into compact vectors, that is, embeddings, and handle these as input features to predict the age of onset of patients with TTR-FAP. Our purpose is to evaluate how information present in genealogical trees can be transformed and used to improve a regression-based setting for TTR-FAP age of onset prediction. Our results show that by combining manual and graph-embeddings features there is a decrease in the mean prediction error when there is less information regarding a patient's family. With this work, we open the way for future work in representation learning for genealogical data, enabling a more effective exploitation of machine learning approaches.

Keywords: Representation learning · Genealogical trees · Regression learning models · Age of onset prediction

1 Introduction

In this work, we approach the medical problem of predicting the age of onset of Familial Amyloid Polyneuropathy (TTR-FAP) patients. This corresponds to

G. Marreiros et al. (Eds.): EPIA 2022, LNAI 13566, pp. 183–194, 2022.
https://doi.org/10.1007/978-3-031-16474-3_16

the moment when a patient starts to feel the symptoms of a disease. Its accurate prediction helps in timely assign appropriate medical resources as well as improving a patient's quality of life.

In two previous works [11], [12] we designed, experimented, and evaluated a regression-based prediction approach that outputs, by using a set of models trained at different ages, for each patient, a vector of future time predictions. It is important to mention that, for each age model, in the training phase, we only consider patients for the time period when they were considered asymptomatic. After they reach the onset age, they are discarded from the pipeline of higher age models. Our approach works with a set of predictors, originated from heterogeneous, complex, and non-structured information collected from genealogical trees and patient clinical records. It operates with a set of regression algorithms whose predictive performance is compared against a clinical baseline. Of note is that it has appropriate pre-processing, model construction, and evaluation steps in order to adequately answer the problem of at which age will a patient feel the symptoms of the disease, called the onset age. In this case, we showed that we were able to improve medical practice.

After that previous work, we were motivated to study whether we were ignoring important information encoded in the genealogical trees, since we had reduced their dimensionality by employing a set of mathematical operators to aggregate different levels of data. Thus, in this work, our motivation is to study the effect of representation learning as a part of feature construction for the problem of predicting of age of onset of TTR-FAP patients.

TTR-FAP is a genealogical hereditary disease, which was first diagnosed in Portugal by Dr. Corino de Andrade [1]. It is life-threatening and transmitted by ancestors in an autosomal dominant trait. Although predicting a patient's age of onset can appear to be of simple determination, it can be influenced by different phenotypic and genotypic attributes. One of the early works that evaluates the age of onset distribution in these families [6] concluded that there was an anticipation component in the age of onset distribution over the years. This indicates that as long as the error subsists, descendants have risks of being afflicted earlier by the disease. It also demonstrates the importance of studying approaches that depend on the type and amount of information regarding a patient's family. Our research questions are: (RQ1) can we improve predictive results for TTR-FAP age of onset, using a representation learning approach; (RQ2) does the combination of learned and pre-defined features obtains useful predictive results; and (RQ3) in what conditions is it useful to employ a representation-learning approach to the prediction of age of onset of TTR-FAP patients. Our experimental methodology corroborates these hypotheses in what is, to our knowledge, the first work exploiting embeddings to represent family trees.

This work is organised as follows: (i) in Sect. 2 we review related works; (ii) in Sect. 3 we explain our approach, both for the feature construction and prediction phases; (iii) in Sect. 4 we present and discuss the results; (iv) while in Sect. 5 we present conclusions and plan on future work directions.

2 Feature Construction and Embedding-Based Network Representation Learning

Machine learning systems must be able to express complex real-world scenarios so as to transform inputs into descriptive, predictive or prescriptive answers. One of its principal phases corresponds to the construction, selection, extraction, and engineering of features [9]. This consists on the application of sets of constructive operators over existing data records in order to learn or generate new sets of predictors [9]. One of its biggest technical advances deals with predicting using network data, where problems acquire a different dimension, since prediction over nodes or edges, sometimes with directionally concerns, requires approaches to handle time-related characteristics [5]. One field of research that deals with different representation learning aspects in these complex scenarios is network embedding (NE).

Network embedding (NE) is a research field that focuses on the representation of complex systems in low dimensional spaces. Since its creation, researchers have dealt with the conceptualisation, development, and application of different solutions, namely: analysis of social networks; language modelling, for example, by studying co-occurrence of words; and networks of communication [4]. NE algorithms focus on utilising the underlying structure present in network data, its vertex content, as well as any other available secondary information [15], while providing answers to intricate questions. Many current works are developed on top of Graph Convolutional Networks (GCN). This is the case in the works of [14] and [7]. In the first reference, authors propose a general framework that learns embeddings of emails and users to improve a classification task over state-of-the-art approaches. In the second case, authors propose a node embedding approach to disentangle the information shared by the structure of a network and the characteristics presented in its nodes, with a multitask GCN Variational Autoencoder. For this, different dimensions of the final embeddings can be dedicated to encode feature information, network structure, and also shared feature-network information.

Embeddings are information/knowledge representation vectors able to represent discrete and relational objects into a fixed set of numerical features. In the early years of its usage, embeddings were useful as a form of dimensionality reduction [2]. These *arrays* of numbers, which lack human meaning, are obtained at a feature construction phase. Further transformation approaches, focused, for example, on retrieving distance or location patterns, also help datamining algorithms in solving problems. Embedding approaches, created in the natural language processing (NLP) field, served as the basis for development of a current new-paradigm that enables the transformation of networks of data with time dimensions that allows the application of traditional machine learning algorithms. In general terms, given a set of independent and identically distributed (i.i.d.) data points, graph embedding algorithms construct an affinity graph, and embed them in a new lower-dimensional space. With this, the algorithm transforms itself into a new model of lower dimensionality while maintaining the main characteristics of the network, since connected vertices are kept closer to

each other in the new embedding space [15]. Current research trends focus on one of two paths: (i) learning the best representation expressing multipurpose scenarios when combining graphs, their sub-components, or sub-parts [10]; and node embedding approaches, where the focus is on representing nodes or their connections [3] in order to express meaningful patterns. In the first case, current works extend the graph2vec algorithm, while in the latter most significant contributions are based on node2vec or edge2vec algorithms. A node2vec model is constructed by learning a mapping of nodes in a low-dimensional space of features that maximises the likelihood of preserving the actual neighbourhood of a node [5]. A graph2vec model, on the other hand, extends document embedding neural networks to learn representations of entire graphs. It forces structurally similar graphs to be closer to each other in the embedding space. With these innovations, it became possible to learn task-agnostic representations of complex networks and to use these features as inputs in different prediction algorithms.

In this study, we then take advantage of a representation learning method that uses feature vectors to encode graphs and represent them in a lower-dimensional space. The algorithm we use, known as Weisfeiler-Leman (WL), transforms our genealogical trees into different embedding structures. This is a combinatorial partitioning algorithm that plays a very important role in the graph isomorphism literature ([8], [15]). The idea behind it is to assign a fingerprint to a graph node based both on its previous fingerprints, and those of its neighbours. For that purpose, the algorithm has a limit k defining the number of dimensions that will be used to represent the new dimensional space. It starts by defining the k-tuples of the vertice list and classifying them according to the characteristics of the individual vertices. In the next step, it aggregates the primary set of results and propagates them between *adjacent* tuples that differ solely in one coordinate, thus collecting local structure information and propagating it along the edges of the meta-model graph. The final output, after a predetermined number of propagations, is a set of feature vectors where each represents a different tree T.

In our work, we then *combine* the final feature embeddings vector of each tree T with different sets of manually engineered features. These are later on used by a set of regression prediction algorithms to model and predict the age of onset of patients diagnosed with TTR-FAP. With this process, we leverage the information of family structures by representing them as genealogical embedded structures over time. Since we express our trees since patients started to be clinically followed, each tree T has a set of outputs that correspond to different time instances I.

3   Model Overview

3.1   Problem Definition

Our aim is to predict the age of onset of asymptomatic TTR-FAP patients, with data sets based on 900 individual genealogical trees and a set of clinical information of patients. These have been followed since 1950 in Centro Hospitalar

Universitário do Porto (CHUPorto). We integrate genealogical and patient data records, namely gender, age of onset, birth and death dates over a set of different age instances, by focusing in different clinical characteristics.

In conceptual terms, we define a function f that takes as input a set of n manual predictors p, and a feature vector e, of d dimensions, which represents the embedding of the genealogical tree for a specific i year. These sets of patients characteristics are fed to a prediction pipeline that conceptualises a virtual scenario accordingly to the patient's age (see Eq. 1 and Fig. 1) in order to predict his future age of onset. Since we expect different progression at different ages, prediction at each age is seen as a specific and individual regression prediction task.

$$y = f(p_1, p_2, ..., p_{n-1}, p_n, e_1, e_2, ..., e_{d-1}, e_d) \tag{1}$$

3.2 Defining and Using Embeddings

In order to learn an optimised vector representation from genealogical trees and the genealogical relations between individuals, we take into account the individual's life events, namely birth and death, to represent on the trees over time. We also take into account disease diagnosis and symptoms onset when the node of the tree represents a clinical patient. In this way, each patient that is matched to a genealogical tree node v has a set of input and output familiar relations r, were relevant relations are depicted in Eq. 2, and it is up to the embedding algorithm to select and maintain the most valuable structural data.

To combine our previously published prediction approach ([11], [12]) with genealogical tree embedding, for each genealogical tree we generated its set of embedding representations, on a yearly basis, since 1950. This was performed with the help of an application programming interface (API) that encapsulates this [13]. Then, and for each tuple (patient, prediction scenario), we considered the genealogical embedding that corresponded to the year prior to patient age instance. For instance, if the prediction task at hand is to predict the age of onset of asymptomatic patients of 20 years old, and if the current patient was 20 years old in 1982, we considered its familiar embedding representation in the year 1981.

With this data alignment, the embedding representation of the tree serves as a meta-model of the most valuable relations with only the most current data at hand, thus preventing data leakage.

$$father_{of}(A, C) \tag{2a}$$
$$mother_{of}(B, C) \tag{2b}$$
$$child_{of}(C, A) \tag{2c}$$
$$child_{of}(C, B) \tag{2d}$$

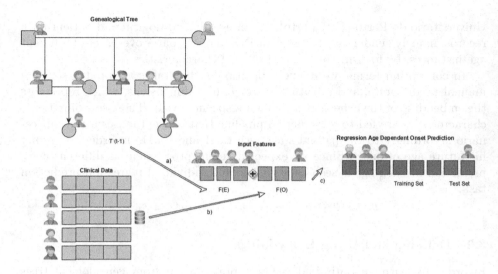

Fig. 1. Conceptual Graph-based Embedding Prediction

3.3 Experimental Setup

The experimental setup was outlined in order to measure the predictive gain of using graph-embeddings over manually engineered features, while also evaluating possible bias associated with the missing data imputation approach, and the chosen graph-embeddings dimension.

To achieve that aim, we defined three important sets of features, namely: (i) a set of original features, henceforth designated as **Original**, combining the features presented in previous works in ([11], [12]); (ii) a set of embedding based features to be used as predictors, henceforth designated as **E**; and (iii) a set of original and embedding features combined, henceforth designated as **O.E.**

In the tasks of evaluating possible bias in the missing imputation approach (k) as well as varying dimensional length (d) of embeddings, we varied these parameters between:

- 5, 10, 15, 20 (parameter k);
- 64, 128 (parameter d).

In the individual regression tasks, we chose to predict the age of onset of asymptomatic patients on ages ranging from 22 to 46 with a step of 3 years (22, 25, 28, ..., 46) (parameter a), while testing the following prediction algorithms: (i) linear regression (lr), (ii) XGBoost (xg), (iii) elastic net (en), (iv) random forest (rf), (v) lasso (la), (vi) support vector regression machine (sv), (vii) ridge (ri) and (viii) decision tree (dt). We separated different models according to whether the patients know their ancestors age of onset or not, thus creating a trio of experimental data sets from now on referenced as: (i) *dataset(a)* for patients with at least one direct ancestor who was previously diagnosed and referenced as symptomatic; (ii) *dataset(b)* for patients without at least one direct ancestor

previously diagnosed as symptomatic carrier with a known age of onset; and, (iii) *dataset(f)*, that combines all patients, independently of the information of their ancestor. Note that this means most patients will disappear from *dataset(b)* and appear in *dataset(a)* as the modelled age increases.

With regards to the estimation and evaluation of the error for the different experiments, we focused on the distribution of the mean absolute error (MAE) over a holdout strategy where the training set holds 80% of the records and the test set considers the most recent 20% of diagnosed patients. In the training phase, we include a nested cross validation operator, in order to optimise the hyper parameters of each algorithm.

4 Results and Discussion

4.1 Overall Evaluation of the Different Embedding Variants

If we consider the best variant in each individual regression task, that is, at each age of prediction, these vary accordingly to the data sets that served as inputs, namely dataset(a), dataset(b) and dataset(f) (see table 1 and Fig. 2).

The top(3) ranking results suggest us that (i) in all the top performers, the best results with only the embedding-based features do not surpass the baselines of human engineered features and (ii) that there is an improvement, especially in dataset(b), when we focus on the E.O.128 or E.O.64 alternative. This leads us to conclude that, when a patient does not have enough information regarding it's ancestor, there is predictive gain in generating and using family tree embeddings as part of the predictors. This is even more clear if we take into consideration the fluctuation of the original best results in dataset(b) and the similarity between the E.O.64 variant and the original results in dataset(f) (see Fig. 2).

Next, we evaluate the prediction of the age of onset of asymptomatic patients by focusing on the 22 years old results for 5 nearest neighbours. We chose this hyper-parameter value for the missing imputation approach by observing the evolution of the prediction results in the best variant compared to the original experiments. In this case (see Fig. 3), it is clear that k(5) experiments are stable in all experimented ages.

4.2 Studying the Effect of Predicting the Age of Onset of Asymptomatic Patients at 22 Years Old

In order to have a clear picture of the variance difference between all the models for all the individual experiments, we compared the error results of all the comparable test sets in a friedman rank test, with a level of significance α of 0.05.

Table 1. Rank of the top(3) best variants. E.O.64 represents the variant that combines embedding and original features with 64 dimensions, while E.O.128 represents the embedding and original features for 128 dimensions. Original represents the variant that only considers original features.

r_i	age		variant	k	alg	mae ± sd		variant	k	alg	mae ± sd		variant	k	alg	mae ± sd
	22		Original	5	ri	2.7 ± 3.2		E.O.128	20	xg	4.2 ± 5.3		Original	20	la	2.8 ± 3.6
	25		E.O.128	10	en	2.4 ± 2.7		E.O.128	5	xg	3.9 ± 4.9		E.O.64	20	la	2.7 ± 3.4
	28		E.O.128	10	en	1.9 ± 2.3		E.O.128	5	xg	3.7 ± 4.8		Original	5	la	2.7 ± 3.1
	31		E.O.128	5	la	2.1 ± 2.5		E.O.64	20	xg	3.7 ± 4.8		Original	10	la	2.6 ± 3.3
1	34		Original	5	la	1.8 ± 2.4		E.O.128	15	xg	4.2 ± 5.4		E.O.128	20	en	3.1 ± 3.9
	37		E.O.128	5	en	2.3 ± 2.4		E.O.128	10	xg	4.5 ± 5.4		Original	5	ri	4.1 ± 4.9
	40		E.O.64	10	la	2.3 ± 2.5		Original	5	xg	4.6 ± 5.1		E.O.128	20	ri	4.6 ± 6.0
	43		E.O.128	10	en	1.7 ± 2.3		E.O.64	15	ri	5.2 ± 5.6		Original	15	xg	3.9 ± 4.4
	46		Original	20	en	2.1 ± 2.6		Original	15	ri	5.2 ± 6.0		Original	15	la	3.5 ± 3.9
	22		Original	20	ri	2.8 ± 3.1		E.O.128	10	xg	4.2 ± 5.3		Original	10	la	2.9 ± 3.6
	25		E.O.64	10	en	2.4 ± 2.7		E.O.128	20	xg	4.0 ± 5.0		E.O.64	15	la	2.7 ± 3.4
	28		E.O.64	5	en	1.9 ± 2.3		E.O.128	10	xg	3.7 ± 4.8		Original	10	la	2.7 ± 3.1
	31	dataset(a)	E.O.64	5	la	2.1 ± 2.5	dataset(b)	E.O.64	10	xg	3.8 ± 4.6	dataset(f)	Original	15	la	2.6 ± 3.3
2	34		Original	5	en	1.8 ± 2.4		E.O.64	15	xg	4.4 ± 5.6		E.O.64	20	en	3.1 ± 3.9
	37		E.O.64	5	en	2.3 ± 2.4		E.O.128	15	xg	4.5 ± 5.5		Original	20	ri	4.1 ± 5.0
	40		E.O.128	10	la	2.3 ± 2.5		Original	15	xg	4.9 ± 5.1		E.O.128	15	ri	4.7 ± 6.2
	43		E.O.64	10	en	1.7 ± 2.3		E.O.64	20	ri	5.3 ± 5.8		E.O.64	20	xg	4.1 ± 4.5
	46		E.O.128	10	en	2.1 ± 2.6		Original	20	ri	5.3 ± 6.1		Original	20	la	3.5 ± 3.9
	22		Original	15	ri	2.8 ± 3.2		E.O.128	15	xg	4.3 ± 5.2		Original	15	la	2.9 ± 3.6
	25		E.O.128	5	en	2.4 ± 2.7		E.O.128	10	xg	4.1 ± 5.1		E.O.64	20	en	2.7 ± 3.3
	28		E.O.128	15	en	1.9 ± 2.3		E.O.128	15	xg	3.8 ± 4.9		Original	15	la	2.7 ± 3.1
	31		E.O.128	5	en	2.1 ± 2.5		E.O.64	20	en	3.8 ± 4.8		Original	20	la	2.6 ± 3.3
3	34		Original	10	la	1.8 ± 2.4		E.O.64	5	ri	4.4 ± 6.1		E.O.64	15	en	3.2 ± 3.9
	37		Original	5	en	2.3 ± 2.4		E.O.128	5	xg	4.5 ± 5.2		Original	15	ri	4.2 ± 5.0
	40		E.O.64	5	la	2.3 ± 2.5		E.O.128	5	xg	5.2 ± 5.5		E.O.64	20	xg	4.7 ± 4.9
	43		Original	10	en	1.7 ± 2.3		E.O.128	20	xg	5.5 ± 5.0		Original	20	xg	4.2 ± 4.7
	46		E.O.64	10	en	2.1 ± 2.6		Original	5	ri	5.3 ± 6.2		Original	10	en	3.5 ± 3.9

The hypothesis results lead us to reject all of the H_0 hypothesis, as there are significant differences (p-value below α and near 0). To have a clear view of the magnitude of the difference between all the experiments, we followed up with a Nemenyi post-hoc test and evaluated the critical difference diagrams (see Figs. 4, 5 and 6). Results show that, for all the experiments, we have different levels of similar variance results, observable on the improvement of O.E experiments for dataset(b) and dataset(f).

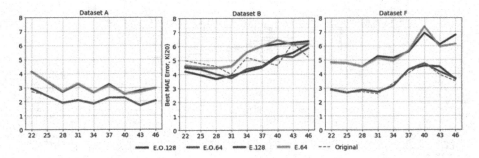

Fig. 2. Best results, for each prediction task, for K(5) experiments. E.O.128 represents the variant that combines embedding and original features for a dimension of 128, while E.O.64 has a dimension of 64. Note that, in each age and according to each variant, we can have different *best* algorithms. For the case of predictions at 22 years, the *best* algorithms are *en* for E.O variants, *sv* for E variants and *ri* for original. In dataset(a) all the records have information regarding the transmitting parent age of onset, while in dataset(b) this is unknown. Dataset(f) combines the patients of dataset(a) and dataset (b).

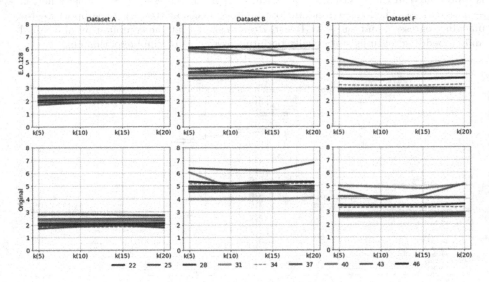

Fig. 3. Influence of k parameter on the best variants: E.O.128 and Original. Each line represents the best values for specific patient age prediction task and the different missing data imputation results are represented by k(n), where n is the number of closest neighbours averaged for imputation. In dataset(a), these values are constant, while in dataset(b) and dataset(f) there is some fluctuation for models starting from the age of 43 years, with values decreasing between k(5) and k(10), and increasing between k(15) and k(20).

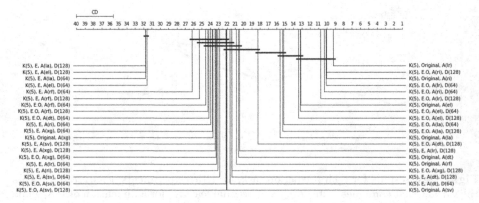

Fig. 4. Nemenyie results for each prediction model for age = 22, k(5) and dataset(a) parameters. D(128) represents results for a dimension of 128, while D(64) represents a dimension of 64. E.O represents the experiments for combining embedding and original features, while E represents experiments only with embeddings features and original represents experiments with only manual features. Each individual prediction algorithm is represented in the A(x) parameter with: lr → linear regression, el → elastic net, la → lasso, ri → ridge, rf → random forest, dt → decision tree, sv → support vector machine regressor, and xg → XGBoost. Results show that the combination of original and embedding features statistically performs as well as original experiments.

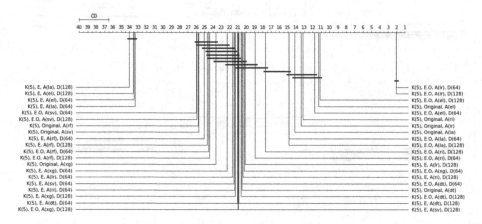

Fig. 5. Nemenyie results for each prediction model for age = 22, k(5) and dataset(b) parameters. Results show that combining original and embedding features statistically performs better than original experiments.

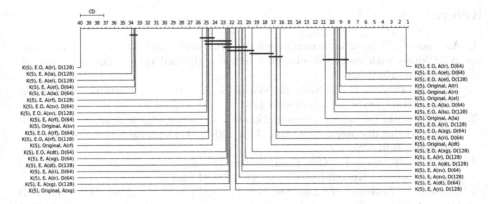

Fig. 6. Nemenyie results for each prediction model for age = 22, k(5) and dataset(f) parameters. Results show that original and embedding features statistically performs better than original experiments.

5 Conclusions and Future Work

The need of studying the applicability of machine-learning based solutions to answer medical problems has never been so pressing. In this paper, we proposed an approach that takes advantage of applying network embeddings as a feature construction method, transforming genealogical trees into a set of numerical feature vectors. These feature vectors are applied to the medical problem of predicting the age of onset of TTR-FAP patients.

We compared prediction results of manually engineered features, i.e. **Original**, with two new set of results, namely individual embedding feature vectors, i.e. **E**, and combined human engineered and embedding feature vectors, i.e. **O.E**. From the results, we can conclude that (RQ1) there is evidence that the application of embedding feature construction methods improves current state of the art prediction approaches for the age of onset of TTR-FAP patients; and (RQ2) combining manually engineered features with graph-embeddings feature vectors is the approach that has greater impact. From the set of results we also conclude that (RQ3) the O.E approach has greater impact when there is no complementary information regarding the familiar history, namely when medical professionals don't have access to a patients transmitting parent data. When this is the case, then manually engineered features shows better results.

In the future, we intend to study other types of embedding algorithms, as well as enhancing the current approach to better work with genealogical structures.

Acknowledgments. This work is financed by National Funds through the Portuguese funding agency, FCT - Fundação para a Ciência e a Tecnologia, within project LA/P/0063/2020 and by Centro Hospitalar do Porto (ChPorto).

References

1. Andrade, C.: A peculiar form of peripheral neuropathy familiar atypical generalized amyloidosis with special involvement of the peripheral nerves. Brain: J. Neurol. **75**(3), 408–27 (1952)
2. Chen, H., Perozzi, B., Al-Rfou, R., Skiena, S.: A Tutorial on Network Embeddings (2018). http://arxiv.org/abs/1808.02590
3. Gao, Z., et al.: Edge2vec: representation learning using edge semantics for biomedical knowledge discovery. BMC Bioinform. **20**(1), 1–15 (2019). https://doi.org/10.1186/s12859-019-2914-2
4. Goyal, P., Ferrara, E.: Graph embedding techniques, applications, and performance: a survey. Knowl. Based Syst. **151**, 78–94 (2018)
5. Grover, A., Leskovec, J.: node2vec. In: Proceedings of the 22nd ACM SIGKDD International Conference on Knowledge Discovery and Data Mining - KDD 2016 (2016). https://doi.org/10.1145/2939672.2939754
6. Lemos, C., et al.: Overcoming artefact: anticipation in 284 Portuguese kindreds with familial amyloid polyneuropathy (FAP) ATTRV30M. J. Neurol Neurosurg Psychiatry. **853**, 326–330 (2014)
7. Lerique, S., Abitbol, J.L., Karsai, M.: Joint embedding of structure and features via graph convolutional networks. Appl. Netw. Sci. **5**(1), 1–24 (2019). https://doi.org/10.1007/s41109-019-0237-x
8. Morris, C., Mutzel, P.: Towards a practical k-dimensional Weisfeiler-Leman algorithm (2019). http://arxiv.org/abs/1904.01543
9. Motoda, H., Liu, H.: Feature Selection, Extraction and Construction. Communication of IICM (Institute of Information and Computing Machinery, Taiwan) **5**, 67–72 (2002). http://www.ar.sanken.osaka-u.ac.jp/motoda/papers/fdws02.pdf
10. Narayanan, A., Chandramohan, M., Venkatesan, R., Chen, L., Liu, Y., Jaiswa, S.: graph2vec: learning distributed representations of graphs (2017). https://arxiv.org/pdf/1707.05005.pdf
11. Pedroto, M., Jorge, A., Mendes-Moreira, J., Coelho, T.: Predicting age of onset in TTR-FAP patients with genealogical features. In: Hollmén, J., McGregor, C., Soda, P., Kane, B. (eds.) 31st IEEE International Symposium on Computer-Based Medical Systems, CBMS 2018, Karlstad, Sweden, 18–21 June 2018, pp. 199–204. IEEE Computer Society (2018). https://doi.org/10.1109/CBMS.2018.00042
12. Pedroto, M., Jorge, A., Mendes-Moreira, J., Coelho, T.: Impact of genealogical features in transthyretin familial amyloid polyneuropathy age of onset prediction. In: Fdez-Riverola, F., Mohamad, M.S., Rocha, M., De Paz, J.F., González, P. (eds.) PACBB2018 2018. AISC, vol. 803, pp. 35–42. Springer, Cham (2019). https://doi.org/10.1007/978-3-319-98702-6_5
13. Rozemberczki, B., Kiss, O., Sarkar, R.: Karate club: an API oriented open-source python framework for unsupervised learning on graphs. In: Proceedings of the 29th ACM International Conference on Information & Knowledge Management, pp. 3125–3132. CIKM 2020, Association for Computing Machinery, New York, NY, USA (2020). https://doi.org/10.1145/3340531.3412757
14. Sun, Y., Garcia-Pueyo, L., Wendt, J.B., Najork, M., A. Broder: Learning effective embeddings for machine generated emails with applications to email category prediction. In: IEEE International Conference on Big Data (Big Data), pp. 1846–1855 (2018). https://doi.org/10.1109/BigData.2018.8622048
15. Zhang, D., Yin, J., Zhu, X., Zhang, C.: Network representation learning: a survey (2017). http://arxiv.org/abs/1801.05852

Cloud-Based Privacy-Preserving Medical Imaging System Using Machine Learning Tools

João Alves, Beatriz Soares$^{(\boxtimes)}$, Cláudia Brito, and António Sousa

INESC TEC & Universidade do Minho, Braga, Portugal
`beatriz.p.soares@inesctec.pt`

Abstract. Healthcare environments are generating a deluge of sensitive data. Nonetheless, dealing with large amounts of data is an expensive task, and current solutions resort to the cloud environment. Additionally, the intersection of the cloud environment and healthcare data opens new challenges regarding data privacy.

With this in mind, we propose MEDCLOUDCARE (MCC), a healthcare application offering medical image viewing and processing tools while integrating cloud computing and AI. Moreover, MCC provides security and privacy features, scalability and high availability. The system is intended for two user groups: health professionals and researchers. The former can remotely view, process and share medical imaging information in the DICOM format. Also, it can use pre-trained Machine Learning (ML) models to aid the analysis of medical images. The latter can remotely add, share, and deploy ML models to perform inference on DICOM images.

MCC incorporates a DICOM web viewer enabling users to view and process DICOM studies, which they can also upload and store. Regarding the security and privacy of the data, all sensitive information is encrypted at rest and in transit. Furthermore, MCC is intended for cloud environments. Thus, the system is deployed using Kubernetes, increasing the efficiency, availability and scalability of the ML inference process.

Keywords: Healthcare application · DICOM images · Cloud computing · Machine learning

1 Introduction

The vast amount of information created and ingested in clinical environments [17] makes the analysis and collection of data with labelled ground-truth a boundless challenge [26]. Thus, the development of technological tools that can assist medical professionals in accessing, processing, and interpreting that data in a timely and accurate manner is a significant concern.

Nowadays, medical images are extensively utilised to diagnose, plan, and guide the treatment and monitoring of disease progression [23]. In this context, systems that enable clinicians to remotely access and evaluate patients' medical

---

J. Alves and B. Soares—These authors contributed equally to this work.

© The Author(s), under exclusive license to Springer Nature Switzerland AG 2022
G. Marreiros et al. (Eds.): EPIA 2022, LNAI 13566, pp. 195–206, 2022.
https://doi.org/10.1007/978-3-031-16474-3_17

imaging information have been increasingly sought-after. Recently, radiologists have collaborated with data scientists to develop web applications for radiological purposes [19, 26]. Web applications allow radiologists to remotely view, share and interpret images within a browser and without additional software installed on their machines [18, 19, 26]. Moreover, cloud computing is becoming an attractive computing model for biomedical research. Hospitals and researchers are shifting to cloud environments to facilitate large-scale data analysis and remote sharing, and web applications are a practical way to interact with such environments [28]. For these reasons, web-based systems have been increasingly valuable for clinicians and researchers. Another fundamental element of the medical imaging field is the Digital Imaging and Communications in Medicine (DICOM) standard. It allows clinicians to view, store, and share medical images independently of their location or the devices they use and is considered the primary standard for image data management in healthcare [22].

There are still some technological challenges regarding medical image analysis to be addressed. Firstly, many users have sensitive clinical data that must be safely stored and retrieved. Therefore, data should be encrypted both at rest and in transit. Secondly, many of the methodological tasks (image registration, localisation, classification, detection, segmentation) involved in a medical image analysis process often encompass manual workflows that can be tedious, prone to observer variation and, most crucially, time-consuming. Artificial Intelligence (AI) is frequently required to enhance these tasks. Constant improvements in AI are helping to identify, classify, and quantify patterns in medical images. For these reasons, some web applications allow the deployment of Machine Learning (ML) or Deep Learning (DL) models to help diagnose clinically relevant results [25]. Current solutions cannot solve such challenges effectively, either by not offering privacy features or not being scalable and high available or not allowing easy integration of new AI algorithms.

To tackle this, we propose MEDCLOUDCARE, a web-based healthcare application. MCC integrates typical DICOM viewer features (*e.g.,* rotation, pan, annotation) with state-of-the-art pre-trained AI models. Due to the large volumes of data, MCC is intended to be deployed in cloud environments. Nonetheless, it also can be deployed locally. Additionally, the system is built for health professionals and researchers. First, it provides a visually appealing interface for health professionals to view and analyse patients' data. Secondly, researchers can add, store, deploy and test their pre-trained AI models on DICOM data.

The outline of the paper is as follows. Section 2 reviews some state-of-the-art medical imaging applications. Section 3 describes the designed system architecture, while Sect. 4 presents some obtained results. Finally, Sect. 5 outlines the main conclusions and the work to be done.

2   Related Work

This section reviews some state-of-the-art medical imaging applications. ePAD [7] is a platform for visualisation, annotation, and quantitative analysis of medical images. Another extensible research platform is 3D Slicer [1], a desktop

application requiring local installation, which is massively adopted for imaging research. RayPlus [27] is a web application for medical image processing developed by Yuan et al. MEDCLOUDCARE distinguishes itself from these applications by offering a cloud-based alternative with security and privacy guarantees.

In the scope of web applications offering AI capabilities, Tesseract-MI supports the deployment of AI models while providing image viewing and reporting [24]. However, Tesseract-MI only supports the deployment of static and pre-defined AI models and requires a connection to a DICOM server to view images since it does not allow users to upload DICOM files in the application. Mehrtash et al. developed DeepInfer [3] as an extension of 3D Slicer. It uses Docker to enable users to run different DL models on their data on a local machine. Similarly, the TOMAAT framework allows users to serve their DL applications over the cloud [15]. Nevertheless, DeepInfer and TOMAAT applications require a client with a specific interface to connect with the server to deploy the DL models.

Distinctively, MCC allows users to upload DICOM files in the application and add and deploy their own AI models, which they can select and apply to those images. Furthermore, it has a visually appealing user interface (UI) while managing multi-users with distinct roles and permissions and having privacy features, scalability and high availability. Moreover, MCC intends to offer straightforward integration of AI models in the medical image analysis workflow, requiring minimal software installation to assure compatibility with clinical standards.

3 MEDCLOUDCARE

The proposed solution intends to provide four main features: user authentication; DICOM image viewing, processing and storage; sharing of imaging data and models between users; and addition and deployment of pre-trained models.

This section describes MEDCLOUDCARE's proof-of-concept (PoC) architecture (Fig. 1). The latter follows the client-server model. The components executed on the server-side create the backend (Django API, PostgreSQL database, Orthanc server and Kubernetes cluster), and the elements executed on the client-side provide the UI, therefore, encompass the frontend (e.g., the OHIF viewer).

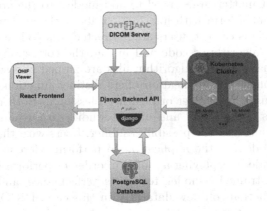

Fig. 1. MEDCLOUDCARE Architecture components.

3.1   React Frontend

The client-side of MCC was developed using the JavaScript programming language, particularly with the React web framework [14]. It is executed in a browser, allowing users to access the backend services by sending API (Application Programming Interface) requests. Since the application is intended for medical and research use, the UI offers different functionalities according to the type of user. Nevertheless, when the application starts, the UI is common to all users, showing an authentication page where they can create an account and sign in. The authentication process can be performed using the users' email or social networks (namely, Google, Facebook, Linkedin, GitHub and Spotify). Once the users are successfully authenticated, they have access to the following features:

- *Image Storage with Orthanc*: the Orthanc DICOM server is currently considered the ubitiquous open-source solution for DICOM image data storage. One of its main strengths lies in its built-in REST API. Such an API gives full programmatic access to all core features of Orthanc, namely, the capability to upload, transfer and retrieve images [10];
- *Image Viewing and Processing with OHIF*: the Open Health Imaging Foundation (OHIF) viewer addresses the demand for open-source web imaging applications [28]. It is based on web technologies, including JavaScript, React [14], and the Cornerstone.js library [2], and can be used as a Single Page Application embedded into third-party applications. It is standards-conforming and relies on DICOMweb [4] for data exchange and connectivity to image archives, e.g., Orthanc. The UI components of the viewer are provided in an independent React library so that developers can customise the UI or use its components in their applications. In reality, the OHIF Viewer has been adopted in various clinical research platforms (e.g., Precision Imaging Metrics [13], XNAT [16]) and commercial applications (e.g., OsiriX [11]) [28]. With this in mind, MCC incorporated a customised version of OHIF to provide DICOM image viewing and processing capabilities;
- *Addition and Deployment of AI models*: MCC provides an interface component that enables the application to use pre-trained, out-of-the-box AI models. To that matter, users need to add models to the application. First, they must fill out a form with information about their AI model. Secondly, if the information is correct, users are redirected to a code editor where they can submit the algorithm's code and upload the corresponding pre-trained model files. Finally, all the algorithm files are zipped and sent to the backend. As mentioned, the application offers distinct functionalities according to the type of user: researcher or health professional. Both groups can view DICOM images using OHIF and upload studies to Orthanc. Nevertheless, from an AI perspective, the possibilities differ. Users with the researcher role may add AI models to the application to perform inference on the images they have uploaded. Deploying a model in order to perform inference means that users have trained a model, tested its performance, and decided to use it to make predictions on new data [21], in this case, DICOM images. This way, researchers test their models on new and undisclosed data. On the other

hand, instead of adding and deploying models, healthcare professionals are perhaps more interested in using available models to aid them in image analysis. With this in mind, MCC enables researchers to add and test their AI models on DICOM images while allowing health professionals to apply models made available in the application and see the outcome results;

– *Sharing of Imaging Data and AI Models*: from a healthcare point of view, there are potential benefits for patients' well-being when health professionals can share patients' medical imaging data. Such data not only includes the image itself. It also comprises measurements and annotations that the health professional user may perform in the patients' study. The ability to share such information with other health professionals that use the application may facilitate the analysis of that data, accelerate the diagnosis procedure and help achieve more accurate clinical results. From a biomedical research perspective, if investigators can get practical insights from their models and make them available to other users, the impact of the models is significantly enhanced. Also, if the model owner concedes access permission to other research users of the application, they can cooperate in editing, improving and testing such a model. With this in mind, MCC allows the creation of user groups, enabling the sharing of studies between health professional users and models between researchers, respectively.

3.2   Django Backend API

The server-side software architecture was implemented using Django, a Python web framework [5]. Since medical data is increasing exponentially, such architecture intends to be efficient, highly available and scalable. Besides, health professionals want to view, store, share and process images independently of their location or devices and with minimum downtime. Django comprises the main endpoint API whose methods allow tasks such as storing data in the database or processing the data model entities of Fig. 2. Each method corresponds to a service, which can be called through Django's REST API.

The chosen database was PostgreSQL [12] since it has plenty of features to help developers build applications and administrators protect data integrity. The database comprises four entities: User, Study, Model and Patient. Each user (researcher or health professional) can upload several DICOM studies to the application. However, each study only belongs to one user (the one who uploaded it). Likewise, every researcher can upload various AI models, but each model only belongs to one user. The latter, however, does not imply that the owner of the study (or model) cannot share that entity with other users. The patient entity can also have several studies associated, but each study only belongs to one patient. Database attributes regarding users' and patients' sensitive clinical information were encrypted using 256-bit AES encryption. These include the user's password, medical certificate, code for two-factor authentication, patient's name and all keys and initialisation vectors for the AES cypher. AES is employed as the chief encryption primitive, which uses the permutation method in a specified number of rounds allowing better security, especially against brute force attacks. Moreover,

an instance of Orthanc was created to store the DICOM studies information in an encrypted state. The metadata related to the physician, hospital, and study modality were encrypted for enhanced privacy and security.

The application has two central users: the health professional and the researcher. Everyone whose intentions are only investigational-driven can be a researcher. In turn, for someone to authenticate as a health professional, must provide a medical certificate, whose validation is done manually by the application administrator. Through the application's authentication system REST API, a user can authenticate himself and ensure that no one can enter his account without the proper credentials. Such authentication system was implemented using Djoser, a library that provides a set of Django Rest Framework views to handle actions such as registration, login, logout, password reset and account activation. When a user signs in, he has an access token, which refreshes itself from time to time, allowing him to remain authenticated. Also, social networks authentication was incorporated with the help of Python Social Auth, using the OAuth2.0 protocol. All API methods are protected as, when a call occurs, an API key (access token) is required to get a valid response from that method. Furthermore, two-factor authentication was enabled to allow better security overall. Therefore, besides providing his credentials, the user needs to insert a secret key, which can be present in a third-party tool such as Google Authenticator.

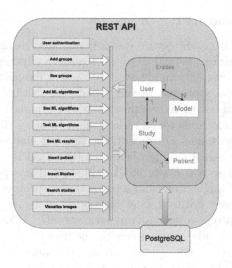

Fig. 2. Backend API.

3.3 Machine Learning Modelling

Machine Learning model deployment is the method by which a model is integrated into an existing production environment to make decisions based on data. One of the typical ways to deploy an ML model is to create a web service for prediction. Usually, the first step is to create an ML model, train it and validate

its performance. Second, the model needs to be persisted. Persistence can be achieved by storing the trained model in a file. Finally, the pre-trained model can be served using a web framework [20]. MCC focus on this last stage of the model's life cycle - using the pre-trained model to make predictions on new data, in this case, medical images.

For that matter, AI models need to be added to the application. In this case, the application accepts algorithms written in Python. To add a model, researchers first need to fill out a form with information about the algorithm, e.g., name, description, model architecture, and task (image segmentation, object localisation, image processing, lesion detection or classification). In the second step, they are redirected to a code editor where they can submit the algorithm's code and upload the corresponding pre-trained model files (Fig. 3a).

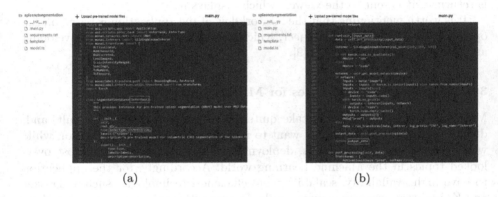

(a)   (b)

Fig. 3. UI of a researcher. Code editor.

The editor also includes a template that users should follow to submit their code. Such a template uses three key Python modules: "InferTask", "InferType", and "Application". Each algorithm is seen as an inference task, so it must correspond to a class that inherits the "InferTask" module. Each task has a "type". For instance, if the model performs image segmentation, its type is "SEGMEN-TATION". Each "type" is defined as shown in Fig. 3a. Finally, the "main.py" file needs another class that must inherit the "Application" module. The latter is what turns the algorithm's code into code that can run on MCC.

The "run" method (Fig. 3b) is mandatory, and it should contain all the code that the user wants to run, i.e., the workflow of the algorithm. All the other methods or functions possibly added to the algorithm's class should be called here. To apply the algorithm, the backend will specifically look for the "run" method and execute its code. Finally, the output will be written in the appropriate format to be displayed in the viewer.

When a "Publish" button is clicked, all the algorithm's files are zipped and sent to the backend, which, first, validates the files, that is, checks if there are no missing files, if the code template was respected and, then, stores the algorithm

in the database. In parallel, a Docker [6] image based on the model API is created for that algorithm. It will be used for the creation of the correspondent deployment with Kubernetes [8].

Once the model is submitted, it is available for the user to perform inference on DICOM images. Since AI is incorporated as a second reader functionality, it is required that AI predictions are available in the same image viewing environment as the images and accessible through a simple click. The user has a choice of multiple models to select from, and the series of images that the user is viewing at that moment is used as input to the chosen model. Once a model is selected, the unique identifier of that series is sent to the backend, which requests those images from Orthanc and caches them. Moreover, the model zip file is retrieved from the database, unzipped, and an instance of the algorithm's class is created. Ultimately, the "run" method of that instance is executed, and once the output is returned, it is sent to the viewer, which displays it.

It is worth mentioning that the AI workflow of the application is based on the open-source MONAI Label project, which provides a framework for developing and deploying AI applications [9].

3.4   Docker and Kubernetes for ML Inference

Machine learning models can take quite a long time to predict a result, and, during that time, the user may want to navigate through the application while waiting for the response. Thus, deployment is perhaps one of the most over-looked topics in the Machine Learning world. Accordingly, for the application to have high availability, scalability and efficiency, technologies such as Docker and Kubernetes are extremely valuable. Docker takes away repetitive, mundane configuration tasks and is used throughout the development lifecycle for fast, easy and portable application development. Kubernetes, in turn, is utilised for automating deployment, scaling, and management of containerised applications using Docker runtime. Such implementation allows the user to update or roll back the version of his models. If he wants to change the model itself, a new image will be created for that model, and the deployment will be updated so that pods can run a container with that updated image. A pod is the smallest and most basic deployable object in Kubernetes. It represents a single instance of a running process (docker container) in the cluster.

As described earlier, each model has its API and runs in a container, where all its dependencies are stored. A Kubernetes cluster with one node was created to orchestrate numerous containers. In such node, each container is allocated to a unique pod and three pod replicas, called a deployment, are constantly running each model API and return the response to the frontend. Each deployment has its service, and each service is exposed to the outside via an ingress. Ingress is a controller that redirects to a specific service depending on the path provided in the URL. Thus, depending on the model that the user selects, the ingress will redirect to the appropriate service, which, in turn, redirects to one of the three pods of the deployment that runs the model API (Fig. 4).

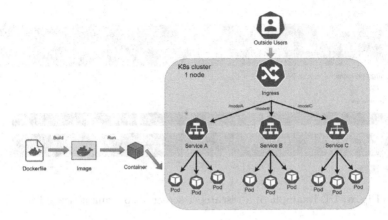

Fig. 4. Kubernetes cluster architecture and pipeline.

4 Results

The proposed web application is in the proof-of-concept stage. Nevertheless, it has been validated from a technical perspective through a set of experiments, such as testing the performance of the backend in terms of scalability, availability, latency, privacy and security; and the efficiency of PostgreSQL database and Orthanc server querying.

The first step that any user must go through to use the application is to authenticate himself with the correct credentials (email and password) as shown in Fig. 5 or pass the two-factor authentication phase.

Fig. 5. Sign in page.

Furthermore, both groups of users, researchers and health professionals, can access a list (Fig. 6) where all the studies they have uploaded (or to which they have been granted access) are displayed. Those studies can be filtered by the information of some DICOM tags, namely, patient name or ID, study modality and date. On this page, users can also upload more studies using the "+" button on the right side of the screen.

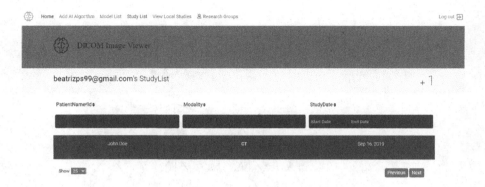

Fig. 6. UI. Example of a researcher screen displaying a study list.

Besides a study list, researchers also have access to a model list, where all the ML models they have access to are displayed. It also allows them to pick a model and be redirected to a page where they can edit its information and code.

When users click on one of the studies from Fig. 6, they are redirected to the OHIF viewer, where they can view the corresponding DICOM images. As mentioned, since AI is incorporated as a second reader functionality, it is required that AI predictions are available in the same image viewing environment as the DICOM images. Therefore, users have access to a panel where they can select and run AI models. Figure 7 shows an example of a user screen where the user chose a model that performed the automatic segmentation of the spleen in a CT series. As noted, sensitive patient information in the DICOM studies must be private and secure. For that matter, data is encrypted at rest in the Orthanc server and at transit over HTTPS. Figure 7 presents an example of a DICOM study in which the metadata tags were encrypted with 256-bit AES encryption.

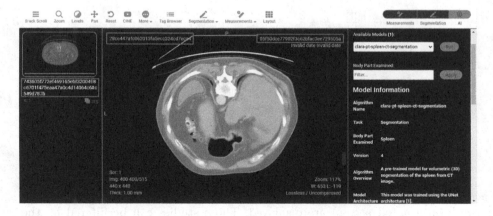

Fig. 7. UI. Example of a user screen displaying images and applying AI to them.

5   Conclusions and Future Work

MEDCLOUDCARE enables healthcare professionals to remotely access and evaluate patients' medical imaging information, which is encrypted to assure security and privacy regarding sensitive information. This platform provides a method for enhancing treatment adherence as it allows health professionals to share medical images and quickly and correctly analyse them. It is also possible to measure biomedical parameters and identify, classify, and quantify patterns in those images with the help of AI.

From a biomedical research perspective, MCC provides research users with a way to add and use pre-trained ML or DL models. The fact that they can test their AI models on medical images and see the result can help them understand if those models have the desired quality.

Additionally, MCC was tested using trials that allow the validation from a technical point of view, assuring that there are no errors. However, besides all the core features and functionalities, there is still work to be done. A core function is the need to encrypt the pixel data of the DICOM files and not only their metadata. Finally, MCC requires validation in third-party cloud infrastructures, namely Google Cloud Platform (GCP). This step will be focused on using the Google Kubernetes Engine (GKE) and will be automated using Terraform.

Acknowledgements. This work is financed by National Funds through the Portuguese funding agency, FCT - Fundação para a Ciência e a Tecnologia, within the project LA/P/0063/2020, and through a PhD Fellowship (SFRH/BD/146528/2019 - Cláudia Brito).

References

1. 3D Slicer. https://www.slicer.org/. Accessed Apr 2022
2. Cornerstone.js. https://www.cornerstonejs.org/. Accessed Dec 2022
3. DeepInfer.http://www.deepinfer.org/. Accessed Apr 2022
4. DICOMweb^{TM}. https://www.dicomstandard.org/using/dicomweb. Accessed Dec 2022
5. Django. https://www.djangoproject.com/. Accessed Apr 2022
6. Docker. https://www.docker.com/. Accessed Apr 2022
7. ePAD - Web-based platform for quantitative imaging in the clinical workflow. https://epad.stanford.edu/. Accessed Apr 2022
8. Kubernetes. https://kubernetes.io/. Accessed Apr 2022
9. MONAI Label. https://github.com/Project-MONAI/MONAILabel. Accessed Jan 2022
10. Orthanc - DICOM Server. https://www.orthanc-server.com/. Accessed Dec 2022
11. OsiriX DICOM Viewer. https://www.osirix-viewer.com/. Accessed Apr 2022
12. PostgreSQL. https://www.postgresql.org/. Accessed Apr 2022
13. Precision imaging metrics. https://www.precisionmetrics.org/. Accessed Apr 2022
14. React - A JavaScript library for building user interfaces. https://reactjs.org/. Accessed Dec 2022
15. TOMAAT. https://tomaat.readthedocs.io/en/latest/. Accessed Apr 2022

16. XNAT. https://www.xnat.org/. Accessed Apr 2022
17. Brito, C.: Cloud-based analytics for monitoring and classification of arrhythmias (2018)
18. Min, Q., Wang, X., Huang, B., Xu, L.: Web-based technology for remote viewing of radiological images: app validation. J. Med. Internet Res. **22**(9), e16224 (2020). https://doi.org/10.2196/16224
19. Min, Q., Wang, Z., Liu, N.: An Evaluation of HTML5 and WebGL for Medical Imaging Applications. J. Healthc. Eng. 2018 (2018). https://doi.org/10.1155/2018/1592821
20. Murallie, T.: 3 ways to deploy machine learning models in production. https://towardsdatascience.com/3-ways-to-deploy-machine-learning-models-in-production-cdba15b00e. Accessed Apr 2022
21. Pinhasi, A.: Deploying machine learning models to production - inference service architecture patterns. https://medium.com/data-for-ai/deploying-machine-learning-models-to-production-inference-service-architecture-patterns-bc8051f70080. Accessed April 2022
22. PostDICOM: Top 25 free dicom viewers for doctors, medical students, and health professionals. https://www.postdicom.com/en/blog/top-25-free-dicom-viewers. Accessed Dec 2022
23. Ramos, A.: Deep Learning Applied to Medical Imaging (2019)
24. Sedghi, A., et al.: Tesseract-medical imaging: open-source browser-based platform for artificial intelligence deployment in medical imaging. Medical Imaging 2019 Image-Guided Procedures Robotic Interventions, and Modeling, vol. 10951, pp. 446–451 (2019) https://doi.org/10.1117/12.2513004
25. Suganyadevi, S., Seethalakshmi, V., Balasamy, K.: A review on deep learning in medical image analysis. Int. J. Multimedia Inf. Retrieval **2021**, 1–20 (2021). https://doi.org/10.1007/S13735-021-00218-1
26. Toshpulatov, Z., Marti, R., Diaz, O.: DeepDraw! developing a web application for medical image annotation and computer aided analysis (2019). http://eia.udg.edu/aoliver/maiaDocs/bookMaia2nd_small.pdf
27. Yuan, R., Luo, M., Sun, Z., Shi, S., Xiao, P., Xie, Q.: RayPlus: a web-based platform for medical image processing. J. Digit. Imaging **30**(2), 197 (2017). https://doi.org/10.1007/S10278-016-9920-Y
28. Ziegler, E., et al.: Open health imaging foundation viewer: an extensible open-source framework for building web-based imaging applications to support cancer research. JCO Clin. Cancer Inf. **4**, 336–345 (2020). https://doi.org/10.1200/cci.19.00131

An Active Learning-Based Medical Diagnosis System

Catarina Pinto, Juliana Faria, and Luis Macedo

CISUC - Centre for Informatics and Systems of the University of Coimbra,
Department of Informatics Engineering, University of Coimbra, Coimbra, Portugal
{fmenino,jcfaria}@student.dei.uc.pt, macedo@dei.uc.pt

Abstract. Every year thousands of people get their diagnoses wrongly, and several patients have their health conditions aggravated due to mis-diagnosis. This problem is even more challenging when the list of possible diseases is long, as in a general medicine speciality. The development of Artificial Intelligence (AI) medical diagnosis systems could prevent mis-diagnosis when clinicians are in doubt. We developed an AI system to help clinicians in their daily practice. They could consult the system to get an immediate opinion and diminish waiting times in triage services since this task could be carried out with minimal human interaction. Our method relies on Machine Learning techniques, more precisely on Active Learning and Neural Networks classifiers. To train this model, we used a data set that relates symptoms to several diseases. We compared our models with other models from the literature, and our results show that it is possible to achieve even better performance with much less data, mainly because of the contribution of the Active Learning component.

Keywords: Machine Learning · Active Learning · Deep Learning · Neural Networks · Medical diagnosis · modAL

1 Introduction

Medicine and Artificial Intelligence (AI) have long crossed paths in different medical fields. These AI technologies have been applied with considerable success in the clinical diagnosis of acute and chronic diseases and breast cancer recurrence prediction, among others [10]. Regarding their performance in medical diagnosis, there is evidence that models in the literature are as good or better than clinicians at this task [10]. The use of AI may allow the optimization of the treatment of common complex diseases, such as cardiovascular diseases. Nevertheless, patients can benefit from a more precise treatment using AI algorithms based on big data. AI may also be an improvement at the financial level.

This work is funded by the FCT - Foundation for Science and Technology, I.P./MCTES through national funds (PIDDAC), within the scope of CISUC R&D Unit - UIDB/00326/2020 or project code UIDP/00326/2020.

By being integrated into hospital management systems, it may reduce the costs associated with logistics and may also reduce time costs [10].

A correct medical diagnosis is crucial. The news of having an illness, the emotional distress and the costs of unnecessary treatment or all the consequences of a diagnosis that wrongly concludes that the patient is disease-free have a massive impact on the patient's life [6]. Unfortunately, there are still many cases of error or long waiting times. This is a problem for the patients since waiting may aggravate their health condition. The development of medical diagnostic models could prevent misdiagnosis when the clinicians are in doubt. They could consult the model to get an immediate opinion and diminish waiting times in triage services since this task could be carried out with minimal human interaction. Since symptoms can provide credible information for disease diagnosis, a symptom-based diagnostic model may be beneficial in achieving the aforementioned goals. Also, the diagnosis decision may become less subjective with the use of an algorithm.

Many of those AI systems rely on Machine Learning (ML) techniques. Such systems are trained with data sets that cross features with diseases to classify diseases correctly. However, these data sets are often difficult to obtain or too short to train ML algorithms effectively, resulting in imperfect models [9]. Active Learning (AL) [7–9] is one of the most selected ML techniques to deal with the problem of scarcity of data. It allows the machine to choose for labelling the most informative instances among many unlabelled samples, reducing to a minimum the time spent by experts in the construction of the data set.

This study aims to help clinicians in their daily practice, especially those dealing with many diseases, as happens in general medicine specialities. We built a medical diagnosis model using AL techniques [9], more precisely the modAL framework [2], and combined it with Neural Networks (NN) as a classifier.

The remainder of this paper is structured as Materials, Methods, Results, Discussion, and Conclusion. In the next section, we describe the related work. In Sect. 3, we describe the materials used, while in Sect. 4 we present the strategy to build the model we propose. We show the results obtained with our model in Sect. 5, and, in Sect. 6, we discuss them. Finally, in Sect. 7, we summarize the work done and make conclusions.

2   Related Work

Shen et al. [10] reviewed papers from the medical context between 2000 and 2019 that compare human clinical performance with that of AI techniques, showing that the performance of AI algorithms is similar to that of clinicians, outperforming them when dealing with inexperienced clinicians.

Regarding the diagnosis problem, to the best of our knowledge, there are only three models that combine several diseases: [4,6] and [3]. In this latter model, the authors used ML and different classifiers for experiments and obtained an accuracy of 84.9% utilising a combination of two modalities.

In [4], a preprocessing of medical texts is performed, and symptomatic entities are identified. For this processing, tools such as MIMIC-III (used to eliminate

the portions of the text where there are no symptoms) and MetaMap (a Natural Language Processing (NPL) tool to identify symptoms extracted from the complete medical texts) are used.

After the preprocessing is done, the authors make a vector representation of the symptoms. The strength of association of each symptom with each disease is obtained (using TF-IDF) and used as a feature in the vector. The data obtained is then used to train a Bi-LSTM multi-label classification model. The preprocessing developed in this work involved assigning different weights to the various symptoms, culminating in a data set with cases given by weighted symptom vectors, ready to be used for model training.

With the 50 and 100 most common diseases being treated, this problem is viewed by the authors as multi-label classification, and the algorithm's performance is evaluated based on four metrics calculated using scikit-learn: precision (also known as positive predictive value), recall (also known as sensitivity), F1-score, and area under the curve (AUC). Our model shares similarities with this one in that we evaluated it using some of these metrics (precision, recall and AUC) and specificity, negative predictive value, and accuracy.

When training the model, the authors use binary cross-entropy loss function and Adam Optimizer. The LSTM model has 100 hidden nodes and uses a dynamical mechanism with 50-time steps and drop-out strategies (where neurons are randomly chosen to be ignored during training).

Another work related to this one relies on automatic ICD-9 coding using Deep Learning [5], which in this case does not use symptoms but the interpretation of medical texts (DeepLabeler model). The model developed by the authors outperforms the DeepLabeler model, showing the importance of symptoms when inferring diseases. Although medical texts have most of the information available, extracting evidence of interest for diagnosis is difficult. Symptoms follow the process from illness to cure and are a significant source of knowledge regarding diagnosis.

Our work shares similarities with this study and with [4], as we use symptoms for diagnosis. In addition, we used a data set that matches a set of symptoms to a medical diagnosis. The preprocessing will be done using only Python, individualizing the symptoms as features.

3   Materials

To build the model, we used the "Disease Symptom Prediction"[1] data set, which includes 41 different diseases and up to 17 symptoms. We have 4920 samples before preprocessing the data to train and test our model. There are 120 cases of each disease, and the data set is balanced. We also have a description of the diseases, the precautions to be taken and the severity of the symptoms. The AL framework used in this work was modAL [2], which is geared towards Python3.

---

[1] https://www.kaggle.com/itachi9604/disease-symptom-description-dataset?select=dataset.csv.

4 Methods

An intelligent model capable of diagnosing several diseases with high performance can turn into a revolution in the medical field. Based on [10], Neural Networks (NN) algorithms are the most used in this type of problem, but to the best of our knowledge it has not been used in conjunction with AL techniques. To unite AL and NN, we followed the following steps. First, we preprocessed the data set, turning the several symptoms into features and attributing weights for each symptom. Next, we built our neural classifier and used it on our AL model. A representation of the developed NN can be found in Fig. 1a. An input layer with 131 neurons (which concerns the total number of symptoms), a hidden layer with 64 neurons and an output layer with 41 neurons (corresponding to the 41 diseases) were used. The layers are all fully connected.

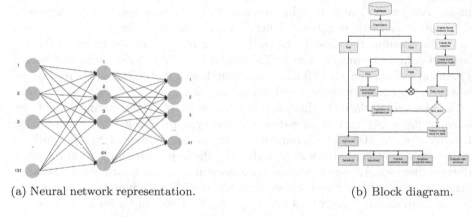

(a) Neural network representation.   (b) Block diagram.

Fig. 1. Methodology: Neural network and block diagram.

Figure 1b presents the flow diagram of the proposed methodology. This study was conducted using Python (4.2.5) and the modAL library (0.4.1) precisely for the AL component.

4.1 Preprocessing

The data set we used comprises a list of symptoms and the correspondent disease. In each case (sample), the number of symptoms varies. We also had a file filled with the information about the severity of the symptoms on a scale of 1 up to 7, being seven the most serious symptom. Considering that each sample had a different number of symptoms and that symptoms were strings, it would be hard to add weight to each one of them, and it would also be more difficult for the classifier to be trained. To overcome these difficulties, we turned the 17 unique

symptoms into features and filled the columns with 0's (if that sample does not have the symptom) and 1's (if that sample has the symptom). After that, we attributed the respective weight (severity) for each column (symptom).

4.2   Active Learning Component

To develop our AL model, we created a classifier and defined some parameters. As a result of the capability of NN to achieve excellent performance and analyze a vast amount of data, we decide to use it as our classifier. The Pytorch library was used to build a simple two fully connected layers classifier, i.e., two linear layers which apply a linear transformation to the incoming data. The loss function chosen for the classifier was the CrossEntropyLoss which computes the cross-entropy loss between input and target. The optimizer used was Adam, a stochastic optimization method.

Beyond the classifier, we also had to define some parameters to our model, such as the query strategy, the number of epochs of the model at its creation (Epochs Learner), and at the Active Learning loop (Epochs AL Loop), the number of instances and queries. Some experiments were done for all those parameters until we got the best values for them, as described in Sect. 4.4. The number of learner epochs defines the number of complete cycles over the training data set at the time the model is created (an object of the ActiveLearner class). The number of AL Loop epochs refers to the number of complete cycles over the training instances passed to the model at the training time.

4.3   Metrics

As stated in previous sections, the model we developed is compared with others already developed and used in the literature. To this end, the model's performance is evaluated based on several metrics: sensitivity, specificity, positive and negative predictive value, and accuracy. The model is also compared and evaluated using the AUC. Sensitivity, specificity, positive and negative predictive value, and accuracy correspond to micro-averaging measurements since it is a multi-class problem where the classes are not equally represented in the data set.

The rationale for choosing these metrics is directly related to the medical domain in which this work lies. Sensitivity is crucial in a medical context since it corresponds to the ability to identify an individual's disease (a late diagnosis or the absence of a diagnosis could lead to the patient's death). On the other hand, specificity in a medical context translates to the ability to exclude disease hypotheses in healthy individuals. While not as striking as the previous metric, it may correspond not to subjecting a healthy individual to unnecessarily invasive or extremely aggressive treatments.

4.4   Experimental Design

The implementation phase began by processing the data set used, as reported in Sect. 4.1. The development of the classifier model using AL and (Pytorch)

followed. Once the model was developed, we made tests to find the best combination of parameters for it. We tried different values for the epoch, instances, and also three different sampling methods: least confident (LC), entropy and margin sampling. The parameters' values chosen were the number of epochs of the model at its creation (30), the number of epochs of the model in the AL loop (40), the sampling strategy (margin sampling), the number of instances that are passed to the model when it is learning in the AL loop (10), the number of queries made in the same loop (10), and the number of layers of the NN in use (two as described at Sect. 4.2). The model was trained and tested ten times for each parameter set (to ensure that the results were statistically significant). Then we evaluated the best parameter set based on the average accuracy for both training and testing.

5   Results

We tested a combination of all parameters described in Sect. 4.4. The best results for a network of 1, 2, and 3 layers correspond to those on Table 1. These results consider the model's performance from the time it is created until it completes the AL loop. In this loop, the model is updated according to the new data it receives, and its performance is successively improved. In many tests, we verified that this performance reached 100% quickly, reflecting that the model was overfitting.

In the tests, it was impossible to have the individual perception since they were done all at once. Although, for these combinations of parameters and when the remaining metrics were assessed (namely sensitivity and specificity), the accuracy was good, leading us to realize that the model should be overfitting. Due to this fact, these were not the parameters adopted for the final version, as seen in Sect. 4.4. Even so, these results showed that the network with the best results was the two layers network (id two and id three). Therefore, from this point on, we focused only on this network to find the best combination of parameters.

The strategy adopted to find the best set of parameters that did not overfit was to go through the combinations from the best to the successively worse ones and evaluate those with good sensitivity and specificity values, not all of which were equal to 1.

We found the best results to arise almost entirely for several instances passed to the model in the AL loop. However, we also found that overfitting almost always (if not always) occurred when that number of instances is 15. Thus, we considered only the best cases for which the number of instances differed from 15. The sets of parameters assessed individually and their respective performances are shown, in order, in Table 2. For all the sets in Table 2, the sampling strategy was margin sampling, the number of instances was 10, and the number of queries was 10.

Table 1. Best combinations of parameters.

Id	Layers	Epochs (Learner)	Epochs (AL loop)	Sampling strategy	Instances to train	Queries	Train accuracy	Test accuracy
1	1	40	20	Margin	10	10	56.02%	54.70%
2	2	10	40	Margin	15	10	61.15%	57.86%
3	2	50	40	LC	15	10	59.31%	60.03%
4	3	40	50	LC	15	10	58.39%	58.37%
5	3	20	50	LC	10	10	57.51%	59.65%
6	3	30	10	LC	10	10	56.77%	58.92%
7	3	40	50	Margin	10	10	58.39%	58.37%

Table 2. More parameters combinations and its respective accuracies.

id	Epochs (Learner)	Epochs (AL loop)	Train accuracy	Test accuracy
1	10	10	55.82%	54.57%
2	50	40	55.55%	54.04%
3	50	30	54.99%	54.10%
4	30	20	54.90%	53.43%
5	30	20	53.05%	52.32%
6	10	40	52.72%	50.91%
7	50	10	52.25%	49.46%
8	50	50	51.65%	50.46%
9	50	20	51.58%	50.92%
10	30	30	51.54%	50.26%
11	30	40	51.49%	49.27%

When evaluating the performance of the first ten models in the previous tables, we realized that the results, although good, could be better without falling into overfitting. We then evaluated them until the 11th model, which appeared to have the best results without overfitting. This was then the model adopted as the final. It should be noted that, in the medical field, the most relevant metric should be the sensitivity, which, for the model in question, reaches values around 90%. Table 4 shows an example of the results generated by the model defined with the previous parameters. We will discuss these results in the following section.

Table 3. Comparison between different models. Guo et al.'s model [4]

	Our model (41 diseases)	Guo et al.'s model (50 diseases)	Guo et al.'s (100 diseases)
Micro-precision	92.07%	50.80%	47.20%
Micro-recall	92.07%	63.20%	52.90%

6 Discussion

The accuracy results at Table 1 are the mean of the models' accuracy during the entire loop. It starts with low values until reaching a great accuracy. Nevertheless, this metric only evaluates the mean, not the final result, considering that the values obtained in Table 4 are consistent with what was expected and closer to the final values of the accuracy of the model.

By analysing the results obtained with the trained model, the variation in classification difficulty between the various diseases is evident. While in diseases such as Tuberculosis, Pneumonia or Heart Attack the model is infallible (that is, it correctly classifies all cases), in cases such as Hepatitis A the model has extreme difficulty in identifying the pathology (the model cannot identify a single case of this pathology).

A small test set can be the reason for the values obtained for some of those metrics, i.e., if we had just one sample of that disease in the test set, a wrong/right classification would lead us to zero/one, and it is not enough to evaluate the model correctly.

Since sensitivity is the most relevant metric in the medical field (it dictates how good the model is at detecting the disease in people who are actually sick), an overall value of 92.07% is quite favourable in general practice since 41 distinct diseases are included here. Even so, the poor results for the illnesses mentioned above indicate that the present model is unsuitable for their classification. Still, the diseases for which the model presents more difficulties can be selected, and we can build one or several new, more specific models for these pathologies. Also, for further study, using a more extensive data set could improve the model's performance.

An average specificity of 99.80% tells us that our model is quite good at identifying negative cases as negative, so it is possible to use it in a medical context which could involve not the detection of the disease but the screening of various illnesses in the diagnosis.

Regarding state of the art in the area (depicted in Sect. 2) and starting with the work of [3], it can be seen that using ML and testing several types of classifiers, the authors obtained a model with 84.9% accuracy, combining these two modalities. As shown in Table 3, our model got an average accuracy of 99.61%, and the added complexity of the work should be highlighted, given the need to test several classifiers (in this work, we used only NN).

Table 4. Metrics for each disease obtained by testing the model created. SS - sensibility, SP - specificity, PPV - positive predicted value, NPV - negative predicted value, ACC - accuracy

Disease	SS	SP	PPV	NPV	ACC
Allergy	1	1	1	1	1
GERD	1	1	1	1	1
Chronic cholestasis	0	1	0	0.979675	0.979675
Drug Reaction	1	1	1	1	1
Peptic ulcer disease	1	1	1	1	1
AIDS	1	1	1	1	1
Diabetes	1	1	1	1	1
Gastroenteritis	1	1	1	1	1
Bronchial Asthma	1	1	1	1	1
Hypertension	1	1	1	1	1
Migraine	1	1	1	1	1
Cervical spondylosis	1	1	1	1	1
Paralysis (brain hemorrhage)	1	1	1	1	1
Jaundice	1	1	1	1	1
Malaria	1	1	1	1	1
Chicken pox	1	1	1	1	1
Dengue	1	1	1	1	1
Typhoid	1	1	1	1	1
Hepatitis A	0	1	0	0.973577	0.973577
Hepatitis B	1	1	1	1	1
Hepatitis C	1	1	1	1	1
Hepatitis D	1	0.952233	0.313433	1	0.953252
Hepatitis E	1	1	1	1	1
Alcoholic hepatitis	1	1	1	1	1
Tuberculosis	1	1	1	1	1
Common Cold	1	1	1	1	1
Pneumonia	1	1	1	1	1
Dimorphic hemmorhoids	1	1	1	1	1
Heart attack	1	1	1	1	1
Varicose veins	1	1	1	1	1
Hypothyroidism	1	1	1	1	1
Hyperthyroidism	1	1	1	1	1
Hypoglycemia	1	1	1	1	1
Osteoarthristis	0	1	0	0.96748	0.96748
Arthritis	1	0.966597	0.448276	1	0.96748
Paroymsal Positional Vertigo	1	1	1	1	1
Acne	1	1	1	1	1
Urinary tract infection	1	1	1	1	1
Psoriasis	1	1	1	1	1
Impetigo	1	1	1	1	1
Micro-averaging measure:	92.07%	99.80%	92.07%	99.80%	99.61%

Regarding the work developed by [4], one can see in Sect. 2 the increased work in data preprocessing compared to our model. The authors do the processing of medical reports, from which they extract symptom entities and, based on this, generate symptom vectors that will then be used in the construction of the model. For this purpose, Guo et al. have to use three different tools. The present work uses a data set that relates several diseases with their respective symptoms, making the preprocessing task much more accessible. Although the most common in clinical settings is still the writing of medical reports, developing an interface that allows the insertion of symptoms in a practical and fast way would allow the direct use of our model and its direct response. Something in common between the work developed by those authors in the literature and the work developed by us is the attribution of weights to symptoms which we consider to be an added value in the detection of the correct pathology. Comparing the models in terms of complexity, one can see that [4] developed a NN as well, but, in this case, a Bi-LSTM with 100 hidden neurons, with a dynamic mechanism with 50-time steps and dropout strategies. The present work developed a NN with a sequential container with two layers, both with a linear activation function.

The metrics obtained for each model are presented in Table 3. As can be seen, the model we developed shows better values both for sensitivity and positive predictive value. The AUC also shows significant differences between our model and Guo et al. models (0.99 vs 0.853 and 0.854). However, we should not directly compare these values since we could not calculate the micro-AUC while Guo et al. did it. It should also be noted that the results mentioned refer to different databases. So, to have a more accurate comparison, it would be interesting to apply the model developed to the database used by the [4].

In Fig. 2, it can be observed the variation of the accuracy obtained in the test based on the number of instances that the model has already used for training. We did this study for the best model found (mentioned before) being presented its performance for each of the three sampling strategies studied.

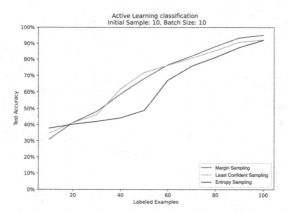

Fig. 2. Evolution of the test accuracy with the number of classified examples.

The margin sampling is the one that presents the best results at the end of the ten queries. This strategy assumes that the most informative data samples are those which fall within this margin, so accordingly to the results is a good option for our problem, which has several classes and, consequently, several support vectors to separate them. Still, we can see that excellent accuracy values are reached with few instances (2.5% of the data set), and, when exceeding this value, the model already tends to enter in overfitting.

In [1] a model was developed using a Support Vector Classifier to predict the same diseases based on the same data set. To train this classifier, the authors use 85% of the data set (which corresponds to 4182 training samples) and obtain a test accuracy of 94.72%. In the present work, only 100 cases are used, and accuracy values of the same order are obtained, which can be considered a remarkable positive consequence of applying AL.

7 Conclusion

The model proved to be quite good and, compared with the models developed so far, gave evidence of surpassing them. These facts make it clear that using AL in this area is an asset since it allows the creation of models with better performance while maintaining simplicity. As can be observed in Fig. 2, with a few instances (100), our model is capable of achieving a high value of accuracy (> 90%). This approach allows us to construct models that demand a lower computational power than usual, as we need to train only with 2.5% of the data set. This achievement becomes even more significant if we also consider the cost for medical experts to build data sets.

As this is a symptom-based diagnostic model, diagnosing the pathology in question in the early stages of the disease or asymptomatic cases may not be easy or even possible. Nevertheless, a model similar to this could be beneficial to assist the physicians in their daily practice.

Since the data set in use has, for each disease, only symptoms that can be associated with the disease (and not extra symptoms that, although not associated with the disease, are often reported by patients), it is thought that this data set already corresponds to the treatment of data in which there should already be some noise component, noise being understood as symptoms not associated with the diagnosed disease. Noise data would be more real than the data set used. Therefore, it may be interesting to evaluate the performance of this classifier with this type of data, or even to re-train the architecture using data with noise.

Each disease is associated with a limited number of symptoms, and the various cases of each disease correspond to combinations of those symptoms. There are then cases of each disease consisting of the same symptoms. On the one hand, it is possible to have quite distinct sets of symptoms among several diseases, making it simple to determine the disease in question. On the other hand, and due to the existence of equal cases, it may happen that there are equal cases in the training and test sets, making them similar (in a very extreme case, it would

be the equivalent to evaluate the classifier with the training set). Therefore, it would be of interest, in future work, to explore data sets with more diversified cases for each disease, with the inclusion of symptoms corresponding to noise, and to evaluate the performance of the classifier developed under these conditions. The addition of noise to cases should add difficulty to classification and a better representation of the real world, in which patients very often report more symptoms than those associated with the disease which they are diagnosed.

Although the data currently used corresponds to real data, we consider that it will be relevant to test the classifier in real-world situations, as well as with different data sets and methodologies, namely, different distributed classes, possibly larger data sets, and different query strategies.

References

1. Disease type prediction using symptoms (2020). https://www.kaggle.com/naga26/disease-type-prediction-using-symptoms
2. Danka, T.: modAL: a modular active learning framework for Python3 (2018). https://modal-python.readthedocs.io/en/latest/. Accessed 29 Oct 2021
3. Faris, H., Habib, M., Faris, M., Elayan, H., Alomari, A.: An intelligent multimodal medical diagnosis system based on patients' medical questions and structured symptoms for telemedicine. Inform. Med. Unlocked **23** (2021). https://doi.org/10.1016/j.imu.2021.100513
4. Guo, D., et al.: Disease inference with symptom extraction and bidirectional recurrent neural network. In: Proceedings of the 2018 IEEE International Conference on Bioinformatics and Biomedicine, BIBM 2018, pp. 864–868 (2019). https://doi.org/10.1109/BIBM.2018.8621182
5. Li, M., et al.: Automated ICD-9 coding via a deep learning approach. IEEE/ACM Trans. Comput. Biol. Bioinf. **16**(4), 1193–1202 (2019). https://doi.org/10.1109/TCBB.2018.2817488
6. Mangiameli, P., West, D., Rampal, R.: Model selection for medical diagnosis decision support systems. Decis. Support Syst. **36**(3), 247–259 (2004). https://doi.org/10.1016/S0167-9236(02)00143-4
7. Ren, P., et al.: A survey of deep active learning. CoRR abs/2009.00236 (2020). https://arxiv.org/abs/2009.00236
8. Settles, B.: From theories to queries. In: Guyon, I., Cawley, G.C., Dror, G., Lemaire, V., Statnikov, A.R. (eds.) Active Learning and Experimental Design workshop, In Conjunction with AISTATS 2010, Sardinia, Italy, 16 May 2010. JMLR Proceedings, vol. 16, pp. 1–18. JMLR.org (2011). http://proceedings.mlr.press/v16/settles11a/settles11a.pdf
9. Settles, B.: Active Learning. Synthesis Lectures on Artificial Intelligence and Machine Learning. Morgan & Claypool Publishers (2012). https://doi.org/10.2200/S00429ED1V01Y201207AIM018
10. Shen, J., et al.: Artificial intelligence versus clinicians in disease diagnosis: systematic review. JMIR Med. Inform. **7**(3), 1–15 (2019). https://doi.org/10.2196/10010

Comparative Evaluation of Classification Indexes and Outlier Detection of Microcytic Anaemias in a Portuguese Sample

Beatriz N. Leitão[1,2], Paula Faustino[2,3], and Susana Vinga[1]

[1] INESC-ID, Instituto Superior Técnico, Universidade de Lisboa, Lisbon, Portugal
susanavinga@tecnico.ulisboa.pt
[2] Departamento de Genética Humana, Instituto Nacional de Saúde Dr. Ricardo Jorge, Lisbon, Portugal
[3] Instituto de Saúde Ambiental, Faculdade de Medicina, Universidade de Lisboa, Lisbon, Portugal

Abstract. Anaemia is often caused by a nutritional problem or by genetic diseases. The world prevalence of anaemia is estimated to be 24.8%, strengthening the need for appropriate discrimination methods between the different types of this disease, an essential step to choosing the best treatment and offering genetic counselling. Several indexes based on haematological features have been proposed to address the challenge of microcytic anaemias classification. However, they have not been tested extensively nor optimised for different countries. Here we test existing binary classification indexes in a Portuguese sample of 390 patients diagnosed with microcytic anaemia and propose novel classification methods to discriminate between the disease classes. We show that existing indexes for the binary classification of Iron Deficiency Anaemia (IDA) and β-thalassaemia trait are well adapted to this sample, with RDWI (red cell distribution width index) achieving a median accuracy of 95.4%, a performance we were also able to achieve using Random Forests. The multi-class classification was also developed to discriminate between three microcytic anaemias and healthy subjects, presenting a median accuracy of 93.0%. In addition, we developed a semi-automatic method to identify outliers, which were shown to correspond to subjects with unexpected features given their class and who may correspond to clinical misclassification that require further analysis. The results illustrate that it is possible to achieve excellent performance using just the information obtained through an affordable Complete Blood Count test, thus highlighting the potential of artificial intelligence in classifying microcytic anaemias.

Partially supported through FCT (UIDB/50021/2020, PTDC/CCI-BIO/4180/2020, DSAIPA/DS/0026/2019) and EU Horizon 2020 (No. 951970). INSEF, developed within the scope of the Pre-defined Project of the Programa Iniciativas em Saúde Pública, was promoted by INSA-DEP and benefited from financial support granted by Iceland, Liechtenstein and Norway, through the EEA Grants.

G. Marreiros et al. (Eds.): EPIA 2022, LNAI 13566, pp. 219–231, 2022.
https://doi.org/10.1007/978-3-031-16474-3_19

Keywords: Microcytic anaemia · Thalassemia · Iron deficiency anaemia · Classification · Machine learning

1   Background

Anaemia is a condition characterized by a decrease of red blood cell mass and low level of hemoglobin, having as principal consequence a diminished oxygen carrying capacity of the blood. The main symptoms are related with lack of oxygen, such as fatigue and shortness of breath [4]. According to the World Health Organization [24] anaemia was estimated to affect 24.8% of the global population, having a bigger prevalence in low income countries. In Portugal, two different studies assessed the prevalence of anaemia obtaining very different results. The first study indicated an anaemia prevalence of 19.9% [7], detecting that subjects with ages between 18 and 34 years old and older adults (≥ 65) had the highest prevalence of anaemia. The most recent study only included subjects with ages between 25 and 74 years old and revealed a prevalence of 5.8% [21].

In microcytic anaemias the red blood cells are smaller than usual due to the decreased production of hemoglobin, a major constituent of these cells. Among the microcytic anaemias the most common are the thalassemias and the Iron Deficiency Anaemia (IDA). IDA is the most common cause of anaemia and is associated with low levels of iron, which is needed for the hemoglobin synthesis in erythropoiesis and essential for the oxygen transport by the red blood cells [3]. Thalassemias are hemoglobinopathies autosomal recessive disorders [17]. The thalassemias, β-thalassemia and α-thalassemia are associated with a deficit in the synthesis of two globin chains, β-globin and α-globin, respectively. These proteins form, in equal quantities, hemoglobin A, which represents about 97.0% of the total red blood cell hemoglobin of a human adult [23]. The distinction between IDA and thalassemia trait is fundamental to prevent iron therapy in individuals with thalassemia trait, which could lead to iron overload, and also to provide genetic counselling to thalassemia carriers and their families and to evaluate the need for prenatal diagnosis of thalassemia.

Anaemia diagnosis is characterized by a hemoglobin concentration $<13\,\mathrm{g/dL}$ for men and $<12\,\mathrm{g/dL}$ for non-pregnant women [24]. Once diagnosed, it is classified into categories based on the mean corpuscular volume (MCV) of the red blood cells as: microcytic (MCV<80 fL), normocytic (80<MCV<100 fL), or macrocytic (MCV>100 fL) [23]. To get information about the MCV, a complete blood count (CBC) test, performed in a haematology analyzer, is required. This test additionally provides information regarding the hemoglobin (Hb), the physical features of the red blood cells: red blood cell (RBC) count, red cell distribution width (RDW), mean corpuscular hemoglobin (MCH); mean corpuscular hemoglobin concentration (MCHC). For the correct diagnosis of IDA the serum ferritin, an indicator of the size of the total body iron store, is normally accessed through enzyme-linked immunosorbent assays or enzyme immunoassays after venous blood collection [25], while DNA testing is mandatory to diagnose thalassemia and to determine the mutation that led to the thalassemic trait.

Due to the clinical relevance of a proper distinction between microcytic anaemias, several indexes based on the blood cell parameters obtained in the CBC test were constructed over the years. In 1973, England et al. [5] published an index to differentiate iron deficiency anaemia (IDA) from β-thalassemia trait. Since then several indexes have been developed to discriminate between the two conditions. For the female Portuguese population, previous studies indicate a good performance of RDWI [6]. However, the performance of these indexes in Portugal for individuals of both sexes is still lacking, contrary to studies in other populations. Indeed, multiple studies performed in other populations have concluded that Green and King (G&K) and RDWI indexes, with an accuracy of 88.4% and 92.0% respectively, provided the highest reliabilities in differentiating β-thalassemia trait from IDA in the Brazilian population [14]. In the Iranian population the index with the better performance was found to be Index26 with an accuracy of 84.7% [10]. In another study, conducted with the Palestinian population, the best indexes were Sirdah, G&K and the RDWI [22]. Accordingly, it is plausible to say that these indexes are better adjusted to specific populations.

The application of statistical learning is not a novelty in disease diagnostics and not even in the classification of anaemia, as in the last decade previous works have already demonstrated its usefulness [11,13,18,20]. These studies referred have presented very exciting results regarding the performance of their models with accuracies ranging from 85% to 99%. Nevertheless, it is important to keep in mind that not all of these studies used the same methodology to assess the accuracy of their models and so a fair comparison cannot be made.

None of the studies mentioned used data from the population living in Portugal which may hamper the correct classification for these patients. Besides this problem, few studies compared and evaluate novel classifiers of microcytic anaemia. Hence, it becomes relevant to test these algorithms in this population as it may allow us to construct new indexes, specifically adjusted to this population, able to differentiate IDA from β-thalassemia trait, and even go further and build a multi-class classifier to discriminate between various microcytic anaemias and, consequently, provide a more efficient, accurate and cost-effective diagnosis.

2   Methods

2.1   Data Description

The data used comprise a total of 390 patients (Table 1) from a sample of the Portuguese population. While all those instances were used in the multi-class models, only 196 (β-thalassemia carriers and IDA patients) were needed in the binary models. In order to address one of the main objectives, which is to reduce the cost of the diagnosis, only the information obtained trough a CBC test (hematological parameters Hb, MCV, MCH, and RDW), the subjects' sex, and his confirmed diagnosis was used. For the IDA patients, the confirmed diagnosis had been obtained through measurement of the serum biomarkers related to iron metabolism (ferritin, total iron binding capacity and transferrin saturation). In the case of the β-thalassemia, the diagnosis had been done through the analysis

Table 1. Data description.

Class	Female	Male	Total
β-thalassemia	68	64	132
α-thalassemia	32	20	52
IDA	54	10	64
Control	97	45	142
Total	251	139	390

of mutations in the β-globin gene and besides that, the serum biomarkers related to iron metabolism were also measured to exclude concomitant IDA. For the α-thalassemia carriers the confirmation had been done with the identification of a common deletion underlying α-thalassemia.

2.2   Classification Indexes Evaluation

The accuracy of the existing indexes was evaluated with the data from β-thalassemia carriers and IDA patients. These indexes accuracy was calculated through the median accuracy of 30 random partitions, each with 30% of the data set, so that it would be more fairly compared with the machine learning models which were evaluated using cross-validation. Then, two different types of machine learning classifiers were created: 1) binary, to distinguish between β-thalassemia carriers and IDA patients, and 2) multi-class, to classify the β-thalassemia carriers, α-thalassemia carriers, IDA patients, and control subjects. Different machine learning algorithms were used to create the predictive models: Logistic Regression (LR), Naïve Bayes (NB), Artificial Neural Networks (ANN), Random Forests (RF), Decision Trees (DT), Support Vector Machines (SVM), and k-nearest neighbors (KNN), implemented in Python 3.8 using libraries sklearn [19], pandas [15], numpy [8], and Matplotlib [9]. The models were evaluated using cross-validation resorting to the median of the accuracy during 30 random partitions, where 70% of the data was allocated to the training set and the remaining 30% to the test set. In addition, for comparison, the models were also evaluated using all data.

To construct the models, multiple different features resulting from the multiplication and division of the original features were also generated. The features used to generate new features refer to blood cell parameters and, therefore, there was no need to avoid multiplication or division by zero, as it is biologically unfeasible. To select the best features' combinations a genetic algorithm adapted from Codes[1] was used. To solve the hyperparameter optimization problem, the random search solution was applied with successive halving [12].

To evaluate the possible presence of outliers, Cook's distance and silhouette analysis were performed using Yellowbrick [2] and sklearn [19], respectively.

---

[1] https://github.com/kiecodes/genetic-algorithms.

The instances that were more often missclassified using the best binary and multi-class models were sought and compared with the outliers found to see if there was any overlap. The gold standard diagnosis of the subjects that make up the data used has already been confirmed by molecular diagnosis. The study of the presence of outliers was not aimed at discarding data, because in this case we would be simplifying the classification task and the performance results would be biased. The objective was to develop a semi-automatic model able to identify instances that present features different from what would be expected according to the attributed disease, and that in the worst case scenario may require a second analysis.

3   Results and Discussion

3.1   Descriptive Data Analysis

A descriptive statistical analysis of the data was performed with all the normalized features per class (Fig. 1). As expected, the median Hb is lower in individuals with microcytic anaemia than in the control group (healthy subjects). However, in the case of α-thalassemia, Hb is higher than in other microcytic anaemias, probably because most of the α-thalassemia data comes from patients with heterozygous mutations, suggesting that these patients must have the α-thalassemia trait 1, or at worst 2, and therefore still have high level of α-globin synthesis. The decreased production of Hb also affects the MCV value, because Hb is a major constituent of the red blood cells. MCH is much lower in individuals with microcytic anaemia, which is expected because it is the average amount of Hb in each red blood cell, so it is also dependent on the production of Hb. The

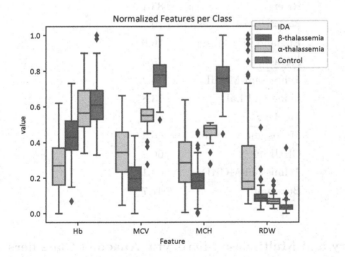

Fig. 1. Boxplot with all the normalized features per class.

RDW represents the coefficient of variation of the red blood cell volume distribution. In the β-thalassemia and α-thalassemia carriers practically all red blood cells are microcytic due to mutations in the globin chain genes and therefore the RDW is consistently low. However, the IDA subjects have the highest RDW. This has been explained in previous studies by the administration of iron therapy in patients with IDA, which results in a rise in the RDW few days after the initiation of the iron therapy and during the next month [1], which also probably explains why IDA patients present the highest variation in all the features.

3.2 Indexes Evaluation

A performance evaluation of all the existing indexes was done to understand which has the higher accuracy in this sample to classify β-thalassemia carriers vs. IDA patients (see Table 2). The results show that the RDWI and G&K are the most reliable indexes in the studied population, as observed in the Brazilian [14] and Palestinian [22] populations. Both indexes have in common the inclusion in their formulas of the MCV, RDW and Hb , suggesting that these three features may be very relevant in the discrimination between β-thalassemia carriers and IDA patients also in this Portuguese sample.

Table 2. Indexes performance with random partitions [10].

Index	Median accuracy %
RDWI	95.4
Green and King (G&K)	92.3
Ehsani	84.6
Ricerca	83.1
Sirdah	79.2
England and Fraser	76.9
Srivastava	75.4
Telmissani-MDHL	75.4
Shine and Lal	73.8
Mentzer	66.2
Matos and Carvalho	66.2
CRUISE	66.2
Telmissani-MCHD	63.1
Bessman	47.7

3.3 Binary and Multi-class Microcytic Anaemia Classifiers

The accuracies of the binary classifiers tested are shown in Table 3. The highest accuracy achieved was 95.4% with RF and ANN, both using the features created

and later selected by the genetic algorithm. These new features contributed significantly to the improvement of the accuracy of most classifiers, i.e., almost all the best classifiers of each algorithm are the ones using the new features. There can be several reasons why this optimization through feature creation and selection did not work in all models. The genetic algorithm used to select the features evaluated the set of features chosen with only on split of the data, which may have introduced a bias, since some splits of the data can result in a test set easier to classify and therefore that group of features is wrongly associated with a high accuracy. In Table 3 the models were evaluated resorting to a median accuracy of 30 different splits of the data and therefore that bias is mitigated. That said some of the features selected were not the best, as the original features actually presented a higher accuracy. This also leads us to think that maybe if these initial features were forced to be in the initial population of the genetic algorithm, they could have been selected. However this genetic algorithm initial population was seeded completely randomly, which may also justify why this optimization did not work in all models. Even if the initial features were in the initial population or had appear through mutations the genetic algorithm may have discarded them due to the penalization on the number of features.

Table 3. Median accuracy of the best machine learning binary classifiers for each algorithm.

Model	Median accuracy %
Random forest (RF)	95.4
Artificial neural network (ANN)	95.4
Logistic regression (LR)	94.6
Decision tree (DT)	93.8
Support vector machine (SVM)	93.8
Naïve Bayes (NB)	92.3

The hyperparameter optimization, despite having improved the performance of some algorithms, did not have as notable an impact as the introduction of the new features, which indeed had the biggest impact, suggesting that the default hyperparameters were already adequate in most of the classifiers. Besides this, this optimization just like the feature selection was done resorting to only one split of the data which may also have introduced a bias. Noteworthy, the accuracy obtained (95.4%) was also the highest, which suggests that there is some difficulty in surpassing this performance. To assess the variation in accuracy across the different partitions of the data, boxplots were constructed with the best binary models (Fig. 2(a)).

RF not only had the highest median accuracy, but also showed lower performance variance in classifying microcytic anaemia across different partitions. In contrast, the Naïve Bayes algorithm obtained the lowest median accuracy and

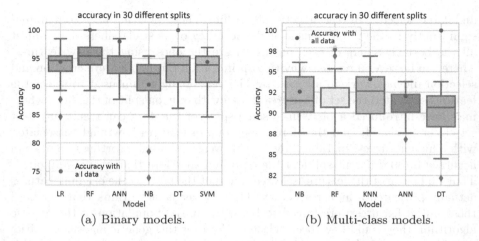

(a) Binary models.   (b) Multi-class models.

Fig. 2. Classification accuracy in the testing sets obtained with 30 data random partitions (boxplots) and using all the data (red points). (Color figure online)

Table 4. Median accuracy of the machine learning multi-class classifiers to discriminate between β-thalassemia carriers, α-thalassemia carriers, IDA patients, and control subjects.

Model	Median accuracy (%)				
	IDA	α-thalassemia	β-thalassemia	Control	Overall
Random forests (RF)	93.4	96.9	95.3	98.4	93.0
k-nearest neighbors (KNN)	93.8	96.9	95.3	99.2	92.6
Artificial neural networks (ANN)	95.3	96.1	95.3	96.9	92.2
Naïve Bayes (NB)	93.4	96.9	94.6	99.2	91.5
Decision trees (DT)	91.5	96.1	95.0	98.1	90.7

a much larger variation. These boxplots also show the accuracy when training and testing the algorithms with all data, for comparison purposes and evaluating which models may be more prone to overfitting, with LR and DT apparently being more robust. Table 4 shows the accuracy of the best multi-class models.

The highest accuracy achieved was 93.0% using RF. As expected, this four-class classification does not achieve the same accuracy as the binary version, although it can still perform very well. In multi-class classification, the best classifiers were seldom the ones that used the selected features, with hyperparameters optimization having a stronger impact on the overall accuracy improvement. As explained before, the feature selection may not have worked due to the bias in the test set, the lack of the initial features on the population that seeded the genetic algorithm, or due to the penalization on the number of features.

Table 4 also presents the accuracy per class of the best microcytic anaemia multi-class classifiers. The control class had the highest accuracy regardless of the algorithm used to create the model; on the other hand, IDA class had the

worst accuracy, which means that with the data used, IDA patients are the most difficult to be identified. As for the binary classifiers, boxplots with the accuracy across the different divisions of the data were also constructed with the best multi-class models (Fig. 2(b)). Within the multi-class models, RF is not only the one with the highest median accuracy, but it also continues to have a low accuracy variability across the different partitions, as already observed with the binary classifiers, which means that it is the most stable method. However, RF and DT are again the classifiers most likely to suffer from overfitting, their accuracy reaches significantly higher values when using all the data, never reaching these values when the data is split in the training and testing set.

Overall, we can conclude that RF reach the best accuracy with low variation, both in the binary classification and in the multi-class classification of microcytic anaemia. Yet, as this algorithm tends to overfit the data, measures must be taken such as using cross-validation to select the hyperparameters.

3.4 Outliers Detection

Considering that the best median accuracy achieved with both binary classifiers and indexes was not able to surpass the value of 95.4% and the best multi-class median accuracy achieved is 93.0%, the suspicion of the presence of outliers arose. For this reason, the consistency within classes as well as the presence of outliers were evaluated using a silhouette analysis (Fig. 3). The α-thalassemia is the class with the highest mean silhouette coefficient. However, it is important to emphasize that it is the class with the lowest number of instances, which will make it difficult to train the models and probably for this reason it is not the class that registered the best accuracy in any of the models. The control class had the second lowest average silhouette coefficient, yet registered the best accuracy in the models, which demonstrates the importance of the number of instances in the performance of the algorithms. IDA is the class with the lowest (negative)

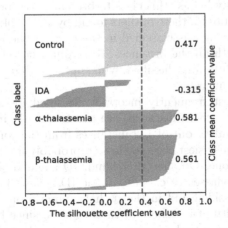

Fig. 3. Silhouette analysis and respective class mean.

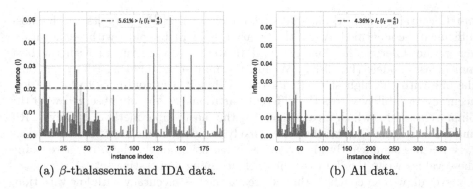

(a) β-thalassemia and IDA data.   (b) All data.

Fig. 4. Cook's distance outlier detection. IDA (blue), β-thalassemia (green), control (yellow) and α-thalassemia (red). (Color figure online)

silhouette value, probably because no information about the iron status was used and also, due to the administration of iron therapy in some patients with IDA. However, this low consistency did not compromise the differential diagnosis between IDA and β-thalassemia in the binary classifiers, most likely because the β-thalassemia class has a very high class accuracy, yet, it had a greater impact on the performance of multi-class models. Since the average silhouette coefficient is 0.37, we can say that the consistency of the classes is, in general, good.

To further evaluate the presence of outliers, the Cook's distance was calculated for all the instances used in the binary (Fig. 4(a)) and multi-class models Fig. 4(b). According to the Cook's distance, the percentage of outliers found was 5.61% in the data used in binary models and 4.36% within all the data, which may partially explain why the accuracy could not surpass the value of 95.4% in the binary models and 93.0% in the multi-class. In both cases the class where most outliers were found was IDA, which is consistent with the results obtained with the silhouette analysis. In opposition, the control class does not have any outliers which certainly helped this class to presented the best accuracy.

In order to understand if these outliers found by the Cook's distance were the instances that were being missclassified in the models, the models were further trained and tested with all the instances. Regarding the IDA class, 6 out of 64 instances were frequently missclassified, while in the β-thalassemia carriers class were 5 out of 132 instances.

Regarding the most frequently incorrect classified instances in the multi-class models, the class whose instances are less frequently incorrectly classified is the control class. Only 1 out of 142 instances from the control class are often misclassified, being the easiest class to classify, probably due to being the largest and most consistent one. On the other hand, IDA and α-thalassemia seem to be the most difficult classes to classify, in the IDA class 3 out of 64 instances are frequently misclassified and in the α-thalassemia 5 out of 52. This can be justified by the scarcity of instances of these classes, since both have less than half of the instances of β-thalassemia and control, and in the case of the IDA

Table 5. Mean feature values per class and some instances' values.

		Hb	MCV	MCH	RDW
Instances	115	12.4	69.9	22.9	32.7
	121	11.6	74.6	25.7	15.2
	139	8.2	68.1	20.6	15.9
Class mean	β-thalassemia	11.8 ± 1.2	65.0 ± 4.3	20.8 ± 1.5	15.0 ± 2.1
	IDA	10.1 ± 1.4	71.5 ± 6.8	22.7 ± 2.9	24.8 ± 12.3
	Control	13.7 ± 1.2	91.4 ± 4.5	31.6 ± 1.9	12.7 ± 1.5
	α-thalassemia	13.5 ± 1.4	81.1 ± 3.2	25.9 ± 1.0	14.1 ± 1.3
	β-thalassemia and IDA	12.3 ± 0.9	60.3 ± 1.5	19.9 ± 0.5	34.6 ± 0.8

class also by the lack of information about the iron status of the body that can have led to the low consistency of the IDA class. Regarding the β-thalassemia class, 5 in 132 instances are often misclassified. Even so, one would expect fewer instances of the α-thalassemia class compared to IDA since the α-thalassemia class did not show any outliers and is the class with the highest consistency.

In the binary classification, three of the instances that were considered outliers (115, 121 and 139, all from individuals with β-thalassemia trait), are also among the ones that are most frequently misclassified. In the case of multi-class classification, only instance 115 was considered an outlier, while it is among the most frequently misclassified instances by multi-class models. Table 5 shows the features' values from these individuals, the mean values of the features in the different classes, and the mean values of a group of five individuals with both β-thalassemia trait and IDA. The data from the individuals with both β-thalassemia trait and IDA were also made available, but due to the small number of instances (only five) with both conditions, it was not included in the multi-class classification.

Regarding instances 121 and 139, some values are a little farther from the β-thalassemia average, such as the MCV in instance 121 and the Hb in instance 139. Although not extreme, it seems to have been enough to lead them to misclassify these instances. In the case of instance 115, the situation is different, as the RDW is more than double the average obtained in the β-thalassemia class. A similar value was only obtained in individuals who had both β-thalassemia trait and IDA, which leads to the suspicion that this subject was misdiagnosed and that, in fact, instead of having the β-thalassemia trait only, he has both β-thalassemia trait and IDA. In general, due to the percentage of outliers detected through Cook's distance, we can admit that some instances may have values a little more distant than what was expected for their class and, therefore, it was not possible to achieve a better accuracy. However, it is also important to bear in mind that the absence of data regarding iron status of the body seems to affect the performance of these classifiers in identifying patients with IDA and that effectively the more data there is to train the classifiers, the better their performance will be.

4 Conclusions

The existing anaemia classification indexes are well adapted to the population living in Portugal, especially the RDWI, which presented a median accuracy of 95.4%. In the present study, even though this performance was not improved with the proposed binary classifiers, we have achieved equivalent accuracy with Random Forests (RF), which exhibited the best accuracy both for binary and multi-class classification. In addition, we develop a semi-automatic method able to identify model-based outliers, i.e., instances that present features' values that significantly deviate from what would be expected according to the attributed disease class and, therefore, may require a more thorough analysis.

As a future work, one should seek to obtain more data from patients with microcytic anaemia, especially from the classes that are less represented, as it could allow to obtain classifiers for microcytic anaemias with a higher accuracy. However, the availability of more data will probably not be enough considering that information about the iron status of the body seems to be important for the identification of IDA patients.

Furthermore, since the latest hematology analyzers are already able to incorporate classifiers, it would be an advantage to add the best multi-class classifier developed in this study, coupled with outlier detection methods, in order to improve the diagnosis of microcytic anaemias.

Acknowledgements. The data used to test the existing indexes and to train and test the predictive models were obtained from the Biobank of the Human Genetics Department of the National Institute of Health Dr. Ricardo (INSA). In addition, some data were added from the INSEF 2015 project [16] carried out by Department of Epidemiology of INSA. The authors wish to thank Marta Barreto, Bárbara Faleiro, and Daniela Santos for their support in the molecular diagnosis of some samples.

References

1. Aslan, D., Gümrük, F., Gürgey, A., Altay, C.: Importance of RDW value in differential diagnosis of hypochrome anemias. Am. J. Hematol. **69**(1), 31–33 (2002)
2. Bengfort, B., Bilbro, R.: Yellowbrick: visualizing the scikit-learn model selection process. J. Open Source Softw. **4**(35), 1075 (2019)
3. Camaschella, C.: Iron-deficiency anemia. N. Engl. J. Med. **372**(19), 1832–1843 (2015)
4. Cascio, M.J., DeLoughery, T.G.: Anemia: evaluation and diagnostic tests. Med. Clin. **101**(2), 263–284 (2017)
5. England, J., Bain, B., Fraser, P.: Differentiation of iron deficiency from thalassaemia trait. Lancet **301**(7818), 1514 (1973)
6. Faleiro, B.D.: Hereditary anemia - characterization of the genetic basis and subjacent mechanisms. Tese de mestrado em Biologia Humana e Ambiente, Universidade de Lisboa, Faculdade de Ciências (2020)
7. Fonseca, C., Marques, F., Robalo Nunes, A., Belo, A., Brilhante, D., Cortez, J.: Prevalence of anaemia and iron deficiency in Portugal: the EMPIRE study. Intern. Med. J. **46**(4), 470–478 (2016)

8. Harris, C.R., et al.: Array programming with NumPy. Nature **585**(7825), 357–362 (2020)
9. Hunter, J.D.: Matplotlib: a 2D graphics environment. Comput. Sci. Eng. **9**(3), 90–95 (2007)
10. Jahangiri, M., Rahim, F., Malehi, A.S.: Diagnostic performance of hematological discrimination indices to discriminate between βeta thalassemia trait and iron deficiency anemia and using cluster analysis: introducing two new indices tested in Iranian population. Sci. Rep. **9**(1), 1–13 (2019)
11. Jaiswal, M., Srivastava, A., Siddiqui, T.J.: Machine learning algorithms for anemia disease prediction. In: Khare, A., Tiwary, U.S., Sethi, I.K., Singh, N. (eds.) Recent Trends in Communication, Computing, and Electronics. LNEE, vol. 524, pp. 463–469. Springer, Singapore (2019). https://doi.org/10.1007/978-981-13-2685-1_44
12. Jamieson, K., Talwalkar, A.: Non-stochastic best arm identification and hyperparameter optimization. In: Artificial Intelligence and Statistics, pp. 240–248 (2016)
13. Kabootarizadeh, L., Jamshidnezhad, A., Koohmareh, Z.: Differential diagnosis of iron-deficiency anemia from β-thalassemia trait using an intelligent model in comparison with discriminant indexes. Acta Informatica Medica **27**(2), 78 (2019)
14. Matos, J.F., et al.: Comparison of discriminative indices for iron deficiency anemia and β thalassemia trait in a Brazilian population. Hematology **18**(3), 169–174 (2013)
15. McKinney, W.: Data structures for statistical computing in Python. In: Proceedings of the 9th Python in Science Conference, pp. 56–61 (2010)
16. Nunes, B., et al.: The first Portuguese national health examination survey (2015): design, planning and implementation. J. Public Health **41**(3), 511–517 (2019)
17. Old, J.: Screening and genetic diagnosis of haemoglobin disorders. Blood Rev. **17**(1), 43–53 (2003)
18. Patel, B.A., Parikh, A.: Impact analysis of the complete blood count parameter using Naive Bayes. In: 2020 International Conference on Inventive Computation Technologies (ICICT), pp. 7–12 (2020)
19. Pedregosa, F., et al.: Scikit-learn: machine learning in Python. J. Mach. Learn. Res. **12**, 2825–2830 (2011)
20. Purwar, S., Tripathi, R.K., Ranjan, R., Saxena, R.: Detection of microcytic hypochromia using CBC and blood film features extracted from convolution neural network by different classifiers. Multimed. Tools Appl. **79**(7), 4573–4595 (2020)
21. Samões, C., et al.: Prevalence of anemia in the Portuguese adult population: results from the first national health examination survey (INSEF 2015). J. Public Health 1–8 (2020)
22. Sirdah, M., Tarazi, I., Al Najjar, E., Al Haddad, R.: Evaluation of the diagnostic reliability of different RBC indices and formulas in the differentiation of the β-thalassaemia minor from iron deficiency in Palestinian population. Int. J. Lab. Hematol. **30**(4), 324–330 (2008)
23. Tefferi, A.: Anemia in adults: a contemporary approach to diagnosis. Mayo Clin. Proc. **78**(10), 1274–1280 (2003)
24. WHO: Worldwide prevalence of anaemia 1993–2005: Who global database on anaemia. World Health Organization (2008)
25. WHO: Serum ferritin concentrations for the assessment of iron status and iron deficiency in populations. World Health Organization (2011)

A General Preprocessing Pipeline for Deep Learning on Radiology Images: A COVID-19 Case Study

Khaoula Echabbi[1], Elmoukhtar Zemmouri[1(✉)] [iD], Mohammed Douimi[1], and Salsabil Hamdi[2]

[1] Moulay Ismail University, ENSAM, Meknes, Morocco
{e.zemmouri,m.douimi}@umi.ac.ma
[2] Institut Pasteur du Maroc, Casablanca, Morocco

Abstract. During the last years, deep learning has been used intensively in medical domain making considerable progress in the diagnosis of diseases from radiology images. This is mainly due to the availability of proven algorithms on several computer vision tasks and the publicly accessible medical datasets. However, most approaches that apply deep learning techniques to radiology images transform these images into a format that conforms with the inputs of conventional learning algorithms and deal with the dataset as a set of 2D independent slices instead of volumetric images. In this work we deal with the problem of preparing DICOM CT scans as 3D images for a machine learning/deep learning architecture. We propose a general preprocessing pipeline composed of four stages for volumetric images processing followed by a 3D CNN architecture for 3D images classification. The proposed pipeline is evaluated through a case study for COVID-19 detection from chest CT scans. Experiment results demonstrate the effectiveness of the proposed preprocessing operations.

Keywords: Radiology image · Preprocessing · Deep learning · 3D CNN · COVID-19

1 Introduction

During the past decade, Artificial Intelligence (AI), especially machine learning/deep learning techniques, has been used intensively to analyze medical data achieving substantial progress in the medical imaging field. IA can support pathologists and radiologists as it is used in medical imaging in diagnosing a broad variety of disease, e.g., heart disease, neurological disease, diabetes, cancer detection [1].

Radiology images are the data format most consumed by machine learning algorithms. A Radiology image represents the internal structure or function of an anatomic region [2], it is captured with dedicated medical hardware and software (scanner) and stored in a specific file format. Computed Tomography (CT) is a type of procedure for capturing radiology images based on x-rays. The CT scan of a patient, as captured by

G. Marreiros et al. (Eds.): EPIA 2022, LNAI 13566, pp. 232–241, 2022.
https://doi.org/10.1007/978-3-031-16474-3_20

a scanner, is a sequence of slices. Each slice is stored in digital imaging and communications in medicine (DICOM) file format. A DICOM file consist of two parts: metadata and pixels data [2].

In the literature, most approaches that apply deep learning techniques to radiology images transform these images into a format that conforms with the inputs of conventional learning algorithms and deal with the dataset as set of 2D independent slices instead of volumetric images.

In this work we deal with the problem of preparing DICOM CT scans as 3D images for a machine learning/deep learning architecture. We propose a general preprocessing pipeline composed of four stages for volumetric images processing that are: (1) Hounsfield units' transformation, (2) CT scan windowing, (3) slices selection and (4) CT scan normalization. Then, to show the importance and the effectiveness of the proposed preprocessing pipeline, we conduct a case study for COVID-19 detection from chest CT scans using a three-dimensional convolutional neural network (3D CNN).

Many related works have treated one or more of the proposed preprocessing operations for a specific learning task. But, to our knowledge, no work has brought all these operations in a comprehensive and detailed pipeline. Rahimzadeh et al. [3] proposed a CT scan selecting algorithm in a deep learning-based network for detecting COVID-19. In this approach, the slices of a CT scan are manipulated independently as 2D image, and the parameters of the section algorithm are more hand crafted. Masoudi et al. [4] proposed an interesting guide on radiology image pre-processing for deep learning applications. This guide misses the slice selection phase that we consider the most import because it allows to clean the data and use computational resources more effectively. In addition, the proposed guide does not put the sequence of preprocessing operations in parameterized pipeline that can be used by novice deep learning users. Zunair et al. [5] proposed techniques to process CT scans with 3D CNN. The only preprocessing proposed technique is slice selection that consist of reducing the number of slices per CT scan to deal with GPU and memory constraints. It proposes also to treat the CT scan of a patient as volumetric 3D image.

The rest of the paper is organized as follows: In Sect. 2 we detail our proposed approach. In Sect. 3 we present conducted experiment and obtained results. In Sect. 4 we draw some conclusions and future work.

2 Proposed Approach

2.1 CT Scans Preprocessing for 3D Deep Learning Architecture

Preprocessing is a crucial step of every machine learning/data mining project. This is particularly the case for machine learning applications using radiology images. In fact, most of available algorithms cannot be directly executed on image from the medical domain. Image preprocessing should also guarantee that the trained model is hardware and software independent. To improve the performance of deep learning architectures on CT scans, we propose the following preprocessing operations:

Hounsfield Units' Transformation. Introduced by Godfrey Hounsfield in 1972, the Hounsfield unit (HU) is a relative quantitative measurement of radio density used by

radiologists in the interpretation of computed tomography (CT) images [6]. It is calculated based on a linear transformation of the baseline linear attenuation coefficient of the x-ray beam, where distilled water is defined to be zero HU and air defined as -1000 HU. The transformation formula is as follow:

$$hu = pixelvalue \times Slope + Intercept \tag{1}$$

The Slope and Intercept values are stored in the metadata part of the DICOM file, generally with the tags Rescale Slope and Rescale Intercept, and typically have values of 1 and -1024 respectively.

CT Scan Windowing. CT images are generally encoded in 16 bits DICOM format. after the HU transformation, pixel/voxel values range within an interval of $[-1024$ HU, 4000 HU]. This interval contains a high number of values that correspond to the density of tissues of organs encountered by the x-ray beams.

Image windowing is a kind of filter used to increase the contrast over a specific organ of interest. The process is also known as grey-level mapping, contrast stretching or contrast enhancement. The brightness and the contrast of the image are adjusted using a window of the initial interval of HU values [7]. The window is defined for each organ with two values: level (denoted L) and width (denoted W). For example, the window for lungs has L $= -500$ Hu and W $= 1500$ Hu. Figure 1 bellow presents the HU scale with typical window width and level values [4, 7]:

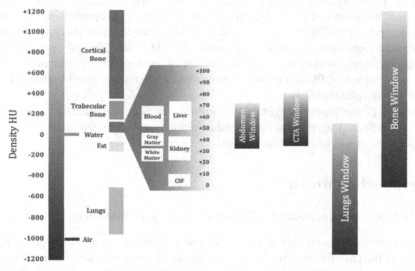

Fig. 1. Hounsfield scale: a schematic representation of the distribution of densities encountered in the organism on the arbitrary density scale, with typical organs' windows.

Given L and W, the formula we used for windowing is:

$$windowing\,(pixelvalue, L, W) = \begin{cases} max \ if \ pixelvalue > max \\ min \ if \ pixelvalue < min \\ pixelvalue \ otherwise \end{cases} \quad (2)$$

$$Where : max = L + \frac{W}{2}, min = L - \frac{W}{2}$$

The visualization of a CT scan is clearly enhanced after the process of Hounsfield unit transformation and windowing as depicted in following figure for a chest CT scan example (Fig. 2):

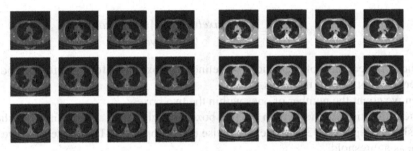

Fig. 2. Visualization of the chest CT scan of a patient before and after windowing.

Slices Selection. The CT scan of a patient, as captured by a scanner (hardware and software parts), is a sequence of slices. Each slice is stored in a DICOM format image. The sequence is generally visualized by radiologists as a video using dedicated software. In this work we will not consider each slice apart, but we consider the whole sequence as a volume or a 3D image. In this 3D image, the organ of interest (we will use the lungs as an example in this paper) or the infected region may appear only in a successive part of the slices, generally in the middle of the CT scan (Fig. 3).

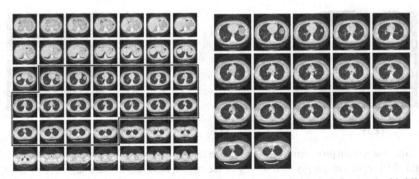

Fig. 3. The CT scan of a patient before and after slices selection. In the left figure, the highlighted sequence of images contains the organ of interest (open lungs), the rest will be automatically dropped out from the 3D image.

The aim of slices selection step is to automatically select the part of the 3D image containing the region of interest and dropout the rest. This will enhance the performance of trained models and optimize the use of computational resources (memory and CPU/GPU). From a data mining perspective, the process of slices selection can be viewed as a data cleansing operation.

The steps of our proposed algorithm for slices selection are as follows (Fig. 4):

- After analyzing the intensity of pixels of a sample of slices that contain open lungs and then closed lungs, we defined two thresholds *tmin* and *tmax*. In the case of CT scan for lungs *tmin* = −900 HU and *tmax* = −300 HU.
- Using the interval *[tmin, tmax]*, we filter each slice of the 3D image using the following formula:

$$pixelvalue = \begin{cases} 1 \ if \ pixelvalue \in [tmin, tmax] \\ 0 \ otherwise \end{cases} \quad (3)$$

- In the obtained mask of each slice, we define two boxes, one for the left lobe and the other for right lobe of the lungs.
- Then we count the number of ones within the two boxes.
- If the proportion of ones within the two boxes is higher than a predefined threshold, the slice is kept in the 3D image, otherwise it is dropped out. In our use case, we use 60% as a threshold.

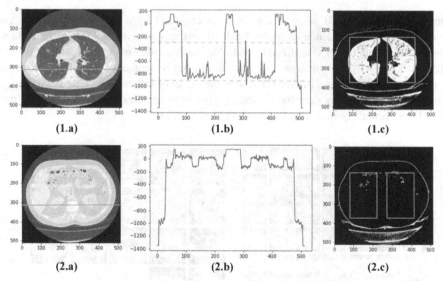

Fig. 4. Slices selection procedure: (1.a) and (2.a) a sample images with visible and invisible lungs, (1.b) and (2.b) represent the pixels intensity of the highlighted line in the images, (1.c) and (2.c) the obtained masks after slice filtering with the boxes bounding the left and right lobes of the lungs.

Our slices selection algorithm is illustrated using chest CT scan and lungs as organ of interest. But this can be easily generalized to other part of the body. In fact, the two thresholds *tmin* and *tmax* are considered as two hyper-parameters of the proposed preprocessing pipeline.

3 CT Scan Normalization

In the domain of machine learning/deep learning, normalization is an important step before feeding the data to a learning algorithm. It allows to have practically the same distribution for each input parameter (pixel/voxel in our case). A common normalization technique used for images dataset is to transform each pixel to the interval [0, 1] using the minimum and maximum pixel values. In the case of radiology images, after the processes of windowing and slices selection, the minimum and maximum pixel values should be L − W/2 and L + W/2 Respectively.

So, given L and W, the formula we used for normalization is:

$$pixelvalue = \frac{pixelvalue - min}{max - min} \qquad (4)$$

$$Where : max = L + \frac{W}{2}, min = L - \frac{W}{2}$$

3.1 Deep Learning Architecture for CT Scan Classification

In this section we present a three-dimensional Convolutional Neural Network (3D CNN) architecture we designed for the classification of chest CT scans from COVID19 patients. This architecture is inspired from the VGG-16 network for image classification [8], but in our case, we use 3D operators instead of 2D. The main objective here is to conduct deep learning case study to evaluate the effectiveness of the previously presented preprocessing steps.

As depicted in Fig. 5, the proposed 3D CNN is composed three main blocks: (1) input layer, (2) features extractor and (3) classifier.

The input layer is a volume with size $512 \times 512 \times D$, where D is the number of slices remaining in the patient CT scan after the process of selection. In our experiments we tested with D = 8 up to 32 depending on the minimum number of slices per patient.

The Features Extraction part consists of four Conv3D + ReLU layers: the first Conv3D have a kernel size of $3 \times 3 \times 3$ and consist of 64 filters, followed by two Conv3D with kernel size $3 \times 3 \times 3$ and 128 filters, then the fourth Conv3D with kernel size $3 \times 3 \times 1$ and 256 filters. Each of these 4 layers is equipped with the ReLU non-linear activation, followed by a max-pooling performed over a $2 \times 2 \times 1$ pixel window with a stride of 2, and ends up with a batch normalization.

The classification block consists of a global average pooling layer followed by two dense layers which are separated by a dropout layer with a rate of 0.5. The last dense layer is equipped with the Sigmoid activation since we have a binary classification problem in our COVID-19 use case.

In the classification block we use global average pooling [9] to minimize overfitting.

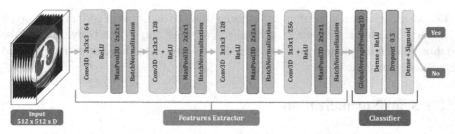

Fig. 5. Proposed 3D CNN architecture for volumetric images classification.

4 Experiment and Results

4.1 Dataset and Preprocessing

The dataset we used in our experiment is the COVID-CTset. It is a large COVID-19 CT scans dataset containing 63849 images from 377 patients [3]. The dataset was gathered from Negin medical center at Sari in Iran during the first wave of the COVID-19 pandemic (March, April 2020).

For privacy concerns, the images in the dataset are not published in DICOM format since the patient's information are easily accessible in this format. Images are converted to 16-bits grayscale TIFF format, which preserve the values of pixels of the origin image and remove personal data. Thereby, a CT scan of a patient consists of a sequence of .tiff files with 512×512 as a resolution. We loaded each patient's sequence of images into a 3D image (volume) in our Python implementation.

The initial loaded dataset is composed of 95 CT scans of confirmed Covid positive patients and 282 normal patients that we stored in two Python lists. We then feed these two lists of CT scans to our preprocessing pipeline: For the first stage HU transformation, we used the default values for Rescale Slope and Rescale Intercept that are 1 and -1024 respectively since we do not have access to the original DICOM files. For the second stage CT scan windowing, the organ of interest is the lungs, so we fixed the level L to be -500 Hu and the width W to be $+1500$ Hu. For the third stage CT slices selection, we defined the thresholds tmin $= -900$ Hu and tmax $= -300$ Hu as explained before. We also defined a minimum number of slices per patients to be 8 slices. Thereby, a CT scan that contains less than 8 slices is removed. If the number of slices is higher than 8, we cropped the 3D image according to the depth dimension. Hence, all remaining 3D images (CT scans) have the size $512 \times 512 \times 8$ which will be the size of the input layer of our 3D CNN architecture we described before.

At the end of the preprocessing pipeline, the two lists are composed of 69 3D images labeled as Covid and 272 3D images labeled as Normal. To train the 3D CNN with a balanced dataset, we kept only 69 3D images as Normal.

Before feeding the data to the deep learning network, we applied data augmentation as a last preprocessing step. For this we performed rotations with angles $[-10, -5, 5, 10]$ on each 3D image of the training set.

4.2   Implementation Details and Model Training

The proposed preprocessing pipeline is implemented in Python. We implemented the
3D CNN architecture in Python using Keras library on Tensorflow backend. The model
is trained on a High-Performance Computing offered by CNRST Morocco [10] which
allocate GPU NVIDIA Tesla V100S with 32 GB memory. We used the binary cross-
entropy loss function, the Adam optimizer, and a batch size of 2. We trained our model
for 25 epochs. After the preprocessing step, the training session of 25 epochs runs in
approximately 53 min.

We provide code and model to reproduce our experiments at https://github.com/zem
mouri-elmoukhtar/medical-imaging.

4.3   Results

To highlight the importance and effectiveness of the proposed preprocessing pipeline,
we compered the performance of the 3D deep learning model when executed with all the
preprocessing stages, and when executed without preprocessing except for 3D images
cropping (to fit the model input size) and normalization.

To evaluate the performance of our model, we used four performance metrics that are:
precision, recall (also referred to as sensitivity), F1_score, and accuracy. The following
equations give the definition of each one of these metrics:

$$Precision = \frac{TP}{TP + FP} \tag{5}$$

$$Recall = \frac{TP}{TP + FN} \tag{6}$$

$$F1\_score = 2 * \frac{Precision \times Recall}{Precision + Recall} \tag{7}$$

$$Accuracy = \frac{TP + TN}{TP + TN + FP + FN} \tag{8}$$

These metrics are calculated for each configuration using the two confusion matrices
depicted in the Fig. 6 below:

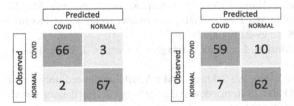

Fig. 6. Proposed 3D CNN architecture.

Table 1 presents the obtained results on the two configurations: with and without preprocessing. The obtained results demonstrate the effectiveness of the proposed
preprocessing stages, even if the number of CT scans of Covid patients is very small
compared to normal patients.

Table 1. Performance metrics of 3D CNN model combined with our proposed preprocessing pipeline.

	Precision	Recall	F1_score	Accuracy
3D CNN without preprocessing	89.39	85.51	87.41	87.68
3D CNN with preprocessing	**97.06**	**95.65**	**96.35**	**96.38**

5 Conclusion

In this paper we addressed the problem of preparing a dataset of radiology images for machine learning/deep learning algorithms. First, we recommend using images in 16-bits grayscale DICOM format instead of 8-bits JPEG or PNG. Second, we recommend manipulating slices of the CT scan of each patient as 3D image (volume) instead of considering each slice apart. Based on these two assumptions, we proposed a preprocessing pipeline for radiology CT scans and a 3D CNN network that we evaluate through a case study for COVID-19 detection from CT scans. The case study demonstrates the effectiveness of the proposed approach in terms of model performance and computational resources' usage. Our preprocessing pipeline was illustrated using chest CT scan. But this can be easily generalized to other types of CT scan. In fact, as future work, we will first define a set of hyperparameters to make the pipeline a fully automated process. We are also evaluating the proposed pipeline on other datasets and learning task (especially 3D segmentation).

Acknowledgement. This work was supported by the «URGENCE COVID-19» fundraising campaign of Institut Pasteur. It was also supported through computational resources of HPC-MARWAN provided by the National Center for Scientific and Technical Research (CNRST), Rabat, Morocco.

References

1. Asha, P., Srivani, P., Rumi, I., Ahmed, A.A.A., Kolhe, A., Nomani, M.Z.M.: Artificial intelligence in medical Imaging: an analysis of innovative technique and its future promise. Mater. Today: Proc. **56**, 2236–2239 (2022)
2. Larobina, M., Murino, L.: Medical image file formats. J. Digit. Imaging **27**(2), 200–206 (2014)
3. Rahimzadeh, M., Attar, A., Sakhaei, S.M.: A fully automated deep learning-based network for detecting COVID-19 from a new and large lung CT scan dataset. Biomed. Signal Process. Control **68**, 102588 (2021)
4. Masoudi, S., et al.: Quick guide on radiology image pre-processing for deep learning applications in prostate cancer research. J. Med. Imaging **8**(01), 010901 (2021)
5. Zunair, H., Rahman, A., Mohammed, N., Cohen, J.P.: Uniformizing techniques to process CT scans with 3D CNNs for tuberculosis prediction. In: Rekik, I., Adeli, E., Park, S.H., Valdés Hernández, M.D.C. (eds.) PRIME 2020. LNCS, vol. 12329, pp. 156–168. Springer, Cham (2020). https://doi.org/10.1007/978-3-030-59354-4_15

6. DenOtter, T.D., Schubert, J.: Hounsfield Unit. 2021 Mar 16. In: StatPearls [Internet]. StatPearls Publishing, Treasure Island (FL) (2022). PMID: 31613501
7. Murphy, A., Baba, Y.: Windowing (CT). Reference article, Radiopaedia.org. https://doi.org/10.53347/rID-52108. Accessed 13 Apr 2022
8. Simonyan, K., Zisserman, A.: Very deep convolutional networks for large-scale image recognition. In: International Conference on Learning Representations (2015)
9. Lin, M., Chen, Q., Yan, S.: Network In Network (cite arxiv:1312.4400 Comment: 10 pages, 4 figures, for iclr2014) (2013)
10. CNRST Morocco High Performance Computing (HPC) Homepage. https://www.marwan.ma/index.php/en/services/hpc

AIPES - Artificial Intelligence in Power and Energy Systems

Automatic Configuration of Genetic Algorithm for the Optimization of Electricity Market Participation Using Sequential Model Algorithm Configuration

Vitor Oliveira[1], Tiago Pinto[1,2]([⊠]), Ricardo Faia[1], Bruno Veiga[1], Joao Soares[1], Ruben Romero[3], and Zita Vale[1]

[1] GECAD, Instituto Superior de Engenharia do Porto, Porto, Portugal
tiagopinto@utad.pt
[2] University of Trás-os-Montes e Alto Douro and INESC-TEC, Vila Real, Portugal
[3] Department of Electrical Engineering, São Paulo State University, Ilha Solteira, SP, Brazil

Abstract. Complex optimization problems are often associated to large search spaces and consequent prohibitive execution times in finding the optimal results. This is especially relevant when dealing with dynamic real problems, such as those in the field of power and energy systems. Solving this type of problems requires new models that are able to find near-optimal solutions in acceptable times, such as metaheuristic optimization algorithms. The performance of these algorithms is, however, hugely dependent on their correct tuning, including their configuration and parametrization. This is an arduous task, usually done through exhaustive experimentation. This paper contributes to overcome this challenge by proposing the application of sequential model algorithm configuration using Bayesian optimization with Gaussian process and Monte Carlo Markov Chain for the automatic configuration of a genetic algorithm. Results from the application of this model to an electricity market participation optimization problem show that the genetic algorithm automatic configuration enables identifying the ideal tuning of the model, reaching better results when compared to a manual configuration, in similar execution times.

Keywords: Automatic algorithm configuration · Electricity markets · Genetic algorithm · Metaheuristic optimization · Portfolio optimization

This work has received funding from FEDER Funds through COMPETE program and from National Funds through (FCT) under project MAS-Society (PTDC/EEI-EEE/28954/2017). This work has been supported by National Funds through FCT - Portugal and CAPES - Brazil, under project 2019.00141.CBM Desenvolvimento de Técnicas de Inteligência Artificial para a Otimização de Sistemas de Distribuição de Energia Elétrica and by the R&D Project "Continental Factory of Future, (CONTINENTAL FoF)/POCI-01-0247-FEDER-047512", financed by the European Regional Development Fund (ERDF), through the Program "Programa Operacional Competitividade e Internacionalização (POCI)/PORTUGAL 2020", under the management of aicep Portugal Global – Trade & Investment Agency.

G. Marreiros et al. (Eds.): EPIA 2022, LNAI 13566, pp. 245–257, 2022.
https://doi.org/10.1007/978-3-031-16474-3_21

1 Introduction

Traditionally, scheduling and planning problems are characterized by their complexity and consequent time-consuming resolution. The objective of an optimization model is to find the optimal value of an objective function, which maximizes or minimizes it, within a domain or space of viable solutions, with n decision variables [1]. The aim is to minimize time, cost and risk or maximize efficiency, profit and quality.

In order to reach a solution in a timely manner, in many cases, combinatorial techniques are used. Artificial Intelligence provides suitable solutions in this domain, namely metaheuristic optimization algorithms [2]. Metaheuristic models are strategies to solve a problem using high levels of abstraction that lead to a heuristic search in a solution space. These metaheuristic algorithms are usually formalized in a generalized way, in order to guarantee their applicability to problems with different characteristics. This requires, however, a demanding work of adaptation and parameterization of the algorithm, in order to obtain adequate results for a specific problem. There are many evidences in the literature that finding adequate configurations of performance optimization parameters of heuristic algorithms requires considerable effort [3, 4].

This work seeks to address the issue of automatic parameterization of algorithms in order to facilitate human effort with manual tests, in addition to avoiding the bias of the combination of parameters chosen for the defined solution. For [5] it is a more robust, powerful and flexible option, in which the Automatic Algorithm Configuration (AAC) automates the task and stabilizes the algorithm parameters.

In this paper, an AAC approach is applied to reach the optimal parameter configuration of a Genetic Algorithm (GA) [6] with the aim of solving an electricity market participation portfolio problem [7]. The AAC is performed using the Sequential Model Algorithm Configuration (SMAC) [8], applying Bayesian Optimization (BO) with Gaussian Processes (GP) and with Monte Carlo Markov Chain.

After this introductory section, Sect. 2 discusses the most relevant related work. Section 3 describes and formalizes the automatic configuration of genetic algorithm for market participation portfolio optimization, and Sect. 4 presents the achieved results. Finally, Sect. 5 finalizes the paper with the most relevant conclusions.

2 Related Work

Optimization problems seek to find the optimal solution considering some objectives. Optimization techniques largely depend on their objective functions and constraints. In the mathematical formulation there are decision variables (Xi), which can be continuous, discrete or boolean, but also functions $fi(x)$ where $i = 1, 2, ..., M$, called objective functions. The space for the decision variables is called the search space, while the space formed by the objective function values is called the solution space. The application of a heuristic method consists of a trial and error approach, based on some previous knowledge about the problem. Also the choice of an algorithm and the multiple options for the components of the algorithm, the selection of which deals with the problem of configuration and solution is commonly referred to as automatic configuration of the algorithm. In the design process, one usually considers multiple options for algorithmic

components, such as different local search procedures or perturbation strategies, and tries to identify the combination that produces the best performance through empirical experiences [5]. This is not a trivial task as components interact with each other in different ways, components may have parameters that need to be fine-tuned, and evaluating a candidate can take a long time, as it usually involves reviewing the candidate on a set of problematic cases.

The reality is that modern algorithms are complex and have many parameters. Adjusting these parameters through manual configuration takes a lot of time and effort. The AAC aims to significantly reduce this effort by making the process more efficient and with better algorithms. According to [9], the AAC often consists of two phases: the training phase and the test phase. The training phase optimizes the configuration of the target algorithm according to a performance metric for a configuration space θ in a given set of training instances. This process corresponds to an optimization problem in which the solution is a configuration and the quality of this solution depends on the objective to be optimized. The test phase evaluates the configuration resulting from the training phase in a set of test instances disconnected from the set of training instances. Since it involves a training phase and a test phase, AAC also corresponds to a machine learning process, involving similar challenges: the configuration returned by the process can readjust to the training instances and, therefore, not be adapted to the instances to solve (test instances). Improving AAC is based on several motivations, being a time-consuming, tedious and error-prone task. In many cases this task is performed manually in an *ad-hoc* way. For [8], the automation of these tasks is of great practical relevance in several contexts. Using automated setup methods can lead to significant time savings and potentially improve results.

The work proposed in [10] considers that the manual adjustment approach is better than no adjustment at all, however it also has a number of disadvantages, as it consumes a lot of time in terms of human effort; it is often guided by personal experience and intuition and therefore biased and not reproducible; algorithms are normally only tested on a very limited set of instances; few design alternatives and parameter settings are explored; the same instances that are often used during the design and parameter tuning phase are also used to evaluate the final algorithm, leading to a biased evaluation of performance. Reference [11] focused on the efficiency in scheduling food deliveries within the restaurant business. Based on current meal delivery patterns in a heavily populated country like China, the authors proposed a model for optimizing delivery schedules in order to minimize delivery distances. For this, a hybrid metaheuristic algorithm was developed, taking into account the strong robustness of the Ant Colony Algorithm (ACO) and the excellent convergence capacity of the Genetic Algorithm (GA). ACO is also used in [12] to provide initial guidance for a simulated annealing metaheuristic model that schedules the charging behaviour of electrical vehicles in a smart grid context. The work of [13] sought to find the best places to place shared bicycle storage/collection stations. To this end, the authors modeled the problem as the p-median problem, which is a large localization problem in optimization. This problem seeks to place a set of facilities (bicycle stations) in order to minimize the distance between a set of customers (citizens) and their nearest facilities (bicycle station). They used a genetic algorithm, local search iteration, particle cluster optimization, simulated annealing and variable neighborhood search to

find the best locations for bicycle stations and study their comparative advantages. The authors used IRACE (iterated racing for automatic algorithm configuration) to parameterize each algorithm automatically, to contribute with a methodology for automatic tuning of the algorithms. They also studied different real data (distance and weights) from different open data sources from a real city, Malaga (Spain), hoping that they will lead to a final smart city application. The results were compared with the solution implemented in Malaga. Finally, it was analyzed how this proposal can be used to improve the existing system in the city, adding more stations.

Multi-objective optimization algorithms are the focus of [14]. These algorithms expose several parameters that need to be tuned to be efficient. Also, the correlation between objective functions is known to affect the search structure and algorithm performance. Knowing the recent success of AAC for multi-objective functions design, the authors raised two questions: the impact of the correlation between optimization objectives on the effectiveness of different AAC approaches and the impact on the designs of optimized algorithms obtained from these automated approaches.

In summary, various methods of AAC can handle the stochastics of the algorithms to be configured, and are able to search algorithms in large parameter spaces with tens or hundreds of parameters of different types. These methods have had different approaches over the last few years, such as ParamILS [10], model-based sequential configuration [8] or gender-based GA. In [15], in addition to the configurator enabling the tuning of parameter definitions or exploring components of alternative algorithms, goes a little further, by asserting a new paradigm for defining an algorithm appropriate to the design space, where choices of design alternatives and number of parameters are encoded. In this way, the application of AAC models for the automatic configuration of metaheuristics when applied to complex problems provides promising perspectives towards the improvement of the achieved results.

3 Automatic Configuration of Genetic Algorithm for Market Participation Portfolio Optimization

This section provides a description of the considered electricity market participation portfolio problem, the GA that is used to solve this problem, and the detail on the AAC model applied to improve the GA performance.

3.1 Portfolio Optimization

The portfolio optimization problem aims at optimizing the investment of a supported player in different electricity market opportunities. Several market opportunities are considered, associated to an expected transaction price per negotiation period. Accordingly, the optimization model aims at finding the optimal combination of trading volume (sale and purchase) that should be performed according to the expected prices and specific market constraints [7].

Equation (1) represents the objective function, which models the optimization of players' market participation portfolio. This function considers the expected production

of a market player for each period of each day, and the amount of power to be negotiated in each market is optimized to get the maximum income that can be achieved [7].

$$(Spow_{M...NumS}, Bpow_{S1...NumS}) = Max \begin{bmatrix} \sum_{M=M1}^{NumM} (Spow_{M,d,p} \times ps_{M,d,p} \times Asell_M) - \\ \sum_{S=S1}^{NumS} (Bpow_S \times ps_{S,d,p} \times Abuy_S) \end{bmatrix}$$

$$\forall d \in Nday, \forall p \in Nper, Asell_M \in \{0, 1\}, Abuy \in \{0, 1\} \tag{1}$$

In Eq. (1) d represents the weekday, $Nday$ represent the number of days, p represents the negotiation period, $Nper$ represent the number of negotiation periods, $Asell_M$ and $Abuy_S$ are boolean variables, indicating if this player can enter negotiations in each market type, M represents the referred market, $NumM$ represents the number of markets, S represents a session of the balancing market, and $NumS$ represents the number of sessions. Variables $ps_{M,d,p}$ and $ps_{S,d,p}$ represent the expected (forecasted) prices of selling and buying electricity in each session of each market type, in each period of each day. The outputs are $Spow_M$ representing the amount of power to sell in market M, and $Bpow_S$ representing the amount of power to buy in session S.

In Eq. (2) is expressed the way in which the negotiation prices are obtained. As one can see, sale prices $ps_{M,d,p}$ and purchase prices $ps_{S,d,p}$ are considered.

$$ps_{M,d,p} = Value(d, p, Spow_M, M)$$
$$ps_{S,d,p} = Value(d, p, Bpow_S, S) \tag{2}$$

The $Value$ is obtained by Eq. (3), and is calculated from the application of the clustering and fuzzy approach.

$$Value(day, per, Pow, Market) =$$
$$Data(fuzzy(pow), day, per, Market) \tag{3}$$

With the implementation of this model, it is possible to obtain market prices based on the traded amount. In order to achieve this, for the modeling of the prices are considered the expected production of a market player for each period of each day. The results of the application of this methodology can be observed in [16]. Equation (3) defines this condition, where Data refers to the historical data that correlates the amount of transacted power, the day, period of the day and the particular market session.

Equation (4) represents the main constraint of this problem. The constraint imposes that the total power that can be sold in the set of all markets is never higher than the total expect production (TEP) of the player, plus the total of purchased power.

$$\sum_{M=M1}^{NumM} Spow_M \leq TEP + \sum_{S=S1}^{NumS} Bpow_S \tag{4}$$

Equations (5), (6) and (7) represent other constraints that can be applied to the problem. This depends on the nature of the problem itself, e.g. type of each market,

negotiation amount, type of supported player (renewable based generation, cogeneration, etc.).

$$TEP = \sum Energy_{prod}, \; Energy_{prod} \in \left\{ Renew_{prod}, Therm_{prod} \right\} \tag{5}$$

$$0 \leq Renew_{prod} \leq Max_{prod} \tag{6}$$

$$Min_{prod} \leq Therm_{prod} \leq Max_{prod}, \; if \; Therm_{prod} > 0 \tag{7}$$

By (5) it can be seen that the energy production may come from renewable sources and thermoelectric sources. If the player is a producer of thermoelectric power, the production must be set at a minimum since it is not feasible to completely turn off the production plant, as can be observed by Eq. (7). If the producer is based on renewable energy, the only restriction is the maximum production capacity, as in (6).

3.2 Genetic Algorithm

The GA technique is based on Darwin theory of natural evolution, where the most capable individuals survive. The GA's search method tries to find solutions based on probabilities, it does not reach an optimal solution, but looks for a well near solution. Besides the natural evolution, other concepts of biology are applied to the GA, such as the crossover, which is the exchange of information from one individual to another, and mutation where the individual suffers a change in its composition. Natural selection is also used [17]. The GA process begins with the formation of an initial population, which may be a random population (as is the case in this study). Then, the population objective functions are assessed, which is done dependently of the problem (in this problem the mathematical formulation presented in Sect. 3.1 is used for fitness function evaluation). After the evaluation is made, the individuals are selected; these are the individuals who will be part of the next stage: the crossover process and also the mutation. The new generation of individuals is then found. Following the diagram, follows the stopping criterion, which in this case may be of various natures. If this criterion is satisfied, the algorithm returns the most suitable solution; if this does not happen, the algorithm goes back to the stage of population evaluation, in order to start a new cycle.

In summary, the purpose of the use of GA is to find the individual from the search space with the best "genetic material". The quality of an individual is measured with an evaluation function, called fitness. GA uses a population formed by a set of individuals. Each individual represents a solution or point in the search space. During the evolution, several points are examined by the individuals.

3.3 Sequential Model Algorithm Configuration (SMAC)

SMAC is an algorithm configuration tool for optimizing the parameters of arbitrary algorithms. The main core consists of a Bayesian optimization in combination with a competitive dispute to decide the most efficient between the two configurations [8]. The predictive models on which SMAC is based seek information about the domain model,

namely knowing which are the most important input variables. With SMAC, it is possible for us to dedicate ourselves more rigorously to the design of algorithms, tasks that are scientifically more interesting than the adjustment of parameters.

Sequential Model-Based Optimization (SMBO), also known as Bayesian optimization, is a general function optimization technique that includes some of the most efficient techniques (in terms of evaluating functions) of currently available optimization methods. Originally developed for designing experiments, SMBO methods are generally applicable to scenarios where a user wants to minimize some function $f(x)$, valued by a scalar, which is expensive to evaluate, often in terms of time or money [18].

The most general view of Hyper Parameters Optimization (HPO) is a "black box" function optimization, where the function c is minimized with respect to its input hyper parameters $\lambda \in \Lambda$. Also [8] considers that it can be framed in this way, as can be seen in Eq. (8), minimizing the loss L in D_{val} validation data of a model trained on D_{train} training data with hyper parameters λ.

$$\lambda^* \in \arg\min_{\lambda \in \Lambda} c(\lambda) = \arg\min_{\lambda \in \Lambda} \mathcal{L}(\mathcal{D}_{train}, \mathcal{D}_{val};)\lambda. \tag{8}$$

Bayesian Optimization (BO) with Gaussian Processes (GP) is the traditional choice for HPO in small continuous spaces. SMAC3 builds on existing GP implementations and offers several acquisition functions, the main ones being: Probability of Improvement (PI) e Expected Improvement (EI) [19] and in variants, for example, EI per second [20] for evaluations with different runtimes and logEI [21] for heavy-tail cost distribution.

Figure 1 shows the Bayesian optimization algorithm, which takes samples and evaluates the initial points (line 1), builds the model (line 3), finds the next point to be evaluated by optimizing the acquisition function (line 4), evaluates the selected point and receives the evaluation value (line 5) and updates the data (line 6). The main components of Bayesian optimization are the surrogate model and the acquisition function.

Algorithm 1 Bayesian Optimization

Require: objective function f, search space $\mathcal{X}$, initial sample size n, surrogate model $\mathcal{M}$, acquisition function $\alpha(\mathbf{x} \mid \mathcal{M})$

1: sample and evaluate initial points: $\mathcal{D}_0 = \{(\mathbf{x}_{0,1}, y_{0,1}), \cdots, (\mathbf{x}_{0,n}, y_{0,n})\}$
2: **for** $t = 1, 2, \cdots$ **do**
3:     construct surrogate model $\mathcal{M}$ by $\mathcal{D}_{t-1}$
4:     find $\mathbf{x}_t$ by optimizing the acqusition function α : $\mathbf{x}_t = \arg\max_{\mathbf{x} \in \mathcal{X}} \alpha(\mathbf{x} \mid \mathcal{M})$
5:     evaluate $\mathbf{x}_t$ and receive: $y_t = f(\mathbf{x}_t)$
6:     update the data $\mathcal{D}_t = \mathcal{D}_{t-1} \cup \{(\mathbf{x}_t, y_t)\}$
7: **end for**

Fig. 1. Bayesian optimization algorithm [22]

SMAC itself offers many design options, some crucial to achieving maximum performance. In this study, we will use the SMAC4BB Facade, using the surrogate model, the Gaussian Process (GP) or the Gaussian Process with Monte Carlo Markov Chain (GP_MCMC) as an acquisition function, EI or PI. The EI represents the amount of expectation of the improvement value for the best evaluation value of the new point candidate, and PI represents the strategy to maximize the probability for the best value.

4 Experimental Findings

Solving the considered portfolio optimization problem requires considering different types of information regarding the electricity markets the support player may participate in. In specific, the following information is needed: (i) the types of markets in which the player can participate; (ii) the expected prices on each market; (iii) information on whether each market is or not available in each period; (iv) expected consumption of the market agent for each period.

Table 1 represents the types of markets (M0 to M7), where each customer or user can participate from a buyer or seller perspective. The volume trading limits are also indicated, in MW, defined by market (e.g. Lim_buy and Lim_Sell).

Table 1. Market transaction limits (MW)

Market	M0	M1	M2	M3	M4	M5	M6	M7
Buyer	1	1	1	1	1	1	1	1
Lim_buy (MW)	1	0.17	0.17	0.17	0.17	0.17	0.17	0.01
Seller	0	1	1	1	1	1	1	1
Lim_Sell (MW)	0	0.17	0.17	0.17	0.17	0.17	0.17	0.01

In Table 2 one is able to see the expected prices per market for each trading period, they are important data to estimate the results and value the objective, which is to achieve the lowest cost for the supported market player.

Table 2. Forecasted market prices (€/MWh)

Period	M0	M1	M2	M3	M4	M5	M6	M7
1	175.28	182.31	190.22	178.58	0	0	0	162
2	172.8	178.84	178.08	168.08	0	0	0	172
...	...	...	...	...	...	...	...	...
24	153.92	168.89	192.65	188.45	192	191.5	189.97	195

Represented in Table 3 by a Boolean variable is the indication whether a user can intervene on each market platform and for each trading period, that is, if he is authorized to buy or sell in each session. The digit (1) indicates availability, while (0) the opposite.

Finally, the last information, provided by Table 4, refers to the consumption expected by the supported player, in each trading period.

The configuration of parameters in SMAC, like many automatic configurators, is done in the form of an interval, which is the main difference for the user, when compared to manual configuration.

Table 3. Market availability in each period

Period	M0	M1	M2	M3	M4	M5	M6	M7
1	1	1	1	1	0	0	0	0
2	1	1	1	1	0	0	0	0
...	...	...	...	...	...	...	...	...
24	1	1	1	1	1	1	1	1

Table 4. Consumption volume per period

Period	Volume (MW)
1	0.469
2	0.064
...	...
24	0.515

These intervals are configurable, which allows SMAC, under associated AI techniques, to indicate a set of parameters, based on a model trained to obtain the best configuration. In addition, we can indicate the number of evolutions (e.g. Function Evolution = 24). This is a stopping criterion for SMAC, as it indicates the possible number of configurations that can be tried, in the search for the best solution. We can also choose the model to use (e.g. GP or GP_MCMC). By default, our solution for the optimization of GA assumes the following parameters and values: Population [50, 1000], Step [1, 4], Mutation [0.2, 0.7], Elistism [0.2, 0.7], Generations [10, 100].

Figure 2 shows the configuration resulting from running SMAC. The solution found (elitism = 0.52, generations = 61, mutation = 0.50, population = 589 and step = 1) results from the minimization of the objective function, with the best result obtained, with no need to indicate specific parameters as in manual configuration. The graph shows the evolution of the GA with Population [500–1000], Step [1, 2], Mutation [0.2–0.7], Crossover [0.2–0.7], Generations [10–100].

Unlike manual configuration processes, SMAC indicates which metaheuristic parameters result from its model, depending on the chosen algorithm and the best value found by the objective function for the addressed problem. However, due to the intrinsic stochasticity of this type of metaheuristic algorithms, in a new execution, based on the configuration of parameters obtained from the SMAC, the result obtained by the objective function may not be exactly the same. From Fig. 2 it can also be seen that there is no clear improvement of the objective function cost throughout the iterations, as the AAC process experiments different combinations of parameters, thus resulting in diversified results throughout the optimal parameter set search process.

In order to analyze the performance of the GA applied to solving the envisaged portfolio optimization problem, a sensitivity analysis is performed, in which, for the manual

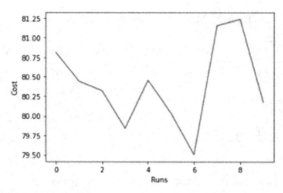

Fig. 2. Objective function cost in different SMAC iterations

configuration, parameters were chosen within the ranges defined in SMAC. SMAC is experimented with both GP and GP_MCMC. The summary from these experiments is presented in Table 5 and Table 6.

Table 5. Summary of results for GA parameterization

Portfolio Problem			
Algorithm (Method)	Configuration (model)	Mean of Mean Cost	Mean of Mean Time (s)
GA	Manual	78,74	2,1794
GA	SMAC	78,63	3,5163
GA	SMAC (gp)	78,74	2,5816
GA	SMAC (gp_mcmc)	78,56	4,8293

As one can see from Table 6, the AAC using SMAC is able to reach lower Best Cost of objective function, namely 78.26 and lower Mean Best Cost, with 78.47. Both of these values are achieved using the GP_MCMC model.

Regarding the execution time, it is verified by Table 5 and Table 6 that the automatic configuration is slower, mainly due to the use of the substitution model (GP_MCMC), because this model seeks a more precise solution in the limit of time. If the option is for GP, the difference between the manual process and automatic configuration is not so significative.

For illustrative purposes, Fig. 3 displays the results of the portfolio optimization for one target period (period 1). Figure 3a) shows that volume (MW) allocated for sale and purchase in each available market for the considered period, while Fig. 3b) shows the expected market prices for the considered period, for all considered markets.

By interpreting the graph from Fig. 3a), some conclusions can be reached, such as considering that M0 is indicated to buy, markets M1 and M2 are allocated to sell and the remaining two: M3 and M7 present perfectly residual values, resulting from the random component of the GA algorithm. Matching these results with the market prices from Fig. 3b) and the information from Table 1, Table 2, Table 3 and Table 4, it is visible that M0 is the market with the lowest price, in which the player is allowed to purchase,

hence the big amount of purchase allocated by optimization process to M0. M1 and M2, in turn, are the markets presenting the highest expected price, hence being allocated to the sale of the allowed volume, within the specified limits for each of these markets.

Table 6. GA parameterization results

			Genetic Algorithm								
Method	Runs	Models	Population	Step	Mutation	Elitism	Generations	Best Cost	Mean Best Cost	Total Time (s)	Mean Time (s)
MC	5		500	1	0,2	0,2	30	78,64	78,80	5,096	1,0192
MC	10		750	1	0,2	0,2	30	78,49	78,68	15,530	1,5530
MC	10		1000	1	0,2	0,2	60	78,50	78,74	39,659	3,9659

SMAC-AC	5	gp	[500-1000]	[1-2]	[0,2-0,5]	[0,2-0,5]	[30-60]	78,31	78,84	11,053	2,2105
SMAC-AC	16	gp	[500-1000]	[1-2]	[0,2-0,5]	[0,2-0,5]	[30-60]	78,30	78,64	94,484	2,9526
SMAC-AC	5	gp_mcmc	[500-1000]	[1-2]	[0,2-0,5]	[0,2-0,5]	[30-60]	78,26	78,47	20,363	4,0726
SMAC-AC	16	gp_mcmc	[500-1000]	[1-2]	[0,2-0,5]	[0,2-0,5]	[30-60]	78,35	78,56	77,296	4,8293

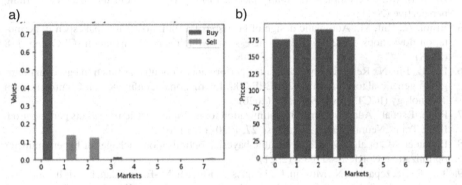

Fig. 3. a) Sale and purchase volume (MW) in each available market; b) Electricity price in each market

5 Conclusions

Metaheuristic algorithms are used as an important tool for solving complex optimization problems. Despite the success of these algorithms, their performance in solving complex problems is directly related to the parameters and meta-heuristics chosen. To obtain the best solution, one should have perfect knowledge about the problem to be optimized and which variation operators best affect its purpose. Even so, considerable effort is required in experimenting with different combinations of parameters in order to obtain the ideal configuration for the problem in hands. ACC models enable reaching optimized config-uration of parameters with minimum effort from the user and at reduced time cost. This paper presents the application of SMAC using BO with GP and GP_GP_MCMC to opti-mize the parameterization of a GA algorithm solving an electricity market participation portfolio optimization problem. Results showed that SMAC improved the robustness of the results as well as a superior performance in identifying the best set of parameters, when compared to manual configuration. SMAC bringsan additional cost in terms of

execution time, which is, however, not significant given the order of these values (few seconds). The superiority verified in terms of results, combined with the simplicity of the configuration process, compared to the exhaustive manual experience, supports the advantage of this model.

References

1. Baghernejad, A., Aslanzadeh, E.: Application of multiobjective optimization in thermal design and analysis of complex energy systems (2022)
2. Kvasov, D.E., Mukhametzhanov, M.S.: Metaheuristic vs. deterministic global optimization algorithms: the univariate case. Appl. Math. Comput. **318**, 245–259 (2018). https://doi.org/10.1016/j.amc.2017.05.014
3. Adenso-Díaz, B., Laguna, M.: Fine-tuning of algorithms using fractional experimental designs and local search. Oper. Res. **54**, 99–114 (2006)
4. Birattari, M.: The problem of tuning metaheuristics: as seen from the machine learning perspective (2004)
5. Brum, A., Ritt, M.: Automatic design of heuristics for minimizing the makespan in permutation flow shops. In: 2018 IEEE Congress on Evolutionary Computation (CEC), pp. 1–8 (2018)
6. Lei, L., Liu, N.: Research on optimization performance of nonlinear function based on multigroup genetic algorithm. In: 2020 IEEE 20th International Conference on Communication Technology (ICCT), pp. 1498–1502 (2020)
7. Pinto, T., et al.: Adaptive portfolio optimization for multiple electricity markets participation. IEEE Trans. Neural Netw. Learn. Syst. **27**, 1720–1733 (2016)
8. Lindauer, M., et al.: SMAC3: a versatile bayesian optimization package for hyperparameter optimization. CoRR abs/2109.0 (2021)
9. Tari, S., Szczepanski, N., Mousin, L., Jacques, J., Kessaci, M.-E., Jourdan, L.: Multi-objective automatic algorithm configuration for the classification problem of imbalanced data. In: 2020 IEEE Congress on Evolutionary Computation (CEC), pp. 1–8 (2020)
10. López-Ibáñez, M., Dubois-Lacoste, J., Pérez Cáceres, L., Birattari, M., Stützle, T.: The Irace package: iterated racing for automatic algorithm configuration. Oper. Res. Perspect. **3**, 43–58 (2016)
11. Sheng, W., Shao, Q., Tong, H., Peng, J.: Scheduling optimization on takeout delivery based on hybrid meta-heuristic algorithm. In: 2021 13th International Conference on Advanced Computational Intelligence (ICACI), pp. 372–377 (2021)
12. Sousa, T., Vale, Z., Carvalho, J.P., Pinto, T., Morais, H.: A hybrid simulated annealing approach to handle energy resource management considering an intensive use of electric vehicles. Energy **67**, 81–96 (2014)
13. Cintrano, C., Chicano, F., Alba, E.: Using metaheuristics for the location of bicycle stations. Expert Syst. Appl. **161**, 113684 (2020)
14. Blot, A., Hoos, H.H., Kessaci, M.-É., Jourdan, L.: Automatic configuration of bi-objective optimisation algorithms: impact of correlation between objectives. In: 2018 IEEE 30th International Conference on Tools with Artificial Intelligence (ICTAI), pp. 571–578 (2018)
15. Stützle, T., López-Ibáñez, M.: Automated design of metaheuristic algorithms. In: Gendreau, M., Potvin, J.-Y. (eds.) Handbook of Metaheuristics. ISORMS, vol. 272, pp. 541–579. Springer, Cham (2019). https://doi.org/10.1007/978-3-319-91086-4_17
16. Faia, R., Pinto, T., Vale, Z.: Dynamic fuzzy estimation of contracts historic information using an automatic clustering methodology. In: Bajo, J., et al. (eds.) PAAMS 2015. CCIS, vol. 524, pp. 270–282. Springer, Cham (2015). https://doi.org/10.1007/978-3-319-19033-4_23

17. Faia, R., Pinto, T., Vale, Z.: GA optimization technique for portfolio optimization of electricity market participation. In: 2016 IEEE Symposium Series on Computational Intelligence, SSCI 2016, Athens, Greece (2017)

18. Bergstra, J., Komer, B., Eliasmith, C., Yamins, D., Cox, D.D.: Hyperopt: a Python library for model selection and hyperparameter optimization. Comput. Sci. Discov. **8**, 14008 (2015)

19. Jones, D.R., Schonlau, M., Welch, W.J.: Efficient global optimization of expensive black-box functions. J. Global Optim. **13**, 455–492 (1998)

20. Snoek, J., Larochelle, H., Adams, R.P.: Practical Bayesian optimization of machine learning algorithms. In: Proceedings of the 25th International Conference on Neural Information Processing Systems, vol. 2, pp. 2951–2959. Curran Associates Inc. (2012)

21. Hutter, F., Hoos, H.H., Leyton-Brown, K., Murphy, K.: Time-bounded sequential parameter optimization. In: Blum, C., Battiti, R. (eds.) LION 2010. LNCS, vol. 6073, pp. 281–298. Springer, Heidelberg (2010). https://doi.org/10.1007/978-3-642-13800-3_30

22. Nomura, M., Abe, K.: A simple heuristic for Bayesian optimization with a low budget. arXiv abs/1911.0 (2019)

Modeling Stand-Alone Photovoltaic Systems with Matlab/Simulink

José Baptista[1], Nuno Pimenta[2], Raul Morais[1], and Tiago Pinto[1(✉)]

[1] Department of Engineering, University of Trás-os-Montes e Alto Douro and INESC-TEC, UTAD's Pole, 5000-811 Vila Real, Portugal
{baptista,rmorais,tiagopinto}@utad.pt

[2] Department of Engineering, University of Trás-os-Montes e Alto Douro, 5000-811 Vila Real, Portugal

Abstract. In the upcoming years, European countries have to make a strong bet on solar energy. Small photovoltaic systems are able to provide energy for several applications like housing, traffic and street lighting, among others. This field is expected to have a big growth, thus taking advantage of the largest renewable energy source existing on the planet, the sun. This paper proposes a computational model able to simulate the behavior of a stand-alone photovoltaic system. The developed model allows to predict PV systems behavior, constituted by the panels, storage system, charge controller and inverter, having as input data the solar radiation and the temperature of the installation site. Several tests are presented that validates the reliability of the developed model.

Keywords: Solar energy · Photovoltaic system · Modeling · Matlab/Simulink

1 Introduction

The sun is the largest source of renewable energy available on the planet, so it makes sense the global effort to develop solutions for its use on a large scale. Until a few years ago, the price of solar technologies and their low efficiency in the conversion were constrains to its growth. However, today, with the price decreasing together with the increasing of PV modules efficiency, the photovoltaic solar energy becomes an interesting solution.

The objective of this paper is to develop of a computational model that predicts the behavior of a PV stand-alone system, knowing the incident solar radiation and the temperature of the site. To achieve this goal, different blocks like PV solar panels, batteries, charge controller and DC/AC inverter were modeled under Matlab/Simulink, which proved to be a robust and versatile tool for this kind of study.

This work was supported by the R&D Project "Continental Factory of Future, (CONTINENTAL FoF)/POCI-01-0247-FEDER-047512", financed by the European Regional Development Fund (ERDF), through the Program "Programa Operacional Competitividade e Internacionalização (POCI)/PORTUGAL 2020", under the management of aicep Portugal Global – Trade & Investment Agency.

G. Marreiros et al. (Eds.): EPIA 2022, LNAI 13566, pp. 258–270, 2022.
https://doi.org/10.1007/978-3-031-16474-3_22

Several authors have studied this topic, mainly the development of models for the photovoltaic system blocks. In the references [1, 2], we can find examples of models for the PV panels developed in Simulink. For the battery block development, there are several types of possible solutions, but the most used are those that use the blocks belonging to the Simulink's library itself, as used in references [3, 4], there is also the option to create new solutions, such as [5, 6]. The model of the inverter block is addressed in several references [7, 8] where different mathematical models of an inverter were created in Simulink.

2 Photovoltaic Systems

The use of solar energy to produce electrical power is done through photovoltaic systems which convert this energy through the photovoltaic effect. This conversion takes place in the photovoltaic cell but its production is low, so it becomes necessary to associate several cells in series and in parallel, forming the photovoltaic panels. The energy produced by these panels can be stored in batteries which in turn needs to be controlled by charge controllers to extend the batteries lifespan. To supply AC loads, photovoltaic systems need an inverter, whose function is to convert direct current to alternating current.

2.1 Photovoltaic Modules

The photovoltaic cell can be approached by a current source in parallel with a diode, where the output is proportional to the incident solar radiation on the cell. The PV current source represents the equivalent current generated by solar radiation and the diode representing the electron exchange at a p-n junction crossing by I_D current, which is dependent of its own saturation current (I_{pv}) and voltage between the photovoltaic cell terminals, given by Eq. 1.

$$I_D = I_0 \left(e^{\frac{V}{mV_T}} - 1 \right) \tag{1}$$

where m is – is the diode ideality factor and V_T – is the thermal equivalent potential, k the Boltzmann constant ($1{,}38 \times 10^{-23}$ J/K), T – cell's temperature, in (°K); q – electron's electric charge ($1{,}6 \times 10^{-19}$ C). To better understand the behavior of photovoltaic cells, many manufacturers provide the values of V_{OC}, I_{SC} and P_{max}, at Standard Test Conditions (STC, cell temperature of 25 °C and an irradiance of 1000 W/m^2). Photovoltaic cells have a limited potential, since the open circuit voltage is independent of the solar cell area and is limited by the semiconductors properties. The maximum power of a cell does not exceed 2 W, which is insufficient for supply most applications, so, the cells are grouped into photovoltaic modules, which in turn are also grouped together forming a photovoltaic panel [9]. The parameters that characterize photovoltaic modules are usually [10]:

- Constant parameters, like the ideality factor (m) given by Eq. 2.

$$m = \frac{V_{max} - V_{OC}}{V_T ln\left(1 - \frac{I_{max}}{I_{SC}}\right)} \tag{2}$$

- Parameters that depend on radiation, like short-circuit current (I_{SC}), given by Eq. 3, where G represents the solar radiation.

$$I_{SC} = I_{SC}^{STC} \frac{G}{G^{STC}} \tag{3}$$

- Parameters that depend on temperature, like reverse saturation current (I_O), given by Eq. 4.

$$I_O = I_O^{STC} \left(\frac{T}{T^{STC}}\right)^3 e^{\frac{\epsilon}{m'}\left(\frac{1}{V_T^{STC}} - \frac{1}{V_T}\right)} \tag{4}$$

2.2 Battery Model

The possibility of storing energy produced by photovoltaic modules for later consumption, during the night or on lower solar radiation days, is one of the great advantages in this type of systems, being the batteries a fundamental part of the solution, because they allow the storage of the electric energy. Photovoltaic systems use rechargeable batteries and the most commonly used are lead-acid batteries; Nickel-Cadmium batteries (NiCd); Nickel-metal hydride batteries (NiMH) and Lithium-ion batteries (Li-ion). The battery capacity is measured by the amount of electrical charge, ie by the number of hours that a given current can be supplied by a fully charged battery, expressed in Ampere hour (Ah), given by the product of the supplied current and the time in hours, corrected for the reference temperature [4]. Many batteries models have been developed, including [11] which developed an equation to describe its electrochemical behavior in terms of the final voltage, the open circuit voltage, internal resistance, discharge current and the state of charge (SOC) that can be applied to both cycles (charge and discharge). The simple electric model that represents a rechargeable battery consists of an ideal voltage source in series with an internal resistance. This model, assumes the same characteristics for the charging and discharging cycles, as shown in the Fig. 1. The controlled voltage source is described by Eq. 5.

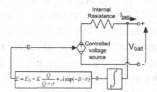

Fig. 1. Equivalent circuit of a battery [8].

$$E = E_0 - K\frac{Q}{Q - it} + Ae^{-B \cdot it} \tag{5}$$

where E – open circuit voltage; E_0 – initial cell potential; K – polarization coefficient in $\Omega\,cm^2$; Q – Battery charge in coulomb; A and B – empirical constants; R – internal

resistance; i – discharging/discharging current. The battery voltage is then obtained from Eq. 6.

$$V_{batt} = E - R \cdot i \tag{6}$$

2.3 Charge Controller and Inverter

The batteries lifetime depends on its charge and discharge profile. The charge controller monitors the battery's voltage by analyzing its voltage during the charging process, helping to increase their life cycle. When the charging is complete, the controller stops supplying current to the battery avoiding the loss of electrolyte and a possible batteries overheating, and typically the state of charge should not exceed 90%. Then, whenever the battery's voltage decreases to a certain value, the charge controller allows a charging current and the charging process starts again. Usually, the charge controllers are chosen according to the system's power and the battery type and can be either series or shunt.

The inverters have an important role in photovoltaic systems, because they establish the link between the DC current generated by the photovoltaic module and the AC grid. The inverter's main function is to convert the DC voltage in a single or three-phase AC voltage, and adjust it to the frequency's characteristics and the appropriate voltage level for its network connection or for use in a stand-alone system. There are two main groups of inverters, the ones corresponding to stand-alone PV systems and those used in grid-connected PV systems.

3 System Modelling

The process developed to obtain the proposed PV system will be presented and analyzed in detail, namely the several system blocks, always showing the simulation results that prove its accuracy.

3.1 Photovoltaic Module

The developed module consists in two inputs, which represents the temperature and the solar radiation and three outputs: current, voltage and generated power. Each PV module has its own characteristics that depend on the manufacturer. These characteristics, are introduced into the system before each simulation. The PV module model was developed with the help of several sets of blocks, called "*Embedded MATLAB Function*", which allow performing mathematical calculations, based on standard values and some introduced parameters. To develop this module were necessary eight blocks:

- **Block 1** – Ideality factor;
- **Block 2** – Equivalent ideality factor;
- **Block 3** – Reverse saturation current;

- **Block 4** – Cell operating temperature: This block is responsible for calculating the cell operating temperature (T_C), using Eq. 7.

$$T_c = T_a + \frac{G(NOCT - 20)}{800} \tag{7}$$

where, G – solar radiation (W/m^2); T_a – ambient temperature (°C); $NOCT$ – normal operation cell temperature (°C).
- **Block 5** – Thermal potential;
- **Block 6** – Output current;
- **Block 7** – Output voltage: this block joins the calculated values obtain in Blocks 1, 2, 3 and 5. The maximum voltage is very dependent of short circuit current, maximum current and reverse saturation current variation with temperature and can be calculated based in Eq. 8.

$$V_{max} = mV_T \ln\left[\frac{\frac{G}{G^{STC}}\left(I_{SC}^{STC} - I_{max}^{STC}\right)}{I_0^{STC}\left(\frac{T}{T^{STC}}\right)^3 e^{\frac{\epsilon}{m}\left(\frac{1}{v_T^{STC}} - \frac{1}{v_T}\right)}}\right] \tag{8}$$

- **Block 8** – Output power: multiplies two signals from blocks 6 and 7, which correspond to the current and voltage of the PV module, respectively.

The entire structure described above is shown in Fig. 2. To verify the accuracy of the developed PV module, several tests were performed based on results obtained in several references [12] and the results confirm the good approximation between the developed model and those previously mentioned.

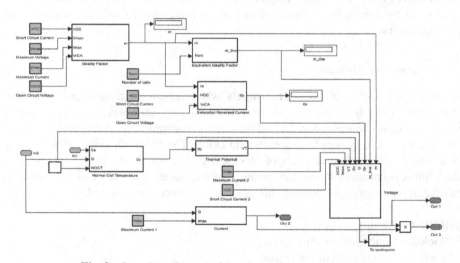

Fig. 2. Complete diagram of the photovoltaic module model.

3.2 Battery

For lead-acid battery model was used a Simulink block approaching. Figure 3 shows the internal structure of the battery, which has as input parameters the current drawn by photovoltaic module/panel (input 1) and ground (input 2) and as output the parameter m. The output parameter m is divided into three parameters of special importance, which are the SOC (state of charge), the discharge current and the output voltage. The Model *Continuous block* is very important because there will result the values of SOC, battery current and voltage.

To test the operation of this block was used the same battery of the reference [13], whose characteristics are presented in Table 1, this is the BP 1.2-12 battery (B.B. Battery, country).

Table 1. Characteristics of BP 1.2–12 battery.

Nominal voltage	12 V
Rated capacity C120	1,2 Ah
Internal resistance	120 mΩ

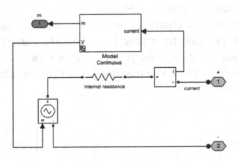

Fig. 3. Battery internal structure.

This model was used to simulate the battery behavior in a charge/discharge test, and the results are shown in Fig. 4.

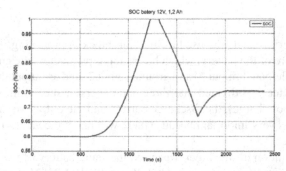

Fig. 4. Charging and discharging test with 12 V and 1.2 Ah battery.

3.3 Charge Controller

The charge controller block was developed with the objective of creating limits to the charging and the discharge processes. For this purpose, upper and lower limits were defined for the SOC parameter. Whenever the SOC value is only 20% or below, the battery will no longer supply the loads, only doing it again when its value exceeds 20%. In the case of the upper limit, the battery charge must not exceed 90% of its capacity, returning to the charging process when it returns to 86% or below. Figure 5 shows the internal structure of the charge controller block.

Figure 6 shows the battery charge current curve and the battery state of charge (SOC). Taking into account that from time t = 12,5 s the battery SOC reaches 90%, thus, between 12,5 s and about 18 s, the battery does not charge, waiting the moment where the SOC reaches 86%. Thus, it is possible to confirm the reliable operation of the developed charge controller.

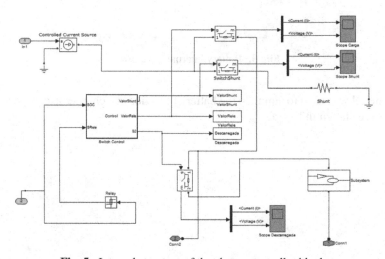

Fig. 5. Internal structure of the charge controller block.

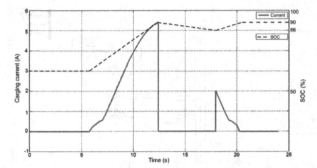

Fig. 6. Example of charge controller operation during the battery charging and discharging processes.

3.4 Inverter

In order to supply AC loads it is necessary to include an inverter block. A Matlab/Simulink model was developed to simulate the inverter, depicted in Fig. 9. To test the inverter behavior, a 12 V DC voltage source was used to simulate the battery output voltage. As can be seen in Fig. 7, the power supply is connected to the *"Universal Bridge"* block, which is a model that can be configured with a series of electronic power devices, such as IGBT, MOSFET and thyristors, among others. The "Universal Bridge" allows to choose the characteristics to use and in addition the choice of the power device, the number of bridges as well others specific parameters. In this study, IGBT's and Diodes with three bridges were chosen in order to constitute a three-phase inverter, and also the values of the damping resistance R_s and the damping capacity C_s are chosen, which when dealing with IGBT devices must be purely resistive, thus choosing $R_s = 5000\ \Omega$ and $C_s = \infty$. The "g" signal is an input parameter to control the electronic power devices, being in this case a six-pulse PWM wave with a frequency of 1080 Hz. The transformer block is used to rise the voltage value to the desired levels and simultaneously filter high frequencies. Figure 8 shows the voltage waveform in the inverter output, in this case voltage value between two phases.

3.5 Loads

The loads will be modeled by a variable resistance R_L that represents the instantaneous power consumed in the circuit (P_L). The resistance value can be calculated through Eq. 9.

$$R_L = \frac{V^2}{P_L} \tag{9}$$

Figure 9 shows the structure of the load block. The input current from the load controller is injected into the input 1 through the equivalent low-values cables resistances. The load supply is controlled by a switch that acts according the load consumption diagram. Therefore, the *"Signal Builder"* block defines the moments when the loads are switched ON or OFF.

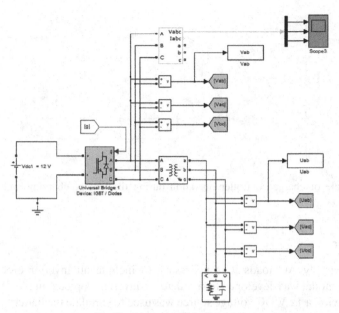

Fig. 7. Inverter block diagram.

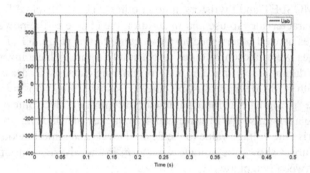

Fig. 8. Three-phase voltage between two phases at the transformer output (U_{ab}).

After the implementation of the different blocks belonging to the PV system (previously described), they were connected in order to work as a complete system, Fig. 10. This model proves to be reliable, flexible and can be used at any time for different number of photovoltaic panels, batteries and loads.

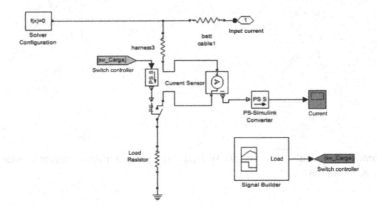

Fig. 9. Load block diagram.

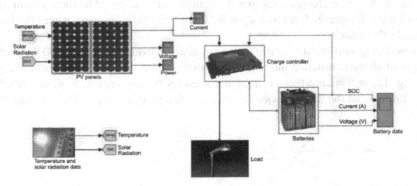

Fig. 10. Complete photovoltaic system modeled in Matlab/Simulink.

4 Simulation Results and Analysis

To test entire model, several simulations were performed under different conditions of temperature, solar radiation and different load regimes. The first test is based on the meteorological data for one day of December in the city of Vila Real, Portugal. The PV system is constituted by 20 photovoltaic modules BP 3230 and 16 batteries OPzS SOLAR 420, 48 V connected. A load with 800 W was considered to be connected between the following ranges: 0–27,000 s and 63,000–86,400 s (00 h 00 min–07 h 30 min and 17 h 30 min–24 h 00 min) to simulate the public lighting behavior. It should be noted that the two intervals at which the load is connected coincides practically with the absence of solar radiation, being the responsibility of the batteries to supply the system. Figure 11(a) shows the daily current produced by the panels on a typical December day while Fig. 11(b) shows the evolution of the batteries state of charge (SOC).

Analyzing Fig. 11(b), it is possible to verify the batteries behavior along the day. The simulation starts at 0 s, corresponding to midnight, so it is clear that the battery will be discharging because at that time there is no solar radiation and the load is supplied,

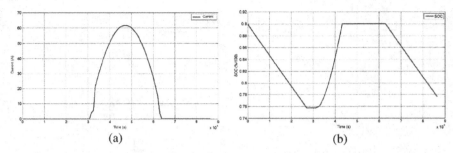

(a)   (b)

Fig. 11. Simulations results with an 800 W load. (a) PV system daily current production. (b) Batteries SOC evolution.

the SOC reaches 78%. Around 26,000 s of simulation time, which corresponds more or less at seven o'clock am, the load is switched OFF and solar radiation appears. At this point, the SOC curve changes, starting the batteries charge and SOC increases until the batteries are fully charged, stabilizing at 90% until 63,000 s, moment where the load is switched ON again.

Considering a different scenario with an increase in load with more 1,000 W, working throughout all the simulation interval, the result would be quite different. As can be seen from Fig. 12, in this case there is a greater need for battery energy, SOC reaches 55% and so throughout the day batteries do not fully charge as in the previous simulation.

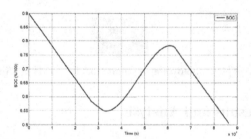

Fig. 12. SOC simulation result with a 1,800 W load.

In order to better verify the reliability of the developed model, another study was carried out for a one-week simulation time, considering a scenario of low solar radiation (typical of winter). The curve describing the solar radiation behavior throughout the week is presented in Fig. 13(a), where the first and last day of the week presents average values and the remaining days present 75%, 50%, 10%, 25% and 50% of daily average radiation. The daily load behavior will be the same as been considered in the previous simulations, switched ON between 0–27,000 s and 63,000–86,400 s. The main objective of this simulation is to test the model over several days and to see how it would behave in a period when the solar radiation is below the normal values.

In Fig. 13(b) it is possible to observe the batteries behavior during the study week and it is observed that even with a significant reduction of solar radiation in this period, the batteries never reach the minimum limit, reaching capacity values close to 21%.

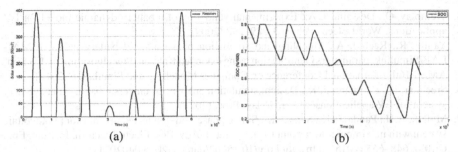

Fig. 13. Simulations results for a week, with an 800 W load. (a) Solar radiation. (b) Batteries SOC evolution.

Comparing Figs. 13(a) and 13(b), the solar radiation influence on the batteries state of charge can be verified. It is visible that on low irradiance days, the batteries SOC has small increments, insufficient to fully charge. This simulation shows that the system for this case would be well-sized. Thus, the developed model demonstrates a benefit to better understand the behavior of the PV systems.

5 Conclusions

With the exponential growth of photovoltaics, expected for the next years, it is fundamental to understand the behavior of the different blocks that constitute PV stand-alone systems, mainly its operation during the different periods of the year. Being the knowledge of the storage systems behavior a fundamental factor to use efficiently the energy produced. In this context, the models developed in this study brings a benefit for the planning and sizing of PV stand-alone systems, allowing understanding the system behavior under different meteorological and load conditions. Five blocks were developed in Matlab/Simulink that reflect the behavior of the photovoltaic panel, charge controller, batteries, DC/AC inverter and the loads. Thus, the results obtained in the performed tests allow to conclude about the good reliability of the developed models. One of the main parameters analyzed was the batteries SOC with different solar radiation conditions and different loads, thus allowing to verify the PV system autonomy, a fundamental reliability aspect for stand-alone systems.

References

1. Krismadinataa, Rahim, N.Abd., Ping, H.W., Selvaraj, J.: Photovoltaic module modeling using Simulink/Matlab. In: The 3rd International Conference on Sustainable Future for Human Security (2014). Published in Procedia Environ. Sci. **17**, 537–546
2. Shevchenko, S., Danylchenko, D., Dryvetskyi, S., Potryvai, A.: Modernization of a simulation model of a photovoltaic module, by accounting for the effect of snowing of photovoltaic panels on system performance with correction for panel cleaning for Matlab Simulink. In: 2021 IEEE 2nd KhPI Week on Advanced Technology (KhPIWeek), pp. 670–675 (2021)
3. Tremblay, O., Dessaint, L.A., Dekkiche, A.I.: A generic battery model for the dynamic simulation of hybrid electric vehicles. In: Vehicle Power and Propulsion Conference, VPPC 2007, pp. 284–289. IEEE (2007)

4. Tremblay, O., Dessaint, L.A.: Experimental validation of a battery dynamic model for EV applications. World Electr. Veh. J. **3**, 289–298 (2009)
5. Yamin, R., Rachid, A.: Modeling and simulation of a lead-acid battery packs in MATLAB/Simulink: parameters identification using extended Kalman filter algorithm. In: UKSim-AMSS 16th International Conference on Computer Modelling and Simulation (2014)
6. Sreedhar, R., Karunanithi, K.: Design, simulation analysis of universal battery management system for EV applications. Mater. Today: Proc. (2021)
7. Mollah, A.H., Panda, G.K., Saha, P.K.: Single phase grid-connected inverter for photovoltaic system with maximum power point tracking. Int. J. Adv. Res. Electr. Electron. Instrum. Eng. **04**(02), 648–655 (2015). https://doi.org/10.15662/ijareeie.2015.0402021
8. Swarupa, M.L., Vijay Kumar, E., Sreelatha, K.: Modeling and simulation of solar PV modules based inverter in MATLAB-SIMULINK for domestic cooking. Mater. Today: Proc. **38**, Part 5, 3414–3423 (2021)
9. Bhaskar, M., Vidya, B., Madhumitha, R., Priyadharcini, S., Jayanthi, K., Malarkodi, G.: A simple PV array modeling using matlab. In: 2011 International Conference on Emerging Trends in Electrical and Computer Technology (ICETECT), pp. 122–126 (2011)
10. So, J.H., Yu, B.G., Hwang, H.M., Yoo, J.S., Yu, G.J.: Comparison results of measured and simulated performance of PV module. In: 2009 34th IEEE Photovoltaic Specialists Conference (PVSC), pp. 000 022–000 025 (2009)
11. Shepherd, C.M.: Design of primary and secondary cells. J. Electrochem. Soc. **112**(7), 657 (1965). https://doi.org/10.1149/1.2423659
12. Wang, N., Wu, M., Shi, G.: Study on characteristics of photovoltaic cells based on matlab simulation. In: Power and Energy Engineering Conference (APPEEC) Asia-Pacific (2011)
13. Salameh, Z., Casacca, M., Lynch, W.: A mathematical model for lead-acid batteries. IEEE Trans. Energy Convers. **7**(1), 93–98 (1992)

A Learning Approach to Improve the Selection of Forecasting Algorithms in an Office Building in Different Contexts

Daniel Ramos[1], Pedro Faria[1], Luis Gomes[1], Pedro Campos[2], and Zita Vale[1(✉)]

[1] GECAD - Research Group on Intelligent Engineering and Computing for Advanced Innovation and Development, LASI - Intelligent Systems Associate Laboratory, Polytechnic of Porto, Porto, Portugal
{dados,pnf,log,zav}@isep.ipp.pt
[2] School of Economics and Management, University of Porto, Porto, Portugal
pcampos@fep.up.pt

Abstract. Energy management in buildings can be largely improved by considering adequate forecasting techniques to find load consumption patterns. While these forecasting techniques are relevant, decision making is needed to decide the forecasting technique that suits best each context, thus improving the accuracy of predictions. In this paper, two forecasting methods are used including artificial neural network and k-nearest neighbor. These algorithms are considered to predict the consumption of a building equipped with devices recording consumptions and sensors data. These forecasts are performed from five-to-five minutes and the forecasting technique decision is taken into account as an enhanced factor to improve the accuracy of predictions. This decision making is optimized with the support of the multi-armed bandit, the reinforcement learning algorithm that analyzes the best suitable method in each five minutes. Exploration alternatives are considered in trial and test studies as means to find the best suitable level of unexplored territory that results in higher accumulated rewards. In the case-study, four contexts have been considered to illustrate the application of the proposed methodology.

Keywords: Energy management · Learning · Load forecast

1 Introduction

The current environmental concerns lads us to the need to optimize the use of energy in buildings, taking into account the consumer needs and the pricing signals from the electricity provider [1]. Demand response plays a very relevant role in the contribution of the consumers to the optimized grid operation [2]. Additionally, forecasting methods [3], and user behavior modeling and learning approaches [4] can contribute to improve the optimization of energy usage.

The forecasting tasks may be enhanced with reinforced deterministic implementations thus achieving more reliable and economic power systems operations [5]. A

G. Marreiros et al. (Eds.): EPIA 2022, LNAI 13566, pp. 271–281, 2022.
https://doi.org/10.1007/978-3-031-16474-3_23

Q-learning technique is used in [6] to obtain more accurate forecasts in the electric vehicle charging station area. The mentioned reinforcement learning technique considers the load profile changes and learns the different charging scenarios to enhance the accuracy of the forecasting algorithms. In [7] a deep Q network application evidences the importance in providing answers to mobile traffic demands compared to similar applications. The uncertainty of distributed renewable energy brings potential problems concerning economic operation of microgrid. An optimization framework uses a model-based RL agent in [8], in order to optimize schedule tasks extracting features from the past renewable generation and load sequences. Reinforcement learning models play an important role in [9] on enhancing the efficiency of response to consumption fluctuations for power requests in urban dense areas. This demand response issue integrated in the smart grids area is valued in [9] considering importance to maintain the desired satisfaction level while dealing with these fluctuation issues.

A deep reinforcement learning algorithm is evidenced the cost reduce for network services in [10] which determine the optimal solution from a large solution space provided by customized forecasting algorithms. An artificial emotional Q learning algorithm proposed in [11] is added along with an emotional deep neural network to enhance the emotional deep learning programming controller which considers the automatic voltage control of power systems. The reinforcement learning algorithm realizes automatic tuning of the controller parameters in order to optimize these thus improving the control performance with smaller voltage deviations. The efficiency and stability of power systems evidence the relevance of anticipated price predictions based on an artificial neural network model in [12]. This model is feed with a multi-agent reinforcement learning that makes optimal decisions for different home appliances in a decentralized manner.

The District Heating mentioned in [13] proposes a model that monitors the buildings' thermal response to energy profile modifications in order to achieve the goal of producing and distributing hot water along the city to head buildings. An agent-based model represents end-users that adapt to variations of temperatures in buildings. The reinforcement learning algorithm anticipated the behavior of energy profiles to reduce the thermal request peak while also learning through trial and error the individual agents' sensitivity to thermal comfort in order to avoid drastic modifications for the most sensitive users. Deep reinforcement learning techniques considered in office building applications as evidenced in [14] are expected to solve nonlinear and complex issues considering the prediction of building energy consumption, thus resulting in lower forecast errors. Incentive demand response programs evidenced in [15] interpret rewards as end users incentives to decrease electricity demand on peak periods. The difficult to optimize balance between energy supply and energy storage for buildings control applications is evidenced in [16] leads to reinforcement learning technique usage in order to optimize the enhance of building performance thus answering much better to energy demands. The energy management system of a microgrid consisting on an energy storage system placed in a wind turbine generator explained in [17] may be enhanced with the support of several deep reinforcement learning algorithms. The minimization of the cost of energy purchased on real-time basis for a storage photovoltaic system installed in a microgrid as evidenced in [18] uses reinforcement learning to deal with non-linear storage charging and discharging characteristics and a non-stationary environment in [18].

The energy sector takes advantage of an historical consumption of customers and additional parameterizations to estimate energy needs for future periods of high energy demand [19]. The mentioned parameterizations are useful to improve the forecasting accuracy relying on adaptive data preprocessing, advanced optimization methods, kernel-based models, and optimal model selection strategies [20]. For example, an hybrid optimization algorithm combines the data preprocessing mechanism, decomposition technology, forecast module with selection and matching strategy and ensemble model to forecast carbon prices [21].

The above-mentioned works deal with forecasting and learning approaches applied to the fields of electricity consumption in buildings. However, these lack the application of learning approaches to select the most reliable forecasting algorithm for the electricity consumption forecast in an office building, which is the main contribution of the present paper. In this paper, the multi armed bandit learning algorithm identifies the most relevant forecast method in each context. Moreover, this paper reuses two forecasting methods from previous research intended on obtaining accurate electricity consumption forecasts including k-nearest neighbors and artificial neural networks [3].

After this introduction, Sect. 2 presents the methodology, Sect. 3 the case study and results, and finally the conclusions are presented in Sect. 4.

2 Methodology

This section describes the different steps of the proposed methodology involved in the process of selecting the best forecasting algorithm for each target context according to an available dataset. The obtained data is extracted from electronic devices located in building offices monitoring different specific measures. This recorded data is taken into account both for the historic and target of data in forecasting tasks. Forecast tasks are supported by forecasting algorithms which are best in different moments and evaluated through reinforcement learning process. The full process is divided in 4 main steps including dataset import, environment customization, learning process and context forecasting algorithm selection as illustrated in Fig. 1.

The methodology starts by the import of data in an appropriated structure to be used for later reinforcement learning operations according to the dataset features. The data consists in an historic of data that is going to be useful on forecasting operations. Thus, the forecasting is supported by two algorithms including ANN and KNN.

This is followed by the environment customization which defines the different aspects involved in the learning process. A similar application shown in [4] assigns workplaces of a building to different users using the building and users data to improve the accumulated reward. Several properties needed from the environment are initialized including the actions dimension, the learning and exploration rate, the upper confidence bound use, an average reward. The exploration rate defines the probability of reselecting other actions for each reward calculation. The confidence bound is a normalized array that updates accumulated values associated to each action. This confidence is supported for the decision making for the forecasting algorithm selection. The criterion for taking an action involves to select the forecasting algorithm that should provide better forecasts, by other words the action with higher confidence bound.

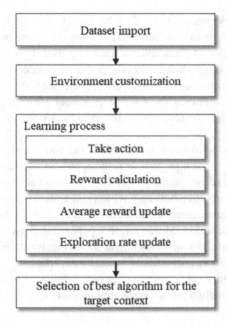

Fig. 1. Proposed methodology.

Therefore, although a higher exploration rate may increase the frequency of applying alternative forecasting algorithms, the disadvantage is that increasing the exploration rate too much may decrease the current knowledge of a particular algorithm evaluation. The confidence bound of each action corresponds to the multiplication between the learning rate and the difference between the reward and the previous confidence bound initialized to zero as represented in Eq. 1.

$$CB(a) = LR * (R - CB(a)) \tag{1}$$

- CB(a) – confidence bound of selected action
- LR – learning rate
- R(a) – reward

The reward calculation analyzes if the selected forecasting algorithm was indeed the best alternative in the respective context. The reward is calculated assigning 1 if the forecasting selection corresponds to the forecasting method with lower error, otherwise the reward is assigned to 0. The reward is added to an accumulated reward which serves to calculate the average reward in each iteration. The exploration rate depending on the number of iterations passed may be updated as means to control higher or lower unexplored actions confidence. Finally, the learning process provides a selection of the best forecasting algorithm in each context, thus allowing to choose in each specific context the best forecasting algorithm.

3   Case Study and Results

This section is structured in two sub-sections, namely Sect. 3.1 Case study, and Sect. 3.2 Results.

3.1   Case Study

The building energy management keeps a storage of data from five-to-five minutes from 22 May 2017 to 17 November 2019 with a weekly pattern as seen in Fig. 2.

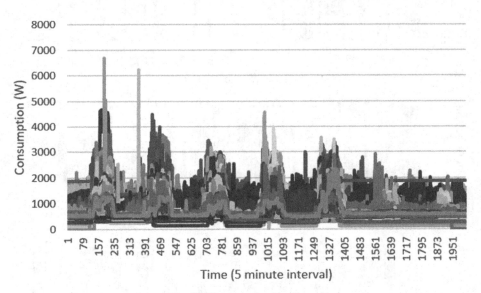

Fig. 2. Consumption profiles.

The data is structured in a total of 130 weeks, each one with a total of 2016 records evidencing each five minutes period. This is the same data as studied in [3]. The case study is organized in four different scenarios to differentiate the different features associated to the sets of five minutes from the data. Therefore data from the twenty four hours is classified in "morning", "afternoon", "night1" and "night2" (alternative as night1). Morning describes all five minutes periods from 9AM to 12PM, afternoon takes all five minutes intervals from 1PM to 6PM, night takes all periods from 8PM to 9AM. While night2 has all the content with a total of 983 records, night1 considers only 359 records the same content as afternoon. Additionally, three exploration rates are tested for each scenario including 0.2, 0.5 and 0.8.

3.2   Results

As said before, four scenarios have been implemented. The actions are kept in an historic of data integrated on contexts described by periods of five minutes corresponding each

context to two possible outcomes. The historic of actions may correspond to 0 or 1 respectively the KNN and ANN algorithms as the selected algorithm for forecast tasks in each context. The historic of actions for each five minutes context as seen in Fig. 3 shows that the algorithms interpret many differences between the several possibilities across the five minutes periods. The average reward progress is in Fig. 4.

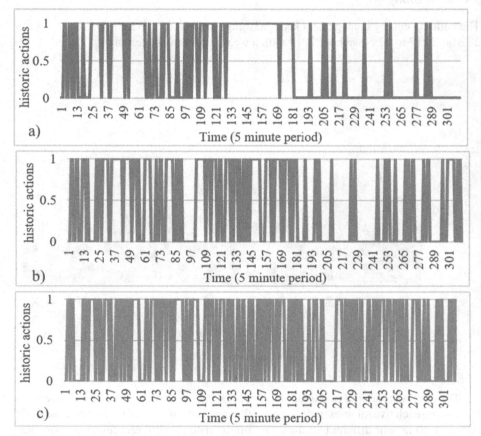

Fig. 3. Historic actions classified in 0 and 1 respectively KNN and ANN in morning scenario: a) exploration rate = 0.2; b) exploration rate = 0.5; c) exploration rate = 0.8.

The exploration rate shows to have some influence in the learning process as lower exploration rates show a high tendency to keep decisions the same for sequences of five minutes when selecting forecasting algorithms. On the other hand, higher exploration rates try to find alternatives for each five minutes context showing a less tendency to being trapped in a particular decision for a long sequence of five minutes. This is an understandable observation as higher exploration rates try to find toggle between ANN and KNN more as they keep focusing more on uncharted region than current knowledge.

The higher issue with an exploration rate of 0.2 shows a sequence of five minutes trapped in ANN decision between 161 and 169 periods of five minutes, while higher

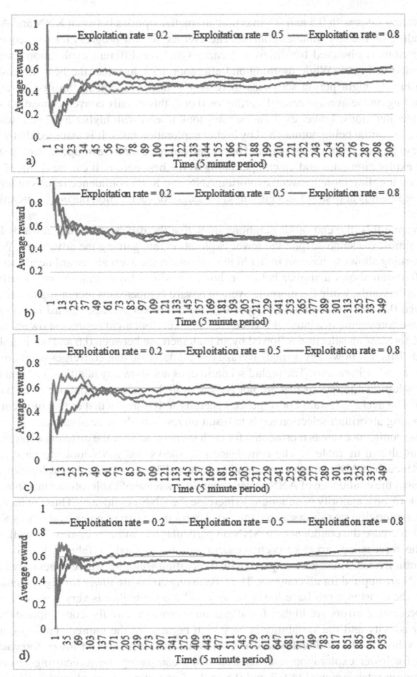

Fig. 4. Average reward in scenario: a) morning; b) afternoon; c) night1; d) night2.

exploration rates with 0.5 and 0.8 interpret alternative options between KNN and ANN depending on the five minutes context. The average reward progress for the sequence of iterations is observed for different scenarios and for different exploration rates as illustrated in Fig. 4. While morning and afternoon look to select the best forecasting algorithm, in night period scenarios there is a wrong selection in the first iteration. Depending on the average reward starting on 0 or 1, this usually converges nearly to 0.6 after few iterations. Lower exploration rates look to end with higher average rewards, despite the initial being outmatched by higher exploration rates. It is assumed that while higher exploration rates have an initial better performance for the average reward in start, lower exploration rates end up compensating as the best option. It can be deduced that while on toggling more between exploring ANN and KNN confidence results in higher average rewards at first, it loses current knowledge for each action during the iterations progress.

Despite this, the end of all iterations show that the different average rewards look to be almost the same despite the lower exploration rate gaining the advantage. While the morning shows to have an initial high decrease in the average reward nearly to 0.2, the afternoon shows a similar behavior, however with a lower impact only nearly to 0.45. Afterwards, while the morning average reward compensates increasing drastically between 0.4 and 0.6 and converging to 0.6, the afternoon average reward has a small decrease converging in a interval between 0.4 and 0.6. Both night regimes show an initial wrong forecasting selection followed by an high increase between 0.6 and 0.8 in a short period. This is followed by a small average reward decrease that converges nearly to 0.6 until the end of iterations. The night2 scenario does not show any additional advantages as the additional iterations that are not present in night1 scenario continue to converge to 0.6. The average reward convergence generally to 0.6 shows that at this moment the forecasting algorithm selection tends to result on rewards above reasonable.

The confidence rate is represented for each scenario and for the different exploration rates as shown in Table 1. The confidence rate shows that KNN looks to have more confidence than ANN on more five minutes context. The increase of the exploration rate decreases the confidence of ANN in any scenario. Increase of exploration rates from 0.2 to 0.8 look on a majority of situations to increase the KNN confidence. Thus, an increase of the exploration rate shows a tendency to classify more five minutes contexts as KNN and to decrease the confidence on ANN on particular five minutes context as well.

The forecasting errors of each scenario are also studied in Table 2 for different exploration rates. These are compared with forecasting scenarios where either only KNN or ANN are applied for all contexts. The forecasting errors are lower for night scenarios where the consumptions have lower activity and the variability is very low. Moreover the forecasting errors are higher for afternoon scenario where the consumptions have higher activity and the variability is very high because of the unpredictability during activity hours. The artificial neural networks algorithms results in lower forecasting errors for lower exploration rates as seen while comparing the forecasting errors of exploration rates assigned to 0.2 and 0.5 to the forecasting errors of exploration rates assigned to 0.8. The k-nearest neighbors results in lower forecasting errors using a lower exploration rate assigned to 0.2 for afternoon and night scenarios, while during morning scenario results in lower forecasting errors using an higher exploration rate

assigned to 0.8. The reinforcement learning application shows that all exploration rate alternatives result in lower forecasting errors using k-nearest neighbors algorithm. It is also noted using artificial neural networks algorithm with reinforcement learning results in lower forecasting errors than no reinforcement learning for at least one exploration rate alternative assigned either to 0.2, 0.5 or 0.8.

Table 1. Confidence rate for each scenario.

Scenario	Exploration rate					
	0.2		0.5		0.8	
	KNN	ANN	KNN	ANN	KNN	ANN
Morning	1.274	0.64103993	1.28437704	0.51420728	1.26276409	0.47323593
Afternoon	0.95506168	0.77442147	0.91544816	0.6591162	1.07098973	0.59035046
Night 1	0.925389	0.91983783	0.88298552	0.83060459	0.92708423	0.69229677
Night 2	1.08235921	0.47986646	0.8811732	0.07628767	1.10907186	0.4108567

Table 2. SMAPE forecasting error for each scenario.

Scenario	Exploration rate						No reinforcement learning	
	0.2		0.5		0.8			
	KNN	ANN	KNN	ANN	KNN	ANN	KNN	ANN
Morning	3.60	3.49	3.98	3.60	3.49	3.98	4.08	3.67
Afternoon	4.59	4.70	4.86	4.59	4.70	4.86	5.01	4.45
Night 1	2.96	3.24	3.69	2.96	3.24	3.69	4.36	3.06
Night 2	2.29	2.60	2.77	2.29	2.60	2.77	2.94	2.70

4   Conclusions

This paper analyzes the forecasting technique that appears to be best suitable in each five minutes context according to two different option: artificial neural networks and k-nearest neighbors. The confidence rates provide a summary analysis stating that on the majority of situations k-nearest neighbor is the algorithm that provides more accurate forecasts. In addition to this it is observed that increases in the exploration rate will result in more confidence in k-nearest neighbor algorithm than artificial neural networks. The graph consisting of an historic of actions support this showing that increases in the exploration rate classify more five minutes contexts as k-nearest neighbors. However, the average reward graphs shows that increases in the exploration rate result in less pragmatic choices in the end, despite the difference not being very significant. It is observed a good aspect in

higher explorations where initial higher rewards are highlighted describing high average increases on short sequences of five minutes.

Acknowledgements. This work has received funding from FEDER Funds through COMPETE program and from National Funds through (FCT) under the project COLORS (PTDC/EEI-EEE/28967/2017), and CEECIND/02887/2017. The authors acknowledge the work facilities and equipment provided by GECAD research center (UIDB/00760/2020) to the project team.

References

1. Faia, R., Faria, P., Vale, Z., Spinola, J.: Demand response optimization using particle swarm algorithm considering optimum battery energy storage schedule in a residential house. Energies **12**(9), 1645 (2019)
2. Faria, P., Vale, Z.: Demand response in electrical energy supply: an optimal real time pricing approach. Energy **36**(8), 5374–5384 (2011)
3. Ramos, D., Khorram, M., Faria, P., Vale, Z.: Load forecasting in an office building with different data structure and learning parameters. Forecasting **3**(1), 242–255 (2021)
4. Gomes, L., Almeida, C., Vale, Z.: Recommendation of workplaces in a coworking building: a cyber-physical approach supported by a context-aware multi-agent system. Sensors **20**, 3597 (2020)
5. Feng, C., Sun, M., Zhang, J.: Reinforced deterministic and probabilistic load forecasting via Q-learning dynamic model selection. IEEE Trans. Smart Grid **11**(2), 1377–1386 (2020)
6. Dabbaghjamanesh, M., Moeini, A., Kavousi-Fard, A.: Reinforcement learning-based load forecasting of electric vehicle charging station using Q-learning technique. IEEE Trans. Ind. Inf. **17**(6), 4229–4237 (2021)
7. Huang, C., Chen, P.: Joint demand forecasting and DQN-based control for energy-aware mobile traffic offloading. IEEE Access **8**, 66588–66597 (2020)
8. Shuai, H., He, H.: Online scheduling of a residential microgrid via Monte-Carlo tree search and a learned model. IEEE Trans. Smart Grid **12**(2), 1073–1087 (2021)
9. Aladdin, S., El-Tantawy, S., Fouda, M.M., Tag Eldien, A.S.: MARLA-SG: multi-agent reinforcement learning algorithm for efficient demand response in smart grid. IEEE Access **8**, 210626–210639 (2020)
10. Pei, J., Hong, P., Pan, M., Liu, J., Zhou, J.: Optimal VNF placement via deep reinforcement learning in SDN/NFV-enabled networks. IEEE J. Sel. Areas Commun. **38**(2), 263–278 (2020)
11. Yin, L., Zhang, C., Wang, Y., Gao, F., Yu, J., Cheng, L.: Emotional deep learning programming controller for automatic voltage control of power systems. IEEE Access **9**, 31880–31891 (2021)
12. Lu, R., Hong, S.H., Yu, M.: Demand response for home energy management using reinforcement learning and artificial neural network. IEEE Trans. Smart Grid **10**(6), 6629–6639 (2019)
13. Solinas, F., Bottaccioli, L., Guelpa, E., Verda, V., Patti, E.: Peak shaving in district heating exploiting reinforcement learning and agent-based modelling. Eng. Appl. Artif. Intell. **102**, 104235 (2021). ISSN 0952-1976
14. Liu, T., Tan, Z., Xu, C., Chen, H., Li, Z.: Study on deep reinforcement learning techniques for building energy consumption forecasting. Energy Build. **208**, 109675 (2020). ISSN 0378-7788
15. Wen, L., Zhou, K., Li, J., Wang, S.: Modified deep learning and reinforcement learning for an incentive-based demand response model. Energy **205**, 118019 (2020). ISSN 0360-5442

16. Wang, Z., Hong, T.: Reinforcement learning for building controls: the opportunities and challenges. Appl. Energy **269**, 115036 (2020). ISSN 0306-2619
17. Nakabi, T., Toivanen, P.: Deep reinforcement learning for energy management in a microgrid with flexible demand. Sustain. Energy Grids Netw. **25**, 100413 (2021). ISSN 2352-4677
18. Kolodziejczyk, W., Zoltowska, I., Cichosz, P.: Real-time energy purchase optimization for a storage-integrated photovoltaic system by deep reinforcement learning. Control Eng. Pract. **106**, 104598 (2021). ISSN 0967-0661
19. González-Briones, A., Hernández, G., Pinto, T., Vale, Z., Corchado, J.M.: A review of the main machine learning methods for predicting residential energy consumption. In: 16th International Conference on the European Energy Market (EEM), pp. 1–6. IEEE (2019)
20. Yang, W., Sun, S., Hao, Y., Wang, S.: A novel machine learning-based electricity price forecasting model based on optimal model selection strategy. Energy **238**, 121989 (2022)
21. Sun, S., Jin, F., Li, H., Li, Y.: A new hybrid optimization ensemble learning approach for carbon price forecasting. Appl. Math. Model. **97**, 182–205 (2021)

AITS - Artificial Intelligence in Transportation Systems

Comparison of Different Deployment Approaches of FPGA-Based Hardware Accelerator for 3D Object Detection Models

Pedro Pereira[1], António Linhares Silva[1(✉)], Rui Machado[1,2], João Silva[1],
Dalila Durães[1], José Machado[1], Paulo Novais[1], João Monteiro[1], Pedro Melo-Pinto[1,3],
and Duarte Fernandes[1,2]

[1] Algoritmi Centre, University of Minho, Guimarães, Portugal
`{asilva,dalila.duraes}@algoritmi.uminho.pt`, `{rui.machado,`
`duarte.fernandes}@dtx-colab.pt`, `{jmac,pjon}@di.uminho.pt`,
`joao.monteiro@dei.uminho.pt`, `pmelo@utad.pt`
[2] Associação Laboratório Colaborativo em Transformação Digital—DTx Colab, Guimarães,
Portugal
[3] Department of Engineering, University of Trás-os-Montes and Alto Douro, Vila Real, Portugal

Abstract. GPU servers have been responsible for the recent improvements in
the accuracy and inference speed of the object detection models targeted to
autonomous driving. However, its features, namely, power consumption and
dimension, make its integration in autonomous vehicles impractical. Hybrid
FPGA-CPU boards emerged as an alternative to server GPUs in the role of edge
devices in autonomous vehicles. Despite their energy efficiency, such devices do
not offer the same computational power as GPU servers and have fewer resources
available. This paper investigates how to deploy deep learning models tailored to
object detection in point clouds in edge devices for onboard real-time inference.
Different approaches, requiring different levels of expertise in logic programming
applied to FPGAs, are explored, resulting in three main solutions: utilization of
software tools for model adaptation and compilation for a proprietary hardware IP;
design and implementation of a hardware IP optimized for computing traditional
convolutions operations; design and implementation of a hardware IP optimized
for sparse convolutions operations. The performance of these solutions is compared in the KITTI dataset with computer performances. All the solutions resort
to parallelism, quantization and optimized access control to memory to reduce the
usage of logical FPGA resources, and improve processing time without significantly sacrificing accuracy. Solutions probed to be effective for real-time inference,
power limited and space-constrained purposes.

Keywords: Hardware accelerator · Light detection and ranging (LiDAR) ·
Object detection

1 Introduction

Over the years, 3D LiDAR has gained increased importance and use on different robotic
platforms, mainly due to its capacity to represent object depth information, long-range

G. Marreiros et al. (Eds.): EPIA 2022, LNAI 13566, pp. 285–296, 2022.
https://doi.org/10.1007/978-3-031-16474-3_24

detection abilities, high resolution and good performance under different lighting conditions. However, the implementation of 3D object detectors that leverage the 3D perspective given by LiDAR technology has been under pressure to reach the end-user, and this sector still embraces many challenges that have been hampering the 3D object detectors from reaching their full potential. The main challenge is related to the fact that LiDAR sensors produce unstructured data in the form of sparse point clouds. To deal with this sparsity, several methodologies have emerged in the literature. Some use the PointNet-based approach [1] to generate dense tensors that represent the point cloud data, and then standard Convolutional Neural Networks (CNNs) are applied [2]. Others offer alternatives by exploring the sparse nature of point clouds by using Sparse CNNs [3] or CNNs based on a voting mechanism [4]. The last solution has appeared as a power-efficient alternative to the first approach. The capacity of such a solution to only compute and process meaningful data reduces the computational cost of object detectors, which is an advantage when there are fewer computational resources.

Implementing these object detectors in-loco using servers is impractical due to power source and space demand implications. Thus, edge devices have increased importance due to the reasonable power source consumption and small space demand constraints. Although it presents limited resources compared with powerful GPU-specific server nodes, it avoids latency in communication, thus reducing susceptibility to failures. Moreover, they provide more compactness, robustness, and flexibility. FPGAs have emerged as one of the most used hardware device accelerator platforms, due to their advances in the currently provided frameworks that facilitate and reduce the time to deploy object detectors. Commercial frameworks are currently available for the deployment of deep learning solutions in FPGA-based accelerators, such as HADDOC2 [5], DNNWEAVER [6], Hls4ml [7], and Vitis AI [8]. In this group, Vitis-AI stands out. It is supported by Xilinx and emerged as an optimal solution for this purpose because it offers a Deep Learning Processor Unit (DPU)-based acceleration and provides a comprehensive integration of tools and libraries optimized to implement neural networks in hardware. It supports the main CNN operations and has direct compatibility with several popular CNNs, such as ResNet [9] and YOLO [10], with ready-to-use solutions. Other CNN-based approaches optimized to point cloud sparsity have been developed and integrated, offering a complete coverage to deep learning operations. These frameworks offer a convenient way of model deployment in edge devices; however, they are often limited in the range of flexibility and parameter configurable. Moreover, the architecture and details of the implementation of the hardware engine are not provided. Some implementations of customized hardware accelerators have been addressed in the literature. Research work [11] and [12] proposed engines that resort to a processing element unit that has a MAC unit and multiply and accumulate operation, while in [13] parallel multipliers to compute all output products in a single clock cycle introduced along with adder tree to aggregate all outcomes; Research [13] and [11] are optimized for processing time, but require redundant on-chip memory access, promoting high energy consumption and resources usage, as model data is fetched from off-chip in an on-demand paradigm, while [12] loads all required data to on-chip memory and as this memory is connected to the processing units, memory access requires lower energy consumption.

This work compares the performance of three different methodologies followed for achieving the implementation of deep learning tasks in resource-constrained devices. We highlight the development of our research team carried out in [14, 15] and [16], and compare for the first time the performance of these three approaches in the current document. Thus we highlight the fine-tuning process on a CNN-based standard object detector and the respective implications of deep learning model hyperparameters in meeting edge device application requirements and discusses the deployment of the resultant model in an edge device resorting to commercial frameworks of model compression and compiling [16]. The object detector selection was based on the literature review presented in [2] and was based on the capability of 3D Object Detection models to provide a better trade-off between accuracy and inference time that simultaneously allows meeting real-time onboard inference. In addition, we will show the advantages of implementing CNN-based approaches optimized to point cloud sparsity instead of standard CNNs by discussing two hardware accelerators optimized for traditional convolutions [15] and convolutions optimized for sparsity [14]. These two solutions take into consideration limitations and insights from deployment based on commercial frameworks conducted in [16] to propose solutions capable of providing accurate models but optimized in inference time. These solutions enable the configuration of all features of a convolution layer: size of the feature map, filter size, stride, number of inputs, number of filters, and the number of hardware resources required for a specific convolution.

2 Design and Implementation

To deploy the deep-learning-based model in a hardware device, we used the four-step methodology according to [2]. (1) The model selection was based on the literature review of existing models for 3D Object Detection, and then compatible frameworks and corresponding hardware devices that accommodate the selected model were studied.

After this step, the selected model [17] was subjected to a training and evaluation pipeline (2), where several optimizations were taken to improve accuracy metrics while granting the inference time requirement less than ~100 ms. This is an iterative workflow that is aimed at granting that the selected model meets the application requirements and achieves the best possible accuracy. The evaluation, comparison and training processes are conducted using KITTI benchmarks on the validation set.

Once completed workflow (2), the models obtained are optimized and compressed (3) using quantization and compression techniques. The compressed model version is evaluated in its performance in terms of accuracy and inference time by analyzing accuracy degradation and speed improvement. An adjustment and transformation phase is carried out to deploy and prepare the model for the target hardware device (4). Next, we analyze and evaluate the model's inference time and accuracy on the KITTI validation set. As pointed out in this article, the bottleneck of the model pipeline is the RPN configuration. Then, after the workflow (4), the final model was chosen to grant application requirements (an optimal balance between inference time and model accuracy), which led to and model with an adjusted RPN.

Proposed solutions are deployed in a hybrid board, FPGA and System-om-chip, as they have been used in the literature for several deep learning-related tasks. These

platforms are known for being energy-efficient and offer high computation speed with regard to their parallelism paradigm. Zynq UltraScale+ MPSoC ZCU102 hardware platform from Xilinx, Inc is the platform chosen, as it comprises a device comprises several processors on a single chip and logic blocks on the Programmable Logic (PL)-side of the chip. This board supports high-level operating systems such as Linux, logic programming in the FPGA fabric and provides several peripherals, some of them crucial for external communication with external devices.

2.1 Proprietary Accelerator Hardware

We selected Vitis AI framework as it supports the most used deep learning frameworks, such as Keras, TensorFlow, Pytorch, and Caffe; provides a kernel called Deep Learning Processing Unit (DPU), while offers a workflow to convert specific deep learning tasks or entire models to the previous mentioned hardware accelerator. Moreover, it allows us to compress networks, reducing the memory footprint and inference time.

In order to compile a model for the target device, we need first to prepare both hardware and software of the target device. Vivado, an IDE from Xilinx, was adopted to integrate the DPU kernel into our board, where aspects such as settling and interrupt connections between PS and PL, defining memory locations for input point cloud, temporary and output were addressed. In relation to the software, a Linux image was generated for our AArch64 hardware architecture, some requirements need to be fulfilled for a successful deployment of the PointPillars model in our platforms. Resources, such as Vitis AI RunTime (VART), Vitis AI Library, Xilinx Runtime (XRT), ZOCL are required for controlling and monitoring the execution of the model by means of an API; utilization of some typical pre and pos processing functions as shared libraries; interface between application code and the DPU Kernel by allocating memory space (DRAM for saving weights, bias and receive input data); FPGA manager integration in fabric by consulting the file that contains the hardware bitstream generated on the hardware configuration step; respectively. In order to compile and generate a Linux image with all these requirements, the tool PetaLinux was adopted. For onboard inference, model-related specific instructions complying with the DPU instruction set are required, being these provided by a xmodel file upon a compilation of our model. Before compiling the model based on the specified DPU microarchitecture, different comprising techniques were adopted, resulting in different versions of the original PointPillars Model.

We updated the RPN for half number of filters when compared with the original model and stride 2 in the first block of convolutional layers, as explained in [16], as the original model was not able to meet the inference time, with runtime higher than 100 ms.

The quantization method is a powerful technique for speeding deep learning tasks at the cost of accuracy reduction. To achieve this goal, our model weights and activations, represented as a 32-bit floating-point, were converted to an 8-bit integer format. Two quantization's approaches were tested in this article, namely post-training quantization (PTQ), where an already trained mode is quantized; and quantization aware training (QAT), here data is quantized during the forward pass of the training process, deliberately incorporating the error due to the lower precision in the loss function, forcing the optimizer to update parameters so that this error is reduced.

2.2 Customized Hardware Accelerator for Traditional Convolutions

From the study of proprietary CNN hardware accelerator frameworks, it was possible to understand the advanced development state of frameworks such as Vitis AI. Extensive integration with deep learning tools and a large set of functionalities makes the presented framework a complete solution for deploying CNNs in hardware. Along with the advantages, some disadvantages can also be recognized as the form of their configuration-wise limitations and also restricted access to specific functionalities. Although a framework is very useful for the quick hardware implementation of neural networks, it is convenient to develop a completely customizable and open-source convolutional module adaptable to any convolution layer. The hardware implementation of a convolutional module, which is configurable according to the typical convolution parameters, allows building a useful tool to implement any convolutional layer in hardware. In addition, through module replication it is possible to build a complete custom CNN, without the implementation or configuration restrictions sometimes found in proprietary hardware accelerators.

Based on the convolution properties and the data access costs for processing, an approach focused on efficient data management was considered. This approach is based on [1] and has the main objective of designing a convolutional module architecture that maximizes energy efficiency by reducing redundant access to on-chip memory through a Broadcast Stay Migration (BSM) scheme as shown in Fig. 1. The general architecture consists of multiple Processing Elements (PEs) that work in parallel. Each PE contains a DSP to perform multiplications and additions, and an internal memory to manage data reuse.

Energy-efficiency is the focus of the BSM architecture thus the execution time is sacrificed. From the data flow diagram Fig. 1, the time required for a complete convolution increases proportionally with the Input Feature Map (IFM) size. While the processing unit core enables a low consumption of both resources and power, parallelism was integrated to increase processing throughput. To parallelize the processing, the module resorts to the allocation of several PEs to operate in different locations of the feature map simultaneously. Equation 1 presents the required processing time as a function of the Input Feature Map size (width + height), number of PEs, input and output channels, and the target board clock frequency.

$$[DenseConv]ProcessingTime(s) = \frac{IFM_w * IFM_h * IFM_{ch} * OFM_{ch}}{Num.Pes * ClockFreq} \tag{1}$$

The instantiation of several sets of PEs enables a filter to be applied in several feature map regions at the same time, however, the memory must allow multiple accesses to the data in the same clock cycles. Given the limitation of data access memory ports several BRAMs are instantiated to distribute the input data, allowing more than one read/write operation to be executed simultaneously. Figure 2 represents an example case of input data distribution over several memories. Moreover, it shows the link between each data and the corresponding PE so that the total processing time is reduced according to the number of PEs allocated.

A CNN layer usually involves a large volume of operations via a large amount of data that needs to be processed. The module architecture was designed to be flexible to the different possible layer requirements and aware of the resources available in the target

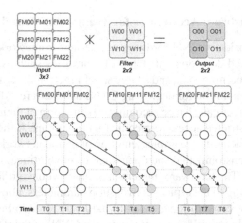

Fig. 1. BSM dataflow for the convolution core.

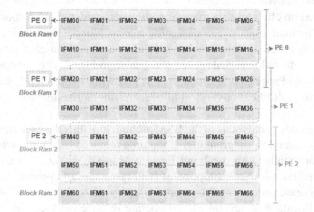

Fig. 2. IFM memory distribution.

platform. Both processing throughput and energy consumption are balanced according to the existing resources. For instance, the number of DSP conditions the number of PEs, consequently affecting the level of parallelism. Regarding the memory, it is used to store the weights and IFM values that are being processed at a given time as well as the Output Feature Map (OFM). As each filter needs one memory to send the output, the amount of available memory will determine how many filters can be applied simultaneously.

Besides the convolutional parameters: stride, padding, and kernel size, as well as the layer parameters: IFM size, OFM size, MaxPooling, and ReLU, the convolutional module also allows the definition of the available resources. From the specification of all these parameters, the module adjusts its base architecture at instantiation time to optimize the processing. Figure 3 (top image) depicts the resultant architecture for a scenario where the user specifies 4 filters, 54 DSPs, and 4 MB of memory available.

2.3 Customized Hardware Accelerator for Sparse Convolutions

Given the success of CNNs in complex tasks such as object recognition, variants have emerged for 3D data processing, however, the sparse and unstructured nature of the point cloud has forced the literature to increase the complexity of 3D models, making their implementation in Edge Devices unfeasible. To counter this problem, novel and more computationally efficient solutions have emerged with faster mechanisms. These solutions aimed at taking advantage of the data sparsity to speed up the convolution operation by reducing the number of points processed, thus decreasing the computational time and resources allocated.

To address these challenges, the first hardware architecture is presented for a sparse convolution named voting scheme-based convolution presented in [2]. Moreover, hardware optimization mechanisms are also integrated in the architecture to take advantage of the architecture specifications and further reduce the time spent on matrix multiplications. This type of convolution, explored only by Dominic Zeng Wang and Ingmar Posner in [2, 3], directs the processing only to feature map regions with relevant information, avoiding the sliding window approach over the entire data adopted by dense convolutions, thus saving the execution time of unnecessary calculations. The voting weights values are obtained by flipping the convolutional weight axis along each dimension and the filter only needs to be applied at each non-null location to return the same result.

Figure 3 (bottom image) illustrates the architecture of the Voting block, highlighting the communication with the memories outside the block. Unlike traditional convolutions, the voting convolution requires information regarding the position of the values to be processed, usually available in models that perform a 2D projection of the 3D data, such as PointPillars [4] and SECOND [5]. This same information is also registered together with the output data, enabling more than one voting block to be instantiated. Within the block, two functional units are distinguished, the Control Unit and the Processing Unit, which are responsible to manage all the data flow and the operations to be made, respectively. Apart from the memories to store the data and its location, a double FIFO is used to save each iteration result and optimize the processing of input values with data dependency by reducing the communication with the output memory.

According to Voting requirements, read and write operations to the output memory are required for each input value to be processed. One of the solutions that allow simultaneous read and write in the same memory is the Dual Port Block Ram. This memory block is composed of two ports, both able to operate as read or write. Given this feature a pipeline processing was adopted to increase performance, thus reducing the number of clock cycles needed to complete the convolution. As can be seen from the figure, there is a possibility of leveraging the data dependency to share data directly between different iterations. The data sharing can be done through a FIFO, represented in Fig. 3 (bottom image) which stores each iteration output. When data dependency occurs, the required data for the next iteration is already inside the block.

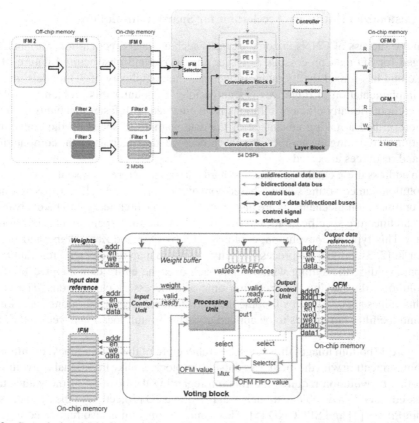

Fig. 3. Convolutional block memory architecture (top image) and Voting block architecture (bottom image) [14].

2.4 Performance Comparison

The model with updated RPN can achieves inferences time near to the maximum allowed, i.e. floating-point model version of the model running on the edge device. In order to speed it up we applied quantization, allowing the on-board inference to achieve inferences time 16.6 ms and 16.7 ms for PTQ and QAT versions.

Regarding the accuracy of the models, as expected the original model pipeline achieves higher results, regardless of the type of quantization approach applied. However, if we only focus on configuration 2, we can conclude that type of quantization has a strong effect on the model performance as shown in Table 1.

As can be seen in Table 1, the reduction of the model parameters resolution due to the PTQ approach incurs a significant penalty on the model precision, in particular for small objects, such as cyclists or pedestrians. On the other hand, the QAT approach is able to significantly reduce the inference time while improving the model performance for certain conditions, as verified on the KITTI 3D BEV for cyclists' detection and KITTI 3D BBOX for Cyclist and Pedestrian. Therefore, this approach not only surpasses the

Table 1. mAP (%) results for KITTI BEV and 3D BBox detection performance for classes Car (IoU 0.70), Cyclist (IoU 0.50), and Pedestrian (IoU 0.50)

	Car	Cyclist	Pedestrian
KITTI BEV			
Floating point	87.22	53.75	53.75
PTQ	85.51	52.27	46.61
QAT	86.93	58.08	45.36
KITTI 3D BBox			
Floating point	68.24	52.26	40.34
PTQ	64.27	46.8	38.04
QAT	68.14	56.41	40.89

PTQ model for all the conditions but while matches the performance of its counterpart floating-point model.

It was reported that the power consumption of the deployed model running in the target device is 15.7W. Previous developments and the performance of the different versions of the same model serve to show that the straight deployment of such heavy computational tasks in edge devices is impractical and that some tradeoffs must be addressed. Vitis AI has proved to be a very convenient way to develop a completely customizable and open-source convolutional module. However, this framework does not cover all the deep learning tasks and functionalities addressed in the literature while having limitations in the DPU configuration and in the fact of the DPU implementation not being open-source. Therefore, in order to achieve a solution fully customized that can be truly customized to any CNN module we proposed two accelerators hardware optimized for convolutions.

One aspect that affects the performance of the voting scheme is the existent of non-null values in the input feature map as it affects the data sparsity level, which can vary from zero to one, according to math Eq. 2. While zero sparsity indicates that all the input values are non-null, a sparsity with value one means that all the values are null. To evaluate the Voting block performance in processing sparse data, several conditions should be created for the block to be subject to different levels of sparsity.

$$sparsity(A) = \frac{count\_nonzero(A)}{total\_elements\_of\_(A)} \tag{2}$$

For a 512×512 feature map (total of 262144 values) with sparsity levels between 80% and 100%, different performance tests were carried out to evaluate the processing time evolution according to the sparsity level variation shown in Table 2.

In comparison with Eq. 1 for the dense convolution, the time consumed by the voting convolution can be described by Eq. 3. The considered parameters are: number of non-null values (x); filter size (y); number of null weights in a given filter (z); stride value

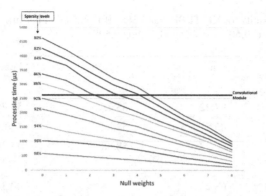

Fig. 4. Null weights effect on processing time [14].

(s).

$$[VotingConv]ProcessingTime(s) = \frac{x * (y^2 - z)}{Stride * ClockFreq} \tag{3}$$

To better evaluate and compare the performance of both hardware accelerators, the PoinPillars model was chosen as a case study. Besides being a state-of-the-art model in 3D object detection, the model meets the requirements for the Voting block integration. As one of the critical requirements is the position of the non-null values in the feature map, that information can be accessed through the data structure that composes the Pillar Index from the PFN stage. Furthermore, the point cloud representation in a pseudo-image ensures high levels of sparsity for 2D data processing, which is ideal for evaluating the performance of a sparse convolution.

Considering the layers where the sparsity level favors the use of the voting scheme-based convolution, the integration in the first three layers of block 1 was carried out, assuming a 200 MHz clock on the board. In each test, the time consumed by the dense convolution and the voting one was measured. Regarding the dense convolution, the parallelism was set to a maximum per filter to improve performance, using all available DSPs. The results are presented in Fig. 4 where it was assumed the worst-case scenario, with each feature map from the PFN stage containing a total of 12k non-null values to process. In addition, the hardware processing time is compared with the software version (Configuration 1) running on the server.

The processing time improvements for the Voting Block, represented in the last column, are only positive for the first two layers, since the sparsity level decreasing across the layers increases the time consumed. As a result, compared with the software version, in the third layer no improvement is verified since the time to process is 10.9% longer, being the dense convolution a better solution. On the other hand, a big improvement can be seen in the first layer of block 1, with the Voting block being 80.44% faster. This great improvement is achieved due to the level of sparsity being higher in the first layer, and also because it is a stride operation, which helps the Voting to achieve substantially lower execution times.

From the integration with the PointPillars model, the performance of both dense and voting convolutions was measured in a real case scenario, showing similar results

Table 2. Processing time comparison between SW version, dense and Voting block

	Software	Dense convolution		Voting block	
	Time (μs)	Time (μs)	Improvement (%)	Time (μs)	Improvement (%)
B1-Conv0	874	654	25.18	171	80.44
B1-Conv1	321	262	18.32	247	23.05
B1-Conv2	321	262	18.32	356	−10.90

in terms of accuracy to configuration ½, but with optimized inferences times compared to these configurations running in the server. The lack of research on custom CNN hardware accelerators opens an opportunity for future work focused on the integration of both dense and voting convolutions in the same hardware module. As shown by the results, both types of convolutions have their potential, however, they should be used under different conditions to complement each other.

3 Conclusions

As demonstrated in our study, we show that the adoption of proposed configurable hardware architecture allows the integration of different type of CNNs, where Sparse CNNs based on the Voting mechanism as the potential to increase accuracy while maintaining inference time requirements. This study shows that there is space for improvements in model architecture to ensure effective object detection running on edge devices by exploring the parallelism paradigm of FPGA-based platforms and its advantages in terms of configurability and modularity.

Acknowledgements. This work has been supported by FCT—Fundação para a Ciência e Tecnologia within the R&D Units Project Scope: UIDB/00319/2020 and the project "Integrated and Innovative Solutions for the well-being of people in complex urban centers" within the Project Scope NORTE-01-0145-FEDER-000086.

References

1. Zhou, Y., Tuzel, O.: VoxelNet: end-to-end learning for point cloud based 3D object detection. In: Proceedings of the IEEE Computer Society Conference on Computer Vision and Pattern Recognition (2018). https://doi.org/10.1109/CVPR.2018.00472
2. Fernandes, D., et al.: Point-cloud based 3D object detection and classification methods for self-driving applications: a survey and taxonomy. Inf. Fusion **68**, 161–191 (2021). https://doi.org/10.1016/j.inffus.2020.11.002
3. Yan, Y., Mao, Y., Li, B.: SECOND: sparsely embedded convolutional detection. Sensors **18**(10), 3337 (2018). https://doi.org/10.3390/s18103337
4. Engelcke, M., Rao, D., Wang, D.Z., Tong, C.H., Posner, I.: Vote3Deep: fast object detection in 3D point clouds using efficient convolutional neural networks (2016). http://arxiv.org/abs/1609.06666

5. Abdelouahab, K., Pelcat, M., Sérot, J., Bourrasset, C., Berry, F., Serot, J.: Tactics to directly map CNN graphs on embedded FPGAs. Comput. Vis. Pattern Recogn. (2017). https://doi.org/10.1109/LES.2017.2743247

6. Sharma, H., et al.: From high-level deep neural models to FPGAs. In: 2016 49th Annual IEEE/ACM International Symposium on Microarchitecture (MICRO), pp. 1–12 (2016). https://doi.org/10.1109/MICRO.2016.7783720

7. Duarte, J., et al.: Fast inference of deep neural networks in FPGAs for particle physics. J. Instrum. (2018). https://doi.org/10.1088/1748-0221/13/07/P07027

8. Xilinx Inc.: Xilinx Vitis Unified Software Platform User Guide: System Performance Analysis (2021). https://www.xilinx.com/content/dam/xilinx/support/documentation/sw_manuals/xilinx2021_2/ug1145-sdk-system-performance.pdf

9. He, K., Zhang, X., Ren, S., Sun, J.: Deep residual learning for image recognition. Comput. Vis. Pattern (2015). http://arxiv.org/abs/1512.03385

10. Redmon, J., Divvala, S., Girshick, R., Farhadi, A.: You only look once: unified, real-time object detection. Comput. Vis. Pattern (2015). http://arxiv.org/abs/1506.02640

11. Chen, Y.-H., Krishna, T., Emer, J.S., Sze, V.: Eyeriss: an energy-efficient reconfigurable accelerator for deep convolutional neural networks. IEEE J. Solid-State Circuits 52(1), 127–138 (2017). https://doi.org/10.1109/JSSC.2016.2616357

12. Jo, J., Kim, S., Park, I.-C.: Energy-efficient convolution architecture based on rescheduled dataflow. IEEE Trans Circuits Syst. I Regul. Pap. 65, 4196–4207 (2018). https://doi.org/10.1109/TCSI.2018.2840092

13. Desoli, G., et al.: 14.1 A 2.9TOPS/W deep convolutional neural network SoC in FD-SOI 28 nm for intelligent embedded systems. In: 2017 IEEE International Solid-State Circuits Conference (ISSCC), pp. 238–239 (2017). https://doi.org/10.1109/ISSCC.2017.7870349

14. Pereira, P., Silva, J., Silva, A., Fernandes, D., Machado, R.: Efficient hardware design and implementation of the voting scheme-based convolution. Sensors 22 (2022). https://doi.org/10.3390/s22082943

15. Silva, J., Pereira, P., Machado, R., Névoa, R., Melo-Pinto, P., Fernandes, D.: Customizable FPGA-based hardware accelerator for standard convolution processes empowered with quantization applied to LiDAR data. Sensors 22(6), 2184 (2022). https://doi.org/10.3390/s22062184

16. Silva, A., et al.: Resource-constrained onboard inference of 3D object detection and localisation in point clouds targeting self-driving applications. Sensors 21(23), 7933 (2021). https://doi.org/10.3390/s21237933

17. Lang, A.H., Vora, S., Caesar, H., Zhou, L., Yang, J., Beijbom, O.: PointPillars: fast encoders for object detection from point clouds (2018). http://arxiv.org/abs/1812.05784

Generating the Users Geographic Map Using Mobile Phone Data

Cláudia Rodrigues[1]([✉]) [iD], Marco Veloso[2] [iD], Ana Alves[3] [iD], Gonçalo Ferreira[1] [iD], and Carlos Bento[1] [iD]

[1] Center for Informatics and Systems of the University of Coimbra, Department of Informatics Engineering, University of Coimbra, Pinhal de Marrocos, 3030-290 Coimbra, Portugal
{cbarodrigues,gfferreira}@student.dei.uc.pt, bento@dei.uc.pt
[2] Instituto Politécnico de Coimbra, ESTGOH, Rua General Santos Costa, Oliveira do Hospital, 3400-124 Coimbra, Portugal
mveloso@dei.uc.pt
[3] Instituto Politécnico de Coimbra, ISEC, Rua Pedro Nunes - Quinta da Nora, 3030-199 Coimbra, Portugal
ana@dei.uc.pt

Abstract. Spatial data on human activity, including mobile phone data, has the potential to provide patterns of how the citizens use the urban space. The availability of this data boosted research on city dynamics and human behavior. In this context, we address the question: Can we generate a sufficiently accurate picture of the main places of individuals from highly noisy and sparse data generated by mobile phone operators?

This paper studies different kinds of anonymized mobile phone data and proposes a model, that uses a density-based clustering algorithm to obtain the geographic profile of customers, by identifying their most visited locations at the antenna level. The individual routine, such as sleeping period and work hours, is dynamically identified according to slots of minimums of activity in the network. Then, based on those slots, areas of Home, Second Home, and Work are inferred. Ground truth is used to validate and evaluate the model.

Keywords: Mobile phone data · Meaningful places · Geo-profile

1 Introduction

Research studies have proved that daily human mobility tends to be largely predictable, with a high degree of temporal and spatial regularity [1,2]. Thus, the study of routines and users' trajectories generally leads to building models for identification of mobility patterns. Nevertheless, this task relies on spatial data, including mobile phone data. Mobile phone data can be used for location analytics to characterize various aspects of human mobility, improve the public transportation systems or deploy new services or infrastructures [3]. At an individual level, the information provided by this data is helpful to understand the

© The Author(s), under exclusive license to Springer Nature Switzerland AG 2022
G. Marreiros et al. (Eds.): EPIA 2022, LNAI 13566, pp. 297–308, 2022.
https://doi.org/10.1007/978-3-031-16474-3_25

behaviors, habits, preferences, and needs by allowing the identification of places that are frequently visited by the user.

Mobile phone tracking refers to the acquisition process of spatial data through these devices. This data can be acquired by several means, including via Global System for Mobiles (GSM), Wi-Fi, Bluetooth, or Global Positioning System (GPS) [4,5]. Most GSM-based data is collected by mobile operators and includes timestamps and geographical references. In particular, Call Detail Records (CDRs) are a type of mobile phone data frequently adopted to study simultaneously individual movements and social interactions [6]. However, due to the temporal and spatial sparseness and irregularity that they present, some companies are extracting and analyzing other types of data sources, such as location updates. This type is mainly produced when a client moves closer to an antenna, even though no call or SMS is made or received. Due to the granularity of the events generated, location updates data can be considered superior to CDRs.

The goal of this research is to understand how mobile phone data can be used to identify the daily life of a citizen, that is, the places frequently visited by the individual. These places are often called "significant places" and can be identified by the frequency with which they are visited [7]. Thus, we study CDRs and location updates from nearly 5 000 clients in Coimbra (Portugal) to produce a model that identifies their geo-profile at an antenna level.

The geo-profile consists of identifying significant places in the individuals' daily life, such as home, second home, and workplaces. The majority of the approaches at the state of the art focus on identifying only one location of home and work based on CDRs generated during fixed time intervals. In our work, we combine this data with location updates data, in order to address temporal and spatial limitations. We also use a more flexible approach that identifies routines and tries to extract from the data second home locations. The geo-profile is created after determining the user's profile according to the activity in the network, which indicates the most probable sleeping period and work hours. The identification of these periods helps identify the significant places.

The article is organized as follows: Sect. 2 presents a brief review of the related work. In Sect. 3, we discuss the datasets used in the analysis. In Sect. 4, we introduce the methodology to identify profiles and geo-profiles of users. Section 5 presents the experimental work and results. In Sect. 6, we discuss the results and highlight the main achievements of this work.

2   Related Work

The study of human movements through the exploitation of mobile phone data has been an active area of research due to the worldwide availability and ubiquity of mobile phones. This data includes, for example, CDRs, and is collected by mobile operators for billing purposes, without requiring user participation, with the advantages of being available for all groups of the population, not intrusive, and anonymized. The analysis of CDRs provides knowledge on the user's

sent and received calls and text messages, as well as about the antenna that received/transmitted the communication.

There are controversial opinions about the use of CDRs to study human mobility due to the considerable challenges presented when they are a source of location information, such as temporal irregularity and spatial sparseness. However, many researchers and institutions are aware of their potential and demonstrated that they might reflect human mobility and significant places. They also consider them representative enough and use them to achieve goals, such as identifying meaningful places [3,8].

Hence, some authors used CDRs to identify homes and workplaces. Some of them rely on the typical behavior of users, using *a priori* assumptions (e.g. criteria with temporal constraints) to determine significant places. Usually, they try to identify home locations based on CDRs generated at night and work locations based on CDRs generated during the day [8–10].

Although rules/criteria are commonly applied to exploit home and work locations, their use implies that subscribers with different routines, such as night workers, are treated the same way as those with common ones. To identify significant places for different types of users with varying habits, some researchers did not make *prior* assumptions about the behavior of users. Lumpsum et al. [7] identified home locations through the determination of a sleeping period and workplaces were identified where individuals used their phone between working hours most regularly in terms of days and hour slots. Mamei et al. [11] presented an approach to identify places that people routinely frequent, using CDRs. In their approach, after using an agglomerative algorithm to cluster CDRs, clusters with a weight greater than a certain threshold were associated to relevant places. Also, Burkhard et al. [12] proposed an approach, based on a density-based clustering algorithm, to extract mobility patterns from CDRs without *prior* assumptions.

Previous research showed that it is possible to identify meaningful places of users with different behavior through the analysis of CDRs. Despite their success, currently, most users are no longer making calls and sending SMSs through the cellular network. Most of the communications are made via Internet Protocol (IP). Consequently, mobile operators that benefit from studying their clients, are also extracting and studying other types of mobile phone data, that attempt to deal with the sparseness and irregularity of CDRs. Thus, we combine CDRs with location updates and attempt to improve the geo-profile identification method, to better understand the users' routines.

3 Dataset Description

The mobile phone data used in this research was collected by a telecommunication company with approximately 40% market share in Portugal. Regarding privacy concerns, all personal information on clients was encrypted by the mobile operator. We have analyzed two datasets, one containing CDRs and another location updates. Both types of registers belong to 5 000 clients from September and October 2021.

CDRs include information on how, when, and where people daily communicate. In our dataset, each CDR represents an event containing the following information: ID of the caller, ID of the antenna, and when the event took place.

Contrary to CDRs, which only provide information on the user's location every time he/she interacts with the network to make/receive a call or a SMS, the location updates include information about the users' movements at the antenna level. This data tries to mitigate some of the challenges of the CDRs, registering the locations visited by the user. Each time the user moves and approaches the boundary of the antenna's coverage area, connects to the network, or receives/transmits a call or SMS, a signal is sent to the nearest antenna, and finally, the location is updated in the company's database.

Although the location updates dataset contain CDRs events (made/received calls or SMSs), there is no attribute column to distinguish CDRs events from displacement events. Consequently, only the CDRs dataset can give information about the real activity/interaction of the user with the network.

Through the antenna ID, both datasets can be linked to a third one that contains information about the antennas. This data gives knowledge on the geographic location of the antenna, coverage radius (in meters), and coverage angle, giving insights into the approximated location of the user.

4   Methodology

4.1   Data Exploration

The telecommunication company owns 48 273 antennas in Portugal, being that 2 093 are in the district of Coimbra. The area studied, the District of Coimbra, can be seen in Fig. 1. Although there are events registered across all country by the clients studied, they had most of their events in this area. Figure 1 also highlights the geographical distribution and density of antennas/cell towers in the district. It is observable that there are areas of higher density.

We use both data types (CDRs and location updates) to identify each user profile based on slots of minimum activity. However, due to the nature of the data, they cannot be treated the same way. While for CDRs we considered each register in the dataset as an activity event and counted the number of CDRs registers throughout different slots of the day, for the location updates we used a different approach. Instead of counting the number of registers in each slot, we count the number of distinct locations visited.

The usage of both types of data allows a more accurate selection of the slots of minimum activity. By adding the real interaction that the user does with the network (CDRs) to the locations visited, it guarantees that selection of the slots can be more accurate when the number of visited locations is the same. That means that CDRs add relevant information to the location updates and vice-versa.

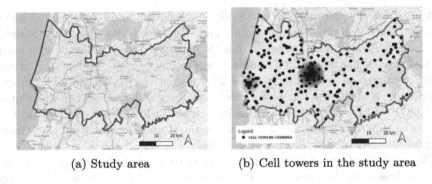

(a) Study area   (b) Cell towers in the study area

Fig. 1. District of Coimbra

As presented in Fig. 2, most of the CDRs and location updates were registered during daytime. This study is related to weekday usage. On average, a client was seen in the network approximately 22 times per day, corresponding to a mean of 3.88 phone calls or SMS made/received and 17.83 visited locations per day. This indicates that the number of CDRs did not keep up the number of movements and many locations visited were not registered in the CDRs mostly because of the continuous growth of VoIP (Voice over IP) communications.

Despite the different proportions, the usage of CDRs matches the movements in terms of hours. Both rise at 7AM and stay at a high level until 7PM, before dropping and reaching a low between 1AM and 5AM.

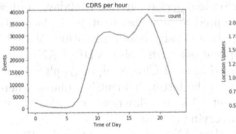
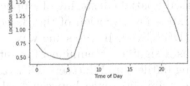

(a) Made/received Calls and SMSs   (b) Locations/antennas visited per
per hour   hour

Fig. 2. Events per hour

4.2 Profile Identification

The identification of homes, second homes, and workplaces is connected with the user profile. In other words, it relies on detecting routines, which include the

most probable sleeping periods and work hours. Thus, homes and second homes are identified based on sleeping periods and workplaces based on work hours.

Assuming that is most probable that there is no activity while the user sleeps and individuals usually sleep at home, the sleeping period consists of finding a period of minimum activity across the 24 h of multiple days [7,13]. The process of finding it, is the following: days of the week are divided into 24 sliding slots of 5 h (12AM–4AM, 1AM–5AM...), then in each slot, the number of CDRs and the number of different locations visited are counted and the slot with a minimum of activity is returned as the sleeping period.

The identification of the sleeping period to predict the home location is achieved based on the events (CDRs and visited locations) registered throughout the weekdays. In order to identify the second homes, the sleeping period is determined based on CDRs registered and locations visited on the weekends, which, typically, is when people dislocate to these places.

The identification of work hours is based on finding a period of less activity in the afternoon on the weekdays. This method was applied based on the assumption that most of the citizens work regularly on weekdays, in a fixed place, and they are not on their phones during their work hours [13]. Then, the same method that is applied to identify sleeping periods is used to identify work hours and a slot of 4 h, from 1PM to 8PM (1PM–4PM, 2PM–5PM...), with minimum activity, is identified. The reason for considering only the afternoon hours is because we intend to include in the study day, night, and shift workers. The latter ones, usually start working at the end of the afternoon.

4.3   Home, Second Home, and Work Locations

After the identification of users' sleeping period on the weekdays and weekends and work hours, these slots are used to infer the mentioned places. To the events in the identified slots, we apply a density-based algorithm, Varied Density Based Spatial Clustering of Applications with Noise (VDBSCAN) [14]. This algorithm is an extension of the Based Spatial Clustering of Applications with Noise (DBSCAN). In the same way as the latter, it identifies places where the user has a significant number of events [15]. In addiction, it is also capable of handling outliers and datasets with varying densities.

The main difference between VDBSCAN and the traditional DBSCAN is that the *eps* parameter is automatically calculated according to the density of the dataset [14]. This parameter defines that two points are considered neighbors if the distance between them is below the threshold epsilon. Other authors used DBSCAN to identify home and work locations [9,12]. However, the necessity of dealing with datasets with varying densities of events (users with events at only one location and users with events registered around the country) and different densities of antennas led us to adopt VDBSCAN.

Another necessary parameter, this time to both algorithms, is the *MinPoints*, which is the minimum number of samples/points in a neighborhood for a point to be considered a core point [14]. Based on the distribution of events, we concluded that a *MinPoints* equal to 500 (mean of registers generated by each user)

is the ideal value for this parameter when dealing with two months of these types of registers. Even though most of the clients in the dataset had more than 500 registers, not every client has this many, so we defined two values for the parameter: for clients that have less than 500 registers of CDRs and location updates, the *MinPoints* was defined as 250, and for clients that have 500 or more registers, the *MinPoints* was defined equal to 500.

For situations in which the client has less than 250 registers, the considered a *MinPoints* parameter equal to the total number of registers that the user made in the period that is being analyzed. Thus, since we are analyzing periods of lower activity, only one register is required during the slot to determine home, second home, or work location. Moreover, in cases where no events occur throughout the defined periods, the impossibility of identifying home locations exists. Though, due to the nature of the location updates, it is very unlikely for this to happen.

4.4 Validation and Evaluation

The final step is the validation and evaluation of the obtained results. To validate the home location results, we use as ground truth the centroid of the ZIP code of 4 170 clients of our dataset. Then based on the information given on the antennas, we calculate the distance between the area of the real home location and the area identified as home by the model and use that to evaluate our results.

The validation and evaluation of work and second home results are made using a survey made by the company to 544 clients that are in the dataset. The survey included questions regarding to their work schedule and, in order to perceive if the clients have a second home, if they have a second home and if they spent their weekends in their home zone or if they usually travel. With this type of ground truth, it was not possible to evaluate our model concerning the locations, however, we could evaluate how the model identifies the slots of work hours and the identification of second homes for those clients who confirmed to visit a second home location at weekends.

5 Experiment and Results

After performing an analysis on the antennas of the district of Coimbra, we observed, that there are antennas with a coverage radius of 23 000 m, which covers a major part of the district. In order to enhance our results, we deleted from each user's dataset events that were registered in antennas with a coverage radius higher than 5 000 m. After this filtering, 7% of the registers were eliminated, leading to the elimination of two users.

The proposed methodology was then applied to the CDRs and location updates of each client. As a result, we were able of identifying home locations for 4 536 clients and workplaces for 4 663 clients which corresponds to 90.07% and 93.26% of the initial dataset, respectively. A reason for the identified home locations being less than the workplaces is that during a sleeping period the activity is more limited than during work hours.

After the identification of the three locations for each user, the algorithm verifies if the second home location is the same as the home location or if the two places are near (<20 km). If one of these situations is observed, it is assumed that the user does not have a second home location. Posterior the verification, a second home location was identified for 847 clients.

Figure 3 presents the distribution of the locations found. Both home and work locations identified are concentrated in an urban area (city of Coimbra), being that the workplaces are more concentrated in the center of the town. Contrary, it is observable that the second home locations are distributed across the district and even in other parts of the country.

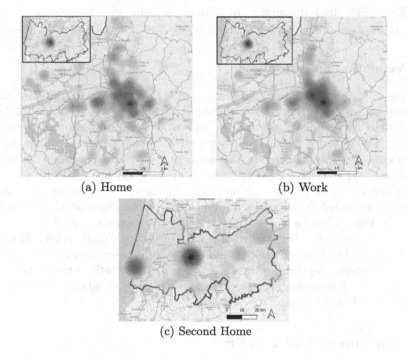

(a) Home   (b) Work

(c) Second Home

Fig. 3. Heat maps of the locations found

5.1   Home Locations

From the 4 170 clients on the ground truth dataset with information about home locations, that are in common with our dataset, we were able of identifying home locations for 4 141 clients (99.03%). Then, to evaluate the results we used a method from Mamei et al. [11] that consists of applying the coverage radius of the antennas to declare if the place was accurately found or not.

To better evaluate our results, we separate areas with a high density of cell towers from areas of low density (Fig. 4). The identification of the areas was

made recurring to DBSCAN. As introduced, this algorithm can recognize areas of elevated density of events [15]. In Fig. 4, it is visible that in urban/dense areas (red color), antennas are more closely located than in rural areas (black color). The urban areas identified correspond to the two major cities of the district (Coimbra and Figueira da Foz).

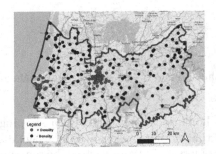

Fig. 4. Rural and urban areas in the district Coimbra (Color figure online)

Once we separated the areas of high density (urban areas) from the areas of low density (rural areas), we calculated the mean coverage radius in each one. So, in the urban areas of Coimbra's district, the mean coverage area of the antennas is 2 246 m and 4 062 m in the rural areas. As predicted, due to the elevated quantity of antennas in urban areas, the coverage radius is lower than in rural areas. Finally, the results are evaluated in a way that if in an urban or rural area, the distance between the antenna found as home and the real home location, is lower than the coverage radius of the respective area, the home location is considered achieved with success.

After performing multiple experiments, we considered that distances between the two places higher than 20 km should be treated as annotation errors. We assumed that users that presented this scenario, were living in the home identified by the model, however, their billing address was registered far away from that place. Thus, these situations were not evaluated. Afterward, we were able of identifying with precision, the home location of 72% of the clients.

Since we have access to such information as the angle and meters that the antennas cover, we used this to boost our model and work with the real coverage of the antenna. So, instead of using the exact location of the antenna as a reference point, we calculated the centroid of the real coverage area of the antennas. The method to achieve the area polygon that accurately represents the coverage of the antenna and its centroid can be observed in Fig. 5. With this technique we raised our percentage of success, identifying with accuracy the home location of 78% of the users.

Comparison. We compared our method's results with the results from Lumpsum et al. [7] which used the last calls before bedtime or the first calls after

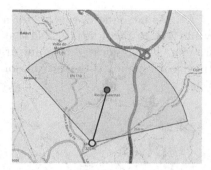

Fig. 5. Centroid of the antenna taking into account angle and coverage radius

waking up to identify home locations based on a sleeping time. In this work, after eliminating users that do not present a daily usage distribution graph that has a U shape, an hour of less activity for each of the remaining users is identified. Then, the CDRs registered 4 h before and after the sleeping hour are obtained and a slot of 9 h is identified as the sleeping period. Next, the events on this slot are used to identify home locations.

Results of the comparison demonstrate that location updates data can increase the accuracy of the results, as the work from Lumpsum et al. [7] reached an accuracy of 69.02% and was able of identifying the home locations of 32.44% of the clients in their dataset. With our method, using both CDRs and location updates, we were able of identifying the home location of 94.48% of the clients with 78% of accuracy. Besides the differences between the two methods, they both used CDRs and looked for a period of less activity (sleeping period). The main discrepancy between the results is the percentage of clients that were geo-profiled. An explanation for these results can be that with our method it is not necessary to make a pre-elimination of clients that do not present a specific distribution of events throughout the days. Concerning the homes found, in both cases, it could be explained because most of the activity occurs during the daytime, and with less activity is more difficult to predict a place.

5.2 Workplace Location

In regards to the work hours, we use a survey made to 544 clients of the mobile operator. From the survey, we use the 170 clients who answer the fields corresponding to their work schedules (check-in, check-out, and lunch break time).

Then, the results of work hours were evaluated in a way that for each user, we verify whether the slot of work hours found by the algorithm corresponds to the period of work mentioned by the user. If we hit at least two hours of the slot indicated by the user, we assume that we got it right. After analyzing the 4-hour slot of minimum activity corresponding to the assumed work hours, we concluded that we were able of identifying the work hours of 119 clients, which corresponds to 70% of the users.

5.3 Second Home Location

In the survey, 79 clients confirmed having a second home location. Of those, from the 38 clients that said that they spend most of their weekends at their first home, we found 8 s home locations. From the 33 clients that said that they occasionally spend their weekends in other locations we found 14 s home locations and from the 8 of them that said that they always spend their weekends out of their first home location zone, we found 5 s home locations. In this evaluation, we assumed that other locations (out of home zone) are the second home location.

6 Conclusions

This paper proposes a model to identify home, second home, and work locations, through mobile phone data. It reaches an accuracy of 78% on the identification of home locations. The remaining 22% we assume are caused by the wrong determination of the sleeping period or the large coverage area of some antennas. We have compared our method for home detection with the one from Lumpsum et al. [7] and concluded that with our method we do not need to go through a pre-elimination process and the usage of location updates seems to increase the accuracy of the results. Thus we could geo-profile most of the users in the dataset with higher accuracy.

This study contributes to proving that it is possible to predict human behavior using mobile phone data with a level of accuracy useful for urban decision makers. Some other aspects of our approach contributed to enhancing the results, such as the usage of varying parameters in the clustering algorithm to deal with different densities of events, the usage of sliding slots to increase the precision of identification of the sleeping periods and work hours, and the method to calculate the centroid of the real coverage area of the antennas.

This work identifies the routines of individuals, which can be a major step to build the citizens' profiles. For future work, the results of this model could be validated and evaluated with a more precise source of ground truth, and be used to infer types of professional activity and commuting flows. This information can give better understanding of the mobility demand in the urban spaces, and be used to improve, for example, urban public transport.

Acknowledgements. This work is funded by the FCT - Foundation for Science and Technology, I.P./MCTES through national funds (PIDDAC), within the scope of CisUC R&D Unit - UIDB/00326/2020 or project code UIDP/00326/2020.

References

1. González, M., Hidalgo, C., Barabási, A.: Understanding individual human mobility patterns. Nature **453**, 779–782 (2008). https://doi.org/10.1038/nature06958
2. Lu, X., Wetter, E., Bharti, N., Tatem, A., Bengtsson, L.: Approaching the limit of predictability in human mobility. Sci. Rep. **3**(2923), 1–9 (2013). https://doi.org/10.1038/srep02923

3. Ranjan, G., Zang, H., Zhang, Z., Bolot, J.: Are call detail records biased for sampling human mobility? ACM SIGMOBILE Mob. Comput. Commun. Rev. **16**(3), 33–44 (2012). https://doi.org/10.1145/2412096.2412101

4. Yuan, Y., Raubal, M.: Exploring georeferenced mobile phone datasets - a survey and reference framework. Geogr. Compass **10**(6), 239–252 (2016). https://doi.org/10.1111/gec3.12269. Characterizing human mobility from mobile phone usage

5. Kasemsan, M.L.K., Ratsameethammawong, P.: Moving mobile phone location tracking by the combination of GPS, Wi-Fi and cell location technology. In: Business Transformation Through Innovation and Knowledge Management: An Academic Perspective, vol. 1–4, pp. 979–985 (2010)

6. Xu, Y., Belyi, A., Bojic, I., Ratti, C.: How friends share urban space: an exploratory spatiotemporal analysis using mobile phone data. Trans. GIS **21**(3), 468–487 (2017). https://doi.org/10.1111/tgis.12285

7. Tongsinoot, L., Muangsin, V.: Exploring home and work locations in a city from mobile phone data. In: 2017 IEEE 19th International Conference on High Performance Computing and Communications; IEEE 15th International Conference on Smart City; IEEE 3rd International Conference on Data Science and Systems (HPCC/SmartCity/DSS) (2017). https://doi.org/10.1109/HPCC-SmartCity-DSS.2017.16

8. Isaacman. S., et al.: Identifying important places in people's lives from cellular network data. In: Lyons, K., Hightower, J., Huang, E.M. (eds.) Pervasive 2011. LNCS, vol. 6696, pp. 133–151. Springer, Heidelberg (2011). https://doi.org/10.1007/978-3-642-21726-5_9

9. Yang, P., Zhu, T., Wang, X.: Identifying significant places using multi-day call detail records. In: IEEE 26th International Conference on Tools with Artificial Intelligence, pp. 360–366 (2014). https://doi.org/10.1109/ICTAI.2014.61

10. Vanhoof, M., Reis, F., Smoreda, Z., Ploetz, T.: Detecting home locations from CDR data: introducing spatial uncertainty to the state-of-the-art. In: Mobile Tartu 2016 Conference (2018). https://doi.org/10.48550/arXiv.1808.06398

11. Mamei, M., Colonna, M., Galassi, M.: Automatic identification of relevant places from cellular network data. Pervasive Mob. Comput. **31**, 147–158 (2010). https://doi.org/10.1016/j.pmcj.2016.01.009

12. Burkhard. O., Ahas, R., Saluvver, E., Weibel, R.: Extracting regular mobility patterns from sparse CDR data without a priori assumptions. J. Location Based Serv. **11**(2), 78–97 (2017). Special Issue: Methodological Aspects of Using Geocoded Data from Mobile Devices in Transportation Research. https://doi.org/10.1080/17489725.2017.1333638

13. Dash, M., Koo, K., Holleczek, T., Yap, G., Krishnaswamy, S., Shi-Nash, A.: From mobile phone data to transport network - gaining insight about human mobility. In: 2015 16th IEEE International Conference on Mobile Data Management, pp. 243–250 (2015). https://doi.org/10.1109/MDM.2015.74

14. Liu, P., Zhou, D., Wu, N.: VDBSCAN: varied density based spatial clustering of applications with noise. In: International Conference on Service Systems and Service Management, pp. 1–4 (2007). https://doi.org/10.1109/ICSSSM.2007.4280175

15. Ester, M., Kriegel, H., Sander, J., Xu, X.: A density-based algorithm for discovering clusters in large spatial databases with noise. In: Proceedings of the Second International Conference on Knowledge Discovery and Data Mining, pp. 226–231 (1996)

Driver Equitability and Customer Optimality in Intelligent Vehicle Applications

Martin Aleksandrov[✉][iD]

Freie Universität Berlin, Berlin, Germany
martin.aleksandrov@fu-berlin.de

Abstract. We consider classical vehicle routing problems with customer costs, vehicle feasibilities, driver profits, and driver responsiveness. We motivate a new template for these new problems, which first returns some feasible matching between drivers and customers and then some feasible plan for routing the vehicles through their matched locations. Thus, by using this template, we show that bounded equitability for drivers and Pareto optimality for customers can always be achieved in isolation but not always in combination. Finally, we give fixed-parameter tractable routing algorithms for fleet equitability and fleet efficiency.

Keywords: Multi-agent systems · Social choice · Vehicle routing

1 Introduction

The 2020 EU Strategy for Sustainable and Smart Mobility has formulated public mobility Transport Policy Flagships, according to which the management of Intelligent Vehicles (IVs) must involve the *preferences* of individuals (e.g. drivers, customers) in addition to information about its state and environment. IVs include autonomous vehicles, connected vehicles, electric vehicles, smart garbage vehicles, and data-driven vehicles. Two ethical principles of Trustworthy AI systems for IVs are equitability and efficiency [12]. They are human factors that are relevant for perceived safety and user acceptance of IVs. In response, we make initial steps in this direction. Our starting point is the following question:

Under driver and customer preferences, how can we model and achieve equitability for drivers and efficiency for customers in applications for IVs?

To model these two goals, we appeal to concepts from computational social choice and economy. Equitability (EQ) [8] is one of the most popular social choice concepts for perceived fairness. In our work for IVs, it encodes the possibility that drivers may receive equal profits from servicing their matched customers. Pareto optimality (PO) [14] is one of the most popular economic concepts for perceived efficiency. In our work for IVs, it encodes the impossibility to make all customers happier than they are with their matched driver services.

G. Marreiros et al. (Eds.): EPIA 2022, LNAI 13566, pp. 309–321, 2022.
https://doi.org/10.1007/978-3-031-16474-3_26

Equitability for drivers and Pareto optimality for customers may not be achieved via a standard routing optimisation approach. Indeed, these properties may be orthogonal to common routing objectives. Examples are minimising the maximum work time of any vehicle (i.e. fleet fairness) and minimising the total work time of all vehicles (i.e. fleet efficiency). This is because these objectives depend on the routing whereas EQ and PO depend on the preferences. We illustrate this for fleet efficiency in Examples 1 and 2.

Example 1 (Equitability for drivers). *Let us consider vehicle v_1 at 0, vehicle v_2 at 1, visit request r_1 at $\epsilon \in [0, \frac{1}{4})$, and visit request r_2 at $2 \cdot \epsilon$. We let each driver derive a profit of 1\$ per visit. Minimising the total work time dispatches v_1 to ϵ and $2 \cdot \epsilon$. Thus, it gives an objective value of $2 \cdot \epsilon$. This outcome is* not *equitable because the driver of v_1 gets a profit of 2\$ and the driver of v_2 gets a profit of 0\$. By comparison, let us first match r_1 to v_1 and r_2 to v_2. Then, dispatching v_1 to ϵ and v_2 to $2 \cdot \epsilon$ gives a total work time of $(1 - \epsilon)$. For $\epsilon \in [0, \frac{1}{4})$, this value is strictly greater than $2 \cdot \epsilon$. This outcome is* equitable *because each driver gets a profit of 1\$.* ∎

Example 2 (Pareto optimality for customers). *In the instance from Example 1, we let the customer of r_1 (r_2) pay a cost of 1\$ for being serviced by v_1 (v_2) and 2\$ for being serviced by v_2 (v_1). Minimising the total work time dispatches v_1 to ϵ and $2 \cdot \epsilon$. Thus, it gives an objective value of $2 \cdot \epsilon$. This outcome is* not *Pareto-optimal because the customer of r_2 pays 2\$ but they can pay a strictly lower cost of 1\$ by being serviced by v_2. Indeed, let us next match r_1 to v_1 and r_2 to v_2. Then, dispatching v_1 to ϵ and v_2 to $2 \cdot \epsilon$ gives a total work time of $(1 - \epsilon)$. For $\epsilon \in [0, \frac{1}{4})$, this value is strictly greater than $2 \cdot \epsilon$. This outcome is* Pareto-optimal *because each customer pays 1\$ and not 2\$.* ∎

To achieve these two goals, it follows that we must solve the matching sub-problem before the routing sub-problem. This is necessary because minimising the routing directly may cause inequality or inefficiency: see Examples 1 and 2. In response, we propose a new template: Template 1. Template 1 returns first a matching between drivers and customers, and then a routing of their vehicles.

Template 1. A MATCH-1ST-ROUTE-2ND algorithm.

Input: *vehicles V, requests R, preferences P, feasibilities F, network N, objective O*
Output: matching $\mathcal{R}$, routing $\mathcal{P}$

1: Given V, R, P, and F, compute $\mathcal{R}$.
2: Given V, $\mathcal{R}$, N, and O, compute $\mathcal{P}$.
3: **return** $(\mathcal{R}, \mathcal{P})$

We give informal preliminaries in Sects. 2 and 3. We review some related work in Sect. 4 and summarise our contributions in Sect. 5. Then, we give formal preliminaries in Sect. 6. We focus on equitability for drivers in Sect. 7 and Pareto optimality for customers in Sect. 8. In Sect. 9, we combine these. In Sect. 10, we look at the routing sub-problem under a few feasibilities per vehicle. Finally, we conclude in Sect. 11.

2   Preferences and Constraints

We first let each driver charge the customer(s) of each request with some cost. The *customer cost* has two components: operating cost and profit cost. For example, FedEx, Lieferando, Wuplo, and Foodpanda drivers charge customers from different districts with distinct service costs for their operations, but customers within the same district with the same cost. DHL drivers in Berlin receive each a profit of five Euros per service. The driver profit for multiple requests is the additive sum of the individual request profits. Additivity is a common assumption in ride-sharing (see e.g. [5]), fair division, and decision (see e.g. [6]).

We next let each given vehicle be *feasible* or not for every request. We can thus encode a second layer of driver preferences, say quality preferences, where we match vehicle type (e.g. regular, luxury) and request type (e.g. commute, business) [10]. We can also model some routing constraints. For example, if a truck is not allowed to enter a given part of the city center due to height restrictions, then we can suppose that it is not feasible for every request with a location within this area. We can furthermore integrate identifying VRP constraints into the matching model. For instance, 1-D vehicle capacities and 3-D package dimensions are two such constraints [13].

3   A Relation to Behavioural Game Theory

In our work, we let drivers (pre-)submit to the (central) planner some but possibly not all of their profit preferences and vehicle feasibilities. If the planner has all this information, then the setting is purely centralised. If they have none of this information, then the setting is purely decentralised. Otherwise, the planner needs to decentralise some but not all of the matching decisions. That is, the setting is semi-decentralised and, whenever some profit preferences or vehicle feasibilities are unknown to the planner, they send some requests to drivers, and drivers may *respond* with private information within some (pre-)specified deadline.

At this point, our model intersects behavioral game theory [7], where rationality is a key concept that is suitable for settings in which agents (e.g. drivers) act in their best interest.

As a first step, if drivers respond to the planner within the deadline, then we assume that they are *truthful* and *profit-maximising*, i.e. they reveal information about their most profitable and feasible request. Otherwise, we assume that they are unresponsive and cannot service requests until the next time they respond. Drivers can be unresponsive for various practical reasons: they depart from and arrive at the market at different times; they have made a sufficient profit in the current day and decide to go home earlier; their vehicles are truthfully infeasible. Finally, we note that the responsive behaviour of drivers can also be seen as preferences about when to participate and for what requests.

4   Some Related Work

Santos and Xavier [16] studied minimising shared taxi costs (not driver profits, vehicle feasibilities, or driver responsiveness) among customers. Li et al. [11] considered a similar setting with people and parcels. These works do not focus on the driver's side of the problem. Rheingans-Yoo et al. [15] analysed matchings with driver location (not profit, feasibility, responsive) preferences. Lesmana, Zhang, and Bei [10] investigated maximising the minimum additive trip profit of any driver (but this may be intractable). These works do not focus on the customer side of the problem. In contrast, we consider both drivers and customers. Additionally, all these works deal with centralised settings. By comparison, we consider customer costs, driver profits, and vehicle feasibilities in semi-decentralised settings. We note that decentralisation is challenging simply because we do not know how drivers might behave in practice. As an initial step, we assume in this work that drivers are truthful and profit-maximising. Furthermore, unlike the above existing works, we propose axiomatic properties that encode driver profit equitability and customer cost optimality in semi-decentralised settings. Also, we give tractable algorithms for achieving each of these in isolation and show that they may not always be achieved in combination. Finally, Aleksandrov [2,3] studied minimising the total and maximum fleet workload by means of the waiting times, tour times, and arrival times of customers. Unlike these two works, we measure the vehicle workload by means of the driver working time. Nevertheless, our brute-force routing algorithms can be used for all these objectives.

5   Our Contributions

We begin with equitability for drivers. In centralised fair division of goods, there are neither vehicle feasibilities nor driver responsiveness. In this setting, one appealing fairness notion is "equitability up to some good" (EQ1). This is because, unlike equitability, EQ1 can always be guaranteed with strictly positive valuations, even in combination with PO [1]. This motivates us to define a version of EQ1 for our semi-decentralised matching model with vehicle feasibilities and driver responsiveness. We refer to it as *responsive FEQ1*. For any fixed pair of drivers, responsive FEQ1 matchings bound the jealousy (i.e. objective profit difference) for their feasible requests for which drivers are responsive. We observe that we can always return such matchings: Theorem 1.

We continue with Pareto optimality for customers. In our setting with vehicle feasibilities and driver responsiveness, we refer to it as *responsive FPO*. As opposed to drivers who aim at maximising their profits for requests, customers aim at minimising their costs for vehicles. We prove thus that minimising the total cost in a feasible and responsive matching satisfies responsive FPO. This can be done quickly: Theorem 2. However, unlike PO and EQ1, none of the responsive FEQ1 matchings may be responsive FPO in some instances, and deciding whether such matchings give total cost, which is bounded from above, is NP-hard: Theorem 3. For NP-hardness, we refer the reader to [9].

In practice, (courier) dispatchers receive only a few requests at a given point in time. We consider therefore a parameter such as the maximum number of feasible requests per vehicle. We discuss that optimising fleet fairness (or $maxWORK$) and fleet efficiency (or $totWORK$) by using naive brute force may take exponential time, even when the parameter admits some constant value. By comparison, with Template 1, we prove that optimising these objectives by using naive brute force is fixed-parameter tractable for any constant value of the parameter: Theorem 4. We can use these brute-force algorithms for customer objectives as well: see e.g. [2,3]. Table 1 contains our main results.

Table 1. Key: n vehicles, m requests, deadline T, f feasibilities. Note: the results hold for matchings that are feasible (i.e. each vehicle services only feasible requests), responsive (i.e. each driver is matched to requests for which they are responsive), and complete (i.e. the number of matched requests is maximised for a responsive behavior).

Template 1	
Goal	Result
Matching sub-problem	
Responsive FEQ1	$O(m\max\{nm, T\})$ (Thm 1)
Responsive FPO	$O(nmT)$ (Thm 2)
Responsive FEQ1 and FPO	NP-hard (Thm 3)
Routing sub-problem	
maxWORK	$O(n(2f)!)$ (Thm 4)
totWORK	$O(n(2f)!)$ (Thm 4)

6 Formal Preliminaries

We let $V = \{v_1, \ldots, v_n\}$ denote the set of driver *vehicles*. Fixed v_i has a start location $s_i \in \mathbb{R}^2$, a finish location $f_i \in \mathbb{R}^2$, and available capacity $q_i \in \mathbb{N}_{>0}$. We let $R = \{r_1, \ldots, r_m\}$ denote the set of customer *requests*. Fixed r_j can have pick-up location $p_j \in \mathbb{R}^2$, delivery location $d_j \in \mathbb{R}^2$, unit demand, and location service delay $\tau_j \in \mathbb{N}_{>0}$. In this case, $r_j = (p_j, d_j, 1, \tau_j)$. Also, fixed r_j can require just a visit at location $l_j \in \mathbb{R}^2$ for a service. In this case, $r_j = (l_j, l_j, 0, \tau_j)$.

6.1 Preferences and Constraints

We let the customer of r_j pay cost $c_j(v_i) \in \mathbb{R}_{>0}$ for being serviced by v_i. We suppose $c_j(v_i) = o_j(v_i) + p_i(r_j)$, where $o_j(v_i)$ is the operating cost for servicing r_j with v_i and $p_i(r_j)$ is the profit of driver i for servicing r_j. Each cost $c_j(v_i)$ can be public or private. Thus, we let $\tilde{c}_{ij} = c_j(v_i)$ if $c_j(v_i)$ is public and $\tilde{c}_{ij} = unk$ if $c_j(v_i)$ is private. The *preference* matrix is $P = (\tilde{c}_{ij})_{n\times m}$. Furthermore, we suppose that drivers have additive profits. That is, for $S \subseteq R$, the profit of the driver of v_i is $p_i(S) = \sum_{r_j \in S} p_i(\{r_j\})$. We let $p_i(\{r_j\}) = p_i(r_j)$. Finally, we suppose that there is some set of constraints for each (v_i, r_j). Thus, we define feasibility indicator f_{ij}: $f_{ij} = 1$ if all constraints of v_i for r_j can be satisfied; $f_{ij} = 0$ otherwise. As for preferences, each f_{ij} can be public or private. We let $\tilde{f}_{ij} = f_{ij}$ if f_{ij} is public, and else $\tilde{f}_{ij} = unk$. The *feasibility* matrix is $F = (\tilde{f}_{ij})_{n\times m}$.

6.2   Matchings and Algorithms

Matching is $\mathcal{R} = (R_1, \ldots, R_n)$, where $R_i \subseteq R$ for each v_i and $R_i \cap R_j = \emptyset$ for each (v_i, v_j) such that $i \neq j$. $(R_1, \ldots, R_n)$ is *feasible* if, for each v_i and each $r_j \in R_i$, $f_{ij} > 0$ holds. Feasible matchings are such that no r_j, s.t. $f_{ij} = 0$ holds for each v_i, is matched. In our work, we consider semi-decentralised matchings algorithms. Each such algorithm returns some $(R_1, \ldots, R_n)$ and *responsiveness* matrix $U = (\tilde{u}_{ij})_{n \times m}$. For each r_j, when r_j is matched to v_i, $\tilde{u}_{kj} = 1$ holds for each driver k (also i) who is not unresponsive and $\tilde{u}_{hj} = 0$ holds for each driver $h \neq k$ who is unresponsive. We say that the returned $(R_1, \ldots, R_n)$ is *responsive complete* wrt matrix U if, for every $r_j \in R$ s.t. $f_{ij} > 0$ and $\tilde{u}_{ij} = 1$ hold for some $v_i \in V$, $r_j \in R_k$ for some $v_k \in V$ with $f_{kj} > 0$ and $\tilde{u}_{kj} = 1$. We consider only algorithms that return feasible such matchings.

6.3   Routes and Plans

The vehicle and request locations form a network source L. For each v_i, we write $t(i, l, l') \in [0, \infty)$ for the shortest travel time of v_i from l to l'. We let D_i denote the matrix $[t(i, l, l')]_{|L| \times |L|}$. Each vehicle matrix D_i defines a quasi metric in real-time environments. The network is $N = (L, [D_1, \ldots, D_n])$. For fixed $v_i \in V$ with $R_i \subseteq R$, route $\rho_i = (l_1(i), \ldots, l_{2 \cdot |R_i|}(i))$ is a strict sequence of the locations of the requests from R_i. We associate each $l_s(i)$ in ρ_i with some $r_j \in R_i$ and weight $cap_s(i) = +1$ if $l_s(i) = p_j$ and $cap_s(i) = -1$ if $l_s(i) = d_j$. Plan $\mathcal{P} = \{\rho_1, \ldots, \rho_n\}$ is a set of routes, where ρ_i is assigned to v_i. Plan $\{\rho_1, \ldots, \rho_n\}$ induces some $R_i \subseteq R$ for each v_i. For each $r_j \in R_i$, we note that $p_j = l_{k_j}(i)$ and $d_j = l_{h_j}(i)$ hold for some $k_j, h_j \in \{1, \ldots, 2 \cdot |R_i|\}$.

We consider the following constraints: (a) Matching constraints insist that the requests cannot be split across multiple vehicles: $\forall r_j \in R, \forall v_i \in V : (r_j \in R_i \Rightarrow \forall v_k \in V, k \neq i : r_j \notin R_k)$; (b) Feasibility constraints ensure that each vehicle services only feasible requests: $\forall v_i \in V, \forall r_j \in R_i : f_{ij} > 0$; (c) Ordering constraints ask that the pickup of each request is executed before its corresponding dropoff: $\forall v_i \in V, \forall r_j \in R_i : k_j < h_j$; (d) Capacity constraints enforce that the capacity of no vehicle can be exceeded while servicing the requests: $\forall v_i \in V, \forall l_s(i) \in \rho_i : \sum_{l=1:s} cap_l(i) \leq q_i$. $\{\rho_1, \ldots, \rho_n\}$ is *feasible* if (a-d) are satisfied. We look only at feasible plans that correspond to responsive complete matchings.

6.4   Fleet Fairness and Efficiency

Let us consider feasible $\{\rho_1, \ldots, \rho_n\}$. The work time of driver i when following route ρ_j is $T_i(\rho_j) := t(i, s_j, l_1(j)) + [\sum_{k=1:(2 \cdot |R_j|-1)} t(i, l_k(j), l_{k+1}(j))] + t(i, l_{2 \cdot |R_j|}(j), f_j) + [\sum_{r_k \in R_j} \tau_k]$. Thus, we can define the routing measures of fleet fairness and fleet efficiency more formally as: maxWORK $:= \min_{\{\rho_1, \ldots, \rho_n\}: \text{feasible}} \max_{v_i \in V} T_i(\rho_i)$ and totWORK $:= \min_{\{\rho_1, \ldots, \rho_n\}: \text{feasible}} \sum_{v_i \in V} T_i(\rho_i)$. The *objective* is $O \in \{$maxWORK, totWORK$\}$.

7   Driver Profit Equitability

In the matching sub-problem, we consider the jealousy among drivers for feasible requests for which they are responsive. For $(R_1, \ldots, R_n)$, this jealousy of driver i for driver k is $j_{ik} = \max\{0, p_k(F_{ik}^U) - p_i(F_{ii}^U)\}$, where $F_{ii}^U = \{r_j \in R_i | f_{ij} > 0, \tilde{u}_{ij} = 1\}$ and $F_{ik}^U = \{r_j \in R_k | f_{ij} > 0, \tilde{u}_{ij} = 1\}$.

$(R_1, \ldots, R_n)$ is equitable whenever $j_{ik} = 0$ for each (v_i, v_k) with $i \neq k$. In instances with r_1 and v_1, v_2 where $f_{11} > 0, \tilde{u}_{11} = 1, p_1(r_1) = 1, f_{21} > 0, \tilde{u}_{21} = 1, p_2(r_1) = 1$, a matching gives r_1 to either v_1 or v_2 and, thus, causes non-zero jealousy. Equitable matchings may therefore not exist in general.

In response, we consider matchings of bounded jealousy. We require to eliminate the jealousy that any driver i might have of any other driver k through the removal of a single request from k's bundle of i's feasible requests, that is assigned to k when driver i is responsive. We define this formally.

Definition 1. $(R_1, \ldots, R_n)$ *is responsive FEQ1 wrt matrix* $U = (\tilde{u}_{ij})_{n \times m}$ *if, for each* $v_i, v_k \in V$ *where* $F_{ii}^U = \{r_j \in R_i | f_{ij} > 0, \tilde{u}_{ij} = 1\}$ *and* $F_{ik}^U = \{r_j \in R_k | f_{ij} > 0, \tilde{u}_{ij} = 1\} \neq \emptyset$, $p_i(F_{ii}^U) \geq p_k(F_{ik}^U \setminus \{r_j\})$ *holds for some* $r_j \in F_{ik}^U$.

Feasible, responsive complete, and responsive FEQ1 $(R_1, \ldots, R_n)$ bounds any j_{ik} from above, where the bound is the maximum request profit, i.e. $\max_{v_i, v_k} j_{ik} \leq \max_{v_i, r_j} p_i(r_j)$. We can compute such matchings in every instance. For this purpose, we can use the *min-max* algorithm from our technical report [4]. This algorithm runs in $O(m \cdot \max\{n \cdot m, T\})$ time.

This algorithm simulates a greedy selection of some minimum (*min*) profit responding driver at each iteration and lets them pick a remaining, feasible, and most profitable (*max*) request. The algorithm encourages drivers to respond actively, supposing that they want to receive more requests and, thus, higher profits at the end of the assignment. We next state the result.

Theorem 1. *There is an algorithm (e.g. the min-max algorithm from [4]) that in* $O(m \cdot \max\{n \cdot m, T\})$ *time returns a matching that is feasible, responsive complete, and responsive FEQ1 wrt the returned responsiveness matrix, supposing that each driver is truthful and profit-maximising whenever they respond.*

8   Customer Cost Optimality

In the matching sub-problem, we consider the impossibility to improve a given matching by weakly decreasing the costs of all customers for feasible vehicles with responsive drivers and strictly decreasing some of these costs. We define this formally.

Definition 2. $(R_1, \ldots, R_n)$ *is responsive FPO wrt matrix* $U = (\tilde{u}_{ij})_{n \times m}$ *if there is no other* $(R_1', \ldots, R_n')$ *such that* $c_j(v_k) \leq c_j(v_i)$ *holds for each* $r_j \in R$, *where* $r_j \in R_i$, $r_j \in R_k'$, $f_{kj} > 0$, $\tilde{u}_{kj} = 1$, *and* $c_h(v_l) < c_h(v_g)$ *holds for some* $r_h \in R$, *where* $r_h \in R_g$, $r_h \in R_l'$, $f_{lh} > 0$, $\tilde{u}_{lh} = 1$.

Feasible, responsive complete, and responsive FPO $(R_1, \ldots, R_n)$ can be computed by iterating over the requests and, for each r_j, assigning r_j to some least cost feasible v_i whose driver is responsive for r_j. We give an algorithm that implements this process in every instance: Algorithm 1.

Algorithm 1. SEMI-DECENTRALISED MIN-COST

Input: V, R, $P = (\tilde{c}_{ij})_{n \times m}$, $F = (\tilde{f}_{ij})_{n \times m}$, $T \in \Omega(\max\{n, m\})$

1: $\forall v_i \in V : R_i \leftarrow \emptyset$
2: $U = (\tilde{u}_{ij})_{n \times m} \leftarrow (1)_{n \times m}$ ▷ responsiveness matrix
3: **while** $R \neq \emptyset$ **do**
4:     pick $r_j \in R$
5:     $N_j \leftarrow \{v_i \in V | \tilde{c}_{ij} \neq unk \wedge \tilde{f}_{ij} \neq unk\}$
6:     **for** $v_i \in V$ s.t. $\tilde{c}_{ij} = unk \vee \tilde{f}_{ij} = unk$ **do**
7:         send $\{r_j\}$ to driver i ▷ decentralisation
8:         **if** within T, driver i replies with $o_j(v_i), p_i(r_j), f_{ij}$ **then**
9:             $\tilde{c}_{ij} \leftarrow o_j(v_i) + p_i(r_j), \tilde{f}_{ij} \leftarrow f_{ij}$
10:            $N_j \leftarrow N_j \cup \{v_i\}$
11:        **else**
12:            $\tilde{u}_{ij} \leftarrow 0$
13:    **if** $N_j \neq \emptyset$ **then**
14:        pick $v_i \leftarrow \arg\min_{v_k \in N_j : \tilde{f}_{kj} > 0} \tilde{c}_{kj}$
15:        $R_i \leftarrow R_i \cup \{r_j\}, R \leftarrow R \setminus \{r_j\}$
16:    **else**
17:        $R \leftarrow R \setminus \{r_j\}$
18: **return** $[(R_1, \ldots, R_n), U]$

Algorithm 1 returns $(R_1, \ldots, R_n)$ that achieves a value of $\sum_{v_i \in V, r_j \in R_i} c_j(v_i)$ that is the minimum possible in any feasible and responsive complete matching wrt the returned matrix. For Taxi, WeShare, ShareNow, DHL, FedEx, Uber, and Lyft vehicles and drivers, the operating and profit costs are correlated positively with the service distances. More formally, for each r_j and each (v_i, v_k) with $i \neq k$ and $o_j(v_i) \geq o_j(v_k)$, this means that $p_i(r_j) \geq p_k(r_j)$ holds.

For such applications, Algorithm 1 returns $(R_1, \ldots, R_n)$ that also achieves overall operating cost $\sum_{v_i \in V, r_j \in R_i} o_j(v_i)$ which is the minimum possible. For the sake of contradiction, suppose the opposite. We can therefore move at least one r_j from some R_i to some other R_k s.t. $\tilde{f}_{kj} = f_{kj} > 0$, $\tilde{u}_{kj} = 1$, and $o_j(v_k) < o_j(v_i)$ hold. This implies $p_k(r_j) \leq p_i(r_j)$ and, therefore, $c_j(v_k) < c_j(v_i)$. But, then $(R_1, \ldots, R_n)$ does not minimise $\sum_{v_i \in V, r_j \in R_i} c_j(v_i)$. This is a contradiction.

As we mentioned, drivers are truthful and profit-maximising. That is, whenever some driver i responds for $r_j \in R$ with $o_j(v_i)$, $p_i(r_j)$, and f_{ij} at a given iteration of the algorithm, we assume that $\{r_h \in R | f_{ih} > 0\} \neq \emptyset$ and $r_j \in \{r_k \in R | p_i(r_k) = \arg\max_{r_h \in R : f_{ih} > 0} p_i(r_h)\}$ hold.

Theorem 2. *There is an algorithm (e.g. Algorithm 1) that in $O(m \cdot n \cdot T)$ time returns a matching that is feasible, responsive complete, and responsive FPO wrt the returned responsiveness matrix, supposing that each driver is truthful and profit-maximising whenever they respond.*

Proof. Pick r_j. Consider the set N_j. Send r_j to each driver of $v_i \in V \setminus N_j$ and wait time T for each of them to reply. If the set N_j is non-empty after that, then each v_i from it is such that $\tilde{f}_{ij} = f_{ij} > 0$, $\tilde{c}_{ij} = c_j(v_i)$, and $\tilde{u}_{ij} = 1$ hold. The algorithm assigns thus r_j to $v_i = \arg\min_{v_k \in N_j : \tilde{f}_{kj} = f_{kj} > 0} \tilde{c}_{kj}$. Otherwise, it removes r_j and proceeds to the next request, if any. Thus, the algorithm returns $(R_1, \ldots, R_n)$ that is clearly feasible and responsive complete wrt the returned matrix U. By the matching rule of the algorithm, it follows that the value $\sum_{v_i \in V, r_j \in R_i} c_j(v_i)$ is the minimal possible within the set of matchings that are feasible and responsive complete wrt U. $(R_1, \ldots, R_n)$ is responsive FPO wrt U. For the sake of contradiction, suppose the opposite. We can therefore move at least one r_j from some R_i to some other R_k s.t. $\tilde{f}_{kj} = f_{kj} > 0$, $\tilde{u}_{kj} = 1$, and $c_j(v_k) < c_j(v_i)$ hold. Hence, $(R_1, \ldots, R_n)$ does not minimise the above sum. This is a contradiction. The algorithm has m iterations. Each of these has $O(n)$ iterations. In each of these, we may have to wait time T. The result follows. ∎

9 Driver Equitability and Customer Optimality

In instances with two or more requests, where driver i responds for every r_j and provides to the customer of r_j a feasible service at the lowest cost, the only way to achieve responsive FPO is to give each r_j to driver i. However, this outcome violates responsive FEQ1 whenever there is another driver k that responds for every r_j, has some strictly positive profit for r_j, and whose vehicle is feasible for r_j. In our semi-decentralised two-sided setting, matchings that are responsive FEQ1 for drivers and responsive FPO for customers may therefore *not* exist in some instances. This result contrasts to centralised one-sided fair division of pure goods, where matchings that are EQ1 and PO for agents exist in every instance [1]. In response, we consider the following decision problem.

Problem: FEQ1 FOR DRIVERS & FPO FOR CUSTOMERS
Data: V, R, P, F, $t \in \mathbb{R}_{\geq 0}$.
Query: Is there feasible, responsive complete, and responsive FEQ1 $(R_1, \ldots, R_n)$ s.t. $\sum_{v_i \in V} \sum_{r_j \in R_i} c_j(v_i) \leq t$?

Theorem 3. FEQ1 FOR DRIVERS & FPO FOR CUSTOMERS *belongs to the class of weakly NP-hard decision problems.*

Proof. We give a Karp reduction from the popular NP-hard partition problem. For multiset $\{c_1, \ldots, c_m\}$ of positive numbers, whose sum is equal to $2 \cdot C > m \geq 1$, this problem asks whether there is an equal partition of $\{c_1, \ldots, c_m\}$ into two multisets, where the sum of each multiset is C. We construct a centralised instance (i.e. $U = (1)_{n \times m}$) with 3 drivers and $(m + 4)$ requests: m number-requests $\{r_1, \ldots, r_m\}$ and four special-requests $\{s_1, \ldots, s_4\}$. We also let $t = 12 \cdot C$. As $2 \cdot C > m$ holds, we note that $t > 0$ holds. We let the planner cover the operating costs and, therefore, drivers charge customers with null such costs. Hence, the difference between a given request profit and cost is zero.

We define the profits of driver 1 as follows: a profit of 1 from servicing every r_j; a profit of $4 \cdot C$ from servicing s_1; a profit of $(8 \cdot C - m)$ from servicing s_2; a profit of $3 \cdot C$ from servicing each of s_3 and s_4. We let v_1 be non-feasible for each r_j and feasible for each of s_1, s_2, s_3, s_4. We define the profits of each of drivers 2 and 3 as follows: a profit of c_j from servicing every r_j; a profit of $2 \cdot C$ from servicing each of s_1 and s_2; a profit of $6 \cdot C$ from servicing each of s_3 and s_4. We let each of v_2 and v_3 be feasible for each r_j and also for each of s_1, s_2, s_3, s_4.

By the structure of the profits and feasibilities, $2 \cdot C > m$, and $C > 0$, a feasible and responsive complete matching gives value t iff s_3 and s_4 are matched to driver 1, whereas $\{r_1, \ldots, r_m\}$ plus s_1 and s_2 are matched to drivers 2 and 3.

1) Let there be an equal partition of $\{c_1, \ldots, c_m\}$. It is possible to give each of drivers 2 and 3 a profit of C from $\{r_1, \ldots, r_m\}$ plus a profit of $2 \cdot C$ from s_1 and s_2. The requests s_3 and s_4 can be matched to driver 1. We let (R_1, R_2, R_3) denote one such matching. This one is feasible, responsive complete, and gives value t. It is also responsive FPO. Driver 1 does not have feasible jealousy up to one request because each of drivers 2 and 3 gets exactly one request for which v_1 is feasible. Drivers 2 and 3 do not have feasible jealousy once any of s_3 or s_4 is removed from driver R_1. (R_1, R_2, R_3) is therefore also responsive FEQ1.

2) Let there be a feasible, responsive complete, and responsive FEQ1 matching, in which the total cost is at most t. Hence, this sum is exactly t because t is the minimum possible value in such a matching. We let (R_1, R_2, R_3) denote one such matching. It is also responsive FPO. Drivers 1 has a profit of $6 \cdot C$ for $R_1 = \{s_3, s_4\}$. Once a request is removed from R_1, their profit for the remaining request is $3 \cdot C$. By responsive FEQ1, we derive that each of drivers 2 and 3 gets a profit of C from $\{r_1, \ldots, r_m\}$ plus a profit of $2 \cdot C$ from s_1 and s_2. It follows that $R_2 \setminus \{s_1, s_2\}$ and $R_3 \setminus \{s_1, s_2\}$ is an equal partition of $\{c_1, \ldots, c_m\}$. ∎

10   Routing Under Few Feasibilities

In the routing sub-problem, we first consider some fixed feasible and responsive complete matching. We also consider $f = \max_{v_i \in V} \sum_{r_j \in R, f_{ij} > 0} 1$ and let f take some constant value. Optimising maxWORK/totWORK by using naive brute force is fixed-parameter tractable.

Theorem 4. *If a feasible matching is fixed where each vehicle is feasible for at most f requests, a brute-force algorithm may need $O(n \cdot (2 \cdot f)!)$ time to return a minimising feasible plan for maxWORK/totWORK.*

Proof. If a feasible matching is fixed, then constraints (a-b) are satisfied. In such a matching, each driver i receives at most f requests. Therefore, for each v_i, there are $O((2 \cdot f)!)$ possible routes. This happens when driver i receives exactly f requests and each of these has some different pickup and delivery locations. Hence, for n vehicles, the overall number of routes is $O(n \cdot (2 \cdot f)!)$. For each v_i, a naive brute-force algorithm iterates over all routes and picks a route that satisfies constraints (c-d) and minimises the work time of v_i. For n vehicles, this gives us a minimising feasible plan.   ∎

We next note that different feasible and responsive complete matchings may give different routing values. To see this, we can observe Examples 1 and 2, where the two matchings, giving one request to each driver, produce different total work times.

We may thus wish to pick a feasible and responsive complete matching that optimises maxWORK/totWORK over all such matchings. However, as some instances admit $O(2^{n \cdot f})$ such matchings, a naive brute-force algorithm for this task may run in time that is exponential in n. We show this in Example 3.

Example 3. *Pick some $n, f \in \mathbb{N}_{>0}$. Suppose that n and f are some even numbers (i.e. 2, 4, 6, etc.). In a centralised instance, let there be n vehicles and $\frac{n}{2} \cdot f$ requests. Define profits as follows: each driver receives 1\$ for servicing a request. Define feasibilities as follows: v_1, v_2 are feasible for the first f requests, v_3, v_4 for the second f requests, and so on. We let the locations of the requests be arbitrary. This instance has $O(2^{n \cdot f})$ feasible and responsive complete (and also FEQ1) matchings. To see this, we observe that the number of such matchings for each (v_i, v_{i+1}) with $i \in \{1, 3, \dots, n-1\}$ is $O((2^f)^2)$. The above bound follows by observing that there are $\frac{n}{2}$ such pairs and the fact that the set of feasible requests of one such pair is disjoint from the set of feasible requests of another such pair. Hence, a naive brute-force algorithm requires $O(2^{n \cdot f})$ iterations.*   ∎

11 Future Work

Our work opens up many directions. As a first example, Template 1 can be used for other social choice concepts as well: e.g. max-min fair share, social efficiency. In the future, we will consider such concepts. As a second example, we considered multi-layer driver preferences and single-layer customer preferences. In the future, we will add multiple layers of customer preferences (e.g. costs, vehicle ETAs, driver locations). As a third example, we considered truthful and profit-maximising drivers. In the future, we will add strategic drivers.

Acknowledgements. Martin Aleksandrov was supported by the DFG Individual Research Grant on "Fairness and Efficiency in Emerging Vehicle Routing Problems" (497791398).

References

1. Aleksandrov, M.: Jealousy-freeness and other common properties in fair division of mixed manna. CoRR abs/2004.11469 (2020). https://arxiv.org/abs/2004.11469
2. Aleksandrov, M.D.: Fleet fairness and fleet efficiency in capacitated pickup and delivery problems. In: Proceedings of the 32nd IEEE Intelligent Vehicles Symposium (IV21), Nagoya, Japan, 11–17 July 2021, pp. 1156–1161. IEEE Xplore, July 2021. https://doi.org/10.1109/IV48863.2021.9576002
3. Aleksandrov, M.D.: Minimising fleet times in multi-depot pickup and dropoff problems. In: Marreiros, G., Melo, F.S., Lau, N., Lopes Cardoso, H., Reis, L.P. (eds.) EPIA 2021. LNCS (LNAI), vol. 12981, pp. 199–210. Springer, Cham (2021). https://doi.org/10.1007/978-3-030-86230-5_16
4. Aleksandrov, M.D.: Fairness for drivers with additive profits in emerging vehicle routing problems. Technical report, AAAI Press, March 2022. https://martofena.github.io/fevrps/publications/2022aaai-symp.pdf
5. Bei, X., Zhang, S.: Algorithms for trip-vehicle assignment in ride-sharing. In: Proceedings of the AAAI Conference on Artificial Intelligence, vol. 32, no. 1, April 2018. https://ojs.aaai.org/index.php/AAAI/article/view/11298
6. Brams, S.J., Taylor, A.D.: Fair Division - From Cake-Cutting to Dispute Resolution. Cambridge University Press, Cambridge (1996). https://doi.org/10.1017/CBO9780511598975
7. Camerer, C.F.: Behavioral Game Theory Experiment in Strategic Interaction, vol. 32. Princeton University Press, Princeton (2003). https://press.princeton.edu/books/hardcover/9780691090399/behavioral-game-theory
8. Dubins, L.E., Spanier, E.H.: How to cut a cake fairly. Am. Math. Mon. **68**(1), 1–17 (1961). https://doi.org/10.2307/2311357
9. Garey, M.R., Johnson, D.S.: Computers and Intractability: A Guide to the Theory of NP-Completeness. W. H. Freeman (1979). https://dl.acm.org/doi/10.5555/574848
10. Lesmana, N.S., Zhang, X., Bei, X.: Balancing efficiency and fairness in on-demand ridesourcing, vol. 32, pp. 5309–5319. Curran Associates Inc., Red Hook, December 2019. https://proceedings.neurips.cc/paper/2019/file/3070e6addcd702cb58de5d7897bfdae1-Paper.pdf
11. Li, B., Krushinsky, D., Reijers, H.A., Woensel, T.V.: The share-a-ride problem: people and parcels sharing taxis. Eur. J. Oper. Res. **238**(1), 31–40 (2014). https://doi.org/10.1016/j.ejor.2014.03.003
12. Llorca, D.F., Gutierrez, E.G.: Trustworthy autonomous vehicles. Technical report, KJ-NA-30942-EN-N (online), EUR 30942 EN, Publications Office of the European Union, Luxembourg, ISBN 978-92-76-46055-8, Luxembourg, December 2021. https://doi.org/10.2760/120385. JRC127051
13. Männel, D., Bortfeldt, A.: Solving the pickup and delivery problem with three-dimensional loading constraints and reloading ban. Eur. J. Oper. Res. **264**(1), 119–137 (2018). https://doi.org/10.1016/j.ejor.2017.05.034
14. Pareto, V.: Cours d'économie politique. Œuvres complètes publiées sous la direction de giovanni busino. tomes 1 et 2 en un volume (1897). https://doi.org/10.3917/droz.paret.1964.01. 9782600040143

15. Rheingans-Yoo, D., Kominers, S.D., Ma, H., Parkes, D.C.: Ridesharing with driver location preferences. In: Proceedings of the Twenty-Eighth International Joint Conference on Artificial Intelligence, IJCAI-2019, pp. 557–564. International Joint Conferences on Artificial Intelligence Organization, July 2019. https://dl.acm.org/doi/abs/10.5555/3367032.3367112
16. Santos, D.O., Xavier, E.C.: Dynamic taxi and ridesharing: a framework and heuristics for the optimization problem. In: Proceedings of the Twenty-Third International Joint Conference on Artificial Intelligence, IJCAI 2013, pp. 2885–2891. AAAI Press, August 2013. https://doi.org/10.5555/2540128.2540544

Assessing Communication Strategies in C-ITS Using n-Person Prisoner's Dilemma

António Ribeiro da Costa[1,2]([✉]) [ID], Zafeiris Kokkinogenis[1,2] [ID],
Pedro M. d'Orey[3,4] [ID], and Rosaldo J. F. Rossetti[1,2] [ID]

[1] Artificial Intelligence and Computer Science Lab (LIACC), Porto, Portugal
[2] Faculty of Engineering, University of Porto, Porto, Portugal
{amrpcosta,kokkinogenis,rossetti}@fe.up.pt
[3] CISTER Research Center, Porto, Portugal
[4] DCC, Faculdade de Ciências, Universidade do Porto, Porto, Portugal
ore@isep.ipp.pt

Abstract. In Cooperative Intelligent Transport Systems, road users
and traffic managers share information for coordinating their actions to
improve traffic efficiency allowing the driver to adapt to the current traffic situation. Its effectiveness, however, depends on i) the user's decision-making process, which is the main source of uncertainty in any mobility
system, and on ii) the ability of the infrastructure to communicate timely
and reliably. To cope with such a complex scenario, this paper proposes
a game theory perspective based on the n-Person Prisoner's Dilemma
as a metaphor to represent the uncertainty of cooperation underlined by
communication infrastructures in traveller information systems. Results
highlight a close relationship between the emergence of cooperation and
the network performance, as well as the impact of the communication
failure on the loss of cooperation sustainment, which was not recovered
after the system was re-established.

Keywords: Game theory · n-Person Prisoner's Dilemma · Advanced
traveller information system · Cooperative intelligent transport
systems · Agent-based simulation

1 Introduction

A transport network is the backbone of urban activities, designed to accommodate the circulation of people and goods in metropolitan areas. The dynamics of
cities and their consequences on traffic flows imply a continuous updating and
readjustment of the system. This must obtain and provide the most appropriate
information to the exact users in a timely manner, at the appropriate place and
to the intended recipient, in order to enable informed decision-making and to
influence users towards an optimal system condition.

G. Marreiros et al. (Eds.): EPIA 2022, LNAI 13566, pp. 322–335, 2022.
https://doi.org/10.1007/978-3-031-16474-3_27

However, uncertainty is inherent to the road traffic domain, populated by boundedly rational agents in a dynamic environment. To cope with such a complex scenario, we propose a game theory perspective based on the n-Person Prisoner's Dilemma as a metaphor to represent the uncertainty of cooperation underlined by communication infrastructures in traveller information systems. The traveller information system is thus one of the participants together with N-1 vehicles in a two-route network setting. This work contributes with a study of information percolation strategies, with both flawless and malfunctioning transmission situations, allowing us to shed light upon the effects of information on the coordination mechanisms. It takes into account the topology of the road network, the characteristics of communication networks, and the composition of transport demand. The proposed approach is leveraged on the assumption that the effectiveness of information is highly dependent on the user's decision-making process, which is the main source of uncertainty in any mobility system. It also depends on the ability of the infrastructure to communicate timely and reliably, which is not always guaranteed. Considering cooperation will perform optimally when no uncertainties are present in the system, i.e. there are no communication failures, the information is clear, the sender is trustworthy and the receiver adopts the information unconditionally, such an ideal scenario becomes rather an utopia.

The remainder of the paper is organized as follows. The next Section reviews the relevant literature. Section 3 presents the formalization in the context of Game Theory, and describes the experimental framework. Section 4 summarizes the results of these experiments. Finally, the main results and future directions are discussed in Sect. 5.

2 Literature Review

Increasing road capacity is not a viable solution for reducing congestion, as the Braess's Paradox has shown (cf. [2]), hence the importance of rational and efficient management of existing resources. Selfish, rational behaviour leads to suboptimal outcomes. The Nash Equilibrium in the Prisoner's Dilemma, obtained with a mutual defection strategy is not socially efficient. However, it is possible for the system to reach an optimum, given the concept of partial cooperation, in which some players are induced to behave cooperatively, while the rest opt for the rational action of defection [10,11]. This is also empirically verified in a route choice experiment [7], with an alternating cooperation emerging between players, previously informed that by coordinating their actions they would be able to achieve maximum time savings.

In the original formulation of the Prisoner's Dilemma, with two participants in a binary choice of different cost and congestion-sensitive routes, equilibrium occurs when both players choose the lowest cost route. However, the social optimum only exists when one player is on the lowest cost route and the other on the complementary route, something hardly achievable by two rational players in a

one-shot game. With repetition, in turn, if players learn to cooperate by alternating between faster and slower routes and share time-saving equally among themselves, partial cooperation can become a game equilibrium [11].

Successive interactions of the same commuter community, by way of social encounter, can define a repeated game [7], which, by promoting cooperation to alternately use better and worse routes, can make each driver's travel costs lower, on average, than in User Equilibrium [8]. With a certain degree of altruism and a sufficient number of route alternations between drivers, there is a self-organizing formation of a fair equilibrium capable of maintaining the network in an optimal state [13].

The benefits of providing rational travellers with journey time information would depend on their knowledge and ability to predict times based on external factors [5], enabling them to make optimal choices, thereby contributing to reducing traffic congestion and improving the level of service provided by road infrastructure. In reality, many travellers rely on information to make their choices, both for its cognitive and affective value, whether in selecting routes or modes of transport [1]. However, increasing the informational burden at the individual level leads to a state of User Equilibrium [9], as rational agents with full knowledge will compete for the least cost paths on the road network. On the other hand, because of the rational traits and cognitive limitations associated with human behaviour, not all drivers would comply with the recommendations [14], particularly when achieving a sub-optimal result [4].

The advent of ATIS has made it easier to provide current or even predictive information on traffic flow to road users (e.g. [18]). If widely accepted by road users, ATIS can contribute to the road network converging towards the System Optimum rather than User Equilibrium by providing the most optimal route for the system [10]. The study of the effects of providing traffic recommendations on driver behaviour, in particular their impact on implicit cooperation in self-interested agents, has demonstrated that optimized route recommendations and extrinsic incentives in a simple two-route network led to more efficient emergence of cooperation [9].

When all agents follow the ATIS recommendations, coordinating actions will allow System Optimum to be achieved by changing suggestions to ensure that all drivers receive the best and worst routes with approximately the same frequency. They will thus be able to learn to cooperate without incentives, although these are useful when cooperation between agents requires a change in behaviour against natural propensities [11]. Accepting the recommendations can be implemented in form of smart contracts, registered by a management blockchain-based infrastructure, and confer reward-based incentives, such as tradable credits to be exchanged for services offered by local administrations [16]. Nonetheless, drivers may mistrust strategic routing heavily relying on incentives [12].

Dissemination of information by the infrastructure to allow drivers to make informed decisions is essential for the performance of the system. It is therefore important to optimize the frequency of message delivery and the efficiency of communication between roadside and on-board units, also articulating its

location with key decision points in the network, but based on a strategy that simultaneously privileges the maximization of coverage and the minimization of transmission failures [3].

In this work, we explore the formalization of the n-Person Prisoner's Dilemma framework to assess the degree of cooperation between driving agents and an ATIS agent, when the latter acts as information provider to the former. To the best of our knowledge, previous works do not consider ATIS as participant in the game.

3   Methodological Approach

The decision-making model is implemented based on the n-Person Prisoner's Dilemma and the payoff matrix was grounded in the social dilemma of the "tragedy of the commons". The participants in the game are the driving agents constituting the population and an information service (ATIS agent), in the form of a road side unit (RSU), which provides a route recommendation to lead the system to an optimal state. Both driving agents population and ATIS agent follow the Multi-Agent System (MAS) paradigm. With a game played between the information system and the driving agents, the two possible actions of *Cooperation* or *Desertion* correspond, respectively, to the options of *Accepting* or *Rejecting* the suggestion provided by the ATIS agent.

3.1 n-Person Prisoner's Dilemma

In the n-Person Prisoner's Dilemma game each of n players has a choice between two actions: to cooperate with the others for the "common good"; or to defect, pursuing their own short-term selfish interests. The participants receive a reward or punishment (the *payoff*) that depends simultaneously on their choice and that of all the others. This paradox of decision-making illustrates that the rational collective acting in self-interest is the opposite of the socially optimum.

For the purpose of this work, the dilemma is formulated as a normal-form game, in which driving agents make a binary decision to *accept* or *reject* the suggestion of the ATIS agent, and the payoff function is based on the socially beneficial outcomes that result from choosing a higher cost route, thus contributing to reduce the total cost to the system.

Within the framework of non-cooperative game theory, the following definitions apply:

Definition 1. *A finite normal-form game is a tuple $\mathcal{G} = \langle \mathcal{I}, \mathcal{A}, (u_i)_{i \in \mathcal{I}} \rangle$, where:*

- $\mathcal{I} = \{1, 2, \ldots, n\}$ *is a finite set of n players, with $n \in \mathbb{N} : n \geq 2$;*
- $\mathcal{A} = A_1 \times \cdots \times A_n$, *where A_i is a non-empty finite set of actions available to player $i \in \mathcal{I}$, whereby $a = (a_1, \ldots, a_n) \in \mathcal{A}$ is an action profile;*
- $u = (u_1, \ldots, u_n)$, *where $u_i : \mathcal{A} \to \mathbb{R}$, is a real-valued payoff function for player $i \in \mathcal{I}$.*

Definition 2. *Let A_i be set of actions available to player i, let $a_j, a'_j \in A_i$ be two actions of player i, and let A_{-i} be the set of all action profiles of the remaining players. Then, a_j strictly dominates a'_j if $\forall a_{-j} \in A_{-i} : u_i(a_j, a_{-j}) > u_i(a'_j, a_{-j})$. An action is strictly dominant if it (strictly) dominates any other action.*

Definition 3. *A player i's best response to the action profile $a_{-j} = (a_1, \ldots, a_{j-1}, a_{j+1}, \ldots, a_n)$ is the action $a^*_j \in A_i : u_i(a^*_j, a_{-j}) \geq u_i(a_j, a_{-j}), \forall a_j \in A_i$. An action profile a is a Nash equilibrium if, for each player i, a_j is a best response to a_{-j}. An outcome of a game is any action profile $a \in \mathcal{A}$.*

Definition 4. *Let $\mathcal{G}$ and $a, a' \in \mathcal{A}$. Then an action profile a Pareto dominates action profile a' if $u_i(a) \geq u_i(a'), \forall i \in \mathcal{I}$, and $\exists i' \in \mathcal{I} : u_{i'}(a) > u_{i'}(a')$*

3.2 Assumptions

Assumption 1. *The participants in the game—the driving agents, in this case—are boundedly rational, meaning that individual players don't have perfect information about the others and try to maximize their expected value.*

Assumption 2. *The ATIS is a participant in the game, playing against all driving agents with a fixed strategy to cooperate (C). The payoff depends on the action of the other players accepting or rejecting its recommendation.*

Assumption 3. *The common resources are the routes of the road network with limited capacity. Each traveller may choose either to travel in a direct route or use an alternative route, thereby not contributing to congestion.*

Assumption 4. *The communication channel for ATIS agents to communicate with the driving agents is reliable and non-lossy.*

Assumption 5. *Driving agents have only knowledge about their experienced travel times and reward.*

Assumption 6. *Each driving agent has a predefined preferred route, which corresponds to the route with the lowest cost.*

Assumption 7. *Each traveller has two possible actions; D (defect) by rejecting the suggestion provided by the infrastructure or C (cooperate) by accepting the recommendation and taking the proposed route.*

Assumption 8. *All players receive a benefit $b \in \mathbb{R}_{>0}$ for their decision to accept the ATIS agent's recommendation and contribute to the social optimum, otherwise pay a cost $c \in \mathbb{R}_{<0}$.*

Considering the payoff-matrix based on the formalization of the n-Person Prisoner's Dilemma (cf. Table 1) for modelling a collective behaviour when users have to compete for the road infrastructure with incomplete information, the payoff function of player i is given by:

Table 1. Payoff matrix structure, where **C** and **D** stand for **C**ooperate and **D**efect respectively. Payoffs are ordered $Benefit > (Benefit + Cost) > 0 > Cost$, assuming a $Cost$ represented by a negative number. Relating to the original matrix of the Prisoner's Dilemma, *Temptation* means getting the *Benefit* without *Cost*, *Reward* is gaining the *Benefit with a Cost*, *Punishment* is not obtaining either (0), and *Sucker's payoff* is paying a *Cost* without realizing the *Benefit*.

	More than n choose **C**	n or fewer choose **C**
C	$Benefit + Cost$	$Cost$
D	$Benefit$	0

$$f_i(a_i, h), a_i = C_i \text{ or } D_i, \ h = \{0, 1, ..., n-1\} \subset \mathbb{N}$$

where a_i is player i's action and h is the number of other cooperators.

In the payoff functions it is assumed:

Assumption 9.

1. The payoff difference $\alpha = f(D, h) - f(C, h)$ is positive and constant for all values of $h = \{0, 1, ..., n-1\} \subset \mathbb{N}$;
2. $f(C, h)$ is monotonically increasing in $h = \{0, 1, ..., n-1\} \subset \mathbb{N}$;
3. $f(C, n-1) > f(D, 0)$.

By the first condition of the above Assumption 9, any player i will get a better payoff by selecting defection (D) than by choosing cooperation (C), regardless of what all other players select, i.e. the dominant action for each player is defection. The payoff difference α is interpreted as the player's incentive to defect. The second condition means that the payoff of a cooperator becomes increasingly larger as more players select cooperation. By the third condition, if all players choose the dominant defection one will have a non-cooperative equilibrium that will be Pareto-inferior to the outcome if they select the cooperative dominated actions.

Considering the payoffs hold the condition:

$$Benefit > (Benefit + Cost) > 0 > Cost$$

for n players, with $n \in \mathbb{N} : n \geq 2$, in view of the general case of a compound symmetric game [6], the following payoff functions result:

$$f(C, h) = \frac{h \cdot (Benefit + Cost) + (n - h) \cdot Cost}{n}$$
$$f(D, h) = \frac{h \cdot Benefit + (n - h) \cdot 0}{n} \tag{1}$$

From Assumption 9:

$$\exists! k^* (2 \leq k^* \leq n) \in \mathbb{N} : f(C, k^* - 2) < f(D, 0) \leq f(C, k^* - 1) \tag{2}$$

where the unique integer k^* is the minimum number of cooperators that guarantees that the cooperative payoff can be greater than or equal to the non-cooperative payoff in case no one selects cooperation, i.e., that the overall utility of cooperators is greater than the utility of those who reject suggestion, hence the social dilemma in this context of traffic recommendation and route selection.

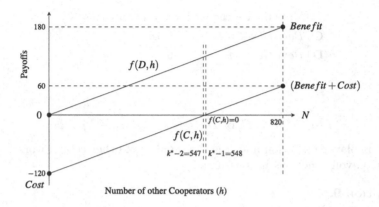

Fig. 1. Graph of the payoff functions for defectors (D) and cooperators (C).

One of the best-known and studied models in game theory, the Prisoner's Dilemma can transition from 2-person to n-person by replacing the two-dimensional matrix by payoff functions [6] (cf. Eq. 1), which can be plotted on the graph in the Fig. 1, along with k^* obtained from Eq. 2.

Parameter Setting. The payoffs chosen were based on the cost of the routes from their travel times in free flow, considering a $Cost = -120$ and a $Benefit = 180$. Given the above formalization and relating it to the outcomes of the original Prisoner's Dilemma matrix, *Punishment* is 0, i.e. not get the benefit nor bear the cost. *Sucker's payoff* is the cost of taking the alternative route, hence the negative value -120. *Temptation*, getting the benefit without bearing the cost (180), is significant for the slope of the payoff functions and, consequently, for the cooperation rates. *Reward*, getting the benefit with a cost, has a value of 60. It results, then, $k^* = 549$ for 820 driving agents plus the ATIS agent, which always cooperates, its payoff being a reflex of the driving agents' cooperation.

3.3 Recommendation Algorithm

The algorithm employed to build the suggestion calculates, for each route, the product of the normalization of occupancies and the average travel time of the last n trips, and reinforces its weight according to the cooperation rate as measured by the RSU (see. Algorithm 1). The weights calculated are then used by the RSU to compose the route recommendations, disseminated in order to distribute the vehicles among routes and lead the system to an optimal state.

Algorithm 1: Calculation of the weight of the routes for recommendation build and dissemination by the RSU.

Input: R – Set of routes, N – Number of vehicles plus ATIS, ρ_r – Occupancy of route r,
$\overline{\Delta t_r}$ – Average of last n travel times for route r, h – Number of other cooperators,
Output: w_r – Route weight

1 **forall** $r \in R$ **do**

2 $\quad w_r = \dfrac{\dfrac{\rho_r}{\sum_{e=1}^{R} \rho e} \cdot \dfrac{\overline{\Delta t_r}}{\sum_{e=1}^{R} \overline{\Delta t_e}}}{\dfrac{h}{N}}$

3 **end**

3.4 Agent Behaviour

As driving agents make several passes through the network, and to observe social and economic behaviour, they were modelled as learning agents, whose probability of electing a particular action changes by an amount proportional to the reward or punishment they received from the environment. If the action is followed by a satisfying state, then the agent's propensity to choose that particular action is reinforced. The Modified Roth-Erev Reinforcement Learning algorithm [17] was implemented (see Algorithm 2). Driving agents choose an action from the set of actions A, which, by Assumption 7, are *Cooperate*, accepting the recommendation provided by the infrastructure, or *Defect*, rejecting that suggestion.

The sensitivity tests with the parameters *Recency* (forgetting) and *Experimentation* of Roth-Erev algorithm evidenced its impact during the initial period on the promptness with which cooperation emerges and the plateau around the analytically calculated value of k^* was established. Therefore, since it was studied the variation of cooperation in case of a system failure, the values $\phi = 0.5$ and $\epsilon = 0.5$ were chosen, for which the plateau was reached more quickly.

Algorithm 2: Modified Roth-Erev Learning Algorithm

Require: $\epsilon \in (0, 1)$ – Exploration rate, $\phi \in (0, 1)$ – Recency (forgetting), A – Set of actions
Input: a_j – Current action choice, $q_{ij}(t)$ – Propensity for action a_j of player i at time t, a_l
$\quad$ – Last action chosen, $P_l(t)$ – Payoff for action a_l at time t, M – Number of actions,
$\quad q_{ij}(0)$ – Initial propensity, ϵ – Experimentation, ϕ – Recency

1 $t \leftarrow 0$

2 initialize $q_{ij}(0) \leftarrow 1$, for all $j \in A$

3 **repeat**

4 $\quad t \leftarrow t + 1$

$\quad$ // calculate the probability that player i chooses action l at time t

5 $\quad \left\{ p_{il}(t) = \dfrac{q_{il}(t)}{\sum_{j=1}^{M} q_{ij}(t)} \right\}_{l \in A}$

6 $\quad$ choose action $a_l \leftarrow l \in A$ randomly, using the probabilities $p_{il}(t)$

7 $\quad$ collect payoff $P_l(t)$

$\quad$ // update the propensity of action l for player i at time $t + 1$

8 $\quad q_{il}(t + 1) \leftarrow (1 - \phi)q_{il} + P_l(t)(1 - \epsilon)$

$\quad$ // update the propensity of all actions j different from the last chosen action l, for player i, at time $t + 1$

9 $\quad$ **forall** $j \neq l$ **do**

10 $\quad\quad |\quad q_{ij}(t + 1) \leftarrow (1 - \phi)q_{ij} + q_{ij}(t)\dfrac{\epsilon}{M-1}$

11 $\quad$ **end**

12 **until** *termination*;

---

4   Results and Analysis

4.1   Simulation Setup

This is an empirical work, based on simulation methods for the implementation and on quantitative methods for the analysis of the results. A microscopic simulation was chosen, using SUMO for traffic modelling [15], externally controlled by modules written in Python, through the TraCI traffic control interface, allowing access to the ongoing traffic simulation, obtain values of the simulated objects and manipulate their behaviour in simulation time. Moreover, this program had also implemented the decision models of driving agents and road infrastructure, as well as the C-ITS service.

Scenario Design. Following a principle of simplification, the designed scenario consists of a binary network (see Fig. 2), with two routes of different cost in free-flow, the one with lower cost being the preferred one for the driving agents. The network is coupled with a 300 m feedback loop and buffer zone, to reintroduce the simulated vehicles and be able to maintain a network overload. The two routes between the origin-destination pair are: *i*) the *direct route* (lower cost) with 6000 m, and *ii*) the *alternative route* (higher cost) with 9000 m. The RSU sector and feedback edge are two-lane roads, while the direct and alternative roads are single-lane. The default maximum speed on the network is 25 m s^{-1} (90 km h^{-1}).

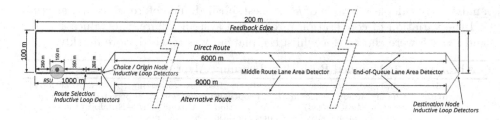

Fig. 2. Network diagram of the scenario, with the two monitored routes

Before the choice node, marked as origin for timing, there is a 1000 m section on which the RSU is located, with a coverage of 150 m, whose zone starts at 250 m of this sector. At 750 m there is an inductive loop detector to carry out route selection, as already chosen by the driving agent. On the destination node side, there are 1000 m lane areas for monitoring traffic density, in the middle of the route and for end-of-queue assessment, as well as inductive loop detectors to record intermediate travel times (in the middle of the route) and time to destination (at the destination node).

Artificial Population. To obtain a heterogeneous simulated population, four different classes of vehicles were inserted in the scenario, capable of travelling at full network speed, as shown in the Table 2, with their respective probabilities. The ceiling on the number of driving agents to be used in the simulation aimed to place the network in a state of congestion on the main (*direct*) route, with traffic moving at a pedestrian-like speed. Thus, the theoretical value were determined analytically considering the passenger class, and then verified in a sensitivity analysis by gradually increasing the number of driving agents, diverting all traffic to the *direct* route, until the average speed of the system dropped to $1.50\,\mathrm{m\,s^{-1}}$ $(5.40\,\mathrm{km\,h^{-1}})$. After the sensitivity analysis, and also taking into account the mitigation of parasitic noise on the network, a ceiling of 820 driving agents was chosen.

Table 2. Different vehicle types used in the simulation, with their respective characteristics and probabilities.

vClass (SVC)	Length width height (m)	a_{max} accel $(\mathrm{m\,s^{-2}})$	b decel $(\mathrm{m\,s^{-2}})$	b_e emergency decel $(\mathrm{m\,s^{-2}})$	v_{max} maxSpeed $(\mathrm{km\,h^{-1}})$	Speed deviation	Probability
Passenger	4.3 1.8 1.5	2.9	7.5	9.0	180	0.1	0.70
Motorcycle	2.2 0.9 1.5	6.0	10.0	10.0	200	0.1	0.10
Truck	7.1 2.4 2.4	1.3	4.0	7.0	130	0.1	0.15
Bus	12.0 2.5 3.0	1.2	4.0	7.0	85	0.1	0.05

Simulation Procedures. The simulation is launched with a warm-up period, for insertion of all driving agents in the network uniformly, after which they make a rolling start and run laps (events) during a simulated period of 24 h, with 0.1 s steps, to allow microscopic simulations in fractions of a second, required by both the RSU dissemination mechanisms and the vehicle insertion manoeuvres at lane changes. Experiments started by determining a baseline, with constant dissemination, to observe the emergence of cooperation and its impact on the network. Then it was proceeded to a progressive degradation of the RSU dissemination, gradually increasing its transmission interval, reaching each time fewer driving agents. Finally, an abrupt increase of this interval was tested, restoring the initial, shorter interval, after a certain period, to analyse the behaviour of the driving agents when faced with a failure and the restoration of the system.

4.2   Scenario Analysis

Baseline Scenario. In the baseline experiment, the emergence of cooperation and the establishment of the plateau occurred after about 5 h (Fig. 3a). The average vehicle speed on the network followed the increase in the number of

cooperators, reaching a plateau around $10.5 \, \text{ms}^{-1}$ ($37.8 \, \text{km h}^{-1}$). Simultaneously, the traffic flow of both routes settled at about 1750 veh/h (Fig. 3b), in line with the travel times on each route, both at about 700 s, a value corroborated by the average speeds registered on each route.

Progressive Degradation Scenario. To analyse the effect of a degradation of the information service, simulations were conducted in which the dissemination time interval doubled every 4 h, in the sequence $\{5, 10, 20, 40, 80, 160\}$ s, during which an increasing number of driving agents stopped receiving suggestions and continued on their default preferred route.

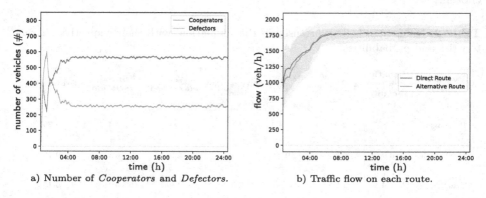

a) Number of *Cooperators* and *Defectors*.   b) Traffic flow on each route.

Fig. 3. Evolution of the number of *Cooperators* and *Defectors,* and traffic flow on each route, in vehicles per hour (veh/h), 4 h Simple Moving Average, over a 24 h period, in which the RSU's dissemination time interval remained constant at 5 s.

During the first 8 h, the evolution was similar to the baseline, both in terms of cooperation emergence (Fig. 4a vs. Fig. 3a) and traffic flow (Fig. 4b vs. Fig. 3b), i.e. up to 10 s interval the ATIS agent was able to deliver recommendation to all driving agents. However, starting at 8 h of simulation, with 20 s interval, there was witnessed a decreasing trend in the traffic flow (Fig. 4b), which followed a drop in the number of driving agents in game (both cooperators and defectors decreased) (Fig. 4a). The traffic flow on both routes, and consequently the mean speed on the network, had a steeper decrease after 12 h, when the interval was increased to 40 s, that of the alternative route tending to zero, as most of the traffic started to converge to the direct route. The cooperation, which had also been decreasing, suffered a strong decline and there was an inversion of trends with an increase in the number of defectors, although the sum diminished, since fewer driving agents were left in game.

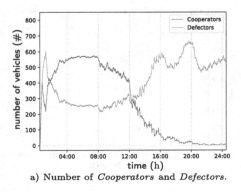
a) Number of *Cooperators* and *Defectors*.

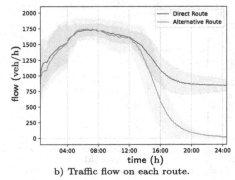
b) Traffic flow on each route.

Fig. 4. Evolution of the number of *Cooperators* and *Defectors,* and traffic flow on each route, in vehicles per hour (veh/h), 4 h Simple Moving Average, over a 24 h period, in which the RSU's dissemination time interval doubled every 4 h, in the sequence $\{5, 10, 20, 40, 80, 160\}$ s (dashed vertical lines).

In subsequent interactions with the ATIS agent, the number of cooperators continued to decrease, tending towards zero, while that of defectors rose, with only part of the population, there being, however, two peaks, which can be explained with the reduction in speed due to the congestion that was forming as more driving agents converged on the *direct* route. In fact, in simulations carried out with a smaller population, which did not generate congestion, after the inversion, the number of defectors reached a peak and then gradually descended in steps.

From the observations, as the recommendations from the ATIS agent became more sparse, the number of cooperators decreased. An analysis of the driving agents' individual history revealed that they began to refuse the few suggestions they were receiving, even those who had been cooperative in the early hours.

Sudden Degradation Scenario. Finally, a sudden degradation of the system was tested, at 8 h of simulation, with the established cooperation plateau, changing the dissemination intervals from 5 s to 160 s during a period of 8 h. The driving agents made successive trips without receiving any suggestion, following the predefined route, and, as expected, there was a significant decrease in the number of participants in the game (Fig. 5a). Similarly to what had happened with progressive degradation, the cooperation status was reversed, with the number of cooperators decreasing, tending to zero. Meanwhile, the number of defectors began a steeper rise, due to the congestion that had commenced to form, keeping the vehicles very slow in the RSU coverage area and, therefore, the number of those who were receiving suggestions was increasing, even with the long transmission interval, also recovering the amount of participants in the game. However, the majority started to reject the suggestion, a behavioural trend confirmed after the 5 s dissemination interval was re-established, at 16 h of simulation, when they were again receiving recommendations at each passage and the number of participants in game grew to the population size.

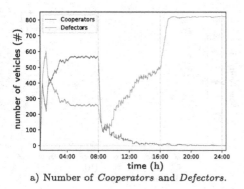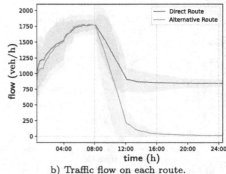

a) Number of *Cooperators* and *Defectors*.   b) Traffic flow on each route.

Fig. 5. Evolution of the number of *Cooperators* and *Defectors,* and traffic flow on each route, in vehicles per hour (veh/h), 4 h Simple Moving Average, over a 24 h period, changing the RSU's dissemination time interval, increased to 160 s at 8 h, and re-established to 5 s at 16 h (dashed vertical lines).

5   Conclusions

In this work, we simulated a binary road network, with routes of different cost, supported by an ATIS that makes en-route recommendations on the best path based on Game Theory, with a formalization of the n-Person Prisoner's Dilemma, in which the ATIS is also a participant of the game along with the driving agents.

With a dynamic network, susceptible to congestion formation in both routes, it was possible to observe the correlation between the cooperation of the driving agents towards ATIS agent and the system performance, namely in the network average speed as well as in the traffic flows in both routes. By causing a degradation of that information service there was a concomitant degradation of the system performance with the formation of congestion in the main route, accompanied also by a loss of cooperation, which tended to zero. Testing full restoration of service after a failure, the trend of declining cooperation continued, even though the number of participants returned to population size, suggesting a loss of credibility of the ATIS.

The simplicity of this road network limits the ability to generalize to more complex networks. Further investigation with more simulations is needed with other traffic patterns and network topologies varying both in number of routes and origin-destination pairs. On the other hand, it is important to account for the trustworthiness of all parties involved, which can be accomplished through modelling a trust factor in ATIS, to understand how cooperation could be restored after a system failure, for instance.

Acknowledgment. This work is a result of project DynamiCITY: Fostering Dynamic Adaptation of Smart Cities to Cope with Crises and Disruptions [reference NORTE-01-0145-FEDER-000073] supported by Norte Portugal Regional Operational Programme (NORTE 2020), under the PORTUGAL 2020 Partnership Agreement, through the European Regional Development Fund (ERDF).

References

1. Ben-Elia, E., Di Pace, R., Bifulco, G.N., Shiftan, Y.: The impact of travel information's accuracy on route-choice. Transp. Res. Part C: Emerg. Technol. **26**, 146–159 (2013)
2. Braess, D.: Über ein paradoxon aus der verkehrsplanung. Unternehmensforschung **12**(1), 258–268 (1968)
3. Costa, A., Rossetti, R.J.F., Kokkinogenis, Z.: Improving route choice: communication issues in moving variable message signs. In: 2020 IEEE International Smart Cities Conference (ISC2), pp. 1–8 (2020)
4. van Essen, M., Thomas, T., van Berkum, E., Chorus, C.: From user equilibrium to system optimum: a literature review on the role of travel information, bounded rationality and non-selfish behaviour at the network and individual levels. Transp. Rev. **36**(4), 527–548 (2016)
5. Ettema, D., Timmermans, H.: Costs of travel time uncertainty and benefits of travel time information: conceptual model and numerical examples. Transp. Res. Part C: Emerg. Technol. **14**(5), 335–350 (2006)
6. Hamburger, H.: N-person Prisoner's Dilemma. J. Math. Sociol. **3**(1), 27–48 (1973)
7. Helbing, D., Schönhof, M., Stark, H.U., Hołyst, J.: How individuals learn to take turns: emergence of alternating cooperation in a congestion game and the Prisoner's Dilemma. Adv. Complex Syst. (ACS) **08**, 87–116 (2005)
8. Klein, I., Ben-Elia, E.: Emergence of cooperation in congested road networks using ICT and future and emerging technologies: a game-based review. Transp. Res. Part C: Emerg. Technol. **72**, 10–28 (2016)
9. Klein, I., Ben-Elia, E.: Emergence of cooperative route-choice: a model and experiment of compliance with system-optimal ATIS. Transport. Res. F: Traffic Psychol. Behav. **59**, 348–364 (2018)
10. Klein, I., Levy, N., Ben-Elia, E.: An agent-based model of a system-optimal ATIS. Proc. Comput. Sci. **109**, 893–898 (2017)
11. Klein, I., Levy, N., Ben-Elia, E.: An agent-based model of the emergence of cooperation and a fair and stable system optimum using ATIS on a simple road network. Transp. Res. Part C: Emerg. Technol. **86**, 183–201 (2018)
12. Kröller, A., Hüffner, F., Kosma, L, Kröller, K., Zeni, M.: Driver expectations toward strategic routing. Transp. Res. Rec. **2675**, 44–53 (2021)
13. Levy, N., Klein, I., Ben-Elia, E.: Emergence of cooperation and a fair system optimum in road networks: a game-theoretic and agent-based modelling approach. Res. Transp. Econ. **68**, 46–55 (2018)
14. Lindsey, R., Daniel, T., Gisches, E., Rapoport, A.: Pre-trip information and route-choice decisions with stochastic travel conditions: theory. Transp. Res. Part B: Methodol. **67**, 187–207 (2014)
15. Lopez, P.A., et al.: Microscopic traffic simulation using SUMO. In: The 21st IEEE International Conference on Intelligent Transportation Systems. IEEE (2018)
16. Martins, S., Costa, A., Kokkinogenis, Z., Rossetti, R.J.F.: Enabling citizen-centric ITS services through blockchain and human incentives. In: Martins, A.L., Ferreira, J.C., Kocian, A. (eds.) INTSYS 2021. Lecture Notes of the Institute for Computer Sciences, Social Informatics and Telecommunications Engineering, pp. 85–94. Springer, Cham (2022). https://doi.org/10.1007/978-3-030-97603-3_7
17. Nicolaisen, J., Petrov, V., Tesfatsion, L.: Market power and efficiency in a computational electricity market with discriminatory double-auction pricing. IEEE Trans. Evol. Comput. **5**(5), 504–523 (2001)
18. Santos, P.M., et al.: PortoLivingLab: an IoT-based sensing platform for smart cities. IEEE Internet Things J. **5**(2), 523–532 (2018)

On Demand Waste Collection for Smart Cities: A Case Study

Saleh A. Alaliyat[1]([✉]), Deepti Mishra[2], Ute A. Schaarschmidt[1], Zhicheng Hu[1], Amirashkan Haghshen[1], and Laura Giarré[1,3]

[1] Department of ICT and Natural Sciences (IIR), NTNU - Norwegian University of Science and Technology, Ålesund, Norway
{alaliyat.a.saleh,ute.a.schaarschmidt}@ntnu.no,
{zhichenh,amirashh}@stud.ntnu.no
[2] Department of Computer Science (IDI), NTNU - Norwegian University of Science and Technology, Gjøvik, Norway
deepti.mishra@ntnu.no
[3] DIEF University of Modena and Reggio Emilia, Modena, Italy
laura.giarre@unimore.it

Abstract. The neat and clean surrounding is the main driving force for any city to be called a smart city. In order to address current societal and business challenges, the objective is to provide a solution to enable collection-on-demand of wastes by connecting waste data and users/customers with the waste management system. In that context, the focus is to improve the waste collection process in terms of collection cost, collection time, and CO2. Within the overall objective, an important goal that needs to be solved is waste collection on demand and the present paper addresses this by tackling the optimization problem related to the routing. Application of the presented solution to a case study with real data collected in the municipality of Ålesund, Norway, is presented. This study also shows a comparison of three popular optimization algorithms for solving vehicle routing problems (VRP) and multiple vehicle routing problems (MVRP), to identify a suitable algorithm for the case study, introducing a data-driven model. Five constraints with alternative objectives of distance and cost minimization are considered.

Keywords: Smart city · Sustainability · Waste management · Optimization · MVRP

1 Introduction

For a sustainable future, addressing the development goals (SDGs) is crucial [1]. In order to transform society into smart circular communities and cities, SDG 11 - Sustainable Cities and Communities, and SDG 12 - Responsible Consumption and Production, are important. Smart cities need smart waste management and an essential step to achieve it is scheduling and planning the collection route.

Supported by NTNU and project IDUN.

G. Marreiros et al. (Eds.): EPIA 2022, LNAI 13566, pp. 336–348, 2022.
https://doi.org/10.1007/978-3-031-16474-3_28

Additionally, enabling optimized management for the collection of the waste gives a significant contribution to the municipalities' budgets and linked environmental hazards. Different constraints (e.g., noise pollution, safety, privacy, etc.) should be considered in planning the collection route(s) since it leads to a sufficient and sustainable system which reflects the inhabitants' needs.

The traditional urban waste collection is mainly done by collecting the waste from all the bins regardless of the status of bins (full or not) considering fixed predetermined routes and schedules and transporting it to the disposal station. This is a vehicle routing problem (VRP). According to the current practices, it is up to the user to move his/her waste bin to a nearby collection point for the next pick up adding more uncertainties.

The waste collection cost is very high and involves many types of costs such as labor costs, maintenance costs, fuel costs, etc. Therefore, the collection process problem has been addressed enormously recently. The proposed solutions range between optimizing the collection routes and collection of selected bins by considering the filling levels. Different researchers solved this problem as a multi-objective optimization problem by considering priorities other than the shortest distance. Mohsenizadeh et al. [2] added the impact of CO_2 emissions from the transportation activities, while Nemachnow et al. [3] added the best service to the shortest distance. Abdallah et al. [4] developed waste collection routes by selecting the waste bins with predicted high filling levels based on historical data. While Mamun et al. [5] used sensor technology to monitor the waste bins and send the filling level in real-time. In [6] the importance of awareness in sustainability in waste collection process is tackled via Cyber-Physical Systems, a mathematical model is described, which incorporates routing, assignment, and scheduling problems. In [7] multi-objective optimization approach to generate a route by minimizing the route distance and maximizing the amount of waste is presented. In [8] the optimization problem of wet waste collection and transportation in Chinese cities is solved in terms of a chance-constrained low-carbon vehicle routing problem, while in [9] a priority considered green vehicle routing problem model in a waste management system is constructed paying particular concern to the possibility of immediate waste collection services for high-priority waste bins, e.g., those containing hospital or medical waste.

The main objective of this study is two-fold:

- To compare various optimization algorithms for standard Multiple Vehicle Routing problems (MVRP) and identify suitable approaches to get optimal collection routes.
- To develop a data-driven optimized routing and scheduling for waste collection and transportation

We consider several objectives linked to Key Performance Indicators (KPIs) such as time consuming, CO_2 producing and financial costs for sustainable smart cities, thereby addressing SDGs 11 and 12. To this purpose, we define single and multi-objective optimization problems to address routing and scheduling under a variety of constraints, identify suitable algorithms to address the optimization problems, and discuss possible gains from using collection-on-demand. The addressed case study is the one of Ålesund municipality, where real data have

been collected. The cooperation between NTNU (Norwegian University of Science and Technology) and local municipalities (i.e., Ålesund Kommune) ensures that the definition of the optimization problem is realistic and adapted to local regulations. The proposed solution is dynamic and interactive.

This paper is organized as follows: Sect. 2 presents the problem and a comparison between different approaches. Section 3 describes a case study of on demand waste collection in Ålesund municipality. Finally, Sect. 4 provides the conclusion of this study.

2   Problem Formulation

A trade-off between conflicting objectives, e.g., environmental and economic goals, motivates multi-objective optimization problems. Additionally, it is required to incorporate constraints, such as number of available trucks, capacities, cost per working hour, time, and distance. Several scenarios can be taken under consideration for optimal routing and trip scheduling as described later.

2.1   Problem Description

The optimization problem is a VRP or MVRP with the goal of allocating a number of filled bins for each truck (i.e., task allocation problem) and finding optimal routes based on the real-time data (e.g., traffic data). The problem can be solved considering several scenarios, such as:

- One vehicle, one disposal center: this is a simple scenario where we have only one vehicle and one disposal station. The vehicle has to start from a starting point and collect the trash from all the filled bins and end up in the disposal station. This is a simple traveling salesman problem (TSP) which can be solved by heuristic algorithms.
- Many vehicles, one disposal center: this is a traditional MVRP, where the bins must be divided between a number of vehicles in order to optimize the objective function (e.g., minimize the cost, minimize the collection time, minimize the travelling distance, ...).
- Many vehicles, many disposal centers: this is a similar problem to the previous one where we add more disposal stations.
- Static problem vs. dynamic problem: static problem is fixed, and the optimal routes are calculated at the beginning of the time window (e.g., in the beginning of the day, midnight). While in the dynamic problem, the routes are subject to re-calculation during the collection process if there is new data such as traffic data, filling level, priority level, inputs from vehicles (drivers).

The data-driven model depends on available GIS data and real-time data:

- Maps: roads, bins' locations, starting points, disposal stations' locations.
- Bin attributes (location, capacity, priority).
- Road attributes (directions, speed limit, noise, safety, real speed).
- Disposal centers (location, capacity, type).
- Vehicles (location (GPS), capacity, cost of use, emission rate).

The waste collection problem and the data flow are depicted in Fig. 1.

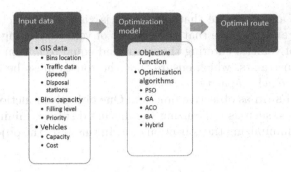

Fig. 1. The optimization problem and the data flow for the waste collection problem

2.2   Problem Representation

The problem can be represented by a graph $G = (V, E)$ with a set of N nodes V and a set of edges E (such that E_{ij} connects node i with node j). Nodes are bins locations, starting points, and disposal stations. Let c the number of vehicles. Hereafter we consider several alternatives for objective functions.

Optimization Problem with Single Objective Function: Following [10], we formulate the optimization problem with a single objective function (e.g., minimizing the total driving distance or cost) and for one depot.

Let d_{ij} the distance or cost for using the path from node i to node j, with depot node $\{0\}$. The binary variable x_{ij} is equal to 1, if the path from node i to node j is part of the solution, and 0 otherwise. $r(S)$ denotes the minimum number of vehicles needed to serve set S of nodes.

$$\min(f) = \sum_{i \in V} \sum_{j \in V} d_{ij} x_{ij}$$

subject to

$$\sum_{i=1}^{N} x_{ij} = 1 \quad \text{for } j = 1, 2, \ldots, N \tag{1}$$

$$\sum_{j=1}^{N} x_{ij} = 1 \quad \text{for } i = 1, 2, \ldots, N \tag{2}$$

$$\sum_{i \in V} x_{i0} = c \tag{3}$$

$$\sum_{j \in V} x_{0j} = c \tag{4}$$

$$\sum_{i \notin S} \sum_{j \notin S} x_{ij} \geq r(S), \ \forall S \subseteq V \tag{5}$$

$$x_{ij} \in \{0, 1\} \quad \forall i, j \in V. \tag{6}$$

Constraints (1) and (2) state that each node is visited by exactly one vehicle. Constraints (3) and (4) state that the number of vehicles leaving the depot {0} is the number of vehicles entering the depot and equal to c. Constraints (5) are the capacity constraints, which ensure that the routes must be connected and not exceed the vehicle capacity.

A weighted sum as objective function: One objective function incorporates several objectives, such as minimizing the driving distance, minimizing the collection time, or minimizing the collection cost. In this case, the objective function can written as,

$$\min(f) = \sum_{i=1}^{n} w_i f_i,$$

where w_i are weights and n is the number of objectives.

Multi-objective Function: In this case, several objective functions are considered simultaneously with the goal of finding Pareto optimal solutions. A Pareto optimal solution cannot be improved in any of the objectives without degrading at least one of the other objectives. The multi-objective optimization problem can be formulated as, $\min(f_1, f_1, ..., f_n)$, where n is the number of objectives.

In the following, we also consider cases of the MVRP with multiple depots as formulated by Kulkarni and Bhave [11, Sect. 4].

2.3 Comparisons of OR-Tools, GA, and DRL for Four Standard MVRP Problems

As depicted in Fig. 1 and discussed in the introduction, a variety of optimization algorithms exist that can be used to address MVRPs such as our waste collection problem. In order to choose an algorithm to be used in the case study, three optimization algorithms are compared in terms of performance when addressing a set of four standard MVRP. We choose three popular algorithms that are relevant to this kind of problems. The first algorithm that is used is based on the OR-tools [12]. This is an open-source library recently developed by Google that can solve combinatorial optimization problems using a Constraint Programming solver with a Local Search implementation on top. It includes a toolbox for solving MVRP, [13]. The CP-SAT solver [14] uses a lazy clause generation solver on top of an SAT solver. OR-Tools is an open source software that suites well for optimization problems in vehicle routing [12]. The second approach is based on Genetic Algorithms (GA) and it is used for solving both constrained and unconstrained optimization problems [15]. GA is a well known meta-heuristic algorithm which can generate high-quality solutions to optimization and search problems. The third approach is based on Deep Reinforcement Learning (DRL) and combines reinforcement learning and deep learning [16]. The DRL concept deals with the problem of learning by trial and error to make decisions on a computational agent. This approach is the most popular among the machine learning techniques for solving VRP [17].

Our experimental setting was conducted on four standard VRP problems that are defined by the number of depots, vehicles, customers and maximum load for each vehicle, see Fig. 2. We consider low numbers of customers, but also

more complex problems with a higher number of customers (20, 50, 100, 120). The problems can be found in the project repository [18]. We address problems with different conditions over three rounds. The minimum cost and minimum calculation time for each solver are given in Fig. 2.

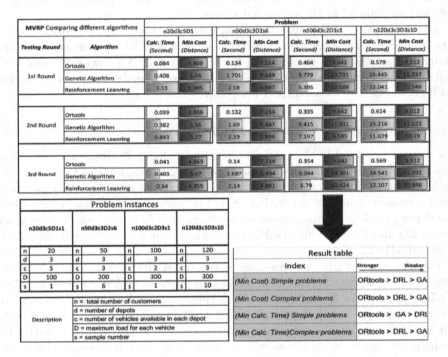

MVRP Comparing different algorithms		Problem							
		n20d3c5D1		n50d3c3D2s6		n100d3c2D3s1		n120d3c3D3s10	
Testing Round	Algorithm	Calc. Time (Second)	Min Cost (Distance)	Calc. Time (Second)	Min Cost (Distance)	Calc. Time (Second)	Min Cost (Distance)	Calc. Time (Second)	Min Cost (Distance)
1st Round	Ortools	0.084	4.869	0.134	7.114	0.464	9.642	0.579	9.512
	Genetic Algorithm	0.408	5.56	1.701	6.689	9.779	10.731	15.445	11.337
	Reinforcement Leanring	1.13	5.385	2.18	6.887	5.395	10.588	12.041	10.546
2nd Round	Ortools	0.039	4.869	0.132	7.114	0.335	9.642	0.614	9.512
	Genetic Algorithm	0.382	5.56	1.69	6.487	9.415	11.031	15.216	11.223
	Reinforcement Leanring	0.843	5.37	2.19	6.896	7.197	9.585	11.639	10.19
3rd Round	Ortools	0.041	4.869	0.14	7.114	0.354	9.642	0.569	9.512
	Genetic Algorithm	0.403	5.67	1.687	6.494	9.044	10.301	14.541	11.291
	Reinforcement Leanring	0.94	4.955	2.14	6.881	5.79	10.424	12.107	10.846

Problem instances							
n20d3c5D1s1		n50d3c3D2s6		n100d3c2D3s1		n120d3c3D3s10	
n	20	n	50	n	100	n	120
d	3	d	3	d	3	d	3
c	5	c	3	c	2	c	3
D	100	D	200	D	300	D	300
s	1	s	6	s	1	s	10

Description	n = total number of customers
	d = number of depots
	c = number of vehicles available in each depot
	D = maximum load for each vehicle
	s = sample number

Result table		
Index	Stronger	Weaker
(Min Cost) Simple problems	ORtools > DRL > GA	
(Min Cost) Complex problems	ORtools > DRL > GA	
(Min Calc. Time) Simple problems	ORtools > GA > DRL	
(Min Calc. Time)Complex problems	ORtools > DRL > GA	

Fig. 2. Comparisons of results with OR tools, GA, DRL algorithms for four standard MVRPs.

In each of the three rounds of the four problem instances considered, ORtools has the shortest calculation time. In eight cases, OR-tools find the best solution, while it finds the second-best solution in one case and the third-best solution in three case. Overall, OR-tools was able to achieve a good decrease of the objective function value with small calculation times, both for problems with 20, 50, 100 or 120 customers in our particular case. Hence, OR-Tools has been chosen as solver for the case study.

3   Case Study: On Demand Waste Collection in Ålesund Municipality

Ålesund in Norway is a small but smart city joined United Nations Cities program, which focuses on the applications of smart innovation and digital technology. We initially consider three trucks (vehicles) and 27 bin stations (locations). The truck drivers utilize Google map and traffic data to choose their routes during the work. The administrative officers plan to find the optimal schedules for

the on demand waste collection, i.e., the set of driving paths with the lowest cost. The cost could be distance, time or the combination with several indicators. The objective function reflects KPI concept by considering minimal distance, time and financial cost. The administrative planners will guide the drivers to collect bins in the bin stations until arriving at the assigned destination (some of 27 bin stations) as planned in the scheduled routes.

The description of the case study is organized as following. We introduce the data and a set of optimization problems in Sect. 3.1. The experimental result for five constraints can be found in Sect. 3.2. In Sect. 3.3, two use cases with multiple constraints are described and addressed. The datasets, source codes, results could be downloaded from here [18].

3.1 A Set of Waste Collection Problems

The dataset provided by Ålesund municipality includes 27 disposal center locations. For the case studies, we assume there is only one kind of trash bin. We track and manually set other problem parameters such as the number of trucks c and numbers of bins at a position (S_d). The parameters are listed in Table 1. The depot positions compose of disposal centers and bin locations. The distance matrix M_d and the time matrix M_t have been obtained using Google map APIs at 2022/03/19 22:52:41.

For the case study, we consider a set of MVRP constraints which we assume to be relevant for the waste collection problem in Ålesund municipality. ① **Multiple starts & ends** means each vehicle might be assigned an individual start depot and stop depot. The start and stop depot lists are saved in S_s and S_e. ② **Capacity Constraints** means each vehicle has limited capacity for the quantity, for example the weight or the volume. In our research this quantity is the maximum bin number for each vehicle by S_c. In this case, we also assign a demand (quantity to be picked up) to each depot position (using S_d). ③ **Pickups and Deliveries** has pairs of pickup and delivery locations in the list S_{pd}. This requires for each pair that the bins in the pickup location should be picked up first and delivered to the delivery location by the same vehicle. It means each item must be picked up before it is delivered. ④ **Penalties and Dropping Visits** introduces a penalty list S_p, it records the extra cost if the depot position is dropped by the vehicle. In this case, the objective function is the total distance together with the sum of all dropped locations' penalties. ⑤ **Time Window Constraints** requires vehicles to arrive at depots within the time period in the list S_{tw}. In this case, vehicles may wait at a location for a waiting time T_w and are assigned a maximum running time T_{max}.

Parameter values for the constraints are presented in Table 2. For all experiments, we let $d = 3$ and $c = 3$. Table 2 also presents our set of optimization problems, which is defined by the set of constraints, combinations of multiple constraints and two baseline experiments. The baseline examples with a single end depot are MVRPs with $S_s = S_e = [3, 3, 3]$ and $S_s = [3, 5, 6]$, $S_e = [3, 3, 3]$, respectively. They are used for comparison. With exception of constraint ⑤ (Time Window Constraints), which requires the time matrix M_t, the constraints only use the distance matrix M_d.

Table 1. List of parameters

	Parameters	Value
M_d	Distance matrix	Each directed edge has a distance
M_t	Time matrix	Each directed edge has a time
d	Number of depots	Each bin position can be a depot
c	Number of vehicles in total	
S_s	Start depots list	Each depot has an index
S_e	End depots list	Each depot has an index
S_d	Demand list	Each location has a demand
S_c	Capacity list	Each vehicle has the maximum quantity that it can hold
S_{pd}	Pairs of pickup and delivery locations	The indexes for the locations
S_p	Penalty list	Each location has a penalty, which is the extra cost if drop this position
S_{tw}	Time window list	Each location has one travel time window with the start and stop time. The unit is minute
T_w	The allow waiting time	(default) 30 mins
T_{max}	The maximum time per vehicle	(default) 30 mins
w_1	Weighted rate for manhour cost, M_t	(default) 10 NOK/min
w_2	Weighted rate for vehicle cost, M_d	(default) 1 NOK/m

Table 2. List of constraints

Constraints No	Parameters with assumed value
Common constraints	$d = 3 \quad c = 3$
One start & end	$S_s = S_e = [3, 3, 3]$
Multiple starts & one end	$S_s = [3, 5, 6] \quad S_e = [3, 3, 3]$
① Multiple starts & ends	$S_s = [3, 5, 6] \quad S_e = [5, 6, 3]$
② Capacity Constraints	$S_d = [1, 3, 2, 0, 4,.., 4] \quad S_c = [25, 25, 30]$
③ Pickups & Deliveries	$S_{pd} = [[19, 2], [10, 11]]$
④ Penalties & Dropping Visits	$S_p = [20, 20, 20, 19,..., 10, 1, 1, 2, 4, 2, 4]$
⑤ Time Window Constraints	$S_{tw} = [[0, 15], [7, 12], [10, 15], ..., [0, 5]]$
⑥ Multiple constraints	① & ②
⑦ Multiple constraints	① & ② & ③
⑧ Multiple constraints	① & ② & ③ & ④
⑨ Multiple constraints	$w1 \times M_t + w2 \times M_d$
⑩ Multiple constraints	⑨ & ⑤
⑪ Multiple constraints	⑨ & ⑤ & ②
⑫ Multiple constraints	⑨ & ⑤ & ② & ③ & ④

3.2   Results for Problems with Simple Constraints

Figure 3(a) presents the results. The total distance in ① **Multiple starts & ends** decreases compared to the baseline experiments because the vehicles could stop more freely. The ② **Capacity Constraints** has higher distance in total, since the vehicles may be full during the work. When requiring ③ **Pickups and Deliveries**, we see an increase of distance due to the given pickup and deliveries sequence. ④ **Penalties and Dropping Visits** allows for dropping some depots and a smaller total distance than in the baseline experiments.

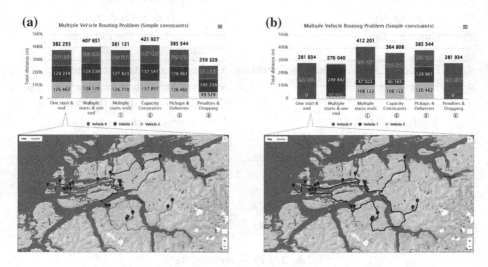

Fig. 3. The experiments result for simple constraints. (a) is with the distance limitation and (b) is without distance limitation

For Fig. 3(a), we set distance limitations for each vehicle to be $(2 \times \max(m_d \in M_d))$, while the vehicles' driving distances are not limited in the experiments whose results are shown in Fig. 3(b). The difference is mostly work load distributed on just one vehicle in the calculation result except the ③ **Pickups and Deliveries**. Therefore, it is critical to set the reasonable distance limitation first to keep the work load balance for each vehicle no matter what's the other constraints.

When our objective is to minimize the time cost instead of the distance cost, time matrix M_t is used to replace the distance matrix M_d as the input of the calculation. In this condition, we marked one start & end (time) in Fig. 4(a) to distinguish the target is to minimize the total time cost, not total distance. This is the baseline compared with ⑤ **Time Window Constraints** result. The total distance is also marked with the total time in different Y axes. The increase of time is much more compared with the increase of distance. Because of the exist of time window, most of the time cost is the waiting time, but not the vehicle running time.

3.3 Results for Problems with Multiple Constraints

In this section, there are two use cases described with the results. The first case is to minimize the distance with a priority list of four constraints, and the second one focuses to find the optimal financial cost with multiple constraints by a weighted sum of distance and time cost.

Case 1. Find an optimal schedule to minimize the distance cost under the multiple constraints with priority

In this case, we assume the officer wish to find the multiple constraints affection on the distance cost for the vehicle schedule. It only relates to the distance matrix M_d and is composed of ⑥ ⑦ ⑧. They are the multiple constraints adding simple constraints ① ② ③ ④ one by one as Table 2.

Figure 4(b) shows sometimes the constraints for the capacity may help to find better solution by chance. Meanwhile, the pickup and deliveries constraints cause much more distance cost compared to the same single constraint ③. And the result of the penalties and dropping in this case is similar with ④ in total value. The multiple constraints for the distribution of vehicles could have more balanced load like compare ④ and ⑧. Sometimes it fails to find the solution if the constraints are more than three kinds and not including penalty constraints.

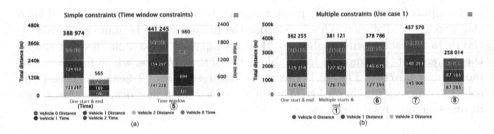

Fig. 4. The experiments result (a) Time window constraint, (b) Multiple constraints use case 1.

Case 2. Explore the lowest financial cost with multiple constraints

In case 2, the officer plans to explore the optimal schedule with lowest financial cost, which happens more often in the real world. The weighted sum (Sect. 2.3) is utilized to compute the financial cost based on the fixed weighted parameters w_1 and w_2 (Table 1). The financial cost is computed by $f = w_1 f_1 + w_2 f_2$, where f_1 is the time objective and f_2 is the distance objective. Therefore, we uses three aspects to reflect the results in Fig. 5(c). They are total financial cost (black), time (orange), distance (blue). The experiment with the constraint ⑨ uses the financial cost as the objective with distance limitation only, and works as a baseline with the rest three multiple constrains configuration. The constraints ⑩ ⑪ ⑫ are the multiple ones adding simple constraints ⑤ ② ③ ④ as Table 2. When ③ is added to ⑪, there is no solution. Therefore, we add ④ together with ③ to to ⑪ as ⑫.

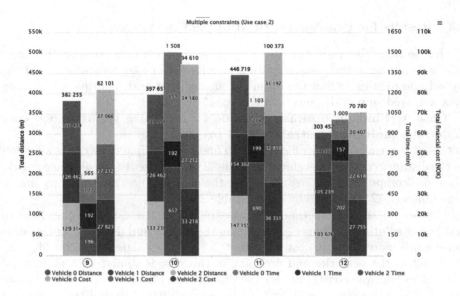

Fig. 5. The experiments result of multiple constraints use case 2.

Compared with ⑨ and ⑩, much more waste of time happens compared with the increase of distance. This is because the financial cost is mainly affected by the distance factor with higher w_1. The ② capacity constraint directly causes the decrease of the time and inevitable rising of the distance, which finally causes more financial cost. The ④ is the main factor to solve ⑫ because there is no solution only adding ③ on ⑪. The results reflect the larger decrease of distance in distance and financial cost.

4   Conclusion, Limitations and Future Work

This study presents a comparison of three optimization algorithms (OR tools, GA algorithm, DRL) for four standard MVR problems and found that OR-tools outperforms others for these specific problems. Further, a data-driven model has been introduced which gives a dynamic interactive solution to the waste collection problem. We propose to use hybrid approaches to improve the performance of the optimization algorithms. The proposed multi-objective cost clarifies how the use of multiple constraints can be addressed and solved in real time. This optimization takes into account KPIs as consumed time, CO2 producing, financial cost in the decision making process. It has been shown how on demand routing is useful for the minimization of fuel consumption and the effectiveness of the data-based management.

We present results for a set of waste collection problems with real data, five constraints, along with the two alternative objectives of distance and cost minimization. Here, we prioritized constraints and included them successively into the problem formulation. We considered single objective functions and a

weighted sum as objective function, representing the financial cost and considering both distance and time. The results also cover all the simple constraints except the multiple starts & ends.

There are several directions for future work building on the presented study. Firstly, parameter values for the constraints have been based on our assumptions (about e.g., capacities or time windows). The optimization algorithm employed for the case study fails to find a solution when constraints are too strict and of many types. The constraints ④ ② ③ ① are negative with higher cost from the strongest to the weakest and ⑤ is strongly positive. ① could be positive sometimes. These classification is made on our experiments by quality and it could be more convincing if we use real world constraints values in the future. It might also be worthy to analyze the result in the quantitative view. A further direction for future work would be to compare results form experiments conducted at several times of the day/week. Ålesund is a small city with minor changes in traffic patterns. Actually, there are more than 30 groups of distance and time matrices collected for the targeted depots list by Google Map API. The comparison of the result shows it brings tiny changes to the result when the temporal changes of raw data are small. In the future, we plan to focus more on the analysis on the traffic data in the large cities. The present solution can be improved by the use of customer satisfaction and real time measurements, such as waste fill-level to dynamically set an adaptive optimal routing. To this purpose data on waste fill-level in a waste bin in real-time, temperature and bin location need to be obtained, i.e. collecting them through IoT devices. Ongoing and future research is addressing these questions.

Acknowledgment. This research has been partially funded by IDUN research project which is funded by the Research Council of Norway Balanse programme, NTNU, and IE Faculty under grant no. 295920.

References

1. UN General Assembly, Transforming our world: the 2030 Agenda for Sustainable Development, A/RES/70/1, pp. 1–35, 21 October 2015. https://www.refworld.org/docid/57b6e3e44.html
2. Mohsenizadeh, M., Tural, M.K., Kentel, E.: Municipal soli d waste management with cost minimization and emission control objectives: a case study of Ankara. Sustain. Cities Soc. **52**, 101807 (2020)
3. Nesmachnow, S., Rossit, D., Toutouh, J.: Comparison of multiobjective evolutionary algorithms for prioritized urban waste collection in Montevideo, Uruguay. Electron. Notes Discrete Math. **69**, 93–100 (2018)
4. Abdallah, M., Adghim, M., Maraqa, M., Aldahab, E.: Simulation and optimization of dynamic waste collection routes, Waste Manag. Res. **37**(8), 793–802. Epub 2019 Mar 8. PMID: 30848721 (2019). https://doi.org/10.1177/0734242X19833152
5. Al Mamun, M.A., Hannan, M.A., Hussain, A., Basri, H.: Theoretical model and implementation of a real time intelligent bin status monitoring system using rule based decision algorithms. Expert Syst. Appl. **48**, 76–88 (2016). https://doi.org/10.1016/j.eswa.2015.11.025. ISSN 0957-4174

6. Bányai, T., Tamás, P., Illés, B., Stankevičiūtė, Ž, Bányai, Á.: Optimization of municipal waste collection routing: impact of industry 40 technologies on environmental awareness and sustainability. Int. J. Environ. Res. Public Health **16**(4), 634 (2019)
7. Ahmad, S., Jamil, F., Iqbal, N., Kim, D.: Optimal route recommendation for waste carrier vehicles for efficient waste collection: a step forward towards sustainable cities. IEEE Access **8**, 77875–77887 (2020)
8. Wu, H., Tao, F., Qiao, Q., Zhang, M.: A chance-constrained vehicle routing problem for wet waste collection and transportation considering carbon emissions. Int. J. Environ. Res. Public Health **17**, 458 (2020). https://doi.org/10.3390/ijerph17020458
9. Wu, H., Tao, F., Yang, B.: Optimization of vehicle routing for waste collection and transportation. Int. J. Environ. Res. Public Health **17**(14), 4963 (2020). https://doi.org/10.3390/ijerph17144963
10. Dantzig, G., Fulkerson, R., Johnson, S.: Solution of a large-scale traveling-salesman problem. J. Oper. Res. Soc. Am. **2**(4), 393–410 (1954). https://doi.org/10.1287/opre.2.4.393
11. Kulkarni, R.V., Bhave, P.R.: Integer programming formulations of vehicle routing problems. Eur. J. Oper. Res. **20**(1), 58–67 (1985)
12. https://developers.google.com/optimization
13. https://developers.google.com/optimization/routing/vrp
14. https://github.com/skatsuta/vrp-solver
15. https://github.com/Lagostra/MDVRP
16. https://github.com/Rintarooo/MDVRP_MHA
17. Czuba, P., Pierzchala, D.: "Machine Learning methods for solving Vehicle Routing Problems. In: Proceedings of the 36th International Business Information Management Association (IBIMA), pp. 4–5, Granada, Spain (2020). ISBN: 978-0-9998551-5-7
18. https://drive.google.com/drive/folders/1PAEEumIzJydlrAXGQBok9eMtxK3PMrek?usp=sharing

AmIA - Ambient Intelligence and Affective Environments

Part 4   Ambient Intelligence
and Affective Environments

LoRaWAN Module for the Measurement of Environmental Parameters and Control of Irrigation Systems for Agricultural and Livestock Facilities

Sergio Márquez-Sánchez[1,2](✉) ⓘ, Jorge Herrera-Santos[1], Sergio Alonso-Rollán[1], Ana M. Pérez Muñoz[2] ⓘ, and Sara Rodríguez[1]

[1] BISITE Research Group, University of Salamanca, Calle Espejo s/n. Edificio Multiusos I+D+i, 37007 Salamanca, Spain
{smarquez,jorgehsmp,sergio.alro,srg}@usal.es
[2] Air Institute, IoT Digital Innovation Hub (Spain), 37188 Salamanca, Spain
am.perez@fiw-consulting.com

Abstract. Recent advances in wireless communication technologies have led to the rapid development of branches of engineering, such as those related to the Internet of Things (IoT) paradigm. IoT interconnects devices with the intention of adding value or reducing costs in production processes. In turn, many productive sectors are benefiting from the advances being made in this field, including the agricultural sector. The IoT for Low-power wide-area network (LPWA) is a perfect fit for sectors whose environments are remote (and therefore have limited access to the power grid) and whose facilities may be located at long distances from each other. This research therefore proposes, the design of a LoRaWAN communications module as part of a modular architecture, compatible with environmental parameter measuring devices and irrigation system controllers. The purpose of this module is to improve the management of agricultural facilities and, therefore, boost the competitiveness of companies in this sector.

Keywords: LPWA · Smart farming · IoT · LoRaWAN

1 Introduction

The agricultural sector is generally a very traditional sector, nevertheless, it is a key sector for the economy. It requires the application of innovative technologies to increase its competitiveness and productivity. Typical processes in this sector, such as irrigation management, are currently carried out with inefficient radio devices—Global System for Mobile Communication (GSM) and proprietary protocols—whose autonomy means that batteries need to be replaced every few months, or with cable-controlled devices that can easily be disconnected from the work of vehicles such as tractors. Among the new long-range, low-power wireless technologies, the LoRaWAN protocol stands out. This new protocol has been very well received by component manufacturers and the community,

G. Marreiros et al. (Eds.): EPIA 2022, LNAI 13566, pp. 351–360, 2022.
https://doi.org/10.1007/978-3-031-16474-3_29

which has led to the recent design and sale of LoRaWAN certified components by semiconductor manufacturers such as Microchip, Murata, etc., enabling and facilitating the development of a multitude of electronic devices using this technology. The great advantage of this technology compared to other similar technologies is its low power consumption (battery life compared to other technologies can be 10 times longer) and that it is long-range (typically 10 km, although communications have been possible for up to 250 km under favorable conditions). In addition, the emergence of public platforms such as The Things Network (which has a wide coverage thanks to a public network of gateways) or Helium, allows for the integration of any type of device developed with this technology, making it possible to easily develop monitoring and control applications for LoRaWAN devices.

2 State of Art

The progressive implementation and success of precision viticulture have given rise to feedback that has led to an increasing number of studies on the subject, with numerous studies relating the effects of climate, irrigation and water stress on the levels of sugars and polyphenols in the fruit, as well as the acidity (pH) of the grapes through the various phenological stages of vegetables and fruits [2, 10, 3, 9, 11].

However, these studies focus on the results in terms of climatology and the water stress, and there are also numerous approaches and advances in irrigation optimization systems in vineyards based on soil studies, Big Data and satellite images [6] or, more recently, images taken by drone flights. However, most studies do not take into account the current problems faced by farmers, which are used to working with different varieties in adjacent plots where water resources and irrigation systems are shared.

Numerous companies in the agricultural field are incorporating weather stations that can measure different soil and environmental parameters to calculate evapotranspiration and make recommendations regarding irrigation [5]. These parameters include ambient temperature, air humidity, rainfall, anemometry (wind direction and direction), solar radiation, leaf wetting (useful in the prediction of secondary infections of fungal diseases that spread from leaf to leaf), soil temperature and humidity, as well as pH and nutrient levels in the soils themselves (NPK sensors for nitrogen, phosphorus and potassium levels). Nowadays, precision agriculture cannot be understood without the Internet of Things (IoT), being applied in multiple scenarios [8, 14] and based on low-cost, energy-efficient transmission techniques (LPWAN or Low Power Wide Area Networks) in rural environments, such as SigFox or LoRa-WAN [1] or even ZigBee.

The application of the Internet of Things is not limited to the filed but can also be extended to the winery through sensors that measure the environmental conditions affecting conservation in warehouses, as well as the electrochemical sensors, measuring the levels of sulphites in barrels [12, 13] in combination with Deep Learning techniques in order to optimize the properties that define the quality of the product in the face of the increasingly demanding consumer. Given their nature, it is common to relate the Internet of Things, Big Data and Data Analytics with computing in the Cloud [7, 15–17]. Big Data is inextricably linked to the Cloud due to factors such as of size, distribution and redundancy, whereas in the Internet of Things, data collection points are usually

located far away from storage and processing systems. The project will integrate all the aforementioned techniques in a distributed computing and storage environment, known as the Cloud Computing paradigm [4].

3   Methodology

The architecture of these devices has been designed in a modular way. In this way, the devices are easily replaceable in the event of failure, reducing repair and maintenance costs, although on the other hand, the design-time increases as the complexity of the device increases. In any case, the savings in maintenance make the additional design cost negligible. The development of this type of modular device makes it possible to improve the features they have, being able to include some type of new sensor in the future or including some type of technology that was not considered at first. All this without having to redesign the entire circuit and architecture. This feature is very important in an area where technology is developing very fast and components become outdated after a few years (Fig. 1).

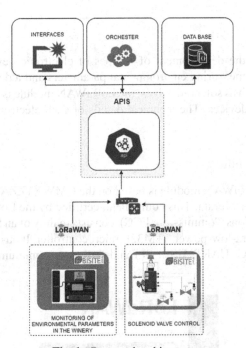

Fig. 1. Proposed architecture

The use of the LoRaWAN wireless communications protocol, being a relatively new protocol, does not have too many developed and certified devices on the market, so competition is low and the differentiating characteristics with respect to other technologies are high.

The main consumption in an IoT device resides in the activation of the device's radio with which to propagate and receive messages. Thanks to the use of LoRaWAN technology, this consumption is drastically reduced, which allows a given battery to have longer autonomy. This is very important for devices deployed in remote or inaccessible locations, as it prolongs battery life and extends battery replacement actions.

By having a microcontroller and a LoRaWAN transceiver under the same component (CMWX1ZZABZ-078), as well as the passive components of the radio frequency circuit, the price is lower than other similar solutions. Moreover, being an FCC-certified component, it is not necessary to submit the device to electromagnetic emission measurement tests (a process that can cost up to €12,000) to obtain the CE marking with which to market the device in the future, thus reducing the costs of market introduction and, consequently, the unit price of the devices, increasing the competitiveness and profitability in the sale of such devices.

Thanks to the use of the LoRaWAN protocol, long communication distances are allowed between the device and the nearest gateway (public or private). This is ideal in applications such as those related to this project, as the devices can be deployed several km away from the nearest facility.

4 Case Study

This work proposes the development of 3 types of electronic devices: a LoRaWAN module, a device for measuring environmental parameters and a device for controlling irrigation systems such as solenoid valves; the LoRaWAN module is compatible with the two aforementioned devices. The technical details of each electronic device are listed below.

4.1 LoRaWAN Module

The design of the LoRaWAN module is based on the CMWX1ZZABZ-078 component from the manufacturer Murata. This component, certified by the LoRa Alliance and the Federal Communications Commission (FCC), consists mainly of an SX1276 LoRaWAN transceiver and an ultra-low-power STM32L microcontroller. It has multiple peripheral interfaces such as I2C, UART, USB, SPI and GPIOs to communicate with any type

Fig. 2. Proposed LoRaWAN module

of component or sensor. It has a power consumption of up to 1.4 uA in sleep mode, which provides long life with the use of a single battery (a typical application such as monitoring environmental parameters, with a small Li-ion 18650 battery can have an autonomy of up to 9.5 years). Thanks to the Real-Time Clock (RTC) functionality, the device will be able to measure times accurately and with low power consumption. A modular architecture is proposed to make this device the backbone of future new devices for the agricultural sector (Fig. 2).

4.2 Environmental Parameter Measuring Device

This device, compatible with the proposed LoRaWAN module, is based on the BME280 component from Bosch. This component, capable of measuring temperature, relative humidity and environmental pressure, has been specifically designed for IoT applications requiring low power consumption and high accuracy. It has a power consumption of up to 1.8 uA in operation and 0.1 uA in sleep mode and communicates with the microcontroller (in our case with the LoRaWAN module) via I2C or SPI interfaces. The device includes a battery, a battery level meter with which the battery level can be monitored and reported when it falls below a certain threshold. Finally, it has a power circuit in charge of maintaining the voltages at the appropriate values for the correct operation of the device (Fig. 3).

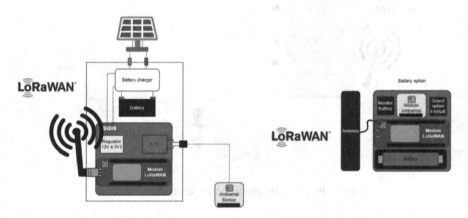

Fig. 3. Proposed Environmental parameter measuring device

The device remains in a "sleeping" state continuously and only wake up on a scheduled basis every "x" minutes/hours, after which it takes the reading of the data from the environmental sensor and the battery monitor and transmits it via LoRaWAN. Once the communication is successful, the device returns to a low power state.

This device is intended to monitor environmental parameters of temperature, humidity and pressure, both indoors and outdoors. The storage and analysis of this type of data is relevant in the agricultural sector, being able to use these parameters as feedback in automated control systems with which to increase productivity and, consequently, the competitiveness of the company in question.

4.3 Irrigation System Controller Device

This device, compatible with the proposed LoRaWAN module, is based on its compatibility with typical irrigation system solenoid valves and, more specifically, with latch-type solenoid valves. These types of solenoid valves stand out for their low power consumption, as they allow for a change of state from "open" to "closed" using a single pulse of a given time, as opposed to the continuous control (which therefore requires higher power consumption) of a typical solenoid valve. In turn, the device will have an analog-to-digital converter circuit to which a pressure sensor can be connected to check that the valve has opened or closed correctly. A power circuit is responsible for maintaining the correct voltage levels and a battery monitor will be used to transmit the battery level of the device (Fig. 4).

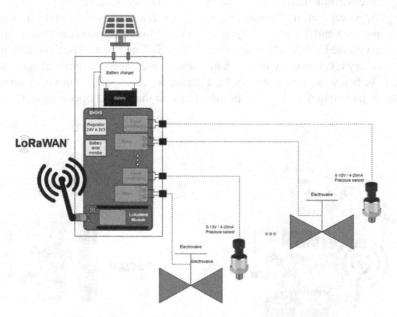

Fig. 4. Proposed Irrigation system controller device

The device shall remain in a dormant state for a programmed period of time, after which it shall wake up and communicate with the irrigation application. If a solenoid valve opening action has been programmed in the application, the solenoid valve shall be operated for the period of time determined by the application. Once this time has elapsed, the solenoid valve shall close. Except for the specific moments of action, the device will remain in a state of low consumption, thus increasing the autonomy of the device.

This device can be used in any irrigation system, as well as to control any type of fluid, for example in animal maintenance tasks, mixing of fluids, control of stopcocks in water circuits in cities or buildings…

5   Results

The development of the electronic devices described above is mainly aimed at improving the competitiveness of sectors such as agriculture and livestock, but also industrial sectors. The technologies that this research has proposed to develop allow to easily automate countless tasks (irrigation, animal handling, heating and air conditioning systems, ventilation, etc.), as well as facilitate the collection of data on important parameters such as environmental parameters, to improve the quality and optimization of processes.

The agricultural sector is a fundamental sector of our country's economy and is subject to strong pressures from countries where labour is cheaper and allows them to sell products at a price with which it is difficult to compete. In today's globalised world of free trade, the solution to this problem lies in the application of innovative technologies that reduce the operating costs and increase the productivity and quality of these sectors. The prototypes of the proposed devices can be marketed to a multitude of companies whose facilities are located in remote places and normally with the problem of being located at long distances from each other. Within this problem, the agricultural sector stands out, a traditional sector that, thanks to the use of this type of technology, can considerably increase its competitiveness and productivity (Fig. 5).

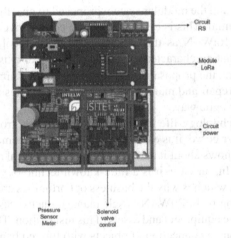

Fig. 5. Developed board designed

The main client will be those agricultural companies, both small farmers and livestock farmers, as well as large distributors and companies, whose production chains have undergone a marked transformation since Spain entered the European Union. This sector is part of the primary sector, which is significant in the rural environment and is made up of the agricultural sector and the livestock and livestock sector, as well as the food industries. It is a vital sector for society as it encompasses those basic products necessary for our sustenance and which, thanks to its technification, allows for higher yields, increased efficiency and productivity. Within the Community agricultural policies, a series of aid packages are established to increase the profitability of the sector, which has a direct beneficial impact on the services offered by our service.

On the other hand, the characteristics of the technology and developments that we work on within the proposal allow us to open sales to other different sectors, such as the manufacturing sector, industrial sector or all those environments in which measurement and communication of parameters in real-time are required, as the proposed architecture makes it possible, for example, to measure and control any irrigation system, control any type of fluid, fluid mixing, control of stopcocks in water circuits in cities or buildings, monitoring of environmental parameters, etc. The functionalities that the development will have to allow its implementation to be considered in all those sectors and industries that carry out technological strategies for the digitization of their processes, monitoring, and control in cities, domestic environments or sectors such as energy, managing to act as enabling technologies for "Industry 4.0", "Smart Grids" or "Smart Cities". The advantage proposed by this work is that, as a modular architecture, its approach allows it to be an effective system for several real use cases. For example, it has been considered for use in the wine industry, where, thanks to the monitoring of vineyards, it is possible to capture all the information about the situation of the plants and predict the quantity and quality of the wines.

6 Conclusions

The devices developed and the modular system proposed to give the project and product great commercial potential. This is evidenced by the competitive advantages provided by the selection of LoRaWAN as the communications protocol, a novel technology with valuable differentiating characteristics concerning other existing technologies on the market. Furthermore, the proposal contemplates a modular architecture and design, which allows for easy repair and maintenance, as well as enables us to carry out future developments in a very agile way.

The LoRaWAN technology life cycle is currently in the growth phase in which, according to the Gartner curve, it is estimated that it could become Mainstream, that is to say, that the sector knows about it and has it as a technological communication alternative for any project. In our case, it is a little-known technology in the market sector that we want to exploit, which is why the business opportunities are very important. The main field of application of LoRaWAN is self-managed networks, where the user can control or monitor all the equipment and assets of his installation. The LoRaWAN infrastructure enables long-range connection of objects with limited bandwidth requirements and low traffic communications, leading to very low power consumption and battery life of a decade or more, using an unlicensed spectrum. To carry out commercialisation, an important task of dissemination and commercial work must be done, since the target market is a very traditional sector, to which we have to make them understand the competitive and productivity advantages that they will obtain by implementing our devices and services in their processes.

In a potential market made up of fundamental sectors for the economy in which there is a large sales potential yet to be exploited, with insufficient technological incursion at present, there is a large gap between the companies specialising in the sector and the needs and demands of potential customers:

The commercialisation of the devices as a product to monitor all kinds of environmental parameters and control actuators. Within the framework of the project, a

LoRaWAN module will be developed, a device for measuring environmental parameters and a device for controlling irrigation systems such as solenoid valves. Thanks to these, the first catalogue of products will be created, aimed at improving the management of agricultural facilities and we will be able to generate easily thanks to the modular design and architecture of the developments. The commercialisation of the devices as an integral support service, in which data collection of the devices, their maintenance over time, as well as the implementation and maintenance of the LoRaWAN communications networks will be carried out. Thanks to this service, the end-user would be able to visualise and analyse the data collected in real-time and, based on this, make productive decisions and feed automated control systems with which to increase productivity and, consequently, the company's competitiveness.

Acknowledgments. This research has been supported by the project "Intelligent and sustainable mobility supported by multi-agent systems and edge computing (InEDGEMobility): Towards Sustainable Intelligent Mobility: Blockchain-based framework for IoT Security", Reference: RTI2018-095390-B-C32, financed by the Ministry of Science and Innovation (MICINN), the State Research Agency (AEI) and the European Regional Development Fund (FEDER).

References

1. Aleixandre, M., Montero, E., Arroyo, T., Cabellos, J.M., Horrillo, M.C.: Quantitative analysis of wine mixtures using an electronic olfactory system. Multi. Digital Publishing Inst. Proc. **1**(4), 450 (2017)
2. Davcev, D., Mitreski, K., Trajkovic, S., Nikolovski, V., Koteli, N.: IoT agriculture system based on LoRaWAN. In: 2018 14th IEEE International Workshop on Factory Communication Systems (WFCS), pp. 1–4. IEEE (2018)
3. Intrigliolo, D.S., Lizama, V., García-Esparza, M.J., Abrisqueta, I., Álvarez, I.: Effects of post-veraison irrigation regime on Cabernet Sauvignon grapevines in Valencia, Spain: Yield and grape composition. Agric. Water Manag. **170**, 110–119 (2016)
4. Delgado Cuzmar, P., et al.: Phenolic composition and sensory characteristics of Cabernet Sauvignon wines: effect of water stress and harvest date. Int. J. Food Sci. Technol. **53**(7), 1726–1735 (2018)
5. De la Prieta, F., Sánchez, A.J., Zato, C., Rodríguez, S., Bajo, J.: .Cloud: unified platform for compilation and execution processes in a cloud. In: Bielza, Concha, et al. (eds.) CAEPIA 2013. LNCS (LNAI), vol. 8109, pp. 219–227. Springer, Heidelberg (2013). https://doi.org/10.1007/978-3-642-40643-0_23
6. González-Briones, A., Castellanos-Garzón, J.A., Martín, Y.M., Prieto, J., Corchado, J.M.: A framework for knowledge discovery from wireless sensor networks in rural environments: a crop irrigation systems case study. Wireless Commun. Mobile Comput. **2018**, 1–14 (2018)
7. Knipper, K.R., et al.: Evapotranspiration estimates derived using thermal-based satellite remote sensing and data fusion for irrigation management in California vineyards. Irrig. Sci. **37**(3), 431–449 (2018). https://doi.org/10.1007/s00271-018-0591-y
8. Lochab, K., Yadav, D.K., Singh, M., Sharmab, A.: Internet of things in cloud environment: services and challenges. Int. J. Database Theory Appl. **10**(5), 23–32 (2017)
9. Bacco, M., et al.: Smart farming: opportunities, challenges and technology enablers. IoT Vertical Topical Summit Agric.-Tuscany (IOT Tuscany) **2018**, 1–6 (2018)
10. Sánchez, S.M.: Integral support predictive platform for industry 4.0. ADCAIJ: Adv. Distrib. Comput. Artif. Intell. J. **9**(4), 71–82 (2020)

11. Merli, M.C., Gatti, M., Galbignani, M., Bernizzoni, F., Magnanini, E., Poni, S.: Water use efficiency in Sangiovese grapes (Vitis vinifera L.) subjected to water stress before veraison: different levels of assessment lead to different conclusions. Funct. Plant Biol. **42**(2), 198–208 (2014)

12. Pérez-Pons, M.E., Parra-Domínguez, J., Chamoso, P., Plaza, M., Alonso, R.: Efficiency, profitability and productivity: technological applications in the agricultural sector. ADCAIJ: Adv. Distributed Comput. Artif. Intell. J. **9**(4) (2020)

13. Ramos, R.M., Brandão, P.F., Gonçalves, L.M., Vyskočil, V., Rodrigues, J.A.: Electrochemical sensing of total sulphites in beer using non-modified screen-printed carbon electrodes. J. Inst. Brew. **123**(1), 45–48 (2017)

14. Jamal, A., Munshi, A., Aljojo, N., Qadah, T., Zainol, A.: Digital information needs for understanding cell divisions in the human body (2020)

15. Gupta, S., Meena, J., Gupta, O.: Neural network based epileptic EEG detection and classification. ADCAIJ: Adv. Distrib. Comput. Artif. Intell. J. **9**(2), 23–32 (2020)

16. Fatima, N.: Enhancing performance of a deep neural network: a comparative analysis of optimization algorithms. ADCAIJ: Adv. Distrib. Comput. Artificial Intell. J. **9**(2), 79–90 (2020)

17. Srivastav, R.K., Agrawal, D., Shrivastava, A.: A survey on vulnerabilities and performance evaluation criteria in blockchain technology. ADCAIJ: Adv. Distrib. Comput. Artif. Intell. J. **9**(2), 91–105 (2020)

Diabetic-Friendly Multi-agent Recommendation System for Restaurants Based on Social Media Sentiment Analysis and Multi-criteria Decision Making

Bruno Teixeira[1]([✉]), Diogo Martinho[1] [ID], Paulo Novais[2] [ID], Juan Corchado[3] [ID], and Goreti Marreiros[1] [ID]

[1] Research Group on Intelligent Engineering and Computing for Advanced Innovation and Development (GECAD), Institute of Engineering, Polytechnic of Porto, Porto, Portugal
{1020504,diepm,mgt}@isep.ipp.pt
[2] ALGORITMI Centre, University of Minho, Guimarães, Portugal
pjon@di.uminho.pt
[3] BISITE Digital Innovation Hub, University of Salamanca, Edificio Multiusos, Salamanca, Spain
corchado@usal.es

Abstract. Lifestyle, poor diet, stress, among other factors, strongly contribute to aggravate people's health problems, such as diabetes and high blood pressure. Some of these problems could be avoided if some of the essential recommendations for the practice of a healthy lifestyle were followed. The paper proposes a solution designed for diabetic people to find restaurants nearby that are more suitable for their health needs. A diabetic-friendly feature that will use a set of criteria, built through a Multi-Agent System (MAS) that using the user preferences initially recorded, will provide the user with three category recommendations that potentially benefit the user lifestyle and health. The solution proposes the use of Case-Based Reasoning algorithm to enable the solution to evolve and improve in each interaction with the user. Sentiment Analysis was also used for identifying the restaurant reviews score, since this is one of the defined criteria for the solution.

Keywords: Recommender system · Diabetic-friendly · Multi-agent system · Sentiment analysis · Multi-criteria decision making · Case-based reasoning · k-Nearest Neighbors

1 Introduction

According with World Health Organization, the number of people with diabetes rose from 108 million in 1980 to 422 million in 2014. Prevalence has increased faster in low- and middle-income countries than in high-income countries. Diabetes is a major cause of blindness, kidney failure, heart attacks, stroke, and lower limb amputation. Between 2000 and 2016, there was a 5% increase in premature mortality from diabetes.

G. Marreiros et al. (Eds.): EPIA 2022, LNAI 13566, pp. 361–373, 2022.
https://doi.org/10.1007/978-3-031-16474-3_30

In 2019, nearly 1.5 million deaths were directly caused by diabetes. Another 2.2 million deaths were attributed to high blood glucose in 2012. A healthy diet, regular physical activity, maintaining a normal body weight, and avoiding tobacco use are ways to prevent or delay the onset of type 2 diabetes. Diabetes can be treated, and its consequences avoided or delayed with diet, physical activity, medication and regular checkups and treatment for complications [1]. Health is one of the global challenges for humanity and computer technological advancements in the latest years, especially with artificial intelligence, gave us the possibility to build solutions more focused on the individual needs of each person, especially if the benefit is health related [2]. Recommender Systems are software tools and techniques providing suggestions for items to be of use to a user [3], and this is the main goal on the proposed solution. The incorporation of user preference information upon multiple criteria to achieve best recommendations, turn this solution into a common Multicriteria decision-making problem. Multicriteria decision-making (MCDM) refers to making decisions in the presence of multiple and usually conflicting criteria. Fuzzy decision-making is used where vague and incomplete data exist for the solution. Fuzzy multicriteria decision-making is one of the most popular problems handled by the researchers in the literature [4]. Multi-Agent Systems (MAS) are already being applied in the development of Recommender Systems and they seem to be a perfect fit to deal also with Multi-Criteria Decision-Making problems. Solutions like [5, 6] and [7] discuss the advantages of integrating multi-agent recommendation system in multicriteria decision making scenarios showing that this approach combined with different algorithms can improve user's satisfaction [6].

Multi-agent systems are made up of multiple agents that exhibit autonomous behavior but at the same time interact with the other agents present in the system using social interaction protocols inspired by the and including at least some of the following features: coordination, cooperation, competition, and negotiation [8]. These agents interact or work together to perform certain tasks or satisfy a set of goals. In our solution we defined that negotiation will be primary, to enable multiple criteria recommendations. The exchange of messages on the JADE platform is carried out using FIPA-ACL messages. JADE provides an asynchronous message mechanism: each agent has a message list (inbox), where this agent decides when to read these posts. At the time desired by the agent, it can read only the first message, or read messages that meet some criteria. This messages exchange between agents will allow negotiation to occur. There is a Feedback agent that will act as a broker for the user and will evaluate each received proposal applying a case-based reasoning algorithm that will provide the system the ability to evolve with time. The solution has one web user interface that allow users to interact with it and is currently in simulation phase.

2 Proposed Solution

The solution proposed is split in three main components as demonstrated in Fig. 1. The user interface is a web-based solution that allow interactions to occur between the user and the recommender system. In the initial survey the user will reply to a sequence of questions, created specifically to gather the initial weights for the pre-defined criteria values, which will work as default settings for the cold start. The second component holds

the negotiation block, in this case, the multi agent system implements an integrative negotiation type, defined by a negotiation where collaboration is the goal along with maximize the resulting recommendations for the user. The dominant strategies in this negotiation type are cooperation, information share and the combined resolution of problems. In current solution the system uses a Feedback agent, which is responsible to analyses each provided proposal, recommendation, by the Multicriteria Decision Making (MCDM) agents. This analysis includes a case-based reasoning algorithm with application of k-Nearest Neighbor to reach the optimal recommendation to be presented to the user. The third component in the solution include a set of agents associated with each criterion defined in the solution, that will be providing their best options to MCDM agent requests.

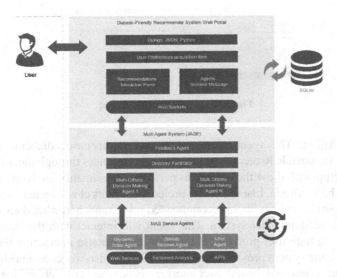

Fig. 1. Proposed solution architecture

2.1 User Interface

The UI component is a web-based portal with a custom designed survey for the initial user preferences setup. It allows the user to interact with the multi-agent system by selecting the preferred recommendation provided. Along with that it is also possible to see a system log message, showing all the messages exchanged by each agent in the system during the negotiation process. In the Fig. 2 it is possible to see the initial prototype version of the user interface with different zones and panels of interaction.

2.2 Multi-agent Negotiation

The multi agent negotiation process is composed by a total of eight agents, with specific characteristics that will be next defined.

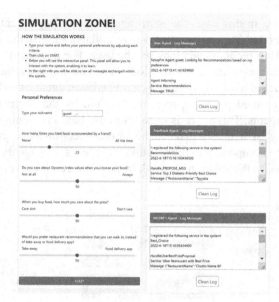

Fig. 2. User interface prototype

User Profile Agent. This agent represents the user, in this case a diabetic patient. The agent will be responsible to record the initial user preferences through the initial survey. This initial setup will allow the system to perform a personality analysis on the user, defining their base criteria, like if the user prefer restaurants closer by his location, if the user values opinion reviews about recommended restaurants and what their confidence level about the recommender system. This agent will interact with the Feedback User agent, improving their user preferences based on the response interaction the user supplied each time the system provide recommendations. It also works as a bridge between the multi-agent system and the web user interface through a set of web service endpoints.

Feedback User Agent. This agent will function as the user representative in the negotiation process. It will be responsible to negotiate which recommendations are the best for a particular user according with the user preferences best interest. During the negotiation process the agent will be capable of accept or refuse suggestions given by the multi-criteria decision-making agents. In this evaluation phase the agent will use a case-based reasoning algorithm to identify the best recommendation for the user based on his case history log. After all this process this agent will provide the User Profile agent with the top 3 best recommendations for the three identified categories and collect the user feedback for the provided recommendations. That information will update the user history log allowing it to evolve over time.

Multi-Criteria Decision-Making (MCDM) Agent. This agent type is the core agent in decision-making process. It will have a specific profile based on the criteria weights, allowing the system to have multiple of these agents each one with different personal objectives, turning the negotiation process more diverse and complex. The MCDM agents will receive requests from the Feedback agent in representation of the user and each of

this MCDM agents will request their preferred service agents for recommendations. Once they receive responses from the service agents, they start negotiating with the Feedback agent. During the negotiation process this agent will use argument-based negotiation providing the capability of explaining each recommendation gave and why it should be considering the best option for the user.

Service Agents. Service agents are responsible to provide MCDM agents the best restaurant option, based on the current user location and the criteria they are specialized in. In this sense we have four service agents, each one representing each criterion in consideration for the proposed solution as mapped in Table 1.

Table 1. Solution criteria for each recommendation category

Recommendation category	Reviews	Glycemic index	Price	Distance
Best Choice		Maximize	Minimize	
Nearby		Maximize		Maximize
Review	Maximize	Maximize		

Those four criteria will have maximization and minimization utility functions and are defined as Reviews (will maximize the score value of restaurants to provide the best resulted one), Glycemic Index (will select restaurants where the foods with lower GI will be preferred for the recommendation), Price (will minimize the cost for the user) and Distance (will optimize the distance and provide recommendations on restaurants that user can walk to, instead of ordering the meal, so in a sense will maximize distance, but in a defined range).

Reviews Agent. This agent is specialized in restaurant reviews. It will receive request from the MCDM agents requesting the best restaurant based on their reviews and in line with the user preferences. The agent has an internal sentiment analysis function that will use the ten closest restaurants and the latest ten reviews for each restaurant to retrieve the best scored one. This result will then be sent to MCDM agents as valid recommendation options.

Glycemic Index Agent. This is the specialized agent for the criteria Glycemic Index. As the other service agents, this one will take in consideration the preferred user foods and present recommendation only if they have meals with their preferred food and if those food are optimal in terms of glycemic index value, providing healthier restaurants for the user.

Uber Price Agent. This agent specialized in the price criterion will provide restaurant recommendation where the price is minimized for the best interest of the user, since this criterion is not related with health it should provide the system indicators of analysis that could influence healthier user decision.

Uber Distance Agent. The purpose of this agent, specialized in the distance criterion is to maximize the distance at which the user is from the recommended restaurant, but in a walkable range. The idea behind is to recommend restaurants the user can walk to, instead of ordering a meal, providing a physical activity to the user that produce health benefits.

2.3   Negotiation Process

As mentioned previously the solution uses an integrative negotiation type, where the system goal is always to provide restaurant recommendations for the user, that could potentially have a health benefit. The following figure below shows briefly the message exchanged in the solution.

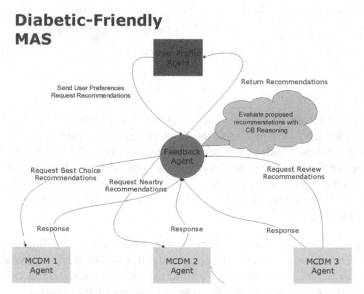

Fig. 3. Diagram with exchanged messages between agents

Accordingly, with Fig. 3 during this message exchange the Feedback agent will receive multiple responses from the MCDM agents, being a response here a potential restaurant recommendation. Internally the Feedback agent holds an evaluation process that takes in consideration previous cases. To enable this evaluation a case-based reasoning algorithm is implemented within the agent. In Table 2 all the classes are defined that characterize one case, being a case in this scenario the record containing the recommendation provided by the system to the user and his/her response.

Case-Based Reasoning and k-Nearest Neighbors. In artificial intelligence and philosophy, case-based reasoning (CBR), broadly construed, is the process of solving new problems based on the solutions of similar past problems. In everyday life, an auto

Table 2. Characteristics of each case

Representation	Name of variable	Variable type	Measurement scale (converted scale)
X1	Id	Numerical	Integer
X2	Recommendation Category	String	String
X3	User Pref - Zomato Review	Numerical	Real Number
X4	User Pref - Glycemic Index	Numerical	Real Number
X5	User Pref - Uber - Price	Numerical	Real Number
X6	User Pref - Uber - Distance	Numerical	Real Number
X7	Recommended Zomato Review	Numerical	Real Number
X8	Recommended Glycemic Index	Numerical	Real Number
X9	Recommended Uber - Price	Numerical	Real Number
X10	Recommended Uber - Distance	Numerical	Real Number
X11	User Action	Numerical	Integer
X12	Created	String	String
R	Similarity Case Score	Numerical	Real Number

mechanic who fixes an engine by recalling another car that exhibited similar symptoms is using case-based reasoning. The proposed CBR approach is composed by four steps, as described in detail in the following sub-sections. During the retrieve phase, the past cases that are similar to the new case are identified and retrieved from the database. This is achieved by applying the k-NN clustering algorithm [9]. By accessing the variables present in Table 2, the k-NN choses the best k neighbors present in the data base (i.e., the most similar cases to the current one). The k-NN requires the specification of the number of k (neighbors). The algorithm will then select the k neighboring that minimizes the sum of the distance between the new case and the k most similar cases (1). Finally, the retain phase determines if the new case should be included in the DB, according to its similarity to the cases that are already part of the data base. In order to apply this model, its required to have a data base that register historic previous cases, meaning, each time the user interact with the system by accepting or rejecting a recommendation, that case will be saved in the database (Fig. 4).

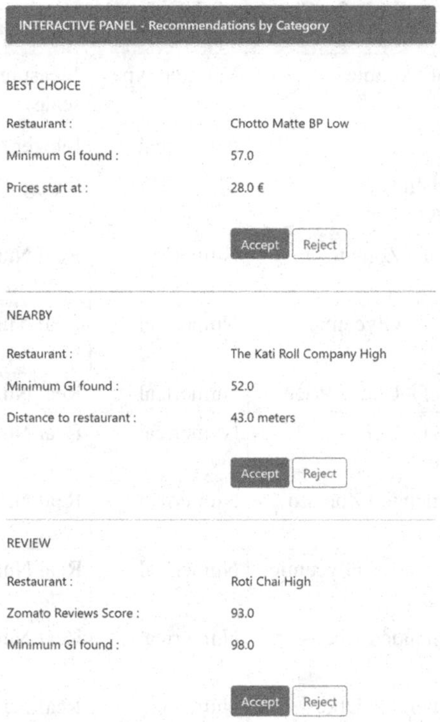

Fig. 4. Interactive panel with recommendations.

The implementation of the CBR inside the multi-agent system was done by using the jCOLIBRI [10]. jCOLIBRI is a framework specifically designed for the development of Case-Based Reasoning Systems, and so, that enabled to speed up the algorithm implementation. With this framework we were able to manage a database of cases and quickly implement the four steps in the algorithm (Retrieve, Reuse, Revise and Retain).

Retrieve. The retrieve step is the most important task of the CBR cycle, and it is the task in which the system selects the most similar cases. In the proposed solution, this process employs the k-NN technique [9], clustering-based method [11], which is utilized to select the most similar cases. For this purpose, the k-NN algorithm uses a distance measure to analyze each case. This measure is the Euclidean distance and is expressed as:

$$d\left(u_i, u_j\right) = \sqrt{\sum_{r=1}^{n} \left((ui) - (uj)\right)^2} \tag{1}$$

where:
n is the dimensionality of the input vector, namely the number of attributes of the examples.

r is from 1 to n.

When $d(u_i, u_j)$ becomes smaller, it means that the two examples are more similar. Equation (2) expresses the prediction that will be the class, and that has the most member in the k-NNs

$$y(d_i) = \arg\max \sum_{u_j \in NN} y(u_j, c_k) \tag{2}$$

where:

d_i is the text example.

u_j is one of its k-NN in the training.

u_j, c_k indicates whether u_j belongs to class c_k.

Reuse. In the reuse task, a solution is obtained from the retrieved cases. This step is completely implemented on the jCOLIBRI framework, being only a set of filters applied, that represent each recommendation type.

Revise. In this paper, the revise task is formulated from the existing knowledge about the problem. A set of hardcoded rules are applied for the comparison between the result retrieved from the previous phases of the CBR cycle and the recommendations received in the meantime by the Feedback agent.

Retain. This is the last task of the cycle, which decides if the new case (recommendation) should or not be added into the data base. The similarity between the new case and the best similar case inside the data base should respect the formula (3). Also, if the difference between the new case result and the CBR result is greater than 0.2, the new case will be excluded, since it does not represent a good enough solution, error is too big.

$$Similarity\{new\ case,\ best\ similar\ case\ in\ data\ base\} \leq 80\% \tag{3}$$

After the revise phase, the Feedback agent will send a recommendation per each category to the user interface, allowing the user to "Accept" or "Reject" the given recommendation. This user action will interact again with the CBR framework to retain the recommendation in the database of cases for that user.

Sentiment Analysis. Sentiment analysis is used to determine whether a given text contains negative, positive, or neutral emotions. It's a form of text analytics that uses natural language processing (NLP) and machine learning. Sentiment analysis is also known as "opinion mining" or "emotion artificial intelligence" [12]. The Reviews agent provide a sentiment analysis implementation on restaurant reviews. As part of this implementation the following methods are applied:

1. Pre-process text reviews by making all words lowercase.
2. Apply tokenization.
3. Remove numbers and punctuation, stop words and lemmatization.
4. Create word-to-vector with TD-IDF to have a rating.

Since this analysis intends only to achieve positive, negative, and neutral reviews scores, the following scale was defined:

1. Positive review – will have a rating above 3.
2. Negative reviews – will have a rating below 3.
3. Neutral reviews – will have a rating of 3.

The metrics used to determine random forest classifiers are precision, recall and accuracy. The list of words that affect the results are ('bad', 'good', 'average', 'best', 'place', 'love', 'order', 'food', 'try', 'nice').

3   Results and Discussion

In order to test and validate the solution here proposed a couple initial simulations were performed. This simulation confirmed that our recommendation system benefits from the CBR algorithm application.

3.1   Scenario I

For this scenario a set of ten (10) simulations were made using the CBR algorithm and then ten different simulations were performed without CBR. Also, these simulations were running under pre-defined set of cases along with the preferences for the user with middle values defined. The only random values were generated by the service agents, when MCDM agents request new recommendation options. The current service agents provide values for Recommended Reviews, Recommended Uber Price, Recommended Uber Distance and Recommended Glycemic Index. All those values are currently being generated randomly and between 0 and 100 since that was the pre-defined scale. Table 3 shows the similarity score percentage between the recommended case and the database cases for that user, by recommendation category. Those values test the application of the CBR algorithm.

Table 3. Simulation results of Scenario I with CBR algorithm

Recommendation category	Restaurant name	Similarity score
Best Choice	Tayyabs High	79,50%
Best Choice	Tayyabs Low	91,67%
Nearby	The Kati Roll Company High	100,00%
Nearby	The Kati Roll Company Low	98,97%
Reviews	Roti Chai High	77,88%
Reviews	Roty Chai Low	95,80%

All the results using the CBR algorithm as we can see in Table 3 obtain a high result in terms of similarity, with all results with values superior to 75% for all the recommendation categories considered. After those initial 10 simulations with CBR, another ten simulations were performed without CBR algorithm application.

Table 4. Simulation results of Scenario I without CBR algorithm

Recommendation category	Restaurant name	Similarity score
Best Choice	Tayyabs High	64,85%
Best Choice	Tayyabs Low	77,45%
Nearby	The Kati Roll Company High	46,95%
Nearby	The Kati Roll Company Low	53,78%
Reviews	Roti Chai High	45,06%
Reviews	Roti Chai Low	51,85%

The results obtained in Table 4 are much lower in similarity score, with worst value being only 45,06%. Table 5 provides an overview of both results, were clearly we can see a better performance, when CBR algorithm is applied.

Table 5. Comparison between similarity score results with and without CBR

Restaurant name	Similarity score with CBR	Similarity score without CBR
Tayyabs High	79,50%	64,85%
Tayyabs Low	91,67%	77,45%
The Kati Roll Company High	100,00%	46,95%
The Kati Roll Company Low	98,97%	53,78%
Roti Chai High	77,88%	45,06%
Roti Chai Low	95,80%	51,85%

3.2 Scenario II

For the second simulation scenario, only ten simulations were performed, but in this case both similarity scores were taken at each simulation. This second scenario confirms also that when a CBR algorithm is applied, the system performance was greater (see Table 6).

After this second set of simulation, we obtained an average score of 91,84% using CBR and 56,94% without CBR, which clearly confirms the advantage of using this technique as part of the solution.

Table 6. Simulation II results with and without CBR algorithm.

Recommendation category	Case	Similarity score with CBR	Similarity score without CBR	Recommended restaurant
Best Choice	1	0,911764706	0,746573898	Chotto Matte BP Low
Nearby	1	1	0,52294686	The Kati Roll Company Low
Reviews	1	0,955223881	0,53814262	Roti Chai Low
Best Choice	2	0,987179487	0,773504274	Tayyabs Low
Nearby	2	1	0,457207207	The Kati Roll Company High
Reviews	2	0,927927928	0,529279279	Roti Chai Low
...	...	...	...	...
Best Choice	10	0,857212476	0,682423652	Chotto Matte BP Low
Nearby	10	1	0,509615385	The Kati Roll Company High
Reviews	10	0,660266257	0,362854461	Roti Chai High
	Average Score	**91,84%**	**56,94%**	

4   Conclusions and Future Work

The paper proposes a recommender system, based on multi-agent systems that implement a set of artificial techniques to allow a diabetic-friendly feature that will recommend the user with healthier options, to improve quality of life and health benefits. The system is currently under development and as the next line of work, different simulations will be performed with different configurations to demonstrate and validate the solution with greater accuracy. The results from the simulation will allow to improve the solution and tackle any identified issues. As future work some key points already been identified that will turn the solution more robust. The complexity of the solution can be increased, specially to the negotiation process, where new types of service agents could be added to the system, turning the multi-criteria decision making a much more powerful component in the solution. Still related with the service agents, there is the potential to improve the Glycose Index agent, by adding for instance object detection functionalities that will allow the user to capture an image of a meal, so that presented food is automatically recognized, and the corresponding Glycemic Index values are measured, making the recommendation done by this agent much more accurate. The solution could also be incorporated within an application like Uber Eats, Zomato or Trip Advisor as a new diabetic-friendly feature in the same sense we can see today for example for vegetarian people. Other methodologies could also be tested and finally, real case scenarios should also provide validation and the applicability of this solution for diabetic people in real life.

Acknowledgments. This research work was developed under the project Food Friend –"Autonomous and easy-to-use tool for monitoring of personal food intake and personalized feedback" (ITEA 18032), co-financed by the North Regional Operational Program (NORTE 2020) under the Portugal 2020 and the European Regional Development Fund (ERDF), with the reference NORTE-01-0247-FEDER-047381 and by National Funds through FCT (Fundação para a Ciência e a Tecnologia) under the project UI/DB/00760/2020.

References

1. World Health Organization: Global report on diabetes. World Health Organization (2016)
2. Bertozzi, D., Dimitrakopoulos, G., Flich, J., Sonntag, S.: The fast evolving landscape of on-chip communication (2014)
3. Ricci, F., Rokach, L., Shapira, B., Kantor, P.B.: Recommender Systems Handbook. Springer, Heidelberg (2010)
4. Kahraman, C., Onar, S.C., Oztaysi, B.: Fuzzy multicriteria decision-making: a literature review. Int. J. Comput. Intell. Syst. **8**, 637–666 (2015)
5. Andronico, A., Carbonaro, A., Casadei, G.: Integrating a multi-agent recommendation system into a mobile learning management system (2003)
6. Morais, A.J., Oliveira, E., Jorge, A.M.: A multi-agent recommender system. In: Omatu, S., De Paz Santana, J.F., González, S.R., Molina, J.M., Bernardos, A.M., Rodríguez, J.M. (eds.) Distributed Computing and Artificial Intelligence. AISC, vol. 151, pp. 281–288. Springer, Heidelberg (2012). https://doi.org/10.1007/978-3-642-28765-7_33
7. Marivate, V.N., Ssali, G., Marwala, T.: An intelligent multi-agent recommender system for human capacity building (2008)
8. Wooldridge, M., Jennings, N.R.: Agent theories, architectures, and languages: a survey. In: Wooldridge, M.J., Jennings, N.R. (eds.) ATAL 1994. LNCS, vol. 890, pp. 1–39. Springer, Heidelberg (1995). https://doi.org/10.1007/3-540-58855-8_1
9. Deng, Z., Zhu, X., Cheng, D., Zong, M., Zhang, S.: Efficient kNN classification algorithm for bid data. Neurocomputing **195**, 143–148 (2016)
10. GOAI Applications. https://gaia.fdi.ucm.es/research/colibri/jcolibri/. Accessed 20 June 2022
11. Faia, R., Pinto, T., Vale, Z.: Dynamic fuzzy clustering method for decision support in electricity markets negotiation, vol. 5 (2016)
12. Zhu, C., Wang, Z., Gao, D.: New design goal of a classifier: global and local structural risk minimization. Knowl.-Based Syst. **100**, 25–49 (2016)

A Review on Supervised Learning Methodologies for Detecting Eating Habits of Diabetic Patients

Catarina Antelo[2]([✉]), Diogo Martinho[1,2], and Goreti Marreiros[1,2]

[1] GECAD – Research Group on Intelligent Engineering and Computing for Advanced Innovation and Development, Porto, Portugal
[2] ISEP – School of Engineering, Polytechnic Institute of Porto, Porto, Portugal
{1150379,diepm,mgt}@isep.ipp.pt

Abstract. Diabetes is a chronic metabolic disease characterized by high blood sugar levels, which over time leads to body complications that can affect the heart, blood vessels, eyes, kidneys, and nerves. To control this disease, the use of applications for tracking and monitoring vital signs have been used frequently. These support systems improve their quality of life and prevent exacerbations, however they cannot help with nutritional control, so several patients with this disease still use the counting carbohydrates method, but this process is not available to everyone and is a time-consuming and not very rigorous method. This study evaluates three approaches including Support Vector Machine, Convolution Neural Network, and a pre-trained Convolution Neural Network called MobileNetV2, to choose the algorithm with the best performance in meals recognition and makes the control nutritional task more quickly, accurately, and efficiently. The results showed that the pre-trained Convolution Neural Network is the best choice for recognizing meals from an image, with an accuracy of 99%.

Keywords: Diabetes · Food recognition · Support vector machine · Convolutional neural networks · MobileNetV2

1 Introduction

According to the World Health Organization [1], diabetes is one of the leading causes of death in the world. About 422 million people worldwide have diabetes and 1.5 million deaths are directly attributed to this disease every year. The use of applications for tracking and monitoring vital signs has been used more frequently to control the disease. Several diabetics use the carbohydrate counting method, which focuses on carbohydrates as the main nutrient that affects the postprandial glycemic response [2]. This method is based on estimating the amount of carbohydrates present in a given meal.

However, this estimate is made by indirect methods so, even being performed rigorously, the calculation is not exact. In addition, both lipids and proteins can have an impact on glycemic control, which makes nutritional control difficult for patients, as there is

G. Marreiros et al. (Eds.): EPIA 2022, LNAI 13566, pp. 374–386, 2022.
https://doi.org/10.1007/978-3-031-16474-3_31

still no evidence of an ideal algorithm that aggregates these particularities. For this reason, it is vital to adopt strategies that allow patients to manage, in a more autonomous way, their health status, to prevent or, at least, control certain diseases. In this context, it is essential to use technological advances and devices that are increasingly present in everyone's daily lives, to automate everyday processes and thus support the user in this management.

This article evaluates the Support Vector Machine, Convolutional Neural Network, and pre-trained Convolutional Neural Network algorithms called MobileNetV2. The best approach will be used in a system that will make the task of nutritional control simpler, faster, and more intuitive. This work is part of the FoodFriend project [3] which is linked to the health area in the topic of monitoring diabetic patients in their day-to-day through the analysis of daily habits (namely diet and physical activity) and the promotion of better behaviors to allow the more controlled and correct management of the disease. For that reason, the implemented prototype is intended to be deployed on a device with limited computing capabilities.

2 Related Work

Several systems of follow-up and monitoring of diabetic patients have been developed over the last years. The Glucose Buddy[1], Diabetes:M[2], Diabetes Connect[3] e MySugr[4] mobile apps allow users to manually record blood glucose levels, insulin doses, other medication intakes, and food input, in grams. Although these applications provide several features to process food intake data, there is no application on the market that, in addition to processing food intake data, also allows recording meals through food recognition.

The Glucose Buddy application does not have this functionality, although it is possible to integrate with the Calorie Mama application so that the user can record their meals more easily, through computer vision. Calorie Mama allows quick food recording via barcode and meal images, as well as visualization of essential macro and micronutrients. Other applications such as MyFitnessPal and SnapCalorie apps also have food recognition. So, the user just needs to take one or more pictures of the meal and the nutritional calculation of the food will be provided. Among these applications, only SnapCalorie does the nutritional calculation considering the volume of food items.

The system presented by Geeta Shroff, Asim Smailagic and Daniel P. Siewiorek [4] makes the food semi-automatic recognition through neural networks. This solution identifies food items from a captured image of the meal with a reference object by its side, which allows the estimation of the volume of food items.

Marios M. Anthimopoulos, Lauro Gianola, Luca Scarnato, Peter Diem and Stavroula G. Mougiakakou [5] developed a solution based on the bag-of-features model to identify homemade food from Central Europe. Eleven food classes were used, three key points were extracted, fourteen image descriptions, two clustering methods for the creation of the visual dictionary, and six classifiers were tested – three Support Vector Machines,

---

[1] https://www.glucosebuddy.com/.
[2] https://www.diabetes-m.com/.
[3] http://www.diabetesconnect.de/en/.
[4] https://www.mysugr.com/en/.

two Artificial Neural Networks, and a Random Forest (RF). The system achieved 78% accuracy.

The article written by Reza Dea Yogaswara, Eko Mulyanto Yuniarno and Adhi Dharma Wibawa [6] reveals a system that calculates the caloric content of food items based on the volume of the food using the Mask Region-based Convolutional Neural Network algorithm. This system proved to be accurate in calculating calories, achieving an average accuracy of 97.48%.

Muhammad Usman, Kashif Ahmad, Amir Sohail and Marwa Qaraqe [7] presented a system that continuously reads glucose through a sensor and controls the food intake of diabetic patients. This solution makes the food recognition with the help of a methodology composed of resource extraction, classification, and fusion. For resource extraction, they used pre-trained models such as AlexNet, VggNet, GoogleNet and ResNet, and trained Support Vector Machine on these resources. They performed early fusion (simple concatenation of feature vectors) and three late fusion methods (Particle Swarm based Optimization, Genetic Algorithm, and simple average of scores obtained in individual models).

These studies showed that the task of recognizing food through images is not easy, however, the algorithms that are most used and that show a better performance is the Support Vector Machines and the Convolutional Neural Networks. The use of pre-trained models is very common in this type of problem and seems to be a good approach when working with a smaller dataset.

Diabetes tracking and monitoring applications are essentially focused on allowing the recording of some vital signs. Although these applications are quite useful, the records are performed manually, so the great advantage of these systems is that they allow the user not to be accompanied by his record book, making them directly in the application, where he can consult and analyze them any time.

It is crucial to create systems that streamline these processes, which in addition to manual registration, also can create records automatically. Controlling carbohydrate intake is extremely important in the routine of diabetic patients, and as already mentioned, this is not an easy task. The creation of systems that make this nutritional reading through an image provided by the user, and that informs the diabetic patient of the meal quality he will eat (good or bad, considering its nutritional values and glycemic index), would make the diabetic life much simpler and carefree.

3   Methods

For the development of the proposed system, studies were carried out with different technologies to evaluate its performance and consequently choose the one that best suited this system. Considering the literature review presented in this article, a Support Vector Machine and two Convolutional Neural Networks were evaluated, as they are the most used technologies in object recognition, presenting good accuracy.

3.1   Support Vector Machines

Support Vector Machine is a supervised learning algorithm type that aims to separate a large amount of dataset using the concept of margins and distance [8]. The Support

Vector Machine performance depends on the hyperparameters that must be adjusted according to the type of data being dealt with. The main ones to pay attention to are:

- C: is a regulation parameter that controls the size of the decision surface margin. The higher the value of C, the smaller the size of the margin, and it is necessary to pay attention to overfitting. On the other hand, the smaller the value of C, the larger the size of the margin, which can cause underfitting.
- Kernel: function used to transform the dataset that defines their similarity. It can be set to linear, polu, rbf, sigmoid, precomputed or provide the callable itself.
- Gamma: defines the weight of the influence of a training data, so low values of γ correspond to a "wide" influence and high values to a "near" influence. This parameter applies to the RBF, sigmoid and polynomial kernel functions.

3.2 Convolutional Neural Networks

Convolutional Neural Networks are widely used in image recognition because they are more accurate than human judgment [9]. Hyperparameter optimization is an economical and convenient way to improve the accuracy of CNN's. The hyperparameters that stand out are the following:

- Number of Hidden Layers: hidden layers are the layers between the input layer and the output layer. Many hidden units within a layer with regularization techniques can increase accuracy. Smaller number of units may cause underfitting.
- Activation function: used to introduce nonlinearity to models, it can be set to Rectified Linear Activation (ReLU), Logistic (Sigmoid), or Hyperbolic Tangent (Tanh).
- Solver: tries to find the parameter weights that minimize a cost function.
- Alpha: controls the weighting of the regularization.
- Max_iter: As the name implies, the maximum number of iterations.

3.3 MobileNetV2

MobileNetV2 uses a Convolutional Neural Network architecture model to classify images and it is special because it uses very less computation power to run, that makes it a perfect fit for mobile devices with limited computing capabilities, embedded systems, and computers to run without GPUs. This model is trained using the ImageNet dataset. The MobileNetV2 architecture utilizes an inverted residual structure where the input and output of the residual blocks are thin bottleneck layers. It also uses lightweight convolutions to filter features in the expansion layer. Finally, it removes non-linearities in the narrow layers [10].

4 Dataset

Although Machine Learning algorithms are used to extract knowledge from a given dataset, their performance largely depends on the data quality [11]. As already mentioned, one of the system objectives is to recognize Portuguese meals. After an extensive

search for datasets that had images of Portuguese meals, it was found that there was no public repository with these characteristics. For this reason, the dataset used was built manually, therefore, at the time of carrying out this study, we only had 11 meal categories, totaling 5528 images. Currently, the dataset has 23 categories, with 6726 images and is available at [12].

Some categories such as Fries, Chocolate Cake, Hotdog, Donut, Ice Cream, Hamburger, Pizza, and Waffles were collected from the dataset provided in [13]. The others – Bacalhau à Brás, Spaghetti Bolognese and Francesinha - were collected from Google Images and restaurant recommendation apps like Zomato, The Fork, and TripAdvisor.

4.1 Data Preprocessing

Before evaluating the algorithms, the images were normalized, as the data set had images of different sizes. Thus, the images were left with a resolution of 224 × 224 pixels, and the colors were kept, as it is a factor of great variance between the different foods.

Since computers read colors as a series of three values – red, green, and blue – and since each pixel has three values to the computer, this resulted in a vector of 224 × 224 × 3, i.e., 150528 attributes for each image. All images were converted to 224 × 224 × 3 size, then converted to a NumPy array and then stored with the appropriate label. To maintain a good performance and reduce the dimensionality of the dataset while preserving as much of the variance, that is, statistical information, the principal components analysis process was used. This technique consists of a linear transformation of data to a new coordinate system so that the largest variance by any data projection is captured along the first coordinate, the second-largest variance along the second coordinate, and so on [14]. To maintain a good performance and try to lose as little information as possible, it was decided to capture at least 90% of the variance.

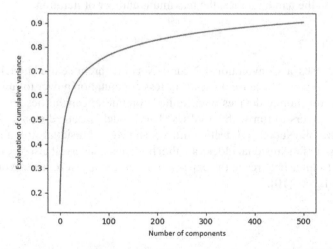

Fig. 1. Graphical demonstration that with 500 components captures 90% of the variance

As can be seen in the Fig. 1, 500 main components were used. From 500 components onwards, the gain of variance per component is residual, so it does not pay to be adding more components.

The dataset was divided into 70% training and 30% testing. As the dataset does not have a large amount of data, mirror images were created temporarily, that is, copies of the originals were created with horizontal rotation.

5 Results

To create a predictive model capable of identifying food items, the Support Vector Machine and Convolutional Neural Networks algorithms were implemented.

5.1 Support Vector Machine

Support Vector Machine's performance is heavily dependent on the defined hyperparameters. To choose the best parameters, the GridSearch method with 5-fold cross-validation was used.

The values used for these hyperparameters are shown in Table 1.

Table 1. Result of the support vector machine hyperparameter optimization process

Hyperparameter	Value
Kernel	RBF
C	10
Gamma	0.0001

Classification metrics were applied to evaluate the performance of the algorithm, namely through the confusion matrix shown in Fig. 2, where it was possible to detect several false positives.

The confusion matrix diagonal shows that some classes such as 'cachorro', 'donuts', 'pizza', and 'waffles' had few correct predictions. In the case of 'waffles', the model correctly predicted 12 images, however, it predicted that another 12 images of waffles were hotdogs. There is no similarity between these two categories, and it is worth remembering that there are no images that have both foods.

Precision metrics allow evaluating performance in terms of detecting false positives, so the higher the result, the better the algorithm's performance. Recall lets you know how many results the algorithm was able to effectively predict, so the higher the result, the better the performance in avoiding false negatives. F1-Score tries to find the balance between accuracy and recall, so false positives and false negatives have a similar cost. The values resulting from the application of these metrics are shown in the Table 2.

As can be seen, the model did not show good precision, obtaining only 38%.

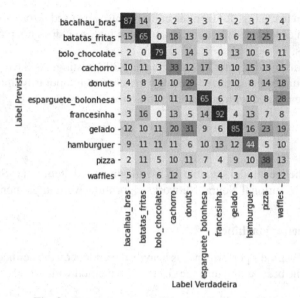

Fig. 2. Support vector machine confusion matrix

Table 2. Result of the support vector machine confusion matrix

Label	Precision	Recall	F1-score	Support
bacalhau_bras	0.71	0.56	0.63	154
batatas_fritas	0.33	0.40	0.36	164
bolo_chocolate	0.54	0.56	0.55	141
cachorro	0.22	0.23	0.23	145
donuts	0.23	0.21	0.22	140
esparguete_bolonhesa	0.38	0.44	0.41	149
francesinha	0.53	0.60	0.56	153
gelado	0.35	0.53	0.42	161
hamburguer	0.31	0.29	0.30	154
pizza	0.32	0.26	0.28	149
waffles	0.17	0.08	0.11	149
accuracy	0.38	0.38	0.38	1659
macro-average	0.37	0.38	0.37	1659
weighted average	0.37	0.38	0.37	1659

5.2 Convolutional Neural Networks

To find out which are the best hyperparameters to use for this model, the GridSeach method with cross validation was used.

As shown in Table 3, three hidden layers were used and for the activation function, ReLu was chosen, because has the same or better performance than the sigmoid and tahn functions [15]. The optimization process chose lbfgs for the solver option and alpha was defined with 1.

Table 3. Result of the CNN hyperparameter optimization process

Hyperparameter	Value
Hidden layer size	(500, 200, 100)
Activation	relu
Solver	lbfgs
Alpha	1
Max_iter	750

As can be seen in Fig. 3, the category 'waffles' had the least correct precisions, as had already happened with the Support Vector Machine algorithm. There are still many false negatives and many false positives that lead to the conclusion that this is not a good model either.

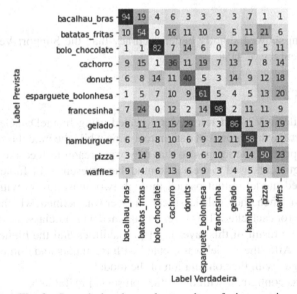

Fig. 3. Convolutional neural network confusion matrix

The class 'batatas_fritas' was correctly predicted 54 times, however, it was incorrectly predicted 110 times, and the 'waffles' class only obtained 16 correct predictions. With this matrix, it is already possible to draw several conclusions, however other metrics presented in Table 4 were evaluated.

Table 4. Result of the convolutional neural network confusion matrix

Label	Precision	Recall	F1-score	Support
bacalhau_bras	0.65	0.61	0.63	154
batatas_fritas	0.35	0.33	0.34	164
bolo_chocolate	0.53	0.58	0.55	141
cachorro	0.26	0.25	0.25	145
donuts	0.29	0.29	0.29	140
esparguete_bolonhesa	0.44	0.41	0.42	149
francesinha	0.52	0.64	0.57	153
gelado	0.40	0.53	0.46	161
hamburguer	0.39	0.38	0.38	154
pizza	0.33	0.34	0.33	149
waffles	0.19	0.11	0.14	149
accuracy	0.41	0.41	0.41	1659
macro-average	0.39	0.41	0.40	1659
weighted average	0.40	0.41	0.40	1659

This algorithm showed slightly better accuracy than the Support Vector Machine, resulting in an accuracy of 41%.

5.3 MobileNetV2

To evaluate MobileNetV2, generators were created using ImageDataGenerator which allows you to increase the amount of data in real-time while the model is training. It was necessary to pre-process the images so that they were ready to feed the MobileNetV2 model and the arguments used to create the model are presented in Table 5.

The pre-trained model output passed through two dense layers with 128 neurons and relu activation. Then, the final classification layer was defined, which stores the real probability values for each class. This layer was defined with 11 classes and with softmax activation [16]. The result of this layer is 11 probabilities and the highest one will be the classification. After the model was created with the inputs and outputs defined, the training phase began with the compilation of the model.

The model was configured with the values presented in Table 6.

For the loss function, the categorical crossentropy was used instead of the sparse categorical crossentropy, because when ImageDataGenerators are used, the classes are

Table 5. Values used in creating the MobileNetV2 model

Argument	Value
input_shape	(224, 224, 3)
include_top	False
weights	imagenet
pooling	avg

Table 6. Values used in model compilation

Argument	Value
Optimizer	Adam
Loss	categorical_crossentropy
Metrics	['accuracy']

coded as vectors, so instead of being passed integers to each class, vectors are passed. In cases where they are passed in the form of vectors, it is more advisable to use categorical crossentropy. Then, the model was trained for 100 epochs and obtained an accuracy of 99%. Some predictions were created, and a confusion matrix was constructed.

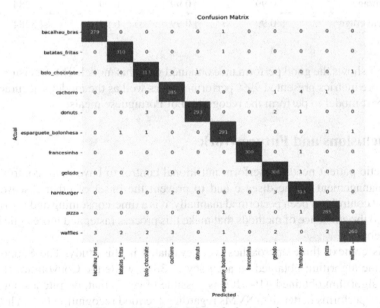

Fig. 4. MobileNetV2 confusion matrix

As can be seen in Fig. 4, the confusion matrix has most of its predictions diagonally. In 3284 images, only 44 images were predicted incorrectly. Right away, is possible to conclude that this will be a great approach to performing food recognition, however, other metrics presented in Table 7 were applied.

Table 7. MobileNetV2 confusion matrix results

Label	Precision	Recall	F1-score	Support
bacalhau_bras	1.00	1.00	1.00	280
batatas_fritas	0.99	0.99	0.99	311
bolo_chocolate	0.97	0.99	0.98	315
cachorro	0.98	0.99	0.98	291
donuts	0.99	0.98	0.98	299
esparguete_bolonhesa	0.99	0.99	0.99	296
francesinha	1.00	1.00	1.00	301
gelado	0.97	0.99	0.98	311
hamburguer	0.99	0.98	0.98	318
pizza	0.99	0.99	0.99	287
waffles	0.97	0.96	0.97	275
accuracy	0.99	0.99	0.99	3284
macro-average	0.99	0.99	0.99	3284
weighted average	0.99	0.99	0.99	3284

Table 7 shows the good performance obtained with this model. The precision, recall, and f1-score metrics presented 99% performance, as well as the model's accuracy. This was the best model to perform the recognition of Portuguese meals.

6   Conclusions and Future Work

The diabetic patient needs to perform nutritional control to have more controlled and correct management of the disease and to prevent the onset of other diseases. This nutritional control has been performed manually, it is a time-consuming and not rigorous process, so the existence of methods that make this process faster and more agile is quite advantageous.

In this context, three approaches were evaluated in this study. The Support Vector Machine algorithm obtained an accuracy of 38%, while the Convolutional Neural Network algorithm obtained 41%. It was possible to verify that, despite a small difference, CNN performs better than SVMs regarding the food recognition task. The results for these two algorithms were not satisfactory, but it is believed that it has to do with the amount of data used. The pre-trained Convolutional Neural Network showed better performance compared to the other approaches, achieving an accuracy of 99%.

Given the results obtained and the methodology chosen, it is intended that the application is ready to recognize all the meals that the user intends to ingest, and, for that reason, it is necessary to add more classes to the dataset. In addition, it is intended that this system makes an estimate of the meal amount present in the image provided by the user and, with these values, gives a more correct estimate of the meal's nutritional values. With all this data, it is expected to build a mobile application that allows the user to capture an image, download it in the application and automatically provide the nutritional values and glycemic index of the meal, as well as an indicator of whether the meal is a good meal for diabetic patient.

Acknowledgements. This research work was developed under the project Food Friend –"Autonomous and easy-to-use tool for monitoring of personal food intake and personalized feedback" (ITEA 18032), co-financed by the North Regional Operational Program (NORTE 2020) under the Portugal 2020 and the European Regional Development Fund (ERDF), with the reference NORTE-01-0247-FEDER-047381 and by National Funds through FCT (Fundação para a Ciência e a Tecnologia) under the project UI/BD/00760/2020.

References

1. World Health Organization. https://www.who.int/news-room/fact-sheets/detail/diabetes. Accessed 10 Nov 2021
2. Fonseca, F., Pichel, F., Albuquerque, I., Afonso, M.J., Baptista, N., Túbal, V.: Manual de Contagem de Hidratos de Carbono na Diabetes Mellitus para profissionais de saúde. Associação Portuguesa dos Nutricionistas, Porto (2015)
3. Itea4. https://itea4.org/project/food-friend.html. Accessed 04 Jan 2022
4. Shroff, G., Smailagic, A., Siewiorek D.P.: Wearable context-aware food recognition for calorie monitoring. In: 12th IEEE International Symposium on Wearable Computers. IEEE Press, Pittsburgh (2008). https://doi.org/10.1109/ISWC.2008.4911602
5. Anthimopoulos, M., Gianola, L., Scarnato, L., Diem, P., Mougiakakou, S.: A food recognition system for diabetic patients based on an optimized bag-of-features model. IEEE J. Biomed. Health Inform. **18**(4), 1261–1271 (2014). https://doi.org/10.1109/JBHI.2014.2308928
6. Yogaswara, R., Yuniarno, E., Wibawa, A.: Instance-aware semantic segmentation for food calorie estimation using mask R-CNN. In: International Seminar on Intelligent Technology and its Applications (ISITIA). IEEE Press, Surabaya (2019). https://doi.org/10.1109/ISITIA.2019.8937129
7. Usman, M., Ahmad, K., Sohail, A., Qaraqe, M.: The diabetic buddy: a diet regulator and tracking system for diabetics. In: International Conference on Content-Based Multimedia Indexing. IEEE Press, Lille (2021). https://doi.org/10.1109/CBMI50038.2021.9461897
8. Towards Data Science. https://towardsdatascience.com/support-vector-machine-introduction-to-machine-learning-algorithms-934a444fca47. Accessed 19 Apr 2022
9. Bergstra, J., Bardenet, R., Bengio, Y., Kégl, B.: Algorithms for hyper-parameter optimization. In: Proceedings of the 24th International Conference on Neural Information Processing Systems, Granada, pp. 2546–2554 (2011)
10. Roboflow. https://blog.roboflow.com/how-to-train-mobilenetv2-on-a-custom-dataset/. Accessed 11 June 2022
11. Medium. https://medium.com/the-ai-technology/understanding-the-importance-of-training-data-in-machine-learning-da4235332904. Accessed 14 Mar 2022

12. Kaggle. https://www.kaggle.com/datasets/catarinaantelo/portuguese-meals. Accessed 14 June 2022
13. Bossard, L., Guillaumin, M., Van Gool, L.: Food-101 – mining discriminative components with random forests. In: Fleet, D., Pajdla, T., Schiele, B., Tuytelaars, T. (eds.) Computer Vision – ECCV 2014. LNCS, vol. 8694, pp. 446–461. Springer, Cham (2014). https://doi.org/10.1007/978-3-319-10599-4_29
14. Medium. https://towardsdatascience.com/a-one-stop-shop-for-principal-component-analysis-5582fb7e0a9c. Accessed 29 Jan 2022
15. Glorot, X., Bordes, A., Bengio, Y.: Deep sparse rectifier neural networks. In: Conference: Proceedings of the 14th International Conference on Artificial Intelligence and Statistics, Ft. Lauderdale (2011)
16. Machine Learning Mastery. https://machinelearningmastery.com/softmax-activation-function-with-python/. Accessed 19 Apr 2022

Visualization of Physiological Response in the Context of Emotion Recognition

Kristián Fodor[⊠], Zoltán Balogh, and Jan Francisti

Department of Informatics, Faculty of Natural Sciences and Informatics, Constantine the Philosopher University in Nitra, Trieda Andreja Hlinku 1, 949 74 Nitra, Slovakia
{kristian.fodor,zbalogh,jfrancisti}@ukf.sk

Abstract. Emotion recognition relies heavily on physiological responses and facial expressions. Using current technology, it is possible to use a set of measuring instruments to create a complex sensory network that is able to acquire physiological response and recognize emotions based on the facial features of the user by using facial recognition software. It is also important to automate these devices and the acquisition of sensory data to make it easy to use without the need of further user input. The aim of this work is to describe an experiment, where physiological functions are collected using low-cost, common and non-invasive Internet of Things (IoT) devices, and the sensory data is automatically sent to a server for further processing. From the measured values a dataset is created and in order to understand the data, descriptive statistics is used. The data are visualized with the help of well-known Python libraries such Pandas, Matplotlib or Seaborn.

Keywords: Sensory monitoring · Physiological functions · Emotion recognition · Visualization

1 Introduction

We are currently making great progress in IoT technology and sensory networks, which can provide affordable sensor devices that are elements of many non-invasive solutions used in a variety of areas. IoT and sensory networks have made significant progress in many applications, including mobility, low costs and high data transfer speeds. IoT technology is used in a variety of areas such as healthcare, transport, video surveillance and the like. In healthcare, there are several sensors that are able to measure physiological functions (heart activity, body temperature, skin resistance, etc.).

It is also possible to use the mentioned IoT technology in face recognition. There can be a number of facial recognition purposes, including the purpose of recognizing an emotional state. Expressing emotions is an important aspect of human life. Facial expression depicts perceptions of various incidents, interpersonal relationships, decision-making cases, and intelligence. Emotions express the psycho-physiological and psychological state of a person [1].

Automated systems capable of recognizing facial expressions to identify emotional state are highly effective in a controlled environment but very unstable in an uncontrolled

G. Marreiros et al. (Eds.): EPIA 2022, LNAI 13566, pp. 387–398, 2022.
https://doi.org/10.1007/978-3-031-16474-3_32

environment, which represents a great effort of research to increase stability even in uncontrollable environments. In recent years, the authors of research [2–4] have focused not only on facial recognition itself but also on the identification of emotions.

A great effort in automated systems is also the evaluation of emotional states on the basis of acquired physiological functions in real time. Physiological functions such as heart activity, skin resistance display autonomic nervous system signals originating from the human physiological system for each emotion [5].

The sensors of the mentioned IoT technology generate a huge amount of data and an important role in research is the method of cleaning and analyzing the obtained data. If it were a non-invasive solution, the data obtained from the sensors would be sent to the central unit for further processing.

The goal of this paper was to describe the methods of acquiring physiological functions and describe the created dataset of physiological functions and classified emotions based on facial recognition. The devices used were mostly non-invasive, low-cost devices where the sensory data was sent to a server and processed automatically. The created dataset is preprocessed and visualized in this paper. In the future, the dataset will be used as an input in machine learning algorithms to classify emotional states.

The paper consists of the following sections: in Sect. 2, we discuss related work and then provide an overview of our materials in Sect. 3. Section 4 describes our proposed methods, while Sect. 5 presents the results of the testing. Section 6 contains the conclusion and the future work in the topic of this paper.

2 Related Work

Emotional health is closely linked to physical health and great emphasis is placed on current care in both categories. Emotional health can be identified by a certain determination of a person's emotional state by measuring and acquiring physiological functions [6].

At present, many researches are trying to classify emotional states in real time by measuring physiological functions using IoT technology. In order to be able to identify changes in a person's emotional state, the speed of sending data from sensors and the processing of acquired data by the central unit is an important task [7–9].

Identifying emotions is relatively easy for people: just listen to the respondents' voice or look at their facial expressions. In recent years, various procedures for automatically identifying emotions have been explored. One of the most popular methods is based on the use of videos and video recordings [10].

In addition to the methods of observing the respondents with a camera, many researchers use the mentioned physiological functions precisely to identify changes in emotional states [11].

In the case of the above-mentioned approach, the area of use of physiological signals represents an interesting area of research, where the effort is to automatically identify changes in emotional states. This is due to the existence of a huge number of different signals that can be detected within the human body [12, 13].

Due to the large number of existing physiological signals, one of the problems is to select the most suitable physiological signals to be used as a way to transform signals

into emotions. For the purpose of measuring physiological signals, it is therefore crucial to use appropriate sensors and it is necessary to achieve high accuracy in order to achieve high reliability [14, 15].

Researchers in the current period are trying to place different sensors on complex devices in order for one device to be able to measure multiple types of physiological functions [16].

In further research, the authors [17, 18] dealt with the design of an architecture designed to detect emotional states. They designed a comprehensive system that is able to link multiple types of information (physiological functions and facial expressions) in order to identify changes in emotional states.

3   Materials and Methods

The measurement priority was to minimize the usage of invasive devices, that would restrict the users in their movement and their daily activates. The second priority included the low-cost of the instrument devices, which doesn't need any special environments and can be easily adapted to any areas, such as education, industrial production or smart homes. The third priority included ease of use. The quality of the sensors was also a topic in our previous work [13].

We cannot expect the users to manually retrieve their data from wearable devices, so it was necessary to develop software for each measuring instrument that automatically sends the sensor data to a specified server location, where the data is then stored in database tables. The measuring instruments together form a complex sensory network, that consisted of common IoT devices, which are able to communicate with the Internet, thus able to send and receive information, such as physiological functions acquired from the sensors.

To test out our solution, we have created a pilot experiment, where we asked students to be part of the experiment. At the first phase of testing, we were able to test the technology on 12 students.

The measuring instruments included a Fitbit Sense smartwatch, where due to an open-source application programming interface (API), we were able to create a software in JavaScript, which automatically sent the heart rate of the user to a server. The frequency of the measurement was 1 s as this is the lowest value we can set in the API and we can consider this real-time monitoring.

The second measuring instrument was an Arduino Uno microcontroller with a Wi-Fi shield connected to a galvanic skin response (GSR) sensor made by Seeed Studio. The measured values were then sent to a server by using the HTTP Client library.

The frequency of the measurement was approximately 1 s. This method was still invasive during our experiment as for the GSR sensor to work, we had to attach 2 electrodes to the fingers of the users and the sensor itself was attached to the microcontroller by cable, however, currently there are already prototypes of solutions, where the invasiveness is eliminated. For example, authors Vavrinsky et al. [19] created a Bluetooth low energy (BLE) device that has a form of a ring and is able to measure electrodermal response and completely eliminates the invasiveness. In the future, we will also try to eliminate the invasiveness of our GSR sensor.

The third measuring instrument was a Raspberry Pi IV microcomputer with a thermal array camera, which was able to measure the temperature of the surface of the user's forehead.

A second camera was added to the Raspberry Pi IV microcomputer, which was used by a facial recognition software. This facial recognition software was able to detect basic emotions defined by Ekman's classification [20]. The frequency of the measurement can be as frequent as every second, however, the software is designed to send the classified emotion based on facial recognition when the software can clearly see and recognize the emotion.

4   Research Methodology

The layout of the used sensors, which were described in the previous section and were used during the experiment can be seen in Fig. 1.

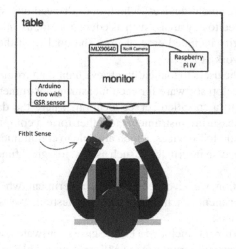

Fig. 1. Visualization of the testing environment

To evoke emotional reactions, the users were tasked to watch a series of movie clips. We used the research from Schaefer et al. [21] to select specific clips that evoke high emotional response. This research (and their created dataset) contained specific movie clips with the valence and arousal levels of the emotions these clips evoked. The clips that were shown to the users in our experiment is summarized in Table 1.

Each clip was about 2 min long making the entire video 9 min and 56 s long. At the beginning we instructed the students to remove their smart watch or fitness tracker if they were wearing one and wear the Fitbit Sense instead. We explained what the experiment was about and reassured the students that their physiological functions and emotions will be collected, but the feed from the cameras will not be saved and no other personal information, such as first name or last name will be saved. In the created dataset each user has a unique identifier (user ID) and the anonymization of the acquired data was

Table 1. Summary of the shown movie clips to the users

Emotion	Happiness	Sadness	Anger	Disgust and surprise	Fear
Movie	Something about Mary	City of angels	Schindler's list	Trainspotting	The blair witch Project
Clip	Hair gel scene	Final scene	Dead bodies scene	Toilet scene	Final scene

an important aspect of our research. After the movie clips, we asked the students how they felt about the experiment. In some cases, the students have already seen the movies and in these cases, we can assume the intensity of the emotional reaction was lower. The length of the experiment was about 15 min per test subject. All text subjects were exposed to the same stimuli (movie clips). Between each clip, there was a 5 s blank screen to avoid contamination.

Since each physiological function and the classified emotion was sent to a different table in the database, we needed to synchronize the data. By using structured query language (SQL), we were able to join these tables on their *date_time* column using *INNER JOIN*. However, because of the different frequencies in the measurement, there were only a few records where we had a measurement of all physiological functions and the output of the emotional recognition software at the exact same time. Missing values in the records contained *NULL* value, so we have created a simple algorithm that complements the missing values by using the last known sensor readings. A simple algorithm was created in PHP that iterated through the dataset and if a sensor value was missing, it replaced the *NULL* value with the last known sensor reading. The final dataset in Comma-separated values (CSV) format contained 2706 records after filtering the records.

To analyze the data, we have created a Jupyter notebook using Google Colab on a personal Google Drive. First, we have visualized the last five records in the dataset (Fig. 2), so we can see the structure of the data.

```
df.tail(5)
```

	gsr	heart_rate	temperature	emotion	date_time	id_user	gender
2701	10	96	29.9	Happy	2022-03-29 13:58:31	1	F
2702	10	96	29.9	Happy	2022-03-29 13:58:31	1	F
2703	22	96	29.9	Fearful	2022-03-29 13:58:30	1	F
2704	32	96	29.9	Happy	2022-03-29 13:58:28	1	F
2705	67	92	31.8	Sad	2022-03-29 13:35:33	1	F

Fig. 2. The last five records in the DataFrame

Then, we have called the describe method from the Pandas library to generate descriptive statistics (Fig. 3).

```
df.describe()
```

	gsr	heart_rate	temperature
count	2706.000000	2706.000000	2706.000000
mean	119.194383	96.686253	29.025684
std	77.936715	10.931523	1.591628
min	1.000000	77.000000	20.900000
25%	71.000000	87.000000	28.300000
50%	99.000000	95.000000	28.900000
75%	184.000000	109.000000	30.300000
max	354.000000	122.000000	32.000000

Fig. 3. Descriptive statistics from the dataset

From the descriptive statistics we can see the number of records, the mean value, standard deviation, min and max value, and the Q1, Q2 and Q3 quartile for each numeric column (physiological functions) of the dataset.

In the GSR column there were extremely low values for one test subject and more analysis is needed to explain this phenomenon. It could have been caused by the fact that the electrodes on the test subject's fingers were touching each other or the test subject was extremely nervous throughout the whole experiment.

5 Testing Results

This section describes and visualizes the results of the pilot experiment by using the exported dataset from the database table. The visualizations were made using Python libraries such as Matplotlib and Seaborn.

From Fig. 4 we can see that for the most part of the experiment, the users were afraid. This phenomenon can be explained by the fact that before the experiment we told the test subjects that the videos they will see might evoke different emotions and they didn't know what to expect. As it was mentioned before, after the experiment most of the time we got feedback that they have seen most of the shown movies before, therefore the proportion of surprised emotional states to the total is very low. In future experiments, it is necessary to find new ways to extend the dataset with more records, where the facial recognition classifies the emotions of surprise and happiness more often.

To understand the shape of the data distribution, we have created histograms, which graphically shows how frequently every value in a dataset occurs. Histograms make it easy to see which values are most common and which values are least common.

The created histogram (Fig. 5) for the GSR readings visualizes a non-symmetric bimodal distribution, where most values are between 70 and 80 (analog reading from Arduino mapped into integer values). The GSR distribution is right-skewed and there are a few outliers which may have arisen from erroneous measurements (the software

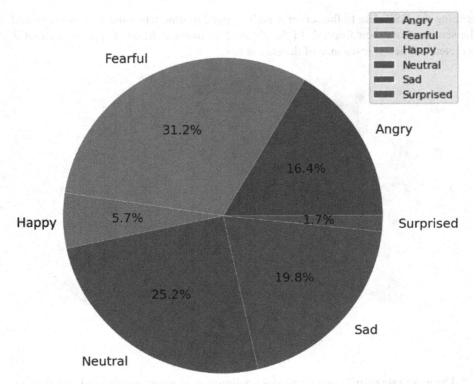

Fig. 4. The proportion of emotions to the total amount of readings

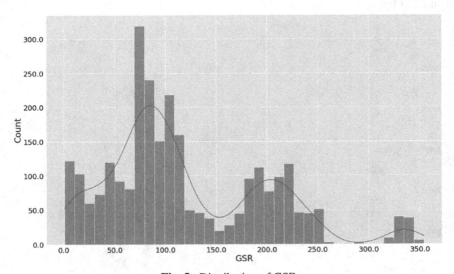

Fig. 5. Distribution of GSR

sending the GSR data to the server wasn't stopped in time when the students removed the sensors from their fingers). In the physical arousal condition of a person, sweat is secreted and hence resistance of the skin is low.

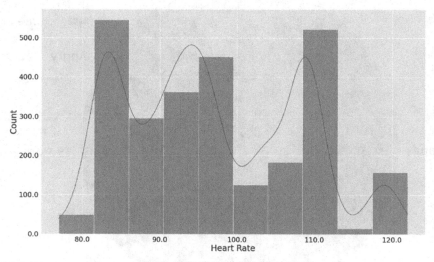

Fig. 6. Distribution of heart rate

The heart rate distribution (Fig. 6) is an almost symmetric multimodal distribution, where most values are between 80 and 85 beats per minute (bpm), 95 and 100 bpm and 110 and 115 bpm.

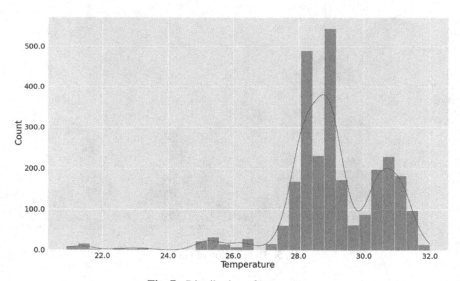

Fig. 7. Distribution of temperature

Most forehead temperature readings (Fig. 7) were between 28.0–28.3 and 28.6–29.0 (Celsius). The distribution is a non-symmetric bimodal distribution. There are a few outlier values (low temperatures), which may have been due to the fact, that the students moved and the central point of the thermal array feed wasn't detecting the forehead of the student.

Next, we also visualized the box plots of physiological functions for each sub-category (emotion).

From the box plot (Fig. 8) we can see the mean values, the interquartile range, the whiskers and the outliers. From the plot it is clear, that the GSR outliers were present, when the emotion recognition software classified the emotion of the user as sad or afraid. The lowest mean value was when the person was surprised, while the highest was in neutral emotional state.

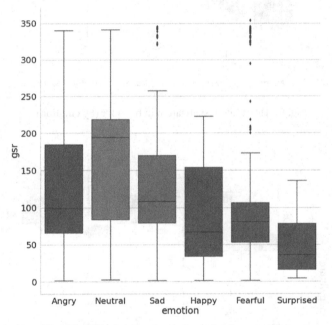

Fig. 8. GSR visualization in box plot (by emotion)

In Fig. 9 we can see the box plot of the heart rate by emotions. Most outlier values were when the test subject was sad according to the facial recognition software. Heart rate was lowest in neutral and angry emotional state and highest when the test subject was happy or sad.

Figure 10 contains the box plot of the temperatures in each sub-category. Highest forehead temperatures were measured when the test subject was sad, lowest temperatures when the test subject was angry.

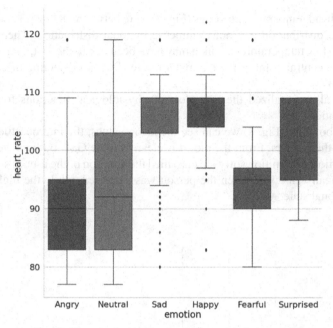

Fig. 9. Heart rate visualization in box plot (by emotion)

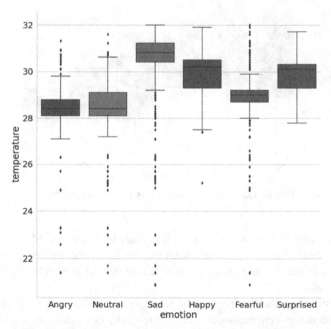

Fig. 10. Temperature visualization in box plot (by emotion)

6   Conclusion and Future Work

In this work we have dealt with the acquisition of physiological functions and described the used methods in the experiment. The created dataset is available on GitHub [22]. The testing results have been processed and visualized by using python libraries such as Pandas and Seaborn. In the future, the dataset can be extended by making new measurements in the same, or similar environment on more subjects in different age groups. This dataset can be then used to train a machine learning model, which will be able to classify emotional states only based on the physiological response of the users without using facial recognition.

The dataset will serve as an input to multiple machine learning algorithms, such as multilayer perceptron, k-nearest neighbors, support-vector machine or Bayesian network, and the algorithm with the best results (highest accuracy) can be selected and implemented in various areas, such as smart housing, where the users would be able to create rules using a mobile application, where they can instruct their smart devices to react to specific emotional states. For example, if the user is afraid during the evening, the user can instruct smart lightbulbs to light up.

In our future work, we want to automatically send the physiological functions to a PHP script on a server, where the machine learning algorithm will use these features to classify the emotional states and store it in a database table. To display the functionality of the proposed method, we want to add another Raspberry Pi microcomputer with LED diodes to our sensory network, which will read the classified emotion in the database table and change the colors of the diodes based on the emotion of the user. Instead of the diodes, a display can also be used to demonstrate the classified emotion to the user.

References

1. Kumar, J., Kumar, J.A.: Machine learning approach to classify emotions using GSR. Adv. Res. Electr. Electron. Eng. **2**, 72–76 (2015)
2. Kaya, H., Gurpinar, F., Salah, A.A.: Video-based emotion recognition in the wild using deep transfer learning and score fusion (2017)
3. Fang, J., Yuan, Y., Lu, X., Feng, Y.: Muti-stage learning for gender and age prediction. Neurocomputing **334**, 114–124 (2019). https://doi.org/10.1016/J.NEUCOM.2018.12.073
4. Zeng, N., Zhang, H., Song, B., Liu, W., Li, Y., Dobaie, A.M.: Facial expression recognition via learning deep sparse autoencoders. Neurocomputing **273**, 643–649 (2018)
5. Ménard, M., Richard, P., Hamdi, H., Daucé, B., Yamaguchi, T.: Emotion recognition based on heart rate and skin conductance. In: PhyCS 2015 - 2nd International Conference on Physiological Computing Systems, pp. 26–32 (2015). https://doi.org/10.5220/000524110026 0032
6. Nandi, A., Xhafa, F.: A federated learning method for real-time emotion state classification from multi-modal streaming. Methods (2022). https://doi.org/10.1016/J.YMETH.2022. 03.005
7. Ayata, D., Yaslan, Y., Kamasak, M.: Emotion recognition via random forest and galvanic skin response: comparison of time based feature sets, window sizes and wavelet approaches. In: 2016 Medical Technologies National Conference, TIPTEKNO 2016 (2017). https://doi.org/ 10.1109/TIPTEKNO.2016.7863130

8. Ayata, D., Yaslan, Y., Kamasak, M.E.: Emotion recognition from multimodal physiological signals for emotion aware healthcare systems. J. Med. Biol. Eng. **40**, 149–157 (2020). https://doi.org/10.1007/S40846-019-00505-7/FIGURES/5

9. Islam, M.R., Ahmad, M.: Wavelet analysis based classification of emotion from EEG signal. In: International Conference on Electrical, Computer and Communication Engineering, ECCE 2019 (2019). https://doi.org/10.1109/ECACE.2019.8679156

10. Sun, Y., Sebe, N., Lew, M.S., Gevers, T.: Authentic emotion detection in real-time video. In: Sebe, N., Lew, M., Huang, T.S. (eds.) CVHCI 2004, vol. 3058, pp. 94–104. Springer, Heidelberg (2004). https://doi.org/10.1007/978-3-540-24837-8_10

11. Canento, F., Fred, A., Silva, H., Gamboa, H., Lourenço, A.: Multimodal biosignal sensor data handling for emotion recognition. Proc. IEEE Sensors. 647–650 (2011). https://doi.org/10.1109/ICSENS.2011.6127029

12. Fodor, K., Balogh, Z.: Process modelling and creating predictive models of sensory networks using fuzzy petri nets. Procedia Comput. Sci. **9** (2021)

13. Fodor, K., Balogh, Z.: Sensory monitoring of physiological functions using IoT based on a model in petri nets. In: Zhang, W., Zou, L., Maamar, Z., Chen, Lu. (eds.) WISE 2021, vol. 13081, pp. 435–443. Springer, Cham (2021). https://doi.org/10.1007/978-3-030-91560-5_32

14. Haag, A., Goronzy, S., Schaich, P., Williams, J.: Emotion recognition using bio-sensors: first steps towards an automatic system. In: André, E., Dybkjær, L., Minker, W., Heisterkamp, P. (eds.) Affective Dialogue Systems, vol. 3068, pp. 36–48. Springer, Cham (2004). https://doi.org/10.1007/978-3-540-24842-2_4

15. Kim, J., André, E.: Fusion of multichannel biosignals towards automatic emotion recognition. In: Hahn, H., Ko, H., Lee, S. (eds.) Multisensor Fusion and Integration for Intelligent Systems, vol. 35, pp. 55–68. Springer, Cham (2009)

16. Munera, E., Poza-Lujan, J.L., Posadas-Yagüe, J.L., Simó-Ten, J.E., Noguera, J.F.B.: Dynamic reconfiguration of a RGBD sensor based on QoS and QoC requirements in distributed systems. Sensors **15**, 18080–18101 (2015). https://doi.org/10.3390/S150818080

17. Castillo, J.C., et al.: Software architecture for smart emotion recognition and regulation of the ageing adult. Cogn. Comput. **8**(2), 357–367 (2016). https://doi.org/10.1007/s12559-016-9383-y

18. Fernández-Caballero, A., et al.: Smart environment architecture for emotion detection and regulation. J. Biomed. Inform. **64**, 55–73 (2016). https://doi.org/10.1016/J.JBI.2016.09.015

19. Vavrinsky, E., Stopjakova, V., Kopani, M., Kosnacova, H.: The Concept of Advanced Multi-Sensor Monitoring of Human Stress (2021). https://doi.org/10.3390/s21103499

20. Ekman, P.: Basic emotions. In: Dalgleish, T., Power, M. (eds.) Handbook of Cognition and Emotion, vol. 39, pp. 125–127. Wiley, Sussex (1999)

21. Schaefer, A., Nils, F., Sanchez, X., Philippot, P.: Assessing the effectiveness of a large database of emotion-eliciting films: a new tool for emotion researchers. Cogn. Emot. **24**, 1153–1172 (2010). https://doi.org/10.1080/02699930903274322

22. Fodor, K., Balogh, Z., Francisti, J.: Emotion Recognition Dataset (GitHub Repository). https://github.com/KristianFodor/EmotionRecognition. Accessed 06 June 2022

GAI - General Artificial Intelligence

Effective Communication in Transition Care During Shift Change

Filipe Fernandes[1,2] ⓘ, Almeida Dias[1] ⓘ, Isabel Araújo[1] ⓘ, Goreti Marreiros[3] ⓘ,
Joana Machado[4] ⓘ, Hossam Dawa[1] ⓘ, Henrique Vicente[4,5] ⓘ, and José Neves[1,4(✉)] ⓘ

[1] Instituto Politécnico de Saúde do Norte, CESPU, Famalicão, Portugal
fernandes.filipe.fa@gmail.com, a.almeida.dias@gmail.com,
isabel.araujo@ipsn.cespu.pt, hdawa@yahoo.com
[2] Universidade Católica Portuguesa, Porto, Portugal
[3] GECAD, Instituto Superior de Engenharia do Porto, Porto, Portugal
mgt@isep.ipp.pt
[4] Centro Algoritmi, Universidade do Minho, Braga, Portugal
joana.machado@algoritmi.uminho.pt, jneves@di.uminho.pt
[5] Departamento de Química e Bioquímica, Escola de Ciências e Tecnologia,
REQUIMTE/LAQV, Universidade de Évora, Évora, Portugal
hvicente@uevora.pt

Abstract. The aim of this study is to examine the effective communication process during shift changes in a transitional care unit; communication should be clear, concise and relevant. The caregivers should be able to understand their mates needs and wants, and they should understand what is happening. Indeed, it will be study if there is inconsistency in the communication process during shift change, since there are some factors that could be affecting the consistency, such as inadequate time for communication, lack of awareness about the needs of other team members and unclear expectations from managers, a process carried out by interviewing employees who have experience in transitional care. The interviewees are asked about their past experiences and what they think are the most important points for effective communication. No doubt this article will discuss the communication challenges and opportunities that arise when a caregiver transfers care from one shift to the next, with effective communication being the key. On the other hand, in this work is also set a *Logic Programming* based framework that nurses may use to optimize their insight into how caregivers may make their communication more effective by understanding the needs of both parties involved in the shift change process.

Keywords: ISBAR method · Transition care · Shift change · Patient's safety · Logic programming · The laws of thermodynamics · Entropy · Computational sustainability

1 Introduction

Cooperation, teamwork, and effective communication among nursing professionals are strategies for the safety and quality of care provided. However, recent studies refer

G. Marreiros et al. (Eds.): EPIA 2022, LNAI 13566, pp. 401–414, 2022.
https://doi.org/10.1007/978-3-031-16474-3_33

to ineffective communication as one of the most commonly cited errors, as a cause of adverse events, putting patient safety at risk [1–4]. Communication failures are presented as the cause of 70% of adverse events that occur during patient care transition moments [5].

The transition of health care is often referred to as handover, it is conceptualized as any moment in the provision of care in which there is a transfer of responsibility for care and information between professionals, whose mission is their continuity and safety [5]. The safe transition of care for the hospitalized patient is considered a challenge for nurses, due to the frequency with which they occur and the amount of information that is shared [6]. At these times, the most regularly identified failures are related to omissions of information, errors in information, and lack of precision and prioritization of activities.

Currently, in health facilities, we are faced with increasingly technologically sophisticated care environments that interfere with efficient communication [1]. Efficient communication is described as timely, accurate, complete, unambiguous, timely and understood by the recipient. In order to guarantee these premises and safeguard patient safety, during shift changes, the use of the ISBAR methodology is recommended, especially during times of transition of care. In the ISBAR mnemonic, the "I" is taken as the Identification of the patient to which the information relates, as well as the identification of the intervenient who make the communication, the "S" is the Current Situation, where the current reason for need for health care, the "B" is the background, where clinical facts or other relevant data, prior to the patient are specified, the "A" is the assessment, which corresponds to information about the general condition of the patient, and the "R" are the recommendations, which are the appropriate attitudes and treatment plan for the patient's clinical situation. This methodology is currently recommended by several health organizations at national and international level, due to its efficiency in the flow of information and patient safety [6–8].

Among the main reasons given for the implementation of the ISBAR methodology, there is the standardization of communication between health professionals, which facilitates decision-making, promotes critical thinking, reduces the time spent in information transfer and rapid integration. of new professionals [6]. The ISBAR methodology is described as being easy to remember and simple to use, as it is flexible, concise and clear to communicate information considered relevant in the transition of care. This leads one to the question, viz.

Does the shift change of nurses with the ISBAR methodology promote patient safety?

This aspect of the problem will be discussed below, and sensitive questionnaires will be object of consideration, viz.

Objectives – Communication is an essential part of every shift change. It is important to understand the goals of the new shift and give them information about what happened *and what to expect. This will help to understand the situation and work effectively* produced with the outgoing team. Indeed, communication has as main goals, viz.

• *Prepare the new team by providing information about patients and their care needs;*

- *To ensure all members are aware of changes in patient status or care needs;*
- *Educating other members of the team about the patient's condition and the treatment plan, if necessary;*
- *Provide new employees with guidance on policies, procedures and work processes to make them more comfortable in their new environment; and*
- *To provide feedback on how good the communication was during this transition.*

Unquestionably, transition care is the care given to patients as they move from a level of care to another. It is a vital component of patient safety and of the quality-of-care.

Background – The *International Organization for Standardization (ISO)* defines patient safety as "the absence of harm to patients from healthcare interventions". The *ISBAR* method is a communication tool used by nurses to evaluate and manage risks during a shift change. Indeed, the transition of care is a crucial time in healthcare environments. It requires the collaboration of many different people with different roles and responsibilities. Communication is the key to success during this time. Below are some points on effective communication for transitional care during shift changes, viz.

- *Clarity of communication is important to ensure that there are no misunderstandings or missed information;*
- *Effective communication involves active listening, asking questions and non-verbal cues;*
- *It is important to be respectful and not to blame or embarrass others;*
- *Non-verbal cues such as eye contact, facial expressions, gestures, tone of voice, and body language can help communicate more effectively;*
- *Providing feedback on what has been communicated can help improve future communication; and*
- *It is important to be respectful and avoid blaming or shaming others.*

It is important to be able to communicate with patients and their families, as well as with other healthcare professionals. Communication can be challenging in a healthcare environment due to shift rotation for caregivers. In this work it is discussed how communication at shift change can be improved by using different strategies, viz.

- *Introduce yourself;*
- *Address concerns or questions;*
- *Check-in on family members or friends who are waiting outside the patient's room;*
- *Provide information about the patient's care plan and next steps; and*
- *Offer reassurance and encouragement.*

To ensure this transition goes smoothly, it is important to have clear expectations for both parties. This includes expectations of how the departing employee should communicate with the new employee and vice versa. It also contains what information must be communicated before, during and after the shift change, viz.

- *Transition care is a process that involves the transition of a patient from one healthcare provider to another and is critical for continuity of care; and*
- *One's goal is to provide healthcare workers with methods for problem solving and decision making during transition care.*

Results – The purpose of this study was to examine the impact of shift change communication on effective transitional care in a geriatric healthcare facility, where nurses and other healthcare providers are expected to communicate effectively with patients and their caregivers, intends to find if there is either difference in rates of adverse events between the two groups, or if there is improvement in nurse-reported communication and workload management practices. Indeed, to fulfill this purpose, the problem will be broken down into three segments, viz.

- *Problem-solving;*
- *Decision-making; and*
- *Communication.*

In fact, the problem-solving methodology presented in this article is based on the laws of thermodynamics and aims to describe the practices of *Knowledge Representation and Reasoning (KRR)* as a process of energy dissipation. It deals with entropy, a property that quantifies the ordered state of a system and its evolution. These properties fit the proposed vision of *KRR* practices as they are to be understood as a process of energy degradation, i.e. energy can be decomposed and used in a sense of devaluation, but never in a sense of destruction [9–12], viz.

- *Exergy*; sometimes referred to as available energy or more precisely available work, which is a measure of a system's entropy;
- *Vagueness*; the corresponding energy values that may or may not have been consumed, and
- *Anergy*; it stands for an energy potential that has not yet been used up, i.e. is available.

2   Methodology

A triangulated study of methodologies was carried out. In the first phase, a qualitative approach was used and in the second phase, a questionnaire with closed questions was applied. The study had the participation of 60 (sixty) students of the degree in nursing. Participants in an initial phase received training on the ISBAR method, later, it were performed simulations of shift changes where they performed different auto scopes (i.e. watch and see). After this training and assessment of the assimilation of knowledge of the ISBAR method, the questionnaires were implemented. The questionnaires were

composed by a group of questions of sociodemographic characterization (e.g. age, sex) and a group with questions of opinion about the ISBAR method. The statements of the questionnaires were elaborated with support from the Psychology Department and were organized into 4 (four) dimensions, viz.

Information Dimension Statements – Two Elements (IDS – 2) (items 1 and 2) that includes the assertions, viz.

Q1 – When changing shifts, do I receive accurate clinical information about patients?

Q2 – During the shift change, is unnecessary information transmitted for the continuity of patient care?

The *IDS* designed to help the patient and their family understand what they can expect during this transition.

Need for Care Dimension Statements – Three Elements (NCDS – 3) (items 3, 4 and 5) that includes the assertions, viz.

Q3 – Does the shift change follow procedures/guidelines/instructions that allow identifying the care needs of patients?

Q4 – Is the changeover time sufficient to collect the information necessary to identify the care needs of patients?

Q5 – Are the nursing people prepared to provide care for patients who are transitioning from one level of care to another.

NCDS are statements that describe the patient's condition, needs, and preferences. They are used by healthcare providers to make decisions about what kind of treatment they should receive. They can also be used by patients themselves to make decisions about their own treatment options.

Background Dimension Statement – One Element (BDS – 1) (item 6), that includes the assertion, viz.

Q6 – When handing over the shift, do I get to know the patient's background, relevant clinical facts?

The *BDS* is a document that provides care for patients who are transitioning from one level of care to another.

Care Recommendations Dimension Statements – Five Elements (CRDS – 5) (items 7, 8, 9, 10, and 11), that includes the assertions, viz.

Q7 – When changing shifts, do I identify the care of patients who are under my responsibility?

Q8 – Could the shift change be performed more efficiently in the replacement of care teams?

Q9 – Could the provision of care for these patients be a challenge to many health care providers?

Q10 – Could the transition from one level of care to another be difficult for patients? They may have to adjust to new routines, new people, and new surroundings.

Q11 – Is it important for the patients to understand what they need to do in order to take care of themselves and their health.

The *CRDS* are a set of statements that provide care for patients. They are used to help the patient understand what they need to do in order to take care of themselves and their health. The goal is for the patient to be able to make informed decisions about their own health and well-being, as well as how they can best manage their condition or illness. On the other hand, the scales used were based on an extension of the Likert scale that was expanded to cover the concept of entropy, viz.

strongly agreeing (4), agreeing (3), disagreeing (2), strongly disagreeing (1), disagreeing (2), agreeing (3), strongly agreeing (4).

In addition, it contains a neutral term *neither agrees nor disagrees* that stands for *uncertain or vague*. On the other hand, the reason for the individual's answers is to be founded in the query, viz.

As a member of a team for shift change, how much would you agree with each one of the statements referred to above?

leading to Table 1, viz.

Table 1. The answers of a team's element to questionnaires' *IDS – 2, NCDS – 3, BDS – 1,* and *CRDS – 5.*

Questionnairs	Question	Scale							
		(4)	(3)	(2)	(1)	(2)	(3)	(4)	*vagueness*
IDS – 2	Q1	×	×						
	Q2						×	×	
NCDS – 3	Q3		×						
	Q4								×
	Q5						×	×	
BDS – 1	Q6				×				
CRDS – 5	Q7				×		×		
	Q8	×		×					
	Q9				×				
	Q10		×						
	Q11								×

Leading to   **Leading to**

Table 6 and 7

The entries in Table 1 are to be read from left to right, from *strongly agreeing (4)* to *agreeing (3)* (with increasing entropy), or from *disagreeing (2)* to *strongly agreeing (4)* (with decreasing entropy). For example, the answer to *Q1* was *strongly agreeing (4)* → *agreeing (3)*, which means that entropy tends to increase. For *Q2* the answer was *disagreeing (2)* → *agreeing (4)*, which means that entropy tends to decrease, while no options are shown for *Q4*, which suggests that one is facing a vague condition, i.e., there is no indication that the element of the team for shift change is aware of his/her undertaking [10]. Figure 1, Table 2 and Table 3 show the evaluation of a *Nurse' Entropic State* according to his/her answers to the *NCDS – 3* questionnaire for the *Best-case Scenario*, viz.

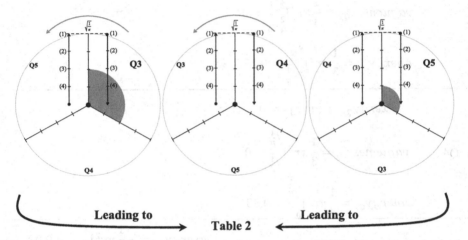

Fig. 1. A pictorial interpretation of a *Nurse's Answers* to the *NCDS – 3* questionnaire in the *Best-case Scenario*.

where the circles denote areas with an amplitude of 1 (one) (i.e. radius $= \sqrt{1/\pi}$); the segments from the middle are marked with the number of statements in a questionnaire; the vertical segments are marked with the number of items of each scale (note that the statements in a questionnaire may be linked to different scales).

Table 2. Evaluation of a *Nurse's Entropic State* in terms of his/her answers to *NCDS – 3* questionnaire in the *Best-case Scenario*.

	(NCDS – 3$_{4\text{-}1}$) – Scale (4) (3) (2) (1)	(NCDS – 3$_{1\text{-}4}$) – Scale (1) (2) (3) (4)
Q3	$exergy_{Q1} = \frac{1}{3}\pi r^2 \Big]_0^{\frac{2}{4}\sqrt{\frac{1}{\pi}}} =$ $= \frac{1}{3}\pi \left(\frac{2}{4}\sqrt{\frac{1}{\pi}}\right)^{-2} - 0 = 0.08$	–
	$vagueness_{Q1} = \frac{1}{3}\pi r^2 \Big]_{\frac{2}{4}\sqrt{\frac{1}{\pi}}}^{\frac{2}{4}\sqrt{\frac{1}{\pi}}} = 0$	–
	$anergy_{Q1} = \frac{1}{3}\pi r^2 \Big]_{\frac{2}{4}\sqrt{\frac{1}{\pi}}}^{\sqrt{\frac{1}{\pi}}} = 0.25$	–
Q4	$exergy_{Q2} = \frac{1}{3}\pi r^2 \Big]_0^0 = 0$	–
	$vagueness_{Q2} = \frac{1}{3}\pi r^2 \Big]_{\sqrt{\frac{1}{\pi}}}^{\sqrt{\frac{1}{\pi}}} = 0$	–
	$anergy_{Q2} = \frac{1}{3}\pi r^2 \Big]_0^{\sqrt{\frac{1}{\pi}}} = 0.33$	–
Q5	–	$exergy_{Q3} = -\frac{1}{3}\pi r^2 \Big]_{\frac{1}{4}\sqrt{\frac{1}{\pi}}}^0 = 0.02$
	–	$vagueness_{Q3} = -\frac{1}{3}\pi r^2 \Big]_{\frac{1}{4}\sqrt{\frac{1}{\pi}}}^{\frac{1}{4}\sqrt{\frac{1}{\pi}}} = 0$
	–	$anergy_{Q3} = -\frac{1}{3}\pi r^2 \Big]_{\sqrt{\frac{1}{\pi}}}^{\frac{1}{4}\sqrt{\frac{1}{\pi}}} = 0.31$

Leading to Table 3 ← **Leading to**

Table 3. Assessing a *Nurse's Entropic State* when responding to the *NCDS-3* questionnaire in the *Best-case Scenario* (Table 1).

	Scale (4) (3) (2) (1)					Scale (1) (2) (3) (4)				
	EX	*VA*	*AN*	*EC*	*QoI*		*EX*	*VA*	*AN*	*EC*	*QoI*
$ncds - 3_{4\text{-}1}$	0.08	-	0.58	0.997	0.92	$ncds - 3_{1\text{-}4}$	0.02	-	0.31	1.0	0.98

Leading to   **Leading to**

→ **Program 1** ←

{

/* *The sentences below state that the extension of predicate ncds* $- 3_{4\text{-}1}$ *is based on explicitly specified clauses and those (i.e. exceptions(...)) that cannot be dropped* */

$\neg\, ncds - 3_{4-1}\ (EX,\ VA,\ AN,\ EC,\ QoI)$

$\leftarrow not\ ncds - 3_{4-1}\ (EX,\ VA,\ AN,\ EC,\ QoI),$

$not\ exception_{ncds-3_{4-1}}\ (EX,\ VA,\ AN,\ EC,\ QoI)$

$ncds - 3_{4-1}\ (0.08,\ 0,\ 0.58,\ 0.997,\ 0.92).$

$\neg\, ncds - 3_{1-4}\ (EX,\ VA,\ AN,\ EC,\ QoI)$

$\leftarrow not\ ncds - 3_{1-4}\ (EX,\ VA,\ AN,\ EC,\ QoI),$

$not\ exception_{ncds-3_{1-4}}\ (EX,\ VA,\ AN,\ EC,\ QoI)$

$ncds - 3_{1-4}\ (0.02,\ 0,\ 0.31,\ 1.0,\ 0.98).$

}

Program 1. Logic program built on the extensions of predicates $ncds - 3_{4\text{-}1}$ and $ncds - 3_{1\text{-}4}$ for the *Best-case Scenario*.

3 Case Study

It is now possible, making use of the procedure employed in the evaluation of a *Nurse's Entropic State* in terms of their answers to *NCDS* $- 3$ questionnaire in the *Best-case Scenario*, get similar values to the remaining predicates, i.e., $ids - 2_{4\text{-}1}$, $ncds - 3_{4\text{-}1}$, $bds - 1_{4\text{-}1}$, $crds - 5_{4\text{-}1}$ and $ids - 2_{1\text{-}4}$, $ncds - 3_{1\text{-}4}$, $bds - 1_{1\text{-}4}$, $crds - 5_{4\text{-}1}$, Table 4, viz.

Table 4. Ids – $2_{4\text{-}1}$, ncds – $3_{4\text{-}1}$, bds – $1_{4\text{-}1}$, crds – $5_{4\text{-}1}$ and ids – $2_{1\text{-}4}$, ncds – $3_{1\text{-}4}$, bds – $1_{1\text{-}4}$, crds – $5_{4\text{-}1}$ predicates' extensions according to the answers given by a nurse to IDS – 2, NCDS – 3, BDS – 1 and CRDS – 5 questionnaires in the Best-case Scenario.

| | Scale (4) (3) (2) (1) | | | | | | Scale (1) (2) (3) (4) | | | | |
	EX	VA	AN	EC	QoI		EX	VA	AN	EC	QoI
IDS– $2_{4\text{-}1}$	0.03	-	0.47	1.0	0.97	IDS – $2_{1\text{-}4}$	0.03	-	0.47	1.0	0.97
NCDS – $3_{4\text{-}1}$	0.08	-	0.58	0.997	0.92	NCDS – $3_{1\text{-}4}$	0.02	-	0.31	1.0	0.98
BDS – $1_{4\text{-}1}$	–	–	–	–	–	BDS – $1_{1\text{-}4}$	1.0	-	-	-	-
CRDS – $5_{4\text{-}1}$	0.06	-	0.54	0.998	0.94	CRDS – $5_{1\text{-}4}$	0.25	-	0.15	0.97	0.75
catch-all-clause	0.06	-	0.53	0.998	0.94	catch-all-clause	0.33	-	0.23	0.74	0.67

Leading to   **Leading to**

⟶ **Program 2** ⟵

where *catch-all-clause* denotes a term that cover all possibilities not covered by the individual ones (e.g. $catch-all-clause_{EX_{4-1}} = (0.03 + 0.08 + 0 + 0.06)/4 = 0.06$.

```
{
/* The sentences below state that the extension of predicates ids – 2₄₋₁ and ids – 2₁₋₄ are
based on explicitly specified clauses and those that cannot be dropped */
```

$\neg\, ids - 2_{4-1}\, (EX, VA, AN, EC, QoI)$

$\leftarrow not\ ids - 2_{4-1}\, (EX, VA, AN, EC, QoI),$

$not\ exception_{ids-2_{4-1}}\, (EX, VA, AN, EC, QoI)$

$ids - 2_{4-1}\, (0.03, 0, 0.47, 1.0, 0.97).$

```
}
```

··· (the dots stand for the remaining *predicates₄₋₁* present in Table 4)

```
{
```

$\neg\, ids - 2_{1-4}(EX, VA, AN, EC, QoI)$

$\leftarrow not\ ids - 2_{1-4}\, (EX, VA, AN, EC, QoI),$

$not\ exception_{ids-2_{1-4}}\, (EX, VA, AN, EC, QoI)$

$ids - 2_{1-4}\, (0.03, 0, 0.47, 1.0, 0.97).$

··· (the dots stand for the remaining *predicates₁₋₄* existing in Table 4)

```
}
```

Program 2. Logic program built on the extensions of predicates $ids - 2_{4\text{-}1}$, $ncds - 3_{4\text{-}1}$, $bds - 1_{4\text{-}1}$, $crds - 5_{4\text{-}1}$ and $ids - 2_{1\text{-}4}$, $ncds - 3_{1\text{-}4}$, $bds - 1_{1\text{-}4}$, $crds - 5_{4\text{-}1}$ for the *Best-case Scenario*.

It is therefore possible to evaluate the *Nurses' Degree of Effective Communication* (*EC*) in the *Best-case Scenario* (which scores from the nurses' answers to the question-naires referred to above) over a period of 5 (five) months (Fig. 2). The nurse' course is gotten by proving theorems 1 and 2, viz.

Theorem 1. Exergy$_{4-1}$.

$$\forall (\{EX_1, VA_1, AN_1, EC_1, QoI_1\}, \cdots, \{EX_4, VA_4, AN_4, EC_4, QoI_4\}),$$
$$(\{ids\text{-}2_{4-1}\,(EX_1, VA_1, AN_1, EC_1, QoI_1)\}, \cdots$$
$$\cdots, \{crds\text{-}5_{4-1}\,(EX_4, VA_4, AN_4, EC_4, QoI_4)\}).$$

Theorem 2. Exergy$_{1-4}$.

$$\forall (\{EX_1, VA_1, AN_1, EC_1, QoI_1\}, \cdots, \{EX_4, VA_4, AN_4, EC_4, QoI_4\}),$$
$$(\{ids\text{-}2_{1-4}\,(EX_1, VA_1, AN_1, EC_1, QoI_1)\}, \cdots$$
$$\cdots, \{crds\text{-}5_{1-4}\,(EX_4, VA_4, AN_4, EC_4, QoI_4)\}).$$

Leading to ⟶ **Fig. 2** ⟵ **Leading to**

in every possible way and according to the timeline (Fig. 2) and Program 2. Indeed, it is shown that it is feasible to monitor and foresee the evolution of the *EC* according to how the nurses judge the state of affairs of the situation along the period of 5 (five) months; to foretell on the basis of a mathematical proof, i.e., all possible sequences that combine the terms or clauses of the predicates being referred to in this work, a number given by the expression, viz.

$$C_1^{Predicates\,extending} + \cdots + C_{Predicates\,extending\,cardinality}^{Predicates\,extending}$$

where $C_{Predicates\,extending\,cardinality}^{Predicates\,extending}$ is a predicate extension combination subset. Thus, one can have a template resulting from a proof of Theorem 1 under *scale$_{4-1}$* and *scale$_{1-4}$* for the different scenarios. Indeed, *Proof Theory* considers the notion of derivability of a sentence in the context of some rules for theorem derivation. We could then work with any set *R* of rules of the form [13], viz.

Derive such a sentence from a set of such sentences or From a set of sentences of that kind, derive a sentence of this kind.

i.e., one could then take any initial set *S* of sentences in LP and by applying different rules in *R* finally derive some new sentences *s* from *S* and/or other derived sentences. This performed, within the given language LP, constructs a *Derivability Relation* symbolized by $\vdash$, $\vdash = \{\langle S, s\rangle\}$, where *S* is a subset of *LP*, *s* is a member of *LP* derivable from *S* using *R*. *R* stands for the the modus ponens inference rule, $\{(A \text{ if } B), B\} \vdash A$, that with the axioms constitute the inference system. Hence a proof from such a system can

be postulated as a sequence, $\langle s_1, \ldots s_i, \cdots, s_n \rangle$, where each s_i is either an axiom or otherwise derivable using R from a subset of the preceding members of the sequence. The sequence is called the proof of theorem s_n, also known as the derivation or deduction. Together with all theorems that can be derived from R, the axioms shape a theory that in our case is gotten as a side effect, via unification, a process inherent to the theorems being object of a proof (that is not given in an analytical form due to the lack of space), but is given in a pictoral form (Fig. 2), viz.

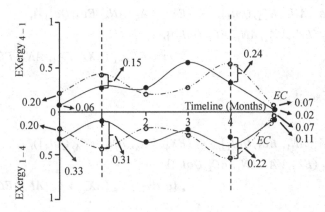

Fig. 2. Evolution of a *Nurses' EC according to the state of affairs of the EC* process in the *Best-case Scenario* along 5 (five) months (Table 4 and Program 2).

According to the diagram of Fig. 2 it is now possible to quantify a nurse perception of the *EC* affair along the timeline. For example, for $t = 0$ one may have, viz.

$$EC_{t=0} = ((EX_{4-1} + VA_{4-1}) + (EX_{1-4} + VA_{1-4}))/2$$

$$EC_{t=0} = ((0.06 + 0) + (0.33 + 0))/2 = 0.195$$

On the other hand, for $t = 5$ one may have, viz.

$$EC_{t=5} = ((EX_{4-1} + VA_{4-1}) + (EX_{1-4} + VA_{1-4}))/2 = (0.02 + 0.11)/2 = 0.065$$

According to Fig. 2, if a nurse entropic state is close to zero (in this case with values of $EC_{t=0} = 0.195$ and $EC_{t=5} = 0.065$ (low entropy)), the *EC* is excellent [1, 2]. On the other hand, an analysis of Fig. 2, in terms of a increase/decrease in entropy between the cutoff lines at times $t = 1$ and $t = 4$, is expressed in the form, viz.

$$I = ((Exergy_{4-1} - \Delta EC_{4-1}) - (Exergy_{1-4} - \Delta EC_{1-4}))_{t=1}$$
$$= (0.15 - 0.31)_{t=1} = -0.16$$

and,

$$J = ((Exergy_{4-1} - \Delta EC_{4-1}) - (Exergy_{1-4} - \Delta EC_{1-4}))_{t=4}$$
$$= (0.24 - 0.22)_{t=4} = 0.02$$

is given as, viz.

$$J - I = 0.02 - (-0.16) = 0.18$$

that reflects a nurse's perception of how much the tendency to system's increase/decrease in entropy can cancel each other out, allowing the trend in systems evolution to be identified. In the present situation $J - I = 0.18$, a value close to zero, meaning that the entropy decreased, and as a consequence an improvement of the nurse's entropic state takes place.

4 Results Analysis

An approach to assessing *EC in Transitional Care During Shift Changes* has a say in *Computational Sustainability* (*CS*) and presents challenges arising from interactions between the natural and human-evolved spheres at the temporal and spatial scales. This has motivated health and informatics researchers to apply their craft to environmental, societal, and sustainable health challenges. In fact, interdisciplinary research teams focus on cross-sectional disciplines such as psychology, economics, mathematical logic, optimization, dynamic modelling, big data, machine learning, citizen science or health. In terms of planning and search technologies, the ability of *CS* to consider many possible outcomes is undeniably a cognitive ability that would greatly benefit human problem solving and decision making. In fact, despite technological developments in several areas of people's lives, few developments in research have been made to meet nurses's expectations. New problem-solving methodologies and methods stemming from the above areas may be used to assess nurses' feelings and sentiments, a way to support their insertion into the system of corporate management; indeed a way to help managers and politicians to back actions that can result in meeting nurses's prospects. This was the main goal of this work, which was achieved by developing a *Mathematical Logic based Computing Environment* in which nurses expectations and concerns can be examined, simulated and solutions provided.

5 Conclusions and Future Work

One of the greatest strategic challenges for heathcare corporations is the management of their nurse staff. A leadership model, emphasizing the flexibility of the health system and the nurses' intrinsic motivations, it is believed that it may not only capture and properly use its nursing staff, but ultimately make them happy. The study objectives were set before the exposed person, i.e. the prioritization of the organization's nurses over factors of *EC*. Long integration times, high workload, professional stress, burnout and others can lead to dissatisfaction and demotivation. In this case of *EC*, one's approach allows for preventive/corrective actions that help create the best conditions for professional development and nurses satisfaction. A continuous and long-term analysis of this problem in this and other contexts, combined with preventive and corrective interventions, will make it possible to retrieve more and more sensitive information. Future work will address nurses' relationships with their peers and other professionals or institutions, and how issues on *Leadership*, *Justice*, and *Power* may affect their empowerment.

Acknowledgments. This work has been supported by FCT – Fundação para a Ciência e Tecnologia within the R&D Units Project Scope: UIDB/00319/2020.

References

1. Alert, S.E.: Inadequate hand-off communication. Sentinel Event Alert **58**, 1–6 (2017)
2. Beigmoradi, S., Pourshirvani, A., Pazokian, M., Nasiri, M.: Evaluation of nursing hand-off skillamong nurses using situation-background-assessment-recommendation checklist in general wards. Evid. Based Care J. **9**, 63–68 (2019)
3. Chapman, Y., Schweickert, P., Swango-Wilson, A., Aboul-Enein, F., Heyman, A.: Nurse satisfaction with information technology enhanced bedside handoff. Medsurg Nurs. **25**, 313–318 (2016)
4. Müller, M., Jürgens, J., Redaèlli, M., Klingberg, K., Hautz, W., Stocket, S.: Impact of the communication and patient hand-off tool SBAR on patient safety: a systematic review. BMJ Open **8**(8), e022202 (2018)
5. DGS. https://www.dgs.pt/directrizes-da-dgs/normas-e-circulares-normativas/norma-n-001 2017-de-08022017-pdf.aspx. Accessed 21 Apr 2022
6. Stewart, K.: SBAR, communication, and patient safety: an integrated literature review. Honors Theses, University of Tennessee, Chattanooga, USA (2016)
7. De Meester, K., Verspuy, M., Monsieurs, K.G., Van Bogaert, P.: SBAR improves nurse – physician communication and reduces unexpected death: A pre and post intervention study. Resuscitation **84**, 1192–1196 (2013)
8. Superville, J.: Standardizing Nurse-to-Nurse Patient Handoffs in a Correctional Healthcare Setting: A Quality Improvement Project to Improve End-of-Shift Nurse-to-Nurse Communication Using the SBAR I-5 Handoff Bundle. The University of North Carolina, Chapel Hill, USA (2017)
9. Neves, J., et al.: A multi-valued logic assessment of organizational performance via workforce social networking. In: Deze, Z., Huang, H., Hou, R., Rho, S., Chilamkurti, N. (eds.) Big Data Technologies and Applications. LNICSSITE, vol. 371, pp. 63–77. Springer, Cham (2021). https://doi.org/10.1007/978-3-030-72802-1_5
10. Neves, J., et al.: Entropy and organizational performance. In: Pérez García, H., Sánchez González, L., Castejón Limas, M., Quintián Pardo, H., Corchado Rodríguez, E. (eds.) Hybrid Artificial Intelligent Systems. Lecture Notes in Computer Science, vol. 11734, pp. 206–217. Springer, Cham (2019). https://doi.org/10.1007/978-3-030-29859-3_18
11. Wenterodt, T., Herwig, H.: The entropic potential concept: a new way to look at energy transfer operations. Entropy **16**, 2071–2084 (2014)
12. Neves, J., et al.: Employees balance and stability as key points in organizational performance. Logic J. IGPL (2021). https://doi.org/10.1093/jigpal/jzab010
13. Neves, J.: A logic interpreter to handle time and negation in logic databases. In: Muller, R., Pottmyer, J. (eds.) Proceedings of the 1984 Annual Conference of the ACM on the 5th Generation Challenge, pp. 50–54. ACM, New York (1984)

PAUL: An Algorithmic Composer for Classical Piano Music Supporting Multiple Complexity Levels

Felix Schön[(✉)] [iD] and Hans Tompits[iD]

Institute of Logic and Computation E192-03, Technische Universität Wien,
Favoritenstraße 9-11, 1040 Vienna, Austria
{schoen,tompits}@kr.tuwien.ac.at

Abstract. *Algorithmic composition* (AC) refers to the process of creating music by means of algorithms, either for realising music entirely composed by a computer or with the help of a computer. In this paper, we report on the development of the system PAUL, an algorithmic composer for the automatic creation of short pieces of classical piano music, based on a neural-network architecture. The distinguishing feature of PAUL is that it allows to specify the desired complexity of the output piece in terms of an input parameter, which is a central aspect towards the designated future usage of PAUL as being part of a tutoring system teaching piano students how to sight-read music. PAUL employs a *long short-term memory* (LSTM) *neural network* to produce the lead track and a *sequence-to-sequence neural network* for the realisation of the accompanying track. Although PAUL is still work-in-progress, the obtained results are of reasonable to good quality. In a small-scale study, evaluating the specified vs. the perceived complexity of different pieces generated by PAUL, a clear correlation is observable.

Keywords: Algorithmic composition · Neural networks · Music education

1 Introduction

Algorithmic composition (AC), in its most general understanding, denotes the creation of music based on formalisable methods. On the one hand, this can refer to music created by humans based on specific rule sets, like counterpoint or dodecaphony, and, on the other hand, to music created fully automatically in terms of algorithms. Although the latter meaning nowadays refers to music created by a computer or with the help of a computer, the origins of algorithmic composition in its strict, automated sense, predate the modern computer as early as Guido d'Arezzo's *Micrologus de disciplina artis musicae*, published around the year 1025, or the well-known *dice game*, commonly attributed to Mozart. While early work in AC using computer programs was pioneered, e.g., by Gottfried Michael

G. Marreiros et al. (Eds.): EPIA 2022, LNAI 13566, pp. 415–426, 2022.
https://doi.org/10.1007/978-3-031-16474-3_34

Koenig [10], modern AC methods encompass techniques including, but not limited to, *Markov models* [8], *generative grammars* [13], *transition networks* [5], *genetic algorithms* [4], *cellular automata* [1], *logic-based approaches* [2,16], and *neural networks* [7,17] (for a detailed overview about AC, we refer, e.g., to *The Oxford Handbook of Algorithmic Music* [14]).

With the growing advancement of techniques in artificial intelligence (AI) and machine learning, AC approaches based on neural networks show particular promise in recent years. Examples in this regard include *MuseGAN* [6], *Music-VAE* [18], and OpenAI's *MuseNet* [17]. Networks employed in several of these approaches are so-called *long short-term memory* (LSTM) units [11], which are powerful recurrent neural network (RNN) architectures particularly useful for processing sequences of data like audio or video signals. Indeed, a particular strength of LSTMs, as far as AC applications is concerned, is their ability to deal with the long-term structure of the generated music.

In this paper, we report on the development of an automatic composer program, called PAUL, for the creation of short pieces of classical piano music, based on LSTM units.[1] PAUL is trained on a dataset of classical piano pieces including works of composers like Mozart, Bach, and Beethoven, taken from the online database at piano-midi.de. The output of PAUL consists of MIDI files containing two distinct tracks, similar to traditional two-handed piano music. While the lead track is generated by means of LSTM units, the accompanying track is taken care of by a *sequence-to-sequence* (seq2seq) neural network [20], depending on the leading track as input. A seq2seq model has the advantage of allowing to map a sequence of one language to a sequence of another, not necessarily of the same length, which is a useful feature for our purpose.

The distinguishing feature of PAUL is that the complexity of the generated output piece can be specified in terms of an input parameter. Here, the term "complexity" refers to the difficulty of playing the generated piece on a regular piano by a human pianist. This is done in order to allow for a future use of PAUL in a tutoring system for teaching piano students how to sight-read without making use of a fixed set of musical phrases to train on. This way, one could make sure that students rely on their sight-reading capabilities rather than memorise a corpus of musical prompts. Furthermore, due to the ability of PAUL to generate music conforming to the above mentioned complexity specifications, one could make sure that the students would be challenged yet not overwhelmed by the tasks. This complexity specification consists of three different levels, each more difficult and demanding than the preceding one. For example, a very demanding piece should be given a "hard" rating while an introductory piece should receive an "easy" rating.

Our initial results on the performance of PAUL show that the obtained pieces are of reasonable to good quality and that there is a clear correlation between the specified input complexity and the complexity of the generated output, which was evaluated in terms of a small-scale user study.

---

[1] The name of the program refers to the famous Viennese pianist Paul Badura-Skoda (1927–2019).

Fig. 1. An assortment of notes and rests of different values.

2 Algorithmic Composition Approach

To start our discussion on the details of PAUL, we lay down the structure and functionality of the system. PAUL was written using Python 3.7.7 and utilises Tensorflow 2.1[2] for the neural network architecture and the MIDI protocol [15] for dealing with digitalised music files, which in turn are handled by the Python library Mido 1.2.9[3].

2.1 A Few Preliminaries

In order to better understand the workings of PAUL, let us first recapitulate some fundamental elements of music notation. For a thorough introduction to music theory, we refer the reader, e.g., to the work of Boone and Schonbrun [3].

In the vocabulary for writing musical scores, *notes* are used to denote pitch. The higher the note on the score, the higher the corresponding pitch will be. These notes have *values*, which tell the reader how long a note lasts. Notes are labeled with letters A through G, and numbers determining the height of the notes, e.g., a G5 is lower than an F6. *Rests* are similar to notes in the sense that they have values, although they tell the player to pause for a specified amount of time. This, in combination with note values, allows for the construction of rhythm.

Figure 1 depicts an assortment of different notes and rests on two tracks. The top track contains a whole note in the first section (called a *bar*), and a half-, quarter-, eighth-, sixteenth-, and thirty-second note in the second bar, in this order. The bottom track contains rests of equal values as the aforementioned notes. The third bar contains two *triplets*, three quarter notes played in the time of two quarter notes, marked by a brace above them.

As pointed out above, PAUL utilises the MIDI format for dealing with digitalised music files. The MIDI protocol is a well-known industry standard for storing and exchanging such files, proposed in 1983 [15]. Roughly speaking, a conventional MIDI file contains a number of *note on* and *note off* messages, which represent, e.g., the pressing and releasing of a piano key. Furthermore, subsequent messages specify how many ticks (units of time) to wait between them. This allows for the construction of rhythm. MIDI is widely used, e.g., to capture piano performances, in digital audio workstations, in the video field, and for many more applications.

---

[2] https://www.tensorflow.org/.
[3] https://mido.readthedocs.io/en/latest/.

2.2   Concept

The aim of PAUL is to create musical pieces of a special nature. The output consists of MIDI files representing the generated composition, which can then be translated into a sheet-music representation using third-party software such as, e.g., Cubase[4]. PAUL supports the handling of two-track piano pieces, where each track corresponds to a score line in the piano score. These tracks are separately encoded in the MIDI file as well. Additionally, the possibility of defining a desired complexity grade is provided by PAUL. Specifying one of the complexity ratings EASY, MEDIUM, or HARD for each of the tracks (not necessarily the same for both) should result in the generation of pieces that conform to the complexity rating as specified later on.

The consideration behind these measures is to eventually use the system in order to create simple musical phrases, used for sight-reading education purposes. Such an educational program would use the generator PAUL in order to dynamically create new pieces based on the skill level of a student. A streak of correctly played notes would, e.g., result in an increase in difficulty level, successive errors in playing in a lowered difficulty. We note that the resolution of the complexity grading as currently realised in PAUL would most likely have to be refined for such a future application.

In order to generate the musical pieces, PAUL employs a *recurrent neural network* (RNN) [9] using *long short-term* (LSTM) units [11] in order to independently generate messages for the right-hand track, and a *sequence-to-sequence* (seq2seq) neural network [20] that takes as input the generated track and outputs a dependent left-hand track. The RNN is then trained to compose a new lead track based only on, e.g., a few input notes, while the seq2seq network is trained in such a way that it correctly encodes the input lead track and, based on this encoding, is able to generate a fitting accompaniment. This way, it is possible to provide piano students musical pieces similar to real-life examples rather than random amalgamations of notes. We note that although recent approaches [12,17] employ the *Transformer* [12,21], a network architecture based solely on an attention mechanism producing promising results, we deliberately opted for a more basic approach. Indeed, the Transformer is particularly well-equipped to handle long-term sequences, but this is not a concern for PAUL since it deals with a fixed size of only four musical bars.

In order for PAUL to be able to generate pieces of varying complexity, we store three different sets of weights for each of the networks. Each set of weights corresponds to a version of the network that is suited to generate pieces of one of the three complexities. These versions are then only trained on pieces of similar complexities. The idea is that this way the versions will be able to pick up on the rules that govern the complexity of a piece. In order to generate a new piece, the requested set of weights can then be loaded.

The networks are trained on a preexisting corpus of classical piano pieces, retrieved from the online database at piano-midi.de. In order to provide the

---

[4] https://www.steinberg.net/cubase/.

Table 1. Internal elements and their representation used in the program.

Message type	Range	Textual representation	Numeral representation
Padding	n/a	n/a	0
Play	21–108	p21-p108	1–88
Stop	21–108	s21-s108	89–176
Wait	1–24	w1-w24	177–200
Start	n/a	m0	201
End	n/a	m1	202

networks with enough data, the pieces are split up into bars, which are then individually judged regarding complexity, independently for the right-hand and the left-hand track. This is done in order to ensure an (approximate) equality of the amount of data available for each complexity class.

2.3 Data Preprocessing

In order to obtain a basis for the training of the neural networks, a collection of different pieces by five different influential classical composers (viz., Beethoven, Chopin, Mozart, Rachmaninoff, and Schubert) was acquired from the database at piano-midi.de. This database is well-fitted for our approach as it exclusively contains sequenced MIDI files rather than pure audio recordings. This fact is essential for the later processing of the data, as otherwise, e.g., quantisation cannot be done consistently. Furthermore, the sequenced files contain separate tracks corresponding to either the lead or the accompanying track.

As neural networks cannot accept traditional MIDI data as input, a conversion from the MIDI file format to one usable by the input layers of the networks has to be done. Musical pieces are hereby represented using three different message types: *play*, *stop*, and *wait*. Table 1 shows the different types of elements of such a representation. Here, every entry corresponds to either a played (or lifted) piano key, the amount of ticks to wait, or an identifier for start and stop messages. The program uses 88 different notes in order to model the entire range of a standard piano, and thus makes use of 88 different play (and stop) messages. A play message signals the start of a note and the corresponding stop message the end.

PAUL allows for note and rest values of down to thirty-second triplets. In order to do so, a *pulses per quarter note* (PPQN) value of 24 was chosen, meaning that a quarter note lasts 24 ticks. Note that the PPQN value is part of the MIDI specification and defines the resolution of a quarter note. This specifies the length of thirty-second triplets and thirty-second notes with 2 and 3 ticks, respectively. In order not to dilute the vocabulary, the longest wait value was set to 24 ticks, corresponding to one quarter rest. Note values are simply constructed using a combination of play, wait, and stop messages, and rests using only wait messages.

The padding, start, and end messages are used exclusively for the neural networks. The padding message is used in order to provide equally sized sequences

Table 2. Amount of complexity classes in the used corpus.

Track	Complexity	Amount	Proportion (rel. to Track)
Right hand	Easy	2263	29.6%
	Medium	3752	49.1%
	Hard	1630	21.3%
Left hand	Easy	2810	36.8%
	Medium	3883	50.8%
	Hard	952	12.5%

within *batches* (groups of bars fed to the neural network). The start and end messages are used by the seq2seq model in the translation of treble sequences to bass sequences.

The pipeline of importing and processing a MIDI file then consists of the following steps:

- **conversion**: converting MIDI messages to the internal format;
- **quantisation**: fitting the start and end of every message to a fixed-size grid;
- **splitting into equal time signatures**: split along time signature changes;
- **adjustment**: ensuring that a sequence represents a valid MIDI file;
- **splitting into bars**: a similar approach to time signatures, splitting messages that linger across two bars;
- **complexity assessment**: assigning a complexity score to each bar; and
- **consolidation of adjacent complexity classes**: consolidating to a maximum length of 4 bars, in order to provide a network with lengthier examples.

For the sake of brevity, in what follows, we will only detail the *complexity assessment* step, covering how bars are assigned a complexity value (further details can be found in the bachelor's thesis of the first author [19]). In this step, each bar is assigned a complexity value from the set {EASY, MEDIUM, HARD}. Note that the complexity is judged separately for each hand; these judgements are not dependent on each other.

The complexity assessment is done on the basis of four different metrics, viz., in descending order of importance: (i) the average time of note and rest values; (ii) the pattern of the elements; (iii) the amount of concurrently played notes; and (iv) the amount of note classes. Table 2 shows the amount of each complexity class per track in the training corpus judged using our criteria. Bars of the complexity rating MEDIUM make for about 50% of all the bars, the other two classes for the remaining half.

We next provide a short description of the four different metrics.

Average Note and Rest Values. This metric is based upon the average time of wait messages in a bar. A lower average wait time implies lower note and rest values, which in turn imply a more complex piece. Pieces with lower note and rest values are arguably harder to play, due to the fact that more notes have

(a) Easy pattern.   (b) More complex pattern.

Fig. 2. Two bars consisting of the same notes in a different arrangement in order to illustrate the influence of patterns on complexity.

to be read and played in the same amount of time. In this assessment, adjacent rests are consolidated, in order not to artificially lower the average wait time (e.g., $(1 + 1 + 4)/3$ is lower than $(2 + 4)/2$, even though the same amount of time is represented). For our assessment, average wait times of greater or equal to 18 (which implies a majority of quarter notes) are evaluated with EASY, while average wait times of greater than 12 ticks are evaluated with MEDIUM and values lower than these with HARD.

Note Patterns. Patterns and repetitions of musical elements can make playing a score considerably easier. Take for instance the two bars depicted in Fig. 2. Both of these bars consist of the same notes, an extract of Beethoven's Opus 27 No. 2, first movement, arranged in two different ways: while Fig. 2a is a one-to-one copy of the mentioned piece, Fig. 2b consist of randomly swapped positions of the elements. Even to the untrained eye, it will be obvious that the second piece is considerably more difficult to play.

PAUL uses regular expressions in order to detect patterns in sequences, and judges their complexity based on these observations.

Concurrent Notes. Playing several notes at the same point in time does not result in a lower average note or rest value, but does increase the complexity of the piece. Reading multiple notes at one time requires recognition of patterns like chords, and the sight-reading of more notes in general.

This metric is based upon the average number of notes played between wait and stop messages. It returns a complexity rating of EASY if the average is less than or equal to 2, MEDIUM if it is less than or equal to 3.5, and HARD otherwise.

Note Classes. Although the sequence represented in Fig. 2b is definitely harder to play than the one represented in Fig. 2a, it still consists of the same notes, and more experienced players will have no difficulties with it. Had the pitches of the sequence changed (in a way that would not result in an easier pattern), the previous metrics would not have estimated it to be more complex. This is why we consider the amount of different note classes played as well. This metric does not consider C3 and C4 for instance to be the same note.

A value of 4 or less note classes in a bar is assessed as EASY, 8 or less as MEDIUM, and everything above that as HARD.

3   Neural Network Training and Generation

As stated previously, two different kinds of neural networks are employed for PAUL: a recurrent network using LSTMs in order to create the treble (or lead) sequences, and a seq2seq model in order to generate the bass (or accompanying) sequences. In what follows, we give a brief discussion on how these networks were generated and trained, as well as an analysis of the created music files.

To begin with, as far as the technical side is concerned, let us note that both networks were created in Python using the Tensorflow framework, and trained on either an NVIDIA GeForce GTX 1060 (6 GB model) locally, or an NVIDIA Tesla K80, made available through Microsoft's Azure platform[5].

Treble Sequences Generation. A three-hidden-layer architecture, consisting of an embedding layer, three LSTM layers with dropout layers prepended after each, and a dense output layer was employed. After embedding an input using 32 dimensions, it gets passed through the hidden layers, each with a size of 1024 nodes per layer. A dropout of 20% is applied after each LSTM layer in order to combat overfitting.

The input data is split into two different sets, consisting of input and target values. The network is then trained to predict the next word in a sequence—in our case, the next play, stop, or wait message in the composition.

After training the network, new sequences can be generated using a primer of one or more start messages. Here, categorical sampling of the predictions was used, where each output has a chance to be drawn proportional to its confidence level. Training this network took approximately 4 to 6 h per complexity rating. Doubling the amount of layers and nodes (like in the seq2seq model) resulted in an exponentially higher training duration and hardware requirement, and exceeded the limits of the employed GPU.

Bass Sequences Generation. As mentioned, a seq2seq model was employed to manage the task of the generation of the bass sequences. In a similar fashion to the conventional model, both the encoder and decoder of the seq2seq unit consist of an embedding layer with 32 dimensions and three LSTM layers with 1024 nodes and a dropout of 20% each. A dense output layer is prepended to the decoder model in order to generate the sequences.

Due to the much larger network size, training this model demanded significantly more resources compared to the traditional one. Training the network on the local GPU was only possible on the EASY rating. Higher complexities had to be trained on a rented virtual machine from the Azure platform. This way, half of an NVIDIA Tesla K80 could be utilised.

The MEDIUM model was trained for around 40 h, resulting in only 10 completed *epochs*, where an epoch consists of feeding the entire dataset to the network once. In comparison, the networks for the treble sequences could be trained for 30 epochs or more.

---

[5] https://azure.microsoft.com/en-us/.

(a) Score representation of an easy instance.

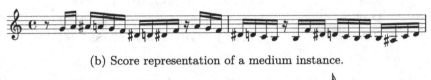

(b) Score representation of a medium instance.

(c) Score representation of a hard instance.

Fig. 3. Two bars consisting of the same notes in a different arrangement in order to illustrate the influence of patterns on complexity.

The generation of sequences works analogously to the treble sequences, with the exception that bass sequences need a full treble sequence as input, rather than a primer consisting of possibly few words.

Discussion and Evaluation of the Generated Music Files. As for an assessment of the music files created by PAUL, we first of all note that a clear difference in quality between treble and bass tracks can be observed. The generated treble (right hand) sequences are of good, sometimes even great quality.

Figure 3 shows different examples generated with the treble model using each of our complexity ratings in a score representation created by LilyPond[6]. The generated MIDI files were not transposed, and no accidental reducing key was chosen. As a result, these excerpts may appear more difficult (regarding conventional standards) than if these measures had been taken. PAUL does not consider accidentals regarding complexity. Apart from the aforementioned metric, a clear correlation between specified complexity and complexity regarding sight-reading can be observed.

One weakness of the network lies in stopping some previously played notes. Sometimes, a few notes drag on until the end of the generated piece, cluttering visual representation. In order to combat this phenomenon, a limit to maximum note length was introduced. For these examples, the limit was set to 24 ticks (the length of a quarter note).

Interesting results regarding the complexity rating can be observed. Table 3 shows the results of generating 80 bars per complexity class and judging these bars regarding their complexity in order to check whether the network is in fact capable of generating pieces that belong to a given complexity.

---

[6] https://lilypond.org/.

Table 3. Amount of complexity classes generated when tasked with a specific class, measured on 80 bars.

Specified complexity	Easy	Medium	Hard
Easy	60 (75%)	19 (23.75%)	1 (1.25%)
Medium	9 (11.25%)	52 (65%)	19 (23.75%)
Hard	2 (2.5%)	11 (13.75%)	67 (83.75%)

A clear trend regarding the specified and the output complexities can be observed: both EASY and HARD complexities generate their respective complexity about three quarters of the time, but almost never complexities on the other end of the spectrum. However, the MEDIUM complexity generation is a bit more scattered as for about two thirds of the time the specified complexity is generated but almost every fourth time a HARD bar is generated.

In order to combat misaligned complexities for practical uses, the bar can simply be generated anew as often as needed in order to produce a bar of the desired complexity. It is important to note at this point that our approach is not deterministic but rather drawing from a set of possible notes with a certain probability determined by the network. Notes that the network deems to be more well-fitted have a higher chance of being drawn, but more unfit notes will be selected from time to time. Independently of whether or not the used metrics accurately describe the "real" complexity of pieces, the networks are capable of generating pieces conforming to the implemented measurements.

In a small-scale study involving 21 participants with varying levels of musical education, we tried to determine whether our complexity metrics accurately reflect the difficulty of the pieces. Persons were provided with audio samples of the respective complexity classes and were asked which of the three complexity levels would best describe the sample. Figure 4 shows a confusion matrix of the results. A clear trend between the actual and the evaluated class can be noted: although EASY and HARD are never evaluated as each other, both of them are sometimes evaluated as MEDIUM. We note that one EASY sample in the set was quite ambiguous and evaluated as MEDIUM almost 50% of the time, which substantially inflates the number of incorrectly categorised EASY instances. Although a clear correlation regarding the MEDIUM samples is visible too, neighbouring classes are predicted more often. We argue that the varying levels of music education of the participants are not significant for this evaluation as the results are quite evident in the first place, especially regarding the HARD class. Although the evaluations of PAUL seem to be quite good according to this survey, future iterations could improve upon the distinctions between MEDIUM and the other two classes.

Currently, the results produced by the bass track generator are not as good as the treble ones. Although a network with three layers for both the encoder and decoder is capable of generating messages, these do not translate well to MIDI. Albeit an unequivocal relationship can be observed of playing one note, stopping it, and then playing another one, only few wait messages are being generated.

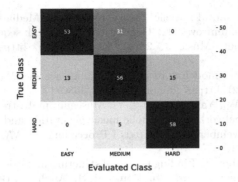

Fig. 4. Confusion matrix of the survey results.

This results in the generated tracks not having sufficient temporal structure. Due to this fact, evaluations of the bass sequences are not yet possible.

4   Conclusion and Discussion

In this paper, we reported on the development and main features of the algorithmic composer PAUL, a system capable of generating classical piano music based on a designated complexity rating. PAUL is work-in-progress and its main aim for future applications is to be used within a tutoring system helping piano students how to sight-read sheet music. PAUL works on the basis of pre-processed MIDI files converted to an internal format, representing musical sequences.

Although the lead track shows already reasonable to good quality, in future work we plan to improve the overall performance of the system, particularly concerning the generation of the bass track. We are currently working on an updated version that eschews the three fixed complexity classes for a more fine-grained difficulty scale. Furthermore, we are planning on employing the Transformer [12,21] as underlying network, since it could produce better results, especially regarding the bass track.

Acknowledgements. The authors would like to thank Wolfgang Schmidtmayr from the University of Music and Performing Arts Vienna for valuable help during the development of this work.

References

1. Bilotta, E., Miranda, E.R., Pantano, P.S., Todd, P.M.: Artificial life models for musical applications: workshop report. Artif. Life **8**(1), 83–86 (2002). https://doi. org/10.1162/106454602753694774
2. Boenn, G., Brain, M., Vos, M.D., Fitch, J.P.: Automatic music composition using answer set programming. Theory Pract. Logic Program. **11**(2–3), 397–427 (2011). https://doi.org/10.1017/S1471068410000530

3. Boone, B., Schonbrun, M.: Music Theory 101. Adams Media (2017)
4. Burton, A.R., Vladimirova, T.: Generation of musical sequences with genetic techniques. Comput. Music J. **23**(4), 59–73 (1999). https://doi.org/10.1162/014892699560001
5. Cope, D.: Computer modeling of musical intelligence in EMI. Comput. Music J. **16**(2), 69–83 (1992). https://doi.org/10.2307/3680717
6. Dong, H., Hsiao, W., Yang, L., Yang, Y.: Musegan: multi-track sequential generative adversarial networks for symbolic music generation and accompaniment. In: McIlraith, S.A., Weinberger, K.Q. (eds.) Proceedings of AAAI, 2018, pp. 34–41. AAAI Press (2018)
7. Eck, D., Schmidhuber, J.: Finding temporal structure in music: blues improvisation with LSTM recurrent networks. In: Bourlard, H., Adali, T., Bengio, S., Larsen, J., Douglas, S. (eds.) Proceedings of NNSP 2002, pp. 747–756. IEEE Press (2002). https://doi.org/10.1109/NNSP.2002.1030094
8. Gillick, J., Tang, K., Keller, R.M.: Machine learning of jazz grammars. Comput. Music J. **34**(3), 56–66 (2010). https://doi.org/10.1162/COMJ_a_00006
9. Goodfellow, I.J., Bengio, Y., Courville, A.C.: Deep Learning. Adaptive Computation and Machine Learning, MIT Press, Cambridge (2016)
10. Gottstein, B.: Gottfried Michael Koenig: Die Logik der Maschine. In: Gottstein, B. (ed.) Musik als Ars Scientia. Die Edgard-Varèse-Gastprofessoren des DAAD an der TU Berlin 2000–2006. Pfau Verlag, Saarbrücken (2006)
11. Hochreiter, S., Schmidhuber, J.: Long short-term memory. Neural Comput. **9**(8), 1735–1780 (1997). https://doi.org/10.1162/neco.1997.9.8.1735
12. Huang, C.A., et al.: Music transformer: generating music with long-term structure. In: Proceedings of ICLR 2019. OpenReview.net (2019)
13. Kitani, K.M., Koike, H.: Improvgenerator: online grammatical induction for on-the-fly improvisation accompaniment. In: Beilharz, K., Johnston, A., Ferguson, S., Chen, A.Y.C. (eds.) Proceedings of NIME 2010, pp. 469–472. nime.org (2010)
14. McLean, A., Dean, R.T. (eds.): The Oxford Handbook of Algorithmic Music. Oxford University Press, Oxford (2018)
15. MIDI manufacturers association incorporated: the complete MIDI 1.0 detailed specification. The MIDI Manufacturers Association (1983)
16. Opolka, S., Obermeier, P., Schaub, T.: Automatic genre-dependent composition using answer set programming. In: Proceedings of ISEA 2015, pp. 627–632. ISEA International (2015)
17. Payne, C.M.: MuseNet (2019). https://openai.com/blog/musenet
18. Roberts, A., Engel, J.H., Raffel, C., Hawthorne, C., Eck, D.: A hierarchical latent vector model for learning long-term structure in music. In: Dy, J.G., Krause, A. (eds.) Proceedings of ICML 2018. Proceedings of Machine Learning Research, vol. 80, pp. 4361–4370. PMLR (2018)
19. Schön, F.: PAUL An algorithmic composer of two-track piano pieces using recurrent neural networks. Bachelor's Thesis, Technische Universität Wien, Institute of Information Systems, E192–03 (2019)
20. Sutskever, I., Vinyals, O., Le, Q.V.: Sequence to sequence learning with neural networks. In: Ghahramani, Z., Welling, M., Cortes, C., Lawrence, N.D., Weinberger, K.Q. (eds.) Proceedings of NIPS 2014, pp. 3104–3112. Curran Associates, Inc. (2014)
21. Vaswani, A., et al.: Attention is all you need. In: Guyon, I., von Luxburg, U., Bengio, S., Wallach, H.M., Fergus, R., Vishwanathan, S.V.N., Garnett, R. (eds.) Proceedings of NIPS 2017, pp. 5998–6008. Curran Associates, Inc. (2017)

Assessing Policy, Loss and Planning Combinations in Reinforcement Learning Using a New Modular Architecture

Tiago Gaspar Oliveira[1,2]($\boxtimes$) and Arlindo L. Oliveira[1,2]

[1] INESC-ID, Lisbon, Portugal
[2] Instituto Superior Técnico, Lisbon, Portugal
{tiagojgroliveira,arlindo.oliveira}@tecnico.ulisboa.pt

Abstract. The model-based reinforcement learning paradigm, which uses planning algorithms and neural network models, has recently achieved unprecedented results in diverse applications, leading to what is now known as deep reinforcement learning. These agents are quite complex and involve multiple components, factors that create challenges for research and development of new models. In this work, we propose a new modular software architecture suited for these types of agents, and a set of building blocks that can be easily reused and assembled to construct new model-based reinforcement learning agents. These building blocks include search algorithms, policies, and loss functions (Code available at https://github.com/GaspTO/Modular_MBRL).

We illustrate the use of this architecture by combining several of these building blocks to implement and test agents that are optimized to three different test environments: Cartpole, Minigrid, and Tictactoe. One particular search algorithm, made available in our implementation and not previously used in reinforcement learning, which we called *averaged minimax*, achieved good results in the three tested environments. Experiments performed with our implementation showed the best combination of search, policy, and loss algorithms to be heavily problem dependent.

Keywords: Deep reinforcement learning · Model-based reinforcement learning · Neural networks · Architecture · Implementation

1 Introduction

In 2016, a program called AlphaGo [13] beat a Go world champion for the first time. Go was seen as the new milestone of artificial intelligence since the former world chess champion, Gary Kasparov, lost to DeepBlue in 1997 [5]. Go was finally mastered using reinforcement learning (RL), neural networks and a search algorithm. Following this achievement, an even more powerful program called AlphaGo Zero [15] was created, learning exclusively from playing against itself, indicating the strong potential of deep reinforcement learning (DRL).

G. Marreiros et al. (Eds.): EPIA 2022, LNAI 13566, pp. 427–439, 2022.
https://doi.org/10.1007/978-3-031-16474-3_35

It is not that any of those elements brought anything completely new to the field, but it was the first time they were assembled together and achieved outstanding results. The search component allowed deep reinforcement learning to reach a completely new level. Following this line of algorithms, two other very successful agents were created: AlphaZero [14], a generalized version of AlphaGo Zero, that became the best player in chess, shogi and Go, and MuZero [12], a program that achieved the same outstanding results, but was not given the rules of the game beforehand. Many other similar contributions happened as a consequence of the success of these algorithms.

These types of model-based algorithms are very complex and involve multiple parts that need to be combined together. There has been some studies varying some of these components trying to improve upon the previous state-of-the-art [3,7,9,16,17]. Another problem associated with this complexity is implementing them. Implementing these algorithms can be very time consuming, one of the reasons being deep learning's proclivity to *fail silently* due to its adaptable nature, which often leads to a large amount of time spent *debugging* and verifying code. It is not practical to refactor and recode the implementation every time one wants to try and study different ideas. We try to help these two problems by 1) Generalizing these model-based algorithms into a modular architecture and then implementing some possible algorithms in each one of the modules. One particular search algorithm, made available in our implementation, which we called *averaged minimax*, achieved good results in our experiments. 2) We present a comparative study of the agents created by combining different modules and show the best agent depends heavily on the nature of the problem being addressed.

2   Background

2.1   Muzero

The agents implementated in this work are similar to Muzero is many ways. Muzero is a model based reinforcement learning (MBRL) agent. It uses Monte Carlo tree search (MCTS) [8] to augment the capacity of its state evaluation by looking ahead in the state-space. In each iteration, the search will descend the tree looking for a leaf node to expand, using a best-first formula that mediates between exploitation and exploration. When expanding, it estimates a value for the leaf node's state, which influences and estimates a policy distribution for the successors. The value estimated is added to the total value of each node in the path descended and the average of these values makes up the improved state value of that node, $V(s)$. The search repeats for a certain number of iterations and, in the end, when it is time to choose an action to use in the *real* environment, the successors of the root node define a policy function, π, using their visit distribution:

$$\pi(a|s) = \frac{N(s,a)^{1/\tau}}{\sum_b N(s,b)^{1/\tau}}, \tag{1}$$

where $N(s, a)$ is the number of visits associated with the transition (s, a) and τ is a *temperature parameter*, influencing the exploration/exploitation trade-off. The lower it is, the greedier the policy becomes.

Muzero learns the environment by interacting with it, and the states learned do not have specific semantics. The environment is learned through a representation function, h_θ, that converts a real observation to a hidden state and a dynamics function, g_θ, that receives a hidden state and an action and returns the next state and reward associated. The policy and value are estimated by a prediction function, f_θ, which receives a hidden state as argument. An observation from a played episode is sampled and is unrolled by applying the representation function, converting it to an hidden state, followed by applying the next k actions used in the episode to the successive hidden states, using the dynamics function. Then, the prediction function is used in each of these hidden states, returning the policy and value estimations. To learn these functions, the rewards obtained are updated to match the observed ones. The policy is updated based on the visit distribution given by the root node of the respective observation and the value function is improved based on a Monte Carlo value or by bootstrapping from an improved state value.

3   Architecture

AlphaGo Zero, AlphaZero, Muzero and other variations of these algorithms [1,7,9] share a common structure and behavior that we generalize into an architecture. This architecture has the objective of facilitating the process of making changes and extensions in each key component, limiting the complexity by using modularity. It identifies key parts in these agents and allows the user to implement them as independently as possible from each other. We propose six different parts, which are called modules: Loss, Model, Search, Policy, Data and Environment. The first four modules determine how the agent acts and learns, while the Data module concerns itself with data storage. Each is designed to have alternative algorithms that can be chosen to accomplish the module's objective. A simple scheme summarizing the structure of the architecture is given in Fig. 1, where the arrows show dependencies between modules.

Briefly, the behaviour of the architecture is as follows. The agent interacts with an **environment** through a **policy**. In each step of the episode, the policy calls a **search** algorithm to *look ahead* into the simulated state-space. After the search algorithm is done, it returns the root node (that corresponds to the current state) back to the policy. Based on the attributes of this root node, the policy decides the next action to take, advancing to the next state. The policy saves the nodes and the data returned by its interactions with the environment using the **Data** module. Then, this stored data can be passed to a **loss** algorithm that calculates a loss value in order to update the model. Lastly, the architecture establishes the relationship between these blocks, but the user is the one who has to instantiate and assemble them according to the desired logic. We describe more details about the behaviour of the architecture and our particular implementation in the next sections.

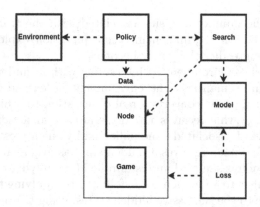

Fig. 1. Basic architecture overview. Each module has arrows pointing toward the modules they depend upon. For instance, the policy needs a search algorithm.

3.1   Environment

The environment is the problem to be solved and it does not depend on any other module. In our implementation, the environment is modeled as a POMDP and the interface is similar to the openAI Gym environment [4]. In each episode's step, the agent executes an action, receiving the next observation and reward. Unlike the Gym environments, ours allows for multiple agents and there can be illegal actions in each state. The specific environments implemented are Tictactoe, Cartpole [2] and Minigrid [6].

3.2   Base Agent

We consider every module except the environment to correspond to the concept of *agent*. Just like in the Environment module, we implement alternative algorithms in the agent's modules, which can compose different agents. There is a base idea behind all of these implemented strategies. We call this common idea the *base agent*. Our base agent learns the model of the environment as it interacts with it and, similarly to MuZero, the hidden states learned do not have a specific semantics. The base agents learns how to estimate the value of each state and the reward associated with each transition. Differently from Muzero, the new idea introduced in this work is to learn to predict the legal actions directly, so that it avoids exploring and conducting updates based on illegal parts of the tree during search. MuZero avoids doing this using a policy function which sets the exploration of the illegal actions to 0. This is unsuitable for algorithms that are non-best first or for those that are but estimate the value of the successors of the leaf expanded, instead of the leaf itself. By predicting the legal actions directly, our agent is much more compatible with different search strategies.

3.3   Model

This module's function is to model not only the environment, but also all the other functions required by the Search module. Different search algorithms might need new functions, so it is important for this component's implementation to be efficient and easily extendable. In this module, for the functions we want to learn, we assume them to be computed using neural networks, but do not make assumptions about their internal structure.

There are five relevant functions used by our base agent. The first, **representation function**, h_θ, receives an observation and returns an encoded hidden state. The next two, **state value function**, v_θ, and **mask function**, m_θ receive an encoded state and return the estimated value for that state and a predicted mask vector for its successors, respectively. Each index in the mask value represents whether the agent estimates the action to be legal or illegal, respectively giving values closer to 1 or to 0. The last two, **reward**, r_θ, and **next state**, g_θ, **functions** receive an encoded state and an action and return, respectively, the predicted reward associated with that transition and the next predicted state. We implement only one specific model that supports the described five functions. Each one of them, internally, is computed by an independent multi-layer perceptron.

3.4   Data

This module stores and transports information between modules. We divide it into the game and node submodules.

Game Submodule. Stores the episode's information: observations, actions, rewards, legal actions, players, and the nodes returned by the search algorithm.

Node Submodule. A node coincides conceptually with an environment state and it is created by the search algorithm to form the search tree. Different types of search algorithms might need different types of nodes. Our implementation has three different types needed for the implemented search algorithms (see Subsect. 3.5). The first one stores: a hidden state s, an improved state value $V(s)$, each successor's hidden state $S(s,a)$ and their validity value $M(s,a)$, according to an action mask, the state's player $Pl(s)$, and the reward per transition $R(s,a)$. The second node implemented is an extension of the first. It is supposed to be used by best first algorithms and it stores, additionally, the number of visits in the tree $N(s)$. Finally, the third node is yet an extension of the second one and it is designed to be used only by a Monte Carlo tree search. It stores a sum of state value estimations, $T(s)$, and it redefines the calculation of the improved state value to be the average of them,

$$V(s) = \frac{T(s)}{N(s)}. \tag{2}$$

3.5 Search

The search explores the state-space, starting from the current state the agent is in. In these, actions mediate transitions between two states. According to each search algorithm, different statistics are calculated and stored (for e.g. action-values, number of visits per node...). Each one might need different functions (for e.g. best first algorithms need some kind of heuristic to estimate the quality of each state). To calculate these functions, the search class receives a (neural) model. How the model works internally is irrelevant, as long as it can calculate all the required functions. This module does not come up with a plan to use during the actual interaction with the environment. It simply creates a state-space graph with different statistics associated in each node that might be used by the policy to come up with a plan. Every time it is called, the algorithm receives the current observation, player and action mask. After the search is done, it returns a (root) node corresponding to the current state. The explored state-space is given by the multiple successor nodes, recursively attached to each other, forming a graph/tree structure. We use interchangeably the term node and state for the rest of the subsection.

We implemented four search algorithms. They all use the five functions discussed in Subsect. 3.3. An encoded state and a mask vector are predicted for every state in the tree. We define the *action-value* as

$$Q(s^k, a) = \begin{cases} R(s^k, a) + V(s^{k+1}) \text{ if } Pl(s^k) = Pl(s^{k+1}) \\ R(s^k, a) - V(s^{k+1}) \text{ otherwise} \end{cases}, \qquad (3)$$

where $s^{k+1} = S(s^k, a)$. When relevant, we use a superscript k to denote that the state s^k was created looking ahead k steps. We can think of it as depth of the state in a hypothetical trajectory. The action-value can be seen as a 1-step bootstrapped value. We define the notion of masked action-value as

$$Q_M(s, a) = M(s, a) \cdot Q(s, a) + \Big(1 - M(s, a)\Big) \cdot c_{\text{penalty}} \qquad (4)$$

For a perfect mask, if the state is valid then the masked action-value is equal to the simple action-value. Otherwise, it is equal to the penalty constant, $c_{penalty}$, which penalizes state invalidity. Without the penalty, an invalid successor has the value of zero, which might still be better than the alternative valid successors. An invalid state should never be chosen so, in theory, the constant c_{penalty} should be minus infinity. However, in practice, we choose a milder value, such as a lower bound of the environment's reward function. The penalty term should only be used to choose an action, not to estimate the value of a state.

The four algorithms implemented start in the same way. They begin by creating the root node and the first encoded state using the representation function, h_θ, based on the observation passed as argument. If the environment has two players, then its children nodes are instantiated with the opposite player. The algorithms start differing after this.

Breadth First. There are two breadth first algorithms: **minimax** and a variation of our own that we call **averaged minimax**. Both incrementally build a

tree until depth d. In each iteration, they gather all the current leaf states and expand them until reaching the maximum depth, one depth level at a time (in a *breadth first* manner). During a node's expansion, the expanded state's mask, the successor's encoded state and the respective transition reward are predicted. If the successor is at maximum depth, their state value is also predicted. After the whole tree has been generated, the values of the leaf states are propagated backwards until the root. These two algorithms differ in the backup rule. For some state s, the update rule in the averaged minimax is given by

$$V(s) \leftarrow \frac{\sum_{a \in A} M(s,a) \cdot Q(s,a)}{\sum_{a \in A} M(s,a)}. \tag{5}$$

For a perfect mask, we can see that the value of each state becomes the average of all its legal successor values. In minimax, however, the best successor is the one that maximizes the masked successor value, but, when updating the actual state value, we assume the successor to be completely valid:

$$V(s) \leftarrow Q(s, \arg\max_a Q_M(s,a)). \tag{6}$$

Best First. The other two implemented algorithms are of type best first: **Monte Carlo tree search** (MCTS) and **best first minimax** (BFMMS), both using a variation of the UCB formula [10] to take into account the mask, resulting in what we call masked upper confidence bound (MUCB). In each step of a best first search iteration, the next action to be selected in a state, s, is given by

$$\arg\max_a \left(Q_M(s,a) + c_{mucb} \cdot \sqrt{\frac{\log(N(s))}{N(S(s,a)) + 1}} \cdot M(s,a) \right), \tag{7}$$

where c_{mucb} is a constant that mediates the intensity of the exploration.

In an iteration, when expanding a leaf node, the successors' states and their state values are estimated. The rewards and mask associated with these transitions are also predicted. The difference between MCTS and BFMMS is also in the backpropagation part. In BFMMS, the update rule is the same as in minimax (Eq. 6). In MCTS, the backpropagation adds, to each node, a path value, G, estimated after expanding the leaf node. The value added to the leaf after its expansion at depth d is the masked average of its newly created successors

$$G^d = \frac{\sum_{a \in A} M(s^d, a) \cdot Q(s^d, a)}{\sum_{a \in A} M(s^d, a)}. \tag{8}$$

For every node in shallower depths after that, the added quantity is given by

$$G^k = \begin{cases} R(s^k, a^k) + G^{k+1} & \text{if } Pl(s^k) = Pl(s^{k+1}) \\ R(s^k, a^k) - G^{k+1} & \text{otherwise} \end{cases}, \tag{9}$$

where $0 \leq k < d$. In simpler words, G accumulates the rewards as it backtracks. This path value is added to each node and their improved state value becomes

$$V(s^k) \leftarrow \frac{\sum_{i=0}^{N(s^k)} G_i^k}{N(s^k)}. \tag{10}$$

3.6 Policy

As explained, the search algorithm returns a graph structure with the explored state-space. The job of the Policy module is to use this state-space and decide the next action (or actions) to take. It then interacts with the environment, applying those actions, and retrieves the next observation and reward from it. Afterwards, it calls the search algorithm again, if necessary. When the episode is over, the policy class stores all the seen data received from both the search (root nodes) and environment, which summarizes the episode, in an object of the Game submodule class. This object can then be returned and used for learning using the Loss module. Each policy receives the instance of the search class to use. Since the policy uses the graph returned by the search to decide its next action, they have to be compatible. For instance, if the policy wants to use the number of times a node has been visited during search (as in MuZero), then the search algorithm needs to store this information in the returned graph nodes.

We implemented three policies. The first is an ϵ-**value greedy**. After calling the search algorithm and receiving the root node, it chooses with 1-ϵ probability the action with the highest action-value and choose a random one otherwise. The second and third policies are only applicable to best first algorithms since they base their choice on the number of visits. The second policy is ϵ-**visit greedy**, which does the same as the first, but, instead of the action-value, it chooses based on the visits of each successor node. The third policy, **visit count**, is given by a visit count distribution just as in MuZero (Eq. 1).

3.7 Loss

After interacting with the environment, the model should be updated to be more accurate and insightful. This is done using the experience that was previously returned by the policy. A loss class receives a set of (root) nodes and calculates a loss value, which is a computational graph that can be used to update the model. Each root node has access to its game class, which means it also has access to all the actions, observations, masks and nodes of its episode in case the specific loss algorithm needs to use them. It is the responsibility of the user to instantiate a policy that returns compatible data instances with the loss.

We implemented three loss algorithms. All of them use the same *unrolling* process as MuZero and Value Prediction Networks [11] to update the reward and mask functions: The state of the respective node is unrolled for k steps (the next k states are predicted using the actions taken during the real episode). The three losses differ in what target value to use to update the model.

- **Monte Carlo loss.** In this loss, the target value, for a specific state, is the (discounted) sum of rewards from that state until the end of the trajectory.
- **Offline Temporal Difference.** This is the one used in Muzero, where the target value is bootstrapped from the state n steps away from the current ones, which is stored in the respective root node.

– **Online Temporal Difference.** If the agent uses a replay buffer and reuses the same nodes for a long time, the value stored in them can easily become outdated. This loss is similar to the previous, but, instead of using the improved state value, $V(s_{t+n})$, it applies the representation function to the observation n steps after the current one, $s_{t+n} = h_\theta(o_{t+n})$, and uses the value function to get a new value to bootstrap from, $v_\theta(s_{t+n})$.

4   Experimental Evaluation

In this section, we assess our implementation by creating different agents for the three environments implemented. For each environment, we look for the best combination of search, loss and policy options, in this order. First. We compare search algorithms and select the most promising one. Then, we use the best search method and choose the best loss. Finally, we do the same for the policy. In the end, we should find a good agent for each environment. For each experiment, the agent plays a full episode, stores it and then conducts 10 updates, each with a batch size of 128 nodes. In each experiment, we select the best algorithm with the highest mean score in the last step. As default, the loss used is the Monte Carlo one and the policy used is ϵ-value greedy, whose parameters can be seen in each environment's second and third experiment, respectively.

4.1   Cartpole

For Cartpole, we limit each episode to a maximum of 500 transitions and report, for each training step, the results as the mean of the last 100 episodes. The Disjoint MLP has one layer, each with 80 neurons, for every function. The encoded state used has size 12. We use a uniform replay buffer with a maximum capacity of 10^5 transitions. The masked penalty is 0 as default. We repeated every experiment 10 times, each for 10^4 training steps. The final results for every experiment for Cartpole can be seen in Table 1.

Table 1. Summary of the final results of the agents tested for Cartpole.

Results for Cartpole					
Search	Loss	Policy	Max	Min	Mean
Avg. Minimax	MC loss	ϵ-value greedy	463.0	188.6	377.4
Avg. Minimax	ON TD	ϵ-value greedy	393.3	255.5	334.4
Avg. Minimax	OFF TD	ϵ-value greedy	**476.5**	**318.7**	**429.6**
BFMMS	MC loss	ϵ-value greedy	450.7	119.5	231.6
Minimax	MC loss	ϵ-value greedy	401.6	258.0	331.1
MCTS	MC loss	ϵ-value greedy	473.1	142.6	311.5

1. **Search.** The best first algorithms use 16 iterations and the breadth first ones explore a maximum depth of 4. The best algorithm was the averaged minimax, which is used in the next experiments.
2. **Loss.** The loss algorithms use 10 unroll steps and a gamma discount of 0.95. For the temporal difference losses, the bootstrapping step is 10. The best loss was the offline temporal difference.
3. **Policy.** There is only one policy that is compatible with breadth first algorithms. So, the averaged minimax with offline temporal difference and ϵ-value greedy is the best algorithm combination discovered.

4.2   Minigrid

We use a 6×6 Minigrid environment. Each episode starts at a random position and is limited to a maximum of 15 steps. The model has one 100 neuron layer per function and the hidden state has size 15. We use a prioritized replay buffer with a maximum capacity of 25000 transitions. The masked penalty used is 0. We repeated every experiment 10 times, each for 20000 training steps. The results are given, per training step, as the mean score of the last 100 episodes. The final results for every experiment for Minigrid can be seen in Table 2.

Table 2. Summary of the final results of the agents tested for Minigrid.

Results for Minigrid					
Search	Loss	Policy	Max	Min	Mean
Avg. Minimax	MC loss	ϵ-value greedy	0.90	0.60	0.76
BFMMS	MC loss	ϵ-value greedy	0.63	0.41	0.54
MINIMAX	MC loss	ϵ-value greedy	0.91	0.71	0.79
MCTS	MC loss	ϵ-value greedy	**0.99**	**0.76**	**0.87**
MCTS	MC loss	ϵ-visit greedy	0.87	0.00	0.62
MCTS	MC loss	Visit dist.	0.33	0.22	0.26
MCTS	OFF TD	ϵ-value greedy	0.91	0.63	0.73
MCTS	ON TD	ϵ-value greedy	0.86	0.52	0.73

1. **Search.** The number of iterations used by the best first algorithms is 27 and the breadth first ones use a depth of 3. MCTS was the best search algorithm.
2. **Loss.** We use 7 unroll steps and a gamma discount of 0.99 in every loss algorithm. For the temporal difference losses, we use a bootstrapping step of 1. The best loss was the Monte Carlo loss.
3. **Policy.** We use 5% exploration for the ϵ-greedy strategies and a temperature of 1 for the visit distribution policy. The best agent found was MCTS with Monte Carlo loss and ϵ-value greedy.

4.3   Tictactoe

The agents are trained in this environment by doing self-play. Every 5000 training steps, we play 100 games against an expert agent (level 1 in our implementation) and report the mean score. When playing against the expert we remove exploration from the policy. The Disjoint MLP has one layer of 100 neurons in every function, except in the next state function, which has 200. The hidden state has a size of 32. We use a prioritized replay buffer with a maximum capacity of 25000 transitions. The masked penalty is -1. Each experiment is ran for 10^5 training steps and repeated 5 times. Table 3 shows the results for this experiment.

Table 3. Summary of the final results of the agents tested for Tictactoe

Results for Tictactoe					
Search	Loss	Policy	Max	Min	Mean
Avg. Minimax	MC loss	ϵ-value greedy	0.28	0.01	0.14
BFMMS	MC loss	ϵ-value greedy	0.48	-0.02	0.29
BFMMS	OFF TD	ϵ-value greedy	**0.54**	0.39	**0.48**
BFMMS	OFF TD	ϵ-visit greedy	0.41	0.14	0.30
BFMMS	OFF TD	Visit dist.	0.53	**0.45**	**0.48**
BFMMS	ON TD	ϵ-value greedy	0.38	0.23	0.29
Minimax	MC loss	ϵ-value greedy	0.21	0.12	0.14
MCTS	MC loss	ϵ-value greedy	0.35	0.02	0.25

1. **Search.** The number of iterations used by the best first algorithms is 25 and the breadth first ones use a depth of 2. The best algorithm was the BFMMS.
2. **Loss.** We use 5 unroll steps and a gamma discount of 0.99. For the temporal difference losses, we use a bootstrapping step of 1. The offline temporal difference was the best loss.
3. **Policy.** The policies use 5% exploration for the ϵ-greedy strategies and a temperature of 1 for the visit distribution policy, when training, and choose always the best action when testing against the expert. There is a tie between two agents, which use BFMMS and offline temporal difference, but differ in policy. One uses the ϵ-value greedy and the other the visit distribution. The combination that uses visit distribution as policy, however, is, throughout the experiment, consistently better than the one with ϵ-value greedy.

4.4   Discussion

Every problem is different and the results captured for these do not automatically guarantee the same for any other. However, these have distinctive characteristics of their own, making them good *testbeds* to see if our implementation works. Cartpole has a strong reward signal, but is very long, as opposed to Minigrid,

which has a sparse reward signal but short episodes. These last two do not have illegal actions, which make them suitable to see if our implementation works in *common* environments. Tictactoe, on the other hand, can be seen as the final challenge since it requires a good use of the mask learned and it uses self-play used during training, a technique known to be challenging in reinforcement learning. In all of these, the best agents found achieved very good results, reaching almost the maximum score in Cartpole and Minigrid. For Tictactoe, the expert is good at defending against obvious plays and it is not good at attacking, so it is expected that a very good agent will win frequently when it starts and tie when the opponent does, leading to a score near 0.5. Our best agent gets very close to this value. The idea of predicting a mask directly and the algorithm adaptations described in this work seem to function well.

The most surprising result is the best search algorithm in Cartpole being the averaged minimax. This algorithm was created in this work based on the very *naive* idea of averaging over all successors in each node. Out of all four algorithms, it is the only one that does not theoretically converge to the minimax function. Still, it was better than all the others in Cartpole, got a better result than BFMMS in Minigrid and had the same result as minimax in Tictactoe.

Regarding the new loss, the online temporal difference, it was not particularly better than the other two, but it was still fairly consistent, achieving better results than Monte Carlo loss in Cartpole and the same in Minigrid.

The most important observation, however, is that, for each component, different algorithms were better according to the environment. For example, the BFMMS, that was the worst in Cartpole and Minigrid, was the best in Tictactoe. Similarly, the visit distribution policy that got poor results in the initial two, achieved the maximum mean score in the third environment. This motivates the existence of flexible, modular, architectures that facilitate the assessement of different choices for policy, loss and search approaches. The existence of architectures that make such assessements easier suggests the possibility of improving state of the art MBRL agents, like Muzero, in certain environments, by modifying their components and finding more suitable algorithm combinations.

5   Conclusions and Future Work

We presented a modular architecture that identifies separate relevant components for MBRL agents that use search algorithms. We provided our own specific implementation of this architecture, capable of searching in domains with a variable set of actions in each state, by learning an action mask directly. We implemented several search algorithms, adapting them to the mask. One of them, called averaged minimax, was proposed in this work and yielded surprisingly good results. Different loss methods, policies and environments were also implemented. We tested this implementation by creating different agents and demonstrated that it works and achieves good results for the environments implemented. The experimentation done seemed to indicate that the best algorithm combination in an agent is strongly problem dependent, motivating the

need for tools and environments that facilitate the implementation and test of variations of the different parts of an agent, like the ones introduced in this work. Our experiments were made comparing different algorithmic strategies. We leave the comparison with other RL algorithms, like MuZero, for future work.

Acknowledgments. This work was supported by the Portuguese Science Foundation, under projects PRELUNA PTDC/CCI-INF/4703/2021 and UIDB/50021/2020.

References

1. Anthony, T., Tian, Z., Barber, D.: Thinking fast and slow with deep learning and tree search (2017)
2. Barto, A.G., Sutton, R.S., Anderson, C.W.: Neuronlike adaptive elements that can solve difficult learning control problems. IEEE Trans. Syst. Man Cybern. **5**, 834–846 (1983)
3. Borges, A., Oliveira, A.: Combining off and on-policy training in model-based reinforcement learning. arXiv preprint arXiv:2102.12194 (2021)
4. Brockman, G., et al.: OpenAI gym. arXiv preprint arXiv:1606.01540 (2016)
5. Campbell, M., Hoane, A., hsiung Hsu, F.: Deep blue. Artif. Intell. **134**(1), 57–83 (2002). https://doi.org/10.1016/S0004-3702(01)00129-1, https://www.sciencedirect.com/science/article/pii/S0004370201001291
6. Chevalier-Boisvert, M., Willems, L., Pal, S.: Minimalistic gridworld environment for OpenAI gym (2018). https://github.com/maximecb/gym-minigrid
7. Cohen-Solal, Q.: Learning to play two-player perfect-information games without knowledge. arXiv preprint arXiv:2008.01188 (2020)
8. Coulom, R.: Efficient selectivity and backup operators in Monte-Carlo tree search. In: van den Herik, H.J., Ciancarini, P., Donkers, H.H.L.M.J. (eds.) CG 2006. LNCS, vol. 4630, pp. 72–83. Springer, Heidelberg (2007). https://doi.org/10.1007/978-3-540-75538-8_7
9. Hamrick, J.B., et al.: Combining Q-learning and search with amortized value estimates. arXiv preprint arXiv:1912.02807 (2019)
10. Kocsis, L., Szepesvári, C.: Bandit based Monte-Carlo planning. In: Fürnkranz, J., Scheffer, T., Spiliopoulou, M. (eds.) ECML 2006. LNCS (LNAI), vol. 4212, pp. 282–293. Springer, Heidelberg (2006). https://doi.org/10.1007/11871842_29
11. Oh, J., Singh, S., Lee, H.: Value prediction network. arXiv preprint arXiv:1707.03497 (2017)
12. Schrittwieser, J., et al.: Mastering atari, go, chess and shogi by planning with a learned model. Nature **588**(7839), 604–609 (2020)
13. Silver, D., et al.: Mastering the game of go with deep neural networks and tree search. Nature **529**(7587), 484–489 (2016)
14. Silver, D., et al.: A general reinforcement learning algorithm that masters chess, shogi, and go through self-play. Science **362**(6419), 1140–1144 (2018)
15. Silver, D., et al.: Mastering the game of go without human knowledge. Nature **550**(7676), 354–359 (2017)
16. de Vries, J.A., Voskuil, K.S., Moerland, T.M., Plaat, A.: Visualizing muzero models. arXiv preprint arXiv:2102.12924 (2021)
17. Wang, H., Emmerich, M., Preuss, M., Plaat, A.: Alternative loss functions in alphazero-like self-play. In: 2019 IEEE Symposium Series on Computational Intelligence (SSCI), pp. 155–162 (2019). https://doi.org/10.1109/SSCI44817.2019.9002814

FIT: Using Feature Importance to Teach Classification Tasks to Unknown Learners

Carla Guerra[(✉)], Francisco S. Melo, and Manuel Lopes

INESC-ID and Instituto Superior Técnico, Universidade de Lisboa, Lisbon, Portugal
carla.guerra@gaips.inesc-id.pt

Abstract. This work introduces an interactive machine teaching approach that teaches classification tasks. But instead of assuming perfect
knowledge about the learner as most machine teaching approaches do,
our adaptive approach—Feature Importance Teaching (FIT)—chooses
the samples to show based on a model of the learner updated online using
feedback about the weights attributed to the features. We run simulations
where there is a mismatch on the prior knowledge and learning model
of the student and the ones assumed by the teacher. The results have
shown that our teaching approach can mitigate this mismatch and lead
to significantly faster learning curves than the ones obtained in conditions where the teacher randomly selects the samples or does not consider
this kind of feedback from the student. We tested using data sets from
two different application domains and the conclusions were the same.
We also tested FIT when the student provides only the most important
feature and it still outperformed the other approaches considered. We
finally conducted a study with real human users, which confirmed the
results obtained in the simulations.

Keywords: Machine teaching · Interactivity · Classification

1 Introduction

A significant amount of teaching relies on providing examples, so the learning efficiency can be greatly improved if the teacher selects the examples that are more
informative for each particular learner. Machine teaching (MT), thus, considers
the problem of finding the smallest set of examples that allows a specific learner to
acquire a given concept, explicitly considering a computational learning algorithm
for the student [15–17]. The optimal amount of training activities needed is known
as the teaching dimension (TD) of that task. A smaller teaching dimension means
less effort required both from the teacher and the student. Thus, minimizing the
TD is the ultimate goal of machine teaching. The main problem with this approach
is its reliance on unrealistic assumptions. MT often assumes that the learner, or
the learning algorithm, is completely known [1,8,13,15]. The very strong assumption that the teacher has perfect knowledge about the learner is seldom (if ever)
satisfied, particularly in the case where the learner is human. In [3] Devidze et al.
formally present the limitations of teaching with imperfect knowledge.

© The Author(s), under exclusive license to Springer Nature Switzerland AG 2022
G. Marreiros et al. (Eds.): EPIA 2022, LNAI 13566, pp. 440–451, 2022.
https://doi.org/10.1007/978-3-031-16474-3_36

Therefore, in this work we propose considering interactivity in the teaching process as the means to solve this problem. Interactivity means allowing the system to ask questions to the students. The idea is to "capture" the learner through a model that can be fine-tuned by asking questions and the goal is that this model gets as close to reality as possible, such that the results obtained through it are as meaningful as possible. This leads us to the main research question addressed in this paper: *how can interactivity be used in machine teaching systems to improve the learning performance of students?*

Our main contribution is a novel interactive approach for a machine teaching system that teaches classification tasks based on feedback from the learner regarding its use of the features of the data. We called this approach Feature Importance-based Teaching (FIT). FIT asks the learner the feature weights used during classification, in order to estimate the learner's prior knowledge, and then selects the samples that minimize the expected future error, based on a model closer to the real model of the learner.

We test our approach against several other approaches—interactive and non-interactive. We start by assuming that the student learning model is known by the teacher (it is a Logistic Regression) and we consider that only the prior knowledge is different between student and teacher. Then, besides different prior knowledges, we also inspect the behaviour of FIT when the learning model assumed by the teacher is different from the one the student follows. To do so, we simulated learners randomly following (with equal probability) one of 3 different learning models: (1) a Logistic Regression; (2) a Random Forest or (3) a Neural Network. In this way we get closer to reality at schools, where the classes are composed of heterogeneous students. We tested in two different domains: 1) a food classification task, where we teach how to classify the nutritional quality of products by looking at their composition; 2) a breast cancer classification task, where we teach how to classify a breast mass image as benign or malign, based on characteristics of the cell nuclei present in the image. The results show that, regardless of the domain and the learning model of the student, our approach teaches faster than the compared approaches. With the end-goal of running an user study, we also tested the case where the student provides information about its most important feature alone, instead of its complete feature weights vector. Such scenario is particularly relevant because in a real world interaction it is not practical to ask the student to discriminate the importance of the complete list of features. The results obtained with only the most important feature reinforce that our approach outperforms the other approaches considered. All these findings contributed to design and conduct an user study to evaluate FIT with real human users, which confirmed the results obtained in the simulations.

2   Related Work

More recently, some researchers started investigating the use of interactivity in the process of teaching, to reduce the strong impact on the teaching dimension of the mismatch between what the teacher assumes about the learners and the

learners themselves [2,4–7,9,10,12,14]. Such works extend the machine teaching algorithms in order to relax the assumptions on how well the learner is known.

Melo et al. proposed to model the learner as a standard learning algorithm, where the variability across learners is explained by different settings/parameters of the algorithm [10]. The teacher could then estimate the necessary parameters using data from the learner. To obtain such data the teacher interacts with the student by asking him questions and then updates its belief of the student by fine-tuning the parameters of the representation considered for him. Their results with Bayesian learning confirmed that an interactive approach reduces significantly the teaching dimension. Other results with inverse reinforcement learners [4,7], forgetful learners [5] and even black-box learners [9] also confirm the advantages of interactivity.

Since our work focus on teaching classification tasks, the teaching approach proposed by Johns et al. is particularly relevant [6] and we used it as comparison against ours. The authors designed an interactive approach for a machine teaching system that teaches an image classification task, which selects teaching samples based on the student's answers. They proposed an algorithm to select the samples—Expected Error Reduction Teaching (EER)—that chooses the teaching sample which, if labeled correctly, would have the greatest reduction in the future error over the samples that were not observed yet.

However, all he work presented regards interactivity by observing the answers given by the learner to a given task and never the weights assigned to the features as we propose in the following section.

3   The FIT Approach

The novel teaching approach we propose teaches a classification task interactively, using feedback given by the student about the relevance that each feature used to classify a given sample has to him. In this way, the teacher does not need to accurately know the student's prior knowledge about the task, because such knowledge is estimated through the information provided by the student. This helps better modelling the student and, therefore, better selecting the samples to show him, reducing the teaching dimension.

3.1   Problem Definition

The problem addressed in this section regards interactively teaching a classification task to one student by providing the smallest number of samples that guarantees he learns the task, i.e., that he reaches a small classification error.

More formally, a sample is an entry from a labeled dataset, $D = \{(x_1, y_1), ..., (x_N, y_N)\}$, where each x_i is an M-dimensional feature vector, and $y_i \in \{1, ..., C\}$ is its corresponding class label. We call teaching set, D_t, to the set composed by the teaching samples selected, which is a subset of D.

To accomplish our goal we propose an interactive system that adaptively selects these samples based on information asked to the learner about the importance he attributes to each feature used to classify a given sample. We refer to

this information as the learner feature weights, encoded as an M dimensional vector $W_l = [w_{f_1}, w_{f_2}, ..., w_{f_M}]$, where each w_{f_i} is the relevance value assigned by the learner to the ith feature when classifying a specific sample. Our goal with this information is to better model the learner and, therefore, choose samples that make him learn faster.

Interactively Updating the Learner's Model. To model the learner we consider two details:

- his learning model, θ_l;
- his prior knowledge, PK_l.

However, since we can not assume perfect knowledge about the learner, the teaching system considers a learner model θ_t and a prior knowledge PK_t.

The learning model is assumed to follow a *Logistic Regression* (LR), thus we define the learner's model by a vector of parameters $\theta_t = [W_t, b_t]$, where $W_t \in \mathbb{R}^d$ is his weight vector and $b_t \in \mathbb{R}$ is a scalar offset term. It solves the problem:

$$\min_{\substack{W_t \in \mathbb{R}^d \\ b_t \in \mathbb{R}}} \sum_{i=1}^{n} \log(1 + \exp\{-y_i(x_i^\top W_t + b_t)\}) + \frac{\lambda}{2}W_t^2 \tag{1}$$

where $\lambda > 0$ is a regularization coefficient, and $(x_i, y_i), i = 1, \ldots, n$, are the teaching samples observed.

The learner feature weights, W_l, are interactively obtained from the student, which makes $W_t = W_l$. This allows us to estimate his prior knowledge, that we encode in the sample set PK_t. At each moment, the vector PK_l can be seen as summarizing the sample set that the student has observed up to that moment. It is composed by the samples the student had seen previously to teaching, $preD_t$ (which are interactively inferred using the learner feature weights), plus the ones showed during teaching, D_t (adaptively chosen by the system). To estimate $preD_t$ we follow the approach of Liu et al. [8] that reconstructs such a training set from the parameter vector $\theta_t = [W_t, b_t]$, with nonzero W_t. To do this we need:

$$n = 2\frac{\lambda||W_t||^2}{2\tau_{max}} \tag{2}$$

training samples, where $x_k = x_+$, $y_k = 1$, for all $k \in \{1, ..., \frac{n}{2}\}$ and $x_k = x_-$, $y_k = -1$, for all $k \in \{\frac{n}{2}+1, ..., n\}$. The samples x_+ and x_- are designed satisfying:

$$x_+^\top W_t = t - b_t, \qquad\qquad x_- = x_+ - 2tW_t||W_t||^{-2},$$

where the constant t is defined by

$$t = \tau^{-1}\frac{\lambda||W_t||^2}{n}. \tag{3}$$

The sample set $preD_t$ can be defined as $\{x_-, x_+\}$. The prior knowledge is then $PK_t = preD_t \cup D_t$. With the learner's learning model, θ_t, and the interactively estimated prior knowledge, PK_t, we can finally (more accurately) estimate the learner conditional distribution over the teaching set, $P_t(y|x)$.

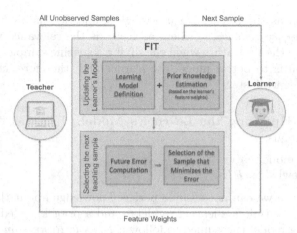

Fig. 1. Diagram illustrating the interaction process in FIT.

Selecting the Teaching Samples. Based on $P_t(y|x)$, we finally select the next sample to show to the student, x_t, using the Expected Error Reduction algorithm—S_{eer}—proposed by Johns et al. [6] and described in detail in the related work section. S_{eer} chooses the teaching sample which would lead to the greatest reduction in the future error of the student over the unobserved samples, D_u:

$$x_t = argmin_{x_p} \sum_{x_i, y_i \in D_u} (1 - P_t^{+(x_p, y_p)}(y_i|x_i)) \tag{4}$$

Here, $P_l^{+(x_p, y_p)}(y_i|x_i)$ is the estimate of the student's conditional distribution if he was shown x_p and would label it correctly after have seen it.

3.2 The Interaction Process

The interaction process followed by the FIT teaching system is illustrated in Fig. 1. The teaching system starts by showing a (random) sample to the student. Before telling him the corresponding label, it asks the student the importance he gives to each feature (in the form of a weight vector) when classifying the given sample. With that information the system estimates the learner's prior knowledge. Having the prior knowledge of the student updated, the system then computes the student's expected future error obtained if each of the unobserved samples was next shown to the student. Finally, it selects the sample that minimizes the expected future error of the student and shows it to the student. This process repeats for a fixed number of samples or until the classification error gets close to zero. With the end-goal of using this system with real human users, we consider also the case where the learner provides only the feature he considers most important to choose a given classification. This is because in a real world scenario would not be practical for the student to give the complete

weight vector associated with the features. We describe that information with an M dimensional weight vector, W_{1F}, that has all entries equal to 0 except from the entry corresponding to the feature chosen by the student to be the most important, which we set to 1. In each iteration we update W_t using the feedback on the most important feature given by the student, W_{1F}, following:

$$W_t = (1 - step) \times W_t + step \times W_{1F}$$

where the step is a scalar parameter that defines how much the feedback obtained from the student influences the feature weights considered.

4 Experiments

We tested our teaching approach against 2 other—one non-interactive, Random, and an interactive approach on the answers level, EER [6]. We present results based on simulations and on a real-world study with human users where we teach a binary classification task. We run the simulations using two different datasets from distinct classification domains: (A) food classification based on its nutritional composition; (B) breast cancer classification based on breast mass images.

4.1 Simulations

We applied the proposed teaching approach on the problem of classifying the quality of a given food based on its nutritional composition by looking at its nutrition label. This is a particular important domain nowadays given the fact that food intake is considered by the World Health Organization (WHO) to be responsible for many non-communicable diseases (e.g. diabetes, cardiovascular diseases, some cancers). Thus, it is urgent to improve food literacy of people.

Data. The data used to teach was taken from the Food Composition Database[1]. It includes information about 42 features of the foods (energy, macronutrients, fatty acids, vitamins and minerals) for 1147 different types of food. We considered 7 of those nutrients as features to describe each food—the amount of lipids, of which the saturated; the amount of carbohydrates, of which the sugars; the amount of salt, fibers and proteins—which is the information usually given in the nutritional table present in the food package. To label the database we defined a set of rules that follow the general recommendations given by the World Health Organization (WHO) and the UK National Health System (NHS) to ensure healthy food choices based on the food labeling information[2,3]. We considered two classes: nutritious (1) or non-nutritious (0).

---

[1] PortFIR webpage with the "Food Composition Table"; 2019. Accessed: 2020-03-26. http://portfir.insa.pt/foodcomp/introduction.

[2] WHO webpage on "Healthy Diet"; 2020. Accessed: 2020-03-26. https://www.who.int/en/news-room/fact-sheets/detail/healthy-diet.

[3] NHS webpage on "How to Read Food Labels"; 2018. Accessed: 2020-03-26. https://www.nhs.uk/live-well/eat-well/how-to-read-food-labels/.

To check if the results are independent of the domain, we considered a second application where we teach how to classify breast mass images based on characteristics of the cell nuclei present in the image. We used the breast cancer Wisconsin (diagnostic) data set[4], comprising 569 instances of breast mass images, each with 30 features that describe characteristics of the cell nuclei present in the image (radius, texture, area, symmetry, among others). The data set is labelled into two classes: malignant (0) or benign (1).

Simulated Learners. To test our approach we simulated different types of learners. We considered 3 types of learning models and each test respected one of the following options:

- All simulated learners have a learning model that follows a Logistic Regression—"LR";
- The simulated learners have different learning models, randomly chosen with equal probability from a Logistic Regression (LR), a Random Forest (RF) or a Neural Network (NN)—"Mix". This option aims at getting closer to the reality, since the learning models of different students can be (and often are) distinct.

Because our teaching system considers a learning model for the learner that follows a Logistic Regression defined by $\theta_t = [W_t, b_t]$, and that uses its feature weights, W_t, to infer the prior knowledge of the learner we need to find a way to obtain this information from learners that have different learning models where this feature weight vector is not directly defined. Therefore, when the learning model considered for the simulated learner was a RF or a NN, we used the Local Interpretable Model-agnostic Explanations (LIME) approach proposed in [11] to get these feature weights. The goal of LIME is to understand why the learner (represented as a black-box model) makes a certain prediction to a given instance, i.e., what are the importances (=weights) given to each feature when attributing a certain class to a given instance. To do so LIME tests what happens to the learner's predictions by probing the learner on a dataset consisting of permuted samples in the vicinity of the instance of interest. On this new dataset LIME then trains an interpretable model, which is then weighted by the proximity of the sampled instances to the instance of interest. The learned model should be a good approximation of the machine learning model predictions locally, but it does not have to be a good global approximation.

Regarding the prior knowledge of the learners, we do not assume that the teacher has any (reliable) estimate for it. Therefore, the learner's prior and the teacher's prior (assumed for the student) are different. In real world scenarios a mismatch between the real prior of the learner and the prior assumed by the teacher for the learner is very often observed, which leads to poor teaching performances. Our approach tries to overcome this mismatch.

---

[4] Scikit-learn webpage on "Breast Cancer Wisconsin (Diagnostic) Dataset"; 1995. Accessed: 2020-03-26. https://scikit-learn.org/stable/datasets/index.html#breast-cancer-dataset.

Conditions. We considered 4 conditions where we compared 4 different teaching approaches:

- FIT (our approach), where the system selects the samples that minimize the expected future error, while inferring the learner's prior knowledge through interactivity on his feature weights vector;
- FIT_1F (a version of our approach more appropriate for real human users), where the system selects the samples that minimize the expected future error, while inferring the learner's prior knowledge through interactivity on only the most important feature to the learner. The step used to update the feature weights vector in Eq. 3.2 given the most important feature feedback equals 0.5;
- EER, where the system follows the approach proposed in [6]), with interactivity on the answers level and a different way of modelling the student that does not attempt to infer its prior knowledge.
- Random, where the system randomly selects the samples (non-interactive);

We run each condition 100 times, varying the learner/teacher priors and the training, validation and testing sets. The following results show the mean of the distributions obtained over all the runs.

Results. The results have shown that, regardless of the domain, when the learning model of the learner and the one assumed by the teacher are the same (Fig. 2), our approach outperforms the other approaches considered, even when the student gives only the most important feature. All the error curves start in a common state, but the FIT curves (conditions FIT and FIT_1F) converge significantly faster. In the food classification task, after 5 samples were shown, the FIT curves are already below a 20% error, while the other two approaches need around 15 samples to reach a similar error. In the breast cancer classification task the FIT curves have an error below 10% after 10 teaching samples, while the other methods stay above that 10% error still after 30 teaching samples were shown. When comparing the FIT curves, as we might expect, getting the complete feature weight vector from the student (FIT) leads to better results than when getting only the most important feature (FIT_1F). However, both FIT approaches, in both tasks, reveal significant differences in their error distributions when compared with the other approaches right after only 3 samples where shown, as confirmed by a statistical Mann-Whitney U test. When the learner's and the teacher's learning model are different (Fig. 3), although less obvious, the conclusions are mainly the same. In the food classification task, our FIT approaches reach an error around 20% with only 3 teaching samples, while the others need 8. In the breast cancer classification task, our approaches reach the 25% error mark with only 1 teaching sample, while the others need 5. Right after the second teaching sample is shown to the student, the FIT approach converges significantly faster than the other teaching approaches considered when compared with a Mann-Whitney U test as before, regardless of the task. The

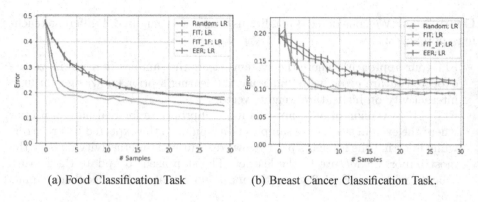

(a) Food Classification Task   (b) Breast Cancer Classification Task.

Fig. 2. Resulting mean error curves when the learning model considered by the system and the learner's are the same ("LR").

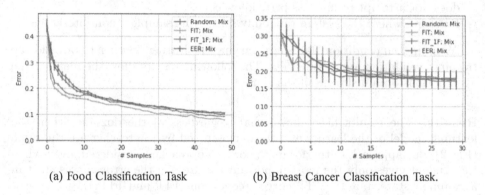

(a) Food Classification Task   (b) Breast Cancer Classification Task.

Fig. 3. Resulting mean error curves when the learning model considered by the system and the learner's are different—"LR" and "Mix", respectively.

difference is significant even when getting only the most important feature from the student, which is a very promising result for the user study with real human users we conducted afterwards (Sect. 4.2).

4.2 User Study

To confirm if the promising results obtained with FIT in the simulations still hold in the real world we conducted an user study on the crowd-sourcing platform Amazon Mechanical Turk with 90 human participants equally distributed across conditions. The scenario regarded the food classification task already considered in the simulations and described in Sect. 4.1.

Conditions. Because it would not be practical for humans to give the complete feature weights vector, the system only asks the learners about the most important feature used to classify each given sample (previously referred as FIT_1F approach). Note that here we refer to FIT_1F as FIT, because in the real world

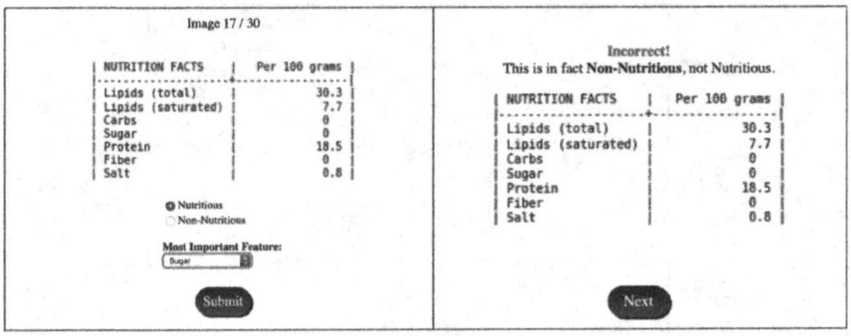

Fig. 4. Interface used on the user study during the teaching phase. Example of one of the questions asked (left) and the corresponding feedback (right).

there is only one feasible approach and, therefore, there is no need to differentiate between them as in the simulations.

Interaction. The study followed a between-subject design, where each participant interacts with a teaching application that follows 3 ordered stages:

1. Pre-testing—where the system pre-tests the participant on his prior classification ability; here the participant is shown a sequence of 10 nutritional composition tables; for each table (that corresponds to a particular food), we ask the participant to select his best estimate of its label (reminding him to choose the label he thinks is the best estimate for people in general and not based on his personal taste or health condition);
2. Teaching—where the system teaches the participant on how to correctly classify 15 items presented; the interaction is similar to the previous stage, but there are two differences: the participant will additionally be asked to select the feature he found most important to choose the label of that particular item (see an example in Fig. 4 (left)); he also is given feedback on the correct solution (Fig. 4 (right)); in the beginning the participant has to guess, but over time he should learn from the computer's feedback;
3. Post-testing—where the computer post-tests the participant on his classification ability after being taught by the teaching system. The interaction is exactly the same as in the pre-testing stage and occurs at three specific times: after 5 teaching samples were shown, after 10 teaching samples were shown and in the end of teaching, after 15 teaching samples were shown.

Results. Before the teaching phase (the first point in Fig. 5, with zero samples, which corresponds to the end of pre-test), a Mann-Whitney U test confirmed that there is no significant differences in the error distributions obtained across conditions (see Fig. 5). This means that any difference found in the post-tests can be attributed to the interaction with the teaching system. After the teaching stage (the other points in Fig. 5 that correspond to the post-tests made after 5, 10 and 15 teaching samples were shown), we performed another Mann-Whitney U test to compare the error distributions obtained at each point) and confirmed

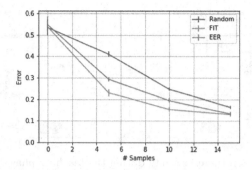

Fig. 5. Resulting mean error curves obtained in the user study.

that the mean error decreases significantly faster when considering our FIT approach. This result confirms the ones already obtained in the simulations, where the FIT approaches outperform the other methods considered.

5   Conclusions and Future Work

In this work we propose a novel interactive teaching approach to teach classification tasks (FIT), that, instead of using the student answers (as most of the work found in the literature), in turn it uses the importance attributed by the student to each feature used to classify a given sample. With this information we can estimate his prior knowledge and, therefore, consider a better model for the student. In this way we partly overcome the common mismatch between the learner and the teacher assumptions of him and we then select better teaching samples that improve the learning rate. We present results with simulated students using data from two different application domains. We also conducted a user study with real human participants. We could confirm that our teaching approach leads to significantly faster learning curves than the ones obtained in conditions where the teacher randomly selects the samples or does not consider the feature weights given by the student. In the future we would like to extend our approach to multiple learners settings, getting even closer to the real world classroom at schools.

Acknowledgments. This work was supported by national funds through Fundação para a Ciência e a Tecnologia (FCT) with reference UIDB/50021/2020 and the FCT PhD grant with reference SFRH/BD/118006/2016.

References

1. Cakmak, M., Lopes, M.: Algorithmic and human teaching of sequential decision tasks. In: Twenty-Sixth AAAI Conference on Artificial Intelligence (2012)
2. Chen, Y., Singla, A., Mac Aodha, O., Perona, P., Yue, Y.: Understanding the role of adaptivity in machine teaching: the case of version space learners. In: Advances in Neural Information Processing Systems, pp. 1476–1486 (2018)

3. Devidze, R., Mansouri, F., Haug, L., Chen, Y., Singla, A.: Understanding the power and limitations of teaching with imperfect knowledge. arXiv preprint arXiv:2003.09712 (2020)
4. Haug, L., Tschiatschek, S., Singla, A.: Teaching inverse reinforcement learners via features and demonstrations. In: Advances in Neural Information Processing Systems, pp. 8464–8473 (2018)
5. Hunziker, A., et al.: Teaching multiple concepts to a forgetful learner. In: Advances in Neural Information Processing Systems, pp. 4050–4060 (2019)
6. Johns, E., Mac Aodha, O., Brostow, G.J.: Becoming the expert-interactive multiclass machine teaching. In: Proceedings of the IEEE Conference on Computer Vision and Pattern Recognition, pp. 2616–2624 (2015)
7. Kamalaruban, P., Devidze, R., Cevher, V., Singla, A.: Interactive teaching algorithms for inverse reinforcement learning. In: Proceedings of the Twenty-Eighth International Joint Conference on Artificial Intelligence, IJCAI-19, pp. 2692–2700. International Joint Conferences on Artificial Intelligence Organization (2019). https://doi.org/10.24963/ijcai.2019/374
8. Liu, J., Zhu, X.: The teaching dimension of linear learners. J. Mach. Learn. Res. **17**(1), 5631–5655 (2016)
9. Liu, W., Dai, B., Li, X., Liu, Z., Rehg, J.M., Song, L.: Towards black-box iterative machine teaching. arXiv preprint arXiv:1710.07742 (2017)
10. Melo, F.S., Guerra, C., Lopes, M.: Interactive optimal teaching with unknown learners. In: IJCAI, pp. 2567–2573 (2018)
11. Ribeiro, M.T., Singh, S., Guestrin, C.: "why should i trust you?": explaining the predictions of any classifier. In: Proceedings of the 22nd ACM SIGKDD International Conference on Knowledge Discovery and Data Mining, pp. 1135–1144 (2016)
12. Singla, A., Bogunovic, I., Bartók, G., Karbasi, A., Krause, A.: On actively teaching the crowd to classify. In: NIPS Workshop on Data Driven Education. No. POST_TALK (2013)
13. Singla, A., Bogunovic, I., Bartók, G., Karbasi, A., Krause, A.: Near-optimally teaching the crowd to classify. In: ICML, vol. 1, p. 3 (2014)
14. Yeo, T., et al.: Iterative classroom teaching. In: Proceedings of the AAAI Conference on Artificial Intelligence, vol. 33, pp. 5684–5692 (2019)
15. Zhu, J.: Machine teaching for Bayesian learners in the exponential family. In: Advances in Neural Information Processing Systems, pp. 1905–1913 (2013)
16. Zhu, X.: Machine teaching: an inverse problem to machine learning and an approach toward optimal education. In: Twenty-Ninth AAAI Conference on Artificial Intelligence (2015)
17. Zhu, X., Singla, A., Zilles, S., Rafferty, A.N.: An overview of machine teaching. arXiv preprint arXiv:1801.05927 (2018)

GANs for Integration of Deterministic Model and Observations in Marine Ecosystem

Gloria Pietropolli[1,2], Gianpiero Cossarini[2], and Luca Manzoni[1(✉)]

[1] Dipartimento di Matematica e Geoscienze, Università degli Studi di Trieste,
Via Alfonso Valerio 12/1, 34127 Trieste, Italy
gloria.pietropolli@phd.units.it, lmanzoni@units.it
[2] National Institute of Oceanography and Applied Geophysics - OGS,
Borgo Grotta Gigante 42/c, 34010 Sgonico, Trieste, Italy
gcossarini@ogs.it

Abstract. Monitoring the marine ecosystem can be done via observations (either in-situ or satellite) and via deterministic models. However, each of these methods has some drawbacks: observations can be accurate but insufficient in terms of temporal and spatial coverage, while deterministic models cover the whole marine ecosystem but can be inaccurate. This work aims at developing a deep learning model to reproduce the biogeochemical variables in the Mediterranean Sea, integrating observations and the output of an existing deterministic model of the marine ecosystem. In particular, two deep learning architectures will be proposed and tested: first *EmuMed*, an emulator of the deterministic model, and then *InpMed*, which consists of an improvement of the latter by the addition of information provided by in-situ and satellite observations. Results show that *EmuMed* can successfully reproduce the output of the deterministic model, while *ImpMed* can successfully make use of the additional information provided, thus improving our ability to monitor the biogeochemical variables in the Mediterranean Sea.

1 Introduction

Improving the capability of monitoring and forecasting the status of the marine ecosystem has important implications (e.g. sustainable approaches to fishing and aquaculture, mitigation of pollution, and eutrophication), especially considering the changes caused by human activities [6]. An unprecedented improvement in monitoring the oceans has arisen from satellite sensors in the 90s and in situ autonomous oceanographic instruments, such as *float* in the 2000s. Floats consist of a two meters long robotic device, that collects marine variable data by diving in the ocean and varying its depth; for more details see the GOOS (Global Ocean Observing System) website [1]. While these instruments do not need human intervention and provide profiles while the battery lasts, however, they are expensive and thus perform relatively few measurements compared to

© The Author(s), under exclusive license to Springer Nature Switzerland AG 2022
G. Marreiros et al. (Eds.): EPIA 2022, LNAI 13566, pp. 452–463, 2022.
https://doi.org/10.1007/978-3-031-16474-3_37

the whole area to cover (Fig. 1 shows the distribution of the float measurement collected during 2015 over the entire Mediterranean sea), which, consequently, cannot be modeled by only relying on these observations. Satellites cover with high resolution the whole marine domain but only at the surface and they suffer from cloud cover. Hence, observational data available are largely spatially sparse, and with a scarcity of series spanning more than a few decades. Deterministic models have been exploited to simulate the marine environment, as they can provide reanalyses and predictions for the whole 3D domain. However, uncertainties in parameterization and input data and high computational costs can impact their reliability and applicability. The current state-of-the-art deterministic marine ecosystem modeling merges observations (e.g. satellite ocean color, BGC argo float, and so on) with ocean model through data assimilation methods [7]. The incorporation of machine learning (ML) techniques offers alternative and stimulant opportunities for advancing the capacity of integrating theory, knowledge and observations to simulate the marine environment [13]. That is, ML is a new way, compared to existing data assimilation methods, of integrating observations and theory. The present work aims to develop a novel deep learning approach to assess spatial and temporal variability of physical and biogeochemical variables in the marine domains, that combines the knowledge provided by the deterministic model and the in-situ and satellite observations. Embedding of ML techniques to physical and biogeochemical oceanography received significant attention in recent years [12], for a comprehensive review of the current state of the art of ML application to this field the reader can refer to [13].

The deep learning method proposed in this work is based on the approach of filling missing pixels of a considered image, which is a well-known and extensively studied computer vision task, often referred to as *image inpainting* [3]. Since this method has been created specifically to synthesize visually realistic, coherent, and semantic plausible pixels for missing regions, our idea was to exploit its architecture to assemble a model capable of skilfully reconstructing the physical and biogeochemical variables and also to fill the information gap provoked by the inhomogeneity of in-situ observation. This novel approach has been implemented in the Mediterranean Sea, a semi-enclosed sea where a rich collection of model, satellite, and in-situ data are already available: a validated model [5], high-resolution satellite data from Copernicus [4] and in-situ BGC-Argo floats [14]. The first ML model that we will introduce, named *EmuMed*, exploits Generative Adversarial Networks (GAN) [8], and is based on an inpainting architecture [9]. *EmuMed* learns spatial and temporal relationship among the marine ecosystem variables starting from the deterministic model *MedBFM* output thanks to the nature of its architecture. The second ML model, that we define is *InpMed*, adds observations to *EmuMed* while maintaining the same architecture of *EmuMed*. We remark that modeling marine ecosystem variables by ML presents several challenges. First of all, marine datasets span four dimensions (i.e., temporal, vertical and two horizontal) which are characterized by different scales and units (e.g., kilometer and meter respectively for horizontal and vertical spatial dimensions). Moreover, unlike many ML applications, in geosciences we cannot rely on ground-truth data. Indeed, the deterministic model is just an

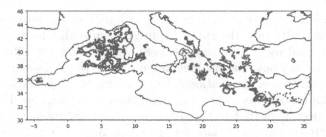

Fig. 1. Map of the *float* measurements over the Mediterranean Sea collected during the year 2015.

approximation itself of the marine ecosystems, with the observations providing only a very sparse and scarce picture of it. These motivations encourage us to select a convolutional-based architecture, as it is naturally suitable for dealing with spatial data. The main idea was to treat horizontal maps of the considered domain as images that capture the marine environment as if it were photography, where the classical RGB channels are substituted with channels representing the marine variables. Indeed, in images, the three colors channels are strongly inter-related and dependent on each other, as they need to collaborate to produce a whole range of colors. Similarly, we aim to introduce an intrinsic strong relation between marine ecosystem variables as they are also naturally correlated. Then, considering that dealing with in-situ measurements leads also to the aforementioned problem of the insufficient spatial coverage of information, an architecture capable of filling areas where measurements are missing becomes essential. These considerations lead us to choose as learning architecture GAN specifically constructed to deal with inpainting tasks to deal with horizontal sections of the marine domain.

The paper is structured as follows: Sect. 2 provides a description of the proposed models. In particular, Sect. 2.1 introduces the deep learning architecture, Sect. 2.2 defines and describes *EmuMed*, while Sect. 2.3 illustrates *InpMed*. In Sect. 3 the experimental settings are provided and experimental results are reported in Sect. 4. Section 5 recalls the main contributions of the paper and provides directions for further research.

2   Material and Method

In this section, we introduce the deep learning architecture employed. In Sect. 2.2 we discuss an intermediary version of the method we build: *EmuMed*. Finally, a final and improved model, *InpMed*, will be presented and discussed in Sect. 2.3.

2.1   Deep Learning Architecture

The deep learning architecture employed will take advantage of Convolutional Neural Network (CNN) [10]. CNN performs proficiently in machine learning problems dealing with multiple dimensional input domains, such as image data,

since they conserve the spatial structure of the input; for further details, the reader can refer to [2]. The models introduced in this work are based on a convolutional inpainting architecture [9], which is in turn based on Generative Adversarial Networks (GAN) [8]. The original purpose of GAN is to train the generative model by using an auxiliary network, called discriminator, which serves to distinguish real images with respect to the one generated by the generative model. The general inpainting architecture consists of the training of a generative network to "fill-in" in the most realistic way possible an image with one (or even more) parts of it masked. In this paper, we will consider an inpainting model composed of three interacting convolutional neural networks: the *completion network* used to complete the image; the *global discriminator*, and the *local discriminator*, which are two auxiliary networks. The completion and the discriminators compete in a two-player game, where simultaneous improvements are made to both of them during the training phase. Thus, while the completion network learns how to fill the holes in a realistic and coherent way, discriminators are trained to understand whether or not the provided input has been completed. The improvement of the completion implies a betterment of the discriminators' performance; and vice-versa, the improvement of the discriminators' capability to recognize completed input implies a rise in the completion performance, to fool the discriminators.

Completion Network. The completion network is a convolutional neural network, consisting of 17 layers, as detailed in [9]. The architecture exploits an encoder-decoder technique that initially decreases the resolution of the input features to reduce the computational effort, and then restores the original resolution. Like in image generation task, the input of the completion network is an RGB image with binary channels, where 1 indicates that a mask is applied to the input pixel, and the output is an RGB image, properly completed.

Discriminator Networks. Two discriminators play against the completion network introduced above: the global discriminator and the local discriminator. The former tests the reliability of the input in its entirety, while the latter focuses on a particular and smaller area, thus paying more attention to details. The discriminators take as input the complete image (adequately re-scaled), both of them are implemented using convolutional neural networks followed by a fully-connected layer producing a real-valued vector as output. Finally, the two resulting vectors are concatenated and passed again as input of a fully-convolutional layer, that returns a continuous value indicating the probability that the provided input is real or fake.

Training. The loss function employed to train the completion network, introduced in [11], is the weighted MSE defined as follows:

$$L(x, M_c) = ||M_c \odot (C(x, M_c) - x)|| \tag{1}$$

where $\odot$ stands for the pixel-wise multiplication and $||\cdot||$ is the Euclidean norm. Furthermore, the GAN loss [8] is used for training together completion and discriminators network. While discriminators aim to maximize the average of the

log-probability of real images and the log of the inverse probability for fake images, the generator aims to minimize the log of the inverse probability predicted by the discriminator for fake images. Therefore, the generator tries to minimize the following function while the discriminator tries to maximize it:

$$\min_C \max_D \mathbf{E}[\log D(x, M_d) + log(1 - D(C(x, M_c), M_c))] \qquad (2)$$

where M_c is the input mask, M_d is a random mask, $D(x, M_d)$ is the discriminator's estimate of the probability for the real input x with mask M_d to be real, $D(C(x, M_c))$ is the discriminator's estimate of the probability for the fake input x to be real, and $\mathbf{E}$ indicate the average over the training input. Finally, taking in account both Eq. 1 and Eq. 2, the resulting loss function is:

$$\min_C \max_D \mathbf{E}[L(x, M_c) + \log D(x, M_d) + \alpha log(1 - D(C(x, M_c), M_c))] \qquad (3)$$

where α is a fixed hyperparameter. The training of the algorithm, which is schematized in Algorithm 1, consists into three main phases: during *phase 1* the completion network is trained among all the features of the training set for T_C epochs; then, during *phase 2*, the completion network is fixed and the discriminator network is trained for T_D epochs; finally, during *phase 3* both the completion network and the discriminators are trained at the same time for T_{CD} epochs.

2.2 EmuMed

The *EmuMed* is the first model that we present in this paper, named after the fact that it behaves as an emulator (meaning that it is learning information from) of the deterministic model *MedBFM* [5,15]. The architecture underlying *EmuMed* is the one presented in Sect. 2.1: a generative convolutional neural network trained through adversarial loss. The input (tensors) employed for the training are obtained from a discretization of data generated through a simulation of the deterministic model. These tensors represent 2-dimensional maps of a fixed region of the Mediterranean Sea (here, with the term map we denote a horizontal section of the region at a fixed depth). The role that pixels accomplished for the image completion task is carried out by rectangles that represent a discretization area of the Mediterranean Sea, while the standard RGB channels are substituted with channels that contain values representing the oceanographic physical and the biogeochemical variables that we aim to reproduce. Thus, *EmuMed* consists of a generative model capable of reconstructing the biological and chemical interactions for the whole Mediterranean Sea domain considered.

2.3 InpMed

InpMed is the second model presented in this paper, obtained starting from *EmuMed* and then performing a further training phase adding both in-situ measurements collected by the float devices and by satellite observations. This additional training phase is performed according, again, to phase 1 of the Algorithm 1

Algorithm 1. Pseudocode of the training steps for the deep learning architecture underlying *EmuMed*, and, consequently *InpMed*.

```
1: for t = 0...T_C do                                                    ▷ phase 1
2:     for all x in the training set do
3:         Generate masks M_c with random holes.
4:         Compute C(x, M_c).
5:         Update completion network weights through Equation 1.
6:     end for
7: end for
8: for t = 0...T_D do                                                    ▷ phase 2
9:     for all x in the training set do
10:        Generate masks M_c with random holes.
11:        Compute D(x, M_d) and D(C(x, M_c), M_c).
12:        Update discriminator network weights through binary cross entropy loss
13:    end for
14: end for
15: for t = 0...T_{CD} do                                                ▷ phase 3
16:    for all x in the training set do
17:        Generate masks M_c with random holes.
18:        Generate masks M_d with random holes.
19:        Compute D(x, M_d) and D(C(x, M_c), M_c).
20:        Update discriminator network weights through binary cross entropy loss.
21:        Update completion network weights through Equation 3.
22:    end for
23: end for
```

described in Sect. 2.1. The weights of *EmuMed* are updated to fit these new data, producing a more reliable prediction that is closer to the real marine ecosystem conformation. *InpMed* ensures an improvement in the simulating capability of the model, as the convolutional structure guarantees a local distribution of information provided by observation also in neighboring areas of these measurements. Another crucial point is that there are certain marine indicators that are not measured either through in-situ devices or via satellite information, such as the primary production, which prediction can be improved anyway by taking advantage of a combination of the ML architecture and of the observed data. In fact, relations between variables are learned through the training of *EmuMed*; subsequently, *InpMed* exploits the information provided by the measured variables and the relations learned from the deterministic model to improve the prediction for both the measured variables and the ones that cannot be measured.

3   Experimental Setting

The geographical area considered in this work is the western Mediterranean portion, specifically, the one with latitude ranging between 36 and 44 and longitude varying between 2 and 9 and the vertical dimension covers a depth ranging from 0 to 600 m. It consists of the portion between southern France and northern

Table 1. Experimental settings values. The table on the left describes the parameters concerning the deep learning architecture. Horizontal lines separate: common parameters, *EmuMed* parameters and *InpMed* parameters. The table on the right represents the parameters referring to the definition of the input structure.

Parameter	Value
Comp. input size	$30 \times 65 \times 75$
Loc. Disc. input size	$20 \times 50 \times 50$
lr_c	0.01
lr_d	0.01
T_c	5000
T_d	200
T_{cd}	1000
α	4×10^{-4}
lr_{float}	0.001
T_{float}	200

Parameter	Value
Time interval	Weekly
Latitude interval	$36°-44°$
Longitude interval	$2°-9°$
Depth interval	0–600 m
Time resolution	weekly
Latitude resolution	12 km
Longitude resolution	12 km
Depth resolution	20 m

Africa, delimited on the east limit by Corsica and Sardinia and on the west limit by Balearic islands. The spatial resolution is 12 km in both latitude and longitude axes and 20 m in the vertical one. The time period covers the year 2015 which is discretized on a weekly basis. Therefore, the 4-dimensional input tensor consists of a horizontal map, of the central-western Mediterranean Sea area, whose dimensions are: length, height, width, and channel. Each channel of the tensor, in turn, collects one marine ecosystem variable. Namely, the variable considered are temperature, salinity, oxygen, chlorophyll-a, and primary production. All the variables can be obtained via the deterministic model *MedBFM*, while only the first four are collected via float measurement (as it is not possible to measure primary production via any sensor), and only chlorophyll-a can be inferred through satellite. Each location in the 3D field has 5 variables associated and a time resolution one week is used (thus, 52 weekly observations are available). Due to their nature, each float provides a 1D profile, where latitude and longitude are fixed and only the depth can change. Finally, since satellites can observe only the surface of the water, they provide 2D data (with holes due to cloud covers). For the training of *EmuMed*, we used the following hyperparameters (summarized in Table 1): the completion network is trained for 5000 epochs, the discriminator network is trained for 200 epochs, and finally the two networks are trained simultaneously for 1000 epochs. These hyperparameters have been fixed after an appropriate preliminary study. The optimizer chosen is ADADELTA [16], which set the learning rate for each weight in the network automatically. The learning rate initial value for both the completion and the discriminator is set to 0.01. Subsequently, *InpMed* is trained for 200 epochs with a learning rate value set initially to 0.01.

4 Experimental Results

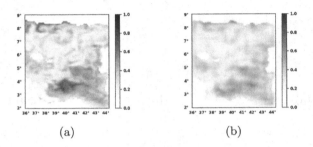

(a)   (b)

Fig. 2. Map of surface chlorophyll produced by (a) *MedBFM* and reconstructed using (b) *EmuMed*.

The Mediterranean case study aims at demonstrating the reliability of ML reconstruction for marine ecosystem variables and at showing how the different components of the ML architecture contribute to the reconstruction quality. To assess the goodness of the proposed reconstruction, the analysis focus on some statistical properties (averages and variances) of the simulated fields. In particular, Fig. 2 reports maps of one of the variables (i.e., surface chlorophyll) demonstrating *InpMed* capability to emulate the intense spatial variability of surface marine fields. Figure 3 shows the vertical profiles of the spatial averages among two given weeks of the year (e.g., one in winter and one in summer), assessing the capability of the technique to simulate different seasonal periods for all modeled variables. These plots compare the original deterministic model *MedBFM* profile with the *EmuMed* and *InpMed* reconstructions, showing the benefits provided by the different architectural components. Finally, Fig. 4 compares, via box-plot, the distributions of the standard deviation of the spatial variability of *MedBFM* and *InpMed*. Four weeks of the year are displayed in order to study how the spatial heterogeneity of the marine proprieties varies throughout the year and how it is handled by the different models.

Results show that the *EmuMed* has learned well to reproduce the typical mean vertical profiles, simulated by *MedBFM*, for all variables but salinity (Fig. 3). Deviations of *InpMed* from *EmuMed* profiles (e.g., orange and green lines in oxygen, chlorophyll, and primary production in Fig. 3) highlight how the inclusion of the observations in the ML architecture introduced possible corrections (i.e., new information) to the *MedBFM* simulated fields. Temperature shows that the inclusion of observations had a marginal effect while salinity shows that observations bring *InpMed* profiles closer to *MedBFM* highlighting a possible inaccurate reconstruction of *EmuMed*, that anyway is corrected in the second phase of the training, confirming the added values of the two-step architecture implemented in *InpMed*. Regarding the spatial variability of horizontal fields of marine variables, maps of Fig. 2 show qualitatively the good performance

Week 2

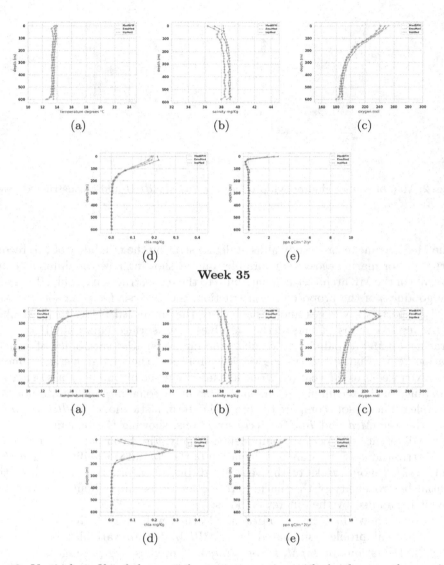

Week 35

Fig. 3. Vertical profile of the spatial averages, varying with depth, over the considered domain. Variables represented are: (a) temperature, (b) salinity, (c) oxygen, (d) chlorophyll, (e) primary production. The gray line represents the deterministic vertical profile *MedBFM*, the orange line represents the one inferred by *EmuMed*, and the green represents the vertical profile predicted by *InpMed*. Above are reported results relative to week 2 (winter), on the right relative to week 35 (summer), in order to demonstrate the capability of introduced models to predict different seasonal periods. (Color figure online)

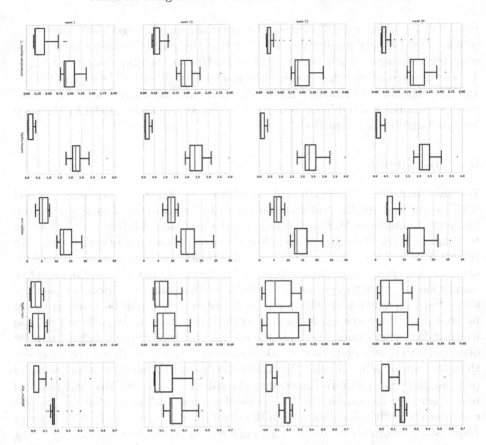

Fig. 4. Box-plots showing the distributions of the standard deviation of the marine variables computed from the spatial maps at different depths. From top to bottom are shown, respectively, temperature, salinity, oxygen, chlorophyll (only layers between 0 and 200 m), primary production (only layers between 0 and 200 m). The box-plot with the median gray line represents deterministic model *MedBFM*, while the box-plot with the green median line represents *InpMed*. From left to right are shown, respectively, week 1, week 10, week 20 and week 30 (Color figure online)

of the ML reconstruction. From a quantitative point of view, the comparison of the standard deviation boxplots (Fig. 4) shows that the spatial variability of *InpMed* is generally higher than *MedBFM* for all variables in all selected weeks. This highlights that, when observations are included in the reconstruction, the ML model *InpMed* simulates horizontal fields characterized by more complicated gradients and spatial structures w.r.t. a possibly too smooth output of the deterministic model.

A separate comment can be done for primary production (i.e., a variable that is not observed). Despite the mean vertical profiles are not substantially changed by ML architecture (Fig. 3), it is possible to notice that the *InpMed* model differs

from the *EmuMed* even if, during the training, no observed data have been provided for primary production. The fact that the variability introduced by the observed variable is clearly propagated by *InpMed* can be also observed in Fig. 4. This evidence confirms that information provided by observed data improves the *InpMed* capability to simulate the unobserved variable, thanks to the relations among variables learned from the output of the deterministic model by the deep learning architecture exploited.

5   Conclusion

We investigated the integration of an existing ecosystem deterministic model with in-situ and satellite information through a convolutional generative deep learning architecture. Merging these two different kinds of information allows us to combine their strengths and exploit them to lessen each other's limits. We remark that a deep learning model can also be less computationally expensive, once trained, with respect to a deterministic one, as it does not require an entire simulation in order to get specific variable estimations (e.g., primary production). Such a comparison will be one of the aspects that will be investigated in future works. Moreover, exploiting the intrinsic structure of the architecture, the learning framework makes possible the spread of information provided from the observed variables (temperature, salinity, oxygen, chlorophyll) also to variables that are not possible to directly collect via in-situ or satellite measurements (e.g., primary production). Experimental results on both *EmuMed* and *ImpMed* have confirmed the validity of the proposed approach, showing that our models can infer correctly information from the deterministic model and, in the case of *ImpMed*, also from observations. This work represents the first step to exploiting deep learning architecture aimed at merging large deterministic model output with observations to reconstruct the marine ecosystem's temporal and spatial variability. Our main goal will be to extend this architecture by inserting a larger number of channels so that it became able to reproduce the whole set of marine ecosystem variables, in particular exploiting this architecture to model unobserved variables (as we did for primary production) also with the information provided by observed data. The extension of the present ML model to the entire Mediterranean Sea represents another important computational challenge given the significant increase in data volume to handle.

References

1. The global ocean observing system. https://www.goosocean.org/. Accessed 22 Mar 2022
2. Albawi, S., Mohammed, T.A., Al-Zawi, S.: Understanding of a convolutional neural network. In: 2017 International Conference on Engineering and Technology (ICET), pp. 1–6 (2017). https://doi.org/10.1109/ICEngTechnol.2017.8308186
3. Bertalmio, M., Sapiro, G., Caselles, V., Ballester, C.: Image inpainting. In: Proceedings of the 27th Annual Conference on Computer Graphics and Interactive Techniques, pp. 417–424 (2000)

4. Colella, S., Falcini, F., Rinaldi, E., Sammartino, M., Santoleri, R.: Mediterranean ocean colour chlorophyll trends. PLoS One **11**(6), e0155756 (2016)
5. Cossarini, G., et al.: High-resolution reanalysis of the mediterranean sea biogeochemistry (1999–2019). Front. Marine Sci. 1537 (2021)
6. Euzen, A., Gaill, F., Lacroix, D., Cury, O.: The ocean revealed (2017)
7. Fennel, K., et al.: Advancing marine biogeochemical and ecosystem reanalyses and forecasts as tools for monitoring and managing ecosystem health. Front. Mar. Sci. **6**, 89 (2019)
8. Goodfellow, I., et al.: Generative adversarial nets. In: Advances in Neural Information Processing Systems, vol. 27 (2014)
9. Iizuka, S., Simo-Serra, E., Ishikawa, H.: Globally and locally consistent image completion. ACM Trans. Graph. (ToG) **36**(4), 1–14 (2017)
10. LeCun, Y., et al.: Backpropagation applied to handwritten zip code recognition. Neural Comput. **1**(4), 541–551 (1989)
11. Pathak, D., Krähenbühl, P., Donahue, J., Darrell, T., Efros, A.A.: Context encoders: feature learning by inpainting. CoRR abs/1604.07379 (2016). http://arxiv.org/abs/1604.07379
12. Sauzède, R., Johnson, J., Claustre, H., Camps-Valls, G., Ruescas, A.: Estimation of oceanic particulate organic carbon with machine learning. ISPRS Ann. Photogr. Remote Sens. Spat. Inf. Sci. **2**, 949–956 (2020)
13. Sonnewald, M., Lguensat, R., Jones, D.C., Dueben, P., Brajard, J., Balaji, V.: Bridging observations, theory and numerical simulation of the ocean using machine learning. Environ. Res. Lett. (2021)
14. Teruzzi, A., Bolzon, G., Feudale, L., Cossarini, G.: Deep chlorophyll maximum and nutricline in the mediterranean sea: emerging properties from a multi-platform assimilated biogeochemical model experiment. Biogeosciences **18**(23), 6147–6166 (2021)
15. Teruzzi, A., Di Cerbo, P., Cossarini, G., Pascolo, E., Salon, S.: Parallel implementation of a data assimilation scheme for operational oceanography: the case of the MedBFM model system. Comput. Geosci. **124**, 103–114 (2019)
16. Zeiler, M.D.: ADADELTA: an adaptive learning rate method. arXiv preprint arXiv:1212.5701 (2012)

The Joint Role of Batch Size and Query Strategy in Active Learning-Based Prediction - A Case Study in the Heart Attack Domain

Bruno Faria⬤, Dylan Perdigão⬤, Joana Brás⬤, and Luis Macedo(✉)⬤

Department of Informatics Engineering, University of Coimbra, CISUC - Centre for Informatics and Systems of the University of Coimbra, Coimbra, Portugal
{brunofaria,dgp,joanabras}@student.dei.uc.pt, macedo@dei.uc.pt

Abstract. This paper proposes an *Active Learning* algorithm that could detect heart attacks based on different body measures, which requires much less data than the passive learning counterpart while maintaining similar accuracy. To that end, different parameters were tested, namely the *batch size* and the *query strategy* used. The initial tests on batch size consisted of varying its value until 50. From these experiments, the conclusion was that the best results were obtained with lower values, which led to the second set of experiments, varying the batch size between 1 and 5 to understand in which value the accuracy was higher. Four query strategies were tested: *random sampling*, *least confident sampling*, *margin sampling* and *entropy sampling*. The results of each approach were similar, reducing by 57% to 60% the amount of data required to obtain the same results of the passive learning approach.

Keywords: Active learning · Heart attack

1 Introduction

Artificial Intelligence (AI) and, more specifically, Machine Learning (ML) have highly contributed to the improvement of prediction tasks in various domains, including critical life situations such as those involving the diagnosis of diseases [2,12,14]. Most of the solutions rely on Passive Learning algorithms. The machine is usually trained with large datasets. A function is learned and then used to predict outcomes in new situations.

A different approach, called Active Learning [8,9], can provide similar performance with fewer data, which is relevant for reducing costs in the acquisition of those data[1]. Active Learning operates with a partially or entirely unlabeled dataset, selecting for labeling only the most informative instances/examples from

---

[1] Active Learning is also used in the ML branch of Reinforcement Learning; in this paper, we are confined to the ML branch of Supervised and Semi-Supervised Learning.

G. Marreiros et al. (Eds.): EPIA 2022, LNAI 13566, pp. 464–475, 2022.
https://doi.org/10.1007/978-3-031-16474-3_38

which to learn based on specific measures such as information gain. In order to label those instances, the algorithm asks for help from the experts, such as medical doctors (Fig. 1). In the end, and in opposition to Passive Learning algorithms, the model is expected to be built with much fewer labeled instances while not losing accuracy in comparison to the Passive Learning counterpart [1].

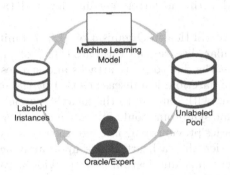

Fig. 1. Active learning cycle.

There are many different scenarios to label data via Active Learning. One of them may consider asking the oracle to label single instances separately or multiple instances simultaneously. For that, we need to define the *Batch Size* that indicates the number of examples that we feed the algorithm at a time. In this case, the dataset is split into multiple batch-sized sets. In a practical scenario, if the dataset were composed of 50 samples and the batch size was set to 5, the data would be split into ten queries, each containing five samples of the original dataset. On the other hand, the *Query Strategy* is the way the oracle chooses the potentially most informative instances of the pool of unlabeled data.

Different performances (efficiency and accuracy) may be achieved with the different query strategies considered for selecting the unlabeled instances to be labeled and with different sizes considered for those sets of unlabelled instances. In this paper, we study the role of this size and the query strategy in the performance of an Active Learning task of predicting heart attacks. The reason for considering our study in this domain is that cardiovascular diseases are the top cause of death globally, and as in other medical domains, acquiring data is a costly task.

The remainder of this paper is organized as follows. Section 2 provides a general review of the state of the art of Active Learning in different application domains and also of the application domain of myocardial infarction. Section 3 explains the tools, dataset, and frameworks used in the experimental tests. Sections 4 and 5 explain the methodologies and the experimental design to achieve the goals proposed previously. Section 6 presents the results obtained which are then discussed in Sect. 7. Finally, Sect. 8 concludes the paper.

2   Related Work

Regarding Active Learning, some progress was made, and researchers found the advantages of using this technique instead of Passive Learning. For example, in [5], a semi-supervised Active Learning approach was used to identify different sounds. After experimenting with both Passive and Active Learning, the best results were obtained with the latter, needing fewer data to achieve a more accurate algorithm.

According to the World Health Organisation [13], 7.9 million people die each year from cardiovascular diseases, an estimated 32% of all deaths worldwide, being 85% of those deaths due to heart attacks and strokes. Heart attack, also known as myocardial infarction, is a disease caused by the interruption of blood circulation in the heart with damage to the heart's muscle. Depending on morphological factors, some symptoms could indicate a risk of myocardial infarction. Considering the statistics previously mentioned, the necessity to quickly and correctly identify if a patient has a heart attack upon arriving at the ICU grows. AI and, more precisely, machine learning can provide a valuable contribution to fast and automatically detecting heart attacks with success. The domain of heart attack diagnostics has been an object of AI. For example, one study done by Chowdhury [3] uses linear classification models to diagnose myocardial infarction in order to prevent road accidents by analyzing electrocardiograms (ECG) waves.

Srinivas's work [11] has some different approaches, beginning with *IF-THEN* branches, turning to more basic machine learning methodologies like ID3 Decisions Trees, Neural Networks, Stochastic Back Propagation Algorithms and Bayesian Networks.

Finding research correlating Active Learning algorithms with heart diseases proved a challenge. However, it is possible to find work with other diseases in which Active Learning was tested. For example, in 2013, Mahapatra [7] studied Crohn's disease detection with Semi-Supervised Learning and Active Learning from magnetic resonances. Semi-Supervised Learning is used to extract from the images' features, and Active Learning classifies each region as "diseased" or "normal".

On that same note, another study was conducted [10] proposing an algorithm that could categorize images in three major groups (images referring to eye fundus, breast and skin cancer). The algorithm also split into two or four sub-categories (the output was binary on images referring to retinal lesions and skin cancer – having a lesion/cancer or not having it – and four categories to distinguish different types of breast cancer – normal, benign, *in situ* and invasive). The researchers concluded that using Active Learning (using a segment of the dataset), they obtained the same accuracy as passive learning (using the whole dataset) with 32 to 40% reduced data. This shows the most significant advantage of using Active Learning rather than the traditional method, which is Passive Learning.

3   Materials

The dataset we used [6] results from merging four databases of clinics and hospitals located in Hungary, Switzerland, and the United States of America. It is composed of 303 samples and 76 attributes. Only 14 of these 76 attributes were used by previous works that relies on the dataset. Those attributes are age, sex, chest pain type, resting blood pressure, serum cholesterol, fasting blood sugar, resting electrocardiographic results, maximum heart rate achieved, exercise induced angina, ST depression induced by exercise relative to rest, the slope of the peak exercise ST segment, number of major vessels and whether the person has thalassemia or not. Previous works have shown that it is possible to predict whether there is a high or low probability of having a heart attack with this relatively small amount of features (more details in Table 1).

ModAL [4] was the selected Active Learning framework. The *ModAL* API allows the user to automate the selection of the best examples in the dataset to constitute a batch. In addition, it is possible to use the different query strategies that will be discussed in Sect. 4.

4   Methods

Active Learning algorithms have various parameters that influence the results according to the dataset. In this paper, the primary focus was on the *query strategy* parameter. We have considered four different query strategies to aid on obtaining the most accurate results with less data: *least confident sampling, margin sampling, entropy sampling,* and *random sampling.*

Both *least confident sampling* and *margin sampling* take into account the probability of the certainty of the output of a given sample. However, they differ in which query is selected next. Margin sampling subtracts the two highest probabilities and selects the query whose result is the lowest, whereas least confident sampling only considers the highest probability. Another query strategy used was *entropy sampling*. The entropy formula is used on each sample, and the sample with the highest value will be selected as the following query. The last approach tested was *random sampling*. This method implies that the following query is selected at random. The code implemented was adapted from [4] and is expressed in Algorithm 1.

Algorithm 1. Random Sampling
___
Require: The *classifier* and the *pool* of examples
Ensure: The index i and the i-th element of the *pool*
1: Let $n =$ length of the *pool*
2: Let $i =$ random integer $\in [0,n[$
3: **return** i, *pool*$[i]$

Table 1. Dataset description

Feature	Type	Description
age	Numerical	Age in years
sex	Categorical	Sex of the individual, 0 represents a female person and 1 represents a male person
cp	Categorical	Chest pain type, 1 is typical angina, 2 is an atypical angina, 3 is non-anginal pain and 4 is for asymptomatic people
trestbps	Numerical	Resting blood pressure (in mm Hg on admission to the hospital)
chol	Numerical	Serum cholesterol in mg/dl
fbs	Categorical	Fasting blood sugar, 1 if greater than 120 mg/dl else 0
restecg	Numerical	Resting electrocardiographic results, if 0 the patient is normal, if 1 the patient is having ST-T wave abnormality (T wave inversions and/or ST elevation or depression greater than 0.05 mV), if 2 the patient is showing probable or definite left ventricular hypertrophy by Estes' criteria
thalach	Numerical	Maximum heart rate achieved
exang	Categorical	The value is 1 if exercise induced angina, else the value is 0
oldpeak	Numerical	ST depression induced by exercise relative to rest
slope	Categorical	Represents the slope of the peak exercise ST segment, upsloping if value is 1, flat slope if the value is 2, downsloping if the value is 3
ca	Numerical	Number of major vessels colored by fluoroscopy
thal	Categorical	If the value is 3 the patient is normal, if the value is 6, that means a fixed defect, and if the value is 7, that means a reversible defect
num	Categorical (target variable)	Diagnosis of heart disease (angiographic disease status) the value is 0 if there is less than 50% diameter narrowing else the value is 1

Algorithm 2 represents the code implemented to obtain the Active Learning algorithm used in the project reported in this paper. First, the number of queries n is computed with the number of instances divided by the batch size. Then, random instances with the batch size are chosen from the training set to initialize the process. Next, a pool is constructed with the remaining instances. Finally, the learner is defined with an estimator and a query strategy. We teach the learner with the initial set of instances, and then a first prediction is made. After that, each query picks instances in the pool to teach the learner again.

Regarding the classifier used, it was implemented the *random forest classifier*, which creates multiple decision trees on various sub-samples of the dataset. The estimator then uses the average prediction of the individual trees to improve the algorithm's accuracy and control overfitting.

Algorithm 2. Active Learning

Require: The $X_{\text{train}}/y_{\text{train}}$ and $X_{\text{test}}/y_{\text{test}}$ examples of the dataset, the *estimator*, the *queryStrategy*, and the *batchSize*

Ensure: The predictions y_{pred} of the *learner*

1: Let $n = \left\lfloor \frac{\text{length}(X_{\text{train}})}{batchSize} \right\rfloor$

2: Let $idx = batchSize$ random integers $\in [0,\text{length}(X_{train})[$

3: Let $X_{\text{init}}, y_{\text{init}} = X_{\text{train}}[idx], y_{\text{train}}[idx]$

4: Let $X_{\text{pool}}, y_{\text{pool}} = X_{\text{train}}, y_{\text{train}}$ without $X_{\text{init}}, y_{\text{init}}$

5: Let *learner* = Active Learner instance defined with an *estimator* and a *queryStrategy*

6: Teach the *learner* with X_{init} and y_{init}

7: Let y_{pred} = predictions of the learner for X_{test}

8: Get and Save metrics using y_{test} and y_{pred}

9: **for** $q = 0$ to $n - 1$ **do**

10:     Let $qidx = batchSize$ indexes of the *learner*'s query

11:     Let $X, y = X_{\text{pool}}[qidx], y_{\text{pool}}[qidx]$

12:     Teach the *learner* with X and y

13:     $X_{\text{pool}}, y_{\text{pool}} = X_{\text{train}}, y_{\text{train}}$ without X, y

14:     y_{pred} = predictions of the *learner* for X_{test}

15:     Get and Save metrics using y_{test} and y_{pred}

16: **return** y_{pred}

---

5   Experiments

The experiments here discussed began by comparing the number of queries and the ideal batch size with *random forest classifier* to obtain results close to Passive Learning. To decide the best batch size to use (amount of data each query contains), the tests contained the batch size value of 1, 5, 7, 10, 20, and 50. However, further examination proved that after a batch size of 5, the accuracy value did not reach 80%. Therefore, the next step consisted of testing batch sizes of 1, 2, 3, 4, and 5. The number of queries varied accordingly to the batch sized, as seen in line 1 of Algorithm 2 until the algorithm analyzed all samples of the dataset (212 random samples of data were used to train the algorithm and the rest for testing, i.e., 70% of the dataset's length used for training). After that, a comparison of the different query strategies was made.

For performance evaluation, several metrics were used, such as accuracy, sensitivity, and specificity:

$$\text{Accuracy} = \frac{TP + TN}{TP + FP + TN + FN} \tag{1}$$

$$\text{Sensibility} = \frac{TP}{TP + FN} \tag{2}$$

$$\text{Specificity} = \frac{TN}{TN + FP} \tag{3}$$

6   Results

In the first experiment, the accuracy for each batch size was compared according to the number of queries. The dashed red line represents the optimal value and the accuracy obtained using the training set with passive learning. That being said, Fig. 2a shows the *random sampling* strategy, Fig. 2b shows the *entropy sampling* strategy, Fig. 2c shows the *margin sampling* strategy, and Fig. 2d shows the *least confident sampling* strategy. The results are very similar. After that, we decided to observe behaviours for batch sizes from 1 to 5 (Fig. 3). For batch sizes 1 and 2, the accuracy of the plateau is above 80%. For batch sizes greater than 2, the accuracy is between 75% and 80%. The difference lies primarily in the rapid growth of accuracy where *entropy sampling* and *least confident sampling* strategies have a higher slope. The boxplots in Fig. 4 show the median and the distribution of the number of samples required to achieve 80% of accuracy. This value increases with the batch size, except for entropy and least confident sampling, where the median decreases for a batch size of 5.

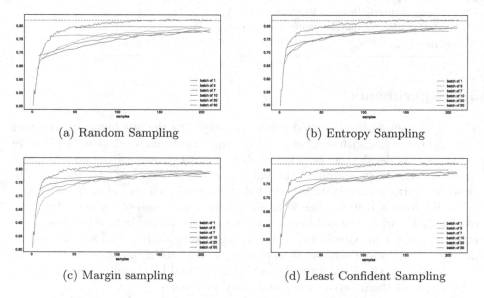

(a) Random Sampling   (b) Entropy Sampling

(c) Margin sampling   (d) Least Confident Sampling

Fig. 2. Accuracy of different query strategies for the *random forest classifier* using batch sizes of 1, 5, 7, 10, 20, 50.

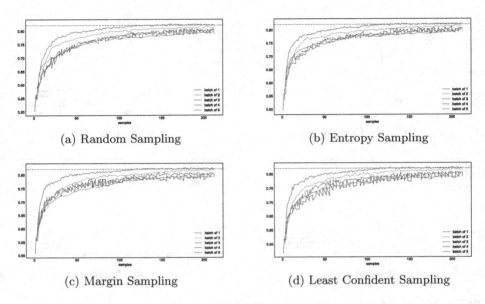

(a) Random Sampling   (b) Entropy Sampling

(c) Margin Sampling   (d) Least Confident Sampling

Fig. 3. Accuracy of different query strategies for the *random forest classifier* using batch sizes of 1, 2, 3, 4, 5.

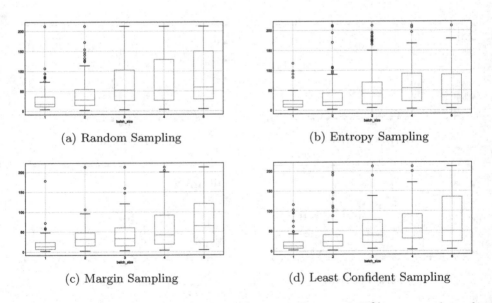

(a) Random Sampling   (b) Entropy Sampling

(c) Margin Sampling   (d) Least Confident Sampling

Fig. 4. Comparison of the number of samples required to reach 80% accuracy depending on various values of batch sizes $\{1, 2, 3, 4, 5\}$ for each query strategy used.

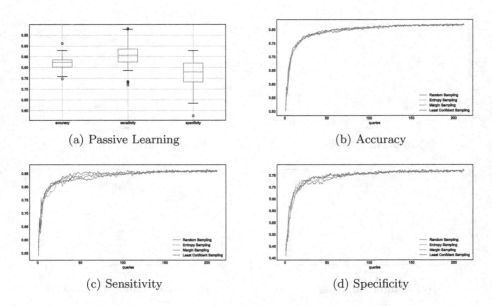

(a) Passive Learning

(b) Accuracy

(c) Sensitivity

(d) Specificity

Fig. 5. Results of the accuracy, sensitivity and specificity using the *random forest classifier* and batch size of 1, comparing the four different query strategies of Active Learning (Figures b, c, and d) with Passive Learning (figure a).

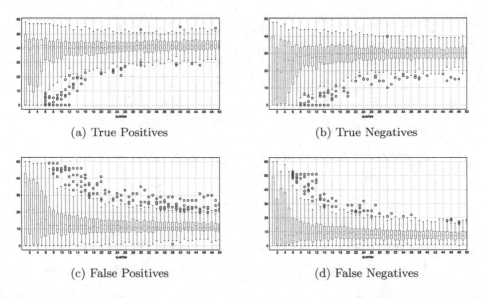

(a) True Positives

(b) True Negatives

(c) False Positives

(d) False Negatives

Fig. 6. Boxplots for true positives, true negatives, false positives, false negatives using *random forest classifier* with *random sampling* strategy and batches of 1.

In the second experiment, the four query strategies were compared with a batch size of 1. The boxplot in Fig. 5a shows the distribution of accuracy, sensitivity, and specificity for passive learning. Figure 5b shows the evolution of accuracy along with the number of queries for each query strategy. With 40 queries (a total of 200 samples of data), it is possible to get near 80% of accuracy. Similarly, Figs. 5c and 5d show, respectively, specificity and sensitivity for each query strategy.

Figure 6 shows in boxplots the distribution for the *random sampling* strategy of *True Positive*, *True Negative*, *False Positive*, *False Negative* for each number of queries, corresponding respectively to Figs. 6a, 6b, 6c and 6d. The number of TP and TN tends to increase. In addition, the number of outliers. decreases. Inversely, cases of FP and FN decrease.

7 Discussion

This paper presented different alternatives to the query strategy and batch sizes in an Active Learning algorithm.

Regarding the batch size, a more general test was made, as described in Sect. 5. As it was explained, the best accuracies were obtained with batch sizes of 1, 2, 3, 4, 5, so these will be the main focus of this section. Considering the results, it was to be expected that using the value of 1 sample per query would produce the best accuracy since it analyzes the influence of each sample individually on the results according to the query strategy rather than the average of the query. Using this batch size, the dataset can be reduced by around 50% of the training set to obtain the same accuracy of Passive Learning.

Using smaller batch sizes increases the computational complexity since more queries are to run, forcing the processor to take a long time to obtain results. However, the only batch sizes that achieved the same accuracy as the value obtained with Passive Learning were 1 and 2. As such, Fig. 4 has the purpose of constituting a middle ground between a good accuracy value and computational time since it indicates that for each batch size ($\{1, 2, 3, 4, 5\}$) and each of the four query strategies, an estimate of the amount of data required to obtain an accuracy of 80%, which all batch sizes ($\{1, 2, 3, 4, 5\}$) achieved. The boxplot corresponding to batch size 1 has the lowest deviation between the lowest and highest quartile across all query strategies, which indicates a lower deviation between data points. Random sampling appears to produce the highest variation between quartiles and, for a batch size of 1, all other three sampling approaches produce similar results. However, when increasing the batch size, there are significant differences between the query strategies, being that least confident sampling has the lowest median (approximately 35 data samples). As such, considering that value, the parameters are chosen previously allow a reduction of the training set by 83%.

Regarding the results obtained using the *random forest classifier*, all the different query strategies seem to obtain similar results across all three metrics analyzed (accuracy, specificity, and sensitivity), with a few discrepancies in

the sensitivity. However, it is still possible to identify in Fig. 5 a higher slope when using the query strategy *least confident sampling* in terms of accuracy and specificity. As it was said previously, this can be since a *least confident sampling* considers the higher probability of the output's class. *Least confident sampling*'s main issue is that it does not consider any other probabilities except the highest one. However, since the dataset only has two classes (binary output – 1 if the patient is possibly having a heart attack and 0 if that possibility is low), having one output class with the highest probability automatically indicates that the other class has the lowest probability. Therefore, this query strategy would be expected to obtain the best results.

Lastly, it is essential to mention that Fig. 6 represents the number of true positives, true negatives, false positives, and false negatives of each query averaged with the previous queries. Ideally, the sum of true positives and true negatives would be 212 samples, which is the amount of data in the training set, and the false positives and false negatives would be 0. As we can see from Fig. 6, the average of the 42 queries is not null for false positives and negatives, although it is a modest number.

8   Conclusions

To summarize, the goal of the work reported in this paper was achieved in some aspects in terms of identifying what query strategies would provide the best results, taking into account also the batch size. The conclusion was that using a batch size of 1 acquires the best accuracy and uses the query strategies least confident and entropy sampling. It was also possible to understand how many samples were required to obtain the same accuracy using Active Learning comparatively with Passive Learning, which is the main focus of using the type of algorithm used in this paper.

The next step would be to use a batch size of 1 preferably and test other parameters, such as the classifier. In this project, the estimator used was *random forest classifier*. However, an idea for future work could be testing shallow or deep neural network-based Active Learning algorithms to increase their accuracy.

Acknowledgements. This work is funded by the FCT - Foundation for Science and Technology, I.P./MCTES through national funds (PIDDAC), within the scope of CISUC R&D Unit - UIDB/00326/2020 or project code UIDP/00326/2020.

References

1. Balcan, M.F., Long, P.: Active and passive learning of linear separators under log-concave distributions. In: Conference on Learning Theory, pp. 288–316. PMLR (2013)
2. Bisdas, S., et al.: Artificial intelligence in medicine: a multinational multi-center survey on the medical and dental students' perception. Front. Public Health **9** (2021). https://doi.org/10.3389/fpubh.2021.795284, https://www.frontiersin.org/article/10.3389/fpubh.2021.795284

3. Chowdhury, M.E., et al.: Wearable real-time heart attack detection and warning system to reduce road accidents. Sens. (Switz.) **19**(12) (2019). https://doi.org/10.3390/s19122780, https://www.mdpi.com/1424-8220/19/12/2780

4. Danka, T., Horvath, P.: modAL: a modular active learning framework for Python. CoRR (2018). https://github.com/cosmic-cortex/modAL. Available on arXiv at https://arxiv.org/abs/1805.00979

5. Han, W., et al.: Semi-supervised active learning for sound classification in hybrid learning environments. PLoS One **11**(9), e0162075 (2016)

6. Janosi, A., Steinbrunn, W., Pfisterer, M., Detrano, R.: Heart disease data set (2020). https://archive.ics.uci.edu/ml/datasets/Heart+Disease. Accessed 03 Nov 2021

7. Mahapatra, D., Schüffler, P.J., Tielbeek, J.A.W., Vos, F.M., Buhmann, J.M.: Semi-supervised and active learning for automatic segmentation of Crohn's disease. In: Mori, K., Sakuma, I., Sato, Y., Barillot, C., Navab, N. (eds.) MICCAI 2013. LNCS, vol. 8150, pp. 214–221. Springer, Heidelberg (2013). https://doi.org/10.1007/978-3-642-40763-5_27

8. Settles, B.: Active learning literature survey. Mach. Learn. **15**(2), 201–221 (2010). 10.1.1.167.4245

9. Settles, B.: From theories to queries. In: Guyon, I., Cawley, G.C., Dror, G., Lemaire, V., Statnikov, A.R. (eds.) Active Learning and Experimental Design workshop, In conjunction with AISTATS 2010, Sardinia, Italy, 16 May 2010. JMLR Proceedings, vol. 16, pp. 1–18. JMLR.org (2011). http://proceedings.mlr.press/v16/settles11a/settles11a.pdf

10. Smailagic, A., et al.: MedAL: deep active learning sampling method for medical image analysis. arXiv preprint arXiv:1809.09287 (2018)

11. Srinivas, K., Rani, B.K., Govrdhan, A.: Applications of data mining techniques in healthcare and prediction of heart attacks. Int. J. Comput. Sci. Eng. (IJCSE) **2**(02), 250–255 (2010)

12. Tengnah, M.A.J., Sooklall, R., Nagowah, S.D.: A predictive model for hypertension diagnosis using machine learning techniques. In: Telemedicine Technologies, pp. 139–152. Elsevier (2019)

13. World Health Organization: Cardiovascular diseases (2021). https://www.who.int/health-topics/cardiovascular-diseases. Accessed 04 Nov 2021

14. Yakar, D., Ongena, Y.P., Kwee, T.C., Haan, M.: Do people favor artificial intelligence over physicians? A survey among the general population and their view on artificial intelligence in medicine. Value Health **25**(3), 374–381 (2022). https://www.sciencedirect.com/science/article/pii/S1098301521017411

Backpropagation Through States: Training Neural Networks with Sequentially Semiseparable Weight Matrices

Matthias Kissel[✉], Martin Gottwald, Biljana Gjeroska, Philipp Paukner, and Klaus Diepold

Technical University of Munich, Arcisstr. 21, 80333 Munich, Germany
matthias.kissel@tum.de
https://www.tum.de/en/

Abstract. Matrix-Vector multiplications usually represent the dominant part of computational operations needed to propagate information through a neural network. This number of operations can be reduced if the weight matrices are structured. In this paper, we introduce a training algorithm for neural networks with sequentially semiseparable weight matrices based on the backpropagation algorithm. By exploiting the structures in the weight matrices, the computational complexity for computing the matrix-vector product can be reduced to the subquadratic domain. We show that this can lead to computing time reductions on a microcontroller. Furthermore, we analyze the generalization capabilities of neural networks with sequentially semiseparable matrices. Our experiments show that neural networks with structured weight matrices can outperform standard feed-forward neural networks in terms of test prediction accuracy for several real-world datasets.

Keywords: Structured matrices · Neural networks · Efficient inference

1 Introduction

In recent years, the trend for neural networks has been towards larger and deeper networks [8,20]. Together with the size of the networks, the demand for computing resources also increased. For example, the number of operations needed to propagate information through the neural network can significantly increase with the network width. This limits the usability of neural networks for many applications, especially for real-time applications or on mobile platforms.

The major computational costs for propagating information through a neural network are typically attributed to matrix vector products. At each layer, the inputs are multiplied with the weight matrix of the layer, which amounts to $\mathcal{O}(nm)$ operations (for a weight matrix $W \in \mathcal{R}^{m \times n}$). These computational costs can be reduced if the weight matrix possesses a specific structure. This is due

© The Author(s), under exclusive license to Springer Nature Switzerland AG 2022
G. Marreiros et al. (Eds.): EPIA 2022, LNAI 13566, pp. 476–487, 2022.
https://doi.org/10.1007/978-3-031-16474-3_39

to the fact that for some matrix structures, there are efficient algorithms for multiplying the matrix with a vector with subquadratic order of operations.

Therefore, if the weight matrices of a neural network are structured, the number of operations for propagating information through the network can be reduced significantly. It has been observed that weights of a neural network tend to be structured after training [3]. Besides observing the structure *after* training, one can also enforce structure in the weight matrices *during* training. This has been shown for example by Sindhwani et al. [12] or Thomas et al. [14] for matrices with low displacement rank.

In this paper, we focus on Sequentially Semiseparable Matrices, which are related to linear time-varying system theory [4]. Our contribution is two-fold. First, we introduce a training algorithm for neural networks with sequentially semiseparable weight matrices. Our algorithm ensures that the weight matrices remain structured while optimizing the training error. Second, we compare the generalization performance of structured neural networks with standard feed-forward neural networks on four real-world datasets.

The paper is organized as follows. We first give an overview over approaches of using structured matrices in neural networks and work connecting semiseparable matrices with neural networks in literature. In the subsequent section, we introduce neural networks with sequentially semiseparable weight matrices. Afterwards, we present our training algorithm *Backpropagation through states*. The results of our experiments are shown and discussed in Sect. 5. Finally, we summarize our findings and draw a conclusion.

2   Literature Review

Several approaches for finding structure in trained weight matrices, or imposing structure constraints during training have been proposed recently. Here, most often matrices of low displacement rank have been used in neural networks. For example, Sindhwani et al. [12] proposed to train neural networks with toeplitz-like weight matrices and Thomas et al. [14] introduced a class of low displacement rank matrices, which can be trained end-to-end including the operator matrices. Zhao et al. [22] proved some theoretical properties for neural networks with weight matrices of low displacement rank.

Another structure, which has been applied to neural networks, are hierarchical matrices [5]. Connecting Hierarchical matrices with semiseparable matrices results in hierarchically semiseparable matrices [2,18].

Finding the right structure for a given problem is difficult, especially since the right structure depends on the problem at hand. Therefore, we regard the previously mentioned approaches not as competitors, but as complementary approaches. For a specific problem, one of the structures from literature might work very good, and for another problem the structure analyzed in this paper might be better. Hence, we think it is crucially important to have several structure-aware training or approximation methods for neural networks, in order to find the best approach for a given problem.

In this paper, we are focusing on sequentially semiseparable matrices. The concept of this structure dates back until 1937 [6,17]. Sequentially semiseparable matrices are closely related to the theory of time varying systems [4], since this structure appears when describing a time varying system. Other definitions of semiseparability have been introduced by Vandebril et al. [18] - for example for quasiseparable matrices.

To the best of our knowledge, (sequentially) semiseparable matrices have not been applied as weight matrices in neural networks yet. Related work, which used semiseparable matrices in the domain of neural networks focused on finding suitable neural network architectures for time-varying system applications. For example, the aim of State-Space Neural Networks [16,21] is to introduce non-linearity into the state space representation of time-varying systems. Another example are Time-Varying Neural Networks (TV-NN) [15], in which the weights of the network change over time in order to adapt to non-stationary input signals. Our method differs from such approaches in that we do not intend to design application specific network architectures. Instead, in our approach we constrain the weight matrices in neural networks to have sequentially semiseparable structure. Our approach refers generically to neural networks, and explicitly not to a specific target application.

3   Neural Networks with Sequentially Semiseparable Weight Matrices

We define neural networks as function $G(u)$

$$\hat{y} = G(u), \tag{1}$$

where u are the inputs to the network and $\hat{y}$ the outputs respectively. G is a composition of layer mappings

$$G(u) = (\mathcal{L}_r \circ \cdots \circ \mathcal{L}_1)(u), \tag{2}$$

where the neural network consists of r layers and $\mathcal{L}_i$ is the mapping of the ith layer. In this paper, we focus on structures in densely connected feed-forward neural networks. For these layers, the mappings are of the form

$$\mathcal{L}_i(u) = \sigma(W_i u + \theta_i), \tag{3}$$

where W_i is a weight matrix and θ_i the biases of the respective layer. σ is the activation function of the layer, which is applied element-wise to its inputs.

We are interested in the special case that the weight matrices W_i are structured. In particular, we want them to be sequentially semiseparable, which allows us to use results from time-varying systems theory [4] to increase the efficiency of information propagation. Sequentially semiseparable matrices can be expressed as

$$\begin{aligned} W_i = D &+ C(I - ZA)^{-1}ZB \\ &+ G(I - Z^T E)^{-1}Z^T F. \end{aligned} \tag{4}$$

Here, I is the identity matrix and Z is a down-shift matrix

$$Z = \begin{pmatrix} 0 & & & 0 \\ 1 & \ddots & & \\ & \ddots & \ddots & 0 \\ 0 & & 1 & 0 \end{pmatrix}. \tag{5}$$

A, B, C, D, E, F and G are block-diagonal matrices, each comprising of k matrices

$$A = diag([A_1, \ldots, A_k]) \tag{6}$$

(B, C, D, E, F and G matrices respectively). In the context of time-varying system theory, the matrices $A, \ldots, G$ define the behavior of a time-varying system. For example, A maps the previous state of the system to the next state, and B maps the previous state to the current output. Note that the dimensions of the $A_k, B_k, C_k, D_k, E_k, F_k$ and G_k matrices are not constant. In general we have $dim(A_i) \neq dim(A_j)$ for $i \neq j$ (B_k, C_k, D_k, E_k, F_k and G_k matrices respectively). This reflects the fact that the state, input and output dimension can change for different k.

In order to apply the results from time varying system theory to our matrix vector products $W_i u$, the input vector u as well as the output vector $\hat{y}$ must be partitioned into p segments

$$u = \begin{pmatrix} u_1 \ldots u_p \end{pmatrix}^T \tag{7}$$

($\hat{y}$ respectively). Note that both, u and $\hat{y}$, must be partitioned into the same amount of segments. However, the segments can be of different size, which means that in general

$$dim(u_j) \neq dim(\hat{y}_j) \quad for \quad j = 1 \ldots p. \tag{8}$$

Finding a good partitioning depends on the problem at hand. In our experiments, we set $dim(u_j) = dim(\hat{y}_j) = 1$ for $j = 1 \ldots p$. This results in $p = n$ for square weight matrices $W \in \mathcal{R}^{n \times n}$.

Exploiting the structure of our weight matrices, the product between W_i and an arbitrary input vector u can be performed in the state-space representation. The corresponding state equations are

$$x_{k+1} = A_k x_k + B_k u_k \tag{9}$$

$$\hat{x}_k = E_k \hat{x}_{k+1} + F_k u_k \tag{10}$$

$$\hat{y}_k^{(1)} = C_k x_k + D_k u_k \tag{11}$$

$$\hat{y}_k^{(2)} = G_k \hat{x}_{k+1} \tag{12}$$

$$\hat{y}_k = \hat{y}_k^{(1)} + \hat{y}_k^{(2)}, \tag{13}$$

where x_{k+1} is the state of the causal part of the matrix, and $\hat{x}_k$ the state of the anti-causal part respectively. The computational graph of these operations is illustrated in Fig. 1.

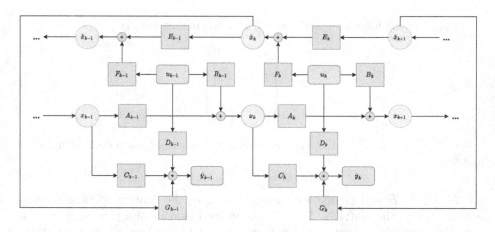

Fig. 1. Computational graph for computing the matrix-vector product in state space. This illustrates the operations described by Eqs. 9–13. In terms of time varying systems, x_k and $\hat{x}_k$ describe the state of the system, u_k are inputs and $\hat{y}_k$ are outputs.

We usually have

$$\max_k\{dim(x_k)\} = \max_k\{dim(\hat{x}_k)\} = d. \tag{14}$$

Moreover, we assume that

$$\max_k\{dim(u_k)\} < d \tag{15}$$

and

$$\max_k\{dim(\hat{y}_k)\} < d. \tag{16}$$

In this scenario, the computational complexity for computing the matrix-vector product for a square weight matrix $W \in \mathcal{R}^{n \times n}$ reduces from $\mathcal{O}(n^2)$ to $\mathcal{O}(pd^2)$. We run experiments with values of d in the range $d = 1, \ldots 5$.

4   Backpropagation Through States

We consider neural networks as defined in Eq. 2 with at least one weight matrix of the form given in Eq. 4. If such a network would be trained with the standard backpropagation algorithm, the structure would most probably vanish during training. That is, after updating a structured weight matrix W according to the gradient taken with respect to the entries of the matrix $W_{e,l}$, the matrix is in general not sequentially semiseparable anymore. To solve this, we propose our training algorithm *Backpropagation through States*, which ensures that the matrix stays sequentially semiseparable after updating the weights. We introduce the necessary steps for a given linear layer with sequentially semiseparable weight matrix W. These steps can be combined with the standard backpropagation steps

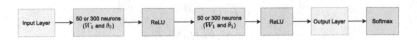

Standard Neural Network

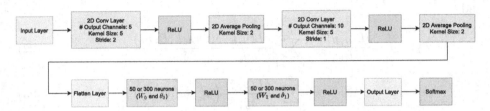

Convolutional Neural Network

Fig. 2. Neural network architectures used in our experiments. The CNN architecture is used for image-based datasets, and the standard architecture in all others. The classifier part consisting of two hidden layers stays the same for our standard networks and convolutional networks. The feature extractor part used for image-based datasets consists of two convolutional layers followed by pooling layers. In our experiments, we focus on the weight matrix W_1. We compare the generalization performance for W_1 being a sequentially semiseparable matrix, a rank 1 matrix or a standard weight matrix.

for the rest of the network, which might as well contain non-fully connected parts like convolutional layers.

The key idea of *Backpropagation through states* is to derive the training error with respect to the entries in the A_k, B_k, C_k, D_k, E_k, F_k and G_k matrices instead of the entries in W. We illustrate the approach in the following exemplary for the setting $dim(u_k) = dim(\hat{y}_k) = 1$ for $k = 1 \ldots p$.

Figure 1 depicts the data flow in the state space model for computing the outputs $\hat{y}$. C_k, D_k and G_k do not influence the state of the system. Therefore, these matrices contribute only to a single output segment

$$\frac{\delta L(y, \hat{y})}{\delta C_k} = \frac{\delta L(y, \hat{y})}{\delta \hat{y}_k} x_k^T, \tag{17}$$

$$\frac{\delta L(y, \hat{y})}{\delta D_k} = \frac{\delta L(y, \hat{y})}{\delta \hat{y}_k} u_k, \tag{18}$$

$$\frac{\delta L(y, \hat{y})}{\delta G_k} = \frac{\delta L(y, \hat{y})}{\delta \hat{y}_k} \hat{x}_{k+1}^T, \tag{19}$$

where $L(y, \hat{y})$ refers to the loss based on the desired output y and the predicted output $\hat{y}$.

In contrast, A_k, B_k, E_k and F_k change the state of the system. By that, they can contribute to past or future outputs (depending if the matrices belong to the causal or anticausal part). During backpropagation, the influence of these matrices for other output segments must also be considered, which results in

$$\frac{\delta L(y,\hat{y})}{\delta A_k} = \sum_{s=k+1}^{p} \frac{\delta L(y,\hat{y})}{\delta \hat{y}_s} \frac{\delta(\tilde{C}(s,k)A_k x_k)}{\delta A_k} \tag{20}$$

$$= \sum_{s=k+1}^{p} \frac{\delta L(y,\hat{y})}{\delta \hat{y}_s} \left(x_k^T \otimes \tilde{C}(s,k) \right) \tag{21}$$

and

$$\frac{\delta L(y,\hat{y})}{\delta B_k} = \sum_{s=k+1}^{p} \frac{\delta L(y,\hat{y})}{\delta \hat{y}_s} \frac{\delta(\tilde{C}(s,k)B_k u_k)}{\delta B_k} \tag{22}$$

$$= \sum_{s=k+1}^{p} \frac{\delta L(y,\hat{y})}{\delta \hat{y}_s} \left(u_k^T \otimes \tilde{C}(s,k) \right), \tag{23}$$

where $\otimes$ denotes the Kronecker product and

$$\tilde{C}(s,k) = C_s \prod_{k+1}^{f=s-1} A_f. \tag{24}$$

The gradients for the anticausal part (E_k and F_k) can be computed analogously.

In order to compute the gradients for A_k, B_k, E_k and F_k, the error gets propagated through the states, which gives our algorithm its name. In our experiments, we used auto-differentiation provided by pytorch[1] to compute the gradients. Our code can be found on GitHub[2].

Empirically, we noticed that initializing the $A_k, B_k, C_k, D_k, E_k, F_k$ and G_k matrices randomly often leads to numerical instability. The resulting weight matrix might have a very big condition number, which led to problems during inference as well as during training (vanishing and exploding gradients). In order to overcome this problem, we propose to initialize the weight matrix W glorot-uniform randomly. The required parameter matrices are then obtained by performing balanced model reduction [4,10] on the randomly initialized weight matrix. By that, the training procedure becomes more stable, while still allowing for indirectly randomly initialized parameter matrices. Note that the weight matrix reconstructed from the parameter matrices obtained by balanced model reduction in general differs from the original glorot-uniform initialized weight matrix.

5   Experiments and Discussion

In our experiments we investigate the prediction accuracy of neural networks with a sequentially semiseparable weight matrix compared to standard neural networks. The architectures of the networks used in our experiments are depicted

---

[1] https://pytorch.org/.
[2] https://github.com/MatthiasKi/statespace_learning.

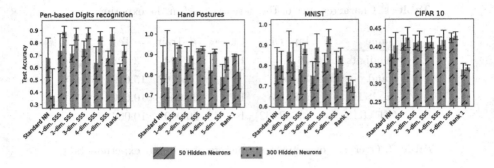

Fig. 3. Generalization performance of standard neural networks, neural networks with one sequentially semiseparable weight matrix, and neural networks with one rank 1 weight matrix on different datasets. Neural networks with semiseparable weight matrices consistently achieve a better test accuracy. This effect is especially visible for models with 300 neurons. In contrast, the rank 1 weight matrix approach could not improve the test prediction accuracy on all datasets.

in Fig. 2. In our comparison, we focus on the weight matrix between the first and the second densely connected hidden layer, corresponding to W_1 in the Figure. We investigate the effect of constraining W_1 to be sequentially semiseparable compared to a non-restricted weight matrix or a weight matrix of rank 1. The number of neurons in the hidden layers was set to 300 so that the parameters in the weight matrix under study account for approximately 90% of the total number of parameters in the neural network (assuming that the parameters in the convolutional layers are shared). In order to compare the results with the scenario where the weight matrix does not represent the dominant part of the parameters, we also perform all experiments with 50 neurons in the hidden layers.

All experiments are repeated 5 times to account for random initialization of the weight matrices and stochastic effects. We chose 5 repetitions, because this was still reasonable considering the computation time. Moreover, we assume that with this number of repetitions the effect of the random initialization can be estimated well. We report the mean and standard deviation of the test prediction accuracy over those runs. Each model has been trained for 200 epochs, followed by training until convergence on a validation set, which comprises 15% of the training data (randomly split at the beginning of the training). Thus, the number of epochs is determined data-driven, and is not set in advance as a hyperparameter. The most important hyperparameters are listed in Table 2.

We train all models on four real-world datasets (see Table 1), inter alia obtained from the UCI machine learning repository[3]:

- The Pen-Based Digit Recognition dataset [1], which contains resampled coordinates of individuals drawing digits.
- The Motion Capture Hand Postures dataset [7], for which the aim is to predict the correct hand posture given the coordinates of 11 markers. There are many

---
[3] https://archive.ics.uci.edu/.

Table 1. Characteristics of the datasets used in the experiments.

Name	Inp. Dim.	Classes	# Train	# Test
Pendigits	16	10	7494	3,498
Hand postures	36	5	62,476	15,619
MNIST	(28, 28)	10	60,000	10,000
CIFAR10	(3, 32, 32)	10	50,000	10,000

Table 2. Overview over hyperparameters used in our experiments.

Hyperparameter	Value
Repetitions per experiment	5
$dim(u_k), dim(a_k) \quad \forall k$	1
Optimizer	Adam ($\beta_1 = 0.9, \beta_2 = 0.999, lr = 1e - 3$)
Training loss function	Cross entropy
Validation set share	15%
Convergence patience	20

missing values in the dataset (which we mask with zeros) and the marker positions have been permuted between different recordings. At each iteration, we randomly split the samples in the datapoint into training (80% of the data) and test (20% of the data) set.
- The MNIST digits classification dataset, which contains grayscale images of handwritten digits.
- The CIFAR10 images classification dataset, which comprises color images from 10 different categories.

We use the proposed split of the data into training and testing data if not stated otherwise.

Our experiments show that the generalization performance can be improved by deploying sequentially semiseparable matrices to neural networks. This effect is visible for the models with 300 hidden neurons as well as the models with 50 hidden neurons. The optimal state space dimension depends on the dataset at hand. For example, for the MNIST dataset the best performance was achieved with $d = 4$, whereas for the hand postures dataset the optimal state dimension was $d = 1$. The results of our experiments are depicted in Fig. 3. Our observations are in line with previous observations in literature. For other structure classes, it has also been observed that in some cases the prediction accuracy can be increased by using structured weight matrices [9, 11, 13, 19].

The results of our 50 hidden neuron model experiments show that the performance gain of our models is not only due to the standard neural network being overparameterized. We suspect that the latter is the case for the model with 300 neurons trained on the pen-based digits recognition dataset as well as the hand postures dataset. The fact that the small model achieved better test accu-

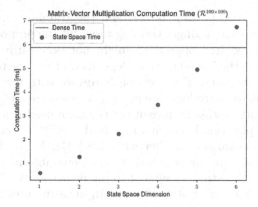

Fig. 4. Comparison of the time needed for computing the matrix-vector product of a 100-dimensional matrix on a STM32F405 microcontroller. When the state dimension is small, the matrix-vector product using a sequentially semiseparable matrix can be performed in a fraction of the time needed for the dense counterpart. However, with increasing state dimension, the time needed for computing the matrix-vector product also increases, finally reaching a break-even point with the dense counterpart.

racies on these datasets suggests that the larger network was overparameterized and thus the training stopped early due to overfitting. In contrast, the models with sequentially semiseparable weight matrix suffered far less from overfitting problems, since these networks inherently comprise fewer parameters. This can, however, not only be attributed to the reduced number of parameters, since the rank 1 weight matrix approach could not consistently outperform the standard neural network.

Interestingly, in our experiments, the inference as well as training times increased for neural networks with sequentially semiseparable weight matrices, even though the number of operations required for inference decreased. This has two reasons. Firstly, we executed our experiments on an AMD Ryzen Threadripper 3990X 64-Core Processor. When computing the matrix-vector product for a standard matrix, the operations could be distributed over 64 available cores. However, computing the matrix-vector product for sequentially semiseparable matrices has fewer parallelization capabilities, since in order to compute the output of timestep $k + 1$, the state of timestep k is required. Therefore, the sequential computation scheme prohibits elaborate parallelization of the operations. The fact that our code is implemented in Python also plays a role here. Our for-loops implemented in Python cannot keep up with the speed of the C-routines used by pytorch. Secondly, computing the computational graph for gradient updates is more complex in our proposed algorithm. As explained in Sect. 4, the training error is propagated through all states. This results in a longer chain of derivatives, similar as obtained in deep neural networks. Constructing and evaluating this computational graph might result in longer training times. Usually, this is not a problem, because for most applications the infer-

ence time is the most important factor, and the training time plays a minor role. In summary, we expect longer training times for the proposed method. The reduced number of required operations might not necessarily lead to reduced inference times, since the inference time depends on the targeted hardware and the implementation at hand. However, on hardware with few processing units (like for example microcontrollers), we can expect speed-ups regarding the inference times. We illustrate this by measuring the time needed for computing the matrix-vector multiplication between a matrix $A \in \mathcal{R}^{100 \times 100}$ and a random vector on a STM32F405 microcontroller with 168 MHz. Figure 4 shows that the matrix-vector product for the sequentially semiseparable matrix can be computed in a fraction of the time compared to the dense matrix. The computation time increases with increasing state dimension, until the break-even point with the dense computation is reached.

6   Conclusion

We introduced an algorithm for training neural networks with sequentially semiseparable weight matrices. The key idea of the proposed algorithm is to backpropagate the training loss to the matrices generating the structured weight matrix, instead of the entries in the weight matrix directly. By that, it is possible to reduce the training loss while maintaining the structure in the weight matrices throughout training. Moreover, our algorithm can be combined with the standard backpropagation algorithm. This allows for training neural networks comprising structured as well as non-structured weight matrices.

To validate our algorithm, we ran experiments using four real-world datasets. Two key findings resulted from our experiments. First, using structured matrices in neural networks can increase the generalization performance of the network. This finding confirms previous observations from literature, but now applied to sequentially semiseparable weight matrices. Second, computing the product between a sequentially semiseparable matrix and a vector can hardly be parallelized without losing the advantages of reduced required number of operations. Therefore, the structure investigated in this paper is mostly relevant to applications running on non-parallelized hardware such as microcontrollers.

References

1. Alimoglu, F., Alpaydin, E.: Methods of combining multiple classifiers based on different representations for pen-based handwritten digit recognition. In: Proceedings of the Fifth Turkish Artificial Intelligence and Artificial Neural Networks Symposium (TAINN 1996). Citeseer (1996)
2. Chandrasekaran, S., Gu, M., Pals, T.: A fast ULV decomposition solver for hierarchically semiseparable representations. SIAM J. Matrix Anal. Appl. **28**(3), 603–622 (2006)
3. Denil, M., Shakibi, B., Dinh, L., De Freitas, N., et al.: Predicting parameters in deep learning. In: Advances in Neural Information Processing Systems, pp. 2148–2156 (2013)

4. Dewilde, P., Van der Veen, A.J.: Time-Varying Systems and Computations. Springer, New York (1998). https://doi.org/10.1007/978-1-4757-2817-0
5. Fan, Y., Lin, L., Ying, L., Zepeda-Núnez, L.: A multiscale neural network based on hierarchical matrices. Multisc. Model. Simul. **17**(4), 1189–1213 (2019)
6. Gantmakher, F., Krein, M.: Sur les matrices completement non négatives et oscillatoires. Compos. Math. **4**, 445–476 (1937)
7. Gardner, A., Kanno, J., Duncan, C.A., Selmic, R.: Measuring distance between unordered sets of different sizes. In: Proceedings of the IEEE Conference on Computer Vision and Pattern Recognition, pp. 137–143 (2014)
8. He, K., Zhang, X., Ren, S., Sun, J.: Deep residual learning for image recognition. In: Proceedings of the IEEE Conference on Computer Vision and Pattern Recognition, pp. 770–778 (2016)
9. Ioannou, Y., Robertson, D., Shotton, J., Cipolla, R., Criminisi, A.: Training CNNs with low-rank filters for efficient image classification. arXiv preprint arXiv:1511.06744 (2015)
10. Kung, S., Lin, D.: Optimal Hankel-norm model reductions: multivariable systems. IEEE Trans. Autom. Control **26**(4), 832–852 (1981)
11. Lebedev, V., Ganin, Y., Rakhuba, M., Oseledets, I., Lempitsky, V.: Speeding-up convolutional neural networks using fine-tuned cp-decomposition. arXiv preprint arXiv:1412.6553 (2014)
12. Sindhwani, V., Sainath, T., Kumar, S.: Structured transforms for small-footprint deep learning. In: Advances in Neural Information Processing Systems, pp. 3088–3096 (2015)
13. Tai, C., Xiao, T., Zhang, Y., Wang, X., et al.: Convolutional neural networks with low-rank regularization. arXiv preprint arXiv:1511.06067 (2015)
14. Thomas, A.T., Gu, A., Dao, T., Rudra, A., Ré, C.: Learning compressed transforms with low displacement rank. Adv. Neural. Inf. Process. Syst. **2018**, 9052 (2018)
15. Titti, A., Squartini, S., Piazza, F.: A new time-variant neural based approach for nonstationary and non-linear system identification. In: 2005 IEEE International Symposium on Circuits and Systems, pp. 5134–5137. IEEE (2005)
16. Van Lint, J., Hoogendoorn, S., van Zuylen, H.J.: Accurate freeway travel time prediction with state-space neural networks under missing data. Transp. Rese. Part C: Emerg. Technol. **13**(5–6), 347–369 (2005)
17. Vandebril, R., Van Barel, M., Golub, G., Mastronardi, N.: A bibliography on semiseparable matrices. Calcolo **42**(3), 249–270 (2005)
18. Vandebril, R., Van Barel, M., Mastronardi, N.: Matrix Computations and Semiseparable Matrices: Linear Systems, vol. 1. JHU Press (2007)
19. Wen, W., Wu, C., Wang, Y., Chen, Y., Li, H.: Learning structured sparsity in deep neural networks. In: Advances in Neural Information Processing Systems, pp. 2074–2082 (2016)
20. Xie, D., Xiong, J., Pu, S.: All you need is beyond a good init: exploring better solution for training extremely deep convolutional neural networks with orthonormality and modulation. In: Proceedings of the IEEE Conference on Computer Vision and Pattern Recognition, pp. 6176–6185 (2017)
21. Zamarreño, J.M., Vega, P.: State space neural network. properties and application. Neural Netw. **11**(6), 1099–1112 (1998)
22. Zhao, L., Liao, S., Wang, Y., Li, Z., Tang, J., Yuan, B.: Theoretical properties for neural networks with weight matrices of low displacement rank. In: Proceedings of the 34th International Conference on Machine Learning, vol. 70, pp. 4082–4090. JMLR. org (2017)

A Generic Approach to Extend Interpretability of Deep Networks

Catarina Silva(✉), António Morais, and Bernardete Ribeiro

Department of Informatics Engineering, Center for Informatics and Systems, University of Coimbra, Coimbra, Portugal
{catarina,bribeiro}@dei.uc.pt

Abstract. The recent advent of machine learning as a transforming technology has sparked fears about human inability to comprehend the rational of gradually more complex approaches. Interpretable Machine Learning (IML) was triggered by such concerns, with the purpose of enabling different actors to grasp the application scenarios, including trustworthiness and decision support in highly regulated sectors as those related to health and public services. YOLO (You Only Look Once) models, as other deep Convolutional Neural Network (CNN) approaches, have recently shown remarkable performance in several tasks dealing with object detection. However, interpretability of these models is still an open issue. Therefore, in this work we extend the LIME (Local Interpretable Model-agnostic Explanations) framework to be used with YOLO models. The main contribution is a public add-on to LIME that can effectively improve YOLO interpretability. Results on complex images show the potential improvement.

Keywords: Interpretable machine learning · Explainable Artificial Intelligence · Deep learning · YOLO · LIME

1 Introduction

Computer vision (CV), more specifically image processing, including classification and object detection, supported by Deep Neural Network (DNN) advances, has become a field where different systems have thrived. Examples range from video security in big cities to fire detection in forests [14]. Different deep models, usually based on Convolutional Neural Networks (CNN) have been put forward with success, among which You Only Look Once (YOLO) [18] is one of the forerunners. Object detection is a CV task that combines two other tasks: object localization, that is, drawing bounding boxes around visual objects, and image classification, which means assigning classes to images. Object detectors can be categorized into one of two types, one-stage and two-stage. Two-stage object detection is separated into two steps: first the model proposes a set of regions or bounding boxes (also called the region proposal phase) and then the class of the proposed regions are predicted by a classifier. Examples of two-stage detectors notably include the R-CNN family (e.g. R-CNN [7], Faster R-CNN [19]). One-stage detectors propose

G. Marreiros et al. (Eds.): EPIA 2022, LNAI 13566, pp. 488–499, 2022.
https://doi.org/10.1007/978-3-031-16474-3_40

bounding boxes in input images directly without the region proposal step. Examples of one-stage object detectors include *YOLO* [18] and *SSD* [12]. Two-stage detectors have high localization and object recognition accuracy when compared to one-stage detectors [10]. One drawback of using two-stage detectors is that they tend to be slower than their one-stage counterparts. Because of their greater inference speed, one-stage detectors are oftentimes utilized in real-time scenarios, where the accuracy of the object detection is not as important as providing a fast detection. Hence, we will focus on one of the most used one-stage object detectors, YOLO [1], focusing on *YOLOv4* interpretability. YOLO divides the input image into an S × S grid. If the center of an object falls into a grid cell, that grid cell is responsible for detecting that object. Each grid cell predicts the bounding boxes and respective confidence scores. Such confidence reflect how confident the model is that the box contains an object and also how accurate it is. This confidence is the product of the probability of finding the object by the Intersection over Union (IoU) (see Fig. 1).

$$IoU = \frac{Area\ of\ Overlap}{Area\ of\ Union}$$

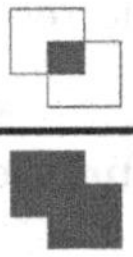

Fig. 1. Intersection over Union (IoU)

For testing, we can multiply the conditional class probabilities and the individual box confidence predictions (see Eq. 1), which gives class-specific confidence scores for each box [18].

$$Pr(Class_i|Object) \times Pr(Object) \times IoU_{pred}^{truth} = Pr(Class_i) \times IoU_{pred}^{truth} \quad (1)$$

These scores encode both the probability of that class appearing in the box ($Pr(Class_i)$) and how well the predicted box fits the object (IoU_{pred}^{truth}) [18]. Notice that this procedure does not include any explainability measures and are being increasingly used in critical scenarios. Hence, underpinning this research is the dominant role played by such models in various critical domains that has sparked fears about human inability to comprehend the rational of gradually more complex approaches, and provoked a demand for model transparency and interpretability [5]. As a consequence, a stream of work in Interpretable Machine Learning (IML)/Explainable Artificial Intelligence (XAI) focusing on making intelligent systems more transparent, and inherently more trustworthy has appeared. The explanations provided by more transparent systems are important to ensure algorithmic fairness, identify potential bias/problems in the training data, and to ensure that the algorithms perform as expected [6]. Distinct challenges are still open in IML. First, the ones related to standardization and assessment that are in an early stage of development. Then, the accuracy/interpretability trade-off that is commonly accepted, but where different research teams are struggling to cope. Finally, the lack of evaluation at scale in real world scenarios is also an open issue.

In this paper, we propose a generic approach to extend interpretability of one of the best known DNN, YOLO, maintaining its performance abilities, by extending the LIME (Local Interpretable Model-agnostic Explanations) framework to be used with YOLO models.

LIME in its standard form is not applicable to YOLO and has not yet been tried, even though both are cutting edge approaches in their domains. The novelty in this paper is a strategy to make it possible by taking advantage of the bounding box that YOLO outputs and using it as input for LIME.

Results on complex images show the potential improvement. The main contribution is a public add-on to LIME that can effectively improve YOLO interpretability and easily be replicated in different scenarios.

2   Interpretable ML/Explainable AI

In this section we introduce IML/XAI and describe the baseline interpretability model that supports the research.

2.1   Background Knowledge

Interpretable Machine Learning (IML), also referred to as Explainable Artificial Intelligence (XAI) [8], constitutes a field that aims at providing intuitive and human-readable explanations of decisions made by ML/AI systems. These explanations can have several formats. One example in the visual field is to map the input pixels that contributed the most to the model output. By turning the model prediction into something that can be understood by humans, we have a way to verify if the model is making decisions based on the parts of the image that we expect it to use.

There are several applications of IML/XAI, but for the purposes of this paper we will only refer to those related to DNN. In [4], there is a categorization of these algorithms according to several properties, namely *scope*, *methodology*, and *usage*. The *scope* of an explanation defines the portion of the predictions made by the model that we intend to explain [2]. Local scope means that we will only create explanations for a single instance of input data. Global scope on the other hand intends to explain every decision the model makes, which means that the explanation map can be used in any number of input data. *Methodology* refers to the fundamental concept of the algorithm that allows it to generate explanations. Backpropagation methods utilize error gradients that are passed backwards from the output to the input layer. These gradients are then used to understand the impact that the different input neurons have on the output. Perturbation methods perform alterations to the input instance such as blocking or substituting some features. In a visual context this could mean omitting some segments of the image. Finally, IML/XAI algorithms can be categorized according to their intended *usages*. If the algorithm is embedded in the explained model, it is called model-intrinsic. On the other hand, if the algorithm can be applied to any model independently, it is called model-agnostic.

This compatibility is of great benefit since it is possible to use any existing model with no limitations in terms of accuracy.

IML/XAI techniques have been applied to image classification tasks. Explainable Object Detection (EOD) is a subfield that is concerned with applying explainability methods to object detectors. There are inherent difficulties to this, since object detectors often have very complex hyperparameters [13]. Some of these IML/XAI methods resort to saliency maps, which highlight the regions of an image that were important for the object detector prediction. One example of a method that utilizes saliency maps is D-RISE [17]. There has also been relevant research in the field of vehicle autonomy [16]. IML/XAI has been successfully applied to multiple critical sectors, such as healthcare [21], cybersecurity [22], and autonomous driving [23]. One critical field that has been lacking research in IML/XAI is forest fire prevention and mitigation and that will be the focus of the case study we present in this paper. In several of these scenarios more traditional approaches exist, but they are often misleading, e.g., confusing the color of the sun with the color of the fire, and do not capture the interpretation of the model's reasoning.

2.2 LIME: Local Interpretable Model-Agnostic Explanations

Local Interpretable Model-Agnostic Explanations (LIME) [20] is a local and model-agnostic IML/XAI technique that uses local approximations of the black box model, by first randomly generating perturbed samples of the original instance we wish to explain. Then, these samples are weighted according to their similarity to the original instance. Lastly, an interpretable model is trained on the perturbed samples.

The end result is a surrogate or replacement model that can be utilized to explain the model prediction in the neighborhood of the original instance. *LIME* can be utilized in tabular data, text or images.

To the best of our knowledge, there have been no prior attempts at applying *LIME* to YOLO-based object detection.

3 Proposed Approach

In this section we describe the approach for enhancing YOLO interpretability with LIME. A scheme of the explanation process is depicted in Fig. 2. The *explain_instance* function from the LIME library is used to create visual explanations for a given set of images. This function receives two mandatory inputs: a list of images to explain; and a classification function, which given a list of images, presents as output the class probabilities for each one.

In object detectors, such as *YOLOv4*, instead of considering the image as a whole, the classification is done for each bounding box. This means that for any given image, the model presents as output the class probabilities for each of the generated bounding boxes. We can obtain the bounding boxes that have the highest confidence by running the model on the image once. Because of the

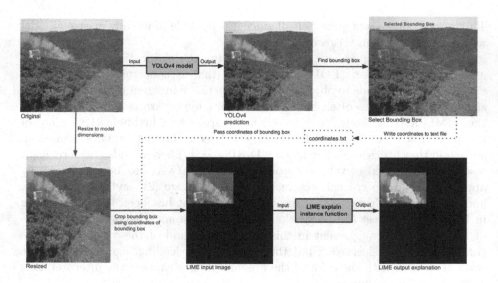

Fig. 2. General proposed explanation schemes (visual explanations are foreseen in a forest fire detection case study)

limitations of LIME, we need to select a specific bounding box and create visual explanations for the object that is contained in that bounding box.

There are several valid ways of doing this selection, which serve different purposes, such as picking the bounding box visually using a Graphical User Interface (GUI) or picking a random bounding box. The proposed process is represented in Fig. 3 and is detailed in the following. The goal is to explain predictions separately for each of the two classes (we want to see the model behaviour for each class). For this reason, in order to select the bounding box, we first select the class we intend to explain, and then we select the bounding box with the highest confidence score, since it is the one that is most likely to contain an object and as such will provide more insightful visual explanations.

The coordinates of the selected bounding box (relative to the resized image) are saved (*coordinates.txt*). These coordinates will later be used by the classification function to find the correct bounding box. Then, we resize the image, so that we can use the bounding box coordinates, and hide everything in the image that is outside the bounding box. This last step is carried out because we want to obtain explanations for the object that is inside the bounding box, and as such do not want other objects to affect the class probabilities. In Sect. 5, we will see a comparison using just the bounding box and using the whole image. Finally, in the part of the algorithm where we are iterating through each bounding box and calculating their respective class probabilities, we first select the one that is closest to the saved coordinates, and then get the values for the class probabilities of the chosen bounding box (*probabilityArray.txt*). This will allow us to

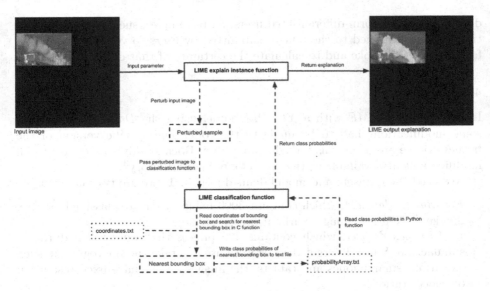

Fig. 3. Proposed instance interpretation process with LIME

return the class probabilities through the classification function that is input to *explain_instance*.

4   Experiments

4.1   Case Study: Forest Fires

Forest fires are a serious issue in countries with meteorological conditions that are susceptible to these incidents. One example is Portugal, where the number of forest fires typically ranges from 15000 to 25000 per year, corresponding to around 150000 to 250000 hectares of burned area [15]. The regularity and extensiveness of these events has adverse consequences in the form of economic and environmental damage, in addition to the risk of injury or loss of human life. For this reason, measures to control forest fires by either limiting their spread, or earlier detection are a benefit to fire departments and to the general population.

There have been several applications of Artificial Intelligence (AI) to forest fire detection and mitigation. One example is the work developed by Castelli et al. [3], where a genetic programming based system was utilized to predict the amount of burned area, effectively reducing uncertainty regarding the progression of the fire and mitigating its negative consequences, with comparable performance to other state-of-the-art ML methods.

Researchers have also combined AI with real-time data collection, utilizing aerial vehicles such as drones [11], and geospacial data [9] to detect fires. FIRE-LOC[1] is a project that utilizes crowdsourced visual and geolocation data to

---

[1] https://fireloc.org/?lang=en.

detect fires and inform differentiated users. AI techniques, such as object detection, are then applied to the images submitted by users to verify if there is in fact fire and/or smoke and to calculate the certainty of that decision.

4.2 Setup

In order to use *LIME* with a *YOLOv4* model using the *Darknet* framework, some modifications had to be made to the code. The specific version of the framework we are using was forked from Alexey Bochkovskiy's repository[2]. All modifications are available at the project's public repository[3].

We used the datasets and model defined in [14]. There are two datasets:

- *Fire-Smoke dataset*[4], which contains 3000 images that are classified as Fire, Smoke or Neutral (images without fire or smoke);
- *Real-Images dataset*, which contains 429 photos that were taken during a simulacrum. Since different devices were used to take the photographs, such as various smartphones and tablets, the images do not have fixed resolution or aspect ratio.

The images that were used for creating explanations in Sect. 5 were retrieved from the portion of these datasets that was used for testing. The code that was developed to fulfill the objectives in Sect. 3 can be accessed in the project repository. For an example of using the code, one can run the *yolime_notebook.ipynb* Jupyter notebook, with further information in the comments. As previously mentioned, we are using the same dataset and weights as in [14], but these parameters can be replaced according to the intentions of the user. To test the explanation on an example image, one needs to input its path (*train.txt*), and then run the following cells. To run the notebook locally, one can clone the repository and install the required libraries. To increase the inference speed of the model, installing *CUDA* is also recommended. The requirements are described in AlexeyAB's repository[5].

5 Results and Analysis

5.1 Comparison Between Original and Cropped Input Images

In Fig. 4 we can see a comparison between using an unaltered input image and hiding everything except the bounding box. The highlighted features are the ones that contribute the most to the more likely class. As we can see in left part of Fig. 4, when we keep the original image, features that are not inside the bounding box will affect the explanation, making it invalid. In the figure on the right, we can see the results when only the bounding box is shown: the only features that contribute to the class are the ones inside the bounding box.

---

[2] https://github.com/AlexeyAB/darknet.
[3] https://github.com/AntMorais/yolime.
[4] https://github.com/DeepQuestAI/Fire-Smoke-Dataset.
[5] https://github.com/AlexeyAB/darknet.

Fig. 4. *LIME* visual explanation not cropping (left) and cropping (right) the image to the bounding box

5.2   Analysis of Visual Explanations

We analyse the visual explanations in the test images containing either smoke or fire. All relevant test data and information is available at https://github.com/AntMorais/yolime.

The test images in the following subsections were selected because it is easy to distinguish the object (either smoke or fire) from the background, so the explanation is more easily interpreted. The bounding boxes that were selected for the explanation belong to the class we are explaining. If more than one bounding box has that class, the one with the highest confidence is chosen. All figures include the following images: (i) output of the *YOLOv4* model; (ii) input image for the *LIME* algorithm. Resized and cropped version of the original image; (iii) zoomed image of the output of the *LIME* algorithm. There are three parameters that affect the visual explanation, as detailed in Table 1. The number of displayed features is the maximum number of features that can be displayed while still belonging to the object. This variable can be thought of as a metric for the model performance that can be used to complement commonly used metrics such as Average Precision (AP) and Mean Average Precision (mAP) [10]. In Fig. 5 and Fig. 6 we can see that the parts of the image that have Smoke are

Table 1. Description of parameters.

Parameter	Description
num_samples	Number of perturbed samples that the algorithm generates The explanation time is directly proportional to this value
num_features	Maximum number of visual features that are present in the explanation
num_displayed_features	Number of features that are visible in the final explanation These features are selected in decreasing order of contribution to the top class, which means that the most important N features will be selected

highlighted. This indicates that the Smoke segments of the image are important when the object detectors classify objects as Smoke. We can also see that in both cases the outline of the highlighted features coincides with the Smoke shape of the Smoke clouds, which means that the model is, as intended, using the parts of the image that belong to the Smoke object.

Fig. 5. *LIME* visual explanation for smoke with 3 features: model predictions (left); cropped input image (middle); Zoomed explanation (right)

Fig. 6. *LIME* visual explanation for smoke with 5 features: model predictions (left); cropped input image (middle); Zoomed explanation (right)

In Fig. 7, the highlighted features correspond to the Fire event, ignoring the parts of the image that are darker. This behaviour is in line with what is expected from the model. Figure 8 has positive features inside the Fire and negative features on the darker parts. In Fig. 9, some parts of the highlighted features have Smoke, which could indicate that the model is classifying the image as Fire not only because there is fire in it, as expected, but also due to Smoke.

From these results we can reach the common analysis that while YOLO outputs bounding boxes, our proposed explainability approach outputs the specific objects/pixels that the model considered relevant for classification, which effectively adds a new layer of interpretability.

Fig. 7. *LIME* visual explanation for fire with 4 features: model predictions (left); cropped input image (middle); Zoomed explanation (right)

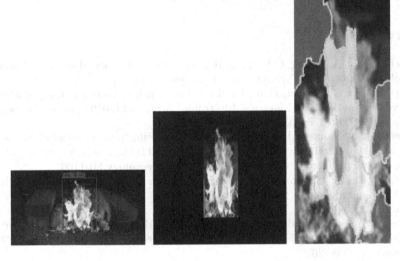

Fig. 8. *LIME* visual explanation for fire with 8 features: model predictions (left); cropped input image (middle); Zoomed explanation (right)

Fig. 9. *LIME* visual explanation for fire with 4 features: model predictions (left); cropped input image (middle); Zoomed explanation (right)

6   Conclusions and Future Work

In this paper, we extended the *LIME* library to a *YOLOv4* model using the *Darknet* framework. The results have shown that the model, which was trained and tested in benchmark data and real data of forest fire images obtained in

a simulacrum, makes use of the expected features of the image. The proposed approach selects specific bounding boxes and creates visual explanations for the object that is contained in that bounding box. The algorithm that was presented is publicly available[6] and can be replicated to improve any model with similar characteristics, by adjusting the training and then testing on the same images to see if the number of relevant features that were selected by the model increased.

We have added a simple yet effective layer of interpretability that adds information to the standard YOLO model, setting an initial path for greater interpretability. In the future we aim to include some of the additional features, e.g., separate different fires, and quantitative metrics. Additionally, this algorithm can be used to increase the trustworthiness of other object detection models which need to be applied to critical scenarios.

References

1. Bochkovskiy, A., Wang, C.Y., Liao, H.Y.M.: YOLOv4: optimal speed and accuracy of object detection. arXiv:2004.10934 [cs, eess] (2020)
2. Carvalho, D.V., Pereira, E.M., Cardoso, J.S.: Machine learning interpretability: a survey on methods and metrics. Electronics **8**(8), 832 (2019). https://www.mdpi.com/2079-9292/8/8/832
3. Castelli, M., Vanneschi, L., Popovič, A.: Predicting burned areas of forest fires: an artificial intelligence approach. Fire Ecol **11**(1), 106–118 (2015). https://fireecology.springeropen.com/articles/10.4996/fireecology.1101106
4. Das, A., Rad, P.: Opportunities and challenges in explainable artificial intelligence (XAI): a survey. arXiv:2006.11371 [cs] (2020)
5. Gade, K., Geyik, S.C., Kenthapadi, K., Mithal, V., Taly, A.: Explainable AI in industry: practical challenges and lessons learned: implications tutorial. In: FAT 2020: Proceedings of the 2020 Conference on Fairness, Accountability, and Transparency, p. 699 (2020)
6. Gilpin, L.H., Bau, D., Yuan, B.Z., Bajwa, A., Specter, M., Kagal, L.: Explaining explanations: an overview of interpretability of machine learning. In: 2018 IEEE 5th International Conference on Data Science and Advanced Analytics (DSAA), pp. 80–89 (2018)
7. Girshick, R., Donahue, J., Darrell, T., Malik, J.: Rich feature hierarchies for accurate object detection and semantic segmentation. Technical report, UC Berkeley (2014). https://arxiv.org/pdf/1311.2524.pdf
8. Islam, S.R., Eberle, W., Ghafoor, S.K., Ahmed, M.: Explainable artificial intelligence approaches: a survey. arXiv:2101.09429 [cs] (2021)
9. Jang, E., Kang, Y., Im, J., Lee, D.W., Yoon, J., Kim, S.K.: Detection and monitoring of forest fires using Himawari-8 geostationary satellite data in South Korea. Remote Sensing **11**(3), 271 (2019). https://www.mdpi.com/2072-4292/11/3/271
10. Jiao, L., et al.: A survey of deep learning-based object detection. IEEE Access 7, 128837–128868 (2019). arXiv: 1907.09408
11. Kinaneva, D., Hristov, G., Raychev, J., Zahariev, P.: Early forest fire detection using drones and artificial intelligence. In: 2019 42nd International Convention on Information and Communication Technology, Electronics and Microelectronics (MIPRO), pp. 1060–1065 (2019). iSSN 2623-8764

---

[6] https://github.com/AntMorais/yolime.

12. Liu, W., et al.: SSD: single shot multibox detector. In: Leibe, B., Matas, J., Sebe, N., Welling, M. (eds.) ECCV 2016. LNCS, vol. 9905, pp. 21–37. Springer, Cham (2016). https://doi.org/10.1007/978-3-319-46448-0_2

13. Longo, L., Goebel, R., Lecue, F., Kieseberg, P., Holzinger, A.: Explainable artificial intelligence: concepts, applications, research challenges and visions. In: Holzinger, A., Kieseberg, P., Tjoa, A.M., Weippl, E. (eds.) CD-MAKE 2020. LNCS, vol. 12279, pp. 1–16. Springer, Cham (2020). https://doi.org/10.1007/978-3-030-57321-8_1

14. Madeira, A.: Intelligent system for fire detection. Master's thesis, University of Coimbra, Coimbra, Portugal (2020)

15. Mateus, P., Fernandes, P.M.: Forest fires in Portugal: dynamics, causes and policies. In: Reboredo, F. (ed.) Forest Context and Policies in Portugal. WF, vol. 19, pp. 97–115. Springer, Cham (2014). https://doi.org/10.1007/978-3-319-08455-8_4

16. Nowicki, M.R., Cwian, K., Skrzypczynski, P.: How to improve object detection in a driver assistance system applying explainable deep learning, pp. 226–231 (2019). iSSN 2642-7214

17. Petsiuk, V., et al.: Black-box explanation of object detectors via saliency maps. arXiv:2006.03204 [cs] (2020)

18. Redmon, J., Divvala, S.K., Girshick, R.B., Farhadi, A.: You only look once: unified, real-time object detection. In: 2016 IEEE Conference on Computer Vision and Pattern Recognition(CVPR), pp. 779–788 (2016)

19. Ren, S., He, K., Girshick, R.B., Sun, J.: Faster R-CNN: towards real-time object detection with region proposal networks. In: Cortes, C., Lawrence, N.D., Lee, D.D., Sugiyama, M., Garnett, R. (eds.) NIPS, pp. 91–99 (2015)

20. Ribeiro, M.T., Singh, S., Guestrin, C.: "Why should i trust you?": explaining the predictions of any classifier. arXiv:1602.04938 [cs, stat] (2016)

21. Tjoa, E., Guan, C.: A survey on explainable artificial intelligence (XAI): towards medical XAI. IEEE Trans. Neural Netw. Learning Syst. 1–21 (2020). arXiv: 1907.07374

22. Wang, M., Zheng, K., Yang, Y., Wang, X.: An explainable machine learning framework for intrusion detection systems. IEEE Access 8, 73127–73141 (2020)

23. Zablocki, E., Ben-Younes, H., Perez, P., Cord, M.: Explainability of vision-based autonomous driving systems: review and challenges. arXiv:2101.05307 [cs] (2021)

Cherry-Picking Meta-heuristic Algorithms and Parameters for Real Optimization Problems

Kevin Martins[iD] and Rui Mendes[(⊠)][iD]

University of Minho, Braga, Portugal
azuki@di.uminho.pt

Abstract. We present an approach that is able to automatically choose the best meta-heuristic and configuration for solving a real optimization problem. Our approach allows the researcher to indicate which meta-heuristics to choose from and, for each meta-heuristic, which parameters should be automatically configured to find good solutions for the optimization problem. We show that our approach is sound using ten well know real optimization problems and five meta-heuristics. As a side effect, we were also able to provide an unbiased way of assessing meta-heuristics concerning their performance to address one or more classes of real optimization problems. Our approach improved the results found for all the meta-heuristics in all problems and was also able to find very competitive results for all optimization problems when given the liberty to choose which meta-heuristic to use.

Keywords: No-free-lunch theorem · Real optimization · Meta-heuristics · Swarm Intelligence · Grammatical Evolution

1 Introduction

A Metaheuristic algorithm (MA) is a stochastic problem-independent algorithm used to find near-optimal solutions for optimization problems. In recent years, MAs have gained popularity as tools for solving a wide array of optimization problems in many different areas of application, including engineering design, digital image processing, computer vision, networks and communications, power, and energy management, machine learning, robotics, medical diagnosis, and others [4].

However, the numerous nature-inspired MAs, i.e., Swarm Intelligence (SI) algorithms, introduced in this era have been subject to intense criticism [1,16] justified, in part, by (i) besides the metaphor, they lack novelty; and (ii) poor experimental validation and comparison.

Nevertheless, the No Free Lunch Theorem for Optimization (NFLT) proposed in [18] establishes that for any algorithm, any elevated performance over

This work has been supported by FCT—Fundação para a Ciência e Tecnologia within the R&D Units Project Scope: UIDB/00319/2020. Kevin Martins thanks FCT for the grant SFRH/BD/151434/2021.

one class of problems is offset by performance over another. Thus, while an algorithm with purposefully configured parameter settings may hold a consistently good performance on a given optimization problem, that configuration will not necessarily ensure it performs well on other problems. In fact, it is challenging to identify efficient algorithms for a new instance of a technologically relevant optimization problem [14].

Since optimization represents a broader research topic with many sub-fields, we frame our study to answer the following questions:

Q1: Is it possible to find a set of parameters $(p_1, \cdots, p_k)$ that it will ensure a very good performance of algorithm A for a single-objective real optimization problem S? And if yes,

Q2: Is it possible to choose the best algorithm among a collection of algorithms $(A_1, A_2, ..., A_n)$ with optimal parameter settings to solve S?

We hypothesize that with an Evolutionary Automatic Programming (EAP) approach it is possible to find an algorithm A with optimal parameters $(p_1, \cdots, p_k)$ from a collection of algorithms $(A_1, \cdots, A_n)$ such that it can provide the best solution for a real optimization problem S. We evaluate our hypothesis by performing two sets of experiments using ten real optimization problems and a subset of five meta-heuristics. Due to the flexibility provided by its modular nature, we opted to use Grammatical Evolution (GE) as the EAP algorithm.

The remainder of the paper is organized as follows. Section 2 provides an overview of the algorithms used in this study. In Sect. 3, we provide an overview of Grammatical Evolution (GE) and a detailed explanation of the procedure used in this study. Section 4 then details the experiments made. The paper closes in Sect. 5 with a conclusion and future work.

2 Meta-heuristics Under Study

This section presents the algorithms that we use in this study. Most of the algorithms used come from Swarm Intelligence (SI) except Differential Evolution (DE). DE was chosen because it shares most of the characteristics of the other algorithms except the SI metaphor.

2.1 Particle Swarm Optimization

Particle Swarm Optimization (PSO) is a meta-heuristic algorithm inspired by the social behavior of animals proposed by James Kennedy e Russell Eberhart in [9]. In this algorithm, the search space is populated with k agents called particles. These particles interact n times to find the best solution possible and, in every interaction, they update their position $x_i^{(t+1)}$ according to the following equation:

$$x_i^{(t+1)} = x_i^{(t)} + v_i^{(t+1)} \tag{1}$$

where $x_i^{(t)}$ represents the particle current position and $v_i^{(t+1)}$ represents the particle calculated velocity. Like the behavior of bird flocking or fish schooling, every particle tries to adjust its velocity according to the swarm. The swarm tends to follow the particle holding the best solution, creating a synchronized movement that balances exploration and exploitation. The velocity is given by:

$$v_i^{(t+1)} = \chi \cdot v_i^{(t)} + c_1 \cdot r_1 \cdot (p_i^{(best)} - x_i^{(t)}) + c_2 \cdot r_2 \cdot (g_{best} - x_i^{(t)}) \qquad (2)$$

Here, the particle holds a local memory of the best position it has ever found, $p_i^{(best)}$, and it knows the global best position g_{best} found by the swarm. Thus, the velocity $v_i^{(t+1)}$ can increase or decrease according to the distance between the particle position $x_i^{(t)}$, the positions $p_i^{(best)}$ and g_{best}.

Several parameters control the velocity of the particle. Random Factors r_1 and r_2 are stochastic parameters randomly generated to introduce variations in the search process. The cognitive factor c_1, the social factor c_2, and the inertia weight w are statically configured. The constriction coefficient χ, also called inertia factor, dampens the velocity in order to ensure that it will not explode [3, 15].

2.2 Bare Bones Particle Swarm Optimization

Bare Bones Particle Swarm Optimization (BB) is a meta-heuristic algorithm proposed by James Kennedy e Russell Eberhart in [8]. It is a modification of the canonical PSO where the velocity formula is eliminated. Instead, to update a particle position, it uses the following:

$$x_i^{(t+1)} = x_i^{(t)} + \mathcal{N}(\mu(x), \sigma^2(x)) \qquad (3)$$

Here, velocity is replaced by a random generated number from a normal distribution $\mathcal{N}$ with mean $\mu = \frac{x_i^{(t)} + g_{best}}{2}$ and standard deviation $\sigma = \left| x_i^{(t)} - g_{best} \right|$. This algorithm has no other parameters besides the population size.

2.3 Artificial Bee Colony

Artificial Bee Colony (ABC) is a meta-heuristic algorithm inspired by the foraging behavior of the honey bee swarm proposed by Derviş Karaboğa in [7].

In this algorithm, the search space is populated with n agents called employed bees. Every employed bee is assigned a food source, i.e., a specific search space region. It's worth noting that other bees have different purposes, as we'll see.

In every interaction, a three-phase process takes place. (1) First, by exploiting neighborhood locations, the employed bees try to find food sources with better quality, i.e., positions in the search space with better fitness. (2) Secondly, the employed bees share the fitness information found with the onlooker bees that, in turn, choose a food source to exploit neighborhood locations using a probabilistic selection mechanism. Higher fitness solutions have a higher probability

of selection. (3) A food source is abandoned if, after *limit* interactions, it was not possible to find better solutions by the bees. In this situation, the employed bee becomes a scout bee and randomly tries to find a new food source in the search space.

Both employed and onlooker bees try to find solutions with better fitness by producing a new food source position with the following:

$$v_{ij} = x_{ij} + \phi_{ij}(x_{ij} - x_{kj}) \qquad (4)$$

Here, the agent i updates its position by randomly picking an index j of the dimensions d of the problem being solved with a randomly selected agent k solution position j. It is worth noting that $k \neq i$.

ABC has the following parameters: the number of the food sources, equal to the number of employed or onlooker bees, and the value of *limit*. To provide a better exploration process, in our experiment, we use the following parameters: Onlooker bees proportion, where $OP \in [0, 1]$; and relative limit where $RL \in [0.5, 1.5]$. As suggested in [7], *limit* can be given by the number of onlooker bees × the number of dimensions d. In order to promote experimentation, in our case, *limit* = Number of onlooker bees × d × RL.

2.4 Cuckoo Search

Cuckoo Search (CS) is a meta-heuristic algorithm inspired by the parasitic behavior of some cuckoo species proposed by Xin-She Yang and Suash Deb in [19]. In this algorithm, the search space is composed of k host nests, and, in every interaction, a cuckoo lays an egg (solution) in a randomly chosen nest. An egg has a probability pa of being discovered by the host. When such a case occurs, a new random solution is generated to replace it. Cuckoo i generates a new solutions $x_i^{(t+1)}$ by performing a Lévy flight,

$$x_i^{(t+1)} = x_i^{(t)} + \alpha \otimes Lévy(\lambda) \qquad (5)$$

where $x_i^{(t)}$ represents the current position. A randomly generated value from the Lévy distribution defines the random walk. Besides the population size, CS has three statically configured parameters: (1) the step size α, (2) the scale factor λ parameters influence the random walk, while (3) the discovery probability pa represents the proportion of worse solutions to be discarded in every generation.

As stated in [20], in the real world, a cuckoo's egg is less likely to be discovered if it is very similar to a host's eggs. Thus, fitness should be related to the difference in solutions. Therefore, it is good to do a random walk with random step sizes in a biased way.

2.5 Differential Evolution

Differential Evolution (DE) is a meta-heuristic algorithm proposed by Rainwer Storn and Kenneth Pricerainer in [17]. In this algorithm, the search space is

populated with k agents that interact n times to find the best solution possible. In every interaction, for every agent i, three other agents a, b, c are randomly selected. A candidate position $y = [y_1, y_2, \ldots, y_d]$ for the agent i is calculated. This is performed by, randomly choosing an index R and to generate a uniformly distributed random number r_j for every y_j that, in turn, is calculated using the equation:

$$y_j = \begin{cases} a_j + F \times (b_j - c_j), & \text{if } r_j < CR \text{ or } j = R \\ x_{i,j}, & \text{otherwise} \end{cases} \quad (6)$$

where $x_{i,j}$ is the agent i vector position j, CR is the crossover probability and F is the differential weight that controls the amplification of the variation $b_j - c_j$. Besides the population size, CR and F are the only statically configured parameters.

3   Cherry-Picking Algorithms and their Parameters

This section introduces the concept of automatically finding a meta-heuristic algorithm and its corresponding configuration so that good solutions for single-objective real optimization problems is consistently found. Thus, this challenge represents an optimization problem that, in turn, we hypothesized that an Evolutionary Automatic Programming (EAP) approach, Grammatical Evolution (GE), would solve. Due to its modular nature [13], our approach would allow the researcher to swap in and out algorithms, parameter values, and even the genetic operators used to evolve the solutions.

3.1   Grammatical Evolution

Proposed by Michael O'Neil and Conor Ryan, GE is an evolutionary algorithm inspired by the biological process of generating a protein from the genetic material of an organism [10]. In GE, this process is simulated by using a genotype-to-phenotype mapping process, which, in turn, is the key idea behind GE modularity.

In GE, there is a separation between the solution and the search space. A Backus-Naur Form (BNF) grammar defines the search space. The terminals of the BNF grammar represent phenotypes used to build the program. A variable-length binary string composed of integers called codons defines the solution space. In an interactive process, each codon G is used to select a production rule P from the BNF grammar using the modulus operation against the number of production rules used in the non-terminal NP, i.e., $P \equiv G \pmod{NP}$. If it runs out of codons, it reuses the genotype.

This process results in a syntactically correct program being constructed that a fitness function can then evaluate. We can then use standard genetic operations to generate end evolve the programs that can optimally solve a specific fitness function. In this study we implemented a tournament selection procedure, a single-point crossover, and point mutation.

3.2   The Search Procedure

The BNF grammar used in this study comprises 20 production rules that specify both the available meta-heuristics and their corresponding parameters. Each real parameter is encoded with a precision of two decimal cases, while the population size can take values in the set $\{10, 20, \ldots, 100\}$. It is possible to change the grammar to use all the algorithms or only a subset, including a single one. Adding new algorithms and/or changing their parameters is simply a matter of modifying the BNF grammar. We include the following productions to illustrate the configuration of a search for five algorithms and add all the parameters for the DE:

```
<expr> ::= barebonesPso(<BB>) | canonicalPso(<PSO>) |
   cuckooSearch(<CS>) | differentialEvolution(<DE>) |
   artificialBeeColony(<ABC>)

<DE> ::= {"populationSize": <populationSize>,
   "crossoverProbability": <crossoverProbability>,
   "differentialWeight": <differentialWeight>}
<crossoverProbability> ::= 0.<int><int> | 1
<differentialWeight> ::= 0.<int><int> | 1.<int><int> | 2
<populationSize> ::= 10 | 20 | 30 | 40 | 50 | 60 | 70 | 80 | 90 | 100
<int> ::= 0 | 1 | 2 | 3 | 4 | 5 | 6 | 7 | 8 | 9
```

In order to provide a fair comparison, each algorithm is allowed to attempt to solve the problem for the same number of function evaluations (NFE). The fitness of a GE individual is given by the best fitness found by the encoded meta-heuristic at the end of its run.

4   Experimental Evaluation

We demonstrate the results of this study through two sets of experiments: Parameter Setting Performance Evaluation and Algorithm Choosing Consistency. These experiments help answer research questions **Q1** and **Q2** respectively.

In Table 1, we detail the benchmark functions used to evaluate the performance of the algorithms described in Sect. 2. These benchmark problems are frequently used to evaluate meta-heuristic algorithm and were used in part or in full by the proponents of these algorithms.

In these experiments, we set the GE parameters as follows: the crossover probability to 0.75, the mutation probability to 0.1, and the population size to 1000 during 100 generations. As for the stop condition of the meta-heuristic algorithm, we used NFE = 50,000 evaluations.

4.1   Parameter Setting Performance Evaluation

To evaluate our approach, we manually set the parameters of the meta-heuristic algorithms used in this study. PSO was configured with $c_1 = 2.05$, $c_2 = 2.05$

Table 1. Benchmark functions used in this study. d is the number of dimensions.

Function	Formula	d
Sphere	$f_1(x) = \sum_{i=1}^{d} x_i^2$	20
Ackley	$f_2(x) = -a\, e^{-b\sqrt{\frac{1}{d}\sum_{i=1}^{d} x_i^2}} - e^{\frac{1}{d}\sum_{i=1}^{d} cos(cx_i)} + a + e^1$	20
Griewank	$f_3(x) = \sum_{i=1}^{d} \frac{x_i^2}{4000} - \prod_{i=1}^{d} cos\left(\frac{x_i}{\sqrt{i}}\right) + 1$	20
Rastrigin	$f_4(x) = 10\,d + \sum_{i=1}^{d}\left[x_i^2 - 10cos(2\pi x_i)\right]$	20
Schwefel	$f_5(x) = 418.9829\,d - \sum_{i=1}^{d} x_i sin(\sqrt{|x_i|})$	20
Rosenbrock	$f_6(x) = \sum_{i=1}^{d}\left[100\left(x_{i+1} - x_i^2\right)^2 + (x_i - 1)^2\right]$	20
Michalewicz	$f_7(x) = \sum_{i=1}^{d} sin\,(x_i)\, sin^{2m}\left(\frac{ix_i^2}{\pi}\right)$	20
Easom	$f_8(x) = -cos\,(x_1) - cos\,(x_2)\, e^{-(x_1-\pi)^2 - (x_2-\pi)^2}$	2
DeJong3	$f_9(x) = \sum_{i=1}^{d}\lfloor x_i \rfloor$	20
DeJong5	$f_{10}(x) = \left(0.002 + \sum_{i=1}^{25} \frac{1}{i+(x_1+a_{1i})^6+(x_2+a_{2i})^6}\right)^{-1}$ where, $\quad a = \begin{bmatrix} -32 & -16 & 0 & 16 & 32 & -32 & \dots & 0 & 16 & 32 \\ -32 & -32 & -32 & -32 & -32 & -16 & \dots & 32 & 32 & 32 \end{bmatrix}$	2

and $\chi = 0.729$. CS was configured with pa $= 0.25$, $\alpha = 1$ and $\lambda = 1.5$. DE was configured with CR $= 0.9455$ and $F = 0.6497$. ABC was configured with $OP = 1$ and $RL = 1$. Except for the population size, these configurations were taken from recommendations in the literature [2,6,11,20]. We set the population size to 40 for all algorithms.

We independently ran our approach for each algorithm and their static settings 30 times each and applied Wilcoxon Signed-Rank Test, detailed in [5], with $\alpha = 0.05$ to check whether there was a statistically significant difference between the standard configuration and the one evolved using our approach. We applied the Holm correction to the p-values because we performed several tests. Whenever there were statistically significant differences, we conducted another batch of tests where we hypothesized that our approach yielded better results. Table 2 presents the results. We concluded that our approach found statistically better solutions in most algorithm × problem combinations.

We couldn't conclude that there was a statistically significant difference in performance between the two settings in some cases. These cases occur for the benchmark problems Easom (f_8) and DeJong3 (f_9). One possible explanation is that the static settings were already particularly effective in these cases. Another one is that these problems are simple, and thus it is easy to find near-optimal (or optimal) solutions. Figure 1 shows the distribution of the fitness ranks, using the mean value for ties, by problem and compares the static versions (with suffix **No**) with the dynamic ones (with suffix **Yes**) and corroborates the results obtained in Table 2.

Table 2. Wilcoxon Signed-Rank Test Results. A value of + means that our approach yields better results than the custom configuration, while a value of o means no statistically significant difference.

Algorithm	f_1	f_2	f_3	f_4	f_5	f_6	f_7	f_8	f_9	f_{10}
ABC	+	+	+	+	+	+	+	+	o	+
PSO	+	+	+	+	+	+	+	o	+	+
BB	+	+	+	+	+	+	+	o	o	+
CS	+	+	+	+	+	+	+	+	o	+
DE	+	+	+	+	+	+	+	o	o	+

We next attempted to check whether some of the meta-heuristics were particularly effective on some of the problems. We ran a Kruskal Wallis test to check whether the choice of the algorithms has a difference in fitness. We ran this test using the results with dynamic parameter configuration (with suffix **Yes**). We found statistically significant differences in all problems except Griewank (f_3), Easom (f_8), DeJong3 (f_9) and DeJong5 (f_{10}). Figure 2 shows the distribution of fitness ranks of each of the 30 runs for every problem.

We may conclude from these figures that even when searching for good configurations for each meta-heuristic, some meta-heuristics are better in some problems, which seems to validate the NFLT. We also performed pairwise Wilcoxon tests, using p-value adjustment for multiple tests as before, to check for statistically significant differences between algorithms on the test problems. ABC is statistically significantly different from all the other algorithms on Ackley (f_2). There are statistically significant differences between all the algorithms except ABC and DE on Rastrigin (f_4). There are statistically significant differences between all the algorithms except ABC and CS on Rosenbrock (f_6). There are statistically significant differences between all the algorithms on Sphere (f_1), Schwefel (f_5) and Michalewicz (f_7). No statistically significant differences were found of Griewank (f_3), Easom (f_8), DeJong3 (f_9) and DeJong5 (f_{10}). Table 3 complements our analysis by giving another view of the comparison between algorithms by presenting the relative ranks of the algorithms for each problem.

4.2   Algorithm Choosing Consistency

We evaluated the consistency of choosing a specific algorithm to solve a target benchmark problem. The GE algorithm evolved both the meta-heuristic choice and its parameters 30 times for all benchmark functions in this study. As shown in Table 4, GE doesn't always choose the same algorithm to solve a particular problem. Nevertheless, according to the results of the previous experiment, the algorithm seems to choose the first and, in some cases, the second contender for

Table 3. Relative ranks of the algorithms per problem using the minimum rank in the case of ties.

Problem	ABC	BB	CS	DE	PSO
Sphere (f_1)	5	2	1	3	4
Ackley (f_2)	5	1	1	1	4
Griewank (f_3)	1	1	1	1	1
Rastrigin (f_4)	1	4	3	1	5
Schwefel (f_5)	2	3	5	1	4
Rosenbrock (f_6)	3	1	2	5	4
Michalewicz (f_7)	2	3	5	1	4
Easom (f_8)	1	1	1	1	1
DeJong3 (f_9)	1	1	1	1	1
DeJong5 (f_{10})	1	1	1	1	1

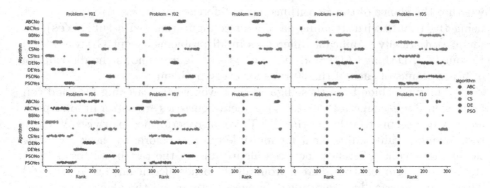

Fig. 1. Distribution of the comparison between algorithms' ranks for each problem. When ties occur, we use the algorithms' mean rank. Each algorithm has two versions: the suffix No means that we are using the fixed version parameter configuration. In contrast, the suffix Yes means that we used our approach to finding good parameter configurations.

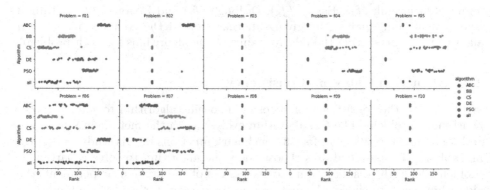

Fig. 2. Distribution of the comparison between algorithms' fitness ranks for each problem with GE choosing both the algorithm and its parameters. When ties occur, we use the algorithms' mean rank.

the problems with clear winners except for Rosenbrock (f_6). In fact, this is the only problem where using GE to choose both the algorithm and its parameters does not yield results as good as selecting the best configuration possible for the best meta-heuristic, which in this problem is BB.

Table 4. Number of times GE chose an algorithm to solve a test problem.

Problem	PSO	BB	ABC	CS	DE
Sphere (f_1)	0	9	0	21	0
Ackley (f_2)	0	21	0	6	3
Griewank (f_3)	1	18	6	1	4
Rastrigin (f_4)	0	0	27	0	3
Schwefel (f_5)	0	0	5	0	25
Rosenbrock (f_6)	4	17	2	6	1
Michalewicz (f_7)	0	0	8	0	22
Easom (f_8)	7	8	5	2	8
DeJong3 (f_9)	4	8	9	3	6
DeJong5 (f_{10})	0	18	2	1	9

Table 5 presents the 95% confidence intervals of the results for all the algorithms that GE tuned. The ALL configuration corresponds to GE choosing both the algorithm and its parameters. In most cases, the amplitude of the intervals is small, which means that the configurations found are consistent. The ALL configuration seems to be a good choice in most cases, except for Rosenbrock (f_6) as mentioned before. However, the results found when choosing both the meta-heuristic and its parameters for this problem are quite competitive, being much better than using each of the meta-heuristics with off-the-shelf configurations. BB can only find good solutions with minimal population sizes since it can spend more iterations fine-tuning since the number of function evaluations is fixed. It is possible that GE could not realize this and thus didn't prefer this algorithm at the beginning of the run and therefore could not fine-tune its parameters during the rest of the evolution process. This is probably due to the non-locality characteristic of GE [12]. Further research is needed using alternatives to GE for the meta-optimization step.

Table 5. Algorithm fitness confidence interval with GE parameter setting. ALL corresponds to using GE to select one of the algorithms and their parameter setting.

Problem	PSO	BB	ABC	CS	DE	ALL
f_1	$1e-64 \pm 2e-64$	$2e-95 \pm 1e-95$	$6e-62 \pm 3e-62$	$2e-89 \pm 5e-89$	$2e-63 \pm 4e-63$	$2e-93 \pm 3e-93$
f_2	$4e-15 \pm 4e-16$	$4e-15 \pm 0$	$3e-13 \pm 3e-14$	$4e-15 \pm 0$	$4e-15 \pm 0$	$4e-15 \pm 0$
f_3	0 ± 0	0 ± 0	0 ± 0	0 ± 0	0 ± 0	0 ± 0
f_4	8.39 ± 0.758	5.01 ± 0.451	0 ± 0	3.92 ± 1.06	0 ± 0	0 ± 0
f_5	643 ± 75.6	619 ± 69.3	$3e-4 \pm 4e-13$	702 ± 90.2	$3e-4 \pm 0$	$3e-4 \pm 5e-13$
f_6	0.092 ± 0.05	$5.3e-4 \pm 3.7e-4$	0.0124 ± 0.0045	0.016 ± 0.013	1.44 ± 0.436	0.013 ± 0.012
f_7	-18.6 ± 0.16	-18.7 ± 0.072	-19.6 ± 0.00012	-18.5 ± 0.15	$-19.6 \pm 1.9e-09$	$-19.6 \pm 4.9e-4$
f_8	-1 ± 0	-1 ± 0	-1 ± 0	-1 ± 0	-1 ± 0	-1 ± 0
f_9	-120 ± 0	-120 ± 0	-120 ± 0	-120 ± 0	-120 ± 0	-120 ± 0
f_{10}	0.998 ± 0	0.998 ± 0	0.998 ± 0	0.998 ± 0	0.998 ± 0	0.998 ± 0

5   Conclusions and Future Work

This work advocates the use of a system that can automatically choose a metaheuristic and calibrate its parameters to solve a real problem optimization. We have chosen to use GE for the meta-optimization step since this gives researchers a lot of freedom in selecting how to configure each algorithm.

We aim to produce a system where it is possible to incorporate other metaheuristics and their parameters and that can find very good solutions for the target optimization problem.

Tests indicate that the approach presented in this work is successful. It was able to find solutions that were competitive with the state-of-the-art in all problems when searching for good values for the meta-heuristic's parameters. Even when choosing both the meta-heuristic and selecting its best configuration simultaneously, it is quite successful.

While the system could not find the best solutions for the Rosenbrock function, the results were quite acceptable. The non-locality problematic of GE may be responsible since BB could only find good solutions when the population size was quite small. Future work will be twofold: exploring other alternatives to GE and producing a publicly available tool that will allow the scientific community to use our tool to solve optimization problems in a semi-automatic manner.

References

1. Aranha, C., et al.: Metaphor-based metaheuristics, a call for action: the elephant in the room. Swarm Intell. **16**(1), 1–6 (2021). https://doi.org/10.1007/s11721-021-00202-9
2. Bratton, D., Kennedy, J.: Defining a standard for particle swarm optimization. In: 2007 IEEE Swarm Intelligence Symposium, pp. 120–127. IEEE (2007)
3. Clerc, M., Kennedy, J.: The particle swarm-explosion, stability, and convergence in a multidimensional complex space. IEEE Trans. Evol. Comput. **6**(1), 58–73 (2002)
4. Dokeroglu, T., Sevinc, E., Kucukyilmaz, T., Cosar, A.: A survey on new generation metaheuristic algorithms. Comput. Ind. Eng. **137**, 106040 (2019)

5. Hollander, M., Wolfe, D.A., Chicken, E.: Nonparametric Statistical Methods, vol. 751. Wiley, Hoboken (2013)
6. Karaboga, D., Basturk, B.: A powerful and efficient algorithm for numerical function optimization: artificial bee colony (ABC) algorithm. J. Global Optim. **39**(3), 459–471 (2007)
7. Karaboga, D., et al.: An idea based on honey bee swarm for numerical optimization. Technical report, Technical report-tr06, Erciyes university (2005)
8. Kennedy, J.: Bare bones particle swarms. In: Proceedings of the 2003 IEEE Swarm Intelligence Symposium, SIS 2003 (Cat. No. 03EX706), pp. 80–87. IEEE (2003)
9. Kennedy, J., Eberhart, R.: Particle swarm optimization. In: Proceedings of International Conference on Neural Networks (ICNN 1995), Perth, WA, Australia, 27 November–1 December 1995, pp. 1942–1948. IEEE (1995)
10. O'Neill, M., Ryan, C.: Grammatical evolution. IEEE Trans. Evol. Comput. **5**(4), 349–358 (2001)
11. Pedersen, M.E.H.: Good parameters for differential evolution. Hvass Labs (2010)
12. Rothlauf, F., Oetzel, M.: On the locality of grammatical evolution. In: Collet, P., Tomassini, M., Ebner, M., Gustafson, S., Ekárt, A. (eds.) EuroGP 2006. LNCS, vol. 3905, pp. 320–330. Springer, Heidelberg (2006). https://doi.org/10.1007/11729976_29
13. Ryan, Conor, O'Neill, Michael, Collins, J.J.: Introduction to 20 years of grammatical evolution. In: Ryan, Conor, O'Neill, Michael, Collins, J.J. (eds.) Handbook of Grammatical Evolution, pp. 1–21. Springer, Cham (2018). https://doi.org/10.1007/978-3-319-78717-6_1
14. Sala, R., Müller, R.: Benchmarking for metaheuristic black-box optimization: perspectives and open challenges. In: 2020 IEEE Congress on Evolutionary Computation (CEC), pp. 1–8. IEEE (2020)
15. Shi, Y., Eberhart, R.: A modified particle swarm optimizer. In: 1998 IEEE international conference on evolutionary computation proceedings. IEEE World Congress on Computational Intelligence (Cat. No. 98TH8360), pp. 69–73. IEEE (1998)
16. Sörensen, K.: Metaheuristics-the metaphor exposed. Int. Trans. Oper. Res. **22**(1), 3–18 (2015)
17. Storn, R., Price, K.: Differential evolution-a simple and efficient heuristic for global optimization over continuous spaces. J. Global Optim. **11**(4), 341–359 (1997)
18. Wolpert, D.H., Macready, W.G.: No free lunch theorems for optimization. IEEE Trans. Evol. Comput. **1**(1), 67–82 (1997)
19. Yang, X.S., Deb, S.: Cuckoo search via lévy flights. In: 2009 World Congress on Nature & Biologically Inspired Computing (NaBIC), pp. 210–214. IEEE (2009)
20. Yang, X.S., Deb, S.: Engineering optimisation by cuckoo search. Int. J. Math. Modell. Numer. Optim. **1**(4), 330–343 (2010)

On Developing Ethical AI

Helder Coelho$^{(\boxtimes)}$ (iD)

LASIGE, Mind-Brain College, Lisbon University, Lisbon, Portugal
hmcoelho@fc.ul.pt

Abstract. Technologies such as Artificial Intelligence (Analytics and Automation) can harm purposely persons (via fake news of social networks, drones, robots, apps, platforms) without any available regulations and forms of protection. We need not only benefits to offer to everybody but responsible ways to develop all new intelligent systems, and agents without high risks and strange behaviours. In many cases, decisions are not intelligible to humans and easy explanations are not available anywhere. We want diverse technologies to aid people and deliver great advantages to society at large.

Keywords: Ethics · Regulations · Governance · Policies · Practical guide to deal with the ethical quandaries

1 Introduction

Many companies, such as Apple, Microsoft, Google DeepMind, Google DeepMind Health, Facebook and Amazon, are discussing Ethics of AI, from 2020, and the same occurs with the European Union (Commission) and UNESCO (SHS/IGM-AIETHICS/2021/JUN/3 Rev.; SHS/IGM-AETHICS/2021/JUN/INF.5 Rev.). Google created an Ethics AI team, yet this initiative was delayed by the output of two scientists, Timnit Gebru and Margaret Mitchell. The manager of the team, Samy Bengio, resigned from Google, and took a senior post, later on, at Apple.

Several big enterprises have now an AI Ethics board to supply thought leadership and guidance on how the organization exploits (and researches) that technology and the connected data. This provide thought leadership, establish policies and procedures, audit and propose overall use, examine proposals, set up a training program, handle any complaints, make decisions, and maintain also an inventory of AI. This can be accountable to another body, be challenged if there are any doubts on the behavior. For example, Lucid AI, based in Texas (USA), provides also a causal reasoning platform, and it announced its internal AI Ethics board.

Regarding the European Union, Google and Facebook are under observation, and the Commission is preparing to intervene by imposing rules. UNESCO is also keen to react on account of education troubles and bad practices. Meanwhile, the Future of Life Institute (FLI) is active observing AI safety (Boylan and Terys 2022).

The increasing use of AI in the development of new medical technologies for healthcare demands also attention to ethical issues. The FLI initiative is a joint project between

G. Marreiros et al. (Eds.): EPIA 2022, LNAI 13566, pp. 512–521, 2022.
https://doi.org/10.1007/978-3-031-16474-3_42

MIT Media Lab and Harvard Berkman-Klein Center for Internet and Society. FLI intends to reduce global catastrophic and existential risks from powerful AI technologies, looking to benefits and advantages of AI. The use of global AI policy resources is now an option, because lethal autonomous weapons (drones able to kill humans) are being tested.

Timnit Gebru was fired from Google on December 2nd, 2021, after an exchange of emails. She was a respected AI Ethics scientist, her termination as controversial as it was sudden. What she hadn't anticipated was becoming a catalyst for labour activism in Silicon Valley—or the subject of a harassment campaign that surfaced alongside her supporters. Later on, Gebru opened the Distributed Artificial Intelligence Research (DAIR) Institute, in South Africa, with the support of funds from many enterprises.

Her firing came weeks after Google managers asked her to retract a paper on the dangers of large language models, like the ones that power the company's search engine. Gebru was pushed back, saying the company needed to be more transparent about the publication process. Employees saw the termination as an act of retaliation, and thousands of workers, researchers, and academics signed an open letter demanding an explanation.

In early December, as media attention mounted and tech workers across the country came to her defence, Gebru waited to see how Google would respond. She didn't have to wait long to find out.

Example of inquiries are underway, such as "can we measure the influence that machine learning, autonomous systems and driver less cars have on public sphere", "what do effective structures of governance and collaborative development look like between platforms and the public" and "can we improve discussions around policy responses to disinformation in empirical research"? For example, a Research Project was launched by professor Sami Haddadin (2021), yet the concept of human centred engineering and embedded ethics was accepted from the start, because it will require explicit laws, codes of conduct and state incentives.

2 Responsible AI

On building AI we need to be attentive with the risks (for example, of large language models (based upon GPT-3) able to generate language from images, for blind people that speak visual descriptions. In facial recognition, the technology is less accurate at identifying women and people of colour, which means its use can end up discriminating against them (Dignum 2019).

Questions have been rising about AI technology and its lucrative work. There are concerns about the environment impact of the AI's, which use amounts of energy and on biases that could entrench existing inequalities, rather than help solve them. Therefore, we need reshape our own ideas about what AI is now and what should be. Definitely, it should be more ethical for everybody (Gautrin et al. 2022). That would aid common people to understand the benefits of AI. The use of Ethics can help enterprises to sell better their products.

Ethical AI research has been recently distributed by several issues: pitfalls of large language models, lack of diversity in the technology, economic power of some enterprises, fear of algorithmic future, or mistreat women and people of colour. We know for years that technology can reflect or magnify society's biases.

Questions were raising about the ethics of language models which seek to understand human language and its use. There are several risks, such as research opportunity costs regarding environment and financial biases, which can entrench existing inequalities, rather than help solve them. The harms can be severe. And, the field needs responsible ways, accountability and transparency in order to mitigate negative impacts. An advice will be advocate diversity and inclusion.

3 Ethics Versus AI

"If many are actively excluded from its creation, this technology will benefit a few while harming a great many."
Timnit Gebru, 2022.

Today, AI is transforming work, organizations, industries and society. Despite the many potential benefits, there are significant challenges and risks, ranging from privacy, security ethics, transparency, regulations and policies implications. The prioritization of ethical (Dubber et al. 2020), legal, and policy considerations requires the integration of engineering, law and ethics approach. AI (and Machine Learning) is working together with neurosciences, within healthcare, for aiding the population (the case of Covid-19). Is there a practical guide to building ethical AI? Do we need more efficient technologies (Ryan and Stahl 2021)?

(Top 9) Ethical Issues in AI (Bossmann 2016):

1. Unemployment. What happens after the end of jobs?
2. Inequality. How do we distribute the wealth created by machines?
3. Humanity. How do machines affect our behaviour and interaction?
4. Artificial stupidity. How can we guard against mistakes?
5. Racist robots. How do we eliminate AI bias?
6. Security. How do we keep AI safe from adversaries?
7. Evil genies. How do we protect against unintended consequences?
8. Singularity. How do we stay in control of a complex intelligent system?
9. Robot rights. How do we define the humane treatment of AI?

AI does not just scale solutions, it also scales risks. Enterprises are leveraging data and AI to create artefacts, and they are also scaling their reputational regulatory and legal risks. The abuse of big data and AI algorithms by companies, to train better models, was not yet properly regulated, and no clear protocols are in place to help identify, evaluate, and mitigate several effects. Risks involve uncertainty about diverse implications of the possibility of something bad happening. In general, tech companies require a plan for avoiding loss, injury, or other adverse and unwelcome circumstances. The difficulty comes always in operationalizing those principles and choosing the varying values of

those companies. What does it mean to be for fairness? Which metric is the right one in any given case, and who makes that judgment? For most tech companies there are no straights answers to these questions.

How to operationalize data and AI Ethics? There are seven steps towards building a customized, operationalized, scalable and sustainable program (Blackman 2020): 1) Identify existing infrastructure that a data and AI Ethics program can leverage; 2) Create a data and AI Ethical risk framework that is tailored to the industry; 3) Change how you think about ethics by taking cues from the successes in health care; 4) Optimize guidance and tools for product managers; 5) Build organizational awareness; 6) Formally and informally incentivize employees to play a role in identifying AI ethical risks; and, 7) Monitor impacts and engage stake holders. Operationalizing data and AI ethics is not an easy task, it requires senior leadership, cross-functional collaboration, more efficient adoption of technologies, and looking for trustworthy.

There is a need for a new regulation for these technologies (EU AI Act with regards to the manipulatory risks of AI) and an EEC Committee is discussing with the European parliament around challenges and shifts, the quest for moral machines, moral agents in society, and moral choice. China is also involved along the regulation of AI.

Along our behaviour we are forced to select one alternative or way out, yet, we need to take care with the scale (quantity of clues that we remember) and the capability of our mind (the forces of our attention) associated with consciousness. Therefore, our mind needs to be supported and enlarged.

Learn about the possibilities of empathetic AI and what it means for our future. Can machines do what we can do with a mind? An answer by Stuart Russell (2020), in his book "Human Compatible", is by "human control of AI". Therefore, themes including privacy, cognitive liberty, self-conception and expression appear to be key areas of ethical concern.

Is AI responsible now? Can we prevent AI from going rogue? The benefits of AI are well established, but organizations using AI-driven systems must be accountable for their actions. Beyond the financial and legal risk of "AI gone wrong", there is a moral obligation (Rocha Costa and Coelho 2019) to improve AI, ie. learn how responsible AI can set higher standards, reduce bias and promote empathy.

4   Understanding Ethics

There is today a promise of AI, supported by several definitions (one, AI is the study of intelligence as computation), what AI can do, the fact that another winter is not coming, and the need of care and fear. However, AI can be extremely disruptive, empowering, challenging and unpredictable.

Developing AI is based upon complementarity, responsibility and sustainability. The global race for AI is based upon ethical guidance, concerted action, and ethics guide lines. The policy changes, with better regulation agenda, liability rules, ad hoc policies. The need of a new strategy, with research, innovation, education, and multiple exchanges with society is desired.

Ethics is considered as a set of moral principles and techniques that govern the behaviour of a group or one individual. Therefore, Computer Ethics promotes the discussion of how much influence computers should have in areas such as AI and Human Communication. Ethical challenges cover biases in AI systems, robot rights, threat to human dignity, liability for self-driving cars, use of weapons plus AI, and opaque algorithms.

Ethics principles can be used to govern technology, including factors like risk management and individual rights. There are basically used to understand and resolve moral issues (Rocha Costa et al. 2019) that have to do with the development and application of different types. attention to integrity, values and respect are mostly required. Also, regulations, principles and policies are needed. A better regulation agenda may involve 1) a set of tools on measuring impacts on innovation and 2) assessing issues related to digital economy and ICT.

Asilomar principles are 23 guidelines, created during a Conference on Beneficial AI in 2017 by the Future of Life Institute (FLI), in Cambridge (Massachusetts, USA), and now directed by Max Tegmark (MIT Media Lab). For example, the safety principle says "AI systems should be safe and secure through out their operational lifetime and verifiably so where applicable and feasible". The principle of judicial transparency establishes "any involvement by an autonomous system in judicial decision-making should provide a satisfactory explanation auditable by a competent human authority". The principle of responsibility says "designers and builders of advanced AI systems are stakeholders in the moral implications of their use, misuse, and actions with a responsibility and opportunity to shape those implications". "The value alignment principle stresses "highly autonomous AI systems should be designed so that their goals and behaviours can be assured to align with human values throughout their operation". Other topics are human values, personal privacy, liberty and privacy, shared benefit, shared prosperity, human control, non subversion, AI arms race, capability caution, importance, risks, recursive self-improvement, and common good. The goal of AI research (Research Goal Principle) should not create undirected intelligence, but beneficial intelligence.

Policies produce sound analytical research leading to constructive solutions to the challenge facing Europe today. The following two examples are: 1) create a regulatory agency for AI, data or machine learning and 2) intervene to facilitate data sharing as a horizontal policy.

Policy issues are necessary when dealing with multiple issues such as personalized genetic tests and personalized medicine, hacking into medical devices, driverless cars, autonomous systems (drones in war/welfare), adaptation to climate change, low-quality and counterfeit pharmaceuticals, human-animal hybrids, cloning, neuro stimulation devices, behavioural biometrics, autonomous translation, seeding trials, suicide machines, insect allies, or data justification of children. An example of three policies are "health promotion", "govern the use and implementation of big data", and "governance".

Benefits are welcome, because attention to business ethics has substantially improved society, and ethics programs help to maintain a moral course in turbulent times, cultivate teamwork and productivity, and support the employees growth and meaning.

We may take care with technologies at large because distributed responsibility in conjunction with a lack of knowledge about long-term or because broader societal tech consequences cause software developers to lack a feeling of accountability or a

view of the moral significance of their work. Especially, economic incentives are easily overriding commitment to ethical principles and values.

Regulations are desired because AI Ethics are often considered as extraneous, as surplus or some kind of "add-on" to technical concerns, as unbinding framework that is imposed from institutions outside of the technical community. Often, no control is enforced on those bad practices, and corporations are almost free on any control.

Care is highly requested in platforms. Not so often, AI software is developed and applied in financial technology, following societal values or fundamental rights: beneficence, justice, and explicability. Many alerts of misuse have been signalled and no arrange was done.

In some areas, efforts are undertaken to improve AI systems, often in fields where technical aids can be found for specific problems, such as accountability, privacy, protection, anti-discrimination and safety. For example, in governing AI, the opportunities and challenges are ethical, legal and technical.

AI, Ethics and Law cover human-centred AI, where we can find combinations of symbolic approaches (KB systems, Argumentation, Autonomous agents and MAS systems) and data-driven approaches (Machine Learning applied in text analytics, predicting outcomes of legal cases, predictive policing, and discovering fraud). We can discover four important actors in AI Ethics, the inter government enterprises, government initiatives, academic drives and private organizations. Enterprises are eager of power and there is a tendency to do big business in a very fast way.

5 Ethical Guidelines for AI

There are clusters of normative principles, including transparency, justice and fairness, non-maleficence, responsibility, privacy, beneficence, freedom and autonomy, trust, sustainability, dignity and solidarity. Ethical behaviour ensures that initiatives of an organization (AI system or entity) maintain human dignity and do not, in any way, cause harm to people.

There are several ethical challenges, including lack of transparency of AI tools. AI decisions are not always intelligible to humans. AI is not neutral: AI based decisions are susceptible to cover inaccuracies, discriminatory outcomes or inserted bias, surveillance practices for data gathering and privacy court users (Ryan and Stahl 2021).

Over the last years the world has deliberated and developed numerous ethical principles and frameworks. For example, legal and ethical issues in AI, privacy and surveillance, bias and discrimination (Jobin et al. 2019).

The Ethics of AI is an important issue when AI-based models are used in decision making. AI Ethics can expose biases that may never been included in the AI applications of engineering and problem solving.

There are plenty of risks of AI, such as automation-spurred job loss, privacy violations, deep fakes, algorithmic bias caused by bad data, socioeconomic inequality, market volatility, weapons automation. Yet, the biggest challenge facing AI is ethical: and, the big problem is the increase of the complexity of the software.

6   Recent Moves of Enterprises

Google, Facebook and Microsoft have all recently (28.08.2020) released technical tools, often free, that developers can use to check their own AI systems, for reliability and fairness. Google offered to help others with the tricky ethics of AI and advice on tasks such as spotting racial bias in computer vision systems, or developing ethical guidelines that govern AI projects.

Longer term, the company may provide to audit customers of AI systems for ethical integrity and charge for ethics advice. Google's new offerings will test whether a lucrative, but increasingly a popular industry, can boost by offering ethical pointers. This company is a distant third in the cloud computing market behind Amazon and Microsoft, and positions its AI expertise as a competitive advantage.

IBM launched a tool last year with a "check fairness" button that examines whether a system's output shows potentially troubling correlation with attributes, such as ethnicity or zip code.

Surveying the safety of a system becomes a greater challenge because we must verify what the system is trying to do, rather than being able to verify the system's safe behaviour in all operating contexts. Ethical cognition itself must be taken as a subject matter of engineering.

Accuracy is also a matter to be controlled. Algorithms may no longer execute in predictable contexts, requiring new kinds of safety assurance and the engineering of artificial ethical considerations. AI's with sufficiently advanced mental states (robots), or the right kind of states, will have moral status, though perhaps persons very much unlike the sort that exist now, and governed by different rules. However, distrust of AI has today a big effect. Use of empathy and intent is increasing to support good interactions with humans. There are still sensitive issues regarding to what extent algorithmic processing may contribute to the decision-making, for example in healthcare: Which data was processed and its source? How parameters were treated and weighted? Which operations were carried out during a treatment?

7   New Bets

Today, AI is viewed as a family of technologies, and when is considered to be used, we are aware of its potential benefits and risks. It can be extremely disruptive, empowering, challenging and unpredictable. The use of AI can create undesirable bias, thus violating key rights and impacts that are perceived to be unfair. In order to defend responsibility and trust we need to look with great care towards bias and value alignment.

AI must be adapted to our legal system. It must be changed in order to contemplate new AI-enabled ways of providing goods and services, organising production and social interaction. Therefore, three directions in which AI should move in order to remain aligned with the interests of mankind: complementary, responsibility and sustainability.

Some examples of applications are: the mechanism of crowdsourcing self-reported preference on ethical dilemmas; revising our current social contracts; ethical decision-making to enable AI to explain its decisions under de framework of human ethics; and, incorporation of ethics into AI systems to influence human-AI interaction dynamics.

No regulations are already known in what concerns digital algorithms (bots), and free from corporate constraints (AI technologies can potentially cause algorithmic bias). Human future is now under watch, even those scientists involved in AI Ethics are being observed.

AI Ethics is a system of moral principles and techniques intended to inform the development and responsible use of artificial intelligence technology. The purpose of an AI code of ethics is to provide stakeholders with guidance when faced with an ethical decision regarding the use of AI.

Consider the long-term consequences of actions and the side effects in the broader population. Some themes may be referred: scale and time; ethical implications: risk of distress, loss, adverse impact, injury or psychological or other harm to any individual; policies and guidelines: benefit of the individual, privacy concerns or issues, complaints about research, coercion, conflict of interest, research design issues. And, the ethics of policy analysis can be viewed from two distinct frameworks: that of the attorney and that of the scientist. Policy analysis and ethics are incompatible.

8 Responsible Autonomous Systems

Let us consider some examples of applying AI techniques to ethical or legal problems. Say, the case of driving a car obeying to traffic laws (Ribeiro et al. 2019). Online information systems have to comply with data protection law. In the case of a robot that can damage the property or the health of the persons they care you. Say the autonomous weapons (drones): they must follow ethical principles or the laws of war, but seldom that occurs. Or, the existential risks when forecasting AI progress without taking into care safety and beneficial development. Many times no big effort is observed when prediction side effects.

Artificially Intelligent software must follow things done by humans and be regulated by law. Autonomous systems can be designed in such a way that their behaviour complies with ethical principles or the law. There are some topics to be taken into account: privacy protection, freedom of speech, responsibility and liability, non discrimination, legal and ethical decision making, and requirements for algorithmic decision making. Questions: Are the regulatory frameworks suffice? Are the innovative forms of regulation necessary?

9 Conclusions

Global consumers are worried about trust, ethics and AI-based engagement. Doubts on AI increased recently, mainly on account of multiple dangers, such as the use of USA planes without human pilots, risks of manipulation from AI systems (Kissinger et al. 2021), the lack of diversity in technology, the fear of algorithmic future, the risk of large language models, and the use of DeepMind when training an AI system (with a learning algorithm) to control nuclear fusion. So, we must combine AI tools with human ethics (and empathy) for better involvement and sustainability. And, we need to design better and responsible appliances (Agarwal and Mishra 2021), built for human change, with more explanations and more help.

The idea is to make ethics an integral part of the research process by integrating ethicists into the AI world development team from day one and without fear. For example, within projects scientists attend team meetings on a regular basis and create a sort of ethical awareness for certain issues. They can also raise and analyse essential ethical and social issues. This concept in practice allows to develop robot assistants capable to help people to live independently in old age. Where the companies at the forefront of AI really listening to the people they had hired to mitigate those harms? In the quest for AI dominance, who gets to decide what kind of collateral damage is acceptable? If AI is trained on data from the real world, who loses out when data reflects systemic injustices?

Therefore, scientists may use AI and be aware of state, business and society, on account of democracy, legitimacy, transparency, bias, inequality, challenges and opportunities. Recommendations for emerging and policymaking for disruptive technologies are required, and, also, guidance will be advised when developing sophisticated AI systems.

Ethical AI has implications for use-cases and governance for any enterprise, namely in what relates with explain ability, bias, reproducibility and accountability, ie. making possible moves from model precision to a more holistic framework, covering organizational strategy, principles and policies. This may help to enlarge AI/ML capabilities enabling natural language processing, computer vision and predictive analytics, ie. use-cases are pervasive, allowing they can be implemented and deployed via a diverse mixture of approaches.

Acknowledgements. I am very grateful to Beatriz Ribeiro by many discussions along the last years on the exploration of ethics in AI, in particular about cars without human drivers, and the related dangers for human beings. Yet, the use of drones in war (Iran, Ukraine) is a recent example of the lack of ethics in taking advantages of AI technology, and on account of that we need to take more attention to our environment.

References

Agarwal, S., Mishra, S.: Responsible Artificial Intelligence: Implementing Ethics an Unbiased Algorithms. Springer, Cham (2021). https://doi.org/10.1007/978-3-030-76860-7

Blackman, R.: A Practical Guide to Building Ethical AI. Harvard Business Review, 15 October 2020

Bonnefon, J.-F., Shariff, A., Rahwan, I.: The social dilemma of autonomous vehicles. Science **352**(6293), 1573–1576 (2016)

Bossmann, J.: Top 9 Ethical Issues in Artificial Intelligence. World Economic Forum (2016)

Bostrom, N.: Superintelligence: Paths, Dangers, Strategies. Oxford University Press, Oxford (2014)

Boylan, M., Terys, W. (eds.): Ethics and Artificial Intelligence, Technology and Information Age. Rowman & Littlefield, Lanham (2022)

Dignum, V.: Responsible Artificial Intelligence. How to Develop and Use AI in a Responsible Way. Springer, Cham (2019). https://doi.org/10.1007/978-3-030-30371-6

Dubber, M.D., Pasquale, F., Das, S. (eds.): The Oxford Handbook of Ethics of AI. Oxford University Press, Oxford (2020)

Fuchtmann, J., et al.: COVID-19 and beyond: development of a comprehensive telemedical diagnostic framework. Int. J. Comput. Assist. Radiol. Surg. **16**(8), 1403–1412 (2021)

Gautrin, P., Mac Andrew, M.: Why Artificial Intelligence Needs Ethics (2022)

Jobin, A., Ienca, M., Vayena, E.: The global landscape of AI ethics guidelines. Nat. Mach. Intell. **1**(9), 389–399 (2019)

Kissinger, H.A., Schmidt, E., Huttenlocher, D.: The Age of AI and Our Human Future. John Murray Publishers, London (2021)

Kuipers, B.: How we can trust a robot? Commun. ACM **61**(3), 86–95 (2018)

Assunção Ribeiro, B., Coelho, H., Ferreira, A.E., Branquinho, J.: Legal implications of autonomous vehicles: what we know so far and what's left to work on. In: Moura Oliveira, P., Novais, P., Reis, L.P. (eds.) EPIA 2019. LNCS (LNAI), vol. 11804, pp. 287–298. Springer, Cham (2019). https://doi.org/10.1007/978-3-030-30241-2_25

Rocha Costa, A.C., Coelho, H.: Interactional moral systems: a model of social mechanisms for the moral regulation of exchange processes in agent societies. IEEE Trans. Comput. Syst. **6**(4), 778–796 (2019)

Russell, S.: Human Compatible: AI and the Problem of Control. Penguin Books, New York (2020)

Ryan, M., Stahl, B.C.: Artificial intelligence ethics guidelines for developers and users: clarifying their content and normative implications. J. Inf. Commun. Ethics Soc. **19**(1), 61–86 (2021)

Sacks, J.: Morality: Restoring the Common Good in Divided Times. Hodder & Stoughton, London (2020)

Sternberg, R.J.: A model of ethical reasoning. Rev. Gen. Psychol. **16**(4), 319–326 (2012)

Veruggio, G., Operto, F.: Roboethics: a bottom-up interdisciplinary discourse in the field of applied ethics in robotics. Int. Rev. Inf. Ethics **6**(12), 2–8 (2006)

IROBOT - Intelligent Robotics

Exploiting Structures in Weight Matrices for Efficient Real-Time Drone Control with Neural Networks

Matthias Kissel[✉], Sven Gronauer, Mathias Korte, Luca Sacchetto, and Klaus Diepold

Technical University of Munich, Arcisstr. 21, 80333 Munich, Germany
matthias.kissel@tum.de
https://www.tum.de/en/

Abstract. We consider the task of using a neural network for controlling a quadrotor drone to perform flight maneuvers. For that, the network must be evaluated with high frequency on the microcontroller of the drone. In order to maintain the evaluation frequency for larger networks, we search for structures in the weight matrices of the trained network. By exploiting structures in the weight matrices, the propagation of information through the network can be made more efficient. In this paper, we focus on four structure classes, namely low rank matrices, matrices of low displacement rank, sequentially semiseparable matrices and products of sparse matrices. We approximate the trained weight matrices with matrices from each structure class and analyze the flying capabilities of the approximated neural network controller. Our results show that there is structure in the weight matrices, which can be exploited to speed up the inference, while still being able to perform the flight maneuvers in the real world. The best results were obtained with products of sparse matrices, which could even outperform non-approximated networks with the same number of parameters in some cases.

Keywords: Neural control · Structured matrices · Fast inference

1 Introduction

Neural networks are universal function approximators [3]. Therefore, they are used in an increasing number of areas. One such area is neural drone control, where a neural network is used to control an autonomously flying drone. In our case, we focus on performing flight maneuvers with a Crazyfly 2.1 quadrotor drone[1]. For that, we train a neural network in simulation using reinforcement learning, and then deploy the network to the real-world (sim-to-real). This training pipeline is explained in detail in [9].

In this paper, we focus on implementing the flying policy in form of the neural network efficiently on the drone. For flying robustly, the neural network

---

[1] https://www.bitcraze.io/products/crazyflie-2-1/.

G. Marreiros et al. (Eds.): EPIA 2022, LNAI 13566, pp. 525–536, 2022.
https://doi.org/10.1007/978-3-031-16474-3_43

must be evaluated on the drone with a high frequency. This is challenging, since we require that all calculations are performed on board of the drone, i.e. on a STM32F405 microcontroller with $168\,MHz$.

Since we use densely connected layers in our policies, the dominant cost for propagating information through the network arises in form of matrix-vector multiplications. For example, to compute the matrix-vector product of a matrix $\mathcal{R}^{n \times n}$ requires $\mathcal{O}(n^2)$ operations. In this paper, we aim to reduce this order of required operations by exploiting structures in the weight matrices of the network. If the weight matrices possess certain structures, the order of required operations needed shrinks to the subquadratic domain. For example, if the weight matrix has many zero entries, the propagation can be made more efficient by exploiting the sparsity in the matrix. For sparse matrices, this results in $\mathcal{O}(k)$ operations for matrices with k nonzero entries. In Sect. 3, we present other matrix structures which can be used for making the inference more efficient.

Our contribution is two fold. First, we introduce several methods which can be used for approximating given weight matrices with structured matrices. Second, we perform extensive experiments for finding structures in the trained weight matrices of a neural network used for neural drone control. This leads to findings regarding the best approximation methods and approximation norms.

The rest of this paper is organized as follows. First, we review approaches in literature that have been used to make neural network evaluation faster. Here, we mainly focus on exploiting structures in the weight matrices of neural networks. In the subsequent section, we introduce the methods we used for approximating weight matrices in neural networks. In Sect. 5, we show the results of our experiments in a simulation environment as well as on our drone flying in the real-world. Finally, we summarize our findings and give a conclusion.

2   Literature Review

There are several approaches in literature targeting to reduce the time required for neural network inference [18]. These include for example optimizing the dataflow [18], quantization techniques [15], using specialized hardware [8], as well as knowledge distillation [10]. For example, many approaches in neural network training or post-processing aim at producing sparse weight matrices [1,14]. Using these approaches, the number of operations needed for computing the matrix-vector multiplication decreases, as explained in the introduction.

In this paper, we focus on structured matrices. Structured matrices can be described with less than $\mathcal{O}(n^2)$ parameters. In contrast to sparse matrices, structured matrices must not contain zeros. Instead, their entries have a relationship to each other, which we denote as *structure*. The research field of structured matrices is fragmented, which means that there are many different special cases of matrix structures. In this paper, we are interested in structures for which the multiplication of the structured matrix with an arbitrary vector requires subquadratic order of operations. Therefore, we focus on four structure classes, namely low rank matrices, matrices of low displacement rank [16], sequentially

semiseparable matrices [7] and products of sparse matrices [4,5,13] (note that the product of sparse matrices is not sparse in general). An introduction to each of these classes is given in Sect. 3.

There are several approaches in literature, where structured matrices have been applied to neural networks. For example, weight matrices in neural networks have been replaced by structured matrices to be trained using the backpropagation algorithm afterwards [4,5,17,19,20]. To the best of our knowledge, there is no extensive comparison of approximating a given weight matrix in a neural net with different kind of structures yet.

3   Methodology

Our aim is to reduce the number of operations required for inference using a trained neural network. For that, we search for structures in the *trained* weight matrices in order to replace the original weight matrices with structured counterparts. Since the application of this paper is neural drone control, our trained network is able to control a quadrotor drone to fly a specific maneuver (in this paper, we investigate the task of flying in a circle). We start from a given neural network J, which is a composition of layer mappings

$$J(u) = (\mathcal{L}_r \circ \cdots \circ \mathcal{L}_1)(u), \tag{1}$$

where the neural network consists of r layers and $\mathcal{L}_i$ is the mapping of the ith layer. We focus on densely connected feed-forward neural networks, i.e. the layer mappings are of the form

$$\mathcal{L}_i(u) = \sigma(W_i u + \theta_i), \tag{2}$$

where W_i is a weight matrix, θ_i are the biases of the respective layer, and σ the activation function of the layer, which is applied element-wise to its inputs.

Given the trained neural network J, we search for structure in its weight matrices W_i. We say that W_i approximately possesses a certain structure, if there is a matrix $\hat{W}_i$ which has the desired structure and

$$||W_i - \hat{W}_i||_N < \epsilon. \tag{3}$$

$||\cdot||_N$ is a matrix norm (for example the Frobenius norm) and ϵ is the maximum error which we tolerate. If the tolerance is chosen too big, the approximated network does not fly in the real world. On the opposite side, if ϵ is chosen too small, we might not find a structured matrix $\hat{W}$ which fulfills the requirements. In practice, we usually do not know the right tolerance beforehand. Therefore, our approach is to find the best approximation $\hat{W}_i$ for a given weight matrix W_i with respect to different structure classes. Afterwards, the approximated weight matrix W_i is evaluated in terms of number of parameters and flying capabilities of the overall network.

We investigate four matrix structure classes in order to find approximations for our given weight matrices W_i. These four structure classes are introduced in the following. The code used for runnning our experiments can be found online[2].

3.1 Low Rank Matrices

The most straightforward matrix structure we investigate are low rank matrices. If our weight matrix $W_i \in \mathcal{R}^{m \times n}$ has rank $r < \min(m, n)$, it can be expressed as

$$W_i = GH, \tag{4}$$

with $G \in \mathcal{R}^{m \times r}$ and $H \in \mathcal{R}^{r \times n}$. Since W_i most likely does not possess a low rank, we are interested in finding a low rank approximation for W_i.

We follow two independent approaches for finding low rank approximations. The first approach uses the singular value decomposition (SVD) of W_i as

$$W_i = USV^T. \tag{5}$$

Using the SVD, we can find the best 2-norm as well as Frobenius norm rank r approximation for W_i by setting all singular values σ_j with $j > r$ to zero

$$\hat{S}_{j,j} = \begin{cases} \sigma_j & \text{if} j \leq r \\ 0 & \text{else} \end{cases}. \tag{6}$$

This results in $G = U\sqrt{\hat{S}}$ and $H = \sqrt{\hat{S}}V^T$. We are also interested in the approximation result if we target other norms than the 2-norm or the Frobenius norm. Therefore, we have a second approach, which consists of glorot-uniform randomly initializing the matrices G and H. Both matrices are then optimized using gradient descent to minimize

$$\min \|W_i - GH\|_N, \tag{7}$$

where N is the norm we aim to minimize (-1, 1, -2, inf, $-$inf or the nuclear norm). We use Adam [11] with the pytorch[3] standard hyperparameters and initial learning rate of 0.1 as step-size optimizer. Each optimization is repeated 5 times taking the best approximation result in order to account for the random initialization of the initial G and H. We train until the loss reduction between two optimization steps is smaller than $1e - 4$.

3.2 Matrices of Low Displacement Rank

Matrices of low displacement rank [16] build on the notion that a matrix might possess low rank after displacing its entries. The displacement rank can for example be measured using the Sylvester type operators

$$L(W_i) = \nabla_{A,B}(W_i) = AW_i - W_iB = GH. \tag{8}$$

---

[2] https://github.com/MatthiasKi/drone_structures.
[3] https://pytorch.org/.

Here, A and B are fixed operator matrices. $W_i \in \mathcal{R}^{m \times n}$ is said to have a low displacement rank, if $L(W_i)$ has low rank, i.e. $G \in \mathcal{R}^{m \times r}$ and $H \in \mathcal{R}^{r \times n}$ with $r < \min(m, n)$.

In this paper, we follow the approach from Thomas et al. [19] and learn the operator matrices A and B jointly with the matrices G and H. For that, we parameterize the operator matrices as tridiagonal plus corner matrices, which includes many well-known standard operators. Therefore, our parameterization inter alia contains toeplitz-like, hankel-like, vandermonde-like and cauchy-like matrices [19].

We formulate the problem of finding suitable A, B, G and H matrices as optimization problem

$$\min_{A,B,G,H} \|W_i - decompress(A, B, G, H)\|_N, \tag{9}$$

where N is the norm we want to minimize (chosen from -1, 1, -2, 2, inf, $-$inf, nuclear or Frobenius norm). The $decompress()$ method recovers the matrix $\hat{W}_i$ from the determined displacement operators

$$\hat{W}_i = decompress(A, B, G, H)$$
$$= \Sigma_{i=1}^{r} \mathcal{K}(A, G_i)\mathcal{K}(B^T, H_i^T)^T, \tag{10}$$

which has a displacement rank at most $2r$ [19]. Here $\mathcal{K}(A, v)$ denotes the $n \times n$ Krylov matrix where the ith column is determined as $A^i v$. We denote the ith column of G with G_i (H_i^T respectively). Note that this approach can only be used for approximating square matrices W_i.

We determine suitable A, B, G and H matrices using stochastic gradient descent. Each approximation run consists of three subsequent optimizations with different learning rates (1, 0.1 and 0.01), whereas each optimization run continues until the minimization loss can not be improved more than $1e - 5$. Each approximation run is repeated 5 times (taking the best approximation result) in order to account for the random initialization of the A, B, G and H matrices.

3.3 Sequentially Semiseparable Matrices

Sequentially Semiseparable Matrices originate from Time Varying Systems theory [7]. This structure naturally arises when describing the input-output behavior of a time varying system, and is defined as

$$W_i = D + C(I - ZA)^{-1}ZB$$
$$+ G(I - Z^T E)^{-1}Z^T F. \tag{11}$$

Here, I is the identity matrix and Z is a down-shift matrix

$$Z = \begin{pmatrix} 0 & & & 0 \\ 1 & \ddots & & \\ & \ddots & \ddots & 0 \\ 0 & & 1 & 0 \end{pmatrix}. \tag{12}$$

A, B, C, D, E, F and G are block-diagonal matrices, each comprising of n matrices

$$A = diag([A_1, \ldots, A_n]) \tag{13}$$

(B, C, D, E, F and G matrices respectively). In the context of time-varying system theory, the matrices $A, \ldots, G$ define the behavior of a time-varying system. For example, A maps the previous state of the system to the next state and B maps the previous state to the current output.

In order to find an approximation of W_i which possesses the sequentially semiseparable structure, we use the time-varying system realization theory in combination with balanced model reduction [7, 12]. We describe our approach for square matrices $W_i \in \mathcal{R}^{n \times n}$ for better illustration. This approach can be straightforwardly extended to non-square cases (for more details we refer to our code). We set the input and output dimensions to 1, which results in $D_j \in \mathcal{R}^{1 \times 1}$. Then, we determine the biggest possible state dimension d which still has less than the allowed number of parameters. This results in realization matrix shapes $A_k \in \mathcal{R}^{d \times d}$, $B_k \in \mathcal{R}^{d \times 1}$, $C_k \in \mathcal{R}^{1 \times d}$, $D_k \in \mathcal{R}^{1 \times 1}$, $E_k \in \mathcal{R}^{d \times d}$, $F_k \in \mathcal{R}^{d \times 1}$ and $G_k \in \mathcal{R}^{1 \times d}$ for $k = 1, \ldots, n$. These realization matrices are obtained by the standard realization approach [7], but cutting out all singular values σ_l for $l > d$ from the Hankel matrices obtained during realization.

3.4   Products of Sparse Matrices

As shown in Sect. 2, there exist many approaches for promoting sparsity in the weight matrices of neural networks. We build on this theory, but in contrast to most existing literature, we investigate *products of sparse matrices*. Recently, interesting results about weight matrices represented as product of sparse matrices have been reported [4–6]. In general, the product of sparse matrices is not sparse. Moreover, the notion of sparsity and structure in linear maps seems to be fundamentally linked [4, 6], which leads to the conclusion that all efficient matrix-vector multiplication algorithms can be factorized into products of sparse matrices [5].

In order to approximate a given weight matrix $W_i \in \mathcal{R}^{m \times n}$ with a product of sparse matrices F_j, we minimize

$$\|W_i - \prod_{j=1}^{k} F_j\|_F, \tag{14}$$

with

$$\sum_{j=0}^{k} nnz(F_j) \leq \psi, \tag{15}$$

where $nnz()$ denotes the number of nonzero elements in a matrix and ψ is the maximum number of nonzero elements in the product. We treat the number of sparse matrices k as a hyper parameter and fix the shapes of F_j

$$F_j \begin{cases} \in \mathcal{R}^{m \times max(m,n)} & \text{if } j = 1 \\ \in \mathcal{R}^{max(m,n) \times n} & \text{if } j = k \\ \in \mathcal{R}^{max(m,n) \times max(m,n)} & else \end{cases} \tag{16}$$

We do not need to optimize the shapes of the factors if they are chosen large enough, because smaller shapes are contained as submatrices of larger shapes.

We use the algorithm proposed by Magoarou and Gribonval [13] in order to find F_j. They proposed to use the Proximal Alternating Linearized Minimization (PALM) [2] algorithm for iterative factorization of a given matrix into sparse factors. The PALM algorithm updates the factors of the sparse product using projected gradient descent steps (in our case we use a projection onto matrices with prescribed sparsity). Based on this, Magoarou and Gribonval proposed to follow a hierarchical approach, where they subsequently add sparse factors to the product in order to approximate a given matrix.

In our experiments, we used this hierarchical approximation algorithm based on PALM for approximating the W_i matrices. We repeated the approximation for different hyperparameters in order to find the best combination for a given weight matrix. For that, we tried different numbers of factors in the product ($k = 1, \ldots, 9$) and different distributions of the number of nonzero elements across the factors in the product. The different distributions were generated by fixing the number of nonzero elements in the last factor $nnz(F_k)$ and determining the number of nonzero elements following a linear

$$nnz(F_j) = floor(\alpha + mj), \tag{17}$$

or exponential distribution

$$nnz(F_j) = floor(\alpha e^{mj}). \tag{18}$$

The parameters m and α can be determined using $nnz(F_k)$ and the constraint given in Eq. 15. In each experiment, we tried different values for $nnz(F_k)$, equally distributed in the range $[0.1\psi, 0.9\psi]$. If $k = 1$, the product over sparse matrices reduces to a single sparse matrix. In this case, we skip the hierarchical optimization scheme and simply use the ψ elements with highest absolute value in the resulting sparse matrix.

4   Experimental Setup

In our experiments, we approximate the weight matrices of two 2-hidden-layered neural networks. We chose to investigate models with 6 and 30 hidden neurons respectively, in order to compare the approximation results for different model sizes. Both models are able to fly in the real world (whereas the bigger model

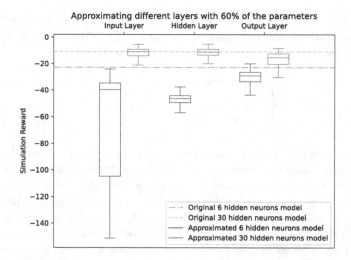

Fig. 1. Comparison of the rewards obtained after approximating certain layers of a neural network for different hidden layer sizes. The approximation tends to be better for networks containing larger weight matrices. For such networks, approximating the input and/or hidden layer weight matrix yields best performance. However, for smaller networks, the effect that approximation errors in early layers of the network might get amplified in later layers becomes apparent. For these networks, it might be better to remove parameters in deeper layers (for example the output layer).

is more robust). For evaluating the models, the original weight matrices are substituted by approximated counterparts in the neural network. The resulting network is evaluated in terms of its flying capabilities in the simulation. For that, we measure the cumulated reward obtained during flying, which was used to train the original model. Hence, the evaluation metric is independent of the matrix norm used during approximation.

Each model is evaluated in terms of its cumulated reward over 500 test trajectories in simulation. The reward takes into account the deviation of the drone position to the ideal position for flying the maneuver, plus terms penalizing undesired flying behaviors such as shaking or drastically changing the motor outputs frequently. We report the mean and the standard deviation of the obtained reward. A reward higher than -25 usually means that the drone is able to fly in the real world (the reward is optimally around -10). If the reward is in the range $[-80, -25]$, this means that the neural network is occasionally able to perform the flight maneuver, but also crashes sometimes. Rewards lower than -80 lead to crashes of the drone in the real world (as well as in simulation) for most times.

5   Results

The approximation results tend to be better for bigger weight matrices than for smaller ones (as shown in Fig. 1). This particularly affects approximating

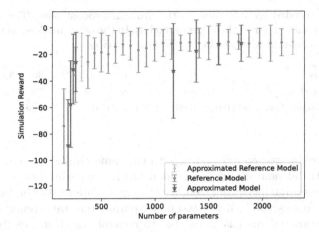

Fig. 2. Rewards achieved by our approximated models compared to models with different number of hidden neurons trained from scratch. Models where we removed a small number of parameters achieved similar rewards like the non-approximated counterparts. If too many, parameters were removed, the models trained from scratch usually outperformed the approximated models.

the output matrix of the network, which leads to worse results compared to the other matrices (depending on the number of hidden neurons). Since our network produces 4 outputs, the size of the output matrix has usually an order of magnitude less parameters. This results in $4z$ parameters (with z being the hidden layer size), compared to z^2 parameters in the hidden layer matrix and $40z$ parameters in the input layer matrix. The network with 6 hidden neurons is less affected by this, because here the hidden layer does not have significantly more parameters than the output layer. Instead, another effect plays a major role here: Errors introduced by approximating the input layer can be amplified while being propagated through the other layers. Hence, in the case of the small network, removing parameters from deeper layers results in better performance.

Therefore, we suspect that more structures are present in the bigger weight matrices. This might be due to overparameterization of the bigger network. Figure 2 shows that a hidden layer size with more than 12 neurons does not result in significant improvements of the obtained cumulated reward. Therefore, we suspect that the model with 30 hidden neurons is overparameterized, which might contribute to the good approximation capabilities.

In order to investigate the tradeoff between parameter reduction and flight capability, we approximated both models with different number of parameters. In the 30 hidden neuron model both, the input layer as well as the hidden layer weight matrix, are approximated with products of sparse matrices. In the 6 hidden neuron model, only the input layer is approximated. The weight matrices are approximated using products of sparse matrices, since this resulted in the best performance. Figure 2 shows the results for the approximated models. Surprisingly, there were even approximated models which performed better than

Table 1. Time needed for inference on the drone microcontroller. The models with 100% parameter share refer to the original models. In the other models, weight matrices have been approximated with products of sparse matrices.

# Neurons	6	6	6	6	30	30	30	30	30
Parameter share [%]	100	80	70	60	100	80	70	60	50
Mean inference time [ms]	0.058	0.068	0.054	0.05	0.4	0.44	0.38	0.34	0.3

their non-approximated counter parts with the same number of parameters. For the model with 30 neurons in the hidden layer, approximation of the weight matrices led to similar performance like training a model with the same number of parameters from scratch, if not too many parameters were removed.

Our approximated models were able to control the drone to fly the circle maneuver even in the real-world. We recorded videos to show the flying performance of the different models compared to the original models[4]. Moreover, we measured the time needed for inference on the drone microcontroller. The results are shown in Table 1. It can be seen, that the time required for inference decreases if there are fewer parameters in the network. However, the computations with sparse matrices also produce an overhead compared to the standard matrix-vector multiplication. Thus, the approximation is only worthwhile in terms of inference time reduction if a certain reduction of the parameters is reached.

A comparison of the performance of the different approximation methods is shown in Fig. 3. Here, we compare the cumulated reward obtained by a model with 30 hidden neurons, for which we approximated the hidden layer weight matrix with 80% of the original number of parameters. It can be seen that the Frobenius and 2-Norm approximation led to the best results for the low rank approximation as well as the low displacement rank approximation methods. Moreover, approximations based on the nuclear norm led to acceptable approximations as well as the 1-norm approximation used in the low rank approach. Using the -1, -2, inf or $-$ inf norms led to consistently bad results.

We would like to point out that for smaller matrices or fewer number of parameters the low displacement rank approach as well as the sequentially semiseparable matrices approach tended to produce poor results. We suspect that this is due to the fact that these matrix structures usually only have advantages for large matrices. Therefore, results might be different for larger neural networks than the ones used in our experiments. However, in some rare cases, the sequentially semiseparable approximation performed very good compared to the other methods.

---

[4] https://youtu.be/PVaTnagaUzs.

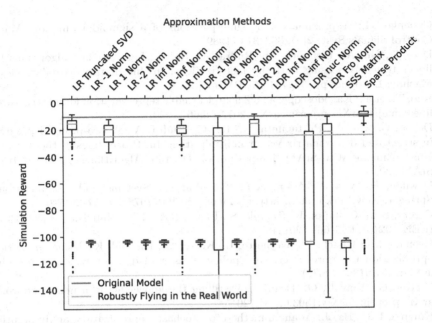

Fig. 3. Comparison of the achieved reward by approximating the hidden layer weight matrix of a model with 30 hidden neurons with 80% of it's parameters. The product of sparse matrices yields the best results. Regarding the low rank and low displacement rank approaches, using the 2-Norm or the Frobenius Norm as optimization objective led to the best results. The nuclear and the 1-Norm also achieved acceptable approximation results, whereas approximating the weight matrix targeting other norms led to bad simulation rewards.

6 Conclusion

We analyzed the weight matrices of a trained neural network used for neural drone control. For that, we approximated the trained weight matrices of the network with structured matrices using four different approaches. Our results showed that the weight matrices possess structure, which can be exploited to speed up the inference. Approximating the weight matrices with products of sparse matrices showed to be the most promising approach in our experiments. With this approach, we could achieve approximations with fewer parameters, which almost had the same flying capabilities as the original model. In the case of very small networks, the approximation could even outperform neural networks with the same number of parameters trained from scratch.

References

1. Blalock, D., Ortiz, J.J.G., Frankle, J., Guttag, J.: What is the state of neural network pruning? arXiv preprint arXiv:2003.03033 (2020)
2. Bolte, J., Sabach, S., Teboulle, M.: Proximal alternating linearized minimization for nonconvex and nonsmooth problems. Math. Program. **146**, 459–494 (2013). https://doi.org/10.1007/s10107-013-0701-9

3. Cybenko, G.: Approximation by superpositions of a sigmoidal function. Math. Control Signals Syst. **2**(4), 303–314 (1989)
4. Dao, T., Gu, A., Eichhorn, M., Rudra, A., Ré, C.: Learning fast algorithms for linear transforms using butterfly factorizations. In: International Conference on Machine Learning, pp. 1517–1527. PMLR (2019)
5. Dao, T., et al.: Kaleidoscope: an efficient, learnable representation for all structured linear maps. arXiv preprint arXiv:2012.14966 (2020)
6. De Sa, C., Cu, A., Puttagunta, R., Ré, C., Rudra, A.: A two-pronged progress in structured dense matrix vector multiplication. In: Proceedings of the Twenty-Ninth Annual ACM-SIAM Symposium on Discrete Algorithms, pp. 1060–1079. SIAM (2018)
7. Dewilde, P., Van der Veen, A.J.: Time-Varying Systems and Computations. Springer, New York (1998). https://doi.org/10.1007/978-1-4757-2817-0
8. Furber, S.B., Galluppi, F., Temple, S., Plana, L.A.: The spinnaker project. Proc. IEEE **102**(5), 652–665 (2014)
9. Gronauer, S., Kissel, M., Sacchetto, L., Korte, M., Diepold, K.: Using simulation optimization to improve zero-shot policy transfer of quadrotors. arXiv preprint arXiv:2201.01369 (2022)
10. Hinton, G., Vinyals, O., Dean, J.: Distilling the knowledge in a neural network. arXiv preprint arXiv:1503.02531 (2015)
11. Kingma, D.P., Ba, J.: Adam: a method for stochastic optimization. arXiv preprint arXiv:1412.6980 (2014)
12. Kung, S., Lin, D.: Optimal Hankel-norm model reductions: multivariable systems. IEEE Trans. Autom. Control **26**(4), 832–852 (1981)
13. Le Magoarou, L., Gribonval, R.: Flexible multilayer sparse approximations of matrices and applications. IEEE J. Sel. Top. Signal Process. **10**(4), 688–700 (2016)
14. LeCun, Y., Denker, J., Solla, S.: Optimal brain damage. Adv. Neural Inf. Processing Syst. **2** (1989)
15. Lee, E.H., Miyashita, D., Chai, E., Murmann, B., Wong, S.S.: LogNet: energy-efficient neural networks using logarithmic computation. In: 2017 IEEE International Conference on Acoustics, Speech and Signal Processing (ICASSP), pp. 5900–5904. IEEE (2017)
16. Pan, V.: Structured Matrices and Polynomials: Unified Superfast Algorithms. Springer, Boston (2001). https://doi.org/10.1007/978-1-4612-0129-8
17. Sindhwani, V., Sainath, T.N., Kumar, S.: Structured transforms for small-footprint deep learning. arXiv preprint arXiv:1510.01722 (2015)
18. Sze, V., Chen, Y.H., Yang, T.J., Emer, J.S.: Efficient processing of deep neural networks: a tutorial and survey. Proc. IEEE **105**(12), 2295–2329 (2017)
19. Thomas, A.T., Gu, A., Dao, T., Rudra, A., Ré, C.: Learning compressed transforms with low displacement rank. Adv. Neural. Inf. Process. Syst. **2018**, 9052 (2018)
20. Zhao, L., Liao, S., Wang, Y., Li, Z., Tang, J., Yuan, B.: Theoretical properties for neural networks with weight matrices of low displacement rank. In: International Conference on Machine Learning, pp. 4082–4090. PMLR (2017)

Deep Learning Methods Integration for Improving Natural Interaction Between Humans and an Assistant Mobile Robot in the Context of Autonomous Navigation

Roberto Oterino-Bono[1], Nieves Pavón-Pulido[1]([⊠]) [iD], Jesús Damián Blasco-García[2], Juan Antonio López-Riquelme[1] [iD], Marta Jiménez-Muñoz[1], Jorge J. Feliu-Batlle[1] [iD], and María Trinidad Herrero[2]

[1] Technical University of Cartagena, Campus Muralla del Mar, Antiguo Hospital Real de Marina de Cartagena, C/Dr. Fleming s/n, 30202 Cartagena, Spain
nieves.pavon@upct.es

[2] Clinical and Experimental Neuroscience (NiCE), School of Medicine, Campus Mare Nostrum, University of Murcia, Murcia, Spain

Abstract. This paper describes a full navigation architecture which includes a set of available Deep Learning-based modules, focused on "speech to text" and "text to speech" translation, and face recognition, for enabling natural interaction between a smart mobile assistant robot and its human users, in a context of autonomous navigation. The system is novel because it allows complex spoken commands to be syntactically analyzed in Spanish and transformed into motion plans, ready to be executed by the robot, by using the well-known Navigation stack included in the ROS ecosystem. A novel computationally efficient approach (to semantically label the free space from raw data provided by a low cost laser scanner device), enables the generation of a labelled polygonal map, which enhances fixed and mobile obstacle avoidance and local planning in real indoor environments. Robot configuration, learned maps, and Deep Learning models adapted to each scenario are safely and privately stored in Google Cloud, allowing the robot to adapt its behavior to different users and settings. The tests which demonstrate the performance of the system, both in simulation and real environments, are also described.

Keywords: Deep learning · Voice and gesture recognition · Mobile robots

1 Introduction

The COVID'19 pandemics has brought out the need of improving Health systems, in general, and the attention of vulnerable people, in particular, through Digital Transformation. The application of Technology in the context of Health attention could be very wide, including emerging technologies such as Cloud Computing, Edge Computing, or Internet of Things (IoT), and other well-known ones such as Artificial Intelligence

G. Marreiros et al. (Eds.): EPIA 2022, LNAI 13566, pp. 537–548, 2022.
https://doi.org/10.1007/978-3-031-16474-3_44

(AI), Machine Learning (ML) or Robotics. The existence of tools and devices, supporting online attention, which help health professionals to make attention easier and more efficient, could be considered as an indispensable requirement, not only during a pandemic as lived, but in a post-pandemic stage, especially when the users are elderly and vulnerable people.

Already in the pre-pandemic era, many research teams were focused on designing and developing solutions in the area of Assistive Robotics (defined as the design of robots capable of sensing, processing sensory information and performing actions that benefit people with any kind of disability), mainly having elderly people and/or disable people as main users [1, 2]. In fact, robotic assistive devices can be very varied, from smart-powered wheelchairs or exoskeletons to independent mobile robots and social robots.

Many advances have been made in the context of autonomous navigation [3–10], in the last 15 years. Some of them has been commercialized. Many vehicles currently include a wide range of tools for helping drivers, for example, parking assistants, smart speed controllers or autopilots [11] with high degree of autonomy in driving, among others. In domestic settings, robotic vacuum cleaners [12] are getting smarter, including new approaches for better carrying out mapping and localization tasks, or smartly detecting objects with the aim of enhancing the clean procedure. However, the success of companion robots is not so obvious. Well-known models as Nao [13] (from Aldebaran Robotics), or Pepper [14] (from SoftBank), aroused great enthusiasm among the Robotics community, but its penetration in Market and in Society, in general, is not as expected. Nevertheless, IoT devices and voice services located at the Cloud, such as Alexa, Siri or that provided by Google [15] are being very successful, predominantly linked to tasks such as surveillance, entertainment or information search, and mainly used by the new generations, considered as digital natives. This technological advances are not so popular among elderly population. In fact, many problems due to lack of digital alphabetization [16, 17] have emerged in the last decade.

Elderly people, especially those with cognitive impairment, are not able to exploit all the possibilities offered by Technology. It is necessary to design technological tools capable of interacting with this segment of population in a natural way and, what is more important, such tools should be able to autonomously go closer users, without an explicit request by such users. Affordable smart mobile assistant robots could be the solution to this problem, but designing such robots is still a challenging research field, particularly when they are deployed in domestic environments, where disable or elderly people live or in elderly residences or similar institutions. A great funding effort from European institutions [18] has been made in the past decade in the context of development of systems for helping elderly people in their daily life. Many works are providing interesting solutions to this purpose [19–27]. However, there is still a long way to go, and many possibilities of contribution in the field of Assistive Robotics, not only in the context of research, but designing proofs of concept as a previous step to transfer results to the market.

The work described in this paper aims to contribute to the development of an economically affordable smart mobile robot capable of interacting with users not familiar with Technology, in a natural manner, considering that the robot should be equipped with

low-cost hardware components and it should be configurable to be adapted to different environments and user profiles by using Cloud Computing techniques.

The outline of the paper is as follows: Sect. 2 presents the system architecture, describing the main features of the robot from the hardware point of view, and detailing which modules are used for natural HRI, and how they are combined for allowing the robot to transform complex spoken commands into navigation tasks directly executed by the navigation modules (localization and path planning). Section 3 shows some experiments carried out and their results. Finally, Sect. 4 addresses the conclusions and future work.

2 System Architecture

This work is part of a current project "Proof of Concept" (named JUNO), which is being developed at the Technical University of Cartagena (UPCT), funded by the Fundación Séneca (an institution in the Region of Murcia, Spain). The final objective of such project is the deployment of a set of economically affordable smart mobile robots in several elderly institutions, for helping elderly people to improve their emotional and mental health by allowing them to carry out several daily tasks focused on cognitive training, through cognitive stimulation exercises. Many of the tasks will require the robot to recognize each elderly people who will be selected as user in the "Proof of Concept", ask him/her information, and acting in consequence. Initial configuration of the robot will be carried out by experts, but the rest of time, the robot will be handled by the institutions' staff (mainly professional caregivers and health professionals). Furthermore, the elderly users could suffer a certain degree of cognitive impairment and they will not be likely familiar with Technology. This means that they will not be capable of using typical well-known applications, such as e-mail, video calls or social networks, among others, or even handling the most basic aspects of an Operating System (OS), such as Windows, iOS or Android.

A very important feature is that related to the communication ability in a natural way with the elderly users, since, as mentioned before, it is assumed that they are not familiar with the use of digital devices. In this case, it is necessary to include software modules capable of performing some key tasks, such as, face detection and recognition, speech-to-text and text-to-speech translation (in Spanish), among others. On the other hand, performing autonomous navigation tasks is also essential. Therefore, the tasks related to navigation are: mapping, localization, path planning and obstacle avoidance.

All the mentioned tasks are performed by a set of distributed software components which have been integrated in the ROS (Robotic Operating System) ecosystem. A method for translating complex spoken commands to activities ready to be executed by the robot has been developed. Some components have been also included for improving the performance of some activities, such as, semantic low-level descriptions of the environment (from raw data acquired by a laser scanner), for enhancing some navigation tasks. Configuration elements (such as, maps or information about users, among others), are stored in the Cloud by using several elements provided by Google Cloud Tools (GCT), always preserving high standards of privacy as current law requires. Figure 1 summarizes the system architecture.

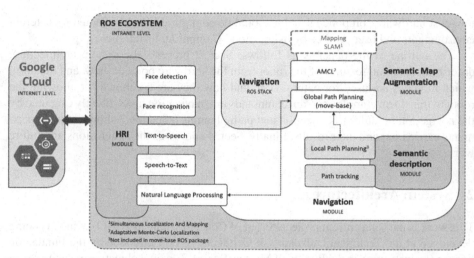

Fig. 1. Outline of the software architecture. ROS ecosystem's intranet modules interact with Google Cloud through the Endpoints Framework. Cloud services are provided by an application implemented under Google App Engine Standard. Data are stored in Google Datastore and Google Storage.

2.1   Operating Scheme

The deployment of the proposed system requires two stages: "first installation" and "daily working". During the "first installation", an expert defines the robot's base location and, taking this pose as the starting position, he/she tele-operates it to create a metric grid-based map of the environment, by using the *gmapping* ROS package. When mapping finishes, the obtained map is manually augmented with high-level semantic data, which allows map cells to be classified according to the meaning of each location. Customized labels for each setting are created for place labelling. Finally, all this information, certain personal data about users and a Deep Learning (DL) model, which will allow face recognition to be carried out, are uploaded to Google Cloud. On the other hand, during the "daily working" stage, the current prototype supports the following tasks: (i) visual recognition of institution's caregivers and elderly users, (ii) visual identification of the users' location, and (iii) understanding of a set of complex spoken commands and transforming them into specific navigation activities. Figure 2 illustrates the described operating scheme.

2.2   Deep Learning-Based HRI Software Modules

Natural HRI is essential in the context of JUNO project, then, it is necessary to include a set of software modules for: (i) "speech-to-text" and "text-to-speech" translation, (ii) face detection and recognition, and (iii) Natural Language Processing (NLP) aimed at enabling transformation of spoken commands to ROS-based navigation tasks. A deep study about already tested free software components, available for integration in the proposed system, has been made.

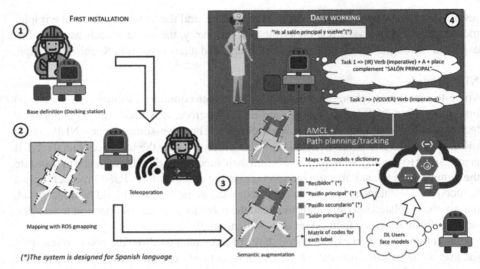

Fig. 2. Operating scheme of the proposed system. The Spanish language is used for communication with the robot. Additionally, users could use a touch screen to send commands to the robot, although the main communication channel should be spoken language.

Speech-to-Text Translation
Cloud-based solutions provided by Google, Apple, Amazon of Microsoft, among others, including services such as Alexa, Siri and Google Assistant have not been used, since they required the continuous connection to Internet. However, the proposed system should work even if Internet fails, in a local mode. Therefore, a DL-based alternative to these solutions named *DeepSpeech* [28, 29] has been selected. It is an open-source engine that uses a model trained by DL-based techniques implemented with TensorFlow. *DeepSpeech* allows the use of pre-trained models or the creation of own ones, and it is compatible with multiple languages, including Python, which has been used for implementation of a ROS node that exposes the functionality of *DeepSpeech* to the rest of components of the proposed system. As the used language in JUNO project is Spanish, the *DeepSpeech-Polyglot* repository [30] has been used for obtaining a Spanish model with 660 h for training.

Text-to-Speech Translation
e conversation with the target users in the context of the tasks that it should perform. One of the requirements is that the robot voice should sound as natural as possible. Several solutions, such as *Festival* [31], *flite* [32] and *SVOX Pico* [33] have been tested, but the obtained results were not appropriate enough, since the voice sounded too artificial. Consequently, the library *pyttsx3* [34] (in combination to the library *talkey* [35]), was selected for text-to-speech translation, since the first one uses idioms' packages already

installed in Linux-based OS and it can work offline, and the last one reduces the implementation effort to a very few code lines. Additionally, the voice sounds as natural as expected in comparison to other tested solutions, and it has support in Spanish language.

NLP Module

Voice-to-text transcription is not enough since spoken commands should be transformed into compatible ROS-based navigation tasks. Therefore, it is necessary to apply NLP techniques for analyzing the transcribed phrases. The open-source Spacy NLP library [36], written in Python, has been used for this purpose. Once the sentence is analyzed, it is necessary to identify some key words and their function inside the sentence to translate the command to the suitable navigation task. In the context of the JUNO project, only a reduced set of sentences (which could be extended in the future), should be understood, mainly those related to commands that lead the robot to go from one location to another, or to perform activities focused on users' attention.

A dictionary and an expert system have been created to allow the robot to interpret the user's requests and translate them to motion actions. The dictionary includes a set of key words (relevant in the context of navigation), classified according to their grammar category, which defines their roles in sentences. The expert system takes a sentence and the labels assigned to each word by Spacy (for verbs the semantic root is taken and the infinitive is considered), and apply a set of rules that extract actions (ready to be executed by the robot), and locations where the robot should go, if such actions involves motion. Table 1 shows some of the relevant Spanish words considered in this work. Table 2 shows some examples of sentences which are translated into navigation tasks.

People Recognition Through Face Analysis

Interaction is only made with those people who have been previously presented to the robot by using pictures or images taken during the installation procedure.

Such information is stored in Google Cloud and downloaded during the "daily working" stage. Thus, the system could work even offline if the Internet connection fails.

People recognition consists of two tasks: face detection and face recognition. The first one is carried out by using the Deep Neural Network (DNN) module provided by *OpenCV* and a *Caffe* model, which obtain information about the regions (rectangles) of the images where possible faces are detected and the probability values assigned to each feasible detected face. The second one is carried out by using a *TensorFlow* module which allow the *TFLite-converted FaceNet* model to be used for inference. The output of the recognition stage is a feature vector of 512 elements. A feature vector obtained after applying the *FaceNet* [37] approach over each recognizable user is stored during "first installation". When a face is detected during "daily working", a feature vector for such face is calculated and compared to each one previously stored by using the Euclidian distance. If such distance is less than a threshold (1.24 has been empirically selected), the user is recognized. Each user is labelled with a specific role: administrator, caregiver, health professional, relative or elderly people. Certain commands are restricted according to such roles.

Table 1. Words in Spanish considered as relevant for translation to navigation tasks. O (Origin) is the current location of the robot and L (Location) represents a possible target location.

Word (Spanish)	English word	Category	Feasible meaning for navigation
Ir	Go	Verb	Go from O to L
Venir	Come		Go from L to O
Traer	Bring		Go and Come
Estar	Be		Find location ("where" is used)
Buscar	Search		Find something
Querer	Want		User's request to do a task
Dónde	Where	Adverb	Waiting for location
A	To	Preposition	For calculating L
Al	To the		
De	From		For calculating origin or belonging
Que	That	Conjunction	

Table 2. Example of sentences understood in this version of the system.

Spanish	English	ROS actions
¿Dónde está la habitación de María?	Where is María's room?	Find position in metric map for María's room, going to room
Quiero que traigas un libro de recepción	I want you to bring a book from reception	Find position in metric map for reception, going to reception. Searching person in reception and ask object. Returning to origin
Lleva la bandeja a la habitación de Juan	Carry the tray to the Juan's room	Find position in metric map for Juan's room, going to Juan's room. Searching Juan and notifying the action. Returning to origin

2.3 Autonomous Navigation Software Modules

The ROS Navigation stack has been selected for endowing the robot with autonomous navigation skills. The ROS *AMCL* package, which implements the adaptive Monte Carlo localization approach, to track the robot pose against the metric map calculated during "first installation", is used. Additionally, the ROS *move_base* package is used for enabling global path planning. As shown in Fig. 2, the metric map is associated to a bi-dimensional matrix that contains codes that represent label of places in a specific setting. Thus, the robot is aware of where it is, not only from a metric point of view, but from a semantic one. This is essential to understand commands such as "go to María's

room", for example. In this case, the target place is one of the map's cells labelled with the code corresponding to "María's room", defined during the "first installation".

Since the performance of the local planner (used by default with *move_base*), was empirically proven to be too unreliable (mainly when the robot navigates through corridors and doors), the method for local path planning described in [38] was used, which enhances the robot's behavior in such circumstances. Such method obtains "a set of linguistically labelled polylines" from raw data acquired by a laser scanner, which "allows to build a compact geometrical representation of the indoor location where a set of representative points (or features) are semantically described" as occlusions (OC), inside angle corners (IAC), outside angle corners (OAC), front wall (FW), lateral wall (LW) and saturated points (SP). A set of feasible local paths are then calculated by taking into account the relation between the detected labelled features. The local path that lead the robot to the global goal is selected at each time. This method is very efficient from the computational point of view, since it represents the local map by using a very compact polygonal representation embedding the calculated semantic landmarks.

2.4 Integration of Modules

Since the robot works in the ROS ecosystem, all the software modules have been implemented as ROS nodes which share information through topics and/or services. The robot waits for "seeing" a known user to start a "conversation". Once a user is recognized, the robot listens to a spoken command and it transforms them to motion, if possible. Then, it performs the required actions. All the HRI modules have been implemented as server nodes: *face detection* node, *face recognition* node, *speech-to-text* node and *NLP* node. They use ROS services for communication and synchronization together with some topics to share data. A *client* node starts the task for attending users by subscribing to the "face/detect" topic, which stores Boolean messages and whose messages are published by the *face detection* node. If there is a message with *true* content, it is necessary to send a request to the service "face_recognition" exposed by the *face recognition* node, which is subscribed to a topic "face/cropped", populated by the *face detection* node. If the image in the topic belongs to a known user, the service response is the name of such user, otherwise a *text-to-speech* function is called for notifying such situation. The *speech-to-text* node provides the service "listening", allowing a spoken command to be recorded and translated to a sentence, which is returned as response. The *NLP* node provides the service "analyzing", which is called if a sentence is available, then it is analyzed and a response is generated, if possible, indicating the action to perform, the place to go and if needed to return to the origin. Finally, such action and the target place are transformed into a "goal" reachable by the robot by using the global planner provided by ROS *move_base*. Once the navigation process starts, all the nodes defined in the ROS *Navigation* stack contributes to reach such goal, except the local planner which is implemented by using the technique described in [38].

3 Results

A reviewed version of the robotic platform described in [39] has been used for real experiments, and its 3D model has been designed for Gazebo/ROS-based simulations. The

real robot, equipped with the Inertial Measurement Unit (IMU) WitMotion WT901C RS232 for enhancing odometry, is non-holonomic with few maneuverability restrictions, since the locomotion system is differential, implemented by a Devantech MD49 controller which controls two Devantech EMG49 DC motors, appropriate for indoor medium sized robots capable of carrying 30 kg. A Raspberry Pi 4 (8 GB of RAM) is used as onboard computer and a Hokuyo URG-04LX-UG01 laser scanner enables obstacle avoidance and mapping and localization tasks, together with an Orbbec Astra Pro RGB-D camera for 3D environment detection.

The system has been tested in a laboratory context, first separately validating each HRI module and then, testing the whole system. HRI modules tests were done with images directly taken by a conventional camera and using conventional speakers and a microphone. Results were as expected, since the DL-based modules are public and they have been already tested by the community. The whole system (including the navigation tasks), was tested in different settings, first in simulation, by using the well-known Gazebo simulator (integrated in ROS), and, finally, in a real environment at the UPCT. Since the objective is to deploy the robot in the context of the JUNO project, several offices and other locations were labelled as places typically found in elderly institutions. Some tests were also performed in a real domestic environment with several rooms, a kitchen and a main room, among others. Researchers and some relatives played the role of potential elderly people and caregivers. Figure 3 shows the results of the "face detection" and "face recognition" nodes. Figure 3 (a) shows 3 persons labelled as elderly users and a caregiver. Detection is made by considering all the faces in the image and only the nearest. Figure 3 (b) shows two patterns used for training when two people act as caregivers. Three images R1, R2 and R3 are correctly recognized by the node as caregiver Roberto. Face detection gets success rates near 100%, and a high rate of success was obtained for face recognition after defining the distance threshold as 1.24. This value was firstly selected by considering the results obtained in [37], and the empirical tests demonstrated that the value is correct for differentiating the users (as shown in Fig. 3 (b)), even when a user is wearing a facemask or light conditions limit the capacity of recognition (see R3 picture). Regarding speech-to-text translation experiments, obviously, the success rate is better in absence of noise. Furthermore, the model used for Spanish language has been trained by the community and it is not so debugged as other official models. In this case, it would be interesting to enhance the model with a customized training process. Figure 4 shows a general view of the whole system working. The caregiver Roberto sends the robot to a room by using the complex spoken command "Quiero que traigas un libro de recepción", defined in Table 2, which leads the robot to reach the goal in the previously built map, to ask for the book when the goal is reached and to return to the origin.

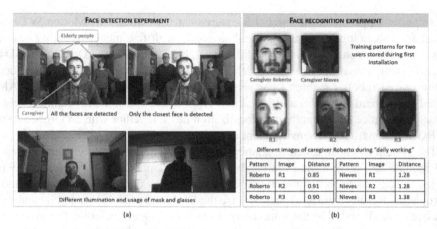

Fig. 3. Results of face detection and recognition tasks.

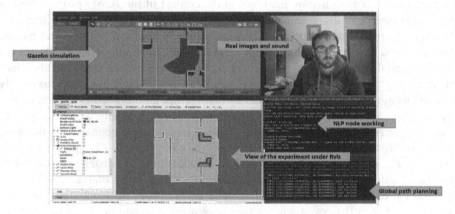

Fig. 4. Global experiment with all the ROS nodes working.

4   Conclusions and Future Work

The system combines a set of DL-based modules in the ROS ecosystem to enable a mobile robot to smartly act in indoor settings and to naturally interact with users. It includes several features that should be found in an assistant smart mobile robot: reasonable cost, skills for performing safe autonomous navigation (including obstacle avoidance, path planning and localization tasks); natural user interfaces for enabling a suitable HRI (including speech-to-text translation, NLP and face detection and recognition), which would lead to a better acceptance of Technology among elderly users. Although the system has been tested both in simulation and in real settings, tests have been made in a controlled laboratory environment. Since the work is part of the JUNO project, a set of real tests in elderly institutions will be carried out in near future. In this case, a new version of the robot will be used, making it cheaper (since a the SLAMTEC RPLIDAR A2M8 laser scanner will be used), and visually adapted by considering usability and

accessibility as main features and with an external design based on the use of materials obtained in a sustainable way, for easily integrating the robot into the furniture. Moreover, NLP module will be improved for allowing the robot to understand more spoken commands related to companion and entertainment tasks, among others. A significance statistical study about system acceptation will also be included since a number of real users enough will be selected for experiments.

Acknowledgements. This work has been partially supported by the project 21668/PDC/21 Program Proof of Concept included in the "Programa Séneca 2021" Region of Murcia, Spain.

References

1. Miller, D.P.: Assistive robotics: an overview. In: Mittal, V.O., Yanco, H.A., Aronis, J., Simpson, R. (eds.) Assistive Technology and Artificial Intelligence, vol. 1458, pp. 126–136. Springer, Heidelberg (2006). https://doi.org/10.1007/BFb0055975
2. Brose, S.W., et al.: The role of assistive robotics in the lives of persons with disability. Am. J. Phys. Med. Rehabil. **89**(6), 509–521 (2010)
3. Thrun, S., Burgard, W., Fox, D.: Probabilistic Robotics, Intelligent Robotics and Autonomous Agents Series. MIT Press, Cambridge (2006)
4. Tzafestas, S.G.: Mobile robot control and navigation: a global overview. J. Intell. Rob. Syst. **91**(1), 35–58 (2018). https://doi.org/10.1007/s10846-018-0805-9
5. Ravankar, A., Ravankar, A.A., Kobayashi, Y., Hoshino, Y., Peng, C.-C.: Path smoothing techniques in robot navigation: state-of-the-art, current and future challenges. Sensors **18**(9), 3170 (2018). https://doi.org/10.3390/s18093170
6. Chandra, R.: Precise localization for achieving next-generation autonomous navigation: State-of-the-art, taxonomy and future prospects. Comput. Commun. **160**, 351–374 (2020). https://doi.org/10.1016/j.comcom.2020.06.007
7. Crespo, J., Castillo, J.C., Mozos, O.M., Barber, R.: Semantic information for robot navigation: a survey. Appl. Sci. **10**(2), 497, 1–28 (2020). https://doi.org/10.3390/app10020497
8. Yasuda, Y.D.V., Martins, L.E.G., Cappabianco, F.A.M.: Autonomous visual navigation for mobile robots: a systematic literature review. ACM Comput. Surv. **53**(1), 1–34 (2020). https://doi.org/10.1145/3368961
9. Zhu, K., Zhang, T.: Deep reinforcement learning based mobile robot navigation: a review. IEEE Tsinghua Sci. Technol. **26**(5), 674–691 (2021). https://doi.org/10.26599/TST.2021.9010012
10. Shishehgar, M., Kerr, D., Blake, J.: A systematic review of research into how robotic technology can help older people. Smart Health. 7–8, 1–18 (2018). https://www.sciencedirect.com/science/article/pii/S2352648316300149
11. Tesla Autopilot. https://www.tesla.com/es_ES/autopilot. Accessed 12 Apr 2022
12. Vaussard, F., et al.: Lessons learned from robotic vacuum cleaners entering the home ecosystem. Robot. Auton. Syst. **62**(3), 376–391 (2014). https://doi.org/10.1016/j.robot.2013.09.014
13. Robaczewski, A., Bouchard, J., Bouchard, K., Gaboury, S.: Socially assistive robots: the specific case of the NAO. Int. J. Soc. Robot. **13**(4), 795–831 (2020). https://doi.org/10.1007/s12369-020-00664-7
14. Pandey, A.K., Gelin, R.: A mass-produced sociable humanoid robot: pepper: the first machine of its kind. IEEE Robot. Autom. Mag. **25**(3), 40–48 (2018). https://doi.org/10.1109/MRA.2018.2833157

15. Këpuska, V., Bohouta, G.: Next-generation of virtual personal assistants (Microsoft Cortana, Apple Siri, Amazon Alexa and Google Home). In: Proceedings of IEEE 8th Annual Computing and Communication Workshop and Conference (CCWC), pp. 99–103. IEEE, Las Vegas (2018). https://doi.org/10.1109/CCWC.2018.8301638
16. Gil, H.: The elderly and the digital inclusion: a brief reference to the initiatives of the European Union and Portugal. MOJ Gerontol. Geriatr. **4**(6), 213–221 (2019)
17. Beaunoyer, E., Dupéré, S., Guitton, M.J.: COVID-19 and digital inequalities: reciprocal impacts and mitigation strategies. Comput. Hum. Behav. **111** (2020). https://doi.org/10.1016/j.chb.2020.106424
18. AAL Programme. Ageing Well in the Digital World. http://www.aal-europe.eu/about/. Accessed 12 Apr 2022
19. engage. Enabling social robots. https://engage-aal-project.eu/. Accessed 12 Apr 2022
20. ReMember-Me. http://www.aal-europe.eu/projects/remember-me/. Accessed 12 Apr 2022
21. AgeWell. http://www.aal-europe.eu/projects/agewell/. Accessed 12 Apr 2022
22. eWare. http://www.aal-europe.eu/projects/eware/. Accessed 12 Apr 2022
23. CAMI. http://www.aal-europe.eu/projects/cami/. Accessed 12 Apr 2022
24. ASSAM. http://www.aal-europe.eu/projects/assam/. Accessed 12 Apr 2022
25. ExCITE. http://www.aal-europe.eu/projects/excite/. Accessed 12 Apr 2022
26. ALIAS. http://www.aal-europe.eu/projects/alias/. Accessed 12 Apr 2022
27. DOMEO. http://www.aal-europe.eu/projects/domeo/. Accessed 12 Apr 2022
28. Hannun, A., et al.: Deep speech: scaling up end-to-end speech recognition. arXiv:1412.5567 (2014). https://doi.org/10.48550/arXiv.1412.5567
29. DeepSpeech. https://github.com/mozilla/DeepSpeech. Accessed 15 Apr 2022
30. DeepSpeech-polyglot. https://gitlab.com/Jaco-Assistant/Scribosermo. Accessed 15 Apr 2022
31. Festival. https://www.cstr.ed.ac.uk/projects/festival/. Accessed 15 Apr 2022
32. CMU Flite. http://cmuflite.org/. Accessed 15 Apr 2022
33. Pico Text-to-Speech. https://www.openhab.org/addons/voice/picotts/. Accessed 15 Apr 2022
34. Text to Speech (TTS) library for Python 2 and 3, pyttsx3. https://pypi.org/project/pyttsx3/. Accessed 15 Apr 2022
35. Talkey Documentation. https://talkey.readthedocs.io/en/latest/. Accessed 15 Apr 2022
36. spaCy. https://spacy.io/. Accessed 15 Apr 2022
37. Schroff, F., Kalenichenko, D., Philbin, J.: FaceNet: a unified embedding for face recognition and clustering. In: Proceedings of the IEEE Computer Society Conference on Computer Vision and Pattern Recognition, pp. 815–823. IEEE. Boston (2015). https://doi.org/10.1109/CVPR.2015.7298682
38. Pavón, N., Ferruz, J., Ollero, A.: Describing the environment using semantic labelled polylines from 2D laser scanned raw data: application to autonomous navigation. In: Proceedings of IEEE/RSJ International Conference on Intelligent Robots and Systems (IROS2010), pp. 3257–3262, IEEE, Taipei (2010). https://doi.org/10.1109/IROS.2010.5650846
39. Pavon-Pulido, N., Lopez-Riquelme, J.A., Pinuaga-Cascales, J.J., Ferruz-Melero, J., Morais Dos Santos, R.: Cybi: a smart companion robot for elderly people: improving teleoperation and telepresence skills by combining cloud computing technologies and fuzzy logic. In: Proceedings of IEEE ICARSC, pp. 198–203, IEEE, Vila Real (2015). https://doi.org/10.1109/ICARSC.2015.40

KDBI - Knowledge D.sicovery
and Business Intelligence

A Comparison of Automated Time Series Forecasting Tools for Smart Cities

Pedro José Pereira[1], Nuno Costa[1], Margarida Barros[1], Paulo Cortez[1(✉)],
Dalila Durães[2], António Silva[2], and José Machado[2]

[1] ALGORITMI Centre, Dep. Information Systems, University of Minho,
Guimarães, Portugal
{pedro.pereira,pcortez}@dsi.uminho.pt, {a89167,a89177}@alunos.uminho.pt
[2] ALGORITMI Centre, University of Minho, Braga, Portugal
{dalila.duraes,asilva}@algoritmi.uminho.pt, jmac@di.uminho.pt

Abstract. Most smart city sensors generate time series records and forecasting such data can provide valuable insights for citizens and city managers. Within this context, the adoption of Automated Time Series Forecasting (AutoTSF) tools is a key issue, since it facilitates the design and deployment of multiple TSF models. In this work, we adapt and compare eight recent AutoTSF tools (Pmdarima, Prophet, Ludwig, DeepAR, TFT, FEDOT, AutoTs and Sktime) using nine freely available time series that can be related with the smart city concept (e.g., temperature, energy consumption, city traffic). An extensive experimentation was carried out by using a realistic rolling window with several training and testing iterations. Also, the AutoTSF tools were evaluated by considering both the predictive performances and required computational effort. Overall, the FEDOT tool presented the best overall performance.

Keywords: Automated machine learning · Time Series Forecasting · Smart cities

1 Introduction

Smart cities collect a huge variety of data variables by using edge sensors (e.g., traffic cameras, meteorological instruments). Since each sensor often performs a regular collection of digital records over time, the collected data tends to assume a time series format. Under this context, Time Series Forecasting (TSF) is a fundamental component. Indeed, TSF can be used to provide valuable insights for city managers and users, allowing to optimize city resources and to support plans. Moreover, TSF can also help to detect anomalies by comparing the real observations with the values predicted by the forecasting algorithms [5]. In effect, several recent studies have applied TSF to smart cities issues, such as: weather conditions [13], city traffic [14] and energy consumption [7].

There are two main TSF approaches used by the related works: Deep Learning (DL), for instance by adopting the Long Short-Term Memory(LSTM) architecture; and AutoRegressive methodologies, such as assumed by the AutoRegressive Integrated Moving Average (ARIMA) methodology. ARIMA was proposed

G. Marreiros et al. (Eds.): EPIA 2022, LNAI 13566, pp. 551–562, 2022.
https://doi.org/10.1007/978-3-031-16474-3_45

in the 70s [2]. Due to its success, several extensions have been proposed and evaluated under the smart cities context [14]. Yet, the ARIMA is a rather rigid model that presents limitations when modeling complex nonlinear relationships. More recently, several studies adopted TSF DL approaches for the smart cities domain, including Recurrent Neural Networks (RNNs) for vehicle parking occupancy [3] and LSTMs for modeling vehicle traffic flow [20].

Nowadays, Machine Learning (ML) is widely used by organizations and individuals. Under this context, there is an increasing focus towards the usage of Automated ML (AutoML) and Automated DL (AutoDL) tools[1] [8]. These tools allow non-experts to more easily design and deploy ML algorithms that are capable of providing value in diverse application domains. As described in [8], there is an increasing number of research works that propose and compare AutoML and AutoDL tools for supervised learning tasks (classification or regression). However, less research and empirical studies have been devoted to the Automated TSF (AutoTSF) task. In [17], a systematic review was performed by comparing 40 Python packages for time series analysis. The packages were analyzed in terms of their functionalities, such as performed tasks (e.g., forecasting, anomaly detection). Yet, the review did not perform any kind of empirical comparison. More recently, the FEDOT AutoTSF tool was empirically compared against the Facebook Prophet [19] and AutoTS [21] tools, outperforming both in terms of predictive performances for a set of 12 financial time series [15].

In this paper, we perform a robust benchmark of eight recent AutoTSF tools (a value that is substantially higher than what was executed in [15]), namely: Pmdarima, Prophet, Ludwig (an AutoDL that is adapted here for TSF), DeepAR, TFT, FEDOT, AutoTs and Sktime. To test the tools, nine time series that can be associated with the smart cities context were used. Within our knowledge, this is the first study addressing the AutoTSF topic within the smart city application domain. The comparison includes the adoption of a robust rolling window evaluation, which performs several training and testing iterations over time. For each iteration, the tools are analyzed in terms of two criteria: predictive performances, set in terms of the Normalized Mean Absolute Error (NMAE); and computational effort, set in terms of training and inference times (measured in seconds and milliseconds).

2   Materials and Methods

2.1   Time Series Data

A time series represents a collection of time ordered observations $(y_1, y_2, ..., y_t)$, each recorded at a specific time (t) [6]. This work addresses multi-step ahead forecasts, meaning that at time t (the last known value) from $t + 1$ to $t + H$ ahead forecasts are performed (H is known as the horizon).

---

[1] Also known as Neural Architecture Search (NAS).

This study considers time series that can be related with the smart cities context, reflecting three city phenomena: meteorology[2], energy consumption[3] and city traffic[4]. For each phenomena, we retrieved three different time series from the Kaggle platform (Table 1). The meteorological data is relative to the maximum daily temperature from three cities (Porto, Lisbon and Madrid), collected from 2008 to 2020. The energy consumption hourly data, measured in Megawatts, was collected from 2004 to 2018. In order to produce a similar time series length (as for the meteorology case), the data was aggregated on a daily basis by summing the hourly values. Each series was recorded by a different North American energy company: American Electric Power (AEP), Commonwealth Edison (COMED); and PJM East Region (PJME). Regarding the traffic data, the series correspond to the hourly number of vehicles passing by three different junctions from a city of the United States of America (USA). The hourly time scale was preserved in order to maintain a series length similar to the meteorology and energy data.

Table 1. Summary of the selected time series (L – series length, K – seasonal period, W – window size, S – step, H – horizon).

Context	Target	Series	Location (years)	L	K	W	S	H
Meteorology	Daily max. temperature (in C$^{\underline{o}}$)	Porto	Porto (2008–2020)	3946	365	1825	105	7
		Lisbon	Lisbon (2008–2020)	3946	365	1825	105	7
		Madrid	Madrid (2008–2020)	3946	365	1825	105	7
Energy	Daily consumption(in MW)	AEP	USA (2004–2018)	5055	7	1825	161	7
		COMED	USA (2011–2018)	2772	7	1825	47	7
		PJME	USA (2002–2018)	6059	7	1825	211	7
Traffic	Hourly no. of vehicles (in units)	Junction1	USA (Jan. to June, 2017)	4344	24	2160	108	24
		Junction2	USA (Jan. to June, 2017)	4344	24	2160	108	24
		Junction3	USA (Jan. to June, 2017)	4344	24	2160	108	24

For the daily time series (meteorology and energy related) the prediction horizon was set to one week ($H = 7$), while for the hourly vehicle traffic the horizon was set to one day ($H = 24$). To set the seasonal period (K) we followed the methodology adopted in [5], which assumes an inspection of the observed values and its autocorrelations. The visual inspection confirmed seasonal periods of $K = 365$ (one year) for the meteorological data, $K = 7$ (one week) for the energy data and $K = 24$ (one day) for the traffic series. As shown in Fig. 1, these K values correspond to higher autocorrelation values within the neighborhood of a time lag and its multiple values (e.g., {12,24} time lags for the AEP dataset). It should be noted that the value of K is often known apriori by the domain user.

---

[2] https://www.kaggle.com/datasets/luisvivas/spain-portugal-weather.
[3] https://www.kaggle.com/robikscube/hourly-energy-consumption.
[4] https://www.kaggle.com/fedesoriano/traffic-prediction-dataset.

Also, the K parameter is only required by the Ludwig tool, to set the number of time lags used by the searched autoregressive models.

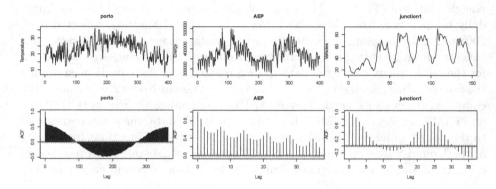

Fig. 1. Examples of time series (top plots) and their autocorrelations (bottom graphs).

2.2 AutoTSF Methods

We compare eight open-source Python AutoTSF tools, summarized in Table 2 in terms of: **Name**, publication **Year**, bibliographic **Reference**, automated **Type**, **Optimization** method used for the TSF model search (when known), domain **License** and **Training Mode**. We selected: three AutoDL tools – Uber Ludwig [12]; Temporal Fusion Transformer (TFT), based on LSTMs [10]; and DeepAR, based on RNNs [16]); three native AutoTSF tools – FEDOT [15]; Auto Time-Series (AutoTS) [21]; and Sktime [11]); and two recent implementations that assume a single TSF model: Auto-Arima [18] and Facebook Prophet [19]). To maintain a fair comparison, whenever possible the tools were executed the default parameters, thus corresponding to a natural choice for an non-expert user. Furthermore, to reduce the computational effort, we limited the models execution time, either by setting a time limitation, selecting a fast execution option or performing the model and hyperparamenter selection only during the first rolling window iteration (Update train mode). This last option assumes fixing the selected model after the first iteration and then only updating it (fit to newer training data) in the remaining iterations. The selected AutoTSF tools are:

1. *Pmdarima*: a recent Python module that implements Auto-ARIMA [18], an extension that automatically chooses the best ARIMA model [1].
2. *Prophet*: Facebook's additive TSF model that is capable to deal with nonlinearity [19]. We used the `prophet` Python package.

Table 2. Summary of the analyzed AutoTSF tools.

Name	Year	Ref.	Type	Task	Opt.	License	Train Mode
Pmdarima	2017	[18]	Auto-Arima	TSF	–	MIT	Train
Prophet	2017	[19]	AutoProphet	TSF	–	MIT	Train
Ludwig	2019	[12]	AutoDL	Reg	–	Apache 2.0	Train
DeepAR	2020	[16]	AutoRNN	TSF	–	Apache 2.0	Train
TFT	2021	[10]	AutoLSTM	TSF	–	Apache 2.0	Train
FEDOT	2022	[15]	AutoTSF	TSF	EA	BSD-3-Clause	Update
AutoTs	2022	[21]	AutoTSF	TSF	GA	MIT	Train
Sktime	2022	[11]	AutoTSF	TSF	GS	BSD-3-Clause	Update

3. *Ludwig*: Uber's open source AutoDL software that uses a DL architecture called Encoder-Combiner-Decoder [12]. The tool is implemented via the `ludwig` Python package. Ludwig was adapted for TSF by converting a time series into a tabular format by using a sliding time window. In particular, autoregressive models are assumed, where $\hat{y}_t = f(y_{t-k_1}, ..., y_{t-k_n})$ is the predicted value, f denotes the learned regression function and $\{k_1, ..., k_n\}$ is the set of time lags used by the sliding window to generate the regression inputs. Similarly to what was proposed in [5], the selected time lags are based on seasonal period (K) heuristics: temperature series – $\{1, 2, 3, 4, 5, 6, 365, 366\}$ (yearly seasonality); energy data – $\{1, 2, ..., 7, 8\}$ (weekly seasonality); and traffic – $\{1, 2, ..., 24\}$ (daily seasonality). To generate multi-step ahead forests, an iterative input feedback of the previous predictions is adopted [5].

4. *DeepAR*: a methodology for probabilistic forecasting that uses autoregressive Recurrent Neural Networks (RNNs) [16]. RNNs do not require sliding windows, since the model is capable of internally memorizing temporal sequences. DeepAR is implemented using the `Gluonts` Python module.

5. *TFT*: similarly to DeepAR, TFT is an AutoDL tool yet with a particular focus in LSTM RNN [10]. This tool was also implemented using `Gluonts` Python module.

6. *FEDOT*: an approach to design ML pipelines based on an Evolutionary Algorithms (EA) and that can be applied to different ML tasks, including TSF [15]. We used the `fedot` Python package with the time series preset setup. Furthermore, the maximum model training time was set to 15 minutes. Since this AutoTSF method is computationally expensive, when compared with the other AutoTSF approaches, the tool was set with the Update training mode.

7. *AutoTS*: an AutoTSF tool based on Genetic Algorithms (GA) [21]. Regarding its implementation, we used the `autots` Python package, assuming the "superfast" model option, which includes a Generalized Least Squares learning and multiple Naive models.

8. *Sktime*: is an unified Grid Search (GS) framework for ML with time series capabilities [11]. We used 4 different models: Theta, Naive, Auto-ARIMA and Auto-ETS. Similarly to FEDOT, the Update mode is assumed.

2.3   Evaluation

In order to perform a robust comparison, we applied a realistic rolling window scheme with a total of $U = 20$ training and testing iterations over time [4]. In each iteration, models are fitted using a training set of a fixed window size W and then performs up to H-ahead predictions. The first iteration assumes that the oldest W data observations are used to fit the TSF model. In the next iteration, the window is rolled by assuming a step size of S, where the S oldest values are discarded from the training set, which is then updated with S newer observations, and so on. In order to set the rolling window parameters, we first adopted a fixed W value for each series type (five years of data for the meteorological and energy series; 90 days of data for the traffic series). Then, the rolling window step was defined as $S = (L - (W + H - 1))/U$.

All selected models were evaluated both in terms of their predictive performances and computational effort. For evaluating the predictive performance, we used the Normalized Mean Absolute Error (NMAE), computed according to $NMAE = \frac{MAE}{y_{max} - y_{min}}$, with $MAE = \frac{\sum_{i=1}^{H} |y_{t+i} - \hat{y}_{t+i}|}{H}$, where y_{t+i} denotes the target values, $\hat{y}_{t+i}$ the predictions (made at time t for the i-th ahead step), and y_{min} and y_{max} the series minimum and maximum values, respectively. The NMAE is a scale independent measure. In terms of computational effort, we measured both the training time, in seconds, and the inference time (when performing one multistep ahead prediction), in milliseconds. For each time series, we aggregated the results for all 20 iterations by using the median for NMAE (which is less sensitive to outliers) and the mean for the training and inference times (one multi-step prediction). The Wilcoxon non parametric statistic [9] is used to check if paired NMAE differences are statistically significant (p-value below 0.05).

3   Results

All experiments were executed using Python code that was run in an Linux Intel Xeon 2.10 GHz server. Table 3 presents obtained results for the meteorological datasets. For the porto series, Ludwig obtained the best predictive performance with 9.56% NMAE, followed by Pmdarima (9.87%) and FEDOT (10.29%). Regarding the lisbon series, Pmdarima achieved the best predictive performance, while FEDOT was the second best AutoTS model, followed by Sktime. For the madrid dataset, FEDOT tool achieved the best predictions, followed by Sktime and then Pmdarima. On the other hand, Sktime obtained the worst NMAE value for the porto series and AutoTS produced the worst predictions for the lisbon and madrid data. Regarding the computational effort, Prophet presents the fastest training process but also the slowest prediction times. As for Pmdarima, it corresponds to the fastest TSF model to perform predictions, achieving the lowest inference times for the same datasets.

Table 3. Comparison results for the meteorological data (best values are in **bold**).

Time series	ML Model	NMAE (in %)	Train time (s)	Prediction time (ms)
Porto	Pmdarima	9.87	87.74	**0.47**
	Prophet	13.76	**0.38**	116.33
	Ludwig	*9.56	5.84	88.74
	DeepAR	10.66	118.13	7.66
	TFT	11.98	291.59	4.74
	FEDOT	10.29	150.80	1.81
	AutoTS	11.34	9.79	7.87
	Sktime	18.67	0.51	4.05
Lisbon	Pmdarima	†5.49	86.61	**0.39**
	Prophet	7.99	**0.22**	115.95
	Ludwig	9.04	5.37	74.96
	DeepAR	8.55	118.44	7.65
	TFT	5.94	291.89	4.75
	FEDOT	5.68	209.46	1.72
	AutoTS	14.76	10.54	9.85
	Sktime	5.80	0.83	1.84
Madrid	Pmdarima	7.26	90.88	**0.37**
	Prophet	13.35	**0.25**	112.84
	Ludwig	7.99	5.88	74.14
	DeepAR	7.70	118.72	7.87
	TFT	8.64	286.85	4.72
	FEDOT	°6.31	150.81	1.53
	AutoTS	22.56	12.85	9.60
	Sktime	6.96	0.49	1.85

⋆ – Statistically significant under a paired comparison with Sktime.
† – Statistically significant under a paired comparison with Prophet and Sktime.
◇ – Statistically significant under a paired comparison with Prophet and AutoTS.

The energy consumption results are presented in Table 4. The DeepAR model achieved the lowest NMAE values for AEP series and COMED while AutoTS selected a TSF model that obtained the lowest NMAE for the PJME data (3.44%). As for Sktime, it presented the worst predictive performances. Similarly to the results obtained with the meteorological data, Prophet is the fastest model in the training stage (less than 1 s), while Pmdarima is the fastest to perform predictions (around 0.4 ms).

Table 4. Comparison results for the energy data (best values in **bold**).

Time series	ML Model	NMAE (in %)	Train time (s)	Prediction time (ms)
AEP	Pmdarima	4.52	128.86	**0.40**
	Prophet	3.93	**0.47**	113.86
	Ludwig	3.75	5.55	77.42
	DeepAR	*3.47	120.58	7.83
	TFT	3.96	292.24	4.65
	FEDOT	3.83	208.16	1.83
	AutoTS	4.83	8.28	6.25
	Sktime	5.30	3.05	3.52
COMED	Pmdarima	4.75	99.86	**0.39**
	Prophet	4.36	**0.39**	115.82
	Ludwig	3.75	6.28	78.23
	DeepAR	**2.45**	119.80	7.74
	TFT	3.96	292.24	4.72
	FEDOT	3.77	150.86	1.47
	AutoTS	4.40	9.41	8.08
	Sktime	6.91	1.29	4.11
PJME	Pmdarima	3.75	97.65	**0.40**
	Prophet	3.62	**0.45**	115.33
	Ludwig	4.63	5.84	78.49
	DeepAR	4.48	119.48	8.45
	TFT	4.06	292.19	4.62
	FEDOT	4.12	207.77	1.40
	AutoTS	*3.44	8.19	6.64
	Sktime	7.31	1.34	4.15

$\star$ – Statistically significant under a paired comparison with Sktime.

Table 5 shows the city traffic results. FEDOT obtained the best predictive performance for two of the three series (junction1 and junction2), while DeepAR achieved the lowest NMAE value for the junction3 data. Similarly to the previous obtained results, the Sktime TSF model presented the highest prediction errors. In terms of the computation effort, the previously detected behavior is repeated (e.g., Prophet is the fastest training method).

The overall results are shown in Table 6 in terms of the tool NMAE median and computational effort average results when considering all 9 time series. The best median predictive performance is obtained by the FEDOT (4.58%), followed by Prophet (5.31%) and DeepAR (5.91%). The obtained results are consistent with the study performed in [15], since in this work FEDOT also outperforms

Table 5. Comparison results for the traffic data (best values in **bold**).

Time series	ML Model	NMAE (in %)	Train time (s)	Prediction time (ms)
Junction1	Pmdarima	12.91	98.10	**0.21**
	Prophet	5.52	**0.39**	34.13
	Ludwig	8.17	8.35	28.28
	DeepAR	6.26	286.20	8.86
	TFT	6.29	711.38	2.25
	FEDOT	*3.44	208.22	0.40
	AutoTS	6.54	13.51	4.49
	Sktime	14.36	1.28	2.59
Junction2	Pmdarima	11.00	145.47	**0.22**
	Prophet	7.13	**0.36**	32.87
	Ludwig	11.34	6.21	28.30
	DeepAR	10.29	286.90	8.13
	TFT	10.70	708.42	2.17
	FEDOT	*5.60	208.13	0.39
	AutoTS	8.95	13.91	5.22
	Sktime	17.19	1.33	3.99
Junction3	Pmdarima	3.82	121.28	**0.18**
	Prophet	2.56	**0.63**	39.20
	Ludwig	2.99	6.98	27.67
	DeepAR	†1.82	279.04	7.65
	TFT	2.58	703.93	2.17
	FEDOT	2.46	208.38	0.43
	AutoTS	2.15	13.70	5.66
	Sktime	4.26	0.59	1.74

⋆ – Statistically significant under a paired comparison with all other methods.
† – Statistically significant under a paired comparison with Pmdarima, Prophet, Ludwig, DeepAR, TFT, FEDOT and Sktime.

the Prophet and AutoTS tools in terms of the obtained median NMAE value. Moreover, FEDOT produces the lowest NMAE values for 3 out of 9 analyzed time series (madrid, junction1 and junction2). For demonstration purposes, some examples of FEDOT forecasts are shown in Fig. 2. While DeepAR also obtains three best results (AEP, COMED and junction3), in terms of the median NMAE, this AutoTSF method is ranked at third place. The other best forecasting results were obtained by: Ludwig – porto series; Pmdarima – lisbon series; and AutoTS – PJME series. On the other extreme, Sktime achieved the worst predictive performances in 7 out of 9 time series. As for the computational cost, Prophet is the

lighter model in terms of training time, while Pmdarima produces TSF models that result in very fast inference times (around 0.34 ms). As for FEDOT, it requires a reasonable computational effort, around 3 minutes for model selection and training with thousands of observations and around 1.22 ms to generate a prediction, which is affordable for the analyzed hourly and daily time scales.

Table 6. Overall comparison results (median NMAE values and average training and prediction times; best values in **bold**).

ML Model	NMAE (in %)	Train time (s)	Prediction time (ms)
Pmdarima	6.54	106.27	**0.34**
Prophet	5.31	**0.39**	88.48
Ludwig	7.99	6.26	61.80
DeepAR	5.91	174.14	7.98
TFT	5.99	430.08	3.87
FEDOT	**4.58**	189.18	1.22
AutoTS	6.74	11.13	7.07
Sktime	8.99	1.19	3.09

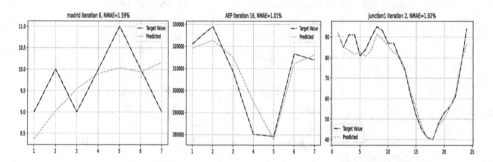

Fig. 2. Examples of multi-step ahead predictions using the FEDOT tool.

4   Conclusions

This paper compares eight recent AutoTSF tools (Pmdarima, Prophet, Ludwig, DeepAR, TFT, FEDOT, AutoTs and Sktime) using nine freely available time series that can be associated with smart city contexts. Using a realistic rolling window scheme, the AutoTSF tools were compared in terms of their predictive performances and computational effort (training and prediction times). Overall, the interesting results were obtained by the FEDOT AutoTSF tool. FEDOT obtained a low average forecasting error (around 4.58%), while requiring a reasonable computational effort, around 3 minutes to generate a new TSF model

and 1.22 ms to produce a single prediction. In terms of future work, we intend to enlarge the comparison study by considering more time series (e.g., public car parking occupation, water consumption levels per district). Furthermore, we also plan to explore more AutoTSF Python modules (e.g., `hcrystalball`, `pyaf`).

Acknowledgment. This work has been supported by FCT - Fundação para a Ciência e Tecnologia within the R&D Units Project Scope: UIDB/00319/2020 and the project "Integrated and Innovative Solutions for the well-being of people in complex urban centers" within the Project Scope NORTE-01-0145-FEDER-000086.

References

1. Alghamdi, T., Elgazzar, K., Bayoumi, M., Sharaf, T., Shah, S.: Forecasting traffic congestion using ARIMA modeling. In: 15th International Wireless Communications & Mobile Computing Conference, IWCMC 2019, Tangier, Morocco, 24–28 June 2019, pp. 1227–1232. IEEE (2019). https://doi.org/10.1109/IWCMC.2019.8766698

2. Box, G.E.: Gm Jenkins Time Series Analysis: Forecasting and control. Holdan-Day, San Francisco (1970)

3. Camero, A., Toutouh, J., Stolfi, D.H., Alba, E.: Evolutionary deep learning for car park occupancy prediction in smart cities. In: Battiti, R., Brunato, M., Kotsireas, I., Pardalos, P.M. (eds.) LION 12 2018. LNCS, vol. 11353, pp. 386–401. Springer, Cham (2019). https://doi.org/10.1007/978-3-030-05348-2_32

4. Cortez, P., Matos, L.M., Pereira, P.J., Santos, N., Duque, D.: Forecasting store foot traffic using facial recognition, time series and support vector machines. In: Graña, M., López-Guede, J.M., Etxaniz, O., Herrero, Á., Quintián, H., Corchado, E. (eds.) International Joint Conference SOCO 2016-CISIS 2016-ICEUTE 2016 - San Sebastián, Spain, 19th-21st October 2016, Proceedings. Advances in Intelligent Systems and Computing, vol. 527, pp. 267–276 (2016). DOI: https://doi.org/10.1007/978-3-319-47364-2_26

5. Cortez, P., Rio, M., Rocha, M., Sousa, P.: Multi-scale internet traffic forecasting using neural networks and time series methods. Expert Syst. **29**(2), 143–155 (2012)

6. Cortez, P., Rio, M., Rocha, M., Sousa, P.: Multi-scale internet traffic forecasting using neural networks and time series methods. Expert Syst. J. Knowl. Eng. **29**(2), 143–155 (2012). https://doi.org/10.1111/j.1468-0394.2010.00568.x

7. Elattar, E.E., Sabiha, N.A., Alsharef, M., Metwaly, M.K., Abd-Elhady, A.M., Taha, I.B.M.: Short term electric load forecasting using hybrid algorithm for smart cities. Appl. Intel. **50**(10), 3379–3399 (2020). https://doi.org/10.1007/s10489-020-01728-x

8. Ferreira, L., Pilastri, A.L., Martins, C.M., Pires, P.M., Cortez, P.: A comparison of automl tools for machine learning, deep learning and XGBoost. In: International Joint Conference on Neural Networks, IJCNN 2021, Shenzhen, China, 18–22 July 2021, pp. 1–8. IEEE (2021). https://doi.org/10.1109/IJCNN52387.2021.9534091

9. Hollander, M., Wolfe, D.A., Chicken, E.: Nonparametric Statistical Methods. Wiley, Hoboken (2013)

10. Lim, B., Arık, S.O., Loeff, N., Pfister, T.: Temporal fusion transformers for interpretable multi-horizon time series forecasting. Int. J. Forecast. **37**(4), 1748–1764 (2021). https://doi.org/10.1016/j.ijforecast.2021.03.012

11. Löning, et al., Arelo, Hongyi: alan-turing-institute/sktime: v0.11.0 (2022). https://doi.org/10.5281/zenodo.6386934,. [Accessed 2022-04-06]
12. Molino, P., Dudin, Y., Miryala, S.S.: Ludwig: a type-based declarative deep learning toolbox. CoRR abs/1909.07930 (2019)
13. Murat, M., Malinowska, I., Gos, M., Krzyszczak, J.: Forecasting daily meteorological time series using ARIMA and regression models. Int. Agrophys. 32(2), 253–264 (2018). https://doi.org/10.1515/intag-2017-0007
14. Nagy, A.M., Simon, V.: Survey on traffic prediction in smart cities. Pervasive Mob. Comput. 50, 148–163 (2018). https://doi.org/10.1016/j.pmcj.2018.07.004
15. Nikitin, N.O., et al.: Automated evolutionary approach for the design of composite machine learning pipelines. Future Gener. Comput. Syst. 127, 109–125 (2022). https://doi.org/10.1016/j.future.2021.08.022
16. Salinas, D., Flunkert, V., Gasthaus, J., Januschowski, T.: Deepar: probabilistic forecasting with autoregressive recurrent networks. Int. J. Forecast. 36(3), 1181–1191 (2020). https://doi.org/10.1016/j.ijforecast.2019.07.001
17. Siebert, J., Groß, J., Schroth, C.: A systematic review of python packages for time series analysis. CoRR abs/2104.07406 (2021). arxiv.org/abs/2104.07406
18. Smith, T.G., et al.: Pmdarima: ARIMA estimators for Python (2017). www.alkaline-ml.com/pmdarima. [Accessed 2022–04-06]
19. Taylor, S.J., Letham, B.: Forecasting at scale. PeerJ Prepr. 5, e3190 (2017). https://doi.org/10.7287/peerj.preprints.3190v1
20. Vijayalakshmi, B., et al.: An attention-based deep learning model for traffic flow prediction using spatiotemporal features towards sustainable smart city. Int. J. Commun. Syst. 34(3), e4609 (2021). https://doi.org/10.1002/dac.4609
21. Wang, C., Chen, X., Wu, C., Wang, H.: Autots: Automatic time series forecasting model design based on two-stage pruning. CoRR abs/2203.14169 (2022). 10.48550/arXiv. 2203.14169

Novel Cluster Modeling for the Spatiotemporal Analysis of Coastal Upwelling

Susana Nascimento[1]($^{(\boxtimes)}$)(iD), Alexandre Martins[1](iD), Paulo Relvas[2](iD),
Joaquim F. Luís[3,4](iD), and Boris Mirkin[5,6](iD)

[1] Department of CS and NOVA LINCS, NOVA University, Lisboa, Portugal
`snt@fct.unl.pt`
[2] Centre of Marine Sciences (CCMAR), Algarve University, Faro, Portugal
[3] Department de Ciências da Terra, do Mar e do Ambiente, Algarve University,
Faro, Portugal
[4] Instituto Dom Luiz (IDL), Lisboa, Portugal
[5] Department of Data Analysis and Machine Intelligence, National Research
University Higher School of Economics, Moscow, Russian Federation
[6] Department of CS, Birkbeck, University of London, London, UK

Abstract. This work proposes a spatiotemporal clustering approach for
the analysis of coastal upwelling from Sea Surface Temperature (SST)
grid maps derived from satellite images. The algorithm, Core-Shell clustering, models the upwelling as an evolving cluster whose core points
are constant during a certain time window while the shell points move
through an in-and-out binary sequence. The least squares minimization
of clustering criterion allows to derive key parameters in an automated
way. The algorithm is initialized with an extension of Seeded Region
Growing offering self-tuning thresholding, the STSEC algorithm, that is
able to precisely delineate the upwelling region at each SST instant map.
Yet, the application of STSEC to the SST grid maps as temporal data
puts the business of finding relatively stable "time windows", here called
"time ranges", for obtaining the core clusters onto an automated footing.
The experiments conducted with three yearly collections of SST data of
the Portuguese coast shown that the core-shell clusters precisely recognize the upwelling regions taking as ground-truth the STSEC segmentations with Kulczynski similarity score values higher than 98%. Also, the
extracted time series of upwelling features presented consistent regulari-
ties among the three independent upwelling seasons.

Keywords: Spatiotemporal clustering · Sequential clustering · Time
window · Coastal upwelling

1   Introduction

Long term spatiotemporal (ST) analysis of coastal upwelling is essential for the
study of ocean dynamics, coastal resource managements and climate models.

G. Marreiros et al. (Eds.): EPIA 2022, LNAI 13566, pp. 563–574, 2022.
https://doi.org/10.1007/978-3-031-16474-3_46

Finding the periodic behaviour of upwelling extension and recession is crucial to derive SST trends and climatological indices [16]. Many studies have been devoted to this topic at various coastal regions of the world (e.g. [13,15]). However, their methodologies are either too complex and/or require too many ad doc parameters.

This paper proposes a novel clustering framework for the spatiotemporal analysis of coastal upwelling. The study area is the Portuguese coast where the upwelling regime, the northernmost branch of the Canary Current Upwelling System, prevails almost continuously typically from April until October. Consistent and reliable data sets from the Advanced Very High-Resolution Radiometer (AVHRR) sensor on board NOAA-n satellite are available for almost 40 years. The data of our study are satellite-derived sea surface temperature (SST) grids being the most suitable data for this type of study [16].

The automatic detection and tracking of upwelling regions from SST data is rather difficult for computerization since they are not "concrete" objects but evolving patterns over space and time with blurred boundaries facing several challenges proper to environmental data [4].

Our work is in the field of spatiotemporal data clustering [4] which "*takes advantage of the fact that in many domains, although the clusters may move, there are "core points" that never change cluster memberships for a given time window.*" [5], p. 2577. However, unlike the approach in [5] which relies on the DBSCAN methodology to capture dense fragments of the data distribution [6], we follow a different methodology to explicitly distinguish between core points and boundary points, which is reflected in the concepts of cluster 'core' and cluster 'shell' proposed in [14].

Using the concept of core-shell structure we assume a (simplified) model for the upwelling recognition and tracking from the SST maps as follows: consider a constant 'core' which forms quite fast and then gradually expands along the offshore waters up to some physical limits, and latter shrinks to the core region.

This allows us to define a clustering criterion and apply the least-squares to approximate the SST data, so that key parameters of the core-shell cluster model are found in an automated way as minimizers of the criterion. This aspect favourably compares our approach with the one in [5] where key parameters like thresholds and the number of clusters to retrieve from data are to be taken ad hoc.

A nice feature of the least-squares clustering criterion is its additivity, which enables to extract clusters one-by-one rather than simultaneously. Such a sequential extraction strategy has two advantages in the context of the issue of upwelling description. First, it is adequate to the nature of the upwelling phenomenon under consideration: at each time instant, there is only one major upwelling region to occur at the coast of Portugal (if any). Second, it allows to apply the Self-Tuning Seed Expanding Cluster (STSEC) algorithm [12], a version of the Seeded Region Growing (SRG) approach in image analysis [2], as a prerequisite to the current core-shell methodology. The STSEC algorithm falls within the same least-squares strategy, so that its application is, in fact, part of the method

being developed in this paper. Moreover, its application to the SST images as temporal data puts the business of finding relatively stable "time windows", here called time "ranges", for obtaining the core clusters onto an automated footing.

Therefore, we propose a three-stage clustering for the spatiotemporal analysis of upwelling. First, the STSEC algorithm is applied to each collection of SST grids (characterizing an upwelling season) producing the segmented upwelling regions. Second, the Iterative Anomalous Pattern (IAP) algorithm [10] unsupervisedly finds time windows, here called time 'ranges', from the STSEC segmentations, to define upwelling intervals along the upwelling season. At the third stage, the STSEC segmentations belonging to each interval T are given as input to the core-shell clustering algorithm to further mine the corresponding upwelling instants into a sequence of core-shell clusters and the corresponding intensities.

The remainder of the paper is structured as follows. We describe the core-shell clustering model and method in Sect. 2. Section 3 is devoted to data preprocessing options needed to balance and straighten the SST image data covering three upwelling seasons (years 2007, 2015, and 2019) of the Portuguese coast. The STSEC based method for deriving stable time intervals, the ranges, is presented in Sect. 4, as well as convincing results of its application. In Sect. 5, we describe and analyze the obtained results. Section 6 concludes the paper.

2   Core-Shell Clustering: Model and Method

Let $A^t(I, J) = (a_{ij}^t)$ be a given preprocessed Sea Surface Temperature (SST) grid, with temperature value a_{ij}^t at point (i, j) where i is the longitude $i = 1, 2, ...I$, j is the latitude $j = 1, 2, ...J$, and t is a time moment within a period T, $t = 1, 2, ...T$.

A core-shell cluster is represented by two non-overlapping sets $R \cup S^t$ of binary values $r_{ij} \in R$, the *core*, and $s_{ij}^t \in S^t$, the *shell* at moment t, such that $r_{ij} \times s_{ij}^t = 0$ always holds for $t = 1, 2, ...T$.

Assume that the shells S^t are characterized by their intensity values λ^t. The intensity of the core should be greater than that for any $t \in T$, that is, the core's intensity is $\lambda^t + \mu^t$ with $\mu^t > 0$. Then, the model to define an upwelling sea surface temperature, a_{ij}^t, at point (i, j) and moment t can be stated as

$$a_{ij}^t = \left(\lambda^t + \mu^t\right) r_{ij} + \lambda^t s_{ij}^t + e_{ij}^t, \tag{1}$$

in which the residual values e_{ij}^t are to be minimized according to the least squares criterion

$$\Delta = \sum_{t=1}^{T}\sum_{i=1}^{I}\sum_{j=1}^{J} \left(a_{ij}^t - (\lambda^t + \mu^t)r_{ij} - \lambda^t s_{ij}^t\right)^2. \tag{2}$$

Consider the first order necessary conditions to minimize function Δ for a moment t:

$$\frac{\partial \Delta}{\partial \lambda^t} = -2 \sum_{i,j} \left(a_{ij}^t - (\lambda^t + \mu^t) r_{ij} - \lambda^t s_{ij}^t \right) \left[-s_{ij}^t - r_{ij} \right] = 0 \qquad (3)$$

$$\frac{\partial \Delta}{\partial \mu^t} = -2 \sum_{i,j} \left(a_{ij}^t - (\lambda^t + \mu^t) r_{ij} - \lambda^t s_{ij}^t \right) r_{ij} = 0 \qquad (4)$$

Solving equations (3) and (4) in order to λ^t and $\lambda^t + \mu^t$, respectively, and after some simplification taking into account the condition $s_{ij}^t \times r_{ij} = 0$, leads to

$$\lambda^t = \frac{\sum_{i,j} a_{ij}^t s_{ij}^t}{\sum_{i,j} s_{ij}^t}, \qquad (5)$$

$$\lambda^t + \mu^t = \frac{\sum_{i,j} a_{ij}^t r_{ij}}{\sum_{i,j} r_{ij}}. \qquad (6)$$

Substituting the intensity values λ^t and $\lambda^t + \mu^t$ derived in (5) and (6) into Eq. (2) leads to

$$\Delta = \sum_{t=1}^{T} \sum_{i=1}^{I} \sum_{j=1}^{J} (a_{ij}^t)^2 - \sum_t \left((\lambda^t + \mu^t)^2 \times |R| + (\lambda^t)^2 \times |S^t| \right), \qquad (7)$$

where $|R| = \sum_{i,j} r_{ij}$ is the number of data points in the *core* and $|S^t| = \sum_{i,j} s_{ij}^t$ is the number of points in the *t*-shell.

Criterion (7) can be written as

$$\Delta = D - G, \qquad (8)$$

with $D = \sum_t \sum_{i,j} (a_{ij}^t)^2$ defining the total data scatter and $G = \sum_t ((\lambda^t + \mu^t)^2 \times |R| + (\lambda^t)^2 \times |S^t|)$ is the core-shell cluster's contribution to that.

Since D is constant, to minimize the least squares criterion (7) is equivalent to maximize criterion G.

We propose an iterative algorithm to build a sequence of T core-shell clusters $\{R \cup S^t\}_{t=1}^{T}$ and corresponding intensity values, finding a suboptimal solution of criterion (8).

The algorithm receives as input a sequence of T SST instant grids (previously pre-processed) each of which is segmented by the STSEC algorithm [12]. The result are T clusters, $C^1, C^2, \cdots, C^T$, corresponding to the T sequential upwelling regions. The output of the algorithm is a sequence of T core-shell clusters $\{R \cup S^t\}_{t=1}^{T}$ and corresponding intensity values λ^t and $\lambda^t + \mu^t$.

The initial core-shell clusters are constructed from those T clusters $C^1, \cdots, C^T$. Since the core cluster is, by assumption, constant and homogeneous, the initial core is defined taking the intersection of T STSEC clusters, C^t, $t = 1, 2, \cdots, T$. Each shell, S^t is defined as the set difference of cluster C^t and core R, covering the upwelling region that may change at moment t along the period T. Then, the initial intensity values λ^t and $\lambda^t + \mu^t$ are calculated by equations (5) and (6).

To connect each initial core-shell cluster with the remaining upwelling region at instant t the set of the grid points forming a 4 neighbourhood, F^t, are merged with them. Thus, sets $B^t = R \cup S^t \cup F^t$ define the initial T core-shell clusters.

After, the algorithm iterates as follows. For each point (i, j) in $B = \cup_{t=1}^{T} B^t$ decide which scenario to take: (A) to make (i, j) to belong to the core, or (B) to belong to any of the T shells, or, on contrary, (C) to remove point (i, j) from any of them, such that the increase of criterion G, δ_{ij} is maximum. This process requires $1 + 2^T$ tentative binary decisions. The process iterates until there is no improvement in criterion G, that is, until $\delta_{ij} \leq 0$.

The algorithm in pseudo-code is presented next.

3   Image Data and Its Preprocessing

Three independent yearly collections of SST images from the Portuguese coast (latitude 36°N to 44°N and longitude 13°W to 8°W) were collected for this study covering the years of 2007, 2015, and 2019. The SST images were downloaded from the OceanColor site (https://oceancolor.gsfc.nasa.gov/) and filtered to use only the best quality data according to the products quality flags. We built SST grids as 401 × 251 matrices, whose entrance is a temperature in degrees Celsius, with a spatial resolution of approximately 2 km × 2 km. Each SST grid represents the average of 8 days. Therefore, each collection of SST grids consists of 46 available weekly SST grids. Since in the Portuguese coast, the upwelling season is typically stronger from March to October [7], we considered SST data from approximately the 30th of March to the 30th of October in a total of 81 SST grids (27 per season).

In order to prepare and improve the quality of the SST grids it was developed a preprocessing pipeline with three stages. First, to remove the North-South temperature gradient due to the Earth sphericity. For this we used the *grdtrend* module from the Generic Mapping Tools (GMT) software [17] to fit and remove a plane to the north-south component of the SST grid. Second, a moving average filter was implemented with a window size W of 5 and a step size of 1. This creates a new set of smoothed SST grids which better exposes the upwelling events to be studied and helps to remove white noise that might be present in the SST data. With the moving average filter applied to each year collection of 27 SST grids, 23 averaged SST grids were produced in this step. In the last stage, the temperature values of each SST grid were normalized using perpendicular lines to the coastline, adapting a method from [3], to avoid the over-segmentation problem [1,3,12]. Since the Portuguese coast has an almost constant longitude, the rows of each SST grid were used as the lines perpendicular to the coastline. Then, each point (i, j) belonging to each line l is assigned with the difference between its temperature and the average temperature, t_{avg}^l, of the points in line l, if its temperature is lower than the average or to zero value in case the point's temperature is higher than the average t_{avg}^l. Considering STSEC clustering criterion [12] is defined by the product of temperatures of pairs of pixels

---

Algorithm 1. Core-Shell Clustering Algorithm

1: **Input:** Preprocessed T SST grids $A^t(I, J) = (a_{ij}^t)$, $i = 1, 2, ..., I$; $j = 1, 2, ..., J$,
   and $t = 1, 2, ..., T$
2: **Output:** Core-Shell clusters $\{R \cup S^t\}_{t=1}^T$, corresponding intensities $\lambda^t + \mu^t$, λ^t
   $(t = 1, 2, \cdots, T)$, and the final clusters contribution G
3: **Initialization:**   ▷ Construct the initial core R and the initial shells S^t from the
   STSEC clusters obtained from SST instant grids A^t at moments $t = 1, 2, ..., T$ as:
4: $R = \cap_{t=1}^T C^t$ with $C^1, C^2, \cdots, C^T$ the T clusters obtained by STSEC algorithm
   over grids A^t
5: $S^t = C^t - R$, $t = 1, \cdots, T$
6: Let $B = \{R \cup S^t \cup F^t\}_{t=1}^T$ with F^t the set of the grid points forming a 4 neighbourhood with the region defined by $R \cup S^t$
7: Calculate the intensities λ^t and $\lambda^t + \mu^t$ by (5), (6);
8: **Iteration:**   ▷ For each point (i, j) in B decide which of r_{ij}, s_{ij}^t should be 0 or 1,
   which requires $1 + 2T$ binary decisions, to maximize the increase δ_{ij} of criterion G
   in (8)
9: **repeat**
10:     **for** each point $(i, j) \in B$ **do**
11:         **if** $r_{ij} \leftarrow 1$ **then**
12:             $s_{ij}^t \leftarrow 0$ for $t = 1, 2, \cdots, T$
13:             calculate the change in criterion G, δ_{ij}
14:         **else**
15:             $r_{ij} \leftarrow 0$
16:             **for** $t = 1, 2, \cdots, T$ **do**
17:                 $s_{ij}^t \leftarrow 0$ .or. $s_{ij}^t \leftarrow 1$
18:                 calculate the (two) change values in criterion G, δ_{ij}
19:             **end for**
20:         **end if**
21:     **end for**
22:     Let $\delta_{i^*j^*}^*$, be the maximum of those $1 + 2T$ δ_{ij} for $i = 1, 2, ..., I$; $j = 1, 2, ..., J$
23:     **if** $\delta_{i^*j^*}^* > 0$ **then**
24:         assign the decision for point (i^*j^*) as $r_{i^*j^*}^*$
25:
26:         **for** $t = 1, 2, \cdots, T$ **do**
27:             assign the decision $s_{i^*j^*}^t$
28:             calculate the intensities λ^t and $\lambda^t + \mu^t$ by (5), (6);
29:         **end for**
30:     **end if**
31: **until** $\delta_{i^*j^*}^* < 0$

---

the former transformation is effective to avoid over-segmentation. Hereafter each SST averaged grid is designated as an *SST instant*.

Figure 2 shows, at top row, five SST instant grids after preprocessing displayed as images with each pixel representing the temperature in degrees Celsius. The continuous white region on the right side of each image corresponds to land, whereas (eventual) white pixels in the ocean part correspond to missing values due to cloud cover.

4   Upwelling Range and Its Modelling

The STSEC algorithm was applied to the preprocessed SST instant grids of the three upwelling seasons resulting in quite effective segmentations, without over-segmentation thanks to the preprocessing transformation.

A careful analysis of the STSEC segmented upwelling regions along each year shown that the upwelling do not gradually evolve through time but instead present several time segments where the upwelling events shown similar behaviors. Empirical analysis of the segmented upwelling regions led to extract four features for each SST instant: the total area, the average temperature, the latitude of the 1% northernmost and the latitude of 1% southernmost upwelled regions.

Thus, given an upwelling season, we want to cluster consecutive SST instants with similar upwelling characteristics respecting the four extracted features. Each group is designated as an *upwelling range*.

4.1   Unsupervised Time Series Segmentation by Anomalous Clustering

To accomplish this goal we applied the Iterative Anomalous Patterns (IAP) algorithm [10]. The IAP is a simple and effective clustering algorithm that sequentially extracts clusters one by one in a manner similar to principal component analysis and, simultaneously, allows to model the number of clusters to be found. This algorithm was originally proposed to initialize K-means leading to the so-called intelligent K-means [10].

So, to find the groups of SST instants as ranges, the IAP algorithm was run taking as input the four features. When running the algorithm, imposing the cardinality of the clusters to be higher or equal to three, it unsupervisedly finds three to four groups of consecutive SST instants for each upwelling season. Figure 1 shows the time series of those features (normalized) obtained from 2019 SST instants STSEC segmentations with the IAP four-cluster partition marked by vertical dash lines.

Table 1 lists the obtained upwelling *ranges* for each year. Each of those series of SST instants are the input of the Core-Shell clustering algorithm.

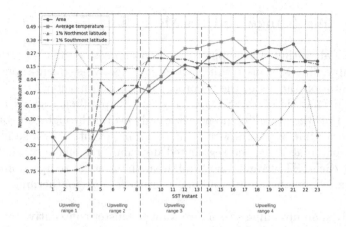

Fig. 1. SST instant ranges obtained by IAP for time series extracted from STSEC segmentations.

Table 1. SST instants forming the upwelling *ranges* for each year.

Upwelling range	Year 2007	Year 2015	Year 2019
1	1 to 8	1 to 3	1 to 4
2	9 to 13	4 to 10	5 to 8
3	14 to 23	11 to 19	9 to 13
4		20 to 23	14 to 23

4.2   The Structure of Core-Shell Clustering Algorithm

An example of the Core-Shell algorithm is illustrated in Fig. 2 taking as input the second series of SST instants of 2007, the instants 9 to 13, after preprocessing. The resulting clusters are visualized as tri-partition maps with the core-shells highlighted with orange-green colors. A supplementary result is the automatic front delineation of the core and the shell structures in the original SST images.

All the experiments were processed in a 15-inch MacBook Pro 2018, with a 2.2 GHz 6-Core Intel Core i7 processor, 16 GB 2400 MHz DDR4 of memory and a Radeon Pro 555X 4 GB graphics card, on the macOS Monterey version 12.2.1 OS. The S-STSEC algorithm took an average of 15.6 s to segment an SST grid. The computation times of the Core-Shell clustering algorithm depends on the cardinality T of the upwelling ranges being processed. The obtained times for $T = 3$ to $T = 8$ were: 00:08, 00:14, 00:26, 00:54, 01:42, 03:43 min, respectively.

4.3   Assessing the Core-Shell Clustering Results

To evaluate the quality of the core-shell clustering segmentations we take as ground-truth the segmentations obtained by STSEC algorithm, i.e. upwelling

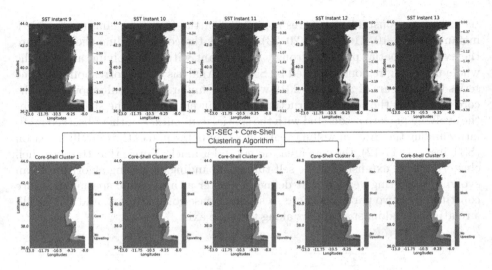

Fig. 2. Core-Shell clustering example.

regions automatically retrieved from SST instants. Those segmentations constitute reliable ground-truth since they obtained excellent evaluation scores when
validated by a team of expert oceanographers.

We used the Kulczynski similarity index [8,18] to measure the concordance
of the segmentation results. In fact, this index had also been proposed in [11],
under the name *Maryland bridge* coefficient, to overcome the drawback of the
popular Jaccard coefficient in underestimating the similarity between two balanced sets with an equally quite balanced overlapping or, contrastingly, when
the cardinality of the sets is quite imbalanced.

We calculated the Kulczynski similarity (with values in the range 0.0 to 1.0)
between each core-shell segmentation and the corresponding STSEC ground-
truth upwelling segmentation. The results correspond to quite perfect matching
with average scores of 0.985 ± 0.004, 0.979 ± 0.007, and 0.984 ± 0.005, for 2007,
2015 and 2019, respectively.

5   Core-Shell Clusters Time Series Analysis

Time series were built from the core-shell clusters to analyse upwelling regular-
ities. For that, the following features were taken: the areas of the cores and the
areas of the shells forming the core-shell clusters characterizing their extent; the
average temperature of each of these structures which are nothing else than the
cores and shells' intensities defined by Eqs. (5) and (6); and yet, the average temperature of upwelling cores against average temperature of offshore ocean waters.

The graphic in Fig. 3 shows the areas of upwelling cores (orange line), the areas
of the corresponding shells (green line) forming each instant core-shell cluster,
as well as the areas of the corresponding whole upwelling regions obtained by S-
STSEC algorithm (blue line) for the SST collection of 2015. One can observe that

the cores are constant structures along each of the four upwelling ranges (SST instants 1–3, 4–10, 11–19, and 20–23), whereas the corresponding shells capture the evolving spatial pattern strongly concordant with the evolving areas of the whole upwelling regions obtained by STSEC. Analysis of the corresponding time series for the years of 2007 and 2019 were very similar. This result shows how the core represents the constant structure of the upwelling while the shells represent the evolving pattern associated with the spatial dynamics. Another observed regularity among the three upwelling years, was that in the mid of the upwelling season (SST instants 11-12), the core areas do not differ much. Notice that the core-shell clustering is an extension of the self-tuning expanding clustering algorithm to an evolving clustering version that defines a cluster as a dynamic spatial structure constituted of two parts: the 'core', a segment-wise constant part, and the 'shell', a relatively random spatial part along the time axis.

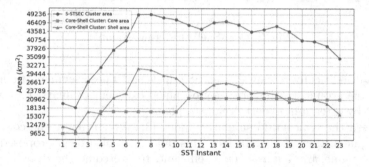

Fig. 3. Areas of the cores, the shells of the core-shell clusters and the areas of upwelling regions by STSEC: year of 2015.

The average temperature of upwelling cores (i.e. their intensities) against the average temperature of the offshore waters at each SST instant of the year 2015 are displayed in the graphic of Fig. 4. The maximum average temperature of core upwelling with value 17.71 °C occurs at instant 11, approximately at the middle of the upwelling season, and the maximum temperature difference occurs at instant 15. We found very much concordant results for the other years. In 2007 the core upwelling with maximum average temperature of 16.97 °C occurred at SST instant 10 while the maximum temperature difference between core and offshore waters occurred at instant 16. A similar pattern is present for the season of 2019 with the maximum average temperature of 17.1 °C for core upwelling occurring at instant 12, the middle of the upwelling season, whereas the maximum temperature difference is achieved at instant 16. These results show that the upwelling events tend to increase in strength around instants 10201312. In fact, these instants coincide with the summer season where the upwelling events tend to have the strongest activity [9]. In summary, the cores' intensities of core-shell clusters very well characterize upwelling reference temperature.

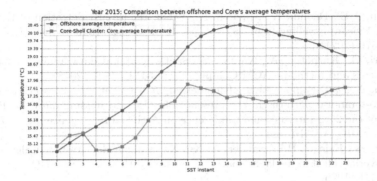

Fig. 4. Comparison of average cores' temperatures against average temperatures of offshore ocean waters: year 2015.

6 Conclusion

The spatiotemporal clustering approach here proposed is aligned with the KDD paradigm on developing *data-driven* methodologies guided by theory to constraint the search space allowing to discover more meaningful patterns and produce more accurate models.

To judge of the merits of the found core-shell cluster structures resulting of the application of the proposed cluster modeling to three yearly collections of SST grids, we are currently left with less rigid tools of which two are of utmost importance: (a) consistence of the results among themselves as well as with existing expert domain knowledge, and (b) oceanographers' judgment. We think that our results are satisfiable on both counts.

Future work comprises the application of the work to the complete Canary current upwelling system.

Acknowledgement. S.N. and A.M. acknowledge the support from NOVA LINCS (UID/CEC/04516/2020), P.R. acknowledges the support through projects UIDB/04326/2020, UIDP/04326/2020 and LA/P/0101/2020, J. L. acknowledges the support through project UIDB/50019/2020, all funded by FCT-Foundation for Science and Technology, through national funds. B.M. gratefully acknowledges support from the Basic Research Program of the National Research University Higher School of Economics. The authors are indebted to the reviewers for their helpful comments that allowed to improve the paper.

References

1. Abidi, Z.E., Minaoui, K., Tamim, A., Laanaya, H.: Delineation of Moroccan coastal upwelling using the principal component analysis fusion algorithm on SSC and SST images. In: 2018 9th International Symposium on Signal, Image, Video and Communications - ISIVC 2018, pp. 174–178 (2018)
2. Adams, R., Bischof, L.: Seeded region growing. IEEE Trans. Pattern Anal. Mach. Intell. **16**(6), 641–647 (1994)

3. Aouni, A.E., Daoudi, K., Minaoui, K., Yahia, H.: Robust detection of the northwest African upwelling from SST images. IEEE Geosci. Remote Sens. Lett. **18**(4), 573–576 (2021)
4. Atluri, G., Karpatne, A., Kumar, V.: Spatio-temporal data mining: a survey of problems and methods. ACM Comput. Surv. **51**(4), 1–41 (2018)
5. Chen, X.C., Faghmous, J.H., Khandelwal, A., Kumar, V.: Clustering dynamic spatio-temporal patterns in the presence of noise and missing data. In: Proceedings of the 24th International Conference on Artificial Intelligence, pp. 2575–2581. IJCAI 2015, AAAI Press (2015)
6. Ester, M., Kriegel, H.P., Sander, J., Xu, X., et al.: A density-based algorithm for discovering clusters in large spatial databases with noise. In: KDD. vol. 96, pp. 226–231 (1996)
7. Fiúza, A.F.G.: Upwelling Patterns off Portugal. In: Suess, E., Thiede, J. (eds.) Coastal Upwelling Its Sediment Record. NATO Conference Series, vol. 10B, pp. 85–98. Springer, US, Boston, MA (1983). https://doi.org/10.1007/978-1-4615-6651-9_5
8. Kulczynski, S.: Die pflanzenassoziationen der pieninen. Bulletin Int. de l'Academie Polonaise des Sciences et des Lettres, Classe des Sciences (1927)
9. Leitão, F., Baptista, V., Vieira, V., Laginha Silva, P., Relvas, P., Alexandra Teodósio, M.: A 60-year time series analyses of the upwelling along the Portuguese coast. Water **11**(6), 1285 (2019)
10. Mirkin, B.: Clustering: A Data Recovery Approach, 2nd edn. Chapman and Hall/CRC Press, Boca Raton (2012)
11. Mirkin, B., Koonin, E.: A top-down method for building genome classification trees with linear binary hierarchies, pp. 97–112. DIMACS series, AMS Providence (2003)
12. Nascimento, S., Casca, S., Mirkin, B.: A seed expanding cluster algorithm for deriving upwelling areas on sea surface temperature images. Comput. Geosci. **85**, 74–85 (2015)
13. Ramanantsoa, J.D., Krug, M., Penven, P., Rouault, M., Gula, J.: Coastal upwelling south of Madagascar: temporal and spatial variability. J. Mar. Syst. **178**, 29–37 (2018)
14. Rodin, I., Mirkin, B.: Supercluster in statics and dynamics: an approximate structure imitating a rough set. In: Polkowski, L., et al. (eds.) Rough Sets, pp. 576–586. Springer International Publishing, Cham (2017). https://doi.org/10.1007/978-3-319-60837-2_46
15. Shi, W., Huang, Z., Hu, J.: Using TPI to map spatial and temporal variations of significant coastal upwelling in the northern south China sea. Remote Sens. **13**(6), 1065 (2021)
16. Siemer, J.P., et al.: Recent trends in SST, Chl-a, productivity and wind stress in upwelling and open ocean areas in the upper eastern north Atlantic subtropical gyre. J. Geophys. Res.: Oceans **126**(8), e2021JC017268 (2021)
17. Wessel, P., Luis, J.F., Uieda, L., Scharroo, R., Wobbe, F., Smith, W.H., Tian, D.: The generic mapping tools version 6. Geochem. Geophys. Geosyst. **20**, 5556–5564 (2019)
18. Zakani, F.R., Arhid, K., Bouksim, M., Gadi, T., Aboulfatah, M.: Kulczynski similarity index for objective evaluation of mesh segmentation algorithms. In: 2016 5th International Conference on Multimedia Computing and Systems (ICMCS), pp. 12–17 (2016)

The Automation of Feature Generation with Domain Knowledge

Tiago Afonso$^{(\boxtimes)}$ and Cláudia Antunes

Instituto Superior Técnico, Universidade de Lisboa,
Av. Rovisco Pais 1, Lisbon, Portugal
{tiago.francisco.a,claudia.antunes}@tecnico.ulisboa.pt

Abstract. AutoML appeared in the last few years as the ultimate challenge in the field of machine learning and data science. However, despite the advances on hyper-parameter optimization, the data preparation step continues to face great difficulties, mainly due to the inability to incorporate human expertise on variables reengineering. In this paper, we present an algorithm able to automate the trivial preparation tasks and to generate features using domain knowledge, represented through entity-relationship (ER) diagrams. Along with the algorithm, we define a set of operators that can be applied to distinct kinds of data, with small human intervention. The algorithm is evaluated over a small set of public datasets, for which we designed basic ER models. The new method shows results comparable to the ones achieved with other automation tools, such as AutoSklearn [4], but with much lower processing times.

Keywords: Feature engineering · Feature generation · AutoML · Domain knowledge · Entity-relationship diagrams

1 Introduction

The success of artificial intelligence and machine learning applications depends deeply on the data to be processed, and its preparation has been shown to occupy between 70% to 80% of the time spent on the knowledge discovery process (KDD process). However, the efforts on the automation of this process have been centered on model selection and hyper-parameter optimization, which kept the problem unsolved regarding the data preparation step.

Data preparation encloses a set of transformations to apply to data, some of them trivial, but other more demanding. Among the trivial ones, we find the imputation of missing values, dummification, scaling and balancing transformations, to name a few. Actually, their automation is simple to implement, and even configurable to be in accordance to data scientists' preferences. Feature engineering, on the other hand, is much more demanding mainly due to the need to explore human expertise.

Recognizing that harnessing domain knowledge improves the KDD process [1], we argue that it is mandatory to represent such knowledge and explore it

G. Marreiros et al. (Eds.): EPIA 2022, LNAI 13566, pp. 575–586, 2022.
https://doi.org/10.1007/978-3-031-16474-3_47

through automation tools. In order to do this, we propose to represent domain knowledge through extended entity-relationship (EER) diagrams, and present an algorithm, DANKFE-II, to automatically generate variables from them. The algorithm receives an EER diagram and a dataset, whose variables correspond to entities in the diagram; it then generates a new variable for each relationship described, and fill its values for each record in the given dataset, following the description and constraints imposed by the diagram. The diversity of the variables to generate only depends on the knowledge made available in the diagram, but by now we present a set of relationship templates, to make it easier to represent the domain knowledge. Among these templates, we propose some for selecting components of single values and others for aggregating records.

The proposal is validated through the analysis of both algorithm's efficiency and efficacy. Given the need to represent some domain knowledge, we collected a small set of public datasets, and created a simple ER diagram representing some common-knowledge for each. From them, extended datasets were generated with the algorithm, in order to compare the performance of the best classifiers trained over the original dataset, the classifiers trained with auto-sklearn [4] over the original dataset, and the best classifiers trained over the extended dataset. Comparisons are made in terms of models accuracy and the time spent on the entire process. Additionally, we present a scalability study, over the average time spent for each kind of feature generated across different datasets' samples. Experimental results show an increase in model performance with the generation of features, with negligible time spent, especially when compared to an AutoML framework.

The rest of the paper is structured as follows: next, in Sect. 2, we provide a brief overview of automatic feature generation procedures. Following this, in Sect. 3, our algorithm is described, addressing its main advantages and difficulties, and defining a small number of relationship templates. Section 4 evaluates the efficiency and efficacy of the new algorithm, by comparing the models learnt over the original data, and datasets enriched with the features automatically generated. The paper concludes in Sect. 5, where a summary of the new approach and its results are presented, along with some guidelines for future work.

2 Background

The strong interest on the automation of the KDD process, usually called AutoML, led to the existence of a large variety of automation frameworks in recent years. Their main goal is to return the best model for a given classification task (pair dataset and target variable) with as little human intervention as possible [8]. In this context, the major advances have been achieved on the hyper-parameterization of machine learning algorithms, with a diversity of methods. However, data preparation is far from reaching similar efficacy. For example, Auto-sklearn [4] uses embeddings, clustering, matrix decomposition and one-hot encoding, as well as meta-features. Auto-Gluon [3] only uses simple data pre-processing techniques, as well as H2O [9]. TPOT [10] uses meta-features and polynomial combinations.

Along with the automation of the discovery process, *explanability* has appeared as one of the key challenges to tackle, and feature engineering, feature generation in particular, is a way to make it approachable. Actually, by creating new variables, models become less complex and easier explainable [12]. However, *feature generation* is usually the most time-consuming step of the KDD process [13], since it requires human interaction and intuition to obtain the best results. This can be subjective, costly and limits the processes repeatability. Its automation is then mandatory, and have been the focus of some research.

There are essentially two paths for the automation of feature generation: with or without domain knowledge. Without domain knowledge, feature generation can follow a *data-driven* approach, that only uses the input data for guidance, and works by applying operators to features (such as logarithm, exponential or extraction of parts of a value, e.g. year and month from a date), by combining features of the same data types through n-ary operators (such as sum and average), or making aggregations (for example count, max, min) [7].

Several works have been published throughout the years researching the incorporation of domain knowledge into feature generation. These approaches go from asking for expert's domain knowledge, to the embedding of that knowledge into dedicated algorithms or by exploring external knowledge representation formalisms. Some authors used a graph-based language for feature generation in linked data, by querying the relations inside the data. Those frameworks allow for extracting information from knowledge bases such as DBPedia [6]. There are also examples of feature generation regarding textual data [5]. Other approaches use already available knowledge repositories, such as ontologies, finding candidate terms that match the dataset to increase the feature space [11].

3   DANKFE-II Algorithm

The desire of exploring domain knowledge across the KDD process is not new, and has been pursued since its origins [1]. However, the different approaches proposed along time did not grasp enough quality to be generally adopted. We can distinguish two main approaches: the embedding of domain knowledge in the mining algorithms or by using external sources explored by general algorithms. Despite the effectiveness of knowledge embedded algorithms, they require a different algorithm for each problem, making it difficult to adapt to new situations. The alternative, however, depends on the availability of knowledge bases, expressive enough to represent the domain expertise.

To our knowledge, ontologies are the most expressive of those formalisms, but their definition for each domain require significant efforts, to take advantage of all their elements. Despite our final goal is to come to use them, we have to recognize that it is not easy to do it nowadays. The availability of semantically rich datasets continues to be a mirage, so we proceed with what is more available, which are databases instead of knowledge bases.

Databases are indeed the most usual data sources, and they are usually designed through *extended entity-relationship* (EER) diagrams [2], formalized

as relational schema a posteriori. EER diagrams have three main elements: rectangles to define concepts, named *entities*, ellipses for *attributes* and diamonds for *relationships* defined between concepts. As an extension of ER diagrams, EERs use the same elements and allow for the representation of three specialized relationships - *inheritance*, *aggregation* and *composition*. Since these diagrams represent the majority of the elements expressible through ontologies, we may say they are simplifications of those formalisms. As a matter of fact, EER diagrams are just not expressive enough to represent axioms - the hardest component to specify. Nevertheless, their generalized use on databases design guarantees their availability for a large number of situations, and a wide number of people able to design them.

In this manner, the *DANKFE-II* algorithm (DomAiN Knowledge based Feature Engineering - II) receives an EER diagram and a dataset, and returns a new dataset by extending the original one, through the generation of new variables from combinations among previous ones.

Before proceeding with the algorithm analysis, we need to specify how the EER diagram and the dataset are related to each other. Given each dataset is just described by a set of variables, the diagram has to represent those variables. The problem to solve is to choose how to represent them - through entities or attributes. This is known as the *reification problem*, and since we want to be able to manipulate the existing variables to create new ones, the solution is easy - we just need to represent every variable as an entity, in order to reason and talk about them. In this manner, our EER diagrams represent all existing variables as entities, and since the new ones shall result from the combination of the existing ones, they are represented through relationships.

We are now ready to define an EER diagram in our context, as a tuple $\mathcal{KB} = (\mathcal{E}, \mathcal{R}, \mathcal{H}, \mathcal{G}, \mathcal{C})$, where $\mathcal{E}$ is the set of `entities`, $\mathcal{R}$ is the set of `relationships` between the entities in $\mathcal{E}$, $\mathcal{H}$ is the subset of $\mathcal{R}$ establishing `inheritance` relations, and similarly $\mathcal{G}$ and $\mathcal{C}$ are subsets of $\mathcal{R}$ defining `aggregation` and `composition` relations, respectively. Moreover, given an EER diagram and a dataset $\mathcal{D}$ described by a set of d variables, for each of those variables there is a corresponding relation in the EER diagram.

In order to explore such diagrams, we translate them into JSON files, following a predefined structure. JSON is a standard text-based format for storing and transmitting structured data, used in plenty of web applications. Other formats could be used, including XML, RDFS and OWL, to name a few. Independently of the choice, the specification of the EER elements must follow a strict definition.

Each entity in an EER diagram is characterised by its *name*, used as an identifier, its *type* to help on determining the possible operations to perform over it and a *description* optionally used to clarify any additional information about the entity.

As relations specify the new variables to generate, they have a much extensive definition. Each *relationship* in an EER diagram is characterised by its *name*, again used as an identifier, but also for naming the new variable to generate, *inputs* for specifying the list of related entities, *operations* corresponding to the sequence of operations to perform over its inputs to generate the new variable,

and the *constraints* its inputs have to satisfy to make the generation possible. Optionally, it may include a *GROUPBY* parameter specifying the variable along with an aggregation may be made and *condition* for specifying which records to aggregate. As special cases of relationships, inheritance, aggregation and composition, just follow the same rules as relationships, for now.

We may distinguish between two different procedures: *record-based generation* involving a single record, and *aggregation-based generation* resulting from the aggregation of more than one record, as specified by the *GROUPBY* parameter.

Considering $\mathcal{D}$ to be a dataset, $\mathcal{F} = \{v_1, ..., v_d\}$ the set of d variables describing $\mathcal{D}$ and $\mathcal{KB} = (\mathcal{E}, \mathcal{R}, \mathcal{H}, \mathcal{G}, \mathcal{C})$ an EER diagram as defined before, we are now able to define how each procedure works.

Definition 1. *Let $r = (\Theta, \Pi, \Psi, \emptyset, null)$ be a **record-based** relation in $\mathcal{R}$, with $\Theta \subset \mathcal{E}$ the set of **input** variables, Π the sequence of **operations**, and Ψ the set of **constraints** to satisfy. The procedure generates a new variable v_r, and each record $x = x_1...x_d$ in the dataset $\mathcal{D}$ becomes $x' = x_1...x_d, x_r$, with x_r filled as follows:*

1. *if $\exists \theta \in \Theta \ \exists \psi \in \Psi$: $x_\theta \not\models \psi$, a null value is assigned to x_r;*
2. *otherwise,*
   (a) *x_r becomes $\pi(x_{\theta_1}...x_{\theta_k})$, where π is the last operation in Π and $(x_{\theta_1}...x_{\theta_k})$ is the projection of x along each variable $\theta_i \in \Theta$;*
   (b) *also, if $|\Pi| > 1$ then x_r becomes $\pi_i(x_r)$ with π_i being each one of the ith operations, with $1 \leq i < j$, and j the number of operations in Π, from the $(j-1)^{th}$ to the first one.*

And for the *aggregation-based* procedure in a similar way:

Definition 2. *Let $r = (\Theta, \Pi, \Psi, \Delta, \phi)$ be a **aggregation-based** relation in $\mathcal{R}$, with $\Theta \subset \mathcal{E}$ the set of **input** variables, Π the sequence of **operations**, Ψ the set of **constraints** to satisfy, Δ the set of variables to specify the **aggregation** and ϕ the **condition** to constraint the aggregation. The procedure generates a new variable v_r, and each record $x = x_1...x_d$ in the dataset $\mathcal{D}$ becomes $x' = x_1...x_d, x_r$, with x_r filled as follows:*

1. *if $\exists \theta \in \Theta \ \exists \psi \in \Psi$: $x_\theta \not\models \psi$, a null value is assigned to x_r;*
2. *otherwise,*
   (a) *a temporary variable γ is created for storing the projections of each x, $(x_{\theta_1}...x_{\theta_k})$, along each variable $\theta_i \in \Theta$ for all records in $\mathcal{D}'$ satisfying the condition ϕ, and aggregated according to all variables $\delta \in \Delta$;*
   (b) *after this, x_r becomes $\pi(\gamma)$, where π is the last operation in Π;*
   (c) *also, if $|\Pi| > 1$ then x_r becomes $\pi_i(x_r)$ with π_i being each one of the ith operations, with $1 \leq i < j$, and j the number of operations in Π, from the $(j-1)^{th}$ to the first one.*

Let $\mathcal{D}$ be a dataset described by a set of d variables, $\mathcal{F}$, and $\mathcal{KB}$ an EER diagram, as defined before, the algorithm generates a new variable v' for each relation r in the EER, extending the set of original features and records, by filling the

Algorithm 1. DANKFE-II algorithm

```
procedure DANKFE-II(𝒟, ℱ, 𝒦ℬ)
    queue ← 𝒦ℬ.relations
    while queue ≠ ∅ do
        rel ← pop(queue)
        if rel.inputs ⊄ ℱ then
            queue ← append(rel)
        else
            for row ∈ 𝒟 do
                if row ⊨ constraint then
                    if rel.groupby ≠ ∅ then
                        row' ← get_rows(row, 𝒟[rel.inputs], rel.groupby,
                                                              rel.condition)
                    else
                        row' ← row
                    end if
                    for operation ∈ reverse(rel.operations) do
                        row' ← operation(row')
                    end for
                else
                    row' ← null
                end if
                𝒟' ← 𝒟' ∪ {row + row'}
            end for
        end if
    end while
    return 𝒟'
end procedure
```

new variables for all records in the original dataset, according to the procedures described in Definitions 1 and 2.

Algorithm 1 illustrates DANKFE-II - our proposal for implementing both procedures. First, the relations are read from the EER diagram, and stored as a queue to be processed; then relations are processed one by one. Whenever their inputs are not yet available, relations are sent to the end of the queue. Otherwise, the algorithm is ready to fill the new variable for each record in the original dataset, as follows:

- If the relation is aggregation-based, i.e., the relation specifies a *GROUPBY* parameter, then we need to collect the rows to perform the aggregation.
- Afterwards, it is possible to apply the list of operations creating the new values for the variable, for all the records satisfying the constraints imposed. The operations are applied as a composition of functions, beginning with the last one and sequentially applying the following ones.
- Whenever any row does not meet the constraints, a null value is imputed.
- When all rows are processed, the relation is removed from the queue.

Since the operation used to generate the new variable is specified in the diagram, we could think this can be any operation imaginable. Unfortunately, that is not the case, since in order to do that we would need an interpreter to decode the operations to apply. Moreover, that would introduce additional processing time and complexity, which we shall avoid.

Among the operations specified by relations in the EER diagram, we may consider several:

- **Decomposition operations** apply an operation on a single variable from each record, extracting some component from its value (*year, month, day* are examples for dealing with dates).
- **Algebraic operations** apply any mathematical operation over a single record, involving one or more variables (examples are *square root* and *division*).
- **Mapping operations** map a variable's value into another one, possibly from different types (*weekday* is an example over dates).
- **Aggregation operations** are applied over a set of records that satisfy some imposed condition similar to the ones achieved with a $GROUPBY$ clause in an SQL query (for example *sum, average, max*).
- **Composition operations** apply a sequence of operations similar to a mathematical composition of functions.

Nevertheless, the implementation of record-based operations, which only encompass a single record (just one row in the dataset), may be directly made through a lambda function in Python. In this case, the function applies each operation in the list of operations in reverse (similarly to a composition of operations) sequentially over the corresponding inputs - the values assumed by each input variable in the record, and return the output value - the value to assign to the new variable for the given record. The input columns are fed to the algorithm for each relation, processing the defined operation row by row.

The DANKFE-II algorithm can also be used as part of a pipeline for preparing a dataset for model training. Data preparation techniques, such as missing value imputation can be performed before the algorithm, and it can be scaled and balanced if needed, after the variables are generated. Additionally, automatic variables that require no knowledge can be added to the EER model, such as automatic decomposition of dates and statistics of variables such as mean, median, standard deviation, etc. This allows the user to be able to enrich a dataset even if there is no domain knowledge available.

3.1 Illustration

In order to better understand the algorithm proposed, consider the knowledge base represented by the EER diagram represented in Fig. 1. Additionally, consider the data on Table 1.

Let them correspond to the data input to the algorithm $\mathcal{D}$, which is then described by the set of variables $\mathcal{F}$,

$$\mathcal{F} = \{current\_date, cases, deaths, country, population, first\_date, high\_risk\_2w\}.$$

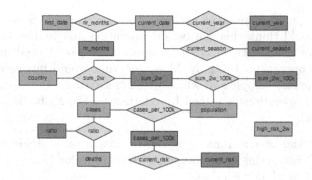

Fig. 1. Example of the ER diagram for feature generation.

We can see that all variables in $\mathcal{F}$ are present in the ER diagram as entities (represented as light blue rectangles). Beside them, we found eight relationships (green diamonds) and eight additional entities (dark blue rectangles), corresponding to the variables to generate.

Note, that each relationship is linked to a set of entities, where the lighter ones correspond to their inputs, and the darker ones to the new variables to generate. Table 2 summarizes the variables generated by our algorithm when applied to the data in $\mathcal{D}$, shown in the previous table, and using the ER diagram in Fig. 1. First, we find *current_year* resulting from a **decomposition** operator, computed by extracting the year from the *current_date* variable. Similarly, we have *current_season* that **maps** the *current_date* to the yearly season. **Algebraic** operations are illustrated by *ratio* that is computed by dividing the number of *deaths* and *cases*, by *nr_months* which results from the difference between *first_date* and *current_date*, and by *cases_per_100k*, which is just the number of *cases* per *population* times 100k.

Table 1. Illustration dataset, labeled by *high_risk_2w*

current_date	Cases	Deaths	Country	Population	first_date	high_risk_2w
2021/02/23	1032	63	PT	10295909	2020/03/03	TRUE
2022/02/14	20360	78	UK	10718565	2020/02/23	TRUE
2021/08/12	223	2	PL	37958138	2020/03/07	FALSE
2020/06/11	22	0	AT	8901064	2020/02/26	FALSE

Table 2. Generated variables extending the data in the same order.

year	Season	Months	Ratio	cases_100k	current_risk	sum_2w	sum_2w_100k
2021	Winter	11	16.4	10.023	FALSE	33692	327.237
2022	Winter	24	261.0	189.951	TRUE	284573	2654.954
2021	Summer	17	111.5	0.587	FALSE	2453	6.462
2020	Spring	3	Null	0.247	FALSE	471	5.292

On the other side, *sum_2w* is an example of a variable resulting from an `aggregation` operation, it results from summing the number of *cases* from the previous two weeks for the country under analysis (the country for the record whose value is being filled). Finally, *sum_2w_100k* and *current_risk* could be seen as `composition` if we had omitted the *sum_2w* and *cases_per_100k*, respectively. Actually, they are just a division by the population and a comparison to a threshold (120 cases per 100k), after computing those previous variables.

4 Validation

In order to validate our proposal, we compared the quality of classification models trained over various public datasets and their extensions, described both by the original and generated variables, using the algorithm proposed. Beside the performance, we studied the impact on the time spent training and predicting those models, as well as the importance given by the models to the generated variables. Additionally, we compared those results with the resulting from training a model for the same problem through AutoSklearn, while also evaluating the algorithm's scalability.

The datasets used were chosen to spread over several different domains[1,2,3,4], allowing for the generation of different kinds of variables. An EER diagram and a target variable were created for each one, similar to the EER diagram on Fig. 1. Two versions of each dataset were tested excluding the baseline. One version only had variables added through domain knowledge present in the EER diagrams, the other also had data preparation steps (scaling and balancing if needed, automatically performed after the DANKFE-II algorithm), as well as automatic decomposition of dates and aggregations of numeric variables.

For each dataset and training technique (Naive Bayes, KNN, Decision Trees, Random Forests and Gradient Boosting, all from sklearn), we found the 10 best models trained over an equal number of random data partitions, and exploring a grid of hyperparameters. While running AutoSklearn, only one model was found. AUC was chosen to assess models quality, due to the existence of some unbalanced datasets among the ones analysed.

Results in Fig. 2 (left) show that on average, all training algorithms benefit from variables generation, increasing their performance over the extended datasets, either with only domain knowledge or with additional automatic variables and data preparation. Additionally, those models always outperform AutoSklearn, with some being better over 5ppt.

Since the datasets under analysis contain different numbers of records, we compared the time spent by each strategy to process each record. So, Fig. 2 (right) shows the average time per record spent by each training technique

[1] https://www.ecdc.europa.eu/en/publications-data/download-todays-data-geograp hic-distribution-covid-19-cases-worldwide.

[2] https://data.world/data-society/city-of-baltimore-crime-data.

[3] https://data.world/data-society/global-climate-change-data.

[4] https://data.world/makeovermonday/2019w32.

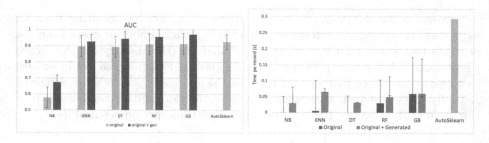

Fig. 2. Comparison of quality (left) and processing times (right) for different models.

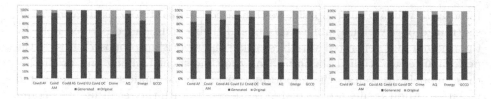

Fig. 3. Average feature importance for original and generated variables for Decision Trees (left), Random Forests (middle) and Gradient Boosting (right).

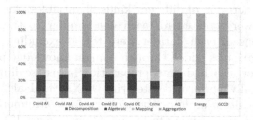

Fig. 4. Time comparison per types of variable generated.

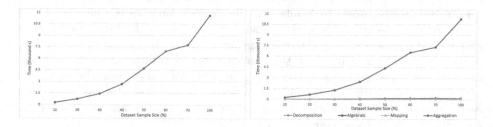

Fig. 5. Scalability: total time on variable generation (left) and per variable type (right).

(including the time spent running DANKFE-II for extending the dataset). In this figure, we can see the time spent by the new approach increases significantly when compared against mining the original dataset. However, this increase depends on the model trained, with a larger increase for Naive Bayes, KNN and Random Forests. We can also see that adding automatic generation only leads

to a small increase (due to the larger feature space), but with a significant improvement in model performance. The results are much better, when compared to AutoSklearn, since it takes a fixed time of one hour to find the best model, which in average corresponds to around 300 milliseconds per record on the datasets used. Using the new approach, in average we spent between 10% and 20% of the time spent by AutoSklearn, depending on the training technique used. The variables generated were also proved useful in increasing the models performance, as seen in Fig. 3. Most datasets and models greatly benefit from the generated variables, making up more than half or almost all features importance used for training Decision Trees, Random Forests and Gradient Boosting.

The type of variables generated also influences the time spent (Fig. 4). On average, aggregation operations take the longest to run (at least 50% of the overall time), due to their need to check other records for the GROUP BY operation. The other 3 types of operations (decomposition, algebraic and mapping) take approximately the same time to run, since these operations do not have any row dependence when computing the value for each record.

The last study performed focused on the DANKFE-II's scalability. In order to analyse it, we took different samples of the covid dataset (originally with 135k records) with progressive sizes, and generated the same variables for each one.

Figure 5 (left) shows the total amount of time spent on feature generation (including the time spent on reading the original and writing the extended datasets). From this chart it is clear that our algorithm presents approximately a linear growth on the dataset size. Additionally, the chart on the right shows that the time spent per record-based operations is residual, and almost all the time is spent on generating aggregation-based variables.

5 Conclusion

Throughout the years, several methods for feature generation have been published, with and without the use of domain knowledge. However, on the last years, the automation of ML processes have not explored this, treating the KDD pipeline as a black-box. In this paper, we propose to exploit domain knowledge, expressed as an EER diagram, to guide the feature generation. The results show that, when trained with the most popular training techniques, its use improves models' quality. Not only did feature generation help increasing the models robustness, but also doing so without a significant time penalty. Additionally, when compared to an AutoML framework, the use of domain knowledge to increase the feature space achieved better classification results, while also taking significantly less time. The next step to follow is to simplify the EER diagram by increasing the number of automatically proposed operations, so that they do not have to be specified in the diagram.

Acknowledgement. The present work was supported by national funds through Fundação para a Ciência e Tecnologia under the VizBig project (PTDC/CCI-CIF/28939/2017).

References

1. Antunes, C., Silva, A.: New trends in knowledge driven data mining. In: ICEIS (1), pp. 346–351 (2014)
2. Elmasri, R., Navathe, S.B.: The enhanced entity-relationship (EER) model, pp. 107–135. Addison-Wesley (2000)
3. Erickson, N., et al.: AutoGluon-tabular: robust and accurate automl for structured data. arXiv preprint arXiv:2003.06505 (2020)
4. Feurer, M., Eggensperger, K., Falkner, S., Lindauer, M., Hutter, F.: Auto-sklearn 2.0: hands-free AutoML via meta-learning. arXiv preprint arXiv:2007.04074 (2020)
5. Gabrilovich, E., Markovitch, S.: Wikipedia-based semantic interpretation for natural language processing. J. Artif. Intell. Res. **34**, 443–498 (2009)
6. Galhotra, S., Khurana, U., Hassanzadeh, O., Srinivas, K., Samulowitz, H., Qi, M.: Automated feature enhancement for predictive modeling using external knowledge. In: 2019 International Conference on Data Mining Workshops (ICDMW), pp. 1094–1097. IEEE (2019)
7. Hu, Y.J., Kibler, D.: Generation of attributes for learning algorithms. In: AAAI/IAAI, vol. 1, pp. 806–811 (1996)
8. Hutter, F., Kotthoff, L., Vanschoren, J.: Automated Machine Learning: Methods, Systems, Challenges. Springer, Cham (2019). https://doi.org/10.1007/978-3-030-05318-5
9. LeDell, E., Poirier, S.: H2o AutoML: scalable automatic machine learning. In: Proceedings of AutoML Workshop at ICML, vol. 2020 (2020)
10. Olson, R.S., Moore, J.H.: TPOT: a tree-based pipeline optimization tool for automating machine learning. In: Workshop on Automatic Machine Learning, pp. 66–74. PMLR (2016)
11. Salguero, A.G., Medina, J., Delatorre, P., Espinilla, M.: Methodology for improving classification accuracy using ontologies: application in the recognition of activities of daily living. J. Ambient. Intell. Humaniz. Comput. **10**(6), 2125–2142 (2018). https://doi.org/10.1007/s12652-018-0769-4
12. Wang, D., et al.: Human-AI collaboration in data science: exploring data scientists' perceptions of automated AI. Proc. ACM Hum.-Comput. Interact. **3**(CSCW), 1–24 (2019)
13. Waring, J., Lindvall, C., Umeton, R.: Automated machine learning: review of the state-of-the-art and opportunities for healthcare. Artif. Intell. Med. **104**, 101822 (2020)

Temporal Nodes Causal Discovery for in Intensive Care Unit Survival Analysis

Ana Rita Nogueira[1,2(✉)], Carlos Abreu Ferreira[1], and João Gama[1]

[1] LIAAD - INESC TEC, Rua Dr Roberto Frias, 4200-465 Porto, Portugal
ana.r.nogueira@inesctec.pt
[2] Faculdade de Ciências da Universidade do Porto,
Rua do Campo Alegre 1021/1055, 4169-007 Porto, Portugal

Abstract. In hospital and after ICU discharge deaths are usual, given the severity of the condition under which many of them are admitted to these wings. Because of this, there is an urge to identify and follow these cases closely. Furthermore, as ICU data is usually composed of variables measured in varying time intervals, there is a need for a method that can capture causal relationships in this type of data. To solve this problem, we propose ItsPC, a causal Bayesian network that can model irregular multivariate time-series data. The preliminary results show that ItsPC creates smaller and more concise networks while maintaining the temporal properties. Moreover, its irregular approach to time-series can capture more relationships with the target than the Dynamic Bayesian Networks.

Keywords: Causal discovery · Bayesian networks · Irregular multivariate time-series

1 Introduction

In hospital and after discharge deaths in Intensive Care Unit (ICU)s are unfortunate but usual, given the severity of the condition under which many of them are admitted to these wings. However, some recent studies show that one in five patients die even after being discharged from the ICU from complications related to the admission, with some deaths being called as "failure to rescue" [10]. Given this, it is crucial to promptly identify and follow these cases closely so that, if possible, the outcome can be changed. The diagnosis of a medical problem can be seen as the relationship between a disease and the symptoms it induces. This notion of causality (finding out what is causing a set of symptoms) is implemented regularly in medicine, although not consciously or through algorithms. The application of causal discovery in the medical field has been debated over the years [6] since the application of this type of technique can help in the fastest diagnosis of certain diseases. However, working with medical data can be challenging since this type of data can be composed of thousands of variables,

G. Marreiros et al. (Eds.): EPIA 2022, LNAI 13566, pp. 587–598, 2022.
https://doi.org/10.1007/978-3-031-16474-3_48

measured only one time or in regular and irregular intervals, depending on the exams performed. Primarily ICU data is characterised by a high flow of information measured in different intervals, usually accompanied by the length of patient's stay as well as their outcome [12]. Moreover, this type of data usually comprises patient data where, for each subject, there is a set of measurements, hence being considered a panel or longitudinal data. This heterogeneity in the sampled data raises the need for specialised methodologies that (1) transform irregular multivariate time-series into stationary or (2) somehow deal with them as irregular time-series.

Causal Bayesian networks are a type of Bayesian Network that captures supposed causal relationships from observational data (data that represents a snapshot of a system) and are known to be an explicable method since their graph-like appearance mimics human decisions. This type of methodology can aid medical staff in performing simple decisions more easily, as the everyday user can easily understand it. PC algorithm [14] is an example of a Bayesian network specifically designed to ensure that every relationship can be assumed as causal. Although Bayesian networks are traditional methods designed for cross-sectional data, since they do not consider time, methods that deal with time have emerged in more recent years. This is the case of the Dynamic Bayesian Network (DBN)s (DBN) [5]. However, these methods have two significant restrictions: they can only be applied in stationary time-series data.

This paper aims to address the problem of ICU patients' non-survival early detection while maximising the data usage by taking advantage of the timing irregularity. To do this, we propose the Irregular time-series PC (ItsPC), a causal Bayesian network-like approach that can model irregular multivariate time-series data. This method models time by incorporating it into the variables' values (instead of creating new variables representing the stages in a particular timestamp). This method combines the time stamp of every instance during the measured value for each temporal variable, thus creating instances that represent both stage and time. To obtain a more accurate depiction of reality, every interval-value is adjusted according to the variables' parents (obtained from the network). Hence it is based on the parents' delayed manifestation and not on the absolute time. In this method, every variable represents a temporal change and every edge a causal, temporal relationship between variables [1].

This paper is organised as follows: Sect. 2 describes some essential definitions. Section 3 illustrates the problem and the used data, Sect. 4 describes the proposed approach, and Sect. 5 the results obtained in the tests.

2   Background

In this section, we introduce some important notations used throughout the document.

2.1   PC

PC is a constraint-based algorithm and was proposed by [14]. This algorithm relies on the *faithfulness* assumption (*"If we have a joint probability distribution*

P of the random variables in some set V and a DAG G = (V, E), (G, P) satisfies the faithfulness condition if, G entails all and only conditional independencies in P" [11]), meaning that all the independencies in a *DAG* (directed acyclic graph) need to respect the d-separation criterion. This algorithm is divided into two phases. The algorithm starts with a fully connected undirected graph in the first phase. It removes an edge if the two nodes are independent, *i.e.* if there is a set of nodes adjacent to both variables in which they are conditionally independent. One of the most applied statistical independence tests is G^2, proposed by [14], and then used in non-causal Bayesian networks by [15]. In the second phase, the algorithm orients the edges by first searching for v-structures ($A \rightarrow B \leftarrow C$) and then by applying a set of rules to create a completed partially directed acyclic graph (*CPDAG*) that is equivalent to the original one, where the faithfulness is respected.

2.2 Temporal Node Bayesian Networks

The Temporal node Bayesian Networks [1] are an extension of the Bayesian Networks, designed to deal with multivariate time-series data. Each node represents a temporal change (based on their relationships) in this method, and each edge represents a temporal relationship. This method first discretises all temporal variables, transforming them into time intervals. Next, it applies the K2 Bayesian network to this new discretised data set. After that, and using the information obtained from the model (such as the parents of each temporal variable), the algorithm adjusts the intervals present in the temporal variables and re-generates the model.

This methodology has an issue: as temporal variables, it only accepts the values that represents the moment where the value was measured, for example, at what time the doctor saw dilated pupils, hence dealing with them as binary variables, where each measurement details if something was measured or not and at what moment was measured. This majorly restrains the number of potential applications, especially in the medical domain, where variables can represent continuous values, or discrete stages, always measured in different intervals of time, consequently representing "hybrid variables" *STAGE A [t1-t2]* or *[interval of continuous measure]/[t1-t2]*. Besides this, the usage of K2 to create the Bayesian model does not ensure the existence of causal relationships between variables (temporal or not), and that can be crucial to identify what is causing changes in the system, as it is not prepared for such a task.

3 Problem

In hospital and after discharge deaths are a well-known problem by ICU practitioners [10]. Specially the death of discharged patients has been considered a problem, with studies showing that potentially one in five patients dies after being discharged from the hospital, with some of these deaths being considered preventable [8]. As some of these cases are considered as a failure of assistance

or "failure to rescue", meaning that, given awareness, they could be addressed and prevented, being their timely prediction a key to saving lives [13]. This problem can also be seen from a cost perspective [9]. After the first discharge, patients who need more care signify more costs for the hospital and the patient. Besides this, the care needed may be more intensive than if the patient had been closely followed after discharge or not been discharged. Machine learning algorithms can be applied to ensure: (1) the timely patient assessment and (2) cost reduction, as this type of methodologies can be more affordable than traditional approaches. This is the case of the work presented by Garcia-Gallo et al. [4], where the authors use a Stochastic Gradient Boosting methodology to model and predict one-year mortality in critical patients diagnosed with sepsis. A different approach was taken by Chia et al. [3], where the authors evaluated the usage of logistic regression, decision tree, and Cox-Proportional Hazards to identify the feature that better help predict the patients' outcomes.

Although there were significant advances in predicting ICU outcomes, none of these studies indeed considered the underlying supposed causes of hospital and after discharge deaths in ICU patients. Moreover, these studies do not consider the lack of regularity in hospital records.

3.1   Data

The physionet data set [7] is a subset of the MIMIC II, a data set with more than 25 000 patients admitted in the Boston's Beth Israel Deaconess Medical Center's ICU, from 2005 to 2008. This subset is composed by 12 000 patients (divided in train set [4000 patients], test set [4000 patients] and scoring set [4000 patients]), that were followed during the first 48 h of their stay in the ICU.

The raw data was cleaned and pre-processed. First, every variable was discretised according to the literature. Next, all the variables whose stages were not defined in the literature (for example, the patient's height) were discretised using equal-frequency discretisation with three bins. Next, all the variables with single values and with at least 50% missing data across all subjects were discarded. Finally, every patient with at least 50% of missing values across all variables was also removed. The new data set is composed of 11 657 patients, split into train and test sets. The following variables are present in the data: Patient identifier, Measurement's time, Height, Age, Weight, Alanine transaminase (ALP), Aspartate transaminase (AST), Alkaline phosphatase (ALP), Lactate, Biliburin, respiration rate, O_2 saturation in haemoglobin (SaO2), Blood urea nitrogen (BUN), Creatinine, Fractional inspired oxygen (FiO2), Glasgow Coma Scale (GCS), Glucose, Bicarbonate (HCO3), Hematocrit (HCT), Heart rate (HR), Potassium (K), Magnesium (Mg), Mean blood pressure (invasive and non-invasive) (MAP, NIMAP), Mechanical ventilation, Sodium (Na), Arterial blood gas (PaCO2, PaO2), Urine, Temperature, Blood pressure (invasive and non-invasive diastolic blood pressure, and invasive and non-invasive systolic blood pressure) (DiasABP, NIDiasABP, NISysABP, SysABP), Haemoglobin saturation, Platelets and Arterial pH, Length of stay and Survival. The target variable of this processed data set is the patient's survival. It is a merge between

Table 1. Mr. Doe's medical tests

Time	Age	Gender	Height	ICUType	BUN	Creatinine	GCS	SaO2	Weight	Length of stay	Survival
0	SENIOR	MALE	80	Surgical ICU	NA	NA	NA	NA	[171.5, 189.7)	[1, 9)	IN HOSPITAL DEATH
2.88	SENIOR	MALE	80	Surgical ICU	NA	NA	NA	NA	[171.5, 189.7)	[1, 9)	IN HOSPITAL DEATH
3.02	SENIOR	MALE	80	Surgical ICU	NA	NA	NA	NA	[171.5, 189.7)	[1, 9)	IN HOSPITAL DEATH
3.18	SENIOR	MALE	80	Surgical ICU	NA	NA	SEVERE	NA	[171.5, 189.7)	[1, 9)	IN HOSPITAL DEATH
4.18	SENIOR	MALE	80	Surgical ICU	NA	NA	SEVERE	NA	[171.5, 189.7)	[1, 9)	IN HOSPITAL DEATH
5.18	SENIOR	MALE	80	Surgical ICU	NA	NA	SEVERE	NA	[171.5, 189.7)	[1, 9)	IN HOSPITAL DEATH
5.85	SENIOR	MALE	80	Surgical ICU	NA	NA	SEVERE	NORMAL	[171.5, 189.7)	[1, 9)	IN HOSPITAL DEATH
6.18	SENIOR	MALE	80	Surgical ICU	NA	NA	SEVERE	NORMAL	[171.5, 189.7)	[1, 9)	IN HOSPITAL DEATH
6.43	SENIOR	MALE	80	Surgical ICU	NA	NA	SEVERE	NORMAL	[171.5, 89.7)	[1, 9)	IN HOSPITAL DEATH
6.85	SENIOR	MALE	80	Surgical ICU	NA	NA	SEVERE	NORMAL	[171.5, 189.7)	[1, 9)	IN HOSPITAL DEATH
7.18	SENIOR	MALE	80	Surgical ICU	NA	NA	MILD	NORMAL	[171.5, 189.7)	[1, 9)	IN HOSPITAL DEATH
8.18	SENIOR	MALE	80	Surgical ICU	NA	NA	MILD	NORMAL	[171.5, 189.7)	[1, 9)	IN HOSPITAL DEATH
8.53	SENIOR	MALE	80	Surgical ICU	HIGH	NORMAL	MILD	NORMAL	[171.5, 189.7)	[1, 9)	IN HOSPITAL DEATH
9.18	SENIOR	MALE	80	Surgical ICU	HIGH	NORMAL	MILD	NORMAL	[171.5, 189.7)	[1, 9)	IN HOSPITAL DEATH
...											
47.18	SENIOR	MALE	80	Surgical ICU	HIGH	NORMAL	SEVERE	NORMAL	[171.5, 189.7)	[1, 9)	IN HOSPITAL DEATH

the *Survival* and *In Hospital Death* variables present in the original data set. This new variable represents whether a patient died in the hospital after the discharge with a problem related to his first hospitalisation (DEATH AFTER DISCHARGE), if he died in the hospital, whether he is still in the ICU or another hospital inpatient unit (IN HOSPITAL DEATH) or is still alive (ALIVE) and is measured after the patients leave the ICU. These classes are distributed as follows: 61.20% (*ALIVE*), 15.51% (*IN HOSPITAL DEATH*) and 23.28% (*DEATH AFTER DISCHARGE*).

3.2 Running Example

A running example representing a patient admitted to the hospital ICU will be used to explain better the proposed methodology and how it is applied to the data. Patient 134432 is a 70 years old male admitted to the surgical ICU. For easier identification, we will call this patient John Doe. Mr Doe was followed for 48h during his stay in the ICU. During this period, several tests were performed and recorded. Table 1 represents part of these tests. This patient was hospitalised for three days and died in the hospital.

4   Methodology

In this section, we present the *Irregular time-series PC* or ItsPC, a causal Bayesian network for irregular multivariate time-series data, designed to deal with data that represents measurements done at specific moments and repeated several times, hence being represented by a value and a timestamp. The model creation process applied by this method can be divided into six steps: state/timestamp conjunction, model generation, first redefinition of state/timestamp conjunction, inexpressive intervals removal, second redefinition of state/ timestamp conjunction and optimal interval selection (Fig. 1).

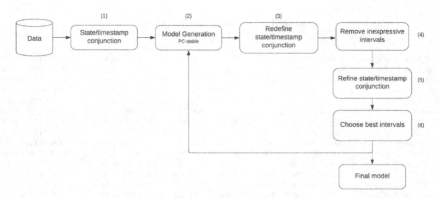

Fig. 1. ItsPC pipeline

Initially, the algorithm starts by merging the temporal states with the respective timestamps (Fig. 2, (1)). As shown in the running example (Table 1), the timestamp is saved separately from the measured correspondent value. For each discrete variable marked as varying over time, the algorithm divides the corresponding timestamps according to their categories (Fig. 2, (2)). For each category, the method discretises the timestamps (Fig. 2, (3)). In the presence of missing data, the unknown value is replaced by the state $UNK[min, max]$, where min and max represent the minimum and maximum timestamp found in that specific variable. In the running example, Mr Doe is grouped with other patients to create the merged states (to ensure (1) the states are meaningfully for the majority of the subjects and (2) the number of generated merged states is low). The result for the GCS (Glasgow Coma Scale) is shown in Table 2.

At this moment, and before we introduce the next step, it is essential to introduce the definition of initial and final cross-sectional variables. As initial variables, we perceive them as variables measured at the study's beginning and not changing over time (for example, age). In contrast, final variables are understood as variables measured only once, but after all, the temporal variables (for example, if a patient survived or not).

After generating the data set, PC (Fig. 3) is applied to create the first model. In this case, the method treats all variables as cross-sectional. To ensure precedence in the model (thus generating a model that genuinely represents time), no temporal variable can cause initial variables, and no final variable can cause initial or temporal variables.

After the network's creation, the model is analysed to discover the parents of the temporal variables. This information is later used to redefine the temporal variables. In Step 3, the Gaussian Mixture Models (GMM) creates new intervals for each partition based on the parent's information. These intervals are created by defining a n number of maximum intervals by partition. With this n value, the algorithm creates 1 to n different time intervals. Therefore, each partition, which represents a configuration of the parent nodes, has n different intervals. It is important to note that the minimum and maximum timestamps in each

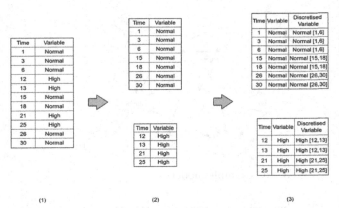

Fig. 2. First discretisation (example)

Table 2. Discretisation for Mr. Doe's GCS measure

Time	GCS
0	UNK [0, 48]
2.88	UNK [0, 48]
3.02	UNK [0, 48]
3.18	SEVERE [3, 23]
4.18	SEVERE [3, 23]
5.18	SEVERE [3, 23]
5.85	SEVERE [3, 23]
6.18	SEVERE [3, 23]
6.43	SEVERE [3, 23]
6.85	SEVERE [3, 23]
7.18	MILD [7, 35]
8.18	MILD [7, 35]
8.53	MILD [7, 35]
9.18	MILD [7, 35]
...	
47.18	SEVERE [25, 48]

interval are given by each cluster's minimum and maximum timestamps. Returning to Mr Doe's example, this patient (grouped with the other patients) has its temporal variables redefined (it is important to note that for this redefinition, we used the original states with no time associated), using the model generated in the previous step, more specifically the parents' information. Using the GCS variable and its respective parent ICUType (this variable is a initial variable that takes the values *Surgical ICU, Medical ICU, Cardiac Surgery Recovery Unit* and *Coronary Care Unit*), the method splits GCS' values and timestamps taking into account ICUType's values. To these subsets, the GMM is applied, resulting in the discretised timestamps presented in Table 3.

Before we move for the next step, it is important to note that from now on a partition is considered as a combination between a value of the parent and a value of the child. In Table 3 we have 4 different partitions (ICUType = SurgicalICU; GCS = SEVERE, ICUType = SurgicalICU; GCS = MILD, ICUType = Medical ICU; GCS = SEVERE and ICUType = MedicalICU; GCS = MILD).

As the number of intervals in each partition can be high but not expressive, depending on the number of parents and their values, a pruning method for removing inexpressive intervals is applied (all intervals with less than β instances are removed):

$$\beta = \frac{number\ of\ instances\ in\ the\ interval}{number\ of\ parent\ nodes \times 2} \tag{1}$$

The partitions are then combined based on common child values (before discretisation) For example, for $GCS = SEVERE$, the method combines the interval

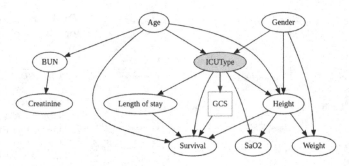

Fig. 3. PC example model

Table 3. Redefinition of GCS values using the parent's information (for simplicity, only two states of GCS and ICUType are used)

ICUType SurgicalICU	GCS SEVERE	[3–48]	ICUType MedicalMICU	GCS SEVERE	[18–35]	
		[3–25][29–48]			[18–21][23–35]	
		[3–16][17–24][29–48]			[18–21][23–26][30–35]	
	GCS MILD	[7–24]		GCS MILD	[7–44]	
		[7–12][14–24]			[7–30][31–44]	
		[7–8][10–12][14–24]			[7–24][26–29][30–44]	

set from *ICUType = SurgicalICU* and *ICUType = MedicalICU*. From these combination nine intervals set result: [3–48][18–35]; [3–48][18–21][23–35]; [3–48][18–21][23–26][30–35]; [3–25][29–48] [18–35]; [3–25][29–48] [18–21][23–35]; [3–25][29–48] [18–21][23–26][30–35]; [3–16][17–24][29–48][18–35]; [3–16][17–24][18–21][23–35] and [3–16] [17–24][18–21][23–26][30–35].

Since many of these intervals overlap, a set of rules is used to combine them: (1) if one interval is contained in another (e.g. [18–35] is contained in [3–48]), the new interval will be *[minimum of the two, maximum of the two]* ([3–48]) and (2), if two intervals partially overlap, ([3–25] and [18–35]), two new intervals are created: *[first interval minimum, average of contained values][average of contained values+unit, second interval maximum]* ([3–21.5][21.6–35]). This process is continuously updating the intervals until all the intervals are adjusted. With this step, the method ultimately tries to instantiate a child node as a delayed occurrence of the parent node and not in absolute time.

After this, another pruning is performed: all partitions that have only one interval or more than n intervals (user-defined) are removed. For example, this means that if we have an adjusted set of intervals for variable V, with the intervals [1–12][12.1–43][45–56][67–70][70.1–90], and n has the value 3, these will be discarded. This pruning ensures that all accepted intervals have a broad representation in the data and are not the representation of only a few examples. Finally, in Step 6, the method chooses the optimal intervals for each temporal variable's value. This selection is made by combining each of the potential intervals' sets for each variable's values. Then, a model is created (with configurations

identical to the first model). These models are then evaluated using the Brier Skill Score, a measure that calculates how precise a probability prediction in a model is (when compared to a reference) and is given by (2) [2] (the higher the value, the more precise is the prediction). In this equation, n represents the number of unmeasured variables in the set, P_i represents the probability obtained from the unseen variables and BS_{ref} represents the reference Brier Score (this value is obtained by calculating the probabilities for the same unseen variables, with the model used in the previous steps). To determine P_i, a random subset of nodes is selected and instantiated with random values based on the original data distribution. With these values, we predict the P_i, probability of the unmeasured variable i, with the measured variables. It is important to note that the Brier Score formula used in this methodology is not the original version (designed for any discrete data) but the binary version instead. We use this equation instead because the algorithm studies, for each event, the probability of a particular value and not all values that the unseen variable can take, hence being a binary *true* and *false* problem. Subsequently, the set intervals chosen is the one that maximises the Brier Skill Score.

$$BSS = 1 - \frac{BS}{BS^{ref}} \qquad BS = \frac{1}{n} \sum_{i=1}^{n} (1 - P_i)^2 \qquad (2)$$

Steps 2 to 6 of Fig. 1 are continually repeated until there are no changes to the model or data set.

5   Results and Discussion

To evaluate the proposed approach and make a comparative study, the following configuration of experiments: we compare the model generated by our approach with a model generated by a DBN [5], in terms of performance (accuracy and F1-score). To do this, we derived ten data sets from the original one, presented in Sect. 3.1, by randomly sampling 70% of the patients for the train set and 30% for the test set. Since the DBNs are a type of model that only deals with regular intervals of time, the data set presented in Sect. 3.1 was transformed. To create this new data set, the mean timestamp interval (t_{mean}), mean minimum timestamp (t_{min}) and mean maximum timestamp (t_{max}) were calculated. With this information, the original data set was transformed. This transformation was done following a set of rules. These rules were: (1) for each subject, the first and last time stamps were t_{min} and t_{max}, (2) all the timestamps are distance exactly t_{mean}, and (3) each new timestamp (for each subject) is filled with the nearest timestamp from the original data. Suppose a particular subject does not have timestamps before the new timestamp is measured. In that case, the values in the new timestamp entrance are filled with missing values and (4) all timestamps from the original data set that is higher than the t_{max} are discarded. The resulting data set is composed of 75 regular timestamps.

To better understand how the algorithms perform in a general hospital situation, where the system encapsulates patients from different services, thus with

Table 4. Results comparison

	Accuracy		F1-score	
	Dynamic Bayesian Network	ItsPC	Dynamic Bayesian Network	ItsPC
ALIVE	59.02 ± 0.70	+68.10 ± 0.45	71.98 ± 0.17	+78.31 ± 0.36
DEATH AFTER DISCHARGE	50.00 ± 0.03	+75.27 ± 0.45	0.02 ± 0.06	+24.08 ± 1.61
IN HOSPITAL DEATH	85.64 ± 0.21	86.43 ± 0.32	10.91 ± 11.71	+33.65 ± 1.61
Overall	53.65 ± 0.40	+64.82 ± 0.51	27.64 ± 3.91	+45.35 ± 0.62

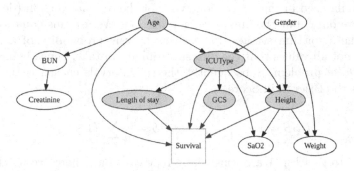

Fig. 4. Simplified model generated be ItsPC

distinct diseases and symptoms, we compared the DBNs and ItsPC (Table 4). If we analyse Table 4, which represents the mean accuracy and F1-score by class and overall accuracy and F1-score, it is possible to see that, in general, the proposed methodology has a better performance than the baseline (DBN).

To further assess the significance of these discrepancies, the performance of ItsPC in each test set was compared to the reference (DBN) using the Wilcoxon signed ranked-test. The sign ± indicates that the algorithm is significantly better/worse than the reference with a p-value of less than 5%. As it is possible to observe in Table 4, the difference between the two methods is significant. Furthermore, considering the proposed practical problem to assess if the patient will parish in the hospital or after being discharged, it is possible to notice that ItsPC is more successful in detecting future dead cases than the baseline. Despite this, both methods demonstrate difficulty in accessing death after discharge patients, which is expectable since, in theory, these patients are not that different from those who survive.

As a final note, it is essential to grasp that ItsPC generates significantly smaller models than DBN (an average of 37 nodes and 30 edges versus 2438 nodes and 4873 edges). Suppose we analyse Fig. 4 and Fig. 5, which represent the simplified versions of the models generated by ItsPC and DBN (with only nodes around the *Survival* node), respectively, we can see that there is a significant difference in size between the models. This happens due to the fact of how the algorithms deal

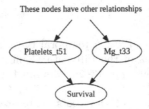

Fig. 5. Simplified model generated by DBN (all the other 2435 nodes not related with *Survival* are omitted)

with temporal variables: while DBN encapsulates time through the creation of new variables that represent each of the temporal variables in each timestamp, ItsPC encodes time in the nodes themselves, thus not creating more variables, instead of creating more states in each variable. This leads to smaller and more interpretable models. Moreover, ItsPC finds relationships between a patient's survival and non-temporal variables, for example, ICU type and age, while DBN only finds relationships with temporal variables. This means that ItsPC's model can partially access the initial potential outcome with non-temporal information from the first moment. From a partitioner's perspective, having a clue right away about the future outcome of a patient, as well as knowing what exams to be more focused on, means that, for example, it is possible to recommend specific treatments that slow or even prevent the potential outcome.

6   Conclusions

In hospital and after ICU discharge, deaths are usual, given the severity of the condition under which many of them are admitted to these wings. Because of this, there is an urge to identify and follow these cases closely. Given their interpretable properties, as they mimic human decision-making, Bayesian Networks, especially methods like PC, can aid in this problem. They can model the supposed causal relationships present in the data. As ICU data is usually composed of variables measured in varying time intervals, there is a need for a method that can capture causal relationships in this type of data. To solve this problem, we propose ItsPC, a causal discovery methodology that can model causal relationships in irregular multivariate time-series data. The results found that ItsPC creates smaller and more concise networks while maintaining the temporal properties that more accurately predict these cases.

In the future, we hope to further address this problem by focusing more on differentiating the death after discharging patients from the other population.

Acknowledgment. This research was supported by the *Fundação* para a Ciência e Tecnologia (FCT), Portugal for the PhD Grant SFRH/BD/146197/2019.

References

1. Arroyo-Figueroa, G., Sucar, L.E.: A temporal Bayesian network for diagnosis and prediction. In: Proceedings of the Fifteenth Conference on Uncertainty in Artificial Intelligence, UAI 1999, pp. 13–20. Morgan Kaufmann Publishers Inc., San Francisco (1999)
2. Brier, G.W.: Verification of forecasts expressed in terms of probability. Monthly Weather Rev. **78**(1), 1–3 (1950). https://doi.org/10.1175/1520-0493(1950)078⟨0001:VOFEIT⟩2.0.CO;2
3. Chia, A.H.T., et al.: Explainable machine learning prediction of ICU mortality. Inform. Med. Unlocked **25**, 100674 (2021). https://doi.org/10.1016/j.imu.2021.100674
4. García-Gallo, J.E., Fonseca-Ruiz, N., Celi, L., Duitama-Muñoz, J.: A machine learning-based model for 1-year mortality prediction in patients admitted to an intensive care unit with a diagnosis of sepsis. Med. Intensiva **44**(3), 160–170 (2020)
5. Ghahramani, Z.: Learning dynamic Bayesian networks. In: Giles, C.L., Gori, M. (eds.) NN 1997. LNCS, vol. 1387, pp. 168–197. Springer, Heidelberg (1998). https://doi.org/10.1007/BFb0053999
6. Giorello, G.: Causality in Medicine (2008)
7. Goldberger, A.L., et al.: PhysioBank, PhysioToolkit, and PhysioNet: components of a new research resource for complex physiologic signals. Circulation **101**(23), E215–E220 (2000)
8. Hamsen, U., et al.: Mortality in severely injured patients: nearly one of five non-survivors have been already discharged alive from ICU. BMC Anesthesiol. **20**(1), 243 (2020). https://doi.org/10.1186/s12871-020-01159-8
9. Katsiari, M., Ntorlis, K., Mathas, C., Nikolaou, C.: Predictors of adverse outcome early after ICU discharge. Int. J. Crit. Care Emerg. Med. **5**(1), 1–6 (2018)
10. Lee, J., et al.: Who dies after ICU discharge? Retrospective analysis of prognostic factors for in-hospital mortality of ICU survivors. J. Korean Med. Sci. **32**(3), 528–533 (2017). https://doi.org/10.3346/jkms.2017.32.3.528. 28145659[pmid]
11. Neapolitan, R.E., et al.: Learning Bayesian Networks, vol. 38. Pearson Prentice Hall, Upper Saddle River (2004)
12. Shillan, D., Sterne, J.A.C., Champneys, A., Gibbison, B.: Use of machine learning to analyse routinely collected intensive care unit data: a systematic review. Crit. Care **23**(1), 284 (2019). https://doi.org/10.1186/s13054-019-2564-9
13. Sparling, J., Bittner, E.A.: Mortality risk after ICU discharge: it's not over until it's over*. Crit. Care Med. **48**(1) (2020)
14. Spirtes, P., Glymour, C., Scheines, R.: Causation, Prediction, and Search, vol. 1, 2nd edn. The MIT Press, Cambridge (2001)
15. Tsamardinos, I., Brown, L.E., Aliferis, C.F.: The max-min hill-climbing Bayesian network structure learning algorithm. Mach. Learn. **65**(1), 31–78 (2006)

MapIntel: Enhancing Competitive Intelligence Acquisition Through Embeddings and Visual Analytics

David Silva[✉][iD] and Fernando Bacao[iD]

NOVA IMS, NOVA University of Lisbon, Campus de Campolide,
1070-312 Lisbon, Portugal
dfhssilva@protonmail.com, bacao@novaims.unl.pt

Abstract. Competitive Intelligence allows an organization to keep up with market trends and foresee business opportunities. This practice is mainly performed by analysts scanning for any piece of valuable information in a myriad of dispersed and unstructured sources. Here we present MapIntel, a system for acquiring intelligence from vast collections of text data by representing each document as a multidimensional vector that captures its own semantics. The system is designed to handle complex Natural Language queries and visual exploration of the corpus, potentially aiding overburdened analysts in finding meaningful insights to help decision-making. The system *searching* module uses a retriever and re-ranker engine that first finds the closest neighbors to the query embedding and then sifts the results through a cross-encoder model that identifies the most relevant documents. The *browsing* module also leverages the embeddings by projecting them onto two dimensions while preserving the original landscape, resulting in a map where semantically related documents form topical clusters which we capture using topic modeling. This map aims at promoting a fast overview of the corpus while allowing a more detailed exploration and interactive information encountering process. In this work, we evaluate the system and its components on the 20 newsgroups dataset and demonstrate the superiority of Transformer-based components.

Keywords: Sentence embeddings · Transformer architecture · Visual analytics · Information retrieval · Topic modeling · Competitive Intelligence

1 Introduction

Competitive Intelligence (CI) is the process and forward-looking practices used in producing knowledge about the competitive environment to improve organizational performance [17]. CI has a fundamental role in helping businesses remain competitive, influencing a wide range of decision-making areas, and leading to

ⓒ The Author(s), under exclusive license to Springer Nature Switzerland AG 2022
G. Marreiros et al. (Eds.): EPIA 2022, LNAI 13566, pp. 599–610, 2022.
https://doi.org/10.1007/978-3-031-16474-3_49

substantial improvements such as the increase of revenue, new products or services, cost savings, time savings, profit increases, and achievement of financial goals.

Competitive Intelligence analysts are responsible for developing the CI task through a combination of gathering data, processing it, and communicating information. The digitalization of the market and the growth of the data economy have pushed the business environment to an online realm where every action and event is public and thus potentially relevant for decision-making. This shift has produced a large volume of data about products, customers, competitors, and any aspect of the business environment that can be used to foresee opportunities and risks. Given the vastness and diversity of this data, it has become necessary to design tools that can aid analysts in the CI gathering and analysis process. Therefore, the goal is to enhance the analyst's task by providing a means to explore, organize and visualize the environmental data present in the array of existing sources.

Traditionally, the most important sources of CI have been news providers, corporate websites, and trade publications, respectively [19]. With the advent of the internet, new sources, such as social networks [7], have emerged, while existing ones have become enriched and easily accessible. Despite the increased availability, CI resources are dispersed through a variety of websites and the underlying data is unstructured and noisy. These characteristics add to the difficulty of the analyst's task and exacerbate the need for tools to support it.

Various studies have attempted to create systems for exploring and gathering intelligence from extensive collections of textual data [5,7,9,14]. These studies have consistently applied Natural Language Processing (NLP) techniques to help users comprehend large volumes of text without requiring to sift through every document. [7] designed a system for CI that captures data from multiple sources, cleans it, uses NLP to identify and tag the relevant content, stores it, generates consolidated reports, and produces alerts on predefined triggers.

Although the previous systems have been used for dealing with large amounts of text successfully, insufficient attention has been paid to the exploratory and serendipitous aspects of the analyst's task. Accordingly, we propose an information environment that supports analysts in having stimulating and productive information encounters [8]. This is achieved by incorporating two types of information acquisition tasks: *searching*, consisting of an information retrieval module that allows *ad hoc* queries on the entire document collection, giving the user the ability to seek information actively, and *browsing*, consisting of a visualization module that equips the user with tools to actively or passively acquire information through the visual exploration of the document corpus (and its thematic cohorts) in a two-dimensional map.

With the recent emergence of the Transformer architecture [28], significant improvements were made in several NLP subdomains, having reached state-of-the-art results in a wide range of tasks [28]. This new architecture is based solely on the attention mechanism, providing parallelization capabilities and thus avoiding the sequential nature of existing Recurrence models. The attention

mechanism allows incorporating information from the input sequence words into the one it is currently being processed, thus providing "context" to the word from the rest of the sequence. Language models like Bidirectional Encoder Representations from Transformers (BERT) [6] leverage this architecture, making up a large part of the modern NLP landscape by providing a powerful off-the-shelf way to create state-of-the-art models for a wide range of tasks. The Transformer flexibility, allied to its reduced training times and improved ability to learn long-range relationships between terms in a sequence, make it one of the pillars of modern NLP research, and we intend to apply this architecture in our work.

This paper explores Transformer-based models for representing documents as semantic vectors. These vectorial representations are commonly denominated as embeddings, and we intend to use them in a CI system as a mechanism for extracting information from environmental data. Furthermore, the system facilitates information encountering by incorporating *searching* and *browsing* mechanisms that leverage the document embeddings. We have named the proposed system MapIntel which derives from (Competitive) Intelligence Map.

2 Related Work

The process of extracting business-related information for anticipating risks and opportunities is an important task for many companies, yet analysts are overwhelmed with extensive amounts of unstructured data. To support CI analysts, we propose an NLP system for exploring and gathering intelligence from large collections of textual data. To situate our contribution, we review existing work on similar systems applied in CI as well as in other domains, in this section.

Arguably, the closest method to ours in terms of domain application is [7]. They formulated a system for acquiring competitive intelligence from different web resources, including social media, using a wide array of text mining techniques. They also showed how the system can be integrated with the business data and adopted for future decision-making. Their goal is to help the analyst in the task of reading, extracting information, and organizing the data. The paper presents an approach for labeling news articles according to CI-related topics by applying Latent Dirichlet Allocation (LDA) [4] clustering. The labeling contributes to the organization of the collection and facilitates the information extraction process.

[14] proposed a method for modeling and mapping topics from bibliometric data and built a web application based on this method. The produced map allows users to read a body of research "at a distance" while providing multiple levels of detail of the documents' topics. They also incorporated a time dimension, allowing users to understand the evolution of the topics over time. They applied Non-negative Matrix Factorization [16] to discover the underlying topics in the data and obtain vectorial representations of the documents, followed by t-distributed Stochastic Neighbor Embedding (t-SNE) [27] for visualizing the documents, resulting in a two-dimensional representation of the corpus. To allow for different detail levels, the authors produced two maps: a coarse map of 9 topics that gives a general overview of the topics within the data and a detailed map

of 36 topics that captures more specific research themes. The web application consists of an interactive dashboard that allows users to explore the map of documents and easily extract information.

We based our *searching* module on the Vector Space Model (VSM) [26, p. 120–126], a common framework in Information Retrieval, consisting of representing a set of documents as vectors in a vector space while also allowing full-text queries to be represented in the same space. The model then ranks each document in decreasing order of their similarity with the query. The fundamental assumption of the model is that similar documents will be placed close together in the vector space, whereas dissimilar documents will be far away. An application of VSM for querying COVID-19 literature can be found in [9]. They proposed Co-Search, an Information Retrieval system that combines semantic search, question answering, and abstractive summarization. The system uses Sentence-BERT (SBERT) [24], a Transformer-based model for representing documents as semantic vectors, combining it with approximate nearest neighbors and cosine similarity to return the relevant results for a query.

A more recent work focusing on the frontier between Computer Graphics and Machine Learning is *Cartolabe* [5]. *Cartolabe* is a web-based, scalable and efficient system for visualizing and exploring large textual corpora, relying on topic modeling algorithms like LDA [4] to represent documents as vectors of topics and on UMAP [20] to produce a 2-dimensional plane that preserves the original topology and neighborhood of the documents. Additionally, they provided an interactive high-level visualization that allows exploration of the corpus in real-time by offloading most of the computations to the data pre-processing pipeline making the system highly scalable to large collections of documents. We intend to apply the same idea of performing the pre-processing offline to improve the system's responsiveness and user interaction. Contrarily to *Cartolabe*, we aim to explore Transformer-based embeddings instead of topic vectors due to the novelty aspect of this architecture and the improved results it has shown in multiple benchmarks in other NLP subdomains.

3   MapIntel

We propose MapIntel - Fig. 1, a system that supports exploring a document collection while promoting serendipity and satisfying emerging information needs by allowing full-text queries over the entire collection. The system is scalable to large amounts of data, is dynamic as it regularly integrates new data, and is fast. It is composed of three main pipelines: Indexing, Query, and Visualization whose objectives are to get documents and their metadata from a source to a database, retrieve the most relevant results to a user query, and produce an interactive interface for exploring the document collection, respectively.

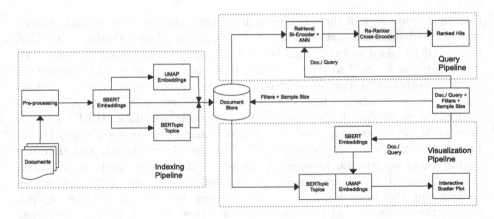

Fig. 1. MapIntel architecture. Composed of three main pipelines: **Indexing**, **Query**, and **Visualization**

3.1 Indexing

In this work we decided to focus on how NLP, particularly sentence embeddings, could help organize, explore, and retrieve text documents in the CI domain. Thus, we have not developed the precedent tasks of data collection and pre-processing. Nevertheless, it is essential to point out that the system's quality is extremely reliant on these steps, as if we feed it non-ideal data, we will get non-ideal results.

Once new documents are fed to the system, their respective embeddings are computed. This process is the basis of our work as it allows the encoding of the semantic identity of the document onto a vector of a given dimensionality. This semantic identity describes the subject of the document, and can be used to compare documents between each other *i.e.*, documents with the same subject will be close in the semantic space and vice-versa. We used SBERT [24], a derivative of the Transformer-based BERT model, to embed the documents using a pre-trained encoder trained on reducing the distance between queries and relevant results in the MS MARCO dataset [2]. This step produced vectors of 768 dimensions, which we then reduced to 2 dimensions using the Uniform Manifold Approximation and Projection (UMAP) [20] algorithm. This aspect is another crucial component of MapIntel as it allows the organization and localization of the entire document collection in a 2-dimensional map, which can be used to explore and interact with the data.

We also applied a topic modeling technique called BERTopic [10], based on the work of [1]. Topic modeling unveils the latent semantic structure of the data and unlike some of the classical techniques such as LDA [4] and pLSA [11], BERTopic leverages the SBERT embeddings and their capacity to encode the semantic attributes of a document to find the most representative topics of a corpus. BERTopic clusters the documents to find the densest areas of the semantic space while identifying outliers. The primary assumption behind BERTopic is

that each dense area in the semantic space is generated by a latent topic shared among the documents that comprise it. Finally, a class-based variant of TF-IDF (c-TF-IDF) is used to extract an importance value of each word for each cluster, which can be used to represent each topic as the set of its most important words. Another advantage of BERTopic over the classical approaches is that we can choose the number of topics by merging less representative topics.

Finally, we loaded the documents including their metadata, SBERT embeddings, UMAP embeddings, and topics into a database. We used Open Distro for Elasticsearch[1]—an open-source, RESTful, distributed search and analytics engine based on Apache Lucene[2]—to store the data, organize it in an index, and perform full-text search on it. We can think of the described approach as an Indexing Pipeline—Fig. 1—that extracts new raw documents from a data source, pre-processes and manipulates them, stores the results in a database, and indexes the documents for future search tasks.

3.2 Query

Finding meaningful information within a large amount of data is a sizable part of the CI task. The ability to retrieve relevant documents from a large collection of news articles through natural language queries empowers the CI analyst with an easy and intuitive interface to scan the environment.

MapIntel provides a searching functionality that can leverage the SBERT embeddings by projecting the query string onto the same vector space as the corpus and computing its k-nearest neighbors *i.e.* finding the k documents whose embedding vectors are closest to the query embedding vector. Since the embedding vectors encode the semantic identity of each document, this method provides semantically relevant results for a given query. Furthermore, we employ a highly performant and scalable similarity search engine by implementing Approximate Nearest Neighbors (ANN) search based on Hierarchical Navigable Small World Graphs [18]. The kNN search can also be combined with binary filters that help the user obtain focused results based on characteristics of the documents such as publication date and topic.

Once again, we can think of the search functionality as a pipeline, illustrated in Fig. 1, where we feed a query string and some binary filters, and obtain documents ordered by their relevance to the query. We employ a Retrieve and Re-rank pipeline based on the works of [13, 21] composed by a "Retrieval Bi-Encoder + ANN" node that performs kNN semantic search, and by a "Re-Ranker Cross-Encoder" node consisting of a BERT model fine-tuned on the MS MARCO dataset that receives a document and query pair as input and predicts the probability of the document being relevant to the query.

The pipeline works by taking advantage of the characteristics of both nodes. The Bi-Encoder, together with ANN search, can retrieve fairly relevant candidates while dealing efficiently with a large collection of records. The Cross-Encoder is not as efficient since it has to be performed independently for each

---

[1] opendistro.github.io/for-elasticsearch.

[2] lucene.apache.org.

document, given a query. However, since attention is performed across the query and the document, the performance is higher in the second node [12]. Therefore, we combined both nodes by retrieving a large set of candidates from the entire collection using the Bi-Encoder, and filtering the most relevant candidates with the Cross-Encoder while removing noisy results.

With this pipeline, we can provide relevant documents to the user given a query and binary filters while ranking them according to a relevancy score. As an additional feature, we can input a document instead of a query, allowing us to search for semantically similar documents within the collection.

3.3   Visualization

We conceptualized a visual interface that organizes and displays the documents to facilitate the environment scanning task, giving the user the ability to browse the data and zoom on particular regions of the semantic space. The interface uses the UMAP algorithm to reduce the dimensionality of the original semantic space to a 2-dimensional representation that reliably preserves the original topology.

The methodology employed to produce the interface is described in Fig. 1 (Visualization Pipeline). It begins by taking the same inputs passed to the Query pipeline: a query, and a set of filters. The common inputs create a connection between the two modules—when the user queries the database, the query text is projected onto the 2-dimensional map and the filters define which documents are displayed in the map. In addition to the common inputs, we require a relative sample size that defines the percentage of randomly chosen documents (after applying the filters) to be displayed in the map. This step is necessary as inter-action with the map is hindered by a large number of data points, resulting in a slow and unresponsive experience. Notice that the sample size does not affect the query results, as the search is always performed on the entire collection.

The map provides a means to explore the documents and the different seman-tic cohorts present within the collection. We color-code the points with the doc-uments' topics identified in the Indexing stage, allowing us to visualize the latent semantic structure of the data, and when hovered, the points display their cor-responding title and content attributes.

4   Evaluation

Our methodology addresses the issues of information dispersion and overload impacting the CI analysts' tasks. The proposed system provides searching and browsing capabilities, contributing to an easier understanding of the business environment by supporting analysts in seeking specific information while pro-moting undirected information encountering. In this section, we elaborate our choices in the design of the MapIntel system with the results of our experiments and analyze the different components of the system individually.

4.1   Experimental Setup

We evaluate our system quantitatively using the 20 newsgroups [23] dataset and the document labels provided. This dataset consists of around 18,000 newsgroups posts on 20 topics divided into 6 main groups: "Computer," "Recreation," "Science," "Miscellaneous," "Politics," and "Religion." We opted to use this dataset because of the presence of labels that describe the semantic meaning of each document, allowing us to have a reference which we can compare the identified topics with.

Given the inherent difficulty of evaluating the system in its entirety, we decided to deal with each component separately, however since every component of our system depends on the vector representation of the documents, we cannot guarantee an orthogonal evaluation of the components. We focus our experiments in comparing 2 of the main components of the MapIntel system: the Sentence Embeddings and the Topic Model. For the former component, we evaluated the Paragraph Vector (or Doc2Vec) [15] and the SBERT [24] models, whereas for the latter we focused on LDA [4], BERTopic [10], and Contextualized Topic Model (CTM) [3].

We use three main metrics to guide our model comparison. To evaluate the quality of the two-dimensional projections, we use the Accuracy of a kNN classifier on the 20 newsgroup labels given these embeddings [20] (we present the average over the range $k = \{10, 20, 40, 80, 160\}$). To evaluate how well the assigned topics correlate with the true labels, we use the Normalized Mutual Information (NMI) - the closer to 1 the value of this metric, the better we can capture the true topical nature of the documents, reflected by their labels. Finally, to measure the quality of the words that describe each topic, we apply the Topic Coherence (C_v) [25] metric, indicating whether the words that compose a given topic support each other.

We performed hyperparameter tuning using a multi-objective approach to optimize the three metrics specified previously. We used the Tree-structured Parzen Estimator (TPE) algorithm [22] for sampling the hyperparameter space at each trial of the optimization process. For each trial, we evaluated the sampled hyperparameters using a 5-fold cross-validation approach where the folds preserve the percentage of samples of each class. In total, 100 trials were evaluated.

4.2   Results

Our results based on the setup described above are shown in Table 1. For each trial, we report the average results and standard deviations over the cross-validation folds. The table contains the best trials for each of the Topic/Embedding model combinations according to the average of the three objective metrics, which we applied MinMax scaling to avoid any impact of the metrics scale on the choice of the best model. We can see that the combination that uses BERTopic and SBERT outperform the others with respect to both NMI and C_v while having a within standard deviation kNN Classifier

Accuracy to the best value. Another interesting observation is that combinations using SBERT have generally better results. To facilitate results reproduction efforts, we open-sourced the code developed for the experiments at github.com/NOVA-IMS-Innovation-and-Analytics-Lab/mapintel_research.

Table 1. Hyperparameter tuning best trials per topic and embedding model according to the MinMax average of the multiple objective metrics.

Topic model	Embedding model	MinMax average	NMI	Coherence C_v	kNN Accuracy
BERTopic	Doc2Vec	0.50	0.11 ± 0.01	0.72 ± 0.02	0.16 ± 0.01
BERTopic	SBERT	**0.94**	$\mathbf{0.36 \pm 0.03}$	$\mathbf{0.76 \pm 0.08}$	0.36 ± 0.01
CTM	Doc2Vec	0.56	0.23 ± 0.02	0.55 ± 0.02	0.24 ± 0.03
CTM	SBERT	0.70	0.33 ± 0.02	0.58 ± 0.02	0.28 ± 0.04
LDA	Doc2Vec	0.58	0.25 ± 0.03	0.53 ± 0.03	0.25 ± 0.01
LDA	SBERT	0.71	0.26 ± 0.03	0.53 ± 0.03	$\mathbf{0.37 \pm 0.05}$

Additionally, we present the UMAP 2-dimensional maps of the documents in the 20 newsgroups dataset. Figure 2 shows the comparison between the distribution of the original labels and the topics assigned by the best performing model according to the MinMax average score for the train data. Likewise, Fig. 3 shows the same comparison for the test data and demonstrates the ability of the model to generalize to unseen samples. We can see that the identified topical cohorts are mostly matching with the original groups, indicating that the embeddings have learned the original labels in a fully unsupervised way. Additionally, it is possible to see that semantically similar topics are located close to each other in the map. This is the case of all the computation related topics such as *window.server.windows.motif.display* and *format.files.graphics.file.gif*. Finally, there is also an agreement between the topic meaning given by the top 5 words describing the topics and the original label description. For example, the same points that have the label *sci.space* also have the topic *space.launch.nasa.orbit.shuttle*.

An important characteristic of BERTopic is that it is able to identify noise, leading to a topic assignment where a portion of the observation are classified as outliers. This produces a cleaner map to explore the documents at the loss of samples that are not given a topic. In Fig. 2 (right) the percentage of documents classified into the aforementioned category is 51.4% - these are the light grey points scattered across the map.

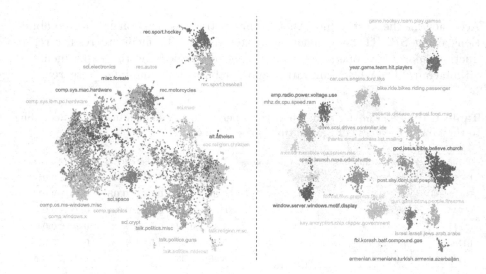

Fig. 2. Comparison between UMAP planes of **train data** with original (left) and topic labels (right).

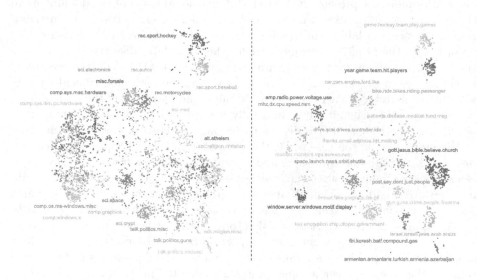

Fig. 3. Comparison between UMAP planes of **test data** with original (left) and topic labels (right).

5   Conclusion

In this paper, we presented MapIntel, a new system for extracting knowledge from large corpora of text documents. MapIntel differentiates from previous systems in that it leverages Transformer-based document embeddings to provide efficient, natural language searching of documents. The use of Transformer-based

embeddings allows to harness the semantic attributes of the documents, which can then be explored in a 2-dimensional map, produced using UMAP. Additionally, MapIntel also organizes the documents in topical cohorts, providing yet another framework for the interaction of the user with the corpus. The system is centered around the concept of information encountering [8], providing *browsing* and *searching* capabilities to acquire information and promote serendipity. MapIntel is aimed at supporting Competitive Intelligence analysts by providing a tool that facilitates the exploration and monitoring of the competitive environment from textual data.

Acknowledgment. This work was supported by the *Fundação para a Ciência e Tecnologia of Ministério da Ciência e Tecnologia e Ensino Superior* (research grant under the DSAIPA/DS/0116/2019 project).

References

1. Angelov, D.: Top2Vec: distributed representations of topics. arXiv:2008.09470 [cs, stat] (2020)
2. Bajaj, P., et al.: MS MARCO: a human generated MAchine Reading COmprehension dataset. arXiv:1611.09268 [cs] (2018)
3. Bianchi, F., Terragni, S., Hovy, D.: Pre-training is a hot topic: contextualized document embeddings improve topic coherence. arXiv:2004.03974 [cs] (2021)
4. Blei, D.M., Ng, A.Y., Jordan, M.I.: Latent Dirichlet allocation. J. Mach. Learn. Res. **3**, 993–1022 (2003)
5. Caillou, P., Renault, J., Fekete, J.D., Letournel, A.C., Sebag, M.: Cartolabe: a web-based scalable visualization of large document collections. IEEE Comput. Graphics Appl. **41**(2), 76–88 (2021). https://doi.org/10.1109/MCG.2020.3033401
6. Devlin, J., Chang, M.W., Lee, K., Toutanova, K.: BERT: pre-training of deep bidirectional transformers for language understanding. arXiv:1810.04805 [cs] (2019)
7. Dey, L., Haque, S.M., Khurdiya, A., Shroff, G.: Acquiring competitive intelligence from social media. In: Proceedings of the 2011 Joint Workshop on Multilingual OCR and Analytics for Noisy Unstructured Text Data, MOCR_AND 2011, pp. 1–9. Association for Computing Machinery, New York (2011). https://doi.org/10.1145/2034617.2034621
8. Erdelez, S., Makri, S.: Information encountering re-encountered: a conceptual re-examination of serendipity in the context of information acquisition. J. Documentation **76**(3), 731–751 (2020). https://doi.org/10.1108/JD-08-2019-0151
9. Esteva, A., et al.: CO-search: COVID-19 information retrieval with semantic search, question answering, and abstractive summarization. arXiv:2006.09595 [cs] (2020)
10. Grootendorst, M.: BERTopic: leveraging BERT and c-TF-IDF to create easily interpretable topics (2020). https://doi.org/10.5281/zenodo.4381785
11. Hofmann, T.: Probabilistic latent semantic indexing. In: Proceedings of the 22nd Annual International ACM SIGIR Conference on Research and Development in Information Retrieval, pp. 50–57 (1999)
12. Humeau, S., Shuster, K., Lachaux, M.A., Weston, J.: Poly-encoders: transformer architectures and pre-training strategies for fast and accurate multi-sentence scoring (2019). https://doi.org/10.48550/ARXIV.1905.01969

13. Kratzwald, B., Eigenmann, A., Feuerriegel, S.: RankQA: neural question answering with answer re-ranking. arXiv:1906.03008 [cs] (2019)
14. Lafia, S., Kuhn, W., Caylor, K., Hemphill, L.: Mapping research topics at multiple levels of detail. Patterns **2**(3), 100210 (2021). https://doi.org/10.1016/j.patter.2021.100210
15. Le, Q., Mikolov, T.: Distributed representations of sentences and documents. In: International Conference on Machine Learning, pp. 1188–1196. PMLR (2014)
16. Lee, D.D., Seung, H.S.: Learning the parts of objects by non-negative matrix factorization. Nature **401**(6755), 788–791 (1999). https://doi.org/10.1038/44565
17. Madureira, L., Popovič, A., Castelli, M.: Competitive intelligence: a unified view and modular definition. Technol. Forecast. Soc. Chang. **173**, 121086 (2021). https://doi.org/10.1016/j.techfore.2021.121086
18. Malkov, Y.A., Yashunin, D.A.: Efficient and robust approximate nearest neighbor search using Hierarchical Navigable Small World graphs. arXiv:1603.09320 [cs] (2018)
19. Marin, J., Poulter, A.: Dissemination of competitive intelligence. J. Inf. Sci. **30**(2), 165–180 (2004). https://doi.org/10.1177/0165551504042806
20. McInnes, L., Healy, J., Melville, J.: UMAP: uniform manifold approximation and projection for dimension reduction. arXiv:1802.03426 [cs, stat] (2020)
21. Nogueira, R., Cho, K.: Passage Re-ranking with BERT. arXiv:1901.04085 [cs] (2020)
22. Ozaki, Y., Tanigaki, Y., Watanabe, S., Onishi, M.: Multiobjective tree-structured parzen estimator for computationally expensive optimization problems. In: Proceedings of the 2020 Genetic and Evolutionary Computation Conference, GECCO 2020, pp. 533–541. Association for Computing Machinery, New York (2020). https://doi.org/10.1145/3377930.3389817
23. Pedregosa, F., et al.: Scikit-learn: machine learning in Python. J. Mach. Learn. Res. **12**, 2825–2830 (2011)
24. Reimers, N., Gurevych, I.: Sentence-BERT: sentence embeddings using Siamese BERT-networks. arXiv:1908.10084 [cs] (2019)
25. Röder, M., Both, A., Hinneburg, A.: Exploring the space of topic coherence measures. In: Proceedings of the Eighth ACM International Conference on Web Search and Data Mining, WSDM 2015, pp. 399–408. Association for Computing Machinery, New York (2015). https://doi.org/10.1145/2684822.2685324
26. Schütze, H., Manning, C.D., Raghavan, P.: Introduction to Information Retrieval, vol. 39. Cambridge University Press, Cambridge (2008)
27. Van der Maaten, L., Hinton, G.: Visualizing data using t-SNE. J. Mach. Learn. Res. **9**(11) (2008)
28. Vaswani, A., et al.: Attention is all you need. arXiv:1706.03762 [cs] (2017)

A Learning-to-Rank Approach for Spare Parts Consumption in the Repair Process

Edson Duarte[✉][ID], Daniel de Haro Moraes[ID], and Lucas Leonardo Padula[ID]

Venturus Innovation Center, Campinas, Brazil
edson.duarte@venturus.org.br
http://www.venturus.org.br/

Abstract. The repair process of devices is an important part of the business of many original equipment manufacturers. The consumption of spare parts, during the repair process, is driven by the defects found during inspection of the devices, and these parts are a big part of the costs in the repair process. But current Supply Chain Control Tower solutions do not provide support for the automatic check of spare parts consumption in the repair process.

In this paper, we investigate a multi-label classification problem and present a learning-to-rank approach, where we simulate the passage of time while training hundreds of Logistic Regression Machine Learning models to provide an automatic check in the consumption of spare parts.

The results show that the trained models can achieve a mean NDCG@20 score of 81% when ranking the expected parts, while also marking a low volume of 10% of the consumed parts for alert generation. We briefly discuss how these marked parts can be aggregated and combined with additional data to generate more fine-grained alerts.

Keywords: Supply chain · Spare parts · Repair process · Alert generation · Information retrieval · Logistic regression

1 Introduction

The repair process of digital devices used by operators in the field is an important part and, sometimes, the main component of the operation of many original equipment manufacturers (OEMs). A device is sent for repair for many reasons, some are non-functional like scratches, but most are functional problems that prevent the device from working properly. A common practice is that the repair process is executed by a partner repair shop of the OEM that sells these devices and their after-sales maintenance. In such cases, it is difficult to validate if the defects reported by the operator and validated by the repair shop are sufficient to explain the spare parts that are consumed in the repair process. Spare parts are an expensive resource, provided by the OEM, and considered a crucial resource to keep track of. Usually, Supply Chain Control Tower (SCCT) solutions are employed to ensure an end-to-end view of the entire process but popular tools

G. Marreiros et al. (Eds.): EPIA 2022, LNAI 13566, pp. 611–622, 2022.
https://doi.org/10.1007/978-3-031-16474-3_50

still lack the support required to validate spare parts consumption. To help check this consumption, the industry is applying Data Science and Machine Learning (ML) to identify possible issues and help improve the repair process.

In this work, we propose a learning-to-rank approach to automatically check the consumption of spare parts in the repair process of digital devices. Using data from an SCCT about each repair service, their identified defects and consumed parts, we train hundreds of Logistic Regression ML models, one for each supported spare part. The trained models generate predictions that tell us which parts should be used in each repair service. We collect these predictions to generate a ranked list of suggestions of parts to be replaced. We show that the trained models obtain a mean NDCG@20 score of 81% when suggesting lists with 20 parts. Next, we use these lists to compare the suggested parts against the list of actual replaced parts. The replaced parts that are not in the suggestions are marked. Finally, we discuss how these marked parts can generate alerts into an SCCT solution to prioritize services that need to be reviewed.

In summary our main contribution is a data-driven method for identifying deviations in the consumption of spare parts in the repair process, these deviations can be integrated and used for alert generation in an SCCT, and the remaining of this paper is organized as follows. Section 2 presents the related work. Section 3 presents details about the data used. Section 4 details the methodology used in this study. Section 5 shows discussion about the results. Section 6 details our conclusions.

2 Related Work

2.1 Spare Parts Supply Chain

A Supply Chain Control Tower (SCCT), or a Service Control Tower (SCT), is an umbrella term for emerging solutions that bring an end-to-end view of the supply chain by acting as a central hub that integrates tools and processes to drive business outcomes. An SCCT solution is a complex set of systems and processes, and an important component of any SCCT is alert generation.

Following the framework proposed by Topan et al. [10], an alert, in this context, is any form of notification that is generated with the intent of triggering any one of their identified interventions into the supply chain processes. Usually, alert generation is based on ad-hoc rules or traditional forecasting techniques, this causes a high number of alerts being generated while a low percentage of them are identified as high priority. And currently, SCCT solutions generate too many alerts and rely in the need for finding arbitrary thresholds.

Specifically, Supply Chain Event Management (SCEM) focuses in real-time monitoring using statistical process control to generate alerts. Still, there is not a common solution for alert generation and, the literature does not address how trends and deviations are identified, how alerts are usually generated, or how to determine interventions.

Also, the identified interventions are divided between reactive and proactive interventions but they are all related to reducing downtime risk or, when a downtime is not avoided, to reduce recovery times. An analysis found out that some interventions are more cost effective than others [4]. Another analysis, combining event-based and periodic interventions, found out that joint interventions can considerably reduce total downtime [11]. Still, there are no proactive interventions related to refining the repair process or improving repair shop efficacy in the consumption of spare parts.

The repair service of capital goods is usually placed as part of after-sales services [2]. When evaluating repair services, top-down frameworks view them as another component in a high-level performance tree [3]. While bottom-up frameworks view the repair services as a subjective component, usually evaluated by customers [1].

2.2 Information Retrieval

Information Retrieval (IR) is defined as dealing with methods that retrieve subsets from data based on the needs of users and it has become popular in the 21st century [6].

The most common way of organizing the results in IR systems is by ranking them. In this context, learning-to-rank are methods that try to learn the ordering of the results [7]. In pointwise methods, when given a document and query pair together with a score or a label, the ranking problem is similar to a regression or a classification problem, respectively.

For classification problems, it is common to use the Logistic Regression or Maximum-Entropy method. Although, when used for learning-to-rank problems, other methods like Support Vector Machines seem to perform better [9].

Multi-label classification is a learning-to-rank extension where each document is assigned to a set of labels. The most common problem transformation method, for multi-label classification, is to learn a binary classifier for each one of the different labels in the set [12].

3   Data

As described in Sect. 1, the repair process is usually performed by a partner repair shop and, to have a coherent SCCT solution, these partners need to report the status of each repair service in a timely manner. A single repair service may have a duration from hours to several days depending on many factors, but at each step in the repair process an update is generated, usually several times during a single day.

A service order registers all the relevant information for a single repair service and may contain hundreds of fields, e.g. the identifier of a client, the start date of the service, the type of product that is being repaired, and many others.

The relevant fields for our study are those specifying the defects validated by a trained technician and the parts replaced by another, or possibly the same,

trained technician. A single device may present, after inspection, several defects that will require the replacement of several parts. Usually, a single defect implies a single part being replaced but this is not a strict rule and a defect may rarely have no parts or two or more parts being replaced. Also, a device may present the same defect multiple times and multiple parts of the same type may be replaced.

Another important aspect and, perhaps, a more difficult issue is that the relationship between defects and parts is not a one-to-one relationship, meaning that a single defect can be addressed by different parts, that may not be of the same type, and that a single part can address different defects. This is common, because a digital device is a really complex piece of machinery that is built from parts from several providers, and a single part can have many similar parts that come from different providers, these providers may have used different materials in the production of similar parts and all these parts have vastly different life expectancy.

We have collected data from an emerging SCCT from a global leader in their sector, the data covers a period of over 14 months, more than 1.5 million repair services, and 23 types of digital devices with over 160 types of defects and more than 350 types of spare parts.

4   Methodology

In this section we show the methodology used to evaluate the efficacy of using a data-driven approach to check the consumption of spare parts for each service order. First we describe the time series setup. Next, we describe the models and the metrics used. Last, we discuss how the consumed spare parts are marked.

4.1   Setup

An important aspect of any solution that will be used in a production setting is that the solution will be in continuous usage. Additionally, when an ML algorithm is employed, this means that a given model must be trained at a given point in time and its use will be spread during a determined time frame that can be days or years.

Because of this, it is usual to frame the setup in terms of a time series with the variables of interest evolving as the time advances. This framing helps reducing problems of data and prediction drift that can happen when future data differs from past data, a common scenario for most ongoing systems. This difference between past and future is usually identified using statistical tests.

Using the data described in Sect. 3, we have divided the data into 18 sequential snapshots, with each snapshot representing the passage of 4 weeks from a previous snapshot. This way the process is simulated with a total retraining of the models every 4 weeks but this time interval is arbitrary and would need to be investigated further. Also, a given snapshot is composed of a train set and a test set. The train set represents the past and is used to train the ML models, while

the test set represents the future and is used to evaluate the models. Further, the test set of a previous snapshot is merged into the train set of next immediate snapshot.

In Fig. 1, we show the total number of samples of each set for all the snapshots. As can be seen, in each snapshot the test set has a variable number of samples and since a previous test set is incorporated into the next train set, this would cause the train set to generate wildly different models with different performances and training times. Because of this, we kept the training size restricted, using close to 17k of its most recent samples.

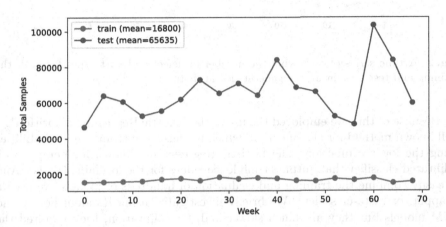

Fig. 1. A time series plot showing the total number of samples for both the training and test sets for all the generated snapshots.

In Fig. 2, we show the total number of types, for both defects and parts, of each set for all the snapshots. As time advances, the number of types varies. This is due to many factors, like seasonal defects because of more rain in a given season of the year, old devices being deprecated or new ones being released, or the low supply of one or more spare parts.

4.2 Models

In this work, we have employed the use of several algorithms available in the scikit-learn Python package [8].

For the base models, we needed a simple, fast and interpretable model but above all, we needed a model that we could combine its predictions with others. Following the discussion from Sect. 2.2, for a multi-label classification problem, we would need to train a model for each label, which means, in our case, training thousands of models.

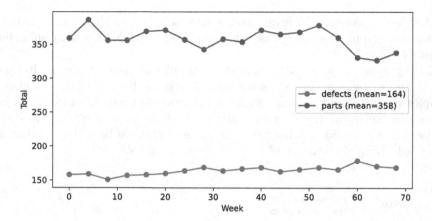

Fig. 2. A time series plot showing the number of defect and part types for both the training and test sets for all the generated snapshots.

Because of this, we employed the use of the Logistic Regression algorithm[1], a well known method for classification, which models its outcomes as probabilities using the logistic function. The Logistic Regression is known for being a well calibrated classifier that outputs confidence values for the available labels[2]. And to easily combine the training and evaluation of hundreds of models, we used a wrapper, or meta-classifier[3]. We briefly investigated using Random Forest and SVM models but they are much slower and, for calibration, they required the training of multiple models, increasing training times even more.

In this study, we have used the Logistic Regression algorithm with all its default values for the hyperparameters because even a small grid-search for just the regularization term would explode the number of models into the tens of thousands of models, and severely increase training times.

4.3 Metrics

An important part of a project employing ML algorithms is the evaluation of the models. To evaluate if a model may perform well when in use, we need a way to measure its performance. For this purpose, we employ the use of different evaluation metrics to assess model performance from different perspectives.

1. Accuracy score[4], in multi-label classification, computes subset accuracy, the set of predicted labels must match exactly the expected labels. It is a common metric for classification problems and is easily adaptable for multi-label

---

[1] scikit-learn.org/stable/modules/generated/sklearn.linear_model.LogisticRegressio n.html.

[2] scikit-learn.org/stable/modules/calibration.html#calibration-curves.

[3] scikit-learn.org/stable/modules/generated/sklearn.multioutput.MultiOutputClassif ier.html.

[4] scikit-learn.org/stable/modules/generated/sklearn.metrics.accuracy_score.html.

classification, still it is a very difficult metric in our case due to the need of matching all the labels exactly. All the models need to match all the labels exactly in all the more than 350 spare parts. That is a really tall order;

2. Coverage error[5] is a measure of how far is needed to go in the ranked scores to cover the expected labels. In our case, it gives us an idea of how long our lists should be to cover all the expected parts. And we use it as a proxy for selecting the parameter k for the next metric;

3. Normalized Discounted Cumulative Gain (NDCG) score[6] considers the top k ranked scores to count the expected labels that were predicted correctly. It is a common metric in IR and multi-label problems [5]. This metric sorts the expected labels by using the predictions, applies a logarithmic discount and, then, sums all the results. And it uses an ideal Discounted Cumulative Gain to normalize the values and keep the metric between 0 and 1.

4.4 Alerts

Having trained and evaluated the ML models using both the identified defects and the consumed spare parts. Now we use their probability outputs to sort and rank the spare parts like a list of suggestions, where the parts with higher probabilities will appear at the top. For each repair service, we generate a list of suggestions with k parts, using the same value used for the k parameter in NDCG.

We compared the suggestions for a service against the actual consumed parts for that same service, if a consumed part does not show up in the list of suggestions, we mark it as a consumption that needs to be checked. Repeating the process for all the services, we mark lots of consumed parts subject for review. Used as is, these marked parts would generate a lot of alerts.

In Fig. 3, we show components of an SCCT solution, mainly how the OEM and repair shops interact to generate and consume data from the SCCT and how our solution can be integrated to provide consumption checks back into the SCCT for use in alert generation. Next, we discuss how to aggregate and filter these parts for more fine-grained alerts.

5 Results

The results obtained are summarized in Table 1. The table shows the results for the Accuracy score, the Coverage error and the NDCG@20 score for both the training and test sets. The values are the averages over all snapshots.

From the results, we can see that, as explained in Sect. 4.3, accuracy is a very difficult metric for our context and the obtained scores are low with a score of 20% in the test sets. Still the scores are high given the difficulty of the task, meaning that for the average 65k samples in each of the test sets with an average of 350 consumed spare parts, the models get correctly all the consumed spare

---

[5] scikit-learn.org/stable/modules/generated/sklearn.metrics.coverage_error.html.

[6] scikit-learn.org/stable/modules/generated/sklearn.metrics.ndcg_score.html.

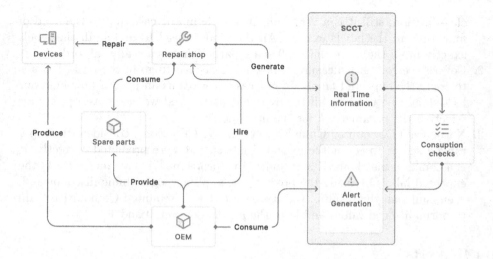

Fig. 3. A diagram highlighting SCCT components and how our solution can be integrated.

Table 1. Results obtained for our multi-label classification problem, values are calculated using all the 18 snapshots for both the training and test sets, with the standard deviation between parenthesis

Metric	Train	Test
Accuracy	0.30 (±0.03)	0.19 (±0.02)
Coverage	10.58 (±0.89)	30.24 (±6.81)
NDCG@20	0.91 (±0.02)	0.81 (±0.04)

parts for 1 in every 5 services, this amounts to more than 4.5 million correct predictions per test set.

For the coverage errors, we got values of 10 and 30 for, respectively, the train and test sets. From our analyses, 95% of the services have less than 10 parts replaced, less than 1% of the services have more than 20 parts replaced, and with such values obtained for the Coverage error, we felt that using a value of 20 for the k parameter in the NDCG score was a good trade-off.

Finally, for the NDCG@20 scores, we obtained a 81% rate for the test set, a really high value given the difficulty of the task. This NDCG@20 score is not a true probability, it is a ratio given an ideal score. Still, it means that given the scale set by the ideal score, the models are ranking the expected parts very high in the predictions.

In Fig. 4, we show the actual values for the NDCG@20 scores for each data set for all the snapshots. As expected, we can see that the training scores are better than the test scores. And since we kept the training sizes constant, we can see that some snapshots are easier than others.

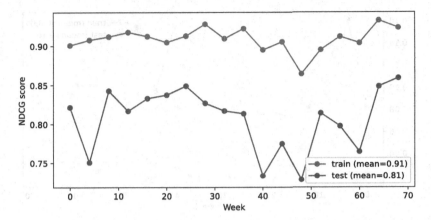

Fig. 4. A time series plot showing the NDCG@20 scores for both the training and test sets for all the generated snapshots.

Having trained the models and evaluated their predictions, we sorted the predictions and compared them with the actual lists of consumed parts. The actual consumed parts that did not show up in the sorted predictions were marked, as discussed in Sect. 4.4.

In Fig. 5, we show the fraction of consumed parts that were marked for use in alert generation. Except for 3 cases where the fraction goes to 16%, most test sets stay below 10%, for an average of 10% of marked parts.

With these parts marked as is, alert generation would create a lot of alerts. Because of this, we investigated some simple ways to group, filter and prioritize these parts to use them for alert generation. It is important to note that alert generation is a feature of the SCCT solution, meaning that the solution has many options of how and when to generate alerts, here we discuss some simple aggregations that should be made by the SCCT solution to generate alerts based on the marked parts and services.

The first simple method is to group and count the marked parts. Table 2 shows the top 10 most consumed spare parts ranked by the total number of alerts for each spare part. And we can see that, in this specific situation, just 4 types of parts generated most of the alerts. Selecting the top parts this way, we can identify the most problematic ones and sample some services for review.

The second simple method is to group the service orders by the number of alerts each service received. Table 3 shows all the services grouped by their number of alerts. We can see that just a few hundreds of services received more than 5 alerts.

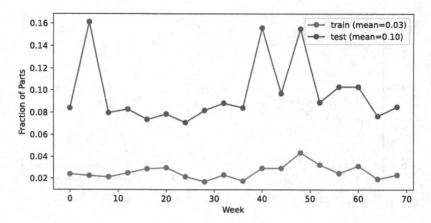

Fig. 5. A time series plot showing the fraction of marked parts for both the training and test sets for all the generated snapshots.

Table 2. Marked parts grouped by part types and sorted by the total amount of alerts

Part	Alerts
Part 01	4405
Part 02	3054
Part 03	3050
Part 04	3040
Part 05	817
Part 06	733
Part 07	537
Part 08	352
Part 09	324
Part 10	312

With the marked parts integrated into an SCCT solution, additional data can be used, fields like parts availability, device type or client, and many other factors could easily be incorporated into more complex schemes to generate fine-grained alerts.

Table 3. Marked parts grouped by service orders and number of alerts per service, sorted by the total number of services per group

Alerts	Services
1	8268
2	2827
3	1704
4	1402
5	633
6	272
7	99
8	30
9	13

6 Conclusion

The repair process is a complex part of many businesses. Investigating how spare parts consumption can be automatically checked allows for the development of better ways to generate alerts that drive supply chain interventions.

In this paper, we proposed a learning-to-rank method to generate alerts in the consumption of spare parts in the repair process. We used data from an SCCT solution about the identified defects that digital devices present when sent to repair and the consumed spare parts used to address these defects.

As a multi-label classification problem, we trained hundreds of Logistic Regression ML models to rank spare parts and automatically check the consumption while simulating the passage of time. From the reported results, the proposed approach achieves a mean NDCG@20 score of 81% and is able to mark a low volume of 10% of the consumed spare parts. And we briefly discussed how the solution can be integrated into an SCCT for alert generation.

The solution and results obtained with this work are promising and for future work, we intend to evaluate how the solution has impacted the real industrial setting, and to explore additional data with an automated solution for selecting the k parameter for the NDCG score.

Acknowledgments. This work is funded by Ingenico do Brasil LTDA using incentive resources by the law 13.969/2019, and in a technical cooperation agreement with Venturus under CATI resolution 135/2020.

References

1. Çevik Onar, S., Oztaysi, B., Kahraman, C.: Dynamic intuitionistic fuzzy multi-attribute aftersales performance evaluation. Complex Intell. Syst. **3**(3), 197–204 (2017)

2. Durugbo, C.M.: After-sales services and aftermarket support: a systematic review, theory and future research directions. Int. J. Prod. Res. **58**(6), 1857–1892 (2020)
3. Gaiardelli, P., Saccani, N., Songini, L.: Performance measurement systems in after-sales service: an integrated framework. Int. J. Bus. Perform. Manag. **9**(2), 145–171 (2007)
4. Gerrits, B., Topan, E., van der Heijden, M.: Operational planning in service control towers-heuristics and case study. Eur. J. Oper. Res. **302**, 983–998 (2022)
5. Järvelin, K., Kekäläinen, J.: Cumulated gain-based evaluation of IR techniques. ACM Trans. Inf. Syst. (TOIS) **20**(4), 422–446 (2002)
6. Liu, J., et al.: Data mining and information retrieval in the 21st century: a bibliographic review. Comput. Sci. Rev. **34**, 100193 (2019)
7. Liu, T.Y., et al.: Learning to rank for information retrieval. Found. Trends® Inf. Retrieval **3**(3), 225–331 (2009)
8. Pedregosa, F., et al.: Scikit-learn: machine learning in Python. J. Mach. Learn. Res. **12**, 2825–2830 (2011)
9. Rahangdale, A., Raut, S.: Machine learning methods for ranking. Int. J. Softw. Eng. Knowl. Eng. **29**(06), 729–761 (2019)
10. Topan, E., Eruguz, A.S., Ma, W., Van Der Heijden, M., Dekker, R.: A review of operational spare parts service logistics in service control towers. Eur. J. Oper. Res. **282**(2), 401–414 (2020)
11. Topan, E., van der Heijden, M.C.: Operational level planning of a multi-item two-echelon spare parts inventory system with reactive and proactive interventions. Eur. J. Oper. Res. **284**(1), 164–175 (2020)
12. Tsoumakas, G., Katakis, I.: Multi-label classification: an overview. Int. J. Data Warehousing Min. (IJDWM) **3**(3), 1–13 (2007)

Uplift Modeling Using the Transformed Outcome Approach

Paulo Pinheiro[1](✉) ⓘ and Luís Cavique[2] ⓘ

[1] Universidade Aberta and Cedis, Lisbon, Portugal
ppinheiro@cedis.pt, luis.cavique@uab.pt
[2] LASIGE, Universidade Aberta, Lisbon, Portugal

Abstract. Churn and how to deal with it is an essential issue in the telecommunications sector. Within the scope of actionable knowledge, we argue that it is crucial to find effective personalized interventions that can lead to a reduction in dropouts and that, at the same time, make it possible to determine the causal effect of these interventions. Considering an intervention that encourages clients to opt for a longer-term contract for benefits, we used Uplift modeling and the Transformed Outcome Approach as a machine learning-based technique for individual-level prediction. The result is actionable profiles of persuadable customers that increase retention and strike the right balance between the campaign budget.

Keywords: Uplift modelling · Causal effect · CATE · Decision trees · Transformed outcome approach

1 Introduction

It is widely accepted that it is a good idea to send a marketing offer to all of its customers, thinking that the customer's likelihood of purchasing a product or service increases. Likewise, when we approach the churn problem, we think that customers identified as most at risk of churn should all be targeted by proactive retention programs.

Some authors [1, 2] argue that since customers respond differently to retention interventions, companies should not seek to intervene with all those at risk of giving up or canceling their subscription but only with those who are more sensitive to the intervention. In this sense, we want to know if a customer will maintain the service if we intervene with him or if he will maintain the service even if we do not intervene. Specifically, we want to know whether or not an intervention influences a client.

In marketing, as in statistics, biomedicine, and other areas, knowing whether and to what extent the value of one variable (the treatment) affects the value of another variable (the outcome) is a crucial issue. This question is a problem in causal inference where two paradigms are known: the paradigm of causal structural models [3] and the potential outcome framework [4].

The paradigm of causal structural models begins by noting that a variable X is a direct cause of the variable Y if X appears in the function that affects a value to Y (Y

© The Author(s), under exclusive license to Springer Nature Switzerland AG 2022
G. Marreiros et al. (Eds.): EPIA 2022, LNAI 13566, pp. 623–635, 2022.
https://doi.org/10.1007/978-3-031-16474-3_51

= f(X)). However, the intervention/treatment T must include a new type of variable in the causality task. In this task, the outcome Y of treatment T is the object of study. For this purpose, test and control data sets are used for treatment performed T = 1 and not performed T = 0. In analogy with f(X, Y), the explanatory function uses three variables, f(T, X, Y). This dichotomy can be found in Pearl and Mackenzie's ladder of causation [5] and the work of Hernán et al. [6].

In this sense, to answer the causal inference question, we need to estimate the causal effect of treatment on outcome. In this work, we use methods of Uplift Modeling that are implicitly designed for data from randomized experiments.

There are several methods to apply Uplift Modelling and find the causal effect we will refer to in related work. This work shows that it is possible to use Uplift Modeling to obtain actionable knowledge concerning finding the consumer profiles most likely to keep their service if subjected to intervention and measure the causal effect of that intervention and its impact on the business. Specifically, based on Telco's dataset, we consider a possible intervention to change the duration of the contracts to find the profile of the customers most likely to maintain the service to maximize return on marketing investment.

The paper is organized into five additional sections. In Sect. 2, related work is presented. Section 3 details the Telco case study. Section 4 discusses the profiles found and those that can be persuadable. In Sect. 5, conclusions are drawn and points out some points that require further investigation and work.

2 Related Work

2.1 What is Uplift?

It is common in marketing to find predictive models to understand which customers will buy if they are intervened. Uplift Modeling seeks to know if the customer will buy only if he is intervened. The difference lies in the fact that in Uplift Modeling, we can predict which customers can be persuaded and who reacts because of an intervention. Siegel [1] points to the Uplift Modeling to predict the influence on an individual's behavior that results from applying one form of treatment over another.

In order to learn to distinguish influenceable clients, those to whom it makes a difference to perform some treatment, the Uplift Model learns from both types of clients, those who were contacted and those who were not, so it is necessary to use two sets of data for training the model. The first group of clients that are intervened or treated, the treatment group, and the second group of clients that do not receive the treatment, is named the control group. Each customer is classified into one of four quadrants, as shown in Fig. 1.

The resulting matrix is created based on the customer's decision to buy (or keep the service in case of a churn problem) depending on whether or not a marketing campaign targeted it. The four quadrants refer to:

- *persuadable* customers who buy when exposed to the marketing campaign (in healthcare are known as *compliers*);

- to secure customers (*sure things*) who buy regardless of whether or not they are the target of a treatment;
- the *lost causes* are customers who, regardless of whether or not they are the target of treatment, will not buy a product or service;
- moreover, the group of clients who should not be treated (*do-not-disturbs,* also known as *sleeping dogs*) under penalty of becoming dropouts.

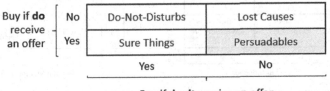

Fig. 1. Conceptual response segments (adapted from [1]).

The aim of Uplift Modeling is thus to identify persuadable customers and avoid treating customers classified as do-not-disturb.

Devrient *et al.* [7] add that Uplift modeling focuses on decision making at the individual level and tries to estimate the causal effect of a treatment on an outcome, thus determining which treatment to apply to each individual to optimize the outcome. On the other hand, it allows determining the success of a campaign by observing customers' behavior in the treatment and control groups in terms of response. It allows the calculation and comparison of the response rate for both groups, and the difference in response rate is the increase due to the campaign.

2.2 Uplift Problem

As mentioned before and illustrated in Fig. 1, the goal of Uplift Modeling is to find persuasive customers and not intervene with do-not-disturb ones. However, the data we have available for building models only contain information on whether or not the client intervened and whether or not he responded, as illustrated on the left side of Fig. 2. The problem that arises is how to frame customers as intended by the Uplift Modeling.

As summarized by Devrient *et al.* [7], given the data obtained in previous interventions, we can group customers into four categories: those who responded and were intervened (TR); in this case, we do not know if they would have responded even if they had not been intervened, reason why they can be *persuadable* or *sure-things*; those who did not respond and were intervened (TN); in this case, we do not know if they would not have responded if they had not been intervened so that they could be *lost causes* or *do-not-disturbs*; those who responded without being intervened (CR); in this case, we do not know if they would also have responded if they had been intervened, so we do not know if they are *sure-things* or *do-not-disturbs*; those who did not respond and were not intervened (CN); in this case, we do not know if they would have responded if they were intervened, the reason why they can be *persuadable* or *lost-causes*.

As it is not expressly possible to separate only persuadable customers, it is not a significant risk to intervene between the categories of those who responded when intervened (TR) and those who were not intervened and did not respond (CN). Although these categories include persuadable clients, lost causes, and sure-things that should not be dealt with, their intervention involves a lower cost than dealing with do-not-disturbs.

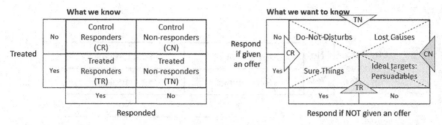

Fig. 2. Conceptual table of what we know and what we want to know (adapted from [7])

After applying techniques that seek to fit clients into these categories, it is possible to find the measure of the Uplift. Ascarza [2] has addressed this problem, then states that the clients to be intervened, the persuadable ones, will be those who have an Uplift measurement above a minimum effect to consider.

2.3 Measuring Uplift

As mentioned by Gutierrez & Gérardy [8], assuming $Y_i(1)$ as the result of person i when he is intervened and $Y_i(0)$ as the result of person i when he is not, the causal effect can be given by:

$$\tau_i = Y_i(1) - Y_i(0) \tag{1}$$

The expected causal effect of an intervention in a subgroup of the population, called Conditional Average Treatment Effect (CATE), is given by:

$$\tau(X_i) = E[Y_i(1)|X_i] - E[Y_i(0)|X_i] \tag{2}$$

where X_i is a vector of random variables (features) that describe the pre-intervention characteristics of the individual. $Y_i(1)$ and $Y_i(0)$ are never observed at the same time because a person i cannot at the same time be and not be intervened. Thus, considering a binary variable T_i that takes the value 1 if the person i is intervened and 0 otherwise, we can write that the observed result Y_i^{obs} is in fact:

$$Y_i^{obs} = T_i Y_i(1) + (1 - T_i)Y_i(0) \tag{3}$$

Assuming that T_i conditional on X_i is independent of $Y_i(1)$ and of $Y_i(0)$ an assumption stated by Rosenbaum & Rubin [9] known as Unconfoundedness Assumption or Conditional Independence Assumption (CIA), expressed by:

$$\{Y_i(1), Y_i(0)\} \perp\!\!\!\perp T_i | X_i \tag{4}$$

we can then consider estimating CATE from observational data by computing:

$$\tau_i = E\left[Y_i^{obs}\middle|X_i, T_i(1)\right] - E\left[Y_i^{obs}\middle|X_i, T_i(0)\right] \tag{5}$$

Zhang et al. [10] mentioned that since Uplift modeling techniques assume that data are obtained from experiments with randomized treatment assignment, the Uplift calculation is equivalent to the CATE calculation as expressed in Eq. (5).

2.4 Uplift Techniques and the Transformed Outcome Approach

Siegel [1] refers to the persuasion effect as the effect obtained in an individual's persuasion by combining the paradigms of comparison of the results obtained in treatment and control groups and applying predictive modeling, namely through machine learning, statistical regression, and other techniques.

There are several approaches to Uplift Modeling through Machine Learning. There are proposals for classifying the methods according to how they approach Uplift Modeling in the literature review. Gutierrez & Gérardy [8] mentions the two-model approach, class transformation, and Uplift direct modeling. Devriendt *et al.* [7] classify them into two large groups: pre-processing data approaches that include transformation approaches, variable selection procedures, net weights of evidence, and net information value; and the data processing approach in which the two-model approach and direct estimation approaches are framed; Finally, Zhang *et al.* [10] mentions methods using existing supervised learning models, and specific methods for Uplift modeling.

In approaches that use existing supervised learning models, we find the S-Learner, T-Learner, X-Leaner, and R-Learner methods based on Deep Learning and the Transformed Outcome. The specific methods for Uplift modeling include approaches based on Decision Trees, SVM, Deep Learning, and Ensemble Methods.

In this work, we will use the Transformed Outcome Approach. We can find this approach in works such as Athey & Imbens [11] and Jaskowski & Jaroszewicz [12]. It lies in transforming the observed result Y into Y^* such that the CATE is equal to the conditional expectation of the transformed result Y^*.

According to Athey & Imbens [11], verifying the Unconfoundedness assumption referred to before in expression (4), the transformed result Y_i^* can be expressed by:

$$Y_i^* = T\frac{Y_i}{e(x)} - (1-T)\frac{Y_i}{(1-e(x))} \tag{6}$$

where $e(x)$ is the propensity score defined as:

$$e(x) = P(T = 1|x) \tag{7}$$

moreover, the CATE can be expressed by:

$$\tau(x) = E\left[Y_i^*\middle|X = x\right] \tag{8}$$

thus, any supervised algorithm that uses Y^* as the target and X as features can be used.

For binary results, Jaskowski & Jaroszewicz [12] propose a transformation of the outcome where $Y^* = 1$ in the cases where ($T = 1$ and $Y = 1$) and where ($T = 0$ and $Y = 0$), and $Y^* = 0$ in all other cases, which results from the following Eq. (9).

$$Y_i^* = Y_i T + (1 - Y_i)(1 - T) \tag{9}$$

It corresponds to the intervention groups mentioned in Sect. 2.2, which we can see on the right in Fig. 2. Considering that Y is binary and that $e(x) = 0.5$ because an individual has an equal probability of being in the treatment or control group, these authors proved that, in this case, CATE could be estimated by transforming Eq. (6) which results in:

$$\tau_{(x)} = 2P(Y_i^* = 1|x) - 1 \tag{10}$$

As pointed out in several literature reviews on Uplift modeling [7, 8, 10], the Transform Outcome Approach is simple. It tends to obtain better results than other approaches based on supervised methods, namely the two-model one. In addition, it has the flexibility to use any supervised method and to calculate the CATE directly. However, they point out as restrictions the dependence of a precise estimate of the propensity score in the case of continuous results. In the case of binary results, the balance between the treatment and control data set.

2.5   Evaluation Metrics

It is a common opinion found in literature reviews [7, 8, 10] that the evaluation metrics of traditional predictive models are not adequate to evaluate Uplift modeling because we can never observe at the same time the effect of intervening or not intervening in an individual. The authors present several metrics that can be used, such as the Gini and Qini coefficients. Devriendt *et al.* [7] also refer to the determination of precision in the estimation of heterogeneous effects (PEHE) and mean absolute percentage error (MAPE) as metrics that can be used with known ground-truth treatment effects.

Gutierrez & Gérardy [8] also prove that, in the case of the transformed outcome approach, the Mean Square Error (MSE) (previously referred to by PEHE), in the form:

$$MSE(\tau_i, \hat{\tau}_i) = \frac{1}{n} \sum_i^n (\tau_i - \hat{\tau}_i)^2 \tag{11}$$

can be approximated by:

$$MSE(Y_i^*, \hat{\tau}_i) = \frac{1}{n} \sum_i^n (Y_i^* - \hat{\tau}_i)^2 \tag{12}$$

Another more visual way of analyzing the quality of the Uplift model is through the use of the Uplift chart, described by Devriendt *et al.* [7]. After building the model, the individuals in the training dataset are scored according to the corresponding uplift value, sorted in ascending order of this value, and grouped into deciles. The response rate increment in each decile is calculated by subtracting the response rate of subjects in the control group from the response rate of subjects in the intervention group. In an ideal model, the graph obtained is similar to that in Fig. 3, where the persuasive individuals will appear in the leftmost deciles and have higher uplift values. However, as they point out, these graphs are never presented so regularly in practice.

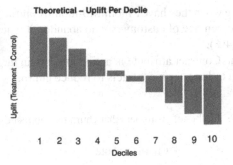

Fig. 3. Uplift chart from an ideal uplift model [7]

3 Finding Uplift

This case study presents the Telco Customer Churn public dataset [13] that contains information on eighteen covariates potentially related to the outcomes of interest (churn or not churn). Our goal is to determine which customers can be influenced by the proposal to change the duration of the contract and the proposed intervention to avoid abandoning or canceling the service. With this in mind, the operations are carried out on Procedure 1.

Procedure 1: Uplift modelling

1. Given a dataset D, define the result Y, the intervention/treatment T to be considered, and the set of available covariates X;
2. After balancing the dataset D, the transformed outcome Y* is obtained, and the feature importance is observed through net information value;
3. After splitting dataset D into train D_t and prediction D_p groups, decision tree algorithm is applied to the training dataset D_t, and a decision tree is obtained. The CATE/Uplift is calculated for each of the nodes and leaves of the tree. The rules that avoid churn can be extracted from the leaf node that have higher CATE/Uplift;
4. In other to calculate performance measures, the model is evaluated by using the prediction dataset D_p.

Finally, we extract the rules with the best Uplift score to identify the persuadable customers.

3.1 Outcome (Y) and Intervention (T) Definition

Each row represents a customer in this dataset, and each column contains the customer's attributes. Those attributes can be grouped in demographic info about customers, attributes that describe customer's account information and attributes that present the services that each customer has signed up for. There is also an attribute, Churn, which indicates whether or not the customer has abandoned services in the last month.

Table 1 shows the number of customers who abandon and do not abandon the service depending on the duration of their contract. As we can see, the percentage of customers

who abandon the service when they have a month-to-month contract (42,71%) is substantially higher than the percentage of customers who abandon it when they have contracts of longer duration (7,24%).

Considering that the Contract attribute is actionable, it can target an intervention to make customers switch to long-term contracts to reduce churn.

Table 1. Number of customers that churn by contract duration

Contract attribute class	Churn attribute		Total
	Yes	No	
Month-to-month	2220	1655	3875
One year, two year	2954	214	3168
Total	5174	1879	7043

An intervention can be planned to improve the recovery rate by increasing the duration of the customers' contract to one or two years. Considering that the Contract attribute is actionable, we can take it as the intervention T to make the customer increase the duration of the contract, Y as the outcome, meaning that the customer may or may not cancel the service and X as the set of features that may be interfering with the outcome.

3.2 Dataset Preparation

To prepare the dataset, we loaded it into the R system and used a set of tools available in the Package 'Uplift' [14], as mentioned by Guelman *et al.* [15].

As shown in Table 1, only 1869 customers continue to use the services, which shows that churn distribution is unbalanced. In order to make the dataset more balanced, we use the **rvtu** (Response Variable Transform for Uplift Modeling) function. This function operates three main changes on the dataset: it creates a new response variable y, with a binary outcome corresponding to the one indicated to the function; it creates a binary variable z corresponding to the transformed outcome Y^* as indicated in the expression (9), and finally creates a new variable to assign each observation to the treatment (ct = 1) or control (ct = 0) group; in this case, the assignment was made by sampling without replacement, in order to distribute the observations among the treatment and control groups proportionally.

The result that relates the duration of the contract with the possible result (churn or not churn) after executing the **rvtu** function in the dataset is presented in Table 2.

To carry out an exploratory analysis of the data and the importance of each of the attributes, we used the **niv** (net information value) function from Package 'Uplift'. This function finds the Net Information Value (NIV) and Net Weight Of Evidence (NWOE) for each of the attributes used in the model. Siegel [1] and Guelman [15] mentioned that the NIV and NOWE are Uplift measurements. The result obtained is shown in Fig. 4.

Table 2. Number of customers that churn by contract duration after **rvtu**

Contract attribute class	Churn attribute		Total
	Yes	No	
(0) Month-to-month	1828	1340	3168
(1) One year or more	2954	214	3168
Total	4782	1554	6336

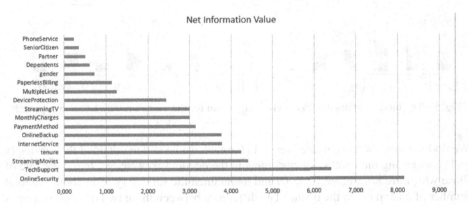

Fig. 4. Net information value by feature

3.3 Applied Model

Initially, and to later assess the quality of the model, the dataset was randomly divided into two parts, leaving 70% of the data for training the model and 30% for testing it.

To create the Uplift model, we use the **ctree** function of the Package 'partykit' [16]. As described in the documentation, **ctree**, short for conditional inference trees, is a binary recursive partitioning function for continuous, ordered, nominal, and multivariate response variables in a conditional inference framework. In this way, the model was built with the target variable Y^* which corresponds to the transformed result of expression (9). The tree obtained is shown in Fig. 5.

For each node and leaf of the tree, the CATE was calculated using the formula defined by expression (10). The values obtained are shown in Fig. 5, in the rectangles to the right and below each node and leaf, respectively.

3.4 Evaluate Model

We used the Uplift chart to evaluate the developed model and calculated the MSE / PEHE as described in Sect. 2.5.

To create the Uplift plot shown in Fig. 6, we score each of the observations in the test dataset with the corresponding uplift value obtained by the model. Then we sort the values obtained in ascending order and group the observations into ten groups (deciles).

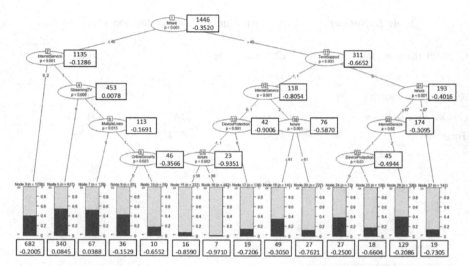

Fig. 5. The model obtained with the **ctree** algorithm for the Transformed Outcome approach

We find the ratio of those treated (ct = 1) for each decile and maintained the service (y = 1) concerning the number of customers in the decile. Likewise, we found the rate of those who were not treated (ct = 0) and maintained the service (y = 1) about the total number of customers in the decile. The difference between these two rates corresponds to the decile Uplift.

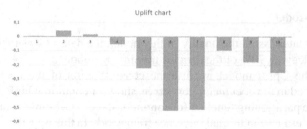

Fig. 6. Uplift chart of the uplift model

To calculate the MSE, we consider the test dataset's Y* and the Uplift value found and described in Sect. 3.3, applied in expression (12). The result obtained corresponds to MSE = 0.67.

As a general appreciation of the model, we found that although the Uplift graph does not present itself in the configuration of an ideal Uplift model, it presents a regularity and a descending curve between the 2nd and the 7th decile that suggests a suitable model. On the other hand, the value obtained for MSE does not correspond to the values of good predictive models. However, the value of MSE is in the same order of magnitude of the values of another works, like the ones in Zhang *et al.* [10].

4 Discussion: Persuadable Profiles

Each branch of the decision tree shown in Fig. 5 forms a division rule, where each node includes one of the attributes used by the algorithm, seeking to optimize the prediction of the target Y^*. Each node has a CATE value calculated as mentioned in Sect. 3.3. Higher CATE values represent a more excellent cause-effect relationship between the intervention and obtained outcome. Therefore, it is expected that we will find the persuadable customers we are looking for in the leaves of the tree with the highest CATE. On the other hand, if we analyze the features and classes that give rise to the splitting of the tree's leaves that present a higher CATE, we can trace the profile of the most persuadable customers. The target of interventions should then be customers who present persuadable profiles above a CATE threshold. The available budget for the intervention should condition the limit above.

In this case study, we define CATE > 0 as a limit. Profiles that have CATE > 0 are shown in Table 3. The table also shows the number of customers for each node, those with month-to-month contracts, and the number of those who canceled the service. The last column considers the average monthly value of contracts of 61.46 dollars to present the maximum value that can be recovered if customers who have monthly contracts and have suspended the service respond positively to the intervention.

Table 3. Persuadable profiles

Node #	Customer profile to target	CATE	Customers			Max recover value
			#	# Drop outs	% Drop out	
5	Tenure $\leq$ 40 and Internet Service = DSL and StreamingTV = No	0.0845	All M-to-m	1041 846	307 296	29.49 34.99	18182.16
7	Tenure $\leq$ 40 and Internet Service = DSL and StreamingTV = Yes and Multiple Lines = No	0.0388	All M-to-m	180 115	37 27	20.56 23.48	1659.42

Given the above, an intervention aimed at customers who have a contract duration of fewer than 40 months, use the DSL internet service without Streaming TV or with Streaming TV but do not use multiple telephone lines in order to switch to annual or biannual contracts can lead to the recovery of 17.67% of dropouts (296 + 27 dropouts in profiles to target dividing by 1828 total dropouts with month-to-month contracts), corresponding to an increase in income up to 19,841.58 dollars per month. This value also represents a maximum estimate for the amount spent on recovering these customers without incurring losses.

5   Conclusions and Future Work

Churn and how to deal with it is a big issue in the telecommunications sector. It has long been an area of research in predictive modeling, trying to predict the greater or lesser probability of a customer becoming a dropout. However, we think that this is just one aspect that can be considered. Within the scope of actionable knowledge, we argue that it is crucial to find effective and personalized interventions that can reduce dropouts and, at the same time, allow the causal effect of these interventions to be determined.

Actionable attributes are attributes that can be manipulated and allow operational changes. Based on the available attributes of the Telco dataset, we consider the contract type as an actionable attribute, as customers with monthly contracts tend to be less loyal, unlike those with longer-term contracts (annual or biannual).

Considering this personalized intervention that encourages clients to opt for a long-term contract in exchange for benefits, we use Uplift modeling as a machine learning-based technique to find actionable profiles and to determine the effects of treatment at the individual level in order to increase retention and find the right balance between the budget allocated to the campaign and the result obtained. The contribution of this work is therefore to find persuasive customer profiles, meaning customers who respond if and only if they are subject to the campaign (treated), through the application of uplift methods in order to obtain actionable knowledge.

However, in order to find a more substantial contribution to the study of Uplift models, it will be useful to carry out further studies to improve the results obtained. More work is needed at the dataset level, selecting subsets of features and pre-processing the data to obtain classes that have higher Uplift values and thus obtain trees that can present more useful actionable profiles. It may also be useful to investigate and experiment with other methods described in the Uplift literature, as well as other ways of evaluating the results obtained, and also comparing results obtained in other similar studies in the area of telecommunications, if available.

References

1. Siegel, E.: Predictive Analytics: The Power To Predict Who Will Click, Buy, Lie, Or Die. Wiley, Hoboken (2016)
2. Ascarza, E.: Retention futility: targeting high-risk customers might be ineffective. J. Mark. Res. **55**(1), 80–98 (2018)
3. Pearl, J., Glymour, M., Jewell, N.P.: Causal Inference in Statistics: A Primer, 1st edn. Wiley, Hoboken (2016)
4. Imbens, G.W., Rubin, D.B.R.: Causal Inference for Statistics, Social, and Biomedical Sciences: An Introduction. Cambridge University Press, Cambridge (2015)
5. Pearl, J., Mackenzie, D.: The Book of Why: The New Science of Cause and Effect. Basic Books, New York (2018)
6. Hernán, M.A., Hsu, J., Healy, B.: A second chance to get causal inference right: a classification of data science tasks. Chance **32**(1), 42–49 (2019)
7. Devriendt, F., Moldovan, D., Verbeke, W.: A literature survey and experimental evaluation of the state-of-the-art in uplift modeling: a stepping stone toward the development of prescriptive analytics. Big Data **6**(1), 13–41 (2018)

8. Gutierrez, P., Gérardy, J.-Y.: Causal inference and uplift modeling: a review of the literature. JMLR **67**, 1–13 (2016)
9. Rosenbaum, P.R., Rubin, D.B.: The central role of the propensity score in observational studies for causal effects. Biometrika **70**(1), 41–55 (1983)
10. Zhang, W., Li, J., Liu, L.: A unified survey of treatment effect heterogeneity modelling and uplift modelling. ACM Comput. Surv. **54**(8), 1–36 (2022)
11. Athey, S., Imbens, G.W.: Machine learning methods for estimating heterogeneous causal effects, April 2015
12. Jaskowski, M., Jaroszewicz, S.: Uplift modeling for clinical trial data. In: ICML 2012 Workshop on Clinical Data Analysis (2012)
13. BlastChar, "Telco Customer Churn" (2018). https://www.kaggle.com/blastchar/telco-customer-churn. Accessed 01 Nov 2021
14. Guelman, L.: Package 'uplift' (2015)
15. Guelman, L., Guillén, M., Pérez-Marín, A.M.: Optimal personalized treatment rules for marketing interventions : a review of methods, a new proposal, and an insurance case study. Research Group on Risk in Insurance and Finance (2014)
16. Hothorn, T., Seibold, H., Zeileis, A.: Package 'partykit' (2021)

A Service-Oriented Framework for ETL Implementation

Bruno Oliveira[1]([⊠]) [iD], Mário Leite[1], Óscar Oliveira[1] [iD], and Orlando Belo[2] [iD]

[1] CIICESI, School of Management and Technology, Porto Polytechnic, Felgueiras, Portugal
`{bmo,oao,8170573}@estg.ipp.pt`
[2] ALGORITMI R&D Centre, University of Minho, Campus de Gualtar, Braga, Portugal
`obelo@di.uminho.pt`

Abstract. The development of analytical systems imposes several challenges related not only to the amount and heterogeneity of the involved data but also to the constant need to readapt and evolve to overcome new business challenges. The data modelling layer represents the mapping between the domain and technical knowledge, however, to organize raw data into a form that can be used for analytics, specific Extract, Transform and Load (ETL) processes should be applied. ETL systems are recognized as a critical and tightly coupled system component that encapsulates data-level requirements that are hard to implement and maintain. In a Big Data era, adaptability and extensibility are important characteristics to hold when developing analytical systems. Thus, to provide more consistent, reliable, flexible, and reusable ETL processes, a service-oriented implementation for ETL development is proposed.

Keywords: Analytical systems · ETL patterns · Service-oriented approach · ETL as a service

1 Introduction

The business world is constantly affected by a volatile environment that imposes several changes on companies and their business processes. The ability to quickly adapt may determine long-term business activity success. As a result, information technology solutions should be constantly adapted to fulfil business changes, not only considering the change of how business operations are driven but also how the services are available to end-users. Recent advances in common software development [1] and specifically in data platform architectures [2, 3], promote decentralization, components decoupling, and abstraction layers over specialized concepts.

In many software development areas, it is common the use of frameworks with pre-built solutions to simplify software development. However, for analytical systems, which historically represent an expensive resource for companies, it is very difficult to reuse software components since each customer has its own manner to support operational requirements, which affects how the data is stored and is available to end-users. As a result, these systems can take months to be set up and present insights to business

G. Marreiros et al. (Eds.): EPIA 2022, LNAI 13566, pp. 636–647, 2022.
https://doi.org/10.1007/978-3-031-16474-3_52

users, which can have a high impact on financial, strategic, and confidence levels. This mainly happens because the "data" team needs to understand the business in which the analytical solution will be deployed. They need to know all the idiosyncrasies of stored data, plan the embody architecture and select the right components and tools to answer the business needs.

Extract, Transform, and Load (ETL) systems are the heart of any analytical system. They represent a workflow of tasks specially designed to deal with common procedures related to data cleaning (to correct, remove or update inaccurate data), summarizing data, or pre-computation (turning raw data into useful measures). A capable ETL system has (naturally) several benefits in ensuring, for example, data consistency, correctness, and validity. All of this contributes to improving the overall system performance and reducing implementation and monitoring costs.

Like any other piece of software, they need to be carefully planned and implemented. However, they are still developed as a system composed of hundreds of tightly coupled components, difficult to implement, maintain, understand, deploy, and scale. One of the reasons for that is related to the ETL nature. They are composed of well-known tasks used typically in SQL language and imperative programming languages that are applied to very specialized data. Even when the procedure is the same (e.g., for handling incremental load) the internal data are different (and potentially heterogeneous), which difficult the reusability between different processes or projects. In many scenarios, general solutions for common problems are still missing.

In a previous work [4], we addressed an approach for ETL development considering the microservice architectural style, coupled with the notion of patterns [5], i.e., standard procedures commonly used in ETL scenarios. The concept of pattern as a service was explored considering its configuration, communication, and data handling. In this paper, a case study is presented to in practice evaluate that ETL services as a way to overcome traditional architectural problems.

The remaining of the paper is organized as follows. Section 2 presents the new trends in ETL development. In Sect. 3, the main architecture and components of the service-oriented ETL are presented, while in Sect. 4 a set of developed services under the notion of software pattern is described. Finally, conclusions and future work directions are given in the last section.

2   Related Work

It is common for companies the need to change their internal business processes to enable data extraction and preparation for analytics. It is a long and risky process that must be carefully managed. Shortcuts can originate errors that can have a tremendous negative impact on tactical and strategic decisions. Such changes have a direct impact on the ETL component. The data processing is handled by ETL activities that must ensure data quality properties for the target analytic system. Thus, ETL engineers must deal with every data detail, implying that they must have a solid understanding of the business activities and the associated data artefacts to minimize ambiguity or misunderstandings.

With the Big Data era, the code-first ETL was popularized resulting in new tools framed under specific infrastructure properties. These trends impose additional challenges to the traditional tasks typically used in ETL development. In most cases, there

is not a clear separation of ETL components, nor a set of design patterns that guide teams in the development process. Typically, the ETL development is guided by *ad-hoc* practices, which contrasts with what traditionally happens with software development. There is not a solid methodology that guides the development process from a conceptual representation to a physical implementation. Some commercial tools and frameworks help in this aspect, providing their notation and methodology for ETL development, normally considering a specific architecture. Although useful, this approach can compromise ETL extensibility and flexibility. Thus, when it is needed to move to another tool, framework, or even reuse components from another framework or language, the developed systems are not extensible. The main reason for this is that the underlying architecture is typically monolithic and dependent on a specific language or infrastructure. As a result, ETL needs to be reimplemented almost from scratch. Moreover, these tools only cover the ETL physical level, lacking in providing conceptual primitives that can be used to describe the ETL system more conceptually [6].

In the last decade, data platforms have been evolving to answer to new data demands related to data growth which naturally affects the underlying models for processing, transforming, and analysing data. Big Data scenarios are related to more unstructured data as developers commonly use NoSQL data stores to store such data in the so-called Data Lakes or to provide additional analytical capabilities using graphs [7] or columnar [8] databases. Using NoSQL technologies makes ETL processes even more complex since dealing with data with implicit/dynamic schema, in opposite to traditional Data Warehouse (DW) architectures in which the target schema topology is known. In [9], the authors propose a two-level approach for DW building under a document-oriented approach. Since an implicit schema is used, the ETL is responsible for schema creation, which imposes new requirements on ETL implementation, mainly related to specific rules for a document-oriented data model. Ali, in [10], addresses an ETL framework for supporting the challenges imposed by Big Data scenarios. The author argues that traditional ETL lacks for support semi-structured data, custom functionality to support complex computations and their consolidation with traditional ETL operators, and efficiency, due to the excessive need for manual intervention both in design and optimization processes. The framework relies on 1) a User Defined Function component used to separate parallelization mechanisms from code, 2) a Recommender component that uses machine learning algorithms to optimize ETL workflow, 3) a Cost Model component used to evaluate the best configuration for execution time and monetary costs in a cloud environment, and 4) a Monitoring Agent component used to monitor ETL executions.

This research work provides a way to separate code related to infrastructure from code that relies on data transformations, and by the definition of different components to support ETL workflow execution. In [11], the authors combine an on-demand data stream pipeline with a distributed, parallel, and technology-independent architecture. The authors address high availability, near real-time latency, and horizontal scalability as requirements for ETL development, which are totally or partially addressed by other research works [12, 13]. Most of the recent approaches focus on specific physical implementations, disregarding a more complete development approach covering from initial design to its physical implementation.

The main idea to expose ETL in a service-oriented approach is not new [14–16] as microservices have become popular in Big Data systems. In [17], the authors report a case study involving the replacement of a legacy (monolithic) system with a microservice-based event-driven system. Despite some drawbacks related to the complexity of data flows and the many technologies involved, they perceived the resulting architecture is easier to maintain and has more fault-isolation. The microservices for Big Data architecture are also explored by [18]. The extensibility behind the integration of new components and the application of best-fitting technology for specific tasks are two examples of success factors that are compared to the proposed architecture for Big Data. Commonly used patterns in a Microservice architecture are studied in [19]. The authors discussed the API Gateway and Service Discovery for supporting a Microservice architecture and addressed event-driven architecture for microservices, proposing a set of possible technologies to support the various aspects of the Big Data stream processing architecture.

3 ETL as a Service

Today, software development is strongly based on design patterns. Patterns are solutions to recurring software problems, avoiding "reinventing the wheel" every time a repeated problem needs to be solved [20]. Typically, design patterns result from past experiences and can be used to conceptualize problems and improve process efficiency.

In the Data Warehouse field, Kimball first explored the conceptualization of ETL tasks with a set of best practices "*required in almost dimensional data warehouse back-room*" [21]. The 34 ETL architectural subsystems represent a set of components covering the data extraction from source systems, the cleaning and conforming subsystems for handling quality errors, for delivering data as dimensional structures to the final Business Intelligence layer and helping to manage the ETL production environment. In [22], a pattern-oriented approach was proposed to support ETL development phases: conceptual, logical, and physical. At the conceptual level, back boxes representing common ETL procedures are identified and framed within a workflow context to create a data transformation pipeline composed only of patterns. In the subsequent phases, each pattern is enriched with additional behavioural metadata to provide pattern instantiation to a target tool or framework. The initial models (conceptual and logical) embody important principles for ETL development:

- To capture expert knowledge and make it available in form of a Domain Specific Language (DSL) specially built to cover each pattern configuration.
- To provide a vocabulary for describing specific procedures and the general solution to them (some of them based on the 34-subsystem identified by Kimball), improving communication, understandability, and development efforts.
- To enable software reuse and flexibility. This is possible since patterns are context-independent and loosely coupled with each other. There is a clear separation between the coordination layer and the data transformation layer.

However, at physical implementation, patterns result in technical tasks used to transform data in a very specific manner. This results in big and complex workflows that are,

in many cases, complex, difficult to develop, maintain and understand. Additionally, the physical implementation normally resides on specific tools or specific frameworks that impose architecture requirements that influence the ETL system's architecture. For that reason, reusability and/or scalability are hard to achieve due to the existence of tightly coupled tasks.

The Microservices architectural style [1] represents an approach for application development based on a suite of small services [23]. Each service can be developed, deployed, and tested independently of the adopted technology. Microservices also empower horizontal scalability, allowing for the creation of new instances of the same service to answer specific execution requirements. Another important aspect of microservices development is related to the empowering of agile development, allowing faster releases, more control, transparency, flexibility, and team collaboration across project development.

Considering the emerging challenges imposed by Big Data scenarios for handling large amounts of heterogeneous and complex data (which contributes to increasing software development complexity), as well the needed computational resources to produce quality data in smaller time windows, the next section presents how ETL patterns can be mapped to a service-oriented approach using a specific case study.

4   Case Study

ETL acronym refers to three steps related to moving data from several data sources to one or a set of destinations while specific data cleaning procedures and transformations are applied. However, due to the amount of data involved, the underlying transformations complexity, and the support infrastructure characteristics, the ETL is a vast concept that requires a substantial amount of understanding. At the top level, the Extraction, Transformation, and Load steps can be drilled down into several detailed tasks that serve specific requirements. For example, the Extraction step can be specialized into batch or stream processing, while batch processing can be specialized in full, differential, and incremental extraction. The latter can be performed using data logs or timestamps, which involves not only specific strategies but also specific technologies. The proposed architecture decomposes each ETL stage into individual components with well-defined communication interfaces. These components are self-adaptative, promoting reusability and process quality to the implementation of well-known design patterns.

Let us consider a real-world based case study, namely "MyCar" as a car glass replacement company. To support the analytical model, data should be extracted from an operational system to a Data Lake holding raw data that should be posteriorly transformed. Based on a set of analytical requirements related to Sales, a dimensional schema consisting of a *Sales* fact table and the dimensions: *Calendar* (supporting the temporal perspective), *Item* (e.g., glass for a given vehicle), *Customer*, the *Branch* (who perform the sale) and *Document* (describing the fiscal operation) was developed. Data extracted from the operational systems are stored in the Data Lake. After applying cleaning and standardization procedures (type conversions, value substitution, value multiplication), the data is moved to the DW.

The ETL system architecture is based on the concept of patterns and micro-patterns. Patterns represent high-level components that act as gateways and mediators to the

underlying micro-services. The system interactions are directly performed to patterns that mediate the necessary steps to accomplish a specific task. That way, the ETL designer doesn't need to know all the existing micro-services available. They only need to know the macro procedures they can use and configure. Everything else is mediated internally, encapsulating complexity and implementation details.

At the logical level, patterns represent software components with a bounded context. They do a particular task considering a specific strategy. For example, for data extraction, several strategies can be applied which are related to several factors (e.g., operational system availability, the analyse frequency or the amount of the handled data.

For that reason, each component should have an interface for interacting with other systems/services, exposing all specificities needed for its execution. The Data Capture (DC) component is responsible for extracting data from one system to another. According to ETL and source system requirements, several possibilities can be followed:

- Using a query: some transactional applications maintain specific metadata for every record, allowing for the identification of new and modified rows (e.g., using a *ModifiedDate/CreatedDate* attribute).
- Differential data extraction, consisting of the comparison between the current state of the data with the previous state of the data to identify the changes.
- Audit tables, storing the entire row to keep track of attribute changes, storing each attribute in which historical data should be kept, a primary key as well as the performed operation.
- Log-Based: typically, transactional databases store all changes in a transaction log (which is useful to recover if some problem occurs).

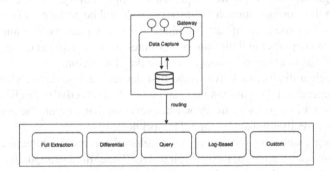

Fig. 1. Data Capture service.

These techniques imply different configurations, not only related to the needed data objects but also to the intermediate operations data that need to be done for a particular strategy. For example, when using the Audit tables approach, data is directly extracted from these tables and a truncate operation is performed for each one.

Depicted in Fig. 1, the DC service acts as an API gateway, providing the routes to each one of the services (presented at the bottom of the image). The API gateway is a middle-tier to interact with services, providing a simpler interface for performing data extraction

procedures. The DC have a database for storing metadata about the process but not the data itself. This component moves data from one repository to another using the strategy encapsulated by one of the services presented in the second-tier. All process is managed by the first-tier service (i.e., the DC) that controls and stores all related information in its internal database. Thus, other processes can access different DC strategies in one place isolated by the DC gateway. It provides flexibility to interact with different strategies as and when the ETL process needs. For example, this component can extract data from a specific data source using different strategies for extracting data from different tables. This way, there is no need to expose all services. Services are independent of each other. While the first-tier service communication is based on REST and has their own endpoints via which they communicate with other first-tier services, the communication between first and second-tier services is performed using a message-based asynchronous communication.

The DC pattern embodies an adaptative behaviour promoted by a specific vocabulary (based on [5]) that specifies what should be done in the data extraction process. The structure defined for each pattern configuration consists of three components: input, core, and output. In the input component, all information about the data input (such as the identification of the source system and related data objects) is defined. The core configuration depends on each service configuration variant, allowing to configure and define the service behaviour and the interactions needed between the second-tier services. The output configuration describes the data destination as well the data properties that are returned after service execution.

The core component is specific to this service and is used to indicate the type of extraction (full or incremental) and the tables to extract (identified by the dataObject tag). Finally, the output component is used to indicate the parts of the data that should be stored in a target repository. Figure 2 represents a simple configuration example for the DC service. In this configuration, a full extraction should be performed from *MyCarDB* (a SQL Server database), specifically in tables: *customer*, *address*, *film* and *rental*. The vocabulary also supports the definition of attributes for each table and the definition of specific conditions to compose a query used for data extraction.

There is a clear distinction between the first tier and second-tier services. The first-tier services represent ETL patterns and can be invoked directly by the ETL workflow. These services act as a gateway to second-tier services that support the first-tier. Thus, they cannot be directly invoked by the ETL workflow.

Figure 3 represents an overview of the developed services architecture. Following the MyCar case study, after data extraction to DL. Then, the Data Quality service will be used to improve data quality through the application of data cleaning procedures (such as string normalization or data uniformization). Then, the Data Conciliation and Integration (DCI) service is responsible for performing the data integration (in major cases, it involves joining operations between data extracted from several data source tables).

Before proceeding to data load to the target repository, new surrogate keys need to be generated for each dimension record, and for fact table records, a Surrogate Key Pipeline service should be used to replace business keys with surrogate keys. Figure 3 only presents a subset of possible first-tier services that can be directly invoked by the

```
<config>
 <name>DC</name>
  <input>
   <database>
    <server>(...)</server>
    (...)
    <type>SQLServer</type>
    <name>MyCarDB</name>
   </database>
  </input>
  <core>
   <extraction>
    <type>full</type>
    <dataObjects>
     <dataObject>customer</dataObject>
     <dataObject>address</dataObject>
     <dataObject>film</dataObject>
     <dataObject>rental</dataObject>
    </dataObjects>
   </core>
   <output>
    <type>DSA</type>
    <database>
     <server>(...)</server>
     (...)
     <type>SQLServer</type>
     <name>MyCarDSA</name>
    </database>
   </output>
</config>
```

Fig. 2. DC configuration example

workflow layer: a specific component responsible to interpret the workflow of tasks that should be executed, ensuring all the dependencies and restrictions needed of its execution. Each one of these services has its own DSL (based on the description presented in Fig. 2) and needs to properly be configured according to its specific requirements.

Figure 3 presents an architecture overview representing the first-tier and second-tier services. Each second-tier service can invoke other second-tier services to support the defined functionality. The first-tier services can be directly invoked by the workflow layer: a specific component responsible to interpret the workflow of tasks ensuring all the dependencies and restrictions needed of its execution. Each one of these services has its own DSL (based on the description presented in Fig. 2) and needs to properly be configured according to its specific requirements. The second-tier services support several specific procedures used by first-tier services. For example, the Data Lookup service is used for data lookups (useful for example in the SKP service or Data Quality Service for data uniformization based on data dictionaries), the Schema Generator service (SG), is used for generate data structures (useful for the generation of intermediate data stores),

or the Data Profiling service (DP) is used to create a data profile (considering the existence of null values, value distribution or integrity constraints) that can be used by other services.

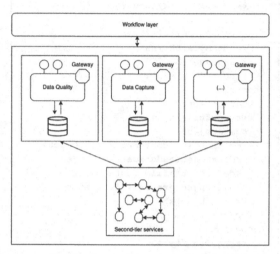

Fig. 3. First and Second-tier services

Each first-tier service runs on a node, representing a process that can host one or many services. Second-tier services are running in several nodes, according to the needs of each first-tier service. All communication is supported by a service broker, presented in each node. A central message broker to exchange messages among nodes using a publish/subscribe messaging pattern (using Kafka) was used. A Gateway service is also used for handling requests made to the system, forwarding them to the service broker (during the development phase we used the Molecular framework[1]). Because we are dealing with very time-consuming operations and the amount of data is considerable, a polling mechanism was implemented that controls the ETL task flow to periodically send requests to the server requesting information about a specific request.

For the developed prototype, the Workflow Layer presented in Fig. 3 was supported by Microsoft Integration Services (SSIS). As such, a control flow component was created with specific tasks to perform HTTP calls to the services with their respective configurations. SSIS defines the order in which service will be called and provide the necessary mechanism to monitor all process (including the pooling mechanism implementation through "for loop containers").

5 Conclusions

During the last few years, several research works have explored new ways to implement and use ETL processes, mainly considering the new demands imposed by emergent

---

[1] https://moleculer.services/docs/0.14/concepts.html.

environments and scenarios (typically involving Big Data scenarios). However, ETL systems still present many challenges. Since specific and low-level tasks/procedures are used to fit analytical requirements, the ETL development process is even more complex, affected by the source data complexity, heterogeneity, and quality. Additionally, analytical requirements also change more frequently (following the changes in operational processes and/or the needs for data analytics), directly affecting the populating processes that are used to fit operational data to the analytical requirements). One of the main problems with ETL development and maintenance is related to its implementation which typically results in monolithic systems. Developed ETL components are highly dependent on each other, resulting in complex systems, difficult to maintain, and directed to specialized personnel to support their implementation.

In this paper, an ETL system prototype was developed following a service-oriented approach. The services composition is based on the notion of subsystems that represent typical procedures applied to ETL implementation. The Surrogate Key Pipeline or Slowly Changing Dimension are typical procedures that can be generalized and applied in almost every case. For example, in a typical scenario, the Surrogate Key Pipeline performs similar tasks for populating DW facts tables. It involves a set of lookup operations to replace business keys with DW surrogate keys. A DSL supporting a set of patterns was used for generalized the behaviour, specifying a set of properties that can be configured to generate specific instances of this procedure.

Considering a specific case study, the developed prototype represents a proof of concept for ETL development considering not only the pattern orientation but also considering some service-oriented architecture specificities. Even considering a subset of the standards that can be implemented and a simplification of the applicability of each one, the prototype allowed for the evaluation of several aspects related to their implementation, namely for the services communication and data persistence for services and among services. The prototype used in the presented case study revealed an interesting performance that is close to the implementation of the same ETL process using a traditional approach based on SSIS. However, is implementation also revealed the complexity of the proposed DSL. It involves several aspects related to the usage of the associated processes, forcing the ETL designer to understand clearly the patterns associated to each service. We believe this problem could be minimized through the implementation of a GUI to guide users in all configuration steps, reducing or avoiding the interaction with long and verbose XML files that support services configuration. The BPMN integration for conceptual representation is also planned, allowing for process abstract description before its implementation. Additionally, BPMN can also communicate with the respective services, providing an interface for the Work-flow Layer (presented in Fig. 3) to represent workflow orchestration, allowing users to monitor and control process execution.

Acknowledgements. This work has been supported by national funds through FCT - Fundação para a Ciência e Tecnologia through project UIDB/04728/2020.

References

1. Newman, S.: Building Microservices: Designing Fine-Grained Systems. O'Reilly Media, Newton (2015)

2. Dehghani, Z.: Data Mesh. O'Reilly Media, Inc., Newton (2021)
3. Armbrust, M., Ghodsi, A., Xin, R., Zaharia, M.: Lakehouse: a new generation of open platforms that unify data warehousing and advanced analytics. In: Conference on Innovative Data Systems Research (CIDR) (2021)
4. Oliveira, B., Oliveira, Ó., Santos, V., Belo, O.: ETL development using patterns: a service-oriented approach. In: Filipe, J., Smialek, M., Brodsky, A., and Hammoudi, S. (eds.) Proceedings of the 21st International Conference on Enterprise Information Systems. pp. 216–222. SCITEPRESS - Science and Technology Publications, Crete, Greece (2019). https://doi.org/10.5220/0007727502160222
5. Oliveira, B., Belo, O.: On the specification of extract, transform, and load patterns behavior: a domain-specific language approach. Expert Syst. **34**, e12168 (2017). https://doi.org/10.1111/exsy.12168
6. El Akkaoui, Z., Mazón, J.-N., Vaisman, A., Zimányi, E.: BPMN-based conceptual modeling of ETL processes. In: Cuzzocrea, A., Dayal, U. (eds.) DaWaK 2012. LNCS, vol. 7448, pp. 1–14. Springer, Heidelberg (2012). https://doi.org/10.1007/978-3-642-32584-7_1
7. Liu, Y., Vitolo, T.M.: Graph data warehouse: steps to integrating graph databases into the traditional conceptual structure of a data warehouse. In: 2013 IEEE International Congress on Big Data, pp. 433–434 (2013). https://doi.org/10.1109/BigData.Congress.2013.72
8. Chevalier, M., El Malki, M., Kopliku, A., Teste, O., Tournier, R.: Implementing multidimensional data warehouses into NoSQL. In: Proceedings of the 17th International Conference on Enterprise Information Systems, vol. 1. pp. 172–183. SCITEPRESS - Science and Technology Publications, Lda (2015). https://doi.org/10.5220/0005379801720183
9. Yangui, R., Nabli, A., Gargouri, F.: ETL based framework for NoSQL warehousing. In: Themistocleous, M., Morabito, V. (eds.) EMCIS 2017. LNBIP, vol. 299, pp. 40–53. Springer, Cham (2017). https://doi.org/10.1007/978-3-319-65930-5_4
10. Ali, S.M.F.: Next-generation ETL Framework to address the challenges posed by Big Data. In: CEUR Workshop Proceedings, vol. 2062 (2018)
11. Machado, G.V., Cunha, Í., Pereira, A.C.M., Oliveira, L.B.: DOD-ETL: distributed on-demand ETL for near real-time business intelligence. J. Internet Serv. Appl. **10**(1), 1–15 (2019). https://doi.org/10.1186/s13174-019-0121-z
12. Debroy, V., Brimble, L., Yost, M.: NewTL: engineering an extract, transform, load (ETL) software system for business on a very large scale. In: Proceedings of ACM Symposium Applied Computing, pp. 1568–1575 (2018). https://doi.org/10.1145/3167132.3167300
13. Ozyurt, I.B., Grethe, J.S.: Foundry: a message-oriented, horizontally scalable ETL system for scientific data integration and enhancement. Database (Oxford) **2018**, 1–13 (2018). https://doi.org/10.1093/database/bay130
14. Awad, M.M.I., Abdullah, M.S., Ali, A.B.M.: Extending ETL framework using service oriented architecture. Procedia Comput. Sci. **3**, 110–114 (2011). https://doi.org/10.1016/j.procs.2010.12.019
15. Akkaoui, Z., El Zimanyi, E.: Defining ETL worfklows using BPMN and BPEL. In: Proceeding of the ACM Twelfth International Workshop on Data Warehousing and OLAP DOLAP 2009, pp. 41–48. ACM, Hong Kong (2009). https://doi.org/10.1145/1651291.1651299
16. Wang, H., Ye, Z.: An ETL services framework based on metadata. In: Proceedings - 2010 2nd International Working on Intelligent System Application, ISA 2010, pp. 0–3 (2010). https://doi.org/10.1109/IWISA.2010.5473575
17. Laigner, R., et al.: From a monolithic big data system to a microservices event-driven architecture. In: Proceedings - 46th Euromicro Conference Software Engineering Advances Application SEAA 2020, pp. 213–220 (2020). https://doi.org/10.1109/SEAA51224.2020.00045

18. Shakir, A., Staegemann, D., Volk, M., Jamous, N., Turowski, K.: Towards a concept for building a big data architecture with microservices. In: Business Information System, pp. 83–94 (2021). https://doi.org/10.52825/bis.v1i.67
19. Zhelev, S., Rozeva, A.: Using microservices and event driven architecture for big data stream processing. In: AIP Conference Proceedings, vol. 2172 (2019). https://doi.org/10.1063/1.5133587
20. Gamma, E., Helm, R., Johnson, R.E., Vlissides, J.: Design patterns: elements of reusable object-oriented software. Design **206**, 395 (1995). https://doi.org/10.1093/carcin/bgs084
21. Ralph, K., Margy, R.: The Data Warehouse Toolkit. John Wiley & Sons, Inc., Hoboken (2013)
22. Oliveira, B., Belo, O.: An ontology for describing ETL patterns behavior. In: Francalanci, C., Helfert, M. (eds.) Proceedings of the 5th International Conference on Data Management Technologies and Applications, pp. 102–109. SCITEPRESS - Science and Technology Publications, Lisboa (2016). https://doi.org/10.5220/0005974001020109
23. Lewis, J., Fowler, M.: Microservices. http://martinfowler.com/articles/microservices.html, Accessed 02 Dec 2019

How are you Riding? Transportation Mode Identification from Raw GPS Data

Thiago Andrade[1,2]([✉]) [iD] and João Gama[1,2] [iD]

[1] Institute for Systems and Computer Engineering, Technology and Science
(INESC TEC), Faculdade de Engenharia da Universidade do Porto, Porto, Portugal
thiago.a.silva@inesctec.pt
[2] Faculdade de Ciências, Universidade do Porto, Porto, Portugal

Abstract. Analyzing the way individuals move is fundamental to understand the dynamics of humanity. Transportation mode plays a significant role in human behavior as it changes how individuals travel, how far, and how often they can move. The identification of transportation modes can be used in many applications and it is a key component of the internet of things (IoT) and the Smart Cities concept as it helps to organize traffic control and transport management. In this paper, we propose the use of ensemble methods to infer the transportation modes using raw GPS data. From latitude, longitude, and timestamp we perform feature engineering in order to obtain more discriminative fields for the classification. We test our features in several machine learning algorithms and among those with the best results we perform feature selection using the Boruta method in order to boost our accuracy results and decrease the amount of data, processing time, and noise in the model. We assess the validity of our approach on a real-world dataset with several different transportation modes and the results show the efficacy of our approach.

Keywords: Transportation mode · Classification · GPS · Boruta · Mobility · Trajectory · Feature selection

1 Introduction

Transportation plays a significant role in human behavior and analyzing the way individuals move is fundamental to understanding the dynamics of humanity. Efforts to learn human mobility patterns were associated with classic social sciences back in the nineteenth century when sociologists proposed studies to measure the time people spend doing different activities throughout the day [2].

More recently the pervasiveness of position-enabled personal devices boosted new disciplines in the direction of studying the mobility behavior of individuals from mobility data. This pervasiveness is strongly related to a hot topic called smart cities which have been the focus of several public policies sustained by research in the most variate fields [2]. Recent studies [12] show that the availability and scale of mobility data are expected to grow exponentially, as more

© The Author(s), under exclusive license to Springer Nature Switzerland AG 2022
G. Marreiros et al. (Eds.): EPIA 2022, LNAI 13566, pp. 648–659, 2022.
https://doi.org/10.1007/978-3-031-16474-3_53

and more physical objects will be connected to the Internet of Things (IoT) in the years to come.

Using these data, which is frequently based on a global positioning system (GPS), offers the scientists the possibility of following individual trips with regard to temporal and spatial characteristics with more detail than the outdated and costly travel diaries and surveys [11].

Many researchers have conducted studies with a focus on trip identification and map matching but still, the important field of transportation mode detection (TMD) research lacks studies [11]. A recent review shows that transport mode detection based on GPS tracking data is still challenging [11], especially when the data is unlabeled, i.e., there is no information regarding the transport mode used during a trip [8].

The most important works referring to transportation modes from trajectory data make use of machine learning approaches to identify the modes from GPS or sensors like accelerometers. However, they still have several limitations like the use of more sensors to improve the performance (gyroscope, rotation vector, other professional devices) generating more accurate data to discriminate better the modes, or the aid of external tools and databases like Geographic Information Systems (GIS) to create more discriminative features. Another key point is that many studies employ traditional machine learning methods such as K-Nearest Neighbors, Support Vector Machines, and Decision Trees while most recent studies point that these approaches perform worse than ensemble methods in terms of overall accuracy and robustness [14].

Based on the mentioned open challenges and limitations, in this paper, we propose a method for multi-class classification of transportation modes from raw GPS data without any external information. The main contributions of this research are:

- *Features generation* based on statistics in order to perform knowledge discovery and find hidden information in the data and use it in the classification problem;
- *Application of machine learning techniques* to classify multiple transportation modes;
- *Application of the Boruta method* for feature importance ranking, classification and selection in order to improve our model's performance resulting in a simpler method that is able to achieve the same results as many state-of-the-art proposals;
- *Evaluation of the method on a real-world dataset* that is used as a reference to many research in transportation mode area to confirm the usefulness of our approach.

The following section presents the literature review and the recent most important related works. The remainder of the paper describes the methodology and the data set utilized to assert the method's validity in Sect. 3, in Sect. 4 we discuss the experiments and results obtained. Finally, the conclusions and future work are presented in Sect. 5.

2 Related Work

Recent studies and surveys show that the interest in methods to analyze mobility data and identify the transportation mode has grown and different methodologies and techniques were applied in many scenarios. In this section, we review some relevant works which leverage the information contained in these data for transportation mode identification.

According to a new review by Sadeghian et al. [11], there are three main methodological approaches for transportation mode detection: statistical methods, rule-based methods, and machine learning methods. Among them, machine learning is by far the most commonly used approach.

These studies commonly detected the modes of walking, car, and bus, reaching a detection accuracy of around 90%. The datasets used in the studies varied from only one user and a few trips up to 1000 users and several trips, having recording movement from a few hours or spanned a period of years.

Lari and Golroo [10] proposed using a Random Forest method to determine the transportation modes in the city of Tehran. They were able to identify a car, bus, and walk by discriminating mostly by instant speed and accuracy of GPS signal. The process of classification was based on two important indices: the Gini index and mean decrease accuracy.

By applying a technique of segmenting raw GPS data into trajectories with single-mode segments, Zhu et al. [17] proposed a framework for the identification of transportation mode. The authors also include modern features in order to discriminate between the different kinds of modes such as car, bus, bike, and walk. A post-processing procedure is then adopted to check the whole trajectory in order to confirm the inferred mode. The Random Forest was the classifier that obtained the best accuracy values reaching around 82% in general with detail of around 91% for the car transportation mode class.

Tree-Based Ensemble Classifiers were used by Xiao et al. [14] in order to infer hybrid transportation modes using only GPS data. The proposal used a statistical method to generate global features and extract several local features from sub-trajectories after trajectory segmentation. These features were then combined in the classification phase. The authors used tree-based ensemble models (Random Forest, Gradient Boosting Decision Tree, and XGBoost) instead of traditional methods (K-Nearest Neighbors, Decision Tree, and Support Vector Machines) to classify the different transportation modes. Their results show that the best model was XGBoost achieving a classification accuracy of around 90%.

A more recent study by Wang et al. [13] used Light Gradient Boosting Machine (LightGBM) classifier to detect seven kinds of transportation modes. They first divided the original trajectories into sub-trajectories to obtain single transportation mode trajectories. Then they create a vector with eight basic and three advanced features. The basics are distance, velocity, and acceleration-related items while the advanced are related to heading change, stop change, and velocity change rates. The authors also used eXtreme Gradient Boosting (XGBoost) and Decision Trees to validate their method being the LightGBM the best model.

In spite of being similar to other proposals listed in the state-of-the-art section, our approach differs from the others as we used fewer features to discriminate between the transportation modes while also using a statistical ground method called Boruta in order to perform the feature selection to keep our model simple, light and noiseless.

3   Methodology

Our proposal is to build a classifier for the identification of the different transportation modes that are available in the mentioned dataset with no help from external data. Among the classes we have: walk, bike, car, subway, taxi, and bus. The steps consist of data preprocessing, features generation and extraction, data balancing, model classification and training, model evaluation, feature selection using Boruta's method, and model reevaluation after feature selection.

3.1   Preprocessing and Data Transformation

The first step is the preprocessing task that is including among other activities, the data cleaning process where we perform outliers and noise removal [3,6]. First of all, we need to look for duplicate data in the dataset and remove it. We also look for null data in the points where we are not able to use the latitude or longitude to create new features in the next step.

The dataset we will use in this study is published with only a few features regarding the position (in the form of latitude, longitude, and a time-stamp) and the user ID. The original GPS Geolife dataset is available in the form of several files per user where some of them are already cut when the user ends a trajectory, others come with a sequence of many trips. In this sense, we have to reprocess all data per user in order to perform the cut accordingly. In this work, we denote a new trajectory every time an individual stops moving or the time delta between points is more than 30 min.

Due to the influence of GPS signal loss and data drift, there are a number of unwanted points in the trajectories set during the data acquisition. Hence, cleaning tasks need to be performed in order to have more trustworthy data. Examples of common situations are individuals appearing very far away from their previous position in a short time, which is quite improbable. This inconsistent data must be deleted. We apply a smoothing median filter to each set of 5 of GPS points to remove the noise as it is more robust to outliers [1,2].

3.2   Feature Generation

One of the most important steps when dealing with classification tasks is the feature engineering [14]. As we are dealing with movements and transitions, one needs to derive new information from the original data to calculate key features to help in the classification task.

In this step, we perform feature engineering creating new fields such as start and stop positions, time of the day, length of trajectory, duration of trajectory, velocity, max velocity, average velocity, the median of velocity, acceleration, max acceleration, average acceleration, and the median of acceleration.

After preprocessing the data and acquiring the new features we can drop the *trajectory id* attribute as it will not contribute to estimating the target variable in our classification task [6]. This field turns out to be irrelevant for the next steps and was used only to calculate the features for each trajectory.

3.3 Classification Models

Here we have a brief but straight definition of the models we used in order to identify the transportation mode of the trips. These are classifiers' versions of algorithms that are widely used in machine learning problems.

K-Nearest Neighbors (KNN) an easy way to vision KNN is to think of the k nearest neighbor algorithm as representing each data point in an *n-dimensional space* which is defined by n features. It calculates the distance between one point to another, then assigns the label of unobserved data based on the labels of the nearest observed data points [6].

Naive Bayes methods are a set of supervised learning algorithms based on Bayes' theorem with the "naive" assumption of independence between every pair of features. In spite of their apparently over-simplified assumptions, naive Bayes classifiers have worked quite well in many real-world situations, famously document classification and spam filtering. The biggest advantage of Naive Bayes is that, while most machine learning algorithms rely on a large amount of training data, it performs relatively well even when the training data size is small [6].

Decision Trees are non-parametric supervised learning methods used for classification. The goal is to create a model that predicts the value of a target variable by learning simple decision rules inferred from the data features. Given a training vector $X(n_{samples}, n_{features})$ and a label vector $Y(n_{samples})$, a decision tree recursively partitions the space such that the samples with the same labels are grouped together [6]. A decision tree builds tree branches in a hierarchical approach and each branch can be considered as an if-then statement. The branches develop by partitioning the dataset into subsets based on the most important features. The final classification happens at the leaves of the decision tree.

Random Forest. As the name suggests, a random forest is a collection of decision trees. It is a common type of ensemble method which aggregates results from multiple predictors leveraging the reason that the combination of simple classifiers performs better than a best single classifier. Random forest additionally utilizes a bagging technique that allows each tree trained on a random sampling

of the original dataset and uses the majority vote from trees to get the final result [6]. In a comparison with a decision tree, it has better generalization, with a trade of having less interpretability, due to the extra layers added to the model. A random forest is a meta estimator that fits a number of decision tree classifiers on various sub-samples of the dataset and uses averaging to improve the predictive accuracy and control over-fitting [6].

Gradient Boosting is a method of converting weak learners into strong learners. In boosting, each new tree is a fit on a modified version of the original data set. Gradient Boosting trains many models in a gradual, additive, and sequential manner and identify the shortcomings of weak learners (e.g. decision trees) by using gradients in the loss function [5]. The loss function is a measure indicating how good the model coefficients are at fitting the underlying data.

XGBoost Classifier is an optimized distributed gradient boosting library designed to be highly efficient, flexible, and portable. XGBoost provides a parallel tree boosting that solves many tasks in a fast and accurate way. It leverages additional regularization terms, second-order approximation of the loss function, and shrinkage to reduce the influence of individual trees [4].

Support Vector Machines (SVM) algorithm finds the best way to classify the data based on the position in relation to a border between positive class and negative class. This border is known as the hyperplane which maximizes the distance between data points from different classes [6]. Similar to the decision trees and random forests, support vector machines can be used in both classification and regression, SVC is the SVM version for classification problems.

3.4 Dataset

Geolife Dataset. This GPS trajectory dataset was collected by Microsoft Research Asia for the Geolife [16] project. It has data from 182 users in a period of almost five years (from April 2007 to August 2012). It is still a reference dataset for many state-of-the-art methods. We used the dataset version 1.2.2. This version contains 17.621 trajectories with a total distance of about 1.2 million kilometers and a total duration of 48.000+ hours. These trajectories were recorded by different GPS loggers and GPS phones, and have a variety of sampling rates. 91% of the trajectories are logged in a dense representation, e.g. every 1 to 5 s or every 5 to 10 m per point [15, 16]. This dataset recorded a broad range of users' outdoor movements, including not only life routines like going home and going to work but also some entertainment and sports activities, such as shopping, sightseeing, dining, hiking, and cycling. In the dataset, a small part of the users labeled their trajectories with their starting transportation mode or when their mode changed. In this version we have 73 users with some of the trips and the corresponding single mode labels, so we use these data to assert the classifiers' results.

Balancing and Pruning the Data in order to maintain just trajectories that may represent some meaningful movements is also an important task. In various real-world datasets, the number of instances varies accordingly to the different classes. This is a common problem in applications where a subset of classes in the data appears more frequently than the rest of the classes. It is known that many classification algorithms perform worse when handling imbalanced data where they tend to classify the instances towards the majority class [6].

To avoid these problems, we employ two techniques for organizing the data. First of all, we prune the data from classes with less than 30 trajectories as they would not be able to represent real scenarios in our data. With the rest of the classes, as we can't generate more data to have a balanced dataset, we have to recur to some techniques for artificially balancing the data so the minority classes become more relevant [6]. In our scenario, we choose to use the oversampling of the minority classes that have more observations than our threshold used in the previous step. The original data distribution has 783 observations for walk, 767 for bike, 593 for car, 377 for bus, 174 for subway, and 81 for taxi. As one can notice, bike and walk represent more than 50% of the data. After performing the data balancing task, we end up with a new and more uniform distribution with roughly 17% of each class.

4   Experiments and Results

In order to obtain unbiased and more reliable results, we employed the K-fold cross-validation for the splitting of the dataset with K equal to 10. In this way, the original data is randomly split into the K parts being one of the K parts used as a validation set, while the other $K - 1$ parts were used for training the model. The process was repeated then for K times, every time with a new and different validation set. We average the accuracy for the K iterations to obtain the final accuracy of the model. One of the great advantages of this technique is that at the end of the process, all samples are used both for training and validation, and each sample is used for validation only once during the whole process.

For this experiment, we consider only the trajectories with more than 50 points and 5 min reasoning that fewer observations than that would not lead to conclusions related to users' transportation modes being too few data to process as other recent works suggest [1,2].

4.1   Evaluation Metrics

Several types of evaluation metrics are commonly used by research communities in multi-class classification problems. To perform a complete evaluation of the method's performance we use accuracy metrics (precision, recall, and F1-score), confusion matrix, ROC, and AUC curves.

Classification Accuracy is used to measure the qualitative performance of the classifiers. The two most popular metrics used to perform the quality of the classifier are Precision and Recall. These measures rely on 4 key components: true positives (TP), true negatives (TN), false positives (FP), and false negatives (FN).

Precision (Eq. 1) is a fraction of items in the query that are relevant. In other words, it is the ratio of results that the user is satisfied with among all the results. The objective is to have few FPs in order to have better results [6].

Recall (Eq. 2) sometimes also referred to as sensitivity, is the fraction of the total relevant items contained in the query. In other words, it is the proportion of classified results that the user is satisfied with among all the items in the query that are desired by the user. The objective is to increase the TP values rather than the FN values [6].

$$Precision = \frac{TP}{TP + FP} \tag{1}$$

$$Recall = \frac{TP}{TP + FN} \tag{2}$$

$$Accuracy = \frac{TP + TN}{(TP + TN) + (FP + FN)} \tag{3}$$

A more balanced metric is the $F1score$, it is designed to obtain the overall score about the performance of the model and considers both precision and recall [6].

$$F1Score = \frac{2 * (Precision * Recall)}{Precision + Recall} \tag{4}$$

In order to have a more visual of the performance of a given algorithm, confusion matrices are employed. The matrix shows error rates as well as precision and recall values. We also use ROC and AUC as they can help with analyzing the results in an even more visual manner. ROC is the graphic representation of true positive rate (TPR) against false positive rate (FPR) at various classification thresholds. AUC is the area under the ROC curve. The higher the AUC indicates the better model performance [6]. The formulas for TPR and FPR are as follows in Eqs. (5) and (6):

$$TPR = \frac{TP}{TP + TN} \tag{5}$$

$$FPR = \frac{FP}{TN + FP} \tag{6}$$

4.2 Using Boruta Method for Feature Selection

Feature selection is an important step in applications of machine learning methods because removing irrelevant features results in a model with better performance, that is easier to understand, runs faster, and with less noise. To perform feature selection we rely on the Boruta [9] algorithm that was designed to

automatically perform feature selection on a given dataset. Modern-day real-life datasets have many features and would be impractical to try every combination of features in order to decide which contributes to the final score and which doesn't. We also have to take into account that non-linear relationships between the features are not easily spotted by the human eye, thus, applying an automated process, especially statistically supported methods is a good practice. One of the main advantages of the Boruta method over other commonly used feature selection techniques such as the *SelectFromModel*[1] used in Python programming language is that these techniques often require the definition of thresholds, thus, excluding bias and arbitrariness from the process.

Boruta adds randomness to the data set by creating shuffled copies of all features generating the so-called *shadow features* Having the engineered data organized the algorithm trains a classifier over the extended data set (original attributes plus shadow attributes) and applies a feature importance measure such as Mean Decrease Accuracy (MDA) [7] to evaluate the importance of each feature. Features with higher importance than the MDA are called *hits*. This process is repeated and at every iteration, Boruta checks whether a real feature has higher importance and removes features that are deemed highly unimportant. The stop criterion is either when all features get confirmed or rejected or when the algorithm reaches a specified limit of the classifier (number of trees for example) [9]. Ideally, the importance of the shadow attributes has to be close to zero and these attributes could play the role of reference values for deciding which attributes are important. After performing the N iterations, the result is three groups of variables: *Rejected:* the features that end up in this group are considered noise, so they should be dropped; *Tentative:* the algorithm is indecisive about the features that are in this group so is up to the user to decide depending on the scenario; *Confirmed:* the features that are considered as predictive, so they are kept.

If one decides to be too conservative about the features, the model could end up having to handle unnecessary data and noise maybe reducing the accuracy of the model and surely requiring more time for it to run. On the other hand, being too aggressive and removing too many features can lead to the loss of useful information.

4.3   Algorithms Results

Here we show the results for the tested models. Table 1 shows the values for precision and recall for all the classes. The number of observations to support the results is the same in all cases: 1097.

The best of the classifiers is the regular Decision Tree, followed by XGBoost. Some classifiers like Naive Bayes and SVM performed below the 50% threshold, which is worse than choosing by chance.

---

[1] https://tinyurl.com/SelectFromModel.

Table 1. Classification report for all the algorithms

Mode	Precision							Recall						
	RF	DT	GBM	KNN	NB	SVM	XGB	RF	DT	GBM	KNN	NB	SVM	XGB
Bus	**0.88**	0.78	0.65	0.59	0.45	0.38	0.73	**0.95**	0.83	0.57	0.52	0.07	0.22	0.66
Walk	**0.91**	0.84	0.78	0.80	0.21	0.57	0.82	0.86	0.88	0.78	0.72	**0.95**	0.64	0.82
Taxi	**0.99**	0.92	0.81	0.75	0.15	0.44	0.87	1.00	0.98	0.85	0.85	0.11	0.68	0.87
Bike	**0.95**	0.93	0.83	0.75	0.53	0.50	0.87	0.89	**1.00**	0.90	0.95	0.06	0.35	0.90
Car	0.95	**0.99**	0.98	0.92	0.93	0.92	0.98	0.91	**1.00**	**1.00**	**1.00**	0.86	0.88	**1.00**
Subway	**0.96**	0.85	0.74	0.81	0.32	0.54	0.81	**1.00**	0.68	0.75	0.56	0.03	0.68	0.83

Fig. 1. Confusion matrix (left) and classification report (right) for the Random Forest classifier. (Color figure online)

Our best model is Random Forest with 100 estimators. This ensemble method obtained an overall accuracy of 0.92% and a ROC x AUC relation of 0.99% being considerably superior over the others.

By looking at the classification report in Fig. 1 is possible to notice that the model can be improved for the classes bus, bike, and walk (the red areas) where it performed slightly worse than the average of the other classes. It is not clear what makes the models not discriminate against these transportation modes so well as the others.

Regarding the application of the Boruta, the recommendations were to keep the features velocity, max velocity, average velocity, the median of velocity, acceleration, max acceleration, average acceleration, the median of acceleration as they were placed in the *tentative* and *confirmed* areas. The method recommends dropping the start position, stop position, time of the day, length of trajectory, and the duration of trajectory as they ranked in lower positions in the *rejected* area.

When comparing the result of the two models we can see that the original random forest with 100 estimators has an accuracy of 92%, which is increased to 94% using the Boruta feature selection. In this way, we have a better model, with a reduced number of features.

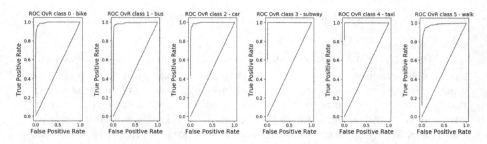

Fig. 2. The ROC and AUC for the Random Forest classifier. We used the strategy One vs. Rest to compare the classes.

The ROC and AUC results for the Random Forest classifier are shown in Fig. 2. We used the strategy *One vs. Rest* to compare the classes. As one can notice, the area under the ROC curve for each of the six classes is close to 1 which means that the classifier is able to clearly separate the instances of each of the different cases.

5   Conclusions and Future Work

In order to understand the dynamics of humanity, is fundamental to analyze the way individuals move and the transportation modes they use to do so.

In this paper, we presented a method for the classification and detection of transportation modes from GPS trajectory without any external data in an automatic manner. The results of the experiments where we compared several other approaches show that the Random Forest classifier is more accurate than the others and the ensemble methods overall perform better for this given task. We achieved the results by performing feature engineering creating new fields from raw GPS data and applying a statistically ground approach for feature selection using the Boruta method which resulted in a simpler and noiseless model with accuracy similar to the others.

For future work, we intend to choose other features and add external information such as closeness to bus stops and bike lanes to boost the accuracy for these classes as they showed to be harder to classify. Hyper-parameter tuning can be also performed over the best-ranked classifiers to obtain even higher accuracy results. We also intend to experiment with our classifiers on other real-world mobility datasets.

Acknowledgement. This work is financed by National Funds through the Portuguese funding agency, FCT - Fundação para a Ciência e a Tecnologia within project: UI/BD/152697/2022.

References

1. Andrade, T., Cancela, B., Gama, J.: Discovering locations and habits from human mobility data. Ann. Telecommun. **75**(9), 505–521 (2020)
2. Andrade, T., Cancela, B., Gama, J.: From mobility data to habits and common pathways. Expert. Syst. **37**(6), e12627 (2020)
3. Andrade, T., Gama, J., Ribeiro, R.P., Sousa, W., Carvalho, A.: Anomaly detection in sequential data: principles and case studies. In: Wiley Encyclopedia of Electrical and Electronics Engineering, pp. 1–14 (2019)
4. Chen, T., et al.: XGBoost: extreme gradient boosting. R package version 0.4-2 1(4), 1–4 (2015)
5. Friedman, J.H.: Greedy function approximation: a gradient boosting machine. Ann. Stat. 1189–1232 (2001)
6. Gama, J., Carvalho, A.C.P.D.L., Faceli, K., Lorena, A.C., Oliveira, M., et al.: Extração de conhecimento de dados: data mining. Edições Sílabo, Lisboa, 3rd edn. (2017)
7. Han, H., Guo, X., Yu, H.: Variable selection using mean decrease accuracy and mean decrease gini based on random forest. In: 2016 7th IEEE International Conference on Software Engineering and Service Science (ICSESS), pp. 219–224. IEEE (2016)
8. Huang, H., Cheng, Y., Weibel, R.: Transport mode detection based on mobile phone network data: a systematic review. Transp. Res. Part C: Emerg. Technol. **101**, 297–312 (2019)
9. Kursa, M.B., Rudnicki, W.R.: Feature selection with the Boruta package. J. Stat. Softw. **36**, 1–13 (2010)
10. Lari, Z.A., Golroo, A.: Automated transportation mode detection using smart phone applications via machine learning: case study mega city of Tehran. In: Proceedings of the Transportation Research Board 94th Annual Meeting, Washington, DC, USA, pp. 11–15 (2015)
11. Sadeghian, P., Håkansson, J., Zhao, X.: Review and evaluation of methods in transport mode detection based on GPS tracking data. J. Traffic Transp. Eng. (English Edition) **8**(4), 467–482 (2021)
12. Toch, E., Lerner, B., Ben-Zion, E., Ben-Gal, I.: Analyzing large-scale human mobility data: a survey of machine learning methods and applications. Knowl. Inf. Syst. **58**(3), 501–523 (2018). https://doi.org/10.1007/s10115-018-1186-x
13. Wang, B., Wang, Y., Qin, K., Xia, Q.: Detecting transportation modes based on LightGBM classifier from GPS trajectory data. In: 2018 26th International Conference on Geoinformatics, pp. 1–7. IEEE (2018)
14. Xiao, Z., Wang, Y., Fu, K., Wu, F.: Identifying different transportation modes from trajectory data using tree-based ensemble classifiers. ISPRS Int. J. Geo Inf. **6**(2), 57 (2017)
15. Zheng, Y., Li, Q., Chen, Y., Xie, X., Ma, W.Y.: Understanding mobility based on GPS data. In: Proceedings of the 10th International Conference on Ubiquitous Computing, pp. 312–321. ACM (2008)
16. Zheng, Y., Xie, X., Ma, W.Y.: Geolife: a collaborative social networking service among user, location and trajectory. IEEE Data Eng. Bull. **33**(2), 32–39 (2010)
17. Zhu, Q., et al.: Identifying transportation modes from raw GPS data. In: Che, W., et al. (eds.) ICYCSEE 2016. CCIS, vol. 623, pp. 395–409. Springer, Singapore (2016). https://doi.org/10.1007/978-981-10-2053-7_35

KRR - Knowledge Representation and Reasoning

Almost Certain Termination for $\mathcal{ALC}$ Weakening

Roberto Confalonieri[1], Pietro Galliani[1], Oliver Kutz[1(✉)],
Daniele Porello[2], Guendalina Righetti[1], and Nicolas Troquard[1]

[1] Faculty of Computer Science, Free University of Bozen-Bolzano, Bolzano, Italy
{roberto.confalonieri,pietro.galliani,oliver.kutz,
guendalina.righetti,nicolas.troquard}@unibz.it
[2] Department of Antiquity, Philosophy, and History, University of Genoa,
Genoa, Italy
daniele.porello@unige.it

Abstract. Concept refinement operators have been introduced to describe and compute generalisations and specialisations of concepts, with, amongst others, applications in concept learning and ontology repair through axiom weakening. We here provide a probabilistic proof of almost-certain termination for iterated refinements, thus for an axiom weakening procedure for the fine-grained repair of $\mathcal{ALC}$ ontologies. We determine the computational complexity of refinement membership, and discuss performance aspects of a prototypical implementation, verifying that almost-certain termination means actual termination in practice.

Keywords: Axiom weakening · Refinement operator · Ontology repair · Almost-certain termination

1 Introduction

The traditional approach to repairing inconsistent ontologies amounts to identifying problematic axioms and removing them (e.g., [4,9,10,18]). Whilst this approach is sufficient to guarantee the consistency of the resulting ontology, it often leads to unnecessary information loss.

Approaches to repairing ontologies more gently via *axiom weakening* were proposed in the literature [2,6,8,19]. In [6], concept refinement in $\mathcal{EL}^{++}$ ontologies is introduced in the context of concept invention. A concept refinement operator to generalise $\mathcal{EL}^{++}$ concepts is proposed and its properties are analysed. This line of work was continued in [19], where the authors define an abstract refinement operator for generalising and specialising $\mathcal{ALC}$ concepts and weakening $\mathcal{ALC}$ axioms. They propose an ontology repair procedure that solves inconsistencies by weakening axioms rather than by removing them. In [2], the authors present general theoretical results for axiom weakening in Description Logics (DLs) and $\mathcal{EL}$ in particular. Refinement operators in Description Logic have also been studied with applications to Machine Learning [5,12–14].

Concept refinement operators come in two flavours [11]. A generalisation operator w.r.t. an ontology $\mathcal{O}$ is a function γ that associates with a concept

G. Marreiros et al. (Eds.): EPIA 2022, LNAI 13566, pp. 663–675, 2022.
https://doi.org/10.1007/978-3-031-16474-3_54

C a set $\gamma_{\mathcal{O}}(C)$ of concepts which are 'super-concepts' of C. Dually, a specialisation operator w.r.t. an ontology $\mathcal{O}$ is a function ρ that associates with a concept C a set $\rho_{\mathcal{O}}(C)$ of concepts which are 'sub-concepts' of C. The notions of 'super', and 'sub-concept' are here implicitly defined by the respective functions, rather than by a purely syntactic procedure. Intuitively, a concept D is a generalised super-concept of concept C w.r.t. ontology $\mathcal{O}$ if in every model of the ontology the extension of D subsumes the extension of C. So for instance, the concept $\exists has\_component.$Carbon is a generalisation of LivingBeing and $= 2\ has\_bodypart.$Legs is a specialisation of LivingBeing (assuming an appropriate background ontology $\mathcal{O}$).

Refinement operators enjoy a few properties that render them suitable for an implementation of axiom weakening [19]. In particular, deciding whether a concept is a refinement of another concept has the same worst-case complexity as deciding concept subsumption in the underlying logic. Refinement operators are then used to weaken axioms, and to repair inconsistent ontologies. Experimentally, it is shown that repairing ontologies via axiom weakening maintains significantly more information than repairing ontologies via axiom deletion, using e.g., measures that evaluate preservation of taxonomic structure. Ontology repairs via concept refinements and axiom weakening have also been used to merge two mutually inconsistent ontologies [17].

In this paper, we fill a gap in the above sketched research landscape and provide a proof of almost-certain termination of the ontology repair procedure based on the axiom weakening proposed in [19]. Since infinite non-stabilising chains of refinements exist in principle, this is the best we could hope for. We also verify in an empirical study that this theoretical result implies actual and robust (that is, reproducible) termination in a number of test scenarios using real world as well as synthetic ontologies.

2   Preliminaries

From a formal point of view, an ontology is a set of formulas in an appropriate logical language with the purpose of describing a particular domain of interest. We briefly introduce $\mathcal{ALC}$; for full details see [1]. The syntax of $\mathcal{ALC}$ is based on two disjoint sets N_C and N_R, concept names and role names respectively. The set of $\mathcal{ALC}$ concepts is generated by the grammar (where $R \in N_R$ and $A \in N_C$):

$$C ::= \bot \mid \top \mid A \mid \neg C \mid C \sqcap C \mid C \sqcup C \mid \forall R.C \mid \exists R.C$$

In the following, $\mathcal{L}(N_C, N_R)$ denotes the set of concepts and roles that can be built over N_C, N_R in $\mathcal{ALC}$. $\mathrm{nnf}(C)$ denotes the negation normal form of concept C. $|C|$ denotes the size of a concept, defined as:

Definition 1. *The size $|C|$ of a concept C is inductively defined as follows. For $C \in N_C \cup \{\top, \bot\}$, $|C| = 1$. Then, $|\neg C| = 1 + |C|$; $|C \sqcap D| = |C \sqcup D| = 1 + |C| + |D|$; and $|\exists R.C| = |\forall R.C| = 1 + |C|$.*

A *TBox* $\mathcal{T}$ is a finite set of concept inclusions (GCIs) of the form $C \sqsubseteq D$ where C and D are concepts. It is used to store terminological knowledge regarding the relationships between concepts. An *ABox* $\mathcal{A}$ is a finite set of formulas of the

form $C(a)$ and $R(a, b)$, which express knowledge about objects in the knowledge domain. An $\mathcal{ALC}$ ontology $\mathcal{O} = \mathcal{T} \cup \mathcal{A}$ is defined by a *TBox* $\mathcal{T}$ and an *ABox* $\mathcal{A}$.

The semantics of $\mathcal{ALC}$ is defined through *interpretations* $I = (\Delta^I, \cdot^I)$, where Δ^I is a non-empty *domain*, and $\cdot^I$ is a function mapping every individual name to an element of Δ^I, each concept name to a subset of the domain, and each role name to a binary relation on the domain; see [1] for details. The interpretation $\mathcal{I}$ is a *model* of the ontology $\mathcal{O}$ if it satisfies all the axioms in $\mathcal{O}$. Given two concepts C and D, we say that C is *subsumed* by D w.r.t. ontology $\mathcal{O}$ ($C \sqsubseteq_{\mathcal{O}} D$) if $C^I \subseteq D^I$ for every model I of $\mathcal{O}$, where we write C^I for the extension of the concept C according to I. We write $C \equiv_{\mathcal{O}} D$ when $C \sqsubseteq_{\mathcal{O}} D$ and $D \sqsubseteq_{\mathcal{O}} C$. C is *strictly subsumed* by D w.r.t. $\mathcal{O}$ ($C \sqsubset_{\mathcal{O}} D$) if $C \sqsubseteq_{\mathcal{O}} D$ and $C \not\equiv_{\mathcal{O}} D$.

We now define the upward and downward covers of concept names and atomic roles respectively. In this paper, their range will consist of the finite set of subconcepts of the ontology $\mathcal{O}$, which is defined as follows:

Definition 2. *For $\mathcal{O}$ an $\mathcal{ALC}$ ontology, the set of* subconcepts *of $\mathcal{O}$ is given by*

$$\mathsf{sub}(\mathcal{O}) = \{\top, \bot\} \cup \bigcup_{C(a) \in \mathcal{A}} \mathsf{sub}(C) \cup \bigcup_{C \sqsubseteq D \in \mathcal{T}} (\mathsf{sub}(C) \cup \mathsf{sub}(D)),$$

where $\mathcal{O} = \mathcal{T} \cup \mathcal{A}$. $\mathsf{sub}(C)$ is the set of subconcepts in C inductively defined over the structure of C.

Intuitively, the upward cover of the concept C collects the most specific subconcepts of $\mathcal{O}$ that subsume C; conversely, the downward cover of C collects the most general subconcepts from $\mathcal{O}$ subsumed by C. The concepts in $\mathsf{sub}(\mathcal{O})$ are *some* concepts that are relevant in the context of $\mathcal{O}$, and that are used as building blocks for generalisations and specialisations. The properties of $\mathsf{sub}(\mathcal{O})$ guarantee that the upward and downward cover sets are finite.

Definition 3. *Let $\mathcal{O} = \mathcal{T} \cup \mathcal{A}$ be an ontology. Let C be a concept, the* upward cover *and* downward cover *of C w.r.t. $\mathcal{O}$ are:*

$$\mathsf{UpCov}_{\mathcal{O}}(C) := \{D \in \mathsf{sub}(\mathcal{O}) \mid C \sqsubseteq_{\mathcal{O}} D \text{ and}$$
$$\nexists . D' \in \mathsf{sub}(\mathcal{O}) \text{ with } C \sqsubset_{\mathcal{O}} D' \sqsubset_{\mathcal{O}} D\},$$
$$\mathsf{DownCov}_{\mathcal{O}}(C) := \{D \in \mathsf{sub}(\mathcal{O}) \mid D \sqsubseteq_{\mathcal{O}} C \text{ and}$$
$$\nexists . D' \in \mathsf{sub}(\mathcal{O}) \text{ with } D \sqsubset_{\mathcal{O}} D' \sqsubset_{\mathcal{O}} C\}.$$

Note that the basic $\mathsf{UpCov}_{\mathcal{O}}$ and $\mathsf{DownCov}_{\mathcal{O}}$ 'miss' a number of relevant refinements, depending on the definition of $\mathsf{sub}(\mathcal{O})$. Consider the following example.

Example 1. Let $N_C = \{A, B, C\}$ and $\mathcal{O} = \{A \sqsubseteq B\}$. Then $\mathsf{sub}(\mathcal{O}) = \{A, B, \top, \bot\}$. According to Definition 3, $\mathsf{UpCov}_{\mathcal{O}}(A \sqcap C) = \{A\}$. Iterating, we get $\mathsf{UpCov}_{\mathcal{O}}(A) = \{A, B\}$ and $\mathsf{UpCov}_{\mathcal{O}}(B) = \{B, \top\}$. Semantically, $B \sqcap C$ is also a generalisation of $A \sqcap C$ w.r.t. $\mathcal{O}$. However, it is missed by the iterated application of $\mathsf{UpCov}_{\mathcal{O}}$, because $B \sqcap C \notin \mathsf{sub}(\mathcal{O})$. Similarly, $\mathsf{UpCov}_{\mathcal{O}}(\exists R.A) = \{\top\}$, even though one would expect semantically that also $\exists R.B$ is a generalisation of $\exists R.A$.

Table 1. Abstract refinement operator for $\mathcal{ALC}$.

$$\zeta_{\uparrow,\downarrow}(A) = \uparrow(A) \qquad , A \in N_C$$
$$\zeta_{\uparrow,\downarrow}(\neg A) = \{\mathsf{nnf}(\neg C) \mid C \in \downarrow(A)\} \cup \uparrow(\neg A) \qquad , A \in N_C$$
$$\zeta_{\uparrow,\downarrow}(\top) = \uparrow(\top)$$
$$\zeta_{\uparrow,\downarrow}(\bot) = \uparrow(\bot)$$
$$\zeta_{\uparrow,\downarrow}(C \sqcap D) = \{C' \sqcap D \mid C' \in \zeta_{\uparrow,\downarrow}(C)\} \cup$$
$$\{C \sqcap D' \mid D' \in \zeta_{\uparrow,\downarrow}(D)\} \cup \uparrow(C \sqcap D)$$
$$\zeta_{\uparrow,\downarrow}(C \sqcup D) = \{C' \sqcup D \mid C' \in \zeta_{\uparrow,\downarrow}(C)\} \cup$$
$$\{C \sqcup D' \mid D' \in \zeta_{\uparrow,\downarrow}(D)\} \cup \uparrow(C \sqcup D)$$
$$\zeta_{\uparrow,\downarrow}(\forall R.C) = \{\forall R'.C \mid R' \in \downarrow(R)\} \cup \{\forall R.C' \mid C' \in \zeta_{\uparrow,\downarrow}(C)\} \cup \uparrow(\forall R.C)$$
$$\zeta_{\uparrow,\downarrow}(\exists R.C) = \{\exists R'.C \mid R' \in \uparrow(R)\} \cup \{\exists R.C' \mid C' \in \zeta_{\uparrow,\downarrow}(C)\} \cup \uparrow(\exists R.C)$$

To address this situation, we introduce generalisation and specialisation operators that recursively exploit the syntactic structure of the concept being refined. Let $\uparrow$ and $\downarrow$ be two functions with domain $\mathcal{L}(N_C, N_R)$ that map every concept to a set of concepts in $\mathcal{L}(N_C, N_R)$. We define $\zeta_{\uparrow,\downarrow}$, the *abstract refinement operator*, by induction on the structure of concept descriptions as shown in Table 1. We now define concrete refinement operators from the abstract operator $\zeta_{\uparrow,\downarrow}$.

Definition 4. *The* generalisation operator *and* specialisation operator *are defined, respectively, as*

$$\gamma_{\mathcal{O}} = \zeta_{\mathsf{UpCov}_{\mathcal{O}}, \mathsf{DownCov}_{\mathcal{O}}} \quad and \quad \rho_{\mathcal{O}} = \zeta_{\mathsf{DowCov}_{\mathcal{O}}, \mathsf{UpCov}_{\mathcal{O}}}.$$

Returning to Example 1, notice that for $N_C = \{A, B, C\}$ and $\mathcal{O} = \{A \sqsubseteq B\}$, we now have $\gamma_{\mathcal{O}}(A \sqcap C) = \{A \sqcap C, B \sqcap C, A \sqcap \top, A\}$ as well as $\exists R.B \in \gamma_{\mathcal{O}}(\exists R.A)$.

Some comments are in order about Table 1. As in [19] the domain of $\gamma_{\mathcal{O}}$ and $\rho_{\mathcal{O}}$ is the set of concepts in negation normal form. In practice it can be extended straightforwardly to all concepts by modifying the clause $\zeta_{\uparrow,\downarrow}(\neg A)$ with $\zeta_{\uparrow,\downarrow}(\neg C) = \{\mathsf{nnf}(\neg C') \mid C' \in \downarrow(C)\} \cup \uparrow(\neg C)$.

Definition 5. *Given a DL concept C, its i-th refinement iteration by means of $\zeta_{\uparrow,\downarrow}$ (viz., $\zeta_{\uparrow,\downarrow}^i(C)$) is inductively defined as follows:*

- $\zeta_{\uparrow,\downarrow}^0(C) = \{C\}$;
- $\zeta_{\uparrow,\downarrow}^{j+1}(C) = \zeta_{\uparrow,\downarrow}^j(C) \cup \bigcup_{C' \in \zeta_{\uparrow,\downarrow}^j(C)} \zeta_{\uparrow,\downarrow}(C'), \quad j \geq 0$.

The set of all concepts reachable from C by means of $\zeta_{\uparrow,\downarrow}$ in a finite number of steps is $\zeta_{\uparrow,\downarrow}^*(C) = \bigcup_{i \geq 0} \zeta_{\uparrow,\downarrow}^i(C)$.

Lemma 1. *$\mathcal{L}(N_C, N_R)$ is closed under $\gamma_{\mathcal{O}}$ and $\rho_{\mathcal{O}}$. If $C \in \mathcal{L}(N_C, N_R)$ then every refinement in $\gamma_{\mathcal{O}}(C)$ and $\rho_{\mathcal{O}}(C)$ is also in $\mathcal{L}(N_C, N_R)$.*

Algorithm 1. RepairOntologyWeaken($\mathcal{O}$)

1: $O^{\mathrm{ref}} \leftarrow$ FindMaximallyConsistentSet($\mathcal{O}$)
2: **while** $\mathcal{O}$ is inconsistent **do**
3:    $\phi_{\mathsf{bad}} \leftarrow$ FindBadAxiom($\mathcal{O}$)
4:    $\Phi_{\mathsf{weaker}} \leftarrow$ WeakenAxiom($\phi_{\mathsf{bad}}, O^{\mathrm{ref}}$)
5:    $\mathcal{O} \leftarrow \mathcal{O} \setminus \{\phi_{\mathsf{bad}}\} \cup \Phi_{\mathsf{weaker}}$
6: **end while**
7: Return $\mathcal{O}$

---

3 Repairing Ontologies

The refinement operators can be used as components of a method for repairing inconsistent $\mathcal{ALC}$ ontologies by weakening, instead of removing, problematic axioms. Given an inconsistent ontology $\mathcal{O} = \mathcal{T} \cup \mathcal{A}$, we proceed as described in Algorithm 1.

We first need to find a consistent subontology O^{ref} of $\mathcal{O}$ to serve as *reference ontology* to be able to compute a non-trivial upcover and downcover. One approach is to pick a random maximally consistent subset of $\mathcal{O}$ (line 1), and choose it as reference ontology O^{ref}; another option is to choose the intersection of all maximally consistent subsets of $\mathcal{O}$ (e.g., [15]). Once a reference ontology O^{ref} has been chosen, and as long as $\mathcal{O}$ is inconsistent, we select a 'bad axiom' (line 3) in $\mathcal{T} \cup \mathcal{A}$) and replace it with a random weakening of it w.r.t. O^{ref} (lines 4 and 5). For added flexibility, a *weakening of an axiom* is a set of axioms.

Definition 6 (Axiom weakening). *For $\mathcal{O} = \mathcal{T} \cup \mathcal{A}$ an $\mathcal{ALC}$ ontology and ϕ an axiom in $\mathcal{T} \cup \mathcal{A}$, the set of (least) weakenings of ϕ is the set $g_{\mathcal{O}}(\phi)$ such that:*

- $g_{\mathcal{O}}(C \sqsubseteq D) = \{\{C' \sqsubseteq D\} \mid C' \in \rho_{\mathcal{O}}(C)\} \cup \{\{C \sqsubseteq D'\} \mid D' \in \gamma_{\mathcal{O}}(D)\}$;
- $g_{\mathcal{O}}(C(a)) = \{\{C'(a)\} \mid C' \in \gamma_{\mathcal{O}}(C)\}$;
- $g_{\mathcal{O}}(R(a,b)) = \{\{R(a,b)\}, \{\top(a), \top(b)\}\}$.

The subprocedure WeakenAxiom(ϕ, O^{ref}) randomly returns one set of axioms in $g_{O^{\mathrm{ref}}}(\phi)$. For every subsumption or assertional axiom ϕ, the set of axioms in the set $g_{O^{\mathrm{ref}}}(\phi)$ are indeed weaker than ϕ, in the sense that – given the reference ontology O^{ref} – ϕ entails them (and the opposite is not guaranteed).

Lemma 2. *For every subsumption or assertional axiom ϕ, if $\Phi' \in g_{\mathcal{O}}(\phi)$, then $\phi \models_{\mathcal{O}} \Phi'$.*

Proof. Suppose $\{C' \sqsubseteq D'\} \in g_{\mathcal{O}}(C \sqsubseteq D)$. Then, by the definitions of $g_{\mathcal{O}}$, $\gamma_{\mathcal{O}}$, and $\rho_{\mathcal{O}}$, it clearly follows that $C' \sqsubseteq C$ and $D \sqsubseteq D'$ are inferred from $\mathcal{O}$. Thus, by transitivity of subsumption, we obtain that $C \sqsubseteq D \models_{\mathcal{O}} C' \sqsubseteq D'$. For the weakening of class assertions, the result follows in a similar way. For the weakening of role assertions, the result simply follows from the definition of $\top$. □

The cases of GCIs and class assertions axioms are rather straightforward. The weakening of a GCI $C \sqsubseteq D$ is obtained by either generalising D or specialising C.

The weakening of the class assertion $C(a)$ is obtained by generalising C. As the refinement operators are reflexive, the choice here is also to make $g_{\mathcal{O}}$ reflexive, so an axiom may be weakened into itself. For the case of the role assertion axiom $R(a, b)$, one should observe that in absence of role hierarchies, nominals, and set constructors, there is nothing weaker apart from a trivial statement. Weakening $R(a, b)$ into the two axioms $\top(a)$ and $\top(b)$ allows us to preserve the signature. To keep $g_{\mathcal{O}}$ reflexive, we also allow $R(a, b)$ to be weakened into itself.

Clearly, substituting an axiom ϕ with one axiom from $g_{\mathcal{O}}(\phi)$ cannot diminish the set of interpretations of an ontology: if I is an interpretation that satisfies the axioms of an ontology before such a replacement, I satisfies the same axioms even after it. Since any concept can be generalised to the $\top$ concept or specialised to the $\bot$ concept (in finitely many steps), any subsumption axiom is a finite number of weakenings away from the trivial axiom $\bot \sqsubseteq \top$. Any assertional axiom $C(a)$ is also a finite number of generalisations away from the trivial assertion $\top(a)$. Similarly, every assertional axiom of type $R(a, b)$ is one step of generalisation away from the set of trivial assertions $\top(a)$ and $\top(b)$ (whilst maintaining the signature of the Abox).

Theorem 1. *If Algorithm 1 returns $\mathcal{O}$, then $\mathcal{O}$ is a consistent $\mathcal{ALC}$ ontology.*

Example 2. Consider the ontology $\mathcal{O}$ containing the following inconsistent set of axioms:

(1)   Vehicle $\sqsubseteq \exists has.$Motor;   (2)   Bike $\sqsubseteq$ Vehicle;
(3)   Bike $\sqsubseteq \neg\exists has.$Motor;   (4)   Motor $\sqsubseteq$ MeansOfPropulsion.

Suppose that FindBadAxiom($\mathcal{O}$) returns axiom (1) as the most problematic one. According to our definitions, a possible weakening of the axiom returned by WeakenAxiom$((1), \mathcal{O}^{\text{ref}})$ may be (1)* Vehicle $\sqsubseteq \exists has.$MeansOfPropulsion. Replacing axiom (1) with its weakening (1)*, the resulting ontology becomes consistent.

4   Iterated Refinements and Termination

Clearly, the set of "one-step" refinements of a concept is always finite, given the finiteness of sub($\mathcal{O}$). Moreover, every concept can be refined in a finite number of iterations to $\top$ (or $\bot$). Nonetheless, an iterated application of the refinement operator can lead to cases of non-termination. For instance, given an ontology defined as $\mathcal{O} = \{A \sqsubseteq \exists R.A\}$, if we generalise the concept A w.r.t. $\mathcal{O}$ it is easy to see that we can obtain an infinite chain of generalisations that never reaches $\top$, i.e., $A \sqsubseteq_{\mathcal{O}} \exists R.A \sqsubseteq_{\mathcal{O}} \exists R.\exists R.A \ldots$. For practical reasons, this may need to be avoided, or mitigated. Running into this non-termination 'problem' is not new in the DL literature. In [3], the problem occurs in the context of finding a least common subsumer of DL concepts. Different solutions have been proposed to avoid this situation. Typically, some assumptions are made over the structure of the *TBox*, or a fixed role depth of concepts is considered. In the latter view, it is possible to restrict the number of nested quantifiers in a concept description to

a fixed constant k, to forbid generalisations/specialisations already picked along a chain from being picked again, and to introduce the definition of role depth of a concept to prevent infinite refinements. If this role depth upper bound is reached in the refinement of a concept, then $\top$ and $\bot$ are taken as generalisation and specialisation of the given concept respectively.

Another possibility is to abandon certain termination and adopt *almost-certain* (or *almost-sure*) termination, that is, termination with probability 1. The idea is to associate probabilities to the refinement 'branches' available at each refinement step. In what follows, we will show that, indeed, if we start from any concept C and choose uniformly at random a generalisation out of its set of possible generalisations (or a specialisation out of its set of specialisations: results and proofs are entirely symmetrical) we will almost surely reach $\top$ ($\bot$) within a finite number of steps. This implies at once that an axiom will almost surely not be indefinitely weakened by our procedure, and that Algorithm 1 will almost surely terminate. The key ingredient of the proof is Lemma 3, which establishes an upper-bound on the rate of growth of the set of possible generalisations (specialisations) along a chain.

Definition 7. *Let $\mathcal{O}$ be an $\mathcal{ALC}$ ontology and let $C \in \mathsf{sub}(\mathcal{O})$. Then let $F(C) = |\gamma_{\mathcal{O}}(C)|$ be the number of generalisations of C, let $F'(C) = |\rho_{\mathcal{O}}(C)|$ be the number of specialisations of C and let $G(C) = \max(\{|C'| \mid C' \in \gamma_{\mathcal{O}}(C) \cup \rho_{\mathcal{O}}(C)\})$ be the maximum size of any generalisation or specialisation of C.*

The upper bound to the size of $\gamma(C)$ and $\rho(C)$ provided in part 1 of the following lemma gives a uniform upper bound to the size of generalisation/specialisation sets, for which we so far only knew that they are always finite.

Lemma 3. *Let $\mathcal{O}$ be an $\mathcal{ALC}$ ontology and let C be any concept (not necessarily in $\mathsf{sub}(\mathcal{O})$). Furthermore, let $k = |\mathsf{sub}(\mathcal{O})|$ and $q = \max(\{|C|, |\mathsf{nnf}(\neg C)| \mid C \in \mathsf{sub}(\mathcal{O}\})$. Then the following two properties hold:*

1. *$F(C), F'(C) \leq 3k|C|$;*
2. *$G(C) \leq |C| + q$.*

Proof. The proof is by structural induction. The intuition behind it is the following: by our definitions, in a generalisation/specialisation step we essentially select a single subcomponent C' of the current expression C and we replace it with some element of $\mathsf{sub}(\mathcal{O})$. But this set is finite, and the number of subcomponents of an expression C increases linearly with the size of C. Thus, the number of possible generalisations/specialisations of C increases linearly with the size of C, and every generalisation/specialisation step increases the size of the resulting expression by some at most constant amount. We next present the main parts of the structural induction on C (leaving out the analogous cases for $\exists R.C$ and $C \sqcup D$), which we assume is in Negation Normal Form.

1. If C is an atomic concept A, $\top$, or $\bot$ then $\gamma_{\mathcal{O}}(C) = \mathsf{UpCov}_{\mathcal{O}}(C)$, $\rho_{\mathcal{O}}(C) = \mathsf{DownCov}_{\mathcal{O}}(C)$ and $|C| = 1$. Thus, $F(C), F'(C) \leq |\mathsf{sub}(\mathcal{O})| \leq k \leq 3k|C|$ and $G(C) \leq q < q + 1$, as required.

2. If C is a negated atomic concept $\neg A$, $\gamma_\mathcal{O}(C) = \{\mathsf{nnf}(\neg C)|C \in \mathsf{DownCov}_\mathcal{O}(A)\} \cup \mathsf{UpCov}_\mathcal{O}(\neg A)$, $\rho_\mathcal{O}(C) = \{\mathsf{nnf}(\neg C)|C \in \mathsf{UpCov}_\mathcal{O}(A)\} \cup \mathsf{DownCov}_\mathcal{O}(\neg A)$, and $|C| = 2$. Thus, $F(C), F'(C) \leq 2|\mathsf{sub}(\mathcal{O})| \leq 2k \leq 3k|C|$ and $G(C) \leq q < q + 2$.

3. $|C \sqcap D| = |C| + |D| + 1$ and $\gamma_\mathcal{O}(C \sqcap D) = \{C' \sqcap D \mid C' \in \gamma_\mathcal{O}(C)\} \cup \{C \sqcap D' \mid D' \in \gamma_\mathcal{O}(D)\} \cup \mathsf{UpCov}_\mathcal{O}(C \sqcap D)$.

   By induction hypothesis, $|\{C' \sqcap D \mid C' \in \gamma_\mathcal{O}(C)\}| \leq 3k|C|$ and $|\{C \sqcap D' \mid D' \in \gamma_\mathcal{O}(D)| \leq 3k|D|$ and furthermore $|\mathsf{UpCov}_\mathcal{O}(C \sqcap D)| \leq k$, and so

$$F(C \sqcap D) \leq 3k|C| + 3k|D| + k \leq 3k|C \sqcap D|.$$

   Moreover, by induction hypothesis if $C' \in \gamma_\mathcal{O}(C)$ then $|C'| \leq G(C) \leq |C| + q$, and so $|C' \sqcap D| \leq |C| + |D| + 1 + q = |C \sqcap D| + q$; if $D' \in \gamma_\mathcal{O}(D)$ then $|D| \leq G(D) \leq |D| + q$ and so $C \sqcap D' \leq |C| + |D| + 1 + q = |C \sqcap D| + q$; and $|C''| \leq q \leq |C \sqcap D| + q$ for all $C'' \in \mathsf{UpCov}_\mathcal{O}(C \sqcap D)$. Thus, for all $C'' \in \gamma(C \sqcap D)$ we have that $|C''| \leq |C \sqcap D| + q$.

   Similarly, $\rho_\mathcal{O}(C \sqcap D) = \{C' \sqcap D \mid C' \in \rho_\mathcal{O}(C)\} \cup \{C \sqcap D' \mid D' \in \rho_\mathcal{O}(D)\} \cup \mathsf{DownCov}_\mathcal{O}(C \sqcap D)$, and a completely analogous argument applies.

4. $|\forall R.C| = |C| + 1$ and $\gamma_\mathcal{O}(\forall R.C) = \{\forall R.C' \mid C' \in \gamma_\mathcal{O}(C)\} \cup \mathsf{UpCov}_\mathcal{O}(\forall R.C)$. By induction hypothesis, $|\{\forall R.C' \mid C' \in \gamma_\mathcal{O}(C)\}| \leq 3k|C|$; moreover, $|\mathsf{UpCov}_\mathcal{O}(\forall R.C)| \leq k$. Thus, $F(\forall R.C) \leq 3k|C| + k \leq 3k(|C| + 1) = 3k|\forall R.C|$. Furthermore, if $C' \in \gamma_\mathcal{O}(C)$, by induction hypothesis $|C'| \leq |C| + q$ and hence $|\forall R.C'| \leq |C| + 1 + q = |\forall R.C| + q$; and if $C'' \in \mathsf{UpCov}_\mathcal{O}(\forall R.C)$ then $|C''| \leq q \leq |\forall R.C| + q$; and so whenever $C'' \in \gamma_\mathcal{O}(\forall R.C)$ we have that $|C''| \leq |\forall R.C| + q$, as required.

   Similarly, $\rho_\mathcal{O}(\forall R.C) = \{\forall R.C' \mid C' \in \rho_\mathcal{O}(C)\} \cup \mathsf{DownCov}_\mathcal{O}(\forall R.C)$, and a completely analogous argument shows that $F'(\forall R.C) \leq 3k|\forall R.C|$ and that $|C''| \leq |\forall R.C| + q$ for all $C'' \in \rho_\mathcal{O}(\forall R.C)$. □

We can now prove our required result by showing that, even though the size of the concept expression – and, therefore, the number of possible generalisations – grows with every generalisation step, it grows slowly enough such that the generalisation chain will almost surely eventually pick an element in the upcover of the current concept which is strictly more general than it. Thus, $\top$ will be almost surely reached in a finite number of steps.

Theorem 2. *Let $\mathcal{O}$ be an $\mathcal{ALC}$ ontology, let C be any $\mathcal{ALC}$ concept, and let $(C_i)_{i \in \mathbb{N}}$ be a sequence of concepts such that $C_0 = C$ and each C_{i+1} is chosen randomly in $\gamma_\mathcal{O}(C_i)$ according to the uniform distribution.*

Then, with probability 1, there exists some $i \in \mathbb{N}$ such that $C_i = \top$.

Proof. Let us first prove that, if $C \not\equiv_\mathcal{O} \top$, there is almost surely some C_i in the chain such that $C_i \equiv_\mathcal{O} \top$ (and, therefore, such that $C_{i'} \equiv_\mathcal{O} \top$ for all $i' > i$).

By the previous lemma, we know that $\gamma_\mathcal{O}(C_i)$ contains at most $3k|C_i|$ concepts. Furthermore, for every concept C_i such that $C_i \not\equiv_\mathcal{O} \top$ there exists at least one $C' \in \mathsf{UpCov}_\mathcal{O}(C_i) \subseteq \gamma_\mathcal{O}(C_i)$ such that $C \sqsubset_\mathcal{O} C'$ (for instance, the $\top$ concept itself): therefore, the probability that the successor of C_i will be

some $C_{i+1} \in \mathsf{UpCov}_{\mathcal{O}}(C_i)$ such that $C_i \sqsubset_{\mathcal{O}} C_{i+1}$ is at least $1/(3k|C_i|)$. Now let $|C_0| = N$: since $C_{i+1} \in \gamma_{\mathcal{O}}(C_i)$, we then have that $|C_i| \leq qi + N$. Therefore, the probability that at step i we do *not* select randomly an element of $\mathsf{UpCov}_{\mathcal{O}}(C_i)$ that is strictly more general than C_i will be at most $\frac{3k(qi+N)-1}{3k(qi+N)} = \frac{i+\ell-\epsilon}{i+\ell}$ for $\ell = N/q$ and $\epsilon = 1/(3kq)$. But then the probability that we *never* select a strictly more general element from the upcover will be at most $\prod_{i=0}^{\infty} \frac{i+\ell-\epsilon}{i+\ell} = 0$,[1] and thus our generalisation sequence $C = C_0 \sqsubseteq_{\mathcal{O}} C_1 \sqsubseteq_{\mathcal{O}} C_2 \ldots$ will almost surely contain some C_i such that $C_{i+1} \in \mathsf{UpCov}_{\mathcal{O}}(C_i) \subseteq \mathsf{sub}(\mathcal{O})$ and $C \sqsubset_{\mathcal{O}} C_i \sqsubset_{\mathcal{O}} C_{i+1}$. By the same argument, the generalisation sequence starting from C_{i+1} will almost surely eventually reach some $C_{j+1} \in \mathsf{sub}(\mathcal{O})$ with $C \sqsubset_{\mathcal{O}} C_{i+1} \sqsubset_{\mathcal{O}} C_{j+1}$, and so forth; and by applying this line of reasoning $|\mathsf{sub}(\mathcal{O})|$ times, we will almost surely eventually reach some concept $D \equiv_{\mathcal{O}} \top$, as required.

Now let us consider a generalisation chain $D = D_0 \sqsubseteq_{\mathcal{O}} D_1 \sqsubseteq_{\mathcal{O}} D_2 \ldots$, where as before every D_{i+1} is chosen randomly among $\gamma(D)$, starting from some concept $D \equiv_{\mathcal{O}} \top$. Now, since $D \equiv_{\mathcal{O}} \top$ we have $\top \in \mathsf{UpCov}_{\mathcal{O}}(D)$, and since $D \sqsubseteq_{\mathcal{O}} D_i$ for all i, $\top \in \mathsf{UpCov}_{\mathcal{O}}(D_i) \subseteq \gamma_{\mathcal{O}}(D_i)$ for all i. Thus, at every iteration step i we have a probability of at least $1/|\gamma(D_i)|$ that $D_{i+1} = \top$; and if we let $N' = |D|$, by the previous results we obtain at once that $|\gamma(D_i)| \leq iq + N'$, and hence that the probability that we do not end up generalising D_i to $\top$ is at most $(3k(iq + N') - 1)/(3k(iq + N'))$, and finally that the probability that we *never* reach $\top$ is $\prod_{i=0}^{\infty} \frac{3k(iq+N')-1}{3k(iq+N')} = \prod_{i=0}^{\infty} \frac{i+\ell'-\epsilon'}{i+\ell'} = 0$ where $\ell' = N'/q$ and $\epsilon' = 1/3kq$. $\qquad \square$

Note that, by our definitions, $\top$ can be further generalized to all elements of its upcover (that is, all concepts of $\mathsf{sub}(\mathcal{O})$ which are equivalent to $\top$ with respect to $\mathcal{O}$), and similarly $\bot$ can be further specialized to other concepts in its downcover. If this behaviour is unwanted, it is easy to force the upcover of $\top$ to contain only $\top$, and likewise for $\bot$.

Corollary 1. *Algorithm 1 almost surely terminates.*

Proof. As long as the ontology $\mathcal{O}$ is inconsistent, Algorithm 1 will select one axiom that appears in some minimally inconsistent subset of atoms and attempt to weaken it. Since the ontology $\mathcal{O}$ contains a finite number of axioms, if the algorithm never terminates then at least one of these axioms must be weakened an infinite number of times without being ever turned into the trivial axiom $\bot \sqsubseteq \top$, or an axiom $\top(a)$ (or a trivial set of axioms $\{\top(a), \top(b)\}$). But this is impossible because of Theorem 2. $\qquad \square$

---

[1] One way to verify this is to observe that the series $\sum_{i=0}^{\infty}(\log(i + \ell - \epsilon) - \log(i + \ell))$ diverges to minus infinity. This in turn may be verified by noting that $\sum_{i=0}^{\infty}(\log(i + \ell - \epsilon) - \log(i + \ell)) \leq \sum_{i=0}^{\infty}(\log(i + \lceil\ell\rceil - \epsilon) - \log(i + \lceil\ell\rceil)) = \sum_{i=\lceil\ell\rceil}^{\infty}(\log(i - \epsilon) - \log(i))$, because $\log(i + \ell - \epsilon) - \log(i + \ell) \leq \log(i + \lceil\ell\rceil - \epsilon) - \log(i + \lceil\ell\rceil)$, and then showing that $-\sum_{i=\lceil\ell\rceil}^{\infty}(\log(i-\epsilon) - \log(i)) = \sum_{i=\lceil\ell\rceil}^{\infty} \log(i) - \log(i-\epsilon)$ diverges to plus infinity by means of the integral method: the terms of the series are all positive, and $\int_{\lceil\ell\rceil}^{U} \log(x) - \log(x - \epsilon)dx$ goes to infinity when U goes to infinity. Since the integral diverges, so does the series, which gives us our conclusion.

It is worth remarking that this proof of almost-sure termination does not imply anything about the *expected time* of Algorithm 1 as a function of ontology size, not even that this expected time is finite. Indeed, note that it is possible for a randomised algorithm to almost surely terminate in finite time and yet have an infinite expected runtime.[2]

Tighter upper bounds than those of Lemma 3 may allow us to make such an estimate; we leave this question to future work.

5   Length of Refinement Chains and Tractability in Practice

We showed that the iterated weakening of concepts almost surely reaches ⊤ and that Algorithm 1 almost surely terminates. But this does not tell the whole story and we next discuss this from a more practical perspective.

The study of [19] provides empirical evidence that axiom weakening is significantly better than axiom removal for ontology repair (gentle vs. coarse repair). Here instead, we focus on the experimental evaluation of the almost-sure termination of our algorithm. For simplicity of exposition we focus on the evaluation of the problem of reaching the top concept by the iterated weakening of a concept. (Axiom weakening and ontology repair tasks are barely more than many repeated iterated weakenings.) The experiments exploit our implementation[3] of the refinement operator w.r.t. various reference (consistent) ontologies.

Ontologies. To better understand the practical aspects of our refinement operators, we performed experiments on real-world ontologies from the Gene Ontology knowledge base[4], and also using synthetic randomly generated ontologies.[5] About the latter, an ontology named C[num-c]_R[num-r]_[pconnect-ratio]_ [cconnect-ratio]_[existconnect-ratio] is an $\mathcal{ALC}$ ontology, with a signature of [num-c] atomic concepts and [num-r] roles. Given two atomic concepts C_1 and C_2, some subset relations $C_1 \sqsubseteq C_2$ and $C_1 \sqsubseteq \neg C_2$ are randomly generated with roughly the probability [pconnect-ratio] and [cconnect-ratio], respectively. Given two atomic concepts C_1 and C_2, and a role R, subset relations $C_1 \sqsubseteq \exists R.C_2$ and $C_1 \sqsubseteq \neg \exists R.C_2$ are generated with probability roughly [existconnect-ratio]. All atomic classes are populated with one individual. For a set of parameters, we generated ontologies until a consistent one was found. Finally, we ran the experiments also on a hand-crafted ontology. a-and-b is a very small manually designed ontology.

---

[2] For example, suppose that the algorithm terminates in exactly n steps with probability $6/\pi^2 \cdot n^{-2}$. Using the fact that $\sum_{n=1}^{\infty} n^{-2} = \pi^2/6$, we have at once that the algorithm terminates in finite time with probability 1. However, the expectation of its runtime would be $6/\pi^2 \sum_{n=1}^{\infty} n^{-1}$, which diverges to infinity.

[3] The implementation is available at https://bitbucket.org/troquard/ontologyutils.

[4] http://geneontology.org/docs/download-ontology/.

[5] These ontologies can be found in the directory ontologyutils/src/master/resources/ Random/ of the implementation.

Table 2. Characteristics of ontologies, and sizes of the chains of generalisation over 1,000 runs of iterated generalisations from $\perp$ to $\top$. (Axioms, $|N_C|$ and $|N_R|$ are the number of logical axioms count, class count, and object property count as given by the metrics of the ontology in Protégé [16].)

Ontology	Axioms	$|N_C|$	$|N_R|$	Min	Max	Average	Median
goslim_mouse	13	44	9	2	14	4.948	5
goslim_plant	49	174	9	3	18	6.385	6
goslim_generic	72	143	9	2	17	5.170	5
goslim_drosophila	160	97	9	2	15	4.628	4
goslim_metagenomics	172	114	9	3	26	6.541	6
goslim_yeast	266	164	9	3	18	5.325	5
goslim_pir	670	514	9	3	22	7.422	7
C50_R10_0.001_0.001_0.001	164	51	10	2	17	4.648	4
C100_R10_0.001_0.001_0.001	413	101	10	2	17	4.925	4
C150_R10_0.001_0.001_0.001	803	151	10	2	17	5.043	5
C300_R10_0.0001_0.0001_0.0001	811	301	10	2	14	4.057	4
a-and-b	3	2	1	3	72	16.142	14

$$A \sqsubseteq A \sqcap B$$
$$B \sqsubseteq A \sqcap B$$
$$A \sqsubseteq \exists R.(A \sqcap B)$$

Clearly, A, B, and $A \sqcap B$ are logically equivalent. It will help to put light on the limitations of the syntactic approach. It also serves to illustrate that despite the likelihood to obtain very large concepts during the iterated refinement of a concept, the process robustly terminates.

Setting and Results. For each ontology, we ran a series of refinements. In each case, we ran 1,000 times the iterated random weakening of the concept $\perp$ until the concept $\top$ was reached. In each case, we recorded the minimum length of the chain of refinements, the maximum length of the chain of refinements, the average length, and the median length. The results are reported in Table 2, alongside the characteristics of the ontologies (number of logical axioms, number of atomic concepts, and number of atomic roles) used in the experiments.

The Case of a-and-b. The ontology is specifically written to trip the almost surely terminating iterated refinement procedure with our operator. When trying to reach $\top$ from $\perp$ in the ontology a-and-b by iterated weakening, first $\top$ is weakened into $\top$, A, B, or $A \sqcap B$. Then at each step, an instance of A or B may be replaced with A, B, or $A \sqcap B$, or with $\exists R.(A \sqcap B)$; and $\exists R.(\ldots)$ can be weakened, possibly replacing the instances A or B as before, or into $\top$.

During the iterated refinement of $\perp$ with the weakening operator, we observed (min, max, average, median): $(3, 42, 17.05, 15)$ with 100 runs, $(3, 72, 16.142, 14)$ with 1,000 runs, $(3, 76, 16.0958, 14)$ with 10,000 runs, $(3, 92, 16.01316, 14)$ with 100,000 runs. We see that long chains of refinements occur, but the procedure robustly terminates.

6 Outlook

We presented a set of refinement operators for $\mathcal{ALC}$, proving the almost-certain termination of their iterated application and verifying their practical tractability via experimental evaluation. Further additions to the general rules of refinements need to be studied, e.g., to deal with more general logics such as $\mathcal{SROIQ}$, as was initiated in [7]. Further directions of research include the study of high-level heuristics and closure conditions (e.g., for $\mathsf{sub}(\mathcal{O})$) to steer, enrich, and accelerate the refinement process.

References

1. Baader, F., Calvanese, D., McGuinness, D.L., Nardi, D., Patel-Schneider, P.F. (eds.): The Description Logic Handbook: Theory, Implementation, and Applications. Cambridge University Press, New York (2003)
2. Baader, F., Kriegel, F., Nuradiansyah, A., Peñaloza, R.: Making repairs in description logics more gentle. In: Proceedings of KR 2018, pp. 319–328 (2018)
3. Baader, F., Küsters, R.: Nonstandard inferences in description logics: the story so far. In: Gabbay, D.M., Goncharov, S.S., Zakharyaschev, M. (eds.) Mathematical Problems from Applied Logic I: Logics for the XXIst Century, pp. 1–75. Springer, Heidelberg (2006). https://doi.org/10.1007/0-387-31072-X_1
4. Baader, F., Peñaloza, R., Suntisrivaraporn, B.: Pinpointing in the description logic $\mathcal{EL}^+$. In: Hertzberg, J., Beetz, M., Englert, R. (eds.) KI 2007. LNCS (LNAI), vol. 4667, pp. 52–67. Springer, Heidelberg (2007). https://doi.org/10.1007/978-3-540-74565-5_7
5. Badea, L., Nienhuys-Cheng, S.-H.: A refinement operator for description logics. In: Cussens, J., Frisch, A. (eds.) ILP 2000. LNCS (LNAI), vol. 1866, pp. 40–59. Springer, Heidelberg (2000). https://doi.org/10.1007/3-540-44960-4_3
6. Confalonieri, R., Eppe, M., Schorlemmer, M., Kutz, O., Peñaloza, R., Plaza, E.: Upward refinement operators for conceptual blending in the description logic $\mathcal{EL}^{++}$. Ann. Math. Artif. Intell. **82**(1–3), 69–99 (2018)
7. Confalonieri, R., Galliani, P., Kutz, O., Porello, D., Righetti, G., Troquard, N.: Towards even more irresistible axiom weakening. In: Borgwardt, S., Meyer, T. (eds.) Proceedings of the 33rd International Workshop on Description Logics (DL 2020) co-located with the 17th International Conference on Principles of Knowledge Representation and Reasoning (KR 2020), Online Event, Rhodes, Greece, 12–14 September 2020. CEUR Workshop Proceedings, vol. 2663. CEUR-WS.org (2020). http://ceur-ws.org/Vol-2663/paper-8.pdf
8. Du, J., Qi, G., Fu, X.: A practical fine-grained approach to resolving incoherent OWL 2 DL terminologies. In: Proceedings of the 23rd ACM International Conference on Conference on Information and Knowledge Management, pp. 919–928 (2014)
9. Kalyanpur, A., Parsia, B., Sirin, E., Cuenca-Grau, B.: Repairing unsatisfiable concepts in OWL ontologies. In: Sure, Y., Domingue, J. (eds.) ESWC 2006. LNCS, vol. 4011, pp. 170–184. Springer, Heidelberg (2006). https://doi.org/10.1007/11762256_15
10. Kalyanpur, A., Parsia, B., Sirin, E., Hendler, J.: Debugging unsatisfiable classes in OWL ontologies. Web Semant.: Sci. Serv. Agents World Wide Web **3**(4), 268–293 (2005)

11. van der Laag, P.R., Nienhuys-Cheng, S.H.: Completeness and properness of refinement operators in inductive logic programming. J. Logic Program. **34**(3), 201–225 (1998)
12. Lehmann, J., Hitzler, P.: Foundations of refinement operators for description logics. In: Blockeel, H., Ramon, J., Shavlik, J., Tadepalli, P. (eds.) ILP 2007. LNCS (LNAI), vol. 4894, pp. 161–174. Springer, Heidelberg (2008). https://doi.org/10.1007/978-3-540-78469-2_18
13. Lehmann, J., Hitzler, P.: A refinement operator based learning algorithm for the $\mathcal{ALC}$ description logic. In: Blockeel, H., Ramon, J., Shavlik, J., Tadepalli, P. (eds.) ILP 2007. LNCS (LNAI), vol. 4894, pp. 147–160. Springer, Heidelberg (2008). https://doi.org/10.1007/978-3-540-78469-2_17
14. Lehmann, J., Hitzler, P.: Concept learning in description logics using refinement operators. Mach. Learn. **78**(1–2), 203–250 (2010)
15. Lembo, D., Lenzerini, M., Rosati, R., Ruzzi, M., Savo, D.F.: Inconsistency-tolerant semantics for description logics. In: Hitzler, P., Lukasiewicz, T. (eds.) RR 2010. LNCS, vol. 6333, pp. 103–117. Springer, Heidelberg (2010). https://doi.org/10.1007/978-3-642-15918-3_9
16. Musen, M.A.: The Protégé project: a look back and a look forward. AI Matters **1**(4), 4–12 (2015)
17. Porello, D., Troquard, N., Peñaloza, R., Confalonieri, R., Galliani, P., Kutz, O.: Two approaches to ontology aggregation based on axiom weakening. In: Lang, J. (ed.) Proceedings of the 27th International Joint Conference on Artificial Intelligence, IJCAI 2018, Stockholm, Sweden, 13–19 July 2018, pp. 1942–1948 (2018)
18. Schlobach, S., Cornet, R.: Non-standard reasoning services for the debugging of description logic terminologies. In: Proceedings of IJCAI 2003, pp. 355–362. Morgan Kaufmann (2003)
19. Troquard, N., Confalonieri, R., Galliani, P., Peñaloza, R., Porello, D., Kutz, O.: Repairing ontologies via axiom weakening. In: McIlraith, S.A., Weinberger, K.Q. (eds.) Proceedings of the Thirty-Second AAAI Conference on Artificial Intelligence, (AAAI 2018), pp. 1981–1988. AAAI Press (2018)

A MaxSAT Solver Based on Differential Evolution (Preliminary Report)

Manuel Framil[1], Pedro Cabalar[1(✉)], and José Santos[1,2]

[1] Department of Computer Science and Information Technologies,
University of A Coruña, A Coruña, Spain
{m.framil.deamorin,cabalar}@udc.es
[2] CITIC (Centre for Information and Communications Technology Research),
University of A Coruña, A Coruña, Spain
jose.santos@udc.es

Abstract. In this paper we present `DeMaxSAT`, a memetic algorithm for solving the non-partial MaxSAT problem. It combines the evolutionary algorithm of Differential Evolution with GSAT and RandomWalk, two MaxSAT-specific local search heuristics. An implementation of the algorithm has been used to solve the benchmarks for non-partial MaxSAT included in the MaxSAT Evaluation 2021. The performance of `DeMaxSAT` has reached results that are comparable, both in computing time and quality of the solutions, to the best solvers presented in MaxSAT Evaluation 2021, reaching the state of the art for non-partial problems.

Keywords: MaxSAT · Differential evolution · Memetic algorithm

1 Introduction

The *Boolean Satisfiability* problem (SAT) is a well-known decision problem that consists in determining whether there exists some interpretation that satisfies a given propositional formula. The *Maximum Satisfiability* problem (MaxSAT) is the optimization version of SAT: given a formula in Conjunctive Normal Form (CNF), the goal is to find an interpretation that satisfies the maximum number of clauses. *Partial MaxSAT* is a more general variant in which all clauses from a given subset (called *hard* clauses) must always be satisfied in any solution. Another generalization is the so-called *Weighted MaxSAT* problem, where each clause has a non-negative weight and the aim is to maximize the sum of weights of the satisfied clauses. Both generalizations can be combined into the *Weighted Partial MaxSAT* problem, whose goal is to maximize the sum of weights of the satisfied soft clauses, while keeping all hard clauses satisfied. The state-of-the-art MaxSAT solvers are yearly evaluated in the *MaxSAT Evaluation* (MSE) [3]. This event witnessed the improvement of MaxSAT solvers in the recent years, going from barely a hundred of clauses and variables in the nineties, up to over 10 millions of variables and 50 million of clauses nowadays.

© The Author(s), under exclusive license to Springer Nature Switzerland AG 2022
G. Marreiros et al. (Eds.): EPIA 2022, LNAI 13566, pp. 676–687, 2022.
https://doi.org/10.1007/978-3-031-16474-3_55

Although most MaxSAT solvers are based today on search algorithms relying on backend SAT solvers, other approaches have also been studied in the literature, including the use of Evolutionary Algorithms (EAs). For instance, several approaches based on classical Genetic Algorithms (GAs) were used for the SAT problem [5,12,16], including also combinations of GAs with local search [14].

Regarding MaxSAT, evolutionary algorithms can be useful when good quality solutions need to be found in moderate time. Examples in this line can be found in [17] (using Extremal Optimization), [2] (Artificial Bee Colony algorithm), [11] (Harmony Search algorithm combined with a flip heuristic and Tabu search), [6] (Scatter Search and GAs), [7] (GAs) and [9] (Bee Swarm Optimization algorithm). These latter works used benchmarks with no more than 200 variables.

In this paper, we define an algorithm, called DeMaxSAT[1], based on a hybrid or memetic version [19] between an evolutionary algorithm (Differential Evolution - DE [23]) and problem-specific heuristics. The goal of this combination is to integrate the global search advantage of the population-based search of the evolutionary algorithm with the local search of the MaxSAT-specific heuristics, the latter allowing fast refinement or exploitation of solutions held in the genetic population. We compare our solver with the state-of-the-art solvers used in the MSE competition, showing the advantages and the problems that appear in the different benchmarks used.

The rest of the article is structured as follows. Section 2 contains the background, starting with a brief introduction to Binary Differential Evolution, and proceeding afterwards with a description of two usual MaxSAT heuristics, GSAT and Random Walk, that we incorporate later on in our algorithm. Section 3 presents the memetic algorithm DeMaxSAT and explains its different parameters. In Sect. 4, we first describe the MSE benchmarks and the scoring scheme used in that evaluation, and proceed then to explain the process of parameter tuning performed on DeMaxSAT. Section 5 presents the results obtained on the benchmarks and compares to other solvers presented to MSE 2021. Finally, Sect. 6 concludes the paper.

2   Background

Differential Evolution is an evolutionary algorithm introduced by Storn and Price [23]. Our choice of DE was motivated by the fact that it is a robust method with proven advantages over other EAs in many optimization problems and also with few defining parameters [8]. DE starts with an initial population of candidate solutions (called *individuals* or *vectors*) so that their *genotypes* encode possible solutions to the optimization or search problem. In each generation of the DE algorithm, new solutions are defined by combining the genotypes of the solutions in the previous generation. Each individual x is assigned a value representing its quality and given by a so-called *fitness* or *objective* function $f_{obj}(x)$ to be optimized.

In order to apply DE to the MaxSAT problem, the DE algorithm must be adapted for its use in a binary domain. We have followed the adaptation defined

---

[1] The code of DeMaxSAT is available at [1].

by Doerr and Zheng [10], which aims to replicate the continuous nature of DE, but with binary variables. Algorithm 1 shows the pseudo-code of the Binary Differential Evolution (BDE) version (integrated with local search heuristics as explained below). The key aspect of DE (and BDE) is the generation of candidate vectors for each solution in the population, candidates that are defined by the difference of (randomly chosen) vectors in the current population. The BDE algorithm has four stages:

1. **Initialization**: This phase initializes the individuals of the first generation. A usual random initialization is employed, with random binary values in each genotype position.
2. **Mutation**: In this phase, in each generation g and for each *target* vector x_i^g of the current population of solutions, a *donor* or *mutant* vector v_i^g (following the standard nomenclature in DE [8]) is created. This vector is defined in line 21 of Algorithm 1: it implies an inversion of the binary value of vector x_1 when vectors x_2 and x_3 have different values at the same bit position in their genotypes. x_1 is called the *base* vector, x_2 and x_3 are randomly chosen vectors and F is the parameter (weight factor) that controls the amplitude of the mutation. The value of F acts as a probability of changing the binary value of the base vector, i.e., it determines the level of exploration.
3. **Crossover**: The crossover operation is the same as in standard DE. The *candidate* or *trial* vector y_i^g (for each target vector x_i^g) is generated by crossing over the genotypes of the target vector x_i^g with the mutant vector (line 24), with CR as the parameter that controls the crossover probability.
4. **Selection**: If the trial improves the target individual (x), that is, its fitness value $(f_{obj}(y_i))$ is higher (when maximizing) or lower (when minimizing) than the target fitness value, the candidate replaces the target vector in the population for the next generation (lines 27–28).

The three last stages are repeated over generations until a stop criterion is satisfied (e.g., a maximum number of generations). The main idea behind this algorithm is that the "difference" between vectors x_2 and x_3 (which determines the number of inverted binary values) will decrease as the evolutionary process advances. In the first generations, this difference tends to be large, leading to larger jumps in the search space and prioritizing the exploration in the search space. As the population concentrates in promising areas of the search space in successive generations, this difference is more likely to diminish with the passage of generations, progressing to a stage where exploitation prevails over exploration. Therefore, the DE algorithm presents an implicit control between exploration and exploitation.

In this work, two heuristics are employed in combination with the BDE algorithm: *GSAT* and *Random Walk (RW)*. GSAT [22] is a greedy local search algorithm that provides suboptimal solutions in a short time. In its adaptation to MaxSAT instances, it starts with a randomly generated truth assignment, and in every step reverses ("flips") the variable that gives the largest increase in the total number of clauses satisfied. This process is repeated until a maximum number of flips is reached. *Random Walk* (RW) [21] consists of randomly choosing a

clause from the set of unsatisfied clauses and inverting the value of one of its variables. This forces the chosen clause to become satisfied (a clause is a disjunction of literals, so if one literal becomes true, the whole clause is satisfied), but could lead to an overall decrease in the total number of satisfied clauses.

Algorithm 1. DeMaxSAT algorithm

1: **for** Individual x $\in$ Population **do**
2:     Individual x $\leftarrow$ RandomInitialize()
3: **end for**
4: **while not** StopCriteria() **do**   ▷ DeMaxSAT evolutionary generation
5:     **for** $i \in 1 : NP$ **do**   ▷ NP defines the population size
6:         **if** isOnHeuristicScope(x_i) **then**
7:             **for** $k \in 1 : LSS$ **do**   ▷ N steps of local search are performed
8:                 $mrand_k \leftarrow$ RandomNumber $\in$ [0,1]
9:                 **if** $mrand_k > PRW$ **then**
10:                     Heuristic $\leftarrow$ GSAT
11:                 **else**
12:                     Heuristic $\leftarrow$ RandomWalk
13:                 **end if**
14:                 $x_i \leftarrow$ Heuristic(x_i)
15:                 $f_{obj}(x_i) \leftarrow$ Re-Evaluate(x_i)
16:             **end for**
17:         **end if**
18:         $x_{r1}, x_{r2}, x_{r3} \leftarrow$ RandomIndividuals(Population) ▷ $x_i \neq x_{r1} \neq x_{r2} \neq x_{r3}$
19:         **for** $j \in 1 : D$ **do**   ▷ D represents the dimensionality of the problem
20:             $mrand_j \leftarrow$ RandomNumber $\in$ [0,1]
21:             $v_{i,j} = \begin{cases} 1 - x_{r1,j} & \text{if } x_{r2,j} \neq x_{r3,j} \text{ and } mrand_j < F \\ x_{r1,j} & \text{otherwise} \end{cases}$
22:   ▷ v defines the mutant vector (v)
23:             $crand_j \leftarrow$ RandomNumber $\in$ [0,1]
24:             $y_{i,j} = \begin{cases} v_{i,j} & \text{if } crand_j <= CR \\ x_{i,j} & \text{otherwise} \end{cases}$
25:                               ▷ y defines the trial vector (y) for the target vector (x)
26:         **end for**
27:         **if** $f_{obj}(y_i) <= f_{obj}(x_i)$ **then**
28:             $x_i = y_i$ ▷ Replace x by y when the trial vector (y) has better fitness
29:         **end if**
30:     **end for**
31: **end while**
32: **return** the best solution found

The combination of GSAT with RW is done to decrease the probability of getting stuck at local maxima and is simply performed by a random choice of one of the two methods at each step, depending on some probability value PRW (Random Walk with probability PRW, GSAT with probability $1 - PRW$). In Algorithm 1, we refer to this combination as GSAT+RW or just LSS (Local

Search Step). Lines 9–12 in Algorithm 1 show this application of LSS search steps on each selected population solution (as described below).

3   DeMaxSAT Solver

The population solutions are truth assignments for the problem variables. Therefore, in DeMaxSAT, individuals are binary vectors where each element represents a variable of the MaxSAT instance, which can be set to 1 (true) or 0 (false). Given any individual or truth assignment, the fitness function will return the sum of weights of the clauses that are not satisfied by that assignment (i.e., the goal is minimizing the fitness value).

Algorithm 1 details the combination between BDE and the two MaxSAT heuristics considered. At the beginning of each generation, a subset of individuals of the population is refined by performing N steps of GSAT+RW, just before the BDE genetic operators (lines 18 and later in Algorithm 1). In each local search step, one variable is flipped, so N variables will be flipped in total. Note that, consequently, for the new truth assignment, it is not necessary to calculate the fitness value of the entire truth assignment, but only of the clauses that have changed (line 15).

The parameters that define the implementation are the following:

- **GEN**: Number of the generations performed by BDE. Given that the MSE evaluation is based on getting the best solution we can after reaching a fixed time limit, we do not set a fixed number of generations.
- **NP**: Population size. Number of solutions in the genetic population.
- **F**: Mutation probability. It controls the probability of inverting a bit of the base vector when creating the mutant $v_{i,j}$ (lines 20–22 of the pseudo-code).
- **CR**: Crossover probability. It controls the probability of passing genetic information from the mutant vector $v_{i,j}$ to the trial vector $y_{i,j}$ (lines 23–25).
- **LSS**: Local Search Step. The local search heuristics (GSAT and RW) are applied N times for each generation and each individual. This parameter adjusts the number of times these heuristics are performed, defining the value of N as a percentage of the number of variables of the MaxSAT instance that is being evaluated. That is, for instance, if $LSS = 0.1$ and the problem has 100 variables, the local heuristics will be run 10 times in each individual. This strategy allows us to automatically adjust the number of local search steps to the size of the problem.
- **PRW**: Probability of Random Walk. This parameter controls the probability of running GSAT or RW. During each local search step, a random number $r \in [0.0, 1.0]$ is generated. If $r > $ PRW, GSAT is applied; otherwise, the heuristic applied is RandomWalk (lines 9–12 of the pseudo-code).
- **HSCOPE**: Heuristic Scope. It controls the subset of individuals on which the local search heuristics is applied. This parameter can be either all, if the heuristics are applied to all individuals, or better_than_mean, in which case the heuristics only affect the individuals whose fitness is lower (better) than the average of the population (the objective is the minimization of the number of unsatisfied clauses).

4   Benchmarks, Scoring and Parameter Tuning

The MSE 2021 dataset is organized into families, which are sets of benchmarks that encode the same problem and therefore share a similar structure, although the size may vary from one instance to another. We have chosen all the families that only contain *non-partial* instances, which in total get to 49 benchmarks (29 weighted and 20 unweighted). We have excluded from the evaluation the SeanSafarPour family, which contains the 10 non-partial largest instances, as DEMaxSat cannot perform enough generations to provide an acceptable solution. This is remarked again in the last paragraph of the following section.

The size (and difficulty) of these instances is very heterogeneous, going from hundreds of clauses up to thousands in the largest instances, as summarized in:

	Min	Max	Mean	Std
#Clauses	432	39k	4,175	5,922
#Variables	40	11k	526	1,735

To evaluate our solver, we have used the scoring scheme proposed by the MSE for the incomplete track, where the optimum may not be reached and the aim is to obtain the best possible solution in a given time limit (either 60 s or 300 s). In fact, in many instances, the optimum is not even known and the best known solution is used as a reference. The solver MSE score corresponds to the formula:

$$\sum_{i \in \text{solved instances}} \frac{(\text{cost of the best known solution for i}) + 1}{(\text{cost of the solution found by the solver}) + 1} \qquad (1)$$

where the cost of a solution corresponds to the sum of the weights of the unsatisfied clauses. This score is divided by the number of benchmarks evaluated. As a result, we obtain a value between 0 and 1 for each solver, representing how close a solver is to the best known solutions, on average, for all instances. That is, the closer the solver's score is to 1, the closer the solutions given by the solver will be to the best-known solutions, so the better the solver will be.

DeMaxSAT has different defining parameters (Sect. 3), so their appropriate values must be adjusted. The parameter tuning of DeMaxSAT was performed with a usual sweep of the defining parameters in an EA: changing the values of one parameter while keeping the other defining parameters at standard or fixed values. We kept $CR = 0.4$ and $F = 0.6$ (whose values have little influence over a wide range around these values), while PRW was set to 0.5 in all subsequent experiments, as this value turned out to be the best in all difficulty partitions discussed below. Instead, the most important effect of NP and LSS was inspected. Note that the former determines how much simultaneous exploration is performed in the search space, while the latter establishes how much exploitation is performed on each solution of the genetic population. We tested as well the effects changing the heuristics scope ($HSCOPE$ in Sect. 3).

For this purpose, we swept the values of the three parameters (NP with six values between 5 and 50, LSS with five values between 0.01 and 0.1, and $HSCOPE$ between `all` and `better_than_mean`), measuring the effect of the combination of these values on the results provided by `DeMaxSAT`. From now on, we will refer to a given combination of values NP, LSS and $HSCOPE$ as a *configuration*. It should be noted that a value $LSS = 0.0$ (pure DE without the use of the heuristics) did not produce competitive results in `DeMaxSAT` so it will not be considered in the following study.

The effect is defined as the average score provided by `DeMaxSAT` in a group of instances considering two limited times, 60 and 300 s. Moreover, given the stochasticity of `DeMaxSAT` (as any EA), for each instance and configuration, 10 independent runs were performed to consider the average score. The non-partial MSE instances were divided into three groups, depending on their "difficulty", estimated as the value $D := \#\text{variables} \times \#\text{clauses}$. The number of variables defines the dimensionality of the search space, since it defines the length of the population vectors. On the other hand, the number of clauses influences the computation time of the heuristics. We considered the following classification: i) instances with low difficulty ($1 \leq D < 2 \cdot 10^5$); ii) instances with medium difficulty ($2 \cdot 10^5 \leq D < 10^7$); iii) instances with high difficulty ($D \geq 10^7$). Note that this categorization makes sense, since the appropriate configuration may be different working with instances of low and high difficulty. Therefore, the experimental determination must be made by working with the different groups of instances.

Figures 1a and 1b show the different configurations considered with the timeouts of 60 and 300 s, respectively.

In the low difficulty benchmarks, best results are achieved by the configurations in which exploitation prevails over exploration (large LSS), while the worst are yielded by those that perform less iterations of the local search heuristics (small LSS, scope `better_than_mean`). However, notice the best solutions are found by the configuration with a medium population size (NP=30), which indicates that it is also important to simultaneously explore several promising areas of the search space. The chosen configurations are: for 60 s timeout (NP=30, LSS=0.05, hscope `all`) and for 300 s timeout (NP=30, LSS=0.1, hscope `all`).

In the medium difficulty instances, time restrictions begins to matter (you can see how score decreases as NP increases in the 60 s timeout). Thus, the highest score is achieved by a configuration with the smallest population size (5). In the 300 s however, the best solutions are reached by the configuration with the largest LSS value but which does not apply the heuristics to all individuals. Consequently, the chosen configurations are: for 60 s timeout (NP=5, LSS=0.025, hscope `all`) and for 300 s timeout (NP=10, LSS=0.1, hscope `better_than_mean`).

Finally, in the high difficulty instances, time is the foremost factor. The best configurations are those that perform more generations, giving enough time to optimize the solutions. This means reducing the population size (NP) and applying the heuristics to less individuals (hscope). Therefore, the chosen configurations are: for 60 s timeout (NP=5, LSS=0.025, hscope `better_than_mean` and for 300 s timeout (NP=5, LSS=0.075, hscope `better_than_mean`). `DeMaxSAT` uses one of these configurations depending on benchmark difficulty and timeout.

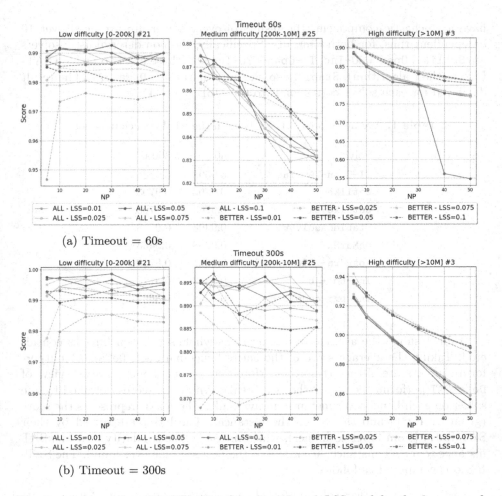

(a) Timeout = 60s

(b) Timeout = 300s

Fig. 1. Average score with different values for *NP* and *LSS*, and for the 3 groups of instances. Both `DeMaxSAT` scopes (`all` and `better_than_mean`) are used.

5   Results

In this section, the `DeMaxSAT` solver is compared to other state-of-the-art incomplete MaxSAT solvers, all of which were presented in the 2021 MSE. These solvers are `TT-Open-WBO-Inc-21` [18], `Satlike` [15], `StableResolver` [20], `Loandra-2020` [4] and `Open-WBO-Inc` [13]. `Satlike` has two versions (`satlike-c` and `satlike-ck`), and so it does `Open-WBO-Inc` (`inc-bmo-jb` and `inc-bmo-complete`). Notice that some of these solvers have not undergone any change since the previous evaluation in 2020. Specifically `Loandra-2020`, `StableResolver` and both versions of `Open-WBO-Inc` were previously presented in the 2020 MSE. The tests have been run with the same benchmark set as in the previous section, with both 60 and 300 s timeouts. As many of the chosen solvers

have a stochastic component, the results of every solver are averaged over 10 independent runs, for both timeouts. Specifically, the non-deterministic solvers are `Satlike`, `Open-WBO-Inc`, `TT-Open-WBO-Inc-21` (those last two include SAT-Like in their algorithm), `StableResolver` and, naturally, `DeMaxSAT`. The result displayed for each solver corresponds to the MSE score (1).

Table 1. Average scores of the solvers in the whole benchmark set.

Solver	60 s	300 s
TT-Open-WBO-Inc-21	0.9698	0.9706
satlike-c	0.9703	0.9703
satlike-ck	0.9703	0.9703
StableResolver	0.9406	0.9588
DeMaxSAT	0.9298	0.9433
Loandra-2020	0.8561	0.8713
inc-bmo-jb	0.8523	0.8727
inc-bmo-complete	0.8238	0.8694

Table 1 shows the average results over the whole set of benchmarks considered. Taking the average score of the entire benchmark set, `DeMaxSAT` outperforms three state-of-the-art solvers. Moreover, to get a more precise view of `DeMaxSAT` performance, Fig. 2 shows a breakdown of the scores obtained by the solver on each benchmark instance, individually. The y-axis represents the score (given by Eq. 1) and the x-axis the instances. The latter are sorted by their SAT-Ratio (from lower to higher), which measures the similarity of a MaxSAT instance to a SAT instance, according to the best solution ever found. The SAT-Ratio is computed as follows:

$$\text{SAT-Ratio} = 1 - \frac{\text{Best solution found (Sum of weights of the unsatisfied clauses)}}{\text{Sum of weights of all clauses}} \quad (2)$$

Thus, when the best solution found satisfies all clauses, the SAT-Ratio has value 1. In the dataset used for this work, the average SAT-Ratio is 0.92. As shown in Fig. 2, `DeMaxSAT` has an excellent performance on the leftmost instances, with lower SAT-Ratio. The three rightmost instances, where `DeMaxSAT` gets its worst scores, actually correspond to those with a SAT-Ratio above 0.999, which means they are very close to being an instance of SAT. These results are far from unexpected, as long as `DeMaxSAT` does not integrate any SAT solver, unlike the rest of the solvers considered.

Figure 2 also shows that, in most of the instances, `DeMaxSAT` outperforms the three solvers `inc-bmo-complete`, `inc-bmo-jb` and `Loandra-2020`, the ones that threw a worse average score for the benchmarks in the study. Moreover, except those three tools, `DeMaxSAT` coincides with the rest of the solvers in getting the maximum score in most of the instances with low SAT-Ratio. Although, as said before, `DeMaxSAT` has low score values in the 3 instances with the highest

SAT-Ratio, it maintains a good overall ranking stability, even as the SAT-ratio increases. In the 3 most difficult instances (regarding difficulty D), whose names are highlighted in bold in Fig. 2, `DeMaxSAT` is only outperformed by `satlike-c` and `TT-Open-WBO-Inc-21`, which are the solvers with the best average performance in the different instances. However, `DeMaxSAT` beats `satlike-c` and `TT-Open-WBO-Inc-21` (both) in 5 instances, and it ties them in 25 instances (rounding scores to 2 decimal places), within the 60 s timeout, whereas `DeMaxSAT` beats both solvers again in 5 instances, and it ties them in 28 instances, within the 300 s timeout.

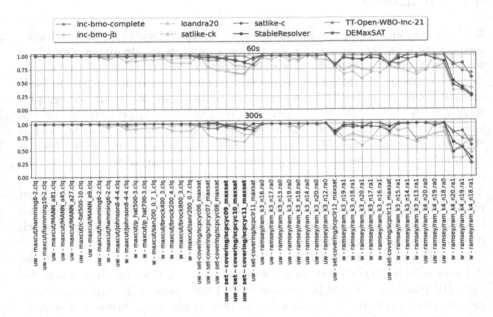

Fig. 2. Scores obtained by each solver in the individual benchmarks, sorted by their SAT-Ratio.

The three solvers with the highest scores rely on algorithms that follow a similar methodology: (1) They start by generating an initial model μ for the hard clauses (if any) with a SAT solver; (2) Then, μ is refined using a local search algorithm (they use `SATLike`, an algorithm that won the incomplete category in 2020); (3) Finally, they switch to a SAT-based algorithm, where μ is used as the initial model. Given this common structure, the solvers differ on the conditions they set to go from step (2) to (3) and in the SAT solver they use.

The most important exception to `DeMaxSAT` good performance is the MSE benchmark family `SeanSafarPour` that, as explained before, has been removed from the current comparison. This family consists of 10 instances with the highest SAT-ratio (all of them above 0.9999) and a huge number of clauses: the smallest instance deals with more than 690K clauses, and the best known solution leaves only 54 of them unsatisfied. This means that, even though these instances are still non-partial, they have the highest resemblance to a regular SAT problem by far.

Given the problem size, timeouts of 60 s and 300 s do not suffice, and `DeMaxSAT` cannot run a sufficient number of generations for an adequate quality evolution. In fact, in some cases, `DeMaxSAT` is unable to run a single generation step within the timeout, so the algorithm is actually *never applied* - thus, comparing its 0 score here with other algorithms does not make much sense. To analyze `DeMaxSAT` on these benchmarks, longer timeouts would be needed, but we postpone that study for future improvements including calls to a regular SAT solver.

6   Conclusions

In this work, an incomplete MaxSAT solver, called `DeMaxSAT`, has been implemented. It uses the Differential Evolution evolutionary algorithm, combined with two MaxSAT-specific local search heuristics, GSAT and RandomWalk, to define a memetic hybridization. The solver has been tested in non-partial MSE instances and measured against other incomplete state-of-the-art solvers presented at the MSE 2021 in a competitive environment, outperforming three of the solvers and reaching a comparable performance to the top tools in most of the benchmark instances. However, with the largest MSE instances (considering the number of variables and clauses), within the time limits of 60 s and 300 s, the memetic algorithm was not able to run for a sufficient number of generations, so higher time limits would be needed to obtain a good solution. Yet, the obtained results are especially remarkable due to the simplicity of the base differential evolution algorithm, with an easy parameterization and adaptability, and which does not rely on a backend SAT solver, like the other tools.

As a first future improvement, other heuristics could be extracted from the different solvers, to embed them in `DeMaxSAT`. Second, if we face a real application, DE parameters could be automatically tuned using self-adaptation mechanisms as in modern DE versions [8], so they would be adjusted not only to general features of the instance and timeout, but also to the specific domain to be solved. Finally, the application to partial benchmark instances must be explored by devising mechanisms that guarantee genetic variability in the population, since the EA will tend to satisfy first the hard clauses with larger weight.

Acknowledgments. Partially funded by the Xunta de Galicia and the European Union (European Regional Development Fund - Galicia 2014–2020 Program), with grants CITIC (ED431G 2019/01) and GPC ED431B 2022/33, and by the Spanish Ministry of Science and Innovation (grant PID2020-116201GB-I00).

References

1. DeMaxSAT Solver (2021). https://github.com/Manuframil/DEMaxSatSolver
2. Ali, H.M., Mitchell, D., Lee, D.C.: MAX-SAT problem using evolutionary algorithms. In: 2014 IEEE Symposium on Swarm Intelligence, pp. 1–8 (2014)
3. Bacchus, F., Järvisalo, M., Berg, J., Martins, R.: MaxSAT evaluation (2021). https://maxsat-evaluations.github.io/2021/

4. Berg, J., Demirovic, E., Stuckey, P.: Loandra in the 2020 MaxSAT evaluation (2020). https://helda.helsinki.fi/bitstream/handle/10138/333649/mse21proc.pdf

5. Bhattacharjee, A., Chauhan, P.: Solving the SAT problem using genetic algorithm. Adv. Sci. Tech. Eng. Syst. J. **2**(4), 115–120 (2017)

6. Boughaci, D., Benhamou, B., Drias, H.: Scatter search and genetic algorithms for MAX-SAT problems. J. Math. Model Algor. **7**, 101–124 (2008). https://doi.org/10.1007/s10852-008-9077-x

7. Chen, W., Whitley, D., Tinós, R., Chicano, F.: Tunneling between plateaus: improving on a state-of-the-art MAXSAT solver using partition crossover. In: Proceedings of the Genetic and Evolutionary Computation Conference, GECCO 2018, Kyoto, Japan, 15–19 July (2018)

8. Das, S., Mullick, S., Suganthan, P.: Recent advances in differential evolution - an updated survey. Swarm Evol. Comput. **27**, 1–30 (2016)

9. Djenouri, Y., Habbas, Z., Djenouri, D., Fournier-Viger, P.: Bee swarm optimization for solving the MAXSAT problem using prior knowledge. Soft. Comput. **23**(9), 3095–3112 (2017). https://doi.org/10.1007/s00500-017-2956-1

10. Doerr, B., Zheng, W.: Working principles of binary differential evolution. Theoret. Comput. Sci. **801**, 110–142 (2020)

11. Doush, I.A., Quran, A.L., Al-Betar, M.A., Awadallah, M.A.: MAX-SAT problem using hybrid harmony search algorithm. J. Intell. Syst. **27**(4), 643–658 (2018)

12. Fu, H., Xu, Y., Wu, G., Jia, H., Zhang, W., Hu, R.: An improved adaptive genetic algorithm for solving 3-SAT problems based on effective restart and greedy strategy. Int. J. Comput. Intell. Syst. **11**(1), 402–413 (2018)

13. Joshi, S., Kumar, P., Rao, S., Martins, R.: Open-WBO-Inc in MaxSAT evaluation 2020 (2020). https://helda.helsinki.fi/bitstream/handle/10138/333649/mse21proc.pdf

14. Lardeux, F., Saubion, F., Hao, J.K.: GASAT: a genetic local search algorithm for the satisfiability problem. Evol. Comput. **14**, 223–53 (2006)

15. Lei, Z., et al.: SATLike-c: solver description (2021). https://helda.helsinki.fi/bitstream/handle/10138/333649/mse21proc.pdf

16. Lovíšková, J.: Solving the 3-SAT problem using genetic algorithms. In: INES 2015 - IEEE 19th International Conference on Intelligent Engineering Systems, pp. 207–212 (2015)

17. Menai, M.E., Batouche, M.: efficient initial solution to extremal optimization algorithm for weighted MAXSAT problem. In: Chung, P.W.H., Hinde, C., Ali, M. (eds.) IEA/AIE 2003. LNCS (LNAI), vol. 2718, pp. 592–603. Springer, Heidelberg (2003). https://doi.org/10.1007/3-540-45034-3_60

18. Nadel, A.: Tt-Open-WBO-Inc-21: an anytime MaxSAT solver entering MSE 2021 (2020). https://helda.helsinki.fi/bitstream/handle/10138/333649/mse21proc.pdf

19. Neri, F., Cotta, C.: Memetic algorithms and memetic computing optimization: a literature review. Swarm Evol. Comput. **2**, 1–14 (2012)

20. Reisch, J., Großmann, P.: Stable Resolving (2020). https://helda.helsinki.fi/bitstream/handle/10138/333649/mse21proc.pdf

21. Selman, B., Kautz, H.A.: Domain-independent extensions to GSAT: solving large structured satisfiability problems. In: Proccedings of the IJCAI-93, pp. 290–295 (1993)

22. Selman, B., Levesque, H., Mitchell, D.: A new method for solving hard satisfiability problems. In: Proceedings of the AAAI Conference, pp. 440–446. AAAI Press (1992)

23. Storn, R., Price, K.: Differential evolution - a simple and efficient heuristic for global optimization over continuous spaces. J. Global Optim. **11**, 341–359 (1997)

A Robust State Transition Function for Multi-agent Epistemic Systems

Yusuf Izmirlioglu[(✉)], Loc Pham, Tran Cao Son, and Enrico Pontelli

Department of Computer Science, New Mexico State University, Las Cruces, USA
{yizmir,locpham}@nmsu.edu, {tson,epontell}@cs.nmsu.edu

Abstract. This paper studies belief correction and state transition for ontic actions in a multi-agent epistemic framework. When a full observer agent observes the execution of an action, he will correct his (possibly wrong) initial belief about the precondition of the action as well as his belief about his own observability. The paper shows that correcting beliefs about precondition and observability is vital for observing the effect of the action and robust state transition, highlighting the risk of yielding counter-intuitive results. The paper proposes a state transition function for ontic actions which integrates correcting beliefs for precondition, observability and realizing the effect of the action. This novel transition function does not require event update models. The paper investigates several properties of the transition function, assessing its robustness in ensuring that beliefs of agents change consistently with their degree of observability of action occurrences. Sample scenarios are provided to illustrate the novel transition function.

Keywords: Multi-agent systems · Epistemic reasoning · State transition function · Belief correction · Belief update

1 Introduction

In a multi-agent epistemic setting, agents have beliefs about the actual state of the world and about the beliefs of other agents. As agents execute actions, the actual state of the world and the beliefs of the agents change. Note that not all agents might observe the occurrence of an action and its effects; some agents may be ignorant or oblivious of the action. Besides agents might initially have incorrect beliefs about the state of the world and about other agents. Thus one of the problems in multi-agent epistemic reasoning is to find out how agents correct or update their beliefs upon an action occurrence, based on their own observability and their belief about other agents' observability.

In this paper, we study the problem of state transition in multi-agent epistemic settings upon an action occurrence. We focus on ontic actions. An ontic action (world-altering action) changes the actual state of the world by changing the value of fluent(s). In a multi-agent context, not all agents might be aware of the execution of an ontic action and its consequences. In this respect, we classify agents into *full observers* who observe the action and its effects, and *oblivious* agents who are unaware of the action occurrence.

G. Marreiros et al. (Eds.): EPIA 2022, LNAI 13566, pp. 688–700, 2022.
https://doi.org/10.1007/978-3-031-16474-3_56

Execution of the action provides information to the full observer agents regarding the action's precondition and observability; this allows them to correct their initial (possibly wrong) beliefs about precondition and their observability. Namely, when an agent observes the action occurrence, he realizes that its precondition holds and he is not ignorant of the action. This correction step is vital for observing the effect of the action and robust state transition; because in possible world semantics whether the effect of the action applies at a world depends on satisfaction of precondition and observability conditions at that world. We will illustrate, by example scenarios, that without correcting beliefs about precondition and observability, the state transition yields counter-intuitive outcomes. We propose a state transition function which performs correction for action precondition and observability and realizes the effect of the action.

Let us first explain the issues with the existing models of state transition for possible world semantics. One approach is to employ *action models*, introduced in [3,4] and later extended to *event update models* in [9,16]. Event update models involve different events and agents have accessibility relations between events depending on their observability. The next state is computed by cross product of the initial Kripke structure with the event update model. However, Example 1 illustrates that the event update model of [7,16], by itself, is not capable of correcting agents' beliefs for precondition or observability.

Example 1. Imagine two agents A, B and a machine which is sound (functional) and initially off ($\neg on$). Agent A believes that the machine is defective. This state of affairs is commonly represented as a pointed Kripke structure, as in Fig. 1(a) (top). Possible worlds are represented by circles. A double line circle represents the actual world. Links between worlds encode the belief accessibility relations of agents. Agent B performs the *start_machine* action, whose precondition is $\neg on \wedge sound$ and effect is on. The condition for full observability of an agent i is *looking_i*; A, B are full observers at both worlds. The event update model for *start_machine* is given Fig. 1(a). σ event denotes the case where the action occurs. Since both agents are full observers, they only consider the σ event. The result of applying this event model to the initial state is given in Fig. 1(a) (bottom). The event model removes the accessibility relation of agent A from world s to u because A considers only σ event and the action is not executable at world u. As a result, A has no accessibility relation at the next state and believes in every formula. Intuitively, when A observes the action, he should understand that the machine is sound and correct his beliefs at world u.

[11] has constructed a model of state transition where agents correct their beliefs about action precondition. However, their transition function does not involve belief correction for observability. Their framework requires two separate operators for belief and knowledge. As the next example suggests, belief correction for agent's own observability as well as other agents' observability is necessary for robust state transition[1].

---

[1] Details of state transition in these examples can be found in our online appendix at https://github.com/yizmirlioglu/EPIA2022.

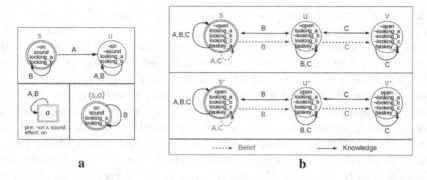

Fig. 1. (a) The first example   (b) The second example

Example 2. Consider another scenario in Fig. 1(b) with three agents A, B, C (top). The knowledge and beliefs of the agents are encoded in a pointed Kripke structure with two accessibility relations: the knowledge and the belief relations. At the actual world, the box is closed and all agents are looking at the box. Agents A, C believe that all agents are looking at the box, B believes that A, C are looking but B is not looking at the box (wrong initial belief). Moreover B believes that C believes that no agent is looking. Suppose that agent A performs the *open_box* action (precondition: *haskey_a*; effect: *open*). The condition for full observability of agent i is *looking_i*. At the next state, we expect agent B to correct his belief at world u about his own observability. Also since B believes that C is a full observer, then B should believe that C will also correct his beliefs at world v about fluent *looking_c*. The next state according to [11] is shown in Fig. 1(b) (bottom): A believes that B is looking but A believes that B believes that B is not looking. Moreover B believes that C is looking but B believes that C believes that C is not looking. This outcome is counter-intuitive.

With these motivations, we investigate the problem of robust state transition with belief correction upon an action occurrence under possible world semantics. Our goal is to develop a novel state transition function for ontic actions that addresses the above shortcomings[2]. It is worth mentioning that due to initial beliefs or observability of action occurrences, agents might have incomplete or incorrect beliefs. As such, given an action occurrence, full observer agents will correct their beliefs about fluents belonging to the precondition of the action as well as the fluents belonging to their observability. It is also important to note that in our framework, agents also correct their beliefs about belief of other agents. In particular, if a full observer agent i believes that another agent j is a full observer, then i believes that j will correct his beliefs about precondition and observability.

---

[2] The proposed approach can be easily extended to cover sensing and announcement actions. We omit it due to space limitation.

2 Preliminaries

A *multi-agent* domain $\langle \mathcal{AG}, \mathcal{F} \rangle$ includes a finite and non-empty set of agents $\mathcal{AG}$ and a set of fluents $\mathcal{F}$ encoding properties of the world. *Belief formulae* over $\langle \mathcal{AG}, \mathcal{F} \rangle$ are defined by the BNF:

$$\varphi ::= p \mid \neg \varphi \mid (\varphi \wedge \varphi) \mid (\varphi \vee \varphi) \mid \mathbf{B}_i \varphi \mid \mathbf{E}_\alpha \varphi \mid \mathbf{C}_\alpha \varphi$$

where $p \in \mathcal{F}$ is a fluent, $i \in \mathcal{AG}$ and $\emptyset \neq \alpha \subseteq \mathcal{AG}$. We refer to a belief formula which does not contain any occurrence of $\mathbf{B}_i$, $\mathbf{E}_\alpha$, $\mathbf{C}_\alpha$ as *a fluent formula*. Let $\mathcal{L}_{\mathcal{AG}}$ denote the set of belief formulae over $\langle \mathcal{AG}, \mathcal{F} \rangle$.

Satisfaction of belief formulae is defined over *pointed Kripke structures* [17]. A Kripke structure M is a tuple $\langle S, \pi, \mathcal{B}_1, \ldots, \mathcal{B}_n \rangle$, where S is a set of worlds (denoted by $M[S]$), $\pi : S \mapsto 2^{\mathcal{F}}$ is a function that associates an interpretation of $\mathcal{F}$ to each element of S (denoted by $M[\pi]$), and for $i \in \mathcal{AG}$, $\mathcal{B}_i \subseteq S \times S$ is a binary relation over S (denoted by $M[i]$). For convenience, we will often draw a Kripke structure M as a directed labeled graph, whose set of labeled nodes represent S and whose set of labeled edges contains $s \xrightarrow{i} t$ iff $(s, t) \in \mathcal{B}_i$. The label of each node has two parts: the name of the world followed by its interpretation. For $u \in S$ and a fluent formula φ, $M[\pi](u)$ and $M[\pi](u)(\varphi)$ denote the interpretation associated to u via π and the truth value of φ with respect to $M[\pi](u)$. For a world $u \in M[S]$, (M, u) is a *pointed Kripke structure*, also called *state* hereafter.

Given a belief formula φ, a Kripke structure $M = \langle S, \pi, \mathcal{B}_1, \ldots, \mathcal{B}_n \rangle$ and a possible state $u \in S$: (i) $(M, u) \vDash p$ if p is a fluent and $M[\pi](u) \vDash p$; (ii) $(M, u) \vDash \neg \varphi$ if $(M, u) \nvDash \varphi$; (iii) $(M, u) \vDash \varphi_1 \vee \varphi_2$ if $(M, u) \vDash \varphi_1$ or $(M, u) \vDash \varphi_2$; (iv) $(M, u) \vDash \varphi_1 \wedge \varphi_2$ if $(M, u) \vDash \varphi_1$ and $(M, u) \vDash \varphi_2$; (v) $(M, u) \vDash \mathbf{B}_i \varphi$ if $(M, t) \vDash \varphi$ for every t such that $(u, t) \in \mathcal{B}_i$; (vi) $(M, u) \vDash \mathbf{E}_\alpha \varphi$ if $(M, u) \vDash \mathbf{B}_i \varphi$ for every $i \in \alpha$; (vii) $(M, u) \vDash \mathbf{C}_\alpha \varphi$ if $(M, u) \vDash \mathbf{E}_\alpha^k \varphi$ for every $k \geq 0$, where $\mathbf{E}_\alpha^0 \varphi = \varphi$ and $\mathbf{E}_\alpha^{k+1} = \mathbf{E}_\alpha(\mathbf{E}_\alpha^k \varphi)$.

For a fluent $f \in \mathcal{F}$, let $\overline{f} = \neg f$ and $\overline{\neg f} = f$; and for a set of fluent literals X, let $\overline{X} = \{ \overline{\ell} \mid \ell \in X \}$. If $\beta = b_1 \wedge \ldots \wedge b_e$ and $\gamma = l_1 \wedge \ldots \wedge l_g$ are conjunctions of fluent literals, $\beta \cup \gamma$ denotes the set $\{ b_1, \ldots, b_e, l_1, \ldots, l_g \}$.

2.1 m$\mathcal{A}^*$ Formalism

In this work, we borrow a fragment of the action language m$\mathcal{A}^*$ presented by [6, 7], to describe actions, observability of agents and initial beliefs. m$\mathcal{A}^*$ is defined over a multi-agent domain $\langle \mathcal{AG}, \mathcal{F}, \mathcal{A} \rangle$, where $\mathcal{A}$ is the set of actions, and contains statements of the form:

$$\textbf{executable a if } \psi \tag{1}$$

$$\textbf{a causes } \varphi \textbf{ if } \mu \tag{2}$$

$$\textbf{i observes a if } \delta_{i,\text{a}} \tag{3}$$

where ψ, μ, $\delta_{i,\text{a}}$ are fluent formulae, φ is a set of literals and $i \in \mathcal{AG}$. A statement of the form (1) encodes precondition of an action a. In this paper, we allow the

precondition to be of the form $\psi = h_1 \wedge ... \wedge h_r$ where h_j are literals, $1 \leq j \leq r$. For the sake of understandability, we do not consider beliefs of the acting agent as part of the precondition. A statement of the form (2) describes the conditional effects of an ontic action a. (3) states the condition for full observability for the action a. We will often say that $\delta_{i,a}$ is the condition for full observability of agent i for the action a. We assume that $\delta_{i,a}$ is in the form of conjuction of fluent literals. An m$\mathcal{A}^*$ domain consists of the statements of the form (1)–(3).

Given an m$\mathcal{A}^*$ domain let $Effects_a$ be the set of (μ, φ) pairs such that "a causes φ if μ" belongs to the domain. We assume that if (μ, φ) and (μ', φ') are in $Effects_a$ then $\mu \wedge \mu'$ is inconsistent. Intuitively, if condition μ holds at a world u, the action replaces the relevant literals in the world with φ. Similar to action language $\mathcal{A}$ [19], $M'[\pi](u') = \phi(a, \pi(u))$ stands for interpretation of the resultant world u' upon applying the action a on the world u. Formally, if $(M, u) \vDash \mu$ and $(\mu, \varphi) \in Effects_a$, then $M'[\pi](u') = (\pi(u) \setminus \overline{\varphi}) \cup \varphi$. If $(M, u) \nvDash \mu$ for any $(\mu, \varphi) \in Effects_a$ then $M'[\pi](u') = \pi(u)$.

Note that entailment of a fluent formula depends on a world thus observability is defined over pointed Kripke structures. In general, an agent may not know true observability of other agents; however the agent can have belief about observability of another agent j, based on his belief about $\delta_{j,a}$.

3   State Transition Function

In this paper, we study state transition due to ontic actions in a domain D. Formally, it is the problem of computing $(M', s') = \Phi_D(a, (M, s))$ given a state (M, s) and the occurrence of a in (M, s). We follow the syntax in Sect. 2 and use ψ, $\delta_{i,a}$, (μ, φ) to denote the precondition, observability and conditional effect of the action a. We assume that the initial pointed Kripke structure (M, s) is given. We also assume that a is executable in (M, s), i.e., $(M, s) \vDash \psi$.

Our state transition function $\Phi_D(a, (M, s))$ corrects agents' beliefs about precondition and observability, and realizes the effect of the action. Namely, full observers observe the effects of the action and correct their beliefs, while oblivious agents remain in the old state. Correcting beliefs is also applicable for beliefs about other agents: If agent i_1 is full observer at the true state and i_1 believes i_2 is full observer, i_1 believes i_2 believes i_3 is full observer, ..., i_1 believes i_2 believes ... i_k is full observer, then i_1 believes i_2 believes ... i_k will correct his beliefs about observability, precondition, and observe the effect of the action.

Note that the effect of the action may alter fluent(s) in the formula of precondition and/or observability. For example, the precondition of open_box action is ¬open and its effect is open. The condition for observability of distract_attention_a action is attentive_a, its effect is ¬attentive_a. Therefore the observing agent should first correct his beliefs about precondition and observability, and then apply the effect of the action.

To illustrate the state transition function definition, we consider the pointed Kripke structure (M, s) in a domain D_{box}, depicted in Fig. 2, with three agents A, B, C and two possible worlds s and u. Agent A performs the open_box action.

The precondition of the action is ¬*open* and its effect is *open*. The condition for full observability of agent i is *looking_i*. At the actual world s, agent A is full observer of this action but he believes that he is oblivious. Agent A also believes that B, C are full observers. Agents B, C are actually oblivious and they know that they are oblivious. To give an idea about how we create the

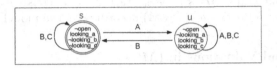

Fig. 2. Initial state (M, s) for $\Phi_{D_{box}}(open\_box, (M, s))$

worlds, their valuation and the accessibility relations at the next state, consider the following cases from our example domain D_{box}. In the first case, as depicted in Fig. 3, agent A is full observer at world s; he considers only world u which violates his observability. Namely, $(M, s) \vDash \mathbf{B}_A \neg looking\_a$. At the next state we shouldn't remove accessibility relation of A from s to u; doing so would cause A considering no world possible. Then we amend the world u by modifying the value of ¬*looking_a* and then apply the effect of the *open_box* action. We call this new world u_A as it is amended for agent A; and create a relation from s' to u_A in M'. This way, agent A corrects his belief for his observability and observes the effect of the action. In the second case, agent B is full observer at

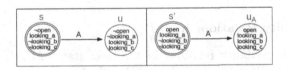

Fig. 3. Case 1 for the transition function

(M, u). At world u, B considers worlds s, u possible (see Fig. 3). u satisfies both action precondition and observability condition of B while s does not. Namely, $(M, u) \nvDash \mathbf{B}_B \neg looking\_b$. In this case, B should keep his accessibility relation from u to u and eliminate the relation from u to s. Hence B should not create the relation from u to amended world s_B because there is already another world he considers possible. At the next state M' when we apply the effect of the action, the new world becomes u' so B has a relation (u', u'). The third case in Fig. 4

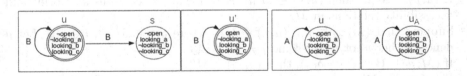

Fig. 4. Case 2 (**left**) and Case 3 (**right**) for the transition function

analyzes the accessibility relation of agent A at world u_A of M'. Since we have created a new world u_A at M', agent A should have beliefs (outgoing relations) at world u_A as well. At world $u \in M[S]$, A considers only world u possible. A is a full observer at world u_A, but (M, u) does not satisfy full observability of A. Thus at the next state, A creates a relation to amended world u_A. That is, a relation from u_A to itself. Let us now provide the formal definitions for the transition function. The next state $(M', s') = \Phi_{D_{box}}(\mathsf{a}, (M, s))$ is constructed from (M, s) and the occurrence of *open_box* (by A) according to the model below.

3.1   Worlds and Valuations in (M', s')

M' contains all worlds and accessibility relations in M, namely, $M[S] \subseteq M'[S]$ and $M[i] \subseteq M'[i]$ for all $i \in \mathcal{AG}$. Valuation of worlds in $M[S]$ also remains the same, i.e., $M'[\pi](u) = M[\pi](u)$ for $u \in M[S]$. Additionally, M' contains new worlds of the form u' and u_i where $u \in M[S]$, $i \in \mathcal{AG}$.

- For each $u \in M[S]$ such that $(M, u) \vDash \psi$, let u' be a new world in $M'[S]$ such that $M'[\pi](u') = \phi(\mathsf{a}, \pi(u))$; this world results from the execution of a in u.
- Let $\lambda_i(u)$ be an interpretation such that $\lambda_i(u) = (\pi(u) \setminus (\overline{\psi \cup \delta_{i,\mathsf{a}}})) \cup (\psi \cup \delta_{i,\mathsf{a}})$. Then u_i is a new world in M' such that $M'[\pi](u_i) = \phi(\mathsf{a}, \lambda_i(u))$. Intuitively, u_i is a new world obtained by agent i first correcting his beliefs at world $u \in M[S]$ about precondition and his own observability, and then applying the effect of a.

We define s' as the actual world in M'.

3.2   Accessibility Relations in (M', s')

We create the accessibility relations in the next state (M', s') such that full observers correct their beliefs and observe the effect of the action whereas oblivious agents remain at the old state. Suppose that $(u, v) \in M[i]$. If agent i is full observer at world $u \in M[S]$, then in the next state he will observe the effect of the action at worlds u' and u_j, $j \in \mathcal{AG}$. In M', we keep only the accessibility relations of agent i from u to the worlds v which satisfy action precondition and observability of i. We apply the effect of the action to obtain v' and create relations from u' and u_j to v'. However if all the v worlds that agent i considers possible at u violate precondition and/or observability, we cannot remove all the edges, thus we amend the worlds to obtain v_i and create relations from u' and u_j to v_i. Formally, for an agent $i \in \mathcal{AG}$,

- If $(u, v) \in M[i]$, then $(u, v) \in M'[i]$. Recall that M' contains all worlds and accessibility relations in M.
- Suppose that $(M, u) \vDash \delta_{i,\mathsf{a}}$, $(u, v) \in M[i]$ where $u, v \in M[S]$, $i \in \mathcal{AG}$. Let $\hat{u}$ denote either u' or u_j for some $j \neq i$, $j \in \mathcal{AG}$.
  If $(M, u) \vDash \mathbf{B}_i(\neg\psi \vee \neg\delta_{i,\mathsf{a}})$, then $(\hat{u}, v_i) \in M'[i]$.
  If $(M, u) \vDash \neg\mathbf{B}_i(\neg\psi \vee \neg\delta_{i,\mathsf{a}})$ and $(M, v) \vDash \psi \wedge \delta_{i,\mathsf{a}}$, then $(\hat{u}, v') \in M'[i]$.

If agent i is a full observer at $u \in M[S]$, then in the next state, i keeps links to those v worlds which satisfy precondition and observability of i and removes links to v worlds which do not satisfy precondition and/or observability. However if all those v worlds violate precondition and/or observability, agent i will amend all these v worlds and create links to amended v_i worlds.

- Suppose that $u_i \in M'[S]$, $(u, v) \in M[i]$ where $u, v \in M[S]$, $i \in \mathcal{AG}$.
  If $(M, u) \vDash \mathbf{B}_i(\neg\psi \vee \neg\delta_{i,a})$ then $(u_i, v_i) \in M'[i]$.
  If $(M, u) \vDash \neg\mathbf{B}_i(\neg\psi \vee \neg\delta_{i,a})$ and $(M, v) \vDash \psi \wedge \delta_{i,a}$ then $(u_i, v') \in M'[i]$.
  Here we construct accessibility relations of agent i at $u_i \in M'[S]$. By definition of u_i, agent i should observe the effect of the action at the world u_i regardless of his observability at $u \in M[S]$. At the next state i keeps links from u_i to those v worlds which satisfy precondition and observability and removes links to v worlds which do not satisfy. However if all those v worlds that i considers possible at $u \in M[S]$ violate precondition and/or observability, agent i will create links from u_i to amended v_i worlds.
- If $(M, u) \vDash \neg\delta_{i,a}$ and $(u, v) \in M[i]$ then $(u', v) \in M'[i]$ and $(u_j, v) \in M'[i]$ where $j \neq i$, $j \in \mathcal{AG}$.
  If an agent i is oblivious at a world $u \in M[S]$, then at worlds u' and u_j, $j \neq i$ of the next state, i will continue to consider the old world v.

The next state according to the transition function is depicted in Fig. 5. We omit the worlds that are not reachable from s' (the actual world in the next state) such as s_A, u_B, and u_C, etc. At the original actual world s, agent A is a full observer and considers only u possible which does not satisfy his observability. Hence in the next state he amends world u,

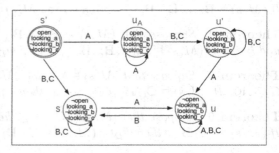

Fig. 5. $\Phi_{D_{box}}(open\_box, (M, s))$

and creates the edge from $\hat{s} = s'$ to u_A. B, C have a loop at s but they are oblivious thus at s' they continue to consider the old world s. B, C are full observers at u, and u satisfies action precondition hence at world $\hat{u} = u_A$, they consider the world u'. Notice that B does not have a relation from u_A to s' or from u' to s' because B is full observer at u_A but not in s (the second part of item 2 applies).

As a result, at the next state (M', s'), A has corrected his belief and A knows that he is a full observer of $open\_box$ action and the box is open. Moreover A believes that B, C believe that they are full observers and the box is open.

4   Properties of Φ_D

This section proves some properties of our transition function: when an action occurs, beliefs of an agent change consistently with his own observability and his

belief about other agents' observability. Theorem 1, 2 describe how first order beliefs of full observer and oblivious agents change due to the occurrence of an ontic action. Full observers observe the effect of the action and update their beliefs whereas oblivious agents remain at the old state. Theorem 3, 4 describe the change in higher order beliefs of an agent about other agents. Theorem 5, 6 describe how common knowledge of agents change upon the action: If G is a group of full observers and it is common knowledge among G that each of them is a full observer then in the next state agents in G commonly observe the effect of the action. If a group G of agents commonly believe that agent i is oblivious then in the next state they commonly believe that belief of i remains the same. The theorems assume that the action a is executable at the true state $((M, s) \vDash \psi)$, "a **causes** φ **if** μ" belongs to D, $i \in \mathcal{AG}$, $\ell \in \varphi$, and η is a belief formula.

Theorem 1. *If $(M, s) \vDash \delta_{i,\mathsf{a}}$ and $(M, s) \vDash \mathbf{B}_i \mu$ then $\Phi_D(\mathsf{a}, (M, s)) \vDash \mathbf{B}_i \ell$.*

Theorem 2. *If $(M, s) \vDash \neg\delta_{i,\mathsf{a}}$ then $\Phi_D(\mathsf{a}, (M, s)) \vDash \mathbf{B}_i \eta$ iff $(M, s) \vDash \mathbf{B}_i \eta$.*

Theorem 3. *Suppose that $(M, s) \vDash \delta_{i_1,\mathsf{a}}$, $(M, s) \vDash \mathbf{B}_{i_1} \delta_{i_2,\mathsf{a}}$, $(M, s) \vDash \mathbf{B}_{i_1} \mathbf{B}_{i_2} \delta_{i_3,\mathsf{a}}$, ..., $(M, s) \vDash \mathbf{B}_{i_1} ... \mathbf{B}_{i_{k-1}} \delta_{i_k,\mathsf{a}}$, $(M, s) \vDash \mathbf{B}_{i_1} ... \mathbf{B}_{i_k} \delta_{i_{k+1},\mathsf{a}}$ hold for some $k \geq 0$.
If $(M, s) \vDash \mathbf{B}_{i_1} ... \mathbf{B}_{i_k} \mathbf{B}_{i_{k+1}} \mu$ then $\Phi_D(\mathsf{a}, (M, s)) \vDash \mathbf{B}_{i_1} ... \mathbf{B}_{i_k} \mathbf{B}_{i_{k+1}} \ell$.*

Theorem 4. *Suppose that $(M, s) \vDash \mathbf{B}_{i_1} ... \mathbf{B}_{i_k} \neg\delta_{i_{k+1},\mathsf{a}}$ holds where $i_k \neq i_{k+1}$ and $k \geq 0$. If $(M, s) \vDash \mathbf{B}_{i_1} ... \mathbf{B}_{i_k} \mathbf{B}_{i_{k+1}} \eta$ then $\Phi_D(\mathsf{a}, (M, s)) \vDash \mathbf{B}_{i_1} ... \mathbf{B}_{i_k} \mathbf{B}_{i_{k+1}} \eta$.*

Theorem 5. *Suppose that $(M, s) \vDash \delta_{i,\mathsf{a}}$ and $(M, s) \vDash \mathbf{C}_G \delta_{i,\mathsf{a}}$ for all $i \in G$ where $G \subseteq \mathcal{AG}$. If $(M, s) \vDash \mathbf{C}_G \mathbf{B}_j \mu$ for $j \in G$ then $\Phi_D(\mathsf{a}, (M, s)) \vDash \mathbf{C}_G \mathbf{B}_j \ell$.*

Theorem 6. *Suppose that $(M, s) \vDash \mathbf{C}_G \neg\delta_{i,\mathsf{a}}$ holds where $i \in \mathcal{AG}$, $G \subseteq \mathcal{AG}$. If $(M, s) \vDash \mathbf{C}_G \mathbf{B}_i \eta$ then $\Phi_D(\mathsf{a}, (M, s)) \vDash \mathbf{C}_G \mathbf{B}_i \eta$.*

Proof of the theorems are omitted due to limited space and collected in the online appendix[3]. Note that the transition function for m$\mathcal{A}^*$ domains defined by [7] does not satisfy the properties in Theorem 3 – 6 because their event update models use fixed observability across worlds. Therefore, the transition function does not respect belief of an agent about other agents' observability. The next theorem describes some properties of our state transition function which are not present in [11]. Theorem 7 states that a full observer agent i, in the next state, believes that he is a full observer. Moreover if i believes that j is full observer, in the next state i believes that j believes that j is a full observer. Considering the belief operator, Example 2 shows that transition function of [11] does not satisfy the property in Theorem 7.

Theorem 7. *Suppose that the conditional effects of the action φ do not involve any fluent in $\delta_{i,\mathsf{a}}$ for any $i \in \mathcal{AG}$. For $i, j \in \mathcal{AG}$, if $(M, s) \vDash \delta_{i,\mathsf{a}}$ then $\Phi_D(\mathsf{a}, (M, s)) \vDash \mathbf{B}_i \delta_{i,\mathsf{a}}$. If $(M, s) \vDash \delta_{i,\mathsf{a}}$ and $(M, s) \vDash \mathbf{B}_i \delta_{j,\mathsf{a}}$ then $\Phi_D(\mathsf{a}, (M, s)) \vDash \mathbf{B}_i \mathbf{B}_j \delta_{j,\mathsf{a}}$.*

---

[3] https://github.com/yizmirlioglu/EPIA2022.

Time Complexity. Checking entailment of the belief formula $B_i(\neg\psi \vee \neg\delta_{i,\mathsf{a}})$ at a world takes $O(|M[S]|)$ time. Observe that in items (1)-(4) of Sect. 3.2, for each accessibility relation in $M[i]$, at most one new accessibility relation is added to $M'[i]$. Hence the running time is at most $O(|M[S]|.|M[i]|)$ for a single agent $i \in \mathcal{AG}$. Since the above procedure is repeated for every agent $i \in \mathcal{AG}$, the total running time is $O(|M[S]|.|\mathcal{R}|)$ where $\mathcal{R} = \sum_{i\in\mathcal{AG}} M[i]$ is the number of accessibility relations in M. Note that in the next state either $(\hat{u}, v')$ or $(\hat{u}, v_i)$ is in $M'[i]$, but not both of them. In the worst case, $M'[S]$ contains v_i for each $v \in M[S]$, $i \in \mathcal{AG}$. Hence the maximum number of worlds (reachable from s') in the next state is $|M'[S]| = (|\mathcal{AG}| + 1).|M[S]|$.

5   Examples

We now demonstrate the benefit of our approach by applying the state transition function on the example scenarios in the introduction. We consider the belief operator of the Kripke structures in Fig. 1. The next state of each scenario is depicted in Fig. 6.

Now the next state is intuitive: In the first scenario, agent A has corrected his belief at world u about action precondition and it is common knowledge that the machine is sound and on. In the second scenario, initially A believes that B is full observer hence in the next state A believes that B has corrected his belief about his observability. Likewise, B initially believes that C is full observer hence in the next state B believes that C has corrected his belief about his observability.

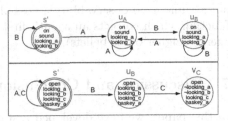

Fig. 6. Solution of example scenarios in the introduction

6   Related Work

In dynamic epistemic logic literature, belief revision and belief update have been studied by [5,8,16,20,22]. Belief revision refers to the change in the agent's belief when he receives an exogenous information about his environment which is static and no action occurs. Hence belief revision models do not involve effect of an ontic action. [1,13,21] have introduced axioms that belief revision functions should satisfy. Various revision functions have been proposed by [10,12,18,24,26]. These functions operate on belief sets or belief bases. [2,14] have defined belief revision function for possible world semantics with plausibility relation. The revision function modifies the Kripke structure upon receiving a belief formula from the outside world. Belief update is similar to belief revision, except that the agent receives information about an outside world which also changes. [20] proposes

axioms and an update operator to modify the knowledge base. [22] studies belief update operation on restricted modal literals.

[15,25] are among the first works which introduce effect of an ontic action in event models. In order to realize action occurrences in the multi-agent context, [7,23] have developed action languages that describe the domain, actions and observability of agents. However, their transition functions do not involve any correction of beliefs about precondition or observability in ontic actions. [7] utilizes a simple belief correction mechanism for sensing/announcement actions where the full observer agents"directly learn the true state of the world".

[11] proposed an alternative state transition function, where full and partial observers correct their beliefs about action precondition, but not about observability. Their model requires two separate operators for belief and knowledge. The authors do not examine whether an agent's beliefs about other agents change due to belief correction. Observability of agents is computed at the actual world and assumed to be fixed across worlds, thus an agent corrects his beliefs even in those worlds where he is not a full or partial observer. Conditional effects are not allowed for an ontic action. In our model, the knowledge operator is not required and the belief operator is sufficient for belief correction. Besides, we do not assume fixed observability across all worlds. We construct a state transition function which corrects an agent's first order beliefs and his beliefs about other agents (higher order beliefs).

7   Discussion and Conclusion

In this paper, we have developed a state transition function for possible world semantics and multi-agent domains where agents may have different observability and may have incorrect initial beliefs. Occurrence of an ontic action does not just alter the value of fluents under the effect of the action; but also helps full observer agents to correct their initial wrong beliefs about action precondition and observability. By examples we have shown that this step is necessary for soundness of the state transition function.

In our transition function, agents correct their beliefs about observability, precondition and effect of the action. Depending on his current beliefs, the agent removes the accessibility relation to a world, or he amends that world. By construction, agents also correct their higher order beliefs about other agents. Our approach does not require event update models.

We proved several properties of our transition function that capture the fact that agents' beliefs change consistently with their observability, even with higher order beliefs of agents. We showed that the newly defined transition function overcomes the shortcomings of earlier approaches, by example and theoretical properties. Furthermore, the transition function has polynomial time complexity.

Acknowledgments. The authors have been partially supported by NSF grants 2151254, 1914635 and 1757207. Tran Cao Son was also partially supported by NSF grant 1812628.

References

1. Alchourrón, C.E., Gärdenfors, P., Makinson, D.: On the logic of theory change: partial meet contraction and revision functions. JSL **50**(2), 510–530 (1985)
2. Aucher, G.: Generalizing AGM to a multi-agent setting. Logic J. IGPL **18**(4), 530–558 (2010)
3. Baltag, A., Moss, L.: Logics for epistemic programs. Synthese **134**(2), 165–224 (2004). https://doi.org/10.1023/B:SYNT.0000024912.56773.5e
4. Baltag, A., Moss, L.S., Solecki, S.: The logic of public announcements, common knowledge, and private suspicions. In: Arló-Costa, H., Hendricks, V.F., van Benthem, J. (eds.) Readings in Formal Epistemology. SGTP, vol. 1, pp. 773–812. Springer, Cham (2016). https://doi.org/10.1007/978-3-319-20451-2_38
5. Baltag, A., Smets, S.: A qualitative theory of dynamic interactive belief revision. In: Proceedings of 7th LOFT. Texts in Logic and Games 3, pp. 13–60. Amsterdam University Press (2008)
6. Baral, C., Gelfond, G., Pontelli, E., Son, T.C.: An action language for multi-agent domains: foundations. arXiv.org p. https://arxiv.org/abs/1511.01960v3 (2020)
7. Baral, C., Gelfond, G., Pontelli, E., Son, T.C.: An action language for multi-agent domains. Artif. Intell. **302**, 103601 (2022). https://doi.org/10.1016/j.artint.2021.103601
8. van Benthem, J., Smets, S.: Dynamic logics of belief change. In: Handbook of Epistemic Logic, pp. 313–394 (2015)
9. van Benthem, J., van Eijck, J., Kooi, B.P.: Logics of communication and change. Inf. Comput. **204**(11), 1620–1662 (2006)
10. Borgida, A.: Language features for flexible handling of exceptions in information systems. ACM Trans. Database Syst. **10**(4), 563–603 (1985)
11. Buckingham, D., Kasenberg, D., Scheutz, M.: Simultaneous representation of knowledge and belief for epistemic planning with belief revision, pp. 172–181 (2020). https://doi.org/10.24963/kr.2020/18
12. Dalal, M.: Investigations into a theory of knowledge base revision: preliminary report. In: Proceedings of the Seventh National Conference on Artificial Intelligence, vol. 2, pp. 475–479. Citeseer (1988)
13. Darwiche, A., Pearl, J.: On the logic of iterated belief revision. Artif. Intell. **89**(1–2), 1–29 (1997)
14. van Ditmarsch, H.: Prolegomena to dynamic logic for belief revision. Synthese (Knowl. Rationality Action) **147**, 229–275 (2005)
15. van Ditmarsch, H.P., van der Hoek, W., Kooi, B.P.: Dynamic epistemic logic with assignment. In: Dignum, F., Dignum, V., Koenig, S., Kraus, S., Singh, M.P., Wooldridge, M. (eds.) 4th International Joint Conference on Autonomous Agents and Multiagent Systems (AAMAS 2005), 25–29 July 2005, Utrecht, The Netherlands, pp. 141–148. ACM (2005)
16. Ditmarsch, H.V., van der Hoek, W., Kooi, B.: Dynamic Epistemic Logic. Springer Publishing Company, Incorporated, 1st edn. (2007)
17. Fagin, R., Halpern, J., Moses, Y., Vardi, M.: Reasoning About Knowledge. MIT press, Cambridge (1995)
18. Fagin, R., Ullman, J.D., Vardi, M.Y.: On the semantics of updates in databases. In: Proceedings of the 2nd ACM SIGACT-SIGMOD Symposium on Principles of Database Systems, pp. 352–365 (1983)
19. Gelfond, M., Lifschitz, V.: Action languages. Electron. Trans. Artif. Intell. **3**(6) (1998)

20. Katsuno, H., Mendelzon, A.: On the difference between updating a knowledge base and revising it. In: Proceedings of KR 92, pp. 387–394 (1992)
21. Katsuno, H., Mendelzon, A.O.: Propositional knowledge base revision and minimal change. Artif. Intell. **52**(3), 263–294 (1992)
22. Miller, T., Muise, C.J.: Belief update for proper epistemic knowledge bases. In: IJCAI, pp. 1209–1215 (2016)
23. Rajaratnam, D., Thielscher, M.: Representing and reasoning with event models for epistemic planning. In: Proceedings of the International Conference on Principles of Knowledge Representation and Reasoning, vol. 18, pp. 519–528 (2021)
24. Satoh, K.: Nonmonotonic reasoning by minimal belief revision. In: Proceedin FGCS, pp. 455–462. Springer, Heidelberg (1988)
25. Van Benthem, J.: Logical Dynamics of Information and Interaction. Cambridge University Press, Cambridge (2011)
26. Winslett, M.: Reasoning about action using a possible models approach. In: AAAI, pp. 89–93 (1988)

Multi-adjoint Lattice Logic. Properties and Query Answering

Maria Eugenia Cornejo[1], Luis Fariñas del Cerro[2], and Jesús Medina[1]([⊠])

[1] Department of Mathematics, University of Cádiz, Cádiz, Spain
{mariaeugenia.cornejo,jesus.medina}@uca.es
[2] University of Paul Sabatier, Toulouse, CNRS, Toulouse, France
luis.farinas@irit.fr

Abstract. Multi-adjoint lattice logic (MLL) has been introduced as an axiomatization of multi-adjoint algebras on lattices. This paper highlights the interest of MLL introducing new relevant properties and some interesting examples of how to reasoning with this logic.

Keywords: Fuzzy sets · Fuzzy logic · Lattice · Multi-adjoint algebra

1 Introduction

Fuzzy sets and fuzzy logic have widely demonstrated their usefulness for modeling vague, imperfect and incomplete information in data sets. Multi-adjoint logic programming [27,29] has been a general and flexible framework in this area, which has generalized different fuzzy logic programming settings [10,12,19,21,25]. However, it was not studied from a syntactic point of view. Following a similar procedure as the ones introduced by Hájek [17], with the basic multi-valued logic BL, the logic for left-continuous t-norms presented by Esteva and Godo in [15], its extension considering right-continuous t-conorms [16], or the logics of subresiduated lattices from Epstein and Horn [14], two new logics associated with the multi-adjoint algebras based on posets [5] and lattices [3] have been presented recently, which have provided a sound and complete axiomatization of these algebras. These logics are called multi-adjoint logic (ML) and multi-adjoint lattice logic (MLL), respectively.

ML and MLL consider a richer language than the one used in basic many-valued logic BL introduced by Petr Hájek in [17] and, with weaker and different axioms. This paper is based on MLL and illustrates the usefulness of this logic for introducing automatic decision methods, whose application to real examples will be studied in the future. In this paper, we will also continue with the analysis

Partially supported by the 2014–2020 ERDF Operational Programme in collaboration with the State Research Agency (AEI) in project PID2019-108991GB-I00, and with the Department of Economy, Knowledge, Business and University of the Regional Government of Andalusia in project FEDER-UCA18-108612, and by the European Cooperation in Science & Technology (COST) Action CA17124.

G. Marreiros et al. (Eds.): EPIA 2022, LNAI 13566, pp. 701–712, 2022.
https://doi.org/10.1007/978-3-031-16474-3_57

of this logic and its comparison with the BL logic. Interesting properties will be studied, such as the "syntactic monotonicity" of the considered operation symbols and the natural translation of different properties of BL into formulas in MLL.

2   Bounded Order-Right Multi-adjoint Algebras

Order-right multi-adjoint algebras were considered in order to define a propositional logic on a bounded poset in [5], and later on a bounded lattice [3]. Since a detailed study of multi-adjoint algebras can be found in [6], here the notions of order-right adjoint pair and (bounded) order-right multi-adjoint algebras are only included. Order-right adjoint pairs are used in general frameworks where the commutativity and associativity properties of the conjunctors are not required.

Definition 1. *Let* $(P, \preceq)$ *be a poset and* $\&, \swarrow : P \times P \to P$ *binary operators in* P *satisfying the following conditions:*

- *The adjoint property holds for all* $x, y, z \in P$, *that is:*

$$x \& y \preceq z \quad \text{if and only if} \quad x \preceq z \swarrow y$$

- $\&$ *is order-preserving in the second argument, that is:*

$$\text{if } x, y_1, y_2 \in P \text{ and } y_1 \preceq y_2, \text{ then } x \& y_1 \preceq x \& y_2$$

Then, we say $(\&, \swarrow)$ *is an* order-right adjoint pair *with respect to* P.

It is convenient to mention that, we can straightforwardly deduce that the conjunctor $\&$ is order-preserving in the first argument, from the adjoint property [6,8]. Consequently, we obtain that the conjunctor $\&$ of an order-right adjoint pair is order-preserving in both arguments. This fact is needed in order to properly capture the semantics interpretation of the fuzzy modus ponens proposed by Hájek in [17].

Below, the algebraic structure associated with different order-right adjoint pairs is introduced. These algebraic structures provides an extra level of flexibility in those frameworks where they are used [7,9,13,23,24,29]. For example, in formal concept analysis [7], considering several adjoint pairs allows to associate different degrees of preference on the attributes/objects of a database.

Definition 2. *Let* $(P, \preceq)$ *be a poset. An* order-right multi-adjoint algebra *is the tuple* $(P, \preceq, \&_1, \swarrow^1, \ldots, \&_n, \swarrow^n)$ *where* $(\&_i, \swarrow^i)$, *with* $i \in \{1, \ldots, n\}$, *is a family of order-right adjoint pairs with respect to* P.

In particular, defining order-right multi-adjoint algebras on a bounded lattice $(L, \inf, \sup, 0, 1)$ instead of a poset $(P, \preceq)$, we obtain the algebraic structure $(L, \inf, \sup, 0, 1, \&_1, \swarrow^1, \ldots, \&_n, \swarrow^n)$, which will be called *bounded order-right*

multi-adjoint lattice and will be the underlying algebraic structure of the propositional logic framework studied in this work. On this structure, we will also consider the characteristic mapping $\nearrow^d$ of the ordering relation defined as:

$$
z \nearrow^d y = \begin{cases} 1 & \text{if } y = \inf\{y, z\} \\ 0 & \text{otherwise} \end{cases} \tag{1}
$$

for all $y, z \in L$. It is important to mention that the consideration of the operator $\nearrow^d$ does not limit the lattice structure, since it can always be defined in every bounded lattice.

The axiomatization of BL-algebras called BL logic, which was proposed by Hájek [17], cannot be straightforwardly applied when bounded order-right multi-adjoint algebras are considered. Hence, a new axiomatization is required considering a richer language and, weaker and different axioms than the ones given to the BL logic.

3 Syntax and Semantics of Multi-adjoint Lattice Logic

This section will show the soundness and completeness of the *multi-adjoint lattice logic (MLL)* with respect to the variety of bounded order-right multi-adjoint algebras. The details appear in [3]. MLL was introduced as a many-valued propositional logic framework defined on a bounded order-right multi-adjoint lattice $(L, \inf, \sup, 0, 1, \&_1, \nearrow^1, \ldots, \&_n, \nearrow^n)$, where the tuple $(L, \inf, \sup, 0, 1)$ is a bounded lattice. A brief summary with the main notions related to the syntax and semantics of MLL will be recalled in this section.

The first formal definition collects the notions of alphabet and language from which the syntax of MLL is built.

Definition 3 (MLL alphabet and language).

- *The alphabet of MLL, denoted as $\mathfrak{A}_{MLL}$, is composed of the set of connective symbols $\{\to, \wedge, \vee, \wedge_1, \ldots, \wedge_n, \to_1, \ldots, \to_n\}$, the logic symbol $\bot$, the auxiliary symbols "(", ")" and "," and a set of propositional symbols Π.*
- *The language of MLL, denoted as $\mathcal{L}_{\mathfrak{A}_{MLL}}$, is given by the set of well-formed formulas (wff), which is inductively defined from an alphabet $\mathfrak{A}_{MLL}$ as follows: $\bot$ and p are wff, where $p \in \Pi$; If φ and ψ are wff, then $(\varphi \to \psi)$, $(\varphi \wedge \psi)$, $(\varphi \vee \psi)$, $(\varphi \wedge_i \psi)$ and $(\varphi \to_i \psi)$ are wff, with $i \in \{1, \ldots, n\}$; Nothing else is a formula.*

The axioms forming the deductive system of MLL are given below.

Definition 4 (MLL axiomatization). *Given the language $\mathcal{L}_{\mathfrak{A}_{MLL}}$, the multi-adjoint lattice logic (MLL) is defined from the following axioms:*

L1. $(\varphi \wedge \psi) \to \varphi$
L2. $(\varphi \wedge \psi) \to \psi$
L3. $(\chi \to \varphi) \to ((\chi \to \psi) \to (\chi \to (\varphi \wedge \psi)))$

L4. $\varphi \to (\varphi \lor \psi)$
L5. $\psi \to (\varphi \lor \psi)$
L6. $(\varphi \to \chi) \to ((\psi \to \chi) \to ((\varphi \lor \psi) \to \chi)))$
L7. $\varphi \to \varphi$
L8. $(\varphi \to \psi) \to ((\psi \to \chi) \to (\varphi \to \chi))$
L9. $(\psi \to \chi) \to ((\varphi \to \psi) \to (\varphi \to \chi))$
L10. $\bot \to \varphi$
L11. $\varphi \to (\bot \to \bot)$
M1. $(\varphi \to (\psi \to_i \chi)) \to ((\varphi \wedge_i \psi) \to \chi)$
M2. $((\varphi \wedge_i \psi) \to \chi) \to (\varphi \to (\psi \to_i \chi))$
M3. $(\psi \to \chi) \to ((\varphi \wedge_i \psi) \to (\varphi \wedge_i \chi))$

and the modus ponens for the implication symbol $\to$ *as inference rule.*

Now, we need to introduce the notion which indicates the degree of truth of any formula, that is the evaluation, in order to define the semantics of MLL. The notion of evaluation is based on the use of the operators considered in a bounded order-right multi-adjoint lattice and the operator $\nearrow^d$ defined in Eq. (1).

Definition 5. *Let* $(L, \inf, \sup, 0, 1, \&_1, \nearrow^1, \ldots, \&_n, \nearrow^n)$ *be a bounded order-right multi-adjoint lattice. An* evaluation *is a mapping* $e \colon \mathcal{L}_{\mathfrak{A}_{MLL}} \to L$ *defined inductively from the propositional symbols of the language, for all* $i \in \{1, \ldots, n\}$, *as:*

$$e(p) \in L, \text{ for all propositional symbol } p \in \Pi$$
$$e(\bot) = 0$$
$$e(\varphi \wedge_i \psi) = e(\varphi) \,\&_i\, e(\psi)$$
$$e(\varphi \to_i \psi) = e(\psi) \nearrow^i e(\varphi)$$
$$e(\varphi \to \psi) = e(\psi) \nearrow^d e(\varphi)$$
$$e(\varphi \wedge \psi) = \inf\{e(\varphi), e(\psi)\}$$
$$e(\varphi \lor \psi) = \sup\{e(\varphi), e(\psi)\}$$

To conclude with the syntax and semantics of MLL, we need to recall that the notions of proof, provable formula and tautology in MLL are defined as in the bounded poset logic (BPL) and the multi-adjoint logic (ML), which were introduced in [5], and adapt the usual notions given in [17,30]. We will also need the notion of provable formula with respect to a *theory* (set of wff).

Definition 6. *Given a theory* Γ, *a* Γ-provable *formula* φ_n, *denoted as* $\Gamma \vdash_{MLL} \varphi_n$, *is any formula at the end of a sequence* φ_1, $\ldots$, φ_{n-1}, φ_n *of formulas such that each* φ_i *is either an axiom of MLL, a formula of* Γ, *or follows from some preceding* φ_j, φ_k $(j, k < i)$ *by modus ponens.*

From now on, we will simplify the notation writing $\vdash$ instead of $\vdash_{MLL}$, when no confusion exists. It is also important to mention that, from now on, the formula $\bot \to \bot$ will be represented in MLL as a new distinguished element denoted as $\top$. Clearly, $\top$ is a provable formula in MLL and it is a tautology. Finally, we include the theorem related to the soundness and completeness of MLL, which was demonstrated in [3].

Theorem 1 (Soundness and Completeness of MLL).

- *Given a formula φ of the language $\mathcal{L}_{\mathfrak{A}_{MLL}}$, if φ is provable in MLL, then φ is a tautology for all bounded order-right multi-adjoint lattice.*
- *For each formula φ of the language $\mathcal{L}_{\mathfrak{A}_{MLL}}$, if it is a tautology for all bounded order-right multi-adjoint lattice, then φ is provable in MLL.*

Continuing with the study of multi-adjoint lattice logic and its comparison with BL logic [17], the following section will present different properties of MLL.

4   Properties of Multi-adjoint Lattice Logic

MLL is defined from the axioms of ML, together with the axioms associated with the connective symbols $\wedge$ and $\vee$ (**L1-L6**), being these symbols directly related to the lattice structure defined from the ordering relation usually defined in [11]. Notice that Axioms **L7-L9**, together with the modus ponens, give rise to a weakly implicative logic, translating them into the framework given in [1,2]. In addition, MLL can be seen as an extension of this logic, with $\rightarrow$ as principal implication. However, MLL is not equivalent to one of the well-known substructural logics, and it is more similar to the well-known BL logic given by Hájek on residuated lattices. Indeed, we can ensure that MLL embeds BL from the construction of the deductive system of MLL and the study of its properties included in [3]. This section is devoted to study more properties of MLL.

To begin with, it is important to mention that the comparative study between BL and ML established in [3,5] can be completely translated into the logical framework of MLL, since this logic is built from the axioms of ML. Specifically, from [5, Section 5] and [4, Section 3], we can guarantee that the axioms given in MLL are provable formulas in BL and there exist different axioms of BL that cannot be proven in MLL. Even more, we can deduce that diverse axioms in BL cannot be properly translated into MLL, because the semantics of MLL does not need to be associated with commutative and associative operators. As a consequence, we obtain that MLL provides an axiomatization of multi-adjoint algebras, which is a more general logic than BL, considering a weaker axiomatization.

Notice that no axiom associated with the monotonicity properties of $\rightarrow_i$ was required for MLL in [3]. The following proposition is introduced to show that the formulas related to the mentioned monotonicity properties are provable in MLL. Specifically, Property **(Pr-OP)** is associated with the order-preserving and Property **(Pr-OR)** with the order-reversing.

Proposition 1. *The following formulas are provable in MLL, for all $i \in \{1, \ldots, n\}$.*

(Pr-OP) $(\varphi \rightarrow \psi) \rightarrow ((\chi \rightarrow_i \varphi) \rightarrow (\chi \rightarrow_i \psi))$
(Pr-OR) $(\varphi \rightarrow \psi) \rightarrow ((\psi \rightarrow_i \chi) \rightarrow (\varphi \rightarrow_i \chi))$

Proof. Formula **(Pr-OP)** arises from the following chain of provable formulas.

$\vdash ((\chi \rightarrow_i \varphi) \wedge_i \chi) \rightarrow \varphi) \rightarrow ((\varphi \rightarrow \psi) \rightarrow (((\chi \rightarrow_i \varphi) \wedge_i \chi) \rightarrow \psi))$ by Axiom **(L3)**

$\vdash (\varphi \rightarrow \psi) \rightarrow (((\chi \rightarrow_i \varphi) \wedge_i \chi) \rightarrow \psi)$ by Proposition 4 **(Pr1)** of [4] and modus ponens

$\vdash (((\chi \rightarrow_i \varphi) \wedge_i \chi) \rightarrow \psi) \rightarrow ((\chi \rightarrow_i \varphi) \rightarrow (\chi \rightarrow_i \psi))$ by Axiom **(M2)**

$\vdash (\varphi \rightarrow \psi) \rightarrow ((\chi \rightarrow_i \varphi) \rightarrow (\chi \rightarrow_i \psi))$ by Axiom **(L3)** and modus ponens

The proof for **(Pr-OR)** is similar to the one given to Proposition 26 of [5].   □

Furthermore, the order-preserving property of the conjunctor in the first argument is also a provable formula in MLL.

Proposition 2. *The following formula is provable in MLL, for all $i \in \{1, \ldots, n\}$.*

(Pr-OP1) $(\varphi \rightarrow \phi) \rightarrow ((\varphi \wedge_i \chi) \rightarrow (\phi \wedge_i \chi))$

Proof. Formula **(Pr-OP1)** holds from the following.

$\vdash (\phi \wedge_i \chi) \rightarrow (\phi \wedge_i \chi)$ by Axiom **P1**

$\vdash ((\phi \wedge_i \chi) \rightarrow (\phi \wedge_i \chi)) \rightarrow (\phi \rightarrow (\chi \rightarrow_i (\phi \wedge_i \chi)))$ by Axiom **M2**

$\vdash \phi \rightarrow (\chi \rightarrow_i (\phi \wedge_i \chi))$ by modus ponens

$\vdash (\phi \rightarrow (\chi \rightarrow_i (\phi \wedge_i \chi))) \rightarrow ((\varphi \rightarrow \phi) \rightarrow (\varphi \rightarrow (\chi \rightarrow_i (\phi \wedge_i \chi))))$ by Axiom **L9**

$\vdash (\varphi \rightarrow \phi) \rightarrow (\varphi \rightarrow (\chi \rightarrow_i (\phi \wedge_i \chi)))$ by modus ponens

$\vdash (\varphi \rightarrow (\chi \rightarrow_i (\phi \wedge_i \chi))) \rightarrow ((\varphi \wedge_i \chi) \rightarrow (\phi \wedge_i \chi))$ by Axiom **M1**

$\vdash (\varphi \rightarrow \phi) \rightarrow ((\varphi \wedge_i \chi) \rightarrow (\phi \wedge_i \chi))$ by modus ponens

□

These previous propositions prove the syntactic properties associated with Lemma 4 in [5]. Now, we will continue with the comparison between BL [17] and MLL. Specifically, we will analyze if the properties given in [17, Lemmata 2.2.8 and 2.2.9] are provable formulas in MLL. Properties (4), (5) and (6) in [17, Lemma 2.2.8], were already studied in [3]. Hence, we will start in this paper from Property (7). One important fact for this analysis is that BL only considers one implication symbol (the one associated with the residuated implication of residuated lattices). However, in MLL two implication symbols are used. Therefore, to carry out the translation of a formula in BL into another one in MLL, we need to determine what implication symbol in MLL must be considered for the implication symbol in BL. For example, Property (7) in [17, Lemma 2.2.8] contains the implication symbol in BL four times. As a consequence, we have different possible translations. Furthermore, the conjunctor symbol in BL is associated with a commutative and associative operator, unlike the one considered in MLL. For example, if the implication symbols in Property (7) are interpreted in MLL as an implication symbol associated with an adjoint implication, except the one in the middle, we obtain the formula

$$((\varphi_1 \rightarrow_i \psi_1) \wedge_i (\varphi_2 \rightarrow_i \psi_2)) \rightarrow ((\varphi_1 \wedge_i \varphi_2) \rightarrow_i (\psi_1 \wedge_i \psi_2))$$

However, in order to prove this formula we need some axioms related to the commutativity and associativity properties. Hence, this translation does not work in MLL. The following proposition shows another alternative.

Proposition 3. *For all $i \in \{1, \ldots, n\}$, given a theory Γ, such that $\{(\varphi_1 \to \psi_1), (\varphi_2 \to \psi_2)\} \subseteq \Gamma$, then we have that*

$$\Gamma \vdash (\varphi_1 \wedge_i \varphi_2) \to (\psi_1 \wedge_i \psi_2)$$

Proof. The proof is obtained from the following chain of deductive formulas:

$\Gamma \vdash (\varphi_1 \to \psi_1) \to ((\varphi_1 \wedge_i \psi_2) \to (\psi_1 \wedge_i \psi_2))$ by $(\mathbf{Pr - OP1})$

$\Gamma \vdash (\varphi_1 \wedge_i \psi_2) \to (\psi_1 \wedge_i \psi_2)$ by hypothesis and modus ponens

$\Gamma \vdash (\varphi_2 \to \psi_2) \to ((\varphi_1 \wedge_i \varphi_2) \to (\varphi_1 \wedge_i \psi_2))$ by Axiom $(\mathbf{M3})$

$\Gamma \vdash (\varphi_1 \wedge_i \varphi_2) \to (\varphi_1 \wedge_i \psi_2)$ by hypothesis and modus ponens

$\Gamma \vdash ((\varphi_1 \wedge_i \varphi_2) \to (\varphi_1 \wedge_i \psi_2)) \to$

$\qquad (((\varphi_1 \wedge_i \psi_2) \to (\psi_1 \wedge_i \psi_2)) \to ((\varphi_1 \wedge_i \varphi_2) \to (\psi_1 \wedge_i \psi_2)))$ by Axiom $(\mathbf{L8})$

$\Gamma \vdash (\varphi_1 \wedge_i \varphi_2) \to (\psi_1 \wedge_i \psi_2)$ applying modus ponens twice

$\square$

Clearly, Property (8) in [17, Lemma 2.2.8], which can be translated to the following formulas

$$(\varphi \wedge_i \psi) \wedge_i \chi \to \varphi \wedge_i (\psi \wedge_i \chi), \quad \varphi \wedge_i (\psi \wedge_i \chi) \to (\varphi \wedge_i \psi) \wedge_i \chi$$

cannot be provable in MLL, since it is related to the associativity of the conjunctor of a right-adjoint lattice and this is another property does not required to adjoint triples. For example, the evaluation of this formula in the right-adjoint lattice $([0, 1], \&_{21})$, we $\&_{21}$ is defined as $x \,\&_{21}\, y = x^2 \cdot y$, for all $x, y \in [0, 1]$, is not valid.

Now, we consider Properties (9)–(12) introduced in [17, Lemma 2.2.9]. Clearly, the two first formulas of Property (9) are Axioms $\mathbf{L1}$ and $\mathbf{L2}$. The third formula: $(\varphi \wedge_i \psi) \to (\varphi \wedge \psi)$ means that the conjunctor associated with $\wedge_i$ is less than the infimum. In the framework of t-norms, this is equivalent to say that every t-norm is less than the Gödel (minimum) one. Notice that the formula $\varphi \wedge \psi$ is equivalent to (indeed it is defined as) the formula $\varphi \star (\varphi \to \psi)$ in BL, which is translated into MLL as[1] $(\psi \to_i \varphi) \wedge_i \psi$. The obtained formula by this equivalence is provable in MLL.

Proposition 4. *For all $i \in \{1, \ldots, n\}$, we have that*

$$\{(\varphi \wedge_i \top) \to \varphi\} \vdash (\varphi \wedge_i \psi) \to ((\psi \to_i \varphi) \wedge_i \psi)$$

---

[1] Notice that the main differences between both formulas are given because the conjunctor in BL is commutative.

Proof. Considering the theory $\Gamma = \{(\varphi \wedge_i \top) \to \varphi\}$, the proof arises from the following chain of deductive formulas:

$\Gamma \vdash (\varphi \wedge_i \psi) \to \varphi$ by hypothesis, Proposition 2 of [4] and modus ponens

$\Gamma \vdash \varphi \to (\psi \to_i \varphi)$ by Axiom (**M2**) and modus ponens

$\Gamma \vdash (\varphi \wedge_i \psi) \to ((\psi \to_i \varphi) \wedge_i \psi)$ by Axiom (**M3**) and modus ponens

□

Property (10) in [17, Lemma 2.2.9], considering the infimum symbol $\wedge$, does not hold in general, due to the symbols $\wedge_i$ satisfy less requirements (less axioms). The formula provable in MLL is the one given by the translation commented above and taking into account that the infimum is commutative.

Proposition 5. *The following formula is provable in MLL, for all $i \in \{1, \ldots, n\}$.*

$$(\psi \to \varphi) \to (\psi \to_i ((\psi \to_i \varphi) \wedge_i \psi))$$

Proof. The proof arises from the following deduction:

$\vdash ((\psi \to_i \varphi) \wedge_i \psi) \to ((\psi \to_i \varphi) \wedge_i \psi)$ by Axiom (**L7**)

$\vdash ((\psi \to_i \varphi) \to (\psi \to_i ((\psi \to_i \varphi) \wedge_i \psi))$ by Axiom (**M2**) and modus ponens

□

The following result shows a special kind of transitivity on provable formulas, which is similar to the one proved in [5, Lemma 13], considering the residuated implication.

Lemma 1. *For every $i \in \{1, \ldots, n\}$, given a theory Γ, satisfying that $\{\chi \to \phi, \varphi \to (\psi \to_i \chi)\} \subseteq \Gamma$, then we have that*

$$\Gamma \vdash \varphi \to (\psi \to_i \phi)$$

Proof. The proof follows from the following chain of deductive formulas.

$\Gamma \vdash (\varphi \to (\psi \to_i \chi)) \to (((\psi \to_i \chi) \to (\psi \to_i \phi)) \to (\varphi \to (\psi \to_i \phi)))$ by Axiom (**L8**)

$\Gamma \vdash ((\psi \to_i \chi) \to (\psi \to_i \phi)) \to (\varphi \to (\psi \to_i \phi))$ by hypothesis and modus ponens

$\Gamma \vdash (\chi \to \phi) \to ((\psi \to_i \chi) \to (\psi \to_i \phi))$ by Property (**Pr − OP**) in Proposition 1

$\Gamma \vdash (\chi \to \phi) \to (\varphi \to (\psi \to_i \phi))$ by Axiom (**L8**) and applying modus ponens

twice from the formulas above

$\Gamma \vdash \varphi \to (\psi \to_i \phi)$ by hypothesis and modus ponens

□

5   Multi-adjoint Lattice Logic for Query Answering

This section shows that MLL can be applied to real problems modelled through a set of rules, which can be written as formulas in this logic. To reach this goal, the axiomatization of MLL must be complemented with a theory (which model the particular problem) and obtaining provable formulas (computing proofs) from the new set of formulas.

It is interesting to highlight that the procedural semantics introduced in different logic programming frameworks, such as multi-adjoint, monotonic and residuated logic programming [10,28] could not compute the correct answer for a program $\mathbb{P}$ and a query A? (as the Morishita's example [20,28], which will be taken into account later), and other techniques (such as the consideration of reductants) need to be used to avoiding this problem [18,28]. Nevertheless, in MLL we can obtain a provable formula associated with the correct answer for a program $\mathbb{P}$ and a query A? in the context of the logic programming paradigms. Next, we will show the well-known Morishita's example [20,28] and how it is handled in MLL.

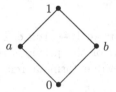

Fig. 1. Lattice $(L, \preceq)$

Example 1. Given the $(L, \preceq)$ depicted in Fig. 1, and a propositional symbol p, if we consider the logic program:

$$\mathbf{R1} : a \to p$$
$$\mathbf{R2} : b \to p$$

where a and b are interpreted as propositional symbols abusing the language. The traditional procedural semantics computes two computed answers for the query p? [20,28], that is, a and b. However, the correct answer is $\top$, which coincides with the value of the least model [28].

By Axiom **L6** and rules **R1**, **R2**, we obtain that $\{a \to p, b \to p\} \vdash a \vee b \to p$ is provable in MLL. Thus, since $\vee$ is interpreted as the supremum operator on $(L, \preceq)$, we obtain the truth value of p is 1, that is, the correct answer for query p? is achieved.   □

Therefore, an axiomatization of multi-adjoint algebras has been introduced, from which automatic decision methods can be developed. This goal will be studied in further extensions of this paper. Now, we will introduce a set of well-formed formulas for representing the behaviour of an engine, which can be seen

as an adaptation of the multi-adjoint logic program considered in [22, 26], and we will show how MLL can be considered to obtain deductions and new knowledge from them.

Example 2. Let Π be the set composed of the elements of the unit interval, the propositional symbols high_fuel_consumption, overheating, rich_mixture, low_oil, low_water, noisy_behaviour, and the connective symbols $\rightarrow$, $\wedge$, $\vee$, $\wedge_G$, $\wedge_P$, $\wedge_L$, $\rightarrow_G$, $\rightarrow_P$, $\rightarrow_L$. Consider a particular language $\mathcal{L}_{\mathfrak{A}_{MLL}}$, on which take into consideration MLL, and the following rules which are well-formed formulas of the mentioned language:

R1 : low_oil $\rightarrow$ noisy_behaviour

R2 : $0.8 \rightarrow$ ((rich_mixture $\wedge_L$ low_oil) $\rightarrow_G$ high_fuel_consumption)

R3 : $0.5 \rightarrow$ (low_oil $\rightarrow_P$ overheating)

R4 : $0.8 \rightarrow$ (rich_mixture $\rightarrow_P$ noisy_behaviour)

R5 : $0.9 \rightarrow$ (low_water $\rightarrow_P$ overheating)

R6 : $0.2 \rightarrow$ low_oil

R7 : $0.2 \rightarrow$ low_water

R8 : $0.5 \rightarrow$ rich_mixture

Notice that, **R1** is equivalent to $1 \rightarrow$ (low_oil $\rightarrow$ noisy_behaviour). Below, we show the theory composed of the previous set of formulas which provide us with an interesting Γ-provable formula related the propositional symbol overheating:

$\Gamma \vdash$ $(0.5 \wedge_P$ low_oil$) \rightarrow$ overheating   by Axiom **M1** and formula **R3** of Γ

$\Gamma \vdash$ $(0.5 \wedge_P 0.2) \rightarrow (0.5 \wedge_P$ low_oil$)$ by Axiom **M3** and formula **R6** of Γ

$\Gamma \vdash$ $(0.5 \wedge_P 0.2) \rightarrow$ overheating   by Axiom **L8** and the two previous formulas

$\Gamma \vdash$ $(0.9 \wedge_P$ low_water$) \rightarrow$ overheating   by Axiom **M1** and formula **R5** of Γ

$\Gamma \vdash$ $(0.9 \wedge_P 0.2) \rightarrow (0.9 \wedge_P$ low_water$)$ by Axiom **M3** and formula **R7** of Γ

$\Gamma \vdash$ $(0.9 \wedge_P 0.2) \rightarrow$ overheating   by Axiom **L8** and the two previous formulas

$\Gamma \vdash$ $(0.5 \wedge_P 0.2) \vee (0.9 \wedge_P 0.2) \rightarrow$ overheating   by Axiom **L6** and the third

and the previous formula

Considering the semantics for this last formula and interpreting the operational symbols $\wedge_P$ as the product t-norm and $\vee$ as the supremum in $[0, 1]$, we obtain the overheating of the motor has a truth value greater than

$$(0.5 \wedge_P 0.2) \vee (0.9 \wedge_P 0.2) = 0.18$$

□

6   Conclusions and Future Work

This paper has shown the possibility of taking into account MLL to design automatic decision methods, for example, we have illustrated that this logic can

be considered for computing correct answers for queries, from a logic program. Moreover, we have proved diverse properties, such as, the "monotonicity" of the implications and conjunctor symbols, and other formulas, which are translations of properties given in BL [17]. In the future, more properties will be studied and an automatic decision method based on tableaux methods will be introduced and tested on (big) real examples.

References

1. Cintula, P.: Weakly implicative (fuzzy) logics I: basic properties. Arch. Math. Logic **45**, 673–704 (2006)
2. Cintula, P., Noguera, C.: A general framework for mathematical fuzzy logic. In: Cintula, P., Hájek, P., Noguera, C. (eds.) Studies in Logic. Mathematical Logic and Foundations, vol. 37 of Handbook of Mathematical Fuzzy Logic, vol. 1, chapter II, pp. 103–207. College Publications, London (2011)
3. Cornejo, M.E., Fariñas del Cerro, L., Medina, J.: Multi-adjoint lattice logic and truth-stressing hedges. Fuzzy Sets Syst. **445**, 43–65 (2022)
4. Cornejo, M.E., Fariñas del Cerro, L., Medina, J.: Basic logic versus multi-adjoint logic. In: 13th European Symposium on Computational Intelligence and Mathematics (ESCIM 2021) (2021)
5. Cornejo, M.E., Fariñas del Cerro, L., Medina, J.: A logical characterization of multi-adjoint algebras. Fuzzy Sets Syst. **425**, 140–156 (2021)
6. Cornejo, M.E., Medina, J., Ramírez-Poussa, E.: Multi-adjoint algebras versus non-commutative residuated structures. Int. J. Approximate Reasoning **66**, 119–138 (2015)
7. Cornejo, M.E., Medina, J., Ramírez-Poussa, E., Rubio-Manzano, C.: Multi-adjoint concept lattices, preferences and Bousi Prolog. In: Flores, V., et al. (eds.) IJCRS 2016. LNCS (LNAI), vol. 9920, pp. 331–341. Springer, Cham (2016). https://doi.org/10.1007/978-3-319-47160-0_30
8. Cornejo, M.E., Medina, J., Ramírez-Poussa, E.: Algebraic structure and characterization of adjoint triples. Fuzzy Sets Syst. **425**, 117–139 (2021). Mathematics
9. Cornelis, C., Medina, J., Verbiest, N.: Multi-adjoint fuzzy rough sets: definition, properties and attribute selection. Int. J. Approximate Reasoning **55**, 412–426 (2014)
10. Damásio, C.V., Pereira, L.M.: Monotonic and residuated logic programs. In: Benferhat, S., Besnard, P. (eds.) ECSQARU 2001. LNCS (LNAI), vol. 2143, pp. 748–759. Springer, Heidelberg (2001). https://doi.org/10.1007/3-540-44652-4_66
11. Davey, B., Priestley, H.: Introduction to Lattices and Order, 2nd edn. Cambridge University Press, Cambridge (2002)
12. Dekhtyar, M., Dekhtyar, A., Subrahmanian, V.: Hybrid probabilistic programs: algorithms and complexity. In: Proceedings of 1999 Conference on Uncertainty in AI (1999)
13. Díaz-Moreno, J.C., Medina, J.: Multi-adjoint relation equations: definition, properties and solutions using concept lattices. Inf. Sci. **253**, 100–109 (2013)
14. Epstein, G., Horn, A.: Logics which are characterized by subresiduated lattices. Math. Log. Q. **22**(1), 199–210 (1976)
15. Esteva, F., Godo, L.: Monoidal t-norm based logic: towards a logic for left-continuous t-norms. Fuzzy Sets Syst. **124**, 271–288 (2001)

16. Godo, L., Sócola-Ramos, M., Esteva, F.: On the logic of left-continuous t-norms and right-continuous t-conorms. Commun. Comput. Inf. Sci. **1239**, 654–665 (2020)
17. Hájek, P.: Metamathematics of Fuzzy Logic. Trends in Logic. Kluwer Academic (1998)
18. Julián-Iranzo, P., Medina, J., Ojeda-Aciego, M.: On reductants in the framework of multi-adjoint logic programming. Fuzzy Sets Syst. **317**, 27–43 (2017)
19. Julián, P., Moreno, G., Penabad, J.: On fuzzy unfolding: a multi-adjoint approach. Fuzzy Sets Syst. **154**(1), 16–33 (2005)
20. Kifer, M., Subrahmanian, V.S.: Theory of generalized annotated logic programming and its applications. J. Log. Program. **12**, 335–367 (1992)
21. Lakshmanan, L.V.S., Sadri, F.: On a theory of probabilistic deductive databases. Theory Pract. Logic Program. **1**(1), 5–42 (2001)
22. Medina, J.: Retículos Multi-adjuntos y teoremas de continuidad para el operador de consecuencias. Ph.D. thesis, Universidad de Málaga (2001)
23. Medina, J.: Multi-adjoint property-oriented and object-oriented concept lattices. Inf. Sci. **190**, 95–106 (2012)
24. Medina, J., Ojeda-Aciego, M., Ruiz-Calviño, J.: Formal concept analysis via multi-adjoint concept lattices. Fuzzy Sets Syst. **160**(2), 130–144 (2009)
25. Medina, J., Ojeda-Aciego, M., Valverde, A., Vojtáš, P.: Towards biresiduated multi-adjoint logic programming. In: Conejo, R., Urretavizcaya, M., Pérez-de-la-Cruz, J.-L. (eds.) CAEPIA/TTIA -2003. LNCS (LNAI), vol. 3040, pp. 608–617. Springer, Heidelberg (2004). https://doi.org/10.1007/978-3-540-25945-9_60
26. Medina, J., Ojeda-Aciego, M., Vojtáš, P.: A multi-adjoint logic approach to abductive reasoning. In: Codognet, P. (ed.) ICLP 2001. LNCS, vol. 2237, pp. 269–283. Springer, Heidelberg (2001). https://doi.org/10.1007/3-540-45635-X_26
27. Medina, J., Ojeda-Aciego, M., Vojtáš, P.: Multi-adjoint logic programming with continous semantics. In: Eiter, T., Faber, W., Truszczyński, M. (eds.) LPNMR 2001. LNCS (LNAI), vol. 2173, pp. 351–364. Springer, Heidelberg (2001). https://doi.org/10.1007/3-540-45402-0_26
28. Medina, J., Ojeda-Aciego, M., Vojtáš, P.: A procedural semantics for multi-adjoint logic programming. In: Brazdil, P., Jorge, A. (eds.) EPIA 2001. LNCS (LNAI), vol. 2258, pp. 290–297. Springer, Heidelberg (2001). https://doi.org/10.1007/3-540-45329-6_29
29. Medina, J., Ojeda-Aciego, M., Vojtáš, P.: Similarity-based unification: a multi-adjoint approach. Fuzzy Sets Syst. **146**, 43–62 (2004)
30. Mendelson, E.: Introduction to Mathematical Logic, 6th edn. Chapman & Hall/CRC, London (2015)

Skill Learning for Long-Horizon Sequential Tasks

João Alves[✉][iD], Nuno Lau, and Filipe Silva

University of Aveiro, DETI-IEETA, Aveiro, Portugal
jbga@ua.pt

Abstract. Solving long-horizon problems is a desirable property in autonomous agents. Learning reusable behaviours can equip the agent with this property, allowing it to adapt them when performing various real-world tasks. Our approach for learning these behaviours is composed of three modules, operating in two separate timescales and it uses a hierarchical model with both discrete and continuous variables. This modular structure allows an independent training process for each stage. These stages are organized using a two-level temporal hierarchy. The first level contains the planner, responsible for issuing the skills that should be executed, while the second level executes the skill. In this latter level, to achieve the desired skill behaviour, the discrete skill is converted to a continuous vector that contains information regarding which environment change must occur. With this approach, we aimed to solve long-horizon sequential tasks with delayed rewards. Contrary to existing work, our method uses both variable types to allow an agent to learn high-level behaviours consisting of an interpretable set of skills. This method allows to compose the discrete skills easily, while keeping the flexibility, provided by the continuous representations, to execute them in several different ways. Using a 2D scenario where the agent has to catch a set of objects in a specific order, we demonstrate that our approach is scalable to scenarios with increasingly longer tasks.

Keywords: Skill learning · Hierarchical model · Reinforcement Learning · Deep learning · Goal-conditioned policy · Sequential tasks

1 Introduction

Exploiting modular structure in tasks can often improve performance across a family of tasks and make the execution of long-horizon ones feasible. Learning individual component skills that solve sub-tasks inside a more extensive one is more efficient because each skill is shorter-horizon, resulting in a substantially easier learning problem and aiding exploration [5]. Each skill can use the internal skill-specific abstraction to focus on only relevant objects and state features, which decomposes a problem that may be high-dimensional, if treated monolithically, into a sequence of low-dimensional sub-tasks. Reusing skills in multiple

G. Marreiros et al. (Eds.): EPIA 2022, LNAI 13566, pp. 713–724, 2022.
https://doi.org/10.1007/978-3-031-16474-3_58

problem settings can avoid the need to relearn problem elements from scratch each time, resulting in faster per-task learning. These component skills can also be organized using a hierarchical structure that offers the opportunity to solve tasks using higher-level states and actions than those in which the task was initially defined.

An agent that needs to perform complex tasks in real scenarios must be able to reason about long-term tasks by inferring the relevant scene aspects and the possible changes that can be done in each moment. One scenario where this capability can be valuable is, for example, when an agent needs to catch several objects sequentially. To solve this task, it must learn how to sequence several simple skills and understand the semantics behind its observations and actions to determine the most appropriate skills. This sequencing requires understanding how to choose, from a poll of simple skills, which one should be used, and also requires the ability to plan their execution in an appropriate order.

Several approaches exist to discover distinct sequences of trajectories (skills) to exploit the modular structure present in the agent's environment: typically, these approaches aim to solve future tasks more efficiently. Usually, they are formulated as a two-level hierarchy composed of a high-level controller and low-level skills. These approaches represent the learned skills as continuous latent vectors, such as goal-conditioned policies [3], or discrete like those who use option-based methods [18]. However, the possibility of combining both discrete and continuous skill representations is still an underexplored area of research. We think that further research on this particular aspect should be performed because these types of representation allow dividing a task into several ones (discrete skills) while allowing multiple ways of executing them with continuous parameterization. We think that besides this advantage, the combined use of both types of representation will also ease continual learning because each skill is associated with a set of representations that could enable incremental learning by using non-parametric methods.

Similar to the Rao et al. [10] work, we also use an approach to learn a hierarchical skill model with three stages from an offline dataset, capturing both discrete and continuous variations at multiple levels of behavioural abstraction. The model comprises a low-level latent-conditioned controller that can perform simple actions. The mid-level controller learns a set of continuous latent skills representing desired transformations in a particular environment. The high-level controller selects among high-level skills using discrete skill representations and composes them to solve a long-horizon task. The architecture proposed in this work can learn skills with variable duration due to the mixed usage of skill type and skill parameterization. This architecture allows us to compose a set of discrete high-level skills and learn continuous mid-level behaviours allowing diversity when executing them.

The main contributions this paper presents are: (1) We present a modular hierarchical approach for skill learning that helps the agent to learn sequential tasks, and it is able to cope with increasingly longer tasks; (2) We show that training the contained models in each hierarchical layer separately allows us to spot failure modes easily while allowing distributed training using different

learning procedures; (3) We present a new form to represent the continuous skill representation based on the difference between the skill's final state and the agent's current state. We show the advantages of this representation and discuss some of its limitations.

2   Related Work

Our work fits inside the field of skill discovery. Work in this area focuses on obtaining prior knowledge about the environment in which the agent is inserted with the expectation of helping him solve tasks that will be presented to him later on. Skill discovery methods can be divided into two groups.

The first encompasses strategies focused on learning skills offline using already collected datasets. These strategies generally obtain trajectories for a collection of tasks and segment these trajectories into a collection of skills that retroactively decompose the input trajectories [3,13,15]. This segmentation is commonly performed using expert demonstration trajectories [15,19]. However, it could also be done on undirected trajectories generated by humans [3] or even trajectories generated by a robot, typically after learning [13]. Some recent approaches in this category use iterative segmentation based on variational autoencoders [4,15]. In these approaches, the trajectory is analyzed n times to sequentially extract its corresponding n skills. These iterative approaches have the advantage of learning variable-length skills compared with non-iterative variational autoencoders based approaches, which learn only fixed length/duration skills [3]. One of the limitations of this type of approach is the restriction in test time to use hard one-hot vectors for a specific skill type, since during training time they are allowed to mix multiple skills due to the continuous approximation used [15].

The methods in the second group of skill learning methods try to learn skills from interaction with the environment only by maximizing the entropy of visited states while keeping skills distinguishable [18]. Approaches from both groups often rely on variational inference, where one or more low-level controllers represent the learned set of skills, and a high-level policy instructs the low-level controller via a latent variable or goal. This hierarchy is typically represented using architectures in which the policy comprises two (or more) levels of hierarchy. Such latent variables can be discrete [2,16] or continuous [8]. The latent variable can represent the behaviour for one timestep, for a fixed number of timesteps [1], or options with different durations [17]. Contrary to the approaches described above that encode a skill as a discrete value, when the high-level encoder produces a continuous latent vector representation, it has the flexibility to encode a whole trajectory [1,3,9] or the current and final goal state [7] in a single latent vector. Despite this type of flexibility, if the user needs to probe the model to check what type of skills were learned, this would be not possible. Another limitation of continuous representation is that it is harder to compose and select learned skills.

Our work is related to methods from the first group that learn robot policies from demonstrations or, more broadly, from logged data (offline RL, e.g. [6]).

Although some approaches learn skills offline that can be transferred online to new tasks [1], in this work, we focused on learning skills regarding only a single task. Our approach consists of learning skills in an offline way, and it is similar to the work of Rao et al. [10].

3 Approach

3.1 Problem Formulation

The Markov Decision Process (MDP) represented by the tuple $(S, A, P, R, \gamma, \rho_0)$ defines a set of problems that contains our specific problem, where S is a continuous world space, A is a discrete set of actions, and P is a deterministic transition probability. R represents the MDP reward, γ is the discount factor, and ρ_0 defines the initial state distribution. Our goal is to find a deterministic policy $\pi : S \mapsto A$, that maximizes the cumulative expected reward $\mathbb{E}\left[\sum_t \gamma^t R(s_t, a_t, s_{t+1})\right]$.

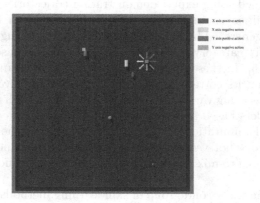

Fig. 1. Scenario used to test the proposed approach.

In this work, we focus on the task of collecting objects in a 2D Scenario that have to be caught in a specific order. In our specific problem, S is the space containing the agent and object positions in a particular scene. Because the agent and the object positions are clearly divided in S, we refer to the agent-related information as the agent space and the object positions as the environment space in the rest of the paper. A is the space composed of all possible combinations of the agents' actions in each scenario dimension (move in the positive/negative direction and stop). π is the policy that will guide the agent when performing a task. Figure 1 shows the scenario simulated environment, where the dark blue box is the agent, the surrounding arrows represent the different actions that can be performed by it, and the remaining objects are the ones that can be caught by the agent. The numbers presented in this figure are objects that visually represent the order from which the objects have to be caught (one before two and two before three). Colours, like numbers, also establish order, but the shapes in

this context are irrelevant. This scenario has the following properties: the input space contains the agent and objects' absolute positions, where each position is represented by a 2D Vector $(x, y$ positions); the agent always starts at the middle of the dark platform presented in the scenario; the objects are positioned at random positions inside the platform at the beginning of each episode; each action leads the agent to move in the desired direction relative to its position. For example, if the agent decides to move positively in the x direction its position (x, y) becomes $(x + i, y)$, where i represent the distance traveled by the agent in each timestep.

The task goal is to catch all the objects presented in the scene, but these must be caught in a specific order. The agent must be near one object and stop during one step to be able to catch it. We considered that these elements are near when both are not separated by more than the distance that the agent is capable of traveling during one timestep. We impose a tight goal region and we do not use collisions as criteria to determine if two objects are close. We made this choice because if a skill does not reach an appropriate end state in a realistic scenario, this can impact future skill execution, leading to compound errors. In our scenario, a skill is represented by a discrete representation $z \in Z$, where Z is the set of all skills, and a continuous one $t \in T$ being these representations related as $T \times S \mapsto Z$. When the agent catches an object, the state space elements representing it's position are zeroed out to indicate that this object was removed from the environment.

3.2 Architecture

We split the policy generation using a two-level temporal hierarchy to solve the long-horizon task presented above. The high level contains a module that acts as a planner that composes a set of learned skills. In this work, we assumed that the numbers of skill increases with the number of objects in the simulated environment as each skill is associated with the trajectory of moving towards a specific object. The lowest temporal level comprises two modules responsible for generating a transformation $t \in T$ and the action a. T is the space containing continuous elements that represent the difference between different state space S vectors separated by n time steps with $n \geq 2$ obtained by computing $s_{t+n} - s_t$. The elements in T represent a relative state-space transformation that can be executed in n timesteps. This transformation t is computed based on a specific skill, as each skill is associated with the trajectory of moving towards a specific object. When seen under the standard formulation of hierarchy policy learning perspective, these transformations provide a way of representing goals. Since the objects are static, the elements in a specific t that are not zeros are those corresponding to the agent space. For this reason, t has the same size as the number of elements in agent space. After the training process of the last module of our architecture, the policy π will know how a specific world change t can be made using a set of n sequential actions.

The architecture introduced in this work allows us to map the agent's current state to actions by decomposing this process into three phases. This architecture,

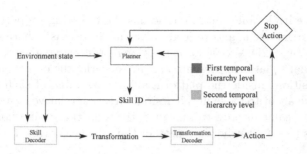

Fig. 2. Hierarchical model with two temporal levels, composed by three modules.

shown in Fig. 2, is composed of three modules, acting on two separate time scales, where each one allows us to perform a specific task. The modules and respective tasks are the following: (1) **Planner** Responsible for learning how to compose skills, mapping the agent's current state to a discrete skill ID; (2) **Skill Decoder** Takes the skill ID and the current state and maps them to transformations (desired environment change); (3) **Transformation Decoder** Based on the computed transformation, this module computes the action needed to achieve the desired environment change;

The Planner's objective is to discover how to compose already learned skills in order to maximize the cumulative sum of rewards given by the environment. In our architecture, this module issues a skill that will be executed by the remaining modules during n timesteps until reaching the skill's final state. Despite being the first intervenient in the entire process, it only acts sporadically. It determines what skill must be executed, but it only makes a new decision when the transformation decoder emits an action that signals the end of the skill. This time interval between the change of skills is not fixed because we do not restrict a skill to have a fixed duration. After the the Planner issues the skill, this is translated to a transformation, which corresponds to a desired change in the environment, and then an action is computed given this transformation. The last two modules (Skill and Transformation Decoder) act in every environment timestep. Figure 3 shows how we deploy our architecture and how the temporal information flow is made throughout the episode.

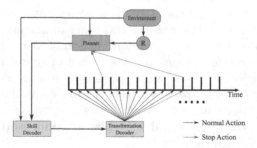

Fig. 3. Temporal view of the hierarchical process using the architecture presented.

In this work, each skill is characterized by a discrete value (skill ID) and a continuous value (transformation). We opt for this type of mixture model for the skill parameterization because having only a continuous representation for a skill makes the process of composing a sequence with several skills infeasible. As a consequence, the usage of both continuous and discrete representations to parameterize skills allows us to have a more general framework as two seemingly different trajectories can be mapped to a single discrete skill with different continuous representations. Besides this advantage, this type of approach can be more robust to a dynamic environment as the agent can learn several ways of executing the same skill. To train the modules contained in our architecture, we used two types of learning procedures. The Planner has learned to compose skills using Reinforcement Learning (RL), which is also used by the Transformation Decoder, while the Skill Decoder uses Supervised Learning.

3.3   Training Procedure

The Planner was trained using a sparse reward mechanism. In the presented scenario, this means that the agent only receives a reward after completing the sequence in the correct order. The Planner input is the environment's current state, and the previous skill represented using one-hot vector encoding. Here, the environment state is normalized to the range $[0, 1]$ to avoid range discrepancies between the input values. This normalization also brings the added benefit of increasing training speed. This fact stems from the time reduction required for the model to understand the data's current mean and standard deviation when the data is not normalized.

By defining the effect that each skill has on the environment, it becomes possible to separate the Planner training process from the remaining ones. To perform this separation, we assume that each time the Planner issue a skill, it's execution is performed correctly by the Skill and Transformation Decoder. In the training process, for example, if the first skill is chosen, the agent reaches the first object position in one timestep. This separation allows faster training times. In each Planner training step, we can simulate the correct execution of each skill and do not need to execute the trained Skill and Transformation Decoders, which would require much more environment steps. Besides this advantage, during inference time if the agent is not correctly reaching the goal, we can easily understand which module is responsible for this faulty behaviour. Moreover, it allows us to distribute the model training process and use different learning procedures for each module.

Having defined the effect of each skill, we used Proximal Policy Optimization (PPO) [12] from stable baselines 31 to train the Planner. Table 1 displays the hyperparameters used during training. We used the default value parameters for the parameters not mentioned in the table[1]. The network architecture used has one hidden layer with a ReLU activation function. The Planner network architecture for the actor and the critic is composed of sixteen units in the hidden

---

[1] Stable baselines 3 PPO.

Table 1. Hyperparameters used to train the Planner using the PPO algorithm.

Hyperparameter	Value
Learning rate	0.0003
Discount factor	0.9
Batch size	64
Generalized advantage estimator lambda	0.95
Gradient maximum value	0.5
Entropy coefficient	0
Value function coefficient	0.5

layer and the output layer has the same number of elements as the number of skills that the agent can execute. As the number of skills increases, the number of hidden units has to grow to allow the agent to learn the right skill sequence.

The Skill Decoder is learned using a purely supervised approach. To gather data to perform supervised training on the presented scenario, we label the data to train the Skill Decoder. This module computes a transformation t, represented by a vector that contains the difference between a state where the agent has the same position as a specific object and its current position. The Skill Decoder input data is a concatenation of the current environment state and the one-hot vector skill ID. The output is the transformation required to reach the skill termination condition, posteriorly fed as input to the Transformation Decoder. Although an analytic computation in our scenario could replace this learning process, we decided to use learning-based approaches because the transformation is generally much harder to compute in a more realistic scenario. Besides that, we wanted to understand if our network architecture could learn the mapping between the current environment state conditioned on a skill ID and a specific transformation.

To train the Skill Decoder, we used a network architecture with one hidden layer with eighteen units with a rectified linear unit(ReLU) activation function. The model has the same number of output units as the number of elements in the agent space because this model outputs a transformation t that has this respective size, as discussed in Sect. 3.2. The model was trained during four epochs using a dataset with 3 276 180 elements, where each element contains the information regarding the environment state and one possible one-hot vector skill ID as input and a transformation t as a label. The hyperparameters used to train the Skill Decoder can be found in Table 2a . We used mean square error and Adam as the loss function and optimizer, respectively.

The Transformation Decoder is learned using Reinforcement Learning. Its input data are the transformations present in the dataset gathered to train the Skill Decoder. To train this module, we noticed that using transformations that could be executed during only three timesteps was enough to allow the agent to generalize to longer sequences. To train the Transformation Decoder,

Table 2. Hyperparameters used to train the Skill and Transformation Decoders

(a) Skill Decoder hyperparameters.

Hyperparameter	Value
Learning rate	0.001
Batch size	1024
Optimizer beta 1	0.9
Optimizer beta 2	0.999
Optimizer weight decay	L2

(b) Transformation Decoder hyperparameters.

Hyperparameter	Value
Learning rate	0.0005
Discount factor	0.95
Batch size	128
Gradient maximum value	0.5
Entropy coefficient	0
Value function coefficient	0.5

we used a network architecture with one hidden layer with twenty-four units and a hyperbolic tangent activation function. The output layer has six units since the agent can execute three discrete actions for each dimension (move in the positive/negative direction and stop). Our scenario has two dimensions, and for this reason, the agent has six output units, being able to perform up to nine different actions. The hyperparameters used to train the Transformation Decoder can be found in Table 2b .

4   Results

Our experiments aim to show, in the above-depicted scenario, how our proposed approach behaves regarding the following question: Can skill decomposition help the learning process when the tasks become longer?

   To better understand if our approach is suitable to handle long-task horizon tasks we perform experiments where the scenario has only one object to have a baseline performance for all tested approaches and then we tested in scenarios with two or more objects. We compared the proposed approach with a behaviour cloning approach [11] that is used as a baseline. To train this algorithm, we collected data composed of one thousand episodes of expert demonstrations. To measure the success rate we get the mean cumulative reward across two hundred episodes. The reward system gives a reward of one when an object is caught and a reward of 10 when all the objects are caught.

Table 3. Normalized success rate for scenarios with different number of objects

		Methods	
	Number of objects	Behaviour cloning	Our aprroach
Tasks	1	0.97	1
	2	0.48	1
	5	0	1

Table 3 shows the results comparing our approach with the behaviour cloning baseline. All the results are normalized between zero and one. As shown in the table, as the number of objects in the scene increases, the behaviour cloning performance tends to degrade. Using our approach, the performance is independent of the number of objects in the scene because the skill informs what the relevant aspects of the scene the agent should pay attention to.

Although after the training procedures, the Behaviour Cloning algorithm is capable of predicting more than 99 percent of all the actions in the validation set correctly, this percentage does not reflect the success in our proposed scenario. This is due to the fact that the agent must learn to stop near the objects. The Behaviour cloning (BC) algorithm struggles in performing this stopping action correctly when the number of objects in the scene is greater than two, although it is capable of moving towards objects. As shown by the table, the BC approach does not scale with the increase of the number of objects, not being able to catch a single object when the task consists on catching five objects.

Due to the modularity of our approach we can treat skill learning and skill composition as two separation learning procedures. In Fig. 4, we show the number of training steps required by the Planner to learn the correct object sequence when the number of skills gets progressively larger.

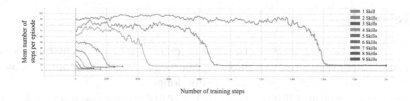

Fig. 4. Number of training steps required by the Planner to learn the correct object sequence

Why Does This Approach Scale? Our approach is scalable in scenarios where the state space is divided into agent space and environment space. For example, in our scenario the agent position is represented in the first elements of the environment state, while the remaining ones represent the objects' positions. This aspect is crucial since the module that determines which action should be executed in our approach (Transformation decoder) has as input a vector that represents a transformation in agent space. For this effect, it is crucial for the transformation to be represented using a continuous representation. This allows learning the Transformation Decoder, which can be reused regardless of the skill being executed and can leverage all the data provided. By defining what is effect that a given skill has in the environment, the second module of our approach can learn to map a discrete skill identifier and the environment state to a continuous representation. For example, in the presented scenario, we associated each skill with a single object and the transformations are the vectors that separate the agent from the objects. To this effect, we also need to define

a suitable representation for the difference between the skill end goal and the current state.

Although this approach scales, it is still restricted by the fact that we need to define manually the desired effect of each skill. Without this assumption, we would not be able to get the desired transformations for each skill. Another potential limitation is the number of steps required by the Planner when the number of skills becomes larger. From Fig. 4, we can see that when we increase the number of skills to be composed the number of training steps needed to learn this composition roughly doubles with each new skill.

5 Conclusions

We present an hierarchical model that enables skill learning to deal with long-horizon tasks with sparse rewards from offline data, and show that our proposed approach can effectively complete them using offline skill composition and learning. We demonstrate that learning skill parameterization using known skill behaviours is valuable and can ease the learning of modular tasks. We also show that a suitable way to learn a goal-conditioned policy is by using the difference between the goal and current state. The results show the robustness of our proposed approach to a simulated scenario where we gradually increase the size of the state space and its duration. As future work, our work can be used with methods that discover discrete and continuous skill parameterization automatically. An interesting avenue to pursue is also skill composition using planning strategies like, for example, Monte Carlo tree search [14].

Acknowledgement. This research was developed in the scope of the PhD grant[2020.05789.BD], funded by FCT - Foundation for Science and Technology. This study was also supported by IEETA - Institute of Electronics and Informatics Engineering of Aveiro, funded by National Funds through the FCT - Foundation for Science and Technology, in the context of the project [UIDB/00127/2020].

References

1. Ajay, A., Kumar, A., Agrawal, P., Levine, S., Nachum, O.: Opal: offline primitive discovery for accelerating offline reinforcement learning. In: International Conference on Learning Representations (ICLR) (2021)
2. Florensa, C., Duan, Y., Abbeel, P.: Stochastic neural networks for hierarchical reinforcement learning. In: International Conference on Learning Representations (ICLR) (2017)
3. Hakhamaneshi, K., Zhao, R., Zhan, A., Abbeel, P., Laskin, M.: Hierarchical few-shot imitation with skill transition models. In: International Conference on Learning Representations (ICLR) (2022)
4. Kipf, T., et al.: Compile: compositional imitation learning and execution. In: Chaudhuri, K., Salakhutdinov, R. (eds.) Proceedings of the 36th International Conference on Machine Learning. Proceedings of Machine Learning Research, vol. 97, pp. 3418–3428. PMLR, 09–15 Jun 2019

5. Kroemer, O., Niekum, S., Konidaris, G.: A review of robot learning for manipulation: challenges, representations, and algorithms. J. Mach. Learn. Res. **22**(30), 1–82 (2021)
6. Kumar, A., Zhou, A., Tucker, G., Levine, S.: Conservative q-learning for offline reinforcement learning. In: Larochelle, H., Ranzato, M., Hadsell, R., Balcan, M.F., Lin, H. (eds.) Advances in Neural Information Processing Systems, vol. 33, pp. 1179–1191. Curran Associates, Inc. (2020)
7. Lynch, C., et al.: Learning latent plans from play. In: 3rd Conference on Robot Learning (2019)
8. Nachum, O., Gu, S.S., Lee, H., Levine, S.: Data-efficient hierarchical reinforcement learning. In: Bengio, S., Wallach, H., Larochelle, H., Grauman, K., Cesa-Bianchi, N., Garnett, R. (eds.) Advances in Neural Information Processing Systems, vol. 31, pp. 3303–3313. Curran Associates, Inc. (2018)
9. Pertsch, K., Lee, Y., Wu, Y., Lim, J.J.: Demonstration-guided reinforcement learning with learned skills. In: 5th Conference on Robot Learning (2021)
10. Rao, D., et al.: Learning transferable motor skills with hierarchical latent mixture policies. In: International Conference on Learning Representations (ICLR) (2022)
11. Ross, S., Gordon, G., Bagnell, D.: A reduction of imitation learning and structured prediction to no-regret online learning. In: Gordon, G., Dunson, D., Dudík, M. (eds.) Proceedings of the Fourteenth International Conference on Artificial Intelligence and Statistics. Proceedings of Machine Learning Research, vol. 15, pp. 627–635. PMLR, Fort Lauderdale, FL, USA, 11–13 Apr 2011
12. Schulman, J., Wolski, F., Dhariwal, P., Radford, A., Klimov, O.: Proximal policy optimization algorithms. arXiv preprint arXiv:1707.06347 (2017)
13. Shankar, T., Gupta, A.: Learning robot skills with temporal variational inference. In: Proceedings of the 37th International Conference on Machine Learning. Proceedings of Machine Learning Research, vol. 119, pp. 8624–8633. PMLR (2020)
14. Świechowski, M., Godlewski, K., Sawicki, B., Mańdziuk, J.: Monte Carlo tree search: a review of recent modifications and applications. arXiv preprint arXiv:2103.04931 (2021)
15. Tanneberg, D., Ploeger, K., Rueckert, E., Peters, J.: SKID raw: skill discovery from raw trajectories. IEEE Robot. Autom. Lett. **6**(3), 4696–4703 (2021)
16. Wulfmeier, M., et al.: Compositional transfer in hierarchical reinforcement learning. In: Proceedings of Robotics: Science and Systems (2020)
17. Wulfmeier, M., et al.: Data-efficient hindsight off-policy option learning. In: Meila, M., Zhang, T. (eds.) Proceedings of the 38th International Conference on Machine Learning. Proceedings of Machine Learning Research, vol. 139, pp. 11340–11350. PMLR, 18–24 Jul 2021
18. Zhang, J., Yu, H., Xu, W.: Hierarchical reinforcement learning by discovering intrinsic options. In: International Conference on Learning Representations (ICLR) (2021)
19. Zhu, Y., Stone, P., Zhu, Y.: Bottom-up skill discovery from unsegmented demonstrations for long-horizon robot manipulation. IEEE Robot. Autom. Lett. **7**(2), 4126–4133 (2022). https://doi.org/10.1109/LRA.2022.3146589

MASTA - Multi-Agent Systems: Theory and Applications

Envy Freeness Up to One Item:
Shall We Duplicate or Remove Resources?

Martin Aleksandrov(✉)

Freie Universität Berlin, Berlin, Germany
martin.aleksandrov@fu-berlin.de

Abstract. We consider a fair division model in which agents have general valuations for bundles of indivisible items. We propose two new approximate properties for envy freeness of allocations in this model: DEFX and DEF1. We compare these with two existing axiomatic properties: EFX and EF1. For example, we give the first result confirming that EFX allocations may not exist with general but identical valuations. However, even when they do exist in such problems, we prove that DEFX (and, therefore DEF1) and PO allocations exist whereas EFX and PO allocations may not exist. Our results assert eloquently that DEFX and DEF1 approximate fairness better than EFX and EF1.

1 Introduction

We study fair division problems where agents have *general* (i.e. positive, zero, or negative) valuations for bundles of indivisible items. Some items are marginally liked by agents. We call these goods. Item o is *good* for agent i with respect to bundle M if the i's marginal valuation for o, when added to M, is non-negative. Other items are marginally disliked by agents. We call these bads. Item o is *bad* for agent i with respect to bundle M if the i's marginal valuation for o, when added to M, is non-positive. We consider three item types depending on combinations of valuations.

We refer to item o as *mixed* if, there is a pair of agents i, j and a pair of disjoint bundles M, N such that the marginal valuation of i for o, when added to M, is strictly positive and the marginal valuation of j for o, when added to N, is strictly negative. Also, we refer to item o as *generally good* for agent i if o is good for i wrt any bundle M. Likewise, we refer to item o as *generally bad* for agent i if o is bad for i wrt any bundle M. We consider three problem types depending on available items.

The first type of problem has only items that are *generally good* and *generally bad* for agents. In other words, each agent considers a given item as generally good or generally bad. From a theoretical perspective, this could be the case whenever we combine a problem with goods and a problem with bads. From a practical perspective, any problem where the valuations are additive (i.e. the valuation for items is the sum of item valuations) has only generally good and bad items. Common applications are paper assignments [13], food allocations [1], and course allocations [5].

Although such problems model some practical settings, there are other practical settings where none of the items is just generally good or just generally bad for a given agent. We illustrate this in Example 1.

G. Marreiros et al. (Eds.): EPIA 2022, LNAI 13566, pp. 727–738, 2022.
https://doi.org/10.1007/978-3-031-16474-3_59

Example 1. *Alice and Bob love playing cricket but suppose that we have only one cricket ball b and one cricket bat r. We let each of them value $\{b, r\}$ at 2, $\{b\}$ and $\{r\}$ at -1, and $\emptyset$ at 0. Giving b and r to Alice and no item to Bob makes Alice happy because she gets a valuation of 2 but giving only b to Alice and only r to Bob makes Alice unhappy because she gets a valuation of -1. This means that Alice's judgment about whether b is good or bad depends on whether she receives r or not. Hence, neither b nor r is considered as generally good or generally bad by Alice.* ◇

This leads us to the second and third problem types: problems *without mixed items* and problems *with mixed items*. Problems without mixed items capture settings where all agents reach a consensus about whether a given item is good or bad with respect to their bundles. For instance, a group of friends benefits from going on a holiday or not given their budgets. Problems with mixed items capture settings with complementarities or substitutabilities. Suppose that we value the right and left shoes together and, otherwise, we have no value or even disvalue just one shoe. Also, suppose that we value one bicycle but disvalue a second one due to the lack of storage space.

An interesting case in our setting is when the agents' valuations are general but *identical* (i.e. for each bundle, the agents' valuations are equal) [2]. For example, people tend to have a similar value for a pair of Nike shoes but perhaps this value differs from their value for a pair of Adidas shoes. Further, students tend to value one module (i.e. a set of courses) identically (e.g. by means of credit points) but they may value differently another module. With identical valuations, the set of problems with generally good and bad items is a strict subset of the set of problems without mixed items and the set of problems without mixed items is disjoint from the set of problems with mixed items.

An allocation exhausts all items by giving to each agent a different bundle. For allocations in the three types of problems, we study approximations of the golden standard in fair division: envy-freeness (i.e. no agent envies another one) [9]. Two such existing properties for our setting are EFX and EF1 [3]. For example, EFX requires that, if agent i envies agent j, 1) hypothetically *removing* any item from agent i's bundle, that is non-zero valued bad for agent i wrt agent i's bundle, makes agent i envy-free of agent j, and 2) hypothetically *removing* any item from agent j's bundle, that is non-zero valued good for agent i wrt agent j's bundle, makes agent i envy-free of agent j. EF1 weakens these conditions to some (possibly zero valued) and not any (non-zero valued) item.

In our work, we propose two alternative properties that aim at restoring envy-freeness by reducing the valuations of envied agents, either through removing goods from their bundles or duplicating bads in these bundles. We refer to them as DEFX and DEF1. For example, DEFX requires that, if agent i envies agent j, 1)′ hypothetically *duplicating* to agent j's bundle any item from agent i's bundle, that is non-zero valued bad for agent i wrt agent i's bundle, makes agent i envy-free of agent j, and 2)′ hypothetically *removing* any item from agent j's bundle, that is non-zero valued good for agent i wrt agent i's bundle, makes agent i envy-free of agent j. DEF1 weakens these conditions to some (possibly zero valued) and not any (non-zero valued) item.

We thus study combinations of each of these fairness properties with an efficiency criterion such as Pareto optimality (PO) [11]. Pareto optimality ensures that we cannot re-distribute items among agents' bundles so that we make all agents weakly happier and some agents strictly happier.

2   Related Work

For indivisible goods, EF1 was proposed by Budish [4] and EFX by Caragiannis et al. [6]. For problems with generally good and bad items, EFX and EF1 were generalized by Aziz et al. [3]. Plaut and Roughgarden [12] proved that an EFX allocation exists in problems with general but identical valuations for goods (i.e. generally good items). At the same time, the existence of EFX allocations in problems with an unbounded number of agents and additive (but not necessarily identical) valuations remained an open question in the last few years. By comparison, we prove that there are problems with general but identical valuations where an EFX (and, therefore, EFX and PO) allocation might not exist. We also prove that a DEFX and PO allocation exists in each problem with such valuations.

The idea of reducing the valuation of an envied agent by duplicating to their bundle a bad from an envy agent's bundle is already used in the literature for another version of EFX: see the work of Chen and Liu [7]. This version requires that each removed item from the envied agent's bundle is non-zero valued good for the envy agent wrt the envied agent's bundle. However, such an item could still be considered as bad by the envy agent wrt their own bundle. We believe that this requirement is counter-intuitive as we would expect the envy agent to be happy that such a bad is not in their own bundle but in the envied agent's bundle. By comparison, our new notion of DEFX requires that each removed item from the envied agent's bundle is non-zero valued good for the envy agent wrt their own bundle. Finally, our notion of DEF1 is also new.

3   Formal Preliminaries

We let $[n]$ denote a set of agents and $[m]$ denote a set of indivisible items, where $n, m \in \mathbb{N}_{\geq 2}$. Further, we let each $i \in [n]$ use some function v_i to specify their *general* valuation $v_i(M) \in \mathbb{R}$ for each $M \subseteq [m]$. We write $v_i(o)$ for $v_i(\{o\})$. The valuations are *additive* whenever, for each $i \in [n]$, $v_i(M) = \sum_{o \in M} v_i(o)$ holds. The valuations have *non-zero marginals* if, for each $i \in [n]$, each $o \in [m]$, and each $M \subseteq [m] \setminus \{o\}$, $v_i(M \cup \{o\}) - v_i(M) \neq 0$ holds. The valuations are *identical* if, for each $M \subseteq [m]$, $v_i(M) = v_j(M) = v(M)$ holds for each $i, j \in [n]$ and some $v(M) \in \mathbb{R}$.

We consider three types of items. We refer to $o \in [m]$ as *mixed* if, there is a pair $i, j \in [n]$ and a pair $M \subseteq [m] \setminus \{o\}, N \subseteq [m] \setminus (M \cup \{o\})$ such that $v_i(M \cup \{o\}) > v_i(M)$ and $v_j(N \cup \{o\}) < v_j(N)$ hold. We refer to $o \in [m]$ as *generally good* for $i \in [n]$ if, for each $M \subseteq [m]$, $v_i(M \cup \{o\}) \geq v_i(M)$ holds. We refer to $o \in [m]$ as *generally bad* for $i \in [n]$ if, for each $M \subseteq [m]$, $v_i(M \cup \{o\}) \leq v_i(M)$ holds.

For each $i \in [n]$, we let G_i, B_i, and M_i denote the sets of generally good items, generally bad items, and mixed items for agent i in a given problem. In a problem *with* mixed items, $G_i \cup B_i \subset [m]$, $M_i \neq \emptyset$, and $G_i \cap B_i = \emptyset$ hold for some $i \in [n]$. In a problem *without* mixed items, $G_i \cup B_i \subseteq [m]$, $M_i = \emptyset$, and $G_i \cap B_i = \emptyset$ hold for each $i \in [n]$. In a problem *with* generally good and bad items, $G_i \cup B_i = [m]$, $M_i = \emptyset$, and $G_i \cap B_i = \emptyset$ hold for each $i \in [n]$.

3.1 Axiomatic Properties

An *(complete) allocation* $A = (A_1, \ldots, A_n)$ is such that (1) A_i is the bundle of agent $i \in [n]$, (2) $\cup_{i \in [n]} A_i = [m]$, and (3) $A_i \cap A_j = \emptyset$ for each $i, j \in [n]$ with $i \neq j$. We write $\overrightarrow{v}(A) \in \mathbb{R}^n$ for the non-decreasing valuation vector wrt A. Agent i envies agent j in allocation A iff $v_i(A_i) < v_i(A_j)$ holds. Thus, A is envy-free iff no agent i envies any other agent j. Envy-free allocations may not exist [3] and, therefore, we consider approximations of envy freeness.

Envy-freeness up to one removed good or one removed bad We first define the existing approximations EFX and EF1.

Definition 1 (EFX). *An allocation A is* envy-free up to any non-zero removed good and any non-zero removed bad *if,* $\forall i, j \in [n]$ *s.t.* $v_i(A_i) < v_i(A_j)$ *holds, 1)* $\forall o \in A_j$ *s.t.* $v_i(A_j) > v_i(A_j \setminus \{o\})$: $v_i(A_i) \geq v_i(A_j \setminus \{o\})$ *and 2)* $\forall o \in A_i$ *s.t.* $v_i(A_i) < v_i(A_i \setminus \{o\})$: $v_i(A_i \setminus \{o\}) \geq v_i(A_j)$.

Definition 2 (EF1). *An allocation A is* envy-free up to some removed good or some removed bad *if,* $\forall i, j \in [n]$ *s.t. i is not EFX of j, 1)* $\exists o \in A_j$ *s.t.* $v_i(A_i) \geq v_i(A_j \setminus \{o\})$ *or 2)* $\exists o \in A_i$ *s.t.* $v_i(A_i \setminus \{o\}) \geq v_i(A_j)$.

By definition, an allocation that satisfies EFX also satisfies EF1. It is well-known that the opposite relation may not be true even with additive valuations [3]. Hence, EFX is strictly stronger than EF1. We write EFX $\Rightarrow$ EF1.

Envy-freeness up to one removed good or duplicated bad We further define the novel approximations DEFX and DEF1.

Definition 3 (DEFX). *An allocation A is* envy-free up to any non-zero removed good and any non-zero added bad *if,* $\forall i, j \in [n]$ *s.t. i envies j, 1)'* $\forall o \in A_j$ *s.t.* $v_i(A_i \cup \{o\}) > v_i(A_i)$: $v_i(A_i) \geq v_i(A_j \setminus \{o\})$ *and 2)'* $\forall o \in A_i$ *s.t.* $v_i(A_i) < v_i(A_i \setminus \{o\})$: $v_i(A_i) \geq v_i(A_j \cup \{o\})$.

Definition 4 (DEF1). *An allocation A is* envy-free up to some removed good or some added bad *if,* $\forall i, j \in [n]$ *s.t. i is not DEFX of j, 1)'* $\exists o \in A_j$ *s.t.* $v_i(A_i) \geq v_i(A_j \setminus \{o\})$ *or 2)'* $\exists o \in A_i$ *s.t.* $v_i(A_i) \geq v_i(A_j \cup \{o\})$.

By definition, an allocation that is DEFX also satisfies DEF1. However, the opposite relation may not hold. To see this, consider a problem with additive valuations. By definition, DEFX coincides with EFX and DEF1 coincides with EF1 in this case. With additive valuations, it follows that an allocation that is DEF1 may violate DEFX. Hence, DEFX is strictly stronger than DEF1. We write DEFX $\Rightarrow$ DEF1.

Pareto-optimality As we mentioned earlier, we also consider a classical efficiency criterion such as Pareto-optimality.

Definition 5 (PO). *An allocation A is* Pareto-optimal *if there is no allocation B that Pareto-improves A, i.e.* $\forall i \in [n]$: $v_i(B_i) \geq v_i(A_i)$ *and* $\exists j \in [n]$: $v_j(B_j) > v_j(A_j)$.

3.2 The Leximin Solution

We consider the *leximin* solution from [8]. This one maximizes the minimum valuation of any agent in an allocation, subject to which the second minimum valuation is maximized, and so on.

Plaut and Roughgarden [12] implemented one total operator for comparing allocations: $\succ$. We write $A \succ B$ (i.e. A *leximin-dominates* B) if there exists an index $i \leq n$ such that $\overrightarrow{v}(A)_j = \overrightarrow{v}(B)_j$ for each $1 \leq j < i$ and $\overrightarrow{v}(A)_i > \overrightarrow{v}(B)_i$. Thus, the leximin solution is a maximal element under $\succ$.

They observed that this solution is trivially PO, since if it were possible to improve the valuation of one agent without decreasing the valuation of any other agent, the new allocation would be strictly larger under $\succ$.

4 EFX: Identical General Valuations

We start with the standard property of EFX. Interestingly, this property might be incompatible with DEFX or PO even in problems where the agents' valuations are identical. This is either because EFX allocations might not exist or because they minimize the valuation of any agent.

4.1 Problems with Mixed Items: Impossibility

We prove the *first* major result. There are problems in our setting, where none of the allocations is EFX. The key rationale behind this is the fact that these problems may contain mixed items.

Theorem 1. *There are problems with mixed items and general but identical valuations whose marginals are non-zero, in which* no *allocation is EFX.*

Proof. Let us consider a problem with 2 agents and 4 items. Define the valuations as follows: $v(\emptyset) = 0$, $v(a) = 5$, $v(b) = 5$, $v(c) = 5$, $v(d) = 5$, $v(\{a,b\}) = 6$, $v(\{a,c\}) = 3$, $v(\{b,c\}) = 3$, $v(\{a,d\}) = 6$, $v(\{b,d\}) = 6$, $v(\{c,d\}) = 3$, $v(\{a,b,c\}) = 7$, $v(\{a,b,d\}) = 8$, $v(\{a,c,d\}) = 7$, $v(\{b,c,d\}) = 7$, and $v(\{a,b,c,d\}) = 9$. Clearly, these valuations are identical.

However, it is not so trivial to see that this problem contains mixed items. To do this, we first show that none of the items is generally good or bad. For item a, $v(\{a,b\}) - v(a) = 1$ but $v(\{a,c\}) - v(a) = -2$. For item b, $v(\{a,b\}) - v(b) = 1$ but $v(\{b,c\}) - v(b) = -2$. For item c, $v(\{a,c\}) - v(c) = -2$ but $v(\{a,b,c,d\}) - v(\{a,b,d\}) = 1$. For item d, $v(\{b,d\}) - v(d) = 1$ but $v(\{c,d\}) - v(d) = -2$.

We conclude that the problem is either with mixed items or without mixed items. To confirm that it is with mixed items, we need to find a single mixed item. For this purpose, we consider the leximin solution $A = (\{c\}, \{a,b,d\})$. In this allocation, item a is bad for agent 1 wrt A_1 (i.e. $v(A_1 \cup \{a\}) - v(A_1) = 3 - 5 = -2 < 0$) but good for agent 2 wrt A_2 (i.e. $v(A_2) - v(A_2 \setminus \{a\}) = 8 - 6 = 2 > 0$).

We can now conclude that the problem has indeed mixed items. We next show that none of the allocations in it is EFX. For this purpose, we consider all allocations in which agent 1 receive a different bundle and give one violation of this property per allocation. By the symmetry of the valuations, one can show that the corresponding allocations where agents swap bundles also violate EFX. The allocations where agent 1 receive a different bundle and the EFX violations are: (1) $A = (\emptyset, \{a, b, c, d\})$: $v(A_1) = 0$, $v(A_2) = 9$, $v(A_2) - v(A_2 \setminus \{c\}) = 1$ and $v(A_1) = 0 < 8 = v(A_2 \setminus \{c\})$; (2) $A = (\{a\}, \{b, c, d\})$: $v(A_1) = 5$, $v(A_2) = 7$, $v(A_2) - v(A_2 \setminus \{c\}) = 1$ and $v(A_1) < 6 = v(A_2 \setminus \{c\})$; (3) $A = (\{b\}, \{a, c, d\})$: $v(A_1) = 5$, $v(A_2) = 7$, $v(A_2) - v(A_2 \setminus \{c\}) = 1$ and $v(A_1) < 6 = v(A_2 \setminus \{c\})$; (4) $A = (\{c\}, \{a, b, d\})$: $v(A_1) = 5$, $v(A_2) = 8$, $v(A_2) - v(A_2 \setminus \{d\}) = 2$ and $v(A_1) < 6 = v(A_2 \setminus \{d\})$; (5) $A = (\{d\}, \{a, b, c\})$: $v(A_1) = 5$, $v(A_2) = 7$, $v(A_2) - v(A_2 \setminus \{c\}) = 1$ and $v(A_1) < 6 = v(A_2 \setminus \{c\})$; (6) $A = (\{a, b\}, \{c, d\})$: $v(A_1) = 6$, $v(A_2) = 3$, $v(A_1) - v(A_1 \setminus \{a\}) = 1$ and $v(A_2) < 5 = v(A_1 \setminus \{a\})$; (7) $A = (\{a, c\}, \{b, d\})$: $v(A_1) = 3$, $v(A_2) = 6$, $v(A_2) - v(A_2 \setminus \{b\}) = 1$ and $v(A_1) < 5 = v(A_2 \setminus \{b\})$; (8) $A = (\{b, c\}, \{a, d\})$: $v(A_1) = 3$, $v(A_2) = 6$, $v(A_2) - v(A_2 \setminus \{d\}) = 1$ and $v(A_1) < 5 = v(A_2 \setminus \{d\})$. ◇

4.2 Problems with Mixed Items: Incompatibility

To understand better the differences between EFX and DEFX, we next consider problems with mixed items where EFX allocations exist. In fact, there are such problems where none of the EFX allocations satisfies also DEFX (see the full version for proof).

Theorem 2. *There are problems with mixed items and general but identical valuations whose marginals are non-zero, in which EFX allocations exist but* none *of the EFX allocations satisfies DEFX.*

We conclude that the set of EFX allocations and the set of DEFX allocations might be disjoint in some problems even under the non-zero marginal assumption. As a result, there are problems where none of the DEFX allocations satisfies EFX.

Further, Plaut and Roughgarden [12] proved that the leximin solution is EFX and PO in problems with general but identical valuations for generally good items, subject to the non-zero marginal assumption.

Interestingly, adding bads to the problem may destroy this compatibility. Hence, as the leximin solution is Pareto optimal, it may no longer be EFX in our setting even under the non-zero marginal assumption.

Theorem 3. *There are problems with mixed items and general but identical valuations whose marginals are non-zero, in which EFX allocations exist but* none *of the EFX allocations satisfies PO.*

Proof. Let us consider again the problem from Theorem 1. Further, let us change only one valuation in this problem: $v(\{a, d\}) = 3$. In this way, the problem remains with mixed items. Next, let us focus on the following two allocations $A = (\{b, c\}, \{a, d\})$ and $B = (\{a, d\}, \{b, c\})$ in it.

By the proof of Theorem 1, each other allocation violates EFX. Each of A and B is such that each agent values their bundle with 3. Hence, agent 1 is envy-free of agent 2, and agent 2 is envy-free of agent 1. A and B satisfy EFX.

Unfortunately, neither A nor B is Pareto-optimal. For example, the allocation $C = (C_1, C_2)$, where $C_1 = \{c\}$ and $C_2 = \{a, b, d\}$ (i.e. leximin) is a Pareto improvement of A and B because $v(C_1) = 5 > 3 = v(A_1)$, $v(C_2) = 8 > 3 = v(A_2)$ and $v(C_1) = 5 > 3 = v(B_1)$, $v(C_2) = 8 > 3 = v(B_2)$ hold. ◇

This result has two insightful implications. Firstly, there are problems with general but identical valuations whose marginals are non-zero, where each EFX allocation is Pareto-improved by any other allocation except the trivial ones that give all items to agents.

Secondly, there are such problems where each EFX allocation minimizes the maximum valuation of any agent. This suggests that maximizing the minimum valuation of any agent, even among those allocations that give to each agent at least one item or the same number of items, might not guarantee EFX.

4.3 Problems Without Mixed Items: Incompatibility

One might hope that removing the mixed items in a given problem will help us restore some of the previous results for EFX. However, our next pair of findings thwart this hope. They hold even for problems with generally bad items and, therefore, for problems without mixed items.

Theorem 4. *There are problems with generally bad items and general but identical valuations whose marginals are non-zero, in which EFX allocations exist but none of the EFX allocations satisfies DEFX.*

Proof. Let us consider 2 agents and their identical valuations for 4 items: $v(\emptyset) = 0$, $v(a) = -4$, $v(b) = -4$, $v(c) = -4$, $v(d) = -6$, $v(\{a, b\}) = -5$, $v(\{a, c\}) = -5$, $v(\{b, c\}) = -5$, $v(\{a, d\}) = -7$, $v(\{b, d\}) = -7$, $v(\{c, d\}) = -7$, $v(\{a, b, c\}) = -8$, $v(\{a, b, d\}) = -8$, $v(\{a, c, d\}) = -8$, $v(\{b, c, d\}) = -8$, and $v(\{a, b, c, d\}) = -9$.

We argue that the way to achieve EFX is to give $\{a, b, c\}$ to agent 1 and $\{d\}$ to agent 2, or to swap these bundles. For each other allocation, one can find a violation of this property as in Theorem 1. However, the allocation $A = (\{a, b, c\}, \{d\})$ violates DEFX: $v(A_1) = -8 < -7 = v(A_2 \cup \{a\})$. ◇

Theorem 5. *There are problems with generally bad items and general but identical valuations whose marginals are non-zero, in which EFX allocations exist but none of the EFX allocations satisfies PO.*

Proof. Let us consider again the problem from Theorem 4. The only two EFX allocations in this problem are $A = (\{d\}, \{a, b, c\})$ and $B = (\{a, b, c\}, \{d\})$. Pick also the allocations $C = (\{a, b\}, \{c, d\})$ and $D = (\{c, d\}, \{a, b\})$. Each of these is the leximin solution. Further, we have that $v(C_1) = -5 > -6 = v(A_1)$, $v(C_2) = -7 > -8 = v(A_2)$, $v(D_1) = -7 > -8 = v(B_1)$, $v(D_2) = -5 > -6 = v(B_2)$ hold. Hence, C Pareto improves A and D Pareto improves B. ◇

We observe that Theorems 4 and 5 do not follow from Theorems 2 and 3 and the latter do not follow from the former. This observation follows because the set of problems with mixed items and the set of problems without mixed items are clearly disjoint.

5   DEFX and PO: Identical General Valuations

We further analyse the new property of DEFX. We prove the *second* major result. That is, DEFX and PO allocations exist in each problem in our setting as long as the agents' valuations are general but identical. For example, the leximin solution satisfies both DEFX and PO.

Theorem 6. *With general but identical valuations, the leximin solution satisfies DEFX and PO.*

Proof. Let A be an leximin allocation. This allocation is PO even with general (but not necessarily identical) valuations. For this reason, we next show that A is DEFX. Assume that A is not DEFX for a pair of agents $i, j \in [n]$ with $i \neq j$. That is, $v(A_i) < v(A_j)$. For our proof, we let $v(A_1) \leq \ldots \leq v(A_n)$ denote the valuation order induced by A. We also let $k = \arg\max\{h \in [n] | v(A_h) \leq v(A_i)\}$. We note that $i \leq k$ and $k < j$ hold. Thus, we can conclude that $v(A_i) = v(A_k)$ and $v(A_k) < v(A_j)$ hold. The violation of DEFX further means that at least one of the following two conditions should hold: (a) $\exists o \in A_j : v(A_i \cup \{o\}) > v(A_i), v(A_i) < v(A_j \setminus \{o\})$ and (b) $\exists o \in A_i : v(A_i) < v(A_i \setminus \{o\}), v(A_i) < v(A_j \cup \{o\})$. We consider two cases.

Case 1: If (a) holds for some $o \in A_j$, then let us move only item o from A_j to A_i. We let B denote this allocation: $B_i = A_i \cup \{o\}$, $B_j = A_j \setminus \{o\}$ and $B_h = A_h$ for each $h \in [n] \setminus \{i, j\}$. We next prove that $B \succ A$ holds.

Wlog, let $v(B_{p_1}) \leq \ldots \leq v(B_{p_n})$ denote the valuation order induced by B. We note that the positions of agents i and j in this order are at least k. As a result, $B_{p_q} = A_q$ for each $q \in \{1, \ldots, k\} \setminus \{i\}$.

We now consider three cases for the kth agent in this order. If $p_k = i$, we derive $v(B_i) = v(A_i \cup \{o\}) > v(A_i)$ by (a). If $p_k = j$, we also derive $v(B_j) = v(A_j \setminus \{o\}) > v(A_i)$ by (a). If $p_k = k + 1$, we conclude $v(B_{k+1}) = v(A_{k+1}) > v(A_k) \geq v(A_i)$ by the construction of B and the choice of k.

To conclude this case, we simple observe that $v(B_{p_q}) \geq v(B_{p_k}) > v(A_i)$ holds for each $q \in \{k + 1, \ldots, n\}$. Gathering the pieces together, it follows that A cannot be the leximin solution. This is a contradiction. Hence, (a) cannot hold.

Case 2: If (b) holds for some $o \in A_i$, then let us move only item o from A_i to A_j. We let B denote this allocation: $B_i = A_i \setminus \{o\}$, $B_j = A_j \cup \{o\}$ and $B_h = A_h$ for each $h \in [n] \setminus \{i, j\}$. We again prove that $B \succ A$ holds.

Consider again the valuation order induced by B, say $v(B_{p_1}) \leq \ldots \leq v(B_{p_n})$. The positions of agents i and j in this order are also at least k. As a result, $B_{p_q} = A_q$ for each $q \in \{1, \ldots, k\} \setminus \{i\}$.

The cases for the kth agent are similar as in the first case. If $p_k = i$, we derive $v(B_i) = v(A_i \setminus \{o\}) > v(A_i)$ by (b). If $p_k = j$, we also derive $v(B_j) = v(A_j \cup \{o\}) > v(A_i)$ by (b). If $p_k = k + 1$, we conclude $v(B_{k+1}) = v(A_{k+1}) > v(A_k) \geq v(A_i)$ by the construction of B and the choice of k.

At the end, we again observe that $v(B_{p_q}) \geq v(B_{p_k}) > v(A_i)$ holds for each $q \in \{k + 1, \ldots, n\}$. Consequently, allocation A cannot be the leximin solution. This leads again to a contradiction. Therefore, (b) also cannot hold. ◇

We can give a "cut-and-choose" protocol for computing a DEFX allocation in problems with 2 agents: (1) agent 1 "cut" the bundle of all items in two, using the leximin solution and supposing that agent 2 has valuations that are identical to those of agent 1, and (2) agent 2 "choose" their most favorable bundle. A similar idea was used by Plaut and Roughgarden [12] for EFX in problems with generally good items.

By Theorem 6, it follows that agent 1 is DEFX of agent 2 for each bundle after the cut. As agent 2 picks their most favorable bundle, they are envy-free of agent 1. This concludes our claim. The interesting part about this simple result in contrast to the one in Theorem 7 is that agents can have general valuations that might not necessarily be disjointly normalised.

6 DEFX: General Valuations

It is well-known that the egalitarian allocation, maximizing the minimum valuation of any agent, might fail EF1 in problems with 3 agents and additive valuations [6]. This holds for the leximin solution and DEF1 in such problems. For this reason, we study the case of 2 agents.

6.1 The Case of 2 Agents

We come to the *third* major result. This one is for general but *disjointly normalised* valuations. That is, for each $M, N \subseteq [m]$ such that $M \cap N = \emptyset$, we have $v_i(M) + v_i(N) = c$ for each $i \in [2]$ and some $c \in \mathbb{R}$. Interestingly, we show that each problem with such valuations admits a DEFX and PO allocation.

A special but very practical sub-case of disjointly normalised valuations is the one of *additive* but not general valuations: for $i \in \{1, 2\}$, $v_i(M) = \sum_{o \in M} v_i(o)$ for $M \subseteq [m]$ and $v_i([m]) = c$ for some $c \in \mathbb{R}$. For example, some applications on Spliddit ask agents to share some pre-defined total valuation for items [6].

Theorem 7. *With general (and not necessarily identical) but disjointly normalised valuations, the leximin solution satisfies DEFX and PO.*

Proof. Let A be the leximin solution. A is PO. Suppose that A is not DEFX. Wlog, let agent 1 be not DEFX of agent 2. Hence, it must be the case that (a) $v_1(A_1) < v_1(A_2 \cup \{o\})$ holds for some $o \in A_1$ with $v_1(A_1 \setminus \{o\}) > v_1(A_1)$ or (b) $v_1(A_1) < v_1(A_2 \setminus \{o\})$ holds for some $o \in A_2$ with $v_1(A_1 \cup \{o\}) > v_1(A_1)$. We consider two cases.

If (a) holds for $o \in A_1$, let us consider bundles $S_1 = A_1 \setminus \{o\}$ and $S_2 = A_2 \cup \{o\}$. If (b) holds for $o \in A_2$, let us consider bundles $S_1 = A_1 \cup \{o\}$ and $S_2 = A_2 \setminus \{o\}$. We construct an allocation B and show $\min\{v_1(A_1), v_2(A_2)\} < \min\{v_1(B_1), v_2(B_2)\}$. We let $B_1 = \arg\min_S v_2(S)$ and $B_2 = \arg\max_S v_2(S)$ where $S \in \{S_1, S_2\}$.

By construction, $v_2(B_2) \geq v_2(B_1)$ holds in B. Moreover, $v_1(S_1) > v_1(A_1)$ and $v_1(S_2) > v_1(A_1)$ hold in each of cases (a) and (b). These inequalities follow because agent 1's marginal valuations for the moved item are non-zero and agent 1 is not DEFX of agent 2. We conclude that $v_1(B_1) > v_1(A_1)$ holds.

We have $v_1(A_1) + v_1(A_2) = c$ and $v_2(A_1) + v_2(A_2) = c$ for some $c \in \mathbb{R}$ by $A_1 \cap A_2 = \emptyset$ and the fact that the valuations are disjointly normalised. As $v_1(A_1) < v_1(A_2)$, it follows $v_1(A_1) < c/2$. By the PO of A, $v_2(A_2) > v_2(A_1)$. Hence, $v_2(A_1) < c/2$ and $v_2(A_2) > c/2$. This implies that $v_1(A_1) < v_2(A_2)$ holds.

Further, B is also such that $B_1 \cap B_2 = \emptyset$ holds. Therefore, $v_2(B_1) + v_2(B_2) = c$. As $v_2(B_2) \geq v_2(B_1)$, it follows that the inequality $v_2(B_2) \geq c/2$ holds. We now derive that $\min\{v_1(A_1), v_2(A_2)\} = v_1(A_1) < \min\{v_1(B_1), c/2\} \leq \min\{v_1(B_1), v_2(B_2)\}$ holds. This is in conflict with the leximin-optimality of A. ◇

It follows that DEFX and PO allocations exist in problems with 2 agents and general valuations. By comparison, Aziz et al. [3] gave a polynomial-time algorithm for computing an EF1 (and, therefore, DEF1) and PO allocations in problems with 2 agents and additive valuations.

7 DEF1: General Valuations

For computing EF1 allocations in problems with generally good items, Lipton [10] gave an envy-graph algorithm. The algorithm allocates the items one by one. If the current item is good for at least one agent wrt their own bundle, the algorithm gives it to an unenvied agent who also considers the item as good wrt their own bundle. The algorithm maintains a graph that encodes the envy relation between the agents and any envy cycle, that forms in this graph after the current item is allocated, is eliminated by letting each agent take the bundle of the agent that they envy.

Unfortunately, this envy-graph algorithm may fail to return an EF1 allocation in problems with mixed items. We demonstrate this in Example 2.

Example 2. *Let us consider 2 agents and the following almost identical valuations v_1 and v_2: both agents value $\{a, b, c\}$ at -1, $\{a, b\}$ at -3, $\{a, c\}$ at -3, a at -2, b at -1, c at -1, $\emptyset$ at 0, but agent 1 values $\{b, c\}$ at 2 and agent 2 values $\{b, c\}$ at -2. We let the initial allocations of agents 1 and 2 be $A_1 = \emptyset$ and $A_2 = \emptyset$, respectively.*

The algorithm allocates the items in an arbitrary order. Wlog, let this be (a, b, c). In the first round, the algorithm picks an unenvied agent and allocates item a to such an agent. Wlog, let $a \in A_1$. In the second round, the algorithm picks an unenvied agent and allocates item b to them. At this moment, only agent 2 is unenvied. Hence, $b \in A_2$.

In the third round, the marginal valuations of the agents for item c wrt their own bundles are strictly negative: $v_1(\{a, c\}) < v_1(a)$ and $v_2(\{b, c\}) < v(b)$. Also, agent 1 envies agent 2 and agent 2 does not have envy of agent 1: $v_1(a) < v_1(b)$ and $v_2(b) > v_2(a)$. Hence, the algorithm picks agent 2 and allocates item c to them, i.e. $c \in A_2$.

At this point, $A_1 = \{a\}$ and $A_2 = \{b, c\}$. Agent 2 does not have envy of agent 1 and agent 1 envies agent 2: $v_2(A_2) = v_2(A_1)$ and $v_1(A_1) < v_1(A_2)$. The algorithm terminates. However, A is not EF1: $v_1(A_1) < -1 = v_1(A_2 \setminus \{b\})$, $v_1(A_1) < -1 = v_1(A_2 \setminus \{c\})$, and $v_1(A_1 \setminus \{a\}) = 0 < v_1(A_2)$. ◇

The issue here is that the envy-graph algorithm allocates the item at the last round to an agent who is envy-free given the partially constructed allocation. This generates strictly positive envy for the agent who is unenvied given the partially constructed allocation at this round.

This is because their marginal valuation for the last item wrt the other agent's bundle is strictly positive. At the same time, their marginal valuation for this item wrt their own bundle is strictly negative. Essentially, this means that the algorithm should select the unenvied agent at the last round.

Unfortunately, the envy-graph algorithm might also fail to return a DEF1 allocation even in problems with generally bad items, where it is guaranteed to return an EF1 allocation. We demonstrate this in Example 3.

Example 3. *Let us consider 2 agents who have the following identical valuation functions:* $v(\{a, b, c\}) = -5$, $v(\{a, b\}) = -3$, $v(\{a, c\}) = -3$, $v(\{b, c\}) = -4$, $v(a) = -2$, $v(b) = -1$, $v(c) = -1$, *and* $v(\emptyset) = 0$. *The algorithm allocates the items in an arbitrary order. Wlog, let this be* (a, b, c).

Also, wlog, suppose that agent 1 receives a. *From now on, the algorithm allocates surely* b, c *to agent 2. Thus, the final outcome is* $A = (\{a\}, \{b, c\})$. *This allocation is not DEF1:* $v(A_2) = -4 < -3 = v(A_1 \cup \{b\})$, $v(A_2) = -4 < -3 = v(A_1 \cup \{c\})$, *and* $v(A_2) = -4 < 0 = v(A_1 \setminus \{a\})$. ◇

8 Conclusions

We considered a fair division model in which agents have general valuations for bundles. We proposed two new axiomatic properties for allocations in this model: DEFX and DEF1. We compared these with two existing properties: EFX and EF1. Table 1 contains our results. They suggest that DEFX and PO allocations exist in each case where EFX and PO allocations do not. Perhaps, this means that DEFX and DEF1 might be favored in practice. We also left open some cases.

Table 1. Key: ✓ - a possibility result, × - an impossibility result, ⋆ - EFX allocations exist, ⋆⋆ - disjointly normalised valuations.

Property	Agents	Problems with mixed items	Problems without mixed items	Problems with gen. good & bad items
Identical General Valuations				
EFX	≥ 2	×, (Theorem 1)	Open	Open
EFX+DEFX (⋆)	≥ 2	×, (Theorem 2)		×, (Theorem 4)
EFX+PO (⋆)	≥ 2	×, (Theorem 3)		×, (Theorem 5)
DEFX+PO	≥ 2		✓, leximin (Theorem 6)	
General Valuations				
DEFX	2		✓, (see after Theorem 6)	
DEFX+PO (⋆⋆)	2		✓, leximin (Theorem 7)	
DEF1	≥ 2		Open	

Acknowledgements. Martin Aleksandrov was supported by the DFG Individual Research Grant on "Fairness and Efficiency in Emerging Vehicle Routing Problems" (497791398).

References

1. Aleksandrov, M., Aziz, H., Gaspers, S., Walsh, T.: Online fair division: analysing a food bank problem. In: Proceedings of IJCAI 2015, Buenos Aires, Argentina, 25–31 July 2015, pp. 2540–2546 (2015). http://ijcai.org/papers15/Abstracts/IJCAI15-360.html
2. Aleksandrov, M., Walsh, T.: Two algorithms for additive and fair division of mixed manna. In: KI 2020: Advances in Artificial Intelligence - 43th Annual German Conference on AI, Bamberg, Germany, 21–25 September 2020, Proceedings, pp. 44–57 (2020). https://doi.org/10.1007/978-3-030-58285-2_1
3. Aziz, H., Caragiannis, I., Igarashi, A., Walsh, T.: Fair allocation of indivisible goods and chores. In: Proceedings of the 28th International Joint Conference on Artificial Intelligence, pp. 53–59. IJCAI 2019, AAAI Press (2019). https://dl.acm.org/doi/abs/10.5555/3367032.3367041
4. Budish, E.: The combinatorial assignment problem: approximate competitive equilibrium from equal incomes. J. Polit. Econ. **119**(6), 1061–1103 (2011). https://doi.org/10.1086/664613
5. Budish, E., Cantillon, E.: The multi-unit assignment problem: theory and evidence from course allocation at Harvard. Am. Econ. Rev. **102**(5), 2237–2271 (2012). https://doi.org/10.1257/aer.102.5.2237
6. Caragiannis, I., Kurokawa, D., Moulin, H., Procaccia, A.D., Shah, N., Wang, J.: The unreasonable fairness of maximum Nash welfare. ACM Trans. Econ. Comput. **7**(3), 1–32 (2019). https://doi.org/10.1145/3355902
7. Chen, X., Liu, Z.: The fairness of leximin in allocation of indivisible chores. CoRR abs/2005.04864 (2020). https://arxiv.org/abs/2005.04864
8. Dubins, L.E., Spanier, E.H.: How to cut a cake fairly. Am. Math. Mon. **68**(1), 1–17 (1961). https://doi.org/10.2307/2311357
9. Foley, D.K.: Resource allocation and the public sector. Yale Econ. Essays **7**(1), 45–98 (1967). https://www.proquest.com/openview/cac1d2d0d079f04d1989726c2c2181fa/1?pq-origsite=gscholar&cbl=18750&diss=y
10. Lipton, R.J., Markakis, E., Mossel, E., Saberi, A.: On approximately fair allocations of indivisible goods. In: Proceedings Fifth ACM Conference on Electronic Commerce (EC-2004), New York, NY, USA, 17–20 May 2004, pp. 125–131 (2004). https://doi.org/10.1145/988772.988792
11. Pareto, V.: Cours d'économie politique. Œuvres complètes publiées sous la direction de giovanni busino. tomes 1 et 2 en un volume (1897). https://doi.org/10.3917/droz.paret.1964.01.9782600040143
12. Plaut, B., Roughgarden, T.: Almost envy-freeness with general valuations. In: Proceedings of the Twenty-Ninth Annual ACM-SIAM Symposium on Discrete Algorithms, SODA 2018, New Orleans, LA, USA, 7–10 January 2018, pp. 2584–2603 (2018). https://doi.org/10.1137/19M124397X
13. Tan, M., Dai, Z., Ren, Y., Walsh, T., Aleksandrov, M.: Minimal-envy conference paper assignment: formulation and a fast iterative algorithm. In: 2021 5th Asian Conference on Artificial Intelligence Technology (ACAIT), pp. 667–674 (2021). https://doi.org/10.1109/ACAIT53529.2021.9731163

Learning to Cooperate with Completely Unknown Teammates

Alexandre Neves[2] and Alberto Sardinha[1,2(✉)]

[1] INESC-ID, Lisbon, Portugal
`jose.alberto.sardinha@tecnico.ulisboa.pt`
[2] Instituto Superior Técnico, Universidade de Lisboa, Lisbon, Portugal

Abstract. A key goal of ad hoc teamwork is to develop a learning agent that cooperates with unknown teams, without resorting to any pre-coordination protocol. Despite a vast number of ad hoc teamwork algorithms in the literature, most of them cannot address the problem of learning to cooperate with a completely unknown team, unless it learns from scratch. This article presents a novel approach that uses transfer learning alongside the state-of-the-art PLASTIC-Policy to adapt to completely unknown teammates quickly. We test our solution within the Half Field Offense simulator with five different teammates. The teammates were designed independently by developers from different countries and at different times. Our empirical evaluation shows that it is advantageous for an ad hoc agent to leverage its past knowledge when adapting to a new team instead of learning how to cooperate with it from scratch.

Keywords: Ad hoc teamwork · Multiagent systems · Reinforcement learning

1 Introduction

As robots become more and more ubiquitous in industrial environments, we also start to see them being deployed in other settings, such as homes [4] and hospitals [14]. In tasks that require cooperation, robots should coordinate to achieve a common goal. However, achieving efficient cooperation may be a complex endeavor when robots come from different origins. One way to address this problem is to endow a robot with the ability to learn *on the fly* how to cooperate by observing their teammates and environment.

Ad hoc teamwork [12] aims to address the problem above and thus design an agent that learns on the fly to adapt to unknown teammates in order to complete

This work was partially supported by national funds through FCT, Fundação para a Ciência e a Tecnologia, under project UIDB/50021/2020 (INESC-ID multi-annual funding), the HOTSPOT project, with reference PTDC/CCI-COM/7203/2020, and the RELEvaNT project, with reference PTDC/CCI-COM/5060/2021. In addition, this work was partially supported by TAILOR, a project funded by EU Horizon 2020 research and innovation programme under GA No. 952215.

G. Marreiros et al. (Eds.): EPIA 2022, LNAI 13566, pp. 739–750, 2022.
https://doi.org/10.1007/978-3-031-16474-3_60

teamwork tasks. Furthermore, these agents must be robust to changes, such as adapting to new teammates and different environments.

Several algorithms for ad hoc teamwork have been proposed over the past few years. The state-of-the-art methods assume an agent has a library of teammate models and/or tasks and propose algorithms that choose on the fly the most appropriate models/tasks to cooperate with the unknown team (e.g., [9,11], and [10]). Other notable examples are the ad hoc agent in [7], where each task within the library is represented as a fully cooperative matrix game, and AATEAM [2] which has a library of teammate models that are learned with attention networks. Probably the most famous algorithm for ad hoc teamwork is PLASTIC-Policy [1], which also resorts to a library of learned policies and teammate models. However, all these algorithms fail to adapt efficiently when an unknown team is very different from the models/tasks within the library.

The main contribution of this work is to address this gap in the ad hoc teamwork literature by combining a transfer learning strategy and PLASTIC-Policy, whereby we use the parameter sharing strategy. Hence, we create a novel ad hoc agent that can efficiently cooperate with an unknown team that differs significantly from the models/tasks within its library.

We also conducted an empirical evaluation in the Half Field Offense simulation domain [5], a modified version of the RoboCup Soccer Simulation 2D sub-league. The results show that an ad hoc agent can indeed take advantage of PLASTIC-Policy combined with a transfer learning method. In our experiments, the ad hoc agent quickly adapts to unknown teammates, exhibiting close-to-optimal behavior from the start.

2   Background

A Markov decision process (MDP) is a mathematical framework for building sequential decision-making algorithms for agents. Formally, an MDP is a 5-tuple (S, A, p, R, γ), where S is a set of states, A is a set of actions, p is the transition probability function for reaching a state s' given that the previous state was s and the action taken was a, $R : S \times A \rightarrow \mathbb{R}$ is the reward received by the agent upon taking an action a from state s, and γ is the discount factor.

Reinforcement Learning (RL) [13] is a subarea of machine learning that aims to learn an optimal policy of an MDP. The most famous RL method is Q-learning [15]. This RL method learns the action-value function directly, $Q_\pi : S \times A \rightarrow \mathbb{R}$, which corresponds to the discounted reward of taking a given action in a given state then following policy π. Q-learning updates its estimate of the Q-value in the following way: $Q(S_t, A_t) \leftarrow (1 - \alpha)Q(S_t, A_t) + \alpha(R_{t+1} + \gamma \max_a Q(S_{t+1}, a))$, where α is the learning rate. Hence, the method interpolates, by a factor of α, the current estimate for a given state-action pair with the reward received by taking the given action in the given state added to the best expected discounted reward possible from the next state onward. With a discrete action space and state space, Q-learning converges to the optimal Q-values (i.e., the Q-values of the optimal policy, $Q_{\pi^*}(s, a)$ or $Q^*(s, a)$) if all actions are sampled a large number of times

in all states. An optimal policy is then derived by simply querying which action maximizes the optimal Q-value for a given state: $\pi^*(s) = \arg\max_a Q^*(s, a)$.

Deep Q-Network (DQN) [8] is a popular RL method for estimating the optimal Q-values with a neural network. An advantage of this approach is that it can handle continuous state spaces in complex environments. DQN approximates the optimal Q-values, Q^*, by using a neural network of parameters θ: $Q(s, a; \theta) \approx Q^*(s, a)$. At each step, the agent adds a transition (s, a, r, s') to a replay memory buffer, from which batches of transitions are sampled in order to optimize the parameters of the network by minimizing the following loss:

$$L(\theta_t) = \mathbb{E}_{s,a,r,s' \sim \rho(.)}\left[(y_t - Q(s, a; \theta_t))^2\right] \text{ where } y_t = r + \gamma \max_{a'} Q(s', a'; \theta_{t-1})$$

Here, y_t is called the temporal difference target, and $y_t - Q$ is called the temporal difference error. ρ represents the behavior distribution, the distribution over transitions (s, a, r, s') collected from the environment. The input to a DQN is a state, s, where each feature of the state space corresponds to an input node, and the output are the various values of $Q(s, a)$ where each output node corresponds to a different action a.

DQNs also resort to *experience replay* to make their updates more stable, by storing each transition (s, a, r, s') in a circular buffer called *the replay buffer* at every time step. Then, instead of using a single transition to compute the loss and back-propagate, a mini-batch of past transitions (randomly sampled) is used instead. This improves the stability of the updates by using uncorrelated transitions in a batch and is called batch learning.

3   OTLPP - Online Transfer Learning for Plastic Policy

In this section, we present our algorithm OTLPP that builds on PLASTIC-Policy [1]. The key aim of this algorithm is to learn to collaborate quickly with unknown teammates that are significantly different from previously encountered teams.

PLASTIC (Planning and Learning to Adapt Swiftly to Teammates to Improve Cooperation) is an algorithm described in [1]. When an ad hoc agent uses PLASTIC, it observes how its team acts and models that behavior to predict the optimal action to take. PLASTIC-Policy is the policy-based version of PLASTIC, which allows it to work in complex and continuous state space domains.

PLASTIC-Policy maintains a probability distribution over all team policies within its library, representing how likely the current team is to its library's team model/policies. The ad hoc agent builds this library from the previous interaction with teammates. To update the distribution, the agent observes the team while it acts and determines which past team is most likely to be the current one. A limitation of PLASTIC-Policy is that it is only effective on a team that resembles a team within its library, meaning the current team must be similar to one of the previously encountered teams so that it can cooperate adequately.

```
 1: function LEARNABOUTPRIORTEAMMATE(t)                                          ▷ t: the prior teammate
 2:     DQN ← a newly initialized Deep Q-Network
 3:     Data ← ∅
 4:     s ← the initial state
 5:     repeat
 6:         a ← DQN(s)
 7:         Take action a and collect (s, a, r, s′)
 8:         Data ← Data ∪{(s, a, r, s′)}
 9:         Add (s, a, r, s′) to DQN's replay buffer and perform batch learning on DQN
10:         s ← s′
11:     until no more transitions are needed
12:     Derive a policy π for t from DQN
13:     Learn a nearest neighbors model m of t using Data
14:     return (π, m)
15: end function
16:
17: function UPDATEBELIEFS(BehaviorDistr, s, s′)      ▷ BehaviorDistr: probability distribution over possible
        teammate behaviors, s: the previous environment state, s′: the new environment state
18:     for (π, m) ∈ BehaviorDistr do
19:         loss ← 1 − P(s′|m, s)
20:         BehaviorDistr(m) ←BehaviorDistr(m)∗(1 − ηloss)
21:     end for
22:     Normalize BehaviorDistr
23:     return BehaviorDistr
24: end function
25:
26: function SELECTACTION(BehaviorDistr, s)  ▷ BehaviorDistr: probability distribution over possible teammate
        behaviors, s: the current environment state
27:     (π, m) = argmax BehaviorDistr                              ▷ select the most likely policy
28:     return π(s)                            ▷ return the action for the given state according to that policy
29: end function
```

Fig. 1. Pseudocode for the policy based implementation of the methods `LearnAboutPriorTeammate`, `UpdateBeliefs`, and `SelectAction` (methods taken from [1] and adapted to use a DQN).

To solve this problem, Sect. 3.2 presents an algorithm that combines a transfer learning algorithm with PLASTIC-Policy, which is the key contribution of our work. In Sect. 3.1, we present the methods from PLASTIC-Policy that have been adapted to use a DQN.

3.1 PLASTIC-Policy Methods

PLASTIC-Policy relies on the `LearnAboutPriorTeammates` function in Fig. 1 to build a team model and policy regarding a previously encountered team. The agent gathers data in the form of the tuple $(s, a, r, s′)$[1] as it plays with a given team. With these tuples, it obtains a policy by using a Deep Q-Network, which is an RL algorithm that uses samples from the transitions to approximate the values of the state-action pairs. It also learns a nearest neighbors model from the same gathered data, to be used later by the PLASTIC-Policy algorithm when making predictions about the new team's behavior.

In `LearnAboutPriorTeammates`, a Deep Q-Network is initialized in Line 2 and the algorithm queries the DQN for which action it should take next (Line 6) and executes it, collecting the tuple $(s, a, r, s′)$ in Line 7. Line 10 adds the tuple to `Data` so that the tuples can be used to build the nearest neighbors model in Line 13. In Line 9, the tuple is also added to the DQN's replay buffer, and the DQN then proceeds to perform batch learning, as described in Sect. 2. Once no more transitions are deemed necessary, the agent derives a policy from the Deep

---

[1] Where s is the original state, a the action taken, r the reward received and $s′$ the resulting state.

```
1: function TRANSFERKNOWLEDGE(BehaviorDistr)   ▷ BehaviorDistr: probability distribution over all known teams
      regarding which one is most similar to the current one.
2:    (π, m) ← argmax BehaviorDistr                                       ▷ get the best policy
3:    DQN_source ← the Deep Q-Network associated with π
4:    DQN_target ← a new Deep Q-Network
5:    Use Parameter Sharing between DQN_source and DQN_target
6:    return DQN_target
7: end function
```

Fig. 2. Pseudocode for the transfer learning algorithm used in this article.

Q-Network (Line 12), which can be done by simply saving a snapshot of the network's weights and later using $DQN(s)$ to select an action, just like Line 6.

PLASTIC-Policy keeps a probability distribution over all previously encountered teams within its library. These beliefs are updated at each timestep as the agent gathers more data regarding the current team. The function UpdateBeliefs, in Line 17 of Fig. 1, presents the pseudocode for updating the beliefs. Line 18 iterates through all team models (i.e., nearest neighbors models) so that, in line 19, it can use the model, along with the original state s, to calculate the probability that the resulting state s' is consistent with the current team. This is done by getting $\hat{s} = m(s)$, where $\hat{s}$ is the closest state in m to s, for some distance measure[2]. Then, the corresponding resulting state, $\hat{s'}$ is obtained from $\hat{s}$[3]. Furthermore, each state feature is compared between s' and $\hat{s'}$ to calculate the probability, where the difference between the two is due to a noise drawn from a normal distribution. These probabilities are then multiplied together to obtain $P(s'|m, s)$. In line 20, the probability distribution is updated for the current team model by a factor of $1 - \eta$loss. The η factor is used to attenuate sporadically incorrect predictions that would otherwise bring the probability of the potentially correct team close to 0. Once all beliefs have been updated, the distribution is normalized (Line 22).

While the agent updates its beliefs, it must also act in the environment to gather further data about the current team. Therefore, it must use one of the policies at its disposal to do so. Choosing which policy to use comes down to simply choosing the team that has the highest belief, according to what the agent has seen so far, as shown in function SelectAction (Line 26 of Fig. 1).

3.2   Combining Transfer Learning and PLASTIC-Policy

Online Transfer Learning for PLASTIC-Policy (OTLPP) is the key contribution of this work, where the ad hoc agent can collaborate with a new team that is significantly different from the team models and policies within its library. OTLPP can effectively leverage the ad hoc agent's past experiences with different teams to quickly adapt to a new one by combining PLASTIC-Policy with Transfer Learning.

---

[2] The only requirement for the distance measure is it to be 0 when $\hat{s} = s$ and close to 0 when $\hat{s}$ and s are considered "similar".

[3] Such association was recorded in LearnAboutPriorTeammates (Fig. 1, line 10).

```
1: function OTLPP(PriorTeammates, HandCodedKnowledge, BehaviorPrior)                    ▷
      PriorTeammates: past teammates the agent has encountered, HandCodedKnowledge: prior knowledge coded
      by hand, BehaviorPrior: prior distribution over the prior knowledge.
2:
3:    PriorKnowledge ← HandCodedKnowledge                    ▷ initialize knowledge from prior teammates
4:    for t ∈ PriorTeammates do
5:        PriorKnowledge ← PriorKnowledge ∪ LearnAboutPriorTeammate(t)
6:    end for
7:    BehaviorDistr ← BehaviorPrior                          ▷ initialize beliefs
8:
9:    Initialize s
10:   repeat                                                 ▷ see which team is the most similar to the current one
11:       a ← SelectAction(BehaviorDistr, s)
12:       Take action a and observe r, s'
13:       BehaviorDistr = UpdateBeliefs(BehaviorDistr, s, s')
14:       s ← s'
15:   until one team has high enough probability
16:
17:   DQN ← TransferKnowledge(BehaviorDistr)                 ▷ use Transfer Learning to adapt to the new team
18:
19:   Initialize s once again
20:   repeat                                                 ▷ begin learning with the jump start from the transferred knowledge
21:       a ← DQN(s)
22:       Take action a and collect (s, a, r, s')
23:       Add (s, a, r, s') to DQN's replay buffer and perform batch learning on DQN
24:       s ← s'
25:   until the agent has learned
26: end function
```

Fig. 3. Pseudocode for OTLPP algorithm, which combines transfer learning with the PLASTIC-Policy algorithm from [1].

One common technique for transferring knowledge between two neural networks is to share the parameters (or part of them) between the source network and the target network [16]. This technique is known as Parameter Sharing, and we used it to transfer knowledge between DQNs. There are several strategies in Parameter Sharing, such as transferring the weights of all layers or just the weights from the shallower (closer to the input) layers. Also, the shallower weights may be frozen, which implies learning will only occur in the deeper layers[4].

The transfer learning algorithm, represented by the function **Transfer Knowledge** in Fig. 2, begins by obtaining the policy that corresponds to the team with the highest probability value, in Line 2. Then, in the following line, it derives a Deep Q-Network from that policy[5], which will be used as the source for the transfer learning algorithm. The target is a newly initialized Deep Q-Network. The final step is to use Parameter Sharing from the source DQN to the target DQN. As mentioned above, all or just a subset of the weights may be transferred, and weight freezing may occur.

In Fig. 3, we present the OTLPP algorithm, which combines transfer learning with PLASTIC-Policy. In Lines 3–7, and much like the original PLASTIC-Policy algorithm, the agent begins by combining some knowledge that may have been hand-coded with knowledge gathered from previously encountered teams by using the **LearnAboutPriorTeammate** function (see Fig. 1). At this point, the ad hoc agent has compiled a library of policies and team models. Therefore, it can reason about the similarities between the current team and each of these past teams.

---

[4] This is done for learning stability reasons.

[5] The policy is actually computed via a Deep Q-Network, so this derivation is straightforward.

In Lines 9–15, the ad hoc agent continuously updates its behavior distribution over the past teams with `UpdateBeliefs` (Fig. 1), while also selecting the next action to take based on the current values of the distribution with `SelectAction` (Fig. 1). Once a certain team reaches some probability threshold of acceptability, indicating that it is indeed the right team, the agent can move on to transferring knowledge (Line 17) from its prior experiences and begin learning a new policy for the new team. In other words, Line 17, obtains a Deep Q-Network whose parameters have been initialized by `TransferKnowledge` (Fig. 2). It can then begin to learn the new policy for the new team, in lines 19–25, with the advantage of not having to start learning from scratch due to the Transfer Learning algorithm.

4   Experimental Setup

This section describes our experimental setup to test the OTLPP algorithm within an agent. We used the Half Field Offense (HFO) simulator [5], a modified version of the RoboCup Soccer Simulation 2D sub-league. In HFO, an offense team tries to score a goal and the defense team tries to prevent it. In addition, only half of the original field is playable, and a defending agent cannot attack nor vice-versa. In following paragraphs, we present the experimental setup in detail.

Test Setting and Agents: All tests were conducted in a 2 vs 2 matches in the HFO, where the ad hoc agent plays with one teammate against two opponents. The opponents are two instances of the `agent2d` and the teammate can be one of the following: `agent2d`, `aut`, `gliders`, `helios`, from 2013, and `receptivity`, from the 2019 RoboCup Soccer Simulation 2D sub-league competition[6] What this means is that the opponents will always act according to the `agent2d` strategy, whereas the teammate can display one of 5 behaviors, according to each of the 5 different types of teammates mentioned above. No behavioral variability was allowed for the opponents, since *ad hoc teamwork* is not concerned with changes in the task (which includes besting the opponents), hence their singular strategy.

State Space: HFO provides two state spaces on the fly: a low-level one and a high-level one. The low-level state space provides $59 + 9T + 9O$ features, where T is the number of teammates (excluding the agent) and O is the number of opponents. These features include the positions and velocities of all agents on the field and of the ball, the sines and cosines of various angles (e.g., goal opening, agent orientation, velocity vector orientation), and other game state variables. The high-level state space provides a higher-level view of the match, which combines the lower-level features into more meaningful ones, exposing only $12 + 6T + 3O$ features. Of these, the following 12 features were selected as the state space for our agent: X position (the agent's X-position on the field); Y position (the agent's Y-position on the field); orientation; ball X (the ball's X-position on the field); ball Y (the ball's Y-position on the field); goal opening angle; proximity to opponent; teammate's goal opening Angle; proximity from the teammate to opponent; pass

---

[6] Agent binaries were downloaded from the following page: https://archive.robocup. info/Soccer/Simulation/2D/binaries/RoboCup/.

opening angle; teammate's X (the X-position of the teammate; teammate's Y (the Y-position of the teammate). We included the agent's position, along with its orientation and the ball's position, for obvious reasons: the agent cannot make the simplest of decisions if it does not know its position and the ball's location. The goal opening angle feature is present so that the agent may decide whether it is worth shooting toward the goal or pass to a teammate, among other scenarios. This is also why we include the proximity to the opponent, the teammate's goal opening and pass angles, and the teammate's position.

Action Space: Although HFO offers action spaces of different levels of abstraction. We decided to use a new action space that resorted almost entirely to delegating to the high-level actions already provided by HFO and preventing some unintended behavior, as explained below. As a result, the following 11 actions were made available to the agent: shoot; short-dribble; long-dribble; pass-to; no-op (the agent takes no action for 4 time-steps); go-to-ball; go-to-goal; go-to-teammate; go-away-from-teammate; go-to-nearest-opponent; go-away-from-opponent.

Reward Function: To create a reward function, we use the status of the game after an action has been taken. The following statuses are available to the agent: in-game (the game is still ongoing); goal; captured-by-defense; out-of-bounds; out-of-time; server-Down. Hence, we use PLASTIC-Policy's reward function [1], which also used the HFO to evaluate the agent's performance. The reward function is the following:

$$R(status) = \begin{cases} 1000 & \text{if } status \text{ is Goal} \\ -1 & \text{if } status \text{ is In-Game} \\ -1000 & \text{otherwise} \end{cases}$$

Deep Q-Network Parameters: The ad hoc agent was first trained using a Deep Q-Network against all 5 different teammate types from scratch. This allowed the agent to have a library of approximately optimal policies for each teammate type. The network has an input layer of 12 nodes to accommodate each of the 12 features from the state space, 3 hidden layers of 512 nodes, an output layer of 11 nodes to indicate the estimated q-value of each of the 11 actions, Rectified linear unit activation functions between all layers, a learning rate of 0.00025, a replay memory capacity of 2.5×10^5 transitions (beginning its use when it has at least 12500 transitions stored), a learning batch size of 64 transitions, an ϵ-greedy action selection (with ϵ having a linear decay that begins at 0.8 and decays to 0.05 after 100000 time-steps), a discount factor, γ, of 0.995, an Adam optimizer [6], a transfer rate of 500 time-steps, and a weight initialization sampled uniformly from $[-\frac{1}{\sqrt{n}}, \frac{1}{\sqrt{n}}]$, where n is the amount of nodes in a given layer.

OTLPP Parameters: Like PLASTIC-Policy, our algorithm relies on a parameter, η, to attenuate sporadic losses on the correct team model. Also, the noise distribution used to compute $P(s'|m, s)$ is a normal distribution of mean 0 and variance σ^2, so σ is also another parameter. The following values were

used in our code: $\eta = 0.10$, and $\sigma = 4.0$. The condition **one team has high enough probability** in Line 15 of Fig. 3 is true at the end of the 25th game, given that at this stage, the agent almost always makes the correct decision regarding its current team. In the `UpdateBeliefs` function (Fig. 1), the probability $P(s'|m,s)$ is calculated by first obtaining the state $\hat{s}$ that is closest to s via the nearest-neighbor model m, obtaining that state's corresponding next state, $\hat{s}'$, and then calculating the distance between the next state and the predicted next state, $d = $ `Distance`$(s', \hat{s}')$. `Distance` can be defined in several different ways, but fundamentally it should be 0 if $\hat{s}' = s'$ and close to 0 if $\hat{s}'$ and s' are considered similar. For this work, and since the intent is to identify which teammate the agent is playing with, the features of the state space that do not pertain to the teammate, such as the opponents' movements or the agent's own movements, should not be considered. Therefore, the only features considered are the teammate's coordinates. Hence, let s_x be the teammate's x-position in a given state s, and s_y its y-position analog. Then, `Distance` is defined as `Distance`$(s', \hat{s}') = \prod_{c \in \{x,y\}}$ `ProbFromNoise`$(s'_c - \hat{s}'_c)$ and `ProbFromNoise`$(\Delta) = 1 - 2 \cdot |F_{N(0,\sigma^2)}(\Delta) - \frac{1}{2}|$, where $F_{N(0,\sigma^2)}$ denotes the cumulative distribution function for a normal distribution of mean $\mu = 0$ and a variance of σ^2. Therefore, `ProbFromNoise` returns the probability that a given value was drawn from a normal distribution. As mentioned before, we use a normal distribution in the equation above because we assume that every transition is affected by the noise of the normal distribution.

Parameter Sharing: During the Transfer Learning stage of the OTLPP algorithm (Fig. 3), the agent uses Parameter Sharing to transfer knowledge between a single source Deep Q-Network and the target Deep Q-Network that will later learn the new policy. We decided to transfer all weights, including those from deeper layers, because the environment and the task remain the same. Therefore, a lot of commonality is expected between how the ad hoc agent should behave when paired with the old teammate and with the new one. However, if the change in teams represents a higher change in the overall problem, perhaps transferring only the shallower layers, which correspond to broader abstractions, could also be used.

5   Results

In our empirical evaluation, the task consists of having our ad hoc agent (with the OTLPP algorithm) cooperate with one of 5 different teammates, namely (`agent2d`, `aut`, `gliders`, `helios`, and `receptivity`). Each teammate was designed independently by developers from different countries for the 2013 and 2019 RoboCup Soccer Simulation 2D sub-league competition. Furthermore, the goal is to score as many goals as possible against a defense team made up of two agents of the type `agent2d`.

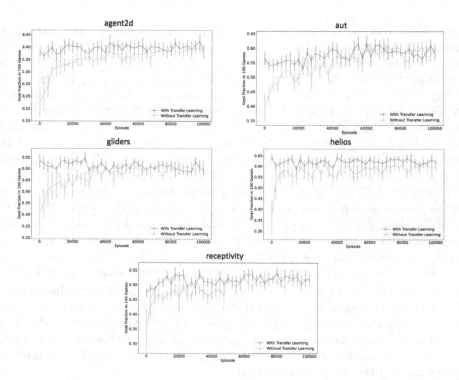

Fig. 4. Comparison between the average goal fraction when the agent uses OTLPP (in red) compared to an RL agent (in green), while playing with each teammate. The vertical bars represent one standard deviation. (Color figure online)

Given that our agent uses a DQN, one way to evaluate the learning procedure at a given point in time is to take a snapshot of its network's parameters at that time and use them to obtain the goal fraction (i.e., the number of goals divided by the number of games). In our experiments, all goal fractions were obtained by running 200 games for the same network parameters and dividing the number of goals scored by that amount. Other metrics may be used, such as the sum of the rewards or the average time to score. However, since the task is ultimately to score a goal, the goal fraction is probably the best metric.

To test the algorithm against each teammate available, we excluded the policy of the teammate from the library, which is the equivalent to calling LearnAboutPriorTeammates (Fig. 1) on all teammates except for the particular one during the execution of OTLPP (Fig. 3). Hence, the ad hoc agent learns the policy of 4 teammates and then uses that knowledge, along with the behavior distribution it maintains over them, to transfer knowledge to a new Deep Q-Network for the 5th teammate.

In Fig. 4, we start showing the ad hoc agent's performance during the learning process, when it resorts to the OTLPP algorithm (red line) with each teammate: agent2d, aut, gliders, helios, and receptivity. We also include the performance of an RL agent (green line), which depicts the performance of an

Table 1. Comparison between the average goal fraction over 100000 episodes when the agent uses PLASTIC-Policy and when it uses OTLPP, for each team.

Team	PLASTIC-Policy	OTLPP
agent2d	0.37	**0.40**
helios	0.61	**0.62**
aut	0.55	**0.58**
gliders	**0.53**	0.51
receptivity	0.47	**0.52**

agent that learns from scratch. From the plots, we can notice that our ad hoc agent with the OTLPP algorithm benefits from a significant boost, when transfer learning takes place at the beginning of learning. In other words, our agent is able to exhibit close-to-optimal behavior from the start.

Finally, Table 1 compares OTLPP's performance with PLASTIC-Policy during run time. In particular, Table 1 compares the average score of an ad hoc agent using PLASTIC-Policy with an ad hoc agent using OTLPP, over 100000 episodes. Each ad hoc agent has 4 policies within its library, and we exclude the policy that corresponds to the current teammate of the ad hoc agent. This evaluation enables us to test the performance of the ad hoc agent with a completely unknown teammate. In bold, we highlight the maximum score between both alternatives. The results show that OTLPP can outperform or perform close to PLASTIC-Policy in every test, showcasing the advantage of our OTLPP algorithm. Hence, OTLPP almost always means an improvement over PLASTIC-Policy.

6   Concluding Remarks

Our paper is the first work to combine a transfer learning method with PLASTIC-Policy in order to create an ad hoc agent that learns to cooperate with a completely unknown teammate. In our empirical evaluation, we show that the combination of a transfer learning method with PLASTIC-Policy can serve as a powerful tool for ad hoc agents. In particular, the results show that OTLPP can outperform or perform close to PLASTIC-Policy. Hence, the ad hoc agent quickly adapts to completely unknown teammates, exhibiting close-to-optimal behavior from the start. As future work, other transfer learning methods may be explored, such as transferring knowledge from multiple sources [3], meaning multiple teams would be a source of transferred knowledge.

References

1. Barrett, S., Rosenfeld, A., Kraus, S., Stone, P.: Making friends on the fly: cooperating with new teammates. Artif. Intell. **242**, 132–171 (2017)
2. Chen, S., Andrejczuk, E., Cao, Z., Zhang, J.: AATEAM: achieving the ad hoc teamwork by employing the attention mechanism. In: AAAI Conference on Artificial Intelligence, vol. 34, pp. 7095–7102 (2020)

3. Ge, L., Gao, J., Zhang, A.: OMS-TL: a framework of online multiple source transfer learning. In: 22nd ACM International Conference on Information and Knowledge Management, pp. 2423–2428 (2013)
4. Iocchi, L., Holz, D., del Solar, J.R., Sugiura, K., van der Zant, T.: RoboCup@Home: analysis and results of evolving competitions for domestic and service robots. Artif. Intell. **229**, 258–281 (2015)
5. Kalyanakrishnan, S., Liu, Y., Stone, P.: Half field offense in RoboCup soccer: a multiagent reinforcement learning case study. In: Lakemeyer, G., Sklar, E., Sorrenti, D.G., Takahashi, T. (eds.) RoboCup 2006. LNCS (LNAI), vol. 4434, pp. 72–85. Springer, Heidelberg (2007). https://doi.org/10.1007/978-3-540-74024-7_7
6. Kingma, D.P., Ba, J.: Adam: a method for stochastic optimization (2014). https://arxiv.org/abs/1412.6980
7. Melo, F.S., Sardinha, A.: Ad hoc teamwork by learning teammates' task. Auton. Agent. Multi-Agent Syst. **30**(2), 175–219 (2016)
8. Mnih, V., et al.: Human-level control through deep reinforcement learning. Nature **518**(7540), 529–533 (2015)
9. Ribeiro, J.G., Faria, M., Sardinha, A., Melo, F.S.: Helping people on the fly: ad hoc teamwork for human-robot teams. In: Marreiros, G., Melo, F.S., Lau, N., Lopes Cardoso, H., Reis, L.P. (eds.) EPIA 2021. LNCS (LNAI), vol. 12981, pp. 635–647. Springer, Cham (2021). https://doi.org/10.1007/978-3-030-86230-5_50
10. Ribeiro, J.G., Martinho, C., Sardinha, A., Melo, F.S.: Assisting unknown teammates in unknown tasks: ad hoc teamwork under partial observability (2022). https://arxiv.org/abs/2201.03538
11. Santos, P.M., Ribeiro, J.G., Sardinha, A., Melo, F.S.: Ad hoc teamwork in the presence of non-stationary teammates. In: Marreiros, G., Melo, F.S., Lau, N., Lopes Cardoso, H., Reis, L.P. (eds.) EPIA 2021. LNCS (LNAI), vol. 12981, pp. 648–660. Springer, Cham (2021). https://doi.org/10.1007/978-3-030-86230-5_51
12. Stone, P., Kaminka, G.A., Kraus, S., Rosenschein, J.S.: Ad hoc autonomous agent teams: collaboration without pre-coordination. In: Twenty-Fourth AAAI Conference on Artificial Intelligence, pp. 1504–1509 (2010)
13. Sutton, R.S., Barto, A.G.: Reinforcement Learning: An Introduction, 2nd edn. MIT Press, Cambridge (2018)
14. Tasaki, R., Kitazaki, M., Miura, J., Terashima, K.: Prototype design of medical round supporting robot "Terapio". In: 2015 IEEE International Conference on Robotics and Automation (ICRA), pp. 829–834 (2015)
15. Watkins, C.J.C.H., Dayan, P.: Q-learning. Mach. Learn. **8**, 279–292 (1992)
16. Zhuang, F., et al.: A comprehensive survey on transfer learning. Proc. IEEE **109**(1), 43–76 (2020)

Bringing Underused Learning Objects to the Light: A Multi-agent Based Approach

André Behr[1]([✉])[iD], José Cascalho[1,2][iD], Armando Mendes[1,2][iD],
Hélia Guerra[1,3][iD], Luis Cavique[4,5][iD], Paulo Trigo[6,7][iD], Helder Coelho[8][iD],
and Rosa Vicari[9][iD]

[1] NIDeS and FCT, University of the Azores, Ponta Delgada, Portugal
`and_behr@hotmail.com`
[2] GRIA and LIACC, Ponta Delgada, Portugal
[3] Centro Algoritmi, University of Minho, Braga, Portugal
[4] Open University, Lisbon, Portugal
[5] LASIGE, University of Lisbon, Lisbon, Portugal
[6] ISEL, Lisbon, Portugal
[7] GuIAA, Lisbon, Portugal
[8] ULisbon, Lisbon, Portugal
[9] Informatics Institute, UFRGS, Porto Alegre, Brazil

Abstract. The digital learning transformation brings the extension of the traditional libraries to online repositories. Learning object repositories are employed to deliver several functionalities related to the learning object's lifecycle. However, these educational resources usually are not described effectively, lacking, for example, educational metadata and learning goals. Then, metadata incompleteness limits the quality of the services, such as search and recommendation, resulting in educational objects that do not have a proper role in teaching/learning environments. This work proposes to bring an active role to all educational resources, acting on the analysis generated from the usage statistics. To achieve this goal, we created a multi-agent architecture that complements the common repository's functionalities to improve learning and teaching experiences. We intend to use this architecture on a repository focused on ocean literacy learning objects. This paper presents some steps toward this goal by enhancing, when needed, the repository to adapt itself.

Keywords: Agent · Multi-agent Systems · Repositories · Metadata · Learning Objects · Analytics

1 Introduction

Due to the advance in e-learning, stakeholders have been employing platforms, tools, and storage widely. At the center of e-learning interactions, the Learning Objects (LOs) have to be concerned with technological and pedagogical aspects for

ⓒ The Author(s), under exclusive license to Springer Nature Switzerland AG 2022
G. Marreiros et al. (Eds.): EPIA 2022, LNAI 13566, pp. 751–763, 2022.
https://doi.org/10.1007/978-3-031-16474-3_61

an effective teaching-learning process [21]. LOs also support the Active Learning concept, where instructional methods engage students in the process of learning.

The development of LOs must consider monitoring different aspects that compose the LO's lifecycle, such as authoring, maintenance, and evaluation [9,21]. Along with these, Learning Object Repositories (LORs) arose to cope with the cited issues. They provide management, discovery, use, and reuse of LOs. Underlying metadata supports LOs' location, dissemination, and harvesting from other applications to handle these subjects [17]. In order to provide some interoperability for repositories, metadata standards also address information for retrieval and exchange. We can cite widespread initiatives to describe LOs at repositories such as Dublin Core [5] as a generic metadata standard, and IEEE-LOM [15] that provides pedagogical aspects.

The advance of open repositories enables the aggregation of several kinds of learning objects that once were at individual websites. With that, it is possible to guarantee the availability of materials, improving the learning experience for students and teachers.

However, Santos-Hermosa *et al.* [17] indicate that most open education-related repositories lack educational metadata and learning goals for LOs. Another issue is that data and metadata fragments have been replicating over repositories, such as authors or intended end-user groups [6]. Furthermore, there is a lack of high-quality services, such as search and recommendation services. Although attempts to automatize quality assessment, they do not rely on models that can predict the quality based on metadata or an intelligent model [19].

In order to improve the user experience, repositories have been incorporating general recommender techniques, such as Content-Based Filtering, Collaborative Filtering, and Hybrid, that focus on the user's behavior (and historical activity) and similarity among users and items [1]. However, they also have to deal with the insufficient existence of data in literature called the Cold Start problem. Besides, some search mechanisms employ ranking metrics to sort results that benefit items with more activity, such as the number of views, downloads, and rates [14]. These approaches can isolate and render obsolete some learning objects in the repository, and users will have difficulty reaching them.

As learning objects are available in a repository, metadata tends to be duplicated or poorly filled. Though, it could bring unsatisfactory services, such as search and recommendations, leading users to use their preferred generalist search engines instead of searching suitable educational material in the repository. These can lead to an underused repository, especially with few accessed learning objects.

Another issue is related to how the users perceive the repository. Most users can consider it just a library of resources and not a place for collaborative learning. So, the possibility of social interaction at repositories does not necessarily entail user participation. Users tend to consume rather than contribute in this kind of environment.

Multi-agent Systems (MAS) are an interesting alternative to deal with these issues, because it is able to model and simulate entities like human behavior. Beyond that, agent-based software systems can be developed in various contexts and interact with several systems [10].

This work combines a repository of learning objects and agents to manage the LO lifecycle in a repository contributing to its proper use. Agent technology is also employed to look at the other side of usage to bring up-to-date underused learning objects in cooperation with their owners. Also, it tries to repackage its metadata to improve its visibility. To evaluate and act on that, we designed the Active-Learning Object Repository (A-LOR) system for learning object repositories improvement, contributing to a more active sharing of LOs, using collaborative agents advising or assisting users in making decisions and reconfiguring metadata.

In the next section, we contextualize this work with our learning object repository Re-Mar. We revise and describe related current works about multi-agent systems and learning objects. The following section presents some technical aspects of the A-LOR based on a multi-agent interaction to provide dynamics in learning object repositories. The paper ends with a discussion and a conclusion to guide future works.

2   Re-Mar: Repository of Marine Learning Objects

Re-Mar[1] [3] is a learning object repository in the context of the multidisciplinary project SeaThings[2]. The project focuses on ocean literacy improvement, providing LOs related to ocean subjects for students and teachers. The repository intends to provide Artificial Intelligence (AI) aspects of LO authoring, recommendations, usage, and searching supported by agent-based tools and ontologies. It is important to note that the marine literacy theme is of primordial relevance in archipelagic regions such as the Azores. Thus, active repository maintenance is a way to introduce this theme in the classroom. Re-Mar follows the MILOS' infrastructure architecture [8] and has a three-layered architecture composed of Ontologies, Agents, and Interface Facilities, as depicted in Fig. 1.

The Ontology level is responsible for the specification of knowledge that the agents will share among them, such as ontologies for the Agent-based Learning Objects (OBAA) metadata, learning domain, and curricular structure. OBAA is a Brazilian metadata standard effort to describe learning objects, compliant with IEEE-LOM metadata that also extends it in several ways to deliver a complete description [20]. Complementary to it, Re-Mar reuses the GEMET[3] thesaurus to provide related marine domain concepts (with Azores terms extension) at searching. A Linked Data repository also stores the LOs' metadata to build a knowledge graph that is machine compliant. Agents could benefit from these machine-understandable artifacts accessed by the Jena[4] framework and Web Ontology Language (OWL) Application Programming Interface (API).

---

[1] http://re-mar.uac.pt.
[2] https://fgf.uac.pt/en/content/sea-things-objetos-de-aprendizagem-para-promover-literacia-oceanica.
[3] https://www.eionet.europa.eu/gemet/en/exports/rdf/latest.
[4] https://jena.apache.org/.

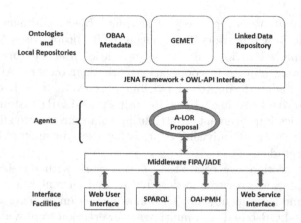

Fig. 1. Overview of Re-Mar infrastructure architecture [4].

The Interface and Facilities level ensures communication with the Agents level by Java Agent DEvelopment Framework (JADE) under the standard Foundation of Intelligent Physical Agents (FIPA) for message exchange. JADE is one of the most widely used tools to create agent-based software systems [10] and supports messages with common understanding through ontology. At this level, e.g., Virtual Learning Environments (VLE), LORs, web servers, and different services can communicate with agents.

At Re-Mar, there is a workflow submission to publish a learning object. After logging, the user uploads the learning object file(s) and thumbnail. Then fill out a form with metadata fields, such as title, description, keywords, learning objectives, and pedagogical strategies. After that, there are the scientific and pedagogical review steps before the learning object is available at the repository.

To monitor the user interaction with LOs, Re-Mar has been storing some useful statistics. Thus, it tracks when a user visualizes, downloads, likes, or rates a LO. As time goes by, the repository naturally separates frequently used LOs from others that are not.

This work will explore the communication among Agents and Re-Mar LOR to get along with this non-generative behavior of users through its use statistics. Agents are employed to cope with the burden of the LO lifecycle, bringing collaborative intelligence between human and computer agents.

3   A Review on Multi-agents Systems and Learning Objects

Diverse techniques can be applied with the agent technology to improve LO reuse, especially in search and recommendation. This section will depict some works related to multi-agents and learning objects.

SIMROAA [13] is a multi-agent system for recommending accessible learning objects. The agents promote the recovery and the recommendation of LOs.

One human agent and another three agents: recommender, analyzer, and data, composed the architecture. The Data Agent leads with the repository metadata. There are no further details on how the Analyzer Agent uses history and knowledge to perceive the environment. The recommender, a content-based model, calculates a similarity measure between the new object and liked objects.

Agents can be used to find suitable partners through conversations and produce a chain-like sequence of LOs. Then, a Multi-Agent Systems (MAS) could automatically create a course content package by remixing LOs based on the input syllabus from different repositories. In the [12] approach, the system has two types of agents: a set of LORs Agents and a single Coordinator Agent. LOs are assigned to the syllabus by a fuzzy coefficient interpreted as a coverage probability.

In the context of learning management systems, the concept of an Intelligent Learning Object (ILO) is presented in [2]. An ILO is an "agent capable of playing the role of a LO, which can acquire new knowledge" of its interaction with students and other ILOs. The system uses the Jadex framework[5] that supports a Belief-Desire-Intention (BDI) agents' architecture. Within this system, additional LOs could be displayed to the student during a learning session, depending on the student's performance. There are no further details about this recommendation.

In [7], a combination of multi-agent systems provides independent services for a LOR. In this work, an ontology-based search engine system has been integrated to catalogue and edit learning object metadata, and assist users without technical knowledge of LO metadata standards.

Learning objects repository and a multi-agent system can also be combined to generate recommendations using clustering learning [11]. LO recommendation results are related to learning style, evaluation by other users, and students' prior knowledge. The clustering agent retrieves numeric metadata from the federation agent to apply the k-means algorithm.

Both tasks of monitoring and incorporating learning object changes can employ Agents. The proposed framework by [18] was composed of Content Change Receptor Agent, Learning Object Change Analyser Agent, Manage Learning Repository Agent, and Learning Content Change Revision Agent. Besides, agents can interoperate through different baseline ontologies for modeling the learning contents, such as lessons, topics, subtopics, and their annotations and instances.

In [16], multi-agents also adapt multimedia documents to users and their devices' interfaces. Agents' cooperation may optimize service plan selection, composition, and execution. Several agents, such as client-server, reasoning, decision, facilitator, and adaptation service, can compose the MAS. The reasoning agent uses ontologies to deduce the adaptation guideline corresponding to one or more context constraints.

All previous works intervene, at some point, in the learning object lifecycle with multi-agents. However, none of them monitor LOs' use and reconfigure

---

[5] https://www.activecomponents.org/.

metadata of unused learning objects. Also, we work with a multi-criteria methodology to analyze not only likes or numeric metadata.

4   Active-Learning Object Repository (A-LOR)

In this section, we present an overview of the multi-agent architecture that supports the A-LOR. It is expected to provide engagement to LOs in their repository lifecycle and to improve their usage by users over time. The main idea is to carry LO's information by agents to furnish a set of features that can turn LOs more proactive in a repository. In this way, the agents will always be concerned about the shared educational resources repository, providing an active ("dynamic") environment.

4.1   A-LOR's Agents Overview

A-LOR has seven agents, as depicted in Fig. 2. They communicate using FIPA Agent Communication Language (ACL) messages and may share an ontology with typed communicative acts. We start by explaining the role different agents have in this architecture. Then we present what we have done regarding achieving the objectives.

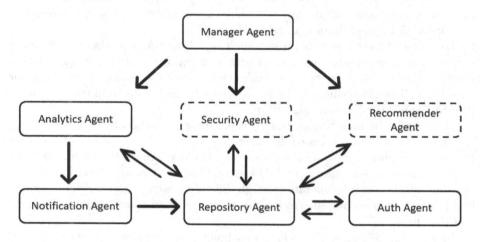

Fig. 2. A-LOR overview of agents' in a communication diagram.

The Manager Agent is the central agent of the social organization. This agent knows the majority of agents and their functions. Its purpose is to act as a "daemon" and enable the other agents' tasks according to a certain period.

One of the seven agents, the main scope of this work, is the Analytics Agent. It is responsible for the evaluation and management of the learning object repository. It reaches all available LOs communicating with the Repository Agent.

After evaluation, it reports to the Notification Agent that calls the Repository Agent to store a notification. Then the LO's owner (who submitted) could show the LO on the Re-Mar's main page, update its metadata, share the LO on social networks, or even do nothing about it at the moment.

Furthermore, this agent can perceive the LO usage and usability statistics. For instance, it can identify the most prolific authors, often LOs used to generate new LOs, main knowledge areas with more examples of LOs, or keywords used by users with scarce LOs examples. In addition, it can understand which LOs are underused and propose to the owners to edit the metadata or make a new classification to improve its use.

The Repository Agent is responsible for the tasks related to the local repository that stores LO's metadata and statistics. Some repository-related tasks are search, store, update, and delete. Before performing these database operations, this agent has to call the Auth Agent to obtain a valid JSON Web Token (JWT) for authorization privileges.

After well-established analytics, a Recommender Agent will interact in the organization. It can assist users while they are filling in metadata for authoring. For example, with title and description, it can suggest suitable keywords. The offered suggestions can concern reusing already described previous metadata fragments. This agent is also responsible to provide LOs suggestions by analyzing users' profiles and ontologies. It can help in LO searching by providing related concepts to terms searched by users through a semantic search in local/external ontologies.

Another concern is related to the security aspects of the learning object repository. Thus a Security Agent could monitor the repository, searching for malicious files or users.

The Recommendation Agent and the Security Agent have not been implemented yet. For this reason they are with dotted ellipses in Fig. 2.

4.2   Analytics from Statistics of Use

The Analytics Agent can process a large volume of data. As depicted in the sequence diagram of Fig. 3, this agent is dynamic, and the Manager Agent can active it with a call after a time window, e.g., each month. In its task, the Analytics Agent evaluates all active LOs by requesting them to the Repository Agent. After the evaluation, it sends a message to the Notification Agent to organize the information stored by the Repository Agent. This stored notification will advise the user in the repository after a new login.

This agent evaluates LO's usage statistics (s_i) in the repository, such as the number of visualizations, downloads, rates, and likes. Re-Mar also monitors the owner's actions in the notification loop, how to show OA on the main page, and edit metadata doing a review. Note that reviews here are the number of times LO stepped back to the workflow submission for the edition. It is natural for recent learning objects to have lower scores, so LOs more recent than the time window is not considered in the assessment.

Due to the previous history of interactions, it is clear that usually are more views than downloads, likes, and rates. To balance these attributes (n), we employ a weighted average score function stated as:

$$Score = \sum_{i=1}^{n} \frac{w_i * s_i}{w_i} \tag{1}$$

Our score function provides a higher weight (w_i) to reviews than other measures such as being on the first page, notifications, rates, likes, downloads, and views. In the current round of tests, we attached 20, 15, 10, 8, 7, 4, and 2 as weight values, respectively. The weights reflect the importance degree of the measures in the final score used for the decision. These can drive underused LOs to gain preference and visibility. This approach uses multi-criteria decision analysis concepts, namely a weighted decision method.

Table 1 exemplifies the learning objects' data (by id) organized by groups and ordered by score. We can note, for example, that the LO with id 53 (LO_{53}) has more downloads and views than the LO_{16}. However, the LO_{53} score is lower than the LO_{16} because of the number of rates and likes. As is common in weighted decision methods, compensations and trade-offs are possible. Another concern is to preferably LOs that have not been notified yet For example, the LO_{37}, even with more balanced usage statistics than the LO_{50}, has a lower score because it has no notifications.

Table 1. Tracking user interactions to score learning objects

w_i	s_i	LO_{54}	LO_{53}	LO_{16}	LO_{47}	LO_{37}	LO_{50}	LO_{38}	LO_{40}	⋯
20	#review	0	0	0	0	0	0	0	1	
15	#atMainPage	0	0	0	0	0	1	1	1	
10	#notification	0	0	0	0	0	1	1	1	
8	#rate	0	1	2	3	5	2	10	21	
7	#like	1	1	5	1	5	3	7	13	
4	#download	1	4	3	5	7	3	16	28	
2	#view	1	7	5	13	15	38	44	51	
Score		0.1970	0.6818	1.1061	1.1667	2.0152	2.2727	4.6364	7.8485	⋯

In this way, we consider an ascending score ranking to underused LOs (with lower scores) in the repository. With that information, the agents can suggest actions to concede more visibility to specific LOs.

4.3   User Notification

When the Analytics Agent completes the evaluation, it generates a list of interactions for each LO in the repository based on the pre-defined weights, as depicted in Table 1. Then it gets the first five items of the list ordered by an ascendant score to deliver to the Notification Agent. Then this agent prepares the data to be stored by the Repository Agent.

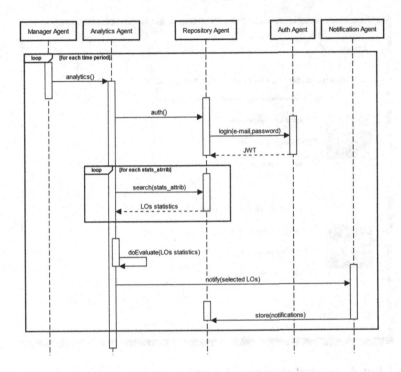

Fig. 3. Sequence diagram for analytics.

In this way, after login, each owner of these five learning objects is notified, as depicted in Fig. 4. The owner can accomplish four static actions related to the LO. (i) Present it on the main page for a while (the same time window that Analytics Agent waits to act). (ii) Edit its metadata to add/modify some information. (iii) Share it on social media. (iv) Do nothing about it this time. When the owner chooses no action, the Notification Agent expires the previous list before storing the new notifications. There is also a limit of three times in sequence with option iv selection.

5   Discussion

The concrete utilization of a learning object is difficult to notice. In the Re-Mar repository, interactions such as rating and likes are measures to understand when a user interacted with the learning object since download and visualization measures may not reflect such attention.

Instead of giving the spotlight to trending learning objects in a repository, A-LOR's focus is on trying to balance proper use. It hopes to reach some key points to promote the dynamism of LOs. (i) Flexibility: with an adjunct agent architecture, it is possible to add or modify agents without affecting the main functionality of the repository. Agents can also communicate with users inside and outside (*e.g.* social networks) the repository, promoting LOs or requesting some LO

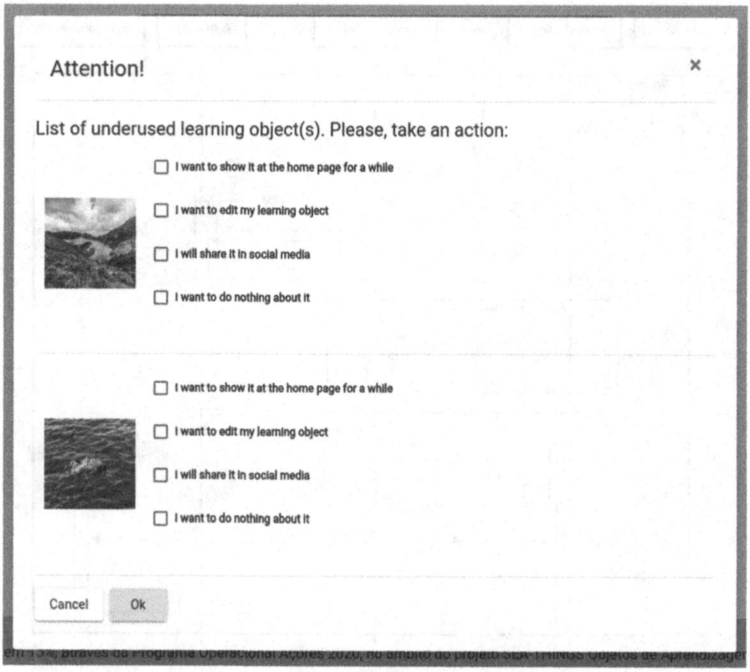

Fig. 4. Notification window for user decision-making in Re-Mar.

improvement. (ii) Advanced search: use the agents' interface to search across multiple linked data endpoints, helping users fill in metadata and search the repository through a knowledge graph. (iii) Feedback: request comments/assessment of users to improve LO recommendations. (iv) Analytics-oriented: wrapper similar group of learning objects to provide helpful new metadata and classification. Also, employ a usage rank for users and LOs based on related search terms, views, downloads, and reuse relations. (v) External repositories: to have more than one repository for searching related material and use agents as a communication interface. (vi) Metadata verification: utilize OBAA metadata ontologies to group close-matching LOs and verify metadata consistency.

The analytics granularity also can be taken into account. Aspects considering a specific LO, LOs groups, or even an entire repository. Some statistics assess the richness of the repository. The need to estimate how the repository's assessment uses some metric is relevant to provide managers feedback continuously. Statistics from the number of users vs. active users, LOs submitted vs. LOs reused, accesses vs. downloads, and knowledge area vs. LO type are possibly related the way LOs disseminate in the user community.

Temporal aspects are also relevant in defining a time window for analysis. How to define when a LO was widely used? How long should be the time window? Do students tend to consume the LOs just in-class semesters? The Analytics Agent could act to answer these questions with gathered statistics. In addition,

it still has to consider a learning process that improves weights and attributes (usage statistics) over time.

With a considerable amount of data and the use of unsupervised learning techniques, such as clustering and other methodologies (*e.g.* analog search), we can predict the usage of new LOs. Using examples of a similar group of LOs that have been in the repository for some time, it is also possible to predict what type of user can utilize a new LO for learning. This information could be sent to LOs producers to improve the construction of new LOs or enhance the ones already in use.

Furthermore, exploring AI techniques can support agents learning through their lifecycle and interaction. Suggest a LO classification within a group could be achieved with Machine Learning techniques. Also, Deep Learning technology with active learning algorithms can explore LOs interactions among them. LO usage and how metadata values are defined could use Reinforcement Learning.

6   Conclusion

General repositories have not achieved their full potential yet. They usually operate as the old libraries where the LO stays, waiting for someone to get interested in it. This behavior, allied to common recommender systems, usually favors just the trending learning objects. In this way, LOs tend to be like immutable artifacts.

This work aims to enhance learning objects in repositories to be more active in their lifecycle through an agent-based auxiliary system. The goal is that agent groups could interact among them to provide new functionalities to the repository to embrace the LO owners' side despite the related works that usually involve the LO users.

The proposed A-LOR system has seven main agents that cooperate in providing LOs with improved performance on LORs. Our approach shows that agents afford a flexible solution and that a multi-criteria decision analysis can be used with agents to deliver a decision method.

The next objective, continuing this work, is that agents could interact and learn among themselves to enhance LORs to be more active. Therefore, agents can help users concerned about the impacts of LO metadata in the environment (repository).

In future work, with the amount of LOs growing in the Re-Mar repository, it is expected to re-evaluate the A-LOR to have a continuously active repository. With a critical mass of data, Artificial Intelligence techniques can play a major role in helping agents to reach their goals.

Acknowledgements. This work is financed by the FEDER in 85% and by regional funds in 15%, through the Operational Program Azores 2020, within the scope of the SEA-THINGS Learning Objects to Promote Ocean Literacy project ACORES-01-0145-FEDER-000110. This study was also financed in part by the Coordenação de Aperfeiçoamento de Pessoal de Nível Superior - Brasil (CAPES) - Finance Code 001.

References

1. Al-Ghuribi, S.M., Mohd Noah, S.A.: Multi-criteria review-based recommender system-the state of the art. IEEE Access **7**, 169446–169468 (2019). https://doi.org/10.1109/ACCESS.2019.2954861
2. de Amorim, J., Silveira, R.A.: ILOMAS: an intelligent learning objects implementation study case. In: Bajo, J., et al. (eds.) PAAMS 2016. CCIS, vol. 616, pp. 428–434. Springer, Cham (2016). https://doi.org/10.1007/978-3-319-39387-2_36
3. Behr, A., et al.: Re-Mar: repository of marine learning objects. In: Anais do XII Workshop de Computação Aplicada à Gestão do Meio Ambiente e Recursos Naturais, pp. 137–146. SBC (2021)
4. Behr, A., et al.: Recommending metadata contents for learning objects through linked data. In: De La Prieta, F., El Bolock, A., Durães, D., Carneiro, J., Lopes, F., Julian, V. (eds.) PAAMS 2021. CCIS, vol. 1472, pp. 115–126. Springer, Cham (2021). https://doi.org/10.1007/978-3-030-85710-3_10
5. DCMI: DCMI metadata terms. Technical report (2020). https://www.dublincore.org/specifications/dublin-core/dcmi-terms/. Accessed December 2020
6. Gabdank, I., et al.: Prevention of data duplication for high throughput sequencing repositories. Database **2018**, 1–10 (2018)
7. Gluz, J.C., Silveira, E.L., Da Silva, L.R.J., Barbosa, J.L.V.: Towards a semantic repository for learning objects: design and evaluation of core services. J. UCS **22**(1), 16–36 (2016)
8. Gluz, J.C., Vicari, R.M., Passerino, L.M.: An agent-based infrastructure for the support of learning objects life-cycle. In: Cerri, S.A., Clancey, W.J., Papadourakis, G., Panourgia, K. (eds.) ITS 2012. LNCS, vol. 7315, pp. 696–698. Springer, Heidelberg (2012). https://doi.org/10.1007/978-3-642-30950-2_126
9. Gluz, J.C., Vicari, R.M.: Rumo a uma plataforma semântica de conteúdos educacionais digitais: o modelo ontológico. In: Brazilian Symposium on Computers in Education (Simpósio Brasileiro de Informática na Educação-SBIE), vol. 25, p. 993 (2014)
10. Kravari, K., Bassiliades, N.: A survey of agent platforms. J. Artif. Soc. Soc. Simul. **18**(1), 11 (2015)
11. Marín, P.A.R., Duque, N., Ovalle, D.: Multi-agent system for knowledge-based recommendation of learning objects. ADCAIJ: Adv. Distrib. Comput. Artif. Intell. J. **4**(1), 80–89 (2015)
12. Mosharraf, M., Taghiyareh, F.: Automatic syllabus-oriented remixing of open educational resources using agent-based modeling. IEEE Trans. Learn. Technol. **13**(2), 297–311 (2019)
13. Mourão, A.B., Netto, J.F.M.: SIMROAA multi-agent recommendation system for recommending accessible learning objects. In: 2019 IEEE Frontiers in Education Conference (FIE), pp. 1–9. IEEE (2019)
14. de Oliveira, M.R., et al.: Open educational resources platform based on collective intelligence. In: 2018 IEEE 4th International Conference on Collaboration and Internet Computing (CIC), pp. 346–353. IEEE (2018)
15. Use at Your Own Risk: Draft standard for learning object metadata. IEEE Standard 1484(1) (2002)
16. Saighi, A., Laboudi, Z.: A novel self-organizing multi agent-based approach for multimedia documents adaptation. In: 2020 International Conference on Electrical, Communication, and Computer Engineering (ICECCE), pp. 1–6. IEEE (2020)

17. Santos-Hermosa, G., Ferran-Ferrer, N., Abadal, E.: Repositories of open educational resources: an assessment of reuse and educational aspects. Int. Rev. Res. Open Distrib. Learn. IRRODL **18**(5), 84–120 (2017)
18. Sarwar, S., Qayyum, Z.U., Safyan, M., Iqbal, M.: A multi agent framework for effective change management of learning contents in semantic e-learning. In: International Conference on Advances in Education and Social Sciences (2018)
19. Tavakoli, M., Elias, M., Kismihók, G., Auer, S.: Metadata analysis of open educational resources. In: LAK21: 11th International Learning Analytics and Knowledge Conference, pp. 626–631 (2021)
20. Vicari, R.M., Ribeiro, A., da Silva, J.M.C., Santos, E.R., Primo, T., Bez, M.: Brazilian proposal for agent-based learning objects metadata standard - OBAA. In: Sánchez-Alonso, S., Athanasiadis, I.N. (eds.) MTSR 2010. CCIS, vol. 108, pp. 300–311. Springer, Heidelberg (2010). https://doi.org/10.1007/978-3-642-16552-8_27
21. Vieyra, G.Q., González, L.F.M.: Learning objects in online education: a systemic approach. Eur. J. Educ. **3**(3), 62–71 (2020)

TeMA - Text Mining and Applications

Expanding UlyssesNER-Br Named Entity Recognition Corpus with Informal User-Generated Text

Rosimeire Costa[1(✉)], Hidelberg Oliveira Albuquerque[2,4], Gabriel Silvestre[3],
Nádia Félix F. Silva[1,3], Ellen Souza[2,3,4], Douglas Vitório[2,4], Augusto Nunes[3],
Felipe Siqueira[3], João Pedro Tarrega[3], João Vitor Beinotti[3],
Márcio de Souza Dias[3,5], Fabíola S. F. Pereira[3,6], Matheus Silva[1],
Miguel Gardini[3], Vinicius Silva[3], André C. P. L. F. de Carvalho[3],
and Adriano L. I. Oliveira[4]

[1] Instituto de Informática, Federal University of Goiás, Goiânia, Brazil
{rosimeire_pereira,matheus_silva}@discente.ufg.br, nadia.felix@ufg.br
[2] MiningBR Research Group, Federal Rural University of Pernambuco, Recife, Brazil
{hidelberg.albuquerque,ellen.ramos}@ufrpe.br
[3] Institute of Mathematics and Computer Sciences, University of São Paulo,
São Paulo, Brazil
{gdalforno7,augustonunes,felipe.siqueira,joao.tarrega,
joaobeinotti,miguelgardini,vinicius.adolfo.silva}@usp.br,
andre@icmc.usp.br
[4] Centro de Informática, Federal University of Pernambuco, Recife, Brazil
{damsv,alio}@cin.ufpe.br
[5] Federal University of Catalão, Catalão, Brazil
marciodias@ufcat.edu.br
[6] Federal University of Uberlândia, Uberlândia, Brazil
fabiola.pereira@ufu.br

Abstract. Named Entity Recognition (NER) is a challenging Natural Language Processing task for a language as rich as Portuguese. When applied in a scenario appropriate to informal language and short texts, the task acquires a new layer of complexity, handling a particular lexicon to the domain in question. In this paper, we expanded the UlyssesNER-Br corpus for NER task with Brazilian Portuguese comments about bills. Additionally, we enriched the annotated set with a formal corpora, in order to analyze whether the combination of formal and informal texts from the same domain could improve NER. Finally, we carry out experiments with a Conditional Random Fields (CRF) model, a Bidirectional LSTM-CRF (BiLSTM-CRF) model, and subsequently, we realized fine-tuning of a language model BERT on NER task with our dataset. We concluded that formal texts helped identification of entities in informal texts. The best model was the fine-tuned BERT which achieved an F1-score of 73.90%, beating the benchmark of related works.

Keywords: Named Entity Recognition · Corpus annotation · Informal text · Legal text

© The Author(s), under exclusive license to Springer Nature Switzerland AG 2022
G. Marreiros et al. (Eds.): EPIA 2022, LNAI 13566, pp. 767–779, 2022.
https://doi.org/10.1007/978-3-031-16474-3_62

1   Introduction

Named-entity recognition (NER) is a task of natural language processing (NLP) that aims to identify and classify all named entities such as person names, locations, among others, in a text. This information is useful by itself or to facilitate other NLP tasks, including text summarizing and automatic translation [31].

The NER task was presented at the 6th Message Understanding Conference (MUC-6), with a focus on the information extraction [17]. In 2015, a Twitter[1] NER shared task was created for Workshop on Noisy User-generated Text (W-NUT) as the majority of NER systems were developed for newswire, not having a satisfactory performance in more colloquial text genres, because of the diverse and noisy user-generated text (UT). For instance, tweets, contrary to formal text genres, have abbreviations, non-trustworthy capitals, etc. [5].

Li et al. 2020 [23] point that one of the greatest challenges for NER task is developing models that achieve a better performance in colloquial text genres, as the best performance observed in the W-NUT-2017 [14] had an F-score slightly higher than 40%. According to the author, having a higher score in informal texts is more challenging compared to formal ones, because of their size (usually shorter), noise and the specific domain to which the UT belongs.

According to [12] and [9], recent studies on NER applied to Portuguese show evidences that the models available for that language still reach the state-of-the-art with difficulty, what can be justified by the low volume of textual information and tools developed to this language when compared to the English language.

There are several NER works focused on the legal domain [3,4,6,8,9,15, 25,32,34], however, only a few of them focus on the Portuguese Language [6, 9,25,32]. Concerning the NER corpus available for formal texts, we identified only two works [6,25] that approach specifically legislative documents written in Portuguese.

Despite the recent NLP task studies on informal corpora for Portuguese [7,10,13,19,20,27], no specific study on NER task was identified.

Given the lack of corpora available to NER in Portuguese added to the absence of works developed for formal texts, the three main contributions of this paper are: **i)** a UT corpus for NER, in Portuguese, in the legislative domain, named C-corpus, which is an extension of UlyssesNER-Br [6]. The C-corpus was collected from an online platform that enables all Brazilian citizens to interact and express their opinions concerning bills being discussed by the parliament; **ii)** an investigation of the hypothesis that models trained using documents of different types (formal and informal texts) can increase the quality of predictions, compared to modeling each genre separately; and **iii)** the training and evaluation of the Conditional Random Fields (CRF), Bidirectional LSTM-CRF (BiLSTM-CRF), and BERT models for the corpora under analysis. All these resources are available for download[2].

The remainder of this paper is structured as follows: Sect. 2 briefly presents the major related studies. Section 3 describes, the process behind the annotation

---

[1] https://twitter.com.

[2] https://github.com/Convenio-Camara-dos-Deputados/ccorpus-epia.

of the dataset, including the different semantic classes annotated. Section 4 describes the C-corpus characteristics, followed by an evaluation. Section 5 presents a discussion about this work, and Sect. 6 brings the conclusion and highlights future works.

2 Related Work

The main channel for disseminating works related to the entity recognition in informal texts is the *Workshop on Noisy User-generated Text (W-NUT)* [5], with the all works focusing on English language. In addition to the works presented at this event, [30] proposed to study this same problem in informal Chinese texts. We detailed these studies in this section.

The first edition of W-NUT Workshop took place in 2015 and presented two Named Entity Recognition shared tasks for *Twitter* messages: one for segmentation and classification (Task 1), and the other only for entity segmentation (Task 2) [5]. This edition attracted eight teams and the winner of both tasks was [40], which obtained an F1 score of 56.41% in Task 1 and 70.63% in Task 2. They used Entity Linking, a method to detect mentions of entities in the text and resolve them to corresponding entries in knowledge bases such as Wikipedia.

In the second edition of the W-NUT, in which the Twitter Named Entity Recognition W-NUT-16 corpus was made available [36], a named entity tagging task with 10 teams participating was proposed. The best result obtained was presented by [24], reaching the F1-score, for segmentation and classification of 52.41% with a Bi-LSTM model, which automatically induces and leverages orthographic features when performing NER. For segmentation only (Task 2) the same team wins with an F1-score of 65.89%.

In 2017, the third edition of the W-NUT took place, and provided the W-NUT-17 corpus [14], focusing on previously-unseen and rare entities in the context of emerging discussions. This corpus includes text from Twitter, Reddit[3], Youtube[4], and StackExchange[5]. The best result was presented by [1], with a F1-score, at the entity level, of 41.86% (task 1). The multitasking neural network architecture proposed by [1] learn higher-order feature representations from strings of words and characters, along with Part-of-Speech tags and information from gazetteers. This neural network acts as a resource extractor to feed a Conditional Random Field (CRF) classifier. For Task 2, the same team wins with 40.24% of F1-score.

More recently, [37] showed that external document-level contexts can significantly improve model performance for W-NUT-16 and W-NUT-17 corpora. They selected a text set through a search engine using the original sentence as the query, and contextual representations were computed on concatenation of a sentence and its external contexts. The authors applied this contextual

---

[3] https://reddit.com.

[4] https://youtube.com.

[5] https://stackexchange.com.

Table 1. NER studies in informal texts.

Study	Corpus	Method	F1-score	Lang.
[40]	W-NUT-2015	Entity linking	56.41%	English
[24]	W-NUT-2016	Bi-LSTM	52.41%	English
[37]	W-NUT-2016	a neural model with a CRF layer	58.98%	English
[1]	W-NUT-2017	Bi-LSTM	41.86%	English
[37]	W-NUT-2017	a neural model with a CRF layer	60.45%	English
[30]	WeiboNER	CRF	56.05%	Chinese
[39]	WeiboNER	FGN with LSTM-CRF	71.25%	Chinese

representation as input in neural model with a CRF layer and achieved 58.98% and 60.45% of F1-Score for W-NUT-16 and W-NUT-17, respectively.

Peng [30] provided WeiboNER, a Chinese corpus for NER, which was built from a Chinese social media platform. The authors evaluated three types of embeddings for informal text, and with the Conditional Random Fields model, they obtained an F1-score of 56.05%.

Xuan et al. [39] proposed a method for Chinese NER, which can extract interactive information between the character distributed representation and the representation of glyphs by a fusion mechanism, named by FGN (Fusion Glyph Network). This method can capture potential interactive knowledge between context and glyph. Experiments have shown that FGN with LSTM-CRF as tagger achieves a new state-of-the-art performance for the dataset WeiboNER, with an F1-score of 71.25%.

We shall remark that our research differs from the existing work due several aspects: (i) We study a legislative domain in open social media platform to the citizen[6] which text is informal and short, having less than 500 characters. (ii) As far as we know, there is no corpus for recognizing named entities in short texts and informal domains for Portuguese. (iii) In addition to providing a corpus of UT to NER, in the legislative domain, we evaluated the benefits of training a model from one formal collection of texts annotated in the same domain, but from different source; and (iv) we experiment CRF, BiLSTM-CRF and BERT models for the corpora, which are a state of the art for many NLP tasks [35]. All these resources are available for download from the project's GitHub (See footnote 2). The Table 1 summarizes the Related Works.

3   Method

The method used in this paper followed the same used by [6], both in the structure of the corpus and annotation process.

---

[6] https://www.camara.leg.br/enquetes/.

Table 2. UlyssesNER-Br: categories and types [6].

Category	Type	Description	Example	#Tokens[a]	#Unique tokens[a]
DATA (Date)	—	Date	01 de janeiro de 2020	45	34
EVENTO (Event)	—	Event	Eleições de 2018	154	72
FUNDAMENTO (Law foundation)	FUNDlei	Legal norm	Lei no 8.666, de 21 de junho de 1993	209	86
	FUNDapelido	Legal norm nickname	Estatuto da Pessoa com Deficiência	180	72
	FUNDprojetodelei	Bill	PEC 187/2016	21	12
	FUNDsolicitacaotrabalho	Legislative consultation	Solicitação de Trabalho n° 3543/2019	0	0
LOCAL (Location)	LOCALconcreto	Concrete place	Niterói-RJ	161	67
	LOCALvirtual	Virtual place	Jornal de Notícias	16	15
ORGANIZAÇÃO (Organization)	ORGpartido	Political party	PSB	12	9
	ORGgovernamental	Governmental organization	Câmara dos Deputados	376	132
	ORGnãogovernamental	Non-governmental organization	Conselho Reg. de Medicina (CRM)	49	38
PESSOA (Person)	PESSOAindividual	Individual	Jorge Sampaio	134	101
	PESSOAgrupoind	Group of individuals	Família Setúbal	7	7
	PESSOAcargo	Occupation	Deputado	272	137
	PESSOAgrupocargo	Group of occupations	Parlamentares	649	200
PRODUTO DE LEI (Law product)	PRODUTOsistema	System product	Sistema Único de Saúde (SUS)	10	6
	PRODUTOprograma	Program product	Programa Minha Casa, Minha Vida	5	5
	PRODUTOoutros	Others products	Fundo partidário	609	167

[a]Quantities referring to the C-corpus.

3.1 UlyssesNER-Br Named Entity Recognition Corpus

The UlyssesNER-Br corpus contains seven semantic classes or categories. Five of them were based on HAREM [33]: *person, location, organization, event,* and *date*. In addition, two other classes were defined for the legislative domain: *law foundation*, which makes reference to entities related to laws, resolutions, decrees, as well as to domain-specific entities such as bills and legislative consultations; and *law product*, which refers to systems, programs, and other products created from legislation. Some of the categories are also divided in types, and Table 2 summarizes them.

The UlyssesNER-Br corpus was built using two types of legislative documents: bills (*Projetos de Lei*[7] - *PL*), public documents available on the Chamber's portal on the Web[8], and legislative consultations (*Solicitações de Trabalho - ST*), internal documents provided by the staff of the Chamber of Deputies. The legislative consultations were not used for this paper due to they contain information classified as confidential. For standardization purposes, we will name the bill corpus as PL-corpus.

As both of the documents types previously used to built the corpus were written in a formal way, we have annotated citizen's comments related to the bills PEC32/2020, PL318/2021, PL2893/2019, PL3019/2020, PL4425/2020, PEC10/2020, EMP5=>PEC10/2020, PL2578/2020, PL591/2021, PL461/2021 and others[9], collected from the polls in the Chamber of Deputies web portal, in order to analyze whether the combination of formal and informal texts from the same domain could improve NER. These polls are an instrument of citizen participation in the law-making process, in which the user can make its participation through a website[10], voting if they are for or against the proposition, as well as formulate a commentary.

---

[7] Portuguese Expression for legislation projects or bills.
[8] https://www.camara.leg.br/buscaProposicoesWeb/.
[9] The bills list of corpus is in project's GitHub.
[10] https://www.camara.leg.br/enquetes/.

3.2   C-corpus

To built this new subset, called C-corpus[11], we followed the same approach from [6], we have annotated the same entities, except FUNDsolicitacaotrabalho. The annotation was performed by three groups of annotators, in which each group was composed of two undergraduate students who were responsible for the annotation, while a graduate student performed the curatorship, and being the disagreements periodically discussed.

This process took place in three phases. In the first one, a training step was carried out, in which 20 comments were annotated by all teams. In the second phase, the documents were sent daily to the teams and, at the end of each day, the monitoring of the Cohen's kappa agreement measure [11] was performed, in addition with frequent meetings being held between curators and annotators. At the end of this phase, 300 comments were annotated. Finally, in the last phase, in which 669 comments were annotated, the meetings were held only when requested by the annotators or curators, and the Cohen's kappa was computed only at the end of the process. Table 2 shows the absolute number of tokens of the entities by type in the C-corpus.

The annotation was performed using the INCEpTION [22][12] tool, which provides an environment for many annotation tasks in written text. Figure 1 shows examples of the entities annotated in the comments. The three teams achieved the following Cohen's kappa coefficient: 65%, 87% and 85%, in the second phase. In third phase they achieved 79%, 86% and 83%, respectively.

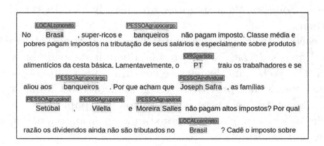

Fig. 1. Entity annotation process using INCEpTION.

4   Experimental Results

The experiments were divided into three parts. In the first, the CRF model was used. In the second part, we use the BiLSTM-CRF model, and finally the fine-tuned BERT model. Subsequently, we evaluated the hypothesis that training NER models using data from documents of different types increases the quality of predictions when compared to modeling each genre independently.

---

[11] The C-corpus is available on the project's GitHub.
[12] https://inception-project.github.io/.

4.1 Experimental Settings

The following features were used for the experiments with the CRF model, with inspiration in [2]. *1) Context words:* Refers to the words surrounding the current word. In this work, was considered the previous and the next word. *2)Lowercase word*: the current word in lowercase. *3) Part of speech (POS) tag*: Returns the grammatical class of the current word. *4) First uppercase character*: Indicates whether the first character of the current word is capitalized. *5)Digit*: Indicates whether all characters are digits. *6)Prefix and suffix*: The suffixes and prefixes of the current word were considered, up to the third position character. *7) First word*: Indicates whether the current word is the first word in the sentence. *8) Last word*: Indicates whether the current word is the last word in the sentence.

Features 2 to 6 of the previous word and the posterior of the current word were also added.

In experiments with BiLSTM-CRF, an open source implementation [16] was used, without changing the hyperparameters proposed by them. We used GloVe word embeddings with 300 dimensions provided by [21, 26].

We used the BERTimbau Base model [35] to realize further pre-training with the C-Corpus sentences. From this specialized model to our texts, we perform the fine-tuning for the named entity recognition task. The hyperparameters for fine-tuning the BERT model for NER were the same used by [18]. The batch size equals 4, the learning rate equals 2e-5, and the choice of the number of epochs equals 3, given that overfitting for higher numbers occurred. We used PyTorch [28] as a Deep learning framework, as well as the tokenizer, pre-trained model, optimizer, and scheduler from HuggingFace [38].

In the experiments with BiLSTM-CRF and fine-tuned BERT model we considered a training-test-validation split of 70%-15%-15%, the sentences were randomly selected for each type with non-overlapping set, and for CRF, we considered train+validation sets in training phase and test in the same setting. Each was repeated 5 times, and the mean and standard deviation of accuracy, recall, and F1-score were reported. We used the CRF implementation from Scikit-learn [29].

4.2 Results

To test our hypothesis, one model was trained for each possible way of joining the training sets and their performance was assessed separately on the validation set. The results of each variation of the CRF, BiLSTM-CRF and fine-tuned BERT model in each test set are shown in Table 3.

Of the three NER models, fine-tuned BERT model achieved the best performance for all training and test set configurations, considering the F1-score. It is also interesting to note that the simplest corpus to model was the PL-corpus, when compared the C-corpus. This is mainly due to the fact that in the PL-corpus the number of sentences available for training the model is much greater. The presence of a less formal language in the C-corpus, significantly hindered the learning of semantic relationships between entities by NER algorithms.

Table 3. Results with dataset aggregation for training the CRF, BiLSTM-CRF+GloVe, and fine-tuned BERT models. P was used for Precision, R for Recall, and F1 for F1-score. PL-corpus was used for legislation projects or bills and C-Corpus for our corpus. The term "All" means the union of PL-corpus and C-corpus in the training set. The best results are in bold.

Results with dataset aggregation for training the CRF model

Level	Training set	Test set	P	R	F1	Level	Training set	Test set	P	R	F1
Categories	PL-corpus	PL-corpus	84.06	80.97	82.48	Types	PL-corpus	PL-corpus	82.78	79.47	81.09
	C-corpus		26.56	22.04	24.09		C-corpus		26.13	19.37	22.24
	All¹		81.76	79.30	80.51		All		80.93	78.63	79.76
	PL-corpus	C-corpus	49.01	24.92	33.04		PL-corpus	C-corpus	26.13	19.37	22.24
	C-corpus		**73.78**	55.89	63.60		C-corpus		74.43	54.88	63.18
	All		69.26	59.93	64.26		All		69.92	57.91	63.35

Results with dataset aggregation for training the BiLSTM-CRF+GloVe

Level	Training set	Test set	P	R	F1	Level	Training set	Test set	P	R	F1
Categories	PL-corpus	PL-corpus	**85.1±0.12**	78.16±0.12	81.48±0.28	Types	PL-corpus	PL-corpus	**85.24±1.17**	74.65±4.83	79.57±3.26
	C-corpus		18.03±1.30	16.19±0.91	17.06±0.91		C-corpus		25.27±1.65	19.53±1.32	22.03±0.72
	All		79.27±2.45	75.37±1.39	78.48±1.69		All		78.31±3.15	75.14±2.22	76.5±1.54
	PL-corpus	C-corpus	36.49±2.63	14.34±0.643	19.54±1.54		PL-corpus	C-corpus	35.99±0.89	13.66±1.64	18.82±1.14
	C-corpus		64.42±3.21	22.65±1.87	33.5±2.36		C-corpus		69.3±2.94	20.89±0.81	32.10±1.17
	All		68.07±3.13	38.05±2.43	48.81±2.43		All		**74.44±2.55**	39.83±1.60	51.89±1.84

Results with dataset aggregation for training the fine-tuned BERT

Level	Training set	Test set	P	R	F1	Level	Training set	Test set	P	R	F1
Categories	PL-corpus	PL-corpus	83.65± 1.63	87.80±0.87	85.67±1.23	Types	PL-corpus	PL-corpus	79.99±1.37	85.03±1.63	82.43±1.49
	C-corpus		33.62±2.19	39.91±4.51	36.46± 3.11		C-corpus		34.57±4.95	43.0±4.30	38.28 ±4.57
	All		83.49±0.92	**88.28± 0.79**	85.82±0.73		All		81.32± 0.88	**86.92± 0.43**	**84.02±0.61**
	PL-corpus	C-corpus	56.22±3.39	56.24±1.77	56.21±2.39		PL-corpus	C-corpus	52.71±4.83	51.96±2.28	52.29±3.38
	C-corpus		68.65±1.64	75.50±2.72	71.89±1.71		C-corpus		64.75±3.13	73.70±3.50	68.88±2.40
	All		70.38±1.81	**77.81±1.32**	**73.90±1.31**		All		68.06±1.74	**74.30±1.95**	**71.05±1.80**

It was observed that the models, when trained only with the C-corpus, obtained bad predictions for the PL-corpus. The poor performance was supposedly due to informal vocabulary and lack of examples for tags. It is still possible to analyze that the fine-tuned BERT trained with the union of the C-corpus with the PL-corpus was the only model that reported gains in the predictions of the PL-corpus tags.

The models trained only with the PL-corpus obtained bad predictions for the C-corpus. Which can be explained by the different examples of entities found in PL-corpus. However, the fine-tuned BERT trained with the union of the C-corpus and the PL-corpus obtained a considerable improvement in the C-corpus predictions, obtaining an F1-score of 73.90%.

5   Discussion

From the results found, it is noticeable that training the NER model with sentences from formal texts added to informal texts was essential for good quality predictions for informal texts. Although the CRF and BiLSTM-CRF model trained with the PL-corpus joined to the C-corpus did not obtain the best result for the PL-corpus test set, it was not far behind the best model in absolute terms, as it obtained greater robustness in all the cases.

Considering the best model in each case, that is, the fine-tuned BERT model trained by joining the PL-corpus to the C-corpus, the performance of each model in each category and type of named entities was analyzed.

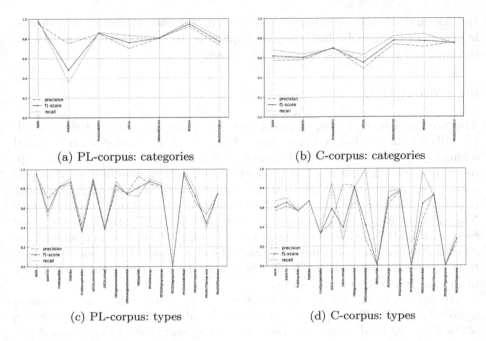

(a) PL-corpus: categories   (b) C-corpus: categories

(c) PL-corpus: types   (d) C-corpus: types

Fig. 2. Fine-tuned BERT model results: chances of success by categories and types.

In the analysis by categories, Fig. 2(a) and Fig. 2(b) shows that, for the PL-corpus, the categories "DATA" and "PESSOA" were more easily identified by the model. We assume that the absence of "EVENTO" examples induced the model to have more difficulties in correctly identifying and classifying entities with this category. For the C-corpus, it was possible to verify a smaller oscillation in the metrics of the categories, varying around 70% in all cases.

As shown in Fig. 2(c), in the analysis by types in PL-corpus, the entities "DATA" and "PESSOAindividual" obtained the best results from the BERT, with F1-score above 90%. The entity "PESSOAgrupoind" was ignored due to its total absence in this type of document.

Finally, the entities "ORGgovernamental", "PESSOAgrupocargo" and "PRODUTOoutros" obtained the best results in the C-corpus, with F1-score above 75% (Fig. 2(d)). The other entities presented a medium performance, confirming what was previously stated, that the comments are slightly more complicated to model due to their linguistic structure. The scarce entities in this corpus were "ORGpartido", "PESSOAgrupoind", and "PRODUTOprograma".

The results found showed that, in the datasets used, the addition of formal texts to informal texts helped the NER models to identify entities in informal texts. It was also observed that the union of the two datasets in the training set helped the BERT model to identify the entities of formal texts. In this sense, some observations can be made: the need for a larger general set of entity samples (for example, in C-corpus, only about 5% of the comments are associated with

entities) and a better distribution among them; the corpora union compensates for the lack of entities in the C-corpus, simplifying the semantic relations between the entities by the presence of more formal sentences.

6 Conclusion

This work presented "C-corpus", a corpus of citizen's comments related to Brazilian bills for Named Entity Recognition. The texts were annotated and curated manually by 3 work teams in 3 phases, and contain named entities that represent organization, people, law products, location, law foundation, event and date. Additionally, we enriched the annotated UlyssesNER-Br corpus in order to analyze whether the combination of formal and informal texts could improve NER. Finally, we trained Conditional Random Fields (CRF), BiLSTM-CRF and fine-tuned BERT models. According experiments, the formal texts improved the identification of entities in informal text. The fine-tuned BERT model has best results, with an average F1-score of 73.90% in analysis by categories, and 71.05% in the analysis by types of C-corpus.

As future work, we asses the effects of applying other deep learning approaches for NER [6,9] in informal text. In addition, there is an expansion of the UlyssesNER-Br corpus in progress, adding texts concerning political discourses in order to increase the number of entities examples.

References

1. Aguilar, G., Maharjan, S., López-Monroy, A.P., Solorio, T.: A multi-task approach for named entity recognition in social media data. In: Proceedings of the 3rd Workshop on Noisy User-Generated Text, Copenhagen, Denmark, September, pp. 148–153. Association for Computational Linguistics (2017)
2. Amaral, D.O.F., Vieira, R.: NERP-CRF: uma ferramenta para o reconhecimento de entidades nomeadas por meio de Conditional Random Fields. Linguamática (Braga) (2014)
3. Angelidis, I., Chalkidis, I., Koubarakis, M.: Named entity recognition, linking and generation for Greek legislation. In: JURIX, pp. 1–10. IOS Press (2018)
4. Badji, I.: Legal entity extraction with NER systems. Master's thesis, Universidad Politécnica de Madrid (2018)
5. Baldwin, T., de Marneffe, M., Han, B., Kim, Y., Ritter, A., Xu, W.: Shared tasks of the 2015 workshop on noisy user-generated text: Twitter lexical normalization and named entity recognition. In: Proceedings of the Workshop on Noisy User-generated Text, Beijing, China, July, pp. 126–135. ACL (2015)
6. Albuquerque, H.O., et al.: UlyssesNER-Br: a corpus of Brazilian legislative documents for named entity recognition. In: Pinheiro, V., et al. (eds.) PROPOR 2022. LNCS (LNAI), vol. 13208, pp. 3–14. Springer, Cham (2022). https://doi.org/10.1007/978-3-030-98305-5_1
7. Capellaro, L., Caseli, H.: Análise de polaridade e de tópicos em tweets no domínio da política no Brasil. In: Anais do XIII Simpósio Brasileiro de Tecnologia da Informação e da Linguagem Humana, Porto Alegre, RS, Brasil, pp. 47–55. SBC (2021)

8. Cardellino, C., Teruel, M., Alemany, L.A., Villata, S.: A low-cost, high-coverage legal named entity recognizer, classifier and linker. In: Proceedings of the 16th Edition of the International Conference on Articial Intelligence and Law, ICAIL 2017, New York, NY, USA, pp. 9–18. ACM (2017)
9. Castro, P.V.Q.d.: Deep learning for named entity recognition in legal domain. Master's thesis, Universidade Federal de Goiás (2018)
10. Christhie, W., Reis, J., Moro, F., Almeida, V.: Detecção de posicionamento em tweets sobre política no contexto brasileiro. In: Anais do VII Brazilian Workshop on Social Network Analysis and Mining, Porto Alegre, RS, Brasil. SBC (2018)
11. Cohen, J.: A coefficient of agreement for nominal scales. Educ. Psychol. Measur. **20**(1), 37–46 (1960)
12. Collovini, S., Bonamigo, T.L., Vieira, R.: A review on relation extraction with an eye on Portuguese. J. Braz. Comput. Soc. **19**, 553–571 (2013)
13. Cortiz, D., et al.: A weakly supervised dataset of fine-grained emotions in Portuguese. In: Anais do XIII Simpósio Brasileiro de Tecnologia da Informaaao e da Linguagem Humana, Porto Alegre, RS, Brasil, pp. 73–81. SBC (2021)
14. Derczynski, L., Nichols, E., van Erp, M., Limsopatham, N.: Results of the WNUT2017 shared task on novel and emerging entity recognition. In: Proceedings of the 3rd Workshop on Noisy User-generated Text, Copenhagen, Denmark, September, pp. 140–147. ACL (2017)
15. Dozier, C., Kondadadi, R., Light, M., Vachher, A., Veeramachaneni, S., Wudali, R.: Named entity recognition and resolution in legal text. In: Francesconi, E., Montemagni, S., Peters, W., Tiscornia, D. (eds.) Semantic Processing of Legal Texts. LNCS (LNAI), vol. 6036, pp. 27–43. Springer, Heidelberg (2010). https://doi.org/10.1007/978-3-642-12837-0_2
16. Genthial, G.: Tensorflow - Reconhecimento de entidade nomeada. GitHub repository. https://github.com/guillaumegenthial/tf_ner. Accessed 24 Feb 2022
17. Grishman, R., Sundheim, B.: Message understanding conference - 6: a brief history. In: The 16th International Conference on Computational Linguistics, COLING 1996, vol. 1 (1996)
18. Guillou, P.: Finetuning of the specialized version of the language model BERTimbau on a token classification task (NER) with the dataset LeNER-Br. GitHub repository. https://github.com/piegu/language-models. Accessed 30 Mar 2022
19. Gumiel, Y., Lee, I., Soares, T., Ferreira, T., Pagano, A.: Sentiment analysis in Portuguese texts from online health community forums: data, model and evaluation. In: Anais do XIII Simpósio Brasileiro de Tecnologia da Informação e da Linguagem Humana, Porto Alegre, RS, Brasil, pp. 64–72. SBC (2021)
20. Hammes, L., Freitas, L.: Utilizando bertimbau para a classificação de emoções em português. In: Anais do XIII Simpósio Brasileiro de Tecnologia da Informação e da Linguagem Humana, Porto Alegre, RS, Brasil, pp. 56–63. SBC (2021)
21. Hartmann, N., Fonseca, E., Shulby, C., Treviso, M., Silva, J., Aluísio, S.: Portuguese word embeddings: evaluating on word analogies and natural language tasks. In: Proceedings of the 11th Brazilian Symposium in Information and Human Language Technology, Uberlândia, Brazil, pp. 122–131. SBC (2017)
22. Klie, J.-C., Bugert, M., Boullosa, B., Eckart de Castilho, R., Gurevych, I.: The INCEpTION platform: machine-assisted and knowledge-oriented interactive annotation. In: Proceedings of the 27th International Conference on Computational Linguistics: System Demonstrations, pp. 5–9. ACL (2018)
23. Li, J., Sun, A., Han, J., Li, C.: A survey on deep learning for named entity recognition. IEEE Trans. Knowl. Data Eng. **34**(1), 50–70 (2020)

24. Limsopatham, N., Collier, N.: Bidirectional LSTM for named entity recognition in Twitter messages. In: Proceedings of the 2nd Workshop on Noisy User-Generated Text (WNUT), Osaka, Japan, December, pp. 145–152. The COLING 2016 Organizing Committee (2016)

25. Luz de Araujo, P.H., de Campos, T.E., de Oliveira, R.R.R., Stauffer, M., Couto, S., Bermejo, P.: LeNER-Br: a dataset for named entity recognition in Brazilian legal text. In: Villavicencio, A., et al. (eds.) PROPOR 2018. LNCS (LNAI), vol. 11122, pp. 313–323. Springer, Cham (2018). https://doi.org/10.1007/978-3-319-99722-3_32

26. Repositório de Word Embeddings do NILC. http://www.nilc.icmc.usp.br/embeddings. Accessed 12 Feb 2022

27. Pardo, T., Duran, M., Lopes, L., Felippo, A., Roman, N., Nunes, M.: Porttinari - a large multi-genre treebank for Brazilian Portuguese. In: Anais do XIII Simpósio Brasileiro de Tecnologia da Informação e da Linguagem Humana, Porto Alegre, RS, Brasil, pp. 1–10. SBC (2021)

28. Paszke, A., et al.: PyTorch: an imperative style, high-performance deep learning library. In: 33rd Conference on Neural Information Processing Systems (NeurIPS 2019), Vancouver, Canada (2019)

29. Pedregosa, F., et al.: Scikit-learn: machine learning in Python. J. Mach. Learn. Res. **12**, 2825–2830 (2011)

30. Peng, N., Dredze, M.: Named entity recognition for Chinese social media with jointly trained embeddings. In: Proceedings of the 2015 Conference on Empirical Methods in Natural Language Processing, Lisbon, Portugal, September, pp. 548–554. ACL (2015)

31. Poostchi, H., Zare Borzeshi, E., Piccardi, M.: BiLSTM-CRF for Persian named-entity recognition ArmanPersoNERCorpus: the first entity-annotated Persian dataset. In: Proceedings of the Eleventh International Conference on Language Resources and Evaluation (LREC 2018), Miyazaki, Japan, May. European Language Resources Association (ELRA) (2018)

32. Quaresma, P., Gonçalves, T.: Using linguistic information and machine learning techniques to identify entities from juridical documents. In: Francesconi, E., Montemagni, S., Peters, W., Tiscornia, D. (eds.) Semantic Processing of Legal Texts. LNCS (LNAI), vol. 6036, pp. 44–59. Springer, Heidelberg (2010). https://doi.org/10.1007/978-3-642-12837-0_3

33. Santos, D., Cardoso, N.: A golden resource for named entity recognition in Portuguese. In: Vieira, R., Quaresma, P., Nunes, M.G.V., Mamede, N.J., Oliveira, C., Dias, M.C. (eds.) PROPOR 2006. LNCS (LNAI), vol. 3960, pp. 69–79. Springer, Heidelberg (2006). https://doi.org/10.1007/11751984_8

34. Savelka, J., Ashley, K.D.: Detecting agent mentions in US court decisions. In: JURIX, pp. 39–48. IOS Press (2017)

35. Souza, F., Nogueira, R., Lotufo, R.: BERTimbau: pretrained BERT models for Brazilian Portuguese. In: 9th Brazilian Conference on Intelligent Systems, BRACIS, Rio Grande do Sul, Brazil, 20–23 October (2020)

36. Strauss, B., Toma, B., Ritter, A., de Marneffe, M.-C., Xu, W.: Results of the WNUT16 named entity recognition shared task. In: Proceedings of the 2nd Workshop on Noisy User-Generated Text (WNUT), Osaka, Japan, December, pp. 138–144. The COLING 2016 Organizing Committee (2016)

37. Wang, X., Jiang, Y., Bach, N., Wang, T., Huang, Z., Huang, F., Tu, K.: Improving named entity recognition by external context retrieving and cooperative learning (2021)

38. Wolf, T., et al.: Transformers: state-of-the-art natural language processing. In: Proceedings of the 2020 Conference on Empirical Methods in Natural Language Processing: System Demonstrations, pp. 38–45. ACL, October 2020
39. Xuan, Z., Bao, R., Jiang, S.: FGN: fusion glyph network for Chinese named entity recognition. In: Chen, H., Liu, K., Sun, Y., Wang, S., Hou, L. (eds.) CCKS 2020. CCIS, vol. 1356, pp. 28–40. Springer, Singapore (2021). https://doi.org/10.1007/978-981-16-1964-9_3
40. Yamada, I., Takeda, H., Takefuji, Y.: Enhancing named entity recognition in twitter messages using entity linking. In: Proceedings of the Workshop on Noisy User-Generated Text, pp. 136–140 (2015)

Neural Question Generation
for the Portuguese Language:
A Preliminary Study

Bernardo Leite[1,2]([✉]) [iD] and Henrique Lopes Cardoso[1,2] [iD]

[1] Faculty of Engineering of the University of Porto (FEUP), Porto, Portugal
[2] Artificial Intelligence and Computer Science Laboratory (LIACC), Porto, Portugal
{bernardo.leite,hlc}@fe.up.pt

Abstract. *Question Generation* (QG) is an important and challenging problem that has attracted attention from the natural language processing (NLP) community over the last years. QG aims to automatically generate questions given an input. Recent studies in this field typically use widely available question-answering (QA) datasets (in English) and neural models to train and build these QG systems. As lower-resourced languages (e.g. Portuguese) lack large-scale quality QA data, it becomes a significant challenge to experiment with recent neural techniques. This study uses a Portuguese machine-translated version of the SQuAD v1.1 dataset to perform a preliminary analysis of a neural approach to the QG task for Portuguese. We frame our approach as a sequence-to-sequence problem by fine-tuning a pre-trained language model – T5 for generating factoid (or *wh*)-questions. Despite the evident issues that a machine-translated dataset may bring when using it for training neural models, the automatic evaluation of our Portuguese neural QG models presents results in line with those obtained for English. To the best of our knowledge, this is the first study addressing Neural QG for Portuguese. The code and models are publicly available at https://github.com/bernardoleite/question-generation-t5-pytorch-lightning.

Keywords: Natural language processing · Neural question generation · Language model · T5

1 Introduction

Question Generation (QG) concerns the task of automatically generating grammatically and semantically correct questions from a range of data sources, such as free text, raw data, or knowledge bases [34]. QG has practical importance in education: it can be used to generate well-formed questions that are crucial for evaluating a student's knowledge and stimulate self-learning, as well as to generate classroom quizzes and assessments [20]. In fact, there is a promising use of QG as a component in adaptive, intelligent tutoring systems [25]. Also, QG helps to improve Question Answering (QA) systems [2]. QA corpora are typically composed of paragraphs and question-answer pairs manually written

© The Author(s), under exclusive license to Springer Nature Switzerland AG 2022
G. Marreiros et al. (Eds.): EPIA 2022, LNAI 13566, pp. 780–793, 2022.
https://doi.org/10.1007/978-3-031-16474-3_63

(human-authored) based on the paragraphs. Following this reasoning, QG assists QA by providing additional question-answer pairs. Conversational and chatbots systems also benefit from QG, as their purpose is to create computer-human dialogue interactions. To achieve this, they require similar datasets containing question-answer pairs. As such, we see QG as a valuable and promising task.

Traditional research in QG mainly relies on linguistic transformation rules for generating factoid questions. More recently, given the significant advances in deep learning, QG research has started to adopt neural techniques [28], focusing on end-to-end neural models and giving rise to the *Neural* QG paradigm. One of the drawbacks related to these neural approaches is their reliance on large-scale quality QA datasets, which are not widely available for languages other than English. SQuAD v1.1 [33] is a reference dataset for both QA and QG systems, consisting of about 100K ⟨*question, answer*⟩ pairs. Because SQuAD v1.1 is originally available in English, it is not straightforward to use it for QA or QG in other languages. To overcome this, some researchers have used translated versions of the dataset to build QA systems [6, 8, 13].

Inspired by this, this study aims to use a Portuguese-translated version [7] of the SQuAD v1.1 dataset for addressing Neural QG, for which no prior work exists addressing Portuguese, to the best of our knowledge. We make use of the pre-trained language model T5 [32], which has been shown to achieve state-of-the-art results in multiple downstream NLP tasks. We fine-tune the T5 model for generating Portuguese open-domain factoid questions given a paragraph and target answer. Figure 1 outlines an illustrative example of five generated questions from the same source paragraph but with different target answers. The contributions of this work are two-fold: (1) the introduction of the Neural QG paradigm in the Portuguese context and (2) the establishment of baseline results for Portuguese Neural QG with the assistance of a (machine-translated) well-known QA dataset.

The rest of the paper is organized as follows. In Sect. 2, we analyze previous studies for QG, and we address previous research that has been performed targeting the Portuguese language. In Sect. 3, we present the methodology followed for Portuguese Neural QG. We describe the experimental setup in Sect. 4. In Sect. 5 we discuss the obtained results and cover an error analysis in Sect. 6. Finally, we put forward final remarks in Sect. 7.

Passage: *Afonso Henriques, também chamado de Afonsinho, e cognominado de "o Conquistador", foi o primeiro Rei de Portugal. Passa a intitular-se "Rei dos Portugueses" a partir de 1140 e reinou de jure a partir de 5 de outubro de 1143, com a celebração do Tratado de Zamora, até à sua morte. Era filho de Henrique, Conde de Portucale e sua esposa Teresa de Leão.*

Question 1: *Quem foi o primeiro rei de Portugal? Afonso Henriques*
Question 2: *Qual era o outro nome para Afonso Henriques? Afonsinho*
Question 3: *Qual era o apelido de Afonso Henriques? "o Conquistador"*
Question 4: *Em que ano foi celebrado o Tratado de Zamora? 1143*
Question 5: *Quem era o pai de Afonso Henriques? Conde de Portucale*

Fig. 1. Examples of Portuguese generated questions from a Wikipedia passage.

2 Related Work

We here look at question generation from a methodological perspective (including both traditional and neural techniques) and its application in the Portuguese context.

2.1 Traditional vs Neural Question Generation

Traditional research in QG has focused on templates [26], syntactic [18] and semantic-based [27] approaches, where well-designed rules and heavy human labor are required for declarative-to-interrogative sentence transformations. In contrast, recent Neural QG approaches motivate the use of end-to-end architectures, where QG is formulated as a sequence-to-sequence (seq2seq) problem [16]. These seq2seq approaches typically use an input text to feed an RNN-based (or transformer-based) encoder and generate questions about the text through a decoder. This way, QG requires less human labor than when using transformation rules, and thus enables better language flexibility compared to question templates [28]. However, as stated earlier, this requires the use of large-scale quality QA corpora in the target language, which may not always be available.

Recent studies have explored fine-tuning methods toward Natural Language Generation (NLG), typically by incorporating pre-trained language models into the seq2seq architecture, and have shown promising results on a range of NLG tasks [15]. For instance, Xiao *et al.* (2020) [37] proposed an enhanced seq2seq pre-training framework called *ERNIE-GEN* incorporating both noise-aware generation and infilling generation mechanisms, resulting in state-of-the-art results for QG. For this task, we aim to fine-tune a pre-trained language model – T5 [32] – which we further describe in Sect. 3.

2.2 Question Generation for the Portuguese Language

While most QG studies focus on English, we focus our study on Portuguese. Some researchers have addressed this problem in Portuguese, following traditional techniques. We provide a general overview of these studies.

Curto (2010) [11] proposed a platform to assist on multiple-choice test items based on two approaches. The first is based on rules that use dependencies and word features. The second uses the web to automatically generate syntactic patterns, given a set of question/answering pairs. Diéguez *et al.* (2011) [14] target factoid questions, by combining a case-based reasoning system and a module for QG. The QG module considers manually built rules that are fed to the case-based reasoning engine, which then selects which of them will be used. Correia *et al.* (2012) [10] have worked on the generation of fill-in-the-blank questions concerning vocabulary. They proposed a supervised machine learning technique (using support vector machines) to define whether a given sentence can be used as a basis for a question. Recently, Gonçalo Oliveira (2021) [19]

employed transformer-based language models for answering these type of questions. Pirovani *et al.* (2017) [30] have worked on the generation of both factoid and fill-in-the-blank questions from named entities, targeting Brazilian Portuguese. The authors' goal is to generate questions for assessing the knowledge acquired by the text reader. Ferreira *et al.* (2020) [17] have exploited chunks, named entities combined with handcrafted rules, as well as semantic role labeling for generating factoid questions. Leite *et al.* (2020) [22] also proposed to generate factoid questions using a rule-based method with respect to three linguistic aspects: syntax, semantic, and dependency features. Finally, for complementing the previous study, Leite (2020) [21] has explored means for generating multiple-choice and fill-in-the-blank questions concerning Portuguese grammar, with difficulty control concerns (the resulting application is available[1]).

Although we do not rule out the usefulness of these studies, they only apply traditional QG techniques, which can be limiting, as their methodologies are confined to the variety of templates and transformation rules exploited. As such, the originality of this proposal is supported by the employment of recent neural models for QG in the Portuguese language.

3   T5 for Question Generation

Text-to-Text-Transfer-Transformer (T5) was proposed by Raffel *et al.* (2020) [32]. As stated by the authors, the main underlying idea for T5 is to treat every text processing problem as a "text-to-text" problem, i.e. taking text as input and creating new text as output. The model was pre-trained on the Colossal Clean Crawled Corpus (C4)[2], which comprises around 750GB of clean English text. In the multilingual version, mC4 is used (includes Portuguese). Interestingly, T5 achieved state-of-the-art results on multiple NLP text-to-text benchmarks, including document summarization and question answering. On this basis, we fine-tuned T5 for QG, which can be seen as the inverse task of QA. By fine-tuning, we mean that the model has been pre-trained in an initial task (e.g., fill-in-the-blanks) using large-scale corpora (C4) and then retrained on a specific dataset (i.e., SQuAD v1.1) and downstream task (QG). Figure 2 illustrates this process. The fine-tuning process focuses on generating questions given a pair $\langle context, answer \rangle$.

Formally, given the context C and answer A, the goal is to generate a question Q that satisfies:

$$\hat{Q} = \underset{Q}{\arg\max}\, p(Q|C, A) \tag{1}$$

where the context C and answer A are both sequences of words, and A is a span in C. We aim to generate Q, which involves reasoning over multiple sentences $S = \{s_i, ..., s_n\}_{i=1}^{n}$, where s_i is a sentence belonging to C. $\hat{Q}$ denotes the Q that maximizes the conditional likelihood given the context C and the answer A.

---

[1] https://github.com/bernardoleite/question-generation-portuguese.
[2] https://www.tensorflow.org/datasets/catalog/c4.

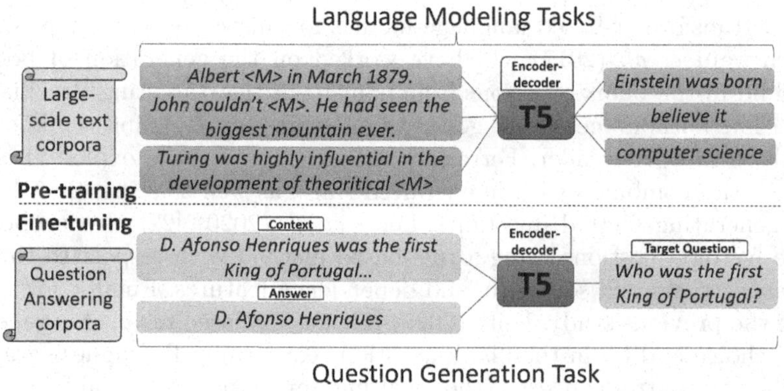

Fig. 2. Pre-training and fine-tuning for neural question generation.

During training, the model parameters θ are optimized considering the sequence cross-entropy loss (which is generically applied for seq2seq models):

$$l(\theta) = -\sum_{t=1}^{T} log\, p(y_t | X, y_{<t}; \theta) \qquad (2)$$

so that the log-likelihood of the training data is maximized. T is the length of the output/target sequence Y (the question), $y_{<t}$ denotes $y_1, y_2, \ldots, y_{t-1}$ and X is the input/source sequence which includes both context C and answer A. Previous ground truth inputs are given to the model when predicting the next index in the sequence [38]. For decoding, we use beam search.

4   Experimental Setup

We experiment with our Neural QG models using the original [33] (English) and Portuguese-translated [7] SQuAD v1.1 datasets. In this section, we first describe the corpus and provide the implementation details behind the fine-tuning process. Finally, we introduce the automatic evaluation method and metrics used to assess the generation performance of the models.

4.1   SQuAD v1.1 Dataset

The Stanford Question Answering Dataset (SQuAD) v1.1 [33] contains around 100K crowd-sourced QA pairs extracted from 536 Wikipedia articles. The questions were elaborated by Amazon Mechanical Turk crowd-workers who were encouraged to write down in their own words and not copy directly from the paragraph. Later, other crowd-workers answered the questions using spans of tokens contained in the reading passages. Each dataset instance is composed of an article's paragraph and multiple ⟨*question, answer*⟩ pairs. Statistically, most questions start with "What" (≈57k), "Who" (≈10k), "Which" (≈7k),

"When" and "How many" ($\approx$6k). Thus, they are mainly factoid questions requiring answers characterized for being objects, things, events, people, times, or quantities—named entities. We use two versions of this dataset. The first is the original English version[3]—we use it for obtaining baseline results for Neural QG in English. The second is the Portuguese-translated version [7] to assess the feasibility of applying Neural QG models in the context of this language. As usual and for the sake of comparability, we use the $\langle train, validation, test \rangle$ splits[4] made originally available by Du *et al.* (2017) [16] for conducting the experiences. We end up with 75,722[5] examples for training, 10,570 for validation and 11,877 for the test set.

4.2 Implementation Details

For experimenting with the T5 pre-trained model, we make use of the PyTorch Lightning framework[6] as our primary programming environment. Depending on the dataset, different versions of the models were employed, all of them available on the HuggingFace[7] platform. For the original (English) SQuAD v1.1 dataset, we make use of *t5-base*[8]. In turn, we take advantage of the PTT5 [5] model (*ptt5-base-portuguese-vocab*[9]) for experimenting with the Portuguese-translated SQuAD v1.1 version. PTT5 was pre-trained in the BrWac corpus [35], an extensive collection of web pages in Brazilian Portuguese. Additionally, we use the multilingual version of T5 [39] (*mt5-base*[10]) in both datasets. We have set 512 and 96 for the maximum token input (answer+paragraph[11]) and output (question) length, respectively. The training process is done under a maximum of 10 epochs, in which we use a batch size of 32. We select the model that achieves the lowest validation error on the validation set. Optimization is performed using *AdamW*, with a learning rate of 1×10^{-4} and Adam's epsilon (for numerical stability) of 1×10^{-6}. Once the models are trained, the inference procedure is performed using beam search (5 beams), for which we return the highest scoring beam obtained. The decoding length is set to a maximum of 96.

4.3 Automatic Evaluation

For evaluating QG systems, the human-expert evaluation has been employed but is typically time-consuming. As such, automatic evaluation metrics such as BLEU 1–4 [29], ROUGE [24] and METEOR [3] are nowadays the rule. It should

---

[3] https://github.com/rajpurkar/SQuAD-explorer/tree/master/dataset.

[4] https://github.com/xinyadu/nqg/tree/master/data/raw.

[5] It seems that Du *et al.* (2017) [16] uses only 70,484 examples after a post-processing step. We use all available instances.

[6] https://www.pytorchlightning.ai/.

[7] https://huggingface.co/.

[8] https://huggingface.co/t5-base.

[9] https://huggingface.co/unicamp-dl/ptt5-base-portuguese-vocab.

[10] https://huggingface.co/google/mt5-base.

[11] Answer and paragraph are separated with the eos_token </s>.

be noted that these metrics have been subject to ongoing criticism. As stated by Amidei *et al.* [1], many studies in NLG show weak correspondence between human judgments and automatic evaluation metrics. Nevertheless, we use them so that the results are comparable with previous work. BLEU is commonly used in machine translation and measures precision: how many of the words or *n*-grams in the machine-generated text were in the human written text. BLEU 1 analyses each token between the human-authored and machine-generated text. Similarly, BLEU 2 analyses each sequence of two words. As such, it can consider different *n*-gram sequences. Additionally, BLEU includes a brevity penalty for overly short sentences. ROUGE, also commonly used in the context of automatic summarization, measures recall: how many words (or n-grams) in the human reference text appear in the machine generated text. We report a widely used variant of ROUGE, called ROUGE$_L$, which considers the longest common sequence between the machine-generated text and the human reference. Lastly, METEOR computes the similarity between references and generations by considering paraphrases, synonyms and stemming. Again, for comparability, we use the same metric implementations[12] as in Du *et al.* (2017) [16].

5   Results and Discussion

Table 1 presents automatic evaluation results on the SQuAD v1.1 *test* set for our models and prior work. As a first note, it is noticeable that the recently proposed pre-trained seq2seq models generally outperform the other models in all metrics. These results evidence that pre-trained models may be favourable for performing downstream QG tasks. In particular, Xiao *et al.*. [37] present not only state-of-the-art results (in terms of BLEU 4, ROUGE$_L$ and METEOR) for neural QG but also introduce a new mechanism called noise-aware generation. This is an effective way to make the model detect mistakes (corrupted text) in training and ignore them. In turn, Chan and Fan [9] achieve the best performance values in terms of BLEU 1–2. The authors introduce three neural architectures built on top of BERT [12] for the QG task.

The English T5 fine-tuned models (our baseline) present results that are slightly below those obtained with recent pre-trained models (except for BLEU 3). In fact, the best values obtained in the original SQuAD v1.1 version have an absolute value difference of 0.85, 0.23 for BLEU 1–2 when comparing them to the best reported scores [9], 4.85 for BLEU 4, 2.63 for METEOR, and 3.28 for ROUGE$_L$ when comparing them to the ones obtained by Xiao *et al.* [37].

Regarding the Portuguese case study, we consider the results to be in line with previous findings. Although the values are below those obtained with the state-of-the-art pre-trained English models (somewhat expected since we are considering a machine-translated version), *ptt5-base* outperform the first two seq2seq models for BLEU 1–4. Also, the largest absolute difference between *ptt5-base* and *t5-base* (English) is 5.92 for ROUGE$_L$. For the BLEU scores, the differences range from 3.01 (BLEU 4) to 5.27 (BLEU 1). A brief empirical

---

[12] https://github.com/xinyadu/nqg/tree/master/qgevalcap

analysis of examples of generated questions can be found in Fig. 3. In general, the models pre-trained in the target language (English and Portuguese) obtain better results than multilingual ones, although the differences are marginal.

Finally, we would like to emphasize that the best reported BLEU 4 score is 25 (scale is 0–100) – low BLEU 4 value. The syntactic distance between generated and ground-truth questions explains the low values. Some intuitions for that syntactic distance might be: (a) the generated questions are valid alternative paraphrases of the ground-truth questions (still, the generated questions are syntactical distant from ground-truth questions) – check the first two examples in Fig. 3; (b) the generated questions have nothing in common with with the ground-truth ones, they are neither valid paraphrases nor suitable for the corresponding input answer – check the last example in Fig. 3. This analysis supports the on-going criticism with the usage of automatic evaluation metrics (see Sect. 4.3).

In general, we claim the suitability of T5 models for performing Portuguese Neural QG and (at least) presenting quantitative results that are in line with prior work for English. We reinforce that this analysis is based on the Portuguese machine-translated version of the original English SQuAD dataset.

Table 1. Question generation results in the test set, following Du *et al.* (2017) [16] splits. "BL" stands for BLEU, "RL" stands for ROUGE$_L$ and "MTR" stands for METEOR. The prior work results are cited directly from the original articles where the methods are proposed. Bold is applied to the best value obtained in each metric. BLEU 1–3 scores were not reported from all papers. The METEOR metric is not available for Portuguese.

	Model		Lang.	BL 1	BL 2	BL 3	BL 4	RL	MTR
Seq2Seq		[16] (2017)		43.09	25.96	17.50	12.28	39.75	16.62
		[40] (2018)		45.07	29.58	21.60	16.38	44.48	20.25
		[23] (2019)		45.66	30.21	21.82	16.27	44.35	20.36
	Prior	[9] (2019)		**49.73**	**34.60**	26.13	20.33	48.23	23.88
	work	[15] (2019)	EN	-	-	-	22.12	51.07	25.06
		[37] (2020)		-	-	-	**25.40**	**52.84**	**26.92**
Pre-trained		[4] (2020)		-	-	-	24.70	52.13	26.33
Seq2Seq		[31] (2020)		-	-	-	23.91	52.26	26.60
		[36] (2020)		-	-	-	21.07	49.14	24.09
		t5-base	EN	48.88	34.37	**26.18**	20.55	49.56	24.29
	Our	mt5-base		48.35	33.73	25.47	19.84	48.76	23.76
	proposal	ptt5-base	PT	43.61	30.04	22.58	17.54	43.64	-
		mt5-base		43.10	29.63	22.20	17.19	43.56	-

Passage (pt-SQuAD version): *Apesar da calamidade e do enorme número de mortes, Lisboa não sofreu nenhuma epidemia e em menos de um ano já estava sendo reconstruída. O novo centro da cidade de Lisboa foi projetado para resistir a terremotos subsequentes. Modelos arquitetônicos foram construídos para testes, e os efeitos de um terremoto foram simulados pelas tropas em marcha ao redor dos modelos. Os edifícios e grandes praças do centro da cidade pombalina ainda permanecem como uma das atrações turísticas de Lisboa. Sebastião de Melo também deu um importante contributo para o estudo da sismologia, concebendo um inquérito que foi enviado a todas as paróquias do país.*

en-SQuAD version: *Despite the calamity and huge death toll, Lisbon suffered no epidemics and within less than one year was already being rebuilt. The new city centre of Lisbon was designed to resist subsequent earthquakes. Architectural models were built for tests, and the effects of an earthquake were simulated by marching troops around the models. The buildings and big squares of the Pombaline City Centre still remain as one of Lisbon's tourist attractions. Sebastião de Melo also made an important contribution to the study of seismology by designing an inquiry that was sent to every parish in the country.*

pt-SQuAD answer: *desenhando um inquérito que foi enviado a todas as paróquias do país*
en-SQuAD answer: *by designing an inquiry that was sent to every parish in the country*
pt-SQuAD question: *Como de Melo contribuiu para o estudo da sismologia?*
en-SQuAD question: *How did de Melo contribute to the study of seismology?*
ptt5-base question: *Como Sebastião de Melo contribuiu para o estudo da sismologia?*
t5-base question: *How did Sebastio de Melo contribute to the study of seismology?*
BLEU 1: 0.91 BLEU 2: 0.85 BLEU 3: 0.83 BLEU 4: 0.81 ROUGE$_L$: 1.0

pt-SQuAD answer: *terremotos*
en-SQuAD answer: *earthquakes*
pt-SQuAD question: *Que tipo de desastre natural o centro da cidade de Lisboa foi projetado para resistir?*
en-SQuAD question: *What type of natural disaster was the city center of Lisbon designed to resist?*
ptt5-base question: *O novo centro da cidade de Lisboa foi projetado para resistir a quê?*
t5-base question: *What was the city centre of Lisbon designed to resist?*
BLEU 1: 0.68 BLEU 2: 0.60 BLEU 3: 0.57 BLEU 4: 0.54 ROUGE$_L$: 0.73

pt-SQuAD answer: *Os edifícios e grandes praças do Centro da Cidade Pombalina*
en-SQuAD answer: *The buildings and big squares of the Pombaline City Centre*
pt-SQuAD question: *Quais são algumas das atrações turísticas de Lisboa?*
en-SQuAD question: *What are some of Lisbon's tourist attractions?*
ptt5-base question: *O que ainda permanece como uma das atrações turísticas de Lisboa?*
t5-base question: *What remains one of Lisbon's tourist attractions?*
BLEU 1: 0.50 BLEU 2: 0.48 BLEU 3: 0.45 BLEU 4: 0.42 ROUGE$_L$: 0.67

pt-SQuAD answer: *marchando tropas em torno dos modelos*
en-SQuAD answer: *marching troops around the models*
pt-SQuAD question: *Como os terremotos foram simulados nos modelos arquitetônicos?*
en-SQuAD question: *How were earthquakes simulated on the architectural models?*
ptt5-base question: *Como os efeitos de um terremoto foram simulados?*
t5-base question: *How were the effects of an earthquake simulated?*
BLEU 1: 0.56 BLEU 2: 0.37 BLEU 3: 0.0 BLEU 4: 0.0 ROUGE$_L$: 0.55

pt-SQuAD answer: *Lisboa não sofreu epidemias*
en-SQuAD answer: *Lisbon suffered no epidemics*
pt-SQuAD question: *Lisboa sofreu alguma epidemia da calamidade?*
en-SQuAD question: *Did Lisbon suffer any epidemics from the calamity?*
ptt5-base question: *Por que a cidade de Lisboa não sofreu nenhuma epidemia?*
t5-base question: *What happened to Lisbon's population during the earthquake?*
BLEU 1: 0.36 BLEU 2: 0.0 BLEU 3: 0.0 BLEU 4: 0.0 ROUGE$_L$: 0.57

Fig. 3. Examples of generated questions (from both Portuguese-translated and English SQuAD v1.1 versions) using a text passage of the *Portugal* article (test set). Both BLEU and ROUGE$_L$ scores concern the comparison between "pt-SQuAD" (ground-truth) and "ptt5-base" (generated) questions. The examples are in descending order of BLEU 4 values.

6 Error Analysis

In order to better understand the quality of the questions generated, we perform two types of analysis: (1) assess the impact of an issue within the machine-translated version of the SQuAD v1.1 (Sect. 6.1) and manually check 100 randomly sampled questions for reporting the main errors found (Sect. 6.2).

6.1 Translation Problem of the SQuAD v1.1 Dataset

As initially pointed out by Carvalho *et al.* [8] (they have studied QA using the same dataset), there is an issue with the Portuguese machine-translated of SQuAD v1.1 dataset. The problem is that 39% of the translated answers are not found in the corresponding translated contexts. This happens because both answers and contexts are translated separately. Therefore, the translation of the individual answer does not always match the answer included in the translated context. For instance, consider the context "...The band entire will play a concert at the steps of Bond Hall..." where the answer is "the steps of Bond Hall". They are correspondingly translated to "...A banda inteira fará um show nos **degraus** de Bond Hall..." and "as **etapas** de Bond Hall...", where the words in boldface are two different translations of the English word "steps", which in this context have different meanings. We assess the impact of these occurrences in QG by first evaluating the model against test set instances where answers can be found in the contexts (7557 from 11877). The results are 44.31 (BLEU 1), 30.98 (BLEU 2), 23.51 (BLEU 3), 18.38 (BLEU 4), and 44.59 (ROUGE$_L$). In contrast, if we evaluate only the test set instances where answers are *not* found in the contexts (4320 from 11877), the results are 42.38 (BLEU 1), 28.37 (BLEU 2), 20.96 (BLEU 3), 16.04 (BLEU 4) and 41.98 (ROUGE$_L$). From the drop in the results, we conclude that this translation problem could potentially influence the quality of the generated questions.

6.2 Manual Sample Analysis

We manually analyze 100 generated Portuguese questions randomly extracted from the *test* set and list the main problems found. Among them, we highlight semantic errors, answer misalignments, syntactic errors, and absence of information:

- **Semantic Errors** (8 occurrences): This happens when the question has logic or commonsense errors, e.g., "Quem Liszt escreveu para Liszt?" or "O que os participantes podem enviar uma audição de vídeo de 40 segundos?".
- **Answer Misalignments** (5 occurrences): This happens when the generated question does not agree with the target answer, e.g., **question** "O terremoto de Sichuan é um dos desastres naturais mais caros da história?" and **answer**: "história chinesa".

- **Syntactic Errors** (3 occurrences): This happens when the question is syntactically incorrect, e.g., "Quem o Carrefour acusou de doar fundos para?" or when the question is not grammatically well-formed, e.g., "O iPod foi aceito como o que?".
- **Absence of Information** (1 occurence): This happens when the question is missing important information, e.g., "Quantos alunos estavam lá quando o terramoto aconteceu?"—What does "lá" refer to?

Regarding the other 83 question occurrences, we found no problems.

7   Conclusions

This study addresses the problem of generating Portuguese factoid questions by fine-tuning a state-of-the-art language model on top of a Portuguese machine-translated QA dataset. Our motivation is supported by recent studies employing neural approaches in QG tasks. We start by creating a baseline by training QG neural models in English to compare with prior work. Then, we apply the same technique in the Portuguese context. We conclude that the results for Portuguese are in line with previous studies, despite the focus of the analysis being based on automatic evaluation metrics, which may not necessarily be consistently good indicators of the quality of the generated text. Relatedly, for future work, we stress the need to perform human-evaluation. That would provide better insights into the quality of the generated questions (formulation, answerability, spelling, semantics). Additionally, it would be interesting to compare the neural QG approach with the traditional ones (rule-based) previously explored in Portuguese. Likewise relevant would be to explore alternative pre-trained seq2seq models. Finally, the development and sharing of quality large-scale Portuguese QA & QG corpora is critical for the NLP community.

Acknowledgments. This work was financially supported by Base Funding - UIDB/00027/2020 of the Artificial Intelligence and Computer Science Laboratory - LIACC - funded by national funds through the FCT/MCTES (PIDDAC). Bernardo Leite is supported by a PhD studentship (with reference 2021.05432.BD), funded by Fundação para a Ciência e a Tecnologia (FCT).

References

1. Amidei, J., Piwek, P., Willis, A.: Evaluation methodologies in automatic question generation 2013–2018. In: Proceedings of the 11th International Conference on Natural Language Generation, pp. 307–317. ACL, Tilburg University, The Netherlands, November 2018. https://doi.org/10.18653/v1/W18-6537. https://aclanthology.org/W18-6537
2. Azevedo, P., Leite, B., Cardoso, H.L., Silva, D.C., Reis, L.P.: Exploring NLP and information extraction to jointly address question generation and answering. In: Maglogiannis, I., Iliadis, L., Pimenidis, E. (eds.) AIAI 2020. IAICT, vol. 584, pp. 396–407. Springer, Cham (2020). https://doi.org/10.1007/978-3-030-49186-4_33

3. Banerjee, S., Lavie, A.: METEOR: an automatic metric for MT evaluation with improved correlation with human judgments. In: Proceedings of the ACL Workshop on Intrinsic and Extrinsic Evaluation Measures for Machine Translation and/or Summarization, Ann Arbor, Michigan, pp. 65–72. ACL, June 2005. https://www. aclweb.org/anthology/W05-0909

4. Bao, H., et al.: UniLMv2: pseudo-masked language models for unified language model pre-training. In: International Conference on Machine Learning, pp. 642–652. PMLR (2020)

5. Carmo, D., Piau, M., Campiotti, I., Nogueira, R., Lotufo, R.: PTT5: pretraining and validating the T5 model on Brazilian Portuguese data. arXiv preprint arXiv:2008.09144 (2020)

6. Carrino, C.P., Costa-jussà, M.R., Fonollosa, J.A.R.: Automatic Spanish translation of SQuAD dataset for multi-lingual question answering. In: Proceedings of the 12th Language Resources and Evaluation Conference, Marseille, France, pp. 5515–5523. European Language Resources Association, May 2020. https://aclanthology.org/2020.lrec-1.677

7. Carvalho, N.R.: squad-v1.1-pt (2020). https://github.com/nunorc/squad-v1.1-pt

8. Carvalho, N.R., Simões, A., Almeida, J.J.: Bootstrapping a data-set and model for question-answering in Portuguese (short paper). In: 10th Symposium on Languages, Applications and Technologies (SLATE 2021). Schloss Dagstuhl-Leibniz-Zentrum für Informatik (2021)

9. Chan, Y.H., Fan, Y.C.: A recurrent BERT-based model for question generation. In: Proceedings of the 2nd Workshop on Machine Reading for Question Answering, Hong Kong, China, pp. 154–162. ACL, November 2019. https://doi.org/10.18653/v1/D19-5821. https://aclanthology.org/D19-5821

10. Correia, R., Baptista, J., Eskenazi, M., Mamede, N.: Automatic generation of *Cloze* question stems. In: Caseli, H., Villavicencio, A., Teixeira, A., Perdigão, F. (eds.) PROPOR 2012. LNCS (LNAI), vol. 7243, pp. 168–178. Springer, Heidelberg (2012). https://doi.org/10.1007/978-3-642-28885-2_19

11. Curto, S.L.: Automatic generation of multiple-choice tests. Master's thesis, Instituto Superior Técnico (2010). https://fenix.tecnico.ulisboa.pt/departamentos/dei/dissertacao/2353642299631. Publication Title: Dissertation for obtaining the Master Degree in Information Systems and Computer Engineering

12. Devlin, J., Chang, M.W., Lee, K., Toutanova, K.: BERT: pre-training of deep bidirectional transformers for language understanding. In: Proceedings of the 2019 Conference of the North American Chapter of the Association for Computational Linguistics: Human Language Technologies, vol. 1 (Long and Short Papers), Minneapolis, Minnesota, pp. 4171–4186. ACL, June 2019. https://doi.org/10.18653/v1/N19-1423. https://aclanthology.org/N19-1423

13. d'Hoffschmidt, M., Belblidia, W., Heinrich, Q., Brendlé, T., Vidal, M.: FQuAD: French question answering dataset. In: Findings of the Association for Computational Linguistics: EMNLP 2020, pp. 1193–1208. ACL, November 2020. https://doi.org/10.18653/v1/2020.findings-emnlp.107. https://aclanthology.org/2020.findings-emnlp.107

14. Diéguez, D., Rodrigues, R., Gomes, P.: Using CBR for Portuguese question generation. In: Proceedings of the 15th Portuguese Conference on Artificial Intelligence, pp. 328–341 (2011)

15. Dong, L., et al.: Unified language model pre-training for natural language understanding and generation. In: Wallach, H., Larochelle, H., Beygelzimer, A., Alché-Buc, F.d., Fox, E., Garnett, R. (eds.) Advances in Neural Information Processing

Systems, vol. 32. Curran Associates, Inc. (2019). https://proceedings.neurips.cc/paper/2019/file/c20bb2d9a50d5ac1f713f8b34d9aac5a-Paper.pdf

16. Du, X., Shao, J., Cardie, C.: Learning to ask: neural question generation for reading comprehension. In: Proceedings of the 55th Annual Meeting of the Association for Computational Linguistics (Volume 1: Long Papers), Vancouver, Canada, pp. 1342–1352. ACL, July 2017. https://doi.org/10.18653/v1/P17-1123. https://aclanthology.org/P17-1123

17. Ferreira, J., Rodrigues, R., Gonçalo Oliveira, H.: Assessing factoid question-answer generation for Portuguese (short paper). In: 9th Symposium on Languages, Applications and Technologies (SLATE 2020). Schloss Dagstuhl-Leibniz-Zentrum für Informatik (2020)

18. Gates, D.: Generating look-back strategy questions from expository texts. In: The Workshop on the Question Generation Shared Task and Evaluation Challenge, NSF, Arlington, VA (2008). http://www.cs.memphis.edu/~vrus/questiongeneration//1-Gates-QG08.pdf

19. Gonçalo Oliveira, H.: Answering fill-in-the-blank questions in Portuguese with transformer language models. In: Marreiros, G., Melo, F.S., Lau, N., Lopes Cardoso, H., Reis, L.P. (eds.) EPIA 2021. LNCS (LNAI), vol. 12981, pp. 739–751. Springer, Cham (2021). https://doi.org/10.1007/978-3-030-86230-5_58

20. Heilman, M., Smith, N.A.: Good question! Statistical ranking for question generation. In: Human Language Technologies: The 2010 Annual Conference of the North American Chapter of the Association for Computational Linguistics, Los Angeles, California, pp. 609–617. ACL, June 2010. https://aclanthology.org/N10-1086

21. Leite, B.: Automatic question generation for the Portuguese language. Master's thesis, Faculdade de Engenharia da Universidade do Porto (2020). https://repositorio-aberto.up.pt/handle/10216/128541. Dissertation for obtaining the Integrated Master Degree in Informatics and Computer Engineering

22. Leite, B., Lopes Cardoso, H., Reis, L.P., Soares, C.: Factual question generation for the Portuguese language. In: 2020 International Conference on INnovations in Intelligent SysTems and Applications (INISTA), pp. 1–7. IEEE (2020)

23. Li, J., Gao, Y., Bing, L., King, I., Lyu, M.R.: Improving question generation with to the point context. In: Proceedings of the 2019 Conference on Empirical Methods in Natural Language Processing and the 9th International Joint Conference on Natural Language Processing (EMNLP-IJCNLP), Hong Kong, China, pp. 3216–3226. ACL, November 2019. https://doi.org/10.18653/v1/D19-1317. https://aclanthology.org/D19-1317

24. Lin, C.Y.: ROUGE: a package for automatic evaluation of summaries. In: Text Summarization Branches Out, Barcelona, Spain, pp. 74–81. ACL, July 2004. https://www.aclweb.org/anthology/W04-1013

25. Lindberg, D., Popowich, F., Nesbit, J., Winne, P.: Generating natural language questions to support learning on-line. In: Proceedings of the 14th European Workshop on Natural Language Generation, Sofia, Bulgaria, pp. 105–114. ACL, August 2013. https://aclanthology.org/W13-2114

26. Liu, M., Calvo, R., Rus, V.: G-Asks: an intelligent automatic question generation system for academic writing support. Dialogue Discourse 3, 101–124 (2012). https://doi.org/10.5087/dad.2012.205

27. Mazidi, K., Nielsen, R.D.: Linguistic considerations in automatic question generation. In: Proceedings of the 52nd Annual Meeting of the Association for Computational Linguistics (Volume 2: Short Papers), Baltimore, Maryland, pp. 321–326. ACL (2014). https://doi.org/10.3115/v1/P14-2053. https://www.aclweb.org/anthology/P14-2053

28. Pan, L., Lei, W., Chua, T.S., Kan, M.Y.: Recent advances in neural question generation. CoRR abs/1905.0 (2019). http://arxiv.org/abs/1905.08949. eprint: 1905.08949

29. Papineni, K., Roukos, S., Ward, T., Zhu, W.J.: Bleu: a method for automatic evaluation of machine translation. In: Proceedings of the 40th Annual Meeting of the Association for Computational Linguistics, Philadelphia, Pennsylvania, USA, pp. 311–318. ACL, July 2002. https://doi.org/10.3115/1073083.1073135. https://www.aclweb.org/anthology/P02-1040

30. Pirovani, J., Spalenza, M., Oliveira, E.: Geração Automática de Questões a Partir do Reconhecimento de Entidades Nomeadas em Textos Didáticos. Brazilian Symposium on Computers in Education (Simpósio Brasileiro de Informática na Educação - SBIE) **28**(1), 1147 (2017). https://doi.org/10.5753/cbie.sbie.2017.1147. https://www.br-ie.org/pub/index.php/sbie/article/view/7643

31. Qi, W.: ProphetNet: predicting future n-gram for sequence-to-sequence pre-training. In: Findings of the Association for Computational Linguistics: EMNLP 2020, pp. 2401–2410. ACL, November 2020. https://doi.org/10.18653/v1/2020.findings-emnlp.217. https://aclanthology.org/2020.findings-emnlp.217

32. Raffel, C., et al.: Exploring the limits of transfer learning with a unified text-to-text transformer. J. Mach. Learn. Res. **21**(140), 1–67 (2020). http://jmlr.org/papers/v21/20-074.html

33. Rajpurkar, P., Zhang, J., Lopyrev, K., Liang, P.: SQuAD: 100,000+ questions for machine comprehension of text. In: Proceedings of the 2016 Conference on Empirical Methods in Natural Language Processing, Austin, Texas, pp. 2383–2392. ACL, November 2016. https://doi.org/10.18653/v1/D16-1264. https://aclanthology.org/D16-1264

34. Rus, V., Cai, Z., Graesser, A.: Question generation: example of a multi-year evaluation campaign. In: Proceedings of the WS on the Question Generation Shared Task and Evaluation Challenge (2008)

35. Wagner Filho, J.A., Wilkens, R., Idiart, M., Villavicencio, A.: The brWaC corpus: a new open resource for Brazilian Portuguese. In: Proceedings of the Eleventh International Conference on Language Resources and Evaluation (LREC 2018) (2018)

36. Wang, W., Wei, F., Dong, L., Bao, H., Yang, N., Zhou, M.: MiniLM: deep self-attention distillation for task-agnostic compression of pre-trained transformers. arXiv preprint arXiv:2002.10957 (2020)

37. Xiao, D., et al.: ERNIE-GEN: an enhanced multi-flow pre-training and fine-tuning framework for natural language generation. In: Bessiere, C. (ed.) Proceedings of the Twenty-Ninth International Joint Conference on Artificial Intelligence, IJCAI-2020, pp. 3997–4003. International Joint Conferences on Artificial Intelligence Organization (2020). https://doi.org/10.24963/ijcai.2020/553. https://doi.org/10.24963/ijcai.2020/553

38. Xie, Z.: Neural text generation: a practical guide. CoRR abs/1711.09534 (2017). http://arxiv.org/abs/1711.09534

39. Xue, L., et al.: mT5: a massively multilingual pre-trained text-to-text transformer. arXiv preprint arXiv:2010.11934 (2020)

40. Zhao, Y., Ni, X., Ding, Y., Ke, Q.: Paragraph-level neural question generation with maxout pointer and gated self-attention networks. In: Proceedings of the 2018 Conference on Empirical Methods in Natural Language Processing, pp. 3901–3910 (2018)

Federated Search Using Query Log Evidence

João Damas[1,2], José Devezas[1,2], and Sérgio Nunes[1,2(✉)]

[1] INESC TEC, Porto, Portugal
`sergio.nunes@fe.up.pt`
[2] Faculty of Engineering, University of Porto, Porto, Portugal

Abstract. In this work, we targeted the search engine of a sports-related website that presented an opportunity for search result quality improvement. We reframed the engine as a Federated Search instance, where each collection represented a searchable entity type within the system, using Apache Solr for querying each resource and a Python Flask server to merge results. We extend previous work on individual search term weighing, making use of past search terms as a relevance indicator for user selected documents. To incorporate term weights we define four strategies combining two binary variables: integration with default relevance (linear scaling or linear combination) and search term frequency (raw value or log-smoothed). To evaluate our solution, we extracted two query sets from search logs: one with frequently submitted queries, and another with ambiguous result access patterns. We used click-through information as a relevance proxy and tried to mitigate its limitations by evaluating under distinct IR metrics, including MRR, MAP and NDCG. Moreover, we also measured Spearman rank correlation coefficients to test similarities between produced rankings and reference orderings according to user access patterns. Results show consistency across all metrics in both sets. Previous search terms were key to obtaining a higher effectiveness, with runs that used pure search term frequency performing best. Compared to the baseline, our best strategies were able to maintain quality on frequent queries and improve retrieval effectiveness on ambiguous queries, with up to ~six percentage points better performance on most metrics.

Keywords: Information retrieval · Federated search · Domain-specific search

1 Introduction

This work was developed in the context of a Portuguese sports website focused on delivering all types of football-related information at national and international level. Our research focused on improving the current search engine by reframing the problem as an instance of Federated Search, as well as proposing changes to the indexing and retrieval processes by incorporating influence from previous searches in order to help predict future relevance. The underlying assumption

© The Author(s), under exclusive license to Springer Nature Switzerland AG 2022
G. Marreiros et al. (Eds.): EPIA 2022, LNAI 13566, pp. 794–805, 2022.
https://doi.org/10.1007/978-3-031-16474-3_64

is that, by incorporating external information, we can positively impact the retrieval performance.

This document is structured as follows. Section 2 presents a definition of Federated Search, as well as relevant proposals on new indexing strategies for similar contexts. Section 3 provides an overview of the available collections, with Sect. 4 detailing the indexing modifications by the introduction of previous search terms. Section 5 provides an overview of how the retrieval process and the overall system work, including our proposed modifications for new relevance formulas. The solution is evaluated in Sect. 6, with Sect. 7 reflecting on the results and potential future work.

2 Related Work

Federated search is a classic information retrieval task that involves querying a set of independent search engines and then centrally merging the results to provide a single result list to the user [14]. This task involves four phases: *Resource Description, Resource Selection, Results Merging* and *Results Presentation* [4], with the first and third being the most relevant in our context. The first phase concerns the indexing process. After resources are selected and their relevant documents retrieved, in the *Results Merging* phase there is the need to order them in a single ranking. Even if they have similarities in the retrieval process, they are not equal and, therefore, query scores for documents from different resources cannot be directly compared [1].

We center our survey on previous research focused on new indexing strategies, particularly those that use past searches to enrich document representations. The motivation is that people might remember the document not by its content, but by some description given by another person other than the author.

Fagin et al. [6] present a system that uses three separate indices to index an intranet's pages: one for their content, one for the title and related metadata, and one that combines all anchor text leading to that page. Ding et al. [5] use a similar approach, but with an index based on previous searches. They reason that a single source of evidence *"is not enough to construct a good website search engine, especially when the page is new or seldom accessed"*. This is an important point that resembles our work closely: we expect to have a heavy tail of pages that are less visited and, therefore, would suffer from a lack of data problem if trying to use solely log data for indexing. In their tests, they compared their proposed approach with a single index with all the combined content and concluded that the former performed better. Moreover, the log index proved most effective in retrieving some top results instead of a full relevant set.

Zhou et al. [17] also use a three-fold index using anchor texts and search log entries, however, their work differs on index construction, with a sliding window to capture surrounding text, as well as term propagation between consecutive pages visited through referrer information. Not all propagated terms have the same importance, as terms from pages closer to the one being processed assume higher weights. Their best results also came when linearly combining the separate indices instead of merging all terms into a single structure.

Oakes et al. [12] take an extreme approach and index documents only by previous search terms. They argue that, in a system with multilingual documents and searches, this strategy allows to merge all previous searches, regardless of language, providing users with easier access to documents in a broader set of languages, as many can be present in the index. Terms are weighted in a TF-IDF like approach. In our case, this strategy alone wouldn't likely work, due to the heavy-tail limitation presented above.

3   Resource Description

The system incorporated four different collections, corresponding to the same amount of distinct searchable entity types within the search engine, amongst the most frequently searched. The first collection stored a sample of 2,000 competitions. Each one had a name stored in a description-like field, as well as, occasionally, an abbreviation. A separate collection stores teams. Each team in our collected sample of 5,000 entries had a unique name stored in a dedicated field. The third collection contains entities of type Manager. Each one of the 3,000 sampled managers had their full name stored. Moreover, there was a keywords field that stored alternative designations, similar to nicknames, for them. However, this field was rarely filled, with only 2.4% of sample entries containing a non-empty value associated. Finally, the last collection holds entities of type Player, which are grouped together to form teams. Our sample contained 10,000 players, storing their name, past teams and in-field preferred positions.

4   Search Term Payloads

We added one extra field to all collections, *searchTerms*, that stored these terms, alongside a search relevance weight for each one. We used the formula provided by Oakes et al. [12] to calculate search term relevance. However, this relevance was complementary to the overall document relevance score instead of a replacement. The difference also shows how the goals between both works differed: in the original proposal, authors aimed at exploring how this technique could aid in multilingual search, while we intended to facilitate previous search pattern recognition for future searchers. More specifically, given an entity e, for each query term t, they defined its search relevance with a TF-IDF like weight as: $Weight(t,e) = TF_{t,e} \times \log \frac{N}{E_t}$ where $TF_{t,e}$ is the number of searches for entity e that use term t, E_t is the number of entities whose term t led to a click in it and N is the total number of documents (here, limited to our samples' size).

Their weighting scheme, despite being based on a traditional relevance formula, allowed to highlight terms that were often used to reach an entity, were seldom used to search others, or ideally both. In order to achieve an optimal weighting scheme, and because term frequency differences between distinct terms for a given entity were sometimes considerable, we implemented two variants. The first is as described, while the second utilizes logarithmic term frequency.

To incorporate this into collection documents, we made use of a Lucene feature that was recently ported to Solr: payloads.[1] The idea is to associate some score to individual terms that, here, represents a relevance confidence weight.

5 Execution Flow

Despite the actual search process responsibility being delegated to Solr, we were not able to implement a fully federated solution within it. The lack of out-of-the-box support for a federated architecture led us to introduce a middleware server, using Python's Flask[2], that interacted with Solr to query collections and then merge results locally. When a user submitted a query, the server would build the request object that was then sent through the Solr API to each collection. Upon receiving all results, score normalization was performed, before sending a final ordered list back to the client.

5.1 Querying Independent Collections

Given the difference in schemas, requests had to be adjusted according to the entity that was being queried. We started by constructing the common core of the request. This included defining the query parser and general options. We opted to use Solr's eDismax query parser[3] due to its flexibility, namely support-ing, e.g., field-dependent boosts. In addition, the *stopwords* parameter was set to false, so that these terms weren't removed during the analyzer pipeline. More-over, despite the existence of a dedicated Payload query parser, that wasn't what met our needs: we intended on calculating document relevance by Solr standards *and* by term payloads, not one or the other. We used eDismax to calculate tra-ditional document relevance and made use of the in-built *payload* function and the possibility of defining custom, calculated fields for each returned document. This function takes a payload field and a term and returns the respective weight or 0 otherwise. Upon receiving a query, the server splits it using a whitespace delimiter and creates one custom field per term. Each term is assigned a sequen-tial field (payload_0, payload_1, ...) that searches the *searchTerms* field common to all entities.

Given this common core, we added the search fields, along with the respective boosts, for each entity, so that we could take advantage of the data structure to value matches on more relevant fields. Furthermore, we replicated these boosts into a phrase search parameter. This way, not only could we boost documents that matched terms in a given field, but also on consecutive term occurrences, much like phrase querying. Boost wise, we valued an entity's main name most over all other fields, followed by other stored designations (e.g., nicknames, abbre-viations), and, finally, other entity-specific fields (e.g., former teams for managers and players).

---

[1] https://lucidworks.com/post/solr-payloads/.

[2] https://flask.palletsprojects.com/en/1.1.x/.

[3] https://lucene.apache.org/solr/guide/8_4/the-extended-dismax-query-parser.html.

5.2   Incorporating Payload Scores

Having queried a collection, the resulting documents all have a *score* field, with the estimated Solr relevance formula result, as well as *payload_* * fields, one for each query term issued. To merge these scores, we use a set of strategies based both on linear scaling and linear combination of factors and terms, respectively. To this end, given a document relevance score *RelS* and payload scores $PL_{0..n}$ for that document, we defined and experimented with 4 strategies. In the first strategy, *Prod*, the document's final score linearly scaled with the matching payload scores, that is: $Score_{Prod} = RelS \times \prod_{i=0}^{n} PL_i, [PL_i \neq 0]$.

On the other hand, the *Sum* strategy performed a linear combination between the relevance score and the sum of the matching payload scores: $Score_{Sum} = \alpha \times RelS + (1-\alpha) \times \sum_{i=0}^{n} PL_i, \alpha \in [0,1]$ where the α parameter could attribute more or less importance to term payloads and defaulted to 0.5. The last two strategies follow from the first ones, but with log-smoothing. The *ProdLog* strategy is similar to *Prod*, but the sequence product of the payloads was log-smoothed. Finally, the *SumLog* incorporation strategy was derived from *Sum*, similarly to *Prod* and *ProdLog*, i.e., the summation component is log-smoothed.

5.3   Results Merging

The last step in the retrieval process was the merging of results from all four collections in order to produce one ordered list. To merge documents, we had to normalize their scores, so that they could be comparable between different collections. One of the most well-known algorithms for this task is CORI [3]. For a given document D retrieved from collection C, CORI defines its normalized score as $FinalScore = S_D * \frac{1+0.4*S_C}{1.4}$, where S_D is the original document score (after term payload incorporation) and S_C is the collection's score, while the normalization constants are a product of experimentation.

An important component in score normalization is the document's origin collection's score. This value should reflect the retrieved documents' overall importance for the final ordered list, thus its value could be the difference between a document placing in the top 10 or much further down. We followed the work of Hawking et al. [10], who, inspired by Rasolofo et al. [13], used a LMS strategy to calculate a collection's score. LMS, short for *"using result Length to calculate Merging Score"* [13], requires no collection metadata or samples, ranking collections based on the result set size for a given query. More specifically, a collection's LMS score is defined as: $LMS_C = \log\left(1 + \frac{|R_C| \times K}{\sum_{i=1}^{n} |R_i|}\right)$ where $|R_i|$ is the size of the result set returned by collection i for the query, n is the number of collections to merge, and K is a scaling constant. In the original proposal, the authors set a value of $K = 600$, which we adopted.

6   Evaluation

To evaluate our solution, we used a collection of real queries and evaluated the performance under several standard metrics. In order to annotate test queries with the correct answers, we used click information as a relevance proxy. The

work of Joachims et al. [8] exposes the potential dangers of using click-through information to this end. To mitigate these problems, a diverse set of metrics was adopted. In order to validate the results, behavior across metrics should remain reasonably consistent. Finally, when possible, work that supports the use of click-through data as an acceptable replacement for manual relevance judgement was cited.

6.1   Datasets

We used two distinct sets of queries to analyze the engine's behavior under different circumstances and scenarios. Queries were mostly short, with a large majority spanning no longer than 2 terms. The first set of queries contained popular queries in terms of frequency. To build it, we collected the 200 most frequently submitted queries and all the entities clicked as a result of that search, keeping only the most clicked one, alongside the number of clicks it received. Liu et al. [11] concluded that, for navigational queries, it was possible to automatically annotate queries with the most clicked result as the correct answer, obtaining over 96% accuracy on the annotation process when compared to manual judgements. In our context, queries were expected to be predominantly navigational, as users mostly sought a specific entity when searching. On average, the top clicked result in each of the 200 queries had an average click share of 85%. Moreover, in nearly 120 queries the top clicked result had over 90% of all clicks for that query. Such skewness towards one result was also a good indicator that helped validate the automation of the annotation process.

The second set of queries consisted of interrogations that produced high variability in clicked results, i.e., different entities were considered the correct answer depending on the search session, and none of them had a noticeable click share majority. In this case, we filtered queries based on individual entity click entropy, using the formula presented by Kulkarni et al. [9]. The building process followed a similar flow to the frequent queries set. We started by collecting the 200 queries with the highest entropy value. However, this time, we considered all results clicked as potential answers. In this case, the top clicked results had an average click share of 36.9%. Thus, due to the ambiguous nature of these queries, we considered multiple possible answers per query. Accordingly, these query sets will be referred to as *Frequent Query Set (FQS)* and *Entropy Query Set (EQS)*.

6.2   Evaluation Metrics

To evaluate the robustness of the system, both query sets were tested against different metrics. As we had no access to a test collection with full relevance judgements for all documents, we avoided measures that directly dealt with recall. More specifically, we used *Mean Reciprocal Rank (MRR)* [16], including a click-weighted variant proposed by Walter Underwood [15], *Mean Average Precision (MAP)* [2], *Success (at N)*, a percentage of queries with at least one correct answer in the top N results, as proposed by Zhu et al. [18] (with values $N = \{1, 5\}$). Moreover, for the Entropy Query Set, we also used *Normalized*

Discounted Cumulative Gain (nDCG) [7], as well as Spearman's rank correlation coefficient, which assesses if the relationship between two variables from dependent samples (here, ranking positions) can be characterized as a monotonic function, i.e., both variables grow in the same direction. Statistical hypothesis testing was performed to assess if coefficient values varied significantly between different strategies in our solution and if there were improvements over the baseline.

6.3   Results and Discussion

We now present the obtained results, partitioned by query set. All metrics were applied with a cutoff at ranking 10. In the following subsections, we consider each independent combination of search term payload score calculation and incorporation as an independent search engine. The engine resulting from the combination of Pure TF (in payload calculation) and the product operator (in payload incorporation) is referred to as *PProd*. *CurrSol* represents the baseline that is the current solution in the product engine. Finally, *NoPayload* refers to a local baseline for our solution, where there was no search term payload in use, i.e., *plain federated Solr*. Regarding Sum and Sumlog strategy variants, we experimented, *a priori*, with α values in the range $[0, 1]$, with a step of 0.1, in order to assess the best linear combination weights. Optimality was achieved when $\alpha = 0.3$, that is, the document's score was made mostly from search term payloads (70%). As we approached both extremes of the tested range, performance tended to get worse, as expected.

Frequent Query Set. Results for the Frequent Query Set are shown in Table 1. For each metric we highlight the strategies that had the highest value. An immediate observation is that the performance of the plain Solr baseline (*NoPayload*) ranks worst in every metric. More specifically, in around 47% of the queries, the engine was able to return the correct result in the first position, and only in a little over two-thirds placed it in the top 5. This was further corroborated by the lower values of weighted and unweighted MRR, reflecting the typically lower ranking positions where correct results were found. Note that, by considering only one correct answer per query, unweighted MRR and MAP values were equal, therefore we show only one designation, in this case the former.

Regarding the different combinations of our solution, it appeared that using Sumlog for search term payload incorporation, regardless of the TF type used for its calculation, lead to worse results. In fact, when using TF Log, results were almost comparable to not using payloads at all. This was likely a sign that both the Sumlog incorporation strategy and logarithmic TF calculation flattened payload values beyond significance. The latter's effect could be seen on the other variants as well: when compared to their Pure TF counterpart, no variant performed better on any metric. In the remaining three strategies (*PProd*, *PSum* and *PProdlog*), performances were more similar and close to the CurrSol baseline. As for the other two, they were almost indistinguishable performance-wise. When compared to the CurrSol baseline, results were also very similar, with a small advantage for the baseline in the Success@5 metric. Indeed, frequently

searched entities already produced good results, as was shown by these results. Therefore, the main conclusion was that some of the combinations of our solution were capable of replicating the good results already provided by the baseline for these situations.

Table 1. Evaluation results for the Frequent Query Set.

Strategy	MRR@10	wMRR@10	Success@1	Success@5
CurrSol	0.84535	0.99580	0.83696	0.87370
NoPayload	0.56864	0.66987	0.47283	0.68478
PProd	**0.84375**	**0.99508**	**0.83696**	**0.85326**
PSum	0.84013	0.99476	0.83152	**0.85326**
PProdlog	0.82201	0.97689	0.79348	**0.85326**
PSumlog	0.66498	0.78311	0.56522	0.78804
LProd	0.80471	0.95340	0.76630	**0.85326**
LSum	0.68554	0.83061	0.59239	0.80435
LProdlog	0.76771	0.91409	0.70109	0.84783
LSumlog	0.60714	0.70529	0.51630	0.73370

Finally, we focused on one metric and looked at its individual values for all queries across one of the top combinations, *PProd*, and the CurrSol baseline. We chose Average Precision (AP) as the metric to observe, not only due to its robustness, but also since it considered multiple answers per query, an important factor so that we could more confidently perform the same analysis later on the Entropy Query Set. Figure 1a shows the obtained values. As expected, values were very close, reflecting what was obtained in their averages. Despite being able to keep a better performance for a short while, the current production engine then had a slower rate of descent for the lowest scoring queries.

Entropy Query Set. Evaluation results for this query set are presented in Table 2. Furthermore, note that, while the NDCG column label reads *NDCG@10*, the values presented are the arithmetic average for all queries, and not individual

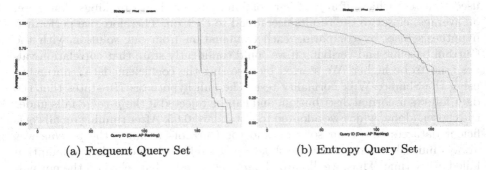

    (a) Frequent Query Set   (b) Entropy Query Set

Fig. 1. AP values per query in descendent order for each query set.

values. Once again, the local baseline of not having search payload incorporation achieves the worst performance of any combination, a repeated behavior. MAP, which was equivalent to MRR in the Frequent Query Set, also follows a similar pattern, though with even lower values. Finally, the newly introduced metric, NDCG@10, also suggests that there wasn't much gain as we moved in the ranking when compared to other strategies. Being a pattern present in both query sets, this confirms that payloads are key for improving retrieval performance.

Sumlog strategy variants are, once again, the ones with the lowest performance, demonstrating the low expressiveness of payloads in that scenario. However, contrary to the Frequent Query Set, there were more strategies that suggest an improvement over the CurrSol baseline. More specifically, both *PProd* and *LProd* surpass other strategies in all metrics (e.g., they are the only ones with a MAP value over 0.8). Moreover, they also present the highest discounted cumulative gain, with NDCG@10 values of around 0.82 each. In terms of correct result presence in the top 1 and 5 ranking positions, other strategies, such as *PSum* and *PProdlog*, perform nearly as well as the former two. In fact, their difference in other metrics is usually small (around 3% points maximum in MAP).

Table 2. Evaluation results for the Entropy Query Set.

Strategy	MRR@10	wMRR@10	MAP@10	Success@1	Success@5	NDCG@10
CurrSol	0.7682	0.9540	0.7492	0.7324	0.8388	0.7451
NoPayload	0.5082	0.7187	0.4822	0.3966	0.6760	0.5198
PProd	0.8304	**0.9955**	0.8011	**0.7989**	0.8659	**0.8201**
PSum	0.8216	**0.9953**	0.7797	0.7933	0.8547	0.8035
PProdlog	0.8233	0.9927	0.7880	0.7933	0.8603	0.8038
PSumlog	0.6974	0.9133	0.6617	0.5978	0.8436	0.6979
LProd	**0.8317**	0.9932	**0.8102**	**0.7989**	**0.8715**	0.8161
LSum	0.7832	0.9683	0.7472	0.7263	0.8547	0.7648
LProdlog	0.8042	0.9865	0.7760	0.7654	0.8547	0.7825
LSumlog	0.6057	0.7458	0.5803	0.4916	0.7709	0.6043

The last metric we used, the Spearman ranking correlation coefficient, was used to assess which, if any, of our combinations produced rankings that were, on average, closer to the results users tend to click on. Therefore, we performed hypothesis tests by comparing each combination from our solution with the CurrSol baseline and verifying if we could confidently state that correlation values tend to be higher. We started by assessing the coefficient data's normality using the Shapiro-Wilk normality test. The null hypothesis $H0$ states that the data follows a normal distribution, and can be rejected if the *p-value* falls under the chosen alpha, which we adopted to a standard 0.05. After running on all coefficient datasets (from our solution and the CurrSol baseline), the *p-value* was always much lower than the threshold set, therefore the normality assumption failed every time. Thus, we discarded parametric tests that relied on the normality assumption. Our choice was then the non-parametric Wilcoxon signed-rank

test. This test is a reliable alternative when there is no support for data normality and can be used to assess if there are significant changes in the distribution of two variables, and if these changes are one or two-sided. Given two variables X and Y, the null hypothesis is $H0 : X \leq Y$. Our interest was then in checking which combinations were able to reject the null hypothesis. Once again, we considered a threshold of $p = 0.05$. Table 3 shows the obtained results. Results below the defined threshold are marked with an asterisk (*). Values lower than 0.001 are highlighted with a double asterisk (**).

Table 3. Wilcoxon signed-rank test *p-values* for Spearman correlation coefficients.

Strategy	p-value
NoPayload	0.922
PProd	1.352e−12**
PSum	1.521e−6**
PProdlog	4.444e−9**
PSumlog	0.036*
LProd	1.311e−7**
LSum	0.007*
LProdlog	3.685e−6**
LSumlog	0.517

Results show that, for both *NoPayload* and *LSumlog* strategies, we can't state that the correlation coefficients are higher than the baseline. Moreover, the *PSumlog* strategy, despite being able to reject the null hypothesis, results in a much higher value (0.036), attributing less confidence to this strategy as well. Otherwise, all strategies' results allow us to say that they produce rankings with higher correlation to typical user result access patterns. Finally, Fig. 1b shows the individual AP values for this query set. Differences are more noticeable in this scenario, also reflecting the enhancement visible when evaluating this query set. There is a sudden break for our strategy towards the worst performing queries. This is likely due to the correct answer inclusion strategy: we consider all queries that had at least one answer present in the samples, no matter how often it was clicked. For queries that closely resemble this edge case, it was not possible for our solution to place them in the top 10 answers. Overall, our solution appears to produce much better results according to user access patterns.

7   Conclusions

In this work, we took an existing sports search engine and proposed reframing it as a Federated Search instance, where each collection corresponds to a searchable entity type. We also indexed previous search terms for a given document, a strategy that was shown to have high discriminative power. Each term's weight

is derived from a TF-IDF adaption, reflecting how often it was used to reach that and other documents. To incorporate payload values, we defined four strategies as a product of two binary variables: score update (linear scaling or linear combination) and previous search term frequency (raw value or log-smoothed). Finally, for merging and normalization, we made use of previous work on CORI variations that used returned result set size as a main signal for collection quality.

Our evaluation process consisted of comparing results from different combinations of our proposed solution and the current production engine. For this, we extracted two query sets from the search logs, one with the most frequents queries and one with the most ambiguous ones (entropy set). To annotate queries with the correct answer, we had to resort to using clicks as a relevance proxy. For the frequent query set, there was one correct answer, the most clicked entity, since they always had a high click share, averaging 85%. As for the entropy query set, a majority was seldom found, hence all entities clicked were considered in a way to reflect graded relevance. In order to mitigate limitations of this approach, we used several distinct IR metrics, including MAP, MRR and NDCG. Results for frequent queries show that we were able to match the current system quality, and, additionally, increase retrieval effectiveness up to six percentage points on most collected metrics for ambiguous queries. Raw search term frequency achieves better results than its counterpart, with both linear scaling and combination providing the best results alongside it, with a slight advantage for the former. In fact, stability was observed across metrics for different strategies, reinforcing confidence on the reliability of the evaluation methodology. This shows how a single, uniform and integrated system was able to provide quality answers for a diverse set of information needs and queries. Moreover, it demonstrates how past searches can be a positive influence in relevance determination for document ordering for future searchers.

As future work, it would be interesting to experiment with other types of incorporation strategies beyond what was tested here. This could lead to a more systematic analysis in order to assess possible patterns concerning optimal strategy types. Another possible continuation includes replicating the behavior of the current system by favoring terms used more recently, so as to avoid wrongful bias of possible search term spikes. Regarding evaluation, quality measurement under real system usage would further aid in testing the solution's quality.

Acknowledgements. This paper would have not been possible without the collaboration of the zerozero.pt team, who kindly provided us continuously refined search logs that were the foundation of the work developed. This work is financed by National Funds through the Portuguese funding agency, FCT - Fundação para a Ciência e a Tecnologia, within project LA/P/0063/2020.

References

1. Arguello, J.: Federated search for heterogeneous environments. Ph.D. thesis, Carnegie Mellon University (2011)
2. Buckley, C., Voorhees, E.M.: Evaluating evaluation measure stability. SIGIR Forum **51**(2), 235–242 (2017)

3. Callan, J.P., Lu, Z., Croft, W.B.: Searching distributed collections with inference networks. In: Proceedings of the 18th Annual International ACM SIGIR Conference on Research and Development in Information Retrieval, SIGIR 1995, New York, NY, USA, pp. 21–28. ACM (1995)
4. Callan, J.: Distributed information retrieval. In: Advances in Information Retrieval, pp. 127–150. Kluwer Academic Publishers, Boston (2005)
5. Ding, C., Zhou, J.: Log-based indexing to improve website search. In: Proceedings of the 2007 ACM Symposium on Applied Computing - SAC 2007, New York, NY, USA, p. 829. ACM Press (2007)
6. Fagin, R., et al.: Searching the workplace web. In: Proceedings of the Twelfth International Conference on World Wide Web - WWW 2003, New York, NY, USA, p. 366. ACM Press (2003)
7. Järvelin, K., Kekäläinen, J.: Cumulated gain-based evaluation of IR techniques. ACM Trans. Inf. Syst. **20**(4), 422–446 (2002)
8. Joachims, T.: Optimizing search engines using clickthrough data. In: Proceedings of the Eighth ACM SIGKDD International Conference on Knowledge Discovery and Data Mining - KDD 2002, New York, NY, USA, p. 133. ACM Press (2002)
9. Kulkarni, A., Teevan, J., Svore, K.M., Dumais, S.T.: Understanding temporal query dynamics. In: Proceedings of the Fourth ACM International Conference on Web Search and Data Mining, WSDM 2011, New York, NY, USA, pp. 167–176. ACM (2011). https://doi.org/10.1145/1935826.1935862
10. Li, P.V., Thomas, P., Hawking, D.: Merging algorithms for enterprise search. In: Proceedings of the 18th Australasian Document Computing Symposium, ADCS 2013, New York, NY, USA, pp. 42–49. ACM (2013)
11. Liu, Y., Fu, Y., Zhang, M., Ma, S., Ru, L.: Automatic search engine performance evaluation with click-through data analysis. In: Proceedings of the 16th International Conference on World Wide Web, WWW 2007, New York, NY, USA, pp. 1133–1134. ACM (2007)
12. Oakes, M., Xu, Y.: A search engine based on query logs, and search log analysis by automatic language identification. In: Peters, C., et al. (eds.) CLEF 2009. LNCS, vol. 6241, pp. 526–533. Springer, Heidelberg (2010). https://doi.org/10.1007/978-3-642-15754-7_64
13. Rasolofo, Y., Abbaci, F., Savoy, J.: Approaches to collection selection and results merging for distributed information retrieval. In: Proceedings of the Tenth International Conference on Information and Knowledge Management, CIKM 2001, New York, NY, USA, pp. 191–198. ACM (2001)
14. Shokouhi, M., Si, L.: Federated search. Found. Trends® Inf. Retr. **5**(1), 1–102 (2011). http://dx.doi.org/10.1561/1500000010
15. Underwood, W.: Measuring search relevance with MRR (2016). https://observer.wunderwood.org/2016/09/12/measuring-search-relevance-with-mrr/. Accessed June 2022
16. Voorhees, E.M., Tice, D.M.: Building a question answering test collection. In: Proceedings of the 23rd Annual International ACM SIGIR Conference on Research and Development in Information Retrieval, SIGIR 2000, New York, NY, USA, pp. 200–207. ACM (2000)
17. Zhou, J., Ding, C., Androutsos, D.: Improving website search using web server logs. In: Proceedings of the 2006 Conference of the Center for Advanced Studies on Collaborative Research - CASCON 2006, New York, USA, p. 22. ACM Press (2006)
18. Zhu, H., Raghavan, S., Vaithyanathan, S., Löser, A.: Navigating the intranet with high precision. In: Proceedings of the 16th International Conference on World Wide Web - WWW 2007, New York, NY, USA, p. 491. ACM Press (2007)

Author Index

Printed in the United States
by Baker & Taylor Publisher Services

T0183258